# TREASURES
# OF
# BRITAIN

## AND
## TREASURES OF IRELAND

**AA**

Published by Drive Publications Limited, for the
Automobile Association,
Fanum House, Leicester Square, London, WC2

TREASURES OF BRITAIN

was edited and designed by Drive Publications Limited
for the Automobile Association

First edition © 1968 Drive Publications

Paper, printing and binding by :

BROWN, KNIGHT & TRUSCOTT LTD, TONBRIDGE; SIR JOSEPH CAUSTON & SONS LTD, EASTLEIGH;
DE SCHUTTER S A, ANTWERP; DORSTEL PRESS LTD, HARLOW;
FAIREY SURVEYS LTD, MAIDENHEAD; HAZELL WATSON & VINEY LTD, AYLESBURY AND CYMMER;
HAZELLS OFFSET LTD, SLOUGH; IMPERIAL CHEMICAL INDUSTRIES LTD, HYDE;
THE INVERESK PAPER CO LTD, MUSSELBURGH; BEN JOHNSON & CO LTD, YORK;
W. & A. K. JOHNSTON & G. W. BACON LTD, EDINBURGH; GEORGE PHILIP PRINTERS LTD, LONDON;
PURNELL & SONS LTD, PAULTON; ROCAPPI LTD, SEVENOAKS;
SCHWITTER LTD, ZURICH; TAYLOWE LTD, MAIDENHEAD;
YATES-DUXBURY AND SONS LTD, BURY

# TREASURES OF BRITAIN

The publishers express their gratitude for major contributions
by the following people and organisations:

Malcolm Aird,
*Aird Taylor Associates Ltd*
John Astrop
Norman G. Barber
John Beale
Claude Blair, M.A., F.S.A.,
*Deputy Keeper of Metalwork,*
*Victoria and Albert Museum*
John Blomfield
Michael Borrie,
*Department of Manuscripts,*
*British Museum*
Broadway Arts Ltd
John Bulmer
Mike Busselle
Norman Cook,
*Director, Guildhall Museum*
A. C. Cooper Ltd.,
*Fine Art Photographers*
George Coral
Maurice Craig,
*Ministry of Public Building and Works*
Anne Cruikshank,
*Trinity College, Dublin*
Catherine Cruft,
*Royal Commission on the Ancient and*
*Historical Monuments of Scotland, Edinburgh*
Roy Dickens
Frank Dowling
Tony Evans
E. C. Fernie,
*School of Fine Arts,*
*University of East Anglia*
Gerald Findlayson
Desmond Fitz-Gerald,
*Department of Furniture and Woodwork,*
*Victoria and Albert Museum*
Christina Gascoigne
Charles H. Gibbs Smith,
*Keeper of the Department of Public Relations*
*and Education, Victoria and Albert Museum*
H. Gordon Slade, T.D., A.R.I.B.A., F.S.A.SCOT.
Charles Green
Paul Grinke
Desmond Guinness,
*President, Irish Georgian Society*
Miles Hadfield
Douglas B. Hague,
*Royal Commission on Ancient Monuments*
*in Wales and Monmouthshire*
John Hayes,
*London Museum*
Leslie Harris

Valerie Howard,
*Department of Public Relations and Education,*
*Victoria and Albert Museum*
Tony Howarth
B. J. Hurren
Philip James
David N. Johnson,
*Office of Public Works,*
*National Monument Branch, Dublin*
Peter Keen
Ann Kings
Sally Kington,
*London Museum*
Alfred Lammer
Andrew Martindale,
*Senior Lecturer School of Fine Arts,*
*University of East Anglia*
John Marmaras
Donald Maxwell
Eric Meacher
Lieutenant Commander George Naish and
the Trustees of the National Maritime Museum
Sydney W. Newbery
John Newman
Richard Ormond,
*National Portrait Gallery*
John Physick,
*Department of Public Relations and Education,*
*Victoria and Albert Museum*
Anthony Radcliffe,
*Victoria and Albert Museum*
L. T. C. Rolt, M.A., F.R.S.L., C.I.MECH.E.
Tom Scott
Edwin Smith
Derek Shrub,
*Department of Education,*
*Victoria and Albert Museum*
Francis Stephens, A.R.C.A.
Dr Roy Strong,
*Director, National Portrait Gallery*
Michael Taylor,
*Aird Taylor Associates Ltd*
Pennie Tweedie
Peter Warner
Martin Weaver
James Wentworth Day
Michael Wynne,
*National Portrait Gallery of Ireland, Dublin*
Doreen Yarwood, A.T.D. (LONDON)
Ian Yeomans
D. Zichy,
*Curator, Chester Beatty Library, Dublin*
Jesse Zierler

Many other people, organisations, and publications
were consulted during the preparation of this book, including those
whose assistance is acknowledged on the last page

# CONTENTS: *A Grand Tour of*

## TREASURES IN THEIR TIME
*How the past has shaped our inheritance*
PAGES 9–48

## GAZETTEER OF THE TREASURES OF BRITAIN
*The Nation's heritage described and illustrated*
PAGES 49–504

PEOPLE AND PLACES : MEN AND WOMEN WHOSE LIVES ARE WOVEN INTO BRITISH HISTORY

## FAMOUS PEOPLE
*Their works and whereabouts*
PAGES 505–535

## MAP SECTION
*Where to find the Treasures of the British Isles*
PAGES 536–576

# Our Most Treasured Possessions

## GAZETTEER OF THE TREASURES OF IRELAND

*The wealth of a unique and little-known land*

PAGES 577–632

PEOPLE AND PLACES

W. B. Yeats, Ballylee 582

## COLLECTIONS INDEX

*Specialised collections in houses, museums and galleries*

PAGES 633–648

## 1000 YEARS OF DESIGN

*How to recognise period styles*

PAGES 649–664

## THE LANGUAGE OF EXPERTS

*The way artists and craftsmen work, and the terms they use*

PAGES 665–679

# THIS LIVELY PAGEANT

by His Grace The Duke of Norfolk KG, GCVO
President of the Automobile Association

This fine book is about the places and things—castles and cathedrals, jewels and paintings—which we treasure as highlights of our national heritage. There is another kind of British treasure of which I have some experience: the lively pageant of national occasions.

They are not all great affairs of state. Few days, I suggest, are quite as splendidly, characteristically British as that Saturday in May when the Australian cricket tourists play my team against a background of spring greenery at Arundel. And Royal Ascot or the colourful bedlam of Derby Day are as much treasures of Britain as the stateliest of our homes—not to mention the Trooping of the Colour and the Changing of the Guard.

The first Coronation I organised as Earl Marshal was King George VI's. I was offered the help of a theatrical producer to ensure the utmost pageantry. I explained, politely, that the sovereign was crowned according to ancient ritual and that the instructions were quite explicit; the pageantry would stem naturally from the personality of the king and the mood of the nation.

So it is with the treasures featured in this book. They are things which stem naturally from their own times and their own settings: tiny Saxon churches which have served lonely parishes for 1000 years to the great house at Blenheim, a gift from the nation to one of its most illustrious heroes.

My home, Arundel Castle, finds a place here not because of great age or magnificence (much of it was rebuilt by my father in Gothic style) but because of the 500 years of history that my ancestors have shared at this spot. Without that Arundel would be a showplace with little meaning.

The editors of this book have put on the map a vast array of evidence that these islands are the world's richest storehouse of achievement, invention and beauty. (And Ireland—and its proud independence—have not been overlooked; its treasures are listed and illustrated separately.)

In my view this AA guide will rank as something of a treasure itself.

*Norfolk.*

# TREASURES
# IN THEIR TIME

---

*The works of builders and artists, from Stonehenge*

*to 20th-century statues, are keys to the understanding*

*of the times in which they were made*

---

Drive into any city in Britain, and you journey backwards in time. First the suburbs of the last half century, then an inner ring of 19th-century building, then the Georgian, Tudor and medieval core, clustering round the soaring spire of a Gothic or Norman cathedral. Buried under the tarmac of the modern highway there may well be the rutted stones of a Roman road. In the country the remains are fewer, but may be still more ancient. A faint bank and ditch in the middle of a field shows where prehistoric men gathered for market or defence; a standing stone marks the spot where generations of their chieftains were buried.

This introductory section of the book relates these objects, large or small, ancient or modern, stone wall or carved jewel, to the men who made them and the times in which they were created. Each period begins with a brief historical sketch, followed by guides to the architecture, sculpture, painting and decorative arts of the period. The treasures described range from medieval manuscripts, Wren churches and Georgian landscape gardens to carved Elizabethan tombs and pinnacled Victorian town halls.

The 20th century, with all its bewildering changes, needs the points of reference given by such treasures. Their slow artistic evolution, in which experiments were adopted only after much trial and error, gives a sense of the continuity of thousands of years of history.

# Ice Age to the Romans

*The Romans in the 1st century* AD
*conquered a land which had seen
many cultures, from primitive hunters
to the princes of the Iron Age*

### THE PALAEOLITHIC PERIOD *c.* 300,000–8000 BC

During the 'Great Ice Age', which is thought to have
lasted about a million years, there were many periods
of tens of thousands of years when the ice-cap which
covered Britain melted away, and the climate became as
warm as it is today. In these interglacial periods primitive
races of men first came to this land as hunters and food-
gatherers. They were merely large families or small clans,
scattered widely over the southern half of Britain. During this period, the Palaeolithic (Old Stone) Age, Britain
still formed, at least at times, a part of the Continent. Each
time the climate worsened and ice-caps began to form in
the hills, the animals and their human predators moved
south.

For most of the period the only archaeological evidence
we have consists of the implements made by chipping
flint nodules or flakes to the required shapes (British
Museum).

Modern man (*Homo sapiens*) is known to have existed
in Western Europe during the last 30,000 years. During
the later cold spells of the Ice Age, his skills enabled him
to clothe himself and to hunt in the areas round the edges
of the ice.

In Britain there are a few caves (like those in Cheddar
Gorge, Somerset) where family groups found conditions
suitable for survival. In some of these the debris of food-
bones and broken implements later became sealed by a
layer of stalagmite, which has preserved many objects
that would otherwise have decayed; so implements of
bone survive as well as of flint.

STONEHENGE, Wiltshire, the
finest Bronze Age sanctuary in
Britain. Built in successive
stages, *c.* 1800–1400 BC. Engraved
by Jan Kip, a Dutchman who
worked in England at the
beginning of the 18th century

### THE MESOLITHIC PERIOD *c.* 8000–3000 BC

A rise in the sea-level, brought about largely by the
melting ice-cap, cut Britain off from the Continent
about 9000 years ago; Ireland had been isolated rather
earlier.

A steady improvement in the climate allowed the
population to increase somewhat; but as long as man
had to rely on gathering food, as opposed to farming it,
his numbers could never grow large.

The improvement of climate was accompanied by a
slow spread of forest from the south, leading to changes
in animal life. The cold-weather herds of the steppes
disappeared, to be replaced by forest animals, and there
was also an increase in the species of fish. This led to
changes of diet and modifications of the old hunting
methods.

STONE CIRCLE, near Tormore,
Arran. A highly romanticised
water-colour by William
Andrews Nesfield (1793–1881)

Of the men themselves of this period we know virtually nothing. All we have are some flint and bone implements. Though many of the occupation sites are known, and have in varying degree been excavated, there are no structural remains.

## THE NEOLITHIC PERIOD c. 3250–1800 BC

Shortly before 3000 BC the first parties of farmer-immigrants established themselves in the chalk Down country of southern Britain. From early beginnings in the Near East, the twin activities of grain cultivation and stock rearing had spread slowly westwards. The visible monuments of this cultural advance are of three kinds—flint mines (Grime's Graves, Norfolk), causewayed camps (Windmill Hill, Wiltshire), and long barrows or long cairns (West Kennet, Wiltshire).

A more regular food supply led to a steady increase of population, which was further increased by the arrival of new settlers and improved farming techniques. During this period, Britain was occupied by many tribes of different cultural levels, probably speaking different languages and certainly different dialects.

The need for open land, both for crop-growing and pasturage, meant that trees had to be felled. On the chalk Downs the woodland was comparatively light and dry, and clearing could be done partly by burning and partly by felling. Tree-felling needed axes, and for these igneous rocks were at first used. Some centuries later, seams of fine flint deep in the chalk were mined.

Causewayed camps, marked by bank-and-ditch rings around hill-tops, have been recognised on a number of sites; the ditches have many causeways for crossing, which correspond with openings in the banks. In this way they can be clearly distinguished from the hill-forts of the Iron Age. They may have been meeting-places for formal communal purposes, and perhaps markets.

The most important monuments are undoubtedly the burial sites. These are called megalithic (from the Greek *mega*-, large, and *lith*-, stone), as the burial-chambers and approach-passages are of large stone slabs; in certain areas, where suitable slabs were not available, drystone walling was used.

Broadly the tombs fall into two main groups—passage-graves, with a passage from the entrance to a circular burial chamber; and gallery-graves, with a long rectangular chamber, the whole of which was used for burials. Some of these have transepts or side-chambers, as in the Cotswold-Severn group. When complete, these structures were concealed below long mounds (although a few are roughly circular) and contained by stone walling. The long ones were usually higher at the entrance end; and here there was often a forecourt, where rites were performed when the tomb was opened for a burial, after which the entrance and forecourt were again masked by a carefully built stone blocking.

In parts of southern and eastern England, long mounds of similar age are to be found, entirely lacking the internal stone structures; excavation has revealed that similar turf and timber structures were often present.

LANYON QUOIT, a Cornish dolmen. The remains of a long-barrow burial chamber after the covering of earth and stones has been removed. The chamber was entered through a passage

CARN EUNY, a 'fogou' near Brane, Cornwall. Primarily associated with Iron Age settlements in Cornwall, fogous were formed by cutting a passage in the soil and concealing it with a covering of stones and earth. Lined and paved with stone slabs, fogous were used either for storage purposes or as escape routes from the village when under attack. The example shown is over 60 ft long

## THE BRONZE AGE c. 1800–550 BC

The division of prehistoric cultures into Stone Age, Bronze Age and Iron Age is a useful time-scale based on the technological skills employed in making important tools and weapons; no hard and fast line can be drawn. The first newcomer to Britain with a small metal knife-dagger began the Bronze Age; but the essentially Neolithic way of life, for most people, was not in the least changed, and it was only slowly that the new metal objects spread to all parts of the island.

The new immigrant group coming in from the Low Countries have been called the Beaker People, because of the characteristic drinking vessels found in many of their tombs (British Museum). They also brought with them the custom of individual burials, under round barrows, much smaller than the large, collective long barrows.

The round barrow slowly became the normal tomb of the Bronze Age, although after a time cremation replaced burial. The commonest visible monuments of the Bronze Age are the many thousands of these round barrows (mainly in Dorset and Wiltshire). A few still stand at about their original height; but most have been reduced, often by later agricultural activity, and an unknown number have been completely destroyed, ploughed flat in the last 2000 years. These are now beginning to be revealed by air photography.

In chalk country, houses of this period can be found only by excavation, and show as a pattern of post-holes. In the West Country, notably on Dartmoor (for example, in the Chagford area), where huts were built of stone, settlements of this date may still be seen. The boundaries of Bronze Age corn plots are sometimes visible as slightly raised banks, known as lynchets.

HILL-FORT, Figsbury, Wiltshire. Iron Age forts provided a commanding view of the countryside and a protected area for livestock. Their ditches and ramparts were an effective defence against the principal weapon of the day—the sling

## THE IRON AGE c. 550 BC–AD 43

This period began with a further strengthening of the farming communities of the Late Bronze Age type in the south-eastern part of the island, and ended in the southern half with the establishment of Roman sovereignty. Military adventurers, traders, refugees and farming migrants all swelled and enriched the cultural variety of British life. The advent of new weapons, such as the sling or the war-chariot, together with the increase in population, led inevitably to tribal warfare. It is this aspect of Iron Age life, represented by fortified villages, hill-forts, and the fortified homesteads of the extreme north, that is most noticeable in our surviving field monuments.

Hill-forts took many forms, Maiden Castle, Dorset, being one of the finest. Some were simply promontories or hill-spurs, cut off by a bank and ditch at the narrowest point; but the most characteristic were those where a whole flattish hill-top was enclosed. At first, a single bank and ditch was thought to be effective, the bank being laced and revetted with timber. Later the weak points were made stronger, and the entrances became more complex—deeply inturned, with gates and guard-rooms. Later still, the number of ramparts was

ROMAN THEATRE Aerial view of the 2nd-century AD theatre at Verulamium (St Albans). The only known Roman theatre in Britain

increased, with as many as three or even four banks and ditches, wide enough to give protection against missiles such as sling-stones. Improved protection of the approaches and gates became common. Forts of this type are the most numerous in the chalk country and the west.

An odd variant is the Scottish vitrified fort, where the stone walls show evidence of molten rock. It is now thought that these were originally timber-laced, that they were set on fire, and the heat of the burning timbers caused the stone to take on a glass-like consistency. These forts are apparently post-Roman in date.

IRISH GOLD COLLAR The Irish were expert at making gold ornaments. This collar dates from the 7th century AD

The last groups of invaders were Belgic warriors and refugees, who established themselves in the south-east, where they built their strong places in valleys rather than on hills. In the century before the conquest of Britain by Claudius in AD 43, their grip on the surrounding tribal areas was increased. Their traders, bringing in goods of Roman origin, began the process of Romanisation before the military occupation took place.

The line between the Forth and Clyde estuaries (later that of the Antonine Wall) seems to have been a racial boundary, north of which the language was different from the 'ancient British' of the south. The eastern area, as far north as the Moray Firth, was the land of the Picts in historic times, and here the vitrified forts are the characteristic defended sites. To the north of Pictland there is a concentration of the defended homesteads known as brochs, and minor concentrations in some Hebridean islands.

Many hill-forts seem to have been no more than tribal refuges, used in times of stress; but the more important ones were permanently occupied, apparently by the tribal chiefs and their followers. These were the *oppida* (Latin *oppidum,* a town), the centres of power in which tribal government was conducted. Though not strictly towns, they foreshadowed in elementary fashion the future towns on which regional government was to be based.

## THE ROMANS AD 43–410

For nearly four centuries the Romans made southern Britain a part of civilised Europe, and almost everywhere there is evidence of the Roman occupation. Much of our road system has a Roman origin. London and other important towns are built on Roman foundations.

MITHRAS, THE BULL-SLAYER Late 2nd- or early 3rd-century relief-carving from the site of the Wallbrook Mithraeum, London. Mithras was the god worshipped by the Roman legionaries

The Roman conquest began in AD 43 (though Julius Caesar had reconnoitred the country a century before), and within a few years the south-east lowlands were subdued. For a time a number of garrisoned forts of timber and earth were sufficient to keep the peace, but by AD 75 permanent legionary fortresses had been established at Caerleon (Monmouthshire), Chester and York; these were rebuilt in stone about 20 years later. By AD 85, the northern Pennines and the Scottish lowlands had also been subdued, and the northern tribes had been defeated at Mons Graupius (near Elgin, Morayshire). Afterwards the troops were withdrawn to a frontier established from Solway to the mouth of the Tyne.

IRON FACE-MASK helmet found during excavations at Trimontium, a late 1st-century Roman fort at Newstead, near Melrose

BRONZE STATUETTE of Mercury from a Roman temple site near Colchester, 2nd century AD

Frontier troubles now led to the building of Hadrian's Wall (c. AD 122–35) to link the forts. This wall, 73 miles long, with stone ramparts 8–10 ft thick, still survives in places. The borders were still not pacified, however; and in AD 142 another wall, the Antonine, was built from the Forth to the Clyde. At the end of the 2nd century, due to a shortage of manpower, this wall was deserted. The troops were stationed along Hadrian's Wall.

Meanwhile Romanisation progressed in the south. *Coloniae* (settlements of retired soldiers) were established, and the beginnings of local government were set up. The tribal areas were marked out and organised as locally-governed cantons, administered from the cantonal towns. By this time the local notables had become Romanised, and from them magistrates were selected. Other towns and posting-stations grew up on the main roads, and large-scale agriculture developed on the estates of the country houses (*villae*). Local disturbances led to these towns being protected, at first by timber-revetted banks and ditches, and soon after AD 200 by stone walls added to the banks.

In the 3rd century barbarians began to raid the coasts. A chain of forts was built from the Wash to Southampton Water against the marauding Saxon long-boats, and also as bases for the Roman fleet. Similar forts were built in the west against the Irish raiders, and signal-stations were built on the Yorkshire coast to counter the threat of the Picts, who sought to outflank Hadrian's Wall by sea.

Towards the end of the 4th century, ambitious Roman generals gradually denuded Britain of most of her troops for a series of continental adventures. In 410, when all the available Roman legions were needed in foreign fields, the British became responsible for their own defence. They engaged Germanic mercenaries, who proved to be a fifth column, opening the doors for the Anglo-Saxon invasion and conquest. During these years many linear earthworks were constructed by the Britons, as regional defences.

PREHISTORIC AND ROMAN ART

Although the Palaeolithic cave paintings of southern France and Pyrenean Spain exhibit remarkable artistic sophistication, Britain has little art to show for the corresponding period. The best we have is a simple incised line-drawing of a hooded man, on a bone from a cave at Cresswell, Derbyshire. Another of these caves has produced engravings of animals on scraps of bone.

The changed way of life of the Neolithic farmers did not at first help the development of the visual arts. Pottery was now in general service; but, as women made the pots for their own household use, they were ornamented only with simple rows of dots or with panels of grooved lines. A few crude sculptures have also been found. In a flint mine at Grime's Graves, Norfolk, where the flint-seam was very thin, a tiny shrine for a crudely carved pregnant woman was found, with offerings thought to be a sacrifice to the fertility goddess. Also at Grime's Graves, fragments of the chalky crust of flint were found, bearing engravings of red deer.

The beakers of the period when Neolithic and early Bronze Ages overlapped show a wider range of decorated pottery; but again the designs are purely geometric, although 'rusticated' decoration was also produced by pinching the wet clay between thumb and forefinger. Later, in the true Bronze Age, small vessels of pottery, amber or occasionally gold are found in the tombs of wealthy Wessex chiefs.

Personal ornaments were also decorated, and the discovery of Irish gold led to its use for such ornaments as the crescent-shaped *lunulae*, worn as collars, which bear simple geometric line decorations. These were copied, in parts of Britain, in elaborate groupings of jet beads. Armlets and torques (twisted bands or belts) were also made in gold and bronze.

Simple designs mark of the best of the pottery and other objects of the first days of the Iron Age, but during this period the decorative La Tène art (named after the Iron Age lake-side settlement at La Tène in Switzerland) was introduced. This was based on the palm-leaf, and had evolved abstract curvilinear patterns.

In Britain this design was to progress to a magnificent climax, but was already deteriorating when the Roman conquest interrupted its course. La Tène art was largely restricted to the weapons, harness-fittings and domestic appointments of aristocratic warriors and their women.

Roman art, on the other hand, was naturalistic, though formal patterns such as the guilloche (two-stranded twist) were commonly used for panel-borders and the like. Architecture, in the real sense of the word, now appeared for the first time. Fine public buildings, both religious and secular, were built and embellished with statues and carved reliefs. The walls were painted and the floors were of *tesserae* (square mosaic tiles) set in various designs. Many town and country houses had these embellishments. The great pavement at Woodchester, in Gloucestershire, for example, shows Orpheus playing his lute to the beasts of the field.

It was in grand, Romanised villas that fine silver and glass were used. The Mildenhall treasure (British Museum) and the looted Roman silver found at Traprain Law, near Edinburgh (National Museum of Antiquities, Edinburgh), show the quality of the silversmith's work.

Nor was the lesser man neglected. Pottery for the table was embellished with a wealth of design; and statues of the gods, cast in bronze or pipeclay as small statuettes, were cheap and plentiful. The coinage, at its best, showed great skill in portraiture. Knife-handles took the form of crouching lions, and the knobs of box-lids were shaped like cocks or eagles.

Though this work was Classical in inspiration, much of it showed its British origin. The Celtic craftsman, deserting his curvilinear patterns for the new style, carried over some of the old tradition. As a result, we have that masterpiece, the gorgon's head, which once stared from the pediment of the temple of Sulis-Minerva at Bath (Bath Museum). Even when the Romans had gone, a mixture of Romano-Celtic designs survived. Modified to suit the Nordic taste, these took their place in the pattern-books of Anglo-Saxon craftsmen.

MOSAIC ARTISTRY at Low Ham Villa, Somerset. Part of a mosaic pavement in a large 4th-century Roman house. It depicts scenes from the Romance of Dido and Aeneas in Vergil's *Aeneid*. One of the first examples where a complete story was told in a series of chronological scenes

# Saxon and Norman

*Between the 6th and 12th centuries
the arts in Britain followed the
rise and fall of kingdoms, culminating
in the great Norman cathedrals*

BAYEUX TAPESTRY 230 ft long
and 20 in. deep, the 11th-century
tapestry tells the story of the
Conquest in 72 scenes, ending
with the defeat of the English at
Hastings. In this scene a
workman is fitting a weather-
vane to the roof of Westminster
Abbey before the funeral of
Edward the Confessor

ROCHESTER CATHEDRAL, Kent.
Over the 12th-century west
doorway the figure of Christ
is surrounded by angels and the
Four Beasts symbolising
the four Evangelists

When St Augustine landed in Thanet, Kent, in AD 597,
under orders from Pope Gregory the Great to convert
the heathen English to Christianity, he brought to
England a new religion and a new way of life.

The worship of Odin and Thor—the religion of the
Anglo-Saxon 'barbarians'—was concerned mainly with
manliness, generosity, loyalty and physical courage, and
did little to promote learning or art. The arrival of the
Christians meant the return of learning to Britain.

The Church, benefiting from the pious gifts of its
patrons, acquired vast lands and wealth. Its great
cathedrals and abbeys dominated the landscape; and,
since the life of Saxon England was centred on the village,
the countless parish churches became the focal points of
village life. Churches monopolised the skill of the builders
until the coming of the Normans in the 11th century,
and artists found their chief source of inspiration and
employment in adorning them.

It was in the north, in the Kingdom of Northumbria
which extended from Edinburgh on the Forth to York
and the Humber, that the arts flourished, reaching their
zenith in the 8th century. Church and state were more
stable in Northumbria than in the surrounding restless
kingdoms, and in this more or less peaceful climate the
Venerable Bede wrote his *Ecclesiastical History* and the
Bishop of Lindisfarne compiled the *Lindisfarne Gospel-
book* with its magnificent illuminations.

The invasion of the Danes in the 9th century brought
cultural disaster. It disrupted the monasteries, where
civilisation had its roots, and the arts barely managed to
survive. It was not until the reign of Alfred the Great
(871–99), scholar, warrior and administrator, who with
his successors made England into one united kingdom,
that men could settle again to more leisurely and cultivated pursuits.

Long before the Norman Conquest of 1066 there had
been a flow of artistic ideas between the Continent and
England. This constant traffic had gone on with few inter-
ruptions for over 200 years. The Norman Conquest in
1066 brought a political revolution which stabilised the
kingdom; but in the arts its effect was not so much a
revolution as an acceleration—sometimes violent, as in
architecture—of already existing trends. Since the kings
of England were also lords of Normandy and later of
Anjou, and constantly travelled to and fro, such continental influences as Romanesque sculpture infiltrated
England. The 12th century and the end of the Norman
period marked a high point in English arts.

## CATHEDRALS, CHURCHES AND FORTRESSES

Anglo-Saxon and Norman architecture is mainly a story of churches, since no secular buildings earlier than the late 11th century survive. Not many Anglo-Saxon churches are left either. Many were built of wood and easily destroyed—there is a solitary example of a 10th-century wooden church at Greenstead, Essex—or else they were demolished by the Normans in the spate of rebuilding that followed the Conquest of 1066. Among the major Anglo-Saxon churches which perished were Canterbury, Winchester and Worcester.

A few of the smaller Anglo-Saxon churches survive. The most important are at Brixworth, Northamptonshire, Bradford-on-Avon, Wiltshire, Deerhurst, Gloucestershire, Great Paxton, Huntingdonshire, Wing, Buckinghamshire, and Stow, Lincolnshire. There are also splendid Anglo-Saxon church towers at Earl's Barton, Northamptonshire, Barton-on-Humber, Lincolnshire, Barnack, Huntingdonshire, and Sompting, Sussex. Architecturally, they fall into two periods—the 7th-8th and 10th-11th centuries. Virtually nothing survives from the Danish invasion in the 9th century.

The early period shows Celtic and Roman influence, rather than any indigenous Anglo-Saxon style. One of the best examples is at Brixworth, Northamptonshire, where bricks from a Roman ruin were used by Anglo-Saxon builders to make a simple, large-windowed rectangular building with a semicircular recess at one end (a Roman apsidal basilica). Other examples are the crypt at Hexham, Northumberland, where the abbey was built by Wilfrid in the 7th century, using stone from the ruined Roman townships of Hadrian's Wall; and the crypt at Ripon, Yorkshire.

Most of the remaining Anglo-Saxon churches belong to the second phase—the 10th and early 11th centuries. Few of the smaller Anglo-Saxon churches survive intact, though more than 200 churches still have pre-Conquest work in them.

The typical Anglo-Saxon church has a simple plan—two rectangles of unequal size linked by an arch, with the smaller rectangle to the east. An additional chamber or *porticus* could be attached to the church; sometimes there was more than one, as at Bradwell, Essex. The buildings tended to be of a much greater height than width, as at Bradford-on-Avon, Wiltshire. The windows were small and round-headed, set high in the walls.

Interiors were often decoratively painted, with little architectural ornament. The external decoration was often elaborate—usually pilaster-work (vertical strips of stone on the outside walls). The exterior might also have round-headed or triangular blank arcading (a series of arches against a blank wall).

The Norman genius found its finest expression in architecture. Although the Conquerors destroyed the great English churches, they raised on their ruins some of the noblest buildings still extant. The Norman influence in building was at work well before the Conquest. Westminster Abbey, built by Edward the Confessor (1042-66), last of the Saxon kings, was Norman in style.

ST MARY'S CHURCH at Dover. A 19th-century engraving depicting one of the few Norman towers still standing with the round-headed arches characteristic of that period. In the background are the ruins of Dover castle

DURHAM CATHEDRAL About 500 years ago the western towers were surmounted by spires; they were made with timber and clad with lead sheeting

This style is characterised by magnificent scale, superb proportions and bold construction. The design was simple yet inventive, and produced an effect of austere grandeur—or so it now seems, though we do not see these churches as they originally were. The bare melancholy now so characteristic of their atmosphere was dispelled by painted interiors, stained glass windows, opulent vestments and furnishings, and the elaborate ceremonial for which the churches formed a setting.

Only three large churches—the cathedrals of Durham, Norwich and Peterborough—remain substantially as they were in Norman times, though fine work can still be seen at Winchester, St Albans, Ely, Gloucester and many smaller churches.

Durham Cathedral, one of the finest Romanesque churches in Europe, was begun by Bishop William of St Carilef in 1093 and completed by 1133. It was the first large building in northern Europe to be rib-vaulted in stone. The ribbed vault was the Normans' greatest contribution to medieval architecture. After passing through all the stages of development and decadence, it ended in the extravagance of the roof of Henry VII's chapel in Westminster Abbey, where the functional ribs evolved into an intricate web of stone decoration.

Though this period saw much splendid ecclesiastical building, the great castles that survive are mainly of later date. The first Norman forts were simple earth mounds with ditches and palisades, and it was not until the 12th century that stone castles began to be built in any numbers. Their characteristic feature is the square Norman keep combining fortress and residence. Two examples survive from the 11th century—Colchester, Essex, and the most famous of all English castles, the White Tower in the Tower of London, completed by 1097. Although the White Tower has been altered, its form is essentially as it was—a four-storey building divided by an internal wall into two parts. One half of the building was again subdivided to the plain but beautiful Chapel of St John, which is the oldest complete Norman church in England.

### SCULPTURE: RISE AND FALL OF STYLES

Monumental carved crosses, erected to commemorate persons or events long since forgotten, are found mostly in the north of England and the Kingdom of Northumbria. Apart from a few crosses in the Midlands, no comparable sculptures of that period can be found anywhere else in western Europe. The finest examples are at Ruthwell, Dumfriesshire, and Bewcastle, Cumberland; they date from the late 7th and early 8th centuries. They are carved with a vine-leaf decoration and figures of Christ and the Saints.

The artistic tradition that produced the crosses declined as the Northumbrian Kingdom declined. The sculpture produced in the south with the rise of the Kingdoms of Mercia and Wessex was different in character. The carved reliefs at Breedon on the Hill, Leicestershire, of 750–850, include a magnificent figure of Christ, with decoration of grotesque beasts and figures intertwined

NORMAN MOULDINGS An unusually varied selection of mouldings on the blind-arcading and pilasters of St Anselm's Tower, Canterbury Cathedral. From John Britton's *Cathedral Antiquities of England* (1814–35)

NORMAN CARVING was usually in low-relief until the axe was superseded by the chisel in the 12th century. The font at St Michael's, Castle Frome, marks the new freedom offered by this change of technique

with vine tendrils. The workmanship is accomplished, and indicates the existence of a flourishing 'Court school' of sculpture in the Kingdom of Mercia.

The same can be said of outstanding works produced in Wessex at a later period. The late 9th-century carved stone at Codford St Peter, Wiltshire, the flying angels at Bradford-on-Avon, Wiltshire, and particularly the great Crucifixion at Romsey, Hampshire (early 10th century), are works of outstanding quality in which can be discerned for the first time a recognisable Englishness— a dignified restraint and lightness of touch.

The Norman churches built immediately after the Conquest had little sculptural ornament. When in the 12th century English craftsmen began to execute extensive architectural sculptures, they got their inspiration from France, where Romanesque sculpture was developing with the brilliance and assurance that was to culminate in the glories of Chartres Cathedral.

The mutilated Madonna at York (early 12th century) is a work of great dignity, and the 12th-century reliefs in Chichester Cathedral, *The Raising of Lazarus* and *Martha and Mary Greeting Christ*, are possibly the finest sculptures produced in medieval England.

No grand sculpture cycles comparable with those of the French cathedrals have survived, but a band of sculptures of biblical scenes on the west front of Lincoln Cathedral serves to indicate the extent of our loss. Smaller-scale architectural sculptures are fairly plentiful. In the crypt and north transept of Canterbury Cathedral, for example, are capitals carved with the strange beasts and monsters dear to the medieval imagination, and all over England there are carved tympana and doorways.

RELIEF CARVING in whalebone. On an 11th century *Adoration of the Magi*, a lower frieze features a hunting scene

## VELLUM AND BURNISHED GOLD

Until the 12th century, graphic art in England is represented solely by manuscripts that were 'illuminated'— that is, painted with pigments whose effect could be enriched by burnished gold laid on the vellum—or else illustrated with line drawings. The subject matter of this art was almost exclusively religious, and its aim was to illustrate and enhance the sacred texts of the Church.

Illuminated manuscripts are the most perfectly preserved of all the works of art left to us by the Middle Ages. Huge numbers of manuscripts were destroyed in the Reformation, when a coloured initial was enough to convict a book of idolatry and condemn it to the flames. But the quality of what has survived shows how the English excelled at this exquisite art.

Outstanding among the earlier manuscript treasures is the *Lindisfarne Gospel-book* (British Museum). Lindisfarne was the great monastery on Holy Island off the coast of Northumberland, founded by St Aidan and his Irish monks from Iona in 635. The *Gospel-book* is the most splendid monument of the Anglo-Irish civilisation which developed in Northumbria after St Aidan's mission and was written by Eadfrith, Bishop of Lindisfarne (698–721). The stylised miniatures of the four Evangelists reflect a Classical influence—evidence of a traffic in books and artistic ideas between England and

THE LINDISFARNE GOSPEL-BOOK A full-page miniature of St Mark from the AD 700 illuminated manuscript by Bishop Eadfrith

CAEDMON'S HYMN Page from the poet's 11th-century book, illustrating the Genesis story of Cain and Abel. The *Hymn* is Caedmon's only surviving work

GOLD BUCKLE with Anglo-Saxon engraving inlaid with niello (sulphur and copper amalgam). Part of the Sutton Hoo Treasure

southern Europe at the time. The decoration derives from contemporary metalwork like the Sutton Hoo buckle (British Museum), and consists of geometric and interlaced ornament, interwoven with strange ribbon-like animals into a complex, many-coloured network. The freshness and delicacy of the colours and the intricacy of the workmanship are unmatched in any other manuscript except the later *Book of Kells* (Trinity College, Dublin), which was possibly written at Iona itself between 760 and 820.

When the Vikings sacked Lindisfarne in 793, the monastic life of the North was disrupted and the production of manuscripts seems to have ceased until southern England became united under the Wessex supremacy of Alfred the Great over 100 years later. The art that revived in the 10th century, though no less brilliant than its Northumbrian predecessor, was different. It drew its inspiration, motifs and techniques from the schools of illumination that flourished in the Holy Roman Empire established by Charlemagne in AD 800.

By the late 900's English artists had adapted these Carolingian ideas to their own taste and talent, and founded the Winchester style of illumination—one of the greatest achievements in the history of English art. Its characteristic features are a luxuriant and finely drawn acanthus leaf motif, usually worked into elaborate foliate borders, and a delicate style of figure-drawing.

The first mature example of the Winchester style is the *Foundation Charter of King Edgar to the New Minster at Winchester*, dated 966 (British Museum). It contains a miniature of the king, between the Virgin and St Peter, offering the charter to Christ. The finest example came ten years later—the *Benedictional* or *Book of Blessings* written for St Aethelwold, Bishop of Winchester.

The Norman Conquest had little immediate effect on the style of English illumination, but there was some influence on detail. Some decorative features became more common, such as 'historiated' initial letters (decorated with figures of men and animals), and 'inhabited scrolls', showing arabesques of foliage with animals 'inhabiting' the branches.

During the first half of the 12th century a new style, the Romanesque, entered the country. This grew up alongside the surviving Anglo-Saxon style. It derived from Byzantium and the East, and its characteristics were firmness of line, boldness of execution, and a rigid, monumental dignity in the portrayal of the human figure. A rare example surviving from this time is the wall-painting of *St Paul and the Viper*, in St Anselm's Chapel, Canterbury Cathedral.

The most important English contribution to Romanesque painting is the development of the technique of pictorial narrative and of a complete cycle of illustrations to the Bible. These appeared in the enormous ceremonial Bibles which were produced in the 12th century, in particular the Winchester Bible (Winchester Cathedral), the Lambeth Bible from Canterbury (Lambeth Palace), and the Bury Bible (Corpus Christi College, Cambridge).

The Winchester Bible, in four volumes measuring 23 in. by 16 in., has claims to be the finest. It was probably begun in 1160–70 and is the work of at least six master illuminators. Its design (not completed) called for an elaborate initial letter at the beginning of each book of the Bible, and several full pages of illuminated illustrations. These magnificent Bibles are the greatest achievements in European painting in the 12th century. At the end of the Norman period they won for England the pre-eminence in the graphic arts which in sculpture belonged to France.

## WHEN BISHOPS WERE METALWORKERS

The metalwork for which England was famous was a monastic craft until the Conquest and was mostly done for the Church. High-ranking churchmen practised these crafts: both St Dunstan, Archbishop of Canterbury, and St Aethelwold, Bishop of Winchester, were skilled metalworkers. Among the best surviving examples of the craft is an elegant silver bowl of c. AD 1000 from Halton Moor, Lancashire (British Museum), decorated with low-relief figures in a Byzantine style; and metal objects decorated with interlace and scroll ornament, found in a hoard at Trewhiddle, Cornwall, c. 875.

Not much early Anglo-Saxon jewellery remains, but the Sutton Hoo Treasure of the early 7th century (British Museum) includes a large and splendid jewelled buckle and other objects. There is little surviving work as good as this, apart from the magnificent Alfred Jewel, of c. 880 (Ashmolean Museum, Oxford), which was perhaps a brooch or part of a sceptre. It is pear-shaped, made of enamel in a gold setting, and has on the obverse a figure bearing two sceptres in fine cloisonné enamel and an inscription in Anglo-Saxon: 'Alfred had me made'. Two other jewels, less fine but still evidence of a vigorous and inventive craft, are the Minster Lovell Jewel of the late 9th century (Ashmolean Museum, Oxford) and the Dowgate Hill Brooch of c. 900 (British Museum).

Among the textiles, the exquisite Anglo-Saxon embroidery known as *opus anglicanum* was prized throughout Europe. Only one example from the Anglo-Saxon period is left—the St Cuthbert Vestments in Durham Cathedral, placed in St Cuthbert's tomb in 934 by King Athelstan. The best-known medieval embroidery is the 11th-century Bayeux Tapestry (at Bayeux, Normandy) —a long strip of linen embroidered in coloured wools with lively, detailed scenes from the life of King Harold, the battle of Hastings and the Norman Conquest.

Carving in ivory of religious objects such as crucifixes or reliquaries was an important craft. Bishop Leofric of Exeter (1050–73) gave his church two crosses, shrines and candlesticks all made of ivory, and two gospel-books bound in ivory. Two early ivories can be seen at the Victoria and Albert Museum, London: a crucifix of c. 950, and a crozier head of the 12th century carved with scenes from the Nativity and the Deposition of Christ from the Cross.

Glass painting was of some importance in the 12th century, but little remains. Canterbury Cathedral has the jumbled remnants of some late 12th-century glass which represents one of the earliest narrative sequences in Europe; there are other fragments at York and Lincoln.

12th-CENTURY PLAQUE A colourful early-English enamel of St Paul being lowered from the wall of Damascus

MUSICAL INSTRUMENT Reconstruction of an Anglo-Saxon harp, with tuning-key in inset, from the Sutton Hoo Treasure, discovered in 1939

# The Gothic Period

*Between the mid-12th and the early 16th century the Gothic cathedrals soared to lofty vaults, while castles evolved from simple keeps to complex palaces*

VIEW OF LONDON from the *Nuremburg Chronicle*, 1493. One of the first publications to use woodcuts, which were often personal interpretations rather than accurate records

15TH-CENTURY BRASS from Felbrigg Church, Norfolk, to Sir Simon Felbrygge and his wife Margaret

The adjective 'Gothic' began as the name of a tribe, but it has come to refer only to a particular style of art. It has nothing to do with the original Goths, whose historical importance waned after the 7th century.

The Gothic style was a North French export of the second half of the 12th century and the first half of the 13th, and the importation of the style into this country was a piecemeal operation moving at a variety of speeds; while the best place to put the end of English Gothic is somewhere between 1500 and the Reformation.

Norman architecture was imported into England, because the new patrons were without exception Normans, who disliked the Anglo-Saxon style. The monastic orders, particularly the Cistercians, introduced a style which made it easier for English architects to accept the Gothic innovations when they came. Westminster Abbey, London, is the first clear case of the influence of the royal house on the development of English Gothic architecture. Due chiefly to the alterations inspired by Henry III (1216-72), the abbey came to resemble French High Gothic cathedrals such as Reims. From the time of Henry III on, the Crown was responsible for most important buildings. The great phase of English late medieval architecture, the Perpendicular, was almost certainly initiated in the early 14th century from Court circles in London.

In any case, money commanded the best workmen, designers and artists, so that one would expect royalty to commission masterpieces. The 15th century saw the rise of a new class of patrons—rich merchants with a penchant for fine building.

## ARCHITECTURE: CATHEDRALS AND CASTLES

The basis of Gothic architecture was the acceptance, in whole or in part, of the new French style, which involved the creation of a structural and spatial unity out of the ribbed vault, the pointed arch, the flying buttress, and slender supports. Sometimes the formulae were accepted wholesale, as in the eastern parts of Canterbury Cathedral; more often they were watered down with Romanesque elements, as at Salisbury Cathedral.

The two great periods of Late English Gothic are loosely called the Decorated (first half of the 14th century) and the Perpendicular (*c.* 1340-1500). The choir of Gloucester Cathedral is one of the earliest and finest manifestations of the Perpendicular style and is also a classic illustration of how little Late Gothic architecture concerned itself with structural function: the revolutionary elements are little more than a veneer of tracery decoration applied to a pre-existing Norman fabric.

The development of English Gothic architecture can be traced in miniature through the changes in the patterns of ribs applied to vaults. In the second half of the 12th century continental Gothic vaults were of the simple four-part or six-part type: the square or rectangular form of the vault was divided up either into four areas by two intersecting diagonal ribs, or into six areas by a further transverse rib cutting through the point of intersection of the diagonals. During this period the English often did not bother to vault, as at Ripon Cathedral, Yorkshire, or Hexham Abbey, Northumberland.

But in the 13th century they accepted and developed with alacrity the embellishment of the basic continental type, on to which ridge ribs were added, running both right down the length of the nave and across each bay. A further rib, the tierceron, was then made to run from the springing point of the vault to these ridge ribs.

This stage is illustrated in the nave of Lincoln Cathedral (early 13th century), the impression being of an undulating, all-over design more or less disguising the original concept of vaults in separate bays. The nave of Lincoln appears almost chaste beside the forest of ribs used at Exeter. If ever there was to be a case for the old idea that Gothic architecture derived from wooden architecture and resembled a row of giant trees in a forest, this nave would justify it.

The next stage was the introduction of short ribs, called liernes, linking the main ribs, ridge ribs and tiercerons and creating star-like patterns in the centre of the vault, as in the nave of York Cathedral (*c.* 1300). The liernes, together with the ogee or reverse-curve arch (excellent examples at Bristol and in the Lady Chapel at Ely), can be said to introduce the Decorated style.

Liernes could be used in two ways—either to make a pattern of odd shapes over the whole surface of the vault, as was attempted at Gloucester in the middle of the 14th century; or to increase the suggestion of a fan already created by the bunches of tiercerons. The second method led to the development of the 'fan-vault', the first example of which appears again at Gloucester, in the cloister, towards the middle of the century. Fan-vaulting only found its full expression when used over main areas in the second half of the 15th century, as at King's College Chapel, Cambridge. Henry VII's Chapel in Westminster Abbey completes the cycle.

The growth of the Gothic style in ecclesiastical architecture has no parallel in castle building. However, the mid-12th century marks a fairly distinct break in the development of castles, in that wooden constructions are as unusual after this date as stone ones were before. Most castles before the 15th century were massive, the spaciousness of Gothic being unsuited to fortification.

Thus the castle of the late 12th and 13th centuries is for the most part the same in form as the Norman one. It is dominated by a heavily fortified keep, generally square but sometimes cylindrical, especially later in the period. There are dungeons and store rooms on the

LINCOLN CATHEDRAL, a 19th-century engraving from Britton's *Architectural Antiquities of Great Britain*. Part of the gable between the two main western towers

HENRY VII'S CHAPEL, Westminster Abbey. An early 19th-century engraving showing the magnificent fan-vaulted ceiling (1503–19). The bronze screen in the foreground encloses the tomb of Henry VII and his queen, Elizabeth of York

ground floor, and an entrance and a great hall with smaller contiguous rooms, often including a chapel, on the first floor. The keep is set on one edge of a large area called a bailey, enclosed by a wall and often a moat, where other buildings and quarters were installed, as with the early arrangements of Dover and Windsor.

The 13th century saw the greatest advance in the development of the castle in England. This was chiefly due to a decline in the importance of the keep, and an increase in the defensibility of the enceinte or perimeter wall, which in turn was made possible by the use of towers on the walls and at the gates. Framlingham, in Suffolk, is an early (13th-century) example of a castle with wall towers. The castle as a whole took on a looser, more rambling quality than previously, and became more like the open layout of a palace. The finest examples of this new stage are found in Wales, as at Caerphilly, Harlech and Beaumaris. The use and enlargement of wall and gate towers reaches such a pitch in this group that it is almost possible to see them as a series of keeps multiplied at intervals around the bailey wall.

There is another way in which one can express this 13th-century development. The keep expands, creating a well and then a courtyard in its centre, and finally evolves into a perimeter on which the old corner turrets become enceinte towers. This results in a symmetrical plan, as at Beaumaris. This type of plan, symmetrical or otherwise, remained the standard of good castle building throughout the period—for example, the late 14th-century Kenilworth, Warwickshire—blurring the difference between military and non-military architecture.

### SCULPTURE: SHARP TRANSITIONS

The dependence of carving on the minor arts, particularly manuscript illumination, is much less marked in these centuries than in the Anglo-Saxon and Norman periods. This is partly indicated by the fact that there was a much sharper transition in sculpture between Romanesque and Gothic than there was in illumination.

Once again, as with church architecture, it is to the Ile de France (the area around Paris) that one must look for the source of inspiration. The portal of Rochester Cathedral, Kent (c. 1170), makes use of the columnar figures used at St Denis and Chartres around 1140.

The revolution carried through at Notre Dame in Paris in the first decade of the 13th century changed Early Gothic into High Gothic—that is, into the style which was going to dominate Gothic figure sculpture until its end. But High Gothic did not make an impact on England until 70 years later, for example in the Angel Choir at Lincoln. This chunky style of sculpture itself soon turned into something elegant and very decorative—for example in the tombs of Edmund Crouchback and Aymer de Valence in Westminster Abbey. Sometimes it is almost frivolous, like the tomb of Edward II in Gloucester Cathedral (1330's). All medieval sculpture was painted in some way or another, which meant a heyday for the decorator. The popularity of small alabaster plaques is a manifestation of the same trend.

RICHARD THE LIONHEART, a statue from the late 15th-century choir-screen at York Minster. One of several Gothic statues depicting a few of the earlier kings of England

## PAINTING: FROM RIGIDITY TO REALISM

The Early Gothic style, from the late 12th to the late 13th century, began, like sculpture, by using a short figure covered in fairly heavy drapery with many folds, and with a well modelled head. Scrolls and other decorative details were still coiled and organised, betraying little of the slight shift towards naturalism made in the figures. The change is nicely illustrated by the superb illuminations of the *Winchester Bible* (c. 1170), in which the artist known as the Master of the Leaping Figures epitomises the extremes of Late Romanesque design, while the style of the Master of the Morgan Leaf is Early Gothic. This style continued in England until the turn of the century, and is also represented by such masterpieces as the British Museum manuscripts of Bede's *Life of St Cuthbert*, and the *Westminster Psalter*. It was at this time and in this medium of illumination that England and many other countries contributed most to a development which was otherwise chiefly French.

In the 13th century this tight, restrained style gave way to something much looser, made up of tall, willowy figures clothed in fine, loose-fitting garments. Good examples of this new style are the *Evesham Psalter* (British Museum), the *Guthlac Roll* (British Museum) and the work of William of Malmesbury. Decorative work of the period still retains a pre-Gothic liveliness.

The century from c. 1270–1370 was characterised by two changes. The tightness of detail was loosened up, so that foliage, for example, moved away from pure design towards naturalism; and there was an increase in the sumptuousness of the decoration (for instance, backgrounds of tooled gold, or small painted repeat patterns), and in the figures themselves, which became almost unbelievably elegant and refined.

This change from Early to High Gothic took place in England during the reign of Henry III (1216–72), just as that reign saw the introduction of High Gothic architecture at Westminster. The change is found in the *Oscott Psalter*, the *de Lisle Psalter* (both British Museum), and the Sion Cope (Victoria and Albert Museum).

Towards the middle of the 14th century there is some evidence of the infiltration of Italian motifs and formulae. This last point is symptomatic of something happening throughout Europe at this time. Countries north of the Alps were being introduced to the intricacies, delights and hazards of the Italian artists' representation of space; while Italy was being educated in the northern traditions of everyday realism and aristocratic flamboyance and manners. The result of this inter-penetration was the emergence, around 1400, of an 'international' style, so-called because of the similarity of its products in different parts of Europe. One of the finest English examples is the *Wilton Diptych* (National Gallery, London).

Parallel to the exploration of space in the international style ran a desire to create scenes with groups of figures, and an interest in portraiture, as exemplified by the portrait of Richard II (1490's) in Westminster Abbey. This makes an interesting comparison with younger and older versions of the same monarch in the *Wilton Diptych* and on the king's tomb in the same abbey.

ILLUMINATED LETTER from a 13th-century manuscript. Certain initial letters were enlarged and embellished with decorative details, in brilliant colour-work. Their treatment was often descriptive of the text

GOTHIC ILLUMINATION from the Evesham Psalter, c. 1250. On this page a tiny figure of the Benedictine abbot, to whom the book belonged, kneels at the foot of the cross

# Tudor and Jacobean

*The adventurers and nobles enriched by Henry VIII and Elizabeth began the English country house tradition, and were lavish patrons of the arts*

In 1509 Henry VIII was crowned king in succession to his father, Henry VII, the founder of the Tudor line. Eighteen years old, with unusual talents of body and brain, he became the patron both of sportsmen and of the men of the New Learning, the Renaissance, which was stirring the universities to a new and vigorous life. Henry was a champion at tennis and a fearless hunter; and his great suit of tilting armour in the Tower of London recalls his exploits in the lists. He was an accomplished musician, and fostered music and poetry at his Court.

In the early days of his reign, Henry employed Cardinal Wolsey as Chancellor and virtual ruler of England. Wolsey flaunted his pride and power in the face of king and nobles, helping to prepare the anti-Church revolution that eventually dissolved the monasteries and dispersed many of their treasures. Wolsey was enormously rich from Church revenues—some said almost as rich as the king. He kept a household of 1000 persons and marched in state with silver pillars borne before him. Wolsey's munificence left its mark on English architecture. Under his patronage Italian architects, painters and sculptors were brought over to assist with two great palaces, Hampton Court and York House (later Whitehall Palace). He endowed Cardinal College (later demolished) at Ipswich, and Cardinal College, now Christ Church, Oxford. Being too rich and powerful, Wolsey was inevitably deposed (1529). Henry VIII, wealthy from confiscations from the Church, became a hectic trendsetter in building for the last 20 years of his reign. He made vast extensions to his London palaces at Hampton Court, Whitehall and St James's. A fantastic palace at Nonsuch, Surrey, later destroyed, was built in direct emulation of the châteaux of the French king.

After the fall of Wolsey, Henry cut England off from Rome and proclaimed himself supreme head of the Church. From 1536 to 1539 he dissolved the monasteries, wrecking the ancient buildings and appropriating their wealth. He brought the clergy and their monies into subservience to the Crown. This seizing of monastic lands meant the biggest change in land-ownership since 1066. Much of the Church property was distributed among Henry's courtiers. Monasteries fell into ruin, became national cathedrals, or were cleared away to have country houses erected on the sites.

When Henry VIII died in 1547, his young son, delicate in health and only nine years old, became Edward VI (1547–53), and the Crown was immediately beset by factions of grasping nobles. Years of strife and upset

ELIZABETH I on her way to Blackfriars. Each year the Queen journeyed throughout the kingdom. In the hope of winning her favour, wealthier subjects built splendid houses in which to entertain her

followed. Protector Somerset, the king's uncle, pushed ahead with the sacking of the guilds and chantries, mostly for his own private interest. Out of his share of the loot the original Somerset House (now destroyed) rose on the banks of the Thames. The royal finances collapsed. As a result, the Crown did not re-establish its role as arbiter of the arts until James I came to the throne in 1603. Instead, this role passed to newly ennobled government officials.

It was these men, many owning land snatched from the monasteries, who sponsored the arts in the years to come. Often building on stolen land with stones from ruined abbeys, they raised the great mansions of Elizabethan and Jacobean England—among them Burghley House, Northamptonshire, Hatfield House, Hertfordshire, Hardwick Hall, Derbyshire, and Audley End, Essex. These were the houses of the new rich—arrogant, bold and spectacular.

From Edward VI's reign onwards ran a strong anti-art current. The Protestant reformers ordered all sculpted or painted religious images to be removed, and the churches whitewashed. This meant the mass destruction of medieval art, and all forms of art came to be regarded with suspicion. On Edward's death, the Crown passed to his Catholic sister Mary (1553-8), whose reign ended in disaster. Although she restored ordered government, she also restored the Catholic faith, began the persecution of Protestants, made an unpopular marriage with Philip of Spain, and lost the war with France, and with it Calais, the English bridgehead on the Continent.

But waiting in Hatfield, Hertfordshire, eager to assume the Crown, was the last and most brilliant of Henry VIII's children, Elizabeth. She was to lead the English back to harmony and prosperity; and on to fresh areas of domination. Foreign artists imbued with Renaissance ideas had attended the court of Henry VIII, and in Elizabeth's reign more were to come. Flemish and German craftsmen settled in the eastern counties, where they influenced the style of the new mansions; and the persecution of Protestants by the Duke of Alva in the Low Countries in the 1560's drove skilled craftsmen to England.

NONSUCH PALACE, Surrey, was the most ambitious building ever undertaken by Henry VIII. It was demolished c. 1860. Contemporary drawings show that it was planned around two courtyards and was lavishly ornamented by foreign craftsmen

The legendary Elizabethan age was one of intellectual brilliance, and of immense commercial prosperity. When Elizabeth died in 1603, Burghley's son, Robert Cecil, saw to it that her cousin James Stuart of Scotland, styled King James VI and I, should succeed smoothly to the throne. The Stuarts brought England into closer touch with the Continent, especially with France and Italy. James I, inept as he was at politics, was a scholar. Through his art-loving wife, Anne of Denmark, he became the pupil of Inigo Jones, the great English architect who was to change the course of architecture and art in England.

The men of Tudor and Jacobean times produced their artistic triumphs almost in spite of themselves. Trouble and upset at home and the anti-art campaign of the Reformers and later of the Puritans cut England adrift from the Continent, where the Renaissance was flourishing in almost every country. The suppression of the visual arts meant that painting was confined to portraits, sculpture to tombs, and building to dwelling-houses.

BURGHLEY HOUSE,
Northamptonshire. One of
the finest houses of the early
Renaissance period in England,
it was formerly the home
of Lord Burghley, Elizabeth I's
minister of state. His design
consultant was the Dutch
architect 'Master Henryk'

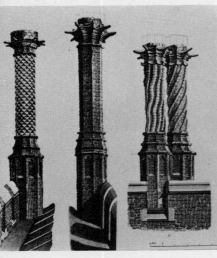

BRICK CHIMNEYS came into
general use early in the 16th
century and were one of the
most characteristic features of
the Tudor house. Often
elaborately carved and
decorated, they offered the
bricklayers the chance to
exploit newly acquired skills

## ARCHITECTURE: THE AGE OF THE COUNTRY HOUSE

Architecturally, the Tudor period (1485-1603) might be
called the age of the country house, because it is at this
time that the country house first emerged as an architectural form. Church building had virtually ceased with
the Reformation, and energies were centred on new
houses.

Tudor architecture, and the Tudor house in particular,
still retained overtones of Gothic from the previous
century, and some of its characteristics persisted until the
middle of the 17th century. Most Tudor houses were still
built round a quadrangular court entered from under a
gate-house. Fortified gateways, grand courtyards, battlemented parapets, towers and turrets lingered on for
ornament rather than defence; and ornamented chimneys
signified comfort within. The hall became a symbol of
grandeur: money and artistic skill were lavished on its
carved fire-places, oak-panelled walls and timber roofs.

Hampton Court, on the outskirts of London, is a
famous surviving example. The original part of the
palace, built of mellow red brickwork in diaper (diamond) pattern, has battlemented parapets, a turreted
gate-house, many courtyards and ornamented chimneys.
The great hall of Henry VIII is its main feature. Later in
Henry VIII's reign, the new Classicism of the Renaissance
came to England from France. Nonsuch Palace, Surrey
(now destroyed), was an embodiment of the new style.

From the death of Henry VIII in 1547 until c. 1570
architecture followed a confused path. The troubles of
the middle years of the century were not conducive to
the long, peaceful task of raising great buildings. Classical
detail, which came to England from France, continued
to be superimposed on Tudor Gothic. Somerset House
(now destroyed) in the Strand, begun in 1547, represented
the first attempt to build a complete Classical façade.

The tradition of French Classicism lingered with some
vitality in Burghley House, Northamptonshire, which
was built by Lord Burghley in the French manner in the
1560's. But already a new influence can be seen at work
there, promoted by Burghley's friend, Sir Thomas
Gresham. Gresham imported from Antwerp a Classicism
more flamboyant than the French style, overladen with
bulbous detail, such as caryatids (female figures used as
pillars), cartouches or scroll ornaments, and strapwork.

After these stops and starts, English architecture quite
suddenly, c. 1570, ceased to be derivative and set out
on a different, startling path. Two great houses epitomise
this. Kirby Hall, in Northamptonshire, now a fairly
intact ruin, was built for Sir Humphry Stafford by John
Thorpe; from its courtyard giant pilasters soar upwards
almost to the skyline. Longleat, Wiltshire, was remodelled from 1573 onwards for Sir John Thynne as the
first spectacular instance of the lantern house—a glisten-
ing acreage of glass and bay windows. These houses of
the 1570's achieve their effects by superimposing Classical
detail on a basically restrained architectural shell.

About 1580 architecture took another course. It rejected the Classical and turned back in time to the glories
of the English Perpendicular style. The effects aimed at by
the builders of King's College Chapel, Cambridge, were

developed in late Elizabethan and Jacobean houses: height, huge windows and a distinctive, striking skyline.

Architects did not really exist as a professional group before Inigo Jones at the beginning of the 17th century. But if any two men may be singled out as superb exponents and creators of a style, it would be Robert Smythson and his son John. Their work, beginning with Robert's Longleat in the 1570's, includes some of the greatest examples of the neo-medieval castle style: Woolaton Hall, Nottinghamshire (1580-8), for Sir Francis Willoughby; Robert Smythson's Hardwick Hall, Derbyshire (1590-7), for Bess of Hardwick, the Countess of Shrewsbury; and John Smythson's Bolsover Castle, Derbyshire (begun 1612), for Sir Charles Cavendish.

These epitomise what the Elizabethans most desired in their buildings. They are impressive, almost melodramatic in their setting, often sited on hill-tops. They rise to a great height, penetrating the skyline in a riot of carved brick and stone, crenellation, balustrading, chimneys and cupolas. Their startling effect is enhanced by symmetry, and by acres of glass, making them lanterns of light twinkling in the sun across the countryside.

ALABASTER MEMORIAL, Elmley Castle. A 17th-century alabaster memorial to William Savage and his wife, Katherine, holding their baby son. Like most other effigies of the period it probably depicts the family as they were in their prime rather than at the time of death

## SCULPTURE: SUMPTUOUS TOMBS

The feverish pace at which the Tudors built was not carried over into their sculpture, which existed only as a complement to building. Sculptors were artificers, employed to overlay and garnish a building, or to carve a tomb with recumbent effigies. They did not sculpt portraits, busts or mythological groups, as in Italy.

Tudor sculpture opened with a brief, spectacular flirtation with Renaissance Italy in the person of Pietro Torrigiano, who worked for the young Henry VIII. The moving effigies on the tombs of Henry VII, his wife Elizabeth of York, and his mother Margaret Beaufort (in Westminster Abbey) represent this fleeting moment. The hands of the aged Lady Margaret, wrinkled and old, laid on each other in prayer, and her tranquil face, are typical of Torrigiano's talents of characterisation.

English sculpture sank back into the rut of the engaging second-rate. Endless tombs were produced, to proclaim for all time the glory of the new gentry. They lie there, with hands clasped, sumptuously dressed and flanked by coats of arms. Near by kneel figures of children ranging downwards in size; and a laudatory epitaph, offset only by skulls, crossbones and bubbles, reminds the spectator that life is transitory. Beautiful examples of this style are the Hoby family tombs at Bisham, Berkshire; the tomb of Robert Cecil, Lord Salisbury, at Hatfield, Hertfordshire; that of Henry, Lord Norris, in Westminster Abbey; and that of Lady Carey at Church Stowe, Northamptonshire.

SIR THOMAS MORE, in the style of Holbein. A political philosopher, humanist and author of the famous *Utopia* (1516), More steadfastly refused to recognise Henry VIII's claim to be head of the church; he was executed at the Tower in 1535

## PAINTING: HOLBEIN AND THE MINIATURISTS

Painting in Renaissance England began quite abruptly with the arrival of a foreigner, the German Hans Holbein the Younger, who lived in England from 1527 to 1529 and from 1531 to 1543. He brought with him all the discoveries of the high Renaissance in Italy: skill in perspective and illusionism, knowledge of Classical antiquity and an acuteness of psychological observation.

Holbein was welcomed by Sir Thomas More, the foremost exponent of the New Learning, and was later patronised by Henry VIII. His style enables us to visualise, by means of his sublime portrait drawings at Windsor Castle, the burly toughs and tight-lipped beauties of Henry VIII's court.

Hans Eworth, an exile from Flanders, was the only painter of any stature to work during the troubled middle years of the century. His portrait called *Mary I* (Fitzwilliam Museum, Cambridge) betrays Holbein's influence.

So, too, does Nicholas Hilliard (1547-1619), Queen Elizabeth I's miniaturist. His is a delicate, flower-coloured world. In an oval the size of a gull's egg, he captures the great Elizabethans: the haughty queen; proud, pouting Leicester; or romantic, curly-headed Raleigh (all in the National Portrait Gallery). Hilliard produced one of the masterpieces of English art, the *Young Man among Roses* (Victoria and Albert Museum).

NICHOLAS HILLIARD miniature (1576) of Robert Dudley, Earl of Leicester. Miniatures were painted on the backs of playing-cards or sheets of vellum, until the superior quality of ivory was discovered in the 18th century

By the turn of the century Hilliard was becoming old-fashioned, and the court took up a new romanticism purveyed in miniature by Isaac Oliver (*c.* 1565-1617) and, larger, by his brother-in-law, Marcus Gheeraerts the Younger (*c.* 1561-1636). Gheeraerts's masterpiece is at Woburn Abbey, Bedfordshire. It is a portrait of Elizabeth's last favourite, Essex, pensive in white and silver against a background landscape. Oliver's large miniature of Lucy Harington, Countess of Bedford, enveloped in billowing gauze veils (Fitzwilliam Museum), is a small-scale counterpart to Gheeraerts's Essex.

## DECORATIVE ARTS: EMBROIDERY AND ARMOUR

In the Middle Ages, England had been famous for her embroidery, and in the reign of Elizabeth there was a remarkable revival of this art. But now it was no longer applied to vestments as in medieval times, but to curtains, bed hangings, tablecloths, cushions and costume. Hardwick Hall, Derbyshire, houses embroideries which are wonderful in the invention of their design.

Little English jewellery survives from this period, but where it does, as in the Armada Jewel (Victoria and Albert Museum), it is exquisite. This is said to have been presented by Queen Elizabeth to Sir Thomas Heneage on the defeat of the Armada in 1588. Vast quantities of silver plate still exist—nefs (silver boats), tazzas (saucer-shaped cups mounted on a foot) and standing cups (British Museum and Victoria and Albert Museum).

In Elizabeth's reign handsome suits of decorated armour were produced, in which her knights would joust in her honour; these can still be seen in the Tower of London.

In Elizabeth's reign, also, tapestry was woven in England for the first time, under the auspices of the Sheldon family of Weston, Warwickshire. Some can be seen at the Victoria and Albert Museum. Hatfield House, too, has a splendid set of tapestries of the Four Seasons.

SUIT OF ARMOUR designed for Sir Henry Lee. From *The Jacobe Album* (1489). The book catalogued the various designs built at the Royal Armouries, Greenwich, during the Tudor reigns of Queen Mary and Queen Elizabeth

# The Stuarts

*The first half of the Stuart period (1625-1714) was dominated by the art of Van Dyck; the second half by the architecture of Wren*

The arts flourished in the early years of Charles I's reign (1625-49), for they were an essential accompaniment to 17th-century absolute monarchy, when the grandeur of princes and aristocracy was measured by the magnificence of their art collections.

When the Crown fell, the arts declined into decadence. The 11 years of the Commonwealth (1649-60), when England was ruled by an oligarchy of republicans, are of little importance in the history of the arts in England. Cromwell's rule as Lord Protector (1653-8) was a virtual dictatorship, with army officers controlling the country. It was not until after Cromwell's death in 1658, and after the short rule of his son Richard, when the Stuarts returned to the throne in 1660 on a wave of popularity, that the arts began to revive.

Charles II made every effort to put the clock back to the gay, carefree days of the 1630's. Theatres reopened, racing started at Newmarket, clothes blossomed out into ruffles and ribbons, and there was ribaldry and excess. Charles's brother, James II, who succeeded to the throne in 1685, had to flee the country in 1688 for promoting the interests of his Catholic supporters. The 'Glorious Revolution' of 1688 set on the throne William of Orange, Stadtholder of the Netherlands, and his wife Mary, James II's daughter, and established Parliamentary monarchy. Under William and Mary, and their successor Queen Anne (1702-14), Britain gained a political and constitutional equilibrium never again upset.

Charles I accumulated an art collection which, if it had survived intact, would have made England the greatest single repository of Renaissance art in the world. Its sale under the Commonwealth was a horrifying artistic tragedy. Now its treasures lie scattered over the great galleries of Europe and America; but enough remains here to evoke some idea of its spectacular opulence. Charles's collection included, for instance, the Mantegna cartoons (Hampton Court), the Leonardo sketchbooks (Windsor Castle), the Raphael cartoons (Victoria and Albert Museum), and the Wilton Diptych (National Gallery).

Charles I was not only an avid collector, but an enthusiastic and discerning patron who wanted England to be in the forefront of artistic taste and achievement. For this reason he welcomed to England Rubens and Van Dyck to put new life into painting, and the sculptors Le Sueur and Fanelli to civilise our lumpish provincial sculpture; and he entrusted the *décor* of the Court, both architectural and theatrical, to the genius of Inigo Jones.

QUEEN HENRIETTA MARIA by Van Dyck. She was the youngest daughter of Henri IV of France, and queen consort of Charles I. An obstinate woman, her zealous Catholicism did little to help her husband throughout a difficult reign

CHARLES II as a boy-commander, by William Dobson (1610-46), who succeeded Van Dyck as Court painter. Dobson was one of the first English artists of this period to achieve distinction

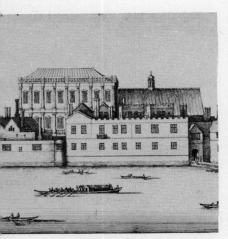

THE BANQUETING HOUSE, Whitehall, is considered to be Inigo Jones's masterpiece. Built as the first stage of a larger palace, which was never completed because of the Civil War, it cost £15,000. The ceiling-panels in the Banqueting Hall were painted by Rubens

CHURCH OF ST MARY-LE-STRAND in London, from an 18th-century water-colour. This building was the first important commission by James Gibbs, a pupil of Sir Christopher Wren, after a protracted tour of study in Italy as a young man

Outside the Court was another great patron and collector, the Earl of Arundel. His antique marbles (Ashmolean Museum, Oxford) give a clue to the quality of his collection, as does Holbein's portrait of Erasmus, the remarkable painting now at Longford Castle, Wiltshire.

After the disruption of the Commonwealth, the Court never quite re-established its position as arbiter of the arts. Charles II and James II, with their Catholic-biased Courts, promoted French baroque in emulation of Louis XIV's palace at Versailles, while Dutch William III brought a flavour of Holland to Hampton Court, with bulbs for the garden and Delftware pottery for the house. Only at the end of the period, in Queen Anne's reign, was there a revival of artistic patronage on the grand scale, when vast baroque palaces were built for the Whig aristocracy by Vanbrugh and Hawksmoor.

The 17th century was a time of disruption and change, and it failed to produce a single, settled standard of taste. But art acquired a status: it became not only respectable but fashionable. Artists, and in particular painters, ceased to be regarded as tradespeople, as they were in Elizabethan days, and became gentlemen. Knighthoods were bestowed on Van Dyck, Lely and Kneller.

The educated upper classes took an acute interest in the arts. The diaries of Samuel Pepys and John Evelyn are full of references to painting, sculpture and architecture. Artistic theory came second-hand through translations from the French and Italian; but by the close of the period Shaftesbury's book *Characteristicks* had launched the notion of a national school of British art. This resulted in the campaign for an academy, a plan that reached fruition three generations later when the Royal Academy was founded in 1768.

### ARCHITECTURE: THE AGE OF INIGO JONES AND WREN

The most important single figure in 17th-century English art was Inigo Jones (1573-1652). He was the judge and dictator of taste at the Stuart Court of James I and Charles I for over 20 years. He was a collector and antiquarian, a connoisseur of painting and antiquities. He designed the fantastic stage designs for the Court ballets (now at Chatsworth House, Derbyshire), as well as being England's foremost architect.

Inigo Jones had worked in Italy and was deeply influenced by Classical tradition and its revival in Renaissance building in Italy. In particular, he admired the work of the 16th-century Venetian architect, Palladio, and introduced into England the new Italianate Classical styles, later called Palladian.

Jones began a revolution: the Banqueting House in Whitehall (1620-35), with its severely Classical façade— tall windows, pediments, columns all strictly symmetrical—arose in the midst of the shambling, black and white timbered houses of Stuart London; his Queen's House in Greenwich (begun 1616), a Venetian villa in the Palladian manner, was built astride the main Deptford-Woolwich Road. Inigo Jones's work and influence affected the whole course of architecture in England. English country houses of the mid-17th century were enlivened by architectural features based on Inigo Jones's work. At the Restoration in 1660, English architects had at last to come to terms with the prevailing European style, the baroque—exemplified particularly by Louis XIV's great palace at Versailles, which inspired Charles II's own artistic taste. The story of art and architecture in the second half of the 17th century is the attempt to adapt the baroque idiom to English taste.

This was crystallised in the career of Sir Christopher Wren (1632-1723), who rebuilt 51 City churches and St Paul's Cathedral after the Great Fire of London in 1666. He was enormously ingenious in planning buildings on cramped sites; and the interiors of some—St Stephen's, Walbrook, especially—are particularly noble.

Under the later Stuarts, Wren worked on frustrating palace projects—Whitehall, Greenwich, Kensington and Hampton Court. Fragments of the last three remain. Greenwich (begun 1694) is his secular masterpiece. Grand blocks form narrowing courtyards which, when viewed from the Thames, lead the eye to Inigo Jones's Queen's House. St Paul's Cathedral, built between 1675 and 1710, is his ecclesiastical masterpiece. In it Wren fulfilled his own creed that 'the glory of that which is good of itself is eternal'.

While Wren was not fundamentally a domestic architect, his followers, Nicholas Hawksmoor (1661-1736) and Sir John Vanbrugh (1664-1726), were particularly interested in great houses. They often worked as a team and developed a more flamboyant, openly baroque style than that of Wren.

INIGO JONES (1573-1651) His brilliant career as an architect at Court was brought to an end by the start of the Civil War. He was imprisoned and forced to pay a heavy fine for being a 'courtier', and died in poverty at the age of 79

## SCULPTURE: ECHOES FROM ITALY

English sculpture throughout the 17th century remained a provincial echo of the great stylistic movements that emanated from Italy. Not that effort was lacking: for Charles I imported foreign sculptors, as well as a hoard of antique statues, to inspire a new generation of artists. But the Frenchman Hubert Le Sueur and the Italian Fanelli did not approach the stature of a Van Dyck. Le Sueur's statue in Trafalgar Square of Charles I on horseback reflects the fairly low level they achieved.

Towards the close of the century Caius Gabriel Cibber and Grinling Gibbons adopted a modified baroque style. The only real sculptural glory of the century was achieved by Gibbons and his followers in their development of wood carving (choir stalls of St Paul's Cathedral, and panelling at Hampton Court). Inspired by Dutch still-life painting, their swags of flowers, fruit, birds and trophies transformed interior decoration.

OLIVER CROMWELL An 18th-century bust by Joseph Wilton, reflecting the reputed sternness of the Lord Protector. Although neither cruel nor tyrannical by nature, Cromwell had a repressive influence on the arts from which they only recovered after the Restoration

## PAINTING: A TRIO OF FOREIGNERS

The history of English painting under the Stuarts can be summed up by three artists, all foreigners: Sir Anthony Van Dyck (1599-1641), Sir Peter Lely (1618-80) and Sir Godfrey Kneller (1646-1723). Between them these three painters cover the 100 years from the accession of Charles I in 1625 to the close of George I's reign in 1727.

The style that Van Dyck brought to England in 1632

SIR CHRISTOPHER WREN painted by Sir Godfrey Kneller, Principal Painter to the Court of Charles II. Wren was the first man to be buried in St Paul's; his tomb bears the inscription: *'Lector, si monumentum requirism circumspice.'* (Reader, if you seek a memorial, look about you)

JACOBEAN EMBROIDERY A detail from a mid-17th-century stumpwork fabric. Stumpwork, or 'embossed' work, was an elaborate form of embroidery which used cotton, wool or hair to achieve raised surfaces. Metal or seed-pearls were used for eyes and hands, and faces were carved in wood or wax

was a muted version of that of Rubens, his master, who had painted for Charles I the ceiling of the Whitehall Banqueting House, one of the finest examples of baroque decoration in Europe. But Van Dyck did not import the rubicund, fleshy, almost coarse writhings produced by his master's studio. Instead he studied the gentler mood of English genteel refinement; he turned every vice of character or appearance into a virtue.

Van Dyck's virtuosity of interpretation and skilful handling of paint are displayed at Windsor Castle—in the portrait of Charles I on horseback riding in triumph through a Classical archway; the triple portrait of this sad-faced little man; the hollow-cheeked Queen Henrietta Maria full face and in profile; and, best of all, the royal children grouped in joyous solemnity.

Van Dyck had a successor—William Dobson, the talented Englishman who painted the Civil War courtiers at Oxford. His portrait of Charles II as a boy commander banishing with a gesture of his baton the snake-haired figure of Rebellion (Scottish National Portrait Gallery) catches the mood of this last outburst of Caroline culture.

After the Restoration in 1660 portraiture was dominated by Sir Peter Lely, who fused the bourgeois style of his native Holland with the refinements of Van Dyck. Lely's studio maintained what can only be described as factory production. At his best, as in the burly *Admirals at Greenwich* (National Maritime Museum), or the *Beauties* (Hampton Court), he was capable of considerable spiritedness; fundamentally he was a superficial recorder of external appearances.

To visualise the Restoration court in depth, it is better to ignore the acreage of Lely and concentrate on the inches of Samuel Cooper (1609-72). Influenced apparently by Rembrandt, Cooper rendered the heavy-lidded ladies and thick-lipped gentlemen with little concern for surface glitter (Victoria and Albert Museum).

Sir Godfrey Kneller, like Lely, maintained a torrential studio production and had a horde of imitators. For 40 years, until his death in 1723, he dominated the scene. The best collection of his portraits is the famous *Kit-Cat Club* series in the National Portrait Gallery.

## DECORATIVE ARTS: TAPESTRY AND EMBROIDERY

The decorative arts were distinguished in the Stuart period by the excellence of their tapestry and embroidery. Furniture and silver, beautiful though they could be, were mere reflections of styles evolved abroad; but English tapestry was an art on its own. In 1620 James I founded a royal tapestry factory at Mortlake. Charles I acquired the Raphael cartoons to inspire these weavers, and examples of their work are in the great houses of England (Belvoir Castle, Leicestershire; Woburn Abbey, Bedfordshire; Chatsworth, Derbyshire).

Surviving embroidery is mostly domestic in character, executed by the children and ladies of the household. The engaging pictorial crudity of these little embroidered pictures and cabinets, worked in coloured silk and metal thread, is in direct contrast to the elegance proclaimed by a Van Dyck or a Lely.

# The Georgian Age

*The reigns of the four Georges, from 1714 to 1830, saw the creation of landscape gardens, the elegance of Georgian houses, and the start of the romantic movement*

The glory of the Georgian age lay in the genius and energy of individuals acting freely, in a community ruled by law and Parliament, not despotism—such men as Wolfe, Clive, Cook, Wellington and Nelson among the soldiers and sailors; Swift, Johnson, Fielding and Wordsworth among the writers; Hogarth, Gainsborough and Blake among the artists; and Handel, Wesley and Watt in music, religion and scientific discovery. The aesthetic principles underlying the arts in this age of rising prosperity and great political families are reflected in its most characteristic achievement, the landscape garden (Stowe, Buckinghamshire; Stourhead, Wiltshire). Gardens were intended to appear natural and irregular, reflecting the 18th-century love of freedom; but in practice they were carefully contrived. Modelled on the landscape paintings of the 17th-century French artist, Claude, they evoked memories of Classical antiquity by means of carefully placed temples and busts. They also aroused feelings of sentiment and melancholy by means of specially built Gothic ruins.

The taste for the elaborate asymmetry of the rococo style was embodied by Capability Brown in his serpentine paths and lakes; and the 'picturesque' school of the latter part of the century, in which open vistas and rolling acres gave way to concealment and surprise, was a foretaste of the romantic and exotic movement which characterised the arts at the end of the Georgian era.

The symbol of Georgian wealth and power was the country mansion, set in acres of carefully landscaped parkland. In order to maintain their status, great landowners felt compelled to live, build and furnish ostentatiously. The state rooms in great houses were designed principally for show, and there were open days when visitors were encouraged to view and admire. Many aristocrats, such as Lord Leicester (Holkham Hall, Norfolk) and Lord Chesterfield (Chesterfield House, London), devoted much of their energy to improving their houses; and some, like Lord Burlington (Chiswick House, and the Assembly Rooms at York) and Lord Pembroke (the Palladian Bridge at Wilton House) even became amateur architects.

Taste was based principally upon the arts and civilisation of Italy and of Classical antiquity. It was customary for the nobility to complete their education with two or three years of travel on the Continent. They were taken to archaeological sites, and to artists' studios, where they bought Classical sculptures, paintings by Canaletto and Pannini, and copies of famous pictures by other artists.

TIMES OF DAY—NOON One of a series of four satirical engravings by William Hogarth (1697-1764), illustrating the uninhibited life of the London streets. The church is St Giles-in-the-Fields

HUNTING SCENE Detail from a landscape by George Stubbs (1724-1806). A great landed aristocrat, the 3rd Duke of Richmond, hunts at Goodwood, surrounded by his retainers

The experience of the Grand Tour led to the foundation in 1734 of the Dilettanti Society, whose membership was confined to those who had been to Italy, and had a general interest in archaeology. The discovery of ancient Herculaneum (near Naples) in 1738, of Baalbek (Lebanon) and Palmyra (Syria) in 1751, and of Pompeii in 1763, and the lavish publications that followed, had an immediate influence on taste and design.

Much of the Classical sculpture bought by 18th-century collectors was fancifully 'restored' by the trade in Rome, but much also was of fine quality. Special sculpture galleries were built in country houses; examples survive intact at Holkham Hall, Norfolk, and at Newby Hall, Yorkshire. Most of the sculpture was Roman; Greek sculpture was little known until the sculptures from the Parthenon (the Elgin Marbles) were bought for the nation in 1816.

ROYAL ACADEMY, 1771 Detail from a work by the mezzotint engraver Richard Earlom (1743–1822), showing prospective buyers of pictures. The bulky figure may be Dr Johnson

Some early 18th-century aristocrats, like Lord Burlington and the Duke of Chandos, had Italian painters to decorate their houses: Amigoni, a Venetian, did fine work for the duke at Moor Park, Hertfordshire. But the taste for painted wall decoration was in decline, and most patrons concentrated on buying old masters in the grand manner—history paintings by Poussin and the Bolognese followers of Raphael, or landscapes by Claude.

Lord Spencer furnished Spencer House, London, with dramatic paintings by Salvator Rosa and Guercino (now at Althorp, Northamptonshire). Other collections in this taste which still exist were formed by Paul Methuen (Corsham Court, Wiltshire) and Sir Nathaniel Curzon (Kedleston Hall, Derbyshire).

With so many rich collectors vying for the best pictures, the art trade in London expanded enormously. Auction rooms were opened: Sotheby's was founded in 1744 and Christie's in 1766. For some enthusiasts like the portrait painters Jonathan Richardson and Sir Thomas Lawrence, collecting drawings became a passion; others collected prints.

An increasing number of middle-class collectors bought pictures and works of art. Charles Jennens, Handel's friend, collected Dutch pictures rather than Italian, in addition to the work of his own countrymen, such as Hogarth; while Jonathan Tyers commissioned Francis Hayman to paint the decorations for Vauxhall Gardens. But this patronage of British painters was uncharacteristic. While British cabinet-makers and silversmiths were widely patronised, in painting only documentary work, portraits, country house views and sporting pictures were commissioned from British artists.

It was not until the end of the century, when the country was fighting Napoleon, that any systematic encouragement of native painting was attempted. The British Institution, which organised exhibitions and awarded prizes, was started in 1805, and collections of British painting and sculpture were formed by Sir J. F. Leicester, Sir George Beaumont, the friend of Constable, and Lord Egremont, the friend of Turner (whose collection may still be seen at Petworth, Sussex).

Patronage and taste under the Georges followed a succession of different fashions. French rococo style

DESIGN BY WILLIAM KENT This pen and ink wash drawing is the design for a side table at Houghton Hall, Norfolk. Kent was an outstanding personality of the Palladian school, and under the patronage of Lord Burlington became the fashionable architect of the 1730's and 1740's. The drawing is dated 1731

began to affect all the decorative arts around 1740, and there was a craze for *chinoiserie*, especially influential in architecture, furniture and gardening, during the 1750's. The feeling for Gothic, stimulated by Horace Walpole's house, Strawberry Hill, Twickenham, was more significant for the future, and reflected a growing interest in British antiquities. The Society of Antiquaries was founded in 1717, and research was begun into Roman as well as medieval Britain. Certain of the cathedrals, Canterbury for example, were cleaned of grime.

Towards the end of the Georgian period there was a Greek revival, foreshadowed by Stuart and Revett's book *Antiquities of Athens* (published in 1762). The Duke of Northumberland was one of the earliest to form a collection of Egyptian sculpture. The collecting of early Italian painting by William Roscoe, Lord Ashburnham and William Fox-Strangways was a development (like the encouragement of contemporary British art and the Gothic Revival), which was to influence Victorian taste.

## THE RISE OF THE ARCHITECT

Early Georgian architecture was anti-baroque, in revolt against the exuberant style of the end of the 17th century. It took its principles and its forms from three sources: from Classical Rome; from Andrea Palladio, the 16th-century Italian whose treatise on architecture was translated in 1715; and from Inigo Jones, who founded Britain's Renaissance style.

The chief exponents of the early Georgian style were Colin Campbell (*d.* 1729), Lord Burlington (Chiswick House), and William Kent (Holkham Hall, Norfolk, and the Horse Guards, Whitehall). The Palladian style they evolved was noble and finely proportioned but austere and sparing of ornament; and it soon penetrated the whole of English architecture. Manor houses up and down the country, as well as streets in London and elsewhere, were built in the simple, unadorned manner which has come to be accepted as typically Georgian. At this period countless pattern-books appeared laying down the 'correct' methods of designing. For the first time designing became dissociated from practical building, and successful practitioners began to call themselves architects. A new profession had come into being.

The most notable architects of the mid-18th century, Sir Robert Taylor and James Paine, were still working in the Palladian tradition. About 1760, however, two greater men appeared on the scene—Sir William Chambers (Somerset House, London) and Robert Adam (Syon House, Greater London; Kenwood, Hampstead; Newby Hall and Harewood House, Yorkshire; Kedleston Hall, Derbyshire). Although Chambers was Palladian in spirit, he used a variety of other architectural sources —a natural consequence of the spate of discoveries of ancient cities, such as Baalbek in the Lebanon.

These discoveries also led to a more flexible attitude among some later 18th-century architects. James Wyatt, for example, did not mind whether he was required to build in Classical or Gothic. Indian (Royal Pavilion, Brighton), Egyptian and other styles were adopted.

ST MARTIN-IN-THE-FIELDS Wooden model of the church built 1722–6 by James Gibbs (1682–1754). His design for what has been called 'the finest parish church of the Grecian style in England' has been widely copied —especially in America

MARBLE FIRE-PLACE at Kedleston Hall, Derbyshire, by Robert Adam (1728–92). Adam designed the interiors of his houses down to the smallest detail. The white stucco figures were made by Joseph Rose

Adam also made use of the new range of Classical forms, but his attitude towards his borrowings was different from that of Chambers. He discarded Classical proportions and used his sources in a personal and inventive way, primarily for the interior decoration of his houses. Adam usually designed all the furniture and accessories for a house, so that the unity of conception was complete (Harewood House, Yorkshire), and he envisaged an interior as a sequence of carefully contrasted rooms (Syon House, Greater London). Similarly his exteriors were designed to show what he called 'movement'—a constant variety of silhouette and of recession and projection (Kedleston Hall, Derbyshire).

The picturesque and dynamic qualities of Adam's architecture were developed by John Nash (1752–1835). In his masterpiece, Regent Street (now rebuilt) and Regent's Park, he gave a complicated piece of town planning the sweep and movement of a house by Adam, and parts of it, in particular Cumberland Terrace, the magnificence of Vanbrugh's architecture.

The most original architect of the late Georgian period was Sir John Soane (1753–1837) (Soane Museum, Lincoln's Inn Fields, London; and Dulwich College Art Gallery). Simplicity, a return to the first principles of building and the pruning of Classical forms to bare essentials were the main characteristics of his work.

BUST OF ALEXANDER POPE The most brilliant poet and wit of England's Augustan Age wears, appropriately enough, a Roman tunic in this sculpture by Louis François Roubiliac

## SCULPTURE: ROMAN NOBILITY, GREEK ELEGANCE

Georgian sculptors had the same dislike of baroque excess as Georgian architects. They were led by a group of Flemish sculptors, all active in England by 1720: Plumier, Delvaux, Scheemakers and, most notably, Michael Rysbrack (Marlborough Monument, Blenheim Palace). Commissions were mainly for monumental tomb sculpture and for portrait busts, the favoured image of the Georgian landowner, and Rysbrack excelled in both.

Louis François Roubiliac (Argyll Monument, Westminster Abbey), who came to England in 1732, created a considerable sensation with the informal design of his statue of Handel for Vauxhall Gardens (1738). In his busts, which were the finest portraiture of the period, he attempted to catch the idiosyncrasies of the sitter.

The sculpture of the second half of the century was influenced by the recent Classical discoveries. The Roman grandeur of Rysbrack gave way to the Grecian elegance of Nollekens, several of whose tombs are in Westminster Abbey, and to the graceful, flowing style of Thomas Banks; while the linear style of Flaxman derived from a study of Greek vase painting. At the turn of the century the principal commissions were for monuments to national heroes, like Nelson, and for outdoor statues.

MONUMENT TO ISAAC NEWTON The great mathematician, sculpted by Michael Rysbrack, broods within his niche in Westminster Abbey

## PAINTING: NATURALISM AND THE GRAND MANNER

Most of the best painters working in Britain up to this time had been foreigners; and wealthy patrons continued to buy or commission foreign rather than British pictures. In 1711 Sir Godfrey Kneller, famous as a portrait painter at the end of the 17th century, started an academy in

London for training British artists; and the St Martin's Lane Academy was revived by Hogarth in the 1730's.

But it remained difficult for painters to find a market for their work. Hogarth started the idea of putting paintings on show at the Foundling Hospital, of which he was a governor; and they are still to be seen there (Brunswick Square, London). However, it was not until the Society of Artists was founded in 1760 that artists had a regular means of exhibiting their paintings.

William Hogarth (*The Marriage à la Mode*, National Gallery, and numerous examples at the Tate Gallery) was a revolutionary influence in many other ways. In *The Analysis of Beauty* he put forward his own theory that painting should be based on a serpentine line; and he evolved a completely new style of painting designed to appeal to middle-class people. His portraits were primarily likenesses, and he introduced the informal group portrait known as the conversation piece—the most popular of all 18th-century genres. He also painted several series of pictures, of which *The Harlot's Progress* was the first, to foster thrift, honesty and hard work.

SIR JOSHUA REYNOLDS A self-portrait of Reynolds (1723–92) as a young man. The painting shows the vitality and confidence that were his trade-marks

Equally important as an influence on British painting was Sir Joshua Reynolds. He came back to England in 1753 after studying for several years in Italy, and established himself as the only rival to the Scottish artist, Allan Ramsay, then the leading portraitist in London.

Reynolds was as determined as Hogarth to raise the status of the British painter. As first President of the Royal Academy, founded in 1768, he delivered a series of annual discourses to the students, in which he taught that history painting was the most important genre. Though he painted few history pictures himself, since they were difficult to sell, he tried to invest his portraits with the characteristics of the 'great style'. He painted the defender of Gibraltar, Lord Heathfield (National Gallery), against storm-laden clouds, with cannon visible beneath; and based his *Commodore Keppel* (National Maritime Museum, Greenwich) on the *Apollo Belvedere* in the Vatican. He was capable of a more informal style. His *Georgiana, Duchess of Devonshire, and Daughters* (Chatsworth) is an incomparable image of motherly love.

The only contemporary of Reynolds to equal him in greatness was a painter opposite to him in every way, Thomas Gainsborough (1727–88) (*Lady Howe*, Kenwood; numerous examples at the National and Tate Galleries). Where Reynolds always generalised, Gainsborough was best at detail—the silks and satins of a lady's dress, or the glitter of a sword hilt. Gainsborough's real love was for landscape. In an age when villagers were beginning to migrate to factories and mills, he painted nostalgic pastoral landscapes of cows being driven home in the evening, or peasants at a cottage door.

By the later 18th century the public had developed a taste for sentiment. Francis Wheatley's *Cries of London*, showing the picturesque and deserving poor, proved more acceptable than the pungent satire of Hogarth. Among other notable contemporaries of Reynolds was Richard Wilson, a landscapist, whose work shows an unusual sensitivity to light and atmosphere (National Museum of Wales, Cardiff).

TINTERN ABBEY, water-colour by Turner (1775–1851). Romantic ruined abbeys and castles were a favourite subject of Turner's early period, and he exhibited water-colours at the Royal Academy from the age of 15

Other leading artists were George Stubbs, the greatest of all English sporting artists (National Gallery, Tate Gallery, British Museum); and Joseph Wright of Derby, who specialised in industrial subjects like the *Experiment on a Bird in the Air-pump* (Tate Gallery).

John Constable (fully represented at the Victoria and Albert Museum) devoted his life to painting the English countryside. Like Wordsworth, he had an almost religious feeling for landscape, and used effects of light and weather to convey different moods and emotions.

J. M. W. Turner (fully represented at the Tate Gallery) was more interested in the wild, romantic aspects of landscape, and specialised in mountain scenes and storms at sea. He was fascinated by effects of light and colour.

Among other romantic painters of the turn of the century who developed often extravagant stylisations of form were Fuseli, Ward, Martin and Danby. The poet William Blake painted religious subjects in a personal, visionary style. Romantic portraiture, in which the sitter was dramatised more than in the Reynolds tradition, was represented in London by Sir Thomas Lawrence and in Edinburgh by Sir Henry Raeburn. In complete contrast were the colourful, descriptive or genre scenes of David Wilkie (1785-1841), which delighted George IV.

GOD JUDGING ADAM William Blake (1757-1827) was almost unknown to his contemporaries; his profundity was utterly opposed to the cold, Classical spirit of the age. This painting illustrates the visionary power that pervades all his work

## DECORATIVE ARTS: GRANDEUR AND GRACE

Grandeur was the keynote to early Georgian style in the decorative arts. The furniture designed by William Kent for Holkham Hall and Houghton Hall, both in Norfolk, was ornate and richly gilded. Walls were covered with damasks and Genoese velvets. Mahogany was replacing oak; and grand, beautifully carved mahogany furniture, whose ornament derived from architectural features, was made by Vile and Cobb in the middle of the century. Silver and glass, though plain, were solid and well proportioned.

By 1740, French rococo, an exuberant, curvilinear style, was influencing all the decorative arts. Graceful, curling ornament and boldly asymmetrical shapes were characteristic of the silverware of Paul de Lamerie, and the gilded wall brackets and mirrors of Thomas Chippendale. French *bombé* (serpentine) shapes were used for commodes, and colourful twisted ornament decorated the stems of wine glasses. The figurines produced by the Chelsea and Bow porcelain factories marked the quintessence of this gay and often whimsical style.

The Gothic and Chinese designs popular in the 1750's were eagerly absorbed by craftsmen, and Chippendale's famous pattern book *The Gentleman and Cabinet-maker's Directory* (published 1754) included designs for chairs and tables in both tastes. Later in the century Classical shapes and patterns, reflecting the Classical revival, were used in glass and silver, most notably in Wedgwood's pottery.

In furniture, influenced by Adam's style of interior decoration, much of the Classical ornament was painted and gilded. Rosewood, satinwood and inlaid and cross-banded furniture became popular. The elegance and straight lines of Hepplewhite and Sheraton furniture matched the simple interiors of Henry Holland.

TWO LOVERS WITH A BIRDCAGE, Bow porcelain, *c.* 1755. Idealised rustic lovers were a recurring theme in the pottery and painting of the Georgian era

# The Victorian Age

*Material expansion during the 19th century was paralleled by artistic upheavals, as 18th-century gaiety gave way to pious high-mindedness*

The coronation of Queen Victoria in 1837 seemed to represent the dawn of a new golden age. Her accession coincided with the beginning of one of the most dramatic periods of national prosperity in the history of the world. Success in the Napoleonic wars had won for England a long period of peace, enabling her to concentrate her wealth and energy on promoting industry. The spirit of the age had changed, too, from the gay exuberance of the 18th century, with its worship of Classical art and culture, its cynicism and immortality, to a more austere, high-minded and religious outlook.

Queen Victoria saw the passing of the Age of Elegance. Her taste for the landscapes of Landseer and for tartan wallpaper was that of her subjects. Oddly enough, Prince Albert had an enthusiasm for early Italian paintings, although his collection was surpassed by those of William Roscoe (Walker Art Gallery, Liverpool) and Thomas Gambier Parry (Courtauld Institute, London). Paintings by the well established masters of the 16th and 17th centuries continued to be popular.

Palladian architecture, introduced from Italy by Inigo Jones in the 17th century, was thought cold and formal, and portraits by Reynolds and Gainsborough changed hands in the sale-rooms for a few pounds. But a more penetrating artistic judgment led to the growing popularity of Botticelli and the 15th-century masters, and also of William Blake (1757-1827).

Taste in the Victorian age was a matter of personal preference and whim: there were no general rules. For example, Pugin, noted as a church architect, built the enormous Alton Towers, Staffordshire, in flamboyant Gothic style, with a cathedral-type tower, in which Lord Shrewsbury inhabited a single whitewashed cell. John Bowes and Baron Rothschild both had elaborate *palazzi* built (Bowes Museum, Co. Durham, and Waddesdon Manor, Buckinghamshire) to house their enormous collections of art treasures.

## ARCHITECTURE: CLASSICAL VERSUS GOTHIC

In previous centuries architecture had evolved gently along traditional lines. The sudden and enormous material expansion of the 19th century and the far-reaching social effects resulting from the new discoveries —steam, gas and electricity—broke up the traditional pattern of life. In architecture, this break-up was symbolised by the so-called 'Battle of the Styles'. Architects reverted to Classical or Gothic. Classical was a hang-over

THE HOUSES OF PARLIAMENT: Sir Charles Barry's design. The style-setting Gothic building was not completed until after Sir Charles's death in 1860. His design won against competition from 96 other architects

CANNON STREET station, an engraving of 1866. The railway stations, practical and awe-inspiring with their great soaring arches, have been called 'the cathedrals of the 19th century'

from the 18th century; Gothic was influenced by the current feeling for medievalism, particularly in literature.

The Classical style continued to be used for public buildings during the first half of the 19th century. Robert Smirke's British Museum (1823), M. L. Elwes's St George's Hall, Liverpool (1839), and Joseph Hansom's Town Hall, Birmingham (1846) were all based on Greek or Roman originals. The battle between Classical and Gothic was particularly heated over public commissions. Sir Gilbert Scott was forced to change from a Gothic to a Classical plan for the Foreign Office in the 1860's and sold the discarded Gothic plan to be used for St Pancras Station; but the designs of Barry and Pugin for the new Houses of Parliament (1836) had been a decisive victory for the Gothic Revivalists.

The Gothic Revival coincided with a revival of religious fervour. Augustus Welby Pugin, a passionate Christian, sought to build in the true spirit of the past. His churches, such as the Roman Catholic Cathedral (St Chad's), Birmingham, show his complete understanding of Gothic architecture. He also built country houses like Alton Towers, Staffordshire, and Scarisbrick, Lancashire, for the older Catholic gentry. The succeeding generation of neo-Gothic architects attempted to use Gothic in an original way. William Butterfield's All Saints, Margaret Street, London (1849 onwards), with its use of multi-coloured bricks, is a good example.

The dominant Victorian style was neo-Gothic, but this did not prevent architects from turning to other styles when it suited them. Barry built the Reform Club, Pall Mall (1837) in an Italianate Renaissance style, while Anthony Salvin's Harlaxton Manor, Lincolnshire (1837 onwards) is modelled on the Elizabethan Hatfield House. In contrast, the factories and warehouses, the great railway stations, or the iron and steel Crystal Palace, built for the Great Exhibition of 1851, express the practical side of Victorian architecture.

Norman Shaw developed a functional and distinctly modern type of domestic architecture, often based on Dutch and Queen Anne styles. The Bedford Park estate at Turnham Green, London, built in the early 1880's, is a good example of this.

Shaw's successors, Charles Voysey, W. R. Lethaby and the early Edwin Lutyens, worked with simpler outlines and made use of projecting wings. The end of the Victorian era was marked by the abrupt buildings of Charles Rennie Mackintosh, whose masterpiece is the School of Arts and Crafts in Glasgow (1896 onwards).

### SCULPTURE: CHASTITY AND PRETTINESS

Victorian sculpture was generally uninventive. Figure compositions were usually reworkings of outworn Classical themes, suitably draped and chaste to conform with Victorian scruples.

John Gibson, who lived in Rome for most of his life, was perhaps the most dedicated and successful of the imaginative sculptors (*The Tinted Venus* and *The Wounded Warrior*, Royal Academy). There were others who followed his example: E. H. Baily, with *Eve at the*

GOTHIC BEDSTEAD, the epitome of the vulgarity and extravagance so often assumed to be typically Victorian. Shown at the Great Exhibition of 1851. It was probably designed especially for the Exhibition and never actually used

HYLAS AND THE WATER NYMPHS, carved by John Gibson (1790-1866), a sculptor much admired by his contemporaries. He interpreted Classical Greek and Roman themes—rather superficially—and revived the Greek practice of colour tinting sculpture

*Fountain* (Bristol Art Gallery) and Richard Wyatt with his *Glycera* (Royal Collection, Buckingham Palace).

Victorian high-mindedness, coupled with a depressing lack of originality, more often led to works of conventional prettiness. An exception is *Paolo and Francesca* (Birmingham Art Gallery), by Alexander Munro, which was influenced by the Pre-Raphaelites. Alfred Stevens produced a few highly inventive works. His most ambitious sculpture was the unfinished Wellington Monument in St Paul's. The only other sculptor of originality in the second half of the 19th century was Alfred Gilbert (the Queen Victoria Monument, outside St James's Palace), who successfully employed sinuous art nouveau patterns and contrasting materials.

## PAINTING: CONFUSION OF STYLES

The first years of Victoria's reign saw no definite line of painting. It was hoped that the grandiose frescoes, begun in 1845, which decorate the Houses of Parliament would foster a native school of history painting. But Daniel Maclise's *Death of Nelson* and the *Meeting of Wellington and Blucher* are the only frescoes with any power and originality.

The most characteristic Victorian school was that of the genre painting—homely renderings of everyday subjects, an expression of an essentially narrative approach to art. Following the success of Wilkie's (1785-1841) early paintings, like *Blindman's Bluff* (Royal Collection), the genre school reached its zenith in William Frith's great scenes of contemporary life: *Derby Day* (1856-8, Tate Gallery), *Ramsgate Sands* (1851, Royal Collection) and *The Railway Station* (1862, Royal Holloway College).

The Victorian era produced no landscape artist of the stature of Constable or Turner. But most early Victorian landscapes have some narrative interest, like Edwin Landseer's *The Monarch of the Glen* (Royal Collection), or William Collins's *The Reluctant Departure* (Birmingham City Art Gallery), and the Pre-Raphaelites fostered a minutely realistic school of landscape painting. Their influence remained strong until the end of the century. Pure landscape painting was largely confined to watercolour such as the Welsh mountainscapes of David Cox or the East Anglian meadows of Peter de Wint.

The Pre-Raphaelite Brotherhood, founded in 1848 as a protest against current academic painting, made the most original contribution to English art. The member painters' meticulous and jewelled canvases have an intense realism that gives a hallucinatory quality to their romantic subjects. D. G. Rossetti's *Girlhood of St Mary Virgin* (Tate Gallery), Holman Hunt's *Awakening Conscience* (collection of Sir Colin Anderson), and J. E. Millais's *Lorenzo and Isabella* (Walker Art Gallery, Liverpool) are works of real power and imagination. The other-worldly pictures of Burne-Jones, based on medieval and Classical legends, owe much to their example, and there were many other followers.

Not all Victorian painters fell under the Pre-Raphaelite spell. G. F. Watts (1817-1904) painted epic allegorical subjects in the manner of the old masters, like *Hope* (Tate

THE LAST OF ENGLAND, painted in 1855 by Ford Madox Brown. Although not a member of the Pre-Raphaelite Brotherhood, he was clearly under their spell. This painting was inspired by the departure of the sculptor Thomas Woolner for Australia, and Brown used himself, his wife and child as models

THE DAY DREAM, by Dante Gabriel Rossetti (1828-82), founder of the Pre-Raphaelite Brotherhood. The precision of detail builds up a romantic, dream-like world

'IMITATION' ANTIQUE VASES, on show at the Great Exhibition of 1851, and imitating the fine-textured white marble obtained from Paros since the 6th century BC. They are made from a mass-produced biscuit porcelain, and illustrate the Victorian taste for anything that appeared 'antique'

WILLIAM MORRIS wallpaper design. Morris (1834–96) founded a firm of artists producing wallpaper, tapestries, furniture and stained glass. He believed that a work of art could not be beautiful unless the artist had enjoyed making it

Gallery) and *The Horsemen of the Apocalypse* (Walker Art Gallery, Liverpool); while running through the second half of the 19th century is a belated Classical revival led by Frederic, Lord Leighton (*Daedalus and Icarus*, Buscot Park, Berkshire), Edward Poynter (*Faithful unto Death*, Walker Art Gallery, Liverpool) and Alma-Tadema (*The Parthenon Frieze*, Birmingham City Art Gallery). Their work was superseded in the 1860's to 1880's by the new ideas flooding in from France. James McNeill Whistler (examples in Glasgow Art Gallery and Tate Gallery), an American, was the first artist to bring an Impressionist technique to England. He concentrated on tone, colour and atmosphere to the exclusion of narrative.

As a challenge to the conventionalism of the Royal Academy and the literary approach of the Pre-Raphaelites, the New English Art Club was founded in 1886. Outstanding among the original members were Wilson Steer (1860–1942) and Walter Sickert (1860–1942).

## DECORATIVE ARTS: ALL FOR COMFORT

The Great Exhibition of 1851 has fostered the misconception that Victorian decoration was over-elaborate and grotesque. In fact, most of the pieces exhibited there, like J. W. Willcox's massive carved sideboard, which is now at Charlecote Park, Warwickshire, were specially designed for the occasion, and do not represent current styles. Early Victorian furniture was relatively simple: it was only towards the middle of the century that the plush, the curves and the twiddles began to come in. Architects often designed the most elaborate pieces, such as the great cupboards of Norman Shaw, William Burges and J. P. Seddon (Victoria and Albert Museum).

Firms like Garrard's and Elkington's continued the tradition of the great Regency silversmith's; but they produced few exciting or new designs. Pugin's church plate, executed by Hardman's of Birmingham, was of much greater quality and originality than most comparable domestic wares. Pottery and glass both followed traditional patterns. Fabrics became increasingly heavy.

William Morris founded his famous firm, Morris & Co., in 1862, as a protest against ugliness and confusion of style. His own designs for wallpapers, chintzes and tapestries, often based on naturalistic flower or bird motifs, are superbly decorative. To everything he produced, whether fabrics, furniture or stained glass, he brought clarity and simplicity. He had a thorough understanding of the materials he used, and a coherent and articulate decorative sense.

The Arts and Crafts movement, headed by Voysey and Gimson, carried Morris's ideas a stage further. It discarded medieval overtones, and produced designs for objects of all kinds that were austerely linear, using simple contrasting materials. William Godwin's geometric and delicate furniture, Whistler's plain, wash-coloured walls, William de Morgan's simple pottery shapes, decorated with designs and colours from the East—all represent a decisive move towards the 20th century. The art nouveau movement of the 1890's, with its swirling and sensuous shapes, marked the final end of Victorian attitudes.

# The Twentieth Century

*Like their fellows on the Continent, British architects and artists have struggled to keep up with the constant changes of the last half century*

In the 20th century the private patron has given way to patronage by museums and the state—for example, the growing collection of modern art at the Tate Gallery, and the travelling exhibitions organised by the Arts Council. The Tate Gallery especially has played a key part in the appreciation of modern art, both British and foreign. The Tate was founded in 1897 as the national collection of British painting, and in 1915 its scope was widened by Sir Hugh Lane's bequest of foreign paintings. In 1946 the gallery received its first Government grant for buying pictures, and the total annual grant now comes to over £100,000. The Tate is to modern art what the National Gallery is to the art of past centuries.

Dramatic new concepts in science and engineering have been echoed in all the arts to the point where the word 'functional', invented by the architects, can almost be applied to modern art. This continuing contact between art and day-to-day life has led to a reciprocal attitude on the part of industry, which is finding increasing employment for artists. It has also achieved the breaking-down or blurring of the traditional divisions between architecture, painting and sculpture, inasmuch as painting frequently becomes three-dimensional, and sculpture tends to make use of architectural and even mechanical structures. The successful sales of abstract art in the auction-rooms have demonstrated its final acceptance on a wide scale.

LEICESTER UNIVERSITY The Engineering Building by architects Stirling and Gowan (1959-63). The wall in the foreground supports the roof trusses over the laboratory. The ends of the trusses have been developed in a sculptural manner to provide top-lighting over the benches

## ARCHITECTURE: FUNCTIONAL STEEL AND CONCRETE

It was almost 30 years before the new image of 20th-century architecture was accepted in Britain. On the Continent and in America, concrete and steel structures were challenging the skies long before they were accepted here. The Victorians had discovered the advantages of prefabrication and the use of glass as a structural element as early as 1851, in Paxton's Crystal Palace; and slowly steel and concrete began to replace bricks and iron for public buildings. But in spite of this, most architects still looked on Georgian housing as ideal.

The one architect from the turn of the century to stand out from his fellows was Charles Rennie Mackintosh, who designed the Glasgow School of Art, begun in 1897; this rock-like building is remarkable for its bold handling of mass.

In the early years the garden city movement developed in London. It originated in Bedford Park, Chiswick, designed by Norman Shaw in the 1880's, and was emu-

WARWICKSHIRE UNIVERSITY The Benefactors' Building by architects Yorke, Rosenburg and Mardall. A characteristic example of modern design where ornament has been sacrificed in favour of elegant proportions, precise detailing and simplicity of form

lated less successfully in Welwyn Garden City (Louis de Soissons and Arthur W. Kenyon, 1918-20), and in Hampstead Garden Suburb (Lutyens, 1908).

The exciting experiments in functional architecture taking place in Berlin and Vienna were looked on with distrust in Britain. The work of Edwin Lutyens, with its return to a simplified Georgian Classicism, in both public and domestic building, typifies the conservatism of the period (Viceroy's House, Delhi, 1920-31; Deanery Gardens, Sonning, Berkshire).

In the 1930's the influx of architects from Hitlerite Germany left an indelible impression on the British architectural scene. Walter Gropius designed the Village College at Impington, Cambridgeshire; Erich Mendelsohn, in partnership with Serge Chermayeff, designed the De la Warr Pavilion at Bexhill-on-Sea, Sussex; and Marcel Breuer planned a garden city (never built) with F. R. S. Yorke. The new functionalism infiltrated British design, and Maxwell Fry's Frognal House, built in 1936, was a perfect example.

The immediate post-war years showed a widening gulf between the new and old generations of architects. The young men were committed to the idea of the Welfare State, put forward by the 1945 Labour Government, and to the revolutionary theories of Le Corbusier in France, and Mies van der Rohe and Frank Lloyd Wright in America, the use of reinforced concrete and fitness for purpose being the key factors. The older generation looked back to indigenous English themes in architecture.

The major projects of the post-war Government were the new schools and the new towns. Only 50 out of 1000 London schools survived the war; and the low-cost single-unit housing of new town projects created not just dormitory suburbs on the old garden suburb plan, but completely new and distinct townships. Stevenage, Harlow, Crawley and Basildon are examples.

The 20th century has seen four major cathedrals built in Britain. Liverpool Cathedral, the earliest, designed by Sir Giles Gilbert Scott, was begun in 1903 and is still not completed. Guildford Cathedral (begun 1936, consecrated 1961) was designed by Sir Edward Maufe; and after the war Sir Basil Spence designed Coventry Cathedral (consecrated 1962). Most recent is Frederick Gibberd's Roman Catholic Cathedral at Liverpool, built in record time and completed in 1967.

New universities, and new colleges at Oxford and Cambridge, have given great scope to architects in the last few years (St Catherine's, Oxford, by Arne Jacobsen; Leicester University Engineering Building, by Stirling and Gowan; and Sussex University, by Sir Basil Spence.

## SCULPTURE: LEADERS FROM BRITAIN

This century is the first to see a really significant body of sculpture in Britain. The work of Sir Jacob Epstein (1880-1959; Tate Gallery, London; also Birmingham, Manchester, Hull) was never accepted by the public during his lifetime. Before moving to massive, often religious, figure subjects in a rough-hewn expressionist

KING AND QUEEN (1952-3) by Henry Moore. Probably the greatest living British sculptor, Moore simplifies the human form in order to emphasise ideas. *King and Queen* illustrates their dignity and repose, yet preserves an anonymity that suggests the present-day decline of monarchy

STANLEY SPENCER (1891-1959) A mystic who spent most of his life in the Berkshire village of Cookham, the setting for many of his paintings. *Swan Upping* was started in 1914 and finished four years later after his return from the war

mould, and a prolific series of portraits, Epstein produced one really remarkable piece of sculpture, *The Rock Drill* (1913-14, Tate Gallery). Henri Gaudier-Brzeska, a Frenchman who lived in London, also produced a handful of important sculptures (Tate Gallery).

Sculpture after the Second World War revolved around one major figure, Henry Moore (*b.* 1898; Tate Gallery), who dominated British sculpture until the late 1950's, by which time he had won an outstanding international reputation. Reclining figures and mother and child groups interested him from the start and have continued to do so both in figurative and non-figurative styles (*Recumbent Figure*, 1938; *Project for Madonna and Child*, 1943; both at the Tate Gallery). Moore's feeling for space was echoed by the work of Barbara Hepworth (*Corinthos*, 1954, Tate Gallery).

Among other sculptors who first began to exhibit in the late 1940's is Reg Butler. He was the prime exponent of the 'rod and wire' school, a linear style which moves away from the masses so skilfully deployed by Henry Moore. His work can best be seen in the *Monument to the Unknown Political Prisoner* (Tate Gallery). Of the later sculptors Anthony Caro and Eduardo Paolozzi stand out (Tate Gallery). Caro's painted metal sculpture and Paolozzi's robot-like, menacing images have a real feeling for the mechanics of the machine age.

LA MITRAILLEUSE (The Machine-gun) by C. R. W. Nevinson (1889-1946). An official war artist during the First World War, his soldiers were depicted as dehumanised components of their fighting machines, expressing 'a life of steel, fever, pride and headlong speed'

## PAINTING: FROM ABSTRACT TO POP ART

In the years before the First World War British painting was still trying to free itself from the dominance of the Royal Academy and its offshoot, the New English Art Club, of which two outstanding members were Wilson Steer (1860-1942) and Walter Sickert (1860-1942). The New English had been formed in 1886 as a protest against academic conventions, but was now losing its impetus as an element of protest.

Meanwhile from the Slade School, a part of the University of London under the direction of Henry Tonks, came a tradition of fine draughtsmanship. From it emerged two remarkable individualists—Augustus John (1878-1961; Tate Gallery), a master of figure drawing; and Stanley Spencer (1891-1959; Tate Gallery), a religious mystic. His painting *The Resurrection*, done in the churchyard of his native village of Cookham, Berkshire, is remarkable both in idea and execution.

In 1911 the Camden Town Group was formed at the inspiration of Walter Sickert, and largely echoed his own delight in the London street scene. At the same time a highly vocal body, stimulated by the painter-critic Roger Fry, formed an aggressive splinter group led by the painter and writer D. B. Wyndham Lewis, with his Vorticist movement and his magazine *Blast*.

The First World War gave English artists first-hand experience of the realities of battle. C. R. W. Nevinson (1889-1946; *La Mitrailleuse*, Tate Gallery) saw war in the field with the Red Cross, and much of his work achieved a semi-abstract quality, as did that of Paul Nash (1889-1946; *Totes Meer*, Tate Gallery), who was commissioned as a war artist. Their stark lunar landscapes of the Flanders

POSTER ART E. McKnight Kauffeur was an American who settled in Britain shortly after the First World War. A successful practitioner of 'persuasive art', he became famous for his London Underground posters. The use of symbols is typified by his 1924 advertisement for Eno's Fruit Salts

battlefields provided a sympathetic climate for the early stirrings of abstractionism in post-war England.

By the early 1930's a handful of major talents had established themselves—Henry Moore, Barbara Hepworth, Ben Nicholson. Nicholson, son of artist Sir William Nicholson, was the outstanding painter of the group. With his balanced geometrical shapes, sensitive line and harmonious combinations of colour, he had dedicated himself to abstractionism since the 1920's.

In 1936 the Surrealist Exhibition demonstrated the freeing of the artist from all the traditional concepts of art. Deeply influenced by this movement was Graham Sutherland (Tate Gallery), hitherto an etcher, engraver and landscape painter. A former pupil of Sutherland, Francis Bacon (Tate Gallery), developed an intuitive style of painting in the 1940's. His distorted images are often taken, like Picasso's, from familiar masterpieces and photographs. Contemporary with Bacon, but quite opposed in style and concept, John Piper (Tate Gallery) also came to the fore, renouncing abstractionism and reverting to romantic architectural subjects.

The 1950's saw L. S. Lowry (Leicester Art Gallery), pursuing a solitary path in his creation of a personal landscape of the industrial north. A new realistic school was recognised in this period, labelled 'the kitchen sink school'. Led by John Bratby, they were concerned with the humdrum things of everyday life. Figurative art has now come back in the shape of 'pop art', which seeks to reflect the images of popular life, and in this field Peter Blake, R. B. Kitaj and David Hockney have established themselves as leaders of the English movement.

BARBARA HEPWORTH *Madonna and Child*. Much of Barbara Hepworth's sculpture is purely abstract; this *Madonna and Child*, carved in 1954, shows the effects of the abstract discipline—the simplified figures creating a basically oval shape without losing their naturalness. The quality of the stone is preserved as if a pebble or a boulder has been animated by the sculptor's art

### THE DECORATIVE ARTS

The influence of William Morris, who revived the idea of the artist-craftsman, lingered on in the firm of Morris & Co. well into the 20th century and did much to raise the level of design. Craft Guilds (co-operatives of artist-craftsmen), founded by A. H. Mackmurdo and C. R. Ashbee towards the end of the 19th century, continued the unification of the arts of design and paved the way for the reception of art nouveau, a style characterised by a sinuous, whiplash line and stylised floral ornament.

The first new movement embracing the decorative arts was Roger Fry's Omega Workshop of 1913—a return to the idea of painted furniture briefly advocated by the Pre-Raphaelites. But it was a painter's movement, and failed because it was essentially decorative and had little grasp of functional design. Its major benefit was to introduce light colours—the palette of the Impressionists—into the home.

ASHBEE PEACOCK PENDANT A piece of art nouveau jewellery in gold, turquoise and enamel, now in the Victoria and Albert Museum. The peacock was a favourite of the art nouveau school and appeared in paintings, fabrics and book decorations

The decorative arts lagged behind the Continent after the First World War, although Sir Ambrose Heal produced well-made English versions of the German Bauhaus furniture designs. After 1933, with the closure of Bauhaus schools, a number of refugee teachers and students gave a new impetus to design. New materials—chrome and glass—began to appear in decoration, as in architecture, and motifs taken from abstract painting made their appearance.

# THE TREASURES
# OF BRITAIN

*A guide to the public and private possessions
which make up the national heritage of
England, Scotland and Wales*

In towns, villages and hamlets, and sometimes in the loneliest corners
of the countryside, heirlooms from the pageant of Britain's past are
liberally scattered. They range from cathedrals and grand houses to
works in museum showcases.

In the following gazetteer pages the most notable of them are
described. The selection has been based on experts' judgment of their
significance, beauty and value. To avoid disappointment visitors are
advised to check beforehand that treasures can be seen when they
wish; some property owners require prior notice of a visit, and
opening times are variable.

All these gazetteer entries are linked to the maps (pages 537–76) by
a simple reference code, and are pinpointed on the map by symbols.

The gazetteer includes picture features on notable people associated
with particular places. Where towns and buildings are rich in treasures
several pages are devoted to illustrating them.

**Abbey Dore** *Herefs.*     *546 Ad*
The monastery was founded in 1147, and the surviving church belongs mainly to the end of the 12th century. The eastern end was added a little later, *c.* 1200, and this part of the building, with its moulded arches and long lancet windows, is particularly striking. A few fragments remain of the nave. The site of the monastic buildings, which lay to the north of the church, has been excavated, and virtually nothing of these buildings can be seen. Work was still continuing on the church in 1260, and it was consecrated *c.* 1270; it eventually became derelict. In 1634 Viscount Scudamore restored what was left, and added the great oak screen. The nave had gone; what remains now are the transepts, crossing and chancel, and the 17th-century tower added on the south side. There are many fragments of sculpture from the ancient church and the monuments include two cross-legged knights of the 13th century.

**Abbotsbury** *Dorset*     *540 Cc*
A village of stone and thatch houses at the foot of the Downs near the Fleet—the lagoon between Chesil Bank and the mainland. In the village are ruins of the 12th-century Benedictine Abbey of St Peter; the Church of St Nicholas was once part of the abbey and so was the great 15th-century tithe barn, 276 ft long. The swannery created by the monks continues today and, like the sub-tropical gardens near by, is open to the public.
CHURCH OF ST NICHOLAS There was once a Benedictine abbey here; ruins of some of its buildings are to be seen, and the great tithe barn, *c.* 1400, is of much interest. The church has a west tower and is to the north of the abbey; it was built mainly in the 14th and 15th centuries. The chancel has a plaster ceiling of 1638, and a large reredos of 1751 completely fills the east wall. There are various monuments including an effigy of an abbot of *c.* 1200 and a fine early 17th-century canopied pulpit.
ST CATHERINE'S CHAPEL Built on a hilltop as a beacon for sailors, the chapel dates from the 15th century; the hill is terraced with lynchets, relics of Bronze Age cultivation.

**Abbotsford House** *Rox.*     *562 Dd*
Sir Walter Scott bought this mansion in 1811 and lived there until his death in 1832. During that time he rebuilt most of the house and planted most of the trees in the grounds. The house contains Scott's relics and a collection of weapons.

**Abbots Langley** *Herts.*     *547 Hc*
CHURCH OF ST LAWRENCE The church has 12th-century arcades to the nave, and a 14th-century south chapel, a west tower, an octagonal Perpendicular font and 14th-century wall-painting of SS Thomas and Lawrence. Among the monuments is one to Lord Raymond (*d.* 1732) by Sir Henry Cheere, with effigy in robes, and seated beside him an allegorical figure holding a portrait medallion. A later monument to the 2nd Lord Raymond (*d.* 1756) is by Peter Scheemakers.

**Aberayron** *Card.*     *544 Ff*
This attractive Georgian port grew until the 1880's, when the coming of the railway ruined coastal shipping. It has survived almost intact to the present day. There is a harbour and a large square. The houses have good fan-lights and are finished with coloured stucco. Its pleasant style has influenced a number of neighbouring villages.

**Aberdeen** *A'deen*     *567 Ge*
ART GALLERY Housed in a modern building with an unusual arcade of polished granite pillars and a fountain group in the entrance court, the gallery has an important collection of paintings including Monet's *La Falaise à Fécamp* and Sisley's *Une Cour aux Sablons.* Works by Boudin, Maris, Forain, Vlaminck, Bonnard and Vuillard can also be seen, along with water-colours by de Segonzac, Kokoschka and others. Scottish painting and sculpture are represented by Ramsay, Nasmyth, Wilkie and Raeburn, and a collection of early English water-colours includes works by Turner and Cozens. Bronzes by Rodin can be seen in the sculpture section with works by Degas, Bourdelle, Henry Moore, Barbara Hepworth, Zadkine and Epstein. Modern tapestry and stained glass are also shown. The Print Room and Art Library has a collection of modern etchings and lithographs, and the J. Cromar Watt Collection of Chinese decorative arts can also be seen.
CATHEDRAL Originally a Norman building, but rebuilt from the 13th century onwards. It is now a relatively small, mainly 15th-century building with two squat west towers. During this century the choir was demolished in preparation for rebuilding, which never took place.
MARISCHAL COLLEGE The present college was started in 1844 when the eastern range of buildings was built to plans by Archibald Simpson. The Perpendicular Gothic façade to Broad Street, built in Kemnay granite to the designs of A. Marshall MacKenzie, was finished in 1906. Together with the Mitchell Tower and the adjoining Greyfriars Church the college forms one of the finest complexes of granite buildings in the country.
MERCAT CROSS This unique cross, designed by John Montgomery of Old Rayne in 1686, was rebuilt in 1821 and moved to its present site in 1841–2. Its central shaft is surmounted by a gilded unicorn rising from a hexagonal platform on a circular, arcaded base. The balustrade has a series of portraits of Scottish sovereigns from James I to James VII and the royal and burgh Arms.
MUSIC HALL One of the finest buildings in Union Street, the construction of which led to the development of the 'Granite City' in the 19th century. Designed with a six-columned portico by Archibald Simpson in 1820 as the assembly rooms, the superb neo-Greek card and supper rooms are noteworthy. The Music Hall was added in 1858–9 by James Matthews.
OLD ABERDEEN Episcopal burgh associated with St Machar's Cathedral, incorporated in 1891 with the 'New Town' to form the present City of Aberdeen. The medieval street lay-out is still visible. High Street, with the town house of 1788 at the head, still retains some 18th-century houses with their gables facing the street. The Chanonry and Don Street, originally containing the manses of the cathedral clergy, now contain simple granite houses, mostly of the 18th and 19th centuries.
PROVOST ROSS'S HOUSE The town house of Provost Ross of Aberdeen, who occupied the building in the early 18th century. The earliest surviving domestic building in the city (1593), it is a three-storey house with the top storey attractively corbelled out.
PROVOST SKENE'S HOUSE Built *c.* 1545, this striking town house was greatly extended *c.* 1670 after George Skene, merchant and Provost of Aberdeen, purchased the property. The building was remodelled, becoming a four-storey rubble block with flat roof. Some interior work survives from all periods, notably a coved ceiling of 1626 painted in tempera representing religious subjects. It is now a museum, containing relics of local history and local social and domestic life.
ROBERT GORDON'S COLLEGE Founded in 1729 by Robert Gordon, an Aberdeen merchant, as a hospital for the education of destitute boys. The

GENERAL WADE'S BRIDGE, ABERFELDY

*General Wade (1673–1748) and his troops, in their campaign to overcome the rebellious Scottish clans and maintain peace for George I, made some 250 miles of roads and bridges, and these are still the main lines of communication in Scotland. Many of the bridges cost* *only £40 to construct, but this one was designed by William Adam and built in 1733 at a cost of £4000. Of the five stone arches, the central one has a span of 60 ft, and the four obelisks crowning the parapets make an unusual feature.*

central block of three storeys, attic, cupola and spire was designed by William Adam and finished in 1746; the advanced wings and colonnade by John Smith of Aberdeen were added 1830–3. The statue of the founder by John Cheere was placed in the niche over the main entrance in 1752. The planning of the early building still survives, with an interesting scale-and-platt stair.

UNIVERSITY ANTHROPOLOGICAL MUSEUM The museum has items of archaeological interest from all parts of the world: the Henderson Collection of classical vases; the Grant-Bey Egyptian Collection including scarabs and mummies; a collection of ancient Chinese art with bronzes of the Shang Yin period, Tang Dynasty horses and carved jade of the Ming Dynasty; and a collection of items made by the native peoples of Australia and America. The collection of local antiquities includes skeletal remains and urns of the Beaker People, who came to Britain from Europe *c.* 1800 BC.

## Aberdour Castle *Fife.* 562Bf
The castle's oldest part is the 14th-century tower which is rhomboidal in plan. Other parts were added in the 16th and 17th centuries. A fine circular dove-cote is well preserved.

## Aberfeldy *Perths.* 566Bb
GENERAL WADE'S BRIDGE This picturesque five-arched bridge, designed by William Adam in 1733, carries Wade's military road to the central Highlands. Raised quoins and voussoirs add architectural finesse to arches and buttresses while tall obelisks dominate the central span.

## Abergavenny *Mon.* 545Jd
ABERGAVENNY AND DISTRICT MUSEUM The museum is housed in a 19th-century stone hunting lodge, built in the moat of a ruined medieval castle; parts of its structure are medieval. The exhibits are mainly items made or used locally, including harness and saddlery, farm tools and equipment, fire-arms, dolls, costumes, a Welsh harp and local archaeological finds. One room is a replica of a Welsh Border farmhouse kitchen as it might have appeared in 1870.
PRIORY CHURCH The church of the Benedictine priory founded in the 12th century, cruciform and with a central tower. Not much Norman work remains, and the building is mainly 14th century. There are canopied choir stalls, a number of monuments, the earliest of which is a lady of *c.* 1270, and a large wooden figure of Jesse.

## Abernethy *Perths.* 562Bg
The capital of the Picts, an early Scottish people who were united with the Scottish Celts under King Kenneth MacAlpin in 844.
CASTLE LAW A fort protected by an inner wall from 18 to 25 ft thick. Excavation has shown that this was laced both across and longitudinally with timber. On the west side there is also an outer wall, in places about 18 ft thick.
ROUND TOWER This 'Irish' round tower is one of only two such structures on the Scottish mainland (the other is at Brechin, Angus); it is 74 ft high and dates from the 12th century.

## Aberystwyth *Card.* 544Fg
NATIONAL LIBRARY OF WALES The library houses collections mostly relating to Wales, comprising topographical prints, water-colours and drawings, including a set of over 50 drawings by Thomas Rowlandson, most of them made during a tour of Wales in 1797; etchings by Augustus John, Whistler, Forain and Zorn; portraits of Welsh celebrities and internationally famous men and women, and a comprehensive library of the fine arts including architecture and archaeology.
UNIVERSITY COLLEGE, ABERYSTWYTH Permanent collections of the museum, which is in the university main building, include examples of Welsh folk art, Welsh pottery, English ceramics and glassware and Oriental artwork (netsuke). Exhibitions of modern work are held whilst the university is in session.

## Abingdon *Berks.* 546Fc
An ancient wool and agricultural town, once the county town of Berkshire, but ceding that distinction to Reading when it refused to accept the introduction of railway services. Abingdon has some famous almshouses, in Long Alley (built 1446), in Brick Alley (1716) and Twitty's Almshouses (1707).
ABBEY Founded in 675 and demolished in 1538, Abingdon Abbey was once important and powerful, but now there are few visible remains. The church has gone and the restored gateway is attached to the Church of St Nicholas. Remaining abbey buildings include a long gallery of stone and timber (*c.* 1500) and the 13th-century Checker (perhaps the Exchequer), a square stone building with an unusual and interesting chimney—the gabled 'roof' of the chimney has triple lancets for the smoke to escape. Several fragments of the destroyed abbey church have been built into an

artificial ruin near the abbey gateway. Adjoining these 15th-century buildings is the Unicorn, an Elizabethan theatre still used for plays and concerts.

ABINGDON BRIDGE Over 150 yds long, it is really three bridges—Abingdon Bridge proper, over a backwater of the R. Thames; Burford Bridge, over the main stream; and Hales Bridge, over a marshy area. The two former were built in 1416, Chaucer's nephew being among the builders, and the third in 1453.

CHURCH OF ST HELEN The splendid 13th-century steeple rises high above this riverside church that is wider than it is long: there are five aisles inside, dating from rebuilding in the 15th and 16th centuries. The north aisle ceiling is panelled and was painted c. 1390 to show the Tree of Jesse. There is interesting woodwork: the pulpit of 1636, the mayor's seat of 1706, and the organ case of 1725. There are monuments from the 15th century onwards; two of the late 18th century are John Hickey's for Elizabeth Hawkins and one by J. Nollekens for Dr John Crossley. The 19th-century stained glass includes some by C. E. Kempe, and the marble font was shown in the Great Exhibition of 1851.

COUNTY HALL (BOROUGH MUSEUM) A fine example of Classical architecture from the reign of Charles II. The Hall, built in 1683, was recently restored, and houses the borough museum and archives including ten borough charters, the earliest of which is dated 1556; relics from medieval Abingdon Abbey; pewter plate; costumes, uniforms and arms from the 16th–19th centuries; children's toys and books; coins and stamps; pottery, implements and ornaments from local Saxon graves, and a collection of fossils from the district.

GUILDHALL Every room was built at a different period. The Roysse Room was the town's grammar school for 300 years. It was built in 1563, the first stone being laid on the 63rd birthday of the founder, John Roysse, who required the room to be 64 ft long to accommodate 63 boys. The courtroom was built c. 1440 as the hospital of the abbey. Today, it houses the Quarter Sessions and two magistrates' benches.

TOWN HALL The town hall at Abingdon was built under the supervision of Christopher Kempster, 1677–82. The architect is unknown, but the building has been attributed to Sir Christopher Wren. The two-storied building has cellars and an attic; the main façade is to the market-place. Giant Corinthian pilasters extend the height of the two main storeys, and pilasters of the Composite order flank the windows on the first floor and the arcade openings on the ground floor. The sloping roof is decorated with a deep cornice and balustraded, with a cupola. At the back a square tower contains the staircase. The market hall occupies the ground floor within the open arcade, and the large courtroom is on the floor above.

**Abington** *Northants.*         *547Gf*
CHURCH A small church on the outskirts of Northampton, with remains of work dating from c. 1200. There is a wide nave, a 15th-century font with cover, and a good late 17th-century pulpit, richly carved. Many memorial tablets by the local family of Cox, and a monument with a robed, standing man by Samuel Cox, c. 1730.

**Achamore** *Isle of Gigha, Argyll*    *560Dd*
Large gardens, with roses and flowering shrubs.

**Ackworth School** *Yorks.*       *558Da*
A Georgian building erected in 1750 as an appendage to the London Foundling Hospital; it is all

that survives of the hospital. Since 1777 it has been owned by the Society of Friends (Quakers) and is now a boarding school for Quaker children.

**Acle** *Norfolk*       *554Eb*
CHURCH OF ST EDMUND The church has an 11th-century round tower, but the octagonal upper stage and battlements are of a later date. Both north and south porches are two storeys high. The font dates from 1410, with carvings of lions, wild men, the Trinity, and emblems.

**Aconbury** *Herefs.*       *546Ae*
CHURCH OF ST JOHN THE BAPTIST Formerly the church of a 13th-century priory of Augustinian canonesses, it is small, consisting of a nave and chancel only, with a later bell-turret of timber. It was restored by Sir Gilbert Scott in 1863.

**Aconbury Camp** *Herefs.*     *546Ae*
An Iron Age oval camp on Aconbury Hill (916 ft).

ABINGDON TOWN HALL

*In many towns the town hall served at least two purposes: the lower part was an open colonnade, used for market stalls, while the upper part served as court and assembly rooms. Abingdon Town Hall is one of the finest examples of the style; the designer is not known, but the influence of Sir Christopher Wren is evident. Under the supervision of Christopher Kempster the hall was completed in 1682. The finely proportioned courtroom on the first floor is 57 ft long and 30 ft wide. The plaster ceiling is a modern restoration.*

**Acrise Place** *Kent*       *542Fe*
An Elizabethan manor with a Georgian entrance front added c. 1790. It contains Georgian, Regency and Victorian costumes.

**Acton** *Cheshire*       *552Ad*
CHURCH OF ST MARY A large 13th- and 14th-century building, the west tower rebuilt after storm damage in 1757. The best of several monuments is a large and canopied knight's effigy, c. 1400, and another, of c. 1660, has two good effigies. There is a Norman font, 17th-century screens and stalls.

**Acton** *Suffolk*       *548Ce*
CHURCH OF ALL SAINTS Originally built c. 1300, but the tower is early 20th century. There is a very good brass of c. 1302, with a life-size figure of a

cross-legged knight wearing chain-mail and holding a shield; also a monument of *c.* 1722, which might be by Thomas Green of Camberwell, with a reclining man against an architectural background, with his wife sitting at his feet.

**Acton Beauchamp** *Herefs.*      *546Be*
CHURCH OF ST GILES The nave and chancel were rebuilt *c.* 1816 in a Classical style; the west tower and the Norman south doorway remain from the original church. An Anglo-Saxon carving of the 9th century is used as a lintel to the tower doorway.

**Acton Burnell** *Shrops.*      *552Ab*
CHURCH OF ST MARY Lying close to the castle, this 13th-century church has much which is architecturally interesting, such as the fine east window and carving on the capitals. The north transept is paved with medieval tiles and the font is also 13th century. The monuments, from the 14th century onwards, include one with alabaster effigies to Sir Richard Lee (1591), and to Sir Humphrey Lee (1632), with figures carved by Nicholas Stone.

**Acton Round** *Shrops.*      *546Bg*
CHURCH Isolated and small, with a pretty, timbered south porch, and a door with 13th-century ironwork. Among the monuments is one of *c.* 1703 by William Stanton; another, of *c.* 1760, incorporates Gothic elements, and seems to owe something to Sir Henry Cheere.

**Acton Round Hall** *Shrops.*      *546Bg*
A Dower House built *c.* 1695 for Aldenham Park; it contains period panelling and a collection of European and Oriental armour and weapons.

**Adderbury** *Oxon.*      *546Fe*
CHURCH OF ST MARY THE VIRGIN A large cruciform church in the Decorated and Perpendicular styles, with a west tower and spire. Outside are many corbels and gargoyles. The chancel is spacious, and there are brasses, a rood screen, and some early woodwork.

**Adderley** *Shrops.*      *552Ad*
CHURCH OF ST PETER A cruciform building of red sandstone, standing on the edge of parkland. It was built in the Gothic Revival style in 1801 (though the tower is older, 1712), and the window tracery is of cast iron, typical of the area at that date. The big carved font is Norman, but the north chapel is mid-17th century, and there is a brass to a 14th-century cleric.

**Addinston and Longcroft** *Ber.*      *562De*
The fort of Addinston crowns a conspicuous hill close to the A68 road north of Lauder. There are two great ramparts, each with an external ditch, the outer having, in places, a counterscarp bank. The enclosed area measures some 280 ft by 160 ft, and the bases of several circular huts are still visible.
The Longcroft fort is less than a mile to the north-east of Addinston and has much more complex defences, which appear to represent more than one period of construction. There are two outer ramparts with an intermediate ditch and, well within the enclosed area, two further concentric ramparts without ditches. The innermost enclosed area has many circular hut-bases and minor enclosures, and a rectangular foundation, probably of a much later date.

**Addlethorpe** *Lincs.*      *554Ae*
CHURCH OF ST NICHOLAS A 15th-century church which lost its chancel in 1706. Some of the medieval glass still remains, and much of the woodwork is original in the screens, pew ends, and angels in the roof.

**Adisham** *Kent*      *542Ff*
CHURCH OF THE HOLY INNOCENTS A cruciform church of Norman origin, with a low central tower capped by a pyramidal roof. There are lancet windows, and a Norman font.

**Adlington Hall** *Cheshire*      *552Be*
Country mansion of mixed architecture, begun in 1315. The great hall was built 1450–1505, and an Elizabethan black and white wing added in 1581. There is a Georgian south front and Palladian portico of 1757. The great hall, in which is installed a Bernard Smith organ, *c.* 1670, has a carved beamed ceiling and fine murals.

**Affleck Castle** *Angus*      *566Eb*
A turreted keep is the main remnant of this 15th-century fortress of the Auchinlecks.

**Affpuddle** *Dorset*      *540Dc*
CHURCH OF ST LAWRENCE Situated on the river bank of the Piddle Valley, this is a church of the 13th century, with aisle and tower of the 15th century. It contains some pleasant mid-16th-century wood benches and a pulpit of the same date; the font is Norman.

**Airlie Castle** *Angus*      *566Db*
The home of the Ogilvy family (Earls of Airlie) since 1431. In 1639 the Earl of Airlie, a strong supporter of Charles I, left Scotland, and during his absence the castle was looted and burnt down. The castle was the scene of further action in the Jacobite rebellions of 1715 and 1745, after which Lord Ogilvy was obliged to take refuge in France. He restored the castle in 1792. In 1961, after it had been used for 70 years as a Dower House, the 12th Earl of Airlie moved in, restored the stone and ironwork, and moved the front entrance to the centre of the house. Topiary work in the garden represents battle formations at Waterloo.

**Alberbury** *Shrops.*      *551Jb*
CHURCH OF ST MICHAEL Close to the castle, St Michael's has a massive tower of *c.* 1300 on the north side. The Loton Chapel is noteworthy; it was built in the 14th century and restored in the 19th, and so has imitation Gothic benches and a chancel of 1840. There are several monuments, especially to the Lyster and Leighton families.

**Albury Park** *Surrey*      *542Af*
John Evelyn (1620–1706), the diarist friend of Samuel Pepys, helped to design the park and gardens here. The mansion was built in Queen Anne's reign; its interior was altered by Sir John Soane in 1802, and the exterior rebuilt in Gothic style by A. W. Pugin in 1847, when more than 40 ornate chimney-pots were added.

**Alcester** *Warks.*      *546Df*
A market town with medieval timber-framed buildings. The Old Malt House was built in 1500. There are several 17th-century buildings; the town hall dates from 1641.

**Alconbury** *Hunts.*      *547Jf*
CHURCH OF SS PETER AND PAUL The fine 13th-century chancel has three lancets at the east and arcading on the north and south walls. The west tower has a broach spire, and inside are fragments of wall-paintings and medieval glass.

**Aldborough** *Yorks.*      *558Dc*
CHURCH OF ST ANDREW A long 14th-century church with low 15th-century tower. Inside, there is a brass of *c.* 1360 and fragments of stained glass from the same period. A Roman sculpture, with the figure of Mercury, is probably from the town of Isurium that once stood here.

# Robert Burns

## ROBERT BURNS, THE PLOUGH-BOY POET

The Ayrshire countryside is rich in associations with the life of her most distinguished son, who wrote of himself 'I have not the most distant pretensions to being what the guardians of the escutchions call a Gentleman. I am simply Robert Burns at your service. I was born to the Plough.' At 14, Burns was already his father's chief labourer and, as the family moved from one unproductive farm to another, he found increasing solace in literature and lassies. His early love poems and country verses were published by William Creech in 1787, making him the toast of Edinburgh at 28. He died nine years later, and his last child was born as he was being buried.

BURNS COTTAGE in *Alloway*, which the poet's father built with his own hands. In the 'butt' or kitchen, his eldest son was born on January 25, 1759, and here spent the first seven years of his life. It is preserved as a museum and contains many relics of the poet's life.

PUNCH BOWL of *Inveraray marble, beaded with silver and engraved 'Come to my bowl, come to my arms, my friends, my brothers'; it is now in the British Museum. It was presented as a wedding gift to the poet, by his wife's father, James Armour. Burns celebrated his love for his wife, Jean, in a poem whose first verse runs:*

> O my Luve's like a red red rose
> That's newly sprung in June:
> O my Luve's like the melodie
> That's sweetly play'd in tune.

POEM engraved on a window-pane from the Globe Inn, Dumfries. These lines from 'Tam o' Shanter' were cut with a diamond by the poet and are preserved at Burns Cottage.

AULD LANG SYNE *manuscript which the Trustees of Burns Cottage bought in 1952 for £1500. Written by Burns to the music of an old Scottish air, it is one of the 350 Scots songs Burns either wrote or revived for inclusion in 'The Scots Musical Museum'. Four volumes of Burns' annotated version of this work remain at the cottage; the manuscript of the fifth volume, published after the poet's death, is in the British Museum. Burns travelled all over Scotland collecting song material for the 'Museum', but never sought payment for this great work.*

> The twa hae run about the braes,
> And pou't the gowans fine;
> But we've wandered mony a weary fitt
> Sin auld lang syne
> We twa hae paidl't in the burn
> Frae morning sun till dine;
> But seas between us braid hae roar'd
> Sin auld lang syne.

In a lane near the cottage there is a plaque with these words: 'One autumn day in 1790 Robert Burns paced up and down this grassy path crooning to himself in one of his poetical moods the words which became the immortal tale of "Tam o' Shanter". In the last field along the path the poet saw the wounded hare which inspired "The Address to a Wounded Hare".'

FIRST EDITION of 'Poems, chiefly in the Scottish dialect', published when Burns was 28. 'Old and young, high and low, grave and gay, learned and ignorant were alike delighted, agitated, transported' by the poems. (Burns Cottage)

BROOCH given by Mrs Dunlop to Burns, who wrote: 'Your criticisms are not the blasting depredations of a canker-toothed, caterpillar-critic, but the judicious observations of animated friendship.' (Lady Stair's House)

MARBLE APPLE given by Burns to his sister-in-law. (Lady Stair's House)

*Had we never lov'd sae kindly*
*Had we never lov'd sae blindly*
*Never met—or never parted,*
*We had ne'er been broken-hearted.*
A silhouette on ivory by John Miers of Clarinda (Mrs Agnes Maclehose) to whom Burns wrote these lines. (Scottish National Portrait Gallery)

CORDIAL GLASS belonging to the poet. In later years 'blue devils' arose to plague Burns and he became a seasoned drinker avowing 'Freedom and Whisky gang thegither'. (Lady Stair's House Museum, Edinburgh)

RELICS of the poet at Burns Cottage. Despite his great triumph as a poet in Edinburgh, Burns returned to the simple life of an Ayrshire farmer. 'I'll be damned if I ever write for money' he said.

PAINTING by W. B. Johnstone of Burns in Sibbald's Circulating Library with distinguished men of the period. 'The man will be spoiled if he can spoil,' said an observer, 'but keeps his simple manners and is quite sober.' (Lady Stair's House)

NRY MACKENZIE       ALEXANDER NASMYTH  JAMES BRUCE        MISS BURNETT        WALTER SCOTT
H BLAIR                        DAVID ALLEN                        JAMES SIBBALD
     ROBERT BURNS                          LORD MONBODDO              DR ADAM FERGESON

**Aldbourne** *Wilts.*     *540Fg*
CHURCH OF ST MICHAEL Standing by the village green the church was originally 12th-century Norman. There were later enlargements and additions, including a fine 15th-century west tower. The south door is Norman with a two-storey Perpendicular porch, and the interior roofs are 15th century. There is an interesting carved Jacobean pulpit, an octagonal 17th-century font and brasses of the 15th and 16th centuries, as well as monuments of a later date.

**Aldbury** *Herts.*     *547Hc*
CHURCH OF ST JOHN THE BAPTIST The church, dating mainly from the 13th and 14th centuries, stands near the village green. The Pendley Chapel, added later, contains a 15th-century monument with recumbent effigies. There is also a 15th-century stone screen, and brasses and a 16th-century wood lectern.

**Aldeburgh** *Suffolk*     *548Ef*
Alde House was the home of Elizabeth Garrett Anderson, one of the first women doctors. The 16th-century Moot Hall dates from the town's most prosperous period; timber-framed with brick, it has an outside staircase leading to an upper floor added in the 17th century. In the council chamber maps and prints are on display.
CHURCH OF SS PETER AND PAUL The church stands on a hill overlooking the town. The west tower is of the 14th century, and most of the building is 16th century. The very long south porch of 1539 has three entrances. Inside is a Norman font, a pulpit of the 17th century, brasses and several 18th- and 19th-century monuments.

**Alderford** *Norfolk*     *554Cc*
CHURCH OF ST JOHN THE BAPTIST The church and its west tower are 14th century and there is no chancel arch. The octagonal seven-sacrament font, typical of East Anglian churches, is carved with a Crucifixion and angels. Some medieval stained glass still remains.

**Aldershot** *Hants*     *541Jf*
AIRBORNE FORCES MUSEUM The museum exhibits all types of equipment used by Airborne Forces.
ROYAL ARMY DENTAL CORPS MUSEUM Dental instruments and records showing the development of dentistry in the army from 1914 to the present can be viewed by appointment.
ROYAL ARMY MEDICAL CORPS HISTORICAL MUSEUM British army medical services are illustrated by uniforms, medals, letters, flags and medical equipment. Relics of Florence Nightingale and Lt.-Col. Martin-Leake, the only man to win the Victoria Cross twice, are included. (By appointment.)

**Aldwincle** *Northants.*     *547Hg*
CHURCH OF ST PETER Norman origin with 13th- and 14th-century additions, and a west tower. Some 14th-century glass remains, while the east window, 1900, is by C. E. Kempe.

**Aldworth** *Berks.*     *546Fb*
High on the Berkshire Downs, this isolated village is near the eastern end of Ridge Way, a prehistoric route along the top of the Downs, which meanders westwards for about 30 miles to beyond Marlborough in Wiltshire. In the Church of St Mary are huge stone effigies of the medieval family of de la Beche. In the churchyard is a yew tree calculated to be 1000 years old.

**Alford** *Lincs.*     *553Je*
CHURCH OF ST WILFRID A 14th-century church, extensively restored and enlarged by Sir Gilbert Scott in 1869. The south porch is chambered; there is a 17th-century pulpit, and a large monument with effigies dated to *c.* 1668.

**Alfred's Castle** *Berks.*     *546Eb*
An Iron Age hill-fort near Ashdown House.

**Alfriston** *Sussex*     *542Cd*
The village lies by the Cuckmere R., overhung by a shoulder of the South Downs on each side. The main street has several fine half-timbered houses, including the Ship Inn with much carving, faces and small figures of priests.
CHURCH OF ST ANDREW A 14th-century cruciform church. Inside is an Easter sepulchre, piscina and triple sedilia. There are some fragments of early glass, but a Jesse window in the south transept is by Kempe & Tower, *c.* 1912.
CLERGY HOUSE This pre-Reformation parish priest's house dates from *c.* 1350. It is half-timbered and thatched, and the living-room has cambered tie-beams and moulded king-posts. It was the first building acquired by the National Trust (1896).

**Allington Castle** *Kent*     *542Df*
A Norman moated castle by the R. Medway, built in the reign of Edward I and altered in Henry VII's reign. It was restored earlier this century and the Norman and Tudor features have been preserved. It contains a collection of Jacobean and Queen Anne furniture, and is now a retreat house for the Order of Carmelites (White Friars).

**Alloway** *Ayrs.*     *561Gc*
BURNS COTTAGE Birthplace of Robert Burns, now a museum of his relics. (See also pp. 54–55.)

**Almondbury** *Yorks.*     *558Ca*
CHURCH OF ALL HALLOWS The church is mainly Perpendicular, with some Early English work and a big west tower. Inside there is a fine ceiling with decorated bosses dated 1522, a good font cover and some early stained glass showing saints and donors.

**Almondsbury** *Glos.*     *540Cg*
CHURCH OF ST MARY THE VIRGIN A large cruciform church, with an Early English chancel and Norman remains. There is a central tower with broach spire, and inside a fine 16th-century tomb with two effigies. The nave was restored in 1834.

**Alne** *Yorks.*     *558Dc*
CHURCH OF ST MARY Basically Norman, with a carved south doorway of that period. The west tower has 18th-century additions. Inside there is a Norman font, and a 14th-century effigy of a lady.

**Alnwick Castle** *Northld.*     *563Gc*
A Border castle, the home of the Percy family since 1309. The site has been occupied since the 12th century; parts of the massive keep and the existing curtain walls enclosing the two baileys date from that time. The main part of the castle dates from

---

## ALNWICK CASTLE

*Throughout the Middle Ages the owners of Alnwick occupied an uneasy political position; nominally subjects of the English king and committed to defending the Border against the Scots, they often allied themselves with the Scottish kings if the occasion suited them. The main part of the castle belongs to the 14th century and the period of the first two Percy lords.*

*The interior was converted into a magnificent Italian Renaissance palace by the director of the Capitoline Museum in Rome for the 4th Duke (1847–65).*
CABINET *The ornate ebony inlay cabinet was made for the apartments of Louis XIV at Versailles. After the French Revolution, it came into the hands of the 3rd Duke, who was Ambassador in Paris in 1825.*

REYNOLDS *Georgiana, Countess Spencer and Lady Georgiana Spencer*

*Sir Joshua Reynolds was the epitome of the successful artist; he was occasionally a great artist. He moved in the best society, and was the first President of the Royal Academy. Reynolds believed greatness in painting only came from observance of rules based on a study of the old masters. He had an extraordinary versatility in composition—far more than Gains-* *borough ever had—and treated his society beauties as material for pictorial organisation rather than as emotive subject-matter. His portraits at Althorp are among his happiest—notably this splendidly composed double portrait painted between 1759 and 1761. Here his characterisation has a sensitivity and intimacy which he never rivalled in his later work. (Althorp)*

the 14th century, but the present building is the result of rebuilding and restoration as successive owners attempted to make the medieval structure conform to later standards of comfort. There were two main periods of restoration—under the 1st Duke of Northumberland (1750–86) who employed Robert Adam as architect, and under the 4th Duke (1847–65) who had Salvin as architect for the exterior. This last work is now most in evidence; the exterior is dominated by the 19th-century Prudhoe Tower. The keep, armoury, guard-chamber, library and other apartments contain heirlooms and relics of the Percys, and the family state coach is also on view. In the castle is a museum of British and Roman antiquities.

**Alrewas** *Staffs.*         *552Dc*
CHURCH OF ALL SAINTS Some of the original Norman work remains, but there is Gothic enlargement, with good 16th-century roofs. The font is of the 15th century and has some carved grotesque heads, and the pulpit is 17th century. There is a monument of *c.* 1707 by Thomas White.

**Alstonefield** *Staffs.*         *552Cd*
CHURCH OF ST PETER A Norman church with later additions; the chancel arch is Norman. There are some good 17th-century box-pews.

**Altarnun** *Cornwall*         *538Ed*
CHURCH OF ST NONNA A church with an imposing, tall west tower, in a pretty hill-side village. There is a carved Norman font, and 79 16th-century bench ends. The rood screen extends across the full width of the church.

**Althorp** *Northants.*         *547Gf*
The home of the Spencer family since 1508, where Queen Anne, the wife of James VI of Scotland, stayed on her way to join her husband in London when he became James I of England in 1603. The mansion, of medieval origin, was altered in 1573, 1660, 1733, and finally by Henry Holland in 1787. Robert Spencer, 2nd Earl of Sunderland (1640–1702) installed paintings by Dutch and Italian masters in the Picture Gallery (115 ft long). A daughter of the 1st Duke of Marlborough and his wife Sarah married one of the Dukes of Sunderland, and their descendants succeeded to the Marlborough title; Sarah, Duchess of Marlborough's personal collection, and portraits by Reynolds and Gainsborough, are in the Marlborough Room.

**Alton** *Hants.*         *541He*
Market town, assumed to have been on the Pilgrims Way. Near the market-place is a house (1590) in which the poet Edmund Spenser lived.

## ALTON TOWERS: THE COLONNADE AND ROMAN BATH

*Charles Talbot, 15th Earl of Shrewsbury, converted thousands of acres of farmland and wild countryside into a huge, fanciful, ornamental park between 1814 and 1827. At enormous expense he directed scores of craftsmen and labourers who laid out terraces and gardens, and created ponds, lakes, fountains and ornamental buildings. The colonnade and Roman bath* *erected in Classical style and the Screw Fountain were some of the many elegant or fantastic monuments built by the earl; these ranged from a Chinese temple in Gothic style to a Swiss cottage. The 16th Earl of Shrewsbury was responsible for 'Her Ladyship's Garden', and erected a monument to his predecessor inscribed, 'He made the desert smile.'*

CURTIS MUSEUM The collections deal with the folk life and natural history of Hampshire; English pottery, porcelain and glass are also displayed.

**Alton Towers** *Staffs.*                                552Cd
A 19th-century neo-Gothic mansion with a splendid park and pleasure gardens.

**Altrincham** *Cheshire*                                552Bf
ART GALLERY AND MUSEUM A collection devoted to local history includes the original charter granted to the borough by Hamon de Massey, *c.* 1290. There is also a small art collection.

**Alvechurch** *Worcs.*                                546Df
CHURCH OF ST LAWRENCE A mainly Perpendicular church; the nave was rebuilt by William Butterfield in the mid-19th century.

**Alveley** *Shrops.*                                546Bg
CHURCH OF ST MARY In a commanding position on a hill, this church was restored by Sir Arthur Blomfield in 1878, but the tower is Norman (with an 18th-century top storey), and there are Norman remains inside, with work from the 13th to the 15th centuries. The 19th-century reredos is painted on zinc, but the embroidered altar frontal is 15th century. There is a brass of 1616, and stained glass by C. E. Kempe of 1882 and 1903.

**Amberley** *Sussex*                                542Ad
Few villages have such a consistent architectural style as Amberley, its brick-trimmed, flint and stone cottages not intruded upon by anything more stately or extreme. At one end stand the church and the mighty ruins of the 14th-century castle, once the palace of the Bishops of Chichester. The church dates from the 12th and 13th centuries, with a Norman chancel arch and a square font. The south doorway of *c.* 1300 has carved foliage capitals. There is an interesting brass effigy of a man (*d.* 1424).

**Amersham** *Bucks.*                                547Hc
CHURCH OF ST MARY A large town church, restored in the 19th century, though originally dating from the 13th–15th centuries. The west tower has a stair turret and spirelet. St Mary's is one of the richest churches in the county for monuments and brasses, especially those in the north Drake Chapel (which is usually locked). The earliest are brasses to Henry Brudenell and his wife, *c.* 1430. There is a beautiful alabaster monument of Henry Curwen (*d.* 1636) by Edward Marshall, and notable 18th-century tombs by Andrew Carpenter, Peter Scheemakers and Sir Henry Cheere. The latest monument of interest is to Thomas Drake by Henry Weekes (1854).

ANTONY HOUSE

*The finest early Georgian house in Cornwall, Antony House was built of granite in 1711–21 for Sir William Carew, whose family had lived at Antony since 1450. In spite of its size and beauty the architect is unknown (though for some time it was thought to be the work of the 18th-century Scottish architect, James Gibbs). The central block is linked to two side wings and square pavilions with fanciful lead roofs by curved screens. On the other side, the north façade has a fine central pediment. The main door, behind a grand porte-cochère (porch for carriages) added in the 19th century, leads into a fine, square, panelled hall, to one side of which is an elegant staircase reached through an arcade.*

**Amesbury** *Wilts.*                    *540Fe*
CHURCH OF SS MARY AND MELOR St Melor was a popular Cornish-Breton saint. The church here, which probably once belonged to the priory (founded 1177), was originally Norman, but now appears chiefly Early English. Its plan is cruciform, with a central tower. The Purbeck marble font is Norman; there are fragments of 13th-century glass and a 15th-century screen. The remains of a Saxon wheel cross can be seen in a case. The church was restored in 1853 by William Butterfield.

**Ammerdown Park Gardens** *Som.*      *540Cf*
Yew gardens, designed by Sir Edwin Lutyens. There are statues, fountains and an 18th-century stone orangery.

**Ampney Crucis** *Glos.*               *546Dc*
CHURCH OF THE HOLY ROOD Cruciform, mainly Early English but with some Norman remains and a 15th-century west tower. In the churchyard is a rare and famous 14th-century cross. Inside the church is a monument of 1584 with effigies of a man, his wife and 12 kneeling children, and a monument of *c.* 1719 by Edward Stanton and Christopher Horsnaile.

**Ampthill** *Beds.*                  *547He*
Ampthill is architecturally one of the most attractive towns in Bedfordshire. Professor Sir Albert Richardson, architect and a past President of the Royal Academy, lived in Avenue House, an 18th-century red-brick dwelling in the main street, for many years. A great enthusiast of Georgian architecture, he was responsible for considerable restoration work in the locality; in particular the 14th-century Church of St Andrew with its 15th-century tower and battlements. It has a curious monument to Richard Nicolls, a local inhabitant who became a Royalist, fought the Dutch in America and finally became the first Governor of Long Island. At the Battle of Solebay in 1672, Nicolls was shot dead and the cannon-ball responsible for 'his mortality and immortality' can be seen mounted on the monument's pediment. Ampthill Park House, now a Cheshire Home, founded by Group-Captain Leonard Cheshire, v.c., was built in 1694 by Lord Ashburnham—a favourite of Charles II. Part of the park is open to the public. The White Hart Hotel is a Queen Anne house incorporating an earlier Tudor building.

About a mile and a half out of the town is the Oxford Hospital or St John's Almshouses, founded by 'John Cross of Oxford, Gentleman' in 1697 to a design by Sir Christopher Wren.

Near by are the atmospheric ruins of Houghton Conquest House, the 'House Beautiful' of Bunyan's *The Pilgrim's Progress*. The house is thought to have been designed by Inigo Jones, or one of his pupils, for Sir Philip Sidney's sister, the Countess of Pembroke.

At nearby Marston Moretaine, there is a half-timbered 16th-century manor house with a moat.
AVENUE HOUSE A red-brick house of 1793, later enlarged by Henry Holland. In the grounds is an 18th-century octagonal garden-house designed by Sir William Chambers, architect of the Pagoda at Kew Gardens. (By appointment.)

**Ampton** *Suffolk*                  *548Cf*
CHURCH OF ST PETER S. S. Teulon restored the church in the mid-19th century. The most interesting feature is the chantry chapel, built after 1479. There are brasses and monuments by John Christmas and Nicholas Stone.

**Ancaster** *Lincs.*                *553Gd*
In the main village street, off the Sleaford–Grantham road, is the site of the south gate of the Roman town of Causennae. In the garden on the left, the bastioned south-west angle of the town wall was recently excavated. In the large field on the right, there is still visible the earthen bank which backed the wall with, in front of it, the half-filled protective ditch. These defences continue round almost to the north-east angle, but surface traces of the north and west walls have disappeared. However, at the north-west angle, a grass

covered mound is believed to contain the base of the angle-bastion. Causennae was the last posting-station for the northward journey along the main road, Ermine Street, from London to Lincoln.

**Angle** *Pemb.*               *544Cc*
THE HALL On the banks of Milford Haven, the gardens contain shrubs, roses, a walled garden, greenhouses and a wishing well.

**Anstey** *Herts.*             *548Ae*
CHURCH OF ST GEORGE A cruciform church, originally Norman, with a central tower, the arches of which are probably from the late 12th century. The remainder of the church dates from the 13th to the 15th centuries. The carved font is Norman, and the stalls have carved misericords.

**Anstruther** *Fife.*            *562Dg*
The burghs of Easter and Wester Anstruther developed independently on either side of the Dreel Burn. There are 17th- and 18th-century houses in Castle Street and Shore Street, fronting the quay, and in the Esplanade, round the miniature harbour and parish church of Easter Anstruther. Most of the two- and three-storey houses display crow-steps and pantiles, features common to the Scottish tradition in Fife.
MANSE The oldest inhabited manse in Scotland, built in 1590.

**Antonine Wall** *Dumb.–Stir.*
The Roman wall running from sea to sea at the narrowest part of Scotland was built *c.* AD 143 during the reign of Emperor Antoninus Pius. It represented the most north-westerly frontier of the Roman Empire, as well as marking the northern limits of Roman Britain, and is the most important remaining Roman work in Scotland.

It consisted of a turf rampart with a stone foundation. The dimensions of this rampart are uncertain, but it was perhaps 10 ft high, and 14 ft wide at the base, tapering to 6 ft at the flattened top. About 20 ft to the north was a large ditch,

some 40 ft wide and 12 ft deep. About 50 yds to the south of the rampart ran a military road 16–18 ft wide. The whole work was 37 miles long, from Bridgeness on the Forth to Old Kilpatrick on the Clyde. It was built not only as a base for military operations into Caledonia but with the political aim of preserving peace by intimidating the enemy barbarians to the north.

Remains of 13 forts on the wall have been excavated, and more probably existed and may yet be found. They were spaced every 2 miles, much closer together than on Hadrian's Wall. Air surveys show there were perhaps also small fortlets between the bigger ones. Small turf platforms, perhaps used for signalling, were built against the back of the wall.

The wall was built by detachments of all three legions stationed in Britain, and 'distance slabs'—inscribed stones—exist showing how many lengths of wall each squad completed. Probably 20,000 men were needed to garrison it and other strongpoints in Scotland. From archaeological finds such as children's shoes it is known that families lived with the soldiers at the wall.

The wall was abandoned *c.* AD 187, so it was used by Rome for less than 50 years. It was mentioned by early chroniclers, including Bede, but systematic excavation only began in 1890 and continues today. The ditch is better preserved than the rampart; the military road is almost obliterated.

Many finds are displayed in the National Museum of Antiquities, Edinburgh, and in the Hunterian Museum, Glasgow.

**Antony House** *Cornwall*         *538Fc*
The finest Georgian house in Cornwall, built of granite for Sir William Carew in 1711–21 by an unknown architect. The main entrance front is on the south side, and has a large columned *porte-cochère* (entrance porch for carriages) added in the 19th century. On either side of the forecourt are wings of red brick linked by colonnades to the

ARBORY HILL

*The earliest relics of buildings for human habitation in Britain are those of the Iron Age Celtic peoples who came from the Continent from about 550 BC to AD 40; they were gradually pushed northwards and westwards by the invading Romans in the 1st century*

*AD. Their habitations (hill-forts) varied in size from small fortified farmsteads to large defended settlements. The fort on Arbory Hill may well have been still inhabited when the Roman legions were passing along their road in the Clyde Valley below.*

## ARBROATH ABBEY

*William the Lion, King of Scotland, lavished endowments on Arbroath, the abbey he founded in 1178 and dedicated to his friend Thomas à Becket, Archbishop of Canterbury. He was buried in 1214 before the high altar—where the Coronation Stone was found in 1951 after it had been taken from Westminster Abbey by Scottish Nationalists.*

central block and terminal square pavilions with fanciful lead roofs. On the north façade is a fine pediment. The house contains the original panelling, and fine furniture, china, needlework, *objets d'art*, and a collection of Carew family portraits including works by Reynolds. Extensive grounds with fine gardens run down to the R. Lynher.

**Apethorpe** *Northants.* 547Hg
CHURCH OF ST LEONARD A Perpendicular church, with a monument to Sir Anthony Mildmay, who died in 1617. The south chapel was built in 1621 to house it. Above the recumbent effigies on a sarcophagus is a huge tented canopy, the drapery of which is held by life-size figures of Charity, Justice, Wisdom and Piety.

**Appleby** *Lincs.* 553Gg
CHURCH OF ST BARTHOLOMEW Originally medieval, this church was largely rebuilt at the beginning of the 19th century. Traces of black on the internal walls date from the time when the church was put into mourning on the death of a former Lord St Oswald. There are fragments of carving from Thornholme Priory. The font is Norman, and there is 19th-century glass.

**Appleby Magna** *Leics.* 552Db
CHURCH OF ST MICHAEL A large, mainly 14th-century church, with many network tracery windows. The plaster vaulting was put in during early 19th-century restoration. The box-pews and west gallery are of the same period. There are fragments of 14th-century stained glass.

**Appleton-le-Moors** *Yorks.* 558Ed
CHRIST CHURCH The architect of this church, with south-east tower and spire, was John Loughborough Pearson, who built it in 1863–5 in Gothic style. The west front has a rose window, and there is stained glass by Clayton & Bell.

**Arborfield** *Berks.* 547Gb
MUSEUM OF THE CORPS OF ROYAL ELECTRICAL AND MECHANICAL ENGINEERS The souvenirs, mementoes, photographs and documents in the museum illustrate the history of the Corps of REME, which was formed in 1942, and the achievements of its personnel.

**Arbor Low** *Derbys.* 552Ce
This is a fine example of a henge monument with two entrances in the containing bank. This bank is still more than 6 ft high and the diameter of the enclosure is some 250 ft. The ditch lies between the bank and the central platform and was originally about 6 ft deep. Some 50 stones—or their fragments—now lie prone, but originally probably stood upright to form an outer circle and a central horseshoe. A Bronze Age barrow overlaps the line of the bank and appears to have been constructed partly with re-used material.

**Arbory Hill** *Lanarks.* 562Ac
This fine fort crowns a hill on the east bank of the R. Clyde, immediately above the Roman road running north along the valley. The centre of the fort is a walled area, about 140 ft across, with two entrances. Well outside this wall are two encircling ramparts, each with an external ditch. There are five entrances through these outer defences. There are traces of hut foundations in the central enclosure. (See p. 61.)

**Arbroath** *Angus* 566Fb
Now an industrial and seaside town, it was of great importance when, in the Regality Chamber in 1320, King Robert de Bruce and the first Scottish Parliament drew up the Declaration of Scottish Independence; a transcript of this document is now in the town library.

**Arbroath Abbey** *Angus* 566Fb
Today only ruins remain of this once powerful monastery, founded in 1178 by King William of Scotland: the church, the abbot's lodging and the gate-house buildings. Arbroath was a wealthy abbey, generally ruled by men distinguished for ambition rather than piety. Bernard de Linton, who was elected abbot in 1307, was also Chancellor of the Kingdom under Robert de Bruce, and in 1396 Pope Benedict XIII granted the abbot the privilege of wearing the mitre, ring and other insignia normal to a bishop. After that date the history of the monastery was undistinguished, and at the end of the 15th century the abbacy came to be granted to laymen. The abbey then became merely a source of revenue, the title of 'abbot' surviving until the 17th century, long after the original purpose of the monastery had lapsed. The Round O of Arbroath is a window—still to be seen in the abbey ruin—from which a beacon gave navigational aid to ships at sea. The mortuary chapel, designed as a mausoleum for the Allan-Fraser family, has many elaborate carvings and enrichments; it was built in 1875–84.

**Arbury Hall** *Warks.* 546Eg
The novelist George Eliot (Mary Ann Cross, 1819–80) was born on the Arbury estate, where her father was the agent. Set in large grounds with landscaped gardens, the Hall is built on the site of an Augustinian priory, and probably follows much of the plan of the former buildings. In 1580 a house was built of which a few details remain—a mullioned window in the courtyard, for instance. The house came into the hands of the Newdegate family in the 16th century, and in 1674 Sir Richard Newdegate consulted Sir Christopher Wren about stables. A few years later he commissioned the new chapel, which contains a magnificent plaster ceiling laden with flowers, fruit and foliage, the work of Edward Martin in 1678. In 1748–96 the Elizabethan house was transformed into a castellated mansion in Gothic Revival style by Sir Roger Newdegate. Inside are collections of family documents and letters, pictures, fine furniture, porcelain and glass.

**Ardersier** *I'ness.* 566*Bg*
FORT GEORGE Constructed after the Jacobite rising in 1745 under the direction of Colonel William Skinner, chief engineer in North Britain, with William Adam and later John Adam as master mason of ordnance. The barrack blocks and chapel comprising the interior are encircled by irregular polygonal walls and six bastions.

**Ardifuir** *Argyll* 560*Ef*
DUN A fine example of a circular galleried dun. Its diameter is 65 ft and its wall is 10 ft thick, still standing in places to a height of 10 ft. This dun has been excavated and, together with some remains of Iron Age type, a fragment of Roman pottery points to its occupation in historic times.

**Ardoch Roman Camp** *Perths.* 562*Ag*
Visible in the grounds of Ardoch House are the earthworks of one of the largest camps in Britain; it was a centre for about 40,000 Roman soldiers during the Emperor Hadrian's time (AD 76–138).

**Ardtornish Castle** *Argyll* 564*Fb*
The 14th-century ruins of a castle overhanging the sea and backed by cliffs; it was the ancient domain of the Lords of the Isles.

**Arkesden** *Essex* 548*Ae*
CHURCH OF ST MARY The church has a 13th-century nave and chancel, and fine effigies.
WOOD HALL A moated mansion, built in 1652 and externally much altered.

**Arlington** *Sussex* 542*Cd*
CHURCH OF ST PANCRAS A little church, with Saxon and Norman remains, Perpendicular font and fragments of mural painting.

**Arlington Court** *Devon* 538*Ff*
A herd of Shetland ponies, a flock of Jacob's sheep, buzzards and ravens are to be seen in the park; by the lake, a sanctuary for wild duck, is a heronry. The Regency house, built in 1822, contains a collection of model ships and pewter snuff-boxes.

**Arlington Mill** *Glos.* 546*Dc*
A 17th-century flour mill, now a museum of old machinery and country crafts and relics.

**Armathwaite** *Cumb.* 557*Jg*
CHAPEL OF CHRIST AND MARY A small chapel consisting only of chancel and nave, rebuilt in the 17th century after falling into ruin and being used as a cattle shed. The east window is a late production by Morris & Co., 1914.

BLAKE *The Circle of the Life of Man*

*A water-colour discovered nearly 20 years ago among rubbish on top of a cupboard in Arlington Court. It seems that it was bought direct from William Blake by the first owner of the house, Colonel J. P. Chichester. Its elaborate composition, its superb condition and its unusual technique make it exceptional in the whole range of Blake's art. In addition to the ordinary technique of water-colour on paper Blake used tempera on canvas, wood or metal. Towards the end of his life, however, he acquired a much greater mastery of his medium and here he used water-colour on a ground of thin gesso on thick paper. The subject is complicated and the title conjectural. It seems to represent the cycle of the life of man, spiritual and material, and according to Sir Geoffrey Keynes 'the two central figures probably represent Albion or Man and his female counterpart Vala, who indicates with her right hand that Man must descend into material existence, and with her left hand that he can ascend again to the regions of the spirit. The creator in his chariot, above, has been stayed in his course by the act of creation. Below, the cord of generative life in the River of Death is cut as it reaches the sea, the circle of symbolic figures, all representing some part of the mystical process of creation, incarnation, death and spiritual restoration.' (Arlington Court)*

**Arreton** *Isle of Wight, Hants.*    *541Hc*
ARRETON MANOR The manor house, which
exhibits a collection of toys, dolls, Jacobean and
Elizabethan furniture and folk items, was built on
the site of an earlier building and completed *c.*
1612. Its carved panelling is over 350 years old and
a 15th-century hall screen is still in position. The
first manor was owned by royalty from the time of
King Alfred to the Norman Conquest, after which
it passed into the hands of the Abbey of St Mary at
Quarr. Henry VIII acquired it at the Dissolution
and it remained a royal possession until Charles I
(whose personal snuff-box is among the exhibits)
granted it to trustees to help pay his debts to the
City of London.
CHURCH OF ST GEORGE The appearance is chiefly
Norman, but St George's also contains Saxon
work: the west front of the original Saxon church
is visible on the west wall, and the door now
concealed by the heavily buttressed 14th-century
tower is of the same period. There are many later
additions, and the church was restored in the 19th
century. Monuments, also of the 19th century,
include two by Sir Richard Westmacott.

**Arundel** *Sussex*    *542Ad*
The distant view of the town from the east is
spectacular, with a French-looking church silhou-
etted against the sky, and the massive grey castle
backed by beech woods. The town, in fact, like
the church, is mostly Victorian. The High Street
is dominated by a splendid coaching inn.
CASTLE For 500 years the home of the Dukes of
Norfolk, Earl Marshals of England. John Howard,
the first Duke of Norfolk of the Howard family,
was killed at Bosworth Field in 1485. The castle,
in a superb position overlooking the valley of the
R. Arun, was begun in the reign of Edward the
Confessor. The crenellated keep on top of the

motte, barbican and drawbridge all date from
Norman times. In 1643 Parliamentary troops
besieged the castle; for 17 days it was bombarded
by cannon from St Nicholas's church steeple, and
suffered much damage. It was rebuilt in the 18th
century, and the 15th Duke carried out much
reconstruction in 1890. The castle contains furniture from the 15th century and portraits by
Gainsborough, Reynolds and Van Dyck.
CHURCH OF ST NICHOLAS A late 14th-century
church, now divided into two by a brick wall, on
one side of which is the Fitzalan Chapel with the
monuments of the family of the Dukes of Norfolk
from the 15th to the 20th century.

**Ascott** *Bucks.*    *547Gd*
A half-timbered hunting lodge built 1870, housing
the collection made by Anthony de Rothschild of
pictures, French and Chippendale furniture, and
ancient Chinese porcelain.

**Ashbourne** *Derbys.*    *552Dd*
CHURCH OF ST OSWALD This cruciform church
has a central spire more than 200 ft high. It is
mainly of the 13th to 15th centuries, but Saxon
foundations have been excavated. It contains a
13th-century font, and 19th-century stained glass.
The monuments include the masterpiece of
Thomas Banks, the sleeping Penelope Booth.

**Ashburnham** *Sussex*    *542Dd*
CHURCH OF ST PETER The west tower is in the
Perpendicular style, but the rest of the church was
rebuilt in 1665. The pulpit, font, box-pews and
west gallery are all 17th century, and so are the iron
screens and panelled wagon-roofs. There is a gilt-
framed painting (*c.* 1676) of the Commandments
and two 17th-century monuments to the Ashburnham family; one by John Bushnell shows a
reclining lady with her husband kneeling by her.

ARUNDEL CASTLE

*For centuries the fortress of the Fitzalan-Howard
family, Dukes of Norfolk, Arundel Castle was begun
in the reign of Edward the Confessor on a bluff
guarding the gap made by the Arun Valley. It had a
stormy history, especially from the time of Henry I.
Roger the 2nd Earl of Norfolk and his son Hugh were
two of the 25 barons elected to see that Magna Carta
was maintained, and the first four Howard Dukes of
Norfolk were all deprived of their estates after their
opposition to the rightful kings of England. Even-*

*tually, at the end of the Civil War the castle was
burnt by Cromwell's troops. However, the fortunes
of the family changed and since the Restoration the
dukedom and office of Earl Marshal of England have
been held without break by the Howard family.
During the 18th century the castle was rehabilitated
and the fine 12th-century stone keep preserved.
Considerable restoration was made during the 19th
century, and today the castle, with its double bailey,
is a smaller version of Windsor Castle.*

CUYP *View on the Maas at Dordrecht*

From his glowing paintings one might think that Cuyp had visited Italy, but he lived all his life in Dordrecht on the Maas and only travelled in his native Holland. The radiant glowing light which we always associate with Cuyp (1620–91) only became an essential part of his painting after the return to his native Utrecht in 1641 of Jan Both, who went to Rome and did landscapes in the style of Claude. There is nothing Claudian in Cuyp's subject matter which, for a Dutch painter, is unusually varied. He did portraits and still-lifes, but it is his landscapes with castle and stolid peasants, and his seascapes and river scenes with their 'amber coloured warmth', which made him so popular with English collectors. *(Ascott)*

---

**Ashby de la Zouch** *Leics.*     *552Dc*
CHURCH OF ST HELEN A 15th-century church, with late 19th-century additions. There is a reredos of 1679, but the main interest lies in the many monuments. Among them is that to the 2nd Earl of Huntingdon (*d.* 1561) with two recumbent alabaster effigies, and that to the 9th Earl, designed by William Kent and carved by Joseph Pickford and J. M. Rysbrack.

**Ashdown House** *Berks.*     *546Eb*
A hunting box built in the late 17th century for Elizabeth of Bohemia by the 1st Earl Craven. The four-storied house, built of chalk blocks, is surmounted by a cupola topped by a golden ball. A notable feature is the great staircase which takes up more than a quarter of the interior. The house is set in fine gardens.

**Ashleworth** *Glos.*     *546Cd*
CHURCH OF SS ANDREW AND BARTHOLOMEW Making a group with Court House and a tithe barn, a small church of varying periods. There is a pre-Reformation holy water stoup in the porch, and inside a 15th-century octagonal font painted with the Arms of Edward VI. The spire is early 14th century.
TITHE BARN A 15th-century barn, 120 ft long, with stone roof, two projecting porch bays and queen-post roof timbers.

**Ashley** *Staffs.*     *552Bc*
CHURCH OF ST JOHN THE BAPTIST The tower is 17th century, but the rest of the church was rebuilt during the 19th century. There is a fine 17th-century monument with effigies, and among memorials of the 19th century are works by Sir Francis Chantrey and Matthew Noble.

**Ashover** *Derbys.*     *552De*
CHURCH OF ALL SAINTS Mainly of the 14th and 15th centuries, the church has a lead Norman font with figures beneath an arcade, a rood screen of *c.* 1500, brasses and an alabaster monument, *c.* 1518, with effigies, saints, angels and weepers.

**Ashridge** *Herts.*     *547Hd*
The children of Henry VIII lived here in a converted 13th-century monastery. In 1808 a new house in Gothic style was begun by James Wyatt for the 7th Earl of Bridgewater, and the 13th-century crypt and Tudor barn are all that remain of the earlier buildings. Wyatt's building has a fine chapel with an apse, and at the other end a square tower which rises above open arcades. In 1928 the house was endowed as a college of citizenship as a memorial to Andrew Bonar Law, Prime Minister in 1922–3. Since 1959 it has been a management training centre for industry. The grounds were laid out by Capability Brown.

**Ashton** *Devon*     *539Hd*
CHURCH OF ST JOHN THE BAPTIST A large 15th-century church with a west tower. Inside are rood and parclose screens of the same period, with painted figures of prophets, the Annunciation and the Visitation. There is an early 17th-century pulpit, a 15th-century wall-painting of Christ, and some original stained glass.

**Ashwell** *Herts.*     *547Je*
A well preserved village, with timber-framed and gable-brickwork houses, representative of some of the finest domestic architecture in England. St John's Guildhall, with its narrowly spaced timber uprights set closely together, is mid-17th century. The town house near by, which contains an excellent museum—originally started by two schoolboys—is 16th century. In St Mary's Church, started in the early 14th century, there is the Latin inscription: 'Miserable, wild and distracted, the dregs of the people alone survive to witness . . .', referring to the Black Death which swept through England killing one man in three. On the inside wall of the tower is scratched a unique 14th-century drawing of old St Paul's Cathedral. Other places of interest are Chantry House, Westbury Farm, with plastered gables, Ducklake Farm in the grounds of Ashwell Bury and Bluegates Farm at Ashwell End. The manor house at Ashwell Bury is a Victorian dwelling internally reconstructed by Sir Edwin Lutyens, the architect and designer of the Cenotaph in Whitehall.
ASHWELL VILLAGE MUSEUM The life of an English village from prehistoric times up to the present day is depicted at this folk museum. The exhibits, which include Stone and Bronze Age implements, Roman pottery and tools used by country craftsmen—farmer, shepherd, blacksmith, wheelwright and coachbuilder—are displayed in a timber-framed, early Tudor building which was originally the Ashwell Tithe Office of the Abbot of Westminster. It later became the town house for

market officials, a meeting place of Dissenters, a straw-plaiting school and a tailor's shop. It was restored in 1930 to house the collection of local bygones, and is now scheduled as an ancient monument. Among a wide variety of exhibits are tradesmen's tokens of the 17th and 19th centuries, a unique 16th-century spectacle frame, and a peep show of the Great London Exhibition.

**Astbury** *Cheshire*     *552Be*
CHURCH OF ST MARY A large battlemented church, of the 14th and 15th centuries, with a detached tower and spire. Inside there are especially good roofs, and screen, lectern and stalls of *c.* 1500. The earliest of the many monuments in the church and churchyard is a 14th-century knight's effigy; an unconventional 17th-century font cover projects from the wall.

**Astley** *Warks.*     *546Eg*
CHURCH OF ST MARY THE VIRGIN This collegiate church of *c.* 1340 was cruciform and had a central tower and spire. After the Reformation, the building fell into disrepair until the tower collapsed *c.* 1600. A few years later the old chancel became the nave of a restored parish church, and a new chancel and west tower were built. The choir stalls, *c.* 1400, have painted figures and misericords. There are brasses and monuments.

**Aston Eyre** *Shrops.*     *546Bg*
CHURCH A small Norman church with a superb carving in the tympanum of the south doorway, depicting Christ's entry on an ass into Jerusalem.

**Aston Upthorpe** *Berks.*     *546Fb*
CHURCH A small building with a Norman window, and remains of a south doorway. The north porch is probably 15th century. The east end was restored during the 1850's, when the bell-turret was added.

**Athelhampton Hall** *Dorset*     *540Dc*
A 15th-century mansion with 16th-century additions, the Hall has a timbered roof, oriel window, heraldic glass, linenfold panels, secret staircases, and a Tudor great chamber. The stables are thatched, and there is a 15th-century dove-cote.

**Atherington** *Devon*     *538Ff*
CHURCH OF ST MARY A Perpendicular Gothic church, with a tall west tower, restored in 1884, whose main attractions are its wagon-roofs and screens, the remains of the rood loft (*c.*1540) in the north aisle, and the series of carved 15th-century bench ends. Much carving of foliage, dating from *c.* 1540. Some monuments, including a cross-legged knight of *c.* 1250, and 16th-century brasses.

**Attingham Hall** *Shrops.*     *552Ab*
A mansion built in Classical style in 1785 for the 1st Lord Berwick to designs by George Steuart. It stands in front of an older house built *c.* 1700. The south front has a portico which rises through three storeys; it is supported by slender Ionic columns. Two wings project behind the remains of the old house on the north side, masked on the south by curved colonnades. The 2nd Lord Berwick commissioned Humphry Repton to landscape the grounds, and shortly afterwards, in 1807, John Nash was engaged to build a picture gallery. Nash originally thought of supporting the ceiling on novel cast-iron frames, to be made at the neighbouring iron-foundry of Coalbrookdale. However, he changed his mind and used instead the present iron frames with glass lights—an early use of these materials in English architecture. The state rooms contain fine furniture and pictures by Caravaggio, Veronese and Spanish masters.

**Attleborough** *Norfolk*     *554Cb*
CHURCH OF ST MARY Formerly cruciform, the church's chancel and apse have disappeared, while the central tower remains. Some Norman work exists and the remainder is mainly Decorated, with a good west window and a two-storey porch. The late 15th-century rood screen has painted decoration. There is a cast-iron lectern of 1816, wall-paintings, and some original stained glass.

**Aubourn Hall** *Lincs.*     *553Ge*
A red-brick 16th-century country house with a fine carved staircase.

**Auchagallon** *Arran, Bute*     *560Ed*
The monument here is a little out of the ordinary. The cairn is a normal rounded mound of stones, but it is surrounded by the stone circle, which consists of 15 standing stones. It stands in the low-lying ground close to the west coast of the island.

**Audley End** *Essex*     *548Ae*
The Benedictine Abbey of Walden stood here, but after the Dissolution the site was given by Henry VIII to Lord Audley, who built himself a house in the grounds. The estate descended to Lord Howard of Walden, created Earl of Suffolk by James I; in 1603 the Earl began an enormous Jacobean house, one of the largest in England, with two great courts. About 1721 the 5th Earl employed Sir John Vanbrugh to work on the house, and the outer court was pulled down and the rest of the house much altered. After that the building gradually deteriorated, and in 1747 it was bought by Lady Portsmouth; her nephew, Lord Braybrooke, succeeded to it in 1762 and between then and his death in 1797 carried out renovations. The house contains a fine collection of pictures.

**Aughton** *Lancs.*     *551Jg*
CHURCH OF ST MICHAEL A Norman church with later medieval work. The 14th-century tower is square at the base, then octagonal, and is surmounted by an octagonal spire. Inside is a 15th-century font, brass plates of 1661 and 1686, and an altar tomb to a 19th-century rector by J. S. Westmacott.

**Aughton** *Yorks.*     *558Eb*
CHURCH OF ALL SAINTS An isolated church on the banks of the R. Derwent, basically Norman with a fine chancel arch, and font. There is a 15th-century brass showing a man in armour.

**Auldearn** *Nairns.*     *566Cg*
BOATH DOVE-COT Built in the late 17th century to house the pigeons which provided the local laird's table with fresh food during the winter months. This circular stone cote, rough cast of lime and small gravel, containing 546 nest holes, occupies a prominent position on a mound that was originally the site of Auldearn Castle. Here James Graham, Marquess of Montrose, defeated the Covenanters, the Presbyterian opponents of Charles I, in 1645.

**Ault Hucknall** *Derbys.*     *552Ee*
CHURCH OF ST JOHN THE BAPTIST The Norman origins of this church, with its central tower, are easily seen, and some even suggest there may be Saxon remains. There is a carved tympanum depicting a centaur, and the Lamb and Cross, while beneath a man is fighting a dragon. A 17th-century monument has some good standing allegorical figures.

**Avebury** *Wilts.*     *540Fg*
Avebury village lies in the centre of this, the largest henge monument in the country. Its enclosing bank of chalk is still 20 ft high and has a diameter of

## THE HALL AT AUDLEY END

The splendid Jacobean house Lord Howard of Walden, 1st Earl of Suffolk, built when he inherited the estate at Audley End in 1603, eventually became one of the largest in England. It was about twice its present size, with two courts built around the ruins of a Benedictine monastery. After the Restoration Charles II acquired the house, but it was returned to the Howards in 1701, when the 5th Earl called in the architect Sir John Vanbrugh. On his advice the outer court was demolished and much of the interior altered. But the graceful exterior of the earlier house, with its roof surrounded by a balustrade and topped by turrets, remains—and so does the great hall, entered through two ornate early 17th-century porches, and containing a flat ceiling embellished with wood and plaster panels, and a screen with a riot of carved decoration.

---

1400 ft. Inside it is the great ditch, cut into the chalk to a depth of 30 ft—as revealed by excavation—with a 15 ft flat base and steeply sloping sides. There were four entrances to the central circle, which is surrounded by more than 100 great slabs of sarsen, a local sandstone. Within this stone ring stood two smaller circles side by side, which may be earlier than the great ring, and of these also many of the stones survive. At the centre of the southern small circle stand some of the stones of what is called a 'cove'. (See p. 68.)

From this monument runs 'The Avenue', a 50 ft wide passage between spaced sarsen pairs. It leads to the smaller site known as The Sanctuary on Overton Hill, more than a mile to the east.

ALEXANDER KEILLER MUSEUM The museum is housed in what was originally a stable block, converted by Alexander Keiller during his excavation and restoration of the Avebury stone circle in the late 1930's. It displays material from the uniquely important complex of prehistoric monuments in the area—Windmill Hill, Avebury, Silbury Hill, and West Kennet Avenue.

AVEBURY MANOR An Elizabethan manor house, with period panelling, plasterwork and collections of porcelain and antique furniture. The park, containing a garden of hedges cut into ornamental shapes, is bounded by the megalithic stone circle.

**Aveley** Essex                    548Ab
CHURCH OF ST MICHAEL Dating from the 12th to 14th centuries, the church has a 12th-century Purbeck marble font and an early 17th-century pulpit. The brasses include one of Flemish type to Ralph de Knevynton (d. 1370).

**Avington** Hants.                    541He
CHURCH OF ST MARY A brick church built c. 1770, with a west tower. The 18th-century interior is unspoilt and contains pulpit, box-pews, family pew, and a west gallery which has an early 19th-century barrel-organ. The 18th- and 19th-century monuments include one to Margaret, Countess of Carnarvon (d. 1768), who ordered the church to be built, but died before it was begun.

**Avington Park** Hants.                    541He
A red-brick country house in the style of Wren, dating from the 16th and 17th centuries.

**Axbridge** Som.                    540Cf
CHURCH OF ST JOHN THE BAPTIST A cruciform Perpendicular church, with a good central tower. There is a fine plaster nave ceiling of 1636, and monuments from the late 15th century.

**Aylesbury** Bucks.                    547Gd
The town has Parliamentarian associations, especially with John Hampden (1594–1643) who in 1635 refused to pay the Ship Money Tax imposed by Charles I. In the main square is a statue to Hampden, who lived at Prestwood Common near by. The 18th-century Prebendal House was the home of John Wilkes (1727–97), satirist and M.P. for Aylesbury from 1757 to 1764. The King's Head Hotel dates from the 15th century and has fine medieval windows, gateway and courtyard.
BUCKINGHAMSHIRE COUNTY MUSEUM The museum is housed partly in an early 18th-century building erected for the grammar school, and partly in a private house rebuilt in the early 18th century but retaining its 15th-century roof. The

collections relate to Buckinghamshire archaeology and history, and include finds from the Romano-British villa at Hambleden, and a collection of Romano-British silver (late 4th–early 5th century AD). Collections of paintings are also on view, including a set of nine oils of the grounds of Hartwell House (1738 and 1749) by B. Nebot, and a portrait by Angelica Kauffmann.

CHURCH OF ST MARY A cruciform church of the 13th–15th centuries, unfortunately over-restored by Sir Gilbert Scott in the 1860's. The spirelet on the central tower is a successful copy of a 17th-century original. The beautiful late 12th-century font is circular, and carved with stiff-leaved foliage round rim and base; it has given its name to a type. Much Victorian stained glass by Thomas Willement and Burlison & Grylls. The monuments include one by Edward Stanton of 1703 and another (1749) perhaps by Peter Scheemakers.

**Aylesford** *Kent*                 542Df
A restored 13th-century friary, with 14th-century cloisters, containing collections of sculpture and ceramics. There is a fine rose garden.

**Aylsham** *Norfolk*               554Dc
John of Gaunt held the Court of his Duchy in the old guildhall of this pleasant market town. There are a number of good 17th- and 18th-century houses in and about the town. Market Place has several, including the Black Boy Inn, probably Queen Anne. On Blickling Road are the Knoll, *c.* 1700, and Aylsham Old Hall, dated 1689, an excellent example of its time, with hipped-roof and pedimented doorway. On the Norwich road

are Bank House, *c.* 1710, and the Manor House, late 17th century. Farther out is Abbots Hall, an early 17th-century brick house.

**Aynhoe Park** *Northants.*         546Fe
A 17th-century country mansion, built on the foundations of a Norman castle. It was remodelled by Sir John Soane in the 18th century and contains collections of paintings and Venetian glass.

**Ayot St Lawrence** *Herts.*         547Jc
SHAW'S CORNER A late Victorian country residence, the home of the playwright, George Bernard Shaw, from 1906 to 1950. It is preserved as he left it. His ashes were scattered in the garden.

**Ayr** *Ayrs.*                     561Gc
The seaport centre of the Robert Burns country. The Auld Brig (Old Bridge) dates from the 13th century, and was renovated in 1910. Loudoun Hall (late 15th century) is the oldest house in the town. In the Wallace Tower (built 1832) is a statue of Sir William Wallace, the Scottish patriot, carved by James Thom, a local sculptor.

CARNEGIE LIBRARY, MUSEUM AND ART GALLERY The one-room museum houses the Auld Ayr exhibition, a historical record of the town. Monthly loan exhibitions are held in the art gallery.

TOWN HALL Thomas Hamilton of Edinburgh, given the commission in 1828 to build a new town steeple and assembly rooms in the town of Ayr, designed this neo-Classical building of Cullaloe stone from Fife. The 210 ft spire, formed by superimposed squares and octagons surmounted by an obelisk, still dominates the town.

## AVEBURY

*The largest stone circle in Europe, probably in the world, this circle of sarsen stones or megaliths in which lies the village of Avebury is 450 yds across; it is surrounded by a bank and ditch enclosing 28 acres. The stones, probably once 100 in all, stand 5 to 20 ft above the ground, but many have been pillaged for use as building material. The monument, approached by an avenue of megaliths, was arranged by Bronze Age peoples about 1800 BC and was probably a form of open temple. Within the main circle are remains of two smaller circles each about 350 ft across.*

# B

**Babington** *Som.* 540Df
CHURCH OF ST MARGARET Grouped with Babington House, the church was built in 1750. It has an apse, and a west tower with a cupola.

**Babraham** *Cambs.* 548Ae
CHURCH OF ST PETER The church is mostly of the 13th century, but contains 18th-century pews and reredos. There is an important monument of *c.* 1658 by the eccentric sculptor John Bushnell—two strange figures in front of a carved drapery.

**Bachwen** *Caern.* 550Ed
Here, close to the sea, stands a typical megalithic burial chamber, with uprights and capstone, from which the circular mound has long since disappeared. The unusual feature here is the wealth of cup-marks which cover the upper surface of the capping. This type of carving, first introduced to Britain at the end of the Neolithic period by the megalith-builders, is fairly well distributed in northern and western Britain, but it is not very commonly found in this position in a grave.

**Backwell** *Som.* 540Cg
CHURCH OF ST ANDREW Dating from the 13th century and with later additions, St Andrew's has a west tower over 100 ft high. Inside, there is a Norman font, a 16th-century screen and a brass.

**Bacton** *Herefs.* 546Ae
CHURCH OF ST FAITH This church was first built in the 13th century; the west tower was added in the late 16th century. Some of the stalls are ornamented with poppy-head carving. The most important monument is to Blanche Parry, a local girl who was Queen Elizabeth's maid of honour. She is shown kneeling before the Queen; the inscription to hers ends: 'Allwaye wythe maeden queene a maede did ende my liffe'.

**Bacton** *Suffolk* 548Df
CHURCH OF ST MARY A Decorated and Perpendicular church with a west tower. There is decorative stone and flint work in the clerestory, and a restored hammerbeam roof in the nave. Inside is a contemporary font with angels; also benches, screen, and medieval mural painting.

**Bacup** *Lancs.* 552Bg
BACUP NATURAL HISTORY SOCIETY'S MUSEUM Collections devoted to local natural history, geology, archaeology and household bygones are exhibited in a former inn of the late 18th century.

**Badbury Rings** *Dorset* 540Ed
This is a conspicuous Iron Age hill-fort by the Wimborne–Blandford road. A steep hill-top has been strengthened with multiple bank-and-ditch defences, through which there are two entrances with rather complicated defence-works. It is probable that this enclosure—or a site just outside the defences—was the Roman posting-station of Vindogladia, for here the main Roman road from Old Sarum to Dorchester, the Ackling Dyke, is crossed by another from Bath to Poole. To the north-west of the site are four mounds presumed to be Roman barrows.

**Baddiley** *Cheshire* 552Ad
CHURCH OF ST MICHAEL A small church, consisting only of nave and chancel; the nave was rebuilt in 1811 but the chancel retains its original

timber construction. The east wall of the nave over the screen is painted with heraldry, the Commandments, Creed and Lord's Prayer, 1663. There are box-pews, west gallery and pulpit of the 18th century, and a large monument of *c.* 1726.

**Badgeworth** *Glos.* 546Cd
CHURCH OF THE HOLY TRINITY An early 14th-century Decorated church, noteworthy for the profusion of 'ball-flower' carving ornamenting the windows and north doorway.

**Badingham** *Suffolk* 548Ef
CHURCH OF ST JOHN THE BAPTIST Originally Norman, with later additions, the church has a pretty hammerbeam roof, and a good example of an East Anglican seven-sacrament font.

**Badminton House** *Glos.* 546Cb
The Palladian mansion home of the Dukes of Beaufort since the 17th century, with alterations in 1740 by William Kent. It contains a collection of Italian, Dutch and English paintings. The annual Horse Trials at Badminton are internationally known and the stables and hunt kennels are open for viewing (as well as the house). William Kent originally laid out the grounds; later the landscaping was extended by Capability Brown.

**Bag Enderby** *Lincs.* 553Je
CHURCH OF ST MARGARET The chancel, nave and windows of this sandstone church date from the 14th century. The font, of the same period, has carvings of a *Pietà*. The tower and porch are of the 15th century, as is the east window. Some medieval stained glass remains.

**Baggrave Hall** *Leics.* 552Fb
The grounds include a water garden and sunken garden.

**Bainton** *Yorks.* 558Fb
CHURCH OF ST ANDREW A fine church, mainly of the 14th century, with a west tower; on the outside are many carved animals and faces. Inside is a Norman font, the brass of a priest, and the effigy of a 14th-century cross-legged knight.

**Bakewell** *Derbys.* 552De
CHURCH OF ALL SAINTS An embattled cruciform church, of Norman origin, with an octagonal central tower and spire. Some Saxon fragments remain. It contains an early 14th-century font, rood screen, and many monuments with effigies and weepers. The most remarkable is that to Sir Godfrey Foljambe (*d.* 1377) with two upright half-figures on a wall.

**Balcaskie House** *Fife.* 562Dg
Hanging terraces and fine hedges are features of the extensive gardens surrounding this house built *c.* 1675 to designs by Sir William Bruce.

**Baldersby** *Yorks.* 558Cd
CHURCH OF ST JAMES A large Victorian church by William Butterfield, designed 1856–8 in the 13th-century style, with a tall steeple and spire. The impressive interior has a tiled floor in the chancel and typical fittings and stained glass of the period.

**Baldock** *Herts.* 547Je
CHURCH OF ST MARY A spacious church, with two-storey south porch and an early 14th-century west tower, embattled, with an octagonal lantern

and small spire. Inside are a 13th-century octagonal font, 15th-century screens, brasses and a monument, of *c.* 1846, by E. H. Baily.

**Ballygowan** *Argyll* 560Eg
A decorated rock-face with a group of the normal Bronze Age cup-and-ring decorations together with several horseshoe-shaped examples.

**Balmerino Abbey** *Fife.* 562Ch
Ruins of an abbey built by Alexander II (1198–1249) at the wish of his mother Queen Ermengarde (widow of William the Lion), who is buried beneath the high altar.

**Balmoral Castle** *A'deen* 566Dd
A private residence of the Queen, used by the Royal Family as a holiday estate. Prince Albert, Queen Victoria's Prince Consort, bought it in 1852 and in the following years had it rebuilt in white granite as a castellated mansion in Scottish baronial style. Only the gardens, first laid out by Prince Albert in the 1850's, and planted with rare conifers and other trees, are open to the public, who may also see Queen Victoria's garden cottage and Queen Mary's sunken garden.

**Balnuarin of Clava** *I'ness.* 566Bf
A ring cairn, an almost circular structure contained in a broad ring of stony rubble, held on the outside by a stone kerb and internally by upright stone slabs. The average thickness of this ring is about 20 ft. The internal area measures 21 ft by 18 ft. Outside the ring are nine standing stones spaced along the circumference of a circle some 100 ft across. These vary greatly in size; the tallest is about 7½ ft high. On either side of the ring cairn is a passage-grave of another type.

**Balsham** *Cambs.* 548Be
CHURCH OF THE HOLY TRINITY The church is mainly 14th century with additions; there is a west tower. Inside is a good rood screen, and traces of medieval stained glass can be seen. Two good brasses to former rectors, 1401 and 1462, and many 14th-century stalls with carving and misericords.

**Bamburgh** *Northld.* 563Gd
CHURCH OF ST AIDAN The church is mainly of the 13th century with later additions, and a west tower. The long, aisle-less chancel has a crypt beneath. There is a monument by Chantrey of 1839; Grace Darling is buried in the churchyard.

**Bampton** *Oxon.* 546Ec
Bampton is a large village that once had a market, and the 19th-century Italianate town hall survives in the market-place. It has a surprising number of good 'gentry' houses, mostly visible from road or churchyard. The castle, west of the village, preserves fragments of the 13th-century castle of Aymer de Valance, but is now a private house. Behind the church the deanery is a rambling house, externally of the early 17th century. Bampton Manor has an 18th-century Classical façade to the garden, and an early 19th-century Gothic-style porch to the drive. Weald Manor, to the southwest, is of *c.* 1700 and is finished with a quality of detail worthy of a much grander house.
CHURCH OF ST MARY THE VIRGIN An impressive cruciform church with central tower and spire, it has Norman and later Gothic work. Inside are brasses, and a monument with an early 17th-century recumbent effigy.

**Banbury** *Oxon.* 546Ee
An ancient wool town, whose castle was twice besieged by Parliamentary forces during the Civil War. The castle was demolished in 1646 and no trace remains. The Banbury Cross of nursery

rhyme fame was destroyed in 1602 by the Puritans as being heretic: the present hexagonal neo-Gothic cross dates from 1860.
The spiced cakes of Banbury were first produced in 1608 but did not find public favour until 1770. The original bake-house still exists at The Original Cake Shop, 12 Parsons Street.
PUBLIC MUSEUM AND GLOBE ROOM A small collection is devoted to local history.

**Banff** *Banffs.* 566Fg
One of the most attractive towns in the north of Scotland, exhibiting a wealth of good architecture. The 16th-century market cross, the tolbooth of 1764–7 by one of the Adam brothers, churches in the Classical form, tall gabled houses and simple artisan dwellings ornament The Shore, Waterpath, High Street and Boyndie Street. Here and there a Classical doorpiece and stone quoins add a note of sophistication. Banff Castle of 1750 and Duff House, magnificent baroque by William Adam, 1725–40, are stalwart reminders of more affluent days.
DUFF HOUSE A great ornate mansion built for the Duke of Fife in 1735 by William Adam in Classical style, based on the style of the Villa Borghese.

**Bangor** *Caern.* 550Ee
CATHEDRAL A small cathedral, originally Norman, which was rebuilt during the 13th and 14th centuries, and much restored by Sir Gilbert Scott in *c.* 1870–8. The building is cruciform with a central tower, and another at the west of the nave. There is a slab with a 14th-century low relief of a lady, and a 15th-century font.

**Bannockburn** *Stir.* 561Jf
BORE STONE A monument, erected in 1964, on the traditional site of the defeat of the English army in 1314 by King Robert de Bruce. A rotunda encloses the Bore Stone site where the Scots standard stood. There is also an equestrian statue to King Robert.

**Banwell** *Som.* 540Cf
CHURCH OF ST ANDREW A Perpendicular church with an imposing west tower. There is a Norman font, a 16th-century rood screen, 19th-century stained glass, and interesting brasses.

**Barden Tower** *Yorks.* 558Bc
Ruins in Wharfedale, all that remains of a house begun in the 16th century as one of six lodges built for keepers' accommodation and the protection of deer in the Forest of Barden. The lodge was completed in 1774. Since then it has fallen into disrepair.

**Bardwell** *Suffolk* 548Cf
CHURCH OF SS PETER AND PAUL Much 15th- and 16th-century building; the south porch has flushwork decoration and Arms, of *c.* 1430. The hammerbeam roof has some of its original colour left, though most of the angels have gone. There is 15th-century stained glass, and a 17th-century monument with kneeling figures and children.

**Barfreston** *Kent* 542Ff
CHURCH OF ST NICHOLAS The small Norman village church at Barfreston is externally ornamented with an unusual amount of carving. The decoration was done *c.* 1180, and is in style similar to other local carving at Rochester and Canterbury. The east end of the church has a row of arcades surmounted by a wheel-window carved with animals, foliage and figures. The arcading is continued round the sides and is topped by a corbel table carved with grotesque figures. There is a less decorated doorway on the south side of the chancel and another on the north side of the nave. The

## BARFRESTON CHURCH

*No explanation has been found for the profusion of rich Romanesque carving on Barfreston Church. (The village church at nearby Patrixbourne is similarly ornamented, but Barfreston is outstanding.) The carving has the same style as other local carving at Rochester and Canterbury, and was probably done by masons with similar training. The manor belonged to the de Port family during the 12th century, but no account has survived to explain the building of such an elaborate little church. The interior is less ornamented, but a curious feature is the carved, raised band which runs horizontally beneath the windows of the nave. The nave and the decoration were partly restored in 1840, and some of the present carving dates from then.*

most impressive carving decorates the south door, which was clearly intended as the main entrance. Carved in the centre of the tympanum is Christ in Glory. The meaning of the remainder of the carving is obscure; many of the roundels on the arches appear to be humorous, particularly those of animals playing musical instruments.

**Barham** *Hunts.* 547Jf
CHURCH OF ST GILES A Norman church, with nave arcade and chancel arch, and a 13th-century chancel. There is a 13th-century font and a 14th-century coffin-lid.

**Barham** *Kent* 542Ff
Seen from the valley road, the village is a cluster of mellow, red-tiled roofs among the trees. Up the hill, along turning and twisting streets, is Barham House, a handsome Queen Anne building, hidden behind a grandiose brick portal contrived in the garden wall by Sir Edwin Lutyens.

**Barking** *Greater London* 548Ab
EASTBURY HOUSE A red-brick, H-shaped manor house of 1572, now in a modern housing estate.
VALENCE HOUSE MUSEUM A 17th-century manor house, still partly moated, with a collection devoted exclusively to local history. The collection includes 17th-century portraits relating to the Fanshawe family.

**Barlaston** *Staffs.* 552Bd
WEDGWOOD MUSEUM TRUST In 1906, many documents and wares were discovered at the Etruria factory, which had been built for Josiah Wedgwood in 1769. This discovery led to the foundation of the museum, which displays only Wedgwood wares and associated documents. Unique exhibits include the 'First Days' vase in black basalt decorated in red, made by Josiah Wedgwood himself on June 13, 1769; a vase in similar style, but decorated in white and green, made for Henry Earle in 1774; a black basalt bust

of Palladio (*c.* 1777); George Stubbs' painting of the Wedgwood family at Etruria Hall (1780); and a plaque in blue and white Jasper, showing the Apotheosis of Homer, made *c.* 1784 and modelled by John Flaxman.

**Barmekin of Echt** *A'deen* 566Fe
Three ramparts form the outer defences of this hillfort, and the five entrances are flanked by walls running well into the enclosure. Inside the enclosure, two more stone walls encircle the innermost area, some 370 ft in diameter. It seems clear that this complex resulted from one or two phases of defence-building.

**Barmston** *Yorks.* 559Gc
CHURCH OF ALL SAINTS The church is mainly of 15th-century work, with a west tower. There is a Norman font with cable-and-diamond decoration, and a 15th-century alabaster effigy.

**Barnack** *Northants.* 547Hh
CHURCH OF ST JOHN THE BAPTIST A Saxon church probably dating from the early 11th century. The west tower has 13th-century additions, including the spire and pinnacles, while the remainder of the church is of the 12th to the 14th centuries. Among the contents are a seated figure of Christ in Majesty (early 11th century), an early English font with leaves (13th century) and monuments dating from the early 15th century.

**Barnard Castle** *Durham* 558Be
The town grew up beside the medieval castle on top of a bluff by a crossing point of the R. Tees. The castle was founded by Guy, Lord of Bailleul, and rebuilt in 1112 by his nephew, Bernard Balliol, from whom it takes its name. It is now in ruins, but remains of the 14th-century great hall and earlier cylindrical, three-storied keep survive. The castle was besieged in 1569 during the Rising of the Northern Earls, and allowed to decay after its capture by Cromwell. The medieval stone bridge

EL GRECO: THE TEARS OF ST PETER *Of all the old masters El Greco seems the most 'modern'. Both in spirit and style his work conforms in its air of unreality and individuality with the art of our own time. Born in Crete in 1541 he clearly reflects his Byzantine heritage but in about 1560 he went to Venice and came under the spell of Titian. Then in 1570 he went to Rome where the gesturings and foreshortenings in the late murals of Michelangelo, only six years dead, had prepared the way for mannerism. In 1577 he settled in Spain for the rest of his life, and in a wealth of portraits and religious works he developed a more and more personal style. A marked elongation of limbs, flame-like forms, pietistic gazes with eyes rolled heavenwards—as in 'The Tears of St Peter'—and a range of predominantly acid colours are the ingredients of his unique visionary intensity. His abstract conflicting planes create a shallow space similar to that in the cubist work of another Spanish painter, Picasso.*

across the river is still in use and on the main street of the town are ancient houses and several inns—in one of which Dickens wrote *Nicholas Nickleby*.

BOWES MUSEUM The building, of French design, was begun in 1869 specifically as a museum, and houses an extensive collection of Spanish paintings, including works by El Greco and Goya, French works by Boucher and Courbet amongst others, and Italian paintings including some by Sassetta and Tiepolo. A series of period settings displays furniture (particularly French 18th century) and also collections of pottery and porcelain. 16th–18th-century tapestries can also be seen, with smaller collections of sculpture, miniatures, jewellery, watches and snuff boxes. There are several objects from royal collections and a number of items belonging to Napoleon. Dolls, dolls' houses and other toys can be seen in a children's room.

**Barncluith** *Lanarks.* 561Je
The house was planned by John Hamilton in 1583; it stands amid fine Dutch gardens on a series of terraces overlooking the R. Avon.

**Barnet** *Greater London* 547Jc
MUSEUM The museum specialises in items of local interest—photographs, maps, brass rubbings—but also contains many varieties of women's dresses,

FRENCH GOLD SNUFF-BOX *Despite the wars and revolutions of the 18th and 19th centuries, French goldsmiths maintained their high standards of work, and this snuff-box is a fine example. Dated on the lid 'May 27, 1853' it was made of several different coloured golds by the Parisian firm of Martial Barnard. The surface is decorated with silver and with opaque and translucent enamels. An inscription around the sides supports legal government as opposed to revolution.*

SILVER SWAN *This swan is an elaborate musical toy, 27½ in. high, with an articulated neck. When set in motion, it bends down to pick up a fish which it appears to swallow while a tune is played. Said to have been made for Thomas Weekes' 'museum' of mechanical novelties in late 18th-century London, it was restored by a London silversmith in the 1860's. The pointed leaves round the 'pool' probably date from then, but the swan itself seems little changed from the 18th century.*

ornaments and children's wear, and a collection of samplers. A Cypriot urn of 900–600 BC can also be seen, with Cypriot figures probably dating from the 4th century AD.

**Barnstaple** *Devon*                                     538Ff
Barnstaple has been a small inland seaport since Norman times. The parish church, consecrated in 1318, has a twisted wood and lead spire, dated 1636. The Long Bridge has crossed the R. Taw since 1273. Queen Anne's Walk (1609–29) was once a meeting place for ship owners and merchants whose bargains were settled on the Tone Stone. The Three Tunes Tavern (1450) has

medieval panelling and fire-places; it was restored in 1947. Horwood and Paiges Almshouses date from the 17th century. The latter has a granite colonnade façade.

PENTECOST-DODDERIDGE PARLOUR Once the town house of a rich merchant it has a collection of plate and ancient seals, and a symbolic Silver Oar showing that the mayor is Water Bailiff holding Admiralty warrant for the post.

ST ANNE'S CHAPEL MUSEUM The upper part of this building probably dates from 1456, but the crypt is much older—it was originally part of a charnel-house. From 1685 the building was used as a place of worship by Huguenots, Protestants who had fled from France to escape religious persecution. The building was a grammar school from the end of the 17th century until 1910; John Gay, who wrote *The Beggar's Opera* in 1728, was a pupil there and items associated with him are in the museum. All the collections are of local interest and include prints, drawings, pottery, seals and fire-arms.

**Barra Castle** *A'deen*                                 567Gf
A partly 17th-century stone mansion with a wing built in the mid-Georgian period.

**Barrington Court** *Som.*                               540Cd
A fine Tudor mansion, built of stone in pure Gothic design by Lord Daubeny between 1514 and 1520. The stable wing was added in 1790.

**Barrowden** *Rutland*                                   553Gb
CHURCH OF ST PETER Mainly 14th century; 15th-century enlargements include the clerestory and east window. There is a west tower with spire. Inside is a late 16th-century monument.

**Barr's Hill** *Dumf.*                                   562Aa
HILL-FORT This hill forms part of the narrow ridge separating the lower reaches of Annandale and Nithsdale and gives a wide view of the approaches on both sides. The outer defences are two ramparts with an intermediate ditch. Within this, enclosing the central area, is a massive bank with an external ditch. Outside, on the north-west, there are traces of additional defences. There is a single entrance on the east side.

**Barsalloch Point** *Wig.*                               556Cf
The tip of a headland is cut off by two ramparts with a broad deep ditch between them.

**Barsham** *Suffolk*                                     548Eg
CHURCH OF THE HOLY TRINITY Norman, with later enlargement, Holy Trinity has a round west tower, and a highly decorated east wall with stone and flint flushwork trellis which incorporates the window as part of the scheme. Two fonts, one Norman, the other Perpendicular; Jacobean woodwork includes the pulpit. The 19th-century east window is by C. E. Kempe. There is a brass, and a 16th-century monument.

**Barton Turf** *Norfolk*                                 554Dc
CHURCH OF ST MICHAEL AND ALL ANGELS With a battlemented west tower, this 14th- and 15th-century church has 15th-century screens with painted figures. A brass dates from c. 1445, and there are monuments from the late 18th century.

**Barton-upon-Humber** *Lincs.*                           553Gg
CHURCH OF ST MARY This magnificent Norman church was once a chapel-of-ease—built for parishioners who lived too far from their parish church for comfort. There are Early English, Decorated and Perpendicular additions, and 14th- and 15th-century brasses.

CHURCH OF ST PETER In what was once an important harbour town, this Saxon church from the middle of the 10th century has a tower and, in the east, Gothic additions from the 13th century onwards. The stonework of an east window has carvings of the Crucifixion, the Virgin and St John.

**Basing** *Hants.*     *541Hf*
A village of brick cottages, with a splendid brick barn at Grange Farm, lying in the marshy valley of the R. Loddon. The Norman earthworks of Basing Castle stand above it, but the great Tudor house inside them was destroyed in the Civil War.
BASING HOUSE RUINS A Saxon fortress, the Old Castle of Basing is referred to in Domesday Book. The Norman New Castle was built on the same site. In 1530 a magnificent Tudor fortified mansion, Basing House, was built on the same spot. Queen Elizabeth I stayed here twice; her second visit lasted 13 days and proved so expensive that her host had to demolish part of his house to pay for it. During the Civil War the house was besieged for three years by Cromwell's troops, and was captured and razed in 1645. Excavations are now in progress on the site and have revealed many items, including Iron Age pottery, Roman coins, 13th- and 18th-century tiles and glassware, 16th- and 17th-century pottery, and relics of the Civil War, all of which are housed in the New Museum. The Old Museum, built over the original powder magazine, contains examples of Tudor and Elizabethan sculpture, Tudor pottery and Elizabethan fire-backs.
CHURCH OF ST MARY A large Perpendicular church near the ruins of Basing House which was destroyed during the Civil War, when the architect, Inigo Jones, was taken prisoner, 1645. The church was also damaged at the same time, but later repaired, and restored again in 1874. There are several monuments of the 15th and 16th centuries, one by John Flaxman.

**Basingstoke** *Hants.*     *541Hf*
WILLIS MUSEUM Local archaeological exhibits, costume and textiles, coins, medals, clocks, watches and watchmakers' tools.

**Basingwerk** *Flints.*     *551He*
ABBEY Basingwerk Abbey, a Cistercian house, was founded during the 12th century; it is now in ruins.

**Baswich** *Staffs.*     *552Bc*
CHURCH OF THE HOLY TRINITY This little church was rebuilt during the 18th century, though the medieval tower was kept. There is a three-decker pulpit and, in the chancel, a double-decker family pew, one with a fire-place.

**Batcombe** *Som.*     *540De*
CHURCH OF ST MARY A 14th–15th-century church with a west tower of 1540. Inside are two Perpendicular fonts, and several mural tablets from the 16th century.

**Bateman's** *Sussex*     *542De*
Rudyard Kipling's home is preserved as it was when he lived there from 1902 until 1936; he described its surroundings in *Puck of Pook's Hill.* The house was built in 1634.

**Bath** *Som.*     *540Df*
The Roman camp established here *c.* AD 44 later became a prosperous spa, Aquae Sulis, based on local warm springs; remains of some of those buildings can still be seen. After 410 the town declined and suffered greatly from Anglo-Saxon raids. Later it became an ecclesiastical centre and wool-manufacturing town. Between 1088 and 1122 the monastic church was rebuilt by John of Tours, but the present abbey dates mainly from

1499–1616. During the 18th century Bath revived as a spa and the many fine Georgian buildings date from this period. The city was badly bombed during the Second World War and has been rebuilt; it is still an important spa and cultural centre. (See also pp. 76–77.)
ABBEY Bath Abbey, founded in 1499, is built in a restrained Perpendicular style and the design is remarkably uniform throughout. The present abbey church, although much smaller than the previous Romanesque building, was obviously intended to be ostentatious. Bishop King, the founder, was a royal servant, and the king's masons whom he employed promised to build him the finest vault in England. Whether the vault was in fact designed by them is uncertain, since it contains heraldic carvings which were probably executed after King's death in 1504, and the vault cuts across the frame of the east window, suggesting that its present curve was not the one originally planned. This striking and elaborate vault, which transforms the whole building, took a long time to complete, and the nave vault was not added until the 19th century. The church is crammed with monuments, and carved decoration on the west front shows angels climbing up and down ladders on each of the turrets flanking the window.
HOLBURNE OF MENSTRIE MUSEUM Built in Palladian style in 1796–7 as part of Sydney Gardens (a place of entertainment similar to Vauxhall Gardens in London) the inside of the house was adapted as a museum in 1913–15. It now houses china, ceramics, silver and glass, fine furniture and

DETAIL OF A 17th-CENTURY EMBROIDERED SILK DRESS

*The dress from which this detail is taken was made about 1660, shortly after the Restoration of Charles II, and is an extremely rare example of a complete dress of the period. On to the linen warp of the fabric silver tissue was woven, and the embroidery work was formed by covering narrow strips of thin parchment with silk; it forms a raised pattern, and was added to the finished dress.*
*(Museum of Costume, Bath Assembly Rooms)*

pictures including some by Gainsborough, Reynolds, Stubbs, Barker of Bath and Guardi.

ROMAN BATHS The Romans early learnt the medicinal quality of the Bath waters and here they established Aquae Sulis, the leading spa and fashionable town of Roman Britain, even as it later became that of 18th-century England. The great bath-buildings with an attached temple stood in the town centre and much of this complex is today incorporated in the modern Pump Room buildings, where there is also a museum of finds from the site.

MUSEUM OF COSTUME In Bath Assembly Rooms is the world's largest exhibition of costume. The period covered is from the 17th century to the present day. All aspects of fashion are covered, from the latest styles to fashionable Victorian costumes displayed against settings of Bath.

VICTORIA ART GALLERY The permanent collection includes *The Adoration of the Magi*, attributed to Hugo van der Goes, 18th- and 20th-century paintings, early English water-colours, the Kimball Collection of etchings, and local topographical prints and drawings. Also on permanent display are Anglo-Saxon, Danish and Norman coins from the Bath Mint, Bath trade tokens, antique watches, 18th-century English glass and ceramics, and examples of Bristol and Brislington Delftware. The frieze of the main gallery is a cast of part of the Parthenon frieze.

## Batley *Yorks.* 558Ca
ART GALLERY A permanent collection of paintings by contemporary artists including Francis Bacon,

FRANCESCO FANELLI
*St George and the Dragon*

*Fanelli was the most accomplished sculptor working at the Court of Charles I. He probably trained in one of the great bronze workshops in Florence and came to England soon after 1610, bringing with him the art of bronze statuette making, for which he was chiefly patronised during his stay until the outbreak of the Civil War in 1642, when he settled in France. With two exceptions all his known bronzes are of equestrian subjects. (Holburne of Menstrie Museum, Bath)*

Max Ernst, Graham Sutherland and Vivian Pitchforth is on view. Temporary exhibitions are held in the museum.

BAGSHAW MUSEUM (WILTON PARK) The archaeology, local history, industry and natural history of the Batley area are the themes of the displays here. There are also collections of Near Eastern antiquities and of Chinese ceramics.

## Battle *Sussex* 542Dd
A small town clustered by the abbey's mighty gate-house; there is a triangular market-place, and the best house, the Deanery, built in 1669, is beside the church.

CHURCH OF ST MARY A Norman building, enlarged during the 12th century, and with later additions. It has a west tower; the font is Norman and has a 15th-century cover. There are brasses, and a 16th-century monument.

## Battle Abbey *Sussex* 542Dd
Before the Battle of Hastings William of Normandy vowed he would build an abbey should the victory be his; he did so, and the remains of the Benedictine house stand on the slopes of Battle Hill, where Normans and English fought.

## Battlesbury Hill *Wilts.* 540Ef
This is one of the finest hill-forts in a county with many fine forts. It has an internal area of nearly 24 acres and most of it has a defence system of three ramparts, though the south-east segment has two only. Excavation has shown that there was permanent occupation late in the Iron Age. Outside the north-west entrance were the burials of men, women and children slain by violence, though whether by Roman soldiers or enemies from another British tribe, could not be determined.

## Baulking *Berks.* 546Ec
CHURCH OF ST NICHOLAS This small rustic church, mainly of the 13th century, has a narrow chancel arch with small side openings. The pulpit is 17th century, and a tie-beam on the roof is dated 1708.

## Bayons Manor *Lincs.* 553Hf
An example of romantic amateurism. Charles Tennyson, a politician and uncle of the Poet Laureate, who had pretensions to be a Peer, built this 'castle' in quasi-baronial style in 1836. The keep, barbican and six gateways are now in a state of decay. When the Duke of Northumberland visited it during Tennyson's life he is said to have observed: 'At Alnwick, I have only three gateways. You have *six!*'

## Beaudesert *Warks.* 546Df
CHURCH OF ST NICHOLAS This Norman church, with later additions, has a Perpendicular west tower, and a Norman chancel arch. The vaulting of the chancel was added by Thomas Garner in 1865. The 19th-century stained glass is by Holland, and Morris & Co., *c.* 1865.

## Beaulieu *Hants.* 541Gd
The pretty village street leads to the bank of the Beaulieu R., where it first opens out as an estuary. Across the river is Palace House, originally the gate-house of the abbey.

ABBEY A Cistercian abbey was founded here in 1204. The 13th-century buildings are now mainly ruined, but the old refectory is now the parish church. Its most important feature is the pulpit reached by way of an open 13th-century arcade in the thickness of the wall; although the present pulpit is new, it rests on the original base decorated with foliage.

MONTAGU MOTOR MUSEUM Founded by Lord Montagu in 1952 in memory of his father, the 2nd

# BATH *Splendour from the waters*

First Iron Age peoples, later the Romans, and later still fashionable society of the 18th and 19th centuries were attracted to Bath, to take the waters. By the time of Agricola (AD 78–84) the town was a thriving spa. In 1705 Beau Nash, leader of London society, went to live there and was soon 'king of Bath'. Once again the town became a major spa and holiday centre, and the finest artists and craftsmen of the time transformed it into a showpiece of Georgian prosperity.

HEAD OF MINERVA *This roughly life-size head is of bronze, hollow-cast and gilded. It had been hacked from the body in ancient times and was found in the 18th century lying in a corner of the Roman bath. The treatment of the back of the head shows that it must originally have worn Minerva's helmet, a separate casting. Here, doubtless, it was the representation of Sulis-Minerva. It was certainly a classical piece and was probably made in a Mediterranean workshop.*

HEAD OF MEDUSA *This frowning, moustached face, radiating locks of hair entwined with snakes, once dominated the temple of Sulis-Minerva at Bath. It was the central figure of a sculpted pediment, and encircled by two oak wreaths. On either side was a Winged Victory on a globe. To the Celts and Romans the head and Victories suggested the healing and evil-averting powers of Sulis-Minerva.*

FAN-VAULTING AT BATH ABBEY *in Prior Bird's Chantry is one of the most majestic features of a building which belongs to neither of the city's principal hey-days. Founded in 1499, it occupies the site of the Saxon abbey in which Edgar was crowned King of England in 972. Transformed into a vast minster by the Normans, the building was destroyed by fire in 1137. The present abbey was restored and altered several times between 1603 and the 1960's, when Second World War bomb damage was finally repaired. The famous west front carvings represent the founder-bishop's dream of angels ascending and descending from Heaven. Inside, 614 memorial tablets make an elaborate mural cenotaph to the many people who have contributed to the grandeur of Bath.*

ROYAL CRESCENT, *a great sweep of 30 houses with 114 Ionic columns supporting a Palladian cornice, was the work of John Wood the Younger. His father began the transformation of Bath by building Queen Square. Other streets followed, and other architects were at work: Thomas Baldwin, who built the guildhall and the Pump Room; Robert Adam, who spanned the R. Avon with the Pulteney Bridge, lining it with shops so that from the road there is no impression of being on a bridge. Meanwhile Ralph Allen, a postal clerk who founded a fortune on his ingenious system for speeding the mail out of Bath, commissioned Sham Castle, a mock Gothic façade which improved the view from his house on North Parade.*

THE EMPEROR HADRIAN *looks down at the Great Bath, 80 ft by 40 ft and 6 ft deep, where Romans bathed in hot mineral-spring water. Once roofed and surrounded by dressing-rooms, the bath is still supplied with water through the lead conduit fitted by a Roman plumber. There are also remains of another rectangular bath and a circular bath with stepped sides. Relics of mosaic pavements and the temple of Sulis-Minerva have been uncovered in the town. Bath was destroyed by the Saxons, and many of its Roman glories lay buried for more than 1000 years.*

CUP AND SALVER *When these magnificent pieces, made of silver heavily plated with gold, were given to the city of Bath in 1739 by Frederick, Prince of Wales, to commemorate his visit of the year before, they were described as being 'of an entire new taste, and much admired'. By then they were already six years old, but fashion travelled slowly in the 18th century. The novelty lay in their asymmetrical, or rococo, style, which was replacing the symmetrical forms established ever since the Middle Ages. The new style had developed in France, and was brought to this country by immigrant French goldsmiths like Lewis Pantin. Both pieces are superbly engraved with the Arms of the Prince of Wales and the city of Bath, and the finial of the cup is in the form of the Prince of Wales's feathers. The gift may have been made at the suggestion of Beau Nash, a personal friend of the Prince of Wales, and the leader of Bath society.*

### RIDLEY GOBLET

*This goblet may have belonged to Bishop Ridley, Henry VIII's chaplain and a friend of Lady Jane Grey. Dating from the 16th century, the jewel-coloured glass shows a possible Venetian influence. Only in the late 17th century, when Ravenscroft's experiments had produced lead-glass, did clear glass become popular in England. The goblet is the earliest piece of English glass in the museum collection.*
*(Cecil Higgins Art Gallery, Bedford)*

### ITALIAN NEEDLE-POINT BORDER

*Early lace was worked on a background fabric which was then cut away, forming a decorated open design. Gradually the ground fabric became less important until eventually the pattern was traced on parchment which was then embroidered with a needle—hence the term 'needle-point'. This border was probably made in the late 16th century, and includes some star-like motifs which originated in lace pattern books first*

Lord Montagu, the museum illustrates the history of motor transport with veteran, vintage and modern cycles, motor-cycles and cars. Among the many exhibits are the 1895 Knight—the earliest petrol-driven car of an all-British design; the 1896 Pennington—a three-wheeler with enormous cylinders and a top speed of about 45 mph, the land speed record of its time; the 1898 Cannstatt-Daimler—a tall motor brougham with a centre-pivot axle like a horse-drawn carriage, a rear engine and a 4-speed belt drive; and the 1920 Stanley steam car. In the motor-cycle section are the 1930 Ascot-Pullin and the 1921 Ner-A-Car—both attempts to produce 'cars on 2 wheels'. Among the bicycles are the 1865 English Bone Shaker, the 1876 Coventry Lever and the 1900 Dursley Pedersen with a unique frame of triangulated tubes and the saddle suspended like a hammock. There is also a national transport library with books, photographs and catalogues.

**Beauly Priory** *I'ness.*      566Bf
In this 'beau lieu' (beautiful place) stand the ruins of a 13th-century foundation, built by French monks for Sir John Bisset of Lovat in 1230; a façade was added *c.* 1530.

**Beaumaris** *Anglesey*      550Ee
The building of Beaumaris Castle was started at the end of the 13th century by Edward I. The castle is situated in open, level country, and since the architect had no natural obstacles to contend with,

the result is a castle of extreme symmetry, unequalled as a piece of military planning and engineering. It was intended that the castle should contain no less than five separate suites of lodgings, each with its own hall, chamber and associated rooms, and it has been estimated that the castle alone cost as much as the town and castle of Conway together. Work on the castle was never completed, and the curiously truncated towers are not, as elsewhere, the result of the activities of the Parliamentarians or of stone robbers, but of lack of interest and money in the 14th century. Building continued until the early years of Edward III's reign, *c.* 1370, and then stopped.

CHURCH A 14th-century building with several monuments, including alabaster effigies of a knight and lady. There are also stalls with misericords.

COURT HOUSE This delightful building was erected in 1614 and was thoughtfully altered early in the 19th century. Many of the fittings and the roof are original and there is an 18th-century canopied pew for the mayor and bailiffs.

NO. 32 CASTLE STREET Now an antique shop and well restored and maintained, it contains the remains of a house of *c.* 1400. The fine woodwork of the medieval roof can be seen from an upper floor inserted during the 17th century.

**Beaupre** *Glam.*      545Hb
The carved Renaissance porch in the inner court of this Elizabethan mansion is certainly the finest in

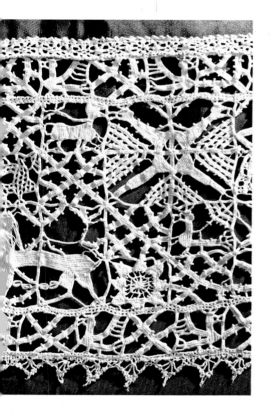

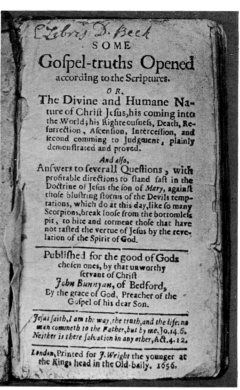

JOHN BUNYAN'S
*Some Gospel Truths Opened*

printed in the mid-16th century. In the pattern are two lions and a ship—one of four in the whole piece—with its occupants hoisting sails. Pictorial motifs of this date were usually of sacred subjects as the lace was intended for ecclesiastical use. Contemporary paintings, however, show that linen tablecloths in rich households were sometimes lace-edged although few now survive. (Cecil Higgins Art Gallery, Bedford)

*Only three copies are known to exist of 'Some Gospel Truths Opened', John Bunyan's first book. An attack on Quaker teaching, it was first published in 1656; four years later he was arrested and imprisoned for Nonconformity. Enforced leisure for 12 years enabled him to produce a spate of books, and during a second term of imprisonment he wrote 'Pilgrim's Progress'. (Public Library, Bedford)*

---

Wales, and in quality equals some of the Northamptonshire examples. The house embodies medieval fabric, built by the Basset family when they first settled in the area, but it took its present form in the second half of the 16th century. The ruins have been consolidated, and it is possible to trace most of the original arrangements. The battlemented courtyard wall and the outer gatehouse were more for prestige than for defence.

**Beccles** *Suffolk* 548Eg
An ancient town on the R. Waveney, with picturesque river reaches. Four fires in the 16th and 17th centuries destroyed much of the old town. It has attractive streets of red-brick Georgian houses. Noteworthy are the old town hall, 1726; St Peter's House, with 18th-century front and 'Strawberry Hill' style Gothic decorations, on the site of a chapel to St Peter; Ravensmere House of 1694; and Leman House on Ballygate Street, a school founded in 1631. On the road to Bungay is Roos or Rose Hall of 1583, a good gabled brick Tudor manor with pedimented windows.

**Bedale** *Yorks.* 558Cd
BEDALE HALL An 18th-century Georgian mansion with a ballroom and museum of domestic arts and crafts.

**Beddington** *Greater London* 542Bf
CHURCH OF ST MARY THE VIRGIN A basically 14th- and 15th-century church, with 19th-century enlargement and restoration. It has a Norman font,

brasses, a 16th-century pulpit, carved misericords, and a 17th-century alabaster effigy of a man in armour lying on his tomb.

**Bedford** *Beds.* 547He
Known in Saxon times as Bedcanford, Bedford was sacked by the Danes in 1010 and granted a charter by Henry II in 1166. It is notable for its connections with John Bunyan—he was born in the nearby village of Elstow in 1628 and imprisoned for religious dissent in 1660. Bunyan Meeting House stands as a memorial to him and contains relics of the writer and a statue by Sir Joseph Boehm; its bronze doors depict in bas-relief ten scenes from *The Pilgrim's Progress*. A statue of John Howard (1726–90), the prison reformer, by Sir Alfred Gilbert, who sculpted Eros in Piccadilly, is in Bedford. The Muniment Room in the town hall has council minutes dating from 1647, and the 'Elizabethan Black Book of Records' of the Court of Common Pleas.
CECIL HIGGINS ART GALLERY Several extensive collections are on view. The collection of watercolours and drawings from the 17th century to the present includes works by Cozens, Rowlandson, Turner, Sickert and Ben Nicholson. There are also collections of prints from Dürer to the present, and of sculpture including bronzes by Epstein and Henry Moore. The collection of English and continental porcelain of the 18th and 19th centuries includes examples from the Chelsea, Bow, Worcester, Meissen and Nymphenburg works, and the

## WOODCARVING AT BELTON HOUSE

*This type of woodcarving reached its height of perfection in England during the 1680's when many Dutch craftsmen emigrated here. One of the most notable carvers was Grinling Gibbons and although there is no documentary evidence to show that he worked at Belton, the style here is very similar to other examples of his work. The carving is of pear and limewood and is almost certainly Dutch or English: the surface is waxed, and French and Italian works of the time were usually gilded or silvered.*

English and continental glass section includes two pieces by George Ravenscroft. The gallery also displays 18th-century furniture, Bedfordshire and Buckinghamshire lace, costumes and embroidery. MUSEUM The collections here are devoted to Bedford and its county, and comprise archaeological finds from Iron Age (Belgic) and Roman sites, Saxon urns and brooches, local traders' tokens, agricultural and domestic bygones, exhibits relating to two local industries—lace-making and straw-plaiting (for hats)—and local animals and birds.

PUBLIC LIBRARY Books and relics devoted to the life and works of John Bunyan are displayed here.

**Bedingfield** *Suffolk*                    548Df
FLEMINGS HALL A fine moated building of *c.* 1550; the ground floor is of brick, the upper floor timber-framed. It has stepped gables, a two-storey brick porch and polygonal chimneys.

**Beeleigh Abbey** *Essex*                    548Cc
An abbey founded for Premonstratensian canons in 1180; at the Dissolution it became a private house, when a timber-framed wing was added and the monastic church pulled down. Of the interesting remains, the most important are the chapter house and the undercroft of the dorter (dormitory), both *c.* 1250; of the same period is a passage with room above. The present windows were made in the 15th century. The chapter house and dorter undercroft are divided by central arcades with Purbeck marble columns having good 13th-century architectural detail. The undercroft, once the abbey warming house, has a large fire-place with a 15th-century mantelpiece. The dormitory houses the outstanding library of William Foyle, the bookseller, and has a fine roof of collarbeams and trussed rafters.

**Beeston** *Norfolk*                    554Bc
CHURCH OF ST MARY The church is mainly of the 14th century, but has a later clerestory and east window. The tower has a Perpendicular top stage with a spire (rebuilt in 1873). Other features include hammerbeam roofs, a pulpit dating from 1592 and a painted rood screen.

**Belas Knap** *Glos.*                    546Dd
This example of the latest stage of development of the chambered barrow has been carefully restored. The horned forecourt at the north end has a dummy entrance and the four chambers are widely spaced round the sides and south end. The rubble of the mound is held in place by walling.

**Belton** *Kesteven, Lincs.*                    553Gd
BELTON HOUSE The home of the Brownlow family for 300 years. The present house, in Wren style, was erected in 1685–8. It is built on an H-plan and has a hipped-roof with dormer windows and, above, an elegant cupola. Between projecting wings a broad flight of steps leads up to the main doorway, above which is a pediment with the Brownlow coat of arms. About 1776 James Wyatt altered the house, and in 1811 his nephew, Sir Jeffry Wyatville, built the orangery. In the house are fine furniture, tapestries and European old masters. There is also an exhibition devoted to the Duke of Windsor which includes the only known portrait of him as Edward VIII.
CHURCH OF SS PETER AND PAUL There were additions and changes to the original Norman church until the 18th century, and in 1816 Sir Jeffry Wyatville designed a chapel. Notable are the many monuments to the Brownlow family, by William and Edward Stanton, John Bacon, Baron Marochetti and many others.

**Belvoir Castle** *Leics.*                    *552Fc*
Formerly a fortress, Belvoir was rebuilt during the
17th century by the 8th Earl of Rutland. In 1779
the 4th Duke asked Capability Brown to improve
the grounds and restore the house. Brown drew up
the plans, but because of the duke's death this work
was not carried out. In *c.* 1800 the 5th Duke asked
James Wyatt to convert the house into a medieval
castle. Wyatt reconstructed the private apartments, rebuilding the south-east range and raising
the Stainton Tower in height. He then added a
new range to the south-west with a large round
tower, and slightly to the south of this he built two
octagonal pinnacled turrets on either side of the
lancet windows which light the chapel. The northern part of the castle was reconstructed following a fire in 1816, by the Duchess of Rutland and
the Rev. Sir John Thoroton, assisted by Benjamin
and Matthew Wyatt. The castle is now roughly
rectangular around a large courtyard. In the
grounds is a mausoleum built in Norman style in
1826–8 by Thoroton. It contains a monument to
the Duchess of Rutland (*d.* 1825) which was carved
by Matthew Wyatt. The castle is noted for its
Gobelins tapestries, *objets d'art* and picture collections which contain works by Holbein, Reynolds,
Gainsborough and Poussin.

**Bembridge** *Isle of Wight, Hants.*          *541Hc*
RUSKIN GALLERIES The largest Ruskin collection
in the world, half on display here, the other half at
Brentwood, Ruskin's former home. The collection consists of drawings and paintings by Ruskin
and some by his friends and associates, and a large
number of his letters, manuscripts, books, etc.

**Bembridge Windmill**                         *541Hc*
*Isle of Wight, Hants.*
The only remaining windmill on the island. The
stone tower with wooden machinery was erected
*c.* 1700, and was last used in 1913.

**Beningbrough Hall** *Yorks.*                 *558Dc*
A large house of stone and brick, built in 1716 for
John Bourchier, possibly by Thomas Archer. It
contains woodwork and carving of a high standard—an oak staircase, friezes and panels.

**Benington** *Herts.*                         *547Jd*
In AD 850 Berthulf, King of Mercia, held a council
of war here when he heard that the Danish fleet
was in the Thames.
     The Lordship, a Georgian mansion, adjoins the
keep of a ruined Norman castle. The large neo-
Norman gate-house 'folly' near by is said to have
been designed by a landscape gardener.

**Benmore** *Argyll*                           *561Gf*
YOUNGER BOTANIC GARDEN A landscaped woodland garden.

**Benthall Hall** *Shrops.*                    *552Ab*
A 16th-century stone house with mullioned windows and moulded chimneys. Interior alterations
were carried out in the 17th century. Notable
features are a carved oak staircase, decorated
plaster ceilings and 16th-century oak panelling.

**Beoley** *Worcs.*                            *546Df*
CHURCH OF ST LEONARD The church is noteworthy for its fine collection of 16th-century
monuments to members of the Sheldon family,
which stand in the chapel on the north of the

THE ELIZABETH SALOON AT BELVOIR CASTLE

*The family of the Dukes of Rutland has lived at
Belvoir since Henry VIII's reign, and the 5th Duke
commissioned James Wyatt to convert the house overlooking the Vale of Belvoir into a romantic Gothic-
style castle in about 1800. The Prince Regent visited
the castle in 1813 and the Regent's Gallery in the
south-west range was named in his honour. It is 130 ft
long and a wide bow in the centre forms part of the
round tower; along the walls is a series of busts by the
sculptor Joseph Nollekens. A disastrous fire in 1816*
*destroyed the northern portion of the castle, and the
Duchess of Rutland and one of the duke's relatives,
the Rev. Sir John Thoroton, employed two of Wyatt's
sons, Benjamin and Matthew, to help them rebuild.
Thoroton designed the east tower containing the
magnificent Elizabeth Saloon, with ceilings painted
by Matthew Wyatt and a life-size statue of the
duchess by him. The room was decorated by Benjamin
Wyatt in French rococo style, soon to become popular
in London and repeated in other houses.*

chancel. Outstanding among these are those to William and Ralph Sheldon and their wives, which display much heraldic ornament.

**Bere Regis** *Dorset* 540Ec
CHURCH OF ST JOHN THE BAPTIST A 12th-century church added to in later styles; the Perpendicular tower has the stone and flint chequerwork typical of the area. Inside, the fine roof with painting and figures dates to the 15th century; the arcades and mid-16th-century seating are also worth noting. There are interesting marble monuments, and a Norman font, with arcading and other decoration.

**Berkeley** *Glos.* 546Bc
CHURCH OF ST MARY THE VIRGIN A fine church with a detached 18th-century tower on the north side. The south doorway and the font are Norman, the rest of the building Gothic, culminating in the lovely Berkeley Chapel on the south side. Inside are many monuments, some mural painting, and fragments of stained glass.

**Berkeley Castle** *Glos.* 546Bc
Edward II was brutally murdered here in 1327; the murder room is as it was at the time of his death. The perfectly preserved stronghold overlooking the Severn has been the home of the Berkeleys since it was begun in 1153. The massive Norman keep, dungeon, great hall and kitchen date from that time, but alterations were made in 1340. The state apartments contain paintings, tapestries, and fine furniture and silver. The grounds include an Elizabethan terraced garden with an ancient bowling alley.

BERKELEY CASTLE

DOORWAY *The door decorated with alternate rows of saints and cherubs was brought to Berkeley Castle from the Continent this century for the doorway of the new clock-tower. Above it are the family Arms supported by two knights. Ten crosses on the shield show that an early member of the family once took part in a Crusade.*
MADONNA AND CHILD *A 15th-century French woodcarving. In his right hand the Infant Christ holds a globe, signifying the world.*

**Berkhamsted** *Herts.* 547Hc
Only earthworks remain of the 11th-century Norman castle to which came Thomas à Becket, Chaucer and the Court of Henry VIII. Berkhamsted is the birthplace of William Cowper (1731–1800), the poet and hymn-writer, whose father was the rector of Great Berkhamsted.
CHURCH OF ST PETER This large cruciform church, originally Norman with later additions, was restored in 1871 by William Butterfield. Fragments of 14th-century stained glass remain. One window is by C. E. Kempe, 1880. There are many brasses and monuments, including a plain one without figures by Nicholas Stone.

**Berkswell** *Warks.* 546Eg
CHURCH OF ST JOHN THE BAPTIST The best Norman church in Warwickshire, probably built in the late 12th century. It has an impressive vaulted crypt under the chancel, with an unexplained octagonal extension westwards beneath the nave. The 16th-century south porch is half-timbered and two-storied. There is a fine Norman chancel and much remaining work of that period in the nave. The monuments include one by John Bacon of 1795.

**Berrington Hall** *Herefs.* 546Af
A country mansion built in 1778–81 by Henry Holland, with fine plasterwork and painted ceilings. The park was landscaped by Capability Brown in 1780.

**Berry Pomeroy Castle** *Devon* 539Gc
Ralph de Pomeroy, who came to England with William the Conqueror, built this Norman castle on top of a wooded cliff. Later a descendant, the Duke of Somerset (1506–52), brother of Henry VIII's wife Jane Seymour, built a great Tudor mansion within the medieval walls while he was Protector Somerset—Regent for Edward VI. The Seymours occupied the castle until late in the 17th century when it was abandoned following extensive damage during the Civil War. Ruins of the mansion, medieval walls and great three-storied gate-house with hexagonal towers remain.

**Berry Ring** *Staffs.* 552Bc
This is an oval area defended by a single bank and ditch. However, on the north side, in the trees, there seems to be a further bank and ditch giving increased protection.

**Berwick-upon-Tweed** *Northld.* 563Fe
During the succession of Border Wars between the Scots and the English, Berwick, founded in AD 870, changed hands 13 times. Since 1482 it has been politically in England. The town is completely surrounded by the 'Elizabethan Wall', some 10 ft thick, completed as a fortification in 1565, and designed specially for gunpowder warfare. Its gates are Scotsgate, Cowport, Ness Gate and Shore Gate. Only fragments of Berwick Castle remain—Bell Tower and Lord Soulis Tower.

Three bridges cross the Tweed: Berwick Bridge, in pink sandstone, opened in 1643; Royal Border Bridge, a viaduct of 28 arches by Robert Stephenson, a mile and a quarter long and 120 ft above water level; and Royal Tweed Bridge, opened in 1928, spanning the river on four arches.
CHURCH OF THE HOLY TRINITY An interesting church of c. 1650, built by John Young of London; there is no tower, but at the west end of each aisle is a forlorn 19th-century turret. Of the galleries inside only that on the west remains. There is a contemporary pulpit.
MUSEUM AND ART GALLERY The art gallery has a collection of pictures given by Sir William Burrell

One of the masterpieces of medieval European art, the tomb with its richly decorated canopy is by tradition that of Lady Eleanor Percy, but was more probably made for her daughter-in-law, Lady Idonea, who died in 1365. As well as the magnificent carving of angels, fruit, leaves and symbolic beasts on the canopy, the minster contains superlative wood and stone carving throughout, especially on corbels, roof bosses, on the nave arcade, in the choir and on and around the great west door, whose panels of the Evangelists and their symbols were designed by Nicholas Hawksmoor. The misericords, carved from Sherwood Forest oak, are some of the best in England; among them can be seen a man shoeing a goose, a pig playing a harp, and men catching a bear in a wicker-work cage. In contrast with these fanciful and expertly worked decorations is the plain 1000-year-old Fridstol or sanctuary chair, a reminder of the minster's ancient Rights of Sanctuary, where fugitives might seek the Peace of St John and at least temporarily gain respite from their pursuers.

including Daubigny's *Cap Gris Nez* and Degas' pastel *Russian Dancer*. The Berwick Room has items of local interest including a 16th-century tempera wall-painting removed from the Old Bridge Tavern, since demolished. The museum contains small collections of silver, bronze, brass, ceramics and glass, mostly from Sir William Burrell's collection, more of which can be seen at the Camphill Museum, Glasgow.

**Besford** *Worcs.*                                 546Ce
CHURCH OF ST PETER The timber and plaster nave is 14th century, rebuilt in the late 19th century with timbers replaced in their original positions. The rood screen is 15th century; the monuments include one in the form of a painted wood triptych, and another by William Stanton.

**Besselsleigh** *Berks.*                            546Ec
CHURCH OF ST LAWRENCE This is a small Norman church, with later rebuilding. At the west end there is a two-bell cote; the church was restored in 1632, and has a 17th-century font and 18th-century canopied pulpit. It is the only church in the county to retain all its box-pews and original seating and ritual arrangements.

**Betchworth** *Surrey*                              542Bf
Hardly more than a hamlet, though the buildings grouped near the church—tarred barns, cottages, a pub behind a semicircle of clipped elms, and a big, plain Georgian house—are typical of old Surrey.

**Betley** *Staffs.*                                 552Bd
CHURCH OF ST MARGARET A church in which a surprising amount of timber was used—not only for the roofs, but for nave piers and arches, and the clerestory.

**Bettws Newydd** *Mon.*                             546Ac
CHURCH This church retains an elegant Perpendicular rood screen with its original gallery decorated with open-work tracery.

**Beverley** *Yorks.*                                559Gb
Once a walled town, there is now only one 15th-century gate surviving from five originals. There are several fine Georgian houses. The guildhall (1762) has excellent plasterwork in the courtroom. The market cross dates from the 18th century.
ART GALLERY AND MUSEUM The gallery includes paintings by F. W. Elwell of Beverley. There is a small collection of folk material.
CHURCH OF ST MARY The second of Beverley's notable churches, St Mary's is overshadowed by the minster. Cruciform, from the 14th and 15th centuries, with some earlier work, it has a pinnacled central tower. Inside are Gothic stalls with misericords and an early 16th-century font. There is a monument by John Bacon the Younger.
MINSTER (CHURCH OF ST JOHN OF BEVERLEY) St John of Beverley (640–721) founded the original Saxon church at Beverley and was buried there. Having been a student at Canterbury under the great Abbot Hadrian, *c.* 687 he was promoted to the bishopric of Hexham and *c.* 703 he ordained the Venerable Bede. In 705 he became Archbishop of York. However, he was a lover of solitude and eventually resigned his archdiocese, and in 717 retired to Beverley where he died in 721. He was canonised in 1037. His church at Beverley became a college of secular canons in the 10th century, but was badly damaged by fire in 1188. Rebuilding did not take place until the 13th century, when a remarkably well unified building was created. A later addition was the west façade, with twin towers, one of the finest late 14th-century façades in England.

**Beverstone** *Glos.*                               546Cc
CHURCH OF ST MARY A small Norman church, rebuilt in the 14th century. The three-bay south arcade of the nave is from *c.* 1200 and the south doorway is Norman. There is a fine nave roof and a restored 15th-century rood screen.

**Bewdley** *Worcs.* 546Bf
TICKENHILL HOUSE The brick façade of this mansion, standing on a hill above the town, was added to the remains of a Tudor royal palace in 1738.

**Bexhill** *Sussex* 542Dd
DE LA WARR PAVILION A long, low, white, concrete block with a balconied bow craning toward the sea; a major example of the international style of its date, 1933–6. Designed by Erich Mendelsohn, whose finest work had been done in Germany.
MUSEUM Permanent displays of local natural history, geology and archaeology, with frequent loan exhibitions on a variety of subjects.

**Bexley** *Greater London* 542Cg
HALL PLACE A flint and brick Tudor house, built by Sir John Champneis, 1537–40, with a 17th-century red-brick extension on the south side. It was once the home (*c.* 1773) of Sir John Dashwood, the notorious rake.

**Bibury** *Glos.* 546Dc
CHURCH OF ST MARY This great Saxon church was enlarged by Norman and Gothic builders, and restored throughout more recently, to clear Sir Gilbert Scott's 19th-century restoration. Inside, the 13th-century font is especially interesting. The churchyard contains the carved altar tombs of 18th-century wool traders, the rococo motifs now coloured by lichen.

**Bicester** *Oxon.* 546Fd
CHURCH OF ST EDBURG The church is basically 12th century, but with considerable later enlargement; the west tower is 15th century. There is a medieval parclose screen, a 13th-century font and an early 18th-century monument with the effigy of a man. Other monuments include ones by Joseph Wilton and Sir Richard Westmacott.

**Bicton Gardens** *Devon* 539Hd
These Italian gardens were originally laid out in 1735. The pinetum has rare trees, which can be viewed from an 18 in. gauge railway.

**Biddenden** *Kent* 542Ee
A beautiful Kent Weald village, with ancient weavers' cottages and a medieval Cloth Hall, famous for the 'Biddenden Maids'—Siamese twins (1500–34) who are commemorated by a distribution of food to the poor on Easter Day.

**Bideford** *Devon.* 538Ff
In the days of sail Bideford was a seaport, and in 1700 was importing tobacco from America on a major scale. Charles Kingsley used the town as the setting for *Westward Ho!* The old town has many medieval streets: in Cunstone, stone cannon-balls were made, and Buttgarden was the site of archery butts. The 24-arch bridge spanning the R. Torridge links the main town with East-the-Water: the original wooden bridge (1280) was replaced by the present stone structure in the 15th century.

**Bigby** *Lincs.* 553Gg
CHURCH OF ALL SAINTS An Early English church, with late 13th-century west tower. There is a sculpture of the Virgin, made *c.* 1300, brasses, and 16th- and 17th-century monuments. One, of 1581, has 22 mourning children.

**Bignor** *Sussex* 542Ad
A large courtyard villa, comparable with those at North Leigh and Chedworth. The main buildings completely enclose the courtyard and there are also some detached buildings outside. Here, too, the establishment as we now see it is the end-process of a long period of remodelling and addition.
It has been calculated that the estate of this villa was upwards of 2000 acres of arable land, together with areas of forest, downland-grazing and marsh.
Its end appears to have been marked by desertion and slow decay of roof and walls. There is no hint of a final catastrophe of fire or slaughter. A museum presents models of a villa of Roman times, with objects found during excavations.

**Billinge** *Lancs.* 552Af
CHURCH OF ST AIDAN Built in 1717 in a mixture of Gothic and Classical styles, with nave arcades of Doric columns, panelled walls and a west gallery.

**Billingham** *Durham* 558Df
CHURCH OF ST CUTHBERT An interesting Saxon west tower, and a nave which was altered during the 12th century. The chancel is modern, dating from 1939. There is a 17th-century font cover.

**Bilston** *Staffs.* 552Cb
CHURCH OF ST LEONARD The church was built in the Classical style by Francis Goodwin in *c.* 1825. The interior is galleried and has contemporary monuments.

MOSAIC FLOOR AT BIGNOR ROMAN VILLA

*This great villa built around a courtyard contains many fine mosaic floors, some of which have portraits in medallions set in surrounds of elaborate formal patterns. This corridor floor, however, is in a very different style, for here a variety of small figure-groups occur.*

*These show stages in a contest of gladiators and, on the right, the 'retiarius', with net and trident, has been felled by his opponent swordsman. Amusingly enough, however, these are not true gladiators, but Cupids dressed for the parts. The floor is late 4th century.*

**Binham Priory** *Norfolk*                    554Cd
The layout of the abbey building at Binham is
reasonably clear, but the main fragment to survive
intact is the west end of the monastic church,
which is now used as a parish church. With the
exception of the west end, the exact date of the
church is not known. It was built mainly during
the 12th century, but evidence suggests that it
remained unfinished for a considerable time.
According to documentary evidence the impressive west front was built between 1226 and 1244,
and the decoration, with its arcading, small
columns and dog-tooth ornament, confirms that
this part of the church was built *c.* 1230. The large
window with its geometric tracery is unusual in an
English church built before 1241, but irregularities
in the masonry suggest that this window was
added at a late date. Inside the building, the join
between the 12th- and 13th-century work is
clearly visible in the arcading on either side of the
west end. There is a Perpendicular seven-sacrament font, and the stalls have misericords. Ruins of
the old priory surround the church.

**Binley** *Warks.*                    546Eg
CHURCH OF ST BARTHOLOMEW Built *c.* 1773 by
Lord Craven, and said to have been designed by
Robert Adam, the church has a western octagonal
cupola, Tuscan columns, and a shallow apsed
chancel, with plaster decoration.

**Binns, The** *W. Lothian*                    562Bf
A country mansion dating from 1478, the home of
the Dalywells, including General Tam Dalywell
who, in 1681, raised the Royal Scots Greys Regiment. The façade has two matching towers and a
castellated parapet.

**Birchington** *Kent*                    543Gg
POWELL-COTTON MUSEUM A large collection of
zoological specimens, including two dioramas
showing African and Indian animals in their
natural habitats, is displayed. There are also collections devoted to native arts, crafts and domestic
objects from Africa, Asia and the Pacific area.

**Birchover** *Derbys.*                    552De
HEATHCOTE MUSEUM Archaeological finds col-
lected by the Heathcote family from local Middle
Bronze Age sites can be viewed by appointment.

**Birkenhead** *Cheshire*                    551Jf
WILLIAMSON ART GALLERY AND MUSEUM A large
group of English water-colours including works
by Turner, Cotman, de Wint, Cozens, Gainsborough, Wimperis and Burne-Jones are displayed with oil paintings by Wilson Steer and
Liverpool artists. The ceramics section includes
Liverpool porcelain. In a separate gallery exhibits,
including ship models, illustrate Birkenhead's
main industry—shipbuilding.

**Birkin** *Yorks.*                    558Da
CHURCH OF ST MARY An almost wholly Norman
building, with west tower and apse. Fragments of
14th-century glass remain and a monument, also
14th century, of a man holding a heart. The font is
dated 1663, and there is an 18th-century pulpit.

**Birmingham** *Warks.*                    546Dg
ASSAY OFFICE Birmingham silverware of the 18th
and 19th centuries, coins, medals and tokens are on
display in the office which is maintained by the
Guardians of Wrought Plate in Birmingham, a
body founded by statute in 1772. There is also a
fine library relating to gold and silversmithing,
and a collection of letters and papers of Matthew
Boulton (1728–1809), the Birmingham engineer
and silversmith, who invented a coin-making

HOUDON *Bust of Anne-Robert-Jacques Turgot*

*One of the great masterpieces of a period when the art
of the portrait bust reached a peak of development, this
terracotta bust was created in 1778 in one of the most
fertile periods of Houdon's life (1741–1828). Turgot
is treated naturalistically and the material is handled
in a vivid way. Turgot was Minister of Finance under
Louis XVI; he tried to initiate sweeping reforms, but
failed and was disgraced.*
*(Birmingham City Museum and Art Gallery)*

machine used for a century at the Royal Mint. (By
appointment.)
ASTON HALL A fine Jacobean house built in 1618–
35 by Sir Thomas Holte, an ardent Royalist, who
in 1642 entertained Charles I at Aston when the
king was on his way from Shrewsbury to relieve
Banbury Castle. Later the house was taken by
Parliamentarians and Sir Thomas was heavily
fined and imprisoned. The Holtes lived at Aston
Hall until 1817; from 1818 to 1848 it was leased by
James Watt, son of the famous engineer. The house
contains a grand balustraded staircase, fine long
gallery and many magnificent plaster friezes and
ceilings. Its rooms are arranged with fine furniture
and pictures dating from the Jacobean to Victorian
periods. The house also contains examples of
needlework by Mary Holte, and local metalwork,
pottery, textiles and furniture.
AVERY HISTORICAL MUSEUM The museum is
owned by W. & T. Avery Ltd., and housed in the
Soho Foundry, built in 1795 by Boulton and Watt.
The exhibits are restricted to the history of
weighing and the museum is open to students.
BARBER INSTITUTE The gallery houses the collection of paintings belonging to the 40 trustees of
the Barber Institute of Fine Arts.
BLAKESLEY HALL (YARDLEY) A timber-framed
yeoman's house built in the late 16th century. The
kitchen and a bedroom which contains its original
wall-paintings are exhibited as period rooms. The
rest of the house contains collections devoted to the
archaeology and history of the Birmingham area.
CANNON HILL A small museum with exhibits
primarily for children and which illustrate the
make-up of plants and animals. Dioramas show
bird habitats and reconstructions of life as it may
have been millions of years ago.

GAINSBOROUGH *The Harvest Waggon*

*Thomas Gainsborough was a painter of landscapes by choice and of portraits by necessity; in one of his letters he talks of being 'sick of portraits'. In stature the equal of Wilson for the development of British landscape art of the 18th century, he owed far less to outside influences. True, he took his cue from French and Dutch sources in his earlier work, but he was an inspired and instinctive painter who created his own version of nature. In 1759 Gainsborough moved from*

*his native Suffolk to Bath, then at the height of its popularity as a fashionable spa, and there he laid aside the clear, dewy freshness of his East Anglian landscapes (which often included a portrait) for a more idealised style which in 'The Harvest Waggon' owes much to Rubens. In colour a range of virtually monochrome tints is brought to life by the introduction of a single note of strong colour in the red shawl.*
*(The Barber Institute, Birmingham)*

CATHEDRAL The baroque Church of St Philip, which became a cathedral in 1905, was begun in 1711. Thomas Archer, designer of the Church of St John in Smith Square, London, was the architect. Archer, unlike any of his predecessors since Inigo Jones, had been to Rome, and the style of the building reflects this. Most of the church was finished by 1719, but the west tower was not completed until 1725. It is a rectangular building with a projection at the east end, added *c.* 1883.

CATHEDRAL OF ST CHAD In 1839 Augustus Pugin began the first Roman Catholic cathedral in England since the Reformation. Pugin, a passionate admirer of medieval architecture, became a Roman Catholic convert in 1834, and his ecclesiastical work culminated with the building of St Chad's. The cathedral was dedicated in 1841.

CITY MUSEUM AND ART GALLERY Outstanding collections of Pre-Raphaelite and European paintings. The sculpture collection includes work by Rodin and Henry Moore; costume from the 17th century onwards is displayed. English ceramics are well represented, and there is a good collection of silver from the 17th–19th centuries. There are also archaeological and natural history collections.

GEOLOGY DEPARTMENTAL MUSEUM (UNIVERSITY) Minerals, including precious stones, rocks and fossils from all over the world, are housed in the museum. Diagrams illustrate the geology of the British Isles and there is a collection of fossils.

MUSEUM OF SCIENCE AND INDUSTRY A variety of heavy engineering exhibits—mill engines, gas engines, steam turbines, electrical generators and various machine tools including a wall planing machine used at Boulton and Watt's Soho Foundry in Birmingham in the 19th century—are housed in the engineering hall. The transport sec-

tion is devoted to cars, motor-cycles and bicycles, and includes the Napier Railton car in which John Cobb reached 394 mph in 1947—a land speed record which remained unbroken until 1964. Also on show are the Liddell Collection of musical boxes; collections of early organs and gramophones; the City Collection of small arms; scientific equipment; and the Charles Thomas Collection of European and Oriental writing implements.

WEOLEY CASTLE Recent excavation has revealed the foundations of a fortified manor house built in 1276–80 on the site of an earlier building surrounded by a moat. Various finds from the excavations are housed in a small museum on the site.

**Birstall** *Yorks.*                                      558Ca
OAKWELL HALL A moated Elizabethan house, the 'Fieldhead' of Charlotte Brontë's novel *Shirley*. In the Civil War it was occupied by Parliamentarians after their crushing defeat at nearby Adwalton Moor on June 30, 1643.

**Birtsmorton Court** *Worcs.*                             546Ce
A moated Tudor house, with Norman work. It has a banqueting hall and great chamber with a secret hiding place used in the Wars of the Roses.

**Bisham** *Berks.*                                        547Gb
CHURCH OF ALL SAINTS Standing beside the Thames, with a 12th-century tower and all the rest 19th-century restoration, All Saints is notable for the Hoby tombs in the south chapel: two brothers, Sir Philip (*d.* 1558) and Sir Thomas (*d.* 1566) lie side by side, semi-reclining, in alabaster. Sir Edward's widow (*d.* 1605) is commemorated by an alabaster obelisk with four swans at its base. Sir Thomas's widow (*d.* 1609) kneels, children behind her, under a canopy and wearing a gold coronet.

**Bisham Abbey** *Berks.*                              547Gb
This is no longer an abbey. The 14th-century parts are included in a modernised building, which is used as a training centre for physical recreation.

**Bishop Auckland** *Durham*                   558Cf
CHURCH OF ST ANDREW The fragment of a Saxon cross, carved with Christ and other figures *c.* 800, may be seen at this late 13th-century church with its west tower and two-storey south porch. Inside sits a cross-legged knight, carved from oak *c.* 1340.

**Bishops Cannings** *Wilts.*                    540Ef
CHURCH OF ST MARY THE VIRGIN An impressive Early English church, cruciform with a central tower topped by a 15th-century spire. A few Norman traces remain. A rare item is a meditation seat (probably 17th century), on which are painted a large hand and Latin inscriptions about sin and death. There is 19th-century stained glass by Wailes in the east window.

**Bishop's Cleeve** *Glos.*                        546Cd
CHURCH OF ST MICHAEL AND ALL ANGELS A magnificent cruciform Norman church, the central tower of which was rebuilt in 1700. The west front is especially impressive, with turrets and a magnificent Norman doorway; and the two-storey south porch is also striking. The Decorated chancel has a good window. There are some interesting monuments with effigies, including a particularly fine one of 1639.

**Bishop's Stortford** *Herts.*                  548Ad
CHURCH OF ST MICHAEL A large 15th-century church with a west tower, heightened in 1812. The pulpit dates from 1658; the 15th-century stalls have carved misericords. There are original roofs. The 15th-century rood screen is richly carved, and the 12th-century font is of Purbeck marble.

BLACKSTONE EDGE ROMAN ROAD

*When they were not fighting, the Roman legions acted as pioneers—building forts, bridges and roads. They covered Britain with a network of straight roads; some stretches are in their original condition today while many more form the basis of roads still in use. This stretch runs north-east from Littleborough in Lancashire, over the moors of Blackstone Edge, and is probably the best preserved section of Roman road in Britain. It goes straight up a steep hill but has resisted centuries of erosion by rain, wind, snow and frost. The surface stones are solidly set on a foundation of sand and rubble, with ditches on both sides. The Romans planned and built with such skill that after they left Britain their roads continued as the chief means of communication for centuries.*

OLD VICARAGE Cecil Rhodes (1853–1902) was born here and the house is now a museum devoted to him; it contains many of his possessions.

**Bishopstone** *Herefs.*                          546Ae
CHURCH OF ST LAWRENCE Originally a Norman building, of which only a blocked south window remains; there are late 13th-century transepts, and a 14th-century timbered south porch. The pulpit is 17th century and there is some 16th- and 17th-century foreign glass, but the east window dates from 1843. One monument is from 1614.

**Bishopstone** *Sussex*                           542Cd
CHURCH OF ST ANDREW An interesting church, originally Saxon with Norman additions and later medieval work. It was restored in the mid-19th century. The west tower is Norman. There is a fine 12th-century coffin-lid with three carved loops of rope enclosing a cross, two birds drinking and the symbols of the Lamb and Cross.

**Bishopstone** *Wilts.*                            546Eb
CHURCH OF ST JOHN THE BAPTIST Standing amid beeches is this large cruciform church with a Perpendicular central tower. The interior is in both Decorated and Perpendicular Gothic styles, with rib-vaulting in the south transept and chancel, carved sedilia and piscinae, and interesting carving. Some traces of Norman work remain. There are several interesting monuments: outside, by the south transept, a small stone cloister of two vaulted bays shelters a decorated tomb chest, perhaps that of the founder of the church. In the north transept is another richly decorated tomb recess, with stone coffin-lids, and in the south transept a mid-19th-century Gothic monument to a former rector by A. W. Pugin. Above this is a window designed by Pugin and executed by William Wailes.

**Bishops Waltham** *Hants.*                    541Hd
The tight-knit little town, mostly with Georgian brick houses, acts as a foil to the enormous grey ruins of the palace of the Bishops of Winchester. It is Norman, remodelled to a large extent in the later Middle Ages.

**Blackburn** *Lancs.*                              557Ja
MUSEUM AND ART GALLERY More than 1200 Japanese prints are contained in the art gallery, together with a collection of English watercolours of the 18th, 19th and 20th centuries. The museum features English, Greek and Roman coins, medieval manuscripts and early printed books, primitive weapons, domestic items and costumes from African tribes, and a small archaeological collection containing Egyptian material. The museum and art gallery are in the public library building at Blackburn.

**Blackbury Castle** *Devon*                    540Bc
This Iron Age single bank-and-ditch fort has an oval interior of 4 acres. The entrance on the south side has a large protective structure. Excavation has shown that the bank was of simple construction without stone or timber revetment, except for a little wattling near the entrance. Both inner and outer openings in the entrance defences had timber gates with a gravelled path between them. The ditch was originally some 8 ft deep, with a wide, V-shaped profile.

**Blackhamar** *Rousay, Orkney*                569Hg
A 'stalled cairn'. The chamber is 42½ ft long by 6 ft wide and is divided by standing slabs into 14 stalls, into one of which the passage leads. The chamber walls, of stone, are very thick. The upper part of the cairn and the roof of the chamber have been removed.

**Blackpool** *Lancs.* *557Hb*
GRUNDY ART GALLERY Paintings and drawings by 19th- and 20th-century British artists are exhibited.

**Blackstone Edge** *Lancs.* *552Cg*
This is perhaps the most remarkable piece of paved Roman road in the country. It formed a part of the road from the fort at Manchester (Mamucium) to that at Ilkley (Olicana) and, as it climbs on to the crest of the Pennines, the paved way, some 16 ft wide, is held in position in the underlying peaty deposits by deeply-set kerbs. The oddest feature is the central paved channel in the roadway. The most likely explanation is that it had a turfy filling which gave a good foothold to horses.

**Blair Castle** *Perths.* *566Bc*
A fortress in the 13th century and home of the Earls and Dukes of Atholl since the mid-19th century. Its key external feature is the Cumming's Tower: in 1269 the crusader Earl of Atholl complained to King Alexander III that during his absence in England a John Comyn or Cumming (grandfather of the John Comyn murdered by Robert de Bruce at Dumfries in 1306) had 'made an incursion into Atholl and had begun building a castle at Blair'.

The present Cumming's Tower was built in 1869, a copy of the former tower with stepped gable and battlements. In the mid-Victorian period the building was re-castellated by Robert Bryce, and the present entrance and ballroom on the north side added. The castle contains many treasures. The Stewart Room has a two-handed sword, 16th- and 17th-century furniture, including an elm chair of 1683, a chittarone (a large lute) made by Melchior of Verona in 1555, and a Regal organ of 1630.

In Earl John's Room is a four-poster bed hung with red velvet, *c.* 1650, and carved walnut chairs of *c.* 1665. There is one of the four copies of the National Covenant of 1638, a document pledging the Covenanters to resist Popery, Prelacy and Superstition.

The Guard Room, once the prison, has a collection of man-traps, handcuffs, locks and instruments of torture.

The small drawing-room, built on the ruins of a former south-east tower in a remodelling phase (18th century) has a Georgian marble chimney-piece supported by Ionic columns and with a carved wood overmantel; walnut cabinets; Queen Anne lacquer 'Union sets' of cabinets; and eight mahogany chairs with fish-scale decoration (supplied in 1756 for 25 gns).

The Tea Room has Chippendale and Sheraton cabinets, and a collection of Sèvres china.

The dining-room was the 16th-century banquet hall, transformed in the 18th century to its present baroque grandeur: the marble chimney-piece with a head of Apollo was made in 1751.

In the Blue Dressing-room is a Louis XV writing-table with ormolu mounts and inlaid Sèvres porcelain panels.

The drawing-room, with modelled ceiling and cornice, is hung with crimson damask and contains a pair of larchwood Regency cabinets, with Glen Tilt marble tops.

The Tullibardine Room is dedicated to the Jacobites: Lord George Murray, son of the 1st Duke, was Lt.-General to Prince Charles Edward in the rising of 1745. The tent bed in this room is covered by a tartan more than 200 years old.

At the foot of the staircase is the suit of tilting armour, horse trappings and banner used by the 6th Duke at the Eglington Tournament in 1839. Two of the cannon recovered from the Spanish

THE TAPESTRY ROOM AT BLAIR CASTLE

*The tapestries in this room were bought when much of Charles I's furniture was sold and the bed, belonging to the 1st Duke of Atholl, was moved here in 1709. From 90 to 100 yds of silk costing from 16 to 21 shillings a yard were needed to cover such a bed—and the crimson silk used here would have cost more because the dye was expensive. The bed was probably made around 1690, when tall beds surmounted by vases of ostrich feathers were the height of fashion, in keeping with the baroque taste.*

# BLENHEIM PALACE

BLENHEIM PALACE *One of the largest mansions in England, the masterpiece of Sir John Vanbrugh, and the gift of the nation to a victorious soldier. Queen Anne rewarded John Churchill, 1st Duke of Marlborough, for his decisive defeat of Louis XIV (1704) with Blenheim Palace; but although a huge sum of money was allocated by Parliament for its erection, the Marlboroughs had to find tens of thousands of pounds to pay for the completion. The headstrong Duchess Sarah lost the queen's favour and quarrelled with Vanbrugh, who left before Blenheim was completed. The greatest artists and craftsmen of the day worked on the interior decoration: the magnificent ceiling and wall-paintings in the great hall, which leads to the saloon and the state apartments, are by Sir James Thornhill and Louis Laguerre; the high relief carvings are by Grinling Gibbons, and Michael Rysbrack designed the huge chapel which contains the duke's tomb. The gardens extend over several acres and were laid out by Henry Wise and Capability Brown, who also created the large lake. In 1874 Sir Winston Churchill was born at Blenheim.*

BRUSSELS TAPESTRY *The Brussels weaving industry still produced many tapestries in the 18th century although it had declined considerably by then. Jos de Vos, a weaver in Brussels from 1703 onwards, wove a set of tapestries depicting the 'Victories of the Duke of Marlborough'. The figure of the duke is taken from a panel showing him receiving the surrender of Marshal Tallard after the Battle of Blenheim.*

Armada galleon sunk in Tobermory Bay are on either side of the entrance archway.

The Terrace Room has a collection of fire-arms; in the ballroom are weapons, drums, chain armour and other trophies of the Sudan Campaign, as well as the Colours of the 77th Atholl Highlanders, later bodyguard of the Dukes of Atholl.

In the Transvaal Room—hung with 18th-century Chinese wallpaper—are cases of personal jewellery and snuff boxes.

The China Room contains an 18th-century oriental service painted with the Arms of the Dukes of Atholl, Wedgwood and Derby ware, and a Sèvres hand-painted dessert service.

The Larch Passage is panelled in larch from a tree brought from the Tyrol and planted by the 2nd Duke at Dunkeld in 1737; the larch forests on the estate were developed by the 4th Duke.

In 1907 the Duke of Atholl, being entitled by ancient statute to maintain his own private army, used this privilege to safeguard the experiments of J. W. Dunne, who built a twin-engined aeroplane at Glen Tilt on the estate. It failed to fly and Dunne later returned to his regular army career.

**Blaise Hamlet** *Glos.*                    540Cg
An eccentric disposition of ten cottages of differing design, built in 1809 by John Nash for John Harford, to house pensioners of the Blaise estate.

BLAISE CASTLE HOUSE A fine house built in the late 18th century and now used as a folk museum. A dairy designed by John Nash stands in the grounds.

**Blakeney** *Norfolk*                    554Cd
A small picturesque port, well known to yachtsmen, wildfowlers and naturalists, built mainly of flint. The guildhall has a brick vaulted undercroft with stone pillars, probably 15th century. At the west end of the quay is the Red House, a pleasant Georgian building, low, with a three-bay pediment. A little to the north of the church, a house called the Friary incorporates parts of a Carmelite friary of *c.* 1296. To the east of this there is a windmill of brick and flint.
CHURCH OF ST NICHOLAS Outside the town and overlooking the sea, the church has two towers, the Perpendicular west tower and a small tower at the north-east angle of the chancel which may have been used as a beacon for Blakeney Harbour. There is a Perpendicular nave, an Early English vaulted chancel with a room above it, and an octagonal font with carved figures.

**Blanchland** *Northld.*                    558Bg
CHURCH OF ST MARY THE VIRGIN The abbey was founded in 1165 for the Premonstratensians, and what remains of their church is the north transept and chancel. There is a tower at the north end of the transept.

BLENHEIM PALACE GARDENS *The ornamental garden below one of the terraces at Blenheim Palace is the work (1900–10) of the French garden designer Achille Duchêne, trained in the formal tradition of André Le Nôtre. The 9th Duke of Marlborough commissioned Duchêne to create the formal garden with its parterres, ponds and fountains—re-creating the original concept of the garden by Henry Wise, which was destroyed by Capability Brown in his quest for the 'natural garden'.*

*Under Brown's direction the grounds were trans-formed into a charming landscape of trees, woods and grass. Brown also produced one of Blenheim's finest features, by skilfully damming the R. Glyme and converting the marshy ground into the present fine lake beyond Duchêne's garden.*

**Blandford Forum** *Dorset*      540Ed
A fine Georgian market town on the R. Stour. There are few antiquities, for the town has a history of destruction by fire. The most disastrous was probably that of 1731 which destroyed most of the town; only 40 or 50 houses, including the almshouses and the Old House, escaped out of a total of more than 500. This was the making of two local men, John and William Bastard, brothers who played a major part in rebuilding the town.
CHURCH OF SS PETER AND PAUL One of the finest Georgian provincial churches, finished in 1739 to John Bastard's design. It is faced with ashlar and has a fine square tower crowned with a cupola. Inside are Ionic nave columns, a font, box-pews, a western gallery and canopied mayor's seat of the period. In the early 19th century obtrusive galleries were added in the nave. In 1893 a chancel was built. The sanctuary apse was raised on rollers and moved away from the nave to new foundations; the chancel was then built between the sanctuary and nave.
TOWN HALL A fine Georgian building designed by the Bastard brothers. Inside is a memorial to Alfred Stevens, born in Blandford in 1818. He was an architect, painter, sculptor and designer, but is best remembered for his magnificent monument to the Duke of Wellington in St Paul's Cathedral, commissioned in 1862.

**Blantyre** *Lanarks.*      561Je
The house in Shuttle Row where David Living-stone (1813–73) was born has been preserved; it contains relics of the missionary and explorer.

**Bledington** *Glos.*      546Ed
CHURCH OF ST LEONARD There is Norman and later work in this church, and Perpendicular windows, some with brilliant contemporary glass. The nave gable still retains its 12th-century bell-cote, and the south arcade is Transitional Norman.

**Bledlow** *Bucks.*      547Gc
CHURCH OF THE HOLY TRINITY A Norman church on a steep slope in the Chilterns. The interior has nave arcades of *c.* 1200 with carved capitals, and a circular Norman font carved with stiff-leaved foliage. Remains of medieval wall-painting include Adam and Eve, and St Christopher; the south door is of the 13th–14th centuries. In the south aisle are a reredos and large candlestick with dummy flame, both 18th century. There is one brass of interest, to the vicar William Hern (*d.* 1525).

**Blenheim Palace** *Oxon.*      546Ed
The nation's gift to the 1st Duke of Marlborough, Blenheim was designed by Sir John Vanbrugh and built in the years 1705–22. The mansion is in

91

baroque style, with two storeys, and is arranged round three sides of an immense courtyard. The large central building has four turrets and a portico supported by Corinthian columns below a rising pediment. Colonnades of Doric columns connect the main building to pavilions on either side, but these massive, castellar buildings tend to over-shadow the central feature. In the state apartments are fine collections of portraits, china, tapestries and furniture. On the ground floor is the small bedroom, with personal relics, where Sir Winston Churchill was born on November 30, 1874.

Henry Wise, gardener to Queen Anne, was the man responsible for the garden designs at Blenheim Palace early in the 18th century. The style was the elaborate formal manner of Le Nôtre, examples of which can be seen in France at Vaux-le-Vicomte and Versailles. The ornamental garden close to the palace consisted of parterres. These were elaborately designed scroll-like patterns with dwarf hedges of clipped box, outlining patterns filled in with brightly-coloured gravels and closely mown turf. Parts of the patterns were planted with flowers, and the whole was punctuated with pyramids and cones of yew. Statuary and fountains were interspersed throughout the design. The kitchen garden was simpler; it was surrounded by thick walls against which fruit trees were trained. Shortly after Wise had finished the ornamental garden, the vogue in garden design changed completely. Formality in the French style was despised, and the natural park-like landscape became fashionable. Except for the kitchen garden, which still exists, Wise's gardens were obliterated by Capability Brown. The grounds, almost up to the palace, were transformed into an idealised scene of trees, woods and grass. One of Blenheim's most singular features was achieved by the same designer. By damming up the little R. Glyme, Brown turned the marshy ground through which it trickled into the present fine lake, spanned by Vanbrugh's triumphant causeway.

**Bletchingley** *Surrey*         542Bf
The village street, curving and falling towards the east, is one of the most pleasant in Surrey. The best houses, however, are a mile away to the north-west, at Pendell, all of red brick: the Court is Jacobean, the House is dated 1636, and is a remarkably restrained design for that date, and the Manor is Georgian.
CHURCH OF ST MARY Norman in origin, the church has 13th- and 15th-century work, and 19th-century restoration. Inside there are a number of brasses and monuments, in particular one by Richard Crutcher, *c.* 1707, with standing figures in contemporary dress. The pulpit is 17th century.

**Blewbury** *Berks.*         546Fb
CHURCH OF ST MICHAEL AND ALL ANGELS Originally a 12th-century building on the cruci-form plan, there were later changes, including the Perpendicular west tower. There is a good parclose screen to the south chapel, and a door to the rood loft; also a late Gothic font and 19th-century glass in the east window. Brasses date from 1496 to one made in 1841 for a 13-year-old boy.

**Blickling Hall** *Norfolk*         554Cc
A fine red-brick Jacobean house built for Sir Henry Hobart by Robert Lyminge in 1616–28. Lyminge's building comprised a large central block with long wings on either side terminated by corner turrets with lead caps like those at Osterley Park, Greater London. During the second half of the 18th century the open ends of the court, left by the two wings, were filled in by Thomas Ivory and

his family of Norwich. The state rooms contain collections of fine furniture, pictures and tapestries. The grounds include an extensive formal garden, a crescent-shaped lake, and an orangery and temple built by the Ivorys.

BLICKLING HALL

*Sir Henry Hobart built Blickling Hall between 1616 and 1628. Although contemporary with Inigo Jones's Palladian Queen's House at Greenwich and Banqueting House in Whitehall, Blickling is very different. Its architect was Robert Lyminge, who had earlier worked at Hatfield House for the Cecils. Lyminge produced a turreted red-brick house in Jacobean style. This was altered in the late 18th century by Thomas Ivory and his family, architects from Norwich. Inside is a fine staircase of the 17th century, altered by the Ivorys, with much carved decorative detail and figures as at Hatfield. Several rooms have ornate chimney-pieces and plaster ceilings, but of those belonging to the original house the most impressive room is the gallery, nearly 130 ft long, lined with windows along one side, and with a decorated plaster ceiling.*

**Blisland** *Cornwall*         538Cc
CHURCH OF SS PROTUS AND HYACINTH A Norman church near the village green, with transepts and a north tower. Inside is a Norman font, and there are wagon-roofs. The 20th-century stained glass is by F. C. Eden, as is the painted rood screen.

**Blithfield** *Staffs.*         552Cc
CHURCH OF ST LEONARD The church adjoins the picturesque Blithfield Hall, and dates from the 13th century. There is some medieval glass, and many monuments, one by William Stanton and another by Sir Richard Westmacott.
MUSEUM OF CHILDHOOD AND COSTUME The museum is situated in an Elizabethan house which has been the home of the Bagot family for 600 years, and which includes a very fine carved oak staircase. Two Victorian dolls' houses are on dis-play with a collection of antique dolls, and child-ren's toys, books, furniture and costumes. Also shown are embroidered Georgian costumes and coronation robes, an embroidered cap given by

Charles I with other Stuart relics, and uniforms of the Victorian Staffordshire Yeomanry and the royal household. In the landscaped gardens are a church, an 18th-century orangery, and the descendants of a herd of goats given by Richard II to Sir John Bagot.

**Bloxham** *Oxon.* 546Ee
CHURCH OF OUR LADY From the pinnacled 14th-century tower of this magnificent large church rises an octagonally based spire. There is some Norman work, and a monument of 1725 by Andrew Carpenter. The church's restoration in 1866 was carried out by George Edmund Street, who also restored Christ Church Cathedral in Dublin, and designed the London Law Courts.

**Blundeston** *Suffolk* 548Fg
CHURCH OF ST MARY A Norman round west tower, and a 14th-century nave; the chancel was rebuilt in the 19th century. The south and north doorways are basically Norman. Inside are the remains of rood screens and benches.

**Blyborough** *Lincs.* 553Gf
CHURCH OF ST ALKMUND An Early English church, with a 13th-century chancel arch and a medieval rood screen. Later work includes the 18th-century tower. There is a reclining effigy of a priest (d. 1434).

**Blyth** *Notts.* 552Ff
PRIORY CHURCH OF SS MARY AND MARTIN A fragment of the original priory church, but the impressive Norman nave remains. The original stone screen across the nave is now built into the east wall behind the altar. There is a medieval monument, and another of the early 18th century.

**Blythburgh** *Suffolk* 548Ef
CHURCH OF THE HOLY TRINITY An interesting church with tall west tower, dating mainly from the later 15th century. There is a contemporary font, carved stalls, and benches with the Seven Deadly Sins instead of poppy-heads.

**Boarstall Tower** *Bucks.* 546Fd
The stone gate-house of a former fortified house, built in the 14th century and altered in the 16th and 17th centuries. It is almost surrounded by a moat. (Interior not open to the public.)

**Bodiam Castle** *Sussex* 542De
Architecturally one of the most satisfying castles, and built during the 14th century. It has a quadrangular plan with the main entrance in the centre of the north side. Although the regular form of the castle follows the development which had already taken place in the 13th century at Harlech and Beaumaris, Bodiam is built on a smaller scale and is intended to combine a high degree of comfort with defence. Before this time there was a tendency for living accommodation to grow up haphazardly inside a castle, but at Bodiam the residential quarters, including the hall and chapel which are still traceable, were carefully planned and built at the same time as the castle itself. The original iron-plated oak portcullis remains.

**Bodmin** *Cornwall* 538Dc
County town of Cornwall. Its features include the Turret Clock which marks the site of the ancient Butter Market; the 144 ft obelisk to Lt.-Gen. Sir Walter Raleigh Gilbert (1785–1853), whose ancestors were the Elizabethan sailors, Raleigh and Gilbert; the assize hall and shire house. In the church of St Petroc is St Petroc's Casket (c. 1170), of Byzantine origin, and the town's four silver gilt maces may be seen on application to the town clerk.

CHURCH OF ST PETROC Mainly 15th century; probably the largest parish church in the county. The tall north tower is of Norman origin and the font is Norman. There is a good monument, with recumbent effigy, to Prior Vyvyan (d. 1533).

BODIAM CASTLE

*The neighbouring towns of Rye and Winchelsea had been attacked and burnt by the French when Richard II granted his supporter Sir Edward Dalyngrydge a licence to build the castle in 1385. But it was never attacked or besieged and, as a result, survives practically unchanged. Bodiam is an interesting monument to the period when considerations of comfort were beginning to weigh equally with those of defence in castle planning, much of the carefully planned living accommodation being still traceable within the walls.*

**Bodnant Gardens** *Denb.* 550Fe
Bodnant, high above the R. Conway, looks out over a valley towards Snowdonia. The magnificent gardens of Bodnant, residence of Lord Aberconway, consist of the upper terrace gardens, and the Dell with a pinetum and a wild garden. The upper garden in front of the house has five formal terrace gardens and lawns with fine specimen trees. The high walls and stairways of the terraces, completed in 1939, are planted with huge banks of hydrangeas, camellias and other ornamental trees and shrubs. Among the terraces are the formal lily pool, with numerous fine hybrid lilies, and the rose terrace whose beds are edged with pinks and dwarf campanulas. There are innumerable and rare varieties of rhododendrons and large plantings of azaleas and magnolias. The pinetum contains huge specimens of Californian silver fir, Douglas fir and Spanish silver fir, planted over the last 100 years. There is a large rockery, and a rockery devoted to dwarf Chinese alpine rhododendrons. Paths in the wild garden lead to flowering shrub borders and an avenue of pleached laburnum and wisteria, bordered by yew hedges. (See p. 94.)

**Bodrhyddan Hall** *Flints.* 551Ge
This has been connected with the Conuy family since the 1280's when Edward I built the nearby Rhuddlan Castle. The name was probably once 'Bodrhuddlan' meaning 'House of Rhuddlan'. The first house was a wooden one, which was replaced in the 15th century by a grey stone version. Most of the south front is of the 17th century, and the big dining-room is 18th century. The west front driveway and major rebuilding were done in 1874. The symbol of the Saracen's Head, dating back to the Crusades, appears on the former entrance gates. There is a collection of arms and armour in the Hall itself. In 1284 the charter of Rhuddlan was signed by Edward I giving it the status of a borough and the protection of a garrison

BODRHYDDAN HALL

**93**

town. There are portraits by de Troy of the Duc d'Anjou and the Duc de Berry, 1696; Reynolds's portrait of Dr Shipley; and Hogarth's of Mrs Shipley. The St Mary's Well building is attributed to Inigo Jones and was possibly used to celebrate clandestine marriages. The Hall managed to be loyal to both Cromwell and the king during the 17th century, and there are several gifts from both Charles I and Charles II. The porcelain collection is mainly 18th-century Chinese with some later pieces. There is also an ornamental garden.

**Bodsey House** *Hunts.*                              547Jg
A moated house, once a hermitage attached to Ramsey Abbey which was dissolved in 1539. The house was later much altered. It has a 14th-century chimney-stack, and a coved and panelled ceiling in one of its rooms.

**Bodwrdda** *Caern.*                              550Dc
This fine-looking house, dated 1621, is notable for being the earliest large brick house in a county where the traditional building material is stone. In fact only the wings are of brick; the main block is of stone incorporating fabric dating from late medieval times. Three small pointed windows of this period light the rear wall.

**Bokerley Dyke** *Dorset*                              540Ed
This fine late Roman and Dark Age linear earthwork is crossed close to its centre by the modern Salisbury–Blandford road and runs for some miles each way. Recent excavations suggest that the first part was constructed during troubles in the 4th century. In AD 367, when Pictish raiders threatened the south country, the check-point opening was sealed and the more westerly arm of the northern half was added. Finally, the north-eastern wing of this northern part was added early in the 5th century, probably because of a threat by Saxon raiders from the north-east. The bank still stands to a good height, particularly to the south of the main road, and is fronted by a now partly silted ditch.

**Bolam** *Northld.*                              562Fa
CHURCH OF ST ANDREW A Norman church with a tall Saxon tower at the west. There is a mutilated wooden effigy of a cross-legged knight.

**Boldre** *Hants.*                              541Gc
CHURCH OF ST JOHN Originally Norman, the church stands on the edge of the New Forest. Later additions include the late 13th-century tower, which has a late 17th-century top stage. A monument of the mid-17th century shows a man's torso. The architect, R. Norman Shaw, built the neighbouring Grange, and shortly afterwards designed the pulpit of 1876.

**Bolsover Castle** *Derbys.*                              552Ee
A castle has stood here since the reign of William the Conqueror, but nothing of the Norman building remains. The present castle was begun during the reign of James I by Sir Charles Cavendish; the keep, with corner turrets, pinnacles and battlements, dates from *c.* 1615. In *c.* 1660, Sir Charles's son, the 1st Duke of Newcastle, added a fine range of terrace buildings in Classical style.

**Bolton** *Westmld.*                              557Jf
CHURCH OF ALL SAINTS Two jousting knights are carved in crude relief over the north doorway of this Norman church, and both north and south doorways have carved Norman capitals. The west turret (with two bells) was built in 1693, and the chancel screen of open tracery is late 18th century.

**Bolton Priory** *Yorks.*                              558Bb
Charming ruins in a delightful setting; the remains give evidence of the mid-12th century, when the priory was founded by Augustinian canons.

**Bonawe** *Argyll*                              565Ha
LORN FURNACE A complete early industrial layout, with stone blast-furnace, sheds for storage of iron ore and charcoal, and housing for workers and manager. Built in 1753 for iron smelting with local birch charcoal.

---

## THE DELL AT BODNANT

*An exotic portion of the Andes, Himalayas and China beside a small stream below the hills of Snowdonia. A great mass of trees, camellias, magnolias, azaleas have been planted beside paths along the sides of the valley. Perhaps the most magnificent of all are the rhododendrons of the 'Grande' series, brought from Asia. Primitive plants unchanged for nearly 50 million years, they flourish outside Asia only in the wetter, sheltered areas of south-west Scotland and Ireland, north-west England and Wales, and California.*

**Bo'ness** *562Af*
**(Borrowstounness)** *W. Lothian*
A stone slab at the eastern outskirts of the town
marks the end of the Roman Antonine Wall.
KINNEIL HOUSE In a cottage on this estate lived
James Watt (1736–1819), and there in 1764 he
developed the condensing steam engine. The
house contains 16th-century wall-paintings.

**Boothby Pagnell** *Lincs.* *553Gc*
MANOR HOUSE A small Norman manor house,
built *c.* 1200 in the grounds of Boothby Hall; it
has a moat for defence and substantial construction
—in places the walls are as much as 4 ft thick—
disguised by ashlar stone dressings. Inside the house
there is a vaulted ground floor with hall and solar.

**Bootle** *Lancs.* *551Jf*
ART GALLERY AND MUSEUM The Lancaster
Collection of English figure pottery and the
Bishop Collection of Liverpool pottery are on
view. Visiting art collections are also displayed.

**Borde Hill Garden** *Sussex* *542Be*
Noted for flowering trees and shrubs.

**Borough Green** *Cambs.* *548Bf*
BOROUGH GREEN HALL With statues of a boy and
girl in the niches it is a splendid Elizabethan house
with red brick and mullioned windows, a porch
with Ionic pilasters outside and an Elizabethan
screen inside. The house dates from 1575 and is
one of the few good small manor houses in the
county.

**Boroughbridge** *Yorks.* *558Dc*
ALDBOROUGH ROMAN SITE MUSEUM Pottery,
coins, inscriptions and bronze, iron, bone and glass
objects found in or near the Roman town of
Isurium Brigantum are displayed.
DEVIL'S ARROWS These are three great standing
stones in a straight line, spaced 200 ft and 370 ft
apart. They stand between 18 and 22 ft high and
were brought, as the stone shows, from a quarry at
Knaresborough, 6½ miles away. Their irregular
surfaces are due to weathering. They were erected
during the Bronze Age.

**Borthwick Castle** *M'loth.* *562Ce*
On June 7, 1567, three weeks after their marriage,
Mary, Queen of Scots and her third husband,
Bothwell, came to live here. But a few days later
they were forced to flee; Bothwell left for Dunbar
and a day later Mary made her escape disguised as a
page. The massive castle, with machicolated
towers dating from 1430, has a great hall containing a huge fire-place and fine vaulting.

**Borwick Hall** *Lancs.* *557Je*
An Elizabethan manor house, set in fine gardens
and unaltered in form since it was built around
portions of an earlier house in 1595.

**Bosbury** *Herefs.* *546Be*
CHURCH OF THE HOLY TRINITY A large, late
Norman church (*c.* 1200) in red sandstone, with a
font of the same date. The detached tower is 13th-
century, but the Morton Chapel was added
probably at the end of the 15th century. Among
the monuments are two Elizabethan ones in the
chancel, one of 1573 by John Guldo of Hereford,
another of 1578 with recumbent effigies.

**Boscobel House** *Shrops.* *552Bb*
Charles II fled here after the Battle of Worcester in
1651. Because of Parliamentary troops it was too
dangerous for him to remain in the house by day,
so he hid in an oak tree. The present Royal Oak
on the spot is said to have been raised from an acorn
of the original tree. The house, built early in the
17th century as a hunting lodge, was later altered.

**Bosham** *Sussex* *541Jd*
CHURCH OF THE HOLY TRINITY In a fishing village
on Chichester Harbour, the church is of Saxon
origin. It features on the Bayeux Tapestry, as it was
from Bosham that Harold sailed to Normandy.
There is a magnificent tall Saxon chancel arch, and
a pre-Conquest tower with later spire. Some 13th-
century additions include the five-lancet east
window. The font is octagonal, and there are some
fragments of medieval stained glass. In the chancel
is a recessed 13th-century tomb with the recumbent figure of a young girl.

**Bossall** *Yorks.* *558Ec*
CHURCH OF ST BOTOLPH Late Norman cruciform
church, with a central tower. The crossing arches
inside are also late Norman, but there are other
additions up to the Perpendicular period. The font,
with 18th-century cover, may be Norman. There
is a brass of 1454, and a 17th-century monument.

**Boston** *Lincs.* *553Jd*
The Peacock and Royal Hotel has a late Georgian
front and some 17th-century panelling in the
ground-floor lounge. Shodfriars Hall in South
Street is a much restored 16th-century timber-
framed house with double overhang and two
gables. From the customs house (1725) there is a
picturesque view of warehouses and old houses
running down to the tidal R. Witham. The ruined
stone shell of the Blackfriars Hall, 90 ft long, is in
Spain Lane. On the Skirbeck Road stand the ruins
of the Hussey Tower, with three floors, a stair-
turret and some ribbed-vaulting on the ground
floor. Boston, Massachusetts, was given the name
by emigrants from the town who left England in
the *Mayflower* in 1620.
CHURCH OF ST BOTOLPH In what was formerly a
notable port, St Botolph's is one of the largest
parish churches in England, with one of the most
famous towers, Boston Stump. The Stump (it has
an octagonal spire) is 272 ft high, a landmark for
travellers and sailors. The church was begun *c.*
1310 and building continued through the Decorated and Perpendicular periods. The style is
sumptuous and unified. The stalls have good
misericords, and among the brasses and monuments is a large slab to a Hanseatic merchant who
died in 1340. There is a 17th-century pulpit, an
18th-century wrought-iron communion rail,
Victorian stained glass, and a font by Pugin.
FYDELL HOUSE The best house in Boston, built
1726, with six bays and giant pilasters, a grand
entablature and balustraded parapet, and a tall
doorway with Doric columns. Internally, there is
an elegant staircase, much rococo decoration,
some first-rate plasterwork and, in a ground-floor
room, an unusually decorative chimney-piece.
GUILDHALL Built 1450, a symbol of medieval
Boston's former prosperity; it has a splendid five-
light window, much Georgian brickwork and a
good example of 15th-century linenfold in the old
council chamber. Several Pilgrim Fathers were
imprisoned there.

**Bothal** *Northld.* *563Gb*
CHURCH OF ST ANDREW A 13th- and 14th-century
church. Many fragments of medieval stained glass
remain, and there are alabaster effigies of the 16th
century.

**Bottesford** *Leics.* *552Fd*
CHURCH OF ST MARY A large church with a
handsome west tower and spire; the building dates
from the 13th century, with many later alterations.
The font is 16th century and the pulpit 17th
century. There are many impressive and important monuments from as early as the 13th century.

The best known are those to the eight Earls of Rutland in the chancel, by Richard Parker, Gerard Johnson, Nicholas Johnson, and to the 7th and 8th Earls by Grinling Gibbons (c. 1684).

**Bottesford** *Lincs.*      *553Gg*
CHURCH OF ST PETER'S CHAINS The dedication itself is one of the most interesting features of this church; others include the many lancet windows and the small bronze 15th-century Sanctus Bell, which was discovered in a wall during the 19th-century restoration. The church is cruciform, with a central tower.

**Bottisham** *Cambs.*      *548Af*
BOTTISHAM HALL Ancient seat of the Jenyns family, rebuilt in 1797 in a comfortable but unpretentious manner. The famous Sarah Jenyns, Duchess of Marlborough, who dominated Queen Anne, was a member of the family. The remainder of the village has pleasant cottages with overhanging upper storeys.
CHURCH OF THE HOLY TRINITY Impressive church of the 13th and 14th centuries, with a west tower and porch. Inside, a clerestory, stone rood screen, and wood parclose screens. There are several interesting monuments, including two seated figures of c. 1740, and one with an urn and *putti*—cherub-like children—by John Bacon.

**Boughton Monchelsea Place** *Kent*      *542Df*
A castellated Elizabethan manor house, set in a deer park; it dates from 1570. Though altered in Regency times, it still has a Tudor kitchen and tithe barn. The house contains tapestries dating from 1680 and manor records going back to 1570.

**Bourne** *Lincs.*      *553Hc*
Home town of Hereward the Wake, last of the Saxon nobles to resist William the Conqueror. His Saxon manor house stood on the site of Bourne Castle, now marked by mounds and part of a moat. The town has a number of good Georgian houses, including the Maltings and the Manor House. The Tudor cottages in South Street, dated 1636, are single-storey structures in brick with stone gable-ends and wooden mullioned windows. Near by is the Free School, of 1768, with six-light windows. The Roman Car Dyke, the earliest canal to attempt to drain the Fens, flows to the east of the town. At Cawthorpe, a mile and a half away, there are two good Georgian houses: Cawthorpe House and Cawthorpe Hall.
CHURCH OF SS PETER AND PAUL Originally the church of the former priory, the present building contains only the nave of the abbey church. The nave arcades are 12th century; of the two west towers that were intended, only one is complete.
RED HOUSE A mansion of c. 1620, with three-gabled bays, a two-storey porch with Tuscan columns, mullioned windows and a good staircase.

**Bournemouth** *Hants.*      *540Fc*
ROTHESAY MUSEUM Collections of 16th- and 17th-century furniture, paintings and ceramics; Victoriana, armour, model ships, butterflies and moths, coins and tokens are displayed, and items associated with the native peoples of New Zealand, Africa and the Pacific Islands.
RUSSELL-COTES MUSEUM AND ART GALLERY Items associated with Napoleon and with Sir Henry Irving (1838–1905), the first actor to be knighted, are on view. The gallery contains collections of oil paintings, water-colours and drawings, mainly from the Victorian period; works by local artists; the Russell-Cotes Oriental Collection representing China, Japan, Burma, Thailand, Tibet and India; South American pottery.

**Bourton-on-the-Hill** *Glos.*      *546Dd*
CHURCH OF ST LAWRENCE Of Norman origin with a west tower, St Lawrence's has Norman cylindrical pillars on the south side of the nave and a Perpendicular font.

**Bow Hill** *Sussex*      *541Jd*
The site of ancient yew plantations, tumuli, and prehistoric flint mines; terracing reveals the pattern of prehistoric cultivation.

**Bowden Hill and Cockleroy** *W. Lothian*   *562Af*
These two forts crown two hills. Each was defended by a single strongly-built stone wall, which enclosed the summit, and each was so disposed that the steeper scarp-slopes aided the defence scheme. It is thought that they were contemporary. The Bowden Hill fort-wall has been robbed in places.

**Bowness** *Westmld.*      *557Hd*
CHURCH OF ST MARTIN The original church was built in the 15th century, and later restored, but the main interest here is in the medieval stained glass in the east window, which came from one of the neighbouring abbeys such as Furness or Cartmel. There is a carved mural monument (without a figure) by John Flaxman, the neo-Classical sculptor (1755–1826), who prided himself on making monumental sculpture in England more Christian.

**Boxford** *Suffolk*      *548Ce*
CHURCH OF ST MARY The church has a 14th-century wooden north porch, which is vaulted, and a Perpendicular south porch, with decoration. The west tower has a small spire. Inside is a 17th-century font cover with doors, an 18th-century pulpit and some medieval mural paintings.

**Boxgrove** *Sussex*      *541Jd*
CHURCH OF SS MARY AND BLAISE Norman remains of Boxgrove Priory, founded c. 1117. The important Early English chancel is of the second quarter of the 13th century. The clerestory has Purbeck marble shafts and rich arcades. Of the monuments the most important is the de la Warr Chantry of c. 1532, with a mixture of Gothic and early Renaissance motifs.

**Boxley** *Kent*      *542Df*
A small village, overshadowed by a green sweep of the North Downs; it consists of a handful of cottages, with some grander houses, each in a luxuriant garden. White weather-boarding and red brick are the characteristic materials here, with one medieval stone house, which is rare for the district.

**Boxted** *Suffolk*      *548Ce*
CHURCH OF THE HOLY TRINITY A flint and stone church, with a hammerbeam roof in the chancel. There is a large pew on the north side for a local family and their household. A monument, c. 1587, has wooden effigies, and another, of the 17th–18th centuries with standing figures of husband and wife, might be by John Bushnell.

**Boynton** *Yorks.*      *559Gc*
CHURCH OF ST ANDREW The present church dates from 1768, when it was rebuilt by John Carr of York, who retained the 15th-century tower. In the Strickland Chapel are a number of 18th-century and later monuments.

**Boynton Hall** *Yorks.*      *559Gc*
A Tudor manor house built by William Strickland in 1550, with Georgian alterations by Lord Burlington and John Carr. (By appointment.)

**Bradfield** *Berks.*      *546Fb*
A village with a boys' public school. The school is built around an 18th-century manor house, and

has an open-air Greek theatre. The Church of St Andrew, in Transitional style, was largely rebuilt by Sir Gilbert Scott in 1847.

**Bradfield St George** *Suffolk* 548Cf
YEOMAN'S ACRE A yeoman's dwelling of pre-Tudor origin. (By appointment.)

**Bradford** *Yorks.* 558Cb
BOLLING HALL The manor of Bolling is mentioned in Domesday Book. It was owned by the Bolling family and their descendants from *c.* 1165 until the end of the Civil War when, having supported the Royalist cause, they were forced to dispose of their property. The earliest part of the present house is the south-east defensive tower which dates from the 15th century. Additions were made in the following centuries, and in 1779–80 the north wing was remodelled by John Carr of York in a style reflecting the Adam brothers. The Hall contains fine panelling and plasterwork, displays of local costume, and items connected with folk life and local history, and its furniture illustrates the development of English furniture from the 16th to the 19th centuries.
CATHEDRAL Formerly the large parish church of St Peter, the cathedral is mainly 15th century, the nave and chancel being dated to 1458, and the tower to 1508. The font and sculpture date from the same period. The notable monuments include one by John Flaxman to Abraham Balme, and others by John Bacon the Younger, J. F. Moore and Peter Scheemakers.
CITY ART GALLERY AND MUSEUM The gallery contains Chinese ceramics, paintings by British and foreign artists including Vasari, Reynolds, Gainsborough, van Os, Romney, Raeburn, Ibbetson, Stark, Corot, Ford Madox Brown, Sargent, Sickert, Pissaro, Orpen, Stanley Spencer, John Nash, Christopher Wood, Ceri Richards. The geology, archaeology, natural history and local history of the West Riding is illustrated by collections which include sections on moths, birds, fish, mammals, Roman coins, the city's electric tram-cars and models of industrial machines.

**Bradford Abbas** *Dorset* 540Cd
CHURCH OF ST MARY THE VIRGIN Mainly of the 15th century, with a good pinnacled west tower. There are 11 canopied niches in the west face, two of which still retain their sculptured figures. There is a good nave roof. Inside is a 15th-century stone rood screen, and a font with figures at each corner, medieval bench ends and a 17th-century pulpit.

**Bradford-on-Avon** *Wilts.* 540Df
A charming small town, in style similar to Bath. It rose to fleeting importance after Dutch spinners arrived to manufacture fine cloth in 1659. Its 12th-century parish church contains the first English Bible to be used in a church—a 1572 reprint of the Bishop's Bible of 1568. The diminutive 8th-century Saxon church is one of the earliest and smallest stone churches in England. The tithe barn, once a granary for Shaftesbury Abbey, dates from the 14th century. It is 167 ft long by 30 ft wide, and is made up of 14 great bays with gabled porches. It is now used as a museum of Wiltshire agricultural implements. The Hall, commonly known as Kingston House after the two Dukes of Kingston who owned it in the 18th century, is an Elizabethan mansion (not open). The Town Bridge is part medieval and part 17th century; it has a small chapel (in being before 1740), surmounted by a weather-vane in the form of a copper gilt fish, known as the Bradford Gudgeon.
CHURCH OF ST LAURENCE The tiny church of St Laurence—the nave height is 25 ft 5 in., 3 in. more

than the length—is one of the few Anglo-Saxon churches to survive intact. It is thought that the church was built by St Aldhelm, a famous scholar and monk, who lived in the late 7th century. The plan and much of the fabric of St Laurence's probably dates from this period, but the external decoration is of a later date. At the end of the 10th century the decorative arcading on the outside was formed by cutting into the stonework of the existing church. At the same time the roof was heightened, and later still the sculptured angels high up in the interior were added. The main loss has been of the south porch, but in essence the church is a near-perfect survival from pre-Conquest times, and—in its oldest part—from the 7th and 8th centuries.
CHURCH OF THE HOLY TRINITY Near the river with visible Norman remains such as the chancel windows, the church has early 14th-century additions, but the west tower with its short spire is of a later date, and there is other Perpendicular work. The squint from the north aisle to the chancel is exceptionally long. There is a medieval wall-painting of the Virgin, and two painted panels of Church Fathers from a former screen. Monuments and brasses include two of the 18th century, by John Nost (*c.* 1701) and Michael Rysbrack (*c.* 1737); 17th- and 18th-century painted glass can be seen in one of the nave windows.
ORPIN'S HOUSE Built in 1720, this was the home of Edward Orpin, parish clerk, whose portrait by Gainsborough is in the Tate Gallery. Considerably restored in 1965, when a stone-arched fire-place with seats and recesses, and a niche with a shell head, both dating from *c.* 1580, were uncovered.

CHURCH OF ST LAURENCE
BRADFORD-ON-AVON

*One of the few Anglo-Saxon churches to remain intact, St Laurence's is a superb survival from pre-Conquest England. Its early history is not known, but after the 12th century the building was not used as a church—by the mid-19th century it was part cottage and part school. At this time William of Malmesbury, an early 12th-century writer, was discovered to have described a small church at Bradford-on-Avon, reputedly built by St Aldhelm—a 7th-century scholar and monk—and it is now thought that St Laurence's, once more a church, dates from his time. The decorative arcading on the outside was probably carved at the end of the 10th century, when the roof was heightened. A little later the sculpted angels were added high up in the interior; these probably flanked a crucifix, now vanished, and they resemble angels that decorated 10th- and 11th-century English manuscripts.*

**Brading Villa** *Isle of Wight, Hants.*  541Hc
This Roman villa was once a fine country house standing on the sheltered southern side of Brading Down, near the east end of the island. Its known buildings stand on three sides of a courtyard, doubtless a farmyard. On the slopes of the Down, north of the house, there is a complex of 'Celtic' fields, probably a part of the villa's estate. As in many Roman villas, the main central rooms must have been lighted by clerestory windows set high in the walls over the penthouse roofs of the front veranda and rear range.

**Bradley** *Staffs.*  552Bc
CHURCH OF ALL SAINTS An interesting church of Norman origin, with 13th-century nave arcades. There is a Norman font, some fragments of medieval stained glass, and monuments with alabaster effigies.

**Bradwell Lodge** *Essex*  548Cc
A small Georgian mansion, much frequented by 18th-century celebrities. There is an Adam wing, an octagon room and a belvedere tower.

**Bradwell-on-Sea** *Essex*  548Cc
CHURCH OF ST PETER'S-ON-THE-WALL Built by St Cedd, Bishop of the East Saxons, in AD 654, this is one of the oldest churches in England. Constructed of Roman materials astride the wall of the Roman fort of Othona, it faces the North Sea. The chancel and porch have disappeared, but the nave with original doorway and west window remain.

**Braemar** *A'deen*  566Dd
BRAEMAR CASTLE Near here in 1715, the Earl of Mar raised his standard in support of the Old Pretender (James Francis Edward Stuart, son of James II) and after James's defeat forfeited his home, Braemar Castle, which was all but destroyed. After Culloden (1746) when the Young Pretender, Bonnie Prince Charlie, was finally defeated, the castle was restored and occupied by English troops, and later came into the hands of the Farquharsons who still own it. Originally built in 1628 it is now a private residence but retains its round central tower with spiral stair, star-shaped curtain wall and underground pit (a prison).

**Brailes** *Warks.*  546Ee
CHURCH OF ST GEORGE The church, with a west tower, dates from the 13th century. In the Decorated chancel are some 14th-century sedilia with stone arms to the seats. The church was restored in the late 19th century.

**Bramall Hall** *Cheshire*  552Bf
The former ancestral home of the Davenport family, the Hall was built mainly in the 16th century with a 'magpie' black and white exterior and many gables. There are portraits dating from 1575, tapestries and murals.

**Bramber** *Sussex*  542Bd
CASTLE The gaunt remains of a Norman castle on the R. Adur, owned by the Dukes of Norfolk from the 14th to the 20th centuries. It was destroyed in the Civil War.
POTTER'S MUSEUM Stuffed animals and birds represent nursery rhyme scenes and figures.
ST MARY'S A 15th-century timber-framed house, with rare 17th-century painted panelling, period furniture and a handicraft museum.

**Bramfield** *Suffolk*  548Ef
CHURCH OF ST MARY The Norman round tower is isolated from a newer Decorated church. There is a screen of *c.* 1500, and one of Nicholas Stone's best-known monuments, of *c.* 1634, which shows Mrs Coke holding a baby.

**Bramham Park** *Yorks.*  558Db
A country mansion, built in 1698 by Robert Benson, 1st Lord Bingley (1676–1731), politician and Chancellor in the reign of Queen Anne; his portrait by Kneller is in the hall. It was damaged by fire in the 19th century and restored with additions in the 20th century. The west front resembles the famous staircase at Fontainebleau near Paris, and the gardens are also in the French style.

**Bramley** *Hants.*  541Hf
CHURCH OF ST JAMES A Norman church with later additions and restorations. It has an early 17th-century brick west tower. Inside are 13th-century wall-paintings, one showing the murder of Thomas à Becket, and an 18th-century pulpit and west gallery. The Brocas Chapel on the south side contains a marble monument of *c.* 1777 which has been attributed to several sculptors, including Thomas Banks and Thomas Carter.

**Brampton** *Hunts.*  547Jf
PEPYS'S HOUSE The picturesque, twin-gabled farmhouse or small manor house where Samuel Pepys's parents lived, and where Pepys, not born here but in London, frequently stayed. In his diary he records how he thanked God he had 'such a pretty spot to retire to'.

**Brancepeth** *Durham*  558Cf
CHURCH OF ST BRANDON Originally 12th century, the church is in the grounds of the castle: it has a west tower. The chancel was rebuilt in the 15th century. Much of the furnishings were given by John Cosin, rector *c.* 1626.

**Brandsby** *Yorks.*  558Dc
CHURCH OF ALL SAINTS Small church designed by Thomas Atkinson, 1767–70, in Classical style. Over the centre a cupola provides unusual light effects inside.

**Brant Broughton** *Lincs.*  553Gd
CHURCH OF ST HELEN The Decorated west tower and tall spire have crockets all the way up; the arcades are 13th century, and there is a Perpendicular clerestory. The church was restored and the chancel rebuilt in 1876 by Bodley, who also installed some wood carving and wrought iron.

**Bratton** *Wilts.*  540Ef
A village containing many 16th- and 17th-century houses, and a Baptist chapel of 1667.

**Bratton Castle** *Wilts.*  540Ef
A fine Iron Age hill-fort on the north-west edge of the Salisbury Plain chalk massif. The internal area is about 24 acres, with two banks and ditches for most of its defences, though one bank is omitted on the east side. A Neolithic long barrow with quarry ditch lies within the enclosure.

There is a white horse carved into the chalk of the hill-side to the west of the fort. This, sometimes called the Westbury White Horse, is more horse-like than the one at Uffington. But we know that this was recarved in 1778 and it has been reported that the outline of the original horse has been seen from the air, when conditions were suitable, and that this resembled the Uffington Horse in outline. If this is accepted, the earlier horse here may also be attributed to the Iron Age.

**Braunton** *Devon*  538Ff
CHURCH OF ST BRANNOC Originally Norman, much of the rest of the building is 13th-century and has later additions. The Norman south tower has a later broach spire. The nave is wide, with a wagon-roof of *c.* 1500; there are many carved bench ends, some as late as 1593.

**Breamore** *Hants.* *540Fd*
BREAMORE HOUSE Built in 1583, this gabled manor house has been the home of the Hulse family for over 200 years; Sir Edward Hulse (1682–1759) was physician to George II. The interior, which was ravaged by fire in 1856, has been restored; its contents include fine furniture, paintings and tapestries.
CHURCH OF ST MARY This important Saxon cruciform church, also displaying Norman and later work, is on the edge of a park close to a red-brick Elizabethan manor house. Over the archway to the south transept is an Anglo-Saxon inscription meaning 'Here the Covenant becomes manifest to thee'. Over the south doorway is a carved stone rood, protected by a later porch, but badly mutilated at the Reformation.

**Brechin** *Angus* *566Fc*
ROUND TOWER Brechin 'Irish' round tower is one of only two such structures on the Scottish mainland—the other is at Abernethy in Perthshire. The Brechin tower, attached to the cathedral, probably dates from the 10th century; it is certainly 200 years older than the oldest part of the cathedral, the spire of which dates from 1360. The tower is about 86 ft high and is capped by a conical roof added in the 14th century.

**Breckles Hall** *Norfolk* *548Cg*
A many-gabled Elizabethan brick house, built in 1583 for the Woodhouse family, and restored by Detmar Blow in 1901 and altered again by Lutyens *c.* 1908. There are two towering chimney-breasts on the original south side, and inside there is a genuine priest's hole.

**Brecon** *Brecon.* *545Hd*
CATHEDRAL The church of the former priory here, raised to cathedral status in 1923. The cruciform building has a central tower, originally Norman, but now mainly Gothic, with a five-lancet east window. There is a monument by John Flaxman. The building was restored by Sir Gilbert Scott during the third quarter of the 19th century.
SOUTH WALES BORDERERS REGIMENTAL MUSEUM The Regiment was founded in 1689, and its activities since that date are recorded in the items on show. The weapons in the armoury include an example of almost every weapon used since 1800.

**Brecon Gaer** *Brecon.* *545Hd*
A mile and a half to the north-west of Brecon, the hill Pen-y-Crug is crowned by a strongly defended hill-fort, of native type, overlooking the junction-point of several radiating valleys. It was probably the strategic importance of this site which led to the Roman commander, in the early days of the conquest, to site a fort a mile higher up the western valley. The first ramparts and buildings were of earth and timber, but some remodelling in stone took place in the 2nd century. Excavation has shown that the civil disturbances which occurred towards the end of the 2nd century led to much damage here. But the fort was restored and occupied, at least intermittently, until towards the end of the occupation of Britain.

**Brede Place** *Sussex* *542Dd*
A country house, built *c.* 1350 in Caen stone, and added to in the 16th century. It contains sculptures by Clare Sheridan, and a pavilion houses the Brede Collection of war posters.

**Bredon** *Worcs.* *546Ce*
CHURCH OF ST GILES Dating in large part from the 12th century, this fine church has a central tower with a tall spire. Inside there is much of interest, including medieval tiles, tombs, early glass, and a heart burial with a slab showing a pair of hands holding a heart. A large 17th-century monument with reclining and kneeling figures, cherubs,

THE ROYAL PAVILION, BRIGHTON

*George IV, as Prince of Wales, first visited the village of Brighthelmstone in 1783 when it was becoming a fashionable resort for the new pastime of sea-bathing. In 1786 he leased a small house in the Steine, a valley running down to the sea; his wife, the former Mrs Fitzherbert, lived in a nearby villa. Soon Prince George commissioned the architect Henry Holland to enlarge his house into a pleasant Classical building with a domed central rotunda. In 1812 George III's mind failed, Prince George became Regent—and the great reconstruction of his Brighton house began. First,* *enormous sums of money were spent on the kitchen, entrance hall, long gallery and state apartments. John Nash, the Regent's Surveyor-general, transformed the exterior by adding to Holland's house the onion-shaped dome, tent-like pavilion roofs, and pinnacles and minarets in the style of a mogul's palace. The lavish interior was much influenced by Chinese decoration. The banqueting room has painted walls, a ceiling resembling a huge palm-tree and a bedragonned chandelier. The music room and saloon are also sumptuous.*

columns and heraldry, an impressive product of the period, is by Michael Sidnell of Bristol, *c.* 1732.
TYTHE BARN A 14th-century barn, 132 ft long.

**Bredon Hill** *Worcs.* 546Ce
Bredon is a great outlier of the Cotswolds, commanding the Vales of Severn and Avon. A spur on the north side of the hill is defended by two ramparts of an Iron Age hill-fort, each with an external ditch. The inner defences came first, and had a simple staggered entrance. Later, the outer bank and ditch were added. This rampart was faced with stone on the outside, and the two entrances through it were inturned to give long narrow passages to the space between the two banks. At the same time a long 'corridor entrance' was made in the inner bank to replace the first simpler one.
   The camp was sacked, and its defenders slain. Thereafter it lay deserted for an indeterminate period before the Roman conquest. The central openings in the outer bank are apparently comparatively modern.

**Bredwardine** *Herefs.* 545Je
CHURCH OF ST ANDREW A large Norman church, with carved north and south doors and a plain Norman font. The chancel is early 14th-century, and the north-west tower was added in 1790. There are two effigies of knights.

**Breedon on the Hill** *Leics.* 552Ec
CHURCH OF SS MARY AND HARDULPH The church is built on the site of a Saxon monastery, commanding a view over the Trent Valley. It is mainly Norman, with later work; the nave was destroyed. High up in the south aisle, and inside the tower, are several magnificent carved fragments with figures dating from *c.* 800, from the monastery. There are late 16th-century tombs with effigies, made by Royleys of Burton upon Trent.

**Breiddin, The** *Mont.* 551Jb
An Iron Age hill-fort overlooking the upper waters of the R. Severn. The site is well defended by multiple ramparts, which link the natural scarp-slopes of the hillside. It was constructed in the latter part of the Iron Age, and occupied until the Roman governor of Britain, Suetonius Paulinus, began the reduction of the Welsh tribes in AD 57, from the new legionary fortress at Wroxeter.

**Brenchley** *Kent* 542De
A picturesque village with splendid Tudor half-timbered houses. An avenue of ancient yews leads to the church, which was built in 1233.

**Brent Eleigh** *Suffolk* 548Ce
CHURCH OF ST MARY A Decorated church with a later west tower, and a 14th-century south door. Inside are a 17th-century pulpit and font cover, 18th-century box-pews and reredos. A large monument to Edward Colman by Thomas Dun, *c.* 1743, is strangely like some of Sir Henry Cheere's designs.

**Brentford** *Greater London* 542Ag
BRITISH PIANO MUSEUM The collection includes a Steinway-Duo-Art reproducing grand piano belonging to Princess Beatrice, youngest daughter of Queen Victoria, a self-playing violin with piano accompaniment, orchestrions, nickelodeons, music boxes, cylinder gramophones, barrel and player pianos, hand organs, and all sorts of old, odd and interesting keyboard instruments.

**Brentwood** *Greater London* 548Bc
ESSEX REGIMENT MUSEUM Weapons and uniforms of various periods, badges, a Victoria Cross and other medals, and special pieces of regimental silver are exhibited in the former officers' mess.

**Brewood** *Staffs.* 552Bb
CHURCH OF ST MARY THE VIRGIN A good church with a spire, dating from the 13th century with later additions. There are several 16th- and 17th-century monuments with effigies.

**Bride Stones** *Cheshire* 552Be
Most of the mound has disappeared, so that the megalithic structure, though somewhat damaged, is visible. There are traces of the semicircular forecourt at the east end and nearly 20 ft of the long gallery is still intact. Originally, the barrow must have been large; it is believed to have exceeded 300 ft in length. This 'gallery grave' belongs to a type known as the Clyde-Carlingford sub-group, the best examples of which are in Ulster and Galloway.

**Bridge of Dun** *Angus* 566Fc
BRIDGE OVER THE R. SOUTH ESK Three wide arches, ornamented with such Gothic motifs as double crosses and quatrefoil columns, span the river; squat obelisks guard the approaches. By Alexander Stevens, it was completed in 1787.

**Bridgnorth** *Shrops.* 546Bg
A town on two levels, one part being called the High Town standing 200 ft above the R. Severn, the Low Town being linked by a bridge across the river. Its oldest dwelling is Bishop Percy's House, built 1580, birthplace in 1729 of Thomas Percy who became Bishop of Dromore (Ireland). The town hall (1652) is a half-timbered building, once a barn in Much Wenlock, standing on an open-arched *piazza* of stonework. In Low Town is the 17th-century Diamond Hall, built by Colonel Roger Pope with the winnings of his racehorse, Diamond.
CHURCH OF ST LEONARD With traces of Norman work in its south tower, this large church was almost entirely rebuilt in the 1860's in Gothic Revival style. The nave roof, of hammerbeam construction, is mid-17th century.
CHURCH OF ST MARY MAGDALENE Begun in 1792 to the design of Thomas Telford the engineer, this church is neo-Classical inside and out. The exterior has large Tuscan columns, a pediment and smooth rustication (the stones smoothly finished, but the joints between them greatly emphasised). The tower is square at first, then octagonal and finally domed. Telford designed the liturgical east end (actually the south end) to be straight but Sir Arthur Blomfield added the apse in 1876. Another Shropshire church by Telford is at Madeley.

**Bridgwater** *Som.* 540Be
An inland seaport and market town, birthplace of Robert Blake (1599–1657), admiral and general-at-sea under Oliver Cromwell; Blake's house is now a museum. The rebel Duke of Monmouth was proclaimed king at Bridgwater in 1685. The medieval steeple of St Mary's Church is a notable landmark, 175 ft high. The town possesses many Georgian houses, especially in Castle Street.
ADMIRAL BLAKE MUSEUM The reputed birthplace of Admiral Robert Blake (1598–1657) and containing relics of his life, including his sea-chest and compass. Also on display are relics of the Battle of Sedgemoor (1685) and of the Duke of Monmouth. Collections of local shipping, industry, archaeology and history, topographical prints, drawings and photographs, and examples of domestic and agricultural bygones.

**Bridlington** *Yorks.* 559Gc
ART GALLERY AND MUSEUM, SEWERBY PARK Amy Johnson's Pilot's Log Book, covering the years 1928–38, is the main exhibit in the Amy

## POSSET POT AND COVER

*Posset was a hot drink of ale, honey and herbs. Refined people spooned their posset out of a silver pot; the less refined sipped it from the spout of an earthenware one. This pot, probably made at Bristol in the late 17th century, is painted with Chinese figures in enamel. (Brighton Museum and Art Gallery)*

## HOVE AMBER CUP

*Found buried in the long-barrow grave of a Wessex Culture chief at Hove in 1857, this cup is nearly 3 in. high. An oak coffin was uncovered and inside with bones were the cup, a stone axe-head and a bronze dagger. The cup was turned on a lathe from a single block of amber. (Brighton Museum and Art Gallery)*

Johnson Room at Sewerby Hall and Park. The famous flier opened the Hall as a museum in 1936 and, today, her trophies, awards and mementoes are collected here. Sewerby Hall was built c. 1720, with later additions dating from 1808–50. It houses a collection of pictures by local artists and an archaeological display of Bronze Age axe-heads and flint implements. Botanical gardens in the park are open to the public.

BAYLE MUSEUM The museum is in the 14th-century stone and brick gate-house of the Augustinian Priory of Bridlington. Structural alterations were made in the 17th century, but some original building remains, including a spiral stair, fireplaces and a groined vault. In its time the manor court-house, a school and a prison, the Bayle is still used for meetings by the Lords Feoffees of the Manor, in whose trust the Bayle has been since 1631. The collections consist of local relics, including weapons, domestic and trade untensils (pipemakers' equipment and farm implements), jewellery, a collection of Valentines, dolls' furniture, model boats and local paintings, prints and maps.

CHURCH OF ST MARY The church is the nave of what must have been an impressive priory church, but after the Dissolution the east end, transepts and central tower disappeared. The two western towers were completed by Sir Gilbert Scott in the second half of the 19th century.

### Bridport *Dorset*                    540Cc
MUSEUM AND ART GALLERY Seven hundred and fifty years of local trade are commemorated in the ropes, nets and lines displayed at the Bridport Museum. Other exhibits include British birds and their eggs, Roman relics from the 1st-century camp near by and items of local history—domestic and agricultural bygones. The collections are contained in a building dating from the early 16th century, which is reputed to have been the house of a chantry priest of St Leonard.

### Brierley Hill *Staffs.*              546Cg
MUSEUM The museum is in the centre of the Stourbridge Flint glass industry; there are items relating to this, and local and foreign glass. Temporary art exhibitions are held.

### Brighouse *Yorks.*                   558Ca
SMITH ART GALLERY A collection of oil paintings and water-colours, mainly by 19th-century artists.

### Brighton *Sussex*                    542Bd
CHURCH OF ST PETER A Gothic building by Sir Charles Barry, later the architect of the Houses of Parliament; it was built c. 1825, and has the tower at the west end. The outside is a mass of pinnacles, and there is much late 19th-century glass inside.

MOTOR MUSEUM Opened in 1961 as an associate to the Montagu Motor Museum at Beaulieu, the museum illustrates the history of motor transport with veteran, vintage and modern cycles, motorcycles and cars. Among the cars shown are the 1901 10 hp Lifu steam-car with a water consumption of 1 mpg, fuel consumption of 5 mpg and requiring one hour to get started from cold; the 1938 Mercedes-Benz with armour-plate and $1\frac{3}{4}$ in. thick glass, weighing over 4 tons and owned by Reichmarschall Hermann Goering; and the 1941 Humber used by Field Marshal Lord Montgomery from El Alamein to the Sangro.

MUSEUM AND ART GALLERY The museum is part of the Royal Pavilion Estate built for George IV, and includes old masters—Flemish, Dutch and English—contemporary oil paintings, English water-colours, prints and drawings. It also deals with archaeology, bones and bone-structure, natural history, musical instruments, English and French furniture, ceramics, glass and bronze.

PRESTON MANOR (AT PRESTON PARK) An early manor house rebuilt in Georgian times and noted for its fine furniture and pictures.

ROYAL PAVILION In 1786 George, Prince of Wales, leased a small house here, and soon afterwards Henry Holland reconstructed it as a Classical building, with a central rotunda and dome. After he became Regent in 1812, Prince George had the house rebuilt; John Nash, his Surveyor-General, transformed Holland's house into something like an Indian mogul's palace by the addition of the great onion-shaped dome, tent-like roofs to the pavilions, numerous pinnacles and small minarets. At this time the royal stables, now the Dome concert hall, were built. William IV and later Queen Victoria stayed at the Pavilion—though she disliked it as new building in Brighton was rob-bing it of privacy. The Pavilion was closed in 1845 and much of the furniture was removed. The building was bought by the town of Brighton in 1850. Since the Second World War it has been restored to its former brilliance, and furnished with most of the original furniture and pictures, returned by the Queen. (See p. 99.)

THOMAS-STANFORD MUSEUM, PRESTON MANOR The house was rebuilt in 1738 on a 13th-century foundation, and was left to the town of Brighton in 1932 by the late owner, Sir Charles Thomas-Stanford, on the understanding that it should be preserved as an English country home. For this reason there are no formal conducted tours or roped-off areas in the house. The collection of silver includes examples from England (some by the famous silversmith Paul Lamerie), Portugal and Scandinavia, and a collection of Russian silver niello snuff boxes (a form of inlay using a black alloy of silver to emphasise the engraved design). There is also a collection of 17th-century Chinese Fukein-ware figures. The furniture is mainly Georgian, with some 16th- and 17th-century pieces, including a cabinet with secret drawers belonging to Queen Anne, and one room contains leather hangings brought from Cordoba by Katherine of Aragon. The 3½ acres of grounds include a walled garden and lily ponds.

**Brightwell Baldwin** *Oxon.*      *547Gc*
CHURCH OF ST BARTHOLOMEW An attractive church, in the Decorated and Perpendicular styles. The stained glass is medieval, the pulpit Jacobean. Inside are brasses and monuments, and a barrel organ made in 1843.

**Brinkburn** *Northld.*      *562Fb*
PRIORY CHURCH OF SS PETER AND PAUL Founded by Augustinian canons *c.* 1135, in an enchanting position by the R. Coquet. It was in ruins until the 19th century, when restoration took place.

**Brinsop** *Herefs.*      *546Ae*
CHURCH OF ST GEORGE An early 14th-century church, with some interesting Norman carving, including a scene of St George and the Dragon. From the 14th century come wall-paintings of the Annunciation and the Crucifixion, and stained glass also showing St George. The ornate reredos was done by Sir Ninian Comper in 1920-8.

**Bristol** *Glos.*      *540Cg*
CATHEDRAL Henry VIII gave cathedral status to what was originally a Norman monastic church in 1542. The cathedral building at Bristol dates from the 12th century, but, apart from the chapter house with its adjoining buildings and the great gate-house, little survives from this period. The chapter house has extremely rich Romanesque decoration of interlaced arcading, and also interlaced chevron patterns carved on its walls. The abbey church, which was started in 1298 and only finished in the 19th century when the nave was built, has many unusual features. In most medieval churches the central aisle rises above those at the side, but Bristol—a hall-church—has aisles of the same height as the central part of the building, while the relationship between the side and central aisles is complicated by the complex system of aisle vaulting. The vaulting of the central aisle itself is unusual and marks a step towards late medieval complexities. Another unusual piece of vaulting, an early 14th-century skeleton vault, appears in the anteroom to the Berkeley Chapel to the south of the choir. The furnishings include stalls with misericords, and many monuments of all periods.
CHURCH OF ALL SAINTS The earliest parts of the church are Norman and 15th century. The north tower, topped by a cupola, is of the early 18th century, and the chancel was rebuilt in the mid-19th century. The most outstanding monument is the Belgian sculptor Rysbrack's to Edward Colston (*d.* 1721), designed by the architect James Gibbs.
CHURCH OF ST MARK (THE LORD MAYOR'S CHAPEL) The chapel originally belonged to St Mark's Hospital, but at the Dissolution became the property of the city corporation (it is the only church in England owned by a corporation) and from 1721 their official place of worship. There have been many alterations to the original 13th-century building: a tower in the Perpendicular style of 1487 and the 16th-century fan-vaulted Poyntz Chapel, floored with Spanish tiles. Amongst a wealth of stained glass is some from the eccentric millionaire William Beckford's Gothic extravagance, Fonthill Abbey. A profusion of monuments, ranging from cross-legged knights of the 13th century to the 19th-century work by Sir Francis Chantrey, make this one of the most important churches for monumental sculpture.
CHURCH OF ST MARY REDCLIFFE A magnificent church, one of the largest in England, dating from the 13th century; the north porch (*c.* 1325) is lavishly decorated. In the 15th century the tall spire was struck by lightning, and was not rebuilt for 400 years. The church contains many monuments and brasses, and among the fittings are candle-sticks, a sword-rest, lectern and wrought-iron screens.
CITY ART GALLERY AND MUSEUM Built in 1899 and presented to the city by Sir W. H. Wills— of the famous tobacco family—it houses a large representative collection of British and European art. The gallery contains old and modern paint-ings, sculpture, water-colours and engravings, some European and Far Eastern ceramics, ivory carvings and embroidery. The museum has a fully documented history of Clifton bridge and an interesting collection of Victorian machinery and vehicles.
CLIFTON SUSPENSION BRIDGE Built by Isambard Kingdom Brunel, 245 ft above the Avon Gorge; it incorporates chains from the old Hungerford suspension bridge in London.
WESTBURY COLLEGE John Wycliffe (1320-84), who instituted the first translation of the whole Bible into English, was a prebend of the College of Priests; the 15th-century gate-house is all that remains.

**Britford** *Wilts.*      *540Fe*
CHURCH OF ST PETA A cruciform church of Saxon origin which contains some important 8th- and 9th-century carvings. There are monuments *c.* 1300, a late 17th-century pulpit and pews, and an 18th-century mausoleum. The church was res-tored *c.* 1875 by G. E. Street.

**Brixworth** *Northants.*      *547Gf*
CHURCH OF ALL SAINTS The church dates from the 7th century and incorporates many Roman tiles. It was monastic until 870 and the belfry and spire were added to the Saxon tower in the 14th century. There is an effigy of a cross-legged knight of *c.* 1300.

**Broad Clyst** *Devon*      *539Hg*
CHURCH OF ST JOHN THE BAPTIST A large church, mainly 14th- and 15th-century, with a tall pin-nacled west tower. The interior has wagon-roofs, and there are several monuments, ranging from a mid-14th-century knight to reclining or recum-bent effigies of 1613 and 1622.

EDWARD BAILY *Eve at the Fountain*

*One of the most successful and prolific sculptors of the first half of the 19th century, Edward Baily is little known today, although his Nelson in Trafalgar Square, London, is one of the most famous statues in Britain. By general consent in his own day 'Eve at the Fountain' was considered his masterpiece. Carved in 1822, it was bought some years later by a general subscription of the citizens of his native Bristol. Strangely enough the model was originally designed as the handle of a silver soup tureen for the Licensed Victuallers Company; the original sketch-model is also at the Bristol gallery.*

*As well as his figure of Nelson, Baily also executed other prominent sculptures in London. Some of the sculptures on the front of Buckingham Palace are by him, and he also worked on the Marble Arch.*
*(City Art Gallery and Museum, Bristol)*

'OLIVER CROMWELL'
PRIVATEER GLASS

*A series of Privateer glasses was made in Bristol to celebrate the commissioning of armed merchant vessels in the Seven Years' War (1756–63). The distinction between privateers and pirates was somewhat academic to their victims. This glass is engraved: 'Success to the Oliver Cromwell Privateer', and 'Paul Flyn, Commander'. Standing 6 in. high, it has an enamel twist stem and a conical bowl; most glasses in the series have bucket-shaped bowls.*
*(City Art Gallery and Museum, Bristol)*

CLIFTON SUSPENSION BRIDGE, BRISTOL

*This bridge was one of the most daring of its kind when designed by Brunel in 1830. The foundation stone of the massive west abutment was laid by Lady Elton in June 1831, but owing to shortage of funds this part alone was completed in Brunel's lifetime. After his death in 1859, the bridge was completed by the engineers Sir John Hawkshaw and W. H. Barlow as a memorial to their late colleague. The suspension chains used were bought cheaply from Brunel's Hungerford Bridge which was then being demolished to make way for the present Charing Cross railway bridge in London. This entailed some alterations to Brunel's original design. The bridge was completed, and opened on December 8, 1864. It has a single* suspended span of 702 ft carrying the roadway 245 ft above the R. Avon.

*Isambard Kingdom Brunel was born at Portsmouth in 1806. When he was only 19 years old he was resident engineer in charge of the Thames tunnel, and at 24 was elected a fellow of the Royal Society. Three years later he became engineer of the Great Western Railway. To extend its services he turned to shipbuilding, and was responsible for the first steamship designed for regular Atlantic crossings, the Great Western. Brunel followed this with the Great Eastern, until then the largest vessel built; its completion almost coincided with his death, probably brought about by overwork on it.*

**Broadstairs** *Kent*     *543Gg*
BLEAK HOUSE Here Charles Dickens wrote *David Copperfield*. The house inspired the title of another work, which he planned while living here in this castellated Victorian house on the edge of the cliffs.

**Broadwater** *Sussex*     *542Ad*
CHURCH OF ST MARY In what was formerly a village, now part of Worthing, the church is cruciform with a central tower. The Norman building was added to, and there was much restoration in the mid-19th century. There are some misericords, a brass to a former rector (*d.* 1432) and monuments to two Lords de la Warr, of 1524 and 1554.

**Broadway** *Worcs.*     *546De*
One of the most famous villages in Britain, with all the best features of Cotswold stone building.

**Broch of Mousa** *Mousa, Shetland*     *568Ee*
This is certainly the best known and, in many ways, the finest of the brochs. It still stands some 43½ ft high and has a 50 ft external diameter at the base. It contains stairs and galleries, and is particularly notable for the thickness of its wall.

**Brockhall** *Northants.*     *546Ff*
An Elizabethan manor house, with a wing by Robert Adam added in the 18th century.

**Brockham** *Surrey*     *542Bf*
A triangular green, with the church, built of white firestone, at one end, and a grand sweep of chalky downland above the houses at the other.

**Brockhampton-by-Ross** *Herefs.*     *546Bd*
CHURCH OF ALL SAINTS A stone and concrete church by W. R. Lethaby, of 1901–2, All Saints has a central tower. The extremely steep arches of the nave spring low from the walls, without brackets. The tapestry was designed by Sir Edwin Burne-Jones and made by Morris & Co., and there is some 20th-century stained glass by Christopher Whall. The two old altar-pieces are 16th-century Flemish and 15th-century Italian.

**Brodick Castle** *Isle of Arran, Bute*     *560Fd*
Set amid fine formal and woodland gardens below bleak Goat Fell, this castle, dating largely from *c.* 1500, was the former home of the Dukes of Hamilton; the west end and tower were added in the 19th century. The castle contains much fine furniture and collections of porcelain, silver and paintings, including sporting pictures.

**Bromham** *Wilts.*     *540Ef*
CHURCH OF ST NICHOLAS Once Norman, most of the building is of a later date with an Early English chancel, and an Early English central tower with Perpendicular spire. The church is notable for the very ornate south chapel with large Perpendicular windows; it was founded in 1492, and has brasses and monuments to the Tocotes-Beauchamp and Baynton families of the 15th and 16th centuries. In the east window is stained glass by William Morris after Burne-Jones, *c.* 1870. The poet Thomas Moore is buried in the churchyard.

**Bromsgrove** *Worcs.*     *546Cf*
CHURCH OF ST JOHN THE BAPTIST There is a mid-14th-century tower with an octagonal crocketed spire, but St John's is chiefly noteworthy for its monuments. These include the 15th- and 16th-century tombs with alabaster effigies to members of the Talbot and Stafford families. On the Talbot tomb evidence was found in 1856 establishing the claim of Lord Talbot of Ingestre to the Earldom of Shrewsbury; Sir Humphrey Stafford was killed in the rebellion against government corruption led by Jack Cade in 1450.

**Broncroft Castle** *Shrops.*     *546Ag*
A centre of fighting in the Civil War (1645), the castle was originally a 14th-century fortress; it was restored and added to in the 19th century.

**Brooke** *Rutland*     *553Gb*
CHURCH OF ST PETER The church dates from Norman times, but much was rebuilt during the 16th century, from which time most of the furnishings survive. There is a fine Renaissance tomb commemorating Charles Noel (1619), which still has traces of the original colouring. The font is Norman.

**Broomend of Crichie** *A'deen*     *566Fe*
This is a circular enclosure with external bank and contained ditch. Its overall diameter is about 110 ft. The two standing stones near the ditch are contemporary with the monument, but that at the centre is a later addition; Pictish symbols are carved on this central stone.

**Brougham** *Westmld.*     *557Jf*
CHURCH OF ST NINIAN There was once a Saxon church on this site, and then a Norman one which Lady Anne Clifford of Brougham Castle rebuilt in 1660. Today the church is as she left it, still with its contemporary furnishing. Near by are St Wilfrid's Chapel, of about the same date, with an interesting screen and stalls, and the castle.

**Broughton** *Lincs.*     *553Gg*
CHURCH OF ST MARY A Norman church, the building has later work and a Saxon west tower with a circular staircase addition. Inside there are interesting monuments of several periods including two fine 14th-century brasses, and two alabaster effigies of the late 14th century. Another effigy of *c.* 1670 commemorates Sir Edmund Anderson, Lord Chief Justice of the Common Pleas.

**Broughton** *Oxon.*     *546Ee*
CHURCH OF ST MARY This spacious church, near the castle, has a 14th-century tower and spire; the stone chancel screen is of the same date, and inside there are wall-paintings and many monuments.

**Broughton** *Staffs.*     *552Bc*
CHURCH OF ST PETER An early 17th-century Gothic church with earlier, medieval stained glass, depicting figures of saints and heraldic shields. Inside are contemporary box-pews, and a monument of *c.* 1813 by S. and T. Franceys, the statuaries of Liverpool.

**Broughton Castle** *Oxon.*     *546Ee*
A moated manor house, with origins dating back to *c.* 1306, the castle was added to and decorated in Elizabethan times. It was owned by William of Wykeham (1324–1404) and passed by marriage to the 2nd Lord Saye and Sele in 1451; the Lords Saye and Sele have lived there ever since. The façade, fire-places, ceiling and panelling were introduced in 1554–99. Features of the house include a collection of Court Rolls of the Manor of Bloxham, dating from 1339, and a collection of pictures, china and Chinese wallpapers.

**Browsholme Hall** *Lancs.*     *558Ab*
The home of the Parker family since 1380. The present Tudor mansion was begun in 1507. It was refronted in 1604, but the top storey of this Elizabethan front was removed and the east wing extension made in 1711. In 1800 Thomas Parker, a friend of the Prince Regent, built the west wing, and later created the landscape garden as a tribute to the Prince and Mrs Fitzherbert. The house contains Elizabethan and Stuart panelling, china, tapestries, fine furniture and pictures.

**Broxbourne** *Herts.* 548Ac
CHURCH OF ST AUGUSTINE A large 15th-century church on the banks of the R. Lea. The builder of the south chapel in 1476 worked also at St Margaret's, Westminster. The nave and chancel are not divided by a chancel arch. The Norman font is octagonal, and there are many interesting monuments and brasses.

**Bryn Celli Ddu** *Anglesey* 550Ee
This fine cairn is a passage-grave of a type limited to the Atlantic areas of Britain and commoner in Scotland and Ireland. The original mound, some 160 ft in diameter, was held within a circle of substantial uprights and, on the north-east side, a long entrance passage led to a 10 ft long chamber near the centre. Only one of the original capstones now remains, but in the chamber there still stands a carefully rounded upright stone set there, not as part of the supports, but for some quasi-religious purpose.

**Bryn Yr Hen Bobl** *Anglesey* 550Ec
A burial chamber contained in a kidney-shaped mound. It is unusual in having a 320 ft long narrow terrace leading off to the south; this has been interpreted as a phallic symbol.

**Buckden** *Hunts.* 547Jf
The Lion Hotel and the George Hotel are notable old coaching inns. The timber-framed manor house was built in 1654 round a 15th-century tower, and has 19th-century additions. The ancient gateway with its bold machicolations overhanging the third storey is probably *c.* 1470, the same period as the chapel, now the great dining-room. The house contains many fine pictures and good furniture.
BISHOP'S PALACE Built 1480–94; there is a massive gate-house, a porter's lodge, battlemented walls, quadrangle and a square tower with four turrets. The Arms over the inner gateway are those of Bishop Russel, who used this as a fortified palace. One of the corner turrets of the main tower was occupied for a short time by Queen Katherine of Aragon before she was removed to Kimbolton Castle, where she died. The palace is now a Roman Catholic school.
CHURCH OF ST MARY The church is near the former bishop's palace, and is mainly Perpendicular with a tower and spire, and a two-storey south porch. There is a 17th-century pulpit, and some fragments of medieval glass and a monument by E. H. Baily may be seen.

**Buckfast Abbey** *Devon* 539Gc
In 1907, Benedictine monks started to rebuild the ruins of a 10th-century abbey which had been dissolved in 1539. The revived abbey was finished in 1938. It is built of local limestone, in Transitional Norman-English style, with a tower 158 ft high.

**Buckingham** *Bucks.* 547Ge
Market town with a Georgian town hall in the market square and, close by, the old gaol, styled as a small castle and built in 1758. There is a 14th-century manor house, while the 16th-century Royal Latin School has a Norman gateway.
CHANTRY CHAPEL Chantry chapels were built with money left by the pious rich to provide places where masses might be sung for them and prayers said. Here the original Norman doorway may still be seen, having survived the chapel's rebuilding in 1475 and its restoration in 1875.

**Buckland** *Glos.* 546De
CHURCH OF ST MICHAEL Mainly Perpendicular in appearance (but with traces of earlier work, such as the late 13th-century nave arcades), it has almost

completely escaped restoration. Outstanding features inside are the 17th-century oak panelling in the south aisle, and the 15th-century glass in the east window, depicting three of the seven sacraments; the tiles in the south aisle and the finely embroidered pall kept in the north aisle are also both of the 15th century.

**Buckland** *Surrey* 542Bf
The main road runs between the pretty church and the prim oblong green, with a black barn on one side and the village school on another.

**Buckland Abbey** *Devon* 538Fc
In 1581, Sir Francis Drake (1540–96) acquired this 13th-century Cistercian monastery from the Grenville family, who had made many alterations in 1576. The monastery nave became the great hall. The abbey is now a museum with relics of Drake and Sir Richard Grenville.

**Buckland Rectory** *Glos.* 546De
A house dating from *c.* 1520; the great hall has a timber-frame roof and stained glass windows of the period.

**Bucklers Hard** *Hants.* 541Gc
This hard (a sloping foreshore) is on the tidal waters of Beaulieu R. Its 18th-century shipyard has now been restored.
The wide, late 18th-century street, which is all there is of the village, runs down to the Beaulieu R. It was the start of a port which the Duke of Montagu meant to develop.
MARITIME MUSEUM The museum contains maps, including a copy of Speed's map of 1611, documents relating to shipbuilding on the Beaulieu R., models of ships including the *Victory,* Nelson's baby clothes and records of Sir Francis Chichester's ocean voyages. Many original shipbuilding drawings by Henry Adams, who designed Nelson's favourite ship the *Agamemnon,* can be seen, and prints of him and his family. There are also paintings and prints of ships built at Beaulieu and the officers who commanded them.

BUILDWAS ABBEY
*The extensive ruins of Buildwas Abbey include the church and the eastern range of the cloister. The ruins of the 12th-century church consist of the nave arcades, the west wall and the choir chapels with their vaults intact. North of the church lie the chapter house and two adjacent rooms, all complete with vaults. The ruins show no signs of enlargements or alterations from the foundation of the abbey in the 12th century until the Dissolution in 1536, a fact which suggests that the house was never powerful or wealthy.*

BURGHLEY HOUSE

One of England's greatest Elizabethan houses, Burghley was begun about *1552* by Sir William Cecil, one of the queen's ministers. Of the earlier part of the building, the grandest room is the great hall, with a double hammerbeam roof incorporating both Gothic and Renaissance elements, especially in the large fire-place with its fluted and bulging supports. Dominating the second stage of the house is the fantastic feature in the courtyard; this is surmounted by a clock on top of which is a huge obelisk held up by two enormous rampant lions, with obelisks behind them. A feature of the interior is the Roman Staircase, based perhaps on one in the Louvre in Paris. Little of the original decoration remains, but there is carved woodwork by Grinling Gibbons, and much wall-painting by Verrio and others, from the subjects of which some of the rooms take their names—the Hell Room and Heaven Room. The building was completed in *1587*.

**Buildwas Abbey** *Shrops.*                    552Ab
Originally a Savignac house, Buildwas Abbey was absorbed into the Cistercian order with other Savignac foundations in 1147. It was founded from Furness Abbey by Roger de Clinton, Bishop of Coventry and Lichfield. A small railway line now separates the immense ruins from the river, but the seclusion of the setting remains intact. The church, built during the second half of the 12th century, is the best preserved part, giving an idea of the simplicity of early Cistercian architecture. (See p. 105.)

**Bunbury** *Cheshire*                    552Ad
CHURCH OF ST BONIFACE A large, formerly collegiate church of the 14th and 15th centuries, with a west tower. It was damaged during the Second World War but successfully restored. Among the monuments is the 14th-century ala-baster tomb, a monument to Sir George Beeston, who fought against the Armada, and a memorial to Sir R. Egerton, Standard-bearer to Henry VIII. The screens and doors are of the 16th century.

**Bungay** *Suffolk*                    548Eg
A small town in the Waveney Valley. A few old houses survived a fire in 1688 but the town is mainly 18th century in character. It has interesting remains of the castle, built by the Bigods in the 12th century and already ruinous in the late 14th century. In the market-place, the Butter Cross of 1689 replaced an older one destroyed by the fire. In St Mary's Street, a 16th-century house has carved woodwork by the windows. There are many pleasant Georgian houses in the town.
CHURCH OF THE HOLY TRINITY With a Norman round tower, the church is Norman with later additions up to 1926, when the chancel was rebuilt. There is 16th- and 17th-century woodwork, and a monument of *c.* 1774 by Thomas Scheemakers.

**Buntingford** *Herts.*                    548Ad
Situated on the R. Rib, with parts of the Roman Ermine Street forming its High Street, is Bunting-ford: a small and architecturally charming little town. Its famous town clock is over 500 years old, but of greater interest are the 17th-century almshouses founded in 1684 by Bishop Seth Ward, the mathematician and astronomer friend of Sir Christopher Wren. The two-storied brick houses with mullioned windows, a pedimented centre and projecting wings forming a three-sided court-yard look like a mansion from the street.

**Bures** *Suffolk*                    548Ce
CHURCH OF ST MARY Of the 13th to 16th centuries, St Mary's has a Perpendicular font with carved angels and heraldry. There are 14th–16th-century monuments, including an early cross-legged knight of wood.

**Burford** *Oxon.*                    546Ed
CHURCH OF ST JOHN THE BAPTIST Recumbent figures and carved projections decorate many of the numerous monuments adorning this church; the complexity of the church is the result of later additions to the original Norman building. The three-storied south porch is in the Perpendicular style, and the central tower carries a spire.
TOLSEY MUSEUM The history of England, from the Norman Conquest to the Industrial Revolution, can be seen here, as reflected in the records of a small town and its neighbouring countryside. The collection is housed in the Tolsey, or toll house, a 16th-century Cotswold building; it contains maces, seals and documents of Burford Corpora-tion, and local industries, past and present, are represented—stone tiling, rope making, bell founding etc. A 16th-century treasure chest and doll's house with furniture can also be seen.

**Burford House Gardens** *Shrops.* 546Bf
The gardens beside the R. Teme are noted for their flowering shrubs and an 18th-century summer-house.

**Burgh Castle** *Suffolk* 548Fh
This is one of the intermediate forts of the Saxon Shore system. The east wall, most of the north and south walls and several of the external bastions, are still standing. Excavation has shown that it was originally planned to have internal turrets in its rounded angles, but these were demolished and the external bastions substituted, before the walls were finished.

The gap in the south wall was made in Norman times, when a motte and bailey castle was built here. The area of the motte at the south can still be seen and its surrounding ditch, now largely re-filled, passed through the wall at this point and is also visible as the external hollow at the south end.

There was also a mid-Saxon monastery within the walls, but no traces of this are now visible.

**Burghley House** *Hunts.* 547Hh
A superb example of Elizabethan domestic architecture, and the home of the Cecil and Exeter families for over 400 years. The house was begun in *c.* 1552 by William Cecil, who had just been knighted. He inherited the manor which had been bought by his father about 30 years previously. Cecil completed the Renaissance building in two stages, because after 1563 he was building another great house, at Theobalds in Hertfordshire. Flemish masons were probably employed on the mansion, which was completed *c.* 1587 after Cecil became Lord Burghley and Elizabeth I's Lord High Treasurer. Built around a central courtyard, Burghley is a square house with rounded corner towers topped by turrets. The main gate-house on one side comprises four more towers with turrets. Inside the state apartments are painted ceilings, silver fire-places, fine furniture, tapestries and over 700 works of art. The house is also noted for its rose garden.

**Buriton** *Hants.* 541Jd
Edward Gibbon, the 18th-century historian, was born here, and lived in the Georgian manor house. The village, round a duckpond, stands below one of the high-points of the South Downs.

**Burleigh Castle** *Kinross.* 562Bg
The ruins of a Balfour stronghold, described in Scott's *Old Mortality*. The lower part of the 15th-century keep remains, and traces of the curtain wall and moat are visible. Later remnants include the tower-house, built in 1582, and southern gate-house.

**Burley on the Hill** *Rutland* 553Gb
CHURCH OF THE HOLY CROSS Although originally Norman, the building was restored by John Loughborough Pearson, *c.* 1870. There is an impressive white marble mourning figure, kneel-ing, by Sir Francis Chantrey, *c.* 1820, on the monument to Lady Charlotte Finch.

**Burnham Norton** *Norfolk* 554Bd
CHURCH OF ST MARGARET The church, of the 13th to 15th centuries, has a round tower which may be of Saxon origin. The rood screen is dated 1458, and there is a fine pulpit with painted panels of the donor and the Latin Fathers of the Church (there is another at St James, Castle Acre). The font is Norman and there is a brass of 1523.

**Burnley** *Lancs.* 558Aa
EAST LANCASHIRE REGIMENTAL MUSEUM (TOWNLEY HALL) The museum has a room of exhibits in the Burnley Corporation museum, Townley Hall. On display are uniforms from 1832, medals, arms and badges, and the Napo-leonic Eagle—the standard of the French 22nd Regiment captured in 1812.
TOWNELEY HALL The fortified home of the Towneley family from the 13th century until 1902. The present house dates from the 14th century and was altered in the 16th, 17th and 19th centuries.

**Burnswark** *Dumf.* 562Ba
HILL-FORT AND ROMAN SIEGE WORKS The hill on which this fort stands is 920 ft high, on the east side of Annandale, with fine views up the dale and down to the Solway Firth and the Cumberland coast. There are multiple defences which indicate more than one period of construction, the fort being finally an area of some 17 acres.

Two opposite flanks of the hill each have the traces of a Roman siege camp and, in the corner of that on the south-east side, there are the remains of an earlier small Roman fort. This dates from *c.* AD 140 and the later siege camps, it is thought, represent the punitive expedition after the revolt of AD 155.

Burnswark has also been identified as the most probable site of the later battle of Brunanburgh (AD 937), where King Athelstan, Alfred's grand-son, defeated Olaf Curan and his Norsemen, who were in alliance with Constantine, King of the Scots.

**Burntisland** *Fife.* 562Bf
CHURCH A square 16th-century church; the gal-lery on all four sides has painted panels of ships, nautical instruments and other devices. In the centre of the church is an unusual early 17th-century pew with three sides.

**Burrough Hill** *Leics.* 552Fb
This four-sided Iron Age hill-fort has an internal area of some 12 acres and crowns the steep slopes of a hill-spur. There is still a substantial bank inside a ditch with small counterscarp bank. Near the south-east angle is the main entrance of the developed inturned type. The fort stands in a position of some importance, overlooking the valley which connects Leicester with Stamford.

**Burry Holms** *Glam.* 544Ec
Recent excavations on the island of Burry Holms have been filled in and none of the pre-Norman buildings can be seen, though the outline of some, including the 12th-century church and the later medieval hall and school-room, can be traced. The square chancel with its small stone altar are 14th-century additions; foundations of the original apse were discovered beneath. Above the low, shel-tered medieval site a deep ditch and bank mark the defences of an Iron Age promontory fort. The island is accessible for about three hours each side of low water.

**Burton** *Sussex* 542Ad
CHURCH Small church of Norman origin near Burton Park. Restored in 1636, it escaped 19th-century alteration. There is a Perpendicular screen with the Arms of Charles I, dated 1636, painted on a wall, and several 16th-century monuments with brasses.

**Burton Agnes** *Yorks.* 559Gc
CHURCH OF ST MARTIN A church dating from the Normans, in a setting near the Hall, with a 15th-century west tower. The chancel was rebuilt in the mid-19th century. There is a Norman font and a fine alabaster monument with effigies of the 15th century.

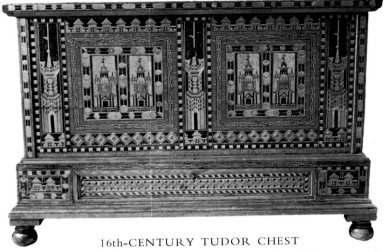

16th-CENTURY TUDOR CHEST

*During the 16th century furniture makers in England copied the practice of marble, metal and timber inlaying developed in Italy during the previous century. Even so, in most English 16th-century interiors, furniture was limited to a few items—chests of drawers and wardrobes were rarely found and the use of the large box was still general. The design of this inlaid wood chest follows the usual pattern of the period, the panels showing the romantic architectural features of Tudor buildings. (Burton Agnes Hall)*

**Burton Agnes Hall** *Yorks.* 559Gc
Mansion, built in 1598–1610 in conventional Elizabethan style except for the bow windows, which were unknown elsewhere at this period. The entrance porch is three-tiered and elaborately decorated. The interior has a carved staircase, Oriental china, and paintings by Renoir, Cézanne, Corot and Gaugin.

**Burton Constable** *Yorks.* 559Gb
An Elizabethan mansion, built in 1570, with castellated towers and oriel windows. Robert Adam, Wyatt, Carr and Lightoler carried out alterations to the interior. The grounds were laid out by Capability Brown.

**Burton upon Trent** *Staffs.* 552Dc
MUSEUM AND ART GALLERY The museum is mainly devoted to local history and traces the history of Burton and district from prehistoric times until the present. There is also a collection of British and foreign birds.

**Burwash** *Sussex* 542De
Here is a long street, made handsome with pollarded trees on one side. Rampyndene, dated 1699, is the outstanding house, with a huge roof and chimney-stacks, and rich carving.

**Burwell** *Cambs.* 548Bf
A large village a mile long on the ancient shore of the once-flooded wilderness of the Old Fen. It has several interesting houses, including the manor house, with notable stone thatched barns, and Maltings Corner, a longstone building with some interesting windows, once part of the ancient Priory of St John. Ramsey Manor is a good 18th-century house, while the Hall, once much larger, contains a recently discovered Perpendicular window. Parsonage Farm, partly pre-Reformation, and Tunbridge, from the 18th century, are both good buildings. The site of the castle, at the siege of which Geoffrey de Manderville, 'the Devil in human form', was slain, is marked by a moat 9 ft deep. There are two tower-mills and a good example of a Fen-draining windmill.
CHURCH OF ST MARY A glorious Perpendicular church, with a west tower of Norman origin. There is a wheel-window above the chancel arch, and much panelling.

**Bury** *Lancs.* 542Ad
ART GALLERY AND MUSEUM The Wrigley Collection contains paintings by British 19th-century artists including Turner, Constable, Landseer, Webster, de Wint, John Crome and Birket-Foster. The gallery also has paintings and sculpture by Lowry, Steer and Epstein. The small museum is devoted mainly to local history, and the displays include Bronze Age items from a recent local excavation.
LANCASHIRE FUSILIERS MUSEUM The collection includes Napoleonic relics from when the Regiment guarded him as a prisoner on St Helena, mementoes of Wolfe of Quebec, and a large collection of medals and regimental relics of the main campaigns of the First and Second World Wars.

**Bury St Edmunds** *Suffolk* 548Cf
Burial place of a martyred king, birthplace of the Magna Carta; both are commemorated in the town's motto granted by King James I, *Sacrarium Regis, Cunabula Legis* (Shrine of a King, Cradle of the Law). Originally a Saxon homestead, known as Beodricksworth, the town was chosen in 636 as a suitable place for a monastery. In 870, King Edmund was brutally killed by the Danes during their raids on eastern England. His mutilated body was buried at Hoxne (4 miles south-east of Diss) where it lay for 33 years. Miracles were attributed to the king; he was canonised, and his body removed to Beodricksworth Monastery. The name of the town was changed to St Edmunds Bury. The Danish-born king, Knut (Canute), who conquered all England in 1016, granted the monastery abbey status in 1032. Edward the Confessor held Edmund's shrine in such reverence that he created the Franchise of the Liberty of St Edmundsbury, approximately modern West Suffolk. At the time of the Norman Conquest the abbot, Baldwin, was a Frenchman, and was able to save Bury St Edmunds from Norman destruction. He planned the town on Roman lines, and built five gates, each with its own chapel and a hostel for pilgrims visiting the shrine. A period of culture followed the appointment of Abbot Anselm in 1121 and the illuminated manuscripts produced by his monks are now in the British Museum, the Metropolitan Museum, New York, the Vatican, at

Oxford and at Cambridge where Corpus Christi College has the Bury Bible. One manuscript, written *c.* 1150–60, is in the form of a diary and gives a picture of daily life in a medieval monastery.

In 1214, ostensibly meeting to honour St Edmund's Day, King John's barons held a secret conference, and swore on the high altar of the abbey church to force the king to sign the Magna Carta—thus the town's claim to be 'Cradle of the Law'.

In 1327, a quarrel between the abbot and the townsfolk reached a violent climax; the monks made an armed attack on the townspeople at their parish church and, in retaliation, the abbey was almost destroyed. The abbey was gutted by fire in 1465, but after rebuilding (completed in 1538), it became one of the architectural glories of England.

The town plan is based on the medieval formula of a square for God and a square for man. The former—just outside the abbey—is now known as Angel Hill; the latter is the market-place, still the commercial heart of the town. Abbot Baldwin's early gates disappeared in the 18th century, but their names are preserved in Northgate, Risbygate, Eastgate, Westgate and Southgate Streets. Athenaeum Lane (formerly Punch Lane), Skinner Lane and Pump Lane date from medieval times. The 12th-century Norman tower was built as a gate to the abbey. The Athenaeum, late 18th-century assembly rooms with 1804 façade and extensions, has a ballroom said to have been decorated by the Adam brothers.

ABBEY The entire precinct of Bury Abbey survives intact, although the buildings themselves are much mutilated. There were formerly three parish churches on the perimeter of the precinct but only two of these medieval buildings have survived. One of them, St James's, has been the cathedral since 1914, the other, St Mary's, has a particularly impressive interior. Of the abbey buildings, the most complete remains are the two gate-houses, one Norman and the other built during the 14th century. All that survives of the immense abbey church is the west front, entirely robbed of its facing stone, a few columns at the east end which have been similarly robbed, and the crypt of the Norman apse which has now been laid open.

ANGEL CORNER A fine Queen Anne house containing the Gershom-Parkington Collection of clocks by such makers as Quare, Tompion, Vulliamy and others. Watches and other time-recording devices are displayed—for example, a ring-dial (a form of sun-dial) in which the sun's rays are cast, through a conical hole, on to the inner side of a brass ring marked off with hour lines. Clock and watch-making flourished in the town in the 18th and 19th centuries.

CHURCH OF ST MARY A great 15th-century church, with a tower at the west end on the north side. There is a very fine nave roof with carved angels, a Perpendicular font, a quantity of 19th-century stained glass, and monuments from the 15th century.

CUPOLA HOUSE A 17th-century house, with cupola, belvedere and a projecting second-floor balcony over the street.

GUILDHALL Built in the 15th century; the doorway has dog-tooth ornament. The two flanking wings were built in 1807.

HENGRAVE HALL Originally built in 1525–38 by Sir Thomas Kyston, of stone and brick, the Hall is now a convent. A complete wing was demolished in 1757, and the moat filled in. The twin turrets to the gate-house are similar to others at Westminster Abbey and King's College, Cambridge. The

oratory has a 16th-century window with 21 lights of biblical scenes. There is a hammerbeam ceiling in the hall and a minstrels' gallery in the restored banqueting hall. (By appointment.)

MOYSES HALL MUSEUM A 13th-century Monk's Chronicle, written in the abbey at Bury St Edmunds, is preserved in the museum, together with items dating from prehistoric, Roman, Saxon and medieval times. Of these, the most interesting is a late Bronze Age founder's hoard, which was found at Isleham, Cambridgeshire, in 1959. Weighing 185 lb, the hoard comprises palstaves, axes, hammers, spearheads, knives, swords, and what appear to be vehicle fittings. It is the largest fully recorded and complete founder's hoard in Britain, and of major archaeological importance because of the presence of decorated mounts (probably used on leather belts or harness), many of which have no parallel in the British Bronze Age, but bear similarity to decorated mounts found in Hungary, the upper Rhine and western France. Moyses Hall is a Norman building, dating from the 12th century, and is possibly the oldest domestic building in East Anglia.

SUFFOLK REGIMENT MUSEUM The museum exhibits items of historical interest connected with the Regiment.

UNITARIAN CHAPEL One of the finest Nonconformist chapels in Britain, built in 1711. It has a double-decker pulpit.

BURY ST EDMUNDS
NORMAN TOWER

*The Norman gateway tower is now the belfry of the nearby cathedral church of St James, the only cathedral in Suffolk. It was formerly the ceremonial gateway for the abbey, once one of the richest monasteries in England, whose abbots exercised considerable power over, and sometimes clashed with, the townspeople. One such clash is commemorated in the abbey gateway, not far from the Norman tower; this was built by the townspeople in 1347, as a punishment for having destroyed the original gateway during a riot in 1327.*

**Buscot** *Berks.*     *546Dc*
BUSCOT PARK An estate of 3853 acres running down to the Thames and including the Cotswold stone village of Buscot. The mansion was built in 1780 in Adam style, but later altered; amongst the contents are Burne-Jones's *Briar-Rose* paintings and pictures by Rembrandt, Murillo and Reynolds. The park, with a lake and gardens, was laid out by Harold Peto.

**Butley Priory** *Suffolk*     *548Ee*
GATE-HOUSE The second greatest medieval gate-house in Suffolk, the first in Europe with a heraldic display in stone. The 14th-century gate-house was once part of the Augustinian priory founded by Ranulf de Glanville in 1171, who travelled with Richard the Lionheart on the Third Crusade. Above this huge gateway are cut in stone the Arms of England and France, the three crowns of East Anglia, the Passion, and the Holy Roman Empire, with Leon and Castile. Below them is the blazonry of many great East Anglian families. The central block of ashlar and blue-grey flints is flanked by huge buttresses. Lancet windows, pierced and foliated, give grace and light. The gate-house is surrounded by one of the oldest forests in England: the pre-Druidic Staverton

Forest. Behind it, in the farmyard, somewhere beneath the ruins of the priory, is said to lie the silver coffin of Michael de la Pole, Earl of Suffolk, killed at Agincourt.

**Butser Hill** *Hants.*     *541Hd*
Butser has an irregularly rounded top joined on the south-west by a narrow ridge to a rather lower hill. The multiple defences, consisting of three widely separated bank-and-ditch structures, cross this ridge at various points to protect the wide top of Butser Hill. There are also minor defence-works at different places on the hill-top itself. To the south-east of the hill-top, the slopes reveal the lynchets of an area of 'Celtic' fields. They were probably cultivated in both Iron Age and Roman times.

**Buxton** *Derbys.*     *552Ce*
An important Roman station built around the natural hot spring known as St Ann's Well on the route from Manchester to Lincoln. The Old Hall by the well was built *c.* 1600 by the Earl of Shrewsbury and was enlarged by the 3rd Duke of Devonshire in 1670. The 5th Duke of Devonshire built the elegant crescent opposite the well in 1780–4, and the assembly room (now the clinic). Many other buildings followed as the repute of the medicinal waters converted the original village to

---

## THE SALOON AT BUSCOT PARK

*Standing in grounds running down to the Thames, Buscot Park was built in Adam style in 1775–80 by Edward Lovenden Townsend. It was carefully restored to its original form by Lord Faringdon in the 1930's. In the house is the 'Briar-Rose' series of art-nouveau paintings by Sir Edward Burne-Jones*

*(1833–98). The magnificent saloon contains the group depicting the story of Sleeping Beauty. Burne-Jones originally intended taking holy orders, but under the influence of Dante Gabriel Rossetti he became a member of the Pre-Raphaelite brotherhood of painters and devoted himself to art.*

a thriving spa in the 19th century. On the southern outskirts of the town is Solomon's Temple, a folly tower, erected in 1896 to honour Solomon Mycock, a farmer who had permitted the excavation of a prehistoric barrow on his land in 1894. MUSEUM Items illustrating local history and geology are on view. There are also collections of ornaments of Ashford Marble (a local stone) and Blue John (a blue mineral found locally), paintings, prints, pottery and glass.

**Byland Abbey** *Yorks.*                      *558Dd*
The remains of this large and prosperous monas-

tery include the west front of the church—the longest Cistercian church in England—and the lay-out of the entire monastic site. Byland Abbey was the final home of a community of monks who had lived temporarily at various other places since its foundation in 1134. The architecture suggests that lay-brothers of the monastery set to work preparing the site before the arrival of the monks in 1177. The west wall has a large rose window. There is medieval tiling in green and yellow geometrical patterns. In a museum near the ruins are preserved the nave capital, decorated with foliage carving.

# C

**Caburn, The** *Sussex*                      *542Cd*
First occupied in Iron Age times without defences; these were later added and consisted of the low inner bank with its external ditch. The much larger outer bank, together with its ditch, was erected at the time of the Roman conquest. This bank was revetted with timber both inside and out, and crossbeams through the bank connected the two. The entrance was also remodelled at this time.

**Cadbury Castle** *Som.*                      *540De*
The fort crowns an isolated hill and is defended by no less than four ramparts, each with its external ditch. The banks were revetted with drystone walling and the internal area is some 18 acres. This is the reputed site of Camelot, the traditional seat of King Arthur's Court. Attempts have been and are being made by excavation to learn its secrets, attempts tinged for many with the romantic hope that the Camelot tradition may be confirmed and that a historical man, perhaps a war chief of the sub-Roman Britons, may have been the original of the knightly king of the story-cycle.

Preliminary excavation has already revealed traces of Neolithic occupation of the hill-top. It has confirmed the construction of the visible defences in the Iron Age. It has found indications of a temple built late in the Roman period and has shown that an additional wall in the defences belongs to the early part of the Dark Ages—the 'Arthurian' period. There is also the promise of what seems to be an early cruciform Christian church and, finally, a late Saxon wall of Ethelred the Unready's day, built over the Dark Age wall. Traces of many other internal buildings also remain to be examined.

**Cademuir Hill** *Peebl.*                      *562Bd*
HILL-FORTS A long spur runs south-west from the central massif of Cademuir, and the larger of these two forts is set upon its south-west end. It has a single stone wall enclosing an 8 acre area and there are traces of the foundations of many Iron Age houses. It is thought to have been deserted soon after the Roman occupation of the Lowlands. The smaller fort lies half a mile to the north-east on the same spur of hill. Its central area is enclosed in a substantial drystone wall and outside this on the east side is an area studded with upright boulders set into the ground, designed to prevent the rush of a body of men.

**Cadney** *Lincs.*                      *553Gf*
CHURCH OF ALL SAINTS There is Early English work here; the body of the church is early 13th

century, and the south arcade is late Norman. There is a Perpendicular east window and screen. The font is Norman, and there is a 12th-century stone coffin-lid.

**Cadzow Castle** *Lanarks.*                      *561Je*
The ruins of a castle visited by Mary, Queen of Scots in 1568. A herd of White Cattle roam the park beside the R. Avon.

**Caerlaverock Castle** *Dumf.*                      *562Aa*
Robert Paterson, 'Old Mortality' of Sir Walter Scott's novel of that name, was buried in the churchyard within the castle, which is triangular in plan and surrounded by a moat. Over the gateway between two round towers is carved the crest of the Maxwells, Earls of Nithsdale, who owned the castle for over 400 years. It was built during the reigns of the Scottish Kings Alexander II and III, destroyed during Border Wars in 1312 and 1356, and rebuilt; it was finally left to ruin after destruction by the Covenanters, Presbyterian opponents of Charles I, in 1640.

**Caerleon** *Mon.*                      *545Jc*
A Norman church largely rebuilt at the end of the 15th century, and again during the 19th century. The west tower is at the end of the south aisle. The organ case was designed by A. E. Caroë. There is a series of 19th-century glass commemorative windows.

The church stands at the centre of Isca, the 50 acre permanent fortress of the 2nd Augustan Legion. Founded by the Romans *c.* AD 75 on the banks of the tidal R. Usk, Isca was a busy seaport; its first clay and timber defences and buildings were rebuilt in stone *c.* AD 100. Parts of this fortress wall and some internal buildings may still be seen. More spectacular, however, is the amphitheatre outside the south-west wall, now fully excavated and preserved. This was the legion's drill-square. Also outside lay the *vicus*, the civilian suburb which grew up as military needs permitted. The fortress was occupied until the end of the 3rd century, when it was partly replaced by the fort at Cardiff, though it was not finally deserted until the latter part of the 4th century.

**Caernarvon** *Caern.*                      *550Ee*
ROMAN FORT Here, on the hill-slopes outside Edward I's castle and the modern town, stand the remains of the Roman Segontium. It had a long history. Placed to overlook the outer end of the Menai Strait and its coastlands, it was first founded in the early days of the Roman occupation. A period of unrest in the second half of the 2nd

CAERNARVON CASTLE

*The first castle at Caernarvon was built during the Norman settlement of Wales, but it was reconquered by the Welsh in 1115 and all traces of any buildings dating from that period have now vanished. The castle was entirely replaced by another begun in 1283–4, during Edward I's conquest of Wales, and completed about 1330. According to ancient Welsh tradition Caernarvon was the birthplace of the Emperor Constantine, and in 1283 it is reported that 'Magnus Maximus', allegedly the father of Constantine, was dug up at Caernarvon and reburied in the church there. In 1284 the future Edward II was created Prince of Wales there and in 1911 the future Edward VIII was also invested with the Principality.*

century AD led to its being rebuilt in stone. Further reconstruction took place at the beginning of the 3rd century and, after the Irish raids of AD 367, yet another reconstruction took place. Its garrison seems finally to have been withdrawn by Maximus in AD 383 to aid in his continental adventure.

SEGONTIUM MUSEUM The museum stands next to the remains of Segontium Roman fort, which was excavated by Sir Mortimer Wheeler in 1921–3, and houses the objects found in the fort.

**Caernarvon Castle** *Caern.*      *550Ee*
Caernarvon Castle was begun in 1283–4 and attained its present form in *c.* 1330. The Eagle Tower was one of the largest single towers built in the Middle Ages. Unlike other Welsh castles of this period, its walls are built of different coloured masonry and the angle-towers are polygonal. These walls in fact bear a striking resemblance to the walls of Constantinople, and in adopting this design Edward I may have been seeking to link the castle with the traditional belief that the Emperor Constantine was born at Caernarvon. Surveys in the 16th century suggest that the castle was neglected and in a ruined state at that period. In the 17th century Caernarvon narrowly escaped demolition after the Civil War, and it was only in the 19th century that the castle was repaired.

In 1284 Edward II was born here and presented to the Welsh people by his father, Edward I, as Prince of Wales—'one who could speak neither English nor Welsh'. The castle was begun in 1283 as part of Edward I's plan for the control of Wales. Here HRH Prince Charles, like previous Princes of Wales, will be invested in 1969.

**Caerphilly Castle** *Glam.*      *545Jb*
Due to the immense reconstructions carried out by the former owner, the 4th Marquess of Bute, and since 1949 by the Ministry of Public Building and Works, Caerphilly Castle, reflected in its great lakes, is a splendid example of early military architecture. Remarkably advanced in plan, it was commenced in 1271. It bristles with ingenious details of internal defence; but its masterpiece is the brilliantly conceived water defence, designed to keep out of range the deadly military catapults, which, at short distance, could batter down the most robust walls.

**Caerwent** *Mon.*      *546Ac*
The Roman city of Venta Silurum, some 9 miles east of Caerleon, was built to house and civilise the conquered native Silures. Originally defended by double earthen banks and ditches, a 30 ft high stone wall was added late in the Roman period as a defence against the raids of Irish pirates. Like Caerleon most of the site of Caerwent is free from modern buildings. Venta was the only walled civilian town in Wales.

**Cairn Holy** *Kirkcud.*      *556Dg*
These are two chambered cairns of the Clyde-Carlingford sub-type, standing about 150 yds apart near the east side of Wigtown Bay. The larger of the two is about 170 ft long and some 50 ft wide. Its great hollow forecourt is outlined by tall standing stone slabs and inside the entrance there is a double chamber, now somewhat ruined. Most of the covering mound has now disappeared.

The northern cairn is smaller, being only some 70 ft long by 40 ft wide. This also has a double burial chamber.

**Cairnpapple** *W. Lothian*      *562Ae*
Cairnpapple Hill is crowned by a complex of henge, cairns and burials. The first structure was a group of three enormous boulders and an arc of

large stones in conjunction with a late Neolithic cemetery. This was superseded by a henge monument with two opposed entrances. Inside the ditch of this henge, stones were set in a great oval. Then came a cairn, 50 ft in diameter, on the site of the henge. This had a stone kerb. Later, the cairn was enlarged; it now had a diameter of 100 ft and received cremations in urns of Middle Bronze Age type. Finally, later burials were intruded, probably in the Iron Age.

**Caisteal Grugaig** *Ross*  565Gf
The remains of this broch are in good condition, and still stand some 13 ft high. A good entrance, wall-chambers, a stair-lobby with part of the staircase and part of a gallery are all evident.

**Caister Castle** *Norfolk*  554Eb
An impressive 15th-century ruin. Built for Sir John Fastolfe in 1432–5, the moated remains include the 98 ft high round tower with stair turret, a gate-house and stretches of wall. It was the home of the Paston family from 1459 to 1599 (except for five years) and some of the 'Paston Letters', which give a vivid account of 15th-century domestic life, were written here. It is now a motor museum.

**Caister-on-Sea** *Norfolk*  554Eb
Here, on the higher land overlooking the former open estuary and harbour, stood a walled town. Much of it has been excavated, but the part preserved for inspection contains part of the south gate with an adjacent length of wall-base, and part of a great building just inside the gate, interpreted as a hostelry, probably for seamen and travellers from the ships. South from this gate, a road led down to the quay and harbour, some 400 yds away. The latter is now the drained marsh-pasture on the south side of West Road, opposite Grange Farm, and the site of the quay is marked here by the new roadway running along the side of this pasture to the new estate. The first occupation began early in the 2nd century and the town survived until the end of the Roman occupation of Britain. Later, a Saxon settlement grew up in its ruins but, at the time of the Danish settlement in AD 880, this was deserted and a new village was formed to become the centre of modern Caister.

**Caistor** *Lincs.*  553Hf
CHURCH OF SS PETER AND PAUL Among the interesting monuments in this church is one in the vestry to Sir Edward Maddison, who died in 1553 at the age of 100. The west tower is Saxon and the nave arcades are 13th century. There are some 13th- and 14th-century stone effigies and a 15th-century brass on the chancel floor. The 19th-century stained glass includes some by C. E. Kempe.

**Caistor St Edmund** *Norfolk*  554Db
Venta Icenorum, the cantonal town of the Iceni, stood on a valley site not far from the confluence of the Yare and Wensum. At first a minor open town, it was walled soon after AD 200, a central area only of some 35 acres being enclosed. On the north side, the outer face of the wall is visible in places, though rather overgrown, but in general the wall today stands no higher than the earthen ramp-remains inside it. The interior, much of which has been excavated, is now under cultivation and, when a suitable dry summer occurs, the whole street plan is visible in the crop-cover from the high point on the main road, nearly a mile away across the valley.

**Cakemuir** *M'loth.*  562Ce
Of 15th-century origin, the house was consider-

ably altered in the 17th century. Of note is a spiral staircase between stone walls 6 ft thick. Two sentry-boxes stand on the parapet around the original tower.

**Calder Abbey** *Cumb.*  557Ge
The remains of a 12-century Cistercian abbey beside a river. The ruins include those of the church and the 13th-century chapter house.

**Callaly Castle** *Northld.*  562Fc
A 17th-century mansion, with Georgian and Victorian additions. Some parts of a 13th-century castle remain.

**Callanish** *Lewis, Ross*  568Bc
STONE CIRCLE AND CAIRN The standing stones form the most imposing feature of the group. A pillar over 15 ft high stands centrally in a circle 37 ft in diameter, formed by 13 tall slabs. North from this circle runs a double avenue of stones for a distance of 270 ft. Ten stones on one side and nine on the other still survive, though originally there may have been 20 on each side. Other shorter stone-lines radiate from the circle, 50 ft on the east and 40 ft on the west.

The remnants of the chambered cairn lie in the eastern part of the circle. There is also another low mound, perhaps another cairn, lying immediately to the north-east of the first.

**Camber Castle** *Sussex*  542Ed
The ruins of one of Henry VIII's coastal defence castles, built in 1539 as a protection against French raids. Originally it was near the sea, but because of silting up of the coast is now over a mile inland. Its fortifications were dismantled in 1647.

**Camberley** *Surrey*  541Jf
ROYAL ARMY ORDNANCE CORPS MUSEUM Cap badges and insignia are among RAOC items displayed. The museum was built in 1916 by Canadian engineers on the log cabin principle and was originally used as a railway station for trains conveying units from the Blackdown area to and from Bisley for training.

**Camborne** *Cornwall*  538Bb
PUBLIC LIBRARY AND MUSEUM The building was given to the town in 1894 by John Passmore Edwards, a philanthropist who founded 70 public institutions. The museum, in one room of the library, houses mainly archaeological, historical, mineral and mining items of local interest. In the archaeological section there are Neolithic and flint implements found on ancient camp sites in the area.

**Cambridge** *Cambs.*  548Af
Much of the charm of Cambridge is in the small streets and passages such as St Edward's Passage off King's Parade. In Botolph Lane off Trumpington Street there is a group of attractive small houses. Little St Mary's Lane, also off Trumpington Street, is a fascinating byway which has been skilfully restored. It overlooks an old churchyard. The Little Rose Inn, in Trumpington Street, *c.* 1600, was probably the last Cambridge inn to have extensive stables. In Chesterton Road No. 2 Wentworth House, an elegant dwelling, dates from *c.* 1720; Nos. 4–10 are attractive one-storey cottages.
ARTS COUNCIL GALLERY Touring exhibitions of British and foreign art are shown here.
BARNWELL ABBEY HOUSE Built 1678, part timber-framed and part brick, with splendid chimney-stacks; it was noted for its alleged population of ghosts, for example the Ghost of Squire Butler who died in 1765; the White Lady; the Ghostly Squirrel; an Astral Hare; a Disembodied Head; a

CLARE COLLEGE GATES AND BRIDGE

*Thomas Grumbold was Christopher Wren's mason for Trinity College Library. When he sketched out his first design for a Classical bridge across the Cam in 1638 he was paid three shillings for his work. Clare College at the time was about to undergo rebuilding and Grumbold's bridge was probably intended to make the transportation of building materials easier. The wrought-iron gateway was made by a local smith named Warren in 1713–15, following a sudden taste for ornamental ironwork stimulated by Mary II and the superb work of the French smith Jean Tijou.*

*Warren also made two other gates for Clare College, replacing ones of timber. The bridge and gates give Clare College access to the Backs, one of Cambridge's chief pleasures. These sweeping lawns beside the Cam, set with willow trees, and affording fine views of the riverside colleges, stretch from St John's College, past Trinity, Trinity Hall and Clare Colleges to King's College and Queens' College. They were largely the work of Richard Bentley, Master of Trinity College from 1699 to 1734, who made them from what was then rough marshland.*

Clanking Chain; and a poltergeist. In recent years the ghosts were solemnly exorcised by a parson with bell, book and candle. This picturesque old house has some fine panelled rooms. Near the corner of Roche Road and Priory Road there are the small but notable 13th-century remains of the Cellarers Chequer House of the original Barnwell Priory, founded 1092 and now vanished, apart from its Chapel of St Andrew the Less.

CHURCH OF THE HOLY SEPULCHRE One of England's few surviving Norman round churches, with a vaulted ambulatory. The building was restored during the 1840's. There is some 19th-century glass.

EAGLE INN Off Bene't Street, the last remaining coaching inn in the city, with a cobbled courtyard and first-floor gallery.

FITZWILLIAM MUSEUM A great Corinthian portico in Trumpington Street is a feature of the entrance to the world-famous museum founded by the 7th Viscount Fitzwilliam of Merrion, who in 1816 bequeathed to the university the sum of £100,000 plus his library and collection of 144 paintings and 134 medieval illuminated manuscripts and other *objets d'art*. The building was begun in 1837, completed in 1875; its interior has a wealth of marblework, statuary, mosaics, friezes, and rococo enrichments in the mid-Victorian taste. Its display rooms include Egyptian and

Western Asiatic Department; Greek and Roman Department; coin room; print room; pottery and porcelain; 600 medieval manuscripts; textiles, many foreign, especially Italian and Turkish; cut velvets; arms and armour; and a library of 25,000 volumes. (See also pp. 120–1.)

HOBSON'S CONDUIT Built between 1610 and 1614 to carry water to Cambridge from Nine Wells near Trumpington, it commemorates Thomas Hobson who died in 1631. He was the famous Cambridge carrier who coined the phrase 'Hobson's Choice', since anyone who wished to hire a horse from his livery stable had to take the first one on the list—and no other. The monument, transferred from Market Hill to the corner of Lensfield Road in 1855, is octagonal with strapwork ornamentation on top and a cupola.

JESUS COLLEGE This college was founded in 1497 by Bishop Alcock of Ely in the buildings of the former Benedictine nunnery of St Radegonds. Alcock suppressed the nunnery and took over the buildings as a working unit—which shows how similar the respective corporate existences of college and convent were. The chapel remained the chapel, but was reduced in size, the prioress's lodging became the Master's lodging, the refectory became the dining-hall, although Alcock enlarged and improved the building. He also added an extra storey to the living quarters. In addition, he made improvements in the outer court, particularly to the attractive main gate of the college.

KING'S COLLEGE CHAPEL The chapel, towering above the surrounding town and university, was the only completed medieval part of this college founded in 1440. The first stone was laid in 1446 and the chapel, in Perpendicular style, was completed in 1515. It is based on Sainte Chapelle, the 13th-century private royal chapel in Paris. Subsequent buildings of the college belong mainly to the 19th century, apart from the Gibbs Building, a fine addition in Classical style, begun in 1723. The whole assembly of buildings stands on a magnificent site on the banks of the R. Cam.

KING'S PARADE Houses and shops of differing styles, heights and periods without a dull frontage among them; they face King's College Chapel, the delicate stone tracery of the college screen, and the Classical lines of the Senate House. No. 17 has a timber-framed and overhanging upper storey. No. 14 is an 18th-century brick house.

LITTLE TRINITY GUEST HOUSE The most handsome private house in Cambridge. Five-bay, c. 1800, with dark brick and a doorcase including Ionic pilasters, it stands back from Jesus Lane behind iron gates and gate piers. No. 32 Jesus Lane is another excellent 18th-century brick house. The Pitt Club, also in Jesus Lane, is an assembly room building with an elegant Ionic portico and a medallion of Pitt above the doorway.

MARKET HILL Dominated by the guildhall, built 1938–9, a plain brick block; behind it the public library contains a richly ornamented fire-place with the initials of the Veysey family (c. 1600), which was removed from No. 1 Market Hill. The gilt Great Mace (1710) and four other gilt maces of 1723 on display here are all large, and of fine workmanship. By comparison, the university maces are austere.

NORTHAMPTON STREET AND MAGDALENE STREET Here are the best medieval houses and cottages in the city—a long range of two- and three-storied plastered and timbered houses, many with oversailing upper floors. This group, with the old houses opposite Magdalene College, are reminders of what medieval Cambridge looked like.

PEMBROKE COLLEGE CHAPEL The first of Cambridge's ecclesiastical buildings in a purely Classical style. Bishop Wren of Ely gave £5000 to Pembroke College in 1663 for a new chapel and this was completed by 1665 to designs by his nephew, Sir Christopher Wren, who probably based his design on drawings of a Roman temple published in a book by the Italian architect Sebastiano Serlio. Serlio's books ran to many editions and were an important source for architectural forms during the early English Renaissance. The street front of the chapel is pedimented, and has four Corinthian pilasters dividing the three bays; above is a small hexagonal wooden cupola. In 1880 George Gilbert Scott enlarged the chapel when he moved the east wall eastwards and rebuilt it.

ST JOHN'S COLLEGE Founded in 1511 by Lady Margaret Beaufort—great-granddaughter of John of Gaunt and grandmother of Henry VIII—St John's has three magnificent red-brick courts with fine gate-tower, a 17th-century library, and a chapel designed by Sir Gilbert Scott. The picturesque 'Bridge of Sighs' crosses the R. Cam.

SCHOOL OF PYTHAGORAS Never a school, and probably never a part of the university; it is, however, the oldest secular building in the city, built of clunch-rubble before AD 1100. It has an undercroft and a hall on the upper floor, a 13th-century solar and 14th-century buttresses. Merton

TRINITY COLLEGE LIBRARY

*Sir Christopher Wren designed Trinity College Library in 1676; it marks a transitional point in his work. Wren first proposed a domed free-standing building, but in the end had to design a building to close off the two arms of Neville's Court, which resulted in this elegant Classical building, some 150 ft long, facing the court on one side and the R. Cam on the other. The library, raised to first-floor level, is a vast hall; bookshelves line the walls beneath the windows and also stand at right angles to form a series of small bays. There is much work by the 17th-century master of woodcarving, Grinling Gibbons. In addition there are busts by Louis Roubiliac, Michael Rysbrack, Peter Scheemakers and John Bacon the Elder.*

Hall, a 17th-century gabled house now belonging to St John's College, is next to the school.

SCOTT POLAR RESEARCH INSTITUTE Established in 1920 as a memorial to Capt. R. F. Scott, RN, and the four companions who died with him on the return journey from the South Pole in 1912, the Institute is part of the Department of Geography of the University of Cambridge, and exists to promote and conduct research in the Arctic and Antarctic. Its museum features relics of Arctic and Antarctic expeditions, among them some 400 water-colours and pencil sketches made by Edward Wilson during Scott's Arctic expeditions on the *Discovery* (1901–4) and *Terra Nova* (1910–13), and others by E. L. Moss and J. E. Davis during 19th-century expeditions. There are also Eskimo soapstone carvings and stone-cuts and other exhibits of current scientific activities in both regions.

SENATE HOUSE James Gibbs, the Scottish architect of St Martin-in-the-Fields in London, designed the Senate House in 1722. It is the only part built of a complex of university administrative buildings designed by him. The building is two storeys high, and nine window bays long. The upper windows are round-headed, but those of the lower level have alternating straight and curved pediments. Between the bays are giant Corinthian columns or pilasters, with the three central bays beneath a pediment. Christopher Cass, a master-mason who died in 1734, was employed to carve much of the decoration. A first-class craftsman, he had also been associated with Gibbs at St Martin-in-the-Fields and with other architects at St Paul's Cathedral.

TRINITY COLLEGE The early college comprised two main elements: King's Hall, founded by Edward II in 1317 and enlarged by his son in 1336, and Michaelhouse, founded in 1323 by Hervey de Stanton, Chancellor of the Exchequer. They occupied adjacent sites, and when Michaelhouse, a religious foundation, was disbanded by Henry VIII at the Dissolution it was possible to consolidate the two buildings to form a single unit in 1546. The founder of Trinity College is therefore Henry VIII, and his Arms decorate the main entrance. Remnants of the college's early buildings are visible: the main entrance was built as part of King's Hall by Henry VIII in 1519–45. Even older is King Edward's Tower, built in 1426–33. It is the earliest of the great Cambridge gate-houses, and is not on its original site, but was taken down in 1601 and rebuilt north of its original position. Thomas Neville, Master of the college in 1593–7 and later Archbishop of Canterbury, succeeded in converting the heterogeneous collection of buildings of different dates into a single great quadrangle by further additions.

TRINITY COLLEGE LIBRARY The library was begun in 1676 to designs by Sir Christopher Wren. It made a fourth side to Neville's Court, previously an open yard facing the R. Cam. A relatively plain Classical building, the library is raised to first-floor level above a ground floor open to the court through a round-arched arcade. On the parapet stand four figures representing Divinity, Mathematics, Law and Physics, for which the 17th-century sculptor Caius Gabriel Cibber was paid £80 in 1681. The river front is plainer than the court side, as there is no open arcade; instead there are windows and three great doorways, one in the centre and one at each end. The door openings are very low because the height of the first floor of the library was dictated by the level of the existing buildings in Neville's Court. (See p. 115.)

UNIVERSITY BOTANIC GARDEN Founded in 1761, the garden covers 40 acres, and has an entrance in Bateman Street and another in Downing Street, and a frontage along Trumpington Road.

UNIVERSITY LIBRARY The origins of the library are probably 13th century: the earliest catalogue, begun c. 1424, lists 122 books. Until 1934, when the new building designed by Sir Giles Scott was opened, the University Library was housed in buildings known as Old Schools, and the collec-

tion had reached a total of 1,250,000 volumes (including 10,000 manuscripts and several hundred thousand maps).

Among the present collections are: Bishop Moore's Library (30,000 volumes) presented to George I in 1715; the Bradshaw Collection of Irish books (1870–86); the Wade Collection of Chinese books (Sir Thomas Wade, 1886); the Acton Historical Library (60,000 volumes) presented by Viscount Morley, 1902; and a collection of incunabula (books printed before 1501). Its treasures include the Codex Bezae manuscript of the Gospels, the only perfect copy of Caxton's *Golden Legend*, and the Gutenberg Bible (*c.* 1450).

The library is entitled (under the Copyright Act) to claim a copy of every work published in the British Isles: it does not necessarily exercise this right, but its resources are continually being enlarged by gifts and purchases of foreign volumes.

The red-brick library is by far the biggest and most overbearing building in Cambridge: the main reading room is 200 ft long on its west side; the front, or east side, is over 400 ft long. At the main entrance are great metal honeycomb-pattern doors beneath a tower that dominates the surrounding landscape.

Admission to the library is open to members of the university, and to the public on completion of formalities that require counter-signature by two members of the Senate.

UNIVERSITY MUSEUM OF CLASSICAL ARCHAEOLOGY A large representative collection of casts of Greek and Roman sculpture is on view.

UNIVERSITY OF CAMBRIDGE COMMITTEE FOR AERIAL PHOTOGRAPHY The Committee for Aerial Photography is a research unit within the university. Its collection of aerial photographs of the United Kingdom can be seen by appointment.

WESTMINSTER COLLEGE The best-looking college building not belonging to the university; built of red brick in the Tudor style in 1899, it has short wings, a good staircase, a turret with a lantern and a dining-hall with a wagon-roof.

WHIPPLE MUSEUM OF THE HISTORY OF SCIENCE Optical and navigational instruments mainly from the 16th–18th centuries are exhibited in the Old Perse Room which dates from 1618.

Good houses on the outskirts of Cambridge include Chesterton Hall close to the highway, a smallish Jacobean mansion, with three big gabled dormers; Fen Ditton Hall behind the famous Ditton Meadow, a charming red-brick house *c.* 1720, with three different types of Dutch gable; Newnham Grange, late 18th century; and the Malting House (1909).

---

## GATEWAY TO ST JOHN'S COLLEGE

*Lady Margaret Beaufort, Duchess of Richmond and Derby, and mother of Henry VII, was one of the great benefactresses of Cambridge. She lived from 1443 to 1509, and in 1505 founded Christ's College. At the suggestion of her confessor and advisor, Bishop John Fisher, she founded a college in honour of St John the Evangelist, but did not live to see it; Fisher continued her work and the college opened in 1511 on the site of a former hospital. The gate-house is a three-storey brick and stone building, the ground floor richly fan-vaulted. It was probably built by the master-mason William Swayne, who also worked at Christ's College and King's College Chapel. The heraldic decoration commemorates Lady Margaret and Henry VII. In the centre the Beaufort Arms are supported by two yales— fabulous beasts with antelopes' bodies, goat-like heads and the ability to swivel their horns about. Above the coat of arms is the Beaufort crest—an eagle's head and*

*wings rising from a coronet, while to the left and right are the Tudor and Beaufort badges—rose and portcullis. All around are strewn daisies and borage, Lady Margaret's flowers. In the niche above is a figure of St John, put there in 1662 to replace the original statue removed during the Civil War.*

*Beyond the gate lies First Court, the original building of St John's College. The doorway at the far side of the court leads to two further courts, the first of them one of the finest in Cambridge. Beyond these is the famous Bridge of Sighs over the Cam, modelled on its Venetian namesake. It leads to New Court cloisters, the Backs, and St John's excellent new buildings. To the right of First Court is the 19th-century college chapel by Gilbert Scott. It contains some of the stalls from the original chapel, and a monument of about 1522 to Hugh Ashton, Archdeacon of York, who is represented by effigies, one in life, the other in death.*

# CAMBRIDGE *Treasures of the Colleges*

The Cambridge colleges have gained their treasures from many sources: from kings and queens, bishops and travellers, craftsmen from the far side of Europe and from the town itself. The quality and variety would be amazing anywhere except in such a great centre of culture as this.

THE TRINITY APOCALYPSE *This is probably the finest of the medieval manuscripts inspired by the visions of the Apocalypse of St John. It was made about 1250. In the upper half St John stands on the left of the Third Beast, or false prophet, which is then shown sitting on a mound faced by the Second Beast and worshippers. Below, three men kill three martyrs and two men worship the Second Beast. (Trinity College)*

PEDESTAL DISH FROM COCLÉ, PANAMA *The Coclé region of Panama has some of the most unusual pottery in a continent notable for its remarkable pottery styles. This dish is decorated with crocodile heads and characteristic pointed hooks. Most Coclé pottery has been found in graves dating from the 14th century to the time of the Spanish conquest, around the 16th century. (Museum of Ethnology)*

KING'S COLLEGE CHAPEL *This chapel, in royal tradition (King's College was founded by Henry VI in 1440), has probably the finest and purest set of fan-vaults in England. They are based on the 14th-century choir of Gloucester Cathedral. The angel stands on top of the organ case. It was modelled in 1859 by Gilbert Scott and is based on an engraving of the chapel made in 1690 which shows the original angels later removed during alteration.*

BERTEL THORVALDSEN: LORD BYRON *The great Danish neo-Classical sculptor Bertel Thorvaldsen (1770–1844) is usually associated with a particularly severe brand of neo-Grecian nude—the museum devoted to his work in Copenhagen makes a chilly impression. But here, suiting the spirit of his statue to its subject, he produced a highly romantic work—one of his masterpieces: Byron sits among the ruins of Athens, composing part of 'Childe Harold'. (Trinity College Library)*

RUBENS: THE ADORATION OF THE KINGS *El Greco's work shows the ingredients of the Mannerist style —asymmetry, deliberate elongation of the human figure and a preference for rather acid and hard colours. In the succeeding baroque period the soaring figures, the exaggerated gestures, the facial contortions were subordinated to a dramatic whole in which the splendour of rich resonant colour played a major part. It was an international, largely Catholic style and Rubens (1577–1640), whose vigour and robustness are unequalled, was the greatest figure in northern baroque; his version of the style was admirably suited to vast canvases glorifying Church and State. This is one of his great altar-pieces painted originally for a convent in Louvain and paid for in 1634. By this time the movement of Rubens's forms had become less energetic and apart from the splash of red which he so often introduces, as here in the robe of the king prostrating himself, the colour range too is quieter.*
*(King's College Chapel)*

THE BETRAYAL OF CHRIST BY JUDAS *A detail from a stained glass window in the Chapel of King's College, the only medieval English church, apart from York Minster, to retain all its original glass. This panel is one of a series portraying scenes from the lives of the Virgin and Christ, designed, painted and glazed by Dirick Vellert of Antwerp and Galyon Hone, a Netherlander, two of the many foreign craftsmen working in England during the reign of Henry VIII. In many great churches splendid windows frequently told the whole history of man from the Creation to the Fall. Those at King's College are the last great example of the medieval glaziers' art in England.*

ST BEDE'S COMMENTARY ON THE APOCALYPSE *The main characteristic of Romanesque art—the portrayal of the human figure in rigid poses expressing abstract qualities— is well illustrated in this drawing from a manuscript written between 1150 and 1155. It shows St John as a bishop with a monk, the writer of the manuscript, at his feet. The Anglo-Saxon technique of coloured outline drawing is adapted to the Romanesque demands with marvellous economy and skill—a striking example of how line was emphasised in English art throughout the stylistic changes of the 10th, 11th and 12th centuries. (St John's College)*

QUEENS' COLLEGE DIAL *The dial in the Old Court at Queens' College is one of the finest examples of sun-dial art in the country, and one of the few moon-dials in existence. It was repainted in the mid-18th century, although records show a dial here in 1642. The small ball on the style is a unique feature of the dial and makes possible many of the calculations. The shadow cast on to the golden Roman numerals is apparent solar time. The table of figures below the dial is an aid to telling the time by moonlight, providing the moon is strong enough to cast a readable shadow. The altitude of the sun can also be observed, the date, the time of sunrise and sunset and the sign of the zodiac in which the sun lies.*

# FITZWILLIAM MUSEUM, CAMBRIDGE

The Fitzwilliam is one of Europe's major museums. Its collections cover Egyptian, Greek and Roman antiquities, coins and medals, medieval manuscripts, painting and drawing of all periods, prints, and the applied arts. Outstanding are the collection of coins and medals, the collection of paintings, and the collections devoted to the applied arts, especially ceramics, glass and armour.

LIMOGES ENAMEL TRIPTYCH *This enamel triptych was made in 1538 in Limoges by Pierre Reymond, who lived from about 1513 to 1584 and was a leading master of the art of enamelling in the Renaissance. Reymond and his contemporaries used coloured enamels applied to a design incised on metal, usually copper. The centre panel here is based on a composition by Raphael. The sides show St Peter and Daniel.*

GREEN JADE BUFFALO *Sculptures of the Chinese Han dynasty (206 BC to AD 220) are rare in Europe; the feeling for flowing curves in this fine example—only $15\frac{3}{4}$ in. long, but unusually large for a jade carving—is typical of the Han period, when sculpture broke away from the more geometrical shapes of earlier styles.*

FIGURE OF OCEANUS *Modelled between 1762 and 1765 by Konrad Linck for the Frankenthal factory in Germany, this figure of Oceanus is an example of the popular 18th-century trend for using gods as the subjects for table centre-pieces. The figures were designed to be seen from all angles and so every detail is carefully finished. Sea-green crêpe paper would have been placed on the table to imitate waves, and figures (originally confectionery but by the 18th century porcelain) representing Neptune, Oceanus and mermaids would be placed on imitation rocks and shells.*

18TH-CENTURY GLASS GOBLET *The Royal Arms of England are painted on this lead-glass goblet, the Prince of Wales' feathers and motto 'Ich Dien' ('I serve') being on the reverse. Made by William Beilby around 1762, the goblet has a bucket-shaped bowl and an enamel-twist stem. The bowl, stem and foot of the goblet were all formed separately and then joined together.*

16TH-CENTURY ITALIAN PARADE HELMET *Bought for a few shillings from a theatrical costumier in 1937, this helmet was probably originally made for a Renaissance prince. Its style is Classical, based on Roman armour, showing that it was designed for show rather than for combat. The visor is in the form of a lion's mask. The skull was beaten out of a single piece of steel, and is embossed in relief with trophies of arms and musical instruments, foliage, and two nude females representing Fame and Victory. Little now remains of the original gold and silver which covered the surface decoration, and one of the cheekpieces has also been lost. Despite these defects it displays the art of the Renaissance metalworker to perfection, and there is little doubt that it is the work of Filippo and Francesco Negroli of Milan, the greatest masters in this field.*

DOMENICO VENEZIANO: THE ANNUNCIATION *One of the four predella panels of the St Lucy altarpiece, painted for a church in Florence by Domenico. He was one of the major painters in 15th-century Florence but few of his works have survived. He* *contributed a feeling for atmospheric colour and the semblance of real light to the development of perspective and the study of anatomy which were the main preoccupations of his fellow Florentine painters, impassioned with a love of abstract ideas and formal relations.*

## CANTERBURY ROMAN GLASS

*Glass-blowing was invented in Roman times, probably in the last century BC. The two-handled flagon is from the 3rd century and was dredged from a lake at Bishopsbourne in 1846. To the right is a 1st-century jug found in a Roman grave at Faversham; it comes from the Rhineland, a great centre of glass-making. The two glass bracelets, found in the 19th century in a field at Milton Regis, may possibly be Anglo-Saxon. (Canterbury Royal Museum)*

---

**Cambuskenneth** *Stir.*      *562Af*
ABBEY Picturesque ruins, beside the R. Forth, of the Augustinian abbey founded in the mid-12th century by King David I. A magnificent 13th–14th-century bell-tower is still intact.

**Cameley** *Som.*      *540Cf*
CHURCH OF ST JAMES A small, isolated church dating from the 12th century, with interesting fittings—pulpit, pews, reredos and communion rail.

**Campsall** *Yorks.*      *552Eg*
CHURCH OF ST MARY MAGDALENE A large cruciform building, of Norman origin with later additions. There is a tall rood screen and a family monument by Flaxman, 1803. There is a chamber above the vaulted west end of the south aisle.

**Camster** *Caith.*      *569Ld*
GREY CAIRNS OF CAMSTER The first of the three cairns in this area is of the long-horned type. It has four horns and is 200 ft long. The entrance is in the long east side and the passage leads to a tripartite main chamber. There is also a minor corbelled chamber reached by another narrow passage.

Two hundred yards to the south-east is a round cairn, a mound of loose stones some 55 ft in diameter. It stands 12 ft high and has a 20 ft long passage leading to a triple chamber, partly roofed by stone slabs and partly by corbelling.

Some 140 yds to the south-west is a third round cairn, 27 ft in diameter and about 2 ft high.

**Cannock** *Staffs.*      *552Cb*
CASTLE RING This is an important fort standing on an isolated elevation to overlook the surrounding country. To the north and west there are two protective banks, each with an external ditch, but on the opposite side, where there is no steep slope,

there are no less than five banks with four ditches. The entrance is on the east side, with the inner bank inturned to provide an entrance passage.

**Cannon Hall** *Yorks.*      *552Dg*
A 17th-century mansion which was rebuilt in the 18th century by Carr of York. It contains furniture and paintings, and stands in a fine park.

**Canon Pyon** *Herefs.*      *546Ae*
CHURCH OF ST LAWRENCE A 13th- and 14th-century church with a south tower. There is an octagonal Perpendicular font, some misericords, and stalls with poppy-head carving. Also a monument (1753) by Louis Roubiliac, the foremost sculptor of his period in this country.

**Canterbury** *Kent*      *542Ff*
During the Second World War bombs destroyed one-third of the old city of Canterbury, and in so doing revealed ancient foundations which enabled archaeologists to trace the story of its occupation from the Stone Age through Roman and medieval times. A settlement of *c.* 300 BC had become a centre of the Belgae tribe when the Romans invaded, and was the Saxon town of Cantwarbyrig when St Augustine arrived on a mission from Rome in AD 597; in 602 Canterbury became the metropolitan city of the English Church. The Normans built a castle, now in ruins, between 1070 and 1094, and in 1067 the cathedral, sacked by the Danes in 1011, was completely rebuilt. In 1170 Thomas à Becket was murdered in the cathedral and, from that date until Henry VIII destroyed the martyr's shrine, Canterbury was the destination of pilgrims from all over Europe. In the late 16th century many Flemish and Huguenot immigrants settled there.

The town is dominated by the long grey pile of the cathedral with its three great towers. The roughly oval plan of the medieval town is easy to make out still, and large stretches of the town walls survive, especially on the east and south sides. The most spectacular building after the cathedral is the West Gate, built in Edward III's time. Since the bombing in the Second World War, the east half of the town has been much rebuilt, but the close medieval texture remains in the streets on both sides of St Peter's Street, especially in the lanes leading to the great Christchurch Gate and the cathedral precincts, with their lofty overhanging houses. The King's School, to the north of Mint Yard in the precincts, has a splendid Norman staircase entrance.

CATHEDRAL Canterbury Cathedral was founded in 597, but of the early buildings nothing survives from before the Conquest. The internal appearance of the present cathedral is dominated by the work of two men—William of Sens, who designed the choir and apse after the fire of 1174, and Henry Yevele, who designed the nave in 1374. The exterior is dominated by the central Bell Harry Tower designed by William Westall in the late 15th century. In the Trinity Chapel, on the south side, is the magnificent tomb of Edward the Black Prince, Edward III's son, who died in 1376; on the north side lie the bodies of Henry IV, who died in 1413, and his queen, Joan of Navarre, in a splendid canopied tomb with elaborate alabaster effigies. Much of the monastic building has survived. The 12th-century monastery had an unusually fine system of sanitation and plumbing; a fresh water supply was piped in from outside and distributed to all the main buildings. The so-called Water Tower still exists although its upper part, which was rebuilt at the beginning of the 15th century, has been converted into a library.

# CANTERBURY CATHEDRAL

CANTERBURY CATHEDRAL *Despite its great antiquity and illustrious origins, the life of Canterbury during the Middle Ages centred on the shrine of St Thomas à Becket. The place of his martyrdom is marked by a plaque on the floor, and the shrine was behind the high altar. Most Archbishops of Canterbury were statesmen. Some, like Becket and Archbishop Sudbury, who became Chancellor and was murdered during the Peasants' Revolt in 1381, came to grief. Henry Chichele, on the other hand, was a great early 15th-century figure and the founder of All Souls College, Oxford, while Archbishop Bourchier, consecrated in 1454, survived to crown in succession Edward IV, Richard III and Henry VII.*

CRYPT *The Norman crypt at Canterbury is the largest in the world; its main feature is the Chapel of our Lady, whose fine stone screens were a gift from the Black Prince, who had intended the chapel to be his last resting place. The Black Prince's Chantry is an early Norman chapel once used by the Huguenots; it takes its name from alterations made by the Black Prince. St Gabriel's Chapel has Byzantine frescoes dating from the early 1100's and pillar capitals carved with figures and animals; some of the original paintwork remains. Opposite the north transept are the two oldest chapels, of St Mary Magdalene and St Nicholas, and in the great east crypt is another superb Chapel of our Lady, the ceiling decorated with crowned 'M's.*

THE BLACK PRINCE'S ACHIEVEMENTS *The armour of noblemen was carried at their funerals and then placed on their tombs as Achievements—emblems of distinction. This is part of the armour of Edward, Prince of Wales—the Black Prince; it was borne at his funeral in Canterbury Cathedral in 1376. The helm has a moulded leather crest in the form of a lion standing on a cap; the loose garment, a surcoat, is embroidered with the prince's coat of arms in gold and silver thread, which also appear in moulded leather on the wooden shield. The gauntlets are of gilded latten— a kind of brass—and the remains of a red leather sword-scabbard are decorated with gilt studs. The buckle is attached to remnants of a linen belt which originally supported either a sword or a shield; and there is a piece of guard chain for the helmet. It is unlikely that the armour was ever used in warfare, although it may have been worn in tournaments.*

# NATIONAL MUSEUM OF WALES, CARDIFF

Prosperity came late to Cardiff. With its bustling streets and docks it seems a child of the Industrial Revolution but its roots stretch back to Roman and Norman times. To preserve this heritage the museum was founded in 1907 'to teach the world about Wales and the Welsh people about their own fatherland', but Welsh achievements are shown against a wider cultural background.

SILVER-GILT TOILET SERVICE *The tray with the Arms of Williams-Wynn, an influential Welsh family, and the ornate box, both belong to a silver-gilt toilet service made in 1768 by Thomas Heming,* the principal goldsmith to George II and George III. *Heming's work reflects the gradual change in design from the elaborate rococo to a more severe Classical style that took place in the late 18th century.*

THE DOLGELLAU CHALICE AND PATEN—*so named because they were discovered by chance in 1890 buried by a road near Dolgellau, Merioneth—are among the earliest examples of church plate in Britain.* *The style of the chalice, the shallow bowl, the lobed knot halfway up the stem and the cusped lobes at the foot, indicate that they were made about 1250. The paten's centre shows Christ enthroned.*

DYNEVOR PLATE *In the second decade of the 19th century, Swansea had one of the best porcelain factories in Britain. This plate, part of the Dynevor service, is of a delicately fragile whiteness. Its hand-painted flower decorations are attributed to a Welsh artist named Evans. The museum porcelain section contains not only Welsh treasures but also English and continental porcelain, and shows Welsh contributions to the main stream of European culture.*

124

THE LLANDAFF DIPTYCH *This ivory carving, originally the right-hand part of a diptych, showing Christ with the Virgin and St John, was discovered accidentally in 1836 when the Old Well House at Llandaff was demolished.*

BRONZE TRITON *One of the greatest treasures of the museum is a bronze triton attributed to Severo da Ravenna, one of the Italian bronze sculptors practising their art in Padua in the late 15th and early 16th centuries. Padua was then leading the world in this art form, and the small bronzes produced by its masters were an inspiration to artists in other lands. Although a Paduan writing at the time listed all the sculptors working in the town and hailed Severo as the greatest master of them all, little is in fact known about him. Only one work, a sea-monster which he signed (now in New York), can with certainty be attributed to him. But as more bronzes in the Severo manner come to light, it should soon be possible to distinguish his work from that of his pupils and imitators.*

ROMAN PAVEMENT The remains of a Roman town house including two mosaic floors and hypocaust have been excavated.

ROYAL MUSEUM (BEANEY INSTITUTE) Items relating to local archaeology and natural history are exhibited with a small collection of china and pictures. Belgic coins, Roman finds including a hoard of silver spoons, Saxon glass and jewellery, and medieval pottery, all from excavations within the city, are on view. (See p. 122.)

ST AUGUSTINE'S ABBEY Canterbury had two great monasteries. The church of one became the cathedral, but its powerful rival is now a ruin of very great interest with Saxon and Norman work, while just to the east is the very early church dedicated to St Pancras. Two of the abbey's gates remain incorporated in the Theological College's mid-19th-century buildings by William Butterfield.

THE BUFFS REGIMENTAL MUSEUM Uniforms, drums, regimental silver and trophies, medals, prints and paintings illustrating the Regiment's history are displayed in the Poor Priest's House, which was built in 1373 by Thomas Wyke.

WEST GATE MUSEUM Collections of arms and armour, both British and foreign, are housed in the West Gate, the only surviving city gate in Canterbury. It was built on the site of a former gate by Archbishop Sudbury and finished in 1380. From 1543 to 1829 it was used as the city gaol.

**Capel Garmon** *Denb.* 550Fd

A roughly wedge-shaped cairn some 140 ft long with a horned forecourt at the east end. This however leads to a dummy portal. The true entrance to the triple chamber is on the south side, from which leads a passage to the central oval chamber, on either side of which is another, roughly circular. The passage and chamber walls are of large stone slabs, with the gaps filled with drystone walling. Only one of the chamber capstones remains, but parts of the passage were also roofed with large covering stones, other parts being corbelled. The stones of the cairn were held by a drystone walling revetment, and the whole structure had a final covering of earth.

**Capel Newydd** *Caern.* 550Dc

Licensed on October 6, 1769, Capel Newydd is the oldest surviving Nonconformist chapel in North Wales. It was carefully restored in 1956–8 when it was on the verge of collapse. The church members' poverty and self-conscious attempt to make their place of worship unlike a church give the building a barn-like appearance. The present two doors were originally windows, and the original earth floor has been retained.

**Capesthorne** *Cheshire* 552Be

A country mansion, originally of 1722, but altered later by Blore and Salvin. It contains collections of paintings, antique vases, furniture, silver, Americana, and figurines. Armour and aeroplane models are also exhibited.

**Cardiff** *Glam.* 545Jb

Cardiff has grown, in little more than 150 years, from a sizeable village to become capital of the Principality of Wales, a major seaport, and a university city. Its prosperity dates mainly from the docks, introduced by the Marquess of Bath in the early 19th century.

CARDIFF CASTLE Robert, Duke of Normandy, was confined here for 28 years following his defeat by his younger brother, Henry I of England, at the Battle of Tenchebrai (Normandy) in 1106 (Normandy remained annexed to the English Crown until the reign of King John). A motte with wooden buildings was raised in *c.* 1093 on the site of a Roman fortification; the present stone keep was erected to replace the wooden buildings in the late 12th century and additions were made in the 15th century and each century following. In 1861 the 3rd Marquess of Bute and William Burges designed additions in the Gothic, Arab and Classical Greek idioms. The Arab Room represents a harem with trellised windows, and throughout the decoration is a riot of inventiveness and allegory, often in exotic materials—lapis lazuli, for example.

NATIONAL MUSEUM OF WALES See pp. 124–5.

ROMAN FORT Adjoining the fine open spaces which surround Cardiff's civic centre, there stands this Roman fort. Built about the end of the 3rd century, it is of the same pattern as the later forts of the Saxon Shore, with rectangular corners and projecting bastions. It was placed here to protect the harbour and coast against the raids of Irish pirates. Its special spectacular interest lies in the fact that a former Lord Bute, its owner, had its curtain wall completely reconditioned, even to the castellation along the wall-top, so that, standing in a modern main street, the exact semblance of a late Roman fort may be viewed.

WELCH REGIMENT REGIMENTAL MUSEUM Military items connected with the Welch Regiment are on display.

**Cardoness Castle** *Kirkcud.*            556Eg
The ruined home of the McCullochs; a 15th-century tower-house on a rocky hill by the Water of Fleet.

**Carew Castle** *Pemb.*            544De
The noble ruins of a 13th-century castle on Milford Haven inlet. The castle was enlarged during the 15th century when the great hall was built, and the fortress became a fine Tudor residence. It was destroyed during the Civil War. Near the entrance to the castle is a carved Celtic cross, 14 ft high.

**Carew Cheriton** *Pemb.*            544Dc
CHURCH A fine, mainly 14th-century church, which is cruciform with a 15th-century tower. There are monuments of the 14th and 17th centuries with effigies. There is also a 19th-century memorial by John Evan Thomas, who exhibited at the Great Exhibition of 1851.

**Carisbrooke** *Isle of Wight, Hants.*            541Gc
CHURCH OF ST MARY A Norman building, formerly the monastic church of the Benedictine priory which was suppressed in 1414. The 15th-century tower is outstanding. The chancel was demolished in the 16th century, but there is a Norman nave and arches, and the south aisle is Early English work. The font and pulpit are 17th century.

**Carisbrooke Castle** *Isle of Wight, Hants.* 541Gc
Roundheads kept Charles I a prisoner here from 1647 until shortly before his execution on January 30, 1649; his children Prince Henry and Princess Elizabeth were imprisoned with him; Princess Elizabeth died here in 1650, aged 15 and still a prisoner. On the site of a Roman fortress the Norman keep was built by William Fitz-Osborn, Earl of Hereford, in the reign of William I. The gate-house was built *c.* 1470. The outworks were added *c.* 1588 when the Spanish Armada threatened England, and a well, 161 ft deep, dates from that time.

**Carlisle** *Cumb.*            557Hg
Near the Scottish–English border, Carlisle occupied an important position for 1700 years, but has few remaining monuments to its turbulent history. A Roman town on Hadrian's Wall, it was abandoned during the Danish invasions and revived by the Normans.

BORDER REGIMENT MUSEUM The keep of Carlisle Castle, which was built *c.* 1092, houses uniforms and documents relating to the history of the Border Regiment. The medals on show include two Victoria Crosses.

CASTLE Built by William Rufus *c.* 1092 and enlarged in the next century. It was a bastion during all the Border Wars, a palace and stronghold: in 1568 Mary, Queen of Scots, came as a guest and stayed as a prisoner. In the Civil War the castle was besieged and captured by Parliamentary forces; in the rising of 1745 it surrendered to Bonnie Prince Charlie. Early in the 19th century large parts were destroyed, including the banqueting hall where Edward I (the 'Hammer of the Scots') held his Parliament and the apartments where Mary, Queen of Scots, was held prisoner. The most important remains are the 14th-century main gate, Queen Mary's Tower and the impressive central keep.

CATHEDRAL Built between 1092 and 1419. First the church of an Augustinian priory, it became the cathedral when the Diocese of Carlisle was founded in 1133. In the Civil War large portions were pulled down and the stones used for military purposes; it is now one of the smallest and most battle-scarred cathedrals in England. It was neglected in the 18th century, and restored in the 19th. The truncated nave is the Border Regiment's chapel. There is a beautiful Early English choir, dominated by the cathedral's chief glory, a huge east window with much original 14th-century glass—perhaps the finest Decorated window in the country. The choir stalls are carved with misericords and tabernacled canopies. There are monuments by Thomas Banks, John Adams-Acton, Hamo Thornycroft and H. H. Armstead. Sir Walter Scott was married in the cathedral.

MARKET-PLACE The centre of Carlisle; here are the 18th-century town hall and 14th-century guildhall.

TULLIE HOUSE A fine Jacobean mansion housing the city's art gallery, library and a museum which displays Roman material from Hadrian's Wall.

**Carl Wark** *Yorks.*            552De
A small enclosure, roughly rectangular, with steep natural scarps on three sides. On the west and south sides there is a stone-faced earth and turf rampart, the stonework in places still nearly 10 ft high. On the south-west is an inturned entrance. Quite probably, this is a hill-fort of the Iron Age, but it is often considered to belong to the Dark Ages.

**Carnasserie Castle** *Argyll*            560Eg
The remains of a fortified house built in the late 16th century by John Carswell, the first Bishop of the Isles after the Reformation. A parapet wall with gun loops and ports connects round corner-towers, and many rooms survive.

**Carneddau Hengwm** *Merioneth.*            550Fc
Here stand two long cairns. Neither is in very good condition, but enough of their essential structure is visible to work out the chambers and the blocked portal at the east end of the south cairn. Close by are the two henge circles known by the same name. Of these two the northern circle, some 120 ft in diameter, was never more than a circular ditch with an earthen bank, for excavation has shown that there were never any upright stones set in the circle. The southern circle, however, still has a few stones in their sockets and the excavation exposed the holes in which the missing stones had stood.

## CASTELL COCH

*A Victorian fairy-tale castle resulted when in 1865 the 3rd Marquess of Bute commissioned William Burges to rebuild his ruined medieval castle on a hill. Burges found only foundations and fragmentary walls and during the next 20 years he created this medieval fantasy of three round towers capped by conical roofs and connected by a curving curtain wall which forms a courtyard. The whole building is a fascinating exercise in late 19th-century romanticism. In the decoration of the hall and the main rooms in the keep, Burges allowed full reign to his imagination of things medieval. The walls and ceilings are covered with painted birds, stars, monkeys, butterflies, scenes from Aesop's Fables and heraldic devices. The chimney-pieces have carved and painted animals, and in the drawing-room are three large carved figures of the Fates. Burges also designed the furniture, and in the bed-rooms, known as the 'Lord's' and the 'Lady's', there are painted beds.*

**Carreg-Cennen Castle** *Carm.*                 *545Gd*
Legend says that one of King Arthur's knights, Sir Urien, had a fortress here on the great rock above the R. Cennen. The present castle was built by a Welsh prince and saw much fighting in the wars between the Principalities. In 1277 it was taken by the English, and John of Gaunt and Henry Bolingbroke were subsequent owners. After the 19th century it fell into disrepair and now only ragged ruins remain.

**Carrock Fell** *Cumb.*                 *557Hf*
In addition to the natural defence provided by the steep scarp-slopes, there is a 5 acre enclosure within a stone wall. This hill-fort is tentatively attributed to the Iron Age, though its inmates may well have not advanced beyond a Bronze Age culture.

Near its east end, the wall encloses a cairn of somewhat earlier date, and there are many more of these in the area to the north of the fell. They may well cover earlier Bronze Age burials.

**Carshalton** *Greater London*                 *542Bf*
Although in the midst of suburbia, Carshalton has a number of Regency cottages around the church and pond, and the splendid Carshalton House, built *c.* 1714, with gardens by Charles Bridgeman and a water house looming above the road, designed perhaps by Vanbrugh.

CASTLE ACRE PRIORY

*Castle Acre is probably the most impressive surviving ruin of an English Cluniac house. The order of Cluny, a reformed type of Benedictinism originally established in Burgundy, was introduced into England by William de Warenne when he founded Lewes Priory in 1077. His son William founded Castle Acre about 1090. The Cluniacs were often criticised for their wealth and ostentation, and the excessively decorated west front at Castle Acre and also the decoration inside the church at the west end probably aroused much criticism. During the Middle Ages there were usually about 25 to 35 monks in residence, but by the Dissolution the number had dwindled to 11, including the prior. A series of scandals suggests that by the 14th century discipline at Castle Acre was slack.*

**Cartmel** *Lancs.*                 *557Hd*
PRIORY CHURCH OF ST MARY THE VIRGIN A great medieval parish church, the building is cruciform and basically of late Norman work, with Perpendicular windows and a diagonally-set upper stage of the central tower added in the 15th century. After the Dissolution the building decayed, and by 1618 was roofless, at which time its restoration began. From this date are the magnificent Renaissance screens and stall-canopies, erected by George Preston of Holker when he was in charge of the restorations. Among many fine monuments is the 14th-century Harrington memorial, with recumbent effigies.

**Cartmel Fell** *Lancs.*                 *557Hd*
CHURCH OF ST ANTHONY A small, early 16th-century church; the attractive interior has two large family pews, a three-decker pulpit and some good medieval glass. A rare figure of Christ from the vanished rood screen has been preserved.

**Castell Coch** *Glam.*                 *545Hd*
A 13th-century castle existed here, but for centuries it was a ruin. In 1865 the 3rd Marquess of Bute asked William Burges to rebuild it. Burges found only foundations and fragmentary walls, and during the next 20 years he created this medieval fantasy of three round towers capped by steep conical roofs and connected by a curving curtain wall forming a courtyard. The castle is approached only by a wooden drawbridge over a dry moat, and at the entrance is a portcullis. (See p. 127.)

**Castell-Y-Bere** *Merioneth.*                 *550Fb*
Beautifully sited and remote ruins of a 13th-century castle with two D-shaped towers—a characteristic feature of Welsh castles. The quality of the carved stonework is high, and it seems likely that Castell-Y-Bere was intended to be a centre of considerable importance to the Welsh princes.

After the English conquest Edward I founded a borough here, but it was abandoned during the 14th century.

**Castle Acre** *Norfolk*                 *554Bc*
The village, lying on a broad street that leads to the R. Nar, has a combination of military and monastic ruins unlike anything else in East Anglia. Castle Acre is one of the few villages on the line of Peddars Way, a prehistoric trackway that crosses Norfolk. To the west of the village is a Saxon cemetery of the 7th century.
CASTLE A motte and bailey fortress, going back to the 11th century, it fell into decay in the 14th century, and was pillaged by local builders. Only the 13th-century gateway with two round towers stands, spanning the village street; there are traces of the keep and ditch. The site covers about 15 acres.
CHURCH OF ST JAMES Near to the castle and the priory, the church was built mainly between the 13th and 15th centuries. There is a west tower, and a Perpendicular pulpit with painted panels of the Latin Fathers of the Church (as at Burnham Norton in Norfolk). The rood screen has paintings of *c.* 1400 and the font has a tall Perpendicular cover with some original colour left. The stalls have misericords.
PRIORY Impressive remains of a Cluniac priory, founded by William de Warenne, 2nd Earl of Surrey, *c.* 1090. The 12th-century arcaded west front of the priory church is built of hewn stone and flint. The sacristy, prior's lodging and chapel with its wooden ceiling of *c.* 1500 and 14th-century murals, and the 15th-century gate-house, also survive.

CASTLE HOWARD

One of the largest and most spectacular houses in the country, Castle Howard was designed in about 1700 for the 3rd Earl of Carlisle by Sir John Vanbrugh, assisted by Nicholas Hawksmoor, one of Sir Christopher Wren's assistants. Vanbrugh's scheme was for a great central domed block, flanked by two smaller side wings, but he died in 1726, long before the work of building was finished, and Sir Thomas Robinson continued the scheme, building one of the side wings. There was a disastrous fire in 1940 which destroyed the central dome, but this has been restored. Beneath the dome is the great hall, 34 ft square, reaching to the full height of the dome; it has arches on huge Composite pilasters, statues in niches, and is flanked by staircases. The charming Temple of the Four Winds in the grounds was designed by Vanbrugh and completed by Hawksmoor, who also erected the circular colonnaded mausoleum on a nearby hill.

**Castle Ashby** Northants.                  547Gf
The Compton family (who became Marquesses of Northampton) have lived in this Elizabethan mansion since it was begun in 1574. It was finished in 1635 and the south wing is attributed to Inigo Jones. The parapet surmounting the house is formed by letters cut in stone. The house contains fine moulded ceilings, panelling, staircases and chimney-pieces dating from 1600–35; fine furniture and Brussels tapestries of 1660–1700; and a collection of Dutch, Italian and English pictures. The grounds were landscaped by Capability Brown.

**Castle Bromwich Hall** Warks.                  546Dg
An early Jacobean mansion, bought in 1657 by Sir John Bridgeman, who added the Restoration-style porch.

**Castlecary** Stir.                  561Jf
CASTLE CARY Remains of a square tower destroyed in 1715.
ROMAN FORT The remains of a stronghold, one of the line of forts along the Antonine Wall.

**Castle Combe** Wilts.                  540Eg
A Cotswold village, elected the prettiest in England in 1962, set in a river valley. There is a 15th-century market cross, stone houses and cottages. The church is mostly Perpendicular; it was restored in 1851 but the original tower still stands.

**Castle Ditches** Cheshire                  552Ae
Iron Age earthworks enclose the whole 11 acre hill-top. The defences have been remodelled more than once. The first was a timber stockade, which was soon replaced by a bank and ditch with counterscarp bank, though these did not include the whole hill-top. The entrance was on the east side, flanked by guard-houses. The bank and ditch were then extended to include the whole area, with a second entrance. Finally, another bank and ditch were added to the complex, outside the earlier ones, and the entrances were remodelled and revetted with stone. In historic times, Aethelfled, Lady of the Mercians, refurbished the defences and made it one of her *burhs*, or strong-points, against the Danes of the Danelaw.

**Castle Dore** *Cornwall*                    *538Dc*
This small Iron Age hill-fort has a roughly circular internal area, protected by two banks and ditches, the outer bank being extended on the east side to make it oval in plan. The elaborate entrance is a passage between inturned banks with a bridge over the wooden gate. There is evidence to support the legend that this was the castle of King Mark of Cornwall, the husband of Tristan's Iseult.

**Castle Haven** *Kirkcud.*                    *556Eg*
This is a galleried dun with a D-shaped plan, and is enclosed in a larger structure of a similar plan. The inner structure encloses a space some 60 ft by 35 ft and has the customary wall-galleries.

**Castle Hedingham** *Essex*                    *548Be*
A small town once dominated by a mighty castle built by the powerful de Veres, Earls of Oxford, in *c.* 1140. The keep still stands, and is one of the best preserved examples of its type in England. It is four storeys high, with square turrets, and walls averaging 11 ft thick. Inside are arches with zigzag decoration, a hall on the second floor, and some original plastering. A late 15th-century bridge crosses the moat. The village below the castle has some attractive medieval and Georgian houses.
CHURCH OF ST NICHOLAS A Norman church with a later clerestory. The tower bears the date 1616. The nave has a double hammerbeam roof. The north and two south doorways are originals of the 12th century and the contents include carved misericords and a 14th-century rood screen.

**Castle Howard** *Yorks.*                    *558Ec*
An obelisk in the grounds is inscribed 'Charles the III, Earl of Carlisle, of the family of the Howards erected a castle where the old castle of Henderskelfe stood, and called it Castle-Howard'. The mansion, which was commissioned by the young Earl of Carlisle, is by Sir John Vanbrugh, who was aided by Nicholas Hawksmoor, an assistant to Sir Christopher Wren. The house was built in 1700–14. The south façade comprises a central block, surmounted by a dome, between two wings. Corinthian fluted pilasters accentuate the height of the central block. The mansion contains a notable long gallery, chapel, hall, and much fine furniture, pictures and statuary; in the Tapestry Room (the dining-room) are paintings by Reynolds, Romney and Gainsborough. An adjacent building houses an exhibition of 17th- to 20th-century costumes in period settings. The grounds include a circular mausoleum designed by Hawksmoor, a Temple of the Four Winds designed by Vanbrugh, and a massive gate-house is crowned with a pyramid. (See p. 129.)

**Castle Leod** *Ross*                    *566Ag*
A turreted castle, built *c.* 1616 by Sir Roderick Mackenzie.

**Castle of Park** *Wig.*                    *556Cg*
A castellated house begun in 1590 and recently restored.

**Castlerigg Stone Circle** *Cumb.*                    *557Hf*
This stone circle is ovoid in plan, with some 38 stones still standing. Its greatest diameter is more than 100 ft. It also has an inner enclosure at its east end.

**Castle Rising** *Norfolk*                    *554Ac*
A small, pretty village that was an important port, until the sea receded.
BEDE HOUSE OR HOWARD HOSPITAL Near the castle, an almshouse founded by Henry Howard, Earl of Northampton in the reign of James I. A one-storey brick quadrangle with a gabled entrance; Jacobean furniture remains. On Sundays the elderly women who live there wear red cloaks with the Howard badge, and the steeple hats worn in the founder's day.
CASTLE Built by William de Albini, mid-12th century. It was acquired by Thomas Howard, Duke of Norfolk, in 1544, and still belongs to the Howards. The main moat is nearly 60 ft deep, crossed by a brick bridge, and there is a gate-house. The impressive hall-keep of two floors is

CASTLE RISING

*Castle Rising stands on some of the most spectacular earthworks in England. The site has not yet been fully excavated, and although the smaller enclosures to the east and west may date back to the Roman occupation, the origin of the main earthworks is uncertain. In the 12th century the property was owned by the Albini family, and the castle itself was built about 1150 by William de Albini, Earl of Sussex, who married the widow of Henry I. The castle was apparently never subjected to any major siege, and only enjoyed one* *brief period of fame when, about 1330, it became the chief residence of Queen Isabella, wife of the murdered Edward II and mother of Edward III. Nominally in disgrace for her liaison with the executed Roger Mortimer and her part in the fall of Edward II, she appears to have lived comfortably at the castle, and was visited there by both Edward III and his son, the Black Prince. In the 15th century the castle decayed, and in 1544 it passed to Thomas Howard, Duke of Norfolk.*

CASTLERIGG STONE CIRCLE

*Surrounded by a rim of mountains two miles east of Keswick is this great prehistoric stone circle known as Castlerigg or Keswick Carles. It is one of a great many such circles in Britain which date from the Neo-lithic and post-Neolithic periods. While many megalithic circles were buried monuments, those as large as this one were probably built as places for religious or ceremonial meetings, the most famous being Stonehenge in Wiltshire. Castlerigg has 38 stones standing or lying to make an oval that is 100 ft to 110 ft in diameter, and a further ten stones beside the circle at the south-east arranged to form a rectangle.*

divided into several rooms with arches and vaulting reached by principal and lesser staircases.

Castle Rising is surrounded by an immense earth rampart about 64 ft high, and the outer ditch which surrounds the wall goes down a further 60 ft below it. The main enclosure is roughly circular and the distance round the circumference is about 1000 yds. This rampart cuts across extensive earthworks on a smaller scale which extend east and west.

TRINITY HOSPITAL Nine 17th-century almshouses of brick and tile, with court, chapel and treasury, the whole forming a 'hospital'—a charitable foundation for the care of the sick and aged.

**Castle Tioram** *Argyll*　　　　564Fc
The ruins of a 14th-century fortress of the MacDonalds of Clanranald, destroyed in 1715.

**Castleton** *Derbys.*　　　　552Cf
A village set charmingly among the hills of the Peak District, near numerous caves and disused lead mines. The Church of St Edmund dates from Norman times and has fine plasterwork and box-pews of the 17th century. The ruined Norman keep of Peveril Castle stands above the village and was the setting of Sir Walter Scott's novel, *Peveril of the Peak.*

**Castletown** *Isle of Man*　　　556Cc
NAUTICAL MUSEUM The museum is housed in a three-storied boat-house, almost 200 years old. Among the exhibits is a schooner-rigged yacht, the *Peggy,* which was built in 1791 and is probably the oldest craft of her kind. There are also models of deep sea vessels and local fishing boats, and a reconstruction of a sailmaker's workshop.

**Castor** *Northants.*　　　　547Hg
CHURCH OF ST KYNEBURGHA A Norman church, with a central tower, which has a 14th-century parapet and spire. The exterior of the tower has two stages of panelling and windows. A carved inscription records the church's consecration in 1124. Wall-paintings in the church date from the 14th century.

**Caterthun, Brown and White** *Angus*　566Ec
Brown Caterthun stands alone with its six lines of defence. The outermost, a rampart with external ditch, encloses an area 1000 ft by 900 ft. This has eight entrances, as has the second line of defence, a ditchless rampart. Then come two more ramparts with an intervening ditch and, close inside these, a greater rampart with a boulder facing. Finally, the innermost line of defence is a stone wall with a single entrance. Its detailed history is not known, but this wealth of defence clearly indicates a history of remodelling and amplifying the defences.

White Caterthun, a mile to the south-west of its neighbour, is a hill-top oval, surrounded by two enormous stone walls, now rather ruinous. Outside these are lesser ramparts with quarry ditches. Again the sequence of construction is unknown, though probably more than one period is represented.

**Cauldside** *Kirkcud.*　　　　556Dg
Here, at the head of the Cauldside Burn, stand the remains of two cairns, two stone circles and a large stone block carved with cup-marks and spirals. The larger cairn is 63 ft across, stands 10 ft high and there is an exposed chamber visible in the top. The second, of which only the foundations remain, lies 150 yds to the north. Each cairn had a stone circle immediately to its south. The first, some 70 ft across, still has ten of its stones standing, but the more northerly one has almost disappeared. The cup-marked stone stands nearly a quarter of a mile north-west of the larger cairn.

**Cavendish** *Suffolk*　　　　548Ce
A pretty village in the Stour Valley, with thatched colour-washed cottages around the green. Nether-hall Farm is a 16th-century timber-framed Tudor house; also from the 16th century are Manor Cottages and the Old Rectory (now the Sue Ryder Home for survivors of concentration camps). A mile from the village is the Regency Cavendish Hall.

CHURCH OF ST MARY The church has a west tower and a clerestory. There is a 15th-century brass eagle lectern, and a 16th-century wooden one.

**Caverswall Castle** *Staffs.*　　　552Cd
The turreted castle, of medieval origin with Jacobean alterations, stands in a dried-up moat; it is now a convent.

**Cavick House** *Norfolk*　　　554Cb
A Queen Anne house with fine interior examples of rococo decoration and plasterwork.

**Cawdor Castle** *Nairns.*　　　566Bg
Picturesque medieval building, with central tower dating from 1454, moat, drawbridge and iron yett (protective gateway grille). It was used by Shakespeare as the setting of Duncan's murder by Macbeth, Thane of Cawdor. (Not open.)

# CHATSWORTH

One of the great mansions of England, Chatsworth dates from 1687 when the 1st Duke of Devonshire employed William Talman, who had also worked at Hampton Court, to rebuild his Elizabethan house in Classical style. When the duke died in 1707 his house was finished.

*THE GREAT CHAMBER The largest room of the state suite and one of the few rooms left unaltered during the 6th Duke of Devonshire's enlargements to the house. Designed in 1690–1700, it has the only ceiling of the suite that was painted by Verrio. The carving of the chimney-piece, although often attributed to Grinling Gibbons, is in fact by Samuel Watson and complements the ceiling. The carved and gilded tables were designed by William Kent, and some were originally part of the Burlington House collection.*

---

**Cawston** *Norfolk*      *554Cc*
CHURCH OF ST AGNES An impressive church with 15th-century additions. The west tower is plain and the nave roof is hammerbeam with widespread winged angels. In the south transept is a piscina with a wild man and a dragon. The octagonal Perpendicular font has decorated panels, and the screen bears painted saints. The stalls have misericords.

**Caythorpe** *Lincs.*      *553Gd*
CHURCH OF ST VINCENT The church dates from the 13th century, with a central tower and tall spire, and has a fine early 14th-century nave arcade. There are fragments of a wall-painting over the tower arch.

**Cedar House** *Surrey*      *542Af*
An H-shaped building of the 15th century, altered in the 17th and 18th centuries. The great hall has a fine timbered roof. (By appointment.)

**Cefntilla Court** *Mon.*      *546Ac*
The home of Lord Raglan, whose ancestor, Lord Fitzroy James Henry Somerset, 1st Baron Raglan

(1788–1855), fought in the Peninsular Campaign as ADC to Sir Arthur Wellesley (later Duke of Wellington), and commanded (1854–5) British troops in the Crimean War. At Cefntilla Court are relics and souvenirs of these two major campaigns. The house was built *c.* 1616 and contains portraits and porcelain collections, and a heraldic frieze painted in 1510.

**Cerne Abbas** *Dorset*      *540Dd*
CHURCH OF ST MARY The church is of mainly 15th- and 16th-century work, with a west tower. There are fragments of 14th- and 15th-century stained glass, and some 14th-century wall-paintings. The canopied pulpit dates from 1640, and the stone rood screen from the 15th century. In the churchyard are the remains of a 15th-century cross. Around the church are the ruins of the Abbey of Cerne.

**Cerne Abbas Giant** *Dorset*      *540Dc*
Carved in outline on a hill-side east of the Dorchester–Sherborne road, close to the village of Cerne Abbas, is the huge figure of the Giant—a

THE GRAND CASCADE *The three great periods of garden design—17th-century formal, 18th-century landscaped, and mid-Victorian—are illustrated at Chatsworth. The garden was first altered in 1688 by George London in the formal style of the Frenchman, André Le Nôtre, and parts that still remain include the canal and fountains, and the temple of the Grand Cascade designed by Thomas Archer in 1696. Capability Brown gave a more park-like aspect to the grounds in the 18th century. They were altered again in 1826 by Sir Joseph Paxton, who in 1843 constructed the second highest fountain in Europe—throwing a jet of water 290 ft high—and also built the giant conservatories. Although none now remain, one was the prototype of the Crystal Palace. The larger flower-beds planted with modern herbaceous plants and roses show 20th-century tastes for less elaborate vistas.*

THE CHAPEL *One of the few rooms of the great house hardly altered since 1694. The altar-piece was designed by Caius Gabriel Cibber although only the two large figures on either side were carved by him. The rest of the altar-piece was carved of the same alabaster by Samuel Watson. The walls and ceiling were painted by Laguerre and Ricard, and the painting above the altar, 'Doubting Thomas', is by Verrio. On the walls are carvings in limewood on cedar by Watson and a group of London carvers. The close collaboration between Laguerre and Cibber is shown in the paintings on either side of the altar-piece—they are an extension of the carved design and not connected with the other wall-paintings.*

naked man bearing a club; it is some 180 ft high. References to 'Helith', apparently its early name, and its relationship to spring-time fertility rites, lead to the belief that it is a representation of the Roman Hercules, identified with some local deity. Similar figures of Hercules are known from Roman times and the Giant is generally considered to be of Romano-British origin.

**Cerrig-y-Gof** *Pemb.*                                    *544De*
A burial chamber of unique design among the many fine monuments, mainly of Bronze Age date, dotted along the North Pembrokeshire coast. In the outer edge of a circular mound are set five megalithic chambers, rectangular in plan, which face outwards, a real departure from the characteristic chamber of uprights supporting a capstone.

**Chacombe Priory** *Oxon.*                               *546Fe*
Bardi, a Saxon lord, lived here until William the Conqueror gave the property to one of his Norman knights. The recently restored chapel was built in 1200. In 1600 the priory was rebuilt following a disastrous fire, and the porch of this period was retained when the Georgian front was added. There is a collection of fine silver, furniture and pictures.

**Chaddesley Corbett** *Worcs.*                           *546Cf*
CHURCH OF ST CASSIAN This is an interesting church with a Norman nave, and later work of the 14th century. There is an early Norman font carved with interlaced work and dragon-like creatures. There are several monuments, including some of the early 14th century. The tower and spire were rebuilt at the end of the 18th century.

**Chalbury** *Dorset*                                     *540Ed*
CHURCH Not a large building, the church is of 13th-century origin, and has plastered walls and timbered bell-cote. The east window is 14th century; the interior has some good 18th-century wood fittings (such as gallery, box-pews, pulpit and a pillared division between nave and chancel).

**Chaldon** *Surrey*                                      *542Bf*
CHURCH OF SS PETER AND PAUL This little church has a south tower with a shingled spire, and dates

from Norman times. It is famous for its great wall-painting, possibly of the early 13th century, showing the Ladder of Salvation. Little naked men and women climb the ladder to Heaven, or go down it to Hell where wait appropriately fearsome demons with great fires into which people are hurled. There is a 12th–13th-century bell hanging in the porch.

**Chalfont St Giles** *Bucks.*                 *542Ah*
MILTON'S COTTAGE The half-timbered house where John Milton the poet lived during the plague in 1665. He finished his epic 'Paradise Lost' here, and began writing 'Paradise Regained'.

**Chalgrave** *Beds.*                          *547Hd*
CHURCH OF ALL SAINTS An interesting church on a hill-top. It has 13th-century and later work, including carved corbels and wall-paintings with saints. There are tombs with effigies, and bench ends. The tower fell during a gale at the end of the 19th century.

**Chanctonbury Ring** *Sussex*                 *542Ad*
A ring of beech trees planted in 1760 around the area enclosed by an Iron Age hill-fort—a small enclosure, surrounded by a single bank and ditch, with a supplementary defence to the west of the enclosure. The remains of a Roman temple, together with other contemporary buildings, stand at the centre of the site.

**Chantry Green House** *Sussex*               *542Bd*
Once the dwelling of a priest, the house dates from 1547. Extensive additions were made in 1705, and after some war damage repair and redecoration took place in 1945. There is a collection of paintings and antique furniture.

**Charing** *Kent*                             *542Ef*
Typical of Kent, Charing seems a tiny town rather than a village. There are no specially grand houses, just a medley of mellow walls and roofs and, by the church, the ivy-covered ruins of a palace of the Archbishops of Canterbury. The barn to the east of these was built in the 14th century as the archbishops' great hall.

**Charlecote** *Warks.*                        *546Ef*
CHURCH OF ST LEONARD A mid-19th-century building in Gothic style, by John Gibson. The stained glass is by O'Connor, Kempe and Willement. The north chapel has 17th-century monuments, with effigies in alabaster, and black and white marble.

**Charlecote Park** *Warks.*                   *546Ef*
An Elizabethan mansion built of stone in 1558. It was altered and reconstructed in the 19th century but the gate-house was left untouched. The grounds were laid out by Capability Brown.

**Charleston Manor** *Sussex*                  *542Cd*
Domesday Book recorded that William the Conqueror's Cup-bearer owned this manor of 'Cerlestone'. A Tudor wing was added to the original Norman house, and a Georgian front was built in the 1770's. There is a tithe barn in the grounds.

**Charlton** *Greater London*                  *542Cg*
CHURCH OF ST LUKE Originally a medieval church; rebuilt *c.* 1630, with later additions. Among its many monuments is one by Nicholas Stone, and there is a bust by Sir Francis Chantrey of Spencer Perceval, Prime Minister from 1809 to 1812, when he was assassinated.

**Charlton Marshall** *Dorset*                 *540Ed*
CHURCH OF ST MARY The 15th-century tower remains, but St Mary's was rebuilt in a Classical style at the beginning of the 18th century. The

pleasant contemporary fittings include a good canopied pulpit and mural monuments.

**Charlton-on-Otmoor** *Oxon.*                 *546Fd*
CHURCH OF ST MARY THE VIRGIN A 13th- and 14th-century church, with an impressive Perpendicular screen; the vaulting of the loft remains, though the gallery has gone.

**Charminster** *Dorset*                       *540Dc*
CHURCH OF ST MARY An aisled 12th-century church with original Norman arcades and chancel arch. It has a 16th-century tower, and late Gothic additions include an attractive 19th-century chancel. There are marble monuments and fragments of mural paintings.

**Charney Bassett** *Berks.*                   *546Ec*
CHURCH OF ST PETER This tiny church, originally 12th century, stands near the local manor house. There is a Norman south doorway with a tympanum showing a man holding two griffins. Rebuilding took place in the 15th century and there is an unusual square 17th-century bell-cote.

**Charterhouse** *Surrey*                      *542Ae*
The school moved here from London in 1872. The buildings, by P. C. Hardwick, make the most complete Victorian group in the area; the skyline is a barrage of steeples, and the lofty chapel was built in the 1920's by Sir Giles Gilbert Scott.

**Chartwell** *Kent*                           *542Cf*
The former country home of Sir Winston Churchill (1874–1965), now kept as a memorial to him with many souvenirs of his eventful life. The grounds include a fine rose garden.

**Chasleton House** *Oxon.*                     *546Ed*
Robert Catesby, a conspirator in the Gunpowder Plot, once owned this fine Jacobean manor house which, like many great houses of the area, also has associations with the Civil War. The house was built in 1603 by Walter Jones; it is unaltered, and an inventory made in 1633 reveals that much of the original furniture survives. The rooms also contain fine ceilings, panelling, glass and tapestries. The gardens, laid out *c.* 1700, are famous for their ornamental hedges clipped into fantastic shapes.

**Chatelherault Lodge** *Lanarks.*             *561Je*
An 18th-century mansion designed by William Adam; it stands on wooded slopes above the R. Avon opposite Cadzow Castle.

**Chatham** *Kent*                             *542Df*
MUSEUM OF THE CORPS OF ROYAL ENGINEERS The development of military engineering is shown in this museum, which covers the history of the Corps, including its orders, decorations, medals and awards.

**Chatsworth** *Derbys.*                       *552De*
William Talman built this Classical mansion for the 1st Duke of Devonshire in 1687–1707. After he succeeded to the title in 1755 the 4th Duke employed James Paine to build the stables and convert the old kitchen into an entrance hall. During this period landscaping of the park began and the duke had most of the buildings visible from the house destroyed. The 6th Duke made further alterations in 1820–30; his architect was Sir Jeffry Wyatville, who built the orangery and an extension on the north-east side of the house, which includes the ballroom and picture and sculpture galleries. The 6th Duke also completed the destruction of Edensor village and rebuilt it where he could see nothing of it. The house contains fine furniture, pictures, sculpture, books and manuscripts.

The extensive gardens at Chatsworth illustrate four periods of garden design. In 1688 George London, leading garden designer of his day, created a formal garden in the valley of the Derwent, laid out with canals, fountains and an orangery. Parts of this early garden remain and include a canal, with a fountain of Neptune with sea nymphs before the south front of the house. A slightly later addition is the great cascade, designed by Thomas Archer and unequalled in Britain. During the 18th century much of London's garden was destroyed when Capability Brown created a woodland park on the banks of the Derwent. Early in the 19th century Joseph Paxton transformed the then neglected gardens into a showplace, building huge but since-destroyed conservatories which were said to be his prototypes for the Crystal Palace. He planted rare conifers, made the large rockery and designed the Emperor fountain which throws a water jet 276 ft high. The modern herbaceous borders and the fine rose garden were laid out in the 20th century. (See pp. 132–3.)

**Chawton** *Hants.*                541He
JANE AUSTEN'S HOME Jane Austen lived in this house from 1809 to 1817, and here she wrote *Emma* and *Persuasion*. The house is now a museum containing the personal effects and other relics of the authoress.

**Chearsley** *Bucks.*                547Gd
CHURCH OF ST NICHOLAS In a pretty setting an unspoilt village church with a 13th-century nave and chancel and a west tower. There is a Norman font, a brass of 1462, box-pews and an 18th-century west gallery. The church is worth seeing, as it seems to have escaped 19th-century restoration.

**Checkendon** *Oxon.*                546Fb
CHURCH OF SS PETER AND PAUL The wall-paintings in this Norman church show how Christ and the Apostles were imagined in the 14th century. The church has post-Norman additions, an apsed chancel that is higher than the nave, and a west tower.

**Checkley** *Staffs.*                552Cd
CHURCH OF ST MARY AND ALL SAINTS An impressive church dating from the Norman period, with later enlargements. There is some medieval stained glass with heraldry and figures, as well as alabaster effigies, screen, stalls and a Norman font. There are the remains of Saxon crosses in the churchyard.

**Cheddar** *Som.*                540Cf
GOUGH'S CAVE This cave was occupied during the last phase of the Ice Age, and excavation revealed large quantities of flint and bone implements and ornaments, as well as much food debris. A burial of this period was also found and this is preserved in the museum on the site. The uppermost layers of the cave floor contained evidence of the cave's occupation in Iron Age and Romano-British times.

**Chedworth** *Glos.*                546Dd
CHURCH OF ST ANDREW Not far from the famous Roman villa of Chedworth, the church conceals its Norman origins on the outside by a fine range of Perpendicular windows. Inside, the north nave arcade and the font with its interlacing arcades are both Norman; the pulpit, of carved stone, is 15th century; and the nave roof is late Gothic.

**Chedworth Villa** *Glos.*                546Dd
This is one of the best preserved Roman villas in the country. Many of the original walls stand several feet high and these have been extended and

PIERCE *Monument to Lady Warburton*

*Edward Pierce was the most sophisticated English exponent of the baroque style; much of his work was done for Sir Christopher Wren. Several monuments reflect his style, but none is certainly by Pierce, except for this one, for which his drawing exists in the Victoria and Albert Museum. The monument was probably begun in or soon after 1693, when Lady Warburton died, and finished after Pierce's death by the Dutch sculptor John Nost. The dramatic motif of a skeleton holding up a shroud was probably inspired by French tombs. (Church of St John the Baptist, Chester)*

roofed so that the buildings may be entered. On the north side is the wing where, in later Roman days, Cotswold wool was processed. The many finds from the site are displayed in a small museum.

**Chelmsford** *Essex*                548Bc
CATHEDRAL Made the cathedral in 1913, the Cathedral Church of St Mary has a 15th-century west tower, with spirelet of 1749, and a south porch containing a 17th-century library in an upper room. Much work dates from the 19th century and there are monuments from the 16th to 18th centuries.

**Chelsworth** *Suffolk*                548Ce
One of the prettiest villages in Suffolk, on the R. Brett. A two-arched bridge crosses the river, and there are attractive timber-framed thatched houses; the Grange is dated 1694 and the rectory was built in the late 18th century.

**Chenies** *Bucks.*                547Hc
CHURCH OF ST MICHAEL Rebuilt in the 15th century and again in the 19th, St Michael's has some interesting fittings—Norman font, 15th- and 16th-century brasses—but is famous for the Russell family tombs in the Bedford Chapel, built 1556. Monuments range from one of the 15th century to a member of the Cheyne family, through elaborate 17th- and 18th-century sculpture, to one to the 9th Duke of Bedford (d. 1891). Though not open to the public except by permission, which can be obtained from the Bedford Estate Offices, London, the chapel is visible through glass screens.

## SIR WINSTON CHURCHILL
### THE ARCHITECT OF VICTORY

'YOU HAVE BEEN SO FAITHFUL AND SO LOVING TO US, YOU HAVE FOUGHT SO STOUTLY FOR US, YOU HAVE BEEN SO HEARTY IN COUNSELLING OF US THAT WE SHALL NEVER FORGET YOUR FAVOUR TOWARDS US'. This tribute to Churchill appears in an illuminated book given him by Members of the House of Commons on his 80th birthday. The book is on view at Chartwell in Kent, his home for 37 years and now open to the public. Churchill was more than 50 years in Parliament and his fighting orations delivered as Prime Minister during the Second World War rank among treasures of the 20th century. His second enduring interest was writing and he won the Nobel Prize for Literature for his four volume work *Marlborough, His Life and Times*. First editions of this and his other works are on view at his home at Chartwell.

PORTRAIT BY WALTER SICKERT *painted in 1927 w Churchill was Chancellor of the Exchequer. At this he wrote 'The World Crisis', a personal account of First World War. (National Portrait Gallery)*

SCHOOLBOY LETTER *written by Churchill from Harrow School to his mother. Churchill made little headway scholastically and said 'Examinations were a great trial to me. The subjects which were dearest to the examiners were invariably those I fancied least.' But failure did not quell his spirit and it is recorded that companions would chase him round the bathing pool until he was out of breath, in a desperate attempt to stop him talking. (Library of Harrow School)*

DETAIL FROM 'DISTANT VIEW OF VENICE' *painted by Churchill and presented to Harrow School in 1966 by Mrs Churchill. His interest in painting began with annexation of his children's water-colour boxes, and developed into a passion. 'If it weren't for painting I couldn't live, I couldn't bear the strain of things', he said.*

GARTER ROBES *belonging to Sir Winston Churchill and Garter Star worn by his ancestor the 1st Duke of Marlborough. Churchill was created Knight of the Garter when he was Prime Minister in 1955. He retired from Office two years later at the age of 80. (Chartwell)*

MODEL OF MULBERRY HARBOUR inset into the library wall at Chartwell. 'He has at least a hundred ideas a day,' said President Roosevelt, 'of which four are good.' This idea is an artificial harbour which was towed across the Channel after D-Day and named Port Arromanches.

WALL AT CHARTWELL demonstrating Churchill's skill as a bricklayer. When invited to join the Union, Churchill sent a cheque for 5s. for registration as an 'adult apprentice'.

DESK with box for cigars (he smoked 3000 a year) and busts of Napoleon and Nelson with family photographs. (Chartwell)

BOER WAR POSTER for Churchill's capture, dead or alive, describing the escaped War Correspondent as '25 years old, about 5 ft 8 in. tall, indifferent build, walks with a forward stoop, pale appearance, red brownish hair, talks through his nose and cannot pronounce the letter 's' properly'. (Chartwell)

FIRST WORLD WAR TANK Derided in 1914, tanks and Churchill's vision led to the army's first decisive victory in 1917. (Hatfield Park, Herts.)

CHURCHILL'S GRAVE in the quiet churchyard at Blaydon. It is within view of Blenheim Palace, where the room he was born in may be seen.

**Chepstow** *Mon.* *546Ac*

CASTLE The Norman fortress, on a cliff above the R. Wye, was a centre of fighting during the Civil War, in 1645; in 1648 it was confiscated by Parliament and used as a prison until 1660. It was built by William Fitz-Osborn in 1067 as a defence for the Roman road leading to South Wales, and was rebuilt and extended by the Clare family in the 13th century. Now a ruin, it has four courtyards dominated by a keep (40 ft high) and surrounded by thick curtain walls, strengthened by towers. The entrance gate-house has two drum towers with a portcullis chamber between.

CHURCH OF ST MARY Formerly a large Norman church with a central tower, but this fell in 1700. The present west tower dates from 1706. There are Norman nave arcades, and the monuments include one to the Earl of Worcester (*d.* 1549), with canopy and reclining figures, and two of the 18th century by James and Thomas Paty, of Bristol. The 17th-century organ came from Gloucester Cathedral.

**Cherry Willingham** *Lincs.* *553Ge*

CHURCH OF SS PETER AND PAUL A small mid-18th-century building with an octagonal lantern at the west end. It has a little apse, and a flat ceiling. In the chancel is a good contemporary reredos

**Chester** *Cheshire* *551Je*

No city in Britain is richer in archaeological and architectural treasures than Chester, which has preserved to this day the walls built in Roman occupation times. It was originally the fortress site of the 20th Legion, the town being known then (*c.* AD 70) as Deva, and it became a major trading port. The Romans withdrew *c.* AD 400, and the prosperous city fell prey to marauding Danes and Saxons to such an extent that it was virtually derelict by 900. The Norman conquerors reached Chester *c.* 1070, and its fortunes revived so that by the 13th century it had again become a ship trading centre, a port serving Scotland, Ireland, France and Spain. The last Norman earl died in 1237, and the earldom passed to the Crown: the eldest son of the reigning monarch now enjoys the title of Earl of Chester. In the 14th century began the Mystery Plays and pageants for which the city became famous. Henry VIII granted a charter in 1541 and made Chester a bishopric.

By the 15th century the Dee began to silt up, and gradually the seaborne trade died. Impoverished by this natural action, further disasters came with fighting in the Civil War. But throughout this chequered history, the Roman walls remained virtually intact. They extend in a 2 mile circuit, and give a vivid reminder of what a medieval fortified town was like. In the Middle Ages several towers and gates to the walls were made: the most important of these was at Eastgate, now astride a main thoroughfare and crowned with an anachronistic clock that commemorates Queen Victoria's diamond jubilee (1897). King Charles's Tower, on the site of the north-east corner of the Roman fortress, retains a medieval appearance after restoration in 1913 and in 1958. From it Charles I is said to have watched the defeat of his forces at Rowton Heath in 1645. The tower now houses an exhibition devoted to the Civil War. The massive Water Tower at the north-west angle of the walls was originally New Tower, built in 1322 by John de Helpston, a mason, for £100. Newgate is modern—it was opened in 1938—but just east of it is the site of a Roman amphitheatre, believed to be the largest in Britain with dimensions of 314 ft by 286 ft, and with an arena measuring 190 ft by 162 ft. The most distinctive medieval feature of the city is The Rows. These are double-level walkways with a continuous line of balconies, and with shops at street and first-floor levels. The Rows are unique and were certainly in being in the 14th century. Throughout the city are splendid Tudor and Elizabethan buildings, the richest example being Bishop Lloyd House. This divine was Bishop of Chester 1604-15; his brother David was mayor 1593-4. Stanley Palace in Nicholas Street is a magnificent half-timbered house built in 1591.

ABBEY SQUARE Opposite the Victorian town hall (1869), and entered through a massive gateway built 1377, Abbey Square was originally the outer court of the Abbey of St Werburgh, and the Chester Mystery Plays were enacted at the gateway.

CASTLE Originally a timber structure of *c.* 1069, the castle was given stone walls and towers by Henry III. It retained its medieval appearance until 1789 when the battlements and defensive walls were removed to be replaced by a severe group of buildings erected 1789-1813. Here is the Regimental Museum of the Cheshire Regiment.

CATHEDRAL A minster existed on the site in the 10th century to hold the remains of St Werburgh (a Mercian princess who died in 707). In 1093 the status was changed by Hugh Lupus, Earl of Chester, a Norman who, with the aid of St Anselm, founded an abbey of Benedictine monks. The abbey was dissolved in 1540, and the cathedral came into being in 1541 as a bishopric. The lay-out of the monastery buildings has hardly changed over the centuries: it still has its consistory court, baptistry, cloisters, chapter house—impressive structures all with superb carvings. A grotesque figure known as the Chester Imp is in the north clerestory of the nave.

CHESHIRE REGIMENT MUSEUM Items associated with the Regiment, including standards and other material captured by General Sir Charles Napier in India in the 1840's, are exhibited in Chester Castle.

CHURCH OF ST JOHN THE BAPTIST This large and impressive Norman building would have been a cathedral, had the See not moved to Coventry. The nave has fine Norman pillars and arcades; the east end is in ruins. In the south aisle a monument, *c.* 1693, shows a shrouded skeleton. (See p. 135.)

GROSVENOR MUSEUM (1885) A fine collection of Anglo-Saxon coins, including the Willoughby Gardner Collection of coins minted in Chester.

**Chesterfield** *Derbys.* *552De*

CHURCH OF ST MARY AND ALL SAINTS The twisted spire is 228 ft high; it is made of lead-covered wood, which has warped through the ages, and caused the curious twist.

**Chester-le-Street** *Durham* *558Cg*

CHURCH OF SS MARY AND CUTHBERT The west tower has an octagonal upper stage, and a spire, and is of *c.* 1400. There is a series of 14 effigies of ancestors of Lord Lumley, who brought them here, or had them carved, *c.* 1590.

**Chesterton** *Hunts.* *547Hg*

CHURCH OF ST MICHAEL Much of the church is of the 14th century, to which has been added an 18th-century chancel. There is a good 17th-century monument with kneeling figures at a prayer-desk, and a host of mourning children.

**Chetwode** *Bucks.* *546Fd*

CHURCH OF SS MARY AND NICHOLAS The body of the church was once the chancel of an Augustinian priory church of *c.* 1250. There is a fine east end with lancet windows, and the 13th- and 14th-century stained glass in the chancel is matched by early Victorian glass in the east window. The piscina and sedilia have dog-tooth carving.

**Chevening Manor** *Kent*                  *542Cf*
A country mansion in Regency style, home of the
7th Earl Stanhope (1880–1967), Knight of the
Garter. In the print gallery is a valuable collection
of portraits of contemporaries of the 5th Earl. The
manor stands in extensive grounds with fine
gardens.

**Chewton Mendip** *Som.*                  *540Cf*
CHURCH OF ST MARY MAGDALENE An originally
Norman church, of which there are still remains
among the later additions. These include the
imposing 16th-century tower. Inside are fragments of medieval glass, and recumbent 14th-
century effigies on a monument.

**Chicheley** *Bucks.*                  *547Ge*
CHURCH OF ST LAURENCE The nave and north
aisle are 14th century, the central tower 15th
century, but the chancel was rebuilt *c.* 1708 and is
all in good Classical style. The architect (perhaps
Thomas Archer) may have built Chicheley Hall
near by. The rood under the tower arch is by Sir
Ninian Comper, 1904. There are two interesting
monuments, the earlier of 1576 with a bizarre
representation of a naked corpse, and caryatids on
either side. The other, 1635, has two kneeling
figures under a canopy.

CHICHESTER CATHEDRAL
*The Raising of Lazarus*

*The Norman cathedral at Chichester was founded on
its present site about 1080. Before that the bishop's
church had been at Selsey, and it was refounded on the
site of a Saxon church at Chichester, a city dating from
Roman times, in accordance with William I's policy
that cathedrals should be moved to the centres of
population. In 1829, two 12th-century panels of
Purbeck stone with scenes from the legend of Lazarus
were found built into the eastern piers of the crossing
of the cathedral. Now re-erected in the south aisle of the
choir, they are perhaps the greatest works of Romanesque monumental sculpture in England. The two
panels are not the work of the same artist—one is more
sophisticated; the other, from which this detail is taken,
is more expressive—but they are both from the same
workshop, and must be the only two surviving sections
from a series. No other sculptures from this workshop
are known, and the panels, because they date from
1125 to 1150, are exceptional for their strong
emotional content. The deeply drilled eyes would
originally have been inlaid with metal.*

**Chichester** *Sussex*                  *541Jd*
A Roman, medieval and Georgian city, Chichester is the administrative centre for West Sussex.
The plan of the Roman town is still evident in the
two long, straight streets that cross at right angles
in the city centre. At the crossing stands the market
cross, one of the most elaborate structures of its
kind in England, erected by the bishop in 1501 to
give shelter to country people selling their produce. The cathedral stands informally against West
Street, not set like most cathedrals within a close.
In the bishop's palace, the chapel and walls of the
great kitchen are 13th century, and the gateway is
14th century. Half the palace is now used by the
bishop and half by a theological college. Westgate
House is dated 1696 and attributed to Wren; it
now houses the county library. But Chichester is
the stateliest town in Sussex because of its Georgian
town houses. The finest of them are at the far end
of West Street, and especially between East Street
and South Street. Best of all is Pallant (or Dodo)
House of *c.* 1712, with dodos on the gate piers. The
Council House was built in 1731; James Wyatt
added the east wing in 1783, and set in the outer
wall by the entrance is a Roman inscription dedi-
cating a temple to Neptune and Minerva.
CATHEDRAL The present cathedral at Chichester
was founded *c.* 1080, and is still substantially the
same building as that begun under Bishop Ralph
de Luffa, who became bishop in 1091. Considerable additions and alterations were made to the
church after a fire in 1187, and changes after that
date included the addition of the central spire to the
earlier tower and the building of a separate bell-
tower in the 15th century. The bell-tower still
stands to the west of the cathedral, but the central
tower collapsed in 1861 and was replaced in 1861–6
by the existing replica. Luffa's building, particularly the nave and choir, bears a striking resemblance to William the Conqueror's foundation of
St Stephen's at Caen, although the stone itself came
from the Isle of Wight and was not imported from
Caen, as was the usual practice at that time. To the
east is the retrochoir, part of the late 12th- and early
13th-century building; the use of shafts and
columns of Purbeck stone in this building was
inspired by the new east end of Canterbury Cathedral which was rebuilt, after a fire, in 1184.
CITY MUSEUM In an 18th-century corn store,
converted into a museum in 1964, collections
devoted to local history and archaeology are on
view; they include Romano-British pottery and
coins, medieval pottery, and a set of stocks on
wheels which used to be pulled around the city
cross in the 18th and early 19th centuries while
onlookers threw refuse and abuse at the offender
locked in them. There is also 17th-century
furniture from the Grange, a demolished house in
the city. Two galleries are devoted to the Royal
Sussex Regiment. Exhibits there tell the story of
the Regiment from the time it was raised in 1701,
and include a diorama of the battlefield of Quebec
(1759) where the Regiment fought. Colours,
drums, portraits and uniforms are also on view.
CORPS OF ROYAL MILITARY POLICE MUSEUM The
first Provost Marshal of the British Army was
appointed in the 14th century. This museum portrays the history and exploits of Provost Marshals
since then, and of the Corps of Royal Military
Police, and contains uniforms and equipment,
medals, flags and documents.
GUILDHALL MUSEUM The building was originally
built in the 13th century as a chapel for Grey Friars
and was later used as a guildhall. It contains a
collection of Romano-British relics, including
pottery from the Roman cemetery at Chichester.

**139**

**Chiddingfold** *Surrey*         *542Ae*
A handsome, spacious village. The church faces a pond, a triangular green and a row of Georgian and tile-hung cottages. To the east is the red-brick manor house, 1762, standing in a dell.

**Chiddingstone** *Kent*         *542Ce*
The whole village belongs to the National Trust, and has a fine group of 16th- and 17th-century half-timbered houses. To the west there is a view across a lake to Chiddingstone Castle, built *c.* 1800. CHURCH OF ST MARY THE VIRGIN Dates from the 13th century, and was later enlarged; it is now quite sizeable, with a Perpendicular west tower, and faces a row of spectacular timbered houses. There is some original stone carving, and a Jacobean font, cover and pulpit.

**Chiddingstone Castle** *Kent*       *542Ce*
An 18th-century restoration of a much earlier manor house, in Gothic style. It contains Stuart and Jacobean pictures and furnishings; an Ancient Egypt collection; Japanese lacquer, and weapons; and Buddha figures. In the grounds are caves and a lake.

**Chilcomb** *Hants.*         *541Ge*
CHURCH OF ST ANDREW A lonely downland church with much Norman work—windows, doorways and chancel arch. The font is in the 18th-century Gothic style, and there is tilework.

**Chilham** *Kent*         *542Ff*
Village squares are rare in South-east England. Chilham is especially delightful, on the top of a hill reached via narrow lanes which lead into the tiny square.

**Chilham Castle** *Kent*         *542Ff*
The gardens and park (with a heronry) overlooking the Stour Valley are open to the public. The house, built in 1616 by Inigo Jones round the keep of a 12th-century Norman castle, is not open.

**Chillingham** *Northld.*       *562Fc*
CHURCH OF ST PETER Originally Norman, there is a crypt below the chancel. Inside is a magnificently decorated monument, *c.* 1443, to Sir Ralph Gray, with 14 small figures of saints in niches.

**Chillington Hall** *Staffs.*       *552Bb*
The seat of the Giffard family since the 12th century, where Charles II rested during his flight after the Battle of Worcester. The house was rebuilt in Georgian style, the south front in 1724 and the rest, including the main front, hall and saloons, to designs by Sir John Soane in 1785.

**Chilworth** *Hants.*         *541Gd*
CHURCH OF ST DENYS Built in a Gothic style in 1812, with transepts; there are lancet windows all down the nave, beneath a plaster vault with roof-bosses. The pews are contemporary with the church, but the font is Norman. There is a medallion of the sculptor R. C. Lucas, carved by himself in 1840.

**Chippenham** *Cambs.*        *548Bf*
A splendid example of a squire's model village with attractive cottages and larger houses, many dating from *c.* 1800. There is a good red-brick school of 1714 and a range of cottages by Professor Sir Albert Richardson. Chippenham Park Mansion, rebuilt in 1886, replaced the earlier 17th-century mansion of the Earl of Orford.

**Chippenham** *Wilts.*        *540Eg*
A stone-built town of the Cotswolds, on the R. Avon, with many fine houses. The timbered town hall dates from the 15th century. There is also a medieval bridge with 20 arches.

WROUGHT-IRON GATES
AT CHIRK CASTLE

*There was a story that these gates were the work of a local smith and his daughter, but in fact they were made by two brothers—Robert and John Davies, Welsh smiths who did most of their work between 1702 and 1755, and who were strongly influenced by the French smith, Jean Tijou. The gates were made for Sir Robert Myddleton in 1718–33, and were probably the brothers' first commission. The work is ambitious; the gates are enclosed by two large square piers of wrought iron, each crowned with a lead wolf representing the Myddleton coat of arms.*

**Chipping Campden** *Glos.*       *546De*
CHURCH OF ST JAMES An imposing church, mainly of the 15th century, with a fine west tower; the chancel is of the 14th century. There are brasses, a 15th-century brass lectern, and several 16th-century monuments with effigies, one of them by Joshua Marshall.
MARKET HALL A fine arcaded Jacobean building with pointed gables.

**Chipping Norton** *Oxon.*       *546Ed*
CHURCH OF ST MARY THE VIRGIN This is one of the largest churches in Oxfordshire. The south porch is hexagonal and two storeys high. The nave is clerestoried, and there is a west tower. Many brasses, and 16th-century monuments with recumbent effigies.

**Chipstead** *Surrey*        *542Bf*
CHURCH OF ST MARGARET A 13th-century cruciform church. Large, and with a central tower, it has late 19th-century additions by R. Norman Shaw. The screen is 15th century, the pulpit 17th, and fragments of medieval glass remain.

**Chirk Castle** *Denb.*        *551Hd*
Sir Thomas Seymour, who married Henry VIII's widow, Catherine Parr, and Robert Dudley, Elizabeth I's favourite, were granted this Border castle, which was in the gift of the Crown for 280 years from its completion in 1310 during the reign of Edward II. The castle, with round towers and battlements, has been lived in continuously ever since; the present owner's ancestor, Sir Thomas Myddelton, acquired it in 1595. Charles I stayed here in 1645. The interior has tapestries and portraits, and decorations and furnishings of the 17th-19th centuries. In the grounds are traces of Offa's Dyke.

**Chislehampton** *Oxon.*       *546Fc*
CHURCH OF ST KATHERINE Urns decorate the roof-line of this pretty, bell-coted little building of 1763. The pews, pulpit, font and other fittings are contemporary with the church.

**Chittlehampton** *Devon*                    *539Gf*
CHURCH OF ST URITH (OR HIERITHA) The saint to
whom the church is dedicated was local, murdered
by pagans. The church is largely late Perpendicular
with a 115 ft high west tower, a stone pulpit,
original wood ceilings, and monuments with
recumbent or reclining figures of the 17th century.
A brass dates from the late 15th century.

**Cholmondeley** *Cheshire*                    *552Ad*
CHURCH OF ST NICHOLAS The chapel of Cholmondeley Castle, originally 13th century, but
rebuilt in the early 18th century. The chancel roof
is probably late 15th century, and there is a good
screen of 1655 with stalls, pulpit and other furnishings of about the same date. A large family pew
extends across the west end.

**Cholsey** *Berks.*                    *546Fb*
CHURCH OF ST MARY A large flint and stone
church standing isolated near the Thames. It is
basically Norman, with interesting architectural
details; the interior was extended in the 13th
century, and the Early English chancel has two
19th-century windows by C. E. Kempe.

**Chorley** *Lancs.*                    *552Ag*
ASTLEY HALL A large mansion, built in 1666. The
great hall is glazed on three sides and incorporates a
massive, original, shuffleboard table. The drawing-room ceiling is so festooned with plasterwork
that it resembles a suspended grotto. The house
contains a collection of fine furniture, pottery,
tapestries and pictures.

**Christchurch** *Hants.*                    *540Fc*
CASTLE The 12th-century keep, now ruined,
stands on a well preserved motte, or artificial
mound; its walls are nearly 10 ft thick.
PRIORY Originally built *c.* 1100 by Ralph Flambard, Bishop of Durham, but added to and completed in 1485–1509. The abbey itself was dissolved
by Henry VIII, but the priory is still as it was
originally built (though part of it has been
restored); the surrounding Norman fortifications
were demolished in the Civil War. Carvings in the
choir are probably 200 years older than those in
Westminster Abbey.
PRIORY CHURCH A magnificent Norman church,
with a 15th-century tower and choir. There is a
fine mid-14th-century reredos with a sculptured
Tree of Jesse, several misericords and many
monuments, including John Flaxman's famous
group to Viscountess Fitzharris of *c.* 1815, and
H. Weekes's monument of 1854 to the poet
Shelley.
RED HOUSE MUSEUM AND ART GALLERY The main
part of the Red House dates from *c.* 1760, when it
was built as a workhouse; the art gallery is housed
in the former stables and coach house, built in
1887. The museum concentrates mainly on displays of the geology, natural history, archaeology
and history of the region. The archaeological section includes material from the Bronze Age (the
Deverel Rimbury phase), from a late Palaeolithic
'Reindeer Hunters' camp site at Hengistbury, and
from the port and settlement which existed there
from the Early Iron Age to Roman times. Special
displays include the Kimmeridge Shale industry—
a prehistoric luxury trade making personal adornments—the Kimmeridge ritual 'beheaded burial',
and pottery from Roman kilns in the New Forest.
An example of local industry is seen in the making
of minute Fusee chains—used in the compensating
mechanism of Verge watch movements and
widely exported—confined almost solely to this
district throughout the 19th century. Smuggling
relics and 19th-century local domestic and dairy
equipment can also be seen, including an original
open hearth fire-place and equipment. Other
Victorian items include lighting, smoking, letter-
writing and needlework materials. Children's toys
and games are on display, and dolls are shown in a
Victorian setting which includes a selection from
the extensive Druitt Collection of 18th- and 19th-
century fashion plates. Some 19th-century costumes and accessories are also shown. The natural
history section includes fossils from the Tertiary
deposits at Barton, and a collection of stuffed birds.
The gardens include roses and a herb garden.

**Christ's Hospital** *Sussex*                    *542Ae*
Often called the Blue Coat School because of the
traditional long, dark blue gown with girdle still
worn by the boy scholars, this school moved here
from London in 1902. It was founded by Edward
VI in 1552 in the buildings of the Grey Friars
monastery in Newgate Street, in the City of
London. A painting, 85 ft by 14 ft, by Antonio
Verrio (*c.* 1639–1707) commemorating the
foundation of the Royal Mathematical School of
Christ's Hospital by Charles II in 1672, hangs in the
school dining-hall.

**Church Crookham** *Hants.*                    *541Jf*
ROYAL CORPS OF TRANSPORT REGIMENTAL
MUSEUM The museum contains items of military
interest covering the period since the formation of
the 'Royal Waggoners' in 1794. The exhibits
include uniforms, manuscripts, etchings and
photographs, as well as items such as belts, buckles
and badges.
    Housed separately from the museum is the
Central Medal Collection of the Corps, which
includes most of the examples of campaign medals
awarded to members of the Corps from the Peninsular War to the present day. (The museum is due
to be rehoused in Aldershot in 1969.)

**Church Eaton** *Staffs.*                    *552Bc*
CHURCH OF ST EDITHA A Norman church, with a
spire added to the tower in the 15th century. The
east window is Gothic, almost filling the wall.
Most of the glass in the church is 19th century,
some showing scenes from the life of Christ.

**Church Hanborough** *Oxon.*                    *546Ed*
CHURCH OF SS PETER AND PAUL Between the lintel
and arch of the south door to this fine church sits St
Peter, holding the keys to the Kingdom of
Heaven. This carving on the tympanum, and the
whole doorway, is Norman workmanship. The
church itself contains later additions to the original
Norman fabric—the Perpendicular west tower,
for example, with its tall spire—and inside is a
14th-century carved font. Amongst its furnishings
are screens, brasses and a carved pulpit.

**Church Stowe** *Northants.*                    *546Ff*
CHURCH OF SS PETER AND PAUL The church is
interesting externally for the Saxon west tower,
and a Norman doorway; there is much later work,
internally renewed. The outstanding monuments
include a cross-legged knight of the 13th century,
Nicholas Stone's monument to Lady Carey, with
a lovely marble effigy of *c.* 1620, and the strange
monument to Dr Turner (*d.* 1714), President of
Corpus Christi College at Oxford. By Thomas
Stayner, it has two life-size figures, one standing
on a celestial globe and the other on a terrestrial
globe. There is a good tablet of *c.* 1757 in
architectural style by John Middleton.

**Chysauster** *Cornwall*                    *538Ab*
A remarkable Iron Age village, with four pairs of
houses each fronting a village street. Each house is
oval in plan, but the rooms are roughly circular, set

CLANDON PARK

*Clandon was built on land acquired in 1641 by the Onslow family, three of whom became Speakers of the House of Commons. In about 1731 the 2nd Lord Onslow commissioned the Venetian architect Giacomo Leoni to build him a new house. Leoni's house is in Classical style. The hall is a single cube, 40 ft by 40 ft*

*by 40 ft. In it are two chimney-pieces, each with a relief carved by Michael Rysbrack, one of the foremost sculptors of the early 18th century. One relief shows the goddess Diana, and the other is a representation of a sacrifice to Bacchus. There is also an ornate plaster ceiling, probably the work of G. Artari.*

in thick walls and all opening to a central courtyard. Now open to the sky, the rooms were apparently roofed with corbelled stone or with thatch, though the courtyards were open. When excavated, querns, pottery and other domestic debris, together with hearths, were found lying on the paved floors. Each house also had a stone-fenced back garden.

**Cilgerran Castle** *Pemb.*                544De
The ruin of a castle standing on a promontory between the Teifi and Plysgog rivers, which was painted by Richard Wilson in the 18th century, and later by Peter de Wint and Turner. The Normans first established a castle here during the 12th century, but the remaining towers and walls date from the 13th century.

**Cirencester** *Glos.*                546Dc
During the Roman occupation, Cirencester, then called Corinium Dobunnorum, served as the administrative centre for a large part of the West Country. The Roman city was the second largest in Britain when its defences, enclosing 240 acres, were set up in the 2nd century. When the Romans left, their town was destroyed piecemeal by Saxon raids, and now only fragments remain. After the Norman invasion, William Fitz-Osborn built a castle, which had disappeared by the end of the Middle Ages, and in 1539 the formerly rich abbey was dissolved. In the 19th century the once thriving wool trade gave place to a considerable market for corn and cheese. In Cirencester Park the 1st Earl Bathurst rebuilt the original Elizabethan house in 1718, and laid out the great park in 1704–35. The house is not open to view, but the public may walk or ride in the park.
CHURCH OF ST JOHN THE BAPTIST It was originally Norman, but as a result of considerable additions during the 14th and 15th centuries by rich local wool merchants, it is now regarded as one of the most beautiful Perpendicular churches in England. There is a three-storey south porch completely covered in Perpendicular tracery, and a west tower. Impressive inside is the high clerestoried nave and the window over the chancel arch; and there is elaborate ornamental stonework over the nave and aisle. Also worth noting is the 15th-century pulpit (one of the few pre-Reformation pulpits in the county), the fan-vaulting in St

Katharine's Chapel, and the monuments in the Lady Chapel, one to Lord Bathurst (*c.* 1776) by Joseph Nollekens.
CORINIUM MUSEUM The museum gets its title from the Roman name for Cirencester, and its exhibits are concerned with that period of British history. Provincial Roman sculpture, architectural detail, mosaic work and domestic items are on display.

**Cissbury Ring** *Sussex*                542Ad
The site of a prehistoric hill-fort of the Iron Age, occupied from 300 BC to 59 BC. It was a centre of flint mining in the early Neolithic period and mine shafts are still visible.

**Clackmannan** *Clack.*                562Af
CLACKMANNAN TOWER On a hill to the west of the town, the tower is 79 ft high, of 15th-century origin with 17th-century additions, and was reputedly built by Robert de Bruce.

**Clandon Park** *Surrey*                542Af
A Classical mansion built by Giacomo Leoni for the 2nd Lord Onslow *c.* 1731–5. It is rectangular in plan, and the roof is hidden behind a balustrade. On the west front is the main entrance, beneath a pediment (and now with a disfiguring porch added during the 19th century). The original gardens were formal, following the fashion of the time, but during the 1770's Capability Brown designed a more fashionable informal arrangement. The house contains splendid plasterwork and rich wallpapers, and fine furniture and pictures.

**Clapham** *Beds.*                547He
CHURCH OF ST THOMAS OF CANTERBURY Noteworthy for its tall Saxon tower, which was incorporated in the Norman church. Inside is a large, 17th-century monument with little *putti*—cherub-like children—one holding a skull.

**Clare** *Suffolk*                548Be
A small ancient town with fragments of a 13th-century shell-keep, part of Gilbert de Clare's castle. The town has houses from all periods, including the Ancient House, *c.* 1473, once the priest's house; the Grove, five-gabled, *c.* 1500, with oriel bracket of huntsmen and hounds; Chapel Cottage or Wentford Chapel, late 12th century; the Bell Hotel, well restored; the Swan Inn; Cliftons, with

splendid 17th-century chimneys; Nethergate Hotel and Stour House, with oversailing upper storey.

CHURCH OF SS PETER AND PAUL A large church, mainly of the 14th to 15th centuries, but with an earlier west tower. There is a Perpendicular font and 17th-century woodwork.

## Claremont Surrey                    542Af

The former house on this site was built by Sir John Vanbrugh for the 1st Duke of Newcastle. It was bought by Clive of India in 1768 and he replaced it with the present Palladian mansion, started in 1770 and built to designs by Capability Brown. The house, on high ground, comprises two floors above a basement. It is rectangular in plan, and the hall is approached by a flight of steps beneath a portico of Corinthian columns, which rises to the full height of the house on the southern side. Henry Holland, assisted by John Soane, was largely responsible for the interior decoration. During the present century the decoration has been much altered, so that not much of the work of Brown, Holland and Soane remains. Claremont is now a girls' school.

## Claverley Shrops.                    546Bg

CHURCH OF ALL SAINTS Founded by Roger de Montgomery, William the Conqueror's cousin (d. 1094). The fine north arcade and the carved font are Norman, but most of the rest of the church was rebuilt between the 13th and 15th centuries. Most important is a large wall-painting in the nave, of c. 1200, showing battling knights on horseback: they represent the Virtues fighting the Vices, and are reminiscent of those in the Bayeux Tapestry. The chancel roof is post-Reformation (1601) and there are two monuments, of 1448 and 1558, the latter with children as the mourners.

## Claverton Manor:                    540Df
## The American Museum in Britain Som.

This mansion contains furnished rooms in the style of 17th- to 19th-century American homesteads, brought complete from across the Atlantic. Also on show are examples of American Indian art, Spanish Colonial rooms from New Mexico and a folk art collection. In the grounds are a reproduction of part of George Washington's flower garden from Mount Vernon, a Conestoga (covered) wagon, a herb garden and herb shop. A maritime section covers aspects of immigration into America, sea battles, the whaling trade and the China traders. The house, in 55 acres of park above the Avon Valley, was built in 1820 in Greek Revival style and was opened as a museum in 1961.

## Claybrooke Leics.                    552Ea

CHURCH OF ST PETER This basically 14th-century church contains a contemporary chancel, and a Perpendicular nave. The windows have flowing tracery, and there are fragments of medieval stained glass.

## Claydon House Bucks.                    547Gd

The Verney family came into possession of land here in 1471, and the family still lives at Claydon. The 16th-century manor house was enlarged by the 2nd Earl of Verney in the middle of the 18th century. Parts of the house were demolished in the mid-19th century, when a new south front was built. In the extensive grounds with fine gardens is a Gothic pavilion which probably dates from the 18th century. Florence Nightingale was a sister of Parthenhope, Lady Verney, and often stayed at Claydon; her bedroom is on view.

## Claypotts Castle Angus                    566Ea

The castle was built between 1569 and 1588. The tower-house plan was unusual—a rectangular

## THE CHINESE ROOM AT CLAYDON HOUSE

*When the 2nd Earl of Verney began the rebuilding of Claydon House in about 1750 his ambition was to outdo Stowe, the home of his rivals the Greville family, in magnificence. The work took nearly 30 years; the architect was Sir Thomas Robinson, and an otherwise unknown Mr Lightfoot designed most of the interior and carved the wooden ceiling of the staircase and north hall. The west front contains a series of magnificent rococo state rooms. Upstairs the Gothic Room has a carved ceiling and next door is the Chinese Room— a riot of English chinoiserie, a style derived originally from imported Chinese porcelain.*

central block with two circular blocks abutting. The central block contains a hall on the first floor, while the extensions contain living accommodation and, on the ground floor, a kitchen. The difficulty of reconciling defence with domestic needs is illustrated by the presence of a gun-port in the back of the kitchen fire-place. The ornament at Claypotts is sparse, but one dormer window has a piece of Italianate decoration over it.

**Cleeve Abbey** *Som.*                             *540Ae*
Founded in 1198, it forms a small but interesting complex of buildings whose main fabric belongs to the 13th century. The church itself has been almost destroyed, but the convent buildings survive in a remarkably complete state. In the late 15th century the refectory was reconstructed, and this medieval hall, with its superb timber roof, is one of the finest surviving in this part of England. Incorporated into the lower floor of the rebuilt refectory are two small sets of rooms, each with its own lavatory or garderobe, which indicate that by the Dissolution in 1537 the monks' dormitory had been split up into cubicles.

**Cleeve Cloud** *Glos.*                            *546Cd*
This Iron Age promontory fort on a Cotswold spur high above the Vale of Severn is small, hardly more than 2 acres in extent. To the west it is adequately protected by the steep slopes of the hill, but on the east it is cut off from the main hill-top by two banks each with an external ditch.

**Clevedon Court** *Som.*                           *540Cg*
Thackeray wrote much of *Vanity Fair* while staying here, and he used the house as a background to his novel *Henry Esmond*. The once-fortified manor house, with additions made in every century since the 12th, has been the home of the Elton family since 1709; it contains the Elton Ware pottery collection and a display of Nailsea glass. The 14th-century chapel is noted for its beautiful window tracery.

**Cley next the Sea** *Norfolk*                     *554Cd*
A picturesque town that was a busy port in the 14th century. It is rich in small, attractive flint houses, some with Dutch gables, and is dominated by a windmill. The old custom house is red brick with Georgian windows. The Maison de Quai has a brick and cobble wall, and a 15th-century doorway.

**Clifton Campville** *Staffs.*                     *552Db*
CHURCH OF ST ANDREW A magnificent, mainly 13th- and 14th-century church, with a tall tower and spire. It has screens, stalls, misericords, remains of wall-paintings, and monuments, including one by J. M. Rysbrack and one by William Behnes.

**Clifton Reynes** *Bucks.*                         *547Ge*
CHURCH OF ST MARY THE VIRGIN Though originally Norman, with a Norman west tower remaining, there were many additions to St Mary's in the 13th to 15th centuries, including the battlemented exterior. Particularly interesting are the 14th-century font with carved figures of the Trinity, the Virgin and saints, and the monuments, with stone and oaken effigies to the Reynes family. One 14th-century tomb chest has little mourners standing round. The tomb of Alexander Small (*d.* 1752) has a terracotta bust by Peter Scheemakers.

**Clipsham** *Rutland*                              *553Gc*
CHURCH OF ST MARY On the edge of a small, well wooded park, St Mary's is large and mainly 14th century, with some 12th-century work. The sturdy west tower has a broach spire of unusual design. Of the original Norman work in the

interior, the font and capitals of the north arcade remain. The window tracery is part of the 14th-century reconstruction.

**Cliveden** *Bucks.*                               *547Hb*
Famous political centre and country home of Lord Astor in the 1930's. This is the third house to be constructed on the site, the great red-brick terrace dating from 1666. The present mansion was built in 1851 by Sir Charles Barry, the architect of the House of Commons; it overlooks the Thames, and in the grounds, designed by Capability Brown, are temples dating from *c.* 1735 by Leoni, and magnificent formal gardens.

**Clodock** *Herefs.*                               *545Jd*
CHURCH OF ST CLODOCK On the edge of the Black Mountains, this church has a Norman nave and chancel arch, a late 17th-century three-decker pulpit and pews, and a west gallery of *c.* 1715.

**Clopton House** *Warks.*                          *546Df*
Begun in Tudor times, altered in the 17th century, this Elizabethan house has associations with Shakespeare and the Gunpowder Plot. Home of the Clopton family, it was remodelled in the 18th century and contains period furniture, and paintings by Reynolds, Romney and others. St Peter's Chapel was built in 1453.

**Clun** *Shrops.*                                  *551Ja*
CHURCH OF ST GEORGE A large church with a massive Norman west tower that has an unusual double pyramid roof. There is more Norman work in the church, but this and work of later centuries was restored by G. E. Street in 1877. The Jacobean pulpit has a tester (horizontal sounding board) and the altar a handsome wood canopy. Outside is a gabled 18th-century lychgate.

**Clyffe Pypard** *Wilts.*                          *546Db*
CHURCH OF ST PETER In a beautiful position on a wooded ridge stands St Peter's, dating mainly from the 15th century (the west tower, nave and aisles with rood and parclose screens are all of that period), but restored by William Butterfield in 1874 when the chancel was rebuilt. There is a Victorian carved font. Among the many monuments is an unusual one by John Deval Junior to a carpenter, dated 1786. The carpenter stands, in white marble, with his tools.

**Clynnog-Fawr** *Caern.*                           *550Ed*
CHURCH OF ST BEUNO This is one of the most impressive churches in North Wales, probably founded by St Beuno (a 7th-century abbot) whose shrine was here. It is a late Perpendicular cruciform building with west tower, joined by a 17th-century passage to St Beuno's Chapel. There is a 16th-century screen and a simple pulpit of *c.* 1700.

**Coalbrookdale** *Shrops.*                         *552Ab*
MUSEUM OF IRONFOUNDING Prominent among the exhibits here, the first centre of iron-casting in Britain, are early castings and some of the first cast-iron wagon rails. There are also early locomotives and stationary steam engines, and other machinery used in the making of iron.

**Coate** *Wilts.*                                  *546Db*
RICHARD JEFFERIES MUSEUM Manuscripts, first editions and personal items of the writer Richard Jefferies (1848–87), are displayed in his birthplace, Coate Farmhouse, together with similar mementoes of another local writer, Alfred Williams.

**Coates-by-the-Stowe** *Lincs.*                    *553Gf*
CHURCH OF ST EDITH A small charming church without aisles. It has a Norman south doorway, font, and a Perpendicular rood screen which still

has its gallery, a great rarity in England. There is a monument of the Commonwealth period to Brian Cook, some fragments of medieval glass, and 15th-century pulpit and bench ends.

## Cobham *Kent* 542Dg
COBHAM HALL The Hall was built in three distinct phases. During the late 16th century it assumed its basic form—a central block with two wings at right angles, each with an octagonal turret. In the mid-18th century the central block was rebuilt, probably by Inigo Jones and John Webb. Further alterations were made at the end of the 18th century by James Wyatt, who also built the mausoleum in the grounds which was never used. At this time Humphry Repton and his son John laid out the grounds and fine gardens. The mansion is now a girls' public school.

## Cochwillan *Caern.* 550Ee
This is probably the best late medieval house in Wales, being built *c.* 1450 by William ap Gruffydd, who later fought at Bosworth and was made High Sheriff for the county for life by Henry VII. The building is used as a barn, but it is possible at times to see the excellent quality of the woodwork, especially the finely carved roof and frieze. There are two-storied parts at each end, separated by wooden partitions; one has been moved and now stands in the middle of the traceried window which would have lit the high table.

## Cockermouth *Cumb.* 557Gf
The ruined castle dates from 1134 and has a good example of an oubliette dungeon—one with entrance only from above by a trap door.
WORDSWORTH HOUSE The house where William Wordsworth and his sister Dorothy were born is preserved and contains relics of them.

## Cockleroy See Bowden Hill and Cockleroy.

## Cogges *Oxon.* 546Ec
CHURCH OF ST MARY The north-west tower is square at the base and octagonal above. Remains of the Norman church include the south doorway and the font. One of the monuments shows a 14th-century lady in a wimple; there are windows with interesting late Decorated tracery, and some medieval glass fragments.

## Coity Castle *Glam.* 545Hb
The ruins of a medieval castle. The 12th-century square keep is surrounded by curtain walls. Later additions include the 13th-century round tower adjoining the great hall, and the 14th-century eastern gate-house. The castle was abandoned and left to decay in the late 16th century.

## Colchester *Essex* 548Cd
There was probably a settlement at Colchester in the 5th century BC, and in the 1st century AD, Cunobelin (Shakespeare's Cymbeline) was king at Camulodunum. Roman invaders occupied Colchester in AD 43 and five years later established a major colony there. In AD 60 the Britons under Queen Boadicea's command revolted against Roman rule, massacred the Roman occupants, and destroyed the temple. In the Dark Ages the Danes frequently raided the town. By *c.* 1085 the Normans had built a castle on and around a former Roman temple. The town's charter was granted by Richard I in 1190. St John's Abbey, of which only the gate-house remains, and St Botolph's Priory, ruined during the Civil War, date from *c.* 1100. The castle keep is now a museum. The Hollytrees Museum, in a Georgian house (1716–18), is the centre for the Essex Archaeological Society.

## TOMBSTONE OF A CENTURION

*One of the finest gravestones from Roman Britain, and possibly the earliest. It commemorates Marcus Favonius Facilis, a centurion of the 20th Legion. Made of Bath stone, the memorial is 6 ft high and was probably carved by a sculptor from the Mediterranean region; it dates from before AD 60, from the military occupation preceding the colonial town of Colchester, for Facilis is not described as a veteran. Traces of plaster on the stone suggest it was once coloured. (Colchester and Essex Museum)*

BOURNE MILL A fishing lodge built in 1591 from material of St John's Abbey, with elaborately stepped and curved Dutch gables. It was later converted into a mill.
CHURCH OF THE HOLY TRINITY A church with a Saxon west tower, and triangular-headed west doorway; its builders made much use of Roman materials.
COLCHESTER AND ESSEX MUSEUM The museum is divided into three parts. Most of the collections are housed in the castle keep, a Norman building of *c.* 1085, constructed on the vaults of the Roman Temple of Claudius, built in AD 50. Here exhibits illustrate local history from the earliest Stone Age to the 17th century; the Roman section includes fine jewellery, coins, pottery, bronzes and statues, glassware, implements and models of Roman Colchester. Items of local crafts, shipping and costume are housed at Hollytrees, a Georgian house near by; exhibits there illustrate local history from the 18th century to the present day. The natural history museum is in the former All Saints' Church; it covers all of Essex and includes a diorama of the Essex marshes.

## WATTS MORTUARY CHAPEL, COMPTON

*An exotic circular chapel, in style part Byzantine, with Tuscan and Norman touches, built in 1896 by a team of amateurs under Mary Watts, wife of the 19th-century artist, George Frederic Watts. After the couple had settled in Compton, Mrs Watts, who had studied art before her marriage, started classes in clay-modelling for local people. Encouraged by the success of the classes, she decided to build the chapel with the help of her pupils, who even made their own*

*bricks. It is 24 ft across with four transepts representing the Circle of Eternity with the Cross of Faith running through it. The outside is plain, but the interior is startling—every inch of walls and vaulting is covered in rich art nouveau decoration, all designed by Mrs Watts with symbolic meaning. Here three winged messengers stand under the Tree of Life. The plaster-work is incised in some places and built up in others to give the effect of light and shade.*

MINORIES A Georgian house, rebuilt in 1776 and now an art gallery; it contains Georgian furniture, pictures, china, 18th-century Colchester clocks, and portraits and drawings by Constable.

**Coldridge** *Devon*                    539Ge
CHURCH OF ST MARY Originally a Norman building, of which some details remain, most of the church now dates from the 15th century. The font is Norman. Other features include rood and parclose screens, bench ends of the early 16th century, and a stained glass figure.

**Coldstream** *Ber.*                    562Ed
BRIDGE OVER THE TWEED This severe but beautifully proportioned five-arched bridge crosses the river between England and Scotland. Designed by John Smeaton and built 1763–6, it still has the Marriage House, famous as the venue of runaway weddings before 1856, on the Scottish side of the R. Tweed.

MARKET-PLACE A tablet here recalls that in this town General Monk raised the Coldstream Guards in 1659.

**Coleford** *Glos.*                    546Bd
This village in the Forest of Dean is of interest to metallurgists: 5125 cu. ft of wood from the forest were needed to produce one ton of iron bar. This deforestation was suppressed in the 17th century, and the local trade declined. A local 'free-miner' named Robert Forester Mushet (1811–91) discovered the value of speigeleisen for restoring the quality of 'burnt iron'. Applying this discovery to the Bessemer process, he produced cast steel, and invented special steel for engineers' tools in 1870.

**Coleridge Cottage** *Som.*                    540Be
Samuel Taylor Coleridge, poet and philosopher, lived here from 1797 to 1800, when he wrote 'The Ancient Mariner' and the dream poem 'Kubla Khan'.

**Coleshill** *Berks.*      *546Ec*
A great estate (3620 acres) adjoining Buscot Park, including the village of Coleshill with its fine Cotswold stone cottages and farmhouses, Bradbury Hill on which is an Iron Age fort, and Great Coxwell village with its fine tithe barn.

**Collacombe Manor** *Devon*     *538Fc*
A late Elizabethan manor house dating from 1574. The window of the great hall has 3000 pieces of glass.

**Colne** *Lancs.*     *558Ab*
CHURCH OF ST BARTHOLOMEW Though mostly late Perpendicular, St Bartholomew's was begun in the 13th century. The 16th-century roof was exposed during restoration in 1856–7. There are noteworthy mid-18th-century monuments to the Emmott family by Sir Robert Taylor.
MUSEUM The public library houses collections illustrating local natural history, geology and geography.

**Combe Bank** *Kent*     *542Cf*
An 18th-century mansion, with Adam-style rooms, now a convent school. It contains decoration by the 19th-century artist, Walter Crane.

**Combe Gibbet** *Berks.*     *546Ea*
This long barrow is apparently one of those without internal megalithic chambers. The quarry-ditches along the sides are still partly visible and the 50 ft wide broader end still stands more than 6 ft high. It lies on Inkpen Beacon, near the village of Combe, and gets its odd name from the fact that, some 300 years ago, a gibbet was erected on the mound on which to hang the murderers of two small children.

**Compton** *Surrey*     *542Af*
CHURCH OF ST NICHOLAS A Norman church with several fascinating and unique features, including a west tower which is probably Saxon; a two-storey chancel, the lower part vaulted, above a Norman wood screen; a Norman nave roof; and a scratched carving on a chancel pillar of a soldier straight from the Bayeux Tapestry.
WATTS GALLERY Featuring the pictures and sculptures of George Frederic Watts (1817–1904), the gallery was founded by Mrs Watts in memory of her husband. Near by is the Watts Mortuary Chapel.

**Compton Acres** *Dorset*     *540Fc*
Seven gardens in English and foreign styles, with statuary in bronze and marble and many rare plants.

**Compton Beauchamp** *Berks.*     *546Eb*
CHURCH OF ST SWITHIN A small cruciform church of chalk near Compton House, dating probably from the 13th century, with a pyramid roof to the tower. The font is late Gothic, and there is 14th-century stained glass in the east windows. The 20th-century reredos, rood, communion rail and some other details are by Martin Travers. There are good monuments of 1737 and 1771.

**Compton Castle** *Devon*     *539Hc*
The house of Sir Humphrey Gilbert (1539–83), founder of Newfoundland, the first British colony in North America, and half-brother of Sir Walter Raleigh. The fortified manor house was built in 1320, added to in the 15th and 16th centuries and restored in modern times.

**Compton Martin** *Som.*     *540Cf*
CHURCH OF ST MICHAEL A Norman church, with a Perpendicular west tower. There is a Norman font.

**Compton Wynyates** *Warks.*     *546Ee*
This fine Tudor house, home of the Comptons who fought on the Royalist side in the Civil War, was taken by Roundheads in 1644; the family got it back two years later after paying a £20,000 fine and agreeing to fill in the moat and dismantle the fortifications. The house, begun by Edmund Compton in 1480 and completed by his son, Sir William Compton, who died in 1528, is surmounted by twisted chimneys. Inside, the plaster ceilings, panelled rooms, furniture and great hall are fine examples of Tudor and Elizabethan craftsmanship. Few alterations have been made to the original house, but several pseudo-Gothic windows were added in the 19th century. The gardens are noted for their hedges and shrubs clipped in fantastic shapes. (See p. 148.)
CHAPEL Attached to Compton Wynyates, the chapel was rebuilt after the Reformation, c. 1665, with box-pews, and a contemporary stone font. Ceiling paintings, painted coats of arms, and 16th- and 17th-century monuments can be seen.

**Condover** *Shrops.*     *551Jb*
CHURCH OF SS MARY AND ANDREW The original Norman north transept remains, but much of the rest of the building is later 17th century, including the west tower. There are many monuments, including one of c. 1746 by Louis Roubiliac, with a reclining man mourned by his seated wife.

**Condover Hall** *Shrops.*     *551Jb*
A gabled and mullioned Elizabethan house, E-shape in plan, built of pink stone and noted for its examples of the mason's craft. It is now a school for the blind. In the large park is a fine yew garden. (By appointment.)

**Congleton** *Cheshire*     *552Be*
CHURCH OF ST PETER The present building of 1742, in Classical style, replaced an old church which had become dilapidated. The lower part of the 14th-century tower remains. Inside there are galleries with box-pews, various 18th-century monuments, coats of arms and a 17th-century pulpit placed centrally before the altar.

**Congresbury** *Som.*     *540Cf*
VICARAGE The house was built in Perpendicular style in the late 15th century; it has fine moulded beams and roof timbers. In 1824–7 a Regency wing was added. (By appointment.)

**Conington** *Cambs.*     *547Jf*
CHURCH OF ST MARY A church of many dates; nave 18th century, chancel late 19th century, and the tower of the 14th century. There is a signed monument by Grinling Gibbons, the great wood-carver of the late 17th century; and earlier work attributed to Joshua Marshall, c. 1658.

**Conisbrough Castle** *Yorks.*     *552Ef*
The present buildings at Conisbrough were probably built by Hamelin Plantagenet, Henry II's half-brother, to whom the estate passed in 1163. The outer bailey is now represented by an earthwork; the inner bailey was surrounded by a stone wall which has mostly survived; on the west and east sides of the wall are projecting turrets (an early instance of the use of round turrets). Dominating the whole site is the 90 ft tall circular keep—interesting because in England before c. 1165 keeps had always been rectangular in shape. The walls of the keep are supported by six heavy buttresses which in effect form small turrets. The planning within the keep is ingenious. The hall is on the first floor, and above it are the solar and chapel. The chapel itself is an unusual shape—an elongated hexagon squeezed into the thickness of the wall and one of the flanking buttresses.

SOUTH FRONT OF COMPTON WYNYATES

Built of unusual pink brick and stone, with tall twisted chimneys, this is one of the finest Tudor houses in England. Edmund Compton, whose family owned an early 13th-century moated house here, began the present house about 1481. His son, Sir William Compton, completed the quadrangular house, the chapel with the fine large window on the south front being finished about 1515. Sir William was a close friend of Henry VIII who often stayed with him; Elizabeth I, James I and Charles I also stayed in the house and their monograms are on the fine plaster ceiling of Henry VIII's room. The Comptons, by then Earls of Northampton, were staunch Royalists and the house was captured by Roundheads after a two-day siege in 1644. Rather than destroy the house attempting to recapture it the family went into exile, and after the Restoration lived largely at their other house, Castle Ashby. Because of this Compton Wynyates survives largely unspoilt by modernisations and additions.

**Coniston** *Westmld.*      557Hd
JOHN RUSKIN MUSEUM Dedicated to John Ruskin who lived at his house, Brantwood, 1¼ miles away, during the last part of his life (1872–1900). The museum contains, among other things, a large part of his mineral collection, engravings of his work, a few original drawings, many of his books, his hand-bells, paintbox and sketchbooks. A corner of the museum is dedicated as a memorial to Donald Campbell, who died on Lake Coniston trying to break the world water speed record.

**Conway** *Caern.*      550Fe
ABERCONWAY A medieval house, built c. 1500.
PLAS MAWR It took from 1576 to 1595 to complete this fine Elizabethan town house, the last addition being the handsome gate-house on the main road. This is one of the few houses of its kind without significant additions and alterations, and almost all the original plasterwork survives. All the ceilings are flat and enriched, although the fine chestnut roof-trusses in the attic space may have been made originally for an open hall. There are two interesting wooden spiral stairs, but most notable is the rich treatment of the elevations with their elaborate crow-stepped gables.
TU HWNT I'R BONT A 15th-century stone building, once a court-house.

**Conway Castle** *Caern.*      550Fe
Conway Castle, built mainly between 1283 and 1287, is one of the outstanding achievements of medieval military architecture in Europe. The castle, with its eight almost identical towers, is built round two wards. The outer ward, which occupies more than two-thirds of the main castle area, contains the remains of the great hall, while the inner contains the royal apartments. Although the timber fittings of the castle have long since perished, the stonework is virtually complete. The town walls were built at the same time as the castle, and neither has been altered in any important detail.

**Conway Suspension Bridge**      550Fe
**and Tubular Bridge** *Caern.*
In 1826 work was completed on the suspension road bridge over the R. Conway. Thomas Telford, architect of the Menai road bridge, here repeated his successful suspension bridge on a smaller scale. Close to the bridge is the medieval Conway Castle, and Telford designed the two castellated tower supports to harmonise with the castle. The original suspension bridge has now been replaced by a new and wider road bridge, but Telford's magnificent achievement has been preserved. Adjacent to the road bridge is Robert Stephenson's railway bridge. It is a tubular iron construction, built in 1848 and, unlike Stephenson's Britannia tubular bridge over the Menai Strait (1850), is in a single span.

**Copford** *Essex*      548Cd
CHURCH A remote Norman church, one of the most impressive in Essex, whose nave, chancel and apse are original. A south aisle was added later. The remains of 12th-century paintings which once covered all the walls—Christ in Glory, signs of the zodiac, and so on—were restored in the 19th century.

FRA FILIPPO LIPPI *The Annunciation*

*In the period of Florentine painting following Masaccio and Donatello, there were two tendencies—one towards a logical and scientific outlook, and another towards a more sensuous reaction to the visible world, which is reflected in Fra Angelico's devotion to the beauty of holiness and his exquisite radiant colours, and in the similar work of Fra Filippo Lippi, who was only a few years younger. Lippi was also a painter-friar, but the story of his life was far different. His seduction of the nun, Lucrezia Buti, and the birth of*

*their son the painter Filippino Lippi indicate a more worldly make-up—and a feeling for human rather than spiritual beauty distinguishes Filippo's later work. His painting became gradually gayer, more decorative and even humorous. His Madonnas have an unusual delicacy and beauty and his cherubs a roguish smile. His luscious colour becomes scumbled, anticipating the development of tonal painting by Leonardo da Vinci. This late 'Annunciation' was painted in 1463. (Corsham Court)*

**Corfe Castle** *Dorset*  540Ec
A village in the Purbeck Hills, dominated by the ruins of a Norman castle. It was besieged during the Civil War.

**Corhampton** *Hants.*  541Hd
CHURCH A Saxon church with long-and-short work. The east wall, however, was rebuilt of brick in the 19th century. The chancel arch is Saxon and there is a Saxon sun-dial. The circular font is Norman, and there are wall-paintings dating from the 13th century.

**Cornworthy** *Devon.*  539Gc
CHURCH OF ST PETER This 15th-century church has a circular Norman font and an 18th-century pulpit with a sounding board. The box-pews and panelling probably date from *c.* 1800. The church was restored in the early 19th century.

**Corrimony** *I'ness.*  565Jf
CHAMBERED CAIRN A passage-grave in a roughly circular mound, some 60 ft in diameter, standing about 8 ft high. There is a stone kerb round its edge. The 23 ft long passage leads to a circular chamber some 12 ft across; the roof was corbelled and then covered by a great capstone with cup-marks. The mound is surrounded by a circle of 11 spaced standing stones.

**Corsham** *Wilts.*  540Eg
CHURCH OF ST BARTHOLOMEW This is a large church oddly restored by G. E. Street. The original building was partly Norman, of which some restored fragments remain. Later Perpendicular additions include a vaulted two-storey south

porch. Street demolished the central tower and built the present south one with its spire. The Perpendicular north chapel has a fan-vaulted stone screen. Monuments from the 15th century onwards include some 19th-century ones to the Methuen family.
CORSHAM COURT An Elizabethan mansion of 1582, with Georgian additions. A collection of old masters hangs in the great picture gallery, which has a fine ceiling and carpet, and is lined with damask made in 1769. The furniture includes suites by Chippendale and mirrors of Adam design. The park was laid out by Capability Brown.

**Cotehele House** *Cornwall*  538Fc
A medieval manor house, dating from 1485–1539, once the home of the Earls of Mount Edgcumbe. Among the contents are furniture, tapestries and armour, and 17th-century needlework.

**Cothay Manor** *Som.*  540Ad
Originally built in 1309 and enlarged in 1481, this manor house beside the R. Tone has a great hall, minstrels' gallery, oratory, Elizabethan dining-room with carved chimney-piece and moulded ceiling, and 15th-century frescoes. The gate-house is now a chapel. The house also contains a rare collection of pre-Crimean War medals.

**Cotheridge Court** *Worcs.*  546Be
A great Georgian mansion incorporating parts of an earlier gabled building. It is approached by a splendid avenue of lime trees planted in 1685. Near by is a 12th-century church with a timber-framed tower and, inside, fine altar rails and box-pews.

COTTERED

**Cottered** *Herts.* 547Jd
Lordship House, surrounded by a moat, is a handsome 15th-century farmhouse with 17th-century additions. The single-storied almshouses in brick with three dormers are mid-18th century.

**Cotterstock Hall** *Northants.* 547Hg
A 17th-century manor house of grey stone. It once belonged to John Dryden's cousin, Mrs Steward; the poet stayed there in the summers of 1698 and 1699. The gardens are noted for their yew trees and herbaceous borders.

**Cottesbrooke** *Northants.* 547Gf
CHURCH OF ALL SAINTS A church of *c.* 1300—originally cruciform, but it has been restored; there is a west tower. Inside is an 18th-century font and cover, and a more recent one by G. E. Street. Fortunately left by the 19th-century restorer are the three-decker pulpit, box-pews and the two-storey pew of the Langham family. Among monuments from the early 17th century are some by Thomas Cartwright, J. F. Moore, and John Bacon Junior.

**Cottingham** *Yorks.* 559Gb
CHURCH OF ST MARY THE VIRGIN The church is cruciform with a central tower, and dates from the 13th to 15th centuries. There is much sculptured decoration, and a 14th-century brass of a priest.

**Coughton Court** *Warks.* 546Df
In 1605, wives of several conspirators engaged in the Gunpowder Plot waited for news of the enterprise in a room of the great central gate-house of this house, the home of the Throckmorton family from 1409 to 1946. The battlemented gate-house dates from 1509 and there are two half-timbered Elizabethan wings and Georgian Gothic additions. The house contains Jacobite relics.

**Coventry** *Warks.* 546Eg
CATHEDRAL The old cathedral, which was the parish church of St Michael until 1918, was built in the 14th and 15th centuries; it was a magnificent example of Gothic church building, with a unique pentagon-shaped east end. The square west tower, built from 1373 to 1394, changes to an octagonal lantern supported by flying buttresses, and is crowned by a spire completed in 1433; this rises to 300 ft and is exceeded in height only by the spires of Salisbury and Norwich Cathedrals. The outside walls and tower are all that remain after the bombing of November 14, 1940. The new cathedral, built on the north side of the old and joined to it by a porch, was designed by Sir Basil Spence and completed in 1962. The great west screen of clear glass by John Hutton enables the old cathedral to be seen from inside the new. The exterior is relatively simple, and the main features are the two free-standing circular chapels, of Unity and of Christ the Servant, the saw-edge elevations of the nave walls and windows, the slender spire which was lowered by helicopter on to the roof, and the large bronze group of St Michael and the Devil by Epstein. (See pp. 152–3.)
CHURCH OF THE HOLY TRINITY A medieval parish church, with one of the famous three spires of Coventry.

**Cowbridge** *Glam.* 545Hb
This small town was originally defended by a circuit of medieval walls, of which only the 13th-century south gate survives. The church is worth a visit, and the main street contains a number of ancient houses.

**Cow Castle** *Lanarks.* 562Bd
This complex contains two settlements, not contemporary with each other. The earlier, which is the larger, occupies the south-west end of a ridge raised above what was once a watery marsh. It had a single rampart and, in places, an external ditch. The smaller, later settlement was built on top of the remains of the earlier one. There are traces of hut-bases visible both of the earlier and later periods. The ridge also shows some evidence of other banks and ditches.

**Cowdray Park** *Sussex* 542Jd
The Cowdray ruins are all that is left of a mansion built *c.* 1530 by the Earl of Southampton, but largely destroyed by fire in 1793. The remains include the east side of a large quadrangular court, and some parts of the west side where the three-storey gate-house, with turrets, stands nearly intact. The hall porch is almost square, with octagonal buttresses: the entrance arch bears a mutilated carving of the Arms of Henry VIII, who visited Cowdray in 1538.

**Cowes** *Isle of Wight, Hants.* 541Gc
The most famous of all yachting centres, Cowes, East and West, is divided by the Medina estuary. West Cowes has the character of a seaside town, but in the 19th century two castellated mansions were built across the estuary; one, John Nash's own castle, has been pulled down, but the other, Norris, makes a splendid sight from the Solent. More famous is Osborne, built by the Prince Consort as Queen Victoria's country home.

**Coxwold** *Yorks.* 558Dd
CHURCH OF ST MICHAEL A 15th-century church with a distinctive octagonal west tower. The 18th-century chancel is by Thomas Atkinson. Among the furnishings is an unusual 18th-century communion rail and pulpit, and monuments to the Bellasis family include one by Nicholas Stone, *c.* 1632, with kneeling effigies.

**Crabtree** *Sussex* 542Be
SOUTH LODGE Garden of flowering shrubs and trees.

**Craigdarroch** *Dumf.* 561Jb
The home of the Fergussons from 1325 to 1923, where Annie Laurie (1682–1761) lived after her marriage to Alexander Fergusson in 1710. The present house was built in 1729, enlarged in 1832 when the grounds were laid out, and further altered in 1932. A tree in the grounds was planted by William IV.

**Craigellachie** *Banffs.* 566Df
SPEY BRIDGE A cast-iron bridge with a single 160 ft span, designed by Thomas Telford in 1815 and built to carry the road south from Elgin. The battlemented abutments with rusticated stonework are set in precipitous wooded banks.

**Craigievar Castle** *A'deen* 566Ee
An example of the Scottish tower-house style, with conical caps to its French château-like turrets. Built in 1626, it has been unaltered and continuously occupied since then. Decorative ceilings are features of the interior and over the hall fire-place an inscription reads 'Doe not vaiken sleiping dogs'.

**Craigmillar Castle** *M'loth.* 562Ce
The central tower of Craigmillar Castle is massive but simple, in plan rather like a squat letter L. On the first floor is the great hall, and adjoining it another smaller room, presumably a living-room or solar. In 1427 the tower was enclosed by a roughly rectangular curtain wall with heavily machicolated parapets which still survives. A gun-port in one of the towers commanding the approaches to the castle is an early instance in

150

CRAIGIEVAR CASTLE

*A tall, dramatic castle, Craigievar is a magnificent Scottish 'tower-house'; it has remained unchanged since it was built between 1610 and 1626 for William Forbes, and his descendants occupied it until 1963. Built on an L-shaped plan, the castle rises straight through seven stories. Its turrets are corbelled, and capped with plain conical roofs like candle-snuffers.*

*Inside there is a fine plaster ceiling in the groined vault of the great hall. This was executed by craftsmen from London and has pendants and portrait medallions, foliage and heraldic devices in relief. Also in the hall are a huge fire-place, a fine wooden screen, a musicians' gallery and, over the grand staircase, the inscription, 'Doe not vaiken sleiping dogs'.*

Scotland of provision for artillery in the defence of a castle. It is not clear whether further domestic accommodation was attached to the curtain wall at this time but such accommodation was certainly added in the 16th century when a range, including a kitchen, was built inside the east wall. Finally, in 1661 more commodious living quarters were added along the west wall.

**Craig Nethan Castle** *Lanarks.*    *561Je*
The ruins of a 16th-century fortress, the 'Tillie-tudlem Castle' of Scott's novel *Old Mortality*.

**Craigston Castle** *A'deen*    *566Fg*
A castle built in 1604–7 by John Urquhart in Renaissance style and still occupied by his family. (By appointment.)

**Crail** *Fife*    *562Dg*
The oldest of the five royal burghs of the East Neuk of Fife. In Marketgate, Rumford and Shoregate are groups of traditional 17th- and 18th-century houses with crow-stepped gables and red pantiled roofs. The 16th-century tolbooth, reconstructed in 1776 and added to in 1814, dominates the south side of the Marketgate. The stone-spired parish church is surrounded by a fine churchyard with mural monuments.

**Cranborne** *Dorset*    *540Ed*
CHURCH OF SS MARY AND BARTHOLOMEW Little remains of the Norman origins, except the fine north doorway; the church is now mostly of the 13th and 15th centuries, with 19th-century restoration in the chancel. There are a 15th-century pulpit, several 17th-century monuments with figures, and a 14th-century wall-painting of St Christopher over the south arcade.

**Cranbrook** *Kent*    *542De*
Cranbrook was the centre of the Wealden cloth-making industry which flourished in the 15th century. The church was built then, but the building which appears at every turn of this intricate little town is the windmill, built in 1816, and set on a high base to help it catch the wind.

**Cranford** *Greater London*    *547Hb*
CHURCH OF ST DUNSTAN An aisle-less church with a west tower; the nave was rebuilt in 1716 after a fire. St Dunstan's was restored in 1895. There are several monuments, the most noteworthy being that to Sir Roger Aston (*d.* 1612) and his wife, by William Cure, with kneeling figures and a large arched canopy on Corinthian columns.

**Crantock** *Cornwall*    *538Cc*
CHURCH OF ST CARANTOC An interesting Norman church which once had a central tower; the tower is now at the west. The chancel is 14th century; there is a Norman font. The church was restored by E. Sedding at the turn of this century.

**Crarae Lodge** *Argyll*    *560Fg*
A woodland garden of rare trees and flowering shrubs by Loch Fyne.

**Crathes Castle** *Kinc.*    *566Fd*
A house built in 1553–96 in Scottish baronial style, with turrets and battlements; a wing was added in the reign of Queen Anne. An iron-studded entrance door gives access to a spiral staircase to the main floor, above ground level. The great hall, with carved Elizabethan fire-place, was built of granite. The house is noted for its painted ceilings, especially those in the Chamber of the Nine Nobles (dated 1602) and long gallery. The Green Lady's Room is reputed to be haunted; it has a painted ceiling and along the crossbeams biblical texts are inscribed.

The garden, dating from the early 18th century, contains some of Britain's finest plant collections. The lime avenues were planted in 1702, as were the dense yew hedges which are now used to divide the garden into units. Each enclosure has a distinctive horticultural personality. The Pool Garden is planted in a colour scheme of purple foliage and red and yellow flowers. The yew borders shelter plants which show off well against the sombre green: yellow-flowered witch hazel and *Eucryphia,* which has blooms of white flowers carrying golden tassels.

# COVENTRY CATHEDRAL

Throughout the night of November 14, 1940, Coventry endured the longest single air raid ever suffered by a British city. During the attack fire bombs destroyed all but the outer walls and tower of the Gothic cathedral. These now form a prelude to the magnificent new cathedral. Work to Sir

Basil Spence's competition-winning design began in June 1954, and the cathedral was consecrated in 1962. The interior, a basilica 270 ft by 80 ft, gives the impression of great space, and this is enhanced by the slender concrete columns supporting a canopy ceiling beneath the concrete roof.

THE NAVE AND HIGH ALTAR *The tapestry of Christ in Glory above the high altar is seen here through the west screen, in whose glass are reflected the ruins of the old cathedral. The tapestry, the largest in the world, takes the place of the traditional east window. It was designed by Graham Sutherland, woven in France, and took 3000 hours to make. The design is based on* *the vision of St John the Divine from the Book of Revelation. The enthroned Christ, Man between his feet, is surrounded by four symbolic creatures—man, eagle, ox and lion; they are worshipping Christ. Above the lion, St Michael casts down the Devil. At the bottom right of the picture, seen as a golden glow, is the Chapel of Christ in Gethsemane.*

PORCH *The ruins of the 14th-century church are linked to the new cathedral by a porch. To the right of it is Sir Jacob Epstein's bronze sculpture of St Michael, the cathedral's patron saint, defeating the Devil in chains. This was Epstein's last religious sculpture before his death. The cathedral is built of Hollington stone from a quarry in Staffordshire.*

THE CHAPEL OF CHRIST IN GETHSEMANE *The golden mosaic by Steven Sykes shows the angel who appeared to Christ during his agony in the garden of Gethsemane, and strengthened him before his betrayal and crucifixion. The chapel is for private prayer.*

BAPTISTRY WINDOW *The largest window in the new cathedral, containing 200 panels, designed by John Piper and made by Patrick Reyntiens. It has alternating panels of stone and of stained glass in a chequer-board pattern. The magnificent range of stained glass windows in the new cathedral culminates in this huge one, which suggests the power of the Holy Spirit at work in the world, reaching up to heaven and down to earth.*

**Crediton** *Devon* *539Ge*
CHURCH OF HOLY CROSS The church (formerly collegiate) is cruciform with a tower over the crossing, which is part of the original 12th-century building. Many additions of the 13th to the 15th centuries include a Lady Chapel. The contents include a Norman font and monuments to Sir John Sully (*d.* 1387) and Sir William Peryam (*d.* 1605).

**Creech** *Dorset* *540Ec*
GRANGE ARCH A folly, built in 1740 of Portland stone, by Denis Bond of Creech Grange; it is also known as Bond's Folly.

**Creech Grange** *Dorset* *540Ec*
A William-and-Mary house, of Tudor origin, with period furniture and paintings. It was redecorated and enlarged in 1738–41.

**Cressing** *Essex* *548Bd*
CRESSING TEMPLE The manor here was given to the Knights Templar in 1135, and was their earliest English possession. It became a private farm in the early 16th century and has two magnificent barns, the Barley Barn of *c.* 1450 and the Wheat Barn of *c.* 1530, both dated much earlier by some authorities. There is another barn of *c.* 1623, a moat, and a red-brick wall of the late 16th century.

**Cresswell Crags** *Derbys.* *552Ee*
In the sides of a cleft in the limestone are several caves which excavation showed were inhabited in Upper Palaeolithic times. Many flint and bone implements were found, as well as fragments with engraved decoration. This early occupation was probably concentrated close to the mouth of each cave. They continued to be occupied into the early Mesolithic period and, after millennia of desertion, use was again made of them in Roman and even early English times. The best caves are Church Hole on the south side and, more important, Mother Grundy's Parlour, Pin Hole Cave and Robin Hood's Cave on the north side of the gorge.

**Criccieth** *Caern.* *550Ed*
A resort on Tremadoc Bay. Earl Lloyd-George, Prime Minister at the end of the First World War, lived at Brynawelon, a house on the hill-side above the town. He was brought up and is buried at the nearby small village of Llanystumdwy. In the town are the remains of a small castle which Edward I rebuilt, and Cefu Isaf, a megalithic tomb or dolmen, known in Wales as a cromlech.

**Crich** *Derbys.* *552Dd*
CRICH TRAMWAY MUSEUM As a form of transport, trams have almost disappeared. At Crich, however, they can be seen in operation. The tramway was built by volunteer members of the Tramway Museum Society and carries a selection of tramcars, including horse, steam and electric.

**Crichton Castle** *M'loth.* *562Ce*
A solid rectangular tower-house, probably built in the late 14th century with a hall on the first floor, was the basis of Crichton Castle. Early in the 15th century the tower's defences were immensely strengthened by the addition of a gate-house tower which had its own hall (on the first floor). The living accommodation in the original tower was probably abandoned at that time, since no communication was provided between the first tower and the gate-house. Further domestic rooms were provided late in the 15th century when an extension was built along the west side of the courtyard. Finally, in the 16th century, a considerable amount of rebuilding along the north side provided a further range of domestic quarters behind an Italianate Renaissance façade.

CRICHTON CASTLE
*Strategically positioned on the banks of Tyne Water about ten miles from Edinburgh, the castle was first a simple rectangular tower-house, probably built in the late 14th century by a John de Crichton. This tower was gradually enlarged, and now reflects the changes in military and domestic design, and architectural fashion, which took place during its development. In the late 15th century Crichton came into the possession of the Earls of Bothwell, one of whom was for a short period the husband of Mary, Queen of Scots. After Bothwell's downfall the castle was forfeited to the Crown, and was later conferred by James VI on Francis Stewart, Earl of Bothwell, who entertained the king there in 1586. Francis Stewart, who himself forfeited the castle in 1593, has been described as 'an eminently cultured ruffian'. He travelled widely in Spain and Italy, and was responsible for the Italianate façade added in the 16th century.*

**Cricklade** *Wilts.* *546Dc*
CHURCH OF ST SAMPSON Dominating this church is the four-pinnacled tower at the crossing of the nave, chancel and transepts. It was built during the 16th century and has a lierne-vault with much heraldry and bosses. The body of the church is of Saxon origin, extended by the Normans and with additions and alterations up to the time the tower was built. St Sampson was a Welsh-Breton saint. Cricklade has another Norman church, St Mary's.
SAXON BURH A large rectangular enclosure surrounded by a defensive bank and ditch. Test excavations have indicated, though perhaps not finally proved, that this was the defensive *burh* established in the last years of King Alfred.

During his campaigns against the Danish armies, Alfred had seen that the ease with which they had overrun the country was largely due to the absence of defensive points which could be garrisoned when necessary. And so, after peace was established, a series of these *burhs*, south of the Thames from Kent to Devon, was set up and finally completed by his son Edward the Elder.

**Croft** *Herefs.* *546Af*
CHURCH OF ST MICHAEL Standing by Croft Castle, and dwarfed by it, this church has an interesting monument to Sir Richard Croft (*d.* 1509)

and his wife, with effigies, a canopy and four figures of saints. There are some medieval tiles and box-pews and a west gallery of the early 18th century. The nave and chancel are of c. 1300.

**Croft** *Lincs.*      *554Ae*
CHURCH OF ALL SAINTS An interesting church, which contains some good 15th-century screens and benches. The pulpit is dated 1615, and there is an impressive eagle lectern in brass, which is late pre-Reformation. Among several fine monuments is a 17th-century piece with kneeling figures, and an early fragmentary brass of a knight in the south chapel.

**Croft** *Yorks.*      *558Ce*
CHURCH OF ST PETER A low church with west tower, originally Norman but now mainly later work. There are some engaging carvings on sedilia and elsewhere, and a fragment of a Saxon cross remains. The massive 17th-century family pew is reached by stairs; there are monuments from the 15th to 18th centuries.

**Croft Castle** *Herefs.*      *546Af*
A Welsh Border castle owned by the Croft family from Domesday until 1957, except for the years 1750–1923. The ancient walls and four round corner-towers of pink stone, dating from the 14th or 15th century, survive, in spite of modifications made to the castle in the 16th and 17th centuries and in the mid-18th century, when the Georgian-Gothic staircase and ceilings were installed.
CROFT AMBREY A spectacular Iron Age hill-fort (on the estate of Croft Castle) used as a military centre from the 4th century BC until AD 50.

**Cromarty** *Ross*      *566Bg*
A unique survival of the 18th century, this burgh contains good houses, a Classical court-house of the 1770's and a parish church of the early 1700's. Two 18th-century buildings represent the past industry of the burgh: a brewery of red freestone and an attractive group of buildings comprising a rope-works. A simple lighthouse and attached dwellings were built near the harbour in 1846.
HUGH MILLER'S COTTAGE The birthplace of Hugh Miller (1802–56), geologist, stone-mason, accountant and author; now a museum devoted to him.

**Cromford** *Derbys.*      *552Dd*
WILLERSLEY CASTLE Built in the late 18th century as the home of Richard Arkwright, who revolutionised cotton mills by using water power at Cromford Old Mill. The castle is known locally as Arkwright Hall.

**Cromford Bridge** *Derbys.*      *552Dd*
A 15th-century bridge across the R. Derwent, with rounded arches on one side and pointed arches on the other. On the south side are ruins of a 'temple' (to be restored) which is inscribed as *Piscatoribus Sacrum* (sacred to fishermen). A stone in the bridge commemorates a feat of 1697 when a man on horseback jumped unharmed into the river some 30 ft below.

**Cromford Old Mill** *Derbys.*      *552Dd*
Here, in 1771, Richard Arkwright first used water power to drive a cotton mill.

**Crondall** *Hants.*      *541Jf*
CHURCH OF ALL SAINTS A church with Norman origins, of which several portions remain. There was once a central tower, but this was pulled down in the mid-17th century, when the present tower was built. The chancel and clerestory are Early English. The church was restored in the second half of the 19th century. There are brasses, and other monuments.

CROOME D'ABITOT CHURCH
*Overlooking Croome Court stands a small early Gothic Revival church, built for the Earl of Coventry about 1761; its architect is unknown. The interior has Gothic plaster ceilings, a fine pulpit with delicately carved canopy, and beautiful Classical font carved with foliage and winged cherub-heads. The monuments are outstanding; they are to the Coventry family and are mostly a century older than the present building. A fine reclining 17th-century lady holds her baby, and on the north side of the chancel is a large work of 1690 by Grinling Gibbons commemorating Lord Coventry. He lies gesticulating on a sarcophagus between two standing allegorical ladies. For many years he wore a coronet placed on his head during a restoration. It was too small for the noble head and looked absurd. The coronet is now back on the cushion where Gibbons intended it to be.*

**Croome D'Abitot** *Worcs.*      *546Ce*
CHURCH OF ST MARY MAGDALENE An early Gothic Revival church, built for the Earl of Coventry, c. 1761, near his country home, Croome Court. The architect is unknown. The church has a fine pinnacled west tower which is attached on the east side only; on the other three sides are large arches at ground level. Inside, the monuments are superb, but one is missing. In 1700 William Stanton carved a monument to the 1st Earl, but because it displayed a false genealogy for his widow—a servant whom the Earl had married in his old age—the 2nd Earl refused to have it in the church. The monument is now in the village church of Elmley Castle, about 4 miles south-west of Evesham.

**Crosby Garrett** *Westmld.*      *558Ae*
SETTLEMENT GROUP Here are three villages set roughly in line, the overall distance being about 1000 yds. The largest of the three is the south-west village; this has sub-rectangular huts and paddocks, and a larger rectangular hut. The middle village, 700 yds from the first, is similar but smaller, and the third compares closely with the second. All three villages are set in a complex of small square fields of characteristic 'Celtic' type, with boundary banks and pathways.

**Crosby Ravensworth** *Westmld.* *557Je*
SETTLEMENT GROUP An excellent group of upland
settlements within a fairly small area. They
probably originated in Iron Age times, but it is
known that Ewe Close continued to be occupied in
the Romano-British period. Burwens has an
enclosing stone wall and comprises almost an acre
of ground with many circular and irregularly
shaped huts. Cow Green lies some distance to the
west, and consists of two groups of huts of rather
different type. Ewe Close is still farther to the west
and is larger than Cow Green, covering about 1¼
acres. There are two main groups of circular huts
and a subsidiary to the south. Ewe Locks lies some
700 yds south of Ewe Close and again has two main
hut-groups, one with an enclosing wall. How-
arcles lies to the north-east of Burwens, and is
grouped on both sides of a roadway. Its huts are
both oval and sub-rectangular in plan.

**Croscombe** *Som.* *540Ce*
CHURCH OF ST MARY A 15th- and 16th-century
church, one of the most interesting in Somerset; it
has a west tower and spire. There are many
Jacobean fittings of 1616, including the rood
screen, stalls, pulpit, pews and parclose screens.

**Crosscanonby** *Cumb.* *557Gf*
CHURCH OF ST JOHN THE EVANGELIST Originally
a Norman church, with later additions. There are
some interesting Saxon and early Norman carvings, and woodwork of the early 18th century.

**Crosswood** *Card.* *545Gf*
The house is surrounded by plantations; the oldest
part, with a good staircase, dates from *c.* 1700; the
Regency library has a richly decorated painted
ceiling of the mid-19th century.

**Crosthwaite** *Cumb.* *557Gf*
CHURCH OF ST KENTIGERN Mainly late Perpendi-
cular of the early 16th century, with a west tower.
Several brasses and monuments, including one by
J. G. Lough to Robert Southey.

**Crowland** *Lincs.* *553Hb*
ABBEY Founded in 716 by King Ethelbald, in
memory of St Guthlac, who had built a cell on the
Fen island. The abbey was burnt by the Danes,
rebuilt *c.* 930, burnt again in 1091, rebuilt in 1114,
shaken by an earthquake in 1117, partly burnt in
1146, completed in 1190 and remodelled *c.* 1281.
The relics of St Guthlac were taken there in 1195.
His cell, at the west end of the south aisle, was
excavated in 1908, but filled in again. The abbey
is now the parish church; the west front is sculptured, and inside there is a 15th-century oak screen.
Hereward the Wake is said to be buried here.
TRIANGULAR BRIDGE Probably unique in Europe,
the bridge consists of three 14th-century stone
arches meeting at an angle of 120 degrees.
They originally spanned three streams of the
R. Welland, but now stand over dry land. The
carved figure on the bridge was put in position in
1720, and probably came from the abbey.

**Croxden** *Staffs.* *552Cd*
ABBEY The abbey was founded in the 12th century,
though most of the ruins are of a later date. The
west front is impressive, with lancet windows.

**Cubert** *Cornwall* *538Cc*
In this village, the manor house of Ellenglaze and
Chenoweth Farm are mentioned in Domesday
Book. To the west, at Trevornick Farm, is the
restored 14th-century holy well of St Cubertus.

**Cuckfield** *Sussex* *542Be*
The village street winds up a gentle hillside,
between houses of all the typical South-east
England materials, brick, weather-boarding, tile-
hanging and, a Sussex speciality, honey-coloured
sandstone.
CHURCH OF THE HOLY TRINITY This is a church of
the 13th and 14th centuries, the west tower having
a broach spire. The roofs, however, are 15th
century. G. F. Bodley and others restored the
building in the second half of the 19th century and
there is much stained glass of this time, including
two good windows by C. E. Kempe. Of the many
monuments one is attributed to Epiphanius
Evesham (17th century) and there are later ones by
Thomas Adye, John Flaxman, Sir Richard
Westmacott and John Bacon Junior.

**Cuddesdon** *Oxon.* *546Fc*
CHURCH OF ALL SAINTS A fine cruciform church
with central tower. Much remains of the original
Norman building, such as the Transitional tower
arches and the font. The medieval west door has its
original iron hinges and binding.

**Cullen** *Banffs.* *566Eg*
CULLEN HOUSE The oldest part of this castellated
country mansion dates from the 13th century and
was once a monastic school; from it an underground passage runs to Cullen parish church. The
house contains a collection of paintings, furnishings and tapestries, and carvings by Grinling
Gibbons. The Second Salon has a fine painted
ceiling.

**Cullercoats** *Northld.* *558Ch*
CHURCH OF ST GEORGE Dating from 1884, St
George's is by John Loughborough Pearson, architect of Truro Cathedral in Cornwall. There is a tall
tower and spire on the south side.

**Cullerlie** *A'deen* *566Fe*
STONE CIRCLE Eight undressed boulders set
equally spaced round the circumference of a circle
32 ft across. Excavation has shown that within the
circle were seven cremation-burials, one at the
centre, the remainder in the space around.

**Culloden** *I'ness.* *566Bf*
On this bleak moor in April 1746 the Jacobite cause
was finally lost—Bonnie Prince Charlie and his
followers were routed by 'Butcher' Cumberland
(the Duke of Cumberland). The Memorial Cairn,
20 ft high, was erected in 1881 by Duncan Forbes
where the bloodiest fighting took place. The
graves of the Clans and the English graves are still
discernible beside the road. Near by are the Well of
the Dead and Old Leanach farmhouse.

**Cullompton** *Devon* *540Ad*
CHURCH OF ST ANDREW An impressive Perpendicular church. The west tower of 1545 has gargoyles and pinnacles. Light interior with clerestory
and an unusual second aisle, fan-vaulted, built *c.*
1525 by wool merchant John Lane. There is no
division between the nave and chancel and the fine
wagon-roof runs the whole length of the church,
while a painted rood screen stretches across its
entire width. The rood beam and parclose screens
remain, and there is a stained glass window of 1904
by Morris & Co.

**Culross** *Fife.* *562Af*
BISHOP LEIGHTON'S HOUSE The Causeways radiating from the market cross contain 17th-century
houses with red pantiled roofs and harled walls. In
Mid Causeway is the house said to have been
inhabited by Bishop Leighton of Dunblane.
PALACE Built (1597–1611) by Sir George Bruce,
whose salt-panning and coal-mining businesses
brought prosperity to Culross and largely created
the lower town below the abbey. Grouped round a

## CULZEAN CASTLE

*A great sham Gothic castle overlooking the Firth of Clyde. Robert Adam began the present huge mansion for the 9th Earl of Cassilis in the 1770's and the work continued until 1790. Adam incorporated the original building—a stronghold of the Kennedy family for centuries—into the south side of his mansion. Next he built the north wing with its massive round tower on the seaward side, which houses the saloon. This left a rectangular house with a central courtyard, and into this Adam built one of his masterly staircases.*

## ENGLISH SIDEBOARD

*Although the sideboard as a single item of furniture existed before the late 18th century, it is at that time that an interesting development occurs. Earlier, rectangular side-tables ornamented with Greek and Roman motifs stood between pedestal cupboards used as storage units and plate warmers, and these were surmounted by urn-shaped water containers. All three components are brought together in this piece of early 19th-century furniture introduced into Britain by Robert Adam. (Culzean Castle)*

courtyard with traditional crow-stepped gables and pantiled roofs, it is one of the finest domestic buildings in Scotland. The interiors contain outstanding 17th-century tempera painting. An attractive terraced garden lies to the north.

STUDY, THE Built *c.* 1600, this fine L-shaped house with projecting stair-tower wing is at the end of the descent from the abbey down the Tanhouse Brae, itself lined with examples of some of the best vernacular burgh architecture in Scotland. One room illustrates three centuries of domestic life in Culross.

TOWN HOUSE The Sandhaven, the old meeting place of the burgh of Culross, is dominated by the town house, originally built in 1626. In 1783 a new front with double forestairs and clock tower with bell-shaped roof was added. A ceiling of 1626, painted in tempera, is to be found in the town council meeting room.

**Culzean Castle** *Ayrs.* 561Gc
In this Gothic-style mansion an apartment is reserved for General Dwight D. Eisenhower, Supreme Commander of the Allied invasion of Europe in 1944 (later President of the U.S.A.). The house, set in magnificent gardens, was designed by Robert Adam and built between 1777 and 1792; it contains an unusual oval staircase, round drawing-room and much fine plasterwork.

**Cuween** *Mainland, Orkney* 569Hf
CHAMBERED CAIRN This cairn had been damaged in the past, but is now repaired for inspection. Its mound is 55 ft in diameter and stands 8½ ft high. An 18 ft long passage leads to the central chamber, a rectangle about 10 ft long by 5 ft wide. The present roof, at 7½ ft above the floor, is a repair, and lies a little lower than the original. Other small cells open off the main chamber.

# D

**Daglingworth** *Glos.* 546Cc
CHURCH OF THE HOLY ROOD The church displays many interesting features of the Saxon church from which it grew. The west tower was added in the 15th century. During the 19th century some of the carvings were found on the site of the nearby priory; three of these are now set on the walls of the nave and aisle: a Crucifixion, Christ in Majesty and St Peter. The chancel was rebuilt in the 19th century.

**Dalhousie Castle** *M'loth.* 562Ce
A castellated castle dating from the 12th century. It has been much altered and converted into a modern mansion, and is now a school for boys.

**Dalkeith Palace** *M'loth.* 514Ce
A 12th-century stronghold here was rebuilt by Vanbrugh *c.* 1700 for the Duchess of Buccleuch, widow of the Duke of Monmouth (executed 1685).

**Dalmeny** *W. Lothian* 562Bf
CHURCH A good example of the Romanesque style in Scotland, dating from the second half of

the 12th century. There is an apse, and the chancel, apse arches and south doorway are impressively carved.

**Dalton** *Lancs.* 551Jg
A 14th-century tower remains in the main street of the village.

**Dalton Holme** *Yorks.* 558Fb
CHURCH OF ST MARY The church is a large mid-19th-century Gothic Revival building, with a lofty central tower and spire; the architect was John Loughborough Pearson. Inside is a late 17th-century monument with an effigy supported on a slab by four Virtues.

**Danby Rigg** *Yorks.* 558Ee
ARCHAEOLOGICAL REMAINS These varied remains are grouped on a steep-sided spur of hill. Close to the tip are several hundred tiny mounds, thought to be related to Bronze Age burial rites, but not with burials below them. These are isolated from the area to the south by a single stony bank crossing the spur. In the centre of the enclosed area is a single

standing stone, all that remains of a former circle. Some 700 yds farther south, the spur is crossed by three banks with two ditches. In the middle of this second enclosed space is another stone and earth circle.

A little to the east is a complex of embanked 'Celtic' fields, which appear to have belonged to the dwellers on this site. They all probably belong to the latter part of the Bronze Age and continued into Iron Age times.

**Danny** *Sussex*  542Bd
A late Elizabethan E-shaped house in red brick, home of the Campion family for centuries. It was built *c.* 1593 by George Gering. In 1728 a wing was added by Henry Campion and part of the interior, including the great hall, was altered. It contains Campion portraits and historical associations.

**Darlington** *Durham*  558Ce
CHURCH OF ST CUTHBERT An important cruciform town church of the 13th century, with central tower and spire. There is a stone screen across the tower arch in the nave. Inside are stalls, misericords, font cover and 19th-century stained glass by Clayton & Bell and others.

**Darrington** *Yorks.*  558Da
CHURCH OF ST LUKE AND ALL SAINTS A Norman church, with additions of the 13th and 14th centuries. There is an unusual arcaded gallery between the vaulted north chapel and aisle. Furnishings include carved bench ends and stalls with misericords, and there are 14th-century effigies of a cross-legged knight and a lady.

**Dartford** *Kent*  544Cg
BOROUGH MUSEUM Devoted to the history and natural history of Dartford and district, including the Darent Valley. Archaeological finds include prehistoric stone implements, and items, including jewellery, from the Roman and Saxon periods. Medieval relics and exhibits connected with past and present industries are on view. The natural history section includes plants, animals and fossils.

**Dartmouth** *Devon*  539Hb
The great international fleet of English, French, German and Flemish ships bound for the Second Crusade assembled at Dartmouth in 1147. In 1341, Edward III granted the first charter. To guard against Breton raids, two castles (which still guard the mouth of the R. Dart) were built between 1490 and 1500, and nine ships from Dartmouth joined Drake against the Spanish Armada. Thomas Newcomen (1663–1729) of Dartmouth produced the first practical industrial steam-engine: one of the originals is preserved in Royal Avenue Gardens. In 1905 the Royal Naval College was built, to train officers for the Royal Navy.
BOROUGH MUSEUM The museum is housed in a merchant's house, one of several 17th-century colonnaded houses on the Butterwalk which were visited by Charles II in 1671. The nautical collection includes fine ship models, relics of famous sailors, including a set of soup spoons owned by Lord Nelson; Newcomen steam-engine models may also be seen.
BUTTERWALK A row of four shops, above which timbered houses, supported by 11 granite columns, project over the pavements. They were built in 1635, damaged by a bomb in 1943, and restored in 1954.

**Deal Castle** *Kent*  543Gf
Built *c.* 1540 by Henry VIII as part of a military defence system against possible invasion by the French. In all 20 forts were probably built by Henry VIII, all of them unlike other medieval castles: in plan they resemble the rose badge of the Tudors. Deal Castle consists of a circular court or keep from which six semicircular bastions radiate, all equipped with guns, with an outer curtain wall of six more semicircular bastions. Altogether there were 145 openings for guns, with an all-round view.

**Dean** *Beds.*  547Hf
CHURCH OF ALL SAINTS The church, with a spire, has portions of the 13th-century building, but was

DEAL CASTLE

*With the close of the Middle Ages fortified castle building came to an end, but the castle at Deal is one of many forts built along the south coast by Henry VIII in about 1540. The king's break with the Church of Rome prompted the Pope to advocate a crusade against England, and Henry VIII built about 20 artillery forts as a precaution against a French invasion. Several of these castles were along the Thames, at Tilbury and Gravesend, for instance, while in Kent there were castles at Deal, Walmer and Sandown. That at Sandown is in ruins and Walmer Castle is the official residence of the Lord Warden of the Cinque Ports. Deal Castle is the most spectacular example of Henry's low, squat forts—with thick walls, rounded parapets, tiers of embrasures for guns and sparse living quarters for the garrison.*

largely rebuilt in the 15th century. The roofs are fine specimens of this period, and there are good screens at the west end of both chapels and also across the chancel arch. The font is 14th century, and there is a pre-Reformation pulpit.

**Deane** *Lancs.* *552Bg*
CHURCH OF ST MARY A spacious Perpendicular church with a Decorated west tower. Like many other churches of the same period, St Mary's has no chancel arch division; the continuous roof of nave and chancel is panelled, and dated 1570. The carved pulpit is Elizabethan, with a canopy.

**Debden** *Essex* *548Ae*
CHURCH OF ST MARY THE VIRGIN AND ALL SAINTS Originally 13th century, but additions were made in 1793 by R. Chiswell from the designs of John Carter. There are 18th- and 19th-century monuments and a Coade stone font of 1789.

**Dedham** *Essex* *548De*
A lovely town in the Stour Valley, one of Constable's favourite subjects. On its two principal streets are some interesting houses: the Sun Hotel, a half-timbered early 16th-century building with stable yard; the Marlborough Head Inn of *c.* 1500; the old grammar school, dated 1732; and Shermans, also Georgian. South of the village is Southfields, timbered and gabled, once the offices, warehouse and living quarters of a prosperous weaver; it was built around a courtyard *c.* 1500. CASTLE HOUSE The former home of Sir Alfred Munnings, containing many of the paintings and unfinished works of this 20th-century artist who specialised in painting horses.

**Deene** *Northants.* *547Hf*
CHURCH OF ST PETER The west tower dates from the 13th century, but most of the remainder is a restoration of *c.* 1868 by Sir M. Digby Wyatt, with some later decoration by G. F. Bodley. The contents include monuments to the Brudenell family, a bust of Anne, Duchess of Richmond (*d.* 1722) by G. B. Guelfi and, in medieval tradition, a monument by Sir J. E. Boehm to the 7th Earl of Cardigan (*d.* 1868).

**Deene Park** *Northants.* *547Hg*
The turreted and towered Tudor home of the Brudenell family since 1514, preserved in its original state. The 7th Earl of Cardigan (James Thomas Brudenell (1797–1868), who ordered the Charge of the Light Brigade at Balaclava, 1854, lived here. The park, with fine gardens and a lake, is noted for rare trees and shrubs.

**Deeping St James** *Lincs.* *553Hb*
CHURCH OF ST JAMES Once the church of a priory founded in 1139, this is a large church which offers a representation of all the architectural styles from Norman to 18th century. The transepts of the original cruciform building have since gone; there is an impressive Norman arcade in the nave, and the late Norman font is adorned with a design of intersecting arches. The west tower and spire are work of the 18th century. There are monumental effigies of the 14th century.

**Deerhurst** *Glos.* *546Cd*
CHURCH OF ST MARY This is an extremely interesting Saxon church, probably of 7th-century origins, with an apsidal east end; it once belonged to the former priory. It retains much of the original tower, though the top is medieval. Inside the nave are the famous triangular-headed windows opening from the tower's east wall. The magnificent Saxon font with its carved decoration is in a remarkable state of preservation.

Near by is Odda's chapel, again Saxon and dated 1056. This, until the 19th century, was part of the farmhouse which has been built on to it.

**Delapre Abbey** *Northants.* *547Gf*
A former Cluniac nunnery which was altered in the 16th and 19th centuries.

**Delgatie Castle** *A'deen* *566Fg*
The 13th-century home of the Clan Hay, the castle was altered in the 16th century and contains fine painted ceilings dating from 1570, and collections of paintings and armour.

**Denbigh** *Denb.* *551Ge*
One of the few Welsh towns set on a hill, and the site of a native settlement before the castle and town walls were commenced in 1282, after the English conquest. The castle gate-house is a more complete example of the three-towered arrangement designed for the King's Gate at Caernarvon Castle. On Castle Green are the remains of an incomplete 16th-century church intended to replace the humble Cathedral of St Asaph.

ST CATHERINE WINDOW

*This panel showing St Catherine holding her wheel is in the west window of the south aisle in the priory church. St Catherine is depicted in the characteristic 'S' pose of the 14th century. The architectural canopy above her is typical of such panels of the period; these were often set half-way up the windows, and surrounded by panes of plain glass and those painted with foliage designs. (Church of St Mary, Deerhurst)*

**Denham Place** *Bucks.* 547Hb
A formal country mansion built in 1688–1700 for Sir Roger Hill. It contains Brussels, Flemish and French tapestries, and friezes by Dutch craftsmen.

**Dennington** *Suffolk* 548Ef
CHURCH OF ST MARY A Perpendicular church, with an earlier chancel, and a west tower. The furnishings include lavish 16th-century parclose screens, 17th-century pulpit and box-pews. The 15th-century bench ends have interesting carving. There is medieval stained glass, and 15th- and 17th-century monuments.

DERBY PORCELAIN ICEPAIL
WITH LINER AND COVER

*Even before the 19th century people wanted to keep ice for cooling their food and drink, and this icepail was painted with overglaze enamels by William Pegg in 1800. The neo-Classical shape and clear colours are typical of Derby porcelain of the time. Glazes were much improved by then, and the wider and more delicate choice of colours imposed far fewer restrictions on the artist. (Derby Museum and Art Gallery)*

**Derby** *Derbys.* 552Dc
A trading centre in medieval times, with a charter (1154) from Henry II and another (1554) from Mary Tudor, Derby was crippled by outbreaks of the plague in 1349, 1592, 1637 and 1645. In 1693 there were only 694 houses in the borough. A change took place in two stages of the Industrial Revolution: first from 1715 to 1850 the silk and hosiery trade flourished and the manufacture of Derby porcelain and chinaware became a major industry; secondly, with the coming of the railway, the town became an engineering centre.

The Old Silk Mill gates are a masterpiece of wrought-iron work (1725); St Mary's Gate was built in 1660.
CATHEDRAL The early 16th-century western tower was part of a medieval church on the site, the rest of which was demolished in the early 18th century, and replaced by a building designed by James Gibbs. Gibbs had studied in Rome, first for the priesthood, and then as a pupil of the late-baroque architect, Carlo Fontana. His church is dwarfed by the massive earlier tower, but like St Martin-in-the-Fields, London, which he also designed, it shows Fontana's influence. The building was completed by 1725; the builder was Francis Smith of Warwick, a member of a family which has great importance in Midland architecture.

Wrought-iron work is by a local smith, Robert Bakewell; pulpit and choir stalls of the late 19th century by Temple Moore; the altar by Sir Ninian Comper. Monuments include that to Bess of Hardwick (Elizabeth, Countess of Shrewsbury, *d.* 1607), and others by Roubiliac, Rysbrack, Nollekens, Chantrey and Westmacott. The church was raised to the status of a cathedral in 1927.
CHURCH OF ST ALKMUND Built in 1846 by H. J. Stevens, in a Gothic style with a tower and flying-buttressed spire. There are two Saxon carved panels, a 14th-century font, and an early 17th-century monument with an alabaster effigy.
MUSEUM AND ART GALLERY A room in the museum commemorates the visit to Derby of Bonnie Prince Charlie during the 1745 rebellion. Other collections cover the archaeology, natural history and history of Derby city and county. In the industrial section is a working model of the Midland Railway, and a collection of Derby porcelain. There are also paintings and drawings by Joseph Wright of Derby (1734–97).

**Devil's Bridge** *Card.* 545Gg
Three bridges span the R. Mynach here, where it enters a deep gorge in a series of waterfalls; they are almost built on top of each other, and the oldest, the bottom bridge, was built in the 12th century by monks from Strata Florida Abbey.

**Devil's Dyke** *Cambs.* 548Bf
This remarkable bank and ditch runs straight across country for a distance of some 7½ miles. It faces south-west and straddles the main road, the A11, which here overlies the Icknield Way, a prehistoric trackway which has served East Anglia for more than 2000 years. The Dyke's north-west end rests on the Fen-edge and its south-east end would originally have reached the virgin forest which at that time lay around the R. Stour basin. Some 6 miles to the south-west, the smaller Fleam Dyke served a similar purpose; it is almost certain that these defences were erected early in the 7th century when East Anglia began to be threatened by its stronger neighbour, the midland kingdom of Mercia.

**Devizes** *Wilts.* 540Ef
A small market town with fine 18th-century houses. The castle, dating from the 19th century, is on the site of a former Norman strongpoint.
MUSEUM (WILTSHIRE ARCHAEOLOGICAL AND NATURAL HISTORY SOCIETY) Collections of finds from Neolithic, Bronze and Iron Age sites in Wiltshire. The most important is the Stourhead Collection of Bronze Age urns, beakers, grave

ROMAN COCKEREL

*A small bronze ornament found on the site of a Roman temple at Nettleton in Wiltshire, not far from Foss Way. The comb and feathers of the bird are represented by boldly marked ornamental hatching, and on its back is a candle holder. (Devizes Museum)*

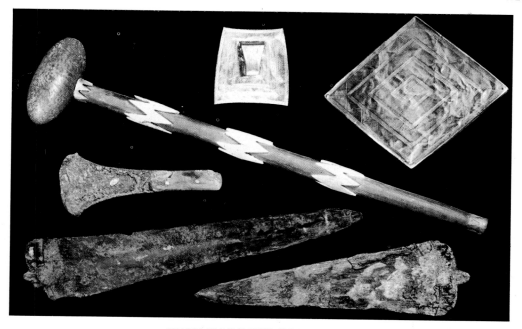

BUSH BARROW CONTENTS

*The Bush Barrow, one of the Normanton Down group close to Stonehenge, was excavated in 1808. The grave, that of a 'tall and stout' man, as the skeleton was described, was so richly furnished and the barrow itself was so prominent, that it has been regarded as belonging to one of the greatest chiefs of the Wessex Culture. Some of the finds—the large lozenge-shaped gold plate which lay over the breast, the two daggers,*

*and a ceremonial mace, as well as a gold scabbard-hook, which were close to the right arm, and the flanged bronze axe found near the right shoulder—are shown here. When first found, the smaller of the daggers had a wooden pommel patterned with thousands of minute gold pins. This fell to pieces, as did a small bronze knife-dagger and what may have been a wooden shield with bronze fittings. (Devizes Museum)*

goods and ornaments excavated from barrows on Salisbury Plain in the 18th century.

WILTSHIRE REGIMENTAL MUSEUM The material in the museum covers the Regiment's life from 1756 when it was raised until 1959 when it became part of the new Duke of Edinburgh's Royal Regiment.

**Dilwyn** *Herefs.* 546Af
CHURCH OF ST MARY A large, light church—only the chancel has stained glass—whose Norman west tower (c. 1200) is surmounted by a small 18th-century spire. The present church dates from the 13th century, with a clerestory and tall rood screen. There is some 14th-century stained glass and tiles, and the tomb of a knight made 1300–10.

**Dinedor Hill Roman Camp** *Herefs.* 546Ae
Site of an Iron Age camp, occupied by the Roman general Ostorius Scalpula, in his operation against the British chief Caractacus.

**Din Lligwy** *Anglesey* 550Ef
This is one of the best preserved and finest examples of its type, a 'native' British village which was occupied throughout Roman times and for some time after. A strongly built wall encloses the settlement-area; within it stand a number of stone-built houses, rectangular or circular in plan. These were not squalid huts but commodious dwellings, built at various periods. The quality of the buildings suggests that Din Lligwy must have been an important settlement, the seat of a person of rank in the native hierarchy.

**Dinmore Manor** *Herefs.* 546Ae
A manor house dating from the 14th century. Only the garden, chapel and music room are open to the public. The medieval chapel was once part of a Commandery (headquarters) of the Knights Hospitaller of St John of Jerusalem.

**Dirleton Castle** *E. Lothian* 562Df
Edward I besieged and took this castle, but in 1311 it was retaken by the Scots. It fell to Cromwell's troops in 1650 and was not rebuilt. Three 13th-century drum towers and part of the walls remain; there is also a 16th-century dove-cote.

**Disley** *Cheshire* 552Cf
CHURCH OF ST MARY THE VIRGIN A 15th-century hill-top church rebuilt in the 19th century. The nave has a timbered roof of exceptional beauty, with bosses and angels. There is German stained glass in the east window, mainly of the 16th century, and a monument to Thomas Legh, of nearby Lyme Park, by the 19th-century Cheshire-born sculptor Alfred Gatley.

**Ditchley Park** *Oxon.* 546Ed
The family of General Robert E. Lee, who fought for the South in the American Civil War, owned this 18th-century mansion for three and a half centuries, and it is now an Anglo-American conference centre. The house was designed by James Gibbs, who entrusted the building work to Francis Smith of Warwick. It is the supreme example of the work of Gibbs, and has magnificent interiors by William Kent and Henry Flitcroft. During the Second World War it was a week-end headquarters of Sir Winston Churchill.

**Ditherington** *Shrops.* 551Jb
In 1796 a flax mill was erected here. The oldest known surviving iron-framed building, it has been adapted as a malt store, and is the first ancestor of the modern skyscraper.

**Doddington Hall** *Lincs.* 553Ge
A gabled gate-house guards the entrance to this Elizabethan manor house crowned with belvederes and cupolas. It was built in 1593–1600 and

contains Stuart and Georgian furniture, tapestries and a collection of china.

### Doddington Moor *Northld.* 562Fd
DOD LOW The western enclosure of these hill-forts is roughly D-shaped, with a double earth and stone bank, and an internal area of about half an acre. On one side is a small annex enclosed within a single bank. In the main enclosure are the remains of stone huts ranging up to 18 ft in diameter. The eastern enclosure is larger, more nearly square and is enclosed within a bank and ditch. The enclosures are late prehistoric, probably of Iron Age date. In the area are many rocks with characteristic Bronze Age cup-and-ring markings.

### Dodington Hall *Som.* 540Be
Tudor mansion containing a great hall with minstrels' gallery.

### Dodington House *Glos.* 540Dg
The Regency-style house was built in 1796–1813 on the site of a 16th-century house; it was designed by James Wyatt for Christopher Codrington. The house is almost square, and on the west side is a portico with huge Corinthian columns, so spaced that a carriage could drive through them to the main entrance. The grounds containing fine gardens and many great trees were laid out by Capability Brown in 1764. Two lakes were created: one is higher than the other, and flows into the lower lake via a Gothic cascade.

### DODINGTON HOUSE

*The Codrington family has lived at Dodington since 1578; an ancestor, John Codrington, was Standard-bearer to Henry V at Agincourt and Harfleur in 1415. In 1796 Christopher Codrington employed James Wyatt to build him a great house in Regency style, and it was completed in 1813. In that year Codrington was indirectly responsible for Wyatt's death: on September 14, he and Codrington were travelling back to London when their coach overturned near Marlborough and Wyatt was killed. The house is almost square. Inside, the spacious entrance hall has scagliola columns, and a marble floor, patterned in black, red and white; the ceiling has sunken panels and is terracotta in colour, enriched with gold. The stair hall rises the full height of the building and is lit by four semicircular windows beneath a dome. The staircase is magnificent; it divides into two flights, to left and right, from the first landing. Mid-18th-century wrought-iron work brought from Fonthill (Wiltshire) which Wyatt was rebuilding was incorporated in the stair railings.*

### Dollar *Clack.* 562Ag
DOLLAR ACADEMY William Playfair of Edinburgh produced a building of great dignity when in 1818–20 he built this school for poor children of the parish of Dollar. The principal façade, dominated by a fine six-columned portico with Tuscan columns, faces south over a magnificent park under the Ochil Hills. The nearby Academy Place contains simple ashlar houses designed by Playfair for the staff.

### Dolwyddelan Castle *Caern.* 550Fd
This was a popular subject for early 19th-century painters. There is a tradition that it was the birthplace of Llewelyn the Great, and the earliest part of the keep may date from the 12th century. It was held for a short time by the English and then abandoned, until occupied by Maredudd ab Ieuan in the late 15th century. Finally it was restored in the mid-19th century.

### Doncaster *Yorks.* 552Ef
MANSION HOUSE This is one of only three mansion houses in England originally provided as mayoral residences (the others being in London and York). It was built in 1745–51 by James Paine, and has a splendid ballroom with ornamental ceiling and Adam-style white marble fire-places.

### Dorchester *Dorset* 540Dc
The history of Dorset's county town goes back to the Stone, Bronze and Iron Ages. It was the Roman stronghold of Durnovaria in AD 70–400. To the west was Poundbury Camp, and Maumbury Rings, a Stone Age stone circle. The Romans adapted this site as an amphitheatre, which even in the Middle Ages was used for bull-, bear- and badger-baiting. Dorchester was a Saxon centre in AD 660, and a Saxon mint town under Athelstan (925–39); it was taken by the Normans, and used by King John as a hunting centre. Puritan emigrants led by John White left the town in the early 17th century to establish a church at Dorchester, Massachusetts. There is a model of their ship, the *Mary and John*, in the council chamber. In 1685, Judge Jeffreys was sent to hold an Assize to punish the Duke of Monmouth rebels after the Battle of Sedgemoor: 300 were tried at the 'Bloody Assize' and 292 sentenced to death. The plague struck Dorchester, and a great fire in 1613 destroyed 300 houses. Dorchester is the setting for Thomas Hardy's novels and 700 volumes of the writer's manuscripts and materials are in the Dorset County Museum. He was born near by at Upper Bockhampton in 1840.
DORSET COUNTY MUSEUM All the collections concern Dorset, and the county's geology, natural history, archaeology and local history are covered. A collection of finds from the Iron Age fort at Maiden Castle is included. The Thomas Hardy Memorial Collection includes manuscripts of his novels and poems, letters, drawings, notebooks and other personal items; much of it is housed in a reconstruction of his study at his house in Max Gate (Dorchester). The museum also contains relics of the Dorset poet William Barnes, and pictures of Dorset by Dorset artists.
DORSET MILITARY MUSEUM The history of the Dorset Regiment (the Dorset Militia, the Volunteers and Queen's Own Dorset Yeomanry) from 1660 is illustrated by pictures, uniforms, medals, weapons and battlefield relics. Hitler's desk from his Berlin Chancellory and relics of Clive of India are on view.
OLD SHIRE HALL Here six men, the Tolpuddle Martyrs, were sentenced to seven years transportation for forming in their village of Tolpuddle,

## EFFIGY OF A KNIGHT

*The dynamism of this powerful figure is unique in English sculpture of its time. Cross-legged effigies are common, but here the whole body of the knight is con-torted by violent action. The figure was probably carved about 1300, and the sculptor may have come from the Abingdon workshops near by. (Dorchester Abbey)*

7 miles north-east of Dorchester, 'The Friendly Society of Agricultural Labourers'; this 'crime', which took place in 1834, is considered to be the start of the Trade Union movement in England. The farmworkers asked for a wage rise from 9s. to 10s. per week, and promptly had their wages reduced to 8s., and, on their complaining, to 7s., to teach them a lesson. The martyrs were given a free pardon two years later.

**Dorchester** *Oxon.*         *546Fc*
ABBEY CHURCH OF SS PETER AND PAUL The church of Dorchester has an unimpressive exterior, and inside is a strange mixture of Norman and Gothic architecture. The church is the only remaining part of an Augustinian abbey founded in 1140. The most interesting features of the abbey church are found in the choir, three windows dating from the early 14th century. The window in the north aisle represents the Tree of Jesse; the designer has made use of the stonework to suggest the branches, and stone and glass were combined in a highly unorthodox style. The large east window is stabilised by a buttress down the centre. The south window has a funeral procession carved on its lower part. Beneath this window is a stone sedilia with rear wall pierced by windows containing 14th-century glass.

**Dorfold Hall** *Cheshire*         *552Ad*
A Jacobean country house, *c.* 1616, with period plaster ceilings and a panelled room.

**Dorney** *Bucks.*         *547Hb*
CHURCH OF ST JAMES A church grouped pleasantly with its house, Dorney Court. Originally Norman, the church has an added Tudor west tower and a porch of 1661, both brick. Inside, the woodwork includes an 18th-century family pew and a west gallery and pulpit of the mid-1600's. Traces of medieval painting show two Annunciation figures. In a chapel is an alabaster monument to Sir William Garrard (*d.* 1607) and his wife, kneeling, with their 15 children, some holding skulls. There is a 12th-century carved font.

**Dorset Cursus** *Dorset*         *540Ed*
This enormous cursus (Neolithic processional way), by far the longest in the country, stretches for some 6 miles across country roughly parallel to and rather more than half a mile south of the Salisbury–Blandford road. Outlined by a bank and ditch, its south-west end is marked on Thickthorn Down by two long barrows, as is the north-east end close to the Bokerley Dyke. Two other long barrows were included in its course. Near the centre it is crossed by the bank of a Roman road.

## Thomas Hardy.

### THOMAS HARDY, THE WESSEX GENIUS

Hardy was only a few months old when his mother found him sleeping in the garden with a snake coiled asleep on his chest. This early affinity with nature was fostered by the isolated situation of his birthplace, which now belongs to the National Trust. Hardy trained as an architect in Dorchester, and his notebooks remain at the County Museum in Dorchester. Also on show are many of Hardy's letters and his reconstructed study. At 22 he travelled to London and in 1863 won the essay prize offered by the Royal Institute of Architects. Writing poetry in his spare time, he now began to write prose. His first novel *Desperate Remedies* cost him £75 to have published, but £60 was returned to him on the sales. Two years later he found success with his fourth novel *Far From The Madding Crowd*. In 1910 Hardy received the Order of Merit and the Freedom of Dorchester. The most astonishing period of his life began at 70 when he launched into a career of lyric poetry, until his death at 87. His poetry was surprisingly original in theme and matter and *The Dynasts* is the fullest expression of his genius. The portrait by R. G. Eves is at the National Portrait Gallery.

HARDY'S TWO WIVES *On the left Emma Lavinia Gifford, to whom he was married for 38 years, and Florence Dugdale whom he married in 1914, when he was 73 and she 35. Hardy was attracted by the concept of the well-beloved migrating from woman to woman. Both portraits at the Dorset County Museum, Dorchester.*

HARDY'S BIRTHPLACE *in the hamlet of Bockhampton, near Dorchester. The boy inherited his love of the country-side from his father, a builder, who liked to lie on a bank in warm weather 'with grasshoppers leaping over him'.*

THE AUTHOR'S PENS *which have on their handles the names of the works he wrote with them. These items can be seen at the Dorset County Museum where Hardy's study has been reconstructed as it was in his home.*

As described by Hardy in his prose and poetry, it is not limited entirely to the county of Dorset but covers the Wessex kingdom of Saxon times, including Berkshire, Wiltshire, Somerset, Hampshire, Dorset and Devon. The author is unique in the way he harnesses nature's atmosphere to heighten the drama of his fiction. For instance, the love of Tess of the d'Urbervilles grew and matured in the lush valley of the Frome, whereas her betrayal took place among the sombre yews of Cranborne Chase. But it is the areas around Dorchester (which has grown to be synonymous with Casterbridge) that Hardy utilises most frequently for his atmospheric settings and some are here illustrated: EGDON HEATH, or 'haggard Egdon' as Hardy called the wild country stretching eastward from the doorstep of his birthplace. This untameable heath-land, with its ancient barrows, rush-filled pools and gaping pits, forms a potent background to violent happenings in 'Egdon Heath', 'Tess of the d'Urbervilles', 'The Dynasts' and 'The Fiddler of the Reels'. GREY'S BRIDGE, which crosses the Frome outside Dorchester, is where the distracted Mayor of Casterbridge saw his own effigy floating down the river and DURDLE DOOR, near to Lulworth Cove, is where Sergeant Troy commits fake suicide in 'Far From The Madding Crowd'.

MEMORIAL WINDOW to Hardy in the church at Stinsford. Hardy was not a religious man and said 'I have been looking for God 50 years and I think if he had existed I should have discovered him.'

HARDY'S DESK, spectacles and blotting paper in Dorset County Museum. He wrote all his work in longhand.

HEART TOMB OF HARDY, whose dying wish was to be buried in his parish churchyard. His fame as an author and poet however, earned him a place in the Poets' Corner of Westminster Abbey. After his death his family compromised by burying his heart at Stinsford and the ashes of the rest of his body at Westminster.

**Dorstone** *Herefs.* *545Je*
ARTHUR'S STONE There are indications that this
barrow may have suffered some disturbance
to its original form. The entrance at the south end
opens to a passage leading into a large oval chamber; this is walled by nine upright slabs which
support an enormous capstone. Other scattered
stones may at one time have formed a part of the
barrow.

**Doune Castle** *Perths.* *561Jg*
Before his murder at Donibristle in 1592, this was
the home of the 'Bonnie Earl of Moray' of the
ballad. Here Bonnie Prince Charlie (Prince
Charles Edward) kept important prisoners after
the Battle of Falkirk in 1745. Restored in 1883, the
castle was built by the Duke of Albany, Regent of
Scotland for James I, in the late 14th century, but
was never finished. It stands on a hill between the
R. Teith and Ardoch Burn, and is surrounded by a
moat.

**Dover** *Kent* *543Ge*
Episodes of invasion and defence make Dover's
history. On a clear day the coast of France, 21 miles
away, can be seen from its White Cliffs. In 55 BC
Julius Caesar landed near Dover with 6000 men of
the 7th and 10th Legions, carried by 80 oar- and
sail-driven boats. In the 650 years following the
Roman occupation, invading Angles, Jutes and
Saxons landed at or near Dover, and at the time of
the Norman invasion, William the Conqueror's
half-brother, Bishop Odo of Bayeux, landed with
the prefabricated parts for a castle stronghold, to be
erected on the heights above Dover. In 1588 two
galleons of the Spanish Armada, the *San Bernard*
and the *Pereira*, were wrecked on the nearby
Goodwin Sands.
Dover Castle inevitably became the most important building in the town. Cromwell's troops
seized it in the Civil War, and it was considerably
fortified against invasion during the Napoleonic
Wars. Inside one of the White Cliffs are cavernous
brick shelters built to hide a large part of the
British army, in case Napoleon invaded England.
In the First World War the town was the centre
for the Dover Patrol, whose job was to safeguard
the Straits, and in the Second World War Dover
endured much bomb damage and shelling by
long-range guns sited in France.
There are many memorials in Dover to heroism
and achievement. The dead of both World Wars
are commemorated by the Dover War Memorial,
and at St Margaret's Bay, 5 miles along the cliffs
to the east, is a granite obelisk commemorating
the Dover Patrol.
CASTLE The main fortifications of Dover Castle
belong to the late 12th and 13th centuries. The
keep was built in the 1180's in the middle of an
inner bailey, and the fortifications of the surrounding outer bailey were begun soon after, although
these were not completed until the reigns of John
and Henry III.
The castle is of particular interest because it is
one of the earliest in England in which the fortifications were arranged concentrically. Much of
the architectural effect of its circuits of enclosing
walls was destroyed during the Napoleonic period
when the tops of many towers were cut off and
the remaining stumps strengthened to provide
gun emplacements.
CHURCH OF ST MARY-IN-CASTRO The church of
St Mary was built in the late 10th and early 11th
centuries, and the Roman lighthouse became a
free-standing bell-tower to this church, which
incorporated a considerable amount of Roman
material. St Mary's was much restored in the 19th

century from a state of ruin, and the interior at least
must rank as a 19th-century building.
CORPORATION MUSEUM A room in the museum,
housed in Maison Dieu Hall, which dates from
1203, is devoted to the history of Dover and includes several dioramas. Other collections include
archaeological finds of the Bronze Age, Iron Age
and Roman period, coins, pottery and glassware,
corporation plate, clocks and watches, furniture,
stitchcraft, British and foreign butterflies and
moths, and British birds.
ROMAN LIGHTHOUSE The Roman *pharos* near the
castle keep is the earliest lighthouse in Britain, and
probably dates from the 1st century AD. The top
floor of this octagonal structure has been removed;
it must have been carried on a stone vault, as the
original light would have been in the form of an
open brazier. In medieval times it was used as a
church tower.
It is comparable to the larger square Roman
tower at Corunna in North-west Spain, which is
almost certainly the oldest lighthouse in the world
still working.

**Dowdeswell** *Glos.* *546Cd*
CHURCH OF ST MICHAEL A cruciform church,
with central tower and broach spire, St Michael's
was considerably rebuilt during the 16th and 17th
centuries. Inside there are several later monuments,
including one of *c.* 1731 by Christopher Horsnaile
the Elder.

**Dowles Manor** *Worcs.* *546Bf*
An 11th-century house with later alterations and
16th-century additions, containing murals and
period furniture.

**Down Ampney** *Glos.* *546Dc*
CHURCH OF ALL SAINTS A cruciform church with
an Early English tower and spire, it was restored
in 1897. The interior, however, retains the 13th-
century arcades and a number of medieval effigies
of knights and ladies, and the south chapel has a
Gothic screen. In the north chapel is a tomb to Sir
Anthony Hungerford.

**Downe** *Greater London* *548Aa*
DOWN HOUSE The home for 40 years of Charles
Darwin (1809–82), the Victorian naturalist, where
he wrote *The Origin of Species*. The house, built
mainly in the 18th century, contains relics of
Darwin and other scientists.
DOWNE COURT A Queen Anne manor house, built
in 1690, and recently restored.

**Downholme** *Yorks.* *558Ed*
CHURCH OF ST MICHAEL The Norman south door
and arcades remain but St Michael's has Early
English and later additions. There are box-pews,
and a Norman font which was converted to the
Perpendicular style in the 19th century.

**Doyden Castle** *Cornwall* *538Dd*
Perched on Doyden Point, the castle is a cliff-edge
folly, built *c.* 1830.

**Drem** *E. Lothian* *514Df*
CHESTERS, THE The interesting feature of this fort
lies in its position. Instead of being sited on a hill
from which it could command the surrounding
country, it is low-lying and is immediately overlooked by a steep scarp from which it could easily
have been assaulted with missiles of any description.
Its internal area is well defended by multiple
ramparts and ditches, which appear to represent
more than one period of construction. There are
indications of circular stone-hut foundations inside
the enclosure. Some of these appear to be later
than the defences, which they overlie.

# DOVER CASTLE

DOVER CASTLE *was constructed mainly in the late 12th and 13th centuries on a magnificent site which shows evidence of occupation or fortification from prehistoric times. The castle commands an important harbour opening on the shortest sea route to the Continent and was for centuries vital to the defence of the kingdom.*

*A 13th-century chronicler described it as the 'Key of England'. The medieval kings spent vast sums of money fortifying the site, and these fortifications have been continuously brought up to date. Within the walls is the Roman lighthouse, the earliest in Britain, probably built in the 1st century AD.*

QUEEN ELIZABETH'S POCKET PISTOL *Despite its popular name, this bronze gun is really a type of cannon, being 24 ft long with a $4\frac{3}{4}$ in. calibre. It was made in Utrecht in 1544—before Elizabeth came to the throne—and the whole surface is decorated in relief with bands of fruit, flowers, grotesques, and figures symbolising Liberty, Victory and Fame. The Tudor*

*coat of arms has beneath it a verse in Dutch, translated as: 'Break, tear every wall and rampart Am I called, Across mountain and valley pierces my ball By me striken.' In 1613–22 the gun was known to be capable of firing a 10 lb ball a distance of 2000 yards: a local rhyme declares: 'Use me well and keep me clean I'll send a ball to Calais Green.'*

**Dreva** *Peebl.*     *562Bd*
This hill-fort commands the valley connecting the Upper Tweed with the Clyde Valley. The top of the prominent crag is encircled by two stone walls. Here also on the south-west is a slope studded with boulders, set in the earth to break the rush of a close body of men. To the north-east are the traces of a later settlement and a similar one may be seen lower down the north-west slopes of the hill.

**Druim An Duin** *Argyll*     *560Ef*
A small galleried dun, some 30 ft by 50 ft. In places its wall is 16 ft thick and stands about 9 ft high. There are two entrances and one of these has a guard-chamber in the thickness of the wall. The dun is on a ridge overlooking Loch Scotnish.

**Drum Castle** *A'deen*     *567Gd*
King Robert de Bruce built the keep of this castle *c.* 1280 and, in 1323, gave it to William de Irvine whose descendants have owned it ever since. A residential wing was added *c.* 1619. The castle, set in extensive gardens, contains collections of fine furniture, antique silver and old masters.

**Druminnor House** *A'deen*     *566Ef*
A 16th-century castle, the former home of the Lords Forbes.

**Drumlanrig Castle** *Dumf.*     *562Ab*
This fine mansion was built to the design of Sir William Bruce in 1645–88 for William, 1st Duke of Queensberry who—horrified by its cost—occupied it for only a day.

**Drummond Castle Gardens** *Perths.*     *562Ag*
Only the gardens of the castle and the armoury are open to viewing.

**Drumtroddan** *Wig.*     *556Dg*
Altogether in this group there are three rock-faces, each one carved with cups, cup-and-ring markings, radial grooves and other channels.

**Dryburgh Abbey** *Ber.*     *562Dd*
Sir Walter Scott and Field Marshal Earl Haig, British Commander-in-Chief in France in 1915, were interred in the abbey. Founded by King David I of Scotland in 1150, and added to in the 12th to 15th centuries, it was several times

damaged by the English during Border Wars; in the 16th century it was left to decay. A memorial to James II of Scotland survives in the grounds.

**Dryslwyn Castle** *Carm.*      *544Fd*
A ruin on a high point overlooking the valley of the Towy, once the fortress of a Welsh prince.

**Dudley** *Worcs.*      *552Ba*
CENTRAL MUSEUM A fine collection of geological specimens features local limestone and coal fossils. Items are also being collected for a museum of Black Country life and industry. There is a permanent art collection, and temporary exhibitions are held in the art gallery throughout the year.
CHURCH OF ST THOMAS THE APOSTLE This is a dominating church in Regency Gothic, designed by W. Brooks, 1817–19, with a good spire and plasterwork of the same style in the interior vaulting and panelling. Above the marble altar is a carving of St Thomas, by Samuel Joseph. Most of the 19th-century glass has now gone, although that in the east window, depicting the Ascension, remains, and is by Joseph Backler, 1821. There are monuments by Peter and William Hollins.

**Dudley Castle** *Worcs.*      *552Ba*
A ruined 13th-century castle, with 16th-century additions, standing in extensive grounds containing a zoo. Near by is a ruined priory.

**Dufftown** *Banffs.*      *566Df*
BALVENIE CASTLE The ruins of a castle owned in turn by the Comyns, Douglas and Atholl families; the Atholl motto is carved on the 15th–16th-century front. A notable feature is the yett (a massive iron grille) guarding the entrance to the tower.

**Duloe Circle** *Cornwall*      *538Ec*
Eight standing stones in a small circle some 37 ft in diameter. It is unique in Cornwall as a megalithic structure, because its builders used quartz instead of Cornish granite. It appears to have been used in the Middle Bronze Age.

**Dumfries** *Dumf.*      *562Aa*
Dumfries was given a royal charter by William the Lion in 1186, and another by Robert III in 1395. It is known especially for its links with Robert Burns and Sir James Barrie. Burns moved into Dumfries from a farm at nearby Ellisland to a house in Bank Street (1791) and then to Mill Street where he died (1796). Burns and his family are buried in a mausoleum (built 1819) in St Michael's churchyard, and the Burns Statue in the High Street was erected in 1882. Sir James Barrie was a pupil at the academy.
Mid Steeple, built 1707, was the town hall and municipal building until 1867.
DEVORGILLA BRIDGE A six-arched stone bridge with massive piers spanning the R. Nith. Steps lead up from the eastern bank to a narrow carriageway still used by pedestrians. Traditionally called Devorgilla Bridge after the foundress of New Abbey in Kirkcudbrightshire, its origins nevertheless are 15th century.
MID STEEPLE In the middle of the High Street this three-storey tolbooth with a square squat tower rising from the north end was designed by John Moffat of Liverpool, and built by Tobias Bachup of Alloa. It was finished in 1708; on its façade is the standard measurement of a Scots ell (37 in., 8 in. less than the English ell).
OBSERVATORY (BURGH MUSEUM) The oldest part of the building is the windmill, built in 1798, which was converted into an astronomical and weather observatory in 1835. A camera obscura was added in 1836, and a hall in 1862. The exhibits cover the natural history and human history of the area from Gretna Green to the Mull of Galloway.

Archaeological finds include an Iron Age plough from Elshielshiels Moss and a Romano-Celtic head from Birrens Roman fort. Robert Burns lived in the burgh and the museum has a collection of his manuscripts.
OLD BRIDGE HOUSE MUSEUM A 17th-century house containing fine furniture from several periods, and period rooms—a Victorian childhood room, a country kitchen of 1850, a town kitchen of 1900 and a bedroom dating from 1870.

**Dunadd Hill-fort,** *Argyll*      *560Ef*
Built upon a rocky hill, the defences of this fort consist of stone walls at different points and levels on the various rocky outcrops, the central area measuring no more than 100 ft by 45 ft. Close to the entrance of this, a rock-face has been carved with various Pictish symbols. The fort may first have been built in the Iron Age, but the symbols are currently attributed to the Dark Ages, probably late 7th–8th century AD. There is a historical reference in an Irish chronicle to Dunadd, for we are told that, in AD 683, a force of Picts and Scots besieged a party of Britons here. This has led to the suggestion that the attacking force was successful and that the symbols were carved to mark the victory.

**Dunaverty Castle** *Argyll*      *560Ec*
Ruins of a castle of the Lords of the Isles, where in 1647 a garrison of 300 men was besieged by Covenanters, Presbyterian supporters of the English Parliament. The defenders were forced to submit because of thirst and were slain to a man by the Covenanters under General Leslie.

**Dunbar** *E. Lothian*      *562Df*
TOWN HOUSE An early 17th-century town house situated on the east side of the High Street. A three-storied main block with a slated irregular hexagonal tower terminates in a slender spirelet. Inside are the usual arrangements of council chamber and prison cells.

**Dun Bharpa** *Barra, I'ness.*      *564Be*
A circular cairn of the passage-grave type. The mound is about 85 ft in diameter and is surrounded by upright stone slabs of heights varying up to 7 ft. The entrance is on the east side and the passage leads to a chamber near the centre. This itself cannot be seen, but its great capstone, 10 ft by 5 ft 8 in. by 1 ft thick, is visible at the top of the mound, which is some 17 ft high.

**Dunblane** *Perths.*      *561Jg*
CATHEDRAL The cathedral was founded in the mid-12th century, but apart from the lower portions of the tower, most of the building dates from the 13th to 15th centuries. Restoration of the nave, which had lost its roof, took place at the end of the 19th century.

**Dun Carloway** *Lewis*      *568Bd*
This fine broch stands on a rocky ridge overlooking the 'black-houses' of the later village. Though robbed, it is still in fair condition and parts of its 11 ft thick wall still stand 30 ft high. The internal enclosure is 25 ft in diameter. The structure displays all the best features of the broch walls. From a wall-chamber at ground level, a staircase ascends to the galleries, the construction of which is clearly displayed.

**Duncombe Park** *Yorks.*      *558Ed*
Formal gardens with two 18th-century temples.

**Dundee** *Angus*      *566Ea*
CUSTOM HOUSE Designed by James Leslie and John Taylor in 1842–3 with a sympathetic addition by C. & L. Ower in 1884. An elegant three-storey

building with four Greek Ionic columns at the upper floor level surmounted by a pediment.

HIGH SCHOOL A portico dominates the façade of this handsome building, built in 1834. The designer, George Angus, based the portico on the style of the Parthenon in Athens.

ORCHAR ART GALLERY Collections of oil paintings by Scottish artists of the Victorian period and of water-colours by such artists as de Wint and Russell Flint are on view. There is also a group of etchings by James Whistler.

**Dundrennan Abbey** *Kirkcud.*    *556Eg*
The ruined Cistercian abbey, founded in 1142, where Mary, Queen of Scots spent her last night in Scotland.

**Dunfermline** *Fife.*    *562Bf*
ABBEY The beautiful Norman church of the Benedictine abbey is only a fragment of the original, but fortunately most of the nave survives intact. The east end and central tower are modern. There are ruins of the abbey buildings.

**Dun Fiadhairt** *Skye*    *564Gg*
The wall of this broch is about 12 ft thick and encloses an area some 31 ft in diameter. There is a guard-room in the wall-thickness on each side of the entrance.

DUNKELD CATHEDRAL

*The early history of Dunkeld Cathedral, on the banks of the Tay, is obscure. The See was revived in 1107, but the existing church dates only from the 13th century when the boundaries of the diocese were redefined and a body of secular canons installed in the cathedral. During the 13th century the Bishops of Dunkeld were frequently involved in affairs of State. Bishop Richard of Inverkeithing was appointed one of Alexander III's guardians, and in 1264 was auditor of accounts in the Exchequer, while Bishop Mathew de Crambeth, elected in 1288, was sent to negotiate with the King of France in 1295. The See survived until its suppression in 1571, although the cathedral had already been 'purged of superstition' in 1560. The choir was ultimately used as a kirk. The cathedral's isolated position dates from the sacking of the town of Dunkeld in 1689 during a battle between government troops and Jacobite supporters. The town was burnt to the ground, and the new town grew up farther to the east.*

**Dungarry and Suie Hill** *Kirkcud.*    *556Eg*
HILL-FORTS Two rather small forts standing nearly 2 miles apart at opposite ends of a hilly ridge.

Dungarry, at the northern end, is enclosed by two stone walls. The outer wall is about 6 ft thick, but the inner has twice this thickness. There is an entrance on the east side with additional external defences, and an annex to the north of the entrance. The fort on Suie Hill is similar to this.

**Dungeness** *Kent*    *542Ed*
LIGHTHOUSE A light was first displayed on this dangerous coast early in the 17th century. In 1792 James Wyatt, who was then architect to Trinity House, designed a handsome tower; this was severely damaged by lightning in 1822 but survived until 1904 when a tower 140 ft high was erected. The keepers' houses built around Wyatt's tower can still be seen, the demolished tower being an open area. Finally, the construction of the atomic power station made it necessary to re-site the lighthouse, and the present slender reinforced concrete tower was built.

**Dun Grugaig** *Skye, I'ness.*    *565Ge*
The dun stands on a cliff-top above the precipitous side of a gorge; its wall does not completely encircle the inner area, but curves from cliff-edge to cliff-edge. This wall is 14 ft thick, with internal chambers and the usual entrance passage with sockets for the bar which held the door. The wall, though somewhat ruinous, still stands some 8 ft high.

**Dun Hallin** *Skye, I'ness.*    *564Dg*
The outer enclosure is surrounded by a 6 ft thick wall and within it stands the broch, still some 12 ft high, with a wall about 11 ft thick. There are two wall-chambers and a stair-lobby.

**Dunkeld** *Perths.*    *566Cb*
A fine seven-arched bridge of 1809, built by Thomas Telford, heralds the approach to late Georgian shops and houses, the only part of a new town planned by the Duke of Atholl in the same year.

CATHEDRAL The plan of Dunkeld is unusual in not being cruciform; the aisle-less choir and long aisled nave make the cathedral look more like an enormous parish church. The earliest parts of the existing church date from the 13th century. The rebuilding of the nave, now a roofless ruin, was begun by Bishop Robert de Cardeny in 1406 and continued by Bishop Thomas Lauder. The design of the nave is also unusual; the arcade is supported on heavy drum columns reminiscent of an earlier period, and the tribune gallery between the arcade and the clerestory, dating from the early 15th century, is an extremely archaic feature for that time. The choir in its present form is largely the result of restorations in 1815 and 1908. No traces of the canons' houses or of the bishop's palace have survived.

DUNKELD LITTLE HOUSES A score of houses in Cathedral Street and High Street, built mainly after 1689 when the town suffered much damage during the siege of 1200 Cameronians in the town by 5000 Highlanders. The houses were restored *c.* 1958.

**Dun Lagaidh** *Ross*    *568Fb*
A fort on the lower ground bordering the south-west shore of Loch Broom. It has a 12 ft thick wall which shows traces of vitrified material. There are additional defences outside the east gate. The broch was later built within the eastern part of the fort, but detailed description is difficult because of the surrounding debris.

# DUNSTABLE

THE FAYREY PALL *Every religious fraternity, City livery company and noble family in the later Middle Ages possessed its own funeral pall (coffin-covering). The Fayrey family gave this pall to the Fraternity of St John the Baptist, which was founded in 1442 and dissolved in 1547. The sides show St John preaching, with barren tree trunks and rocks representing the wilderness. Henry Fayrey, who died in 1516, is leading members of the fraternity to the Baptist from one side, and from the other, Henry's wife Agnes presents a row of women. The centre portion (bottom right) is of rich crimson cut Florentine brocaded velvet on cloth-of-gold. St John is depicted in his rough coat* of camel's hair, and the Arms shown are those of the Fayrey family and the ancient Arms of the Mercers' Company (a demi-figure of Our Lady, crowned). The silk is Italian, the style Flemish, but the workmanship undoubtedly English. (Dunstable Priory)

DUNSTABLE SWAN BADGE *These gold-and-enamel badges were probably awarded at tournaments, and were worn by kings and nobles who claimed descent from the legendary Knight of the Swan, who appears in medieval romance in a boat drawn by a white swan, then vanishes for ever in the same boat. The example shown, made in the late 15th century, is in the British Museum.*

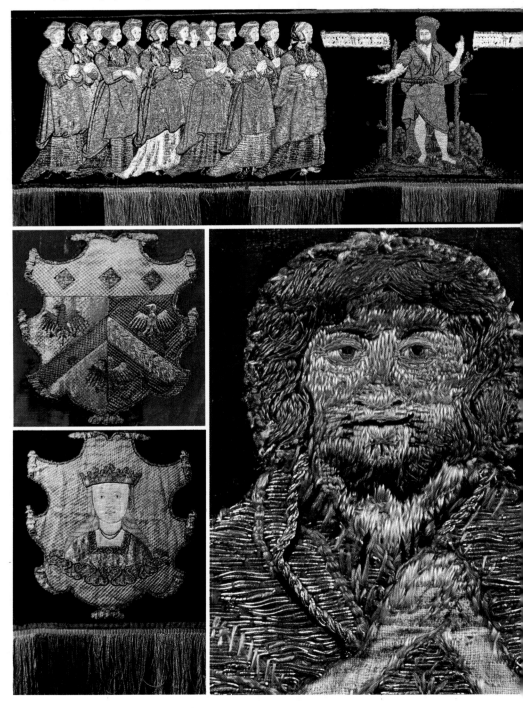

**Dunlossit** *Isle of Islay, Argyll*   560Ce
An extensive flower garden.

**Dunnottar Castle** *Kinc.*   567Gd
In 1652 this castle was the only one in Royalist hands and here the crown and sceptre of Scotland were taken for safe-keeping. After eight months of siege the castle fell to Cromwell's troops and was plundered, but the regalia were smuggled to safety. Records show that in 1685 167 Covenanters were held in the dungeon. The castle was dismantled after the Jacobite rebellion of 1715; the ruins, with tower and chapel dating from the 14th century, and gateway of *c*. 1590, stand on top of a rocky cliff, 160 ft above the sea.

**Dunrobin Castle** *Suth.*   569Jb
The castle, overlooking the Moray Firth, has parts dating back to 1401, plus additions made in the 18th and 19th centuries. A wing, destroyed by fire in 1915, has been restored. Part of the castle is now a boys' school; but the principal rooms on view house Louis XV furniture, tapestries and paintings. Collections of uniforms and court dress, and of wild animals shot by the 5th Duke of Sutherland, are also on view. The 19th-century gardens are laid out in the style of Versailles.

**Duns** *Ber.*   562Ee
CASTLE Noted for its great avenue of lime trees, the present modern building has only a 14th-century tower remaining from the past.

**Dunsinane** *Perths.*   566Da
The internal area of this conspicuous fort is enclosed by a strong rampart, which may have been timber-laced. Additional ramparts add to its strength. Inside the fort was a small earth-house (souterrain). This is reputedly the site of Macbeth's castle.

**Dun Skeig** *Argyll*   560Ee
This oval fort crests a steep hill overlooking West Loch Tarbert, and has a heavily vitrified ('melted') wall. Outside the fort, the dun is roughly circular, some 45 ft in diameter with a 13 ft thick wall. There is a single entrance.

**Dunsland House** *Devon*   538Ee
From the Norman Conquest until 1947 the ownership of this house was solely by inheritance, sometimes through the female line. The east wing is of Tudor origin but was altered *c*. 1630; the stately north wing was added *c*. 1680. Both wings contain fine plaster ceilings of the period.

**Dunstable** *Beds.*   547Hd
CHURCH OF ST PETER The magnificent Norman nave of 1150 survives from the priory church; the east end has disappeared since the Dissolution. The west front includes both Norman and Early English work, and the north-west door has rich ornamentation of the 13th century. There are screens; one of the monuments is by Thomas Green of Camberwell, and there is a late 15th-century embroidered pall.

**Dunstaffnage** *Argyll*   565Ga
Home of the Scottish kings before they removed their capital and Coronation Stone (now in Westminster Abbey) to Scone, the castle was later the fortress of the MacDougalls, but was stormed and taken by King Bruce who gave it and the hereditary title of Captain to the Campbells. Flora Macdonald was imprisoned here after leading Bonnie Prince Charlie to safety following his defeat at the Battle of Culloden. Ruins of three round towers and walls forming a four-sided stronghold dating from the 15th century are all that remain.

**Dunstanburgh Castle** *Northld.* *563Gc*
The remains of an extensive castle standing on high cliffs above the North Sea. The castle was begun in 1313 by the Earl of Lancaster, and enlarged by John of Gaunt in the 14th century. It was surrounded by defensive walls, even on the seaward side, and covered 11 acres. It was taken by the Yorkists in the Wars of the Roses and afterwards dismantled.

**Dunster Castle** *Som.* *540Hg*
This crenellated hill-top castle dominates the little market town. Dating from 1070 and modified in the 17th and 19th centuries, it has been the home of the Luttrell family since 1376. It contains a bedroom once occupied by Charles II, a fine carved staircase installed in 1681, and a banqueting hall with hanging leather panels embossed to show the story of Antony and Cleopatra.

**Dun Suledale** *Skye, I'ness.* *564Eg*
Similar to the broch Dun Hallin, for again the outer wall is some 6 ft thick. The broch wall is 12½ ft thick and the internal area about 42 ft in diameter. The western entrance has a guard-chamber. Also in the wall-thickness are other cells and a gallery.

**Dun Telve and Dun Troddan** *I'ness.* *565Ge*
These two brochs stand close together in the glen below Dun Grugaig. They are regarded as the best preserved of their type on the mainland of Scotland. Dun Telve has an inner area 32 ft across, surrounded by a wall 13¼ ft thick at its base. In places it stands more than 33 ft high. It contains the usual galleries and chambers. Dun Troddan, a little higher up the glen, is slightly smaller. Its internal space is 28 ft in diameter, surrounded by a wall 13½ ft thick, which still stands 25 ft high in parts.

LEATHER HANGINGS

*One of six magnificent leather panels in fine condition, richly coloured and relieved in places with impressed designs made by iron tools. The panels tell the story of the Roman, Mark Antony and the Egyptian queen, Cleopatra. Originally made in Spain or Portugal about the middle of the 17th century, the panels must have been intended for a particular house, as they vary greatly in size. (Dunster Castle)*

**Duntisbourne Rous** *Glos.* *546Cc*
CHURCH OF ST MICHAEL A small church of Saxon origin, with Norman additions. The 15th-century west tower has a saddle-back roof. Under the chancel is a Norman crypt. Inside the church are a fine Norman font and medieval misericords.

**Dun Torcuill** *North Uist* *564Bh*
The wall of this dun is rather variable in thickness, ranging from 7½ ft to 12½ ft. It encloses a space some 38 ft in diameter. In the wall are cells and galleries. In places it still stands some 12 ft high.

**Duntreath Castle** *Stir.* *561Hf*
A 15th-century fortress, in which are preserved medieval stocks and dungeons.

**Dun Troddan** See Dun Telve and Dun Troddan.

**Duntroon Castle** *Argyll* *560Ef*
A modernised Scottish baronial fortress on the shores of Loch Crinan.

**Dunvegan** *Isle of Skye, I'ness.* *564Dg*
The home of the chiefs of the Clan MacLeod since 1200, the castle has a 15th-century dungeon, a 16th-century tower, and was restored in the 19th century. Among its treasures are relics of Bonnie Prince Charlie, manuscripts of Sir Walter Scott and Dr Johnson, the Rory More drinking-horn and the 'Fairy Flag of Dunvegan'.

**Dunwich** *Suffolk* *548Ff*
Once a considerable port, with monastic houses, hospitals and many churches, Dunwich now lies at the bottom of the still-encroaching sea. All that remain are the 19th-century Church of St James, and by it the apsed chapel of the Norman leper hospital. There are some ruins of the Franciscan friary, a few houses and crumbling cliffs.

**Durham** *Durham* *558Cf*
Ancient and modern buildings jostle for space on a natural fortification site, for here the R. Wear makes a hairpin bend, almost encircling a great sandstone outcrop. In 1072 William the Conqueror built the castle on the narrow neck of land commanding the approach to the city. This was founded in 995 when a Saxon church was built on the river-girt rock. The Norman cathedral and monastery were begun on the same site in the 11th century. Around the cathedral and castle are many fine 17th- and 18th-century houses. There is little industry in the city, which now straddles the river; the university was founded in 1832, and the city is the administrative centre of County Durham. It has always been a route focus—it lies on the Great North Road—and four bridges span the Wear: the Elvet and Framwellgate bridges are preserved as ancient monuments; Prebends' Bridge (foot-bridge) dates from 1778, and Baths Bridge (foot-bridge) leads to a former House of Correction. On the western outskirts of the city a cross marks the position of the left flank of the English forces who defeated the Scots and captured King David II in the Battle of Neville's Cross, 1346.
BISHOP COSIN'S HALL AND ALMSHOUSES Built *c.* 1660 on Palace Green near the cathedral.
CATHEDRAL AND CASTLE Durham Cathedral, one of the most outstanding examples of Romanesque architecture in Europe, stands on a great rock surrounded on three sides by the R. Wear. The complex of buildings at the summit is dominated by the cathedral and castle. The cathedral was begun by Bishop William of St Calais in 1093, and the Norman work was finished by 1133. This part of the church, which has survived almost intact apart from the east end, shows the first use of ribbed vaulting on an extensive scale in a church.

The main additions after 1133 were the Chapel of the Nine Altars at the east end in the middle of the 13th century, Le Puiset's Gallilee or Lady Chapel at the west end in the late 12th century, and the central tower in the last half of the 15th century. The interior of the cathedral, which is richly ornamented, contains many interesting tombs and furnishings, including a magnificent screen behind the high altar (1372–80) and the north door's famous 12th-century knocker. (See pp. 174–5.)

Durham Castle lies to the south of the cathedral and the earliest of its existing buildings date from c. 1070. Of the magnificent buildings erected by Hugh le Puiset, who became bishop in 1153, only the main entrance to his hall survives. This entrance is the most extravagant piece of Norman work to survive in the county and, in the nearby Constable's Gallery, is another piece of striking decorative arcading. Much of the rest of the castle was renewed at a later date. The great hall was probably built in Bishop Bek's time (1284–1311), while the keep is the work of Bishop Hatfield (1345–81). All these buildings were restored in the 19th century and later adapted for use by the university.

GRAMMAR SCHOOL Founded in 1541 by Henry VIII; the present building dates from 1660.

GULBENKIAN MUSEUM OF ORIENTAL ART The only museum in Britain devoted wholly to Oriental art. The many treasures on view include the Hardinge Collection of Chinese carved jade, Tibetan paintings and sculpture, the Macdonald Collection of Chinese pottery and porcelain, Chinese paintings and textiles, and the Northumberland Collection of Egyptian antiquities. The museum also houses temporary exhibitions of ancient and modern Eastern art. (See p. 176.)

UNIVERSITY OF DURHAM A collegiate university founded in 1832. Parts of it are housed in the castle, a nearby monastery and the Old Shire Hall.

**Durisdeer** Dumf.                           562Ab
CHURCH A 17th-century church with the mausoleum of the Dukes of Queensberry on the north side. A monument to a duke who died in 1711, by John Nost, has columns, flying cherubs, and the duke reclining beside his dead wife. Nost's original design is in the Bodleian Library, Oxford.

**Durrington Walls** Wilts.                 540Fe
This great circular structure is almost bisected by the Amesbury–Marlborough road. The bank, now largely eroded, enclosed a ditch some 80 ft wide and 20 ft deep. There were two entrances. New road construction led to an emergency excavation being made on part of the site in 1967. This showed that, within the circle, there stood at the south end a series of six concentric rings of post-holes, very similar in pattern to the Woodhenge monument which stands close by to the south-west. It is fairly clear that this complex at Durrington was an important religious centre before this was transferred to Stonehenge at the very end of the Neolithic period.

**Dwarfie Stane** Hoy, Orkney              569Hf
A great block of sandstone, 28 ft long by 14 ft wide by 8 ft deep. Into it a passage has been cut, 7½ ft long by 2 ft 4 in. high and 2 ft 10 in. wide. On either side there is a cell cut into the rock. Each is about 5 ft wide by 3 ft deep and 2½ ft high. The square block which now lies outside the entrance was originally used to stop it. No other such rock-cut tomb is known in Britain, though a comparable one is at Glendalough in Ireland.

DUN TELVE BROCH

*One of the best preserved brochs on the mainland of Scotland, situated in the picturesque glen above Glenelg. These drystone circular structures were built as defensive dwelling-places some time between 100 BC and AD 100, usually beside cultivable land, and are peculiar to Iron Age Scotland. At Dun Telve the hollow central tower, enclosing an area 32 ft across at its base, had a wall 13½ ft thick at the bottom and which tapered inwards. As buildings of strength these*

*towers with their single entrance were perhaps the greatest in prehistoric Europe. Inside the thickness of the walls was a series of galleries and living chambers reached by stairs; the chambers or cells had no windows on the outside of the tower. Parts of the outer wall with its one defended entrance still survive around the tower-like inner structure, and the enclosed space would probably have included a number of defended small out-buildings.*

# DURHAM CATHEDRAL

Durham is no stranger to power. For centuries its mighty Norman cathedral and castle, sited on a rock 70 ft above the R. Wear, have dominated one of Britain's arteries, the Great North Road; its coalfields—among the richest in England— and its manufacturing industries still give it immense economic strength. William the Conqueror, when he first visited it in 1072, immediately saw its importance, and he and his successors made certain of the loyalty to the Crown of its prince-bishops.

DURHAM CATHEDRAL AND CASTLE *According to legend, the first church on the site of Durham Cathedral was built in the 10th century AD by the guardians of the remains of St Cuthbert who were guided to the spot by a maiden searching for her lost cow. The Norman cathedral was not planned until 100 years later. By then William the Conqueror had ordered the construction of the castle and had, in order to stabilise the North, conferred special powers on the Bishops of Durham who as a result became important political figures. The castle is now part of Durham University.*

ANGLO-SAXON STOLE *Durham Cathedral is the home of one of the oldest surviving embroidered stoles in Western Europe. Originally made for Bishop Frithestan of Winchester who died in 931, and later presented by King Athelstan to the shrine of St Cuthbert, it is now extremely fragile, and the coloured silks used to embroider the figures of saints on it are faded. The prophets Daniel and Jonah who are still recognisable are embroidered in Byzantine tradition.*

THE CARILEF BIBLE *One of the most splendid works in Durham Cathedral's library is an illuminated Bible in two volumes bequeathed by William of St Carilef or St Calais, Bishop of Durham from 1081 to 1096, who not only founded the Norman cathedral we know today but also its library. As in all illuminated manuscripts, the initial letters are most elaborately decorated and in this instance none more than the letter B. In the upper part of the B the stylised foliage customary in illuminated manuscripts merges with a grotesque creature, also made of foliage and in the lower part King David sits playing his harp.*

THE CONYERS FALCHION *A falchion, a broad, curved, convex-edged sword in use in the Middle Ages, and one of the treasures preserved at Durham, had to be presented by the head of the Conyers family who held their lands from the Bishops of Durham, to every new prince-bishop as he first entered his diocese. Failure to do so was tantamount to refusing to render military service to their feudal overlord and entailed forfeiture of their lands.*

THE SANCTUARY DOOR KNOCKER at *Durham Cathedral* recalls the days and nights in medieval times when debtors and other fugitives from the law could seek protection from arrest in places of worship like Durham Cathedral. The Rights of Sanctuary which went back to Old Testament times were eventually, because of blatant abuse, abolished in *1540*.

DURHAM CATHEDRAL, proudly dominating its surroundings, is one of the finest examples of the Romanesque style of architecture. Though the style varied in different countries, the round arch and ever more ambitious experiments in vaulting were common features everywhere. The ribbed vaulting in the north and south aisles of the choir of Durham Cathedral is the earliest of its kind in Europe.

IRON HORSE *The Chinese preferred such small-headed horses of South Russia to their own large-headed ones,* *and fine iron casting became one of their skills during the 10th century AD when this statue was made.*

EGYPTIAN BOXWOOD FIGURINE *A servant-girl of 1580 –1314 BC; such statues were put in tombs in the belief that the persons portrayed became real in the next world.*

18TH-CENTURY TIBETAN TANKA *showing a compassionate being, reborn to help end suffering; he is with a goddess, surrounded by Buddhas, saints and deities.*

**Dyce** *A'deen* 567Ge
CHURCH OF ST FERGUS Here are two fine Pictish symbol stones of different types, bearing many kinds of symbol.

**Dynevor Castle** *Carm.* 544Fd
In the grounds of this modern castle are the ruins of a Norman castle which was built on the site of a fortress made in AD 870 by Rhodri Mawr, a great leader among the princes of Wales.

**Dyrham** *Glos.* 540Dg
CHURCH OF ST PETER Mainly in Perpendicular style, but a late Norman arcade survives in the nave. A tower stands over the west end. Inside the church is a fine Norman font; there is also a large late 16th-century monument with recumbent effigies, mourning children and heraldry.

**Dyrham Park** *Glos.* 540Dg
A country mansion built *c.* 1698 to designs by William Talman by William Blathwayt, politician and Secretary of State to William III in Flanders. It contains portraits and tapestries, and furniture used by Pepys and Evelyn, the diarists; and rooms panelled in oak, walnut and cedar.

# E

**Eaglesham** *Renf.* 561Hd
An interesting 18th-century village lay-out. The plan conceived by Alexander, 10th Earl of Eglington, in 1769 takes the form of an elongated triangle. One- and two-storey traditional harled houses frame the large grassy area in the centre, some being distinguished by Classical details such as fan-lights and pilastered doorways.

**Eardisley** *Herefs.* 545Je
CHURCH OF ST MARY MAGDALENE Originally a Norman building, with later additions, most interesting for its cup-shaped font of *c.* 1150, whose carvings show men fighting with spear and sword, the Harrowing of Hell, a large lion, and other figures and ornaments.

**Earls Barton** *Northants.* 547Gf
CHURCH OF ALL SAINTS The tower of this church was probably built in the 10th or 11th century, and must at some time have been incorporated into the defences of the nearby Norman castle. The decoration of the tower includes a row of arches and two rows of chevron decoration set between narrow pilaster strips. The origin of this type of decoration is obscure, but it may derive from timber construction or it may have been an imitation of building techniques on the Continent. The original west entrance survives at the base, a massive and clumsy piece of Saxon architecture. It is popularly believed that the doors which open out of the first floor were used for access when the church was used for defensive purposes, but this is unlikely since there were three external doorways—in the west, south and east faces. The upper storey contains openings separated by characteristic Saxon baluster-shaped pillars. The Normans added a small nave and chancel to the Saxon tower, and the church was further enlarged in the 14th and 15th centuries. The tower battlements were added in the 15th century.

**Earl Stonham** *Suffolk* 548Df
CHURCH OF ST MARY A cruciform church of various dates, with a west tower. There is a magnificent hammerbeam nave roof with angels, and another in the chancel; carved octagonal font, a 17th-century pulpit with hour-glasses, and interesting bench ends.

**Earn's Heugh** *Ber.* 562Ee
These hill-forts and settlements stand on the cliff-edge, not far from St Abb's Head; owing to marine erosion, they have suffered some loss. They were probably originally roughly circular enclosures. The eastern site is defended by a single bank and external ditch with an entrance on the west.

The other, clearly later, as its defences partly cover those of the first, has a double rampart with an intermediate ditch. The settlement, itself defended by a single rampart without a ditch, is sited within the earlier fort, and contains the foundations of several circular huts. The evidence suggests that the original forts were of the Iron Age and that, some time after they had been disused, a settlement of the later Roman period was sited within the earlier defences.

**Easby** *Yorks.* 558Ce
CHURCH OF ST AGATHA Stands near the ruins of a 12th-century abbey, and is basically of the same period, with 13th-century additions. Sir Gilbert Scott made restorations in 1869. The medieval wall-paintings are of biblical scenes, but the finest piece from St Agatha's, the Saxon Easby Cross, has been removed to the Victoria and Albert Museum.

**Easington** *Durham* 558Dg
CHURCH OF ST MARY THE VIRGIN Originally Norman with later enlargements, the church has a west tower. There are pews with poppy-heads, and two 13th-century monuments with effigies, one of a lady, the other of a cross-legged knight.

**Eassie** *Angus* 566Bb
A fine Pictish symbol stone stands in the ruins of Eassie church. It is carved on one side with a cross and figures; the other has an 'elephant' symbol, disc and Z-rod symbols, together with men and animals.

**East Barsham Manor** *Norfolk* 554Bc
A notable early Tudor house of coloured brick, built by Sir Henry Fermor between 1520 and 1530. The two-storied gate-house is adorned with royal Arms carved in brick, and the house itself has a long embattled front with eight great buttresses, twisted and decorated chimneys and a porch also bearing the royal Arms carved in brick. Much restoration has been done this century. It is said that Henry VIII stayed here on his way to the Shrine of Our Lady of Walsingham. The house contains a collection of early English and European furniture.

**Eastbourne** *Sussex* 542Cc
TOWNER ART GALLERY The house was built *c.* 1760 and was later used as a manor house. The collections include the works of British 19th- and 20th-century painters; contemporary original prints by artists such as John Piper, Ceri Richards, Picasso, Michael Rothenstein; sculptures by Elizabeth Frink and Henry Moore; works by Sussex artists, and a set of Georgian caricatures including some by Henry Cruickshank. Frequent temporary exhibitions are held here.

**East Dereham** *Norfolk*      *554Cb*
CHURCH OF ST NICHOLAS The church is cruciform, with a lantern tower over the crossing and a
detached bell-tower. Work dates from all periods
from Norman to Perpendicular. The seven-sacrament font cost £12 in 1468. St Nicholas's contains
a brass lectern, c. 1500, 19th-century stained glass
and a monument by John Flaxman to the poet
Cowper, 1802.

**East Grinstead** *Sussex*      *542Be*
In the main street is a group of fine houses: Cromwell House, 16th century and timber-framed as
was standard at that time, and an 18th-century red-
brick building, Dorset House, dated 1705. Opposite these is Sackville College, a generous piece
of philanthropy by the Earl of Dorset. The
buildings, of local sandstone, are dated 1619, and
lie around a quadrangle.

**East Guldeford** *Sussex*      *542Ed*
CHURCH OF ST MARY Standing on the fringe of the
Romney Marsh, below Rye, this brick church,
with no tower, has the appearance of a barn. Built
in the first years of the 16th century, it has immense
triangular buttresses at the west end. Inside there
are early 19th-century box-pews and a pulpit.

**East Hagbourne** *Berks.*      *546Fc*
CHURCH OF ST ANDREW The church is of the
13th–15th centuries; the north chapel can be dated
exactly from brass plates commemorating the
founder and his wife (d. 1403 and 1414). Some
good 14th-century glass shows the Nativity, and
Our Lady and Child, and there are the large
painted Arms of George III in the church.

**East Ham** *Greater London*      *548Ab*
CHURCH OF ST MARY MAGDALENE A Norman
church, with an early 16th-century west tower,
fragments of 13th-century wall-painting and some
good 17th-century monuments, including one to
Edward, Earl of Westmorland.

**East Harling** *Norfolk*      *554Ca*
CHURCH OF SS PETER AND PAUL The west tower
has a small spire surrounded by flying buttresses,
with pinnacles. Other features include a clerestory,
a hammerbeam roof to the nave, an octagonal font
with decorated panels, remains of screens and some
original stained glass in the east window. Some
15th- and 16th-century monuments with effigies
are dedicated to the Harling and Lovell families.

**East Horndon** *Essex*      *548Bc*
CHURCH OF ALL SAINTS A cruciform church with
a 17th-century west tower, 12th-century decorated font, and several monuments, one by Joseph
Nollekens.

**East Lambrook Manor** *Som.*      *540Cd*
A 15th-century house with 16th-century additions
and a notable minstrels' gallery. The gardens are in
cottage style.

**Eastleach Martin** *Glos.*      *546Dc*
CHURCH OF SS MARTIN AND MICHAEL A Norman
church with a low west tower and fine Norman
doorways. There is later Early English work, a
14th-century font and medieval carved benches.

**Eastleach Turville** *Glos.*      *546Dc*
CHURCH OF ST ANDREW A small church with a
fine Norman south doorway which has several
rows of zigzag ornament, and a carving of Christ
over the door.

**East Linton** *E. Lothian*      *562Df*
PHANTASSIE A mansion where John Rennie, the
bridge engineer, was born in 1761. In the grounds
is a 16th-century rubble-built beehive dove-cote,

now harled and colour washed. Thick walls taper
to a slated roof and attractive stone hood sloped to
the north. Pigeon entries situated below the eaves
on the south side are also found in a wooden
dormer. Fixed ladders inside enabled the 544 stone
nests to be reached.
PRESTON MILL A picturesque rubble-built pantiled
corn mill of the 18th century, containing a circular
drying kiln with conical roof, a cast-iron wheel
made by the Carron Iron Co. in 1760, and
machinery in working order; the mill-pond also
remains.

**East Looe** *Cornwall*      *538Eb*
CORNISH MUSEUM Housed in one of the few
remaining old fish-storage cellars in Looe, the
museum illustrates the life and culture of Cornwall. Its collections deal with Cornish arts and
crafts, local history and folklore, mining and fishing, early travel, games and pastimes, and literature. There is also a unique collection of charms
and relics of Cornish witchcraft and superstitions.

**East Markham** *Notts.*      *552Fe*
CHURCH OF ST JOHN THE BAPTIST A large church
of the 15th century. There are some fragments of
early glass, and a late 19th-century window by Sir
Ninian Comper. There are also monuments, and a
brass to a lady, c. 1419.

**East Meon** *Hants.*      *541Hd*
The village is compact and well tended. The High
Street has a rivulet running along it, and one fine
red-brick William-and-Mary house.
CHURCH OF ALL SAINTS A Norman cruciform
church, with a central tower with lead spire, and
much Norman work inside. The magnificent
black Tournai marble font dates from the mid-
12th century, and is carved with the Creation,
Temptation, Expulsion from Eden, dragons, birds
and animals. A similar font is in Winchester Cathedral. The pulpit is early 18th century, and the east
window has stained glass by Sir Ninian Comper.

**Eastnor** *Herefs.*      *546Be*
CHURCH OF ST JOHN THE BAPTIST A 14th-century
tower and some 12th-century work remain, but
the rest of the building is by Sir Gilbert Scott, who
used the 'Middle Gothic' style in 1852. The east
window is by C. E. Kempe. There is a monument
of 1778 by Thomas Scheemakers, from a design by
James 'Athenian' Stuart, the painter and architect
whose accurate accounts of the monuments in
Athens helped to introduce the Greek style of
architecture to London, and an effigy, c. 1883, by
Sir J. E. Boehm, who designed the Wellington
Statue at Hyde Park Corner.

**Eastnor Castle** *Herefs.*      *546Be*
A castellated mansion, built in 1814; it contains
collections of armour, tapestries and paintings, and
stands in spacious grounds.

**Easton Maudit** *Northants.*      *547Gf*
CHURCH OF SS PETER AND PAUL Mainly of the
Decorated period, the church has a tower with a
spire, pinnacles and flying buttresses. Two large
monuments with effigies, and children kneeling at
the bottom of them, date from the early 17th
century.

**Easton Neston House** *Northants.*      *547Ge*
The only country house devised by Nicholas
Hawksmoor, it was built as a miniature palace in
1696–1702 for Lord Leominster. Its style was influenced by Wren (to whom Hawksmoor was a
young assistant). The fine plasterwork in the
drawing-room was carried out by a local craftsman in the mid-18th century.

EASTNOR CASTLE

*A huge pile of towers, which could be a Norman and Gothic castle. But Eastnor is a sham castle dating only from the beginning of the 19th century; it was built in 1812–15 by Sir Robert Smirke for the 1st Earl Somers—probably to demonstrate the antiquity of the* *owner's lineage. Smirke's finest work to survive is the British Museum, with its great Ionic colonnades. At Eastnor the central room is the great hall, 60 ft high. Another room was decorated by Augustus Welby Pugin in mid-19th-century Gothic style.*

**East Riddlesden Hall** *Yorks.*                         *558Bb*
A clothier's mansion, built in 1640, with a Gothic rose window and battlements to one wing. It contains oak furniture, armour and pictures. A fine medieval tithe barn stands in the grounds.

**Eastrington** *Yorks.*                         *558Ea*
CHURCH OF ST MICHAEL A magnificent church, originally Norman, but enlarged, with a west tower. There is a monument of *c.* 1456 to a judge, who wears armour, robes, and has a pigtail.

**East Wellow** *Hants.*                         *542Gd*
CHURCH OF ST MARGARET Dating from the 12th century and later, the church has some 13th-century wall-paintings of St Christopher, a knight and the murder of Thomas à Becket. The pulpit dates from the early 17th century, and there is other good woodwork.

**Eaton Bishop** *Herefs.*                         *546Ae*
CHURCH OF ST MICHAEL AND ALL ANGELS A spacious church, enlarged in the 13th century. The Norman west tower remains, with a later broach spire. There is a clerestory of lancet windows, and a window above the chancel arch. Stained glass of the early 14th century has figures of the Virgin, saints, and a representation of the Crucifixion.

**Eaton Bray** *Beds.*                         *547Hd*
CHURCH OF ST MARY THE VIRGIN Externally, the 15th-century reconstruction and a simple modern west tower belie the original 13th-century interior, with carved foliage capitals on the nave arcade. The font is also of the 13th century: a large bowl with four columns at the corners, rich with foliage carving. The 13th-century ironwork of the south door is by Thomas of Leighton.

**Ebberston Hall** *Yorks.*                         *558Fd*
A small house built in 1718 by Colin Campbell in the Palladian style which became popular in this country largely through Campbell's own work.

**Ebrington** *Glos.*                         *546De*
CHURCH OF ST EADBURGHA A mainly Perpendicular church, but Norman work remains in the north and south doorways. Of interest inside are wall monuments, benches, a canopied 17th-century pulpit and medieval glass.

**Ecclefechan** *Dumf.*                         *562Ba*
CARLYLE'S HOUSE The birthplace of Thomas Carlyle (1795–1881), essayist and historian; it contains Carlyle relics and some of his manuscripts.

**Eccles** *Lancs.*                         *552Af*
MONKS HALL MUSEUM Housed in a Tudor building with 17th-century additions, the museum opened in 1961 and has items of local interest. The Nasmyth Room contains early machine tools, notably a steam hammer made at the local Bridgewater foundry by the engineer James Nasmyth. Pottery and historic transistors can also be seen, and a collection of paintings emphasising the work of northern artists.

**Ecclesfield** *Yorks.*                         *558Df*
CHURCH OF ST MARY A spacious church, mainly Perpendicular, with crossing tower and battlemented exterior. Inside, there are carved stalls and benches, medieval and 19th-century glass, a monument with effigy of *c.* 1640, and a font of 1662.

**Eccleshall** *Staffs.*                         *552Bc*
CHURCH OF THE HOLY TRINITY A magnificent church with a tower nearly 100 ft high. Holy Trinity is of Norman origin, but much of the building is Gothic work. There are many monuments.

**Eccleston** *Lancs.*                         *552Ag*
CHURCH OF ST MARY A 14th-century church with later additions, including the late Perpendicular south aisle. It was restored in the 18th and 19th centuries. A 15th-century table-tomb has a brass of a priest, and there are 18th-century wall monuments.

EDINBURGH CASTLE

*Castle Rock was probably the site of an Iron Age fort which was rebuilt in the 7th century by Edwin, King of Northumbria. In the 11th century the castle was used as a residence by Malcolm III and his pious English queen, Margaret, who was eventually canonised. The Scottish kings continued to use the castle during the following century, and by the late 13th century the state records and royal treasures were* *kept there. James VI of Scotland and I of England was born there, and it was in the apartments used by Mary, Queen of Scots, that the Casket Letters, which were used to prove her complicity in Darnley's murder, were found. After the kingdoms of England and Scotland were united in the 16th century, the castle was only occasionally visited by the kings of Scotland, and it was used mainly as a fortress.*

**Eckington** *Derbys.*　　　　552Ee
CHURCH OF SS PETER AND PAUL The church, with its massive tower and spire, has 13th- to 15th-century work. Parts of the interior were Classicised during the 18th century but made Gothic again in the 19th.

**Edgcote House** *Northants.*　　　　546Fe
Mid-18th-century Palladian mansion with rococo interior, good fire-places and plasterwork.

**Edgehill** *Warks.*　　　　546Ee
Scene of the Battle of Edgehill (October 23, 1642), marked by an octagonal stone tower (now the Castle Inn Hotel) erected in 1750 on the position of Charles I's royal standard at the start of the fight.

**Edinburgh** *M'loth.*　　　　562Be
CALTON HILL An area set with Grecian buildings in Classical style.
CANONGATE TOLBOOTH Built 1591, it is now a city museum, with the J. Telfer Dunbar Collection of Highland Dress.
CASTLE Edinburgh's principal building, dominating the city. It is perched on a basalt rock, that juts up 443 ft above sea-level and has been a fortress site since the 7th century. No 11th-century castle buildings survive, but St. Margaret's Chapel, named after Malcolm III's wife, remains from the 12th century. In 1314 all the other early buildings were destroyed to make the castle useless to the invading English. King David's Tower—a large L-shaped keep at the south-east corner of Castle Rock—was built in 1367, and a fragment of this tower, which was later greatly reduced in height and incorporated into Half Moon Battery (1574), still survives. Many alterations have been made, especially in the 17th century, to the King's Lodging and the great hall, which were built in the 15th and early 16th centuries. The palace buildings inside the castle precincts form three sides of a square, the fourth being the impressive Scottish National War Memorial. The United Services Museum is at the west end of Palace Yard. On the south side is the great hall, former Parliament meeting place and banqueting hall: it contains a collection of weapons and armour. On the east side are the royal apartments.

The Scottish regalia—crown, sceptre, sword of state—is kept in the castle, in the stone-vaulted Crown Room. The crown (dated 1540) is of Scottish gold, set with 94 pearls, 10 diamonds, 33 gems.
CATHEDRAL The Cathedral Church of St Giles is large, mainly of 14th and 15th century date, and has a central tower crowned by a lantern supported on flying buttresses. There are monuments with effigies, and the ornate Chapel of the Order of the Thistle, added at the beginning of the 20th century, with the knights' stalls and banners.
CHAMBERS STREET The University of Edinburgh, founded in 1582, has a number of buildings here, notably the Heriot-Watt University founded in 1854. The old college buildings of Edinburgh University are in South Street, and were erected between 1789 and 1834.
GENERAL REGISTER HOUSE Built mainly between 1774 and 1789 to Robert Adam designs, and completed 1822–7 by Robert Reid. Its documents go back to the 13th century.
GLADSTONE'S LAND A 1620 house, with outside stairway, crow-stepped gables, painted ceilings and period furniture.
HOLYROOD ABBEY The abbey was founded in 1128 by King David I, in thanksgiving, it is said, for his escape from an enraged stag after the sudden appearance of the Cross between himself and the animal. Very little can now be seen of the original buildings. Parts of the nave are 12th century, but the surviving arcade belongs to the first half of the 13th century. As frequently happened, the nave was kept as a parish church; its present ruined state dates from the collapse of its vault in 1768.
HUNTLY HOUSE Built 1517, it is a museum of local history, with a collection of 19th-century glass.
JAMES COURT David Hume, the philosopher and historian (1711–76) lived here, and here James Boswell entertained Dr Samuel Johnson.
JOHN KNOX'S HOUSE Built 1490, and occupied by the famous preacher 1561–72. Many religious items are in this museum, which has a splendid Oak Room with a painted ceiling, of *c*. 1600.
KIRK OF GREYFRIARS Here the National Covenant was signed in 1638. 'Greyfriars Bobby' is a statue of a dog which lingered near its master's grave for 14 years after his death in 1858.

LADY STAIR'S HOUSE Built in 1622, now a literary museum with manuscripts of Scottish writers.

MAGDALEN CHAPEL Once a mortuary, it has exceptional pre-Reformation stained glass. The steeple dates from 1618.

MERCAT CROSS Originally of the 14th century, but the present building was opened by W. E. Gladstone; it is the appointed place for reading royal proclamations by the Lord Lyon King of Arms, and was once an execution site.

MUSEUM OF CHILDHOOD A collection of toys, mainly post-1850 but some are 4000 years old.

NATIONAL GALLERY OF MODERN ART The gallery was opened in 1959, and contains European, Scottish and English paintings of the 20th century.

NATIONAL GALLERY OF SCOTLAND Amongst the artists represented in this collection of European painting, sculpture and drawing are Gainsborough, Constable, Turner, Rembrandt, Watteau, Goya and Velasquez; the collection of Scottish painting is unrivalled. (See pp. 186–7.)

NATIONAL LIBRARY OF SCOTLAND Founded in 1682, this is one of the four largest libraries in Britain, containing over 2,000,000 books and a large collection of manuscripts.

NATIONAL MUSEUM OF ANTIQUITIES OF SCOTLAND The collections deal with Scottish history from the Stone Age to modern times. As well as Bronze Age amulets, Roman silver, Viking and Highland weapons, there are personal relics, including some of Robert de Bruce and James IV. In the same building is the Scottish National Portrait Gallery. (See p. 183.)

OLD TOLBOOTH Built in 1466, it no longer remains but is commemorated near St Giles' Cathedral by a heart-shaped pattern of cobble-stones laid in 1817. This old tolbooth provided the opening scene in Scott's novel *Heart of Midlothian*.

PALACE OF HOLYROODHOUSE James IV of Scotland began this palace adjacent to the Abbey of Holyroodhouse in 1501, with the building of the north-west tower. During his son's reign additions were made, but much was destroyed by fire in 1650 while Cromwell's troops occupied the building. The damage was made good, but when Charles II was restored to the thrones of England and Scotland, he undertook a major reconstruction of the palace. Sir William Bruce was the architect and in 1671–9 the south-west tower was built to match that of James IV, and the apartments behind the west façade were added. George V and Queen Mary had the throne room and state rooms renovated and redecorated; they were refurnished with period furniture and hung with tapestries and portraits of Scottish kings and queens.

PARLIAMENT HOUSE The Scottish Parliament met here 1639–1707. It is now the Supreme Court, Court of Session and High Court. In Parliament Hall the south window depicts the inauguration of the Court of Session by James V in 1532. In Parliament Square is Edinburgh's oldest statue, of Charles II, completed in 1685.

PRINCES STREET At the west end of Princes Street is New College and, near by, the Assembly Hall. In May each year the ministers and elders of the Church of Scotland meet here for conference.

REGIMENTAL MUSEUM OF THE ROYAL SCOTS The British army's oldest and most senior regiment has since 1960 displayed its collection of campaign medals and decorations, uniforms, equipment, silver, prints and portraits in Edinburgh Castle.

ROYAL COLLEGE OF SURGEONS OF EDINBURGH The building was erected in 1835 to designs by Playfair. Collections in the museum have the history of surgery and pathology as their theme, and can be viewed by appointment.

THE GUTENBERG BIBLE

*Until the 15th century the need to copy books by hand was a barrier to the rapid spread of knowledge; but with the invention of cast metal type by Johan Gutenberg of Mainz, Europe entered the modern age. The Gutenberg or Mazarine Bible, produced about 1456, was the first substantial work to be printed with cast type. (National Library of Scotland)*

ROYAL SCOTTISH ACADEMY The Academy is the Scottish counterpart of the Royal Academy of Arts in London. It was constituted by royal charter in 1826 and has held annual summer exhibitions of works by living artists ever since. During the Edinburgh Festival special exhibitions of works by masters from all over the world take place.

ROYAL SCOTTISH MUSEUM In the natural history section is material collected by early explorers, and a children's gallery. The geology section has fossil and mineral collections, and in the department devoted to technology are scale models which can be operated by visitors, exhibits devoted to shipping, navigation and mining, and much historical material. There is a fine collection of prehistoric Japanese pottery, and African, Egyptian and Mexican works are also shown. (See pp. 184–5.)

SCOTTISH UNITED SERVICES MUSEUM The only museum in the United Kingdom dealing with all three services at all periods of their history. The displays of uniforms, head-dresses, arms and equipment, medals, portraits, engravings and prints, housed in the castle, illustrate the history of the armed forces of Scotland. There is also an extensive library on military affairs.

SCOTT MONUMENT A memorial to Sir Walter Scott, it was completed in 1844 to the design of George Meikle Kemp. This neo-Gothic edifice has a statue of Scott under a canopy of arches and tiers, with niches in which are 64 statuettes of characters from Scott's novels. The monument is 200 ft high.

STENHOUSE MANSION Built in 1623, and now adapted as a centre for tempera paintings.

WHITE HART INN Frequented by Burns and Wordsworth. In the adjoining Tanners Close lived Burke and Hare, the murderers hanged in 1829, who sold the bodies of their victims for surgery.

# ROYAL EDINBURGH

Edinburgh has long been the capital of Scotland. By the reign of Malcolm Canmore (1057–93) the castle included the royal palace where the Celtic and Stuart kings often resided. Here the Scottish Regalia is now kept. About 1500 James IV began the Palace of Holyroodhouse, beside the abbey founded by David I. Linking castle and palace is the Royal Mile, a series of narrow streets—the centre of Edinburgh life until the elegant New Town was built in the 17th century.

PALACE OF HOLYROODHOUSE *These magnificent 20th-century wrought-iron gates lead to the official residence in Scotland of the reigning monarch.*

SCOTTISH REGALIA *The crown, of Scottish gold, was remodelled for James V in 1540. The sword of state, from Italy, was given by Pope Julius II to James IV.*

# NATIONAL MUSEUM OF ANTIQUITIES

Situated in the same building as the Scottish National Portrait Gallery, the National Museum of Antiquities contains the most comprehensive collection in existence of the history and everyday life of Scotland from the Stone Age. Launched in 1781 by the Society of Antiquaries of Scotland, the collection at first set out to attract antiquities from all over the world but in time it became progressively more specialised, concentrating on exhibits to illustrate the story of Scotland and her people.

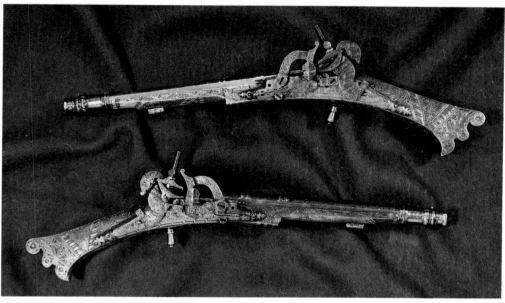

PAIR OF SCOTTISH BELT-PISTOLS *King Louis XIII (1601–43) may be regarded as the first gun-collector, in the modern sense of the term. At the age of 12 he owned 50 guns, and by the time he died many hundreds, both ancient and modern. The collection was catalogued, and pieces from it can still be identified. Among them is this pair of pistols; they may have been presented to Louis by his Scots Guard. Apart from the silver tubes under the barrels for the missing ramrods, and the iron working parts, they are made entirely of brass, engraved with scrolling foliage and originally gilt. The barrels are engraved with the date 1611, the French royal Arms, the inscription* LOUIS XIII ROY DE FRAC, *and a maker's mark ascribed to John Low of Dundee.*

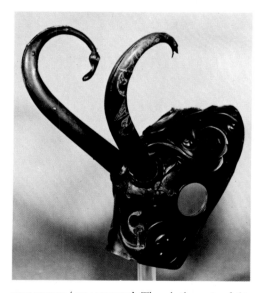

THE TORRS 'CHAMFREIN' *Though the parts of this piece are certainly ancient and genuine relics of the Iron Age, it was a puzzle until recent study revealed the truth: Somebody had made a 'fake' piece of three fine genuine pieces by cutting two holes in what was a pony-cap, and attaching horns to them, probably the terminals of two drinking horns. The chamfrein was discovered in 1829.*

ST NINIAN'S TREASURE: THE HANGING-BOWL *In 1958 a hoard of treasure was discovered below the nave of a ruined medieval church on St Ninian's Island in the Shetlands. As well as the hanging-bowl, brooches, shallow bowls, belt-attachments, strap-ends, a sword pommel, and a spoon and ladle were found, 29 objects in all made of an alloy of silver and copper. They were buried late in the 8th century, probably to avoid the Viking raids on the islands which were just beginning. It is thought that the pieces were made in Scotland. This hanging-bowl is in many ways similar to those found in Anglo-Saxon graves.*

# ROYAL SCOTTISH MUSEUM

Situated in Chambers Street, immediately to the west of the Old College of the University of Edinburgh, the Royal Scottish Museum, founded in mid-19th century, combines collections of exhibits which reflect human endeavour not only in Scotland, but in other countries. Though rich in Scottish examples from many fields, it is representative of all the world. It is the largest comprehensive museum of science and art (excluding painting) in the British Isles.

13TH-CENTURY CIBORIUM *Medieval craftsmen gave their time and skill lavishly to make liturgical vessels like ciboria, in which the Host is prepared for the celebration of mass. This ciborium, made at Limoges in central France, shows the splendidly ornate enamel decoration traditional for such objects in the 13th century. It is however incomplete. Its lid is missing, and the foot of the vessel is a replacement from a similar ciborium of contemporary date. The foot shows a type of cast pierced design in which Limoges goldsmiths particularly excelled. The bowl's decoration allows it to be dated to the early 13th century.*

MEISSEN LION *In the 1730's Meissen porcelain was of an extremely high quality—as shown by this model of a lion. Copied from a figure by Kirchner about 1732, it was probably made for the Japanese Palace in Dresden of the Elector Frederick I of Saxony (1694–1733).*

SWORD OF BATTLE ABBEY *Like most medieval swords, the Battle Abbey sword is a straight, two-edged weapon with a simple cross guard and a shaped knob—the pommel—at the top to counter-balance the blade. Made between 1417 and 1435, the steel pommel and cross are overlaid with silver which was originally gilt, and engraved with Gothic foliage. The pommel is engraved with the Arms of Battle Abbey in Sussex, and with the letters 't.L', the initials of Thomas de Lodelowe, Abbot of Battle. The abbey's Arms include a sword to symbolise the right of administration of justice granted by William the Conqueror.*

EMBROIDERED BOX *This box, made about 1670, with its fine silk thread laid in graded colours with animals and floral motifs worked in satin-stitch, is typical of the needlework boxes in which young English ladies kept their small personal belongings; it is lined with silk. The ladies did their own embroidery and, having first practised the craft on samplers and, perhaps, on embroidered pictures, they worked the strips and panels for their boxes. These were then assembled by a cabinet-maker who added handles, and fitted secret drawers for jewellery, and mirrors. The edges of the boxes were often trimmed with silver braid.*

MOSQUE LAMP *An enamelled mosque lamp dating from about 1340, containing an oil vessel; such lamps were suspended by chains from the ceilings of Egyptian mosques. Most were inscribed with names and titles of the Mameluke Sultans of Egypt or their officers and until about 1400 were made in Syria. The museum also contains a small but important collection of antiquities from Ancient Egypt.*

BLACKWORK PANEL *This panel dates from the 16th century, when blackwork was used mainly as a decoration on undergarments, sleeves and cuffs, and head-dresses of both men and women. Such examples of its use appear in portraits by Holbein. The formal pattern is made up of running stitches worked entirely by the thread of the linen. The flowing black outline is then filled in with various stitches.*

GREAT HELM OF SIR RICHARD PEMBRIDGE *This great helm made about 1360 for Sir Richard Pembridge, who fought beside the Black Prince in France, is constructed from five riveted plates with rounded and oblique surfaces to deflect and resist sword and lance thrusts. It is made of steel so hard that a modern penknife cannot scratch its surface, and was worn over a smaller helmet during battle.*

# NATIONAL GALLERY OF SCOTLAND

The National Gallery of Scotland was designed in the Grecian style and opened to the public in 1859. It contains one of the most exquisite collections of paintings in the world. It boasts some of the most important and intriguing groups of works by masters such as Raphael, Titian, Rembrandt, Gainsborough, Poussin, Degas and Cézanne as well as a section devoted to Scottish artists.

WATTEAU: FÊTES VÉNITIENNES *The 18th century in France produced two great masters of painting, Watteau and Chardin. Their worlds were poles apart. Chardin's scenes come from the nursery and kitchen: Watteau created a make-believe world of gallants and their ladies dancing, play-acting or love-making in enchanted gardens. The ingredients of his art were the vigour and precision of his draughtsmanship, his keen observation, and the beauty of his tones and colours.*

DEGAS: DIEGO MARTELLI *The portrait of Martelli, a Florentine art critic, seen in his study, carpet-slippered, in his shirt-sleeves and amid a confusion of papers, gave Degas the chance to display his psychological penetration of the sitter's character and surroundings and for his superb draughtsmanship and gift for colour. Although Degas helped to organise the first Impressionist exhibition in 1874, and consistently exhibited with Impressionists, he was not really one of them. He hated the word 'Impressionist' and tried to prevent its adoption by the group. But he approved of their sense of immediacy and their choice of subjects from everyday life.*

TITIAN: THE THREE AGES OF MAN *The cornerstone of Venetian art was colour and the artist's gift, which is particularly noticeable in Titian's paintings, to make his work come alive by his superb handling of oil paint. 'The Three Ages of Man' belongs to Titian's early period. Its composition is simple and uncomplicated:* immature childhood is represented by the three putti, old age by the man with the skulls in the background and the earthly paradise of requited love by the boy and the girl. The radiant sensuousness of the glowing flesh tints reveals the maturing Titian's master touch.

GAINSBOROUGH: THE HONOURABLE MRS GRAHAM *Mrs Graham was one of the many society beauties Gainsborough painted in order to make a living, although he preferred painting landscapes. He has been called the only true rococo artist England has produced. His feeling for the medium is French; indeed his impassioned brushwork in Mrs Graham's carmine skirt looks forward to Renoir's art. Unlike Sir Joshua Reynolds, his contemporary and fellow portrait painter of high society, Gainsborough did not belong to the world of his sitters. His real friends were musicians, actors and other painters.*

*Joseph Lister*

## JOSEPH LISTER, THE MAN WHO MADE SURGERY SAFE

Joseph Lister came from a gentle but industrious background, and his father's lively scientific interests led him to delight in experiments—at first into the causes of inflammation, which often led to gangrene. 'Having got a frog from Duddingston Loch I proceeded last night to the investigation, and a most glorious night I had of it', wrote Lister from his house at 11 Rutland Street, Edinburgh. The Infirmary where he worked is now the geological department of Edinburgh University. Lister acted on the results of his experiments when he moved to Glasgow as Professor in 1860, insisting on cleanliness and the dressing of wounds with carbolic acid gauzes; as a result, his wards remained entirely free of hospital diseases, when others were frequently closed because of gangrene. Relics of this period in his life may be seen at Glasgow University. In 1877 he moved to London and a memorial bust in Portland Place, near his house in 12 Park Crescent, recalls the man who brought about an incalculable saving of human life suffering.

PRESCRIPTION BOOK *written up by Lister when Professor at the Glasgow Royal Infirmary. The death-rate in unhealthy wards was drastically reduced by his Antiseptic System. (Wellcome Historical Medical Museum, London)*

UPTON HOUSE *Lister's birthplace in East London, now derelict. His early resolve to be a surgeon is borne out by his description: 'When Mamma was out I was by myself and had nothing to do but draw skeletons.'*

LADY LISTER *at the time of her marriage in 1856. She was the daughter of Lister's chief in Edinburgh, Professor Syme, and was of great practical help to her husband. Nearly all his early notebooks of experiments are in her handwriting.*

CARBOLIC ACID *was the liquid chosen by Lister as an antiseptic in surgery, after reading that it had been used to purify sewage in Carlisle. This liquid, used on gauze to cover wounds after an operation, prevented putrefaction and gangrene. (Glasgow University Museum)*

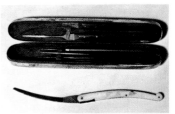

SURGICAL INSTRUMENTS *used by Lister, a great practical surgeon. The first man to dare to open the abdominal cavity, he occupied the Chair of Clinical Surgery at King's College, London, for 15 years. (Glasgow University and Wellcome Institute)*

CARBOLIC SPRAY *introduced by Lister to purify the air, this one operated by steam.*

LISTER PERFORMING AN OPERA-TION *For some years he alone could safely perform the operations he had devised. (Both at Wellcome Institute)*

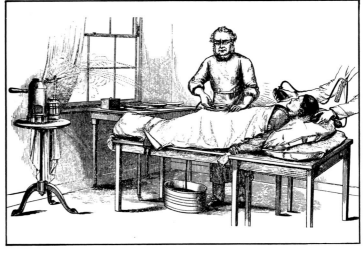

LISTER'S MEDICINE CHEST AND MICROSCOPE *The companions of 'his faultless patience, his unyielding will, beautiful gentleness and splendid skill'. (Royal College of Surgeons)*

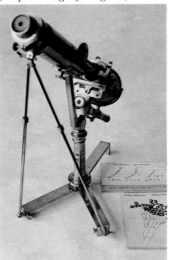

QUEEN VICTORIA'S DEDICATION *on the flysheet of her book on Balmoral, presented to Lister after his success in lancing an abscess in her armpit. (Private collection)*

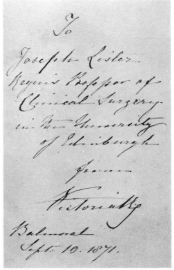

EILDON HILLS

*The Selgovae, an Iron Age tribe of Scotland, made this hill-top their chief settlement. The snow clearly picks out the third rampart they built for their hill-fort; it encloses an area of 40 acres. When the Romans* *occupied the area in AD 79 the Selgovae fled. The Romans built their fort of Trimontium near the foot of the hill at Newstead, and a small signal-station on top, within the remains of the hill-fort.*

**Edington** *Wilts.* 540Ef
CHURCH OF SS MARY, KATHERINE AND ALL SAINTS A 14th-century collegiate church, cruciform in plan with fairly low embattled central tower and battlements all round. The college was founded by William of Edington in 1351, and the church consecrated ten years later. The Perpendicular font has a Jacobean cover of 1626. There are numerous monuments from the 15th century onwards, including a fine one of *c.* 1630 with recumbent effigies, children and angels, and another of *c.* 1815 by Sir Francis Chantrey. The nave has a 17th-century panelled plaster ceiling.

**Edin's Hall** *Ber.* 562Ee
A complex and unusual group of monuments. The fort, which is the earliest feature, does not crest the hill, Cockburn Law, but is on its sloping north-east side. It is defended by two banks with external ditches and has an entrance at the west end.
The broch is large and circular, some 55 ft in diameter, with 17 ft thick walls, within which are groups of chambers and guard-rooms.
The settlement is sited in the western half of the fort and extends in part over the original defences, which here it has virtually levelled. It consists of many stone foundations of circular huts and the walling of minor enclosures.
The time covered by the three settlements extends from the later Iron Age to perhaps the end of the Romano-British period.

**Edlesborough** *Bucks.* 547Hd
CHURCH OF ST MARY Standing isolated on a mound, this large church is 13th century in its oldest part, was added to in the two following centuries and restored in Victorian times. It has fine Gothic woodwork: a delicate Perpendicular pulpit with tester, fine rood screen and carved misericords on the stalls. The Victorian contributions include stained glass by Warde & Hughes, and Kempe, and painting in the nave. There are also good brasses dating from 1395 to 1540.

**Edmondthorpe** *Leics.* 553Gc
CHURCH OF ST MICHAEL A Decorated church with a 13th-century west tower that was finished in the 15th century, when the clerestory was added to the building. Inside are several monuments of the 17th and 18th centuries.

**Edzell Castle** *Angus* 566Fc
Ruins of a 16th-century castle. The walled Renaissance garden was laid out in 1604; its walls have carvings of the 'cardinal virtues'.

**Eggardon** *Dorset* 540Cc
This fine Iron Age hill-fort has three banks with intermediate ditches and additional defences at the east and north-west entrances. The visible hollows in the 20 acre internal area are grain storage-pits. Also within the defences are two Bronze Age round barrows.

**Egilsay (Isle of)** *Orkney* 569Hg
The ruined 'Irish' round tower stands by the church where St Magnus was murdered, *c.* 1115. Both tower and church date from the 11th century. The tower, now roofless and 48 ft high, was probably at least 60 ft high when first built.

**Egleton** *Rutland* 553Gb
CHURCH OF ST EDMUND The chief interest of this mainly Norman church is the richly carved south doorway and west tower.

**Egmanton** *Notts.* 552Fe
CHURCH OF ST MARY One of the best churches in which to see the work of Sir Ninian Comper, who reconstructed the rood screen and designed the pulpit and organ case for the Duke of Newcastle, *c.* 1898. There is Norman architecture in the nave, but the glass in the east window is also by Comper.

**Eildon Hills North** *Rox.* 562Dd
HILL-FORT AND SIGNAL-STATION This great fort shows evidence of three structural periods. It began with the building of a rampart to enclose the top of the hill, a structure which is now almost obliterated. It was followed by a new work which included the first area and additional ground on the north and north-east slopes of the hill. Finally, two strong ramparts were thrown round the hill to enclose a 40 acre area. This was the chief settlement of the Selgovae tribe. It appears to have been evacuated in AD 79 when the Romans occupied this area and built their fort at Newstead close to the foot of the hill. A small signal-station, used by the Roman garrison, was erected close to the top of the hill, and the shallow circular ditch, broken by a causeway, which lies just to the west of the hill-top, is the last trace of it.

**Eilean Donan Castle** *Ross* 565Gf
Built in 1220 by Alexander II of Scotland, on an islet where Lochs Duich, Aish and Long meet, to ward off Danish raiders; it later passed to the Clan Mackenzie (Earls of Seaforth). In 1719 it was held by Spanish Jacobite troops and bombarded by the *Worcester*, an English warship. It remained a ruin for 200 years before being rebuilt.

**Elford** *Staffs.* 552Db
CHURCH OF ST PETER There is a 16th-century tower, but the rest is mostly a restoration by G. E. Street, *c.* 1870. However, it is full of interesting monuments, many with effigies; outstanding is the mid-15th-century figure of a boy holding a tennis ball, pointing to his head to indicate where the ball had struck and killed him. There is also good ironwork on the door to be seen, and interesting carved work in the corbels and capitals.

**Elgin** *Moray* 566Dg
ANDERSON'S INSTITUTION Founded in 1831 by Lt.-Gen. Anderson as the Elgin Institute for Support of Old Age and Education of Youth. Designed by Archibald Simpson of Aberdeen in the Greek Revival style with recessed two-column Ionic portico surmounted by a tall dome dominating the north front. A six-column Doric portico adds interest to the west elevation.
CATHEDRAL Elgin Cathedral, now in ruins, belongs mainly to the 13th century, although the Diocese of Moray had been founded in 1107. The oldest existing fragments of the building, the choir and transepts, are usually dated after 1224, although their style suggests an earlier period. The presbytery has a great eastern façade composed of rows of lancet windows similar to buildings in England of *c.* 1240–50, although it is usually dated after a great fire of 1270. On the north side is an octagonal chapter house, built in the 13th century but re-roofed and repaired after a further great fire in 1390. The See was dissolved in 1560 and the cathedral no longer required. The lead was stripped from the roof in 1567 and gradual ruination followed. A monument to the Duchess of Gadon survives; the original design by Peter Scheemakers is in the Victoria and Albert Museum.
GRAY'S HOSPITAL Occupying a superb position at the west end of the High Street, this hospital, endowed by Dr Alexander Gray in 1815, was designed by James Gillespie Graham of Edinburgh. A central cupola with octagonal base surmounts a three-storied building with impressive four-column portico.
NO. 7 HIGH STREET Dated 1694, this three-storey house with dormers, crow-stepped gables and stone slated roof was from 1702 to 1722 the home of William Duff of Dipple and Braco, Bankers. The ground floor has an arcade or *piazza* to the street, once a feature of the Elgin street scene.

**Elie** *Fife.* 562Dg
A spacious burgh with attractive kirk of 1726 on the north side of the High Street. Houses in the Scottish native tradition front South Street, some with carved doorpieces and pediments. The Castle, a fine L-plan house of the 17th century in South Street, is the most notable building in the burgh.

**Elkstone** *Glos.* 546Cd
CHURCH OF ST JOHN THE EVANGELIST A Norman church, the Perpendicular west tower with musician gargoyles. Over the south doorway is a sculpture showing Christ in Glory; it is surrounded by rows of grotesque carvings. There is a dove-cote over the east end of the church. Inside is a fine Perpendicular font.

**Ellisland Farm** *Dumf.* 562Aa
In Robert Burns's former granary a collection of folk material is exhibited.

**Elmley Castle** *Worcs.* 546Ce
CHURCH OF ST MARY At the end of a pretty street, beneath Bredon Hill. Here one can see the change in English sculpture during the 17th century. An early work of the century in alabaster, still in the medieval tradition, with recumbent effigies, heraldry, weepers and so on, faces a large marble creation by William Stanton. This has columns, pediment, reclining figure, and standing angels with gilded wings, and is of 1700. Both are beautiful, but quite different.

**Elmore Court** *Glos.* 546Bd
A country mansion with Elizabethan, Stuart and Georgian features. It contains collections of period furniture and tapestries, and a selection of historical manuscripts; it has a 16th-century staircase and fine chimney-pieces.

**Elmswell** *Suffolk* 548Cf
CHURCH OF ST JOHN The west tower has flush-work decoration. The chancel and aisles were rebuilt in the 19th century. There is a carved font, and a monument to Sir Robert Gardner, Lord Chief Justice, ascribed to Maximilian Colt (1619).

---

ELGIN CATHEDRAL

*The Diocese of Moray was founded in 1107 when the Scottish Church was reorganised under Alexander I, but the cathedral at Elgin was not established until 1224. The See was dissolved in 1560 and the buildings gradually disintegrated after 1567 when the lead was stripped from the roof. The stones of the cathedral were used for local building until preservation measures were taken in the 19th century. Many of the Bishops of Moray were employed in the royal service. Bishop Richard (1187–1207) was chaplain to William the Lion, who was one of Elgin's great benefactors. David Murray (1299–1325) was an ardent opponent of Edward I; in 1304 he preached, as though for a crusade, that those who supported Robert de Bruce would acquire as much merit 'as if they had set out from the Holy Land against the Pagans and Saracens'.*

# ELY CATHEDRAL

ELY CATHEDRAL *Originally the monastery and town of Ely were situated on an island in the midst of an immense expanse of marshy Fenland; even today, Ely Cathedral rises clear of the surrounding countryside— the now-drained Fen. The cathedral was probably founded in 673 by St Etheldreda. The present building dates from 1083. There are two heavily carved but very mutilated chantry chapels at the east end of the church. One is dedicated to Bishop Alcock who died in 1501; and the other, dedicated to Bishop West who died in 1534, is particularly interesting for its early use of Renaissance motifs.*

**Elsdon** *Northld.* 563Fb
CHURCH OF ST CUTHBERT A mainly 14th-century church. Inside is a Roman tombstone, brought from a Roman fort at neighbouring High Rochester.

**Elsing** *Norfolk* 554Cc
CHURCH OF ST MARY The church was built by Sir Hugh Hastings, *c.* 1330, with a battlemented west tower. The nave has no aisles, but is nearly 40 ft wide. The octagonal font has a good canopied cover, with some original colouring. Figures in stained glass date from the 14th century. A magnificent brass to the founder, who died in 1347, shows small representations of some of his relatives, including Edward III, on either side of the armoured figure.

**Elstow** *Beds.* 547He
Famous principally for its associations with John Bunyan, who was born there in 1628. His cottage home has, however, since been demolished. The Moot Hall, a splendid red-bricked half-timbered 16th-century building was once a meeting-place for Bunyan's followers. The ground-floor doors and windows, now blocked up, were originally used as shops and stalls.

William the Conqueror's sister founded a nunnery at Elstow which, among other things, celebrated a two-day fair every year. This involved a considerable amount of merry-making among trenchermen and became notorious throughout the country; Bunyan used it in *The Pilgrim's Progress* as the model for his 'Vanity Fair' and Thackeray as the title of a novel nearly 200 years later.

CHURCH OF SS MARY AND HELEN Of Norman monastic foundation, this originally cruciform church has lost its eastern portion. Begun in the 13th century, it was never finished, but there has been good restoration work on the remains. There is a detached tower at the south-west, Norman nave arcades, font, door and brasses; also a 16th-century monument with effigies. John Bunyan was baptised in the church.

To the south of the church are the remains of a lovely Renaissance house called Elstow Place; attributed to Inigo Jones, it is said to incorporate part of the 11th-century nunnery.

**Elton Hall** *Hunts.* 547Hg
The 15th-century gate-house and vaulted crypt are all that remain of a house destroyed during the Commonwealth period. The present Jacobean house was built by Sir Thomas Proby in 1662–89, and his descendants still live there; it has 18th-century alterations and additions. There is a fine library containing early English Bibles and prayer books, including Henry VIII's prayer book with his signature and that of Mary Tudor. There is also a collection of pictures including works by Constable, Reynolds and Frans Hals.

SOUTH TRANSEPT *The magnificent painted roof.*

LANTERN *Inside the unique octagonal lantern tower, built to replace the Norman crossing tower that collapsed in 1322.*

NAVE *The majestic Norman nave, 208 ft long; its roof was painted by le Strange and Perry in the 19th century.*

## Ely *Cambs.* 548Ag

Ely, the Capital of the Fens where Hereward the Wake, 'The Last of the English', held out against William the Conqueror, has some good domestic buildings. They include the half-timbered St Mary's Vicarage, also known as Cromwell House or the Steward's House; a few attractive Georgian houses in St Mary's Street; St John's Farmhouse, 16th century with a good monastic barn of the early 13th century; the small 12th-century remains of the chapel of St John; a good half-timbered 16th-century house, No. 22 Fore Hill; the White Hart Inn, part 15th century with a first-floor gallery; and a charming jumble of small cottages on Waterside, the most picturesque street in the town. Stuntney Hall across the river is a small, early 17th-century squire's house of brick, with gables, a tall gabled porch and two big chimney-breasts. The prior's house, now part of the King's School, has 14th- and 15th-century work with some large windows. The Treasury, or Audit Chamber, was added in the 14th century. Near by is Prior Crauden's Chapel. Recently restored, it is a classic example of the Decorated style, built *c.* 1325. The carved figures in the east window are said to have come from Cologne Cathedral.

BISHOP ALCOCK'S PALACE Built in the late 15th century, of which the east tower and parts of the west tower remain. It has much good red brick-work.

BISHOP'S HOUSE Built into the former great hall of the monastery, which has a 13th-century vaulted undercroft with 13th-century buttresses outside. It was partly rebuilt in the 18th century.

CATHEDRAL The present cathedral was begun in 1083. The choir was rebuilt in the 13th century to provide a more adequate setting for St Ethel-dreda's shrine, and in the 14th century a very elaborate Lady Chapel was added to the north transept. In 1322 the Norman crossing tower collapsed, and was replaced by a larger, octagonal tower surmounted by a timber vault carrying an octagonal lantern. This crossing tower is unique in medieval English architecture and is the cathedral's most characteristic feature. The 12th-century decoration on the exterior of the north wall of the nave is the cathedral's finest carving. Three door-ways of *c.* 1130 survive—originally they opened into the cloister which is now destroyed—and the quality of the carving and its excellent state of preservation place them among the most important survivals of Norman architecture.

CHANTRY The Chantry lies on the north side of Palace Green, with a high brick front wall incorporating an 18th-century wrought-iron gate. The front dates from Charles II's reign; the rear from about 40 years later. Interior features are a rococo ceiling (18th century), made of papier-mâché, and an Ionic chimney-piece of stripped pine.

ELY PORTA The great south gate-house, which was begun in 1397, is unusually broad with square rooms on either side of the gateway and square angled turrets. The long 14th-century barn is now the gymnasium of the King's School. Powchers Hall has an early 16th-century third storey; Walsingham House, built for Alan of Walsingham in 1335, has a late 12th-century Norman doorway, and the Black Hostelry opposite, once a hostel for visiting Benedictine monks, is partly mid-13th century. The rest of the cathedral precinct includes the almonry with a vaulted 12th-century undercroft and the sacristy which was once Alan of Walsingham's offices.

KING'S SCHOOL HEADMASTER'S HOUSE Has a splendid late Norman doorway in the part known as the Storehouse. There are flat 12th-century buttresses on the street front.

**Empingham** *Rutland*                    *553Gb*
CHURCH OF ST PETER A church of grand proportions, it has a west tower with crocketed spire, west front of notable 14th-century work, and a mainly Early English interior, with the arcades and south transept retaining traces of mural paintings. There are fragments of early stained glass.

**Enfield** *Greater London*                *547Jc*
CHURCH OF ST ANDREW Parish church dating from the 13th century; St Andrew's was later enlarged with a 14th-century nave, choir and (probably) west tower. Good monuments include a 15th-century brass with canopy and a standing monument to a Lord Mayor of London (*d.* 1646): he and his wife recline on shelves, the family kneeling below; and a wall tablet with symbolic figures of Faith and Charity by Nicholas Stone, *c.* 1617.

FORTY HALL Built in 1629–32 for Sir Nicholas Raynton, Lord Mayor of London, the museum has a courtyard archway attributed to Inigo Jones. The interior contains 17th-century strapwork ceilings, a carved screen, and moulded medallions of 1787. On permanent display are 17th- and 18th-century paintings, water-colours, pottery and furniture, and there is also a collection of silver plate on loan from the Victoria and Albert Museum. Modern art is occasionally exhibited.

**Enstone** *Oxon.*                         *546Ed*
HOAR STONE This much-denuded long barrow has lost virtually all its mound, so that the roughly rectangular megalithic chamber at the east end stands exposed. Three of its sides are still extant, and fallen stones close by doubtless comprise the capstone and additional parts of the chamber and its entrance structure.

**Epworth** *Lincs.*                        *552Fg*
OLD RECTORY John Wesley (1703–91), the founder of Methodism, and his younger brother Charles, the hymn writer, were born here while their father was Rector of Epworth. Early in 1709 the rectory was burnt down by a mob of people opposed to their father's political views; the house was rebuilt later that year, and was restored in 1957.

**Erith** *Greater London*                  *548Ab*
MUSEUM The exhibits are concerned with local and natural history.

**Erwarton** *Suffolk*                      *548De*
Built *c.* 1549, the house has a red-brick Jacobean gate-house, with rounded arch, buttresses and pinnacles, and four semicircular gables. The house itself was built in 1575 by Sir Philip Parker and has an impressive façade of mullioned windows and gables. Tradition has it that after Anne Boleyn was

ETON COLLEGE

*Eton College was founded in 1440 by Henry VI as a chantry chapel with a school and almshouse attached. It is one of the few great medieval scholastic foundations whose buildings, provided mainly by the founder, survive. The planning passed through several stages, becoming steadily more ambitious; but in 1461 Henry was deposed and the existence of the college was endangered. The present chapel is no more than the choir of the church as originally conceived. Inside is a set of 14th-century wall-paintings which are the finest of their kind surviving in England (one is shown above). In 1463 Edward IV secured a Papal Bull which annexed the college to St George's Chapel, Windsor Castle. However, the provost succeeded in getting the Bull revoked in 1467, and the school was fully established by the reign of Henry VIII.*

beheaded in the Tower in 1536 mourning sympathisers surreptitiously removed her body at night and buried her heart in Erwarton's church. Whether true or not, in 1836 a heart-shaped casket was found buried in the chancel wall.

**Escomb** *Durham* 558Cf
CHURCH OF ST JOHN THE EVANGELIST One of the most striking features of Escomb church is the quality of the masonry—squared ashlar, varying slightly in size, laid in regular courses—which may originally have been Roman. The church, which is one of the most important survivals of early Christian architecture in Britain, consists of a nave and small chancel separated by an arch with carefully fitted Saxon long-and-short work on the side supports. Some of the original windows, small with large embrasures inside, can still be seen.

**Escrick** *Yorks.* 558Eb
CHURCH OF ST HELEN A mid-Victorian Gothic Revival church by F. C. Penrose, who held the appointment of Surveyor to St Paul's Cathedral. There are monuments sculpted by Matthew Cotes Wyatt and by Prince Victor of Hohenlohe-Langenburg, as well as one of a medieval knight.

**Esher** *Surrey* 542Af
CHURCH OF ST GEORGE A delightful 16th-century church, with additions of the 18th and 19th centuries, such as the brick transept and upper west gallery. A marble monument commemorates Princess Charlotte of Wales (George IV's daughter), who died at nearby Claremont in 1817.

**Essendine** *Rutland* 553Gb
CHURCH OF ST MARY A small church, largely Norman, consisting of nave and chancel. Once the chapel of the adjoining castle, which has disappeared, it has been considerably restored and rebuilt. The south doorway has a fine carving of Christ.

**Etchingham** *Sussex* 542De
CHURCH OF SS MARY AND NICHOLAS A former collegiate church, a good example of the Decorated style, built by Sir William de Etchyngham, who died in 1389 and is buried here. The church has a tall central tower, and inside the stalls have interesting misericords. Original tiles and fragments of stained glass remain, but the east window is of 1857, by J. Clayton. There are brasses of the 15th century to the Etchyngham family.

**Eton College** *Bucks.* 547Hb
The present chapel and dining-hall and the east and west sides of the cloister remain from the original medieval buildings built during the reign of Henry VI. In Henry's lifetime the planning of the college passed through several stages, but practically none of the final stage was executed. The famous Long Building and Lower School—the original school buildings—were probably added in the late 15th century, while the west range of the cloister with the big gate-house known as Lupton's Tower was completed in the early 16th century. No further important building took place until the 17th century. By that time the school was firmly established and, at the end of the century, the range known as Upper School was built. The most notable 18th-century buildings are the brewhouse and the library.

**Ettington** *Warks.* 546Ee
CHURCH OF THE HOLY TRINITY In the church is a good example of the work of the London sculptor John Francis Moore. It is the monument to Earl Ferrers, *c.* 1775, and admirably illustrates Moore's love of coloured marbles with cold white contrasting with grey or black as was the fashion.

TOMB OF ALICE DE LA POLE

*In 1437 William de la Pole, Duke of Suffolk, and his wife, Alice, founded an almshouse near the Perpendicular church at Ewelme. In the church is Alice's tomb, with a splendid alabaster effigy. Alice, who died in 1475, was the daughter of Thomas Chaucer, lord of Ewelme Manor, and granddaughter of Geoffrey Chaucer the poet. (Church of St Mary the Virgin, Ewelme)*

**Euston** *Suffolk* 548Cg
CHURCH OF ST GENEVIEVE The church was rebuilt in the late 17th century by an unknown architect incorporating an earlier tower. There is a high-quality carved wood pulpit and reredos, attributed by some to Grinling Gibbons.

**Evesham** *Worcs.* 546De
ABBEY Benedictine abbey of pre-Conquest foundation, though little now remains above ground-level of the 11th-century and later buildings. The most prominent remaining part is the early 16th-century bell-tower.
ALMONRY A 14th-century half-timbered building on the site of the Benedictine abbey.

**Ewelme** *Oxon.* 546Fc
CHURCH OF ST MARY THE VIRGIN The church is a well preserved Perpendicular building. It contains a good but much restored rood screen, and a very striking late 15th-century font cover. There are two magnificent tombs within the church. One, a plain chest with 24 heraldic shields painted on it, is the tomb of Thomas Chaucer. The son of Geoffrey Chaucer, the poet, he was lord of the manor of Ewelme, and a soldier who fought at Agincourt. Alice de la Pole, Duchess of Suffolk, was his daughter, and it was through her marriage that the de la Poles became connected with Ewelme. Alice's tomb is near that of her father. It has a splendid alabaster effigy, carved in a first-class workshop, probably in London. Beneath, behind arcading, her corpse is represented by a repulsive rendering of the shrunken body of an elderly female. Alice died in 1475 and the monument may have been erected by her son, John.
GRAMMAR SCHOOL AND ALMSHOUSE The original buildings of the pre-Reformation almshouse survive. The almshouse is built around a small courtyard at the west end of the church. It was founded in 1437 by William, Duke of Suffolk, and his wife Alice for two chaplains and 13 poor men. Originally one chaplain was to be Master of the almshouse, the other a Grammar Master of the school alongside it. There is now no Grammar Master, and in 1605 the mastership of the almshouse was combined with the Regius Professorship of Medicine at the University of Oxford. The almshouse still functions and the school building survives near by.

**Ewenny Priory** *Glam.* *545Hb*
A monastery with serious military defences. The priory was established in 1141 as a cell of the Benedictine abbey at Gloucester. The walls are mostly 13th century, but there is evidence that they replaced earlier defences. The nave of the mid-12th-century church is still used for services, but the transept and chancel have been cleared for use as a museum. The crude vault of the chancel, which was heightened at an early date and lengthened, is the best Norman work in the county. There are a number of medieval sepulchral slabs with Norman French inscriptions cut in Lombardic characters. Little is left of the convent building which stood to the south on the site now occupied by a modern mansion, whose private grounds extend to the south walls of the church.

**Ewerby** *Lincs.* *553Hd*
CHURCH OF ST ANDREW A fine example of Decorated Gothic architecture, the church has a west tower and an impressive broach spire. The font, which is contemporary with the church, incorporates Norman work. There are some good screens and a late 14th-century effigy in the north aisle.

**Ewloe Castle** *Flints.* *551Je*
This small castle with a D-shaped tower is a well preserved example of a native Welsh castle built before Edward I's conquest at the end of the 13th century.

**Exeter** *Devon* *539Hd*
The Roman city founded in AD 50–55 later became capital of the West Saxon kingdom. The Danes sacked the city in 1003. After the Norman invasion, Exeter was a centre of West Country resistance, but William secured its submission in 1068. A Parliament was held at Exeter in 1286. The impostor Perkin Warbeck led 6000 rebels against the city in 1497, but was forced to withdraw. The Devon sea captains—Drake, Frobisher, Hawkins, Gilbert, Raleigh, Carey—frequented Mol's Coffee House in the Close.

Many Exeter men joined in the Duke of Monmouth's rebellion against James II: Chief Justice Jeffreys held one of his 'Bloody Assizes' in the city, and 80 rebels were hanged (1685).

Exeter's correct title is 'The county and city of Exeter', deriving from the terms of a charter granted by Henry VIII in 1537. With county status, Exeter has its own Sheriff and its own Assize Court.

Near the town centre is a small port, to which sea-going ships of up to 300 tons have access by means of a 5½ mile canal, cut in 1563 by John Trew of Glamorgan. The canal became necessary after Isabel, Countess of Devon, built a weir across the R. Exe in Henry III's reign, thus starting 300 years of litigation.

CATHEDRAL Exeter Cathedral, situated in the centre of the city, was established as a cathedral church in 1050. The two large transept towers are the main remnants of the Norman church; the position of the towers is unusual for the period, and the plan may have come from the Continent. The outer nave walls appear to be Norman as well, but the present cathedral is, in fact, the result of a rebuilding which was begun *c.* 1275. Almost the entire church was remodelled from east to west, the façade being finished *c.* 1360. In spite of the length of time involved, the cathedral has a remarkable unity of style; the main differences occur in the treatment of details, such as the carving of foliage and the design of window tracery.

DEVONSHIRE REGIMENT MUSEUM The Devonshire Regiment was raised in 1685 as The Duke of

EXETER CATHEDRAL
FIGURES ON THE WEST FAÇADE

*The largest surviving array of 14th-century sculpture in England graces the west façade of Exeter Cathedral. The cathedral interior, remodelled in the 13th century, is ornate, with multiplication of mouldings on the arches and piers. The vaulting has more ribs than any other 13th-century church in England, and great cones of descending ribs resemble palm branches. The bishop's throne has some of the most impressive woodcarving of 14th-century Europe. Bishop Stapleden was Edward II's Treasurer; associated with an unpopular ruling clique, he was murdered by a London mob in 1326.*

THE EXETER BOOK OF
OLD ENGLISH VERSE

*This book, the longest single source of Anglo-Saxon poetry, was written between 950 and 1000 and given by Bishop Leofric of Exeter to the cathedral library. This poem, 'The Wanderer', is an exile's lament: 'Oft a solitary mortal wishes for grace, his Maker's mercy. Though sick at heart he must long traverse the watery ways, with his hands must stir the rime-cold sea, and tread the paths of exile.'*
*(Exeter Cathedral Library)*

Beaufort's Musketeers, to help fight the Duke of Monmouth, a natural son of Charles II, who landed at Lyme Regis to claim the English Crown; he was defeated at Sedgemoor (Somerset), captured and beheaded on Tower Hill. The Regiment amalgamated with the Dorset Regiment in 1958. Its history is told in the museum's collection of uniforms, medals, weapons and documents.

GUILDHALL Claimed to be the oldest municipal building in England; it is referred to in a document of 1160. The main hall and roof were completed in 1466, and the mayor's parlour—with a portico overhanging the pavement—in 1595.

ROYAL ALBERT MEMORIAL MUSEUM AND ART GALLERY Founded in 1865, and later extended. The archaeological section includes the Montague Collection of Classical Antiquities. The art gallery concentrates on Devon artists; many works date from before 1800. The Harry Hems Collection of woodcarvings of the Decorated and Perpendicular periods contains specimens from churches in various parts of the country. There is also a collection of British and European lace.

### Exmouth *Devon*      *539Hd*
A LA RONDE A house of circular plan, with a shell gallery, built in the style of the Villa San Vitale, Ravenna, in 1798.

### Exton *Rutland*      *553Gb*
CHURCH OF SS PETER AND PAUL Extensively rebuilt in the mid-19th century after lightning damage, the church contains an impressive series of monuments from the 14th to 18th centuries; there are fine 16th-century tombs with effigies, and work by Grinling Gibbons, Joseph Nollekens, and some attributed to Nicholas Johnson.

### Eyam *Derbys.*      *552De*
In 1665 a box of clothes was sent from London to the village tailor, and thus the great plague (then raging in London) was brought here. The villagers voluntarily isolated themselves to stop the plague spreading farther, and within a year some 259 of the 350 villagers were dead. Their graves are mostly in the churchyard. Seven of the Hancock family, who died between August 3 and August 10, 1665, are buried in Cucklet Dell. Each year on the last Sunday in August the Eyam Plague Commemoration Service, including a procession to Cucklet Dell, takes place.

### Eye *Suffolk*      *548Df*
Once surrounded by water, and named after the old Saxon word for island, this agricultural town received its first charter from King John in 1205. Its Norman castle reverted to the Crown five times, and was finally demolished by Cromwell's army in 1655. Stones from the castle were used to make a castellated house on the original site in the 19th century. Only the old guest house and fishponds remain of the Benedictine monastery founded in 1066. The guildhall is early 16th century and there are some good 18th-century houses.

CHURCH OF SS PETER AND PAUL The 15th-century west tower is one of the best in the county; there is flint and stone panelled decoration from ground to battlements. The rood screen has painted figures, and was restored, together with the rood and loft, by Sir Ninian Comper, *c.* 1925.

### Eye Manor *Herefs.*      *546Af*
A 17th-century Renaissance manor house, built by Ferdinando Gorges, a slave-trader of Barbados. Its fine plaster ceilings resemble those of Holyroodhouse. It contains an exhibition of costumes and books, and the Beck Collection of costume dolls.

### Eynesbury *Hunts.*      *547Jf*
CHURCH OF ST MARY THE VIRGIN Originally Norman, the church was altered in the 13th century and later; the tower on the south dates from the later 17th century. There are many 16th-century benches with carved poppy-heads, and an 18th-century pulpit.

# F

### Faenol Fawr *Flints*      *551Ge*
This Elizabethan house has the date 1597 on a fireplace, and also has a fine stair. It was built by John Lloyd, who was registrar of the Diocese of St Asaph, and has attractive elevations with crow-stepped gables and dormers.

### Fairford *Glos.*      *546Dc*
CHURCH OF ST MARY THE VIRGIN A late 15th-century church with a good central tower, reflecting the prosperity of local wool merchants. The church has 28 windows with magnificent contemporary stained glass illustrating biblical stories; there are also screens, monuments, misericords, and fine roofs. (See p. 198.)

### Falkirk *Stir.*      *562Af*
ROUGH CASTLE The site of a large Roman fort, one of a line of strongholds built by Agricola in AD 80; the forts stretched across the narrow neck of Scotland from Bowling on the Clyde to Bo'ness on the Forth, and 60 years later were linked by the Antonine Wall.

STEEPLE An elegant steeple surmounted by a tapering octagonal spire. It was designed by David Hamilton of Glasgow and built 1813–14 on the foundations of a steeple of 1697, demolished in 1803. It is square in plan and built in four stages.

### Falkland *Fife.*      *562Cg*
Lying in the Fife hills this burgh, with its palace completed in 1542 by James V as the centrepiece, possesses many buildings of interest. Key House of 1713, thatched Moncrieffe House dated 1610, and Cameron House, also thatched, are the best of the houses of some pretension in the High Street. The Classical town house of 1801 with octagonal belfry is another notable building.

Some 18th-century weavers' houses, many built using the solid rock as a foundation, border the narrow streets leading from the Bruce Fountain of 1856.

FALKLAND PALACE A 16th-century hunting palace of the Stuart Kings until the death in 1625 of James VI of Scotland (James I of England). The palace, which was frequently used by Mary, Queen of Scots, is now owned by the Queen. The gardens have been restored to the original royal plan.

### Falkland Memorial *Berks.*      *546Ea*
A 19th-century monument to Lucius Cary, 2nd Viscount Falkland (1610–43) who fell at the first Battle of Newbury.

### Falmer *Sussex*      *542Bd*
The new University of Sussex is one of the most dramatic groups of modern buildings. It was

begun in 1960, and Sir Basil Spence was the architect. The dominant motif, which recurs again and again in different sizes and proportions, is of red brick and exposed concrete lintels, arched on their undersides.

**Falmouth** *Cornwall* 538Cb
The great natural harbour of Falmouth only began to be developed as a maritime port in 1688 when it was selected as a station for the Mail Packet Service. By 1827 this service had 39 vessels conveying mail to America, the West Indies, South America and the Mediterranean; but when steam replaced sail the service was transferred to Southampton and Falmouth declined.

**Fareham** *Hants.* 541Hd
The old High Street has the longest and most varied stretch of Georgian architecture in Hampshire, a relic of the days when it was fashionable for naval officers from Portsmouth to retire here. The locally made red bricks glow with colour. The Kintyre Hotel, one of the best houses, is dated 1756.

**Faringdon** *Berks.* 546Ec
CHURCH OF ALL SAINTS A large, cruciform church, with low central tower that has lost its spire. All Saints dates from the 12th to 19th centuries, with the 13th predominating. The font is Perpendicular, and the 13th-century south door has decorative ironwork with dragon monuments, including those to the Unton (16th century) and Pye (18th century) families. There is also a typical work by Edward Stanton of Holborn (*c.* 1706).

**Farleigh Castle** *Som.* 540Df
The ruins of a castle built *c.* 1383 by Sir Thomas Hungerford. The inner bailey containing the domestic buildings is surrounded by a curtain wall with round towers. There are monuments to the Hungerford family in the chapel, which was originally a parish church.

**Farnborough Hall** *Warks.* 546Ee
A country mansion, mainly rebuilt in the 18th century, with fine plasterwork designed to harmonise with Italian paintings and sculptures. The grounds contain a long terrace walk and two temples.

**Farnham** *Surrey* 541Jf
There are two fine streets in the town. West Street has two sumptuous Georgian houses, Willmer House of 1718, and Sandford House of 1757. Castle Street, a picture of domestic variety, leads to the castle.
CASTLE The building of Farnham Castle was begun by Henry of Blois, Bishop of Winchester (1129–71). In 1155 Henry II ordered everything built by Henry, who was King Stephen's brother, to be destroyed, although the foundations of the massive central tower can still be seen on top of the existing (artificial) mound; the present shell wall was built soon afterwards. Immediately behind the wall lies the castle court, and beyond that parts of a further perimeter wall with a gate-house. Both the court and the wall date from the late 12th and early 13th centuries, although they have been extensively repaired and altered. The castle keep is the most interesting and impressive part of the remains. Farnham Castle has been continuously occupied, apart from a short period during the Civil War, and the main buildings round the castle have been considerably altered. The great hall has been much reduced in size.
WILLMER HOUSE MUSEUM This early Georgian house has a façade of cut and moulded brick dated 1718, and contains fine carving and panelling. Its collections cover life in the district from earliest

STAINED GLASS OF A DEVIL'S HEAD
*The parish church at Fairford is the only one which has kept its complete set of medieval stained glass windows. These were painted between 1495 and 1505 when the present church was built. This devil's head is a detail of the western window depicting the Day of Judgment. In the north clerestory window other devils stand above the Persecutors of the Church. The series of 28 windows also shows events from the Gospels, saints and martyrs from Church history, and prophets of the Old Testament. The strong Flemish influence suggests that some of Henry VII's men were employed here. The king himself was the owner of the manor and many of his glaziers were of Flemish origin. (Church of St Mary the Virgin, Fairford)*

times and include archaeological finds, 17th- and 18th-century furniture and clocks, costumes, folk material, and items associated with local artists, architects and inventors. There is also a collection of 19th-century English and French glass paperweights.

**Farningham** *Kent* 542Cf
Once an important stop for coaches on the Dover Road, hence the handsome 18th-century houses, and the splendid red-brick Lion Inn.

**Farnworth** *Lancs.* 552Af
CHURCH OF ST LUKE Originally 12th-century, but now mainly Decorated and Perpendicular Gothic, with 19th-century restoration. There are many monuments, some to the Bold family by Pietro Tenerani, Sir Francis Chantrey and the firm of Franceys of Liverpool, who employed as an apprentice John Gibson, one of the most successful 19th-century English sculptors.

**Faversham** *Kent* 542Ef
A quiet old town. It was once a flourishing port, and the best street, Abbey Street, has wharves behind it. Recently well restored, Abbey Street perfectly expresses modest Georgian prosperity.
ARDEN'S HOUSE A 15th-century house, sometimes called the Old Abbey because of its 12th-century abbey remains. It commemorates the name of Thomas Arden, who was murdered here in 1550.
FREEMASON'S·HALL The hall of Queen Elizabeth's Grammar School, founded in 1576.

**Fawsley** *Northants.* 546Ff
CHURCH OF ST MARY Mainly Decorated, the church has 13th-century details in the arcade. There is a west tower. Main interest lies in the many monuments to the Knightley family, which include brasses. A magnificent coloured altar-tomb of *c.* 1619 has recumbent effigies. Two large urns on pedestals of *c.* 1681 and *c.* 1715 might possibly be the work of William Stanton and his son Edward, and there is also a mid-19th-century work by John Gibson.

**Fedw Deg** *Caern.* 550Fd
Part of this 16th-century house has been destroyed, but the surviving section has been restored. Typical of this slate area is the arched door-head, which is cut out of a single slab; also of interest is the primitive 'pre-glazing' wooden mullioned window. The parish of Penmachno in which the house stands is rich in 16th- and 17th-century houses.

**Felbrigg** *Norfolk* 554Dd
CHURCH OF ST MARGARET The church, which has Decorated and Perpendicular work, is remarkable for its many 14th-century monuments. These include the brass to Simon de Fellbrigg (*d.* 1416), Standard-bearer to Richard II. Other monuments are to William Windham (*d.* 1686), for which Grinling Gibbons was paid, and William Windham (*d.* 1813) by Joseph Nollekens. Other features of the church are a 14th-century octagonal font, box-pews and a fire-place in the tower.

**Felmersham** *Beds.* 547Hf
There are many stone-built houses of great charm here, a great buttressed tithe barn opposite the 13th-century Church of St Mary the Virgin, and the picturesque Six Ringers Inn.
CHURCH OF ST MARY THE VIRGIN An impressive 13th-century church, and a fine example of Early English work, especially the west façade. There is a central tower; during the 15th century the nave walls were raised to give a flat-pitched roof and clerestory. A delicate screen of the same period contrasts strongly with the massive piers of the crossing.

**Fenny Bentley** *Derbys.* 552Dd
CHURCH OF ST EDWARD A Gothic church with a restored west tower. There is a good early 16th-century rood screen still with its vaulting. From slightly later in the same century come the two macabre tomb-effigies.

**Fenstanton** *Hunts.* 547Jf
The home of Capability Brown, the famous landscape gardener. Brown, his wife and their eldest son are buried in the church.

**Fettercairn** *Kinc.* 566Fc
In the main square is the shaft of the old Kincardine Tower Cross (1670) which is notched to show the length of the Scottish ell (37 inches).

**Ffestiniog Railway** *Caern.–Merioneth.* 550Fd
This 13 mile long narrow-gauge railway connecting the slate quarries of Ffestiniog with Portmadoc was opened in 1836, first as a horse-drawn tramway; then, in 1863, steam engines were introduced. This was in many ways a pioneering railway, and on it ran the first articulated locomotive in the world (1869) and the first bogie coach (1872).

**Ffynnon Gybi (St Gybi's Well)** *Caern.* 550Ed
Set in a valley immediately north of the church, the two well chambers with attached cottage and a small privy, although simple in style, form the most elaborate establishment of its kind in the

county. To the north of the larger well is a smaller one of the kind adjacent to many old churches in the area. Although archaic in appearance the larger building is most likely to be the work of a Merioneth squire, who *c.* 1750, 'caused proper conveniences for Bathing, and other improvements to be made'.

**Filkins** *Oxon.* 546Dc
FILKINS AND BROUGHTON POGGS MUSEUM Over 150 years of village life is reflected in the display of items made and used in the farms, workshops and cottages of Filkins and the surrounding district. The museum is housed in a small Cotswold stone cottage and village lock-up.

**Finavon** *Angus* 566Eb
VITRIFIED FORT A long, rather narrow fort which excavation showed had a wall about 20 ft thick, still standing some 16 ft above its original ground surface. This wall had been timber-laced and it is thought that the burning of these timbers resulted in heavy vitrification, or 'melting' of the stone.

**Finchale Priory** *Durham* 558Cb
Finchale Priory was founded in 1237 on the banks of the R. Wear and laid out on the normal monastic plan. This plan proved unsuitable for the revised establishment of the 14th century, when Finchale became the holiday house for the monks of Durham Cathedral Priory, and the church was drastically reduced in size; the refectory seems to have been abandoned in the 15th century, when part of it was turned into chambers for the monks. The life of this small community centred on the prior's lodgings, a well developed domestic residence, with its own hall, chamber, chapel and kitchen.

**Finchingfield** *Essex* 548Be
An unspoilt village, with a charming street of varied houses climbing the hill from the green and duckpond to the church. There is a guildhall of *c.* 1500; a late 18th-century hexagonal thatched cottage, the Round House; and a windmill. One mile north is Spains Hall, a red-brick house of *c.* 1570 with a two-storey porch and seven gables on the front.

**Finlarig Castle** *Perths.* 566Aa
The ruined stronghold of the Earls of Breadalbane at the head of Loch Tay, built in 1621–9. Near the entrance tower is the beheading pit where executions were carried out by means of a crude form of guillotine—called The Maiden or sometimes The Widow. The castle is described in Scott's *Fair Maid of Perth*.

**Firle Place** *Sussex* 542Cd
The home of the Gage family since the 15th century. General Thomas Gage was Commander-in-Chief of the British army at the beginning of the American War of Independence (1775–81) and the house contains items he brought from America. The original Tudor house was reconstructed in Georgian style *c.* 1730 and contains French and English furniture, Sèvres porcelain and old masters from the Cowper Collection.

**Fishbourne** *Sussex* 541Jd
ROMAN VILLA Situated near Chichester, this great Roman house contains a fine mosaic floor, laid early in the 3rd century AD. (See p. 200.)

**Fishlake** *Yorks.* 552Fg
CHURCH OF ST CUTHBERT Originally a Norman church, with alterations up to the 15th century. There is a fine Norman south door with lavish carving. Inside are a medieval carved font, screens and a monument of *c.* 1505.

**Five Knolls** *Beds.* *547Hd*
This is an unusual barrow group with a triple bell barrow and two normal bowl barrows. In addition, there are what may be two of the rare pond barrows. Excavation of the mounds showed them to belong to the Early Bronze Age, but with some surviving Neolithic traces. Mutilated human remains found in one mound suggest that 2000 years later several Anglo-Saxons were killed in a skirmish near by.

**Flamborough** *Yorks.* *559Gc*
CHURCH OF ST OSWALD Rebuilt during the 19th century, it has a Norman chancel arch and font. There is a 15th–16th-century screen with one of the two surviving Yorkshire rood lofts, which still has some of its original colouring; there are parclose screens as well, and some monuments.

**Flamstead** *Herts.* *547Hd*
CHURCH OF ST LEONARD The church was originally Norman, but it is now mainly of the 13th and 14th centuries. It contains a number of 13th- and 14th-century mural paintings—St Christopher, Christ in Glory, the Last Supper—and monuments by William Stanton, late 17th century, and an early work by John Flaxman.

**Flatford Mill** *Suffolk* *548De*
One of the 18th-century water-mills owned by the father of John Constable (1776–1837), landscape artist. Flatford Mill figures in his painting *The Hay Wain.* Near by is Willy Loft's Cottage, an early 17th-century house, beautifully sited beside the mill stream. (Interiors not open.)

**Fleet** *Dorset* *540Dc*
CHURCH OF THE HOLY TRINITY An attractive Gothic church with a west tower, built in 1827–9 to replace the old church which was badly damaged by a gale in 1824. The apsidal chancel has a good vaulted plaster roof, and contains a large marble monument with mourning figures, *c.* 1818.

**Fleet** *Lincs.* *553Jc*
CHURCH OF ST MARY MAGDALENE A 14th-century Fenland church, with tower and spire detached from the main building. Apart from the chancel, rebuilt in 1862, the remainder of the church is in the Decorated style, except for Early English arcades and the Perpendicular west window.

**Flint Castle** *Flints.* *551He*
The ruined Flint Castle has a great round tower or donjon outside the circuit of the walls. It is the only example of this plan used by Edward I, who in all his other castles used the more 'modern' form of great, independently defended gate-houses.

**Flitton** *Beds.* *547He*
CHURCH OF ST JOHN THE BAPTIST The church is mainly 15th century, and is noted for its many monuments to Earls and Dukes of Kent; the later ones are in a family mausoleum. Among sculptors whose work is represented are Thomas Banks and Matthew Noble. There is also a number of brasses.

**Floors Castle** *Rox.* *562Ed*
A large 18th-century mansion, originally designed in 1718 by Vanbrugh but later altered by Playfair, with an abundance of capped turrets surmounting a façade that shows Tudor influence.

MOSAIC FLOOR AT FISHBOURNE ROMAN VILLA

*There were several phases of construction at this great Roman house, and early in the 3rd century this fine floor was laid. On the panel, roughly 17 ft by 17 ft and surrounded by a chequered border, the central medallion shows a winged boy astride a dolphin, and the semicircles show sea-horses and sea-panthers.*

## Fochabers *Moray* 566Eg
The 4th Duke of Gordon replaced the old burgh of Fochabers, *c.* 1780, by a new planned village at a respectful distance outside the castle walls. Laid out by Thomas Mylne, his surveyor, the traditional two-storey houses and church with portico and steeple were designed by John Baxter in 1798. The village was planned on the rectilinear principle with main street and parallel back streets and large open space in the centre. Milne's Institute, designed by Thomas MacKenzie of Elgin in 1843, is a notable later building.

## Folkestone *Kent* 542Fe
Until the railways acquired the port in 1842 for the sum of £18,000, the town had little significance except as a smuggling centre, which flourished *c.* 1800. It is now a holiday resort and cross-Channel port. Just to the north is an ancient fortification called Caesar's Camp. On the Leas, a shrub and floral coastal walk, is a statue of William Harvey, the great anatomist who discovered the circulation of blood, born in Folkestone in 1578.

## Folkingham *Lincs.* 553Hc
CHURCH OF ST ANDREW An interesting church, with an outstanding Perpendicular tower, it retains evidence of its Norman origins. Inside are 14th-century arcades, early 15th-century windows, a good screen, and an Early English chancel.

## Forde Abbey *Som.* 540Bd
A Cistercian monastery, founded in 1138, notable for its collection of tapestries and 15 acres of fine gardens.

## Fordham *Norfolk* 554Ab
SNORE HALL A little-known house built of brick *c.* 1480–90. It has buttresses with pinnacles, an embattled porch, and on the west side a gable and panelled shafts running up the middle. On the south side are Elizabethan (or Jacobean) windows and a big chimney-stack of the same period. The house has a secret chamber, 3 ft by 6 ft.

## Fordwich *Kent* 542Ff
Once a town, now a tiny village, Fordwich has kept its half-timbered town hall, on the quay-side by the R. Stour.

## Foremark *Derbys.* 552Dc
CHURCH OF ST SAVIOUR Built in 1662, it has a Gothic exterior with an embattled west tower. The interior is Renaissance with a 17th-century screen, a three-decker pulpit and box-pews. The iron communion rails are probably by Robert Bakewell, who made the screens in Derby Cathedral.

## Forfar *Angus* 566Eb
MEFFAN INSTITUTE MUSEUM Devoted to the history of Forfar from earliest times, and to its geology and natural history. A bridle used during the burning of witches in 1650–62 is included.

## Forrabury Common *Cornwall* 538Dd
A unique survival of the Celtic (pre-Saxon) system of land tenure—stitchmeal. There are 42 'stitches' or small fields grouped at the edge of the common, each field containing a portion of better soil and not so good soil.

## Forse *Caith.* 569Ld
SETTLEMENT COMPLEX The remains of this homestead are complex, and their sequence obscure. The first structure was probably the circular enclosure, some 45 ft across, with a 4 ft thick wall. This may have been sited within an outer enclosure measuring about 40 yds by 35 yds, formed by an earthen bank. The complex is of Iron Age type.

## Fort Augustus *I'ness.* 565Je
Built in 1715–30 to help quell the Jacobite rebellion, the fort is named after William Augustus, Duke of Cumberland—'Butcher' Cumberland of Culloden. The site was given to the Benedictine order in the 19th century and the abbey, with cloisters and tower designed by Pugin, was built.

## Fort George *I'ness.* 566Bf
REGIMENTAL MUSEUM OF THE SEAFORTH HIGHLANDERS, THE QUEEN'S OWN CAMERON HIGHLANDERS AND QUEEN'S OWN HIGHLANDERS The history of these regiments is reflected in the uniforms, medals, weapons, silver, prints and pictures displayed in a building erected over 200 years ago to designs by Robert Adam.

## Forth Railway Bridge 562Bf
The first plans for a bridge over the Forth, to link Edinburgh with the north of Scotland, were drawn up by Sir Thomas Bouch. However, following the disastrous destruction of his bridge over the Tay in 1879, these were dropped. Sir John Fowler and Sir Benjamin Baker drew up new plans, and in 1882 work began on the present enormous cantilever construction, with 1700 ft main spans—a world record for many years. The bridge, about 5300 ft long altogether, and 360 ft above high water, was opened in March 1890.

## Forton *Staffs.* 552Bc
CHURCH OF ALL SAINTS An interesting combination of Georgian and medieval work, All Saints was begun in Norman times, enlarged during the Gothic period, and altered in the 18th century. An 18th-century south wall and nave link the squat medieval tower with the Decorated east end.

## Fort William *I'ness.* 565Hc
The base for climbers ascending Ben Nevis, the highest mountain in the British Isles (4406 ft).
THE FORT The stronghold was built in 1655 to restrain the Highlanders; it was rebuilt by General Wade in 1715, but the fortifications were dismantled in 1855.

## Foss Dyke *Lincs.* 553Ge
Still a navigable canal with a tow-path which can be walked from end to end, this waterway links the R. Witham at Lincoln with the R. Trent at Torksey. It formed part of a system of water-transport designed by the Romans, probably to convey the corn of East Anglia to the garrison at York and thence north by road. Much of the first part of that system, the Car Dyke, which ran from the R. Cam near Cambridge to the central river-system of the Fens and then from the Nene to the Witham, is now filled in or incorporated in the Fenland dyke-drainage system. But the Foss Dyke was reconditioned in post-Roman times and still provides a route by water from Lincoln to the Trent and so down to the Humber and up the Yorkshire Ouse.

## Foston Old Rectory *Yorks.* 558Ec
Designed and built of pink brick in 1813–14 by Sydney Smith, the Rector of Foston. An essayist noted for his wit, Smith later became a canon of St Paul's.

## Fotheringhay *Northants.* 547Hg
CHURCH OF ST MARY AND ALL SAINTS Part of a college founded in 1411, the church was partially demolished after the Dissolution when the chancel was pulled down. All that remains is the nave and aisles. The west tower becomes a pinnacled octagonal lantern at its upper stage. There are flying buttresses from the high clerestory and a Perpendicular pulpit with a vaulted tester. The contract for the nave survives and is dated 1434.

# MARIE R

## MARY QUEEN OF SCOTS, SCOTLAND'S TRAGIC QUEEN

Mary Stuart, 'the fairest and most cruel queen on earth' became Queen of Scotland at eight days old. She married the Dauphin of France at 15, sending a miniature of herself to her cousin Elizabeth, which remains in the Royal Library, Windsor. In 1558 Mary became heir apparent to the English throne and in 1559 Queen of France as well. Her troubles began when her young husband died and the 18-year-old Papist queen returned to Protestant Scotland. Her personal apartments at Holyroodhouse can be visited and a brass plate marks the spot where her favourite secretary was murdered at the instigation of her jealous second husband, Lord Darnley. At the Castle of Loch Leven Mary was held after the mad episode of her abduction and marriage to the Earl of Bothwell and the disaster of the Battle of Carberry Hill. At 26 Mary fled to England, where she was imprisoned for 19 years. Her embroideries can be seen at Holyrood and Hardwick Hall.

LE DEUIL BLANC *(white widow) portrait, after a sketch by Clouet or Jehan de Court, painter to the King of France. It gives an accurate map of the features of Mary without catching anything of the vivacity and charm of the 18-year-old queen in her white widow's weeds. (National Portrait Gallery)*

GOLD DUCAT *of extreme rarity struck for the wedding of Mary and the Dauphin of France, with the arched crown of Scotland suspended between them. They became king and queen when Henri II died after being accidentally struck in the eye at a tournament. (British Museum)*

CHILD PORTRAIT *of Mary's son who was crowned James VI of Scotland on the abdication of his mother, when he was 14 months old. In 1603, he was also crowned James I of England. (Scottish National Portrait Gallery)*

HENRY, LORD DARNLEY *and* MARY STUART. *Mary's headlong infatuation and marriage to her 19-year-old cousin culminated in his murder 18 months later at Kirk o' Field. (Engraving at the British Museum)*

SILVER CASKET *said to be identical with the one discovered at Kirk o' Field after Darnley's murder. It contained love letters from Mary to Bothwell and other documents incriminating the queen in the murder of her husband. It is not certain whether these are authentic or forgeries.*
*(Lennoxlove Museum, East Lothian)*

SCOTTISH PENNY, *about 1554, with the earliest likeness of the queen as a five-year-old child. Aged six she went to be educated with the French royal children, having been engaged to the Dauphin. Her mother remained in Scotland as Regent. (British Museum)*

THE PENCUIK JEWELS AND FAN *which belonged to Queen Mary. She was greatly loved by her attendants and during the last hours before her execution, divided her exquisite treasures amongst them. These possessions she gave to one of her maids of honour. The locket, known as the Pencuik Jewel, opens to show a tiny miniature of the queen. On the back is a miniature of her son as a boy of about ten. (Scottish National Museum of Antiquities)*

GOLDEN ROSARY, CRUCIFIX AND PRAYERBOOK *carried by Mary Queen of Scots to her execution. On the steps of the scaffold she spoke to the assembly 'with joyous countenance' saying 'I have been brought before a company who will witness that I die a Catholic.' (Arundel Castle, Sussex)*

MARY'S SIGNET RING, *the shoulders ornamented with leaves and flowers and engraved with the emblem of Mary. In the hoop at the back are the marks of Mary and Francis, her first husband. (British Museum)*

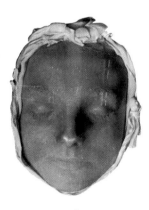

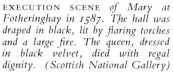

EXECUTION SCENE *of Mary at Fotheringhay in 1587. The hall was draped in black, lit by flaring torches and a large fire. The queen, dressed in black velvet, died with regal dignity. (Scottish National Gallery)*

HIGHLAND HARP *or clarsach said to have been given by Queen Mary to Beatrix Gardyne. This fine Celtic harp was probably made about AD 1500. (Scottish National Museum of Antiquities)*

DEATH MASK *of Mary. When the executioner held up the head crying 'God Save the Queen', the coverings fell off showing it to be 'as grey as if she had been three score years and ten, polled very short'. The head was placed in the castle window for an hour so that the crowd could see it. (Lennoxlove, East Lothian)*

FOUNTAINS ABBEY

*Fountains Abbey was founded in 1132 on a site which was later described as 'fit more for the dens of wild beasts than for the uses of man'. At first the monks suffered considerable privations and hardship, but the abbey ultimately became the richest Cistercian house in England, although its inmates were not especially distinguished either for holiness or scholarship. The ruins of the abbey form one of the most complete sets of Cistercian buildings to survive the Dissolution of the monasteries.*

**Foulden** *Ber.*       *562Fe*
TITHE BARN One of the few remaining tithe barns in Scotland, situated in the north-east corner of the churchyard belonging to the parish church of 1786; it has two floors with crow-stepped gables and outside stone stairs leading to the first floor.

**Fountains Abbey** *Yorks.*       *558Cc*
The buildings of Fountains Abbey, founded in 1132, were reconstructed between 1148 and 1179 after enemies of the abbot had broken in and destroyed the abbey by fire. The only major additions after 1179 were the north tower, built by Abbot Huby (1479–94), and the Chapel of the Nine Altars at the east end of the church, built between 1203 and 1247. The whole ground plan has survived, and the positions of the refectory and the lay brothers' quarters (peculiar to Cistercian monasteries) can be clearly seen. The abbey also possesses the most imposing surviving medieval provisions for waterworks and drainage, most of the 12th-century tunnelling constructed to conduct the R. Skell along the chosen course being still visible. The house is now approached through the beautiful grounds of Studley Royal.

**Fountains Abbey Garden** See Studley Royal.

**Fountains Hall** *Yorks.*       *558Cc*
Built in the late 16th century from abbey stones, the Hall was begun by Sir Richard Gresham (connected with the merchant bank in London) and sold, in 1597, to Sir Stephen Proctor, who completed the building by 1611. There is a fine oriel window in the great chamber.

**Fowlis Easter** *Angus*       *566Da*
CHURCH A mid-15th-century church, which retains some of the painted panels of its former rood screen. There is also a tabernacle with a sculptured representation of the Annunciation.

**Fowlis Wester** *Perths.*       *566Ca*
A fine Pictish symbol stone, 10 ft high, stands railed within the village. Its carvings are elaborate

examples of Pictish work, but today it is weathered.

**Foxdenton Hall** *Lancs.*       *552Bf*
A Stuart mansion, reconstructed in 1700 and restored in 1965.

**Fox's Hospital** *Wilts.*       *540Fe*
A group of 12 red-brick, Flemish bond almshouses, designed by Wren and modernised in the 20th century. They were built in 1681–2 through the bounty of Sir Stephen Fox, Paymaster to the Armed Forces of Charles II.

**Framlingham** *Suffolk*       *548Ef*
An old market town with some pleasant domestic architecture on Castle Street and Market Hill; also the late 17th-century Ancient House with pargetting, and two sets of almshouses of 1654 and 1703.
CHURCH OF ST MICHAEL Rebuilt from mid-15th century, it has a west tower and a magnificent nave roof. It is famous for its 16th-century monuments to the Duke of Richmond (1536), and to members of the family of the Dukes of Norfolk, with carved recumbent effigies. From the mid-18th century is a minor work by Louis Roubiliac.
CASTLE When built by Roger Bigod, the 2nd Earl of Norfolk, *c.* 1190, it was the most modern type of defence then known. The keep and bailey plan was being abandoned in favour of a uniform curtain wall with projecting towers, and Framlingham is an early English example of this style, built before square towers had been replaced by round ones. The rebellious medieval owners of Framlingham frequently forfeited the castle to the Crown. It was attacked and taken by King John's forces in 1215 but underwent no other siege. In 1553 when it was held by the Crown, it was the home of Mary Tudor, and became a rallying point for her supporters at the beginning of her reign, when her succession to the throne was in doubt. In the 17th century Pembroke College, Cambridge, received the castle as a bequest, and was instructed to build a Poor House, which still exists on the site of the Bigod great hall (fragments of which are embedded in the present building).

**Frampton** *Dorset*       *540Dc*
CHURCH OF ST MARY Later additions to the original 15th-century church include the 17th-century west tower, the 18th-century north aisle, and the south aisle, added in 1871. Monuments include 17th-century recumbent effigies, and a large wall monument of *c.* 1750 with a bust and flying cherub, probably by Sir Henry Cheere.

**Frampton Court** *Glos.*       *546Bc*
Built in 1731 in the style of Vanbrugh, it has fine panelling and 18th-century furniture. An ornamental canal leads to an orangery of 'Strawberry Hill' style Gothic design. (By appointment.)

**Frampton-on-Severn** *Glos.*       *546Bc*
CHURCH OF ST MARY This church, with its pinnacled west tower, is mainly Decorated and Perpendicular Gothic. The lead font is Norman. Monuments with effigies of a knight and lady date from the 14th century; the pulpit is dated 1622.

**Freiston** *Lincs.*       *553Jd*
CHURCH OF ST JAMES The remains of the church of the former 12th-century priory; the present building shows Norman work. Inside are good screens, and a Perpendicular font with cover.

**Fressingfield** *Suffolk*       *548Eg*
CHURCH OF SS PETER AND PAUL A Decorated and Perpendicular church, with west tower, clerestory and vaulted two-storey south porch. Inside are good benches with carving.

FRAMLINGHAM CASTLE

By the middle of the 12th century Framlingham was one of a group of castles in the eastern counties held by the powerful Bigod family, Earls of Norfolk. Framlingham was destroyed in 1174, but Roger, the 2nd Earl, built a new and stronger castle about 1190. The layout of the rooms is now almost completely lost, although the house was still inhabited in the 16th century when it had passed to the Howard family. The destruction seems to have occurred in the 17th century when the castle was bequeathed to Pembroke College, Cambridge, which was instructed to pull it down 'saving the stone building'.

FURNESS ABBEY

Originally a Savignac house, this abbey was taken over by the Cistercian order in 1147, and became the second richest Cistercian house in England after Fountains Abbey, acquiring extensive property in northern England and the Isle of Man. The piscina and sedilia in the presbytery are among the finest to survive from the 12th and 13th centuries. The 'bays' to the right are the sedilia, and the piscina at the left formerly had a basin with towel recesses on each side.

**Freston Tower** *Suffolk*                    548De
A slim, dramatic, six-storied tower-house with a spiral staircase linking each floor, it was built of red diapered brickwork *c.* 1550. Thought to have been designed by one of the Latimers, the early English Church reformers, as a school for his daughter, it has six rooms set one above another. This strange design is said to have represented the successive stages of her education.

**Fritton** *Suffolk*                    548Fh
CHURCH OF ST EDMUND The church has a thatched nave, a circular Norman tower, and a Norman apse. Inside is a three-decker 17th-century pulpit, and some medieval mural painting.

**Frome** *Som.*                    540Df
A town of Saxon origin, and the scene of brutal executions following the Duke of Monmouth's rebellion in 1684. A waterway runs along the centre of Cheap Street, emerging from paving stones at one end and disappearing at the other.

**Froyle** *Hants.*                    541Je
CHURCH OF THE ASSUMPTION The brick nave, dating from the early 19th century, is by James Harding, but the chancel is part of the original church and dates from the late 13th century, while the west tower is of *c.* 1720. Fragments of medieval heraldic stained glass remain, and the windows of 1874–97 are by C. E. Kempe.

**Furness Abbey** *Lancs.*                    557Ac
Furness Abbey was founded in 1123, but the present buildings belong almost entirely to the period after it became a Cistercian house in 1147. A great deal of the abbey survives, including the east end of the church and the transepts up to roof level, and the east side of the cloister with the adjoining 13th-century chapter house. The surviving parts of other monastic buildings make it possible to appreciate the size of the abbey. The dormitory was over 200 ft long, the infirmary 126 ft, and the refectory nearly 150 ft (at Fountains Abbey the refectory is about 100 ft long and the dormitory about 110 ft). The abbey's great size created problems, and the refectory in particular seems to have been made smaller, possibly *c.* 1500.

# G

**Gaddesby** *Leics.*         *552Fb*
CHURCH OF ST LUKE An impressive medieval church, primarily late 14th-century work. The south side is lavishly decorated with stone carvings of the same period. There has been some restoration on the interior. In the chancel is a life-size statue of Colonel Cheney on horseback at Waterloo, by J. Gott.

**Gainsborough** *Lincs.*      *552Ff*
A market town identified with 'St Ogg's' in George Eliot's *Mill on the Floss*. The 15th-century Old Hall in the town centre is traditionally the scene of the assassination of Sweyne, King Canute's father.
OLD HALL The original medieval Hall was wrecked during the Wars of the Roses; the present house, partly of brick and partly in half-timbering, was built *c.* 1500. In the late 16th century it was the meeting place of the early Dissenters, later known as the Pilgrim Fathers. John Wesley, the founder of Methodism, preached at the Hall several times. It is now a folk museum which also has collections of furniture, paintings, coins, china, dolls and period dresses.

**Garn Bodfean** *Caern.*     *550Dd*
A mile from the sea, south of Nevin, stands an isolated hill, on the crown of which is this Iron Age hill-fort. The defences, though originally of some strength, are no longer in good condition, but relics of its occupation still survive in the form of many round stone-built huts, still quite well preserved. The crest of the hill is marked by rubble remains which may have been at one time the motte of an early castle of the English conquest.

**Garthewin** *Denb.*        *551Ge*
A Georgian mansion overlooking the Elwy Valley, built in 1730 and altered in 1772. Near the main house is an 18th-century barn now used as a small theatre. Period furniture, armorial china and a collection of portraits of the Wynne family are displayed in the house.

**Garway** *Herefs.*        *546Ad*
CHURCH OF ST MICHAEL AND ALL ANGELS This was one of the round churches of the Knights Templar, an order of the knighthood founded *c.* 1118 to guard pilgrims on their way to Jerusalem; it dates from the late 12th century. Part of the original round nave is visible, but the present nave is 13th century. The Norman chancel arch remains. The early 13th-century west tower was once detached from the church. The stalls, benches, communion rails and panelling are all of the 16th and 17th centuries. South of the church is a dove-cote dated 1326.

**Garynahine** *Lewis*      *568Bc*
STONE CIRCLE The stones comprise a central slab surrounded by a ring of boulders. Outside these is a second ring composed of upright stone slabs, the tallest rising to a height of 9 ft. Five of these uprights remain, the sixth having disappeared.

**Gatehouse of Fleet** *Kirkcud.*    *566Eg*
A pleasant burgh of two-storey traditional stone houses with symmetrical three-window elevations distinguished here and there by pedimented doorways and window surrounds painted in a darker colour. High Street and Fleet Street run from east to west. A wide street to the south leads to the gates of Cally Palace, designed by Robert Mylne in 1763–5.

**Gatton** *Surrey*        *542Bf*
Gatton was a 'rotten borough', and the houses were all swallowed up in a gentleman's landscaped park. The so-called town hall is a tiny Classical temple with an urn in front. It was built in 1765, and two Members of Parliament were solemnly elected there, although there was hardly anyone to vote for them.

**Gawsworth** *Cheshire*     *552Be*
CHURCH OF ST JAMES Gawsworth is a picturesque village, and St James's is a fine 15th-century building with a tall pinnacled west tower, decorated with heraldic shields. There are good roofs in the nave and chancel, and several 17th-century monuments to the Fylton family, who lived at the Hall near by.

**Gawsworth Hall** *Cheshire*   *552Be*
A 16th-century Elizabethan half-timbered manor house, the former home of Mary Fitton (*c.* 1600), who may have been the 'Dark Lady' of Shakespeare's sonnets. The park encloses a medieval jousting ground.

**Gawthorpe Hall** *Lancs.*    *558Ab*
The home of the Shuttleworth family since 1330. The present mansion was built around an earlier house in the late 16th century and houses a collection of textiles and craft tools.

**Gayhurst** *Bucks.*      *547Ge*
CHURCH OF ST PETER A complete rebuilding in 1728 of an older church by an unknown architect. It stands next to Gayhurst House, a 16th–17th-century house. The square west tower is crowned with a cupola. It is rusticated below, and there are Ionic pilasters around the exterior. The pleasant interior has been almost untouched in the intervening centuries, having giant pilasters, and decorated plaster ceiling, while panelling, box-pews, two-decker pulpit and reredos are all woodwork of the time. The showpiece is the monument to Sir Nathan Wright and his son (*c.* 1728) with two standing figures in contemporary dress and wigs, the architectural background with looped curtains, all in marble; it has been implausibly attributed to Louis Roubiliac.

**Gayton Manor** *Northants.*   *547Gf*
A cross-shaped Tudor house, perhaps built in 1540. The interior has much good 16th-century detail, and includes a fine staircase.

**Gedding** *Suffolk*      *548Cf*
GEDDING HALL A partially moated Tudor mansion, with a fine turreted gate-house and a successful extension of 1897, all in red brick. For long a farm, it has been restored in recent years. The drawbridge mechanism still exists.

**Gedney** *Lincs.*       *553Jc*
CHURCH OF ST MARY MAGDALENE The Early English tower has an unfinished Perpendicular spire. There are remains of 14th- and 15th-century glass in the north aisle, and the south porch has an upper storey. Monuments include a 14th-century brass of a lady, some coloured alabaster effigies, and a 13th-century figure of a knight.

GLAMIS CASTLE

*During the 1715 Jacobite rebellion, James Francis Edward Stuart, the Old Pretender, was entertained in this magnificent 'tower-house' castle; since 1372 it had been the home of the Lyon family, later Earls of Strathmore and Kinghorne, and forbears of Queen Elizabeth the Queen Mother. It was also visited by Mary, Queen of Scots, and was occupied by Cromwell's troops. The original tower dates from the 15th century,*

*but in 1650 the 3rd Earl began enlargements in French-château style—the wings and rounded turrets, castellations and corbels were added, eclipsing the nucleus of the castle. Inside, delicately worked plaster ceilings, also showing Renaissance influences, were installed. About this time, several castles, including Craigievar and Caerlaverock, also 'flowered' in this way, and the style became known as Scottish baronial.*

**Gibside** *Durham*                                    558Cg
CHAPEL In the grounds of Gibside House, an interesting building now a ruin, the chapel, now used as a church, was designed by James Paine in 1760; it was originally intended as a family mausoleum. A gracious Classical building, converted to a church in 1812, it has a good interior and fittings.

**Gifford** *E. Lothian*                               562De
YESTER HOUSE A fine Adam mansion built *c.* 1745. Near by are the ruins of Yester Castle, which has an underground chamber known as the 'Goblin Ha' of *c.* 1267; it is referred to in Scott's *Marmion*.

**Giffords Hall** *Suffolk*                            548Ce
An early Tudor house with a two-storey brick gate-house leading into a courtyard with timber-framed buildings. A porch leads into the great hall, which has a hammerbeam roof and gallery. Parts of the house were added in the 18th and 19th centuries, but blend well with the earlier fabric.

**Gilfach** *Caern.*                                   550Fe
A small garden specialising in shrubs.

**Gilling Castle** *Yorks.*                            558Ed
An Elizabethan house with a front added in the early 18th century. The Elizabethan great chamber has ceilings supported on columns and arches, and its original frieze, oak panelling and stained glass were rescued from a London warehouse, to which they had been sent by the American millionaire, William Randolph Hearst, and re-installed. The grounds include fine terraced gardens.

**Glamis** *Angus*                                     566Eb
GLAMIS CASTLE This castle, the scene of Duncan's murder in Shakespeare's *Macbeth*, has been the home of the Lyon family since the 14th century. The head of the family, forbears of Queen Elizabeth the Queen Mother, was made Earl of Strathmore and Kinghorne in 1606; Princess Margaret

was born here. The castle was remodelled in French-château style by the 3rd Earl in 1650–96, but the tower dates from the 15th century. It is reputed to contain a secret chamber, which is known only to each heir.
KIRK WYND (ANGUS FOLK MUSEUM) Agricultural and domestic equipment, cottage furniture, hand looms and workmen's tools, all collected in Angus, are displayed in a row of five cottages, built between 200 and 300 years ago.

**Glandford** *Norfolk*                                554Cd
MUSEUM OF SHELLS A collection of shells from all over the world. The museum also includes jewels, pottery and relics of Pompeii.

**Glasgow** *Lanarks.*                                 561He
St Mungo the missionary founded this city on the R. Clyde in the 6th century; he is its patron saint and the 12th-century cathedral is dedicated to him. In 1451 Bishop William Turnbull founded the university. During the Border Wars Glasgow was a rallying point for Scottish armies engaged in feuds and battles with England, in particular with the city of Carlisle. It remained a small port, and market and university city, until the 18th century. Then the dredging of the Clyde improved navigation and the city's trade, shipbuilding and manufacturing increased rapidly. The city grew, quickly expanding beyond the limits of the old town centred round the cathedral; today it is Scotland's largest city. Around the old centre are many fine streets and squares of 18th- and 19th-century houses.
BOTANIC GARDENS Kibble Palace within the gardens was rebuilt in 1872; it houses rare ferns.
CALEDONIA ROAD CHURCH. A fine Grecian-style church built in 1857 by Alexander 'Greek' Thompson, with a tall, thin unadorned tower and a fine Ionic portico. It has fallen into disrepair but is now being restored.

# GLASGOW CITY ART GALLERY AND MUSEUM

Glasgow is fortunate to have the finest municipal collection in Britain—enriched by the gift of the Burrell Collection in 1944. The art gallery and museum is especially famous for its armour.

COURT LADIES OF THE CHINESE T'ANG PERIOD *The most characteristic products of the T'ang dynasty of China, lasting from AD 618 to 906, were naturalistic reproductions of animals and figures. These court ladies date from the early T'ang period and wear the elaborate costumes and head-dresses of the time. Tomb figures of animals, birds and humans were made of bronze, terracotta, or a glazed earthenware.*

SET OF THREE STEEPLE CUPS *This set is the only existing group of three steeple cups made by the same maker at the same date. The cups were made in 1611 by a London silversmith with the monogram TB. The two smaller cups have identical decoration, but the larger one has slight variations. Inspired by church spires or more probably by Tudor obelisks, steeple cups seem to have been an English innovation.*

15TH-CENTURY MILANESE ARMOUR *The earliest complete suit of armour which can be seen in Britain, made about 1440 for a member of the Matsch family of Churburg in South Tyrol. It is also one of the earliest and finest surviving examples of Italian Gothic-style armour. It was designed for a mounted knight—the holes to the right of the breastplate were used for attaching a lance-rest. Carefully tailored to its owner's figure like a well-made suit, it gives the effect of 'sculpture in steel' while preserving practicality.*

208

GIORGIONE: THE ADULTERESS BROUGHT BEFORE
CHRIST *Giorgione died in 1510 at the early age of 33
and there are perhaps no more than a dozen pictures in
the world which can be assigned to him without
question; but he brought to Venetian painting a rare
poetic quality. Some of this he inherited from his
teacher Giovanni Bellini and he passed it on to his
fellow pupil Titian to such an extent that it is difficult
to decide which artist did some paintings. The 'Adulteress' is one of these, but the balance of opinion is in
favour of Giorgione, if only because it has that particular
gift of his—a sort of melancholy grace. Being a
Venetian, Giorgione creates his ideal world out of
colour rather than form.*

FRENCH TAPESTRY OF THE 15TH CENTURY *The
popular medieval millefleurs motif—a field of flowers
forming the background to unlikely scenes and strange
events—greatly influenced designers of a later age,
such as William Morris. This tapestry, probably made
in the late 15th century, mixes legend and fact
indiscriminately: Charity, on an elephant, strikes
down Envy dressed as a knight.*

ENAMEL SPUR *This crane-neck spur is the product of
a short-lived fashion for enamelled brass that arose at
about the beginning of the Restoration. The brass was
cast with a low-relief design, after which opaque
enamels, usually blue and white in colour, were
applied in the recessed sections.*

PAIR OF FLINTLOCK PISTOLS *These pistols were
designed to be carried in holsters slung on either side of
a horse's saddle. Because of their decoration it is
unlikely that they were intended to be taken into battle,
but they were probably used for self-defence or for
hunting. The pistols bear the mark of the city of
Augsburg in southern Germany, and a partly illegible
date—probably 1661.*

209

CHARDIN *The Scullery Maid*

*Chardin (1699–1779) gives each subject its own special quality. Forsaking the brilliance of high society, he records the dignity of simple people and humble occupations with a superb mastery of form, an exquisite eye for colour and an exceptional feeling for paint. His technique gives to the full the different textures of wood, a coarse apron, or a kitchen maid's rough, red hands. (Hunterian Museum)*

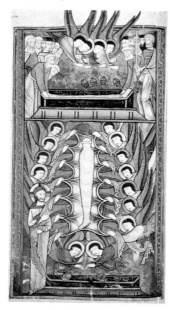

THE YORK PSALTER

*The York Psalter was written and illuminated about 1175, perhaps in the Diocese of York, and the pages illustrating the death and Assumption of the Virgin Mary mark an important stage in the cult of the Virgin in England. They contain the earliest surviving pictorial statement on the bodily Assumption of the Virgin. In the upper part of the miniature shown here, the Apostles and others lay Mary in the tomb while angels perfume the shrouded corpse with incense. In the lower part Christ points at the body as it is lifted from the tomb. The Romanesque technique of composing a picture by using related masses of colour is seen here at its finest. (Hunterian Museum)*

CATHEDRAL Dedicated to St Mungo, the well preserved cathedral was built between the 12th and 15th centuries. It is cruciform in plan, with a low central tower and spire. Beneath the east end is a crypt. Most of the fittings are 19th century.

CITY ART GALLERY AND MUSEUM (KELVINGROVE) A collection of old masters and modern works including Salvador Dali's *Christ of St John of the Cross* is kept here with the Burrell Collection of art treasures.

HUNTERIAN MUSEUM, UNIVERSITY OF GLASGOW The museum, besides containing one of the four major British coin collections in the Hunter Coin Cabinet, also has Roman relics from the Antonine Wall and archaeological finds from the Mediterranean area including Egypt, Jericho and Jerusalem. The ethnographical material includes some from the South Sea Islands brought back by Captain Cook, and in the geological collection of minerals, rocks and gemstones is a set of casts of fossil footprints. A model of James Watt's Newcomen engine is displayed. The York Psalter is on view in the manuscript collection, and amongst the paintings are works by Rembrandt, Rubens, Chardin and Whistler, and a selection of prints.

HUTCHESON'S HOSPITAL Built in 1802–5 and designed by David Hamilton in the neo-Classical style with a traditional Scottish 'town house' steeple. Statues of the founders George and Thomas Hutcheson made in 1649 by James Colquhoun are those from the original hospital building.

MERCHANT'S STEEPLE Built into the Fish Market of 1873, this relic is all that remains of the guildhall and hospital built by the Merchants of Glasgow in 1665. Gothic and Renaissance details add charm to the 164 ft steeple. Originally it stood as part of the garden frontage entered from the Bridgegate.

MUSEUM OF TRANSPORT (EGLINTON TOLL) Here a collection of the city's old tramcars is housed.

PROVAND'S LORDSHIP The oldest house in Glasgow, built in 1470 as part of the Hospital of St Nicholas. It is now a museum housing collections of 17th-century furniture, stained glass, tapestries and paintings.

ROYAL BANK OF SCOTLAND AND ROYAL EXCHANGE SQUARE A fine unit, comprising a central block of two storeys with Greek Ionic portico and pediment. Archways set in coupled Ionic columns link the bank with the symmetrical flanking buildings, whose first and second floors are fronted by the Ionic order. Archibald Elliot of London designed the bank in 1827. David Hamilton and James Smith designed Nos. 1–29 and 2–40 in the square.

ST VINCENT STREET CHURCH Alexander 'Greek' Thompson built this delightful Grecian church in 1859. Its elaborate tower is a hill-top landmark, and the church itself rises sheer from a great podium. Originally built for the United Presbyterians, it is now used by Spiritualists. Outside are magnificent Ionic porticos. The interior of the church is spacious, with galleries and two tiers of strange columns tricked out in Pompeian red, blue, white and gold.

SCHOOL OF ART In 1895 a competition was held to choose designs for a new, larger School of Art. The competition was won by a Glasgow firm with designs by Charles Rennie Mackintosh. Building began in 1897 and the first portion was finished within two years; there was then a pause of some years and the remainder was not completed until 1909. The school is practically designed with large windows. Some of it is decorated in the flowing art

## INTERIOR AT GLASGOW SCHOOL OF ART

*Charles Rennie Mackintosh (1868–1928) was a Scottish art nouveau architect who designed the interiors, furniture and fabrics for many of his buildings. The Glasgow School of Art, built 1897–*

*1909, shows his preference for black-and-white colour schemes. He is remembered for his high-backed chairs —some were made about 5 ft tall; but in their surroundings Mackintosh designs do not look incongruous.*

nouveau style which had recently become fashionable, but much of it is simply designed and forms a link between Victorian architectural style and the modern trends of the 20th century.

STIRLING'S LIBRARY David Hamilton, one of the principal architects of the new town of Glasgow, designed the Royal Exchange in 1829, incorporating the earlier Cunningham Mansion of 1778. A massive portico of the Corinthian order surmounted by a tower dwarfs the equestrian statue of Wellington by Marochetti which stands in front.

TOLBOOTH STEEPLE Erected in 1626. Originally a handsome tolbooth of five storeys fronting the north side of the Trongate, with the surviving seven-storey steeple at the east end. An open cross with balustrade crowns the steeple, and the lintels are embellished with carved strapwork containing emblems of St Mungo and royalty.

UNIVERSITY OF GLASGOW The second oldest university in Scotland, founded in 1451. The original buildings were in the High Street, but in 1870 the university moved to Victorian Gothic buildings in Kelvingrove Park, designed by Sir Gilbert Scott, who also designed the Albert Memorial, London.

UNIVERSITY OF STRATHCLYDE Founded in 1964 and formerly the Royal College of Science and Technology.

**Glassenbury Park** Kent                    542De
A moated manor house, dating from 1472.

**Glastonbury** Som.                    540Ce
ABBEY The most substantial remains at Glastonbury, apart from two great columns where nave and chancel meet, are of the Lady Chapel (at the west end). The ruins of the chapel, which stands on the site of the 7th–8th-century church, date from 1184 when rebuilding began after a fire had destroyed the earlier buildings. The chapel is remarkable for its sculptured doorways and elaborate late Norman architectural decoration; the sculpture appears to date from the late 13th century. Near by, the abbot's kitchen, dating from the late 14th century, is the chief monastic building still visible. It is one of the most complete medieval kitchens to survive in Europe, and contains a small museum. The monastic gate-house can also still be seen at the entrance to the precinct.

LAKE VILLAGE MUSEUM Glastonbury was once—from the 2nd century BC to the Roman conquest—

an important trading site, built near navigable water on artificial islands or platforms of brushwood or timber; archaeological finds from the Iron Age Celtic lake village are now housed in a 15th-century building, thought to have been the abbey courtroom.

**Glenapp Castle** Ayrs.                    560Fa
The castle, set in grounds including a walled garden with lily ponds, contains a collection of paintings.

**Glencoe** Argyll                    565Hc
A tall stone cross marks the scene of the massacre of February 1692 when a party of Campbells led by their Captain killed 40 Jacobites of the Macdonald clan. To this day the glen is known as the Glen of Weeping.

**Glencorse** M'loth.                    562Be
CASTLE LAW FORT AND EARTH-HOUSE This interesting fort has been excavated, and the sequence of its various defences determined. Its first enclosure was a simple timber palisade, soon succeeded by a timber-laced rampart which did not quite coincide with the line of the first stockade. Later, two ramparts, each with an external ditch, were constructed outside the first, so that finally there was a trivallate hill-fort shortly before the early Roman expeditions reached southern Scotland. The earth-house (souterrain) is a small underground apartment entered from the inner of the two later ditches; it may be of the 3rd century AD.

**Glendurgan Garden** Cornwall                    538Ca
The garden at Glendurgan lies in a small wooded valley which drops down to the fishing village of Durgan. At the head of the garden stands the house. On the front lawn tropical succulents such as giant agaves flower in Cornwall's temperate climate. A path down one side of the valley is planted with exotic flowering shrubs, and branches off to a group of giant camellias. There is a water garden surrounded by primulas and bluebells. The path to the house on the other side of the valley runs beside an extremely rare Bunya-bunya tree from Australia and an unusual maze.

**Glenesk** Angus                    566Ec
FOLK MUSEUM In a converted shooting lodge, it is part of a community centre sponsored by Lord

211

# GLOUCESTER CATHEDRAL

TOMB OF EDWARD II *In 1327 Edward II was murdered. The body of a murdered king is a difficult thing to find a home for, but it was finally taken for burial by the Abbot of Gloucester. Within a few years the new king, Edward III, began to make a cult of his father's memory, and this magnificent tomb was his first move in establishing it. With its elaborate stone canopy, it dates from soon after 1330, and was the work of London Court sculptors. The alabaster head is not a portrait but an idealised symbol of saintly majesty. The rather effeminate style of this period is appropriate to the subject.*

TOMB OF ROBERT, DUKE OF NORMANDY, *the eldest son of William the Conqueror, is carved in oak painted to represent life, and dates from the end of the 12th century; but the chest under it is 15th-century. The figure was broken during the Civil War but was later restored. Robert was his father's natural successor but he twice revolted against William, so that when the Conqueror died he named his second son Rufus heir to the throne of England. The dissatisfied Robert eventually died a prisoner in Cardiff Castle in 1134.*

THE MONKS' LAVATORIUM *The Abbey of St Peter at Gloucester was founded before the Conquest but, like many English abbeys, was reformed soon after the arrival of the Normans. The first Norman abbot, Serlo, began the existing church in 1089, and the main work was complete by the consecration of 1128. In appearance, Romanesque Gloucester is similar to the neighbouring cathedral of Tewkesbury. The origin of the design of these buildings, which both have cylindrical columns in the nave, can be found in Burgundy and Italy rather than in Normandy. The east end was remodelled after the interment of Edward II. The king was murdered at Berkeley Castle in 1327, and some effort was made to have him recognised as a royal martyr and saint. Edward is buried in a magnificent tomb on the south side of the high altar, and it seems certain that Edward III allowed masons from London to go to Gloucester to begin transforming the building around the monument.*

and Lady Dalhousie. It contains folk material, period rooms and a reference library.

**Glenfinnan Monument** *I'ness.* 565Gd
A tall, narrow tower, on which the statue of a Highlander stands, was erected in 1815 on the site where Prince Charles Edward (Bonnie Prince Charlie) raised his standard for the Jacobite rebellion on August 19, 1745.

**Glenluce Abbey** *Wig.* 556Cg
The abbey, founded in 1190, is now a ruin, but the vaulted chapter house remains intact.

**Glenquicken** *Kirkcud.* 556Dg
STONE CIRCLE This circle, with a 50 ft diameter, comprises 28 boulders set with their narrow edges outwards (radially). In the centre of the circle is a larger rectangular stone which stands almost 6 ft high.

Another similar circle of nine stones in the circumference and a central stone $5\frac{1}{2}$ ft high, lies $1\frac{1}{2}$ miles to the south-east.

**Gloddaeth Hall** *Caern.* 550Fe
Gloddaeth Hall was greatly extended in the 19th century, but most of the older parts are concentrated around the entrance front. Although dating from the 16th century, the Hall with its open roof is medieval in inspiration; of particular interest is the coved ceiling at the end where the high table would have been set. Behind this are two rooms, both lined with Elizabethan wainscoting, the

upper room or solar having a roof similar to that over the hall. The wing to the north-east has a fine late 17th-century staircase.

**Gloucester** *Glos.* 546Cd
CATHEDRAL Gloucester Cathedral was begun in 1089 and completed by 1128. The east end was remodelled by London masons after Edward II was buried there in 1327, and although much of the Romanesque work survives, the internal face was covered with a skin of masonry in the new Perpendicular style. To the east, the Norman apse was removed and replaced by one of the largest Perpendicular windows in England. This window retains its original 14th-century glass. The cloisters were also rebuilt in the 14th century. They contain the earliest surviving fan-vaulting and, down the south walk, the carvels (miniature studies used by the monks for reading and working).
CHURCH OF ST MARY-DE-CRYPT A cruciform church, of Norman origin, with a central tower. It contains brasses, and several 17th- and 18th-century monuments, including one (the design for which is in the Victoria and Albert Museum) by Peter Scheemakers, who carved Shakespeare's bust in Westminster Abbey.
CITY MUSEUM AND ART GALLERY The archaeology and natural history of the area are featured, one of the most important archaeological items being the late Iron Age bronze Birdlip mirror from *c.* AD 25. English furniture, pottery, silver, glass and costume can be seen, and temporary art exhibitions are held throughout the year.
FOLK MUSEUM AND REGIMENTAL MUSEUM Housed in a group of 15th- and 16th-century timber-framed houses, the museum illustrates past crafts and industries of the region, such as the different fishing methods used on the R. Severn. The history of the Gloucestershire Regiment from its formation in 1694 to the present day is also depicted.

**Glyn Cywarch** *Merioneth.* 550Fc
The earliest part of this attractive Welsh country house dates from the mid-16th century. It is an example of the curious custom seen in this part of Wales, of an extension (dated 1616 in this case), taking the form of a separate house joined at one point to the original; this is thought to be connected with the practice of gavelkind, the equal division of property among heirs, as opposed to the English custom of primogeniture, by which property is inherited by the eldest son. Set opposite the entrance to the 1616 house is a tall gate-house which is of a kind added to about half a dozen houses in North Wales during the 17th century. This one is unusual in being tall, but rather less formal than some, as its entrance is off centre.

**Glynde** *Sussex* 542Cd
CHURCH OF ST MARY THE VIRGIN A Classical church, built in 1765, probably to the designs of Sir Thomas Robinson. The interior, with its 18th-century furnishings—pulpit, box-pews, gallery—is somewhat spoilt by the big 19th-century screen. There is some 16th- and 17th-century Netherlandish stained glass, as well as some late 19th-century stained glass by C. E. Kempe.

**Glynde Place** *Sussex* 542Cd
Richard Trevor (1701–71), Bishop of Durham, lived in this 16th-century quadrangular mansion built of flint and brick; in 1752 he rebuilt much of the house and added the stable block. The house contains a long gallery with 17th-century panelling, a collection of bronzes by Soldani, fine needlework, and paintings by Rubens, Kneller, Hoppner, Lely, Weenix and Zoffany.

MEISSEN PORCELAIN GROUP
*During the mid-18th century the Meissen porcelain factory began producing groups of figures and these gradually became quite complex, often including pieces of furniture with elaborate decoration. The group illustrated is of a lady at her dressing table, and the intricate details of costume and ornament show the high technical standards then achieved. (Glynde Place)*

**Glynllifon** *Caern.* 550Ed
This large mansion is mainly in the early 19th-century Classical style. It is at least the fourth house to stand on the site, and the kitchen block contains some work of 1751, but the greatest parts were built between 1836 and 1848, with a final extension at the end of the century. The architecture is not distinguished and may have been designed by the owner, Lord Newborough. There are lavish period gardens which include a grotto, waterworks, a 'Druidical Sanctuary', a lighthearted fort and an incomplete mausoleum.

**Glyn Pits** *Mon.* 545Jc
At Glyn Pits are preserved the only two early beam-engines in Wales. The smaller building houses the pumping engine and is dated 1845; opposite is the winding engine, which lifted cages in the two shafts, now filled in. This engine, with its large overhead drum, has interesting manually-operated valve gear. It dates from *c.* 1850.

**Gnosall** *Staffs.* 552Bc
CHURCH OF ST LAURENCE The impressive cruciform building was begun by the Normans, whose tower arches still remain. There is work of all periods to the 15th century. The east window has some good Decorated tracery and 20th-century glass. There is also an effigy of a knight.

**Godalming** *Surrey* 542Ae
The polygonal white market hall, built in 1814, with arcades and a cupola, is the focal point of the long street. There is also a fine coaching inn, the King's Arms, built in 1753.
BOROUGH MUSEUM The museum is housed in the old town hall or Hundred House, built in 1814 to replace an earlier building on a site which was a centre of local government for over 1000 years. The exhibits are arranged to show the story of the town and the Godalming Hundred (a medieval county division) from prehistoric times.
CHARTERHOUSE SCHOOL MUSEUM The school's collection of local antiquities, classical pottery, ancient Peruvian pottery, natural history, and

GOODRICH CASTLE

*Goodrich Castle is set on an outcrop of red sandstone overlooking the R. Wye, and throughout the 12th and 13th centuries its importance lay in the fact that it was a Welsh Border castle. It came into the possession of the Crown in the 12th century and was granted to William Marshall, Earl of Pembroke, who had made his fortune by winning prize money in tournaments. In 1245, on the death of his son, the property passed to William de Valence, a half-brother of Henry III, whose enamelled tomb can still be seen in Westminster Abbey. The castle has not been inhabited since the 16th century.*

relics of the school, are housed in two Victorian Gothic halls, built in 1890.

CHURCH OF SS PETER AND PAUL A cruciform church with a central tower and spire; it stands on a Saxon site, and contains work of all periods—from Norman times to the restorations of the 19th century.

**Godinton Park** *Kent*      *542Ee*
A Jacobean gabled mansion containing carved panelling, particularly in the hall and on the staircase, fine furniture, paintings and china. The grounds, laid out in the 18th century by Sir Reginald Blomfield, contain formal gardens with fine topiary work.

**Godmanchester** *Hunts.*      *547Jf*
Twin town of Huntingdon, with several 16th- and 17th-century half-timbered houses, some of them thatched. In 1964 a hoard of more than 1000 English and foreign coins of the 15th and 16th centuries was found during the construction of Longstaff Way.

CHURCH OF ST MARY THE VIRGIN A 13th- and 14th-century church, with a 15th-century clerestory. The 17th-century tower has a spire. Inside are noteworthy 15th-century choir stalls, with carving, and a series of misericords.

**Godolphin House** *Cornwall*      *538Ba*
The country mansion home of the Earls of Godolphin. It is partly of Tudor date, with Elizabethan and Stuart additions; the colonnaded façade was added in 1635.

**Godshill** *Isle of Wight, Hants.*      *541Hc*
CHURCH OF ALL SAINTS Conspicuous on its hilltop site, a church of the 14th and 15th centuries. In the south transept is a contemporary wall-painting of Christ crucified on a tree. Among several interesting monuments, from the 16th to 19th centuries, the best is to Sir John Leigh and his wife.

**Goodmanham** *Yorks.*      *558Fb*
CHURCH OF ALL SAINTS A Norman church, with Gothic additions, which is believed to be on the site of a pagan temple destroyed during the 7th century after its priest was converted to Christianity. There is a Norman chancel arch and doorways, and a Perpendicular font.

**Goodrich Castle** *Herefs.*      *546Bd*
Goodrich, or 'Godric's', Castle is first mentioned in a document of 1101 or 1102, but the existing buildings are all later. At the centre stands a square Norman keep built in the second half of the 12th century. Any 12th-century outworks there may once have been have now vanished, and the keep is surrounded by late 13th-century walls; these were designed to bring the defences up to date, and in fact made the keep militarily almost unnecessary. During the conquest of Wales by Edward I, William de Valance, half-brother to Henry III, made extensive additions to Goodrich, which had passed to him in 1245. He gave the castle an almost square inner ward, an outer ward covering two sides, a barbican covering the main gate and, inside, a suite of living rooms including a great hall, upper chamber, chapel and kitchen.

**Goodwood House** *Sussex*      *542Jd*
Home of the Dukes of Richmond and Gordon, the house was built in Sussex flintwork in 1780–1800 by Charles Lennox, the 3rd Duke (1735–1806), with James Wyatt as architect. It contains paintings by Canaletto, Van Dyck, Romney and Lely, sporting pictures by Stubbs and Wootton, furniture of the Louis XV period, and a collection of Sèvres porcelain.

**Gop Cairn** *Flints.*                    *551Hc*
Crowning Gop Hill, the largest prehistoric cairn in Wales. Over 60 ft high, it was partly excavated in 1866 when it was found to be built entirely of dry-stone.

**Gorhambury** *Herts.*                    *547Hc*
The home of the Earl of Verulam, a descendant of the great Elizabethan essayist and scholar, Francis Bacon. The house was designed by Sir Robert Taylor and completed in 1784; it contains portraits and books belonging to the Bacon family. The older 16th-century manor house, home of Francis Bacon, is now a ruin in Gorhambury Park.

**Gorsey Bigbury** *Som.*                    *539Cf*
The base of this site is a circular bank some 200 ft in diameter surrounding a ditch cut into the under-lying rock. In places, this ditch was more than 20 ft wide. There is an entrance on the north side only. There are no visible upright stones and nothing is known of any in the past.

**Gosfield** *Essex*                    *548Bd*
GOSFIELD HALL A Tudor courtyard house, much altered in the 18th century, and added to and restored in the 19th century by the Courtauld family. It has a Tudor panelled long gallery, ballroom and hidden room.

**Gowthorpe Manor** *Norfolk*                    *554Db*
Sir William Boleyn, grandfather of Anne Boleyn, acquired this Tudor manor between 1494 and 1505. It passed to Thomas Aldrych, twice Mayor of Norwich, in 1525. The west wing dates from *c.* 1530. The great chamber was shortened by 26 ft in 1669, and the oak framing by the spiral stair and the fire-place in the south room are additions, *c.* 1550. In 1669, Thomas Berney cased the oak-framed west wing with brick; and his son Thomas (1674–1720), introduced the 18th-century fire-places in the drawing-room and a bedroom, and also built a walled garden with new entrance gates. The Steward family bought the property in 1810; it was used as a farmhouse until 1908, when John Henry Steward moved the main front door from the west to the east of the house, at the same time building a new kitchen wing.

**Goxhill Priory** *Lincs.*                    *553Hg*
Often regarded as a mystery building, since there is doubt about its religious origins. The records of the Wentworth family show that Marjorie, the last heiress of the le Despensers, whose family seat was at Goxhill, married Roger Wentworth of Nettle-shead (*d.* 1452), and that Goxhill was a Wentworth possession until Sir Richard Wentworth's death in 1528. This 14th-century house, therefore, seems likely to have been a Despenser manor house, and not a priory. The main doorway carries shields and spandrels and there is a spiral staircase in the south-west corner, a three-light Perpendicular window on the west side and three wide blank arches on the north and south. It adjoins a charming five-bay brick house of 1700, with Queen Anne panelling.

**Grantham** *Lincs.*                    *553Gc*
Originally a staging point between London and Lincoln, the town was sacked in 1461 during the Wars of the Roses. In 1483 at the 14th-century Angel Inn, Richard III signed the death warrant of the Duke of Buckingham. In 1643, Cromwell made Grantham his centre of operations. The Early English church has a spire 272 ft high. Notable buildings are the elegant George Hotel of 1780, Vine House in Vine Street (1764), and Grantham House, dating from 1380 but with Elizabethan additions of *c.* 1570. The Beehive Inn in Castlegate has as its sign a beehive actually used

18th-CENTURY FRENCH WRITING CABINET OR SECRETAIRE

*Made by one of the leading 18th-century Parisian cabinet makers, Bernard van Risenburg, this cabinet may have been at the Palace of Versailles, as it is similar to other pieces made by Risenburg for Louis XV and Madame de Pompadour. It shows Risenburg's taste for the exotic in the Oriental lacquer and porcelain plaques. Louis wanted smaller rooms within the grand salons of Versailles and so smaller furniture was required. Risenburg achieved this diminution in size without offending the French taste for grandeur. (Goodwood House)*

COMPOTIÈRE AND COVER

*Made in 1756, the year when the French porcelain factory moved from Vincennes to Sèvres, this compotière (dessert-dish) and cover were probably decorated by Armand Aine. He used the popular 'bleu céleste' or 'heavenly blue' glaze, and the panel is painted with birds in overglaze enamels. The collection of Sèvres porcelain at Goodwood was accumulated by the 3rd Duke of Richmond when Ambassador to Louis XV. (Goodwood House)*

by bees. In front of the guildhall is a statue to Sir Isaac Newton, who was born in 1642 at Wools-thorpe Manor by Colsterworth, about 6 miles south of Grantham.
ANGEL AND ROYAL HOTEL The inn dates from the 13th century. At the front of the decorated two-storey structure two bay windows flank a central archway. The medieval windows were at some later date replaced by sash windows. However, the inn, like the George Inn at Glastonbury, is a fine 13th-century survival.
CHURCH OF ST WULFRAM A magnificent church,

with work of all periods. The tower and spire are fine work of the 14th century, and the main body of the church is of the same period; the north aisle, however, is earlier. Beneath the south chapel is a vaulted 14th-century crypt. There is late Decorated work in the north porch, and the chantry chapel in the north aisle is late Perpendicular. The font, which is Perpendicular, is richly carved with figures and biblical scenes.

GRANTHAM HOUSE Princess Margaret, daughter of Henry VII, stayed here in 1503 on her way north to marry James IV of Scotland. The original house, including the hall used by the princess, is late 14th century; it was enlarged in the 16th century and extensively altered in the 18th century.

LIBRARY AND MUSEUM Sir Isaac Newton was educated at Grantham Grammar School, and items associated with him are included in the collections which reflect the social and industrial history of the town from the Bronze Age onwards. Relics of the Beaker People, who came to Britain *c.* 1800 BC, and Romano-Britons are included.

**Grasmere** *Westmld.* 557He
DOVE COTTAGE Home for 13 years of the poet William Wordsworth. His house and personal belongings are preserved; there is also a Wordsworth Museum. The poet is buried in St Oswald's churchyard, near the grave of Samuel Taylor Coleridge.

**Gravesend** *Kent* 542Dg
CHURCH OF ST GEORGE A fine Georgian church of red brick with stone facings, built *c.* 1731 on the site of a medieval church destroyed by fire. Its architect was probably Charles Sloane. The building was enlarged during the 19th century, and is now no longer used as a church. Pocahontas, a Red Indian princess who came to England from North America during the early 17th century, died at Gravesend in 1617; she was buried in the churchyard here and commemorated by a life-size statue.

**Great Amwell** *Herts.* 548Ad
CHURCH OF ST JOHN THE BAPTIST A Norman church, with an apse and a 15th-century west tower. It also has two brasses, a 17th-century pulpit and several large 18th-century monuments in the churchyard.

**Great Badminton** *Glos.* 546Cb
CHURCH OF ST MICHAEL AND ALL ANGELS Standing in the park of the Dukes of Beaufort, for whom it was rebuilt in 1783, the church is in the Classical style of the period. Inside, there are notable contemporary fittings, including box-pews and canopied pulpit, and a great number of marble monuments to the Beaufort family by J. M. Rysbrack, of the mid-18th century.

**Great Bardfield** *Essex* 548Bd
CHURCH OF ST MARY THE VIRGIN A 14th-century church, with west tower and a stone rood screen of the same date. Some fragments of late 14th-century stained glass remain.

**Great Barrington** *Glos.* 546Dd
CHURCH OF ST MARY THE VIRGIN Of Norman origin, with work of the Early English and Perpendicular periods, the church has a pinnacled west tower; inside, the nave roof is a fine example of 15th-century work, and the chancel arch is Norman. The monument to two children who died of smallpox in 1711 and 1720 may be by Christopher Cass, who carved the coat of arms over the portico of St Martin-in-the-Fields, London. The designs for this and for the large mourning figure by Joseph Nollekens are both in the Victoria and Albert Museum.

**Great Bookham** *Surrey* 542Af
CHURCH OF ST NICHOLAS Originally a Norman building; most notable of the later additions are the chancel, built by John Rutherwyke, Abbot of Chertsey in 1341, and the south aisle, widened in the 15th century. There is a timber tower, with shingled spire, on a stone base. Restorations took place in the second half of the 19th century. There are brasses and monuments of all periods.

**Great Brington** *Northants.* 546Ff
CHURCH OF ST MARY A large church with a west tower, mainly of the Decorated and Perpendicular periods. The north chapel, dating from the early 16th century, was built by Sir John Spencer as a chapel for his family. The series of Spencer monuments includes work by Jasper Hollemans, Nicholas Stone, Joseph Nollekens and John Flaxman.

**Great Bromley** *Essex* 548Dd
CHURCH OF ST GEORGE A mainly 15th-century church, it has a fine west tower, a south porch with flushwork panelling, a clerestory to the nave and a double hammerbeam roof. There is a 15th-century brass to a priest.

MONUMENT TO
SIR EDWARD SPENCER

*Carved in marble by John Stone—probably the third son of the famous mason Nicholas Stone (1586–1647) —the monument shows Sir Edward's effigy emerging from an urn. (Church of St Mary, Great Brington)*

**Great Budworth** *Cheshire* 552Ae
CHURCH OF ST MARY AND ALL SAINTS The church and its imposing west tower both date from the 14th and 15th centuries. Inside there are some original roofs, medieval stalls and chest, and a 15th-century font. The monuments include one to Sir Peter Leycester, Cheshire historian (*d.* 1678) and the alabaster figure of Sir John Warburton (*d.* 1575).

**Great Casterton** *Rutland* 553Gb
CHURCH OF SS PETER AND PAUL A large 13th-century church, with a west tower added in the 15th century. The font is Norman; there are traces of 13th-century mural painting and a carved effigy of a priest.

**Great Chalfield** *Wilts.* 540Ef
CHURCH OF ALL SAINTS Small, with a square bell-turret, the church stands with the manor house built by Thomas Tropenell. He also added a chapel

to the church in 1480, where wall-paintings of the life of St Katherine and a heraldic stone screen still remain. The church contains a 17th-century three-decker pulpit.

**Great Chalfield Manor** *Wilts.*                    540Ef
A moated house built *c.* 1480; an example of domestic Gothic architecture, with a fine great hall.

**Great Coggeshall** *Essex*                    548Cd
PAYCOCKE'S HOUSE Great Coggeshall has several interesting houses, such as the gabled Wool Pack Inn, late 15th century, but this is its most noted building, a complete, richly ornamented merchant's house of *c.* 1500. It has a remarkable façade with oriel windows, a slightly overhanging second storey, and a carved frieze with the builder's initials, T.P. Inside the house there are rooms with carved and moulded beams, and the original fire-places.

**Great Coxwell** *Berks.*                    546Ec
TITHE BARN The monks of Beaulieu built this enormous tithe barn of stone in the 13th century. Its size indicates the productiveness of the local tithe, or levy, on crops. The roof is of unusual timber construction with stone tiles. The barn, considered by many the finest in England, is 152 ft long, 44 ft wide and 48 ft high.

**Great Cressingham Priory** *Norfolk*                    554Bb
The remains of a once great house built of brick in 1545. It has been partly rebuilt, but the original south front exists, showing ornate brickwork with a frieze of arches and leaves, and above it brick panelling decorated with such emblems as a hawk on a fist and a wreath with monogram. There is also the Perpendicular stone arch of the former gateway.

**Great Dixter** *Sussex*                    542De
A half-timbered manor house, built *c.* 1450 and recently restored; it has a fine great hall and oriel windows. The gardens were laid out by Sir Edwin Lutyens.

**Great Dunmow** *Essex*                    548Bd
A small market town with some good buildings. The town hall was built in the 16th century, but enlarged subsequently, and the brick and timber Clock House of *c.* 1600, with a square clock turret, is a good example of its time. Bigods, a late 16th-century house, has an attractive Elizabethan summer-house. In the Doctor's Pond, Lionel Lukin tested one of the first lifeboats, 1785.

**Great Gaddesden** *Herts.*                    547Hd
CHURCH OF ST JOHN THE BAPTIST A 12th-century church with later, mainly 15th-century, additions; the north-east chapel dates from 1730. The monuments, mainly of the 18th century, include one of *c.* 1782 by John Flaxman.

**Great Gidding** *Hunts.*                    547Hg
BAPTIST CHAPEL Built in 1790, the chapel contains nearly all its original furnishings.

**Great Glemham** *Suffolk*                    548Ef
CHURCH OF ALL SAINTS A west tower with flush-work decoration, and a good roof with bosses. Inside is a seven-sacrament font, and fragments of medieval stained glass. All Saints was restored in the 19th century.

**Great Hormead** *Herts.*                    548Ad
BRICK HOUSE A small manor house in red brick, built shortly before 1576. Two tower-like wings (north-east and south-west corners) have in the upper rooms small slit windows, 9 in. long by 3 in. wide, inserted for no identifiable reason.

**Great Malvern** *Worcs.*                    546Bc
PRIORY CHURCH OF SS MARY AND MICHAEL A beautiful, mainly 15th-century building, containing tiles, some good choir stalls and magnificent 15th-century glass. Earlier work, of the 12th and 13th centuries, can also be seen, and there are Norman nave arcades. A kiln discovered locally in the 19th century gives weight to the suggestion that all the tiles were made *in situ*.

**Great Milton** *Oxon.*                    547Cc
CHURCH OF ST MARY THE VIRGIN A fine church with work of the Early English to Perpendicular periods, but also with traces of Norman work. The large west tower has a stair-turret capped by a spirelet, and the south porch is two-storied. The choir roof is Perpendicular; fragments of medieval glass and an imposing tomb of *c.* 1618 remain.

**Great Packington** *Warks.*                    546Dg
CHURCH OF ST JAMES This late 18th-century church is the work of Joseph Bonomi (1739–1808). With a plain brick exterior, it has four small towers, one at each corner. The stone-faced, vaulted interior has Greek Doric columns. The altar-piece is a painting by J. F. Rigaud, set into a frame of marble columns and pediment. An 18th-century organ is reputed to have been played by Handel.

**Great Salkeld** *Cumb.*                    557Jf
CHURCH OF ST CUTHBERT An austere battle-mented tower was added to the Norman nave of St Cuthbert's during the 14th century, obviously as a defensive measure against raids from the neighbouring Scots. There is a good Norman south doorway, and a 14th-century effigy of a priest.

**Great Sampford** *Essex*                    548Be
CHURCH OF ST MICHAEL Most of the church dates from the 14th century when it was rebuilt by the Knights Hospitaller, though the south chapel remains from an earlier building. It has a 14th-century font.

**Great Snoring** *Norfolk*                    554Bc
RECTORY Part of an old manor house, built 1525. It is of brick, with decorative friezes; the main front is flanked by panelled turrets, the ornate side front with original 16th-century windows.

**Great Staughton** *Hunts.*                    547Jf
The village cross, erected in 1637, has a complicated sun-dial on three of its four faces.

**Great Warley** *Essex*                    548Bc
CHURCH OF ST MARY THE VIRGIN An outstanding example of an art nouveau church, built in 1904; there is a screen with angels standing beneath foliage. The architect was Harrison Townsend, the designer of the Whitechapel Art Gallery, London, and most of the interior fittings are by Sir William Reynolds Stevens.

**Great Witcombe Villa** *Glos.*                    546Cd
A fine Cotswold Roman villa which nestles in a sheltered combe of the scarp and looks out over the Vale of Gloucester. When first excavated, some of the walling still stood to a height of about 6 ft. The remains contain tessellated pavements and there is a bath wing. The fabric of the remains has been renovated.

**Great Witley** *Worcs.*                    546Bf
CHURCH OF ST MICHAEL AND ALL SAINTS There was a medieval church here beside Witley Court, once the home of Lord Foley, but early in the 18th century the decision was made to rebuild it. In 1735 the present rococo church, of the same size as the old building, was consecrated. It is a hall-like

GREAT WITLEY CHURCH

*This elegant parish church of St Michael and All Saints stands beside gaunt Witley Court, a roofless ruin with trees growing inside. The church is a surprising excursion into rococo style in such a remote place. It dates from the 18th century, when the decision was made to rebuild the medieval church. Much of it has its origins near London. In the suburban wilderness of Edgware once stood Canons, the palatial house built for the 1st Duke of Chandos, who had amassed a colossal fortune as Paymaster-General to Marlborough. After the duke's death, his heir was forced to sell the property and later the mansion was demolished. Lord Foley of Witley Court bought from the chapel the stained glass windows, made about 1719 by Joshua Price from designs by Sebastiano Ricci, and the magnificent plaster and painted ceiling panels, probably the work of Louis Laguerre, and installed them in the church at Great Witley. The organ-case may also once have been at Canons. In the north transept is a towering monument to the 1st Lord Foley by Michael Rysbrack, the foremost sculptor in England during the first half of the 18th century.*

building with transepts at the east end, and a tower over the western end where the entrance is. But it is the interior, with its magnificent stained glass, and painted and plaster ceilings, which makes the church the important building that it is.

**Great Wymondley** *Herts.* 547Jd
An attractive village linked with the 16th-century kings of England, who granted the lord of the manor the right to be Cup-bearer at coronations. DELAMERE HOUSE Built *c.* 1600, named after one of these lords, it is a three-storied brick building occupying the site of a dwelling where Henry VIII was once entertained by Cardinal Wolsey.

**Great Yarmouth** *Norfolk* 554Eb
A great herring port, a 19th-century resort and now a popular holiday centre, Yarmouth is a long town stretching north–south on a gridiron plan. Already settled at the time of the Conquest, it was granted a charter by King John in 1208.
ELIZABETHAN MUSEUM An Elizabethan-style house with a Georgian front. There are fine 16th-century panelled rooms with period furniture and exhibits illustrating domestic life, mainly that of the 16th and 17th centuries. Lowestoft china and glass decorated by William Absolon is shown.
MARITIME MUSEUM FOR EAST ANGLIA The displays depict the maritime history of East Anglia.
MARKET-PLACE A large open space merging into Church Plain, with the Fishermen's Hospital or almshouse of 1702. A fine one-storey building around a courtyard, it is picturesquely gabled with a cupola, a pediment with relief and a statue of Charity in the yard. Near here stood the Benedictine priory of St Nicholas, *c.* 1100, of which the refectory remains. Close by is the vicarage of 1718, which has an elegant doorway with shell-hood, and then the great parish church of St Nicholas. King Street is a shopping street with some good buildings, including the Elizabethan White Lion Inn, the early Georgian house (No. 51), and other 17th- and 18th-century houses.
QUAYSIDE On the R. Yare; over a mile long, one of the finest quays in England. Hall Quay has the Victorian town hall of 1882, the Duke's Head Hotel dated 1609 and the Elizabethan Star Hotel. South Quay has a sequence of notable houses: Nos. 1 and 2 are of 1700; No. 4 was built in 1596 and has a panelled Elizabethan room with an excellent plaster ceiling. Nos. 5, 20 and 74–75 are all early 18th century; No. 20 is now the customs house, the most ambitious house on the quay, with big porch and Doric columns. The Old Merchant's House (museum) is of 17th-century brick with later west front. Off South Quay are the remains of the Franciscan (Greyfriars) friary of the 13th century, and near these the old tolhouse of 1362, badly bombed but restored, with Early English doorways. The narrow streets here called the Rows were also badly bombed.

TOLHOUSE A 14th-century civic building restored in 1961 after bomb damage in the Second World War. There is a series of dungeons and the house contains displays depicting local history.

TOWN WALLS Of the 13th to 14th centuries, they enclosed the town until the 17th century. They had 16 towers and ten gates, and well preserved stretches of wall and towers can still be seen from Blackfriar's Road to Rampart Road.

To the south of the town is the large St Nicholas Hospital (a naval hospital, built in 1809–11), and beyond that the Nelson Column, erected in 1817, and 144 ft high. North and east of the hospital lies seaside Yarmouth, with piers, pavilions, the Marine Parade, and Victorian hotels and squares.

### Greaves Ash *Northld.* 562Fc
A group of three settlement-units. That on the west is enclosed within a double stone wall, roughly circular in plan, and with occasional cross-walls between. There are over 20 circular huts within the area. The other groups, to the north-east, are smaller and unprotected, but are composed of similar circular huts. The settlements are late prehistoric, presumably of the Iron Age.

### Greenock *Renf.* 561Gf
MCLEAN MUSEUM AND ART GALLERY James Watt, who perfected the steam engine, was born in the port of Greenock; the museum contains his tools and other items associated with him. There are sections devoted to geology, natural history and shipping, with model ships and engines. Collections of British pewter and of arms from China, Japan and West Africa are also on view.

### Greensted-juxta-Ongar *Essex* 548Ac
CHURCH OF ST ANDREW One of the best-known churches in England because of its pre-Conquest log nave. The chancel was built in the early 16th century. The church was restored in the mid-19th century, when the nave roof was added.

### Greenwich *Greater London* 542Cg
BOROUGH MUSEUM The main collections are of local and natural history. There is also the Dawson Collection of foreign butterflies and moths.

CHAPEL, TRINITY HOSPITAL Almshouses on the Thames, near Greenwich Hospital and a power station. Founded in 1613 by Henry, Earl of Northampton, they have been much altered. A monument to the founder in the chapel, a now fragmentary work, is by Nicholas Stone; transferred from Dover Castle in 1696, it has a kneeling figure of the earl and other good figures.

CHURCH OF ST ALFEGE Designed by Wren's assistant, Nicholas Hawksmoor, this massive Portland stone church of *c.* 1715 has a tower by John James. The fine woodwork of the interior was destroyed by fire during the Second World War.

QUEEN'S HOUSE At the beginning of the 17th century Greenwich Palace was a conglomeration of Tudor buildings on the south bank of the Thames, with the Woolwich–Deptford road running alongside just to the south. In 1616 Inigo Jones was commissioned to build a house for Queen Anne, wife of James I; it was to be Palladian, on either side and bridging the Woolwich road. Two years later work stopped and was not resumed until 1630—for Henrietta Maria, wife of Charles I; it was completed *c.* 1635. The house is of brick with Portland stone dressings; as the road went through at ground level, the H-shape of the plan appeared only at first-floor level. It is now masked, as a little later John Webb, Jones's assistant, built two other bridges over the road at each end of the house, which now give it the appearance of a rectangular building. On the south side is an open loggia with

six Ionic columns, overlooking Greenwich Park. The roof is flat and surrounded by a balustrade. Later the colonnades at either side of the house were added. It now forms part of the National Maritime Museum.

NATIONAL MARITIME MUSEUM The exhibits, arranged chronologically, range from Tudor times to the Second World War, and include a collection of portraits and seascapes, including some by Turner, Hogarth and Reynolds. There are also nautical instruments and charts, model ships and relics of Nelson, including the uniform worn by him at Trafalgar. In the Barge House, the barges of Mary II (1689) and Frederick, Prince of Wales (1732) can be seen.

ROYAL NAVAL COLLEGE A rambling Tudor building, Greenwich Palace (known also as Placentia) stood on this site. It was demolished in 1662 and all that remains today is the vaulted crypt beneath the present Queen Anne's Block. In the same year the foundations of King Charles's Block, designed by John Webb, Inigo Jones's assistant, were laid; this building near the Thames was finished in 1669. At the end of the 17th century Mary II planned to build a hospital for disabled men of the Royal Navy. After the death of William III, Sir Christopher Wren was appointed architect for the new hospital, although at that time he was fully employed with St Paul's Cathedral, Hampton Court and churches in the City of London. Wren incorporated the existing King Charles's Block and Inigo Jones's Queen's House in a single grand design. By 1814 Queen Anne's Block near the river, and Queen Mary's and King William's Blocks nearest to the Queen's House, were complete. Although the whole conception was Wren's, he was assisted by Nicholas Hawksmoor, and his successor as surveyor to the hospital, Sir John Vanbrugh. In 1873 the hospital was given over to the Royal Naval College.

VANBRUGH CASTLE In 1692 Sir John Vanbrugh, the author of Restoration comedies, and architect of Castle Howard in Yorkshire, was imprisoned in the Bastille by Louis XIV on a charge of spying. In 1717 he built Vanbrugh Castle in the style of his former prison, its original name being Bastille House. Some of the rooms are still decorated in the style of Vanbrugh's time. It is now a school for boys whose fathers were in the RAF.

### Greystoke *Cumb.* 557Hf
CHURCH OF ST ANDREW A large church, mostly of the 15th century, with a west tower. Inside are misericords, brasses and alabaster effigies. There are stained glass fragments, of the 15th century, in the east window. Near by is Greystoke Castle, rebuilt by Anthony Salvin in the 19th century.

### Grime's Graves *Norfolk* 554Ba
Of the hundreds of filled mine-shafts in this immediate area, 16 have been excavated and two are kept open for inspection, though covers have been placed over them as a protection from the weather. Layers of flint occur naturally in chalk, the quality varying considerably. Here and there in the sides of this ancient valley, the best flint, the floorstone as it is known, outcrops. Neolithic man, knowing its approximate depth, dropped these shafts to reach it, sometimes as deep as 40 ft. From the central shaft, he ran out galleries in all directions. The waste material from a new shaft was then thrown into the adjacent exhausted mine. The 'altar' to a little chalk goddess may still be seen in one of the open pits.

Nearby Brandon is the last centre of the flint-knapping ˅industry, and from here flints are exported all over the world.

JOHN HARRISON'S CHRONOMETER *Before 1736 there were no time-pieces accurate enough to be used for calculating longitude successfully. In 1714 the English government offered a prize of £20,000 for the discovery of a method of determining longitude to within 30 miles, and between 1735 and 1770 John Harrison built five* successful chronometers—but did not receive his prize money until 1773. The large clock is Harrison's first; it was encouragingly tested on a voyage to Lisbon in 1736. The dial at the top indicates seconds, those below minutes (on the left) and hours, while the bottom dial indicates days. (National Maritime Museum)

**Grimsby** Lincs.                                   551Jg
The coming of the railway in 1848 transformed this medieval fishing port into a great trading centre. Today, Grimsby's 3000 fishermen supply a market handled by 350 merchants and one fresh filleting factory deals with up to 200,000 lb of whole fish a day.

Grimsby's old buildings include the Augustinian abbey of Wellow, founded 1100–35; the nunnery of St Leonard, c. 1184; Greyfriars in Cartergate, 1240; Austin Friars, 1293; Hospital of St Mary Magdalene, in Bargate, 1291.
DOUGHTY MUSEUM More than 60 ship models include some made by French prisoners of war in the 18th and 19th centuries, and a large group of fishing vessels. The Doughty Collection of china and a small group of paintings, mainly of local interest, are also exhibited.

**Grimspound** Devon                                 539Gd
In the *Hound of the Baskervilles*, Sir Arthur Conan Doyle gave Sherlock Holmes the remnants of a hut in a prehistoric settlement in which to bivouac; his model was this ancient village. Surrounding a roughly circular 4 acre area is a stone wall some 9 ft thick, and in it are the remains of 24 circular huts of about 15 ft diameter. A raised stone bed-place was a luxury that several enjoyed. The inhabitants made sure of a water supply by enclosing part of a stream with the wall.

**Grimsthorpe Castle** Lincs.                        553Gc
Of 13th-century origin, the castle was considerably enlarged c. 1540. A north front was added by Sir John Vanbrugh in 1722 and further alterations were made c. 1810. The castle contains paintings, coronation robes and plate.

ROYAL NAVAL COLLEGE *By the time Charles II was restored to the throne in 1660, the old Tudor buildings of Greenwich Palace, where Henry VIII and Elizabeth I were born, had been so neglected that it was decided to demolish them. In 1662–9 they were replaced by King Charles's Block which was designed by John Webb, Inigo Jones's assistant. At the end of the 17th century Mary II proposed the foundation of a hospital for disabled men of the Royal Navy, and Sir Christopher Wren was appointed architect. Not far from the site was Inigo Jones's Queen's House, and this Wren decided to make his central feature. He designed two magnificent colonnades leading towards the house and away from the existing palace, and above each colonnade he placed an elegant dome. The colonnades form the sides of Wren's Queen Mary's and King William's Blocks. Since 1873 the hospital has been the home of the Royal Naval College.*

FREEDOM BOX *Enamelled boxes like this were made in Great Britain and Ireland during the 18th century to contain the written grant of the freedom of a town or city. This box is not only a superb example of its kind but also has great historical interest. It is of two-colour gold, decorated with a scene in painted enamel showing the Battle of the Nile. The sides are set with four plaques which bear coats of arms, the initials of Captain Edward Berry, trophies, and the British lion and Egyptian crocodile on either side of a pyramid. The box contained the freedom presented to Captain Berry, captain of the admiral's ship under the command of Nelson at the Battle of the Nile on August 1, 1798, by the City of London to thank him and his fellow sailors for 'their gallant services . . . manifesting to the world an additional instance of the superior Discipline and irresistible Bravery of the British Seamen'.*
*(National Maritime Museum)*

From A. K. Snowman's '18th Century Gold Boxes of Europe' (Faber)

## Grinton *Yorks.* 558Bd
CHURCH OF ST ANDREW St Andrew's was built by the Normans, but is now mainly in the Perpendicular style. There is a carved Norman font, and fragments of medieval stained glass; also screens and an early 18th-century pulpit.

## Groombridge *Kent* 542Ce
There was no medieval village here, but the brick church was built in 1625, and round it grew up rows of tile-hung cottages on two sides of a sloping green.
THE MANOR A Restoration country house built in 1660 with interior panelling from the Elizabethan manor which once stood on the site. The old moat was retained for decorative purposes to harmonise with the stone-walled garden which was constructed during the 15th century.

## Guildford *Surrey* 542Af
The High Street is one of the finest streets in southern England. Abbot's Hospital, the great almshouses begun in 1619, and the town hall, of 1683, with a cupola and its great clock riding out over the street, are both of an unforgettable self-confidence. The mighty keep of the Norman castle lies to the south, nearer the valley bottom.
CATHEDRAL The Second World War held up the building of the cathedral. Sir Edward Maufe's design was accepted in 1932 but the building was not consecrated until 1961. The style of the building is simplified Gothic, the exterior being of red brick with Clipsham stone dressings. Among those whose work decorates the building was Eric Gill, whose *St John the Baptist* stands outside the south transept; he also designed the sculpture around the circular east window. Other sculpture is by

Vernon Hill, and by Alan Collins, who carved the font. There is stained glass by Moira Forsyth and Rosemary Rutherford, and glass engraved by John Hutton, who engraved the glass screen at Coventry Cathedral. The sanctuary carpet was designed by Sir Edward Maufe.

CHURCH OF THE HOLY TRINITY A large church, rebuilt in the mid-18th century, but having a late 19th-century east end. Michael Rysbrack may be the sculptor of the man in Roman dress on the monument to Speaker Onslow (d. 1768).

MUSEUM AND MUNIMENT ROOM The museum is housed in a 17th-century brick building adjoining the medieval Castle Arch. Lewis Carroll (Charles Dodgson) often stayed with his family in Guildford, and died there in 1898; his letters and other relics are preserved in the museum. Other exhibits show items from the 6th-century Saxon cemetery at Guildown, medieval tiles from Chertsey Abbey, examples of Wealden ironwork, needlework and needlework implements. Over 100,000 documents relating to Guildford and district are kept in the Muniment Room.

WOMEN'S ROYAL ARMY CORPS MUSEUM On display are women's uniforms of the First World War, of the ATS of the Second World War, and of the WRAC. Also shown are photographs, decorations and medals.

**Guisborough** *Yorks.*                    *558Ee*
CHURCH OF ST NICHOLAS This late 15th-century church, restored c. 1905, stands near the ruins of a 12th-century priory. There are fragments of the original glass, and a good early 16th-century monument brought from the priory at the Dissolution, with carved figures of knights and saints.

**Gunby Hall** *Lincs.*                    *553Je*
Tennyson's 'haunt of ancient peace' was built of red brick and stone dressings by Sir William Massingberd in 1700. It is a fine example of William-and-Mary architecture, and reflects the influence of Wren. Inside are panelled rooms containing fine furniture and portraits by Reynolds.

**Gunton** *Norfolk*                    *554Dc*
CHURCH OF ST ANDREW The church, designed by Robert Adam in 1769, has a portico of Tuscan columns. The organ is in the west gallery, which is supported by Corinthian columns.

**Gunwalloe** *Cornwall*                    *538Ba*
CHURCH OF ST WINWALLOE An isolated church on a sandy beach. The detached tower is built into a rock. St Winwalloe's is mainly of the 14th and 15th centuries. Inside are rood screen fragments with painted panels.

**Gurness** *Mainland, Orkney*                    *569Hg*
The archaeological remains are a complex of several occupations, but the site is very close to the sea and parts of the outworks have been eroded.

First came the broch, which stood within a walled area. Much of this outer wall has now disappeared. Outside this was a ditch and other ramparts and ditches farther out were probably contemporary. The broch building has a double skin, touching in places, some 14 ft thick overall.

Later, after the broch had ceased to be occupied, the outer space between it and the ditch was filled with many other small buildings and occupation seems to have persisted until Viking times.

**Guthrie Castle** *Angus*                    *566Fb*
A 15th-century castle on the site of an earlier fortress. The square tower dates from 1468 and additions were made in the 19th century. It contains 15th-century wall-paintings. In the grounds are a fine walled garden and 'wild' garden.

**Gwydir Castle** *Caern.*                    *550Fe*
This romantic building, wrongly called a castle, was for many years the principal seat of the influential Wynn family. Its founder, Maredudd ab Ieuan, moved into the area in the late 15th century, and after living at Dolwyddelan Castle came to Gwydir and built the tall block opposite the entrance c. 1500. Many additions were made during the next 100 years; medieval stonework from the dissolved abbey at Maenan was used during that period, and also re-used and copied in the 19th century. The building was burnt out in this century, and restored to its present appearance. A muster of 50 peacocks lives in the grounds.

**Gwydir Uchaf Chapel** *Caern.*                    *550Fe*
The small private chapel of Gwydir Uchaf, built by Sir Richard Wynn in 1673, has a painted ceiling which is one of the most complete examples of this robust class of vernacular art to be seen anywhere in Britain. There is a similar chapel at Rug, near Corwen, Merioneth, of 1637.

# H

**Hackness** *Yorks.*                    *558Fd*
CHURCH OF ST PETER The church was begun in the 12th century and added to later; the chancel arch, however, may be Saxon, and fragments of a Saxon cross may be seen. There is a Perpendicular font cover, the stalls have misericords, and there are 19th-century monuments by Sir Francis Chantrey and Matthew Noble, who was born at Hackness.

**Haddenham** *Bucks.*                    *547Gc*
CHURCH OF ST MARY A 13th-century church with a good west tower with arcades. Inside is an early 19th-century plaster ceiling, which masks the 14th-century timber roof. There is a Norman font, and medieval glass in the north chapel. Two brasses show 15th-century priests.

**Haddenham** *Cambs.*                    *548Af*
Haddenham, the highest village in the Fen country, 120 ft above sea level, has an air of spacious dignity, enhanced by three or four good houses including the red-brick Porch House of 1657 with a central porch, and Vine House and The Limes, both of the 18th century.

**Haddington** *E. Lothian*                    *562De*
CHURCH A large cruciform church, with a central tower, of the 14th and 15th centuries. The nave is still in use, but the tower and building east of the crossing are in ruins.

**Haddo House** *A'deen*                    *567Gf*
For over 500 years the home of the Gordons of Haddo, who became Earls of Aberdeen; the 4th Earl was Prime Minister from 1852 to 1855. The present mansion was designed by William Adam in 1731 but altered in the 1880's. It contains fine furniture, portraits of the Gordons, and a chapel designed by G. E. Street, and is the centre for the Haddo House Choral Society.

HADDO HOUSE

*Like Hopetoun House near Edinburgh, Haddo House is basically the work of the Scottish architect William Adam, whose sons John and Robert were to become famous architects during the second half of the 18th century. The house, begun for the 2nd Earl of Aberdeen in the 1730's, was a simple but elegant building with a central block and a curving flight of steps up to the first-floor entrance; on either side two* *wings were connected to the main house by single-storey corridors. In the 1880's the house was enlarged by Lady Aberdeen. The entrance hall was brought down to ground level and an extra storey was added to each of the wing corridors. All the new decoration was carefully chosen in keeping with Adam's work. The drawing-room is a magnificent example of this late 18th-century decoration.*

---

**Haddon Hall** *Derbys.*                    552De
This famous manor house is a 20th-century restoration. The same basic materials were used as when the Hall was originally built. Devoid of brickwork or ornamental frills, the oldest parts of Haddon Hall date from the 13th century. Among the special features are the long gallery (110 ft), panelled in oak and walnut, with a decorative ceiling that has an acoustic function. Haddon Hall passed to the Dukes of Rutland when Dorothy Vernon eloped with Sir John Manners, but by the 18th and 19th centuries the Rutland family were using Belvoir Castle as their main country residence and Haddon Hall was abandoned. Detailed restoration, begun in the early 20th century, was not completed until the 1930's. The house is a fine example of change from an original fortified dwelling, although its battlements were never used by archers.

**Hadleigh** *Suffolk*                    548De
A market town which was once a centre of the East Anglian cloth trade, it has a remarkable grouping of buildings by the church. The 15th-century guildhall is timber-framed with two overhanging storeys. There are several attractive medieval and Georgian houses throughout the town.
CHURCH OF ST MARY A spacious 14th- and 15th-century church with tower and spire. Inside is a 14th-century font, with modern cover, screens and bench ends, and a fine early 18th-century organ-case. There are brasses, and monuments by Charles Regnart, *c.* 1793, and Eric Gill, *c.* 1935.
DEANERY The house has an early Tudor brick gateway. The Deanery Tower of 1495 is the surviving gate-house of an archdeacon's palace. It is of brick, with panelled and embattled turrets six storeys high, a splendid survival. The interior has a Georgian panelled room, an octagonal oratory with brick vaulted ceiling, and remains of a secret hiding place.

**Hadrian's Wall** *Cumb.–Northld.*        557Cg
As a barrier against infiltration by barbarians from Scotland and as a base against attack by them, a great wall was built by order of the Roman Emperor Hadrian in the years AD 122–30. It ran for 73 miles, from Wallsend-on-Tyne in the east to Bowness on the Solway Firth in the west, taking advantage of every natural point of strength and, at its highest, following ground 1230 ft above sea level. It is the chief monument of the Roman occupation in Britain, and the most remarkable of all Roman frontier works.
   Built of stone and 20 ft high in its eastern part, and of turf and 12 ft high in its western sector, it had 17 large forts about 5 miles apart, and a line of smaller forts each a Roman mile apart. Between each pair of these 'milecastles' were built two signal towers 20 ft square. On the northern side of the wall ran a continuous protective ditch, averaging 27 ft in width and 9 ft in depth. On the southern side was the *vallum*, a flat-bottomed ditch about 20 ft wide and 10 ft deep, with earthworks on either side; it ran straight from point to point like a Roman road and therefore often deviated from the course of the wall. This ditch seems to have served as the civil boundary. A road, now known as the Military Way, was built later between wall and *vallum* and was about 20 ft wide.
   The wall was garrisoned by infantry and cavalry, usually auxiliaries from all parts of the Empire under Roman officers. Detachments from the three Roman legions always stationed in Britain were sent to the wall only for special duties, for example when it was under attack. Garrisons were lodged in the forts and the milecastles. The wall was abandoned in AD 197 and a century later, but each time was rebuilt and re-garrisoned. It was finally abandoned in AD 383.
   The first important survey was made by William Camden, scholar and historian, who first published his *Britannia* in 1586. Archaeological

research has continued from his day to the present. The wall suffered much destruction after the Jacobite rebellion of 1745, the stones being used to build a new road from Newcastle to Carlisle; and even in the Second World War 300 yds of it were quarried for military use. There are museums at Housesteads and at Chesters Fort, and the museums in Carlisle and Newcastle also have excellent collections from the wall. Among these are votive stones and altars dedicated to many different deities—Jupiter, Fortune, Germanic gods, the Mother Goddesses, and the soldiers' god, Mithras. On the wall at Carrowburgh (Brocolitia fort) a Mithraic temple has been excavated.

**Hadstock** *Essex*                                   *548Ae*
CHURCH OF ST BOTOLPH This Saxon church, with transepts, has 14th-century additions and a 15th-century west tower. There is a 15th-century screen across the south transept. A great rarity is the wooden Saxon south door. This may, indeed, be the church built by King Canute in 1020 to commemorate a victory.

**Hafodty** *Caern.*                                   *550Ed*
Gardens in Snowdonia which include the Nant Mill waterfalls, and rock and water gardens.

**Hafotty** *Anglesey*                                 *550Ee*
Now abandoned, this stone building is a 14th-century house with alterations of the 16th and 17th centuries. These include the insertion of a floor in the medieval open hall, together with a carved fire-place; some were probably added by Henry Norris, who was Constable of Beaumaris Castle early in the 16th century.

**Hailes** *Glos.*                                     *546De*
CHURCH There was a Cistercian abbey here, founded in the 13th century, and its ruins are not far from the Norman parish church. This houses 15th-century glass, 14th-century wall-paintings with figures of saints, screen, benches, medieval tiles and a 17th-century oak canopied pulpit. A small museum contains abbey relics.

**Hailes Castle** *E. Lothian*                         *562Df*
James Hepburn, 4th Earl of Bothwell, abducted and married Mary, Queen of Scots and brought her here in 1567; the dungeon (with a water-gate) where she was kept still remains. The ruined castle comprises 13th-century masonry with 14th- and 15th-century additions.

**Hale Park** *Hants.*                                 *540Fd*
A Palladian-style Georgian country mansion, designed by Thomas Archer and built for his use in 1715; it was altered by Henry Holland in 1770. The house contains fine furniture, pictures and Aubusson tapestries.

**Halifax** *Yorks.*                                   *558Ba*
CHURCH OF ST JOHN A large building, mainly of the 15th century, but with some 12th-century fragments. The west tower is Perpendicular. Inside are medieval stalls and font cover.
SHIBDEN HALL A 15th-century timber-framed house, maintained by Halifax corporation as a folk museum.
TOWN HALL Erected in 1861-3 to designs by Sir Charles Barry, architect of the Houses of Parliament. The tower, 180 ft high, is decorated with sculptures by John Thomas representing Europe, America and Africa. He died before finishing the work; the final group, Asia, was completed under the supervision of the painter Daniel Maclise.

**Hallaton** *Leics.*                                  *552Fb*
CHURCH OF ST MICHAEL There are Norman fragments, including a tympanum in the porch depicting St George and the Dragon, but the body of the church is 13th century, including the west tower with broach spire. The aisles are a 14th-century addition; at the east end of the north aisle there is an elaborately decorated turret, surmounted by a little spire. Some good 13th-century ornamentation remains in the chancel. There is a small crypt in the north aisle, and some good 19th-century stained glass.

**Hall-I'-Th'-Wood** *Lancs.*                          *552Bg*
A black and white timbered manor house, built in 1483. A stone wing was added in 1591, and alterations made in 1648. The spinning-mule, an improved version of Hargreaves' spinning-jenny for fine cottons, was developed here by Samuel Crompton (1753–1827). The house is now a folk museum.

**Halsall** *Lancs.*                                   *551Jg*
CHURCH OF ST CUTHBERT A 14th-century church, one of the best in Lancashire. The 15th-century octagonal tower rises from a square base, and has a spire. There is a good chancel, with a fine medieval doorway and the original oak door with traceried top. A 14th-century tomb recess contains a later effigy, and a table-tomb of *c.* 1523 also has effigies.

HADRIAN'S WALL

*The greatest monument of the Roman occupation of Britain. The wall, shown near Housesteads in Northumberland, was first built in AD 122–30 by order of the Emperor Hadrian, to act as a defence against the Celts from Scotland. Built of stone in the east and turf* *in the west, it stretched 73 miles, from Wallsend-on-Tyne in the east to Bowness on the Solway Firth, and ran from one natural vantage point to the next. It was garrisoned by troops from all over the Roman empire, but was finally abandoned in AD 383.*

## HAM HOUSE

HENRY BONE: MINIATURE OF LADY DYSART *This
enamel miniature by Henry Bone (1755–1834),
Painter in Enamel to the Prince of Wales, copies a
portrait of Lady Dysart as Shakespeare's heroine
Miranda painted by Sir Joshua Reynolds in 1775.
Bone, one of the last and best practitioners of enamel-
painting in miniature, specialised in miniatures of
portraits by great contemporary artists. He achieved
the fine detail and delicate modelling first seen on
enamel miniatures in about 1630.*

QUEEN'S BEDROOM *Decorated in 1675 for use by
Catherine, Charles II's wife, this room is hung with
tapestries made of silk and wool by the English master
weaver, Bradshaw. These show scenes taken from the
painters, Watteau and Pater, and were made between
1730 and 1750.*

---

**Halstead** *Essex* 548Cd
CHURCH OF ST ANDREW Mainly of the 14th to
15th centuries, but restored in the 19th century, the
church has a reredos of 1893 by Sir Arthur Blomfield and several monuments to the Bourchier
family, including a brass and effigies.

**Hambledon** *Hants.* 541Hd
The cradle of cricket, the village lies in a valley-
bottom, half-way along which a charming short
street opens up, with the church at the top. Cricket
was first played a mile or so away, on Broadhalf-
penny Down.

**Hambledon Hill** *Dorset* 540Ed
The centre of three radiating hill-spurs is occupied
by the single bank and ditch of a partly obliterated
Neolithic causewayed camp, which also had
additional earthworks on the adjoining spurs.
There is a long barrow outside the main area on the
south-western spur and another lies within the
earthworks on the northern spur. These earthworks were the defences of a major hill-fort,
which was remodelled two or even three times,
and now show double or triple banks with
additional defences at critical points.

**Ham House** *Greater London* 542Ag
HAM HOUSE The original Ham House was built in
1610 as a modest country residence by Sir Thomas
Vavasour. In the middle of the century it was
bequeathed to Elizabeth, Countess of Dysart, by
her father. After her marriage to the Duke of
Lauderdale, Minister at the Court of Charles II, the
house was enlarged and redecorated in 1673–5 in
the flamboyant baroque style of the period. Much
of the original furniture and interior ornament has
been retained. Paintings include works by Kneller

and Van Dyck in the great hall, works by the
Dutch, Venetian, Roman and Flemish schools
elsewhere in the house, and a fine collection of
miniatures in the room over the chapel, including a
Nicholas Hilliard, Isaac Oliver's portrait of an
unknown man against a background of flames,
and a Samuel Cooper. Also in this room is an
interesting collection of ancient costumes and
other textiles, including a complete 'wedding set'
all of tissue of blue silk and silver thread, of early
18th-century French work.

The rest of the textile collection consists of furnishing fabrics, carpets, and a large collection of
tapestries of English, French, Dutch and Italian
manufacture. Particularly notable among these are
the 17th-century Flemish tapestries in the Volary
Roome, or aviary, after paintings by Poussin in the
Louvre depicting incidents in the life of Pyrrhus,
King of Epirus in the 3rd century BC.

There is also a rich display of furniture mainly of
the 18th century, particularly Dutch and French
work. A plasterer named Joseph Kinsman seems to
have been extensively employed in the 1630's to
provide ornate decoration on ceilings and walls;
and outstanding work of the same period is the
handsome staircase with carved and pierced panels
depicting trophies of arms.

**Hampton Court** *Greater London* 542Ag
Thomas Wolsey, Archbishop of York and subsequently Cardinal and Lord Chancellor of England,
began this enormous palace in the early 16th
century. He fell from power in 1529, having
already in 1526 offered Hampton Court to Henry
VIII in an attempt to regain favour. Its size and
splendour made it suitable as a royal palace and
with additions and alterations it remained a royal

# HAMPTON COURT

TIJOU SCREEN *Decorative ironwork flourished in England in 1685 to 1740 as never before, and the acknowledged master of the art was the Frenchman Jean Tijou, who came to England in 1688 with William III and stayed until 1712. At Hampton Court Tijou made wrought-iron gates, balustrades, and a magnificent screen for the Fountain Garden (now in the Privy Garden). Above is a detail of one of the 12 decorative panels which are connected by plainer palisades. These panels are typical of Tijou's work; he liked elaborate flowery effects, and used much repoussé work such as the mask at the top here.*

HAMPTON COURT *Cardinal Wolsey started to build the largest house in England in 1514. The magnificent result and the cardinal's ostentation, however, irritated the king and Wolsey, in an unsuccessful attempt to stave off his displeasure, thought it prudent to 'present' the house to him. Between 1531 and 1536 Henry VIII added the great hall, with its magnificent hammerbeam roof, and various other buildings. He lavishly embellished the chapel with a fine fan-vaulted wooden ceiling, which looks like stone. After that no significant additions were made until William III, who ascended the throne in 1689, and who disliked living in London, employed Sir Christopher Wren to enlarge the palace. The cloistered Fountain Court dates from this period, and the Cartoon Gallery was built to house a set of great tapestry designs by Raphael. Wren also decorated the chapel, designing the paintings and the oak reredos carved by Grinling Gibbons.*

*After William's death from a riding accident in 1702 there were no more major changes to the building. The state apartments in Wren's building (shown here) contain painted decoration by Laguerre, Verrio and Sir James Thornhill, and works by leading sculptors of the late 17th century, such as John Nost, Grinling Gibbons and Caius Gabriel Cibber. The French smith Jean Tijou was responsible for a great deal of the ornamental ironwork. In the gardens, mainly designed for William and Mary by Henry Wise and George London, are the vinery with the Great Vine planted in 1768, and the maze, planted in the reign of Queen Anne. The Lower Orangery, built for Anne, now houses the magnificent series of cartoons by Mantegna depicting 'The Triumph of Caesar'.*

residence up to the death of George II in 1760; five of Henry VIII's wives lived there. The palace is roughly symmetrical, and there is some Italianate detail, showing the influence of Renaissance ideas from the Continent. But in general, the building is still a large rambling medieval palace built around a series of courtyards. Much of Wolsey's building survives in the Tudor portions of the complex, although the great hall was built for Henry VIII. The astronomical clock in Clock Court was made for Henry in 1540—the dial remains, but the mechanism was renewed in 1879. Adjoining the palace is the closed tennis court built by Henry

in 1529, and to the north-west lie the Tiltyard Gardens, laid out on the site of the Tudor tiltyard where, in Henry's time, tournaments were held.

**Hanbury** *Staffs.* 552Cc
CHURCH OF ST WERBERGH A 13th-century church, restored during the 19th century. It contains several good and interesting monuments of the 16th and 17th centuries, as well as a cross-legged knight in alabaster of the 14th century.

**Hanbury Hall** *Worcs.* 546Cf
A red-brick house, built in 1701 in Wren's style. The staircase and hall were painted by Thornhill. The Long Room contains good plasterwork.

MANTEGNA: CAESAR'S CHARIOT FROM 'THE TRIUMPH OF CAESAR' *Mantegna was the most important 15th-century North Italian painter and the 'Triumph of Caesar' may well be his masterpiece. Even today, after centuries of neglect and crude repainting, it is still possible to recapture some of its original glory, thanks to the most recent restoration. The nine paintings, each 9 ft square, were painted for the Gonzaga family at Mantua to whose court Mantegna was attached for the rest of his life after he left Padua. The panels were begun before 1486 and completed soon after 1492. In 1629 they were bought by Charles I, and fortunately withdrawn from the sale of his collection by Cromwell in 1679; they were then removed to Hampton Court, and have remained there ever since. The scene is a continuous Roman triumphal procession moving from right to left—against the movement of the eyes which instinctively enter on the left. A cumulative effect and avoidance of any anti-climax is achieved by placing Caesar on his triumphal car in this last panel. Mantegna spent two years in Rome during the period covered by the Triumph, and his work teems with allusions to Roman architecture, costume and reliefs which deeply influenced his style.*

**Harberton** *Devon* 539Gc
CHURCH OF ST ANDREW A battlemented church of the 14th and 15th centuries, with long wagon-roofs. There is a fine rood screen (with 19th-century painted panels said to depict young ladies of the congregation) and some parclose screens. The 15th-century stone pulpit (one of the best in Devon) has 17th-century figure carving, and the circular Norman font has carved decoration in Byzantine style.

**Hardingstone** *Northants.* 547Gf
On high ground stands a fine stone cross, one of several erected by Edward I in 1291–4 to mark sites where the body of Queen Eleanor rested on its way from Harby (Nottinghamshire) to Westminster Abbey. The cross was restored in 1840 and 1884.
CHURCH OF ST EDMUND The church has a 13th-century tower and 14th-century nave arcades. There are two 17th-century monuments to the Harvey family, one with kneeling figures in two tiers, and a large wall monument with portrait medallions by J. M. Rysbrack, *c.* 1760.

**Hardwick Hall** *Derbys.* 552Ee
This magnificent Elizabethan house was begun in 1591 by Elizabeth, Countess of Shrewsbury (Bess of Hardwick). Work progressed incredibly

## HARDWICK HALL

*'Bess of Hardwick', a much married lady and one of the most powerful personalities of Elizabeth I's reign, built herself this magnificent house. Bess, who was born in 1520, was first married at the age of 12, and as each of her husbands died she became richer and richer. Her fourth and last husband was George, Earl of Shrewsbury, for many years the custodian of the imprisoned Mary, Queen of Scots. The Countess of Shrewsbury eventually tired of this arrangement and left her husband; he died in 1590, leaving her yet more money. Assisted by Robert Smythson, she at once started on the building of Hardwick and by 1597 it was ready for her to move into. Inside the house are large ornate chimney-pieces and a rambling staircase. In the High Great Chamber is a splendid elaborate plaster frieze showing such scenes as Diana and Venus with the infant Cupid, based on 16th-century engravings.*

quickly for that time, considering the size of the house. Within three years the structure had been completed and by 1597 the house was decorated and furnished ready for occupation. It has four great towers, one at each corner, and huge windows which increase in size the higher they are. Parapets incorporating the initials E. S. (Elizabeth Shrewsbury) stand against the sky and proclaim the builder. It is thought that Robert Smythson was the architect. The house contains fine furniture, needlework, tapestries and portraits, and is set amid extensive gardens with yew hedges and borders.

**Hardwick Park** *Suffolk*                    548Cf
Noted for its cedar trees, said to be the finest in Britain.

**Hardy Monument** *Dorset*                    540Dc
A tall column on a hill near Portesham commemorates Vice-Admiral Sir Thomas Masterman Hardy (1769–1839), who was Flag Captain in the *Victory* at the Battle of Trafalgar, and with Lord Nelson when he died; the column was erected in 1846.

**Hardy's Cottage** *Dorset*                    540Dc
A thatched cottage where the novelist Thomas Hardy (1840–1928) was born.

**Harefield** *Greater London*                    547Hc
CHURCH OF ST MARY There is a low embattled tower at west end of the north aisle here, and an impressive array of monuments, the most sumptuous being to the Countess of Derby (d. 1636). Others are by Grinling Gibbons, William Stanton

and John Bacon Junior. There is also some splendid woodwork.

**Haresfield Beacon** *Glos.*                    546Cc
South of Gloucester, a great spur of the Cotswolds projects far into the Vale of Gloucester; its outer part bears a fine Iron Age hill-fort of double construction. The outer end of the spur, the Beacon, has a single bank-and-ditch defence. The enclosed area was later greatly increased by a further series of defences on the east.

From here may be had perhaps the best view across the Vales of Gloucester and Berkeley to the Forest of Dean and, when visibility permits, to the Black Mountains and Brecon Beacons.

**Harewood** *Yorks.*                    558Cb
CHURCH OF ALL SAINTS A Perpendicular church, altered in the 19th century by Sir Gilbert Scott. There is an impressive series of 15th-century alabaster effigies lying on tomb chests, on which are angels, heraldry and figures of weepers. There is an oak communion-rail in memory of George V.

**Harewood House** *Yorks.*                    558Cb
The home of HRH The Princess Royal, Countess of Harewood, until her death in 1965, this fine country mansion was built in 1759–71 by John Carr of York for Edwin Lascelles, whose heir became the 1st Earl of Harewood; Robert Adam decorated the interior. In 1843 Sir Charles Barry carried out alterations which changed the Classical balance of the house. The great gallery has an Adam ceiling, and the ceiling in the music room by Zucchi is set with ten medallions above a similarly

patterned carpet. Much of the furniture was designed by Adam and made by Chippendale especially for Harewood House, which also contains paintings by old masters, Sèvres porcelain and fine silver. The park and gardens were laid out by Capability Brown, but the formal terrace gardens were added later.

## Harlech Castle *Merioneth.* 550Ec

One of Edward I's Welsh castles, built of local grey sandstone in 1283–90 on a rocky spur near the sea. It was fruitlessly defended so many times that it is sometimes called the Castle of Lost Causes. It was taken by Owen Glendower in 1401 and occupied by him until 1409. During the Wars of the Roses it was besieged by Yorkists for eight years until 1468, and this long struggle inspired the song 'Men of Harlech'. By Elizabethan times all but the gatehouse was in ruins, but even so Harlech was the last Royalist stronghold in Wales during the Civil War. The castle is rectangular in plan with two concentric sets of walls. On the east side the massive four-towered gate-house—the focal point of the castle where the living-quarters were—leads into the inner courtyard which has a round tower at each corner. (See p. 230.)

## Harlington *Beds.* 547Hd

HARLINGTON MANOR A many-gabled 17th-century house in the village of Harlington, it contains the panelled room in which John Bunyan was brought before Francis Wingate, Justice of the Peace, and committed to Bedford gaol for Nonconformist preaching. The architrave of an upstairs door is dated 1633.

## Harlington *Greater London* 547Hb

CHURCH OF SS PETER AND PAUL A small Norman church, with a fine south doorway and 15th-century south porch. There is a 12th-century nave, 14th-century chancel, and a tower added in the next century. A recessed monument of *c.* 1545 was also used as an Easter sepulchre. Brasses include one of a 15th-century priest with half-effigy; the tomb chests of the mid-19th century are by R. C. Lucas. A wall monument of *c.* 1695 incorporates winged cherub-heads and three portrait busts.

## HAREWOOD HOUSE

THE GREEN ROOM *The home of the late Princess Royal, Countess of Harewood and daughter of George V, the magnificent mansion at Harewood was begun in 1759 by Edwin Lascelles, 1st Earl of Harewood, who employed John Carr of York as architect. Robert Adam assisted Carr and was responsible for the Classical interior decoration of the house; he also designed much of the furniture. The entrance hall has a splendid plaster ceiling and decoration by Joseph Rose, and the long gallery has painted panels by Angelica Kauffmann.*

CARVED PELMET *An illustration of baroque illusionism, this pelmet is carved in wood to imitate the gathered cloth of the curtains. Probably designed by Robert Adam, it was made with great skill by Thomas Chippendale's workshop, and shows the high standards they achieved. Illusionism was never generally popular in England, but a few patrons of the arts who had been on the Grand Tour of Europe favoured it. A series of these pelmets adorns the windows of the gallery at Harewood, and show fine craftsmanship, wealth and imagination.*

**Harlyn** *Cornwall* 538Cc
HARLYN BAY MUSEUM An Iron Age cemetery of 130 slate coffins with skeletons was discovered near the beach between 1900 and 1906. Relics of this 3000-year-old burial site, including urns, weaving combs and bobbins, clothes pins and jewellery, are in the local museum

**Harpswell** *Lincs.* 553Cf
CHURCH OF ST CHAD The Saxon tower of this church has an inscription which records that the clock that once stood there was given to commemorate the Battle of Culloden. There is a Norman font, and a 14th-century south aisle. In 1891 the effigy of a priest was found in the floor, and there are also two other effigies, of the 14th and 17th centuries.

**Harrogate** *Yorks.* 558Cb
A spa town, famous for its sulphur and iron springs, which was a fashionable watering-place of the 18th and 19th centuries. The Royal Baths are still used by sufferers from rheumatic illnesses. The Royal Pump Room over the main spring was erected by Lord Rosslyn in 1786: it is now a museum.
HARLOW CAR GARDENS The Northern Horticultural Society's gardens—40 acres of ornamental gardens and woodland.

**Harrow** *Greater London* 547Jc
CHURCH OF ST MARY The spire at the west end of St Mary's is a prominent landmark. The church is of Norman origin and there are 12th-century remains in tower. There were 13th- to 15th-century additions, and restorations in the 19th century. There is some 19th-century glass, and an east window by Sir Ninian Comper. Among the monuments is that by Flaxman to Dr Lyon of Harrow School, with boys said to be the sons of Spencer Perceval, the murdered Prime Minister.

**Harrow Hill** *Sussex* 542Ad
Here is a representative group of Neolithic flint-mines, one of which, when excavated, proved to be 22 ft deep, with six radiating galleries at its base. Close by, and partly overlying some of the mine-shafts, is a small enclosure with a single bank and ditch. The bank was strengthened by the use of timber and the western entrance had a substantial timber gateway. There was apparently no regular occupation, so this was doubtless a stronghold intended for use in emergency.

**Hartford** *Hunts.* 547Jf
This picturesque village has a number of charming cottages, the 17th-century manor house on the main road and the 18th-century Hartford House. In August 1964, workmen here dug up 1108 English and foreign silver coins of the 15th and 16th centuries, ultimately declared Treasure Trove. The vicarage is said to have been part of the marriage settlement of Oliver Cromwell's wife.

**Hartington** *Derbys.* 552Ce
A small town near Beresford Dale. In the market-place are old cottages and a town hall dating from the 19th century. Hartington Hall is a gabled mansion with mullioned windows, of 14th-century origin but largely rebuilt early in the 17th century.
FISHING TEMPLE A fishing lodge of 1674 in Beresford Dale, used by Charles Cotton and Izaak Walton, who wrote *The Compleat Angler* in 1653.

**Hartland** *Devon* 538Ef
CHURCH OF ST NECTAN Standing in a commanding position, looking out to the Atlantic, with a pinnacled west tower 130 ft high, St Nectan's was begun in the 14th century, and has later additions. The wagon-roofs are partly plastered and coloured, and the finely carved rood screen goes right across the church. The Norman font has carved decoration, and the bench ends were given in 1530. There are monuments, and a brass of *c.* 1610.

**Hartlebury** *Worcs.* 546Cf
CHURCH OF ST MARY While parts of the medieval chancel still remain, and the west tower is of 16th-century construction, the body of the church was restored in the 19th century in Gothic Revival style, with slender nave columns and a plaster vault.

**Hartlebury Castle** *Worcs.* 546Cf
The residence of the Bishops of Worcester for more than 1000 years. The present mansion was erected in 1675 on the site of a moated medieval castle, and carefully restored in 1964. The state rooms include a great hall with portrait gallery and

HARLECH CASTLE

*One of Edward I's great military projects in his conquest and settlement of Wales, Harlech Castle was begun in 1283 and virtually complete by 1290—an extraordinarily rapid achievement made possible by an enormous expenditure of money for an army of workmen. It has been estimated that, in modern terms, Harlech Castle cost nearly £1,000,000. The labour force at its greatest was about 950 men, and the weekly average during the summers of 1286 and 1287* *was about 850. Like the other castles of this period, Harlech is not merely a fine example of military design but a considerable achievement in administration: workmen were brought from all over England. This was not voluntary service—the King of England then had the right to impress labour for his service. But the cost was prodigious—in modern terms the bill for Beaumaris, Conway, Caernarvon and Harlech together was over £8,000,000.*

## MONUMENT TO ROBERT CECIL, 1st EARL OF SALISBURY

*The effigy of Sir Robert Cecil, holding the white staff of Lord Treasurer, lies on a slab of black marble supported by four kneeling Virtues; underneath is a skeleton. The monument was carved by Maximilian Colt (or Poutrain) a Huguenot who carved Elizabeth I's tomb at Westminster. He also carved river barges for the Royal Family and, besides money, received an annual suit of broadcloth and fur for life. Cecil's tomb was ordered before his death to ensure a good likeness, a common practice in 16th-century England—'thereby to prevent the negligence of heirs and to mind him of his mortality'. Colt made a model of the tomb for Cecil in 1609, although he did not die until 1612. (Church of St Etheldreda, Hatfield)*

an 18th-century rococo saloon. The castle also contains the library of Richard Hurd (1720–1808), a noted divine. The Worcester County Museum is housed in the north wing.

**Hartlepool** *Durham*                    558Df
CHURCH OF ST HILDA An impressive 13th-century church, with a battlemented west tower. The chancel was rebuilt in 1870, and restored by W. D. Caroë in 1931. The font is from 1728 and there is 19th-century glass.

**Hartwell** *Bucks.*                    547Gd
CHURCH OF ST MARY THE VIRGIN Henry Keene, surveyor to Westminster Abbey and an exponent of Gothic Revival in the mid-18th century, built St Mary's in 1753–5. It is a most important example of the 18th-century Gothic style— though much of the detail is not correct. It stands in the grounds of Hartwell House and is octagonal in plan, with twin pinnacled towers at east and west. Inside there are rose windows; the lovely fan-vaulting has collapsed through neglect.

**Harvington Hall** *Worcs.*                    546Cf
A moated Tudor manor house, associated with religious persecution of Catholics and featuring priests' hiding places, and painted walls.

**Harwich** *Essex*                    548Ed
LIGHTHOUSE During the 17th century the great increase in coal shipments from Newcastle to London caused demands for many coastal lights, and in 1665 two were built at Harwich. These were crude structures, the upper light being a coal fire displayed in an open room above the town gate; the lower, which was a primitive candle-lit wooden tower on the shore, figures in a painting by Constable. These functioned until 1818, when they were replaced by octagonal brick towers, interesting examples of early cavity-wall construction. Owing to movement of the channel both had to be replaced in 1862 by the Dovercourt Lights, which in their turn became redundant.

**Hascombe Court** *Surrey*                    542Ae
The house is surrounded by flower gardens, particularly beautiful in spring.

**Haslemere** *Surrey*                    541Je
There are several generously scaled Georgian houses in the wide main street, which slopes downhill and up to the back of the town hall. Behind the town are the woods of Blackdown.
EDUCATIONAL MUSEUM Started in 1888 by a surgeon, Sir Jonathan Hutchinson, who saw the function of a museum to be not merely the display of random collections of rare or extraordinary objects, but a means of explaining the story of the earth and its life. The exhibits here are mainly concerned, therefore, with geology, zoology and human history. In the geology gallery the display of rocks and fossils is supplemented by an analysis of local geological history through relief-models, maps and diagrams, and by show-cases dealing with such themes as the story of fossils, the story of coal, and precious stones. There is a display of minerals which, when lit by an ultra-violet lamp, fluoresce in spectacular colours. In the history gallery there are illustrations of life in each period, a collection of prehistoric tools, and panels indicating the phases through which people in Britain were passing relative to other civilisations. The zoology gallery covers vertebrates, invertebrates and insects. Particularly notable are the collection of British mammals, an exhibit on bird biology and the collection of British birds.
JESSES Only the gardens of this house, which contains the best collection of early English musical instruments in the country, are open to the public.

**Haslingfield** *Cambs.*                    548Ae
CHURCH OF ALL SAINTS A church of the 14th century, but with earlier work. The west tower has embattled pinnacle turrets. There is a Perpendicular pulpit and a Jacobean font cover. Fragments of stained glass, and a standing figure of a man in contemporary dress, *c.* 1675, possibly by William Stanton of Holborn.

**Hastings** *Sussex*                    542Dd
The old town of Hastings was one of the Cinque Ports. The Battle of Hastings, when Harold was defeated by William the Conqueror in 1066, actually took place at Battle, known to the invaders as Senlac, about 6 miles to the north-west.

To record the history of the Norman invasion, Matilda, the wife of the Conqueror, ordered the weaving of the 213 ft long Bayeux Tapestry. To mark the 900th anniversary of the Norman invasion, the Royal School of Needlework embroidered a similar strip of tapestry, the Hastings Embroidery, 243 ft long, recording in detail 81 of the great events of British history since 1066.

PELHAM CRESCENT With the church of St Mary-in-the-Castle at the centre of the arc, the crescent was built in 1824–8 by a little-known architect, Joseph Kay. The architecture is more distinguished than any of the contemporary terraces at Brighton.

**Hatchlands** *Surrey*                     *542Af*
Admiral Boscawen, who defeated the French fleet at Louisberg (1758), built the exterior of the mansion *c.* 1756. In 1759 Robert Adam carried out the fine interior decoration—his earliest known work in England.

**Hatfield** *Herts.*                     *547Jc*
Fore Street has a charming row of small Georgian dwellings that were stepped up the hill to exploit the slope. At the bottom, on the corner of Park Street, is the timber-framed and gabled Eight Bells Inn, *c.* 1630. Dick Turpin is said to have leapt from one of the upper windows on to his horse Black Bess, and galloped away as the Bow Street runners entered the place. Several other houses of interest, with oversailing upper floors, are in Park Street, and a good group of half-timbered late 16th-century houses can be found in Church Street.

CHURCH OF ST ETHELDREDA Most of the church was rebuilt by David Brandon in 1872, with the east end, chancel and transepts from an older building. The north chapel was built in 1618 as a family chapel for the Cecils. Monuments include the work of Maximilian Colt, Nicholas Stone, Rysbrack and others, the latest being by Goscombe John of the early 20th century. Of the 19th-century stained glass, one window is by Morris & Co. from a design by Burne-Jones. (See p. 231.)

**Hatfield Broad Oak** *Essex*                     *548Ad*
CHURCH OF ST MARY THE VIRGIN Formerly a priory founded by Aubrey de Vere in 1135, the church consists only of the nave. There is much 15th-century work, including the west tower and south porch. In 1708, a library was built to the east of the south chapel. The contents include a 15th-century screen, an 18th-century reredos by John Woodward, and several monuments, of which one is by J. F. Moore, another by John Flaxman.

**Hatfield House** *Herts.*                     *547Jc*
The original palace here was completed in 1497 for Bishop Morton of Ely. After the Dissolution it became a royal residence, but James I exchanged it for the home of Robert Cecil, 1st Earl of Salisbury. The remains of the palace, including the banqueting hall, still stand in the west gardens. In 1607 Salisbury asked Robert Lyminge to design a new house. This Jacobean building kept to the usual E-plan of Elizabethan houses and was completed in 1611. In size it is impressive—it is nearly 300 ft long and 150 ft wide. The wings are wide and have square turrets at each corner. Still the home of the Cecil family, it contains fine portraits, including the Rainbow portrait of Elizabeth I by Zucchero, and manuscripts and relics of her. There are fine gardens and an extensive park.

**Haughley Park** *Suffolk*                     *548Cf*
An Elizabethan manor built in 1620, set in a park.

**Haughmond** *Shrops.*                     *552Ac*
ABBEY One of the impressive Shropshire abbey ruins, Haughmond was founded by the Augustin-

THE HALL AT HATFIELD HOUSE

*At the Dissolution Henry VIII seized the palace of Hatfield which belonged to the Bishops of Ely. His daughter, Mary Tudor, lived there and during her reign her half-sister, the Princess Elizabeth, was kept virtually a prisoner at Hatfield. There in 1558, while in the park, Elizabeth heard of her accession to the throne. James I coveted Theobalds, the nearby home of Robert Cecil, 1st Earl of Salisbury, and he exchanged houses with Salisbury. From 1607 Salisbury set about building a great new Jacobean house at Hatfield. Inside is the two-storey hall with a carved screen at one end; at the other end a door leads to the magnificent carved wooden staircase, much decorated and with standing figures of boys and heraldic lions. The long gallery runs the entire length of the south front, 180 ft long. In King James's Drawing-room is a large chimney-piece, probably by Maximilian Colt, with a painted statue of James I. The chapel retains its contemporary stained glass.*

ians at the beginning of the 12th century. Most of the church has gone, but there are remains of the various monastic buildings dating from the Normans.

**Haughton-le-Skerne** *Durham*                     *558Cg*
CHURCH OF ST ANDREW A Norman church, including the chancel arch, but the transepts are from the 19th century; there is a west tower. Inside are 17th-century furnishings—box-pews, font cover and pulpit. There are some Saxon carved fragments.

**Hawkshead** *Lancs.*                     *557Hd*
In Ann Tyson's cottage the poet William Wordsworth (1770–1850) lodged when a scholar at the 16th-century grammar school; the cottage has an outside staircase. The medieval gate-house of Hawkshead Hall survives almost intact.

**Haworth** *Yorks.*                     *558Bb*
BRONTË PARSONAGE MUSEUM The home of the Brontë sisters from 1821 until 1849, where Anne, Charlotte and Emily Jane wrote their novels. Manuscripts and personal effects of the sisters are exhibited in the bleak Georgian house, which is preserved as it was in their day.

**Hawstead** *Suffolk*                     *548Cf*
CHURCH OF ALL SAINTS Norman and later; the west tower is Perpendicular, with flushwork decoration. The nave has hammerbeams and angels,

HATFIELD HOUSE: DETAIL FROM A TAPESTRY OF 'SPRING'

*This tapestry is one of a set of four depicting 'The Seasons', a favourite subject for a tapestry room. The engravings of a Flemish artist, Marten de Vos (1531–1603), provided the main theme of the gods surrounded by seasonal activities. The detail here shows hunts in progress through fields and woods, with much incidental detail around the central subjects. Made about 1611, the tapestry also shows the signs of the zodiac for each season, and emblems with their Latin tags fill the borders.*

but was restored in the mid-19th century. There are attractive furnishings—benches, 16th-century pulpit, lectern—a large number of brasses, and monuments by Nicholas Stone, the two John Bacons and others from the 13th century onwards.

**Hawthornden** *M'loth.* 562Ce
A mansion rebuilt in 1638 by the poet William Drummond (1585–1649), who is buried in the churchyard of the nearby Norman church in Lasswade. In the grounds is a tree commemorating a visit by Ben Jonson in 1618.

**Hawton** *Notts.* 552Fd
CHURCH OF ALL SAINTS The interest here is nearly all centred in the magnificent chancel built by Sir Robert de Compton before 1330; he is buried in it near the richly ornamented Easter sepulchre, opposite which is an equally richly decorated sedilia.

**Heaselands** *Sussex* 542Be
The gardens contain flowering shrubs and trees, and a water garden.

**Heath Hall** *Yorks.* 558Ca
A mid-Georgian house with fine interior wood-work, carvings and plasterwork.

**Heaton Hall** *Lancs.* 552Bg
Built by James Wyatt in 1722, the Hall was formerly a residence of the Earls of Wilton. It contains one of the few surviving Etruscan rooms, with painted walls and ceiling by Biagio Rebecca. Other contents include an organ built by Samuel Green (1790), furniture and paintings of the 18th century, the Assheton Bennett Collection of English silver, and paintings (mostly 17th-century Dutch).

**Heckington** *Lincs.* 553Hd
CHURCH OF ST ANDREW One of the best Decorated churches in Britain, with a tall tower and spire. Inside there is a very fine Easter sepulchre with carved figures, including a mermaid and a man playing bagpipes. The loss of the chancel screen detracts from the medieval proportions, but the tracery work in the east window is a masterpiece.

**Hedon** *Yorks.* 559Ga
CHURCH OF ST AUGUSTINE A cruciform church which is mainly of the 13th century at the east end, and has a 14th-century nave. The central tower is 15th century. G. E. Street restored St Augustine's during the third quarter of the 19th century. There is fine tracery in the windows, lancet arcading, and a 14th-century font with carved angels.

**Hellen's** *Herefs.* 546Be
A stone manor house dating from 1292, with a stone table at which the Black Prince dined. The pigeon house dates from 1641.

QUEEN ELIZABETH *painted by Nicholas Hilliard.* (*National Portrait Gallery*)

## ELIZABETH I, THE GREAT GLORIANA

'In my opinion', said the Mantuan envoy, 'she exceeds the bounds of gravity and decorum.' The subject of his displeasure was a young queen, 'as tall as a door', as she described herself, with tawny hair and clothed in cloth-of-gold, who was 'very cheerful and smiling and giving everyone a thousand greetings' on her progress through the streets of London to her coronation. In a few weeks Elizabeth had captured the devotion of the City and established herself as her own Prime Minister, a position she was to maintain, in peace and war, through nearly 45 years. In her reign Shakespeare wrote *Hamlet*, Drake circumnavigated the globe, and England rose from a second-class nation to the dominant power of the 16th-century world. Her tomb is at Westminster Abbey.

MEDAL *commemorating the defeat of the Spanish Armada.* (*British Museum*)

ESSEX RING *given by the queen to Essex to return if he were ever in danger.* (*Westminster Abbey Museum*)

MINIATURE BY NICHOLAS HILLIARD, *and its original case, of Elizabeth, with her hair flowing loose in token of her maidenhood. 'I will never marry', she is reported to have said as a child of eight, when Catherine Howard, the step-mother whom she loved, was beheaded.* (*Victoria and Albert Museum*)

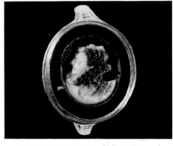

ARMADA JEWEL. (*Victoria and Albert Museum*)

THE OLD PALACE AT HATFIELD, *Elizabeth's residence before she became queen. At 15 she wrote to her brother 'The face, I grant I may well blush to offer, but the mind I will never be afraid to present.'*

BUCKSKIN RIDING BOOTS AND EMBROIDERED GLOVES *belonging to the queen, a superb horsewoman. She was very proud of her long, slim hands and had the habit of constantly drawing her gloves on and off when she was thinking.* (Ashmolean Museum, Oxford)

WHITE HORSE *which the queen rode to review her troops before the Armada.* (Hatfield House)

ANCIENT OAK TREE *standing in the grounds of Hatfield Park and traditionally the place where Elizabeth was sitting when messengers from London pronounced her queen. She had long been out of favour with Mary I, and four years earlier had been charged with treason. Her sister's death gave Elizabeth both the Crown and her freedom.*

ELIZABETH'S VIRGINALS. *One day she was alone, and playing these virginals, when she was surprised by the envoy of Mary, Queen of Scots, and she jealously asked him if she played better than her cousin Mary, if she danced better, and which of them was fairer. The envoy told her that she was 'the whiter' but that her cousin was very lovesome.* (Victoria and Albert Museum)

QUEEN ELIZABETH DANCING WITH ROBERT DUDLEY, EARL OF LEICESTER, *at sight of whom 'her whole body was suffused with desire' during the early days of her reign.* *Their close friendship endured until his death in 1588. The dance is thought to be the French 'la volta'. The picture, oil on panel.* (Penshurst Place)

**Helmingham** *Suffolk*                                    *548Df*
The Tudor Hall stands within a deer park; it is
moated, with a functioning drawbridge, and has
crenellation added by Nash in the 18th century. It
was built by the Tollemache family, to whom
there are many monuments in the church (which
has a good Perpendicular tower).

**Helpston** *Hunts.*                                       *547Hh*
A memorial to John Clare (1793–1864), known as
the Peasant Poet, stands at the cross-roads in this
village in which he was born. The son of a Northamptonshire labourer and without education, his
poems about the countryside and those written
during his confinement in Northampton asylum
are among the finest in the language.

**Helston** *Cornwall*                                      *538Ba*
BOROUGH MUSEUM In the old Butter Market folk
collections illustrating all aspects of local life in the
Lizard Peninsula are displayed. In 1901 Marconi
successfully transmitted the first wireless message
across the Atlantic from Poldhu Point, just south
of Helston, and a small section of the museum is
devoted to the early days of wireless.
CHURCH OF ST MICHAEL Built during the second
half of the 18th century. The west tower has
obelisk pinnacles; inside the church is a gallery on
iron columns.

**Hembury** *Devon*                                         *540Ad*
When excavated, this fine hill-fort was seen to
cover an earlier Neolithic causewayed camp. The
hill-fort itself had been remodelled. At first it had a
single bank and ditch with two entrances. The
bank was held by a timber revetment with an external palisade, and the entrances had timber gates
with bridges over. Later, additional banks and
ditches were constructed to deepen the defences
and, finally, more banks and ditches were put in,
crossing the interior of the fort and blocking the
west gate. The entrances are fine examples of the
inturned type. This most westerly of the causewayed camps appears to link its builders with the
tribes of the Salisbury Plain area.

**Hemel Hempstead** *Herts.*                                *547Hc*
CHURCH OF ST MARY A large, mainly Norman,
cruciform church with a central tower and tall
spire. The chancel, decorated by G. F. Bodley in
the 1880's, has a mid-12th-century ribbed vault.
The church contains a 14th-century brass and some
19th-century stained glass.

**Hemingbrough** *Yorks.*                                   *558Ea*
CHURCH OF ST MARY A splendid cruciform
church, of the 13th to 15th centuries, with a squat
central tower and lofty spire. There is good
medieval woodwork in the roofs, screens, bench
ends and misericords. The pulpit dates from 1717.

**Hemingford Grey** *Hunts.*                                *547Jf*
MANOR HOUSE This moated stone-built house, of
12th-century origins in a picturesque riverside
village, is claimed to be the oldest inhabited house
in England. Two storeys high, with a first-floor
entrance door, now turned into a window, and
Norman windows, it has a fire-place and a 16th-
century chimney-stack.

**Hendon** *Greater London*                                 *547Jc*
CHURCH OF ST MARY The original church dates
from the mid-13th century, but was greatly
enlarged in 1914–15. There are interesting furnishings and a fine square Norman font carved
with intersected arcading on all sides. Monuments
include a bold heraldic slab of 1677 and one of
*c.* 1703 with a reclining bewigged figure.

HENDON HALL The home of David Garrick, the
celebrated actor-manager, in 1756, the porticoed
house has a painted ceiling by Tiepolo.

**Henley-on-Thames** *Oxon.*                               *547Gb*
A small town set in beautiful wooded country in
the Thames Valley. The bridge dates from the 18th
century and there are many fine Georgian houses.

**Hereford** *Herefs.*                                      *546Ae*
CATHEDRAL A cruciform cathedral dating from
the 12th century, but with much alteration. There
was, besides the central tower, one at the west end
as well; this fell in 1786, knocking down part of the
Norman nave. James Wyatt restored the west end,
and this again was rebuilt at the beginning of the
20th century. The central tower dates from the
14th century, and is studded with ball-flower decoration. Inside are many brasses and monuments,
and some fine 14th-century stalls with misericords.
CHURCHILL GARDENS MUSEUM The collections
of costume, accessories, dolls, jewellery, furniture
and paintings date from 1750 to 1950.
CITY MUSEUM AND ART GALLERY Historical
exhibits include a Bronze Age burial, finds from
Iron Age hill-forts and discoveries made at the
Roman town of Magna (Kenchester). There are
also natural history and geological displays, collections of agricultural and domestic bygones,
military costume and accessories, English china
and glass and water-colours by local artists,
including David Cox and Joshua Cristall.

**Herefordshire Beacon** *Herefs.*                         *546Be*
This Iron Age hill-fort is marked by its com-
manding position and complex earthworks. In
the centre are the first defences, a single ditch with
bank and counterscarp bank. Later, the internal
area was extended to some 32 acres by a great
ditch with bank and counterscarp. This incorporated the earlier bank on the west, but stretched
away outside it on the east. In Norman times, a
castle was built at the centre of the original works
and its earthworks add to the complexity.

**Hergest Croft** *Herefs.*                                *545Jf*
Only the garden and park, noted for their flower-
ing shrubs and woodland, are open to the public.

**Hermitage Castle** *Rox.*                                *562Db*
A Border castle owned by the Earl of Bothwell,
the lover of Mary, Queen of Scots, who rode 40
miles there and back from Jedburgh to visit him.
Four great square towers are linked by curtain
walls which date from the 14th century.

**Herstmonceux** See Hurstmonceux Castle.

**Hertford** *Herts.*                                       *547Jd*
CASTLE Built *c.* 1100, the oldest building in Hertford, which until the reign of Elizabeth I was
closely connected with royalty. When Edward
III's mother Queen Isabella died, he recruited a
guard of 14 poor persons at twopence a day, for
three months, to watch over her body. The King
of Scotland, David Bruce, was imprisoned there,
as was King John of France, after the battle at
Poitiers. Here also Henry Bolingbroke, Duke of
Lancaster, drew up the charges against Richard II,
which subsequently dethroned him in 1399. James
I's son, Prince Charles, sold the castle to William
Cecil, Earl of Salisbury, whose family have owned
it ever since. The present building includes the
Mount, some of the 12th-century curtain wall, a
postern gate and an octagonal tower. The late
15th-century gate-house was considerably altered
*c.* 1800. Castle Street has timber-framed cottages,

## HEREFORD CATHEDRAL

RICHARD OF HALDINGHAM'S MAPPA MUNDI
*This map of the world (mappa mundi) is one of the largest (65 in. by 53 in.) and most elaborate medieval maps in Europe. Richard, who died about 1313, was Treasurer of Lincoln Cathedral and Prebendary of Hereford, and the prominence given to Lincoln on the map, together with the sketchy impression of Hereford, suggest he painted it in Lincoln about 1275. The map, worked on vellum, embodies all the Middle Ages' fundamental beliefs about the shape and nature of the world, which is drawn centred on Jerusalem; east is at the top.*

CHAINED LIBRARY *The largest library of its kind in the world, with nearly 1500 books, handwritten and printed. Each has a chain attached to the front edge of one cover and to a rod on the bookcase; only by turning a key to free the rods can books be removed or added. The oak bookcases were made in 1611. Seventy books were printed before 1500, two by Caxton.*

THE ENTRANCE HALL AT
HEVENINGHAM HALL

*Sir Robert Taylor designed this, the loveliest Palladian house in England, for Sir Gerald Vanneck in 1779. Taylor had started his career as a sculptor and had been an assistant to Sir Henry Cheere; he did not turn to architecture until the mid-18th century. He carved the sculpture in the pediment of the Mansion House in London—a commission he won as the result of a competition in which there was stiff opposition from his former master, Cheere, and Louis Roubiliac. The interior decoration at Heveningham was entrusted to James Wyatt. The superb hall has screens of columns at either end, and in the saloon the ceilings and walls were painted by Biago Rebecca.*

and in Water Lane Nos. 4–16 are thought to be former outbuildings of the castle.

FORE STREET Many of the buildings have splendid pargetting or ornamental stucco work including a variety of floral decoration. Shire Hall is a simple and unpretentious building designed by Robert Adam's brother James, in 1768–9. Nos. 3–13 have excellent 17th-century pargetting.

LOMBARD HOUSE On Bull Plain, the 17th-century home of Henry Chauncy, the Hertfordshire historian and judge, who presided over one of the last witchcraft trials in England. The façade facing the R. Lea retains the original brick, timber and plasterwork; the remainder is later restoration.

MUSEUM A half-timbered town cottage of the mid-17th century houses objects of local origin: archaeological finds, geological specimens, paintings, photographs and prints of Hertfordshire, the collections of the Hertfordshire Regiment, and a collection of Hertfordshire mosses. There is also Japanese armour and Turkish swords.

ST ANDREW'S STREET No. 43, the Old Verger's House, is a half-timbered structure with oversailing upper storeys dating from the 15th century.

**Hessett** *Suffolk* 548Cf
CHURCH OF ST ETHELBERT A 15th-century church, with a west tower and porch with flushwork decoration. There is an early 16th-century font, and a screen and benches. Mural paintings of the Seven Deadly Sins, St Christopher and St Barbara, and a monument by John Stone, *c.* 1653.

**Hetty Pegler's Tump** *Glos.* 546Bc
This transeptal gallery barrow was excavated in the 19th century, and has been consolidated and kept open so that its structure and some of the interior chambers may be seen. A deep forecourt leads to an entrance, inside which is a gallery with two chambers on either side (two of which are now sealed) and a fifth at the inner end. Half a mile south lies Uley Bury, a fine Iron Age hill-fort.

**Heveningham Hall** *Suffolk* 548Ef
Sir Gerald Vanneck inherited this estate with its small 18th-century house in 1777, and had a great new house built. He employed as architect Sir Robert Taylor, who left to the University of Oxford £180,000 with which the Taylorian Institute was founded. Taylor's Palladian house is a pillared centre block rising from an arcaded basement, with a pedimented wing on either side. James Wyatt decorated the interior of the house and also built the orangery. The grounds, containing a lake, were laid out by Capability Brown *c.* 1780. The entrance hall, Etruscan Room and library have their original furniture and contents. The estate still belongs to the Vanneck family.

**Hever** *Kent* 542Cf
CHURCH OF ST PETER A good example of 14th-century work, with west tower and spire, and barrel roof. There is a 15th-century brass to a lady in the chancel, but more important is one on an altar-tomb in the north chapel to Sir Thomas Boleyn (*d.* 1538), the father of Anne Boleyn. He wears full Garter robes, and lies with his head resting on his helmet.

**Hever Castle** *Kent* 542Ce
The girlhood home of Anne Boleyn (1507–36) second queen of Henry VIII and mother of Queen Elizabeth I. The late 13th-century moated castle was altered in the 15th century. The grounds contain a formal garden in Italian style with topiary work, fountains and statues.

**Hexham** *Northld.* 558Bg
A town famous in Saxon times when, under the name of Hagulstad, it became a bishopric in AD 678. However, it was largely destroyed by the Danes in 810. From those times the priory church dates, though much reconstruction took place in the 13th century; its treasures include a wooden pulpit, a pre-Conquest stool which gave sanctuary to anyone seated upon it, a crypt and fine choir screen. In 1464 the Yorkist army of Edward IV routed the Lancastrian forces of Henry VI at the battle of Hexham. The bridge across Haglut Burn dates from the 13th century. The 14th-century prison has the deceptive name of Manor Office. There is a 15th-century Moot Hall, and an unusual market-place or *piazza* dating from 1766.

**Hexham Abbey** *Northld.* 558Bg
Hexham Cathedral, founded *c.* 675–80, survived until 821. The town was sacked in 876 and there are no records of the church until the Archbishop of York refounded it as a house of Augustinian canons in 1113. The church is the main building to survive from the refoundation, but the external view from the east is dominated by the 19th-century façade, built *c.* 1858. Behind this stands a church begun *c.* 1180, which is an excellent

ITALIAN GARDEN *William Waldorf Astor, who had been American Minister to Italy, acquired Hever in 1903. He restored the building to its Tudor glory, and created the Italian Garden as a setting for Classical sculptures he had collected in Italy; it has a pergola, bath and grottoes—one is shown here.*

PARADE ARMOUR OF HENRI II OF FRANCE *A suit of armour probably designed about 1550 by Giovan Paolo Negroli of the Milanese armour-making family, whose skill in embossing steel has never been surpassed. Made for Henri II of France (1547–1559) it was worn only on ceremonial occasions to show the wealth and importance of its owner. The surface is covered with embossed and gilded tendrils of acanthus foliage and grotesque masks. This gilding may be a later addition, as contemporary portraits show the armour in the king's colours of silver and black only.*

HIDCOTE MANOR GARDENS

*Lawrence Johnston, an American, bought this estate in 1907 and created a series of delightful gardens, both formal and informal. The site was inhospitable: the soil was limestone, limiting the choice of plants, and there was little shelter from the wind in the wide Cotswold valley with its small stream. Johnston planted protective hedges and these were often unorthodox—red-leaved beech was mixed with the usual kind, and golden-leaved with green yew. They form a series of compartments with plants from all over the world, and each garden has a particular quality— one is full of red-foliaged and flowered plants.*

example of Early English style, with its long lancet windows and clustered column shafts. One outstanding feature is the massive staircase in the south transept, which led up to the canons' dormitory, and was used by them to descend directly into the church to sing the night offices. Inside is a Roman tombstone and a chair called Wilfrid's Throne, dating probably from the 7th century; beneath the buildings is Wilfrid's crypt of the same date, which utilises Roman stones in its construction. There are choir stalls with poppy-heads and misericords, and mural paintings.

**Heysham** *Lancs.*          557Hc
CHURCH OF ST PETER The church is mainly of the 13th and 14th centuries, but there are Saxon relics, including the base of a 9th-century cross with carved decoration in the churchyard.

**Heytesbury** *Wilts.*          540Ee
CHURCH OF SS PETER AND PAUL A large cruciform church with a central tower, collegiate in the 12th century. Its origins are Norman, but there is much 13th-century work and additions up to the 15th century. There is a fine stone screen to the north transept with fan-vaulting on both sides. It was restored by William Butterfield in 1866–7.

**Hidcote Manor Gardens** *Glos.*      546De
These gardens in the Cotswolds have been called the most beautiful gardens of the 20th century. In 1907 an American officer, Lawrence Johnston, began to transform what was virtually a wilder-

ness into a series of superb gardens. A cedar of Lebanon, a clump of fine beech trees, barren fields and a stream trickling through a small valley were the raw materials. First, the limestone windswept Cotswold scarp was converted into broad terraces. Along these unusual hedges were planted to form a series of compartments linked by a central vista. Each compartment has a special quality, such as the garden of plants all with red foliage and flowers. The gardens contain many rare and exotic plants and lime-hating rhododendrons, camellias and magnolias are grown in beds of sawdust. From the last terrace an alleyway of pleached hornbeam leads through a gate into a holly-grove.

**High Banks** *Kirkcud.*          556Eg
There is a rock-face exposed about a mile southeast of High Bank Farmhouse. This 100 ft surface bears groups of cup-and-ring markings, remarkable for the unusual grouping-patterns they display.

**High Bridestones and Flat Howe**     558Fe
*Yorks.*
The Bridestones are the remains of two circles of standing stones, each originally nearly 40 ft across. A few stones only remain upright; more have fallen, and the rest have disappeared. There are also single standing stones outside the circles.
   Flat Howe is a round barrow about a quarter of a mile to the east of the circles. Its mound has a visible kerb of stones.

HITCHIN

**Highdown Hill** *Sussex* 542Ad
The site of a Bronze Age settlement, overlaid by an Iron Age hill-fort. Remains of a Roman bath-house and a Saxon cemetery have been found by excavation. Finds from the site are in Worthing Museum.

**High Melton** *Yorks.* 552Ef
CHURCH OF ST JAMES Some Norman work, but St James's is mainly a Perpendicular church; the west tower is of that period. There is a parclose screen and some medieval stained glass, and a 20th-century screen and reredos by Sir Ninian Comper.

**High Wycombe** *Bucks.* 547Gc
MUSEUM AND EXHIBITION ROOMS Since the end of the 18th century High Wycombe has been a major centre of the chair-making and furniture trades; up to the First World War, it was almost the town's sole source of employment. The museum, which stands on the site of an Iron Age hill-fort, displays an extensive collection of the domestic chairs (mainly Windsors) and chair-making equipment that are part of this local craft. A small collection of local bygones is also shown.

**Hillesden** *Bucks.* 547Gd
CHURCH OF ALL SAINTS A lonely and most interesting church, all late Gothic though the west tower was built somewhat earlier than the rest. The walls are impressively battlemented, and there is a two-storey north vestry with a delicate canopy to the tower. Below the chancel roof is a row of carved stone angels holding music scrolls. The rood and parclose screens have linenfold panelling, and the 16th-century stained glass shows stories of St Nicholas. There are several monuments, one of marble to Sir A. Denton and wife (*d.* 1733) by Sir Henry Cheere. Sir Gilbert Scott made a thorough restoration in the 19th century.

**Hillingdon** *Greater London* 547Hb
CHURCH OF ST JOHN THE BAPTIST Mainly 14th century, with a west tower of 1629; restoration by Sir Gilbert Scott in 1848. There are several brasses and monuments, those of 1657 and 1743 with kneeling or reclining effigies.

**Hill Top** *Lancs.* 557Hd
Beatrix Potter lived here and wrote the *Peter Rabbit* books. The 17th-century house contains her pictures, china, furniture and some of her original drawings.

**Hilton** *Dorset* 540Dd
CHURCH OF ALL SAINTS A 15th-century church, typical of the Dorset country churches. After the Dissolution, several windows from the cloister of Milton Abbey were fitted in the north aisle; it is thought that the fan-vault of the porch may also have come from there. In the tower are 12 tall panels with painted figures of the Apostles, also from Milton, of the early 16th century; there is a 17th-century pulpit and a Norman font.

**Hindley** *Lancs.* 552Ag
CHURCH OF ALL SAINTS In 1766 the earlier church here was rebuilt in the Classical style. All Saints is brick with traceried windows; the galleried interior contains panelling and woodcarving.

**Hingham** *Norfolk* 554Cb
A small, unspoilt town between Norwich and Watton. Samuel Lincoln, weaver and ancestor of Abraham Lincoln, was baptised here in 1622 in the splendid medieval church. Shortly before Lincoln left England the Puritan rector, Robert Peck, fled to America and with others founded Hingham, Massachusetts. A bronze bust of Abraham Lincoln is in the church.

MARKET PLACE Has a number of elegant houses: Beaconsfield House, early Georgian; the Admiral's House with embattled wings; Quorn House with a Tuscan porch and pediment; Southernwood with imposing end gables and chequered brickwork.

**Hintlesham Hall** *Suffolk* 548De
A mid-Tudor mansion with additions in Queen Anne style made in 1842, scene of an annual Festival of Arts.

**Hinton Blewett** *Som.* 540Cf
CHURCH OF ALL SAINTS Mainly 15th century, with a later north aisle of *c.* 1530. Inside is a Norman font, and a canopied pulpit of 1638; there are some fragments of stained glass.

**Hinwick House** *Beds.* 547Hf
The Orlebar family have lived here since 1230. The present Queen Anne mansion was built in 1710; adjacent buildings date from 1430. The house contains paintings by Van Dyck, Lely, Kneller and Pieter Breughel, Mortlake tapestries and 17th- and 18th-century furniture.

**Hirwaun Iron Works** *Glam.–Brecon.* 545Hc
The works closed down early in the last century, and the furnaces fell into decay, but sufficient remains above the surface to see that the builders worked in a grand manner. Particularly interesting is the use of wrought-iron reinforcement bars, in the furnaces and in the slender tram-road embankment; some stone sleepers are still *in situ*.

**Hitchin** *Herts.* 547Jd
CHURCH OF ST MARY A large embattled church, mostly dating from the 14th and 15th centuries. The west tower is earlier. The stone font dates from the 15th century. Of the monuments, one of *c.* 1697 appears to be typical of the style of William Stanton of Holborn.

ST NICHOLAS WINDOW

*There are eight panels in this 16th-century window illustrating stories from the Miracles of St Nicholas, and here is a detail of a scene from the 'Boy and the Gold Cup'. A rich nobleman promised that if he had a son, he would present a gold cup to the altar of St Nicholas. A son was born and the cup was made, but only a duplicate was offered to the Saint. During the voyage to the church the boy fell into the sea with the cup. Part of the medieval ship and sailors are depicted here. The glass is rich in colour, and the drawing style shows a strong Flemish influence. (Church of All Saints, Hillesden)*

241

### HOLKHAM HALL

*Thomas Coke succeeded to the Holkham estates when he was ten years old. In 1712, when he was 15, he set out on the Grand Tour and did not return to England until 1718. During this time, his most impressionable years, he met the Earl of Burlington, a great advocate of the Palladian style of architecture which became so fashionable in mid-century. Burlington had befriended a remarkable man who was painter, architect, interior decorator and designer of sculpture and furniture—William Kent. Coke, later the Earl of Leicester, employed Kent to design his new house at Holkham, built in 1734–61. The interior is sumptuous and ornate. The main hall is 50 ft high— the full height of the building—and occupies most of the central block; it has a superb coffered plaster ceiling. Much of the furnishings and decoration of the state rooms, including the saloon (above) and state bedroom (right), was designed by William Kent.*

**Hoarwithy** *Herefs.* 546Ad
CHURCH OF ST CATHERINE An Italianate Romanesque church of the late 19th century by J. P. Seddon, with a bell-tower and a cloister walk on the south side. Inside is a Byzantine east end with gold mosaic work by Italian and local craftsmen.

**Hod Hill** *Dorset* 540Ed
Across the valley from Hambledon Hill lies this second great Iron Age hill-fort, with an internal area of 50 acres. Again there are multiple defences with well protected entrances. Remodelled three times, this hill-fort was one of the settlements reduced by Vespasian and his 2nd Legion in the early days of the Roman conquest. Shortly afterwards, the Romans erected a small fort in one corner and this was occupied for a time by both legionaries and some auxiliary cavalrymen.

**Hodnet** *Shrops.* 552Ac
CHURCH OF ST LUKE An unusual church, for the present wide south aisle was originally the nave, and the present nave the former north aisle; the octagonal tower is battlemented. The font is probably 17th-century, in a pseudo-Norman style, with carving. 19th-century restoration included the addition of the Heber Chapel in 1870. Interesting 18th- and 19th-century tombs include one

by John Carline, one to Bishop Heber (*d.* 1826) by Sir Francis Chantrey, and one of *c.* 1752 attributed to Sir Henry Cheere.

**Hodnet Hall** *Shrops.* 552Ac
Hodnet Hall, a large red-brick mansion designed in the 19th century by Salvin in the Tudor style, stands on the bank of a small valley. It contains fine furniture, silver and pictures. An adjacent hall houses a collection of big game trophies. The surrounding Victorian garden was of no great merit, but the countryside abounded with streams and pools. In 1921 Brigadier Heber-Percy created the first water garden in the valley and added a lake in 1923, but work was then halted until 1953. A chain of many pools covering 60 acres now fills the valley; massed primulas, irises, giant gunneras and other moisture-loving plants grow beside the water. The water gardens are linked to the house on the bank by formal terraces covered with lawns and massed rhododendrons and azaleas. There is a fine shrubbery and a large rose garden; daffodils and early flowering shrubs provide brilliant spring colours.

**Hoghton Tower** *Lancs.* 557Ja
Relics of James I's visit to this house in 1617 are preserved here. The house, rebuilt in 1565 and re-

stored during the late 19th century, contains 17th-century panelling and pictures of local interest.

**Holbeach** *Lincs.*                                   553Jc
CHURCH OF ALL SAINTS A large decorated church with west tower and spire, which shows features of the transition from Decorated to Perpendicular. There are brasses, and a magnificent 14th-century monument with effigy of a knight.

**Holcombe Court** *Devon*                         540Ad
An early Tudor mansion, with fine ceilings, chimney-pieces and a long gallery. It contains a collection of 18th-century furniture.

**Hole Park** *Kent*                                   542De
The grounds are noted for their formal and 'wild' gardens, water garden and bluebell wood.

**Holker Hall** *Lancs.*                               557Hd
Former residence of the Dukes of Devonshire, the Hall was built in the 17th century and restored in 1873 after a fire. The interior has woodcarvings by local craftsmen, period furniture and paintings. In the grounds are rare shrubs and a deer reserve.

**Holkham Camp** *Norfolk*                         554Bd
This is a camp or fort lying on an island of solid ground in a surrounding drained salt marsh. It is defended by one or two banks and a single ditch, except where the natural slope and the water which formerly surrounded it gave adequate protection. It has never been excavated and its date is very uncertain, but it is generally thought to belong to the latter part of the Iron Age.

**Holkham Hall** *Norfolk*                         554Bd
A Palladian mansion, built in 1734–59, which symbolises planned progress as seen in the 18th century. It was built near Wells by Thomas Coke to show how an area of dunes and salt marshes could be reclaimed and utilised, and how the style of an Italian palace could be harmoniously introduced into an English setting. Coke's plans were crystallised after discussions with Lord Burlington and William Kent; the result was a mansion of H-plan, with four wings to a central section: the overall front is 340 ft, with a great central portico. The interior became as lavish as the exterior is arid: a marble pillar and galleried entrance hall leads to a saloon of dark red velvet and gold with the Rubens painting of *The Return from Egypt* as its dominant theme. All the main rooms have a full measure of 18th-century magnificence—ceilings, paintings, tapestries and statuary. The interior at Holkham was planned to give

long vistas—landscapes of connecting rooms. The long library has a notable collection of 18th-century books acquired by Coke in Italy during his Grand Tour in 1715.

**Hollingbury** *Sussex*                    542Bd
Very early in the Iron Age, a simple defensive fort was built here, traces of which remain. But more than a century later, the present main structure was built in substitution. Its rampart was revetted with substantial timbering and there was also timbering enclosed within the ramp. The west gate has an inturned entrance, but that on the east side was of much simpler construction.

Like the fort on Harrow Hill, this was apparently used only in times of emergency.

**Holme Cultram Abbey** *Cumb.*                557Gg
This was a Cistercian foundation of the mid-12th century, and the nave survives as the parish church of St Mary. This has a good Norman west doorway, and a 16th-century west porch. The east window appears to be a 17th-century form of Perpendicular.

**Holme Lacy** *Herefs.*                    546Be
CHURCH OF ST CUTHBERT An interesting church with 14th-century arcade dividing the nave and south aisle, which are almost of the same width. The late 17th-century font is carved, and the stalls have misericords. There are many monuments to members of the Scudamore family from the 16th century, that of 1571 with alabaster effigies, and there are two (1861 and 1871) by Matthew Noble.

**Holme Pierrepont** *Notts.*                552Fd
CHURCH OF ST EDMUND A Gothic church of the later 17th century, with a west tower. There is a 15th-century font, and many monuments, from *c.* 1300 up to early 19th-century work by John Flaxman.

**Holt** *Wilts.*                    540Ef
THE COURTS Local weavers brought disputes to this house for adjudication until the end of the 18th century. Its decorated façade dates from 1700.

**Holt** *Worcs.*                    546Cf
CHURCH OF ST MARTIN This mainly Norman church, with the 14th-century castle near by, stands remote from all other buildings. It has rich 12th-century decoration on the doorway and chancel arch; there are some fragments of medieval glass of fine quality, a number of monuments and some good 19th-century mosaics.

**Holt Castle** *Worcs.*                    546Cf
Only the 14th-century tower and medieval hall are open to view.

**Holtye** *Sussex*                    542Ce
It has been shown by excavation that the Roman roads crossing and linking sites in the Weald were often paved with slag from the iron-smelting works in the area. Many of the minor roads, indeed, appear to be have constructed largely to serve these sites. At Holtye a section of such a road has been excavated and left open for inspection. Its surface of slag has consolidated with the passage of time and it still shows the ruts and wear of the traffic which passed along it.

**Holyhead** *Anglesey*                    550Df
CAER GYBI Holyhead was an important harbour as early as Roman times. Here, in the latter part of the Roman occupation, when the Irish were raiding and settling on the Welsh coast, a tiny fort was built. Its pattern resembles those later forts of the Saxon Shore in South-east England, and two of its projecting bastions still stand. It was this Irish

threat which led the British authorities, at the beginning of the 5th century, to move the leaders of the Votadini, and many of their tribesmen, from the Lothians of Scotland to settle in North Wales as a bulwark against invaders. The little church of St Gybi is set within the fort's curtain wall.
CHURCH OF ST GYBI A cruciform church, with a west tower. Much of the building is the 15th- and 16th-century enlargement of the earlier church whose chancel dates from the 13th century.

**Holy Island** *Northld.*                    563Gd
LINDISFARNE CASTLE A small castle on a high rock above the sea. It was built in 1549 as a protection against Scottish raids; stones from the nearby ruined abbey founded in 635 were used in its construction. From the Civil War until 1900 the castle was in ruins; it was made habitable again by Sir Edwin Lutyens, who designed the Cenotaph in Whitehall, London.
LINDISFARNE PRIORY St Aidan founded a monastery here in 635, but this was destroyed in the 9th century by the Danes. It was not until the 11th century that the present building was begun for the Benedictines of Durham. Now only ruins remain, but they are impressive and atmospheric.

**Holywell** *Flints.*                    551He
ST WINIFRED'S CHAPEL This well chapel and well chamber, built in the late 15th century, is one of the most perfect buildings of its kind in Britain. The well forms the basement of the chapel and consists of a large stone basin with steps for pilgrims to descend into the water.

**Homme House** *Herefs.*                    546Bd
The present house, built in 1600–23 on the site of an original Tudor building, was refaced *c.* 1820.

**Honeychurch** *Devon*                    539Ge
CHURCH OF ST JAMES A remote Norman church, with chancel arch and wagon-roofs in the nave. The Norman circular font has cable and zigzag carved decoration and a Jacobean cover. The west tower and bench ends are of the 15th century.

**Honington Camp** *Lincs.*                    553Gd
Hill-forts are almost unknown in Lincolnshire, but this small Iron Age fort must have been placed here for much the same reason that the early Roman defences at Ancaster, which preceded the civilian town of Causennae, were established. Both lay on the southern slopes of Ancaster Gap, an ancient channel eroded through the upland of Lincoln Edge. Honington stands on the hill-slopes at its south-west end and commands the Witham Valley at its junction with the Gap. Its internal area of about an acre is guarded by no less than three banks with two intermediate ditches.

**Honiton** *Devon*                    540Ad
Once famous as a wool town, Honiton suffered disastrous fires in 1672, 1747, 1754 and 1765: its houses are mainly Georgian and Victorian. It is noted for its pottery and its lace which is similar to Brussels lace, and which was worn by Queen Charlotte, Queen Adelaide and Queen Victoria.
HONITON AND ALLHALLOWS PUBLIC MUSEUM The museum is housed in what was probably the chancel of the oldest church in Honiton, whose tower and nave were demolished in the 1850's to build the present church of St Paul. The original shape of the building and some of the original windows can still be seen. The display centres around a collection of bones of straight-tusked elephant, hippo, ox and deer, all about 100,000 years old. A small version of a Devon kitchen can also be seen, and relics of the First and Second World Wars.

## HOPETOUN HOUSE

*An enormous house on the south bank of the Firth of Forth, not far from the Forth Bridges. In 1721 William Adam, father of the two famous architects and decorators, John and Robert, began enlarging the existing house, built by Sir William Bruce for the 1st Earl of Hopetoun. Work went on for 30 years and when their father died in 1748, the Adam brothers* *carried on, finished the house and decorated the new building with its two flanking wings joined to the main block by colonnaded quadrants. The interior is magnificent with woodcarving and plasterwork. The chimney-piece in the Red Drawing Room is the work of Michael Rysbrack, one of the most successful sculptors of the first half of the 18th century.*

**Hopes, The** *E. Lothian*      562De
One of the many large hill-forts scattered on the northern edge of the Lammermuir Hills. Built at one end of a ridge, its many ramparts appear to indicate at least two phases of construction. The inner area is protected by three ramparts without intervening ditches. Outside these are various lengths of rampart with external ditches, which do not encircle the whole area but curve from one steep scarp to another.

**Hopetoun House** *W. Lothian*      562Bf
The house was begun in 1699 by Sir William Bruce and completed by Robert Adam; it has a central building and two flanking wings surmounted by towers and cupolas, and is richly furnished. The grounds were laid out in the style of Versailles.

**Horham** *Norfolk*      548Df
THORPE HALL This 16th-century brick house has an interesting stack of four ornamental octagonal chimneys. The mullioned windows are of brick, rendered to simulate stonework. (By appointment.)

**Horham Hall** *Essex*      548Bd
A fine pre-Reformation brick mansion of *c.* 1515, with an even earlier south wing. Built by Sir John Cutte, Treasurer to Henry VIII's household, it has vari-coloured brickwork, a battlemented parapet, and a hexagonal turret; its showpiece is a bay window in the great hall, reaching the full height of the façade.

**Hornby Castle** *Lancs.*      557Jc
A conspicuous landmark above the R. Lune with a keep erected by Sir Edward Stanley (1460–1523) who became 1st Baron Monteagle after the Battle of Flodden Field (1513).

**Horncastle** *Lincs.*      553He
A small market town on the site of the Roman station at Banovallum, with traces of Roman walls and other relics remaining. The parish church, St Mary's, is notable for the excellent brasses of the Dymoke family—Hereditary Champions of England. There are some good Georgian houses, principally Rollestone House, No. 2 West Street, the naturalist Sir Joseph Banks's old house, a nine-bay block in the High Street, and No. 28 East Street. The Fighting Cocks Inn in West Street still has a cockpit in the yard. Bull-baiting was practised in the Bull Ring until 1835. Horncastle was once famous for its annual horse-fairs, considered to be the largest of their kind in the world.

**Horningsham** *Wilts.*      540De
In the village is the Old Meeting House, built in 1566, with a thatched roof. It is the oldest Nonconformist chapel in England, erected by Scottish workmen engaged on the mansion of Longleat.

**Horton Court** *Glos.*      546Bb
A Cotswold manor house, altered in the 19th century but with a 12th-century Norman great hall and early Renaissance features. In the garden is an unusual late-Perpendicular ambulatory.

**Horwood** *Devon*      538Ff
CHURCH OF ST MICHAEL A small, remote, church in the hills above Bideford Bay. There is a low west tower with pinnacles. There is only one aisle, on the north side, the south side having a transept instead. The Norman font is square, and the piscina is distinguished by its curling horn-shaped drain. There is some 15th-century stained glass, 16th-century bench ends and a pulpit of 1635. A mid-15th-century alabaster monument shows a woman in horned headdress, with children.

**Hough-on-the-Hill** *Lincs.*      553Gd
CHURCH OF ALL SAINTS The west tower is Saxon, with an exterior circular stair turret. Inside, the pillars of the aisle arcades are Early English, and the arches on the north side of the chancel leading into a chantry chapel are 13th century.

**Houghton and Wyton** *Hunts.*      547Jf
Houghton and Wyton, 2 miles from St Ives, have many picturesque cottages and riverside views. Houghton Water-mill, believed to be the oldest on the Great Ouse, is now a youth hostel. The 'Gothic' village pump on the green, an elaborate cast-iron affair, is unique. Magdalene College Farm in Wyton was built in 1600, and an adjoining farmhouse is dated 1648. There are some wall-paintings of 1622 in the Three Jolly Butchers Inn.

**Houghton-le-Spring** *Durham*      558Cg
CHURCH OF ST MICHAEL AND ALL ANGELS A large cruciform church, with a central tower; originally Norman, now mainly of the 13th to 15th centuries. There is pretty tracery in the east window, and effigies of 13th-century cross-legged knights.

**Houghton Regis** *Beds.*                           *547Hd*
CHURCH OF ALL SAINTS A large 14th- and 15th-century building, with a west tower. It possesses brasses, a monument of a knight in armour, a Norman font, and a 15th-century screen.

**Hougue Bie** *Jersey*                           *540Ea*
A prehistoric burial ground containing a tomb dating from the New Stone Age (*c.* 2000 BC). Great stones dragged from the nearby beach were arranged to form a central chamber reached by a passage with three side chambers. The whole was then covered by earth and rubble. When opened in 1924 the tomb was found to have been plundered. The hill is crowned by the 12th-century Chapel of Notre Dame de la Clarté (Our Lady of the Dawn), probably built to banish pagan associations still clinging to the mound. The Jerusalem Chapel was added *c.* 1520 by Dean Mabon on his return from a pilgrimage to Jerusalem; in the crypt is a replica of Christ's tomb in the Church of the Holy Sepulchre in Jerusalem.
AGRICULTURAL MUSEUM A small museum with a collection of old farming implements. An old manual fire engine is also displayed.
GERMAN OCCUPATION MUSEUM An extensive German underground installation contains a large collection of Nazi relics and samples of food, clothing and personal effects used by the civilian population during the Second World War.

**Howden** *Yorks.*                           *558Ea*
CHURCH OF ST PETER A magnificent cruciform church, formerly collegiate, with a very tall central tower; the building dates mainly from the 14th century. The chancel has been in ruins since the end of the 17th century, and just to the south are the ruins of a charming octagonal chapter house. There are a number of medieval and later monuments.

**Howell** *Lincs.*                           *553Hd*
CHURCH OF ST OSWALD There is much Norman work here, with additions in the Transitional and Decorated styles. Some fragments of medieval stained glass remain, and the font and bell-gable are 14th century.

**Huddersfield** *Yorks.*                           *558Ba*
CHURCHES OF ST THOMAS THE APOSTLE AND OF ST JOHN Two 19th-century churches, the former built in 1858–9 by Sir Gilbert Scott, with a tower and broach spire at the south-west. St John's was designed by William Butterfield in 1852–3, in the style of *c.* 1300, with a tall spire.

**Hughenden Manor** *Bucks.*                           *547Gc*
The home from 1847 to 1881 of Benjamin Disraeli, Earl of Beaconsfield, whose portrait by Sir Francis Grant is on show. Disraeli (1804–81) has a monument in Westminster Abbey but is buried at Hughenden.

**Huntingdon** *Hunts.*                           *547Jf*
Linked by a bridge across the R. Ouse, the twin towns of Huntingdon and Godmanchester lie at the intersection of three Roman roads. Huntingdon suffered from Danish raids, endured the Normans, but was nearly wiped out by the plague in 1348. From 1205 to 1686 it was granted 18 charters of privileges. Its bridge was built in 1332.
Oliver Cromwell and Samuel Pepys were pupils at the grammar school, converted from the Hospital of St John the Baptist in 1565. The building is now a museum of Cromwelliana.
HINCHINBROOKE A mainly mid-16th-century dwelling which was first founded as a Benedictine convent. It later became the home of Sir Henry Cromwell, great-uncle of the Protector, who

entertained Queen Elizabeth here in 1564. Sir Henry's son frequently received King James here before selling the house to Sir Henry Montagu in 1627. It has a notable gate-house and altogether represents a typical stately home of the period.

**Huntly Castle** *A'deen*                           *566Ef*
This castle was once the home of the Gordon family, the Marquesses of Huntly, after whom the 'Gay Gordons' dance was named. Now derelict, it dates from 1600 when it replaced the medieval Palace of Strathbogie.

**Hurlers, The** *Cornwall*                           *538Ec*
This is a group of three Bronze Age stone circles set in a straight line. They range from 105 ft to 135 ft in diameter. Perhaps half of the original number of uprights has been lost. These uprights appear to have been carefully shaped and are of equal height. The central circle also had a single stone at its centre. The north-east circle appears originally to have had the unusual refinement of a paved floor.

**Hursley** *Hants.*                           *541Ge*
CHURCH OF ALL SAINTS The church (all but the tower) was rebuilt by John Keble, *c.* 1848. Keble, the poet, essayist and designer in whose memory Keble College, Oxford, was founded in 1869, is buried in the churchyard. So too is Richard Cromwell, son of Oliver, known as 'Tumble-down Dick', who preferred being lord of the manor at Hursley to being Lord Protector of the Realm.
MERDON CASTLE Remains of the castle, built *c.* 1129 by Bishop Henry de Blois, are in Hursley Park.

HURSTMONCEUX CASTLE

*Sir Roger Fiennes, who received licence to build Hurstmonceux Castle in 1440, was a civil servant under Henry VI and was Lord Treasurer from 1439 to 1446. The massive gate-house was the main feature. The castle was dismantled in 1777 and remained a ruin until it was extensively restored in 1933. During the restorations many of the present fittings were brought to Hurstmonceux from other houses, so that the interior now bears little resemblance to that of the original castle. In 1948 the castle became the home of the Royal Observatory after its move from Greenwich, where it was established in 1675.*

**Hurstbourne Tarrant** *Hants.* 541Gf
A picturesque valley village, with many thatched cottages, and a prim white Regency house by the church.

**Hurstmonceux Castle** *Sussex* 542Dd
Hurstmonceux Castle, built of brick and surrounded by a moat, is, with its towers and battlements, one of the most picturesque castles in England. It was built during the 15th century, and has an external regularity reminiscent of the earlier castle at Bodiam.

Although termed a castle, Hurstmonceux is more properly a fortified residence, since it possesses innumerable large windows and comparatively thin walls. Gate-houses were at that period becoming architectural showpieces and symbols of prestige, and the gate-house at Hurst-monceux is the main architectural feature. The space inside the walls was divided into a number of courtyards of unequal size; these were cleared away in 1933 when the castle was restored, to leave one large courtyard. (Interior not open.)

**Hythe** *Kent* 542Fe
CHURCH OF ST LEONARD In a commanding position on the side of a steep hill, this large church is celebrated for its soaring 13th-century chancel, rising 13 steps above the nave. There are Norman remains in the nave and transepts. Below is a crypt containing thousands of human bones and a tunnelled processional way beneath the altar. The 13th-century tower fell in 1739 and was replaced in 1750 when the south aisle was rebuilt. The altarpiece in the south choir aisle is by Henry Armstead the sculptor (1828–1905).

# I J

**Ickleton** *Cambs.* 548Ae
CHURCH OF ST MARY An interesting church, with Romanesque nave incorporating several Roman columns. Formerly cruciform (the north transept has gone), there is a crossing tower with a spire, and a vaulted south porch.

**Ickwell Green** *Beds.* 547Je
In this beautiful village the green has a maypole, and there is a burnt-out 17th-century mansion and many picturesque cottages. Nearby Old Warden has a number of charming cottages, some with thatched roofs, dormer windows and Elizabethan chimneys.

**Ickworth** *Suffolk* 548Cf
A 700 ft long building devised and begun by the eccentric Frederick Augustus Hervey, 4th Earl of Bristol and Bishop of Derry. From an oval rotunda housing a central hall the main rooms are reached via two curved corridors. The rotunda is 100 ft high with a shallow dome; round the outside is a frieze of reliefs by Casimiro and Donato Carabelli from Milan, after John Flaxman's designs based on Homer. The house, designed in 1794 but not completed until 1830, contains Regency furniture, magnificent silver, paintings and *objets d'art*. The park was landscaped by Capability Brown. (See p. 248.)

**Idsworth** *Hants.* 541Jd
CHURCH OF ST HUBERT This small chapel stands in a field, and has a nave and chancel with an 18th-century bell-turret at the east end. Though basically of the 12th century, the chapel, after years of neglect, was restored c. 1912 by H. Goodhart-Rendel. Some of the fittings are of the 18th century—box-pews, and a pulpit with sounding board. The 14th-century wall-paintings may represent the legend of St Hubert, or perhaps the life of St John the Baptist. In the chancel are the painted figures of SS Peter and Paul.

ICKWORTH

*An eccentric bishop with a taste for travel had the idea of building this unusual house to display his fine collection of paintings and sculpture—but he lost most of the collection before the house was completed. The bishop was Frederick Hervey, 4th Earl of Bristol and Bishop of Derry, who decided in 1792 to build a house with an oval ground plan on land which his family had owned since the 15th century. Five years later, with the building still in its early stages, the bishop was unlucky enough to be in Rome when Napoleon occupied the city. He was imprisoned, and his collection confiscated. Back in England he saw work on the house progress under the architect Francis Sandys, but the bishop died in 1803 with the building only half completed. After a halt of several years, the 1st Marquess of Bristol completed the house and furnished the main rooms. Antonio Canova, the great Italian sculptor, carved the chimney-piece in the library.*

**Iffley** *Oxon.* 546*Fc*
CHURCH OF ST MARY One of England's most famous Norman churches, dating from the late 12th century. It has a nave, tower and chancel; the later sanctuary is Early English. There is a spectacular west front with doorway, a circular window and three arched windows, all with zigzag decoration. The south doorway and the tower arches inside are also richly decorated, and there is a Norman font.

**Ightham** *Kent* 542*Cf*
CHURCH OF ST PETER A historically interesting church in a picturesque village; the main fabric of St Peter's is 14th century, but some Norman work remains. There are box-pews, embroidery work of the 17th century, and some Dutch glass depicting Henry VII and his queen. Two interesting monuments are the 14th-century effigy of Sir Thomas Cawne, who lived at Ightham Mote, and one by Edward Marshall, one-time assistant to Nicholas Stone, to Dorothy Selby (*d.* 1641) who, according to the epitaph, deciphered the letter warning of the Gunpowder Plot.

To the south-west of the village are ancient habitations, the prehistoric hill-fort and Stone Age rock dwellings on Oldbury Hill.

**Ightham Mote** *Kent* 542*Cf*
A moated manor house, almost unchanged outwardly since it was built in 1340, though there were additions and interior alterations in 1520. Its name derives from the Anglo-Saxon word 'moot', a local discussion place. The house has been in almost continuous occupation since its erection. The great hall (1340) has its original oak ceiling, the entrance tower (1480) its original wood doors, and the chapel (1520) its original roof.

**Ilam** *Staffs.* 552*Cd*
In the churchyard there are two Saxon crosses; in the church itself is a carved font showing St Bertram, and a tomb designed by Sir Francis Chantrey. St Bertram's 13th-century shrine is in the grounds of Ilam Hall.

**Ilford** *Greater London* 548*Ac*
CHURCH OF ST MARY Originally Norman, St Mary's has later additions. There are fine roofs, a rood screen fragment with painted figures, and a brass, *c.* 1483. Pride of the church is the magnificent telescopic font cover, which rises to the roof in a mass of pinnacles. There are also carved 15th-century bench ends.

**Ilfracombe** *Devon* 538*Fg*
LIGHTHOUSE The tiny medieval chapel of St Nicholas crowns Lantern Hill. The first reference to the display of a light is in 1522, but one may have been shown when the building was erected in the 14th century. The light was originally shown from a projecting window on the north side; after the Reformation the chapel became a house, and a lantern was devised on the west gable.

SILVER ICE-PAIL

*One of a pair, this ice-pail was made about 1715 by the Huguenot silversmith Philip Rollos. Driven out of France by Louis XIV's persecution, Rollos settled in London, and was patronised by William III. But like many of his exiled compatriots, he still followed French developments in taste. The ice-pail is decorated in régence manner, a later elaboration of the baroque style of Louis XIV's reign. (Ickworth)*

This was replaced by the present one in 1819; it still carries a light. Although there are several records of medieval chapels showing coastal lights, this is one of the few to survive.

**Ilkley** *Yorks.* 558Bb
MANOR HOUSE MUSEUM AND ART GALLERY The Romans built a fort on this site and a section of its wall has been excavated beside the house. Anglo-Saxon invaders founded the original manor house, using stones from the Roman fort. The house escaped pillage by Danish, Norman and Scots invaders, and early in Elizabeth I's reign it was rebuilt and enlarged. It has been faithfully restored, and its contents illustrate the history of Ilkley from prehistoric times until the present. Exhibitions of sculptures, paintings and pottery are held.

**Ilkley Moor** *Yorks.* 558Bb
On Rombald's Moor are many scattered rocks carved with the characteristic Bronze Age cup-and-ring ornamentation. Many of the best have been brought down and now stand in the gardens facing Ilkley parish church, St Margaret's. With them is another, the Swastika Stone, which may belong to the Iron Age.
    On the moor are also several stone circles, three of which, the Twelve Apostles Circle, the Grub-stone Circle and the Horncliffe Circle are of some importance. The others lie to the east of the Grubstones.

**Inchcolm** *Fife.* 562Bf
ABBEY The ruins of the abbey are on an island in the Firth of Forth, and are extensive and well preserved, due no doubt to their isolation. The buildings date from the 12th century onwards.

**Ingatestone** *Essex* 548Bc
The village has a 16th-century inn, The Bell, and a number of pleasant Georgian brick houses. There are some good mock-Tudor houses built in the 19th century by George Sherrin.
CHURCH OF SS EDMUND AND MARY With a 15th-century diapered brick west tower, the church was originally Norman, but has later additions. The Perpendicular font is octagonal. Several monuments with effigies are dedicated to 16th- and 17th-century members of the Petre family.
INGATESTONE HALL The Hall was built *c.* 1540 for Sir William Petre, Tudor Secretary of State, and since 1953 the north wing has been used for a display of Essex archives. Each annual exhibition is based on a theme of Essex history. The archives contain over 3,000,000 documents, including manuscript estate maps dating from the 16th century, and prints, paintings and old photographs. The permanent display in the Long Gallery includes a rare 16th-century virginal (William Byrd, the Elizabethan composer, was a frequent visitor to the house), late 18th- and early 19th-century furniture and Essex armorial china. The Garden Chamber has some original panelling and contains Tudor and early Stuart furniture.

**Ingestre** *Staffs.* 552Cc
CHURCH OF ST MARY The design of this Classical church is attributed to Sir Christopher Wren, *c.* 1676. The magnificent interior has four-cluster columns in the nave, plaster roofs, a good screen with royal Arms, and monuments by Sir Francis Chantrey, Richard Westmacott the Younger, and others.

**Ingestre Hall** *Staffs.* 552Cc
Of early 17th century origin, the Hall was rebuilt in neo-Gothic style following a disastrous fire in 1820. The church is probably the work of Sir Christopher Wren.

IGHTHAM MOTE

*The forecourt leading to this bridge is guarded by peacocks, and swans occupy the spring-fresh water of the moat. The door leads into the spacious medieval kitchen of the mid-14th-century manor house.*

**Inglesham** *Wilts.* 546Dc
CHURCH OF ST JOHN THE BAPTIST This is a small church near the Thames, without a tower but with a bell-cote. It is interesting because, although repaired in 1888–9, it was saved by William Morris from the prevalent over-restoration or falsification. Mainly of the 13th century, it has a 16th-century pulpit and 17th-century box-pews.

**Ingoldmells** *Lincs.* 554Ae
CHURCH OF SS PETER AND PAUL Situated near the sea, this is a large and impressive church with a 15th-century porch. Of interest inside is much woodwork, and carvings of angels in the roof; an interesting brass of the 16th century depicts a man named William Palmer with his 'stylt' or crutch at his side. There is a fine Perpendicular font; the chancel was demolished in the early 18th century.

**Inveraray Castle** *Argyll* 560Fg
The home of the Dukes of Argyll and headquarters of the Clan Campbell since the 15th century. The present castle, greatly admired by Sir Walter Scott, was built in the late 18th century by Roger Morris and Robert Mylne in French château-style, with corner towers and conical turrets. The great hall, armoury and state rooms are open to view. The castle, set in extensive gardens, contains old masters, tapestries, fine furniture and plate, and early Scottish armaments.

**Inveresk Lodge** *M'loth.* 562Ce
A garden created by the National Trust for Scotland with the object of demonstrating plants suited to the smaller garden and the interesting varieties now available. In the conservatory is a small aviary of exotic birds.

**Inverewe Gardens** *Ross.* 568Ea
In 1862 Osgood Mackenzie built a house on a rocky peninsula in Loch Ewe, and three years later

INVEREWE GARDENS

*Osgood Mackenzie began these superb gardens in 1865, on barren, rocky moorland beside Loch Ewe.*

*Now a wide variety of trees and plants from the world over flourish in the almost sub-tropical climate.*

he began to create these Highland gardens, now famous for rare and sub-tropical plants. A large shelterbelt of pines was planted to break the Atlantic gales, and tons of pebbles were replaced by fertile soil. In these sheltered gardens, warmed by the Gulf Stream, thrive tender rhododendron species, Himalayan and Chinese magnolias, daisy bushes and, from New Zealand, *Hoherias* with fragrant, pure white flowers. There are giant eucalyptus and tree-ferns, and the extremely rare giant forget-me-nots and many other plants from Australia and South America.

**Inverness** *I'ness.* 566Af
A beautifully situated town on the R. Ness, with mountains to the east and west, the Moray Forth to the north and the Caledonian Canal and Loch Ness to the south. St Andrew's Cathedral was built in the 19th century; its font is a copy of the famous angel font in Copenhagen. There are many 18th-century town houses, and the museum houses a collection of Jacobite relics.
ABERTARF HOUSE A 16th-century house, now restored. It is the headquarters of the Highland Association.

**Inverurie** *A'deen* 566Fe
MUSEUM The museum has a display of local archaeology, including a Neolithic bowl, a 'cushion' mace-head and a large collection of arrowheads, polished stone axes, flint knives, etc. The geology section has a collection of Scottish minerals and fossils, and local bygones can be seen, including snuff boxes, communion tokens and mortsafe tackle. (A mortsafe was a heavy stone lowered on to the coffin as a temporary measure to protect it from grave robbers. When the grave itself was filled in, the mortsafe was raised.)

**Iona** *Argyll* 564Da
The island of Iona has been associated with the spread of Christianity in northern and central Britain since the 7th century. St Columba, the missionary from Ireland, landed on this island in AD 563 and built a monastery, but it was constantly ravaged by raiding Norsemen. One of its most famous monks was St Aidan, who later founded a bishopric at Lindisfarne. In *c.* 1203 an abbey and nunnery were founded by Benedictines and these were restored early in this century. St Columba's cell, with the stone slab on which he slept, has been excavated. Eight Norwegian kings and many

Scottish kings, including Macbeth, were buried in the graveyard. Three of the 360 tall crosses that once stood here remain: St John's Cross (9th century), St Martin's Cross (10th century) and Maclean's Cross (15th century).

**Ipswich** *Suffolk* 548De
An ancient port on the Orwell estuary, pillaged by the Danes in 991 and again in 1000. A borough before the Norman Conquest, its first charter was given by King John in 1199. It reached its zenith as a wool port in the 16th century, declined in the 17th and 18th centuries, but revived after harbour improvements in the 1840's. Much of the town was built or rebuilt in the 19th century, but 12 medieval churches and several 16th-century

CELTIC HIGH CROSS, IONA

*One of three stone crosses left standing on Iona after the Reformation; its circle symbolises Eternity.*

IRON-BRIDGE

*Abraham Darby built this, the first iron bridge, in 1777–9. The delicate, airy, cast-iron structure over* *the R. Severn is nearly 200 ft long, with the largest semicircular span being 100 ft, and is 45 ft high.*

buildings survive. Cardinal Wolsey was born here *c.* 1475, and Thomas Gainsborough, the painter, was a resident. The Great White Horse Inn was the scene of some of Mr Pickwick's misfortunes. Today the town is a thriving port and industrial centre, and the county town of East Suffolk.

ANCIENT HOUSE Charles II hid in the chapel of this house, built in 1567 and owned by the Sparrowe family from 1603.

CHRISTCHURCH MANSION A Tudor mansion begun in 1548 on the site of the 12th-century Augustinian Priory of Holy Trinity and altered after a fire in the 1670's. It contains period rooms dating from the 16th–19th centuries, and also contains a collection of paintings including works by Gainsborough, Constable and Steer, and porcelain, glass and domestic bygones.

CHURCH OF ST MARY-LE-TOWER The civic church, rebuilt in the late 19th century with a tower, 176 ft high. It contains fine carvings.

MUSEUM All the material exhibited here relates to Suffolk, and includes Stone Age flint implements; weapons and jewellery from the pagan Saxon cemetery at Hadleigh Road, Ipswich; replicas of the Mildenhall and Sutton Hoo Treasures (now in the British Museum); and collections of fossils and of birds.

OLD CUSTOM HOUSE A handsome house in miniature Palladian style, built on the quay in the 1840's.

WOLSEY'S GATEWAY The sole remains of a College of Secular Canons founded by Cardinal Wolsey in 1536.

**Irnham** *Lincs.* 553Gc
CHURCH OF ST ANDREW A large church dating from Norman times, it has a woodland setting and represents architectural styles of the 13th–15th centuries. Among the 14th- and 15th-century brasses is an interesting one to Sir Andrew Luttrell, of 1390.

**Iron Acton** *Glos.* 546Bb
CHURCH OF ST JAMES THE LESS A handsome church, mainly of the 14th and 15th centuries; it has a pinnacled west tower and, in the churchyard, a rare 15th-century memorial cross. Interesting features inside include a canopied 17th-century pulpit, 19th-century mosaic floors, and attractive modern reredos and side chapel screen. Some of the stained glass and a series of effigies of the Poyntz family date from the Middle Ages.

**Iron-Bridge** *Shrops.* 552Ab
The bridge over the R. Severn, from which the town takes its name, was the first iron bridge constructed in England. This was beginning of industrial architecture's use of iron, which culminated in the great spans of the 19th-century railway stations such as Paddington, and the glory of the Crystal Palace housing the Great Exhibition in Hyde Park in 1851. The bridge was built between 1777 and 1779 with iron from the Coalbrookdale foundry. The original furnace used to make the iron for it is now in the Museum of Ironfounding at Coalbrookdale. In 1934 the bridge was closed to vehicles: today the river banks are moving together and gradually forcing the centre of the bridge upwards.

**Isel** *Cumb.* 557Gf
CHURCH OF ST MICHAEL A 12th-century Norman church, containing some fragments of 10th-century carved crosses.

**Isleham** *Cambs.* 548Bf
CHURCH OF ST ANDREW A spacious, cruciform, 14th- and 15th-century building. The hammer-beam roof, of 1495, is embellished with angels. Inside are stalls, misericords, a font, brasses, and effigies of knights. There are two big monuments of *c.* 1590 and 1616.

**Isle of May** *Firth of Forth* 562Eg
LIGHTHOUSE Although reduced in height, this strange structure gives an excellent idea of the appearance of an old coal-fired beacon. A carved panel over the door is dated 1636, and there is a carved fire-place bearing the Arms of the owner. The survival of the building was due to Sir Walter Scott, who in 1814 persuaded the engineer Robert Stevenson, who was engaged on the present 'Gothic' tower, to 'ruin it *à la pittoresque*'.

**Iver** *Bucks.* 547Hb
IVER GROVE Elaborately painted cornices and pediments decorate this slate roofed brick house, built by Sir John Vanbrugh, the dramatist turned architect, in 1722–4. The house was enlarged in the late 18th century. (By appointment.)

**Iwerne Minster** *Dorset* 540Ed
CHURCH OF ST MARY Details may still be seen of the original Norman church; later additions include the 19th-century south chapel designed by J. L. Pearson.

**Ixworth Abbey** *Suffolk*        *548Cf*
An 18th-century house incorporating the 12th-century crypt of the original abbey. Abbey documents and manuscripts and the adjacent ruined priory church are on view.

**Ixworth Roman Camp** *Suffolk*    *548Cf*
Here are the remains of an important Roman settlement.

**Jarrow** *Durham*            *558Cg*
CHURCH OF ST PAUL The church contains a unique dedication tablet of the monastery founded in 684. The tower and chancel are still standing—tall and narrow. There was a Norman nave west of the tower, but in 1786 it was destroyed, and rebuilt in the 19th century by Sir Gilbert Scott.

**Jedburgh Abbey** *Rox.*       *562Dc*
David I of Scotland founded this Augustinian abbey, built of local red sandstone beside Jed Water, *c.* 1138. As a result of Border Wars, little but the church now remains; the abbey was suppressed in 1559. The church dates mainly from the period 1150–1220, when first the Romanesque choir and transepts, followed by the Transitional nave, were built. In addition, *c.* 1200 the choir was extended eastwards. In the choir and transepts the design of the main arcade and triforium is unusual. The triforium is contained within the giant main arcade which springs from ground level. The nave, on the other hand, is arranged after the more usual manner in clearly distinct rows of arcading, one on top of the other. Jedburgh also has a magnificent west door and another (heavily restored) leading out to the cloister.

**Jervaulx Abbey** *Yorks.*      *558Cd*
The abbey was of the Cistercian order, who moved here during the second half of the 12th century; now in ruins.

**Jullieberrie's Grave** *Kent*    *542Ff*
An unchambered Neolithic long barrow, far from others of the type, with a now-filled quarry-ditch. One end of the barrow has been mutilated, but what is left is still nearly 150 ft long and some 7 ft high. Romano-British burials have been found in the filling of the quarry-ditch at its south end.

JEDBURGH ABBEY

*Many times in its history this retreat of Augustinian monks has been wrecked and burnt by invading armies —the price it has had to pay for being so close to the Scottish border with England. It was ransacked in 1297 by Edward I's army under Sir Richard Hastineg, burnt in 1523 and again only 11 years later. Little has survived this devastation apart from the church, built between 1150 and 1220, nearly a century after the foundation of the abbey by David I. Parts of the building were still being used in Victorian times as a place of worship for the surrounding parish. When a new church was founded in 1875 the remains of the abbey were conscientiously restored.*

# K

**Kedington** *Suffolk*       *548Be*
CHURCH OF SS PETER AND PAUL Dating from the 13th century and later. The Barnardiston family pew is constructed from a 15th-century screen. There are Perpendicular benches, 18th-century box-pews, and a three-decker 17th-century pulpit and screen. Also interesting is a Saxon carved Crucifixion, and several monuments to the Barnardiston family with effigies, 16th to 18th centuries.

**Kedleston Hall** *Derbys.*     *552Dd*
The home of the Curzon family for over 800 years. The present mansion was originally designed *c.* 1757 by Matthew Brettingham for Sir Nathaniel Curzon. But Curzon then turned to the most prominent architect of the mid-18th century, James Paine, to remodel his Stuart house in a Classical and more fashionable style. Paine had built the north front by 1761. It has a noble portico of six Corinthian columns above a ground storey, on either side of which is a double staircase. There

are no windows between the columns, but niches for statues instead. In 1760 Curzon called in Robert Adam to continue work on the new house, and for a while he and Paine worked amicably together. The south front is Adam's, and is based on the triumphal arch of Constantine in Rome. The house, set in extensive gardens, contains fine furniture and a collection of old master paintings. In the grounds is the 12th-century church containing the Marquess Curzon of Kedleston Memorial Chapel.

There is also a museum containing the silver-ivories, weapons and works of art collected by the Marquess when he was Viceroy of India in 1898–1905.

**Kegworth** *Leics.*        *552Ec*
CHURCH OF ST ANDREW A mainly early 14th-century church, with west tower and chapels at the east end of the aisles adding to the impressive external view. The interior has fragments of medieval stained glass.

**Kelham** *Notts.* 552Fd
CHURCH OF ST WILFRID A good example of 18th-century sculpture is the monument to Lord Lexington (*d.* 1723) who reclines with his wife, in marble, back to back on a free-standing tomb. She died in 1703.

**Kelmscot** *Oxon.* 546Ec
CHURCH OF ST GEORGE A cruciform church whose south doorway and font remain of the original Norman work. Inside there are carved corbel heads, medieval glass, and wall-paintings. William Morris lived near by at Kelmscot Manor, and is buried in the churchyard.

**Kelmscot Manor** *Oxon.* 546Ec
William Morris, poet, craftsman and socialist, made this gabled Cotswold Tudor house, in the Thames-side village of Kelmscot, his home from 1871 until his death in 1896. The house probably dates from the late 16th century.

**Kelso** *Rox.* 562Ed
ABBEY The abbey, in Norman and Gothic styles and probably the largest of the Border abbeys, was founded by Benedictine monks from Tiron (in Picardy, France) in 1128; it was destroyed during the Border Wars of 1523–45.

**Kempsford** *Glos.* 546Dc
CHURCH OF ST MARY THE VIRGIN Originally Norman, St Mary's has a fine central tower built by John of Gaunt, with large Perpendicular north and south windows in the lower stage, and weather-vanes on all the crocketed pinnacles. The vaulting within has carved and painted heraldic shields as bosses. Victorian stained glass contributes to the effect of darkness; some of it is by Kempe.

The chancel was enlarged by G. E. Street in 1858. On the walls of the nave are framed Puritan texts.

**Kendal** *Westmld.* 557Jd
A fine town in the Lake District. In 1189 Kendal was made a barony by Richard Coeur de Lion. In 1331, under the protection of Edward III, Flemish weavers set up a woollen industry which gave the town its motto: *Pannus mihi panis* (Wool is my bread). In the Norman castle, now a ruin, was born Katherine Parr, last queen of Henry VIII. The castle dairy, rebuilt in 1564, is a fine example of Tudor domestic architecture. In the town hall are seven paintings by Romney, and Katherine Parr's book of devotions, exquisitely penned and bound in solid silver.
ABBOT HALL ART GALLERY The house, built in 1759 by John Carr of York, retains its original *décor* on the ground floor, which exhibits period furniture. The upstairs rooms contain a growing collection of modern paintings and sculpture.
BOROUGH MUSEUM Collections devoted to the natural history and local history of the Kendal area are on view.

**Kenilworth Castle** *Warks.* 546Ef
Elizabeth I was entertained here by her favourite, Robert Dudley, Earl of Leicester, for 18 days in July 1575 at a cost of £1000 per day. The enormous ruins of Kenilworth Castle suggest importance as a fortress during the Middle Ages. It was founded by Geoffrey de Clinton *c.* 1122, and within the next few decades the immense keep was built. In the 14th century John of Gaunt turned the fortress into a palace by adding large domestic quarters. Much of John of Gaunt's banqueting hall survives, together with other domestic offices.

KEDLESTON HALL

18TH-CENTURY MIRROR *Using an exotic design of palms, this mirror was probably designed by John Linnell, a cabinet-maker employed by Robert Adam. Within the frame of carved and gilded wood, several sizes of glass were used; this allowed the framework to be fragile in appearance, yet not overwhelmed by an unrelieved area of mirror—in any case, at that time it was expensive to produce single sheets of glass in such a large size. Mirrors of this type were usually placed above side-tables, opposite or between windows, so as to give the illusion of a larger room.*

18TH-CENTURY SOFA *Made of carved, gilded wood, this sofa is primarily a work of art, but it is also functional. The extravagant design is reminiscent of the 17th-century sculptor Bernini and contrasts with the Classical interior of Kedleston designed by Robert Adam. The sofa, however, is probably not by Adam but by John Linnell, a cabinet-maker employed by him. Unlike Adam, Linnell tended to emphasise the sculptural rather than the architectural form in his work; he is comparatively little known as, unlike Chippendale, he did not publish his designs.*

KENILWORTH CASTLE

*This fortress has stood for over 800 years, a stronghold for the kings and lords of England capable of withstanding attack from mighty armies. It was founded about 1122 by Geoffrey de Clinton, royal Treasurer to Henry I, but within 50 years it had become too important to be left in private hands, and was taken over by Henry II. It stayed the property of the kings of England until 1244 when it passed to Simon de Montfort, Earl of Leicester, later a leading rebel against Henry III. In 1266 Henry's army surrounded Kenilworth, but its fortifications withstood the siege until famine forced the defenders to surrender. The fortress was later turned into a medieval palace by the addition of living quarters, and flourished in the late 16th century as the home of Robert Dudley, Earl of Leicester, a favourite of Elizabeth I, who was frequently entertained there at great expense. The castle has been unoccupied for 300 years.*

During the reign of Elizabeth I the Earl of Leicester added more living quarters and the great northern gate-house. The keep was partially destroyed in the Civil War, and the castle was never re-occupied after the Restoration.

**Kentchurch Court** *Herefs.* 546Ad
A fortified manor house on the Welsh border, with a 14th-century great gateway and tower built by Owen Glendower, the Welsh hero who fought against the English. The interior has Grinling Gibbons carvings.

**Kentisbeare** *Devon* 540Ad
CHURCH OF ST MARY The west tower of this 14th- and 15th-century Perpendicular church is chequer-patterned in red and grey stone. There are wagon-roofs, that of the chancel plastered in 1757, a good rood screen, and a pulpit and desk of *c.* 1737. OLD PRIEST'S HOUSE A medieval house with a minstrels' gallery and oak screens.

**Kenton** *Devon* 539Hd
CHURCH OF ALL SAINTS An impressive 14th-century red sandstone church, built entirely between 1360 and 1370. The west tower is about 120 ft high, and the two-storied south porch is embattled. The massive rood screen has painted panels, with some restoration. There is a 15th-century carved pulpit, and a monument of 1628 with seated figure of a woman. The 19th-century stained glass in the east window is by Clayton & Bell.

**Kent's Cavern** *Devon* 539Hc
A Palaeolithic cave-dwelling first investigated in the early 19th century, when evidence of human occupation from the Middle Palaeolithic Age onwards could not be accepted because it clashed with the prevailing views on the date of the Creation (biblical calculation suggesting that Adam had lived only about 4000 years before). The finds are in the Torquay Museum and the Natural History Museum, London.

**Kersey** *Suffolk* 548Ce
A picturesque village with the R. Brett running through it. Kersey cloth probably originated here, and the timber-framed houses date from the village's days of greatness in the wool trade. Priory Farm has remains of a 13th-century Augustinian priory.
CHURCH OF ST MARY In a picturesque village, St Mary's has a 15th-century west tower, but the church was restored in the mid-19th century. There is a Perpendicular font with carved angels, and painted panels to the rood screen; also a mural painting of St George and the Dragon.

**Kettles, The** *Northld.* 562Fc
A promontory hill-fort with somewhat complex defences, ranging from one to three stone ramparts in different parts of the perimeter. The total internal area is some 4½ acres. No huts are visible.

**Kettlethorpe Hall** *Lincs.* 553Ge
The 14th-century embattled stone gateway and moat are all that remain of Kettlethorpe Hall, home of Sir Hugh Swynford. His widow, Katherine Swynford, was first mistress to and later wife of John of Gaunt. Katherine's brother-in-law was the poet Chaucer. The new Hall was built in 1863.

**Ketton** *Rutland* 553Gb
CHURCH OF ST MARY A large church, mainly early 13th century, with late 12th-century work on the west front, and some 14th-century work. The

KEW GARDENS

*Kew's connections with royalty begin with Frederick, Prince of Wales, who leased the property from the Capel family in 1730. Frederick himself had a hand in laying out the grounds, but it was his widow, Augusta, and son, George III, who really developed Kew. Their work was aided by botanists such as the Aitons and Sir Joseph Banks, who began to bring plants to Kew systematically from all over the world. The architect Sir William Chambers decorated the royal estate with*

*pavilions, temples and other follies in the then fashionable style. Much of his work was pulled down when Capability Brown redesigned the garden, but some examples were left—including the Chinese Pagoda, built in 1761. The pagoda, 163 ft high, contains only a staircase. Originally, it was decorated with 80 dragons on the eaves and roofs. George IV allowed the gardens to decline, and in 1840 the Royal Botanic Gardens were taken over by the nation.*

transepts have gone, and the building is dominated by the impressive central tower and spire. The chancel was rebuilt in the 19th century, and the panelled roof was repainted in colours closely resembling the medieval originals.

**Kew** *Greater London*                   547Jb
The 18th century is dominant at Kew, in the church on the spacious green and in the terraces of houses round it. Kew Gardens, however, contain, at the north end, the Dutch House, dated 1631, and the world-famous botanical gardens, 300 acres in extent, landscaped by Capability Brown for Princess Augusta, George III's mother, and made a public garden in 1841. The Palm House, forerunner of the Crystal Palace, was erected in 1844.
CHURCH OF ST ANNE Originally an early 17th-century church, St Anne's has late 18th- and 19th-century enlargements by J. J. Kirby and Robert Browne. There is a mausoleum *c.* 1850 to the Duke and Duchess of Cambridge, and other 18th- and 19th-century monuments.
PAGODA, ROYAL BOTANIC GARDENS The royal park at Kew became a national property in 1840. The gardens had been laid out, under the auspices of George III and his mother, to designs by Sir William Chambers. The orangery and most of the small Classical temples and pavilions are examples of Chambers's early work. He also designed the Chinese Pagoda (1757–61) which took only six months to complete and shows the influences of Chambers's travels in the Orient as a young man.
PALM HOUSE, ROYAL BOTANIC GARDENS This great glass house was built in 1844–8 to designs by Decimus Burton, who also built the Athenaeum Club in Waterloo Place at the corner of Pall Mall. The Palm House is plain and functional. The iron-

work for it was constructed by Richard Turner at his Hammersmith Works in Dublin. The building is 362 ft long, and at the centre 100 ft wide and 66 ft high, and required 45,000 sq. ft of glass. The boiler house was built nearly 500 ft away in order not to impair the graceful lines of the building. A tunnel was constructed to the boiler house, where the chimney was disguised as an architectural feature, and also contained the water tanks.
ROYAL BOTANIC GARDENS MUSEUMS OF ECONOMIC BOTANY The General Museum contains collections of plants useful to man, their products, portraits of botanists and pictures of plants in their natural settings throughout the world. The Wood Museum, displaying timber of the world, is housed in Cambridge Cottage, which was used by the Royal Family in the reign of Queen Victoria.

**Kidwelly Castle** *Carm.*                   544Ec
A fortress built by Edward I *c.* 1275–1325; it has a 14th-century gate-house. The outer curtain wall follows the line of the earlier Norman earthworks and the courtyard is enclosed by four round towers. The castle is now in ruins.

**Kilbarchan** *Renf.*                   561He
WEAVER'S COTTAGE A handloom weaver's house, built in the 18th century; restored as a museum.

**Kilchurn Castle** *Argyll*                   565Ha
A ruined castle, built in 1440, and altered and extended in the 16th and 17th centuries by Sir John Campbell (1635–1716), 1st Earl of Breadalbane and Holland.

**Kildoon** *Ayrs.*                   561Gb
VITRIFIED FORT This fort crowns a rocky ridge overlooking the valley of the R. Girvan. Here a

more modern monument has been erected and this has destroyed a part of the fort's defences. The size is about 150 ft by 100 ft, and its rampart is vitrified. In addition, there are two ramparts with external ditches on the west side which give additional protection along the approach-route.

**Kildrummy Castle** *A'deen* 567Ge
Imposing ruins of a fortress of the Earls of Mar in the Don Valley, so old that it had to be rebuilt in 1303; it was reduced to a pathetic pile after the Jacobite rebellion of 1715. The hall, chapel and 14th-century gate-house remain.

**Kilkhampton** *Cornwall* 538Ee
CHURCH OF ST JAMES A large church, with a west tower, and a Norman south doorway. Inside are carved bench ends and wagon-roofs; the organ is reputed to be from Westminster Abbey.

**Killerton Gardens** *Devon* 539He
Hill-side gardens noted for rare trees and shrubs.

**Killiecrankie** *Perths.* 566Cc
URRAND HOUSE Here on July 27, 1689, a Jacobite force under Viscount Dundee defeated the English troops of William III. Dundee was killed in the battle and a stone in the grounds marks the spot where he received his death-wound.

**Killochan Castle** *Ayrs.* 561Gb
A 16th-century fortified house, containing a collection of Stuart and Napoleonic relics.

**Kilmartin** *Argyll* 560Eg
In the churchyard are a badly damaged Celtic cross and medieval sculptured stones.

**Kilmuir** *Isle of Skye, I'ness.* 564Eh
An Ionic cross stands in the churchyard to mark the grave of Flora Macdonald (1721–90), the Jacobite heroine who aided the escape of Bonnie Prince Charlie after the Battle of Culloden.

**Kilpeck** *Herefs.* 546Ad
CHURCH OF SS MARY AND DAVID A small Norman church, one of the finest in Britain. Built *c.* 1145, it is now well preserved and noted for its carving. This is extremely interesting, as none of it can be traced back directly to Normandy—the motifs of the carving on the chancel arch have been traced to the transept façade of St James's at Compostela in northern Spain. Outside is a series of carved corbels running round the church. But the main decorative feature is the south door. Perhaps nowhere in Europe is it possible to find such a strange mixture of ideas and motifs—fruit, flowers, warriors, serpents and dragons intertwine in a mass of detail. A corner of the nave is Saxon, several windows date from late medieval times and the bell-cote was restored in the 19th century, but apart from these the church is purely Norman in style. A. W. Pugin designed the stained glass of the apse window in 1849.

**Kilpheder** *South Uist, I'ness.* 564Be
This round-house, or wheel-house, has an outer wall enclosing a circular area 29 ft in diameter. Within its circle stand 11 drystone pillars free of the wall, with a central space 18 ft across.

**Kilphedir** *Suth.* 569Kc
BROCH The outer enclosure is protected by a bank and external ditch and a second ditch to the north-east. The broch wall is 15 ft thick and encloses a space some 32 ft in diameter. There is a wall-chamber.

**Kimbolton** *Hunts.* 547Hf
CHURCH OF ST ANDREW A 13th-century church, with a west tower and spire of a century later.

CHURCH OF SS MARY AND DAVID, KILPECK : SOUTH DOOR

*Nowhere in Europe is there such a strange mixture of ideas and motifs as in the decoration around the south door of this little church; another decorative feature is the chancel arch. Oliver de Merlimont founded nearby Shobdon church about 1140, and Kilpeck probably followed in the next ten years. Oliver had made a pilgrimage to St James's at Compostela in Spain and the figures that decorate the Kilpeck chancel arch are similar to those on the transept façade of St James's. Almost nothing in the decoration of the church can be traced back directly to Normandy—a reminder that 12th-century architecture and carving in England was not always Norman in origin. Other examples of decoration by what is now known as the Herefordshire School of carving may be found at Brinsop and Stretton Sugwas near by.*

Inside are painted medieval screens, some fragments of glass, carved roof bosses, and 17th-century monuments with figures.

**Kimbolton Castle** *Hunts.* 547Hf
The original medieval mansion here was re-modelled in the reign of William and Mary. In 1707 part of the building collapsed and the owner, the 1st Duke of Manchester, commissioned Sir John Vanbrugh to rebuild the castle. Vanbrugh's building is quadrangular around an inner court-yard, and has a medieval battlemented exterior. The south front was completed *c.* 1708 and the rest by 1714. In *c.* 1766 Robert Adam added the outer gate-house and the gateway on the north side. The castle is now a school.

**King Arthur's Cave** *Herefs.* 546Ad
Site of the discovery in 1870 of flints fashioned by Early Man, and remains of hippopotamus, elephant, and other animals long extinct in Britain.

**King Arthur's Round Table** 557Jf
**and Mayburgh** *Westmld.*
The Round Table is an embanked circle, some 300 ft across, with an internal ditch. There were once

two entrances, though that on the north side has disappeared. Here there were once two standing stones and another stone structure stood near the centre of the circle.

Mayburgh lies a few hundred yards to the west. It is a circular enclosure slightly larger than the Table and has a single entrance on the east. The bank here is higher than usual. Near the centre is a single standing stone, of which there were once four, with others at the entrance.

**Kings Langley** *Herts.*         *547Hc*
CHURCH OF ALL SAINTS Most of the church is of the 15th century, but the piscina in the chancel dates from the 13th century. There is a 17th-century pulpit and several 19th-century stained glass windows by Clayton & Bell and Ward & Hughes. Monuments include one to Edmund of Langley, with heraldry (14th century) and another altar-tomb to Sir Ralph Verney, *c.* 1500, with effigies.

**King's Lynn** *Norfolk*         *554Ac*
An ancient port on the R. Ouse, near the Wash; it is still a busy harbour for agricultural produce, and a beautiful small town. Before the bishop's manor became royal property it was called Bishop's Lynn, and was linked to the Continent through trade, principally in wool, and by pilgrims on their way to the shrine at Walsingham. It was once a walled city, but now only a small part of the wall and the south gate remain. Many monastic orders were settled there, and are remembered in the names of streets and buildings: Greyfriars, White-friars, Blackfriars and Augustine Friars. There are notable merchants' houses and municipal buildings.
BRIDGE STREET This street contains the Greenland Fishery House, built 1605 as a merchant's house, with a cruck-based roof, 17th-century wall-paintings and an overhanging upper floor. At the end of Bridge Street is the stone and brick 14th-century gateway to the former Whitefriars' house, one of King's Lynn's many vanished monastic buildings.
CHURCH OF ST MARGARET One of the few parish churches with two western towers (mid-12th century). Much of the interior of the building is 18th-century Gothic by Matthew Brettingham, *c.* 1745. The outstanding possessions are two brasses of *c.* 1349 and *c.* 1364, which are the largest in England, and minutely detailed.
CHURCH OF ST NICHOLAS Very large, it was founded in 1146, but built in the 15th century. The tower at the south-west is earlier, but has a spire of 1869. St Nicholas's has many interesting fittings and monuments.
CLIFTON HOUSE The façade is Georgian, and there is a portal decorated with barley-sugar columns; a 15th-century undercroft remains. A tall Elizabethan tower gives good views of the town.
CUSTOM HOUSE Designed by the local architect Henry Bell in 1683; a small and charming building on the quay reminiscent of Dutch styles. There is a statue of Charles II in a niche, and the building is surmounted by a lantern tower.
GUILDHALL OF THE HOLY TRINITY Built in chequer-board pattern of flint and stone, it dates from 1421; there were additions in the 18th century and in 1895 municipal offices were added to make it the modern town hall. The Treasury here contains city regalia, including King John's Cup, gilded and embossed with enamelled panels showing hawking and hunting scenes of the mid-14th century; King John's Sword; the notable Mayoral Chains of the late 15th and 16th centuries;

the Nuremberg Cup of *c.* 1600, an elaborate piece by a German Court goldsmith; and various 17th- and 18th-century treasures. Another guildhall is that of St George, which is a fine medieval guildhouse.
HAMPTON COURT A 14th-century former warehouse on the river, converted to dwellings in the 17th century and one of the best of the town's merchant buildings. The others include the Hanseatic Warehouse (1428), a depot for the German commercial league known as the Hansa; Greenland Fishery House (1605), a merchant's dwelling that became an inn and then a museum; and Clifton House, a medieval dwelling modernised in 1708, from whose Elizabethan tower there is a good view of the town.
KING STREET The best street for pleasing Georgian and 19th-century houses; also includes St George's Guildhall, the largest and oldest example in England of a medieval Merchant Guild's house. Built in the early 15th century, it was restored and adapted as a theatre in 1957.
MUSEUM AND ART GALLERY Displays relating to local natural history, archaeology and geology are on view with coins, costumes and local folk material. In the art gallery are water-colours, oils, local prints and a collection of English drinking glasses and pottery.

### KING JOHN'S CUP

*This cup is the earliest surviving piece of English medieval secular plate. It is decorated in translucent enamel, which is fragile and tends to flake. The cup was restored four times between 1692 and 1782 but the enamels on the bowl, showing men and women hunting, are mostly original. Tradition says the cup was among the treasure lost by King John in the Wash, but its style shows it to date from a century later. Translucent enamelling came into fashion late in the 13th century; the design was engraved on silver and showed clearly through the enamel. A play of light and dark was obtained by varying the depth of the engraving. (Guildhall, King's Lynn)*

KINGSTON LACY

*This is the building that has survived to show how Sir Roger Pratt designed country houses. Pratt, one of the most important 17th-century architects, designed only five country houses, and four have since disappeared. His major work was helping to redesign London after the Great Fire of 1666. When Pratt built Kingston Lacy in 1663–5 it was a fine example of the Restoration style, but during the 1830's the house was drastically altered by Sir Charles Barry, architect of the Houses of Parliament. One of his additions was the sumptuous marble staircase. The house's founder was Sir Ralph Bankes, who built Kingston Lacy after his previous home, Corfe Castle, had been destroyed by Cromwell's troops after withstanding weeks of siege during the Civil War.*

HALS *Portrait of a Lady*

*In 1624, Frans Hals painted one of the most popular portraits—the 'Laughing Cavalier'—in which his brushwork can be compared with the touch of the Impressionists, although it had none of their atmospheric quality. The paint is laid on thickly; his sitters have extrovert expressions and the swagger of their poses is enhanced by a low viewpoint. From the 1640's onwards Hals developed a more restrained style, but what he lost in panache he gained in intimacy. To this demure young woman the painter has brought an unusually profound sympathy of observation. The paint surface is now thin, and the treatment of the costume is summary but this serves only to emphasise the exquisite modelling of the face.*
*(Ferens Art Gallery, Kingston upon Hull)*

QUEEN STREET AND SATURDAY MARKET Four contiguous buildings of different dates and styles: the guildhall (1421) of chequer-board flint and stone with low ground-floor windows and a tall seven-light upper window beneath a gable; next to it the fanciful Elizabethan extension in the same flint chequer. Behind these are the assembly rooms of 1766, plain but containing a magnificent rococo mirror. The Victorian town hall of 1895 also uses flint chequer work, and in it are exhibited the city regalia.

RED MOUNT CHAPEL Built in 1485, it stands in a park area known as The Walks. The chapel has three storeys inside an octagonal shell, the top storey being a cruciform chapel with beautiful fan-vaulted roof. This Chapel of Our Lady of the Mount was a stopping place for the many pilgrims to Walsingham.

ST MARGARET'S LANE Has two interesting timber-framed warehouses with overhangs, one of them known as the Hanseatic Warehouse.

ST NICHOLAS CHAPEL Almost entirely 15th century, with a beautiful south porch and carved angel roof.

SOUTH GATE The only surviving town gate, embattled, dating from 1520. Remains of the wall that encircled the town can be seen in Kettlewell Lane, Wyatt Street, The Walks and St Ann's Street.

THORESBY COLLEGE Founded in 1500 for priests of the Trinity Guild; it now mostly consists of 17th-century work, but an original archway and door survive.

TUESDAY MARKET-PLACE A fine open space dominated by the Duke's Head Hotel (1683–9), probably by the same Henry Bell who designed the custom house; unusual but of a commanding design.

**King's Norton** *Leics.*  552Fb
CHURCH OF ST JOHN THE BAPTIST An impressive Gothic Revival church rebuilt entirely between 1760 and 1775 by J. Wing the Younger of Leicester. The interior is dominated by the centrally placed pulpit, and the fittings are all 18th century. The spire was destroyed by lightning in 1850.

**Kingston** *Dorset*  540Ec
CHURCH OF ST JAMES The Church of St James was built in 1880 by G. E. Street, and has an imposing central tower. The fittings are also by Street, and include some good ironwork.

**Kingston Lacy** *Dorset*  540Ed
The home of the Bankes family for 300 years. Sir Roger Pratt designed the Restoration house for Sir Ralph Bankes in 1663; it was completed by 1665. Pratt also laid out the extensive grounds. In the 1830's Sir Charles Barry, who designed the Houses of Parliament, carried out major alterations to the mansion. The stone building is surmounted by a cupola and lantern, and has a main front with a great porch and a fine pediment. In the grounds is an Egyptian obelisk similar to Cleopatra's Needle on the Embankment in London, which was set up in 1827 and is probably the only one in private possession. The house contains a collection of old masters and other works of art.

**Kingston upon Hull** *Yorks.*  559Ga
Originally a trading settlement of 1160 known as Wyke upon Hull. It was acquired from the Abbots of Meaux (France) by Edward I in 1293, and the name changed when its first charter was granted in 1299. It prospered sufficiently to have a mayor in 1331; the first was William de la Pole, whose statue is at the Victoria Pier. In 1321 the town was

enclosed and fortified, with a moat and walls of brick. In 1447 the aldermen won the right to elect 'one suitable and discreet man to be Admiral of the Humber', and this title is held today by the current lord mayor.

Among the ancient buildings are Holy Trinity Church (Early English and Perpendicular); St Mary's at Lowgate (a Knights Hospitaller foundation, *c.* 1325); the Old Grammar School (1583), its upper hall being used by the Hull Merchant Adventurers; and the Maison Dieu, founded in 1384 by Sir Michael de la Pole (later Earl of Suffolk).

CHURCH OF THE HOLY TRINITY One of the largest parish churches in England; it is cruciform with a grand central tower, and is mainly 14th and 15th century, with some early brickwork and huge windows. Inside are medieval roofs, screens and benches, and a carved font.

FERENS ART GALLERY Opened in 1928, the gallery has an important collection of old masters including works by Frans Hals, Guardi, Canaletto, Maffei and Philippe de Champaigne. Sculpture by Henry Moore, Barbara Hepworth and Paolozzi can be seen with a wide selection of modern paintings by Victor Pasmore, David Hockney, Allen Jones and Alan Davie, among others. There is also a special collection of marine paintings, mostly from Hull and Humberside.

HULL TRINITY HOUSE Founded as a religious body in 1369, the organisation responsible for pilotage in the Humber. In 1787 the brethren established a Navigation School, and the characteristic uniform of the Trinity House boys, patterned on that of the R.N. midshipman of the period, is a familiar sight in Hull. The headquarters building dates from 1753, and is of elegant simplicity, richly furnished.

MAISTER HOUSE A mansion rebuilt in 1744 with a Palladian hall and staircase, and ironwork by Robert Bakewell.

MARITIME MUSEUM The maritime history of the area is shown by exhibits dealing with shipping, fishing, and the whaling industry.

WILBERFORCE HOUSE A 17th-century merchant's house where William Wilberforce (1759–1833) was born. It contains a museum of material from his anti-slavery and philanthropic activities, and a collection of dolls and toys.

## Kingston upon Thames *Greater London* 542Bg

CORONATION STONE Seven Saxon kings were crowned at this ancient market town during the 10th century, and the traditional coronation stone (King's Stone) now stands in front of the guildhall.

QUEEN'S ROYAL SURREY REGIMENT MUSEUM Military uniforms, arms and collections of medals belonging to the Queen's Royal Regiment and the East Surrey Regiment, which amalgamated to become the Queen's Royal Surrey Regiment, are the principal exhibits. Military paintings and prints are also displayed.

## King's Weston *Glos.* 546Cg

At Sea Mills, 2 miles away on the Avon estuary, was Abone, a small port at the end of the road from Silchester (Calleva Atrebatum). From here travellers could ferry across to Caerwent (Venta Silurum) and Caerleon (Isca). Considerable excavation of this Roman villa has been made and the remains are on display. The skeleton of a man, killed by the sword, was found in the ruins of a hypocaust.

## Kingussie *I'ness* 566Bd

HIGHLAND FOLK MUSEUM Here, among exhibits showing all facets of the past life in the Highlands—dress, furnishings, etc.—is a replica of the 19th-century farm-shed and mill of a crofter.

## Kinlet *Shrops.* 546Bg

CHURCH OF ST JOHN THE BAPTIST Standing in the grounds of Kinlet Hall (1729, now a school), but isolated from other buildings, this Norman church has many later additions including the Early English west tower with Perpendicular top. Also Perpendicular is the timber-framed clerestory (restored by Oldrid Scott, 1892). There is stained glass of 1814 in the east window. Among many interesting monuments (the oldest date from the early 1400's) there is one of 1584 to Sir George Blount and his wife: arches into the tomb chest reveal a carved effigy of a corpse inside.

## Kinneff *Kinc.* 567Gc

CHURCH The Honours of Scotland (the crown jewels) were temporarily concealed in this church for safety in 1652. They had been daringly smuggled from Dunnottar Castle by the minister's wife just before the castle fell to besieging Roundheads.

## Kinross *Kinross.* 562Bg

KINROSS HOUSE Built in 1685–92, and one of the best period works by Sir William Bruce. The house is set in beautiful gardens on the shores of Loch Leven.

## Kintraw *Argyll* 560Eg

CAIRNS AND STANDING STONES These monuments stand at the roadside close to the head of Loch Craignish. There are four cairns, three of which are quite small. The fourth, 8 ft high and nearly 50 ft across, has been excavated. When built, it was heaped round a central post fixed in the ground. The burial chamber was double and close to the cairn's edge. The mound is contained by a stone kerb. Close by stands the upright stone, some 13 ft high.

## Kirby Hall *Northants.* 547Hg

A house begun in 1570 by an unknown architect. In 1575 it came into the hands of Sir Christopher Hatton who added to the building. Kirby is of architectural significance, though now a ruin, because it incorporates motifs occurring in French architecture; this appears to be the only instance of their use in England and they were probably based on books of engravings. Later, in the first half of the 17th century, more building was undertaken, it is said, by Inigo Jones; this is not confirmed although it is known that one of the leading sculptors of the period, Nicholas Stone, was employed here. The Hall remained in the possession of the Hatton and Finch-Hatton families but had become ruinous by the 19th century. (See p. 260.)

## Kirkby Lonsdale *Westmld.* 557Jd

CHURCH OF ST MARY THE VIRGIN Ruskin praised the view from the churchyard here, and Turner painted it; it is one of the finest in Westmorland, embracing Howgill and Casterton Fells, and the R. Lune.

Much remains of the original Norman church, and the interior is impressive, with massive pillars in the north arcade alternating with piers of clustered shafts. There is a 17th-century six-sided pulpit, and many 18th-century mural tablets.

## Kirkby Malham *Yorks.* 558Ac

CHURCH OF ST MICHAEL A Perpendicular church with a west tower. There is a Norman font, and 17th- and 18th-century pews.

## Kirkcaldy *Fife.* 562Cf

The picturesque ruins of Ravenscraig Castle, built *c.* 1440 and inhabited until the Restoration, overhang the sea near by. Adam Smith (1723–90), the political economist, was born here; the house

KIRBY HALL

*Kirby Hall was begun in 1570 for Sir Humphrey Stafford. The architect is unknown, but the mason was Thomas Thorpe; and his seven-year-old son John, who later became an architect, laid the first stone—as he himself recorded in one of his later drawings. When Stafford died in 1575 the estate was bought by Sir Christopher Hatton, who continued the building work. Further additions were made in the 17th century and then the architect may have been Inigo Jones. The house, now a ruin, combines elements of early Renaissance architecture of Elizabeth I's time with elements of Inigo Jones's period.*

in the High Street where he wrote *The Wealth of Nations* may still be seen. In 1816 the historian Thomas Carlyle was a master at the burgh school.
MUSEUM AND ART GALLERY The museum was founded as a First World War memorial by John Nairn, a local linoleum manufacturer. The collection is devoted to the history, industries, and natural history of Fife and includes many pieces of Wemyss ware, a distinctive, finely crazed pottery, originally made *c.* 1883 at Robert Heron's Fife Pottery in Gallatown by Karel Nekola, a Bohemian immigrant. Other items include duelling pistols used in Fife in the 19th century; the inkstand used by Kirkcaldy-born Adam Smith when writing *The Wealth of Nations*; and paintings by Sickert.
SAILOR'S WALK A harbour-side group of 17th-century houses. (Not open to visitors.)

**Kirkleatham** *Yorks.*                    558Jf
CHURCH OF ST CUTHBERT An earlier church was rebuilt in 1763 to make St Cuthbert's; the mausoleum was designed by James Gibbs in 1740. There are delightful 18th-century fittings and many monuments, some by Peter Scheemakers and Sir Henry Cheere.

**Kirknewton** *Northld.*                    562Ed
CHURCH OF ST GREGORY Mainly a 19th-century rebuilding which contains two important examples of primitive building: a transept and chancel which appear to be vault only—the walls are so low that they are hardly apparent. There is

also a crude stone-carving depicting the Adoration of the Magi, which probably dates from the 12th century.

**Kirkoswald** *Ayrs.*                    561Gb
SOUTER JOHNNIE'S COTTAGE The home of John Davidson (Souter Johnnie), the village cobbler of Burns's 'Tam O'Shanter'. The cottage contains Burns relics.

**Kirkoswald** *Cumb.*                    557Jf
CHURCH OF ST OSWALD A church of various dates, with a 16th-century chancel built by Lord Dacre when he founded a college here. There is a detached tower some distance away, which was built in 1897, and several coffin-lids.

**Kirkstall** *Yorks.*                    558Cb
ABBEY One of Yorkshire's ruined Cistercian abbeys, Kirkstall was founded in the 12th century; much of its building survives surprisingly well, even the seemingly precarious wall of one side of the church's central tower.

**Kirkstead** *Lincs.*                    553He
CHURCH OF ST LEONARD Once the 13th-century south chapel of the former Cistercian abbey of Kirkstead, founded during the 12th century, and now surrounded by the ruins of various abbey buildings. There is an early effigy of a knight, *c.* 1250.

**Kirkwall** *Mainland, Orkney*                    569Hf
The capital of Mainland and the Orkneys. The Cathedral of St Magnus dates mainly from the 12th century: its nave is notable, and there are many memorials of different periods.

**Kirkwhelpington** *Northld.*                    562Fa
CHURCH OF ST BARTHOLOMEW A 12th- and 13th-century church, originally cruciform, with a west tower. Inside is a large architectural-type monument of the mid-18th century.

**Kirriemuir** *Angus*                    566Eb
This town was described by Sir James Barrie, author and playwright, as the town of Thrums in *The Little Minister* and *Window in Thrums*. The house where he was born and his grave are here.

**Kirtling** *Cambs.*                    548Bf
CHURCH OF ALL SAINTS Originally Norman, All Saints has a good south doorway, with a carving of Christ in Majesty. The rest of the fabric is of various dates, up to *c.* 1500. There are many monuments to the North family, including two big and ornate ones of the 16th century.

**Kirtling Tower** *Cambs.*                    548Bf
The best and finest tower gate-house in the county. It dates from 1530 and is of red brick, with blue diapers, two tall polygonal outer turrets, slender turrets behind and a superb semicircular oriel window squashed in between. The whole unifies the architectural features of the Middle Ages and the Renaissance.

**Kirton in Lindsey** *Lincs.*                    553Gf
CHURCH OF ST ANDREW The huge Early English west tower has pilaster buttresses; the south door is contemporary with it. There are remains of Norman work, including the priest's door in the chancel, which has a tympanum of knot work. Restoration was carried out in the mid-19th century.

**Kisimul Castle** *Isle of Barra, I'ness.*                    564Ad
A castle on a sea-girt rock, begun in 1030; it has been the stronghold of the chiefs of the Clan Macneil since then, except for the years 1838–1937, and has been greatly restored.

**Kit's Coty House** *Kent*     *542Df*
These are the remains of the most spectacular of the small group of Kentish Neolithic chambered barrows. The covering mound has now disappeared.

Of the megalithic structure, there survive uprights on which the great capstone still rests, probably what is left of a burial chamber, though it has sometimes been interpreted as a false entrance.

**Knap Hill** *Wilts.*     *540Fg*
This Neolithic camp crowns a hill in the ridge bordering the north side of the Vale of Pewsey. The external ditch has causeway crossings corresponding with openings in the inside bank, which encloses a 4 acre area. Half a mile to the west, on the opposite hill, stands a prominent long barrow. Adjoining the causewayed camp on its eastern side, a smaller earthwork may be traced. This is of a later date, having been erected as the outer protection of an Iron Age farmstead.

**Knaresborough** *Yorks.*     *558Cc*
CHURCH OF ST JOHN The church was once cruciform, but the transepts disappeared in 15th-century rebuilding; the former central tower has a small spire. Inside is a Perpendicular font with a later cover, a 17th-century screen and monuments, one with a standing figure under an arch.

**Knebworth** *Herts.*     *547Jd*
CHURCH OF ST MARY AND THOMAS OF CANTERBURY Norman, with later enlargements, the church stands in the grounds of Knebworth House. The monuments include two (1800–10) by Edward Stanton, and one with the standing figure of Lytton Lytton (*d.* 1710) which has been attributed to Thomas Green of Camberwell, an outstanding statuary of the early 18th century.

**Knebworth House** *Herts.*     *547Jd*
The Victorian statesman and romantic novelist, Sir Edward Bulwer-Lytton (1st Lord Lytton) who wrote *The Last Days of Pompeii*, succeeded to this property in 1843. He lived here until his death in 1873, and was visited by Disraeli, Charles Dickens and other literary friends. The house was begun in 1492 by Sir Robert Lytton; it was partly demolished in 1812, but the Tudor great hall survives. The exterior was redecorated in Gothic style by the 1st Lord Lytton in 1843. The house, set in fine gardens, contains 17th- and 18th-century furniture, portraits, and relics and manuscripts of Bulwer-Lytton.

**Knockderry Castle** *Dunb.*     *561Gf*
On the east side of Loch Long this castle replaced and stands on the dungeons of a much older castle called Knock Dunder, described in Scott's novel *Heart of Midlothian*.

**Knole** *Kent*     *542Cf*
One of the largest private houses in England, Knole was built by Thomas Bourchier when Archbishop of Canterbury (1454) and used as a retreat by bishops until Archbishop Cranmer released it to Henry VIII, from whom it passed to Queen Elizabeth I. Elizabeth granted it to her courtier, the politician and poet Thomas Sackville, 1st Earl of Dorset, who extended the property in 1603–8.

The house contains pictures, tapestries, rugs and silver up to the 17th century. The Brown Gallery has portraits and 17th- and 18th-century English furniture. The fire-place in the great chamber resembles a high altar, and the ornamental great staircase, introduced by Sackville, set a fashion previously unknown in private houses. The great hall dates from *c.* 1460. (See also p. 262.)

KIT'S COTY HOUSE

*On the side of the Downs above Aylesford stand these relics of the most spectacular of the barrows in Kent that date from the Neolithic period. Such earth burial mounds were oval in plan, and contained chambers made from drystone walling and megaliths—or great stones. The Neolithic peoples were the first farmers in Britain and came from the Continent to the chalk uplands of south-eastern England about 3700 BC. They interred their dead in these chambered barrows in groups, possibly in families, often with their pots and stone implements. The earth mound at Kit's Coty House has now disappeared, leaving the remains of the burial chamber, with the great capstone which formed the roof, and the stone supports.*

EARLY 17th-CENTURY CHAIR

*Upholstered chairs with X-shaped legs enjoyed a period of popularity during the early 17th century. Their design recalls the folding chairs of ancient Rome, but they were made with broader seats and backs for greater comfort, and were covered in rich fabric. The entire framework of this chair is covered in patterned silk, and the fringe, made of strands of silk, is attached to the frame by nails with decorated heads. The cushion, covered with silk and stuffed, is another concession to rising standards of comfort after the austerity of the carved wooden chairs which were the fashion in Elizabethan times. (Knole)*

THE VENETIAN AMBASSADOR'S ROOM AT KNOLE

*Nicolo Molino, a Venetian ambassador at the court of James I, once occupied this room, and it is named after him; his portrait, painted by Mytens about 1640, hangs by the bed. The furniture and bed, decorated with cupids and the letters JR, may have belonged to James II. Thomas Roberts, cabinet-maker to Charles II and James II, made the chairs and stools. The tapestries, depicting landscapes with mythical figures, are Flemish, and were woven by Francis Spierinck in the late 16th or early 17th century.*

**Knowe of Laird** *Rousay, Orkney* 569Hg
A long four-horned cairn. It is about 180 ft long, 16 ft high above the chamber, which is tripartite, and with an entrance passage 18 ft long.

**Knowe of Yarso** *Rousay, Orkney* 569Hg
A small 'stalled cairn' of four compartments.

**Knowlton Circles** *Dorset* 540Ed
Here are three henge-circles in a row. The largest, some 800 ft in diameter, is roughly bisected by the Cranborne–Wimborne road, and the other two lie to the north. A ruined Norman church with later additions stands in the middle of the central circle. To the east of this circle is an enormous round barrow, and smaller barrows are grouped close by.

**Knutsford** *Cheshire* 552Be
CHURCH OF ST JOHN THE BAPTIST A brick Classical church, it was built in 1744. The west tower has urns at each corner of the parapet, as does the body of the church; the windows have stone dressings. There is a monument of *c.* 1823 by Sir Richard Westmacott.

**Kymin, The** *Mon.* 546Ad
In 1804 Lord Nelson dined in the many-windowed Round Tower. It stands on the Kymin Hill overlooking the Wye and Monnow Valleys and was built in 1794 by a dining club which, in 1802, erected a 'naval temple' near by in honour of the Royal Navy.

# L

**Lacock** *Wilts.* 540Eg
One of the most beautiful villages in England, with houses dating from the 15th to 18th centuries.
CHURCH OF ST CYRIAC Built mainly in the 14th and 15th centuries, the church is cruciform with a west tower and spire. The north-east chapel was built *c.* 1430, has a notable lierne-vault with pendants, and an outstanding monument to Sir William Sharington, who converted Lacock Abbey into his dwelling after its dissolution. His tomb is a decorative example of mid-16th-century work.
LACKHAM SCHOOL OF AGRICULTURE: AGRICULTURAL MUSEUM Tools and implements, farm machinery and granaries are exhibited.
LACOCK ABBEY Here in 1839–41, William Henry Fox Talbot perfected his talbotype technique which laid the foundations of modern photography. About 1540 Sir William Sharington, one-time Treasurer of the Mint at Bristol, acquired the abbey overlooking the Avon and adapted it as a Tudor mansion, adding an octagonal tower and twisted chimneys and retaining the 13th- and 15th-century cloisters, chapter house and nuns' parlour. The house was altered in neo-Gothic style in 1753 and further alterations were made in 1828.

**Ladle Hill** *Hants.* 541Gf
The special interest of this Iron Age hill-fort lies in the fact that its defences were never completed and that what was done shows well the method of construction. A shallow marking-ditch enclosing some 7 acres was first dug, and used in part a length of a Bronze Age ditch. Gangs thereupon began

work by scraping off the topsoil and dumping this in heaps inside the line of the future rampart. They then widened and deepened the marking-ditch by cutting into the chalk and piling the rubble spoil inside the ditch-line to form the core of the bank. Apparently the threat which had led to the beginning of the work soon passed. The site was thereupon deserted.

Several disc, bell and saucer barrows of Early Bronze Age date may also be seen on the hill-top.

**Laindon** *Essex*                    548Bc
CHURCH OF ST NICHOLAS A small church, mainly of the 14th and 15th centuries, with carved wood decoration in the south porch. Attached to the west end is a two-storied priest's house of the 17th century. The font is 13th century.

**Lamberts Castle Hill** *Devon*       540Bc
Site of an Iron Age fort, and a round barrow. From the hill are superb views to Chesil Bank in the east and Dartmoor in the west.

**Lambourne** *Berks.*                 546Eb
SEVEN BARROWS This famous barrow group is one of the finest in England. 'Seven' is a misnomer, for there are 26 in the whole group, which today is split by a minor road. Those to the north of this road lie in two straight rows with a few outliers. South of the road, the grouping is irregular and more scattered. These barrows are of various types, including bowl, disc, bell and saucer, as well as an earlier long barrow. Some have almost disappeared, but others still stand to heights of 10 ft.

**Lampeter** *Cards.*                  544Fe
ST DAVID'S COLLEGE Founded in 1822, it was built to the pattern of an Oxford college in 1827, in neo-Gothic, by architect Charles Cockerell. At the north gate of the old building is a Norman motte: the college site was known as Castle Field.

**Lamphey** *Pemb.*                    544Dc
BISHOP'S PALACE This small palace was a rural retreat of the medieval Bishops of St David's. As at St David's, most of the building took place between the 13th and 15th centuries; here, too, is a great hall built by Bishop Gower, using the same kind of arcaded roof parapet as appears at St David's and Swansea Castle. After the Reformation, Lamphey was for a time a private house and some of the alterations can still be seen; but it was soon abandoned and used as a stone quarry.

**Lamport Hall** *Northants.*          547Gf
The Hall was built in two stages: the central block by John Webb c. 1655, the wings by Francis Smith in 1730–8. The music hall contains 18th-century plasterwork. (By appointment.)

**Lancaster** *Lancs.*                 557Hc
An old town and port on the R. Lune. Its medieval castle stands on the site of a Roman military station; John of Gaunt, Duke of Lancaster and father of Henry IV, stayed there in 1385 and again in 1393. The town gave lodging to Bonnie Prince Charlie and his army on their ill-fated march south during the Jacobite rebellion of 1745. Lancaster is the county town of Lancashire and contains many fine old buildings. The Friends' Meeting House dates from 1690. The custom house was built in the 18th century; at its front stand graceful Ionic columns, each carved from a single block of stone. Skerton Bridge was constructed c. 1787.
CASTLE In 1102 the Normans built a great square stone keep to replace the Saxon wooden tower on Castle Hill, the site of Roman fortifications. King John built a curtain wall with round towers and a massive gateway around the keep, enclosing a

roughly circular area, 380 ft by 350 ft. Under Edward III's son, John of Gaunt, the gateway towers were added and banqueting halls and fine apartments were built. The castle was a Parliamentary stronghold in the Civil War. George Fox, founder of the Friends (Quakers), was imprisoned there in 1663–5. Besides being a prison the fortress has also been a judge's lodging, and Crown court was opened there in 1796. The Shire Hall within the castle contains over 600 heraldic shields. The keep, 78 ft high with walls 10 ft thick, is surmounted by a beacon tower known as John of Gaunt's Chair; from it the approach of the Spanish Armada was signalled.
LANCASTER CITY MUSEUM The museum is in Lancaster Town Hall, built in 1781, and contains archaeological and historical exhibits, including Corporation weights and measures dating from 1588. It is also the museum of the King's Own Royal (Lancaster) Regiment. Works by local artists, topographical paintings, drawings and prints make up the museum's art collection.
PRIORY CHURCH OF ST MARY The church dates from Saxon times, but all that remains of the Saxon church is a doorway at the western end. Most of the present Perpendicular church was built in the late 15th century; the belfry was added in 1754. Inside are elaborate oak choir stalls, carved c. 1340, and a Jacobean pulpit; there is also a monument by Louis Roubiliac.

**Lanchester** *Durham*                558Cg
CHURCH OF ALL SAINTS A Norman and Early English church, with a good Norman chancel arch. Later additions include the Perpendicular clerestory and windows in the south aisle. There is a Roman altar in the porch. The church also has some 13th-century stained glass.

**Landwade** *Cambs.*                  548Bf
The comparatively new Hall incorporates some part of the old mansion built in 1445. The treasures of this remote and quiet hamlet, consisting of Hall, church and a few cottages, are superb tombs in the little church, of the Cotton family, who first settled in Landwade in the 15th century.

**Laneast** *Cornwall*                 538Ed
CHURCH OF SS SIDWELL AND GULVAL Originally Norman, and with a west tower, the cruciform church has later additions. Inside is a Norman font, carved bench ends, rood screen, and fragments of stained glass.

**Lanercost Priory** *Cumb.*           557Jg
Founded in 1169 for Augustinian canons by Robert de Vallibus, the priory is approached by a Tudor bridge. In the aisle of the ruined priory church is the Lanercost Celtic cross (1214).

**Langham** *Rutland*                  553Gb
CHURCH OF SS PETER AND PAUL An imposing church, mainly of the 14th century, when a Decorated spire was added to the 13th-century west tower. Inside there is a Perpendicular clerestory, and some early 20th-century stained glass by Sir Ninian Comper.

**Langley Marish** *Bucks.*            547Hb
CHURCH OF ST MARY There are vestiges of Norman work, but the varied architecture has much of the 17th century, including the brick tower, the Kederminster Chapel (south transept), and a surprising library to the west. These were added by the Kederminster family in the 1600's. In the chapel there is a painted wooden screen and, leading into the chapel, a later Coade (artificial) stone screen of 1792; panelling in the library is painted with landscapes of Windsor and Eton.

## THE GUILDHALL AT LAVENHAM

*In the Market Square stands this fine early Tudor timber-framed building. It was the former Hall of the Guild of Corpus Christi and was erected shortly after the guild's foundation in 1529. A full-length figure of the founder of the guild, the 15th Lord de Vere, is carved on an elaborate corner-post. The early guilds were formed for the benefit of trade, yet they had strong religious connections, and in their halls traditional miracle plays and pageants were performed. Lavenham, a thriving centre of the wool trade in the 16th century, had three guildhalls; that of the Guild of Corpus Christi was the first to be built.*

There are monuments to the Kederminster family dated 1599, and one of David Harvey (d. 1788).

**Langport** *Som.*     *540Ce*
A small market town whose architectural curiosity is the Hanging Chapel—a chapel over an archway.

**Langwell** *Caith.*     *569Lc*
HOMESTEAD Buildings of this type are not uncommon in the northern part of Scotland, but very little is known of them or their purpose.

The main structure is a 6 ft thick wall enclosing a circular area some 27 ft across. There is an entrance from the outside and another into an adjoining rectangular structure enclosed by a similar wall and measuring about 48 ft by 14 ft. This rectangular building is halved by a cross-partition wall. Also inside it are three stone pillars which supported roofing slabs also resting on the walls.

**Lanhydrock House** *Cornwall*     *538Dc*
Overlooking the R. Fowey, the house was begun by Lord Robartes in the 17th century. The gatehouse and north wing are original, but the remainder was built mainly in the 19th century, following a fire. The picture gallery (116 ft long) has a plaster ceiling with scenes from the Old Testament. In the grounds (424 acres) are formal gardens (1857) with a number of bronze urns from the Château de Bagatelle, which were designed by Louis XIV's goldsmith, Louis Ballin. The formal gardens include a typical Cornish sycamore avenue-approach to the house.

**Lanteglos-by-Fowey** *Cornwall*     *538Db*
CHURCH OF ST WILLOW A somewhat isolated, mainly 14th–15th-century church. The west tower has openings into nave and both aisles. There are fragments of early stained glass.

**Lanyon Quoit** *Cornwall*     *538Ab*
A huge granite slab, 17 ft by 9 ft, and 18 in. thick, rests on three upright stones—all that remains of a New Stone Age long barrow.

**Lapworth** *Warks.*     *546Df*
CHURCH OF ST MARY The battlemented tower with a steeple is detached from the main body of the church, which has Norman remains. The nave is tall, with a clerestory of Perpendicular square-headed windows. There is a two-storey west porch. Inside, the features include an early 14th-century octagonal font, and a carved monument, *c.* 1928, by the sculptor, wood-engraver and type-designer Eric Gill.

**Largs** *Ayrs.*     *561Ge*
SKELMORLIE AISLE A building erected in 1636 as a mausoleum for Sir Robert Montgomerie, in Italian baroque style with elaborate paintings and carvings.

**Lasborough Manor** *Glos.*     *546Cc*
A Cotswold manor house, built in 1609, with a garden noted for herbaceous borders and shrubs.

**Laugharne** *Carm.*     *544Ed*
This attractive village is strategically set at the mouth of the R. Taf, where its medieval castle could be serviced from the sea; evidence of its later use by coastal shipping can be seen in the ruined wharf buildings. There is an interesting courthouse, where a corporation still meets under its port reeve. Laugharne was the home of the poet Dylan Thomas (1914–53) and the possible inspiration for his play *Under Milk Wood.*

**Launcells** *Cornwall*     *538Ee*
CHURCH OF ST ANDREW Set in an attractive position in a valley, with a delightful unrestored

interior, St Andrew's has carved bench ends, a wagon-roof, and some 15th-century tiles. There is a monument *c.* 1644, with effigy.

**Launceston** *Cornwall*                                     538Ed
CHURCH OF ST MARY MAGDALENE This church was built in 1511–24 by Sir Henry Trecarrel. It has a 14th-century south-west tower, and is noted for extravagant carving all over the granite exterior. There are many early fittings and monuments.

**Lavenham** *Suffolk*                                        548Ce
Lavenham has superb timber-framed houses dating from the prosperous 15th century when wool was practically as valuable as gold itself (today the Lord Chancellor still sits on the Woolsack). Its exquisite houses include: the Old Wool Hall, *c.* 1500, the Tudor shops, the superb De Vere House, Nos. 11, 12, 13 and 15 Church Street, the old grammar school, Mullet House, Shilling Old Grange, the Swan Hotel, the guildhall, *c.* 1529, Woolstaplers, and the Little House. Of particular interest is some of the finely executed pargetting work on house façades.
CHURCH OF SS PETER AND PAUL A very well-known church, it is mainly from the 15th century, with a tall west tower, and has a nave, clerestory, chancel and chapels with very large windows. There is a 14th-century rood screen, and good screens to the chapels. Also interesting are the stalls and carved misericords, and there are some 15th- to 17th-century monuments with effigies. Some of the glass is medieval, some mid-19th century.
GUILDHALL A timber-framed building of 1529, originally the Hall of the Guild of Corpus Christi.

**Laxton** *Notts.*                                            552Fe
CHURCH OF ST MICHAEL A large late 15th-century church, with clerestory, tall chancel and west tower. The north aisle screen is of 1532. There are many monuments from the 13th century.

**Layer Marney** *Essex*                                       548Cd
CHURCH OF ST MARY THE VIRGIN Standing near a Tudor gate-house, the church was rebuilt in brick by the 1st Lord Marney at the beginning of the 16th century. It has a west tower and a 15th-century mural of St Christopher. There are monuments which show the mingling of Perpendicular and Renaissance motifs.

**Layer Marney Towers** *Essex*                                548Cd
This mansion, which was never completed on its original scale, consists of an enormous gate-house with smaller ranges of buildings clinging to it. As an example of a phase in the development of English domestic architecture it is both impressive and interesting. The house dates from the early 16th century, and the main part of it was intended to face south. Only the seven-storied gate-house, with its adjacent small buildings, was finished. This was clearly intended as the showpiece of the mansion. The gate-house had emerged, centuries earlier, as a dominant feature of castle building, and the trend was continued in domestic building. At Layer Marney this architectural feature was developed almost to excess: it is the largest of all gate-houses of its kind. The decorations in terracotta on the battlements and windows are typical early Renaissance motifs of Italian character.

**Leamington Spa** See Royal Leamington Spa.

**Learable Hill** *Suth.*                                      569Kc
Several stone-rows stand on the hill-slope down to the R. Helmsdale. Many cairns are also scattered over the area and a standing stone with a cross carved on its face stands on the hill-top. The relationship of cairns to stone-rows is unknown.

LAYER MARNEY TOWERS

*A folly-like building, this enormous gate-house—the largest of its kind—is the only completed part of a magnificent 16th-century mansion. The original intention was to build the main part of the house to the south, but this never materialised. The 1st and 2nd Lords Marney died in 1523 and 1525 and the gate-house probably dates from that period. Since Edward I's time it had become the fashion to make the gate-house instead of the keep the aggressive and dominating component of a castle; the trend also became a feature of domestic building, and at Layer Marney the idea was developed to excess. The terracotta decoration on the battlements and windows is one of the earliest uses in England of Italian Renaissance motifs.*

16th-CENTURY MARNEY TOMBS

*John, 2nd Lord Marney, in black marble, lies on a table-tomb of terracotta—the newly fashionable Italian material. This tomb and that of Henry, 1st Lord Marney, are probably by Italians working on Layer Marney Towers. (Church of St Mary the Virgin, Layer Marney)*

## 18th-CENTURY SHIP'S CANNON

*This bronze cannon, one of a pair, was made in 1747, probably by José Solano in the royal cannon-foundry at Seville. The guns were almost certainly made for the Spanish navy and captured in 1762 by the British fleet in Havana; they are 41 in. long and have a calibre of 3¼ in. (Council Offices, Leatherhead)*

**Leatherhead** *Surrey* 542Af
Among Leatherhead's interesting houses is Kingston House where, in 1791, John Wesley preached his last sermon. The council offices house two 18th-century cannons. Anthony Hope, author of *The Prisoner of Zenda*, is buried in the churchyard.

**Lechlade** *Glos.* 546Dc
CHURCH OF ST LAWRENCE A Perpendicular church of the 15th century, with west tower and spire. Inside there is a curious roof boss depicting wrestlers, similar to one in Lincoln Cathedral. The font is embellished with carved panelling, and there is a monument (*c.* 1769) by Nicholas Read.

**Leckhampton** *Glos.* 546Cd
This is one of the best of the Cotswold Iron Age promontory forts, remodelled many years after its first construction. Its single ditch, cut into the limestone, was flat-floored and originally rather wide and shallow. When remodelled, the inner third of the ditch was considerably deepened, thus leaving a 'step' in its floor. The bank was at first of rubble, held by timber-lacing, and later a stone revetment was built on the outer face. Outside the entrance is a round barrow with a four-sided defence-bank, of uncertain date.

**Ledbury** *Herefs.* 546Be
CHURCH OF ST MICHAEL AND ALL ANGELS A church of Norman origin, but now mostly of the late 13th and early 14th centuries. There is a detached 13th-century tower, with a spire built 1727–34. There is early stained glass, and windows by C. E. Kempe of 1895–1904. Monuments and brasses, mainly from the 15th to 19th centuries, include work by Charles Regnant (1800), John Flaxman (1803) and J. G. Lough (1857), but the finest of all is perhaps a praying priest of the late 13th century.

**Ledsham** *Yorks.* 558Da
An essentially Saxon church, with a good carved Saxon doorway in the tower. There is also Norman and Gothic work and, inside, a Norman font and some medieval glass. There are 17th-century monuments with effigies, and one of *c.* 1739 by Peter Scheemakers.

**Leeds** *Yorks.* 558Cb
Many natural routes lead to and from Leeds; in the Middle Ages it was a market centre, and in 1626 Charles I created it a municipal borough

to protect and regulate the wool trade. By the 19th century it was an obvious focal point for the Industrial Revolution's developing road, rail and canal system, and was raised to the status of a city in 1893. In 1933 George V opened the new municipal offices.
ABBEY HOUSE MUSEUM The building was originally the great gate-house of Kirkstall Abbey, founded in 1152 by Cistercian monks from Fountains Abbey.

At the Dissolution of the monasteries John Ripley, the last abbot, converted the gate-house into a private dwelling and continued to live there; it was occupied for 800 years. Now a folk museum, it contains—as well as items of costume, dolls and toys, musical instruments and domestic bygones—three 'streets', with houses, cottages and shops, removed from the Leeds area and rebuilt in the museum.
CITY MUSEUM The collections are mainly of geology, natural history and archaeology, the main emphasis being on Yorkshire, but with displays from all over the world.

Also in the museum is a model coal pit, which shows in minute detail all the workings of a full-scale mine.
CHURCH OF ST PETER A large 19th-century church which replaced the medieval one, but which contains effigies of knights and monuments by Andrew Carpenter, John Flaxman and Baron Marochetti. There is also a Saxon cross.
CITY ART GALLERY Exhibitions of old masters, modern painting and sculpture, water-colours, prints, pottery and silver.
THORESBY SOCIETY A collection of books, pictures, maps and other material illustrating the history of Leeds and the surrounding district.
TOWN HALL As a result of a competition held in 1853 and judged by Sir Charles Barry, Cuthbert Brodrick's design for a new town hall at Leeds was chosen.

His building, with a many-columned exterior, has a columned clock tower over 200 ft high. Work began in 1855, and the new town hall was opened by Queen Victoria in 1859. The building was decorated with sculpture by Matthew Noble and John Thomas. To commemorate the opening, Noble carved an 8 ft high statue of Queen Victoria as part of the decoration.

**Leek** *Staffs.* 552Cd
ART GALLERY The gallery exhibits work of the Leek Embroidery Society, and houses temporary exhibitions of paintings.

**Leez (or Leighs) Priory** *Essex* 548Bd
A 13th-century priory here was rebuilt by Lord Rich in 1536. The greater part of the house was razed in 1753, leaving only outer and inner gate-houses and parts of the outer quadrangle, all in richly ornamented red brick. Foundations of the priory church have been excavated.

**Legis Tor** *Devon* 538Fc
This Bronze Age settlement covers more than 4 acres. There are four walled enclosures with accompanying huts. The enclosure-walls were of stone-faced earth, and the huts had low stone walls with timber and thatched roofs. The settlement was doubtless that of a tribe of herdsmen, who built the enclosure-walls to protect their animals from wolves and bears.

**Leicester** *Leics.* 552Eb
BELGRAVE HALL A small Queen Anne house and gardens, with 18th- and early 19th-century furniture, and a collection of agricultural implements and equipment.

COURBET *Les Demoiselles de Village*

*Courbet was a 19th-century revolutionary and a realist. He disowned both the clichés of academic art and the heroic scenes from history or legend often set in exotic surroundings. He wanted to paint ordinary people in their natural surroundings and always intended to shock: he succeeded with two early testaments of realism, the 'Burial at Ornans', a peasant funeral, and the 'Stone Breakers', a glorification of physical labour and stark poverty. These pictures outraged both public and critics and earned Courbet the reputation of being a dangerous socialist. But he was more than a propagandist; he was a fine painter with a great feeling for solidity—achieved by rich colour, especially greens, often applied with the palette-knife. In this picture of an upland scene near his native Ornans, he introduces his three sisters, with the characteristic addition of a bare-footed village girl. (City Art Gallery, Leeds)*

CATHEDRAL Formerly a parish church, raised to cathedral status in 1927. Originally Norman, there was much rebuilding until the 19th century, when Brandon, Street and Bodley did work there. There is a monument of 1656, which was signed by Joshua Marshall.

CHURCH OF ST MARGARET The south doorway and south arcade of the nave are 13th century, the rest of the building is of the 14th and 15th centuries; there is a large west tower. It was restored twice in the 19th century, once by Sir Gilbert Scott and then by G. E. Street. The stained glass, of c. 1840, is by T. Willement.

GUILDHALL A medieval building containing a hall, mayor's parlour, library and cells.

JEWRY WALL In Roman times here stood Ratae Coritanorum, the cantonal town of the Coritani. Most of it is buried below modern Leicester, but the substantial fragment known as the Jewry Wall can be seen. It was the ornate façade of a great public baths-building and its covered exercise hall, which stood close to the centre of the Roman town.

JEWRY WALL MUSEUM Has a mosaic pavement, and is responsible for the upkeep of the Roman Jewry Wall and baths. It is also a museum of archaeology.

MUSEUM AND ART GALLERY It contains English paintings, examples of modern art, ceramics and sculpture. There is also an aquarium.

NEWARKE HOUSES MUSEUM Presents a social history of the city and county from 1500 to the present day, and is also the museum of the Royal Leicestershire Regiment.

**Leighton Bromswold** *Hunts.*      547Hf

CHURCH OF ST MARY THE VIRGIN A medieval cruciform church, with nave and tower rebuilt in the early 17th century; the west tower has obelisk-pinnacles. On either side of the nave are twin pulpits. The church contains 16th-century monumental effigies.

**Leighton Buzzard** *Beds.*      547Hd

CHURCH OF ALL SAINTS A large and impressive church, dating from the 13th century, it has a central tower and lofty spire completing its cruciform composition. Inside there is much to see, including a 13th-century font, misericords, brasses and a medieval brass lectern. The magnificent timber roofs have the flat pitch typical of 15th-century construction; the collegiate chancel dates from the same period and its screens and seating are still intact. The fine ironwork decoration on the west door is by Thomas of Leighton, who was also responsible for the grille on the tomb of Eleanor of Castille, the wife of Edward I, in Westminster Abbey. An interesting feature of the interior is the *graffiti* on piers and walls, all medieval. Many of the windows have good 19th-century glass by C. E. Kempe.

*Samˡ Johnson*

## DR SAMUEL JOHNSON, THE GREAT LEXICOGRAPHER

'Cut out the cant' is perhaps the central theme of the man who has gone down in history as the embodiment of a typical Englishman. Johnson was the son of a Lichfield bookseller; his birthplace is now a museum, and the Dame's School and Grammar School where he was educated can still be seen in Lichfield. At 28, Johnson rode to London to make his fortune. 'No man but a blockhead ever wrote except for money', he said, but in the following 18 years of hack-writing he barely made enough to live on. His articles in *The Rambler* made his name, and the publication of his dictionary confirmed his reputation as the most formidable figure in literary London.

SAMUEL JOHNSON *by Sir Joshua Reynolds (1756), a close friend who painted him several times. Johnson stood 6 ft among his contemporaries, whose average height was 5 ft 5 in., and such was his humanity that he would hoist sick beggars on to his back and carry them home to food and comfort. (National Portrait Gallery)*

TABLE AND PORTABLE DESK *belonging to Johnson, who said 'a man may write at any time if he set his mind doggedly to it'. (Johnson Birthplace, Lichfield)*

DICTIONARY OF THE ENGLISH LANGUAGE *published in 1775 after eight years work. The entry under 'Lexicographer' reads 'a writer of dictionaries—a harmless drudge'. (First edition at the British Museum)*

THE GARRET *where Johnson compiled the dictionary can be seen at 17 Gough Square, London. When the messenger who carried the last sheet of the dictionary to the publisher returned Johnson asked him 'Well, what did he say?' 'Sir', answered the messenger 'he said—"Thank God I have done with him."' 'I am glad,' answered the doctor, with a smile, 'that he thanks God for anything.'*

A TAVERN SCENE by Samuel Percy, made out of wax. It shows Dr Johnson holding court among members of 'The Club', which met once a week at the Old Cock Tavern. This Literary Club was founded in 1773 by Joshua Reynolds—no mean conversationalist himself—'in order to give Dr Johnson unlimited opportunities for talking'. The figures are traditionally identified, from left to right: a servant holding a mop in mock homage, Dr Johnson, Reynolds with his ear trumpet, an unidentified man, Thomas Gainsborough the painter, General Paoli, the Corsican leader who was lionised in London at this time and Charles James Fox the statesman. Johnson had many close friends, and in 1763 rescued the author and dramatist Oliver Goldsmith from a debtors' prison. (London Museum)

JOHNSON'S CHAIR, used during last illness. 'Sir, you cannot ceive with what acceleration I ance toward death', he said to a nd; he died on December 13, 1784. hnson Birthplace, Lichfield)

WEDDING RING belonging to Mrs Johnson. 'Marriage has many pains but celibacy has no pleasures', wrote the doctor. He was a 26-year-old hack writer when he married a well-to-do widow almost twice his age, with three children. Johnson was not inclined to discuss his 'beloved Tetty' with his young friends, but the marriage was one of strong affection. Mrs Johnson died in 1752, two years after Johnson had become recognised as a writer with his twice-weekly essays in 'The Rambler'; her husband took this ring from her finger and wore it thereafter himself. His grief was profound; but work, good company and talk helped to keep melancholia at bay. (Johnson Birthplace, Lichfield)

DR JOHNSON'S TEAPOT He was a 'hardened and shameless tea drinker ... who with tea amuses the evening ... and with tea welcomes the morning'. Like talk, it was a passion with him. (Johnson Birthplace, Lichfield)

OLDE CHESHIRE CHEESE, a 300-ar-old inn, with sawdusted floor, in ine Office Court, close to Johnson's use in Gough Square. The doctor ieved 'a tavern chair is the seat of nan felicity', and is said to have quented this inn. The seat he is pposed to have favoured is marked th a brass plate. On one wall hangs aricature of Johnson and Boswell by sley, an American artist of the early h century, which was discovered ently in the cellars. James Boswell t Johnson in 1763, and though the st sentence the great man spoke to n was a snub, the persistent Scot an to make notes of Johnson's versation almost at once, with a w to writing his life. This 'Life of nuel Johnson', which occupied the xt 20 years of his life, was published e years after Johnson's death, and it both he and Boswell owe their mortality.

## THE WEST FAÇADE OF LICHFIELD CATHEDRAL

*Lichfield is the only English cathedral to preserve three stone spires—though the central one was destroyed during the Civil War and was rebuilt. Lichfield also has the distinction of having once been the seat of an archbishopric. The See was established by the missionary, St Chad, in 669, as the main centre of Christianity in the Kingdom of Mercia. In the 8th century, during the reign of Offa, Mercia became the dominant English kingdom and Offa obtained papal permission to have his bishop elevated to the dignity of archbishop in 785. However, Offa died in 796 and his successors quickly lost Mercia's pre-eminence, and in 803 Lichfield was down-graded again to the status of bishopric. The existing cathedral dates only from the 13th century. From 1200 to 1240 the choir, transepts and chapter house were built, and the nave followed about 1250. The west façade, built about 1300, has the appearance of a magnificent screen filled with sculpture, and dominates the small doorways at its base.*

**Leighton Hall** *Lancs.*      557Jc
In *c.* 1800 a neo-Gothic façade was superimposed on this Classical house, set in extensive grounds with fine gardens.

**Leiston** *Suffolk*      548Ef
ABBEY Leiston is an industrial town; a mile away is Leiston Abbey, founded 1182 and transferred to its present site and rebuilt 200 years later. The remains are extensive but fragmentary; there is an early 16th-century gate-house with turrets. The abbey is now a Diocesan retreat house. (On application.)

**Leith** *M'loth.*      562Cf
LAMB'S HOUSE A merchant's house of *c.* 1600; it originally combined a residence and warehouse and was renovated in the 18th century.

**Leith Hall** *A'deen*      566Ef
The country home of the Leith family since 1650, the Hall has numerous conical towers capped in the fashion of French châteaux. It contains many family and Jacobite relics and in the grounds is a fine rock garden.

**Lennoxlove** *E. Lothian*      562De
Formerly Lethington Tower, the home of the Maitlands; William Maitland (1528–73) was secretary and counsellor to Mary, Queen of Scots—the lime avenue in the grounds is called 'Politician's Walk' after him. The mansion has a 15th-century tower, and the entrance door dates from 1626.

**Leominster** *Herts.*      546Af
CHURCH OF SS PETER AND PAUL The priory was built in the 12th century, but most of the buildings disappeared after the Dissolution of the monasteries. The nave survives with a Norman arcade and triforium on the north side, a west doorway, and the north aisle. The south aisle is of the 14th century. The 19th-century windows are by C. E. Kempe and Mayer & Co. of Munich.

**Leonardslee Gardens** *Sussex*      542Be
Spring-flowering gardens famous for camellias, magnolias and the Loderi rhododendron.

**Leonard Stanley** *Glos.*      546Cc
CHURCH OF ST LEONARD The cruciform church, largely 12th-century Norman, was originally part of the Augustinian priory. The massive central tower has a fine stair turret. Perpendicular windows have been inserted on the north of the nave, and all have clear glass. There are some good Norman doorways and tower arches. The original cloisters are now in a local farmyard.

**Lerwick** *Shetland*      568Ea
SHETLAND COUNTY MUSEUM The history of the Shetlands and man's life there is the theme of the museum. Archaeology, folk life, shipping and seafaring, and textiles and art are among the themes of the collections.

**Leuchars** *Fife.*      562Ch
CHURCH A modern church built on to a magnificent chancel and apse dating from the 12th century—one of the best examples of Norman work in Scotland. Above the apse is a 17th-century bell-turret.

**Levens Hall** *Westmld.*      557Jd
An Elizabethan mansion, converted from a medieval tower refuge against the Scots, and completed *c.* 1586. The famous gardens were originally laid out in 1689–1700, and feature shrubs trimmed into ornamental shapes.

**Leverington** *Cambs.*      553Jb
LEVERINGTON HALL One of the better houses in the county, partly Elizabethan and partly of 1660–75. It has two chimney-breasts, mullioned windows, straight gables of the 18th century and a good staircase. The parish has several other 17th- and 18th-century houses, including Hallcroft and Lancewood. Beechwood, half a mile south of the church, has a dove-cote of 1600 or earlier. Park House and the rectory, half a mile north-west of the church, are good 18th-century houses.

**Lewes** *Sussex*      542Ce
The county town of Sussex, and one of the most worth-while towns in the county to walk around. The High Street contains most of the best work. Georgian houses dominate, mostly in chequered red and blue brick. At the top of the street, the medieval castle lies back, protected by a massive preliminary tower, or barbican, built *c.* 1300.

ANNE OF CLEVES HOUSE Built in 1559, the house is now a folk museum of Sussex crafts, especially ironwork.

BARBICAN HOUSE Elizabethan house, with later adaptations, now an exhibition centre for prehistoric, Roman and Saxon items; it also contains a collection of Sussex paintings and prints.

### Lewknor *Oxon.*     *547Gc*
CHURCH OF ST MARGARET A small church, with a mainly Gothic west tower. There is a good Norman font with sculptured roundels, and some 17th- and 18th-century monuments, one by Sir J. E. Boehm of *c.* 1882.

### Lichfield *Staffs.*     *552Cb*
Lichfield has been given six royal charters, the earliest granted by Richard II in 1387. The charter of Mary I in 1553 made the city a county in its own right, separate and distinct from Staffordshire, electing its own sheriff. Its outstanding feature is the cathedral, built in the years 1195–1325: it is the only English cathedral to retain its group of three spires, which are known as the Ladies of the Vale. In the close, the canons' houses are splendid examples of Tudor domestic architecture.

Ancient buildings include the friary and friary gardens, with links with the Grey Friars of 1229, and Dame Oliver's School where Dr Johnson was a schoolmaster. The Vicar's Close has buildings of the 14th and 15th centuries. Milley's Hospital, founded in 1423 and endowed in 1504 by Dr Thomas Milley, has a fine gateway. Lichfield, for long a centre of pilgrimage to St Chad, was the birthplace of Dr Samuel Johnson (1709–84), the great lexicographer, whose childhood house in the Market Square is now a museum. Other famous men of Lichfield were Joseph Addison (1672–1719), essayist, poet and statesman, and David Garrick (1717–79), the actor who was Dr Johnson's first pupil.

ART GALLERY AND MUSEUM The museum specialises in local history and the art gallery has temporary exhibitions, usually concentrating on local artists.

CATHEDRAL England's only medieval three-spired cathedral, originally of Saxon foundation, and dedicated to St Chad, appointed Bishop of Mercia in 669. Chad lived at Lichfield, which became a place of pilgrimage, and the cathedral was built with money donated by the pilgrims. The present church suffered badly at the hands of Cromwell's troops: they shot down the central tower, and pillaged lead and other metals. After the Restoration of the Monarchy in 1660, the long task of rebuilding began. In the 18th and 19th centuries restorers were more keen to replace than to preserve. On the west front there are more than 100 carved statues. The cathedral contains what is probably the most famous of Sir Francis Chantrey's monuments, *The Sleeping Children*, which he completed in 1817. Other monuments are by E. H. Baily, Edward Stanton and Richard Westmacott the Elder.

STAFFORDSHIRE REGIMENTAL MUSEUM This amalgamation of the former North and South Staffordshire Regimental Museums consists of uniforms, weapons, battle trophies, medals, documents and pictures, including reproductions of uniforms from 1705 onwards. Relics of Field Marshals Wolseley and Colin Campbell can be seen, along with items connected with the American War of Independence.

### Liddington Bede House *Rutland*     *547Gg*
Thomas Cecil, son of Elizabeth I's Lord High Treasurer, Lord Burghley, converted the medieval palace of the Bishops of Lincoln into a bede house (almshouse). The former banqueting hall in the upper floor contains a fine ceiling and wooden panelling. The building has been restored.

### Lilleshall *Shrops.*     *552Bc*
In the 13th-century church is the extravagant Leveson Monument, which dates from 1764. Near by are the remains of a 12th-century abbey with a fine carved Norman arch.

### Lilleshall Abbey *Shrops.*     *552Bc*
Impressive ruins of a house founded for Arroasian canons *c.* 1148. The main survival is the church, which is entered through a large round-headed door of the late 12th century. Remains of the façade exist, with some Early English arcading. The church was aisle-less, a feature commonly found in Augustinian churches. The canons' choir lay to the east, under the crossing. Much of the transept is destroyed, but the two chapels off the south transept still exist. Probably the best surviving piece of architecture is the south door from the church to the cloister—a fine example of late 12th-century Norman decoration. The main surviving monastic quarters lie to the east and south of the cloister court. Still traceable to the east are the chapter house and slype (the dormitory would have been above these), and to the south, the refectory.

### Lincluden Abbey *Dumf.*     *562Aa*
A red sandstone ruin, the remains of a 12th-century convent, noted for its heraldic adornments.

### Lincoln *Lincs.*     *553Ge*
The Ancient Britons' town of Lindon was renamed Lindum by the Roman occupation forces, and, on development, was raised to colony status, giving Lindum Colonia as the root for the present name. In AD 48 a Roman military garrison was set up to command the meeting of two great highways, Ermine Street and Fosse Way.

WEST FRONT FRIEZE,
LINCOLN CATHEDRAL

*The west front of Lincoln Cathedral, one of the earliest Norman cathedrals in England, was built by Bishop Remigius between 1072 and 1092. It was enlarged in the following century, and a sculptured frieze showing scenes from the Old and New Testaments was added at the same time. This detail from the frieze, which runs above the niches, is from the panel of Noah building the ark, axe in hand.*

LINCOLN CATHEDRAL

*Lincoln became the centre of a bishopric in 1072, when the See was transferred from Dorchester (Oxfordshire). A cathedral was begun at once, but much of the present church dates from after an earthquake in 1185. It has been little altered since its completion about 1280. Lincoln has had one of the most varied successions of bishops of any English See. Among them were Alexander the Magnificent (1123–48), the illegitimate son of the influential royal servant, Bishop Roger of Salisbury, who was probably responsible for the Romanesque parts of the west front; St Hugh of Avalon (1186–*

*1200), an ascetic Carthusian, brought unwillingly from his monastery; and Robert Grosseteste (1235–53), a strong supporter of Oxford University in its early years, when it fell within the Diocese of Lincoln. Inside the cathedral, St Hugh's choir and the nave are impressive examples of early Gothic architecture, with fine columns of Purbeck stone; over the choir is a complicated system of arches—the 'crazy vaults of Lincoln'. To the east, the Angel Choir is one of the most heavily decorated of its period. The whole interior is dominated by the immense traceried window in the east end.*

CARDINAL'S HAT Situated at the corner of Grantham Street and High Street, a splendid example of a late 15th-century house. Named after Cardinal Wolsey, it was restored in 1953. Near the lower end of the Strait is a row of good timbered houses.

CASTLE Built on a Roman site by William the Conqueror in 1068; the surrounding ditches and banks enclosed nearly 14 acres of land. Entry was through the surviving eastern gateway, a structure which has a Norman tunnel-vault internally but a 15th-century façade. The castle's remains include a Norman gateway, part of a barbican and an early 19th-century inner gateway. The gaol, *c.* 1780, is now the Lincolnshire Record Office and has the largest collection of local records in England. The castle walls carry three interesting towers: to the south-east the Observatory Tower, *c.* 1400 (built by a prison governor for observing the stars as well as possible escapees); the Lucy Tower, a Norman shell-keep standing on a separate mound, *c.* 1200; and Cobb Hall, the small north-east tower *c.* 1400.

CATHEDRAL The original Norman cathedral was begun in 1072, and parts of this building remain at the west end of the present church, where three elaborate Norman portals are surmounted by a magnificent sculptured frieze which dates from *c.* 1145. The main cathedral is in Gothic style; the rebuilding of the choir was begun in 1192, and rebuilding of the western part of the church followed. The Angel Choir—so-called from its interior decoration—was added in 1256–80. Thereafter only small additions were made to the cathedral, which dominates the city and surrounding country; for instance, the towers were height-

ened. On the south side is a fine sculptured porch. The decagonal chapter house, on the north side, is the earliest Gothic polygonal chapter house in England. Great Tom of Lincoln—a sonorous 5 ton bell—hangs in the central tower. (See also p. 271.)

CATHEDRAL TREASURY Sponsored by the Worshipful Company of Goldsmiths and Silversmiths, the Treasury was opened in 1960 in the renovated 'Medicine Chapel' of the cathedral. It shows a changing collection of gold and silver plate from the diocese as well as a few permanent exhibits. The latter include medieval chalices and patens taken from the graves of the Bishops Grosseteste, Sutton and Gravesend. The Treasury also contains the cathedral's original of Magna Carta and the foundation charter of William the Conqueror.

CITY AND COUNTY MUSEUM The museum, which displays collections of armour, local archaeological finds with emphasis on Roman Lincoln, and natural history, is in an early 13th-century building, originally a church for the Greyfriars.

HIGH BRIDGE Built on one side of the bridge spanning the R. Witham are 16th-century timber-framed houses and shops; the bridge is one of the few examples of its kind in England.

HOUSE OF AARON THE JEW Situated at the corner of Steep Hill and Christ's Hospital Terrace, this 12th-century house is said to be the oldest inhabited dwelling in England; it takes its name from the original owner, a rich merchant. Lower down the hill is the better known Jew's House, of the same date, and one of the best known houses of its period in England.

JAMES STREET Contains two notable houses: Deloraine Court, whose Georgian façade hides a

NOLLEKENS *Venus and Cupid*

*Joseph Nollekens (1737–1823) carved this marble statue of Venus chiding Cupid for one of his chief patrons, Lord Yarborough. Nollekens, one of England's greatest portrait sculptors, worked for ten years in Rome, and it is for his severely Classical busts, like that of Dr Johnson in Westminster Abbey, that he is chiefly remembered. Much less well known are his statues of goddesses, but he probably considered them to embody his best work. Nollekens was probably the shrewdest businessman of English art, and amassed a fortune of £200,000. (Usher Art Gallery, Lincoln)*

Norman undercroft and a well panelled room dated 1602; and No. 7, the Burghersh Chantry, founded in 1485 for five priests, but now mainly mid-18th century.
JEW'S HOUSE In 12th-century England Jews could often afford to build themselves modest town houses of stone, for in the English economy then, Jews were essential as money-lenders and financiers because Christians were forbidden to lend money at interest. One of the greatest of the Jewish businessmen was Aaron the Jew of Lincoln. His operations were known to have extended over 25 counties from Kent to Cumberland. His clients included the King of Scotland and the Archbishop of Canterbury. It is not certain whether Aaron lived at the Jew's House, since a further 12th-century building traditionally attached to his name survives. Both houses are interesting reminders of the presence of Jews in 12th-century England. These stone houses were symbols of power and wealth, and they were also places of strength. The Jews were only too useful, but in return they were hated and up to their expulsion under Edward I in 1290, periodic anti-Jewish riots occurred.
ROMAN TOWN GATE Roman Lincoln (Lindum) began as a legionary fortress in the middle of the 1st century AD. By AD 77 the soldiers had gone and, *c.* AD 90, it was made a *colonia*, a settlement of time-served soldiers who formed a self-governing local community of importance. This *colonia* covered the site of the earlier fortress on the hill-top to the north of the Witham. Fragments of its stone wall are still visible. But the most important fragment, unique in Britain, is the Newport Arch which straddles the main road to the North out of the

town. The south face of this arch is the original Roman stone, though behind it there is much medieval reconstruction and the original north (outer) face has disappeared. The area of the *colonia* was later extended down the slope to the south. This too was walled, and the new south gate stood only a little way above the still-visible medieval gateway, the Stonebow. The city museum contains many remains from the Roman occupation.
STONEBOW AND GUILDHALL The Stonebow is a 13th- and 16th-century gateway with the guildhall above it: the whole is surrounded by a three-storey building. The hall is partly panelled with a magnificent open-timbered roof, contains good portraits and carries on the roof the Mote Bell. The oldest bell of its type in the country, dated 1371, it is still rung. The civic insignia and royal charters include a 14th-century fighting sword which may have belonged to Richard II.
USHER ART GALLERY The Usher Collection of watches, miniatures and porcelain, and the Peter de Wint Collection of oils, water-colours and drawings are the principal exhibits in the gallery. There are also portraits, relics, first editions and manuscripts of Alfred, Lord Tennyson. (See also pp. 274–5.)

**Lindisfarne Castle** See Holy Island.

**Lindisfarne Priory** See Holy Island.

**Lindores Abbey** *Fife.*      *562Ch*
The ruins of a Benedictine abbey founded in 1178.

**Lingfield** *Surrey*      *542Be*
CHURCH OF SS PETER AND PAUL 15th-century, but with slightly earlier work in the south-west of the building. The fittings are contemporary: font, screens, stalls with misericords, and lectern with a chained Bible. Among many brasses and monuments with effigies there is a good series of monuments to the Cobham family.

**Linlithgow** *W. Lothian*      *562Af*
CHURCH OF ST MICHAEL A large 15th-century building, with a west tower, transepts and three-sided apse. There are several sculptured slabs, two of which depict the Mocking of Christ and the Agony in the Garden.
PALACE The ruined palace where Mary, Queen of Scots was born on December 8, 1542. A royal manor has existed on this site since early in the 12th century. During the campaigns of Edward I in the early 14th century the area was fortified by a ditch and palisade. Edward used Linlithgow as a base of operations, particularly during the siege of Stirling Castle. However, it was retaken by the Scots *c.* 1313, and the fortifications were demolished. James I of Scotland began the present building in 1424 and the work continued into the 16th century, particularly under James V. By the late 16th century parts of the palace had become derelict and in 1607 the north side collapsed; it was repaired in 1618–20.

**Little Bytham** *Lincs.*      *553Gc*
CHURCH OF ST MEDARD The church incorporates Saxon work from the original building (in the south-east corner of the nave), and there is Norman work too. In the south chancel doorway is an interestingly carved tympanum, with a sunken circular medallion in its centre, which is said to have once contained the skull and arm-bone of St Medard, the patron saint of the church. On either side of this medallion is carved an eagle within a circle.

**Little Casterton** *Rutland*      *553Gb*
CHURCH OF ALL SAINTS A small church with a west bell-cote. It dates from the 12th century, and

An early 19th-century watch made by James Rigby of London. The gold and blue enamel case has a double border of half pearls set with brilliants and diamonds.

A French repeater watch of the late 18th century. The engine-turned case has an enamelled dial with a pierced design showing Venus receiving an apple from Cupid.

The chased gold outer case of this quarter repeater is set with diamonds, rubies and moss agate plaques; an early 18th-century watch made by Ferron of London.

The enamelled outer case of this watch depicts Venus rising from the sea. Made in Vienna in the late 17th century, the watch has a gilt and champlevé enamel dial.

This watch dates from the late 18th century; it was produced by Gregson of Paris. The outer case has an enamelled design showing Narcissus at the pool.

The gold outer case of this watch, made by Baillon of Paris in the late 18th century, has an enamelled miniature, 'Abraham offering Isaac', on its front.

has carvings of that date. Some 14th-century wall-painting remains, and there is a good medieval brass in the chancel of a man and his wife.

**Little Chesterford** *Essex* 548Ae
MANOR HOUSE FARM A rare surviving manor house of the early 13th century, with thick stone walls and arched doorways inside. An aisled timber-framed hall was added later, and there were 16th-century alterations.

**Little Coggeshall** *Essex* 548Cd
The remains of a Cistercian abbey of *c.* 1140, interesting for the early use of brickwork. The church has disappeared, and after the Reformation a house was built into the monastic ruins, dated 1581. The Abbey Gate Chapel of St Nicholas survives as a rectangular building of *c.* 1225.

**Littlecote** *Wilts.* 541Gg
A gabled Elizabethan manor house, of Tudor origin (1490–1520), Littlecote has a splendid great

hall displaying Cromwellian armour, and a long gallery. It contains period panelling and plaster-work, tapestries and carpets. There are walled gardens in the grounds.

**Little Dunmow** *Essex* 548Bd
CHURCH OF ST MARY The remnants of an early 12th-century Augustinian priory church, which was once cruciform with a central tower; all that remains is the 13th-century south chapel, or Lady Chapel. The arcade along the north wall would have been the south arcade of the chancel of the former church. Monuments include one by Thomas Adye, 1753.

**Little Gaddesden** *Herts.* 547Hd
A turreted, stone Elizabethan house of 1576, with stone-mullioned windows, fine fire-places and wall-paintings of the period. The house contains a collection of early keyboard musical instruments. The gardens are particularly noted for their ornamental yew hedges.

A French musical watch of the late 18th century. The gold case is set with pearl borders and on the back is an enamelled design of moving figures on a stage.

This late 18th-century French watch is in the form of a mandolin. The gold case is embellished with pearls and enamels.

A late 18th-century French repeater striking on wire gongs. The gold case has mechanical figures in vari-coloured gold on the face and an engine-turned back.

A quarter repeater made by Justin Vulliamy in London during the late 18th century. An enamelled miniature of 'Hope nursing Love', after Reynolds, decorates the case.

W. Ilbery of London made this early 19th-century watch for the Chinese market. Its gold case has an enamelled miniature of girls and a youth butterfly hunting.

This watch, hall-marked London, 1824/5, was made by Viner and Co. The chased vari-coloured gold case is set with 54 emeralds and the watch has a cylinder movement.

**Little Gidding** *Hunts.* 547Hg
Outside the door of the small church in the village is the table-tomb of Nicholas Ferrar, whose family manor house (now destroyed) stood near by. Nicholas Ferrar (1592–1637) was a friend of religious poets John Donne and George Herbert. He founded a religious community known as the Protestant Nunnery, which was used by T. S. Eliot as an example of achieved spiritual life in the last of his 'Four Quartets' entitled 'Little Gidding'.

**Little Malvern** *Worcs.* 546Be
CHURCH OF ST GILES There was a 12th-century Benedictine monastery here, and the adjoining court incorporates part of its domestic buildings, but all that remains of the church is the central tower and east end, dating from the 15th century. The 15th-century stained glass in the east window depicts Edward IV and his family. Much of the 15th-century floor tiling remains, and there are also misericords.

**Little Maplestead** *Essex* 548Ce
CHURCH OF ST JOHN THE BAPTIST One of the five round churches of England, built *c.* 1340 by the Knights Hospitaller. The chancel projecting towards the east has an apse, and dates from the same period.

**Little Moreton Hall** *Cheshire* 552Bd
A tall, moated house, built between 1559 and 1580, and scarcely changed since. The outside is a mass of carved gables; ornate windows project from the upper storeys, and door and corner posts are carved. Inside, the fireplaces are heraldically carved, and the long gallery retains its original panelling; contemporary oak furniture and pewter may be seen.

**Little Sodbury Manor** *Glos.* 546Bb
A 15th-century mansion built for Sir John Welsh; its outstanding feature is the great hall. The northwest wing was destroyed by fire in 1702.

# THE ANGLICAN CATHEDRAL, LIVERPOOL

EXTERIOR *When it is finished—possibly in the mid-1970's—this cathedral will be the second largest in the world, surpassed in size only by St Peter's, Rome. Standing on high ground overlooking the Mersey, the massive, towering cathedral is the overpowering achievement of one man: Sir Giles Gilbert Scott, grandson of Sir George Gilbert Scott, architect of the Albert Memorial. Scott was 22 when, in 1901, he won a competition to design it. Building began in 1903, but two World Wars and rising costs delayed progress, and by the time Scott died, in 1960, his original design had been modified several times.*

THE HIGH ALTAR *The interior of Scott's cathedral lacks the rich ornamentation of Victorian Gothic architecture; he has re-interpreted Gothic forms to create an atmosphere of vastness, grandeur and silence, rather than of gloom. The massive piers seem to lose themselves in the darkness as they soar uninterrupted towards the lofty vaults. The windows, set in thick walls, admit only glimmerings of light. Liverpool will probably be the last cathedral in Britain to be built entirely of stone; it may also, perhaps, turn out to be the finest ecclesiastical building of the 20th century—economic difficulties and the decline of the mason's craft have put a stop to cathedral-building on such a gigantic scale.*

**Little Stanmore** *Greater London* 547Jc
CHURCH OF ST LAWRENCE (WHITCHURCH) There is a 16th-century west tower, but the rest of the church dates from the early 18th century when it was rebuilt by the Duke of Chandos, whose great house by Talman was near by. There are wall-paintings by Louis Laguerre and Antonio Bellucci, and monuments in the Chandos Mausoleum, the largest being that of the duke by Andrew Carpentier. The furnishings include contemporary pews, a west gallery, and an organ on which Handel is supposed to have played.

**Littleton** *Surrey* 542Af
CHURCH OF ST MARY MAGDALENE The church is of the 13th century, with additions right through to the 18th century. The west tower is brick. There are good furnishings from the 15th to the 18th century.

**Little Walsingham** *Norfolk* 554Bc
The site of the famous Shrine of Our Lady of Walsingham, one of the two chief centres of pilgrimage in England from 1153 until the Reformation. The ruins of the Augustinian priory which took care of the shrine include the gateway of *c.* 1440 and the east window of the priory church, *c.* 1380. The exact site of the shrine was probably just north of this church. A revival of pilgrimage in recent times has centred on the Slipper Chapel, a mile to the south of the village, and on the Anglican shrine built 1931–7.
The village has many worthwhile houses in the Common Place (which has a Pump House of *c.* 1550 topped by a brazier), High Street and Market Place. In part of the priory ruins is Abbey House, late 18th century. On the Fakenham road are the ruins of the Franciscan (Greyfriars) friary of 1347.

**Little Wymondley** *Herts.* 547Jd
WYMONDLEY HALL An early 17th-century timber-framed house with a fine group of Elizabethan chimneys.
WYMONDLEY PRIORY A medieval barn 100 ft long and 40 ft wide, with the remains of 13th-century arches in the farmhouse alongside.

**Liverpool** *Lancs.* 551Jf
The city holds a charter granted by King John in 1207. It had a Norman castle (on the site of the present Queen Victoria memorial) the ruins of which were removed in 1725. At the time of the first Stuarts the population was only 1000, but by the early 18th century the town had a thriving trade mainly connected with the West Indies, and was also concerned with the slave trade. The coming of the railways altered Liverpool entirely, and it was from this port that the first ocean steamship line operated across the Atlantic in 1840.
Sudley Gallery, an early 19th-century merchant's house, supplements the treasures of the Walker Art Gallery. The Picton, Hornby and Brown libraries together have more than 200,000 volumes. Liverpool University originated with University College (1881), which was raised by royal charter in 1903 to full university status. The city has two cathedrals, Anglican and Roman Catholic.
ANGLICAN CATHEDRAL The red sandstone cathedral of Liverpool was begun in 1903 by Sir Giles Gilbert Scott. More than half a century later the cathedral is still incomplete; the west end and one bay of the nave have still to be built. Although the style is Classical Greek, Scott's design is essentially original, the dominant feature being the large central tower. In 1925 Scott himself laid the last stone of the 173 ft high tower, which has double transepts on either side. The first part of

THE ROMAN CATHOLIC
CATHEDRAL, LIVERPOOL

*This cathedral to Christ the King, the newest cathedral in the British Isles, was consecrated in May 1967. A vast circular building set on a hill, it was achieved at the third attempt. Augustus Welby Pugin designed the first cathedral in 1853, but only the Lady Chapel was built. In 1928 Sir Edwin Lutyens conceived an enormous Classical domed building; work started but was abandoned at the outbreak of the Second World War when only the crypt was completed. After the war, Lutyens' design was simplified but abandoned because of the astronomical cost involved. About 1960, Cardinal Heenan, Archbishop of Liverpool, revived the idea of a cathedral and Sir Frederick Gibberd's design was chosen from 300 competition entries. The building rises from a large concrete base over Lutyens' crypt. The altar is in the centre and the congregation is able to participate in services to a greater extent than in a conventional cathedral.*

the cathedral to be finished was the Lady Chapel, which was consecrated in 1910. It is estimated that completion will be in the 1970's.
BLUECOAT CHAMBERS An example of Queen Anne architecture, built in 1717, the house was acquired in 1927 as a centre for painters, sculptors, musicians and the arts generally under the supervision of the Bluecoat Society of Arts. (By appointment.)
CITY MUSEUM The original building, designed by John Weightman, was destroyed by fire in 1941. Phase one of the rebuilding, opened in 1966, includes some of the museum's treasures, an aquarium and items of local history. (See p. 279.)
HORNBY LIBRARY Poems by Johnson and Cowper, letters from Nelson, Byron, Gladstone and Verdi, and signatures of many British monarchs, are part of the autograph collection in this extensive library. The book collection contains about 8000 rare books, and there are many manuscripts, book illustrations (the collection is especially rich in French illustrated books), prints and examples of bookbinding and printing.

ERCOLE: PIETÀ *Ercole de Roberti, who lived about 1450–96, belonged to the northern Italian school at Ferrara; but he softened the harshness of the Ferrarese style—the petrified landscapes, grimacing faces, contorted figures. However, the style has still left its mark here, in for example the hard, jagged outline of the Virgin's robe. The Pietà—Christ's body lying across His mother's knees—is a theme which originated in Germany in the 13th century. Ercole's painting, which was in the Church of San Giovanni in Monte at Bologna, is similar in arrangement to the marble Pietà at St Peter's, which was the masterpiece of Michelangelo's early period. It is tempting to assume that Michelangelo saw this painting during his stay in Bologna in 1494–5. (Walker Art Gallery)*

LE HONGRE: CUPID *This intimate, informal bronze figure is one of the rare examples of French baroque sculpture in Britain. It is by Étienne le Hongre (1628–90), one of the small army of artists employed on the decoration of Versailles for Louis XIV. Le Hongre lived and had his workshop in the Palace of the Louvre in Paris. (Walker Art Gallery)*

JOHN THE BAPTIST *A striking Byzantine ivory,
[sho]wing the Court style of Constantinople at its most
[refi]ned. The Baptist holds a scroll which says, in
[Gr]eek: 'Behold the Lamb of God, who taketh away
[the] sins of the world.' The figure and scroll date from
[the] early 11th century, but the background is modern
[as t]he original one was lost. (City Museum)*

KINGSTON BROOCH *This great gold brooch, 3·3 in.
across, is the finest example of the work of the 'Kentish
School' of Anglo-Saxon jewellers. It belongs to the
second half of the 7th century, and the technique is
known as 'cloisonné'—the jewels, flat pieces of red
garnet and blue lapis lazuli, are set in small prepared
cells, the cloisons. (City Museum)*

[MA]RTINI: CHRIST DISCOVERED IN THE TEMPLE
*[Th]e 14th-century Sienese school reached its zenith in
[the] work of Simone Martini (1284–1344). His figures
[hav]e a new suppleness and grace. This picture, dated
[134]2, was painted after he had reached Avignon, then
[the] seat of the Papacy. His work there had an important
[infl]uence on the development of the sophisticated
['Int]ernational Gothic' style. (Walker Art Gallery)*

HAMADA VASE *Shoji Hamada (b. 1892) is a
Japanese potter whose stoneware, drawing on Japanese
peasant traditions, combines formal vigour with highly
sensitive brushwork. He worked in England from 1920
until 1923, and on returning to Japan, despite a growing
reputation, hired himself out as a pottery worker in the
village of Mashiko. It was not until 1931 that he
established his own kiln. (Walker Art Gallery)*

## PLAS NEWYDD, LLANGOLLEN

*Famous as the home of the 'Ladies of Llangollen', two Irishwomen who left their native land in 1778 with their maid, Mary Carryl, and settled in Wales. They lived in the house for some 50 years, and their powers of conversation, coupled with a reputation for eccentricity, drew scores of interesting visitors. The playwright Sheridan, the statesmen Burke, Castlereagh and Canning, emigrés from the French Revolution, the Duke of Wellington, Sir Walter Scott and William Wordsworth were all drawn to this beautiful but out-of-the-way spot by the fascination of the 'Ladies'. The ruined castle on the hill is Dinas Bran.*

ROMAN CATHOLIC CATHEDRAL The circular cathedral was consecrated in 1967; its dominant feature is the central lantern tower with slender, spiky pinnacles, some 290 ft high, above an aluminium roof. This lantern, with stained glass by John Piper and Patrick Reyntiens (who also worked on Coventry Cathedral) illuminates the interior of the cathedral with a pool of light over the central altar. Radiating from the walls are chapels of various shapes, with stained glass windows and austere ornament. At the west is a wedge-shaped belfry-cum-porch, 90 ft high, forming the principal entrance. (See p. 277.)

ST GEORGE'S HALL Liverpool possesses one of the great Victorian Classical buildings—St George's Hall, masterpiece of the young architect, Harvey Lonsdale Elmes. He began work on it in 1842, but died at the age of 34 in 1847, long before the project was finished. The great vault was the work of Sir Robert Rawlinson, to Elmes's designs, and C. R. Cockerell completed the exterior and the interior decoration. St George's Hall, inaugurated in 1854, stands in the centre of the city. The Hall is of Classical Greek design; the façade has a great portico of Corinthian columns, and is further decorated with partly free-standing square piers of the same order. There is another, smaller portico of columns at the south end of the Hall, while the north end is semicircular.

SPEKE HALL One of the finest Elizabethan half-timbered houses in the country. It was built around a courtyard in 1530–98 and was formerly moated. Internally it is like a maze, with secret chambers and hideaways. The great hall contains elaborate 16th- and 17th-century plasterwork, and in the great parlour is a representation of a local giant, reputed to have been nearly 10 ft tall. The house was built by the Norris family, who owned it until 1797. Between 1720 and 1797 it was rented to local farmers, but was restored and refurnished by 1812.

TOWN HALL The present building was completed in 1754 to the design of John Wood of Bath. The original building was largely destroyed by fire in 1795; immediate rebuilding on the original idea was begun, a council chamber being added in 1811. On a newly devised dome, Felix Rossi's statue of Minerva was mounted in 1802.

WALKER ART GALLERY Named after Sir Andrew Barclay Walker, who donated the money for its construction. It has a notable collection of European and English paintings, including work by the Pre-Raphaelites; there are 20th-century paintings and sculptures. (See pp. 278–9.)

**Llananno** *Rad.*                                545Hf
CHURCH A little church with an extravagant Perpendicular rood screen with much carved foliage decoration; the gallery has a row of canopied niches containing carved figures.

**Llandaff** *Glam.*                               545Jb
CATHEDRAL The first church here was probably built in the 6th century, but the present building was founded during the early 12th century. There are some remains of this early work, but most of the present cathedral is Early English and Decorated Gothic. After the Reformation the building lost its roofs, and the south-west tower collapsed. In the 19th century the building was restored, and a new tower and spire built, but even then the cathedral's troubles were not over, for it was bombed during the Second World War. This damage has now been repaired. A new feature of the interior is the great concrete arch in the nave supporting the organ, and a figure of Christ by Sir Jacob Epstein.

**Llandegai** *Caern.*                             550Ee
A model village built by Lord Penrhyn during the first half of the 19th century. *Cottages ornée* and two school-rooms are grouped round the entrance to the medieval parish church.

**Llandegley** *Rad.*                              545Jf
THE PALES There are few old Quaker Meeting Houses in Wales, and this tiny building, dated 1745, is one of the most attractive. A simple rectangular building is divided by a screen into a school-room and meeting-room. Most of the seating is original, and the roof is still covered with thatch.

**Llandrindod Wells** *Rad.*                       545Hf
The small red-brick town of Llandrindod Wells is one of three adjacent small inland spas which were popular and prosperous in mid-Victorian Britain. The town has a good museum and an excellent small private art gallery.

**Llandwrog** *Caern.* 550Ed
CHURCH OF ST TWROG A mid-19th-century
church, but among its 18th-century monuments is
one of *c.* 1749 with a good bust—almost certainly
the work of Sir Henry Cheere.

**Llanegryn** *Merioneth.* 550Eb
CHURCH The pride of the church is its rood screen
with the original wide gallery on top, decorated
with a wealth of delicate carving, *c.* 1520. There is
also a Norman font.

**Llanengan** *Caern.* 550Dc
CHURCH This beautiful and large church stands on
the route to Bardsey Island for pilgrims from the
south. Doubtless it became wealthy as a consequence, and in the later medieval period, from
which most of the building dates, it became a place
of pilgrimage itself. Many of the churches in Lleyn
have double aisles (one, Llangwnadl, has three):
this has in addition a fine tower dated 1534, and a
porch. Internally the original roofs survive, as does
one of the rood screens and lofts; the second screen
has lost its loft. In addition there are medieval stalls
and good communion rails. A quaint feature is the
outlet of a latrine which was set in the tower.
Buried outside the east wall is a Roman Catholic
priest, Fr Hughes, who attempted to re-establish a
monastery on St Tudwal's East Island some 2 miles
off Abersoch. This island has been partly excavated, but all that can be seen is the plan of a
medieval hall similar to that found on Burry
Holms, Glamorgan, and an 18th-century building
which was erected across the west end of the
medieval church.

**Llangollen** *Denb.* 551Hd
An old town on the R. Dee in the beautiful Vale of
Llangollen, described by George Borrow in *Wild
Wales.* The river is spanned by a fine 14th-century
stone bridge built by a Bishop of St Asaph. Every
summer since 1947 the International Eisteddfod
has been held in the town. The roof of St Gollen's
church is carved with angels, flowers and animals,
and is reputed to have been brought from nearby
Valle Crucis Abbey—a 13th-century Cistercian
foundation now in ruins. On a hill overlooking
the town are the remains of Castell Dinas Bran.
PLAS NEWYDD An 18th-century black and white
house, once the home of the 'Ladies of Llangollen'.

**Llanmelin** *Mon.* 546Ac
Llanmelin stands on a spur of hill close to and
overlooking Caerwent. Defended by stone-faced
multiple banks, with additional earthworks at one
point, it was occupied for some two centuries. It
was probably the chief settlement of the Silures
tribe and, after the firm establishment of Roman
government in South Wales, the new cantonal
town was placed in the open country below, as was
done in so many tribal areas.

**Llanrhydd** *Denb.* 551Hd
CHURCH OF ST MEUGAN A simple church about a
mile from Ruthin. There is a 15th-century roof
and screen, and a 17th-century pulpit. Monuments
include one of the 17th century, with kneeling
figures, and there is 19th-century stained glass.

**Llanrwst** *Denb.* 551Hd
CHURCH The church was damaged during the late
15th century and rebuilt towards the end of the
17th century. Like some other Welsh churches it
possesses a good rood screen with its original gallery. There is a 17th-century mausoleum containing monuments.

**Llanrwst Bridge** *Caern.* 550Fe
Until 1826, when Telford's suspension bridge at
Conway was opened, this was the major bridge

over the R. Conway. It consists of a central
segmental arch 60 ft high, flanked by slightly
lower ones, 44 ft high. The most beautiful bridge
in North Wales, it was built in 1636, and the
western arch, which has a poorer foundation than
that on the Denbighshire side, has been rebuilt at
least once.

**Llanthony Priory** *Mon.* 545Jd
The ruins of a priory founded *c.* 1108 for Augustinian canons in the Honddu Valley in the Black
Mountains. The present buildings are early 13th
century, and much of the church remains.

**Llantwit Major** *Glam.* 545Hb
The centre of this small town contains a number of
attractive stone houses dating from medieval times
to the 18th century. The parish church, a complicated building, stands on or near the site of an
important Celtic monastery, and in it are preserved some good pre-Conquest memorials.

**Llanvihangel Crucorney** *Mon.* 546Ac
LLANVIHANGEL COURT A gabled Elizabethan
manor house, the front of which was rebuilt in
1559. The interior was remodelled in 1660. In the
gardens is a long avenue of fir trees.

**Lochinch Castle** *Wig.* 556Bg
A 19th-century building in Scottish baronial style
set in landscaped gardens on a peninsular flanked
by the White and the Black Lochs. Near by are the
ruins of Castle Kennedy, the Kennedy Clan's
stronghold, which was erected in the reign of
James IV (1473–1513).

**Loch Leven Castle** *Kinross.* 562Bg
Rugged ruins of a 15th-century fortress set on an
island in Loch Leven. William Douglas helped
Mary, Queen of Scots escape from it in 1568 after a
year of imprisonment.

**Lochnaw Castle** *Wig.* 556Bg
This is the ancient home of the Agnew family,
who were hereditary sheriffs of Galloway for 300
years. It is a picturesque building, originally built
in 1426, in an area famous for its rhododendrons.

**Lockington** *Yorks.* 558Fb
CHURCH OF ST MARY THE VIRGIN Originally
Norman, with later additions, the church has a
17th-century pulpit and an 18th-century screen.
There is a Norman chancel arch and doorway.
Inside is much display of heraldry, some old glass
and a 17th-century monument.

**Lockleys** *Herts.* 547Jc
A red-brick Georgian mansion (*c.* 1720) now used
as a school.

**Loddon** *Norfolk* 554Db
CHURCH OF THE HOLY TRINITY A 15th-century
church, with large clerestory, west tower, vaults
and a two-storey south porch with stair-turret.
The pulpit is Jacobean. Of the monuments and
brasses, the most notable is the reclining Lady
Williamson (*d.* 1684) in marble.

**Logan Gardens** *Wig.* 556Bf
Logan House lies half-way down the Mull of
Galloway. The proximity of the Gulf Stream and
the sheltered position on Luce Bay create a temperate, frost-free climate. During the last century
the old walled gardens were developed into a sub-
tropical garden, first by the McDouall brothers
and then by R. O. Hambro. There is a collection,
rare in the British Isles, of sub-tropical shrubs and
trees. Near the lily pond are clusters of giant New
Zealand palm trees and tall species and hybrids of
rhododendrons. Elsewhere Australian tree-ferns
thrive together with fine Chinese hydrangeas, notable for their exquisite foliage.

# LONDON

## *Proud pageant of the nation's wealth*

At the heart of the sprawling London conurbation are two cities which had distinct beginnings and have always had different roles, characters and styles. The City of London is the crowded centre of Britain's trade and finance; Westminster is the home of the Court, government and high society.

Underlining them both is the Thames, England's major outlet to the sea, and the reason why the capital is where it is.

A little lump of a hill (later Cornhill), after miles of marshland along the river banks, gave the invading Romans in AD 43 a first defensible stronghold at the lowest point where the river was narrow enough to be bridged; there has been a London Bridge near by ever since. Roman London grew with astounding speed, though it

was sacked in its infancy, in AD 60, by Queen Boadicea. Less than 100 years later it was a walled city, with its own forum and the largest known basilica outside Rome, on the site of the modern Leadenhall Market. None of the original wall survives above ground level, but excavations have revealed some important Roman remains, including the Temple of Mithras, unearthed on a Walbrook building site in 1954.

After the Roman evacuation, London was settled by the Saxons, sacked by the Danes and rebuilt by Alfred—only to be sacked again by the Danes. Little of Saxon London remains above ground, though traces of a recently-discovered Saxon church can be seen in the crypt of St Bride's, Fleet Street.

To find the medieval City of London is almost an archaeological pursuit. Most of it was destroyed in the Great Fire in 1666, giving a young inventor and astronomer, Christopher Wren, the chance to show his genius as an architect. As the builder of St Paul's Cathedral, the Monument to the Fire, and 51 City churches, Wren inspired a new generation of architects and craftsmen.

The City today is a complex of modern sky-scrapers and imposing Victorian and Edwardian masonry—the handsome cladding of affluent commerce; but the ground plan of medieval London still shows through, with some of the streets little wider than alleys. North of the Fire area a few churches of the Middle Ages and the Tudor period can be found more or less intact, such as Great St Helen's. But some churches which had survived the Fire were gutted in the later tragedy of the Blitz.

The Tower of London was the most notable building to survive the Fire. Built by the Normans —and built to last—as fortress, prison and palace all in one, the Tower is now the oldest major monument in London.

Most of the City's great public buildings have tended to re-shape themselves through the centuries. The Royal Exchange, for example, built in 1565, was burnt down twice, and finally rebuilt in 1844 to present a portico of gigantic columns as the proud face of the Victorian empire.

Most of the Halls of the City Livery Companies, originally guilds of master craftsmen, have been rebuilt several times since the Middle Ages; but they still house a wealth of antique furnishings, pictures and plate. Particular streets came to be associated with particular crafts and trades. The Grocers were to be found in Soper's Lane (now Queen Street), the Merchant Taylors in Birchin Lane, the Drapers in Candlewick. The Fishmongers were at Billingsgate, and the Fishmongers Company still controls Billingsgate market, with officers known as 'fish meters' checking on the freshness of the wares.

The Goldsmiths had the authority of a royal proclamation for their presence in Cheapside and Lombard Street. This was a form of medieval 'window dressing': Cheapside was the highway into London for foreigners coming from the

docks, and the idea was to impress them with the taste and wealth of the capital.

In cracks in the present commercial masonry more convivial needs are met by the lively City chop-houses and taverns. Such are Simpson's, down Ball Court, and the George and Vulture (Mr Pickwick's pub, but Chaucer knew it too, when it was only the George).

The border between the City and Westminster is marked by a strip of gardens, courts, lawns and passages running north from the Thames for about three-quarters of a mile. This is legal London, the Inns of Court where the lawyers work—and some still live.

To the west is Westminster, with an antiquity almost as venerable as that of the City. There was a small Roman settlement there, but its national importance began with Edward the Confessor, who started rebuilding Westminster Abbey *c.* 1050. For nearly 1000 years, and almost without a break, Westminster has remained the site of the Court and the seat of government. William III moved his court to Kensington, but the Georges moved back to Westminster—to St James's Palace. And Queen Victoria finally settled at Buckingham Palace.

By the mid-18th century the Prime Minister was established in what is now Downing Street; and in time, the apparatus of government, the Civil Service, absorbed virtually the whole of Whitehall. The present buildings housing the great departments of State, such as the Home Office and the Foreign Office, mostly date from the confident mid-Victorian era.

About half of London is built on land held under lease—a system begun by the 4th Earl of Southampton in 1660, when he laid out Bloomsbury Square as a speculative development.

Speculative building had started 29 years earlier, when the Earl of Bedford was granted a licence to build on Covent Garden, once the garden of Westminster Abbey's convent. The earl commissioned Inigo Jones as his architect; London acquired its first square, and the Russells an investment that remained in the family until 1914.

After the Restoration (1660), the high servants of the Crown moved into the area around St James's. The Earl of St Albans developed St James's Square, the first of the great squares of the West End. Grosvenor Square was started in 1725, on land which had been the country estate of Sir Thomas Grosvenor. Lord Edward Harley and Lady Henrietta Cavendish developed Cavendish Square with the help of John Prince, the self-styled 'Prince of Builders'. Among other West End squares of this period were Hanover, Soho and Bedford. In the 19th century, a further expansion created the stuccoed opulence of Belgravia.

What Wren had been to the City, John Nash (1752–1835) was to the West End. In an age of patrons he had the greatest patron of all—the Prince Regent (later George IV), who gave Nash the chance to set about town-planning on an ambitious scale. Between 1810 and 1830 he planned Regent's Park (from a rough heathland belonging to the Duke of Portland), Waterloo Place, Carlton House Terrace and Regent Street.

Nash's buildings in Regent Street have vanished almost entirely, but the theatrical scale of his conception can be assessed from surviving terraces at Carlton House and round Regent's Park. With Wren, he is perhaps the greatest of those artists and craftsmen who, finding that London has always offered them the best patronage and livelihood, have responded generously to make it the unique and fascinating city it is.

# LONDON GAZETTEER

The sites described here are all in the main
metropolitan area, and are listed alphabetically
with their addresses. At the end of the section are picture spreads
on the major museums and art galleries.

ALBERT MEMORIAL (KENSINGTON GARDENS, W8) The vast monument to the Prince Consort of Queen Victoria was designed by George Gilbert Scott, who was later knighted for this achievement. Scott based his design for the huge tabernacle on the Eleanor crosses (crosses erected by Edward I to mark his wife's funeral route from Nottingham to London) and nearly ten years were spent on erecting the 175 ft high memorial. The shrine is a metal construction, lavishly ornamented with mosaics, gilt, precious metals and enamels, and embellished with extravagant sculptures by the foremost artists of the Victorian period. The monument was completed in 1876.

APOTHECARIES' HALL (BLACKFRIARS LANE, EC4) The Apothecaries' Society, one of the City livery companies, was founded in 1606 under a charter from James I and had the monopoly of buying and selling drugs within the City of London. Their hall was built in 1670 and renovated in 1786. Through the entrance arch, with its red and gold coat of arms, is a charming courtyard, quiet in

contrast to the noise of Blackfriars traffic outside. Inside the brick building the courtroom has some fine old panelling and some interesting pictures, including a life-size sketch of John Hunter the surgeon, by Sir Joshua Reynolds, and portraits of James I and Charles I.

APSLEY HOUSE See Hyde Park Corner and Wellington Museum.

ARTS COUNCIL GALLERY (ST JAMES'S SQUARE, SW1) The house where the Arts Council holds temporary exhibitions of British and foreign art is a reconstruction—following a fire in 1725—of a house built in 1675 by Nicholas Barbon. It contains 18th-century mouldings and plasterwork.

BANQUETING HOUSE (WHITEHALL, SW1) Cardinal Wolsey's house by the Thames was appropriated by Henry VIII after the cardinal's fall from power. It was enlarged by Henry and remained a royal residence until the late 17th century when William III preferred life away from London at Kensington Palace or Hampton Court. After a fire in 1619, Inigo Jones built the present Banqueting

## ALBERT MEMORIAL

*In 1861 the Prince Consort died and Queen Victoria invited proposals for a national monument. The winning design by Gilbert Scott includes a bronze figure of the Prince holding a catalogue from the Great Exhibition.*

## BANQUETING HOUSE

*The Double-cube Room in the Banqueting House is 110 ft long, 55 ft wide and 55 ft high. The magnificent ceiling was painted by Peter Paul Rubens for Charles I in 1635. Rubens received £3000 for the work and was knighted four years later. The subjects of the ceiling panels represent the 'Apotheosis of James I' and the 'Union of England and Scotland'.*

House on the site. The building is in severe Classical style, with a flat roof surrounded by a balustrade. George I converted it into a royal chapel, and in 1894 the building became the Royal United Services Museum. It has been restored, and has reverted to its original purpose.

BEDFORD PARK (W4) London's first garden suburb, which influenced all similar developments in the country. It was begun in the late 19th century by Jonathan Carr, a merchant, who disliked the current outward spread of London in rows of streets and houses. Carr chose Edward Godwin, the architect who designed Northampton Town Hall, and Norman Shaw, designer of London's former police headquarters at New Scotland Yard, as his architects. They laid out the site to take advantage of the existing trees; houses, a church, an inn and an art school were built, centred on South Parade.

BRITISH MUSEUM (MUSEUM STREET, WC1) Perhaps the world's greatest museum, founded in 1753, and having as its basis the collections of Sir Robert Cotton, the antiquary and book collector (*d.* 1631); it is responsible for the national library (a copyright library to which a copy of every book, periodical, newspaper and pamphlet must by law be sent). With the space restricted in the building designed by Sir Robert Smirke and built between 1823 and 1850, many priceless parts of the vast archaeological and ethnographical collections are held in storage and only rarely displayed to the public. (See pp. 313–17.)

BRITISH MUSEUM (NATURAL HISTORY) (CROMWELL ROAD, SW7) Opened in 1880 in a building designed by Alfred Waterhouse, the museum contains five principle collections embracing the history of plants, minerals and the animal kingdom. These range from the Whale Gallery's 91 ft model of a blue whale to the Botanical Gallery's section on insect-eating plants. A special exhibit also illustrates the evolution of Man. (See pp. 318–19.)

BRITISH THEATRE MUSEUM Concerned with all aspects of the theatre, the museum contains a very wide selection of letters and original manuscripts from actors, writers and theatre-managers, prompt scripts, records, diaries, address books and scrap books. One of the most complete of the collections devoted to individual actors, actresses and dramatists is the Henry Irving archive, consisting of some 4000 items, among them telegrams of condolence to the great actor from the Royal Family at the time of his illness. Other figures similarly treated include Herbert Beerbohm Tree, Sir James Barrie, Harley Granville-Barker and Diaghilev. Among the costumes displayed is that worn by Nijinsky for the Diaghilev Ballet's first performance of *Les Biches* in Monte Carlo, 1924. There are photographs of stage personalities and of all Old Vic productions of 1931–9. Among many theatrical articles is the dressing table designed for Sarah Siddons by Sheraton in 1760.

BROOMFIELD HOUSE MUSEUM (BROOMFIELD PARK, N13) A late 17th-century building, which has since been altered, containing a mural painting and ceiling by Gerard Lanscroon (early 18th century). Collections of local and natural history are on exhibition.

BUCKINGHAM PALACE The Queen's London residence, where James I's mulberry orchard once grew. It was built by the Duke of Buckingham and Chandos, and bought by George III in 1761; in 1826–30 John Nash made alterations for George IV, and further alterations were made for Queen

Victoria and George V, who employed Sir Aston Webb to reface the east front in 1913. The state apartments are never open to the public.

The Queen's Gallery, once the chapel of Buckingham Palace, shows a selection of paintings and other works of art from the royal collections.

CARLYLE'S HOUSE (CHEYNE ROW, SW3) This house, built in 1708, is a fine example of an 18th-century town house. It is much as it was when Thomas Carlyle and his wife Jane lived there from 1834 to 1865 and were visited by Dickens, Thackeray, Browning, Tennyson and other eminent Victorians. Many of the Carlyles' letters, personal possessions and furniture are preserved, including an early piano played by Chopin and the desk at which Carlyle wrote all his books.

CENOTAPH, THE (WHITEHALL, SW1) The National Memorial to the dead of both wars was designed by Sir Edwin Lutyens, and unveiled in 1920. Its name in Greek means 'the empty tomb'.

CHARLES II STATUE (CHELSEA HOSPITAL, SW3) In the main court a bronze statue by Grinling Gibbons honours the founder of the hospital. On May 29 (Oak Apple Day and also Charles II's birthday) the statue is decorated with oak leaves in memory of the day after the Battle of Worcester (1651) when Charles escaped capture by hiding in an oak tree at Boscobel House.

CHARTERHOUSE, THE (CHARTERHOUSE SQUARE, EC1) Founded as a Carthusian monastery in 1371, the buildings became a private dwelling after the Dissolution of the monasteries in 1537. Thomas Sutton bought them in 1611 and endowed them as a charitable foundation; part of the foundation became a school and part a 'hospital' for gentleman pensioners. The school moved to Godalming, Surrey, in 1872, but about 40 'brethren'—single men over 60 who were formerly officers or professional men—remain at Charterhouse. The buildings, mainly of 16th-century origin, were badly bombed in 1941. In 1947-9 excavations were possible around them and the original monastic plan, much overlain since the Dissolution, was discovered. The buildings themselves, which formed the 16th-century manor house, have been carefully restored. They include an Early English great hall and a great chamber dating from 1571. In the chapel is the tomb of Thomas Sutton. Wash-House Court is the best preserved of the earlier monastic buildings. (Interior by appointment.)

CHISWICK HOUSE (BURLINGTON LANE, W4) Chiswick House was built in 1725 for the Earl of Burlington to his own designs. Lord Burlington became the patron of the Palladian school of architecture, whose most prominent members were the architects Colin Campbell and William Kent.

The partnership of Lord Burlington and William Kent produced the Palladian villa, Chiswick House, in 1725-9. Of two storeys, the upper is the principal floor, and is approached through a great portico, supported by columns and with a pediment above the entablature. Near the portico are decaying statues of Palladio and Inigo Jones, carved by Rysbrack from designs by Kent. In 1788 two wings were added by James Wyatt.

The villa contains interior decorations by William Kent, and paintings by Kneller, Ferdinand Elle, Guido Reni, Anthonie Schooyans, Danielo da Volterra, Dobson, Kent and Sebastiano Ricci; adjoining it is the Summer Parlour, built some time before the villa by Colin Campbell, the Earl of Burlington's first guide and tutor. In the 18th century the house was a popular meeting place for poets, artists, aristocrats and statesmen.

CHRIST CHURCH (COMMERCIAL STREET, E1) Built between 1723 and 1729, this is one of Nicholas Hawksmoor's East London churches, and has a huge tower with spire. Among the monuments is a statue of a former Lord Mayor of London by John Flaxman.

CHURCH OF ALL HALLOWS BARKING BY THE TOWER (GREAT TOWER STREET, EC3) Of Saxon origin, this church survived the Great Fire of London in 1666, but was bombed during the Second World War, allowing some of the early church to be uncovered. It was rebuilt in 1955-8 by Lord Mottistone and Paul Paget. In the crypt are remains of a Roman pavement and a magnificent font cover of 1689.

CHURCH OF ALL SAINTS (MARGARET STREET, W1) The site on which William Butterfield in 1849 began to build the Victorian Gothic Church of All Saints was so narrow and cramped that the only way in which Butterfield could express his love of massed shapes was by building towards the sky. The church was highly original—and controversial—for its day, and a century later it still appears startling. Butterfield used red bricks, which were then unfashionable; both the exterior and interior brickwork is decorated with geometrical patterns and horizontal bands of black brick and stone. The narrow 230 ft tower ends in an octagonal steeple. The church, completed in 1859, was an early example of Butterfield's highly individual style, which reached its perfection with his polychrome design for Keble College Chapel, Oxford.

The effect of space and size in the interior is amazing, and so is the riot of colour, gilding, mosaics and painting. The church is on a strictly Tractarian plan—one altar visible from all parts of the church, no screen, light from the west end, and the chancel extremely sumptuous.

CHURCH OF ALL SAINTS (OLD CHURCH STREET, SW3) Chelsea 'Old Church' was almost entirely destroyed during the Second World War, but has since been rebuilt. There are monuments from the 16th century onwards, including one designed by Pietro Bernini (1672), son of the famous sculptor.

CHURCH OF ALL SOULS (LANGHAM PLACE, W1) Designed by George IV's favourite architect, John Nash, as a feature of the new Regent Street, the church was completed by the end of 1824. Nash's circular Ionic portico is surmounted by the tower with a slender spire, now somewhat overshadowed by neighbouring new buildings. The interior has recently been restored.

CHURCH OF ST ANNE (COMMERCIAL ROAD, E14) Designed by Wren's assistant Nicholas Hawksmoor, the building was started in 1712 and consecrated in 1730. The tower is famous as a landmark from the Thames; the church was restored in the 19th century.

CHURCH OF ST AUGUSTINE (KILBURN PARK ROAD, NW6) This is a large, red-brick, cruciform church, with a spire over 250 ft high, designed by J. L. Pearson in 1870. There are windows by Clayton & Bell, and contemporary paintings and ironwork.

CHURCH OF ST BARTHOLOMEW THE GREAT (SMITHFIELD STREET, EC1) The impressive remains of a Norman priory church, founded by Rahere in 1123, the same year he founded St Bartholomew's Hospital. Only the east end and crossing remain, as the long nave, originally of ten bays, was demolished after the Dissolution. The church was restored during the late 19th century

## CHISWICK HOUSE

*Lord Burlington designed this villa for himself after his first Grand Tour in 1714–15. In Italy he became greatly impressed by the work of the 16th-century architect Andrea Palladio, who had influenced Inigo Jones so much a century earlier. Chiswick House was inspired by Palladio's Villa Capra (The Rotunda) near Vicenza. The interior decoration was by William Kent, and the most important room is the central domed hall, round which all the other rooms are built. The magnificent gallery (above), completed in 1729, runs the length of the house; it was designed as a setting for part of Burlington's art collection.*

by Sir Aston Webb. The most important monument is that of *c.* 1500 on the north side to the founder Rahere, with a recumbent effigy.

CHURCH OF ST BENET (PAUL'S WHARF, EC4) First mentioned in the early 12th century, this church was rebuilt by Wren after the Great Fire, in 1677–85. It has an almost Dutch exterior of red and blue brickwork, and a hipped-roof. The tower has a lead spire on a lead dome. The interior has galleries to the north and west between Corinthian columns. Henry Fielding was married here in 1748.

CHURCH OF ST BOTOLPH (ALDERSGATE, EC1) A medieval church that was rebuilt in 1754, and altered again in 1788–91 by Nathaniel Wright. The exterior is modest red brick with a small west tower. The well preserved interior is late 18th-century, with two coffered apses and three dark wooden galleries with Corinthian columns. In the

west gallery is an organ-case of 1778; the east window of 1788 shows the Agony in the Garden. There are some monuments from the old church, and a simple monument with portrait medallion, by Louis Roubiliac, to Elizabeth Smith (*d.* 1750).

CHURCH OF ST BOTOLPH (HOUNDSDITCH, EC3) Built 1741–4 by George Dance the Elder, the interior was considerably altered by J. F. Bentley, who redecorated it in 1889. There are galleries on three sides and an unusual embossed ceiling by Bentley. Among 16th- and 17th-century monuments are two to victims of Henry VIII, who were beheaded in 1537 and 1538. The tower and main entrance at the south end (the liturgical west end) are flanked by domed side entrances.

CHURCH OF ST BRIDE (FLEET STREET, EC4) The church, dating from the 12th century, was rebuilt by Christopher Wren in 1670–84, but was burnt

287

out during an air raid in 1940; it was restored in 1956–7 by W. Godfrey Allen, who was able to make use of Wren's original drawings. Inside is much good woodwork, including a carved oak reredos. The font of 1615, in which Samuel Pepys was baptised, and which survived the bombing, has been replaced in the church.

CHURCH OF ST CLEMENT DANES (STRAND, WC2) The church was rebuilt after the Fire of London by Wren, only to be destroyed again during the air raids of 1941. But the walls and James Gibb's elegant tower survived, and the church has now been restored as that of the Royal Air Force.

CHURCH OF ST ETHELBURGA (BISHOPSGATE, EC2) A small but ancient church, built of ragstone and brick, a survivor of the Great Fire that destroyed so many of the original City churches. It has a small square bell-turret, probably 18th century. The modest interior is mainly 14th century, but there are panels of heraldic 17th-century stained glass.

CHURCH OF ST HELEN'S (BISHOPSGATE, EC2) A large and interesting church, the remains of a Benedictine nunnery founded c. 1210. The nun's church was built on to an existing parish church, and hence there are two naves. The exterior has embattled gabling and a 17th-century bell-turret. There are many architectural features of the 13th to 15th centuries, and some later furnishings, including a Jacobean pulpit and marble font of 1632. St Helen's is rich in monuments and brasses to leaders of English commerce. There are the tombs of Sir John Crosby of Crosby Hall (d. 1476),

CHURCH OF
ST MARTIN-IN-THE-FIELDS

*There has probably been a church here since before the 13th century when fields stretched between the City and Westminster. A 16th-century church had become unsafe by 1720, and James Gibbs was asked to build the present one—his masterpiece—with his name and the completion date (1726) carved on the pediment.*

Sir Thomas Gresham (d. 1579), Sir John Spencer and his wife (c. 1609) and one to Sir Julius Caesar Adelmare (d. 1636) by Nicholas Stone.

CHURCH OF ST JAMES (CLERKENWELL ROAD, EC1) Designed by James Carr c. 1790, St James's replaced an earlier building. It still has galleries in spite of restoration in the late 19th century. The monuments date from the 16th century.

CHURCH OF ST JOHN (CAMBRIDGE HEATH ROAD, E2) Built c. 1825 to Sir John Soane's design; the church is of brick with an unconventional stone bell-cote. During the latter half of the 19th century St John's was remodelled by G. F. Bodley.

CHURCH OF ST KATHARINE CREE (LEADENHALL STREET, EC3) On the site of a vanished Augustinian priory (Christchurch, whence Creechurch), the body of this church was built in 1628–31, a rare period for church building in England. It was consecrated by Archbishop Laud. The tower is older, 1504. The interior is a mixture of Classical and Gothic styles, containing Corinthian columns, plaster vaulted ceiling and a large east window incorporating a Catherine wheel in the tracery. The organ of 1686 is by Father Schmidt.

CHURCH OF ST LEONARD (SHOREDITCH HIGH STREET E1) An unpretentious, somewhat ponderous church by George Dance, Senior. Completed in 1740, it is in red brick and Portland stone. The gilt clock case in the gallery, and an unusual monument by Francis Bird to Elizabeth Benson (d. 1710), on which two carved skeletons tear apart an oak tree, are among the features inside.

CHURCH OF ST LEONARD (STREATHAM HIGH ROAD, SW16) Built on the site of a medieval church, St Leonard's was rebuilt in the 19th century. Inside there are several monuments from the 14th century onwards, including some to Dr Johnson's friends, the Thrales. A 19th-century brass commemorates the painter William Dyce.

CHURCH OF ST LUKE (SYDNEY STREET, SW3) Designed by James Savage c. 1820 in the Gothic style, St Luke's is faced with ashlar, and has a stone vault. The galleries are worth noting, as is the stained glass by Hugh Easton.

CHURCH OF ST MARK (COBURG ROAD, N22) Designed by R. Norman Shaw in 1879, it was not completed until 1932. During the Second World War the church was badly damaged.

CHURCH OF ST MARTIN-IN-THE-FIELDS (TRAFALGAR SQUARE, W1) The present church, built 1722–6, is the most prominent work by the Scottish architect, James Gibbs. A disciple of Wren, Gibbs evolved his own architectural style, and his designs for St Martin-in-the-Fields influenced ecclesiastical architecture beyond Britain, especially in the U.S.A. Many churches in different American states are erected in accordance with Gibb's arrangement of St Martin's. The rectangular church is approached by a broad flight of steps and has a great Corinthian portico. The large carved armorial achievement of George I in the pediment is the work of Christopher Cass. The steeple, which rises above the portico, is in Ionic pilaster form; above the clock Corinthian columns are capped by the actual spire. Gibbs, architect of the Radcliffe Camera, Oxford, also designed monuments. His use of a figure leaning on a large urn set a long-lasting fashion in sculpture.

CHURCH OF ST MARY (BATTERSEA CHURCH ROAD, SW11) Rebuilt c. 1775 by Joseph Dixon in brick, the church contains 17th-century glass and, among its numerous monuments, one by Louis Roubiliac, c. 1751. It stands on the bank of the Thames opposite Lots Road power station.

**CHURCH OF ST MARY (MARYLEBONE ROAD, W1)**
This is the parish church of Marylebone. The medieval church was rebuilt in the first half of the 18th century, but soon proved too small. Sir William Chambers produced plans for a larger building, but nothing was done until the 19th century, when the present church was designed by Thomas Hardwicke and consecrated in 1817. An expensive Corinthian church built in Portland stone, its portico and steeple terminate Nash's stucco York Gate leading out of Regent's Park. The galleried interior, over-decorated in Victorian times, has 19th-century wall monuments.

**CHURCH OF ST MARY ABCHURCH (ABCHURCH LANE, EC4)** A rebuilding by Sir Christopher Wren (in 1686) of a church first mentioned in the 12th century. The plain brick exterior has stone dressing and the tower in the north-west bears a pretty lead spire. The domed interior was restored by Lord Mottistone after bomb-damage in the Second World War. The carved wooden altar-piece of 1686 is by Grinling Gibbons, and the marble font of the same date is by Christopher Kepster, one of Wren's masons at St Paul's Cathedral.

**CHURCH OF ST MARY ALDERMARY (ALDERMANBURY, EC2)** First mentioned in the 11th century, St Mary Aldermary's was rebuilt by Wren after the Fire of London, the money supposedly given on condition that the new building was a copy of the old. Certainly this is in Perpendicular Gothic style, with plaster fan-vaults in aisles and nave. The tower has large polygonal buttresses ending in tall pinnacles. Interesting furnishings include the pulpit, and the font and sword-rest, both of 1682.

**CHURCH OF ST MARY-AT-HILL (LOVE LANE, EC3)** Rebuilt by Wren soon after the Great Fire, in 1670–6, it replaced a church first mentioned in 1177. The exterior is plain and has a projecting clock. The interior is domed and vaulted, the central dome supported by Corinthian columns that form a cross shape. There is much good woodwork, and box-pews. There are elaborate wrought-iron sword rests, and a sculptured relief of the Resurrection, c. 1600, from the old church.

**CHURCH OF ST MARY-LE-BOW (CHEAPSIDE EC4)** The bells ('Bow Bells') were installed in the church in the 15th and 16th centuries, partly to guide travellers to the City of London, partly to signal the end of a day's work. The church was largely destroyed (except for the tower) in an air raid in 1941 and the original bells were lost.

**CHURCH OF ST MARY-LE-STRAND (STRAND, WC2)** James Gibbs (1683–1774), a follower of Sir Christopher Wren, studied architecture in Italy, and his Italian training shows clearly in St Mary-le-Strand, built 1714–17. The church stands on an island site, like its near neighbour, St Clement Danes; it was gutted during an air-raid in the last war, but has now been rebuilt. The nave and chancel have rich, vaulted ceilings.

**CHURCH OF ST MARY MAGDALENE (BERMONDSEY STREET, SE1)** Dating from the end of the 17th century, there was rebuilding c. 1830 by George Porter, in stucco Gothic. The interior is mostly late 17th century; there is a font of 1808.

**CHURCH OF ST MARY WOOLNOTH (KING WILLIAM STREET, EC3)** A church built by Wren's assistant, Nicholas Hawksmoor, in 1716–26. The unusual tower divides at the top into two small turrets. The façade is heavily rusticated. The interior was restored by William Butterfield in 1875 and the galleries were then removed, but much of Hawksmoor's woodwork remains. Corinthian columns in groups of three are arranged in each corner, and above are semicircular clerestory windows and a moulded plaster ceiling. There is an organ by Father Schmidt.

**CHURCH OF ST PANCRAS (EUSTON ROAD, NW1)** A fine example of Greek Revival architecture, designed by Henry Inwood and his son Henry William, and built in 1819–22. At the west end is an impressive Ionic portico with three huge doors. Above, following the example of St Martin-in-the-Fields built 100 years before, projects the steepled tower; this comprises a tower with a smaller edition of the same tower on top, and incorporates elements freely taken from the Temple of the Winds in Athens. The rest of the church is based on the Erechtheum in Athens. At the east end, on either side of the Ionic apse, are two small vestries which incorporate versions of the caryatids of the Erechtheum temple on the Acropolis. In Athens H. W. Inwood made plaster casts of the original figures and these were turned into terracotta copies by J. C. F. Rossi and his son Henry. These were then built up in sections around the true supports, cast-iron columns. The flat-ceilinged interior contains galleries supported by columns.

**CHURCH OF ST PAUL (OLD TOWN, SW4)** Rebuilt in the 19th century, but inside there are monuments from the earlier church. These include one to Sir Richard Atkins (d. 1689), his wife and children (with lying, seated and standing figures), which could be the work of the Holborn mason-sculptor, William Stanton.

**CHURCH OF ST PETER (LIVERPOOL GROVE, SE17)** Designed by Sir John Soane, c. 1823. His steeple rises above four large Ionic columns. The interior retains its galleries.

**CHURCH OF ST STEPHEN WALBROOK (WALBROOK, EC4)** Rebuilt by Wren in 1672–7, the church has a plain exterior with a tower and steeple finished in 1717. The interior, however, is elaborate, with a large dome supported at ground level by Corinthian columns, three in each corner. Contemporary furnishings include the organ, pulpit and reredos.

**CLEOPATRA'S NEEDLE (VICTORIA EMBANKMENT, SW1)** A 68½ ft high obelisk of granite given to the nation in 1819 by Mohammed Ali of Egypt. It did not reach England until 1878, when it was erected on the Embankment. The monument has no connection with Cleopatra, Queen of Egypt (69–30 BC), but was carved in honour of Thothmes III, King of Egypt c. 1500 BC. It originally stood with a companion obelisk (now in New York) outside the temple at Heliopolis.

**COLLEGE OF ARMS (QUEEN VICTORIA STREET, EC4)** A plain brick building which replaced one burnt down in the Great Fire of London of 1666, it was built in 1671 to be the headquarters of the Royal Officers of Arms, incorporated by Richard III in 1484. The College has exclusive powers to grant armorial bearings. The large wrought-iron gates were added in the late 19th century.

**CORAM FOUNDATION FOR CHILDREN (BRUNSWICK SQUARE, WC1)** This charity, founded in 1739 by Thomas Coram, the mariner, empire-builder, philanthropist and pioneer in child welfare, with the aim of helping unwanted children, was known until 1954 as the Foundling

## HANDEL'S KEYBOARD AND COPY OF 'THE MESSIAH'

*Written at great speed between August 22 and September 14, 1741, Handel's 'Messiah' was first performed in Dublin in 1742. The organ (shown right) was used by him for performances of the oratorio before large audiences throughout the country. In Handel's lifetime all performances of the work were for charity, many for the Foundling Hospital, now the Thomas Coram Foundation. The manuscript copy, one of several still in existence, is open at the passage: 'And the Angel said unto them, "Fear not, for behold I bring you good tidings of great joy"'. Blind for the last eight years of his life, Handel died in 1759 at the age of 74. He was buried in Westminster Abbey. (Coram Foundation for Children)*

Hospital. It has always enjoyed the support of artists, and William Hogarth, a founder member, was more than anyone else responsible for fostering this link. He gave to the foundation a full-length portrait of Thomas Coram, which hangs on the first landing. His example was followed by many other artists, prominent amongst whom were Allan Ramsay, Thomas Gainsborough and Sir Joshua Reynolds. Another Hogarth painting was won in a lottery with a ticket presented by the artist himself. In the picture gallery hangs *The Massacre of the Innocents*, a portion of one of twelve cartoons for a tapestry depicting scenes from the life of Christ. This has been attributed to Raphael, though the style suggests that it is the work of his pupil Giulio Romano.

The organ in the chapel was presented by Handel, and an original manuscript of his *Messiah* is displayed in the picture gallery. Both the oak staircase and the courtroom to which it leads on the second floor are from the original hospital, though the latter has been moved from the ground floor to its present position. Today, the Foundation has in its care between 200 and 300 children, all of whom live in foster homes.

COURTAULD INSTITUTE GALLERIES (WOBURN SQUARE, WC1) A collaboration between Viscount Lee of Fareham and Samuel Courtauld, an art collector and a textile manufacturer, led to the foundation of the Courtauld Institute of Art in 1932. Their aim was to create an art gallery for the benefit of London University, and to this end they both bequeathed their art collections to the university. Other bequests make up the main part of this collection, namely the Roger Fry Collection, the Sir Robert Witt Collection of old master drawings and, most recently of all, the Gambier-Parry Collection of Italian Renaissance paintings and other *objets d'art*.

The Samuel Courtauld collection is the most representative selection of Impressionist and post-Impressionist paintings in the country and centres around a collection of paintings by Cézanne that includes his *Lac d'Annecy, Mont Ste-Victoire* and *Card Players*. Manet's *Déjeuner sur l'Herbe* and Renoir's *La Loge* are notable in a collection which includes works by Degas, Pissarro, Monet, Seurat, Bonnard, Modigliani and Utrillo.

The Lee Collection of old masters is shown in rooms decorated with furniture and other works of art in the collection. The most outstanding painting is probably Rubens's *Descent from the Cross*, which was the model for the high altarpiece in Antwerp Cathedral, but works by Lely, Veronese, Bellini, Botticelli, Gainsborough, Goya, Van Dyck and Tintoretto may also be seen.

The 20th century is represented by the Fry Collection, which illustrates the most advanced English taste in the years preceding the First World War. It includes works by Seurat, Renoir, Sickert, Bonnard, Marchand, Rouault and Roger Fry, and also examples of African sculpture.

The recent bequest of the Gambier-Parry Collection adds a fine selection of 14th- and 15th-century Italian paintings along with splendid collections of majolica and Venetian glass, medieval ivories and Limoges enamels. Examples of early 16th-century Turkish 'Rhodian' pottery and inlaid Islamic metalwork are also displayed. (See pp. 320–1.)

CROSBY HALL (CHEYNE WALK, SW3) A remarkable medieval hall, of great interest to scholars, is incorporated in this building on Chelsea Embankment. The original Crosby Hall was part of a 'large and sumptuous building' known as Crosby Place, built in Bishopsgate in 1466 by Sir John Crosby, alderman of the City of London and a rich merchant. He owned it from 1466 until his death in 1475. Richard, Duke of Gloucester, lived there in 1483, and in this connection, Crosby Place is mentioned three times in Shakespeare's *Richard III*. Sir Thomas More bought it in 1523 and then sold his 41-year lease to a rich merchant, Antonio Bonvisi, for £200. The house was burnt down in the 17th century, but the great hall survived. In 1910, as a result of an appeal to preserve it, the hall was transferred to Chelsea and rebuilt exactly as the original on part of the site of Sir Thomas More's Chelsea garden. The hall is still used as a dining-hall; of particular interest is the lofty oriel window occupying the whole of one bay, with the Crosby crest in the vaulting, and the magnificent oak roof.

CUMING MUSEUM (WALWORTH ROAD, SE17) The collection was originally built up by the Cuming family from the 18th century onwards, and was bequeathed to Southwark Borough Council in 1902. The museum now concentrates mainly on local history and archaeology and has added many finds from Roman and medieval Southwark. There is also a coin collection, a selection of London charms and superstitions, and some items associated with Dickens in 18th- and 19th-century Southwark—the Dog and Pot inn sign from Lant Street, and the pump from Marshalsea Prison.

CUSTOM HOUSE (LOWER THAMES STREET, EC3) The headquarters of the Collector of Customs for the Port of London, this early 19th-century building has a fine neo-Classical façade to be seen from the river. In the Long Room (190 ft long), ships' masters and agents come to register the arrival and departure of ships. (By appointment.)

DICKENS HOUSE (DOUGHTY STREET, WC1) In this house, the only survivor of his London residences, novelist Charles Dickens completed *Pickwick Papers* in 1837-9. It is now the headquarters of the Dickens Fellowship, with a museum and the world's most comprehensive library on Dickens.

EMBROIDERERS' GUILD (WIMPOLE STREET, W1) A society founded to encourage the art of embroidery. The collection contains English items, including lace, from the 16th century to the present, and international work of various periods.

FENTON HOUSE (HAMPSTEAD GROVE, NW3) A small mansion, built 1693. It contains old furniture, porcelain and the Benton-Fletcher Collection of early musical instruments, including a harpsichord used by Handel.

GEFFRYE MUSEUM (KINGSLAND ROAD, E2) Originally built c. 1715 as almshouses by Sir Robert Geffrye, a Lord Mayor of London (1685-6), it contains furniture and woodwork from the Elizabethan period to the present, and panelling and staircases from demolished London houses.

GEOLOGICAL MUSEUM (EXHIBITION ROAD, SW7) Precious and ornamental stones, dioramas of past and present landscapes of outstanding geological interest, British fossils and rocks, and minerals from all parts of the world form the museum's permanent exhibition. Exhibits showing the use of minerals and gems in industry are also on view. (See p. 292.)

GEORGE INN (BOROUGH HIGH STREET, SE1) The only surviving galleried inn in London, built in 1677. It was a famous coaching terminus in the 18th and 19th centuries, and is mentioned in Dickens's *Little Dorrit*.

GRAY'S INN (HIGH HOLBORN, WC1) Dates from 1370, but was damaged in 1941 and most buildings are modern restorations. The Elizabethan essayist and philosopher Sir Francis Bacon lived and worked here for 50 years, and is said to have laid out the gardens. The hall was the scene of the first performance of Shakespeare's *Comedy of Errors* in 1594.

GUILDHALL (EC2) The City of London's Hall where the Court of Common Council, which administers the City, meets, and where the Lord Mayor and Livery Companies (Guilds) of the City entertain famous visitors to London. The original building dates from 1411, but little is left of that

## PORCELAIN GOATHERD AND MILKMAID

*Porcelain was originally imported from China, but was so expensive and difficult to obtain that some European potteries were encouraged to copy it. Started in 1709 at Meissen, Germany, porcelain production eventually reached England during the 1740's. In 1749 the famous 'soft-paste' pottery at Bristol was founded by William Miller and Benjamin Lund. By this time the Meissen potteries were producing small porcelain figures, enamelled with colour, as replacements for the*

*sugar and wax table-decorations used by the rich at their banquets. At first the figures were modelled to be seen from all sides, but the growing practice of using them as ornaments on mantelpieces and side cabinets resulted in the figures being set against a leafy bower or background feature. This pair of Bristol porcelain figures, the Goatherd (left) and the Milkmaid, date from 1775. Eleven in. high and enamelled in several colours, they incorporate a background or bocage. (Fenton House)*

## JEWELS IN THE GEOLOGICAL MUSEUM

*The Geological Museum contains one of the largest and finest collections of gems and ornamental stones in the world. The picture shows:*

1　green demantoid garnet
2　oval aquamarine
3　emerald cabochon
4　lilac-coloured kunzite
5　rich red spinel
6　drop-shaped brown topaz
7　yellow sapphire
8　purple amethyst
9　olive-green zircon
10　brown zircon
11　carved tourmaline pendant
12　brilliant colourless danburite

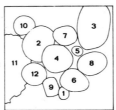

period, for the Guildhall suffered both in the Great Fire, and in the Blitz when the original council chamber and the roof of the great hall were destroyed. The building has been restored; the interior was completed to designs by Sir Giles Scott in 1952. The Corporation Art Gallery, within the Guildhall, has paintings of great state occasions over the past 100 years. The Guildhall Library, also badly bombed in 1940, contains such treasures as the First, Second and Fourth Folios of Shakespeare's plays, a map of London of 1591 and a deed of sale for a house, signed by Shakespeare.

GUILDHALL ART GALLERY (EC2) The collection started in 1670 with the commissioning of portraits of the judges who dealt with property claims after the Great Fire. The gallery opened in 1886. It exhibits selections from the permanent collection that includes E. W. Cooke drawings of London Bridge, W. Alister Macdonald water-colours of London and the Charles Cassiot Bequest of English 19th-century paintings.

GUILDHALL MUSEUM (55 BASINGHALL STREET, EC1) Many items from Roman London, some of them finds from the Temple of Mithras uncovered in Walbrook in 1954, are on display in this museum. They range from domestic articles to iron picks and trowels, spearheads and arrowheads. Of more artistic interest are the Samian bowls, the glassware and the figures of Mercury and Mithras. From the Temple of Mithras there is also a collection of medieval London pottery, including a 13th-century jug in human form, and examples of medieval and 16th-century shoes. The museum will soon be amalgamated with the London Museum, to form the Museum of London.

GUY'S HOSPITAL (ST THOMAS STREET, SE1) Founded in 1721 by Thomas Guy, a bookseller with a licence to print the Bible, who also made a fortune out of South Sea stock. The iron gates and railings at the entrance are original, and much of the present building, including the façade, dates from 1773. A statue of Guy leading a sick man into hospital, sculpted by John Bacon in 1779, stands in the 18th-century chapel. The medical school was set up *c.* 1769 and the poet John Keats was a student there from 1814 to 1816.

HEALTH EXHIBITION CENTRE (ROYAL SOCIETY OF HEALTH, BUCKINGHAM PALACE ROAD, SW1) The country's only permanent public exhibition concerned with health includes sections on clean air, food, water, vital statistics (those relating to births, deaths, disease and health), radiation, pest control, diseases and occupational health.

HORNIMAN MUSEUM (LONDON ROAD, SE23) Built in 1902 to designs by C. H. Townsend, the museum has extensive ethnographical collections. There is a fine collection of musical instruments, and a library.

HOUSES OF PARLIAMENT OR PALACE OF WEST-MINSTER (SW1) In deference to nearby Westminster Abbey, a Gothic design by Sir Charles Barry was chosen when the Palace of Westminster was rebuilt following a fire in 1834. Work on the new building began in 1840. The palace comprises a central hall and corridor with the two Chambers (Houses of Lords and Commons) to the north and south, with identical projecting pavilions at either end of the river façade. There are strong vertical features in the massive Victoria Tower, the clock tower and the spire over the central hall. This Classical plan is masked by Gothic detailing, nearly all produced by Augustus Pugin. The clock tower, housing Big Ben, the bell named after the first Commissioner of Works, Sir Benjamin Hall, was completed in 1858 and the Victoria Tower two years later. The stone chosen for the building did not stand up to London's atmosphere and has been gradually replaced by a more durable type. In 1941, during the Second World War, the House of Commons was destroyed by a bomb; a new Chamber was opened in 1950.

HYDE PARK Its 360 acres, originally known as the Manor of Hyde, first belonged to the Abbey of Westminster who acquired it in 1066 and held it until Henry VIII appropriated it to the Crown *c.* 1536 and used it as a royal deer park. It was first opened to the public by Charles I in 1635, when it was used for horse-racing and quickly became a rendezvous for society people; it was also a popular place for duels. The mile-long track of Rotten Row was used for riding and was a favourite parade of the fashionable in their horse-carriages.

The Serpentine, an artificial lake formed from the R. Westbourne, was constructed at the order of Queen Caroline in 1730. A fine bridge built in 1826 by the Rennie brothers and known as Rennie's Bridge crosses the lake between Hyde Park and Kensington Gardens.

In 1850 Joseph Paxton began building the Crystal Palace in the park for the Great Exhibition of 1851. The building remained there for a year and was subsequently removed to Sydenham. Twenty years later the Albert Memorial was put up slightly west of the site.

In the Victorian age the park became a centre for popular orators; for years meetings were forbidden, until a serious riot led to a special place, now known as Speakers' Corner, being designated for assemblies in 1872.

## GUILDHALL

*This medieval hall was once the centre of administration and court for the City. Here kings and distinguished visitors were received—in 1419 the lord mayor, Sir Richard (Dick) Whittington received Henry V, the victor of Agincourt. Today ceremonies granting the Freedom of the City, and the election of the lord mayor, still take place here. The annual lord mayor's banquet is a reminder of the great medieval feasts. Around the walls are monuments to the two Pitts, Wellington and Sir Winston Churchill, and two mythical giants, Gog and Magog—the last survivors of Albion—stand guard on either side of the gallery and screen at the far end.*

## SCULPTURES FROM THE
## ROMAN TEMPLE OF MITHRAS

*The head of Seraphis (left) was imported into Britain from an Italian workshop. Seraphis, of Greco-Egyptian origin, was equated with the true Egyptian Osiris, the consort of the goddess Isis. He was lord of the underworld and god of fertility. His head-dress, the modius, was characteristic of a giver of prosperity in this world and the next. The life-size head of Mithras (right) is the only certain British example. Mithras is usually shown on a relief panel—as a handsome youth wearing a Phrygian cap, slaying a bull, his head turned to the front. The posture of this head suggests it came from a free-standing representation of the same scene. It is of Italian marble, but the rest of the group, in the apse at the west end of the temple, was probably locally made of inferior material. (Guildhall Museum)*

HYDE PARK CORNER (SW1) Until the beginning of the 19th century London ended here and the country began; Apsley House was known as 'No. 1 London' and many of the distances to England's towns were measured from the Corner. Near Apsley House is the screen at the entrance into Hyde Park, and the Constitution Hill Arch. Apsley House was built by Robert Adam for Lord Apsley during the 1770's, and was later acquired by the 1st Duke of Wellington, the victor of Waterloo, who employed Benjamin Wyatt to enlarge the building c. 1828. At this time the Waterloo Gallery was built facing Hyde Park and the statue of Achilles—erected by women's subscription to commemorate Wellington's victories. Apsley House was given to the nation by the 7th Duke of Wellington after the Second World War; now the Wellington Museum. (See p. 296.)

The screen and arch were designed by Decimus Burton c. 1825, and when the arch was erected it was much nearer the screen than it is today. The sculptured frieze on the screen is the work of John Henning and his sons John and Samuel, and is based on the Elgin Marbles, now in the British Museum. In 1846 a huge equestrian statue of Wellington was hauled to the top of the arch. It was ridiculed for years and when the arch was moved further down Constitution Hill in the 1880's, the statue was moved to Aldershot, where it still towers over the trees. The Arch now supports a bronze group, *Victory*, by Adrian Jones.

On the central traffic island are the statue of Wellington by Sir Edgar Boehm; the Royal Artillery war memorial in the form of a huge stone gun, by C. Jagger; and *David*, the war memorial of the Machine Gun Corps by Francis Derwent Wood—there is an even more nude version on the Chelsea Embankment.

IMPERIAL INSTITUTE TOWER (PRINCE CONSORT ROAD, SW7) The Imperial Institute in South Kensington was built behind the Royal Albert Hall to mark the celebration of Queen Victoria's Jubilee. In 1887 the queen had reigned for 50 years, and the architect T. E. Collcutt began the construction of the great Imperial Institute. Never a popular museum, the institute later became part of Imperial College, London University, and in recent years the original buildings have been demolished and replaced by a modern glass complex. Towering over the new buildings of the Imperial College of Science and Technology is the elegant central tower of the Imperial Institute. The 280 ft high copper-domed tower is built of white stone and houses a peal of bells; it is all that now remains of the Imperial Institute.

IMPERIAL WAR MUSEUM (LAMBETH ROAD, SE1) The building, originally the home of Bedlam (Bethlehem Hospital for the Insane), dates from c. 1812, and suffered bomb damage in the Second World War. The exhibits are divided into two main sections. One shows, by means of both models and real tanks, aircraft and armaments, the development of warfare on land, sea and in the air. The other section, the picture gallery, has paintings by official artists of both World Wars, including works by John Singer Sargent, Sir William Orpen and Wyndham Lewis.

INDUSTRIAL HEALTH AND SAFETY CENTRE (HORSEFERRY ROAD, SW1) The Centre is an exhibition (probably the most comprehensive in the world) of methods and appliances that are used for ensuring the safety and well-being of industrial workers. Exhibits keep pace with new developments in this field.

## ARTHUR WELLESLEY, DUKE OF WELLINGTON, HERO OF WATERLOO

Arthur Wellesley joined the army at 19, and as a colonel in India defeated the notorious Tippoo Sahib, whose sword and tent hangings can be seen at Apsley House, where Wellington lived for 50 years; now a museum. In July 1808 he sailed from Cork with 9000 men, to pit himself against the legions of Napoleon. 'They may well overwhelm me,' he said 'but they will not out-manoeuvre me.' Six weeks after landing on Portuguese soil he had won two decisive victories, and in the end he chased the French across the Pyrenees. The two great soldiers faced one another on the field of Waterloo on June 18, 1815. The duke rose early that morning, wrote three letters before 3 a.m. and was in the saddle of his horse Copenhagen by 8 a.m. It was dusk when the 'Saviour of Europe' rode back through a battlefield littered with 45,000 dead and dying soldiers.

PORTRAIT BY GOYA *at the National Gallery; this famous portrait was founded on a sketch by Goya now in the British Museum. The haunting drawing records an exhausted and unshaven Wellington riding back to headquarters in the village of Alba de Tormes, after victory at Salamanca on a summer night in 1812.*

WELLINGTON SHIELD *shows the duke mounted, and surrounded by a group of officers, with the figure of Victory flying above and carrying a laurel wreath. The ten compartments of the shield show scenes of the duke's campaigns. After the Battle of Waterloo, honours were showered on the 46-year-old duke and in the years which followed he acted as administrator, diplomat, and even Prime Minister during 1828–30. The shield was given to him by the merchants and bankers of the City of London and designed by Thomas Stothard. (Apsley House)*

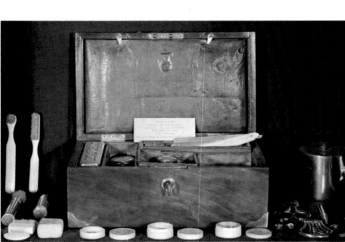

DRESSING CASE *illustrating the duke's Spartan habits. He often slept in his clothes and ate when convenient. 'I conceived a horror for the two words "cold meat" and "daybreak"', said one of his officers. (Apsley House)*

PENCILLED ORDERS *sent by the duke to unit commanders at Waterloo. The writing could be erased and the skin used again. During the battle he spent 13 hours in the saddle. (Apsley House)*

THE AGONY IN THE GARDEN *by Correggio;
carried by the duke on all his campaigns, it was
one of the masterpieces captured in Joseph
Bonaparte's baggage train at Vittoria.
(Apsley House)*

WELLINGTON'S FUNERAL CARRIAGE *in the
crypt of St Paul's. One and a half million
mourners lined the streets at his funeral.*

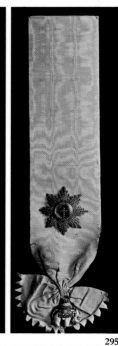

PORTUGUESE SERVICE *Items from
the famous service of silver plate
presented by the Regent of Portugal
to the duke in gratitude for delivering
his country from the French. The
service is one of the major examples
of silversmithing of the neo-Classical
period. It took 142 craftsmen three
years to make, and was delivered in
1816. (Apsley House)*

A WELLINGTON BOOT *A caricature
of the duke as Commander-in-Chief
of the Army. He wore such boots, and
the style has since been named after
him. On each point of the spur is an
initial of one of the duke's many
orders. (Apsley House)*

THE GOLD BATON *presented to
Wellington by the Prince Regent in
return for Marshal Jourdan's baton,
captured on the field of the Battle of
Salamanca, and* THE ORDER OF THE
ELEPHANT, *Denmark's supreme
order, given to the duke for his great
victory at Waterloo. (Apsley House)*

VELASQUEZ *The Water-seller of Seville*

Velasquez, one of the greatest portraitists of all time, began his career as a painter of religious subjects and scenes of peasant life. His needle-sharp eye for the appearance of things, his ability to subject his appetite for detail to the overall wholeness of the picture, his sheer technical skill in defining the unique texture of glass, fabric, metal or wood, and his restraint as a colourist all combine to make these early works masterpieces of realism. In the 'Water-seller', painted about 1619 when Velasquez was only 20, the high-lights and strong shadows bespeak a debt to Caravaggio, whose style had a strong influence outside Italy in the early 17th century. The old water-seller was a Corsican and a well-known character in Seville where Velasquez was born, and the youth was a studio boy who served as a model several times. Four years later Velasquez showed the picture to King Philip in Madrid, and he kept it and the artist—who became Court painter for the rest of his life. (Wellington Museum, Apsley House)

INNS OF CHANCERY These Inns, of lesser importance than the Inns of Court, have largely disappeared. Staple Inn, Holborn, a fine survival of an Elizabethan house, is no longer connected with the legal profession. The other former Inns of Chancery were Clement's Inn, Clifford's Inn, Barnard's Inn, Lyon's Inn, Furnival's Inn, Thame's Inn, Strand Inn and New Inn; none survives except in some cases as names of modern buildings.

INNS OF COURT Lincoln's Inn, the Inner Temple, the Middle Temple, and Gray's Inn are the four great Inns of Court which largely govern the practice of barristers in England and Wales. The Inner and Middle Temples adjoin each other between Fleet Street and the Embankment, an area that was once the seat of the Knights Templar.

IVEAGH BEQUEST See Kenwood.

JEWEL TOWER (OLD PALACE YARD, SW1) A surviving fragment of the medieval Old Palace of Westminster, built in 1365 as a moated treasure house for Edward III. It now houses a museum of relics of the Old Palace.

JOHNSON'S HOUSE (GOUGH SQUARE, EC4) A house of the late 17th century where Dr Samuel Johnson, the critic and lexicographer, lived (1748–59) and where he compiled his *Dictionary*. The house contains many of his relics.

KEATS HOUSE (KEATS GROVE, HAMPSTEAD, NW3) Keats, with his friend Charles Armitage Brown, lived in half of the house at Wentworth Place, John Street, as it was then called, from December 1818 to September 1820. In the other half lived the Brawne family. It was then that Keats fell in love with the eldest girl, Fanny Brawne, and it was there that he wrote some of his best work—the 'Ode to a Nightingale', 'The Eve of St Agnes' and 'Hyperion'. A unique collection of Keats relics are to be seen in the house and in the museum and library adjoining; among them are Keats's letters, Fanny Brawne's portrait and her engagement ring, books belonging to Keats and annotated by him, and early editions of his poems. In the garden is the mulberry tree under which it is thought that Keats wrote the 'Ode to a Nightingale'.

KENSINGTON GARDENS Adjoining Hyde Park, they were originally part of the 26 acre garden of Kensington Palace, laid out by William III in the formal manner of the time. They were extended by Queen Anne and later by Queen Caroline, and now cover 275 acres. In the early 19th century they were open to the public from spring to autumn and it was at this period that Shelley was seen sailing paper boats on the Round Pond.

Features of the garden are the modern sunken garden with its lily pond and pleached lime walks, and Queen Anne's Orangery designed by Wren, 1704–5, an elegant brick building. Also in Kensington Gardens is the popular statue of Peter Pan designed by Sir George Frampton in 1912 in honour of J. M. Barrie's play of that name.

KENSINGTON PALACE (W8) The country home of the Earl of Nottingham was in 1689 acquired by William III, who commissioned Sir Christopher Wren to carry out numerous alterations and additions. The palace was further enlarged during the reign of Queen Anne, for whom Wren designed the orangery. The brick building is roofed with green slates, and Grinling Gibbons decorated the interior with carved panels, fluted columns and flower-bedecked archways. William Kent fashioned the interior of the palace for George I, and walls and ceilings are painted in

profusion. Kent also laid out the gardens. In 1951 the London Museum, previously housed in Lancaster House, was moved to Kensington Palace.

KENWOOD (IVEAGH BEQUEST, HAMPSTEAD, NW3) Kenwood is in a large park of beeches, oaks and chestnuts. The original 17th-century house was owned at various times by the Duke of Argyll and the Earl of Bute before coming into the possession of the 18th-century politician, the Earl of Mansfield. Robert Adam then remodelled the present mansion in Classical style. The principal façade, facing north, has two projecting wings, one of which contains Adam's splendid library. The portico on the north front has a decorated pediment supported by four fluted Corinthian columns. In 1922 the 6th Earl of Mansfield sold the contents of the house by auction, and the furniture was dispersed. The mansion itself was in danger of being demolished, but in 1925 Lord Iveagh bought the property. On his death in 1927 the estate was left to trustees for the nation, and Kenwood was opened to the public the following year. It contains a collection of paintings by Rembrandt, Vermeer, Van Dyck, Aelbert Cuyp, as well as English masters—Gainsborough, Reynolds, Romney, Lawrence and Turner. (See p. 298.)

LAMBETH PALACE (LAMBETH PALACE ROAD, SE1) The official home of the Archbishops of Canterbury, built when the Thames was the great highway of London, and it was convenient to have a large riverside residence with its own water-gate. The red-brick exterior dates from the late 15th century, the main gate being the work of Archbishop Morton *c.* 1495. The chapel, much restored, dates probably from *c.* 1230; it was rebuilt after war damage, and has modern stained glass by Powell and Edwards. Under the chapel the crypt, the earliest part of the palace (*c.* 1200), has Purbeck marble pillars. The main medieval buildings are of the 15th and 16th centuries. Apart from a considerable amount of rehabilitation in the 19th century, the main post-medieval building is the hall, erected *c.* 1660–3 to replace one destroyed under Cromwell's Commonwealth. It is 93 ft long and has a hammerbeam roof. The Lambeth Conferences of Anglican bishops are held in the hall, which contains a magnificent library, including illuminated manuscripts and early printed books.

LANCASTER HOUSE (STABLE YARD, SW1) Lancaster House is one of the finest surviving examples of early Victorian architecture. The town mansion was designed in 1821 for the Duke of York by Benjamin Wyatt, architect of Apsley House, the Duke of Wellington's town residence. When the Duke of York's mansion passed into the possession of the Dukes of Sutherland in 1827, the house was enlarged by Sir Charles Barry.

LEIGHTON HOUSE (HOLLAND PARK ROAD, W14) The house was built in 1866 by Lord Leighton, one-time President of the Royal Academy, with help from architect George Aitchison, and was his home until his death in 1896. The house, with its entire contents, was given to Kensington Borough Council in 1926 and is crowded with collector's pieces, many of them from the Middle East. The Arab Hall, with its Persian tiles of the 14th–16th centuries, has damascene stained glass windows, and a mosaic frieze by Walter Crane; William de Morgan designed some of the wall-tiles. In the studios are paintings by Lord Leighton and other contemporary artists.

LINCOLN'S INN (WC2) Has been on its present site near Chancery Lane since at least 1422. Its name may come from the Earl of Lincoln, legal

REMBRANDT *Portrait of the Artist*

Rembrandt Harmenszoon van Ryn was born in Leyden in the Netherlands and lived from 1606 until 1669. His autobiography is unique in its sincerity and humanity. It was not written but painted, drawn and etched in over 100 self-portraits. Every change in his features and his fortunes is dispassionately reflected. Sometimes he is in armour or a fur-trimmed robe or some other richly embroidered garment from his store of studio properties, or again in a beggar's rags. In his last period—that is, from about 1650—his self-portraits reach a monumentality, a poignancy and a maturity which remind us of the last of other great creative artists—the last quartets of Beethoven or the final religious works of Titian. In the portrait at Kenwood, usually dated 1663, we see Rembrandt old before his time—he was only 57. He shows himself not dressed up but as a painter in a composition of majestic simplicity and almost Classical geometry. The baroque flourish has gone and the pyramidal figure is set off by a background relieved only by two large arcs which presumably symbolise a pair of looped curtains. The expression is not tortured. He was now bankrupt but had been saved from ruin by his son Titus and second wife, who made him their employee. He could paint his last masterpieces in peace for his own satisfaction. His brushwork, becoming steadily freer, took on a vitality of its own and the surfaces of his pictures seem to vibrate. The paintings show his increasing detachment from the throes of the world. (Kenwood)

adviser to Edward I. The Old Hall, dating from 1492, the Victorian New Hall and the library (founded in 1497 and the biggest law library in England) are open on application. The quadrangle and gardens are open to the public at midday. Among many famous men connected with Lincoln's Inn are Sir Thomas More, John Donne, William Penn, Disraeli and Gladstone.

LINCOLN'S INN FIELDS (WC2) A large open space with trees, lawns, tennis courts and band concerts in summer. The Royal College of Surgeons stands on its south side, Sir John Soane's Museum to the north, and there are many handsome houses around the square.

LONDON BRIDGE (SE1) A bridge across the Thames at the site of London Bridge has existed for almost 2000 years. An unknown number of wooden bridges were built by the Romans, by the Anglo-Saxons, and after the Norman Conquest. In 1176, at the instigation of Henry II, work was begun on the first stone bridge, which was finished 30 years later in the reign of King John. Until 1750 when Westminster Bridge was built, this Old London Bridge was the only bridge across the Thames. It became the centre-point of London life and one of the wonders of the Middle Ages. It was lined by houses and shops, had a chapel dedicated to St Thomas of Canterbury, and was often decorated at each end by traitors' heads stuck on spikes. Old London Bridge stood until 1832, when it was taken down after construction of the New London Bridge in 1825–31. John Rennie and his sons designed and built this outstanding piece of 19th-century engineering, which has had 137 years of service. Because it is too narrow for modern traffic requirements and cannot conveniently be enlarged, it is to be replaced by a modern bridge.

LONDON MUSEUM (KENSINGTON PALACE, W8) Opened in 1912, it soon moved to Lancaster House, but in 1951 moved back to Kensington Palace. The collections show the history and life of London from earliest times to the present, and include paintings, drawings and prints. Other sections contain displays of royal personalia, 18th- and 19th-century toys, and material relating to the theatre. (See pp. 322–3.)

LORD'S CRICKET GROUND (ST JOHN'S WOOD, NW8) Named after Thomas Lord (1735–1832), a groundsman to the White Conduit Club, in 1780, Lord's has been the headquarters of the Marylebone Cricket Club—the governing body of cricket—since 1814. Lord's Cricket Museum includes the urn for the original Ashes.

MANSION HOUSE (EC4) The official residence of the Lord Mayor of London was originally designed in Palladian style by George Dance the Elder, in the years 1739–53, but has been altered since. A suite of state rooms in 18th-century style, including the 90 ft long Egyptian Hall, can be visited on written application.

MARBLE ARCH (W1) Originally the main gateway to Buckingham Palace, which John Nash designed when he repaired and enlarged the palace in 1825–36. It was moved to its present position in 1851, and in 1908 was closed to traffic and has been purely ornamental since then. A small tablet on the traffic island at the junction of Edgware Road and Bayswater Road marks the site of Tyburn Tree, London's former place of execution. The gallows and public galleries stood here from 1196 until 1783; thereafter executions took place at Newgate.

MARLBOROUGH HOUSE (SW1) Marlborough House was the home of Queen Mary until her

THE RAMILLIES STAIRCASE
AT MARLBOROUGH HOUSE

*A magnificent staircase, with wrought-iron balustrade and black marble steps, decorated with scenes from the Battle of Ramillies (1706), one of the Duke of Marlborough's most notable victories over the French. Louis Laguerre, a Frenchman who settled in England in 1684, completed pictures depicting most of the duke's battles about 1711, for the house designed by Wren.*

death in 1953. It was built by Sir Christopher Wren for the victorious Duke of Marlborough, owner of Blenheim Palace (Oxfordshire), c. 1705. The red-brick house had certain additions made to it during the 19th century, when it was the home of Edward VII when he was Prince of Wales. Inside are superb wall-paintings by the French painter Louis Laguerre, depicting famous battles of the duke—Blenheim, Ramillies and Malplaquet.

MAYFLOWER INN (ROTHERHITHE STREET, SE16) This Thames-side inn juts out into the river and is named for the famous ship which in 1620 carried the Pilgrim Fathers to America. The Master, Christopher Jones, is buried in the nearby churchyard of St Mary's.

MIDDLE TEMPLE HALL (EC4) Elizabethan, but most of the buildings date from after the reign of Elizabeth I or the Great Fire. Extensive damage was done in the Second World War, but has been repaired. The Temple has been the home of many famous men, among them Thackeray, Dr Johnson and Charles Lamb; Shakespeare placed the incident that began the Wars of the Roses in its gardens *(Henry VI, Part I)*.

MOCATTA MUSEUM (UNIVERSITY COLLEGE, WC1) Synagogue ritual silverware of the 17th–19th centuries is exhibited with other items of Anglo-Jewish historical interest such as medallions and pottery. (By appointment.)

MONUMENT (FISH STREET HILL, EC4) Wren's fluted Doric column, surmounted by a golden globe rising from flames, commemorates the Great Fire of London in 1666, which started in

## QUEEN VICTORIA'S SALOON

*Designed by Richard Bore and built by the London and North Western Railway at Wolverton in 1869, this carriage, with ceiling of quilted silk, was in use for 13 years. Servants travelled in an annexe and were summoned by an electric bell. The queen gave respectability to rail travel on her first journey in 1842, but she never allowed her drivers to exceed 40 mph. (Museum of British Transport)*

nearby Pudding Lane. Built in 1671–7, it is 202 ft high; a spiral staircase of 311 steps leads to the balcony near the top.

On the high square base are three panels recording in Latin the story of the fire and the subsequent rebuilding of London. The fourth side (to the west) has a sculptured bas-relief by Caius Gabriel Cibber showing Charles II giving protection to the devastated City.

MUSEUM OF BRITISH TRANSPORT (CLAPHAM HIGH STREET, SW4) The collections cover all aspects of transport and include royal railway coaches, locomotives, trams, buses and vintage vehicles.

MUSEUM OF LEATHERCRAFT (52 BASINGHALL STREET, EC2) The use of leather through the ages is demonstrated in a collection of some 2000 objects. These include medieval caskets, sheaths, and other containers: the most important is the 'Charles V casket', so-called because of the representation of a figure thought to be Charles V, the Holy Roman Emperor, on the lid, with the date 1532. There are also collections of 'Cordoban' leather (mainly gilt leather hangings) and leather footwear, and many examples of the industrial use of leather. Military equipment is displayed, including a rare shield of *c.* 1500. There are fine 17th- and 18th-century coffers and saddles, including one used by Queen Victoria. Flasks, bottles, gloves, clothing, and tannery and leather-working tools, are also on show. Contemporary leather objects are regularly added to the collection.

MUSEUM OF THE CHARTERED INSURANCE INSTITUTE (ALDERMANBURY, EC2) The museum has a large collection of British and foreign fire marks and a small collection of objects associated with the history of insurance.

NATIONAL GALLERY (TRAFALGAR SQUARE, WC2) The building was designed by William Wilkins and was built between 1834 and 1837. The collections deal with aspects of European painting and are particularly rich in works of the Italian schools of the 15th and 16th centuries and of the British school; the paintings are a comprehensive national collection, although not all are on display, many being kept in store. (See pp. 324–9.)

NATIONAL PORTRAIT GALLERY (ST MARTIN'S LANE, WC2) Adjoining the National Gallery the collection was founded in 1856 to illustrate British history with 4000 paintings, drawings and sculptures. The pictures are there more for the fame of the subject than of the artist, although there is good work by Millais, Romney and Reynolds.

NATIONAL POSTAL MUSEUM (NEWGATE STREET, EC1) Priceless documents and stamps comprising one of the world's greatest philatelic collections are on show in this new museum specially designed for the purpose. It houses the Phillips Collection of British postage stamps worth £275,000, and recently presented to the Post Office by the collector Reginald M. Phillips. The collection documents the conception, planning and issue of this British invention, the world's first postage stamp. It consists of 45 volumes which together illustrate the history of 19th-century stamps in Great Britain, and among the rare documents is the original draft letter of Rowland Hill, written in November 1839 to the Chancellor of the Exchequer advocating postal reform. The collection also traces manufacturing and design developments in British stamp production during the 19th century.

Also in the museum is the Post Office's own unique collection of stamps and documents. This includes essays or first proofs, registration sheets (final proofs), designers' sketches, original artwork, documents and letters relating to the execution of the designs.

NELSON'S COLUMN See Trafalgar Square.

PASSMORE EDWARDS MUSEUM (ROMFORD ROAD, E15) Built in 1896–8 in a way which made use of every possible architectural style then current, the museum has an important research collection of skeletal material from archaeological sites from the Pleistocene period to the present day. The natural history collection includes material relating to British deer, in which the museum specialises, Lord Lister's herbarium, and an aquarium and vivarium (where living animals are kept in conditions as natural as possible for purposes of interest or study). Also on display are items of local archaeological and historical interest, and a collection of Bow porcelain.

PERCIVAL DAVID FOUNDATION OF CHINESE ART (GORDON SQUARE, WC1) The collection is devoted to Chinese ceramics of the 10th–18th centuries. Most of the pieces were made for or collected by the emperors and the nobility. The Foundation also has a reference library on Chinese art.

PHARMACEUTICAL SOCIETY'S MUSEUM (BLOOMSBURY SQUARE, WC1) Displays of crude drugs, plants used in medicine, poisonous plants and apparatus used in the preparation of medicines in the past are on view. The library contains works on medicine and botany, including a Latin herbal published in 1485. (By appointment.)

PUBLIC RECORD OFFICE (CHANCERY LANE, WC2) The home of the nation's state papers, records and documents dating from the time of the Norman Conquest. The museum's collection includes the

Domesday Book (1086), two 13th-century editions of Magna Carta, papers connected with the Gunpowder Plot of 1605, Shakespeare's will and the log of the *Victory* at the Battle of Trafalgar. The building—a neo-Classical palace erected in 1857–66—was designed by Sir James Pennethorne.

QUEEN ELIZABETH'S HUNTING LODGE (RANGERS ROAD, E4) The early Tudor building was erected to serve as a base for royal hunting expeditions into Epping Forest. It contains displays illustrating the animal, bird and plant life of the forest.

QUEEN'S CHAPEL (ST JAMES'S, SW1) An exquisite small chapel opposite St James's Palace, built by Inigo Jones between 1623 and 1627 for the wife of Charles I, Henrietta Maria, though it had been intended for the Spanish princess whom it was hoped Charles would marry. It is in Classical style and was Jones's first ecclesiastical building. Inside there is a fine coffered ceiling and a west gallery (with a fire-place), originally a royal pew.

REGENT'S PARK Probably the most beautiful and certainly the most elegant of all London's royal parks. It was designed by John Nash in 1812 for the Prince Regent, after whom it was named. The park was the culmination of Nash's plan for Regent Street, which begins at Carlton House Terrace in the Mall, where the Regent lived, and sweeps in a broad curve to Portland Place, whose wide straight road, flanked on either side by elegant houses, terminates in Regent Crescent and the great green open space (410 acres) of the park. It was the Prince Regent's original intention to build a palace in the north-east corner of the park, but this came to nothing.

The park is surrounded by a carriageway, the Outer Circle, connected by two roads with the Inner Circle, originally a sawdust and sand track for horse-riding, but now a tarmac road. This encloses the beautiful garden now known as Queen Mary's Garden, which was taken over from the Royal Botanic Society in 1932 and re-planned. A small lake includes an island rock garden devoted to alpines and miniature perennials.

On the north side is the open-air theatre, where Shakespeare's plays are performed in the summer; in the Zoological Gardens are the huge artificial rocks of the apes' Mappin terraces, the aviary designed by Lord Snowdon and the concrete elephant-house by Sir Hugh Casson. Regent's Canal, opened in 1820, connects the Grand Junction Canal at Paddington with the Thames at Wapping.

ROOSEVELT MEMORIAL (GROSVENOR SQUARE, W1) A statue of the American President, Franklin Delano Roosevelt (1882–1945) by Sir William Reid Dick, was erected in 1948, near the site of the American Embassy (designed by Eero Saarinen and opened in 1960).

ROYAL ACADEMY (BURLINGTON HOUSE, PICCADILLY, W1) Founded in 1768 by George III; the Academy's first president was Sir Joshua Reynolds. The Summer Exhibition is of works by living artists, but loan exhibitions are held during the rest of the year. (See p. 302.)

ROYAL ALBERT HALL (KENSINGTON GARDENS, SW7) The Hall, completed in 1871, was erected in memory of Prince Albert to designs by General H. Scott. It is in the form of a huge oval arena, surrounded by tier upon tier of boxes and galleries, and roofed by a shallow metal and glass dome. Encircling the exterior below the dome is a terracotta frieze which illustrates man's progress in the arts and sciences through the centuries.

ROYAL COLLEGE OF MUSIC: THE DONALDSON MUSEUM (PRINCE CONSORT ROAD, SW7) Musical instruments from all parts of the world are displayed in various parts of the college. The extensive library includes printed music and original

CHARLES V CASKET

*This superb casket, dated 1532 on the lid, was probably made in the Low Countries and associated with Charles V, the Holy Roman Emperor in 1519–56. Its wooden base was covered with brown vellum covered with gold leaf; incised designs were then cut in the vellum, and red, blue and green tempera added. On the front are depicted St Michael combating the Devil (left) and St Francis and the Miracle of the Stigmata (right). A representation of Charles V appears on the lid, together with a woman's head, probably that of his wife, Isabella of Portugal. On the back are the Hapsburg Arms and the same impaled with those of Portugal. The casket is lined with sheepskin tanned red with oak. (Museum of Leathercraft)*

MICHELANGELO *The Virgin and Child with the young St John the Baptist*

*By common consent Michelangelo is regarded as the greatest sculptor who ever lived, and this beautiful marble roundel is the only major work of his in Britain. Probably carved about 1503 for Taddeo Taddei, it was bought in Rome in 1823 by Sir George Beaumont, who presented it to the Royal Academy.*

*Its unfinished state is not unusual, for Michelangelo failed to carry many of his greatest works to completion, but Michelangelo's statue of the Virgin and Child in Bruges, carved about the same time, gives an indication of the kind of surface it would have had if he had completed it. (Royal Academy)*

manuscripts, concert programmes and portraits of musicians.

ROYAL COLLEGE OF SURGEONS' MUSEUM (LINCOLN'S INN FIELDS, WC2) John Hunter (1728–93), the British surgeon, began this collection of specimens and preparations to illustrate his views on animal physiology and anatomy. (By appointment.)

ROYAL COURTS OF JUSTICE (STRAND, WC2) Following the successful result of the collaboration between Augustus Pugin and Sir Charles Barry over the new Gothic Palace of Westminster, the style of George Edmund Street's Royal Courts of Justice, built in 1868–82, was again Gothic. However, this time an adaptation of the more austere 13th-century style was used. The centrepiece is the stone-vaulted great hall, about 80 ft high, whose roof is surmounted by a tall, narrow spire, best seen from the distance, rising above the roof-line; in the gable is a fine rose window. The Strand stone-faced façade has a tower with a

hipped-roof and a clock projecting over the roadway, open screens of pointed arches, and small turrets with pointed caps clinging to the walls. The back of the building in Carey Street also has a tall tower, but here the emphasis is on exposed brick with bands of stone as decoration.

ROYAL EXCHANGE (ROYAL EXCHANGE, EC3) The Royal Exchange was destroyed by fire twice and was rebuilt for the third time in 1842 by Sir William Tite, whose building still stands. It was first instituted and built in Elizabeth I's reign by Sir Thomas Gresham, the richest London merchant and financier of his time, and son of the lord mayor. The Exchange was built in Classical style round a quadrangle where the merchants transacted their business, and was surrounded by two colonnades; the upper one, called The Pawn, was lined with 100 small shops. Statues of all the English monarchs, from Edward the Confessor onwards, stood in niches looking down on to the quadrangle. The first meeting of merchants in the new Exchange was held on December 22, 1568. When Gresham died in 1579 he entrusted the Exchange to the City Corporation and to the Mercers, his livery company. It was destroyed in the Great Fire, rebuilt by Edward Jarman and again burnt down in 1838.

The foundation stone of the third building was laid by the Prince Consort in 1842. A broad flight of steps leads up to the sheltered portico, with its eight Corinthian pillars, which could be used as a meeting place; above it, a sculpture in the tympanum by Sir Richard Westmacott represents Commerce, in the form of British and foreign merchants and City worthies. Like its predecessors the Renaissance-style building surrounded an open quadrangle, which was roofed over in 1882. In front of the Exchange is a statue of the Duke of Wellington by Sir Francis Chantrey (1844) and a war memorial to Londoners who served in the two World Wars. Paintings presented by Lord Leighton in 1893 led to the quadrangle being used as an art gallery. For the last 40 years no exchange business has been done there.

ROYAL FUSILIERS MUSEUM (EC3) The museum, in the Tower of London, has uniforms including those worn by George V as Colonel-in-Chief, regimental silver and china, four dioramas of famous battles, and campaign medals, among them five Victoria Crosses including the prototype approved by Queen Victoria.

ROYAL GEOGRAPHICAL SOCIETY (KENSINGTON GORE, SW7) A private society founded in 1830, dedicated to the diffusion of geographical knowledge and to aiding exploration and discovery. The Society's house includes a library, and map room (open to the public) containing over 500,000 maps, as well as mementoes of famous explorers.

ROYAL HOSPITAL (CHELSEA, SW3) The Royal Hospital, founded by Charles II in 1682, houses over 400 veteran and invalid soldiers, known as Chelsea Pensioners. The building was designed by Christopher Wren and took ten years to build. It is of brick with stone cornices, cornerstones, door and window dressings. Charles II spent £20,000 on its erection and endowed it with £5000 a year. Although Robert Adam and Sir John Soane made alterations and additions, the main building remains virtually unchanged. The pensioners' uniform today—a scarlet frock-coat in summer and blue greatcoat in winter—dates from the time of Marlborough in the early 18th century. One of the Soane buildings has a collection of historical material relating to the hospital.

ROYAL INSTITUTE GALLERIES (PICCADILLY, W1) Exhibitions of works by members of the Royal Institute of Painters in Water-colour, the Pastel Society, the Society of Women Artists, the London Group and other bodies are held here.

ROYAL MEWS (BUCKINGHAM PALACE, SW1) The Gold State Coach, with its panels painted by the Florentine artist Cipriani, is the most spectacular exhibit at the Royal Mews. It was made in 1762, and has been used for every coronation since that of George IV in 1820. Other state coaches and carriages are on display, including a miniature barouche, presented to Queen Victoria's children in 1846, and now used by the present royal children, and the Irish Coach normally used by the Queen for the State Opening of Parliament. Royal sleighs are also on display, including Queen Victoria's State Sledge. State harness, probably the finest collection in existence, and items of saddlery can be seen, as well as the Windsor Grey and

THE IRISH STATE COACH

*A Lord Mayor of Dublin, M. Hutton, built this coach in 1852. It was bought by Queen Victoria when she visited Dublin, and she used the coach on the only two occasions on which she opened Parliament during her widowhood, in 1887 and 1897. Later sovereigns have driven to the opening of Parliament in the coach and it is also used at royal weddings and funerals. The wooden body was originally painted maroon but successive varnishings have given it a black appearance. The coach is drawn by four or six horses. (Royal Mews)*

THE GOLD STATE COACH

*Made of gilded oak, this coach was completed in 1762 used at the coronation of George IV, and has been for every coronation since. Four Tritons support the coach body. Eight palm trees form its framework and nine painted panels depict allegorical scenes. On the roof are three cherubs representing the genii of England, Scotland and Ireland. The coach weighs 4 tons, and the harness is of red morocco. (Royal Mews)*

Cleveland Bay carriage horses, which are kept in the stables. The royal motor cars may be seen. The stables and coach houses were designed by John Nash and completed in 1825.

ROYAL OPERA HOUSE (COVENT GARDEN, WC2) The chief theatre for grand opera and ballet in London, originally opened in 1732 and twice destroyed by fire. The present building was designed by E. M. Barry in 1858.

ST BARTHOLOMEW'S HOSPITAL (WEST SMITH-FIELD, EC1) London's oldest hospital, founded in 1123 by Rahere at the same time as the priory church of St Bartholomew the Great; both were erected as a thank-offering for Rahere's recovery from malaria while on a pilgrimage to Rome. The hospital, facing Smithfield meat market, is still on the original site, and the gate-house, built in 1702, still makes a fine entrance. Above its arch is a statue of Henry VIII, who refounded the hospital in 1546 after suppressing the priory. Through the archway is the hospital church of St

# ST PAUL'S CATHEDRAL

WEST FRONT *The old St Paul's, one of England's largest and finest Gothic buildings, was destroyed in September 1666 during the Great Fire. Sir Christopher Wren prepared a first design for a new cathedral in 1670. A second design in the form of a Greek cross, usually called the Great Model design, was submitted in 1673, but was also rejected by the Church Commissioners. Wren's third design, on which the present cathedral is based, was a compromise between Wren's insistence on a Classical cathedral with a dome and the clergy's preference for a cruciform plan. This design received the Royal Warrant in 1673, and the foundation stone was laid during the same year. In 1708 the last stone in the lantern above the dome was laid by Wren's son, and by 1711 the cathedral was complete.*

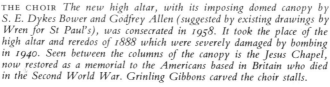

THE CHOIR *The new high altar, with its imposing domed canopy by S. E. Dykes Bower and Godfrey Allen (suggested by existing drawings by Wren for St Paul's), was consecrated in 1958. It took the place of the high altar and reredos of 1888 which were severely damaged by bombing in 1940. Seen between the columns of the canopy is the Jesus Chapel, now restored as a memorial to the Americans based in Britain who died in the Second World War. Grinling Gibbons carved the choir stalls.*

MONUMENT TO JOHN DONNE *Donne, the great English poet and Dean of St Paul's, died in 1631, and this monument to him by Nicholas Stone (1587–1647) was carved in the same year. Towards the end of his life Donne was obsessed by death, and Stone's carving was made from a painting which Donne posed for in a shroud shortly before he died. The monument, although discoloured, was the only complete figure to be salvaged after the Great Fire and was re-erected in Wren's new cathedral. Stone, one of the most successful sculptors of his day, was the son of a Devon quarryman.*

Bartholomew the Less where Inigo Jones was christened in 1573. It was rebuilt by Dance in 1787 and by Hardwick in 1823. When the hospital was rebuilt, from 1730 to 1760, the quadrangle and buildings round it were designed by James Gibbs; he also designed the great hall (1730–4), giving it a decorated ceiling and incorporating a 'charter' window of the 17th century showing Henry VIII handing a charter to the Lord Mayor of London. Portraits of famous medical men painted by Kneller, Reynolds, Thomas Lawrence, Millais and Herkomer hang on the walls.

ST JAMES'S PALACE (PALL MALL, SW1) Charles I spent his last night here before walking through St James's Park to his execution in Whitehall in January, 1649. Built by Henry VIII in 1530–6 on the site of a leper hospital dedicated to St James the Less, the palace was the official royal residence for only 140 years, but foreign ambassadors are still accredited to the 'Court of St James'. The gatehouse with clock remains from the original building; the many courts and the Chapel Royal where Queen Victoria was married are later additions and are open to the public. Much of the palace comprises 'grace and favour' residences granted by the Sovereign, and apartments of the Royal Family

ST JOHN'S WOOD CHAPEL (WELLINGTON ROAD, NW8) On the crest of a hill, this building, with its Ionic Portland stone portico and turret above, is seen to good advantage. It was begun in 1813 after designs by Thomas Hardwicke, who had in the same year started building the parish church of St Mary. The interior, which is all white, has monuments of the 19th century by Sir Francis Chantrey, W. Behnes, E. Physick, S. Nixon and others.

ST PANCRAS STATION (EUSTON ROAD, NW1) One of the three great 19th-century railway stations in North London; the other two were Euston and King's Cross. Along the main road spreads Sir Gilbert Scott's Gothic Revival hotel, designed in 1865–71, with spires and pinnacles. Behind is W. H. Barlow's splendid station-shed. This is roofed by a magnificent iron span of nearly 250 ft —a world record at the time of its construction.

ST PAUL'S CATHEDRAL (EC4) A great Gothic cathedral stood on this site. Its spire was nearly 500 ft high, but this was destroyed by fire in 1561. The building was generally neglected at that time and by 1600 there was concern for its safety. Inigo Jones patched up certain parts, but the cathedral was neglected again during the Commonwealth. After the Restoration in 1660, Christopher Wren put forward proposals for renovating the cathedral, the most important of these being his intention to demolish the central tower and build a dome instead. However, the building was virtually destroyed in September 1666 during the Great Fire of London. The present magnificent domed building was erected to Wren's designs in 1675–1711. During recent years the exterior has been cleaned of two and a half centuries' accumulation of soot, revealing the carved decoration by Francis Bird, Caius Gabriel Cibber, Edward Pierce and Grinling Gibbons.

ST THOMAS'S HOSPITAL (LAMBETH PALACE ROAD, SE1) Founded in the 13th century in Southwark by the canons of St Mary Overy's Priory as a result of distress caused by a great fire, it was dedicated to St Thomas à Becket. Henry VIII took it over in 1538 on the Dissolution of the monasteries, and in 1553 Edward VI, regarded as the founder, granted it a royal charter; a statue of him by Scheemakers, erected in 1739, was transferred to the new site when the hospital was

GEORGE STEPHENSON'S 'ROCKET'

*In 1829 the owners of the unfinished Liverpool and Manchester Railway offered a prize of £500 for the most improved locomotive. Three engines—the 'Rocket', the 'Sans Pareil' and the 'Novelty'—competed in the trials held at Rainhill in October 1828. The 'Sans Pareil' and the 'Novelty' failed to finish the course, but the 'Rocket', drawing three times its own weight (4¼ tons), completed the 35 mile course at an average speed of 14 mph, and became the forerunner of the steam-driven passenger train. (Science Museum)*

moved to the Albert Embankment in 1871. The new building was opened by Queen Victoria and cost half a million pounds. The Nightingale Training School for Nurses was set up in St Thomas's to commemorate the work of Florence Nightingale.

SCIENCE MUSEUM (SOUTH KENSINGTON, SW7) First established in 1856, the Science Museum building was designed by Sir Richard Allison. The collections cover all aspects of science including industrial and technological developments. Many working models, as well as actual locomotives, planes, machinery of both historical and contemporary interest, combine to give an all-embracing panorama of science through the ages.

SOANE MUSEUM (13 LINCOLN'S INN FIELDS, WC2) Founded by Sir John Soane, RA, in the house he originally built for himself in 1812, it contains collections for 'the promotion of the study of Architecture and the Allied Arts'. It includes Hogarth's famous paintings of *The Rake's Progress*.

SOMERSET HOUSE (STRAND, WC2) Old Somerset House was begun in 1547. Its architecture probably derived from the work of contemporary architects such as Philibert de l'Orme; later additions were made by Inigo Jones and John Webb, but the building was completely demolished in the 18th century and replaced by the present palace, designed by Sir William Chambers. This frames a courtyard about 350 ft by 300 ft, and originally reached to the river. The river front, now nearly 800 ft long, was raised on a high base because of the slope of the land towards the Thames, and there were entrances from the river. These have now lost their significance, and are not usually recognised for what they were since the construction of the Victoria Embankment and the roadway over the underground railway. The sculptured decoration of the exterior of the building is by Agostino Carlini, Nathaniel Smith, Joseph Caracchi, John Bacon, Joseph Nollekens and others. To the west side is the 1856 extension made by Sir James Pennethorne, while to the east is King's College (London University) designed by Sir Robert Smirke and built in 1829–35.

SOUTHALL DISTRICT LIBRARY (OSTERLEY PARK ROAD, W7) Salt-glazed stoneware made by the Martin Brothers of Southall is on display.

SOUTH LONDON ART GALLERY (PECKHAM ROAD, SE5) The gallery was started as a private venture in 1868 by William Rossiter in a shop in the Camberwell Road. Supported by leading figures in the art world, notably Lord Leighton, G. F. Watts and the actor Henry Irving, Rossiter obtained the present site and the gallery was built in 1891.

The gallery's main collection is of some 300 paintings from the Victorian and earlier eras, including works by Hogarth, Millais, Leighton, G. F. Watts and John Opie, and with drawings by Ruskin. There is a small but growing collection of modern British paintings including works by Sickert, Piper and Christopher Wood, and an artistic record of the London Borough of Southwark shown by paintings dating from the 18th century to the present day. There is also an important reference collection of 20th-century original prints, and ten varied loan exhibitions are held throughout the year.

SOUTHWARK CATHEDRAL (LONDON BRIDGE, SE1) The design of this fine Gothic church contains a mixture of English and French ideas. The parish church, which became Southwark Cathedral in 1905, was originally the church attached to the priory of St Mary Overy, founded in 1106. Early in the 13th century a fire destroyed much of the first church of the priory. An old chronicle gives 1208–9 as the year in which rebuilding began, but the exact dates are not known. The low eastern retrochoir with four aisles, and the broad simple proportions of the choir, are reminiscent of the Gothic style of other English ecclesiastical buildings, such as Salisbury Cathedral and the Temple Church, London. But the detail of the choir, for example the vaulting and the use of a triforium passage, were doubtless the mark of a man acquainted with contemporary French architecture. The medieval nave was demolished in 1838, and the present nave, designed in the style of the medieval choir, was built in 1890–7.

STAPLE INN (HOLBORN, WC1) A medieval inn, dating from the 14th century when it got its name from the Merchants of the Staple (wool merchants) who used it as a hostelry where wool was weighed and excise duty collected. A wool-pack is still to be seen on the wrought-iron gate of the garden. Its quaint half-timbered façade with overhanging gables, said to be the oldest in London, was added in 1586 by the Benchers of Gray's Inn, who bought the building in 1529, and is the only surviving example of Elizabethan domestic architecture in London. The Inn was built round two irregular courtyards in 1545–89 but rebuilt to a large extent in the 18th century. Dickens describes it in *The Mystery of Edwin Drood* as 'one of those nooks turning into which out of the clashing street imparts to the relieved pedestrian the sensation of having put cotton in his ears and velvet soles on his boots'. Nathaniel Hawthorne had the same impression: 'In all the hundreds of years since London was built it has not been able to sweep its roaring tide over that little island of quiet.' It was there that Dr Johnson in 1759 wrote *Rasselas*, in the evenings of one week, to defray his mother's funeral expenses.

TATE GALLERY (MILLBANK, SW1) Sir Henry Tate, the sugar refiner, commissioned the gallery to which he donated his own collection of paintings.

SOMERSET HOUSE

*Designed by Sir William Chambers (1723–96)—one of the founder members of the Royal Academy—Somerset House in the Strand had a Thames-side frontage 600 ft long. Built expressly to house government offices, the Royal Academy and other learned societies, it was the first office building of its kind in England. The rooms on the Strand front contain painted ceiling panels by Giovanni Battista Cipriani, left behind when the Academy moved to the National Gallery in 1836. Started in 1776, the building took ten years to complete. It stands on the site of the former Somerset House built about 1547 for Protector Somerset, Regent for Edward VI.*

The building, in Classical style, was designed by S. R. J. Smith and was opened in 1897. Works by Turner and Constable figure predominantly in a vast collection, only a small percentage of which is displayed at any given moment. The British paintings cover all important artists for the past 450 years and there is also much sculpture; the foreign collections include a representative selection of work by French Impressionists and Post-Impressionists. (See pp. 330–2.)

TEMPLE BAR (EC4) From 1301 a bar (gateway) stood at the boundary of the Cities of London and Westminster. In 1672 a fine gateway designed by Wren was erected. This was removed in 1878 and now stands at Theobald's Park in Hertfordshire; a pedestal surmounted by a griffin marks its former site at the junction of the Strand and Fleet Street. The sovereign may not enter the City of London in state without permission from the lord mayor. At the bar on state occasions the Sword of the City is presented to the sovereign by the lord mayor, and immediately returned; formerly the gate was kept closed until after this ceremony.

TEMPLE CHURCH (EC4) This church, which dates from the 12th century, is the finest monument in England to the Knights Templar. The earliest part of the church is the circular nave, erected c. 1160–85. The circular shape is common to most churches associated with the Templars. The Knights were the self-appointed guardians of the Church of the Holy Sepulchre in Jerusalem, and their round English churches are reminders of this duty and privilege. The design combines Gothic and Romanesque architectural characteristics. Purbeck marble, which centuries later became a favourite decorative material with English masons, was used for the main columns. To the east of this Romanesque church a chancel was added in the 13th century in the form of a three-aisled hall.

THOMAS CORAM FOUNDATION See Coram Foundation for Children.

TOWER BRIDGE (E1) London's best-known bridge. Its centre span is formed by two drawbridges which are raised several times a day to allow ships to pass to and from the Pool of London. Farthest downstream of the Thames bridges, it was opened in 1894.

TOWER OF LONDON (TOWER HILL, EC3) The Tower of London has been a fortress, palace and prison, and it is one of the most important works of medieval architecture to survive in England. It was intended as a royal fortress from which to control the City of London, and represents a system of medieval defences frequently brought up to date. At the core of the whole system stands the White Tower, a massive Norman keep built under William I and William II, and probably finished by 1097. This was built just within the Roman city walls, and it is likely that these were utilised in the original fortress. In the 13th century, following developments in military thought and planning, the White Tower was encircled by two lines of walls and received substantially the form in which it is today. The palace buildings have now all disappeared but evidence for the use of the Tower as a prison is plentiful. Many of the towers have inscriptions carved by former inmates and the records provide a list of illustrious names, including those of Sir Thomas More, Archbishop Laud, Lady Jane Grey and Anne Boleyn, Henry VIII's second wife. (See pp. 308–9.)

TOWER OF LONDON (ARMOURIES) Great Britain's national collection of armour and arms, based on the arsenal of Henry VIII (1509–47), is housed in the 11th-century White Tower of the Tower of London, and in the 17th-century building known as the New Armouries. The collection has been added to over the years and now illustrates the evolution of weapons and defensive armour in Europe from the Middle Ages to 1914. The Armouries, the oldest national armoury still in its original home, can claim to be the oldest museum in Britain.

TOWER OF LONDON (CHAPEL OF ST PETER-AD-VINCULA) The present building dates from 1520, and is small, with nave and north aisle, and small west tower. Here were buried many famous victims of the executioner, some of whom are listed on a tablet. Monuments include an elaborate one to the Duke of Exeter (d. 1447); the organ-case, 1676, was originally made for Whitehall Palace.

TRAFALGAR SQUARE (SW1) London's most famous square was designed by John Nash early in the 19th century, and was named for the great naval victory of 1805. Its chief monument is the column with Nelson's statue, the base of which is guarded by Landseer's four bronze lions. On its north side stands the National Gallery.

VICTORIA AND ALBERT MUSEUM (CROMWELL ROAD, SW7) The vast Victoria and Albert Museum was built as a result of the Great International Exhibition in 1851. Contrary to popular expectations the exhibition, staged by Prince Albert, was a great success, and made so large a profit that a commission was set up to administer the money. The commission bought land south of Hyde Park, commemorated by Exhibition Road in South Kensington, and gradually a cultural and educational centre came into being. The Victoria and Albert Museum was the first establishment of this centre; it was designed haphazardly over many years. Sir Henry Cole, Francis Fowke and H. Scott, an army engineer, were among the architects associated with the series of buildings grouped round a central garden. Lord Leighton, Godfrey Sykes and Reuben Townroe did much of the interior decorations. Sir Edward Poynter, Philip Webb and William Morris decorated the restaurant, which has been preserved as one of the museum's period rooms. By the end of the 19th century the rapidly growing collections had taken up all available space, and in 1899 Queen Victoria laid the foundation stone for the main galleries facing Cromwell Road. Sir Aston Webb, who designed the Victoria Memorial (in front of Buckingham Palace) and the Admiralty Arch, was the architect of the new building. It is dominated by the richly ornamented doorway below a crown-shaped tower. The façade is decorated in the Renaissance style with sculptures and figures set in niches. (See pp. 333–8.)

WALLACE COLLECTION (MANCHESTER SQUARE, W1) The collection is housed in a building begun in 1776 by the 4th Duke of Manchester, which later became the Spanish Embassy and passed to the Hertford family in 1797. On the death of the 4th Marquess in 1870, it passed to his natural son Sir Richard Wallace, who altered it considerably to house his father's art collection and also added many new works—Renaissance and medieval paintings and European arms and armour. The collection was bequeathed to the nation in 1897 by Sir Richard's widow Lady Wallace.

The collection includes paintings by such masters of the Flemish and Dutch schools as Rembrandt, Rubens, Van Dyck and Frans Hals. French schools are well represented with works by

# TOWER OF LONDON

Tradition points to Julius Caesar as the founder of the Tower of London, but its fame begins with the Normans. The White Tower, the massive keep at its heart, was built under William I and William II as a fortress from which to control London. The two outer walls were added in the 13th century. The Tower is famous for its Yeomen Warders, or Beefeaters, resplendent in their Tudor uniforms; its magnificent collection of medieval armour; and as the home of the Crown Jewels. It is even more famous as the 'Bloody Tower', a reputation acquired in the centuries when it filled the treble role of fortress, palace and prison. Cromwell ordered the demolition of the palace buildings, but there is ample evidence of the use of the Tower as a prison—including the inscriptions scratched by former inmates. The story of the murder of the Princes in the Tower is perhaps an example of Tudor propaganda, but there is poignancy enough in the list of those known to have spent their last days there. State prisoners were commonly admitted through the Traitors' Gate in St Stephen's Tower, and executions took place both on Tower Hill and inside the Tower. Among the illustrious prisoners in the Tower were Sir Thomas More, Sir Walter Raleigh, Archbishop Laud, Lady Jane Grey and Anne Boleyn, the second wife of Henry VIII.

ST EDWARD'S CROWN *Edward the Confessor, who died in 1066 and was the only English king to be canonised, is said to have placed regalia in Westminster Abbey for the use of his successors. But most of what still survived of these early Crown Jewels by the time of Charles I, was destroyed by order of Parliament after his execution in 1649. The frame of St Edward's Crown is possibly one of the few pieces which escaped destruction; but it more probably derives from the old Imperial Crown of Henry VII, which in turn incorporated earlier materials. The crown is of gold, and it was re-worked and set with diamonds and other precious and semi-precious stones after the Restoration of the Monarchy in 1660. With the minever-trimmed purple velvet Cap of Estate inside, it is traditionally used to crown English sovereigns. (Jewel House)*

STATE SALT *This silver-gilt salt was presented to Charles II by the City of Exeter in thanks for the Restoration. It was used during the coronation banquets of all the monarchs from Charles II to George IV, and has been re-gilded and repaired several times. The condiment was placed in boxes along one side and in receptacles on the tops of the towers. The salt may have been bought second-hand and embellished for presentation to the king. The decoration of lizards and frogs on the base, and the gems and enamelling, suggest that it was made on the Continent in the late 16th or early 17th century. The feet and other details appear to date from 1660. (Jewel House)*

ST JOHN'S CHAPEL *Probably the oldest of the Tower's four chapels, built about 1080 under William I and improved by William Rufus. Henry III added the splendid mosaic floor. Knights of the Bath spent all-night vigils in the chapel before being dubbed. Later, the chapel became neglected, and under Charles II it was dismantled and used as a storehouse for records. Prince Albert, the Prince Consort, restored it to its former glory, and it is still used as a chapel.*

HENRY VIII'S GUN *The king had this gun—one of the earliest recorded breech loaders—made in 1537. It is almost certainly the gun referred to in accounts of the setting up of targets at Greenwich Palace and Windsor Castle 'for the Kynge to shotte at with his handgoune'. The royal monogram is incorporated in relief ornament on the barrel. (Armouries)*

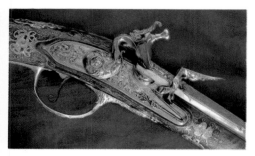

SPORTING GUN *It is almost certain that this gun was commissioned by Louis XIV to present to Charles Lennox, 1st Duke of Richmond and Lennox, an illegitimate son of Charles II. It was made by Bertrand Piraube, gunmaker to Louis, probably in the early 1680's and is unique in having a solid silver barrel. It is unlikely that it was intended for use. (Armouries)*

HENRY VIII'S ARMOUR *(left) In 1515 Henry set up the Almain Armoury at Greenwich Palace. Staffed by Almains (Germans and Flemings)—expert armourers —it made armour for the upper classes only, maintaining a high standard of work. This set of foot-tournament armour was made in 1540. Of bright steel, it has etched and gilded borders probably designed by Hans Holbein the Younger. (Armouries)*

ARMOUR OF ROBERT DUDLEY, EARL OF LEICESTER *This armour of Elizabeth I's favourite was made at the Almain Armoury at Greenwich about 1575, when he entertained the queen at his castle of Kenilworth. A tilt-armour with reinforcing pieces, it has finely etched scrollwork with the initials RD. (Armouries)*

Watteau, Boucher, Fragonard, Lancret, Pater and Nattier. Spain and Italy are represented by Velasquez, Murillo and Titian among others, and the British school includes works by Reynolds, Gainsborough, Romney, Hoppner and Lawrence.

Most of the furniture is 18th-century French, much of it from the royal palaces of France, and includes works by some of the greatest French craftsmen—A. C. Boulle, Riesener, Oeben, Weisweiler and Carlin. There is a large collection of Sèvres porcelain, and of Italian maiolica, mostly from the 16th century. Bronze and gold work of the Renaissance and the 18th century are well represented. There is also an Oriental armoury and a European armoury with many decorated pieces of the 16th and 17th centuries. (See p. 339.)

WELLCOME HISTORICAL MEDICAL MUSEUM AND LIBRARY (EUSTON ROAD, NW1) The Wellcome Trust, by which this museum and library (the largest of their kind in the world) are maintained, was established by the American founder of a great pharmaceutical firm—Burroughs Wellcome and Co.—to advance medical research throughout the world. The library contains approximately 500,000 items: manuscripts and printed books from the 11th to the 20th century, the original letters, notebooks and documents of medical and scientific pioneers—including the laboratory notebook of Mme Curie, who first isolated radium—and a selection of Oriental and American texts. The museum (approximately 400,000 items) includes some 1500 paintings from the 15th century onwards, 100,000 prints and drawings, ceramics—3000 drug jars, some from the 9th century—glass, carved ivories, coins, medals and sculpture. The scientific apparatus ranges from Ancient Egyptian to 19th century, and non-scientific medicine is illustrated by a large collection of ethnographical objects from Africa, Asia and the Pacific Islands. In the entrance hall there are re-creations of original 17th- and 18th-century pharmacies, with their furnishings, drug jars and equipment.

WESLEY'S HOUSE AND CHAPEL (CITY ROAD, EC1) John Wesley, 1703–91, the founder of Methodism, lived the last years of his life in this late-18th-century house in City Road, where relics of his life are collected. His furniture and books are there, his bedroom and study, and the room reserved for private prayer. Next to the house is Wesley's chapel, opened by him in 1778; it was burnt down and rebuilt in 1899. In front of the chapel is a statue of Wesley, who is buried in the chapel graveyard. Books on the history of Methodism are housed in the chapel crypt.

WESTMINSTER ABBEY (SW1) Built during the 13th and 14th centuries, this church with its great rose window, its outstanding height, and its flying buttresses, is closer to French Gothic architecture than any other English church. The design of the building seems to have been particularly inspired by the cathedrals of Rheims and Amiens, and the palace chapel of the Kings of France in Paris, Sainte Chapelle. Henry III did not complete the abbey, and the nave was finished only after 1375. However, the Master of the King's Works at that time, Henry Yevele, followed the design of the 13th-century building so closely that the abbey, apart from the Hawksmoor towers, has the appearance of a building designed and built at one period. The 13th-century sculpture on Westminster Abbey is of an extremely high quality. The best-known pieces are probably the figures of angels high up in the interior of the transepts, although much more survives on the lowest

# WESTMINSTER ABBEY

Since the 11th century Westminster Abbey has been the usual place for the coronation of English monarchs, and most of the medieval English kings from the time of Henry III were buried there. The present abbey was begun by Henry III (1216–72) on the site of the 11th-century building erected by the royal saint, Edward the Confessor, whose body lies in the great 13th-century shrine at the east end of the church. Henry III never finished the building and the nave was only completed after 1375; but the French Gothic style of the previous century was adhered to, so that most of the abbey gives the impression of a building designed and built as a whole. The latest major addition was Henry VII's Chapel, begun in 1503; it is the chapel of the Order of the Bath and the banners of the knights of the order hang there. The west front gives the appearance of having been constructed during one period, but it represents 600 years of alterations and restorations. In the 18th century, both Christopher Wren and Nicholas Hawksmoor worked on its two main towers.

CORONATION CHAIR *Since the reign of Edward II, all but two English sovereigns have been crowned on the Coronation Chair in Westminster Abbey. It was made of English oak to hold the Stone of Scone, the coronation seat of Scotland's kings, which was seized by Edward I in 1297 to demonstrate Scotland's subservience.*

HENRY VII'S CHAPEL *Raised above the general level of the abbey and approached by a broad flight of steps, the chapel (above) contains the magnificent tomb of Henry VII and his wife, Elizabeth of York. Enclosed by a Gothic screen, the white and black touchstone tomb is the work of the famous Florentine sculptor Torrigiani (1472-1528). Commissioned by Henry VIII in 1512, Torrigiani was paid £1500 and took six years to complete the work. The chapel roof with its intricate and lace-like fan-vaulting is one of the finest of its kind.*

ELEANOR OF CASTILE *This effigy of Edward I's wife, cast in gilt and bronze by William Torel, a London goldsmith, in 1291, is the earliest of its kind in England. It lies on a tomb of Purbeck marble in the Chapel of Edward the Confessor.*

311

arcading round the walls in the Chapel of St Faith and elsewhere. Henry VII's Chapel, built 1503–c. 1512, is the Chapel of the Order of the Bath. Also used as a royal burial place, it is among the most brilliant and ostentatious works to survive from the Middle Ages; it has an extremely elaborate fan-vault and an unequalled amount of surviving figure sculpture. The latest additions to the abbey are the west towers designed by Nicholas Hawksmoor, which were built from 1735–40.

WESTMINSTER CATHEDRAL (ASHLEY PLACE, SW1) A Roman Catholic cathedral in Byzantine style, built in 1895–1910. John Francis Bentley, the architect, did not live to see the building finished. The dominant feature of the exterior is the tall thin campanile (bell-tower), which rises without ornamentation except for bands of stonework contrasting with the brick, to a graceful octagonal lantern. The tower was for years a prominent feature of the London skyline, but it is now dwarfed by neighbouring office blocks.

WESTMINSTER HALL (HOUSES OF PARLIAMENT, SW1) The scene of many famous trials, including those of Sir Thomas More (1535) and Charles I (1649), the Hall was the chief law court of England from 1224 until 1882. Since then monarchs and famous men have lain in state there before burial. The Hall, part of the medieval Old Palace of Westminster, was built by William Rufus in 1097. It was rebuilt in its present form for Richard II in 1394–1402 by Henry Yevele; the fine hammer-beam roof was the work of Hugh Herland.

## WESTMINSTER CATHEDRAL

*A great Byzantine-style cathedral, the achievement of Cardinal Vaughan. Built in 1895–1910, it is a large church, impressive in scale inside, the nave and sanctuary comprising four square, domed bays. Originally there was no decoration and the large areas of brickwork were austere. But now marble and mosaic are being added to the walls and domes, as in this Chapel of the Blessed Sacrament. Some of the earlier mosaics were by R. Anning Bell.*

## THE 'WOODPECKER' TAPESTRY

*In 1881, William Morris (1834–96) the poet, designer, art critic and political thinker, bought Merton Abbey, once a silk factory. There he set up looms for carpets and tapestries, and workshops for other crafts. He revived the 17th-century Gobelins method of high-warp tapestry weaving, and also studied medieval and later tapestries. The 'Woodpecker' tapestry, woven in 1885, was his second full-size tapestry; his friend Philip Webb drew the birds. The design was inspired by the 16th- and 17th-century 'verdures' from Enghien (near Brussels) which usually consisted of a field filled with scrolling leaves similar to acanthus, sometimes with flowers but more usually with birds and insects. Later Morris tapestries included human figures drawn by Sir Edward Burne-Jones.*
*(William Morris Gallery and Brangwyn Gift)*

WHITTINGTON MEMORIAL (HIGHGATE HILL, N19) London's most famous lord mayor, Sir Richard Whittington, is commemorated by a stone at the foot of Highgate Hill. Here, legend says, the runaway boy heard the sound of Bow Bells three times calling him back to be lord mayor. At his death in 1423, he was buried in the City church of St Michael Paternoster Royal, bombed during the Blitz.

WILLIAM MORRIS GALLERY AND BRANGWYN GIFT (FOREST ROAD, E17) A specialised collection of work by William Morris and the Morris firm, and by his contemporaries and forerunners of art nouveau is exhibited in Morris's boyhood home. The house is Georgian, has been altered very little, and has much of its original panelling.

# BRITISH MUSEUM

The nucleus of the British Museum, established by an Act of Parliament in 1753, was the collection of scientific books and manuscripts bequeathed to the nation by Sir Hans Sloane, the fashionable 18th-century physician. As other valuable collections were rapidly acquired, either as gifts, bequests, purchases or copyright deposits, the museum's original premises had to be substantially enlarged. The present building, designed by Sir Robert Smirke and built in successive stages between 1823 and 1847, has since become the home of priceless man-made objects from all over the world, some of which are more than 3000 years old. In addition to its 6,000,000 books, the museum's contents range from medieval manuscripts to sheet-music, postage stamps, the log-book of Nelson's *Victory* and a 1623 First Folio of Shakespeare's plays. Many thousands of prints and drawings illustrate the history of graphic art from the 15th century onwards, and statues, tombs, mummies and fragments of architectural antiquities link the Assyrian, Egyptian, Greek and Persian with his Romano-British and Anglo-Saxon counterpart.

MILDENHALL TREASURE: THE GREAT DISH *In 1942 a group of silver vessels was found buried near Mildenhall on the borders of the Fens; the hoard was probably hidden for safety and never recovered. This great dish is perhaps its finest piece. Inside the beaded rim, the figure-frieze depicts the triumph of Bacchus over Hercules. The figures include Bacchus (the god of wine), Hercules, Silenus (a foster-father of Bacchus), Pan, satyrs and priestesses of Bacchus.*

*Inside this is a zone of sea-nymphs riding on sea-monsters and, in the central medallion, there is a bearded mask, probably of Oceanus, a sea-god. The dish, possibly dating from the 3rd century, is approximately 2 ft in diameter and weighs more than 18 lb. It was made in a workshop in the Mediterranean area, probably in Rome itself, and was buried during the troubled years that saw the end of Roman rule in Britain, when the Anglo-Saxons were invading.*

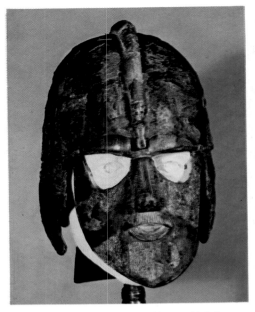

THE SUTTON HOO HELMET *Reassembled from a mass of fragments, this Anglo-Saxon helmet consists of an iron cap, to which are attached visor, cheek-pieces and a neck-guard of iron. It was padded internally and further protection from blows was given by the tubular crest of silver-cased iron on the outside. The eyebrows are bronze, edged below with garnets, each with a gilt boar's head at the outer end. A single bronze-cast, with silver and niello decoration, forms the nose and mouthpiece of the visor. The cap was covered with tinned bronze sheeting, stamped in relief.*

BRONZE HEAD *Head of a queen mother found in the wood and mud palace at Benin, one of the old negro empires. Almost the entire art of Benin, about 3000 objects, was brought here in 1897 after the palace was burnt by a British punitive expedition. The head is probably the finest piece of cast-bronze discovered there.*

CODEX SINAITICUS *The great 4th-century manuscript of the Bible, in Greek capitals, was bought from the Soviet Government in 1933 for £100,000. The name Sinaiticus is derived from St Catherine's Monastery on Mount Sinai, the former home of the manuscript where, in 1844, a German scholar found a basket filled with old parchment, about to be burnt as rubbish. In this basket were 129 leaves of the Codex. He was allowed to take away 43 leaves, now in the Leipzig University. The remainder, together with others, were bought by the Imperial Government for 9000 roubles and later sold to Britain. The reproduction shows the end of St John's Gospel from chapter 21.*

THE SNETTISHAM TREASURE *Hoards of metalwork and coins were found at Snettisham, Norfolk, during 1948–50. This Iron Age gold torque consists of eight strands, each of eight twisted wires soldered into decorated terminals, and is the only complete torque found in Britain.*

IRON AGE SHIELD *One of several Iron Age shields found in Britain, this was recovered from the Thames at Battersea. Its gleaming golden-bronze surface is decorated with patterns hammered into relief from the reverse side and embellished with a series of small, quartered, red enamelled studs. The pattern on the shield reveals an unusual symmetry of design, rarely seen in British work of this period.*

THE HORSE OF SELENE *from the east pediment of the Parthenon, the great temple of the goddess Athene. This marble horse was one of the four (two are in Athens; one is lost) that drew the chariot of Selene across the night sky until dawn, when her chariot sank into the ocean, while the chariot of her brother Helios, the sun-god, emerged from the ocean to bring a new day. The Selene and Helios groups stood on opposite sides of the Parthenon's east pediment, in striking contrast—Selene's horses weary after their journey, Helios's fresh and ready to begin. These and a number of other architectural fragments from the Parthenon were brought to England in 1802–11 by Lord Elgin, Ambassador to Turkey. He had seen the neglect many of the sculptures were suffering following the partial destruction of the Parthenon by a Turkish shell during the Turko-Venetian war of 1687. The British Government paid Elgin £35,000—half the cost of bringing the sculptures to England.*

FROISSART'S CHRONICLE *A page from a 15th-century copy of the chronicle, written and illuminated in France, covering the events of the last ten years of Richard II's reign. It starts with the entry of Richard's wife, Queen Isabella, into Paris in 1389 and finishes with Richard's deposition in 1399. The jousts depicted took place at St Inglevert soon after the queen's entry into Paris. Three French knights of great renown are said to have jousted for 30 days. Froissart was born in Valenciennes, France, about 1337 and came to London in 1361, where he gained the favour of Queen Philippa, Edward III's wife, who came from the same town. He stayed five years as the official chronicler at the English Court during the Hundred Years War—already a quarter of a century old. Froissart fell from favour on the death of the queen and returned to France to become a priest. He died in 1404.*

SEAL OF KING JOHN *The original seal of wax attached to the document submitted by the barons to King John at Runnymede in 1215. The document was later developed into the Magna Carta, the great charter of English liberties. Four copies of the Magna Carta survive: two at the British Museum, one at Lincoln Cathedral and one at Salisbury. The obverse of the seal (above) shows John seated in his coronation robes and with regalia.*

315

ROYAL GOLD CUP *Made about 1380 for the Duc de Berri, this solid gold cup, decorated with brilliant enamels, has been part of both the French and the English royal treasures. In a chequered career, it was once sold by a Spanish convent for £100; now worth more than £200,000, it is probably the most valuable piece of goldsmith's work in Britain.*

PAINTED WOODEN COFFIN *of Pen-sen-Heru, a Libyan who died in Egypt during the 26th Dynasty, about 500 BC. Below the pectoral, or breastplate, is a brightly-painted judgment scene in three sections, culminating in the dead man adoring the god Osiris.*

GOLD COIN OF CHARLES I *The troubled reign of Charles I is reflected in his coinage, which is more varied than that of any other English monarch. This gold unite, or 20-shilling piece, was struck at the Tower Mint in 1631–2. As the king's quarrel with Parliament grew worse, local mints were set up throughout the country to supply him with money to continue the struggle. During the Civil War coins were issued in towns and castles under siege.*

GREEK SILVER COIN *One of the masterpieces of Greek colonial coinage, this tetradrachm of 460 BC comes from Naxos, a vine-growing district near Mount Etna, and the oldest Greek colony in Sicily. Appropriately, it carries a portrait of Dionysus, god of fertility and the vine; his great black beard overlaps the frame of the coin. The Greeks made their coins by hand, re-heating the metal after it had been cast while molten, and impressing the design with a bronze or iron stamp.*

GOLD CORONATION MEDAL *Henry Basse, chief engraver to the Mint in 1544–9, made this medal to mark the coronation of Henry VIII's son, the boy-king Edward VI, in 1547. Known only from castings, in both gold and silver, it is England's first official coronation medal. The art of casting portrait medals was introduced in Italy by Renaissance artists, and developed in France, Germany and the Netherlands; but it had little vogue in England until the 17th century.*

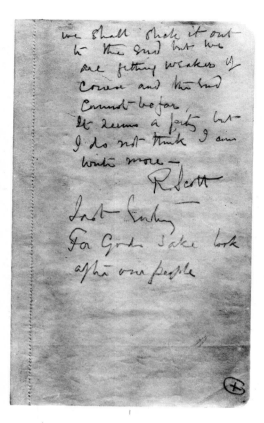

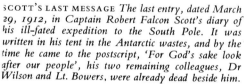

SCOTT'S LAST MESSAGE *The last entry, dated March 29, 1912, in Captain Robert Falcon Scott's diary of his ill-fated expedition to the South Pole. It was written in his tent in the Antarctic wastes, and by the time he came to the postscript, 'For God's sake look after our people', his two remaining colleagues, Dr Wilson and Lt. Bowers, were already dead beside him.*

THE ROSETTA STONE *From the inscriptions on this slab of black basalt, found in the Nile delta in 1799 by one of Napoleon's officers, the French scholar Champollion cracked the code of Egyptian hieroglyphics, or picture-writing, and formulated the system of decipherment which is in use today. The inscriptions are in two languages, but in three scripts—the hieroglyphs in the top section were the form used by priests; the centre section is in the demotic script, a popular form of hieroglyphic writing; and the lower portion is in Greek, a language known to the Ptolemies. The text on the stone is a copy of a decree passed by the council of Egyptian priests in the ninth year of the reign of Ptolemy V (204–181 BC).*

HEAD OF APHRODITE *This bronze head, roughly 15 in. high, is from a statue roughly twice the size of life, found at Satala (now Sadagh) in Armenia Minor. The head and the left arm, holding a fragment of drapery, are all that remain of the statue, which is believed to have been a copy of the celebrated Aphrodite, goddess of love, by the 4th-century BC Greek sculptor Praxiteles. Like most of his work, this masterpiece is known only by copies. Praxiteles set a standard of Classical beauty which was often imitated, but never surpassed, by the later Greeks and the Romans, and was to inspire the sculptors of the Renaissance. With his Aphrodite he set himself no less a task than to capture Hellenistic beauty in its most perfect form; for she was the one chosen by Paris, prince of Troy, to receive the apple as the most beautiful of all the goddesses. The eyes in this copy were at one time inlaid with precious stones or enamel.*

**317**

# BRITISH MUSEUM (NATURAL HISTORY)

The lofty halls of the Natural History Museum provide nearly four acres of gallery space where exhibits relating to the products of nature and of early man are on display. Properly, the museum should be called the British Museum (Natural History), for it is an offshoot; the natural history departments were moved from Bloomsbury in 1881, when the parent British Museum was bursting at the seams for lack of space—a condition which has become almost routine. The vast natural history collections are based on the original collection of Sir Hans Sloane (1660–1753), a physician who built his fortune on a rich marriage, a fashionable practice and an early appreciation of the value of quinine. The specimens on display are, in fact, only a small selection from the museum's riches. Unseen to the general public are the laboratories, workshops and libraries where the museum's scientific and technical staff are engaged in research. As part of the museum's educational work, schoolchildren are encouraged to study and draw exhibits.

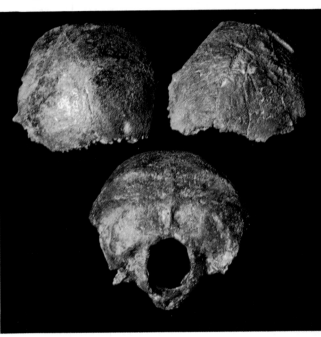

THE SWANSCOMBE FINDS *In 1925–6 two fragments of a human skull (right) were found in a gravel-pit at Swanscombe in Kent. In 1955, not many yards away from the original find, a third fragment was unearthed; the three pieces fitted together perfectly. The skull was associated with flint axes and other implements (above) dating back some 200,000 years, and is probably that of a young woman who died in her twenties. The hand-axe was a general-purpose tool used for cutting meat, scraping flesh from bones, and digging up roots.*

HIBISCUS DRAWING *(left) by Sydney Parkinson. Originally a draper by trade but with a passion for drawing, Parkinson was enlisted by Sir Joseph Banks as an assistant. Together they accompanied Captain Cook, on the Endeavour, on a voyage to the South Seas in 1768. Parkinson, as natural history draughtsman, was paid a salary of £80 a year. He made numerous drawings, many of which are also preserved in the British Museum. Parkinson contracted a fever on the voyage and died at sea, aged 26. Botanical and natural history studies flourished in the 18th century and many foreign expeditions were made, most of them carrying a skilled artist to make drawings of the flowers, plants and birds of the countries visited.*

CHELIDONIUM DRAWING *(right) by George Dionysius Ehret. Born in 1708 in Heidelburg, the son of humble parents, Ehret spent much of his youth as a gardener's apprentice, practising drawing in his spare time. After a period of study and travel on the Continent when he made hundreds of drawings, he finally settled in England in 1736. Here he met Dr Mead, the Royal Physician, who bought 200 of his paintings and introduced him to Sir Hans Sloane and the Duchess of Portland. By the middle of the 18th century Ehret dominated botanical drawing and was contributing to Linnaeus's 'Genera Plantarum'. In 1750 he was elected to the Botanic Gardens at Oxford as a draughtsman and was finally made a Fellow of the Royal Society in 1757—the only foreigner then so honoured.*

*glaucium.*

CHELIDONIUM *pedunculis unifloris,*
*foliis amplexicaulibus sinuatis, caule glabro.* Linn.

# COURTAULD INSTITUTE GALLERIES

In 1932 Samuel Courtauld and Viscount Lee of Fareham founded the Courtauld Institute of Art for London University. They both gave their magnificent art collections to the Institute, and these formed the nucleus of the present collections, enlarged by further bequests to the university.

GAUGUIN: NEVERMORE *Gauguin reacted against Impressionism, introducing into his paintings simple outlines of form and large areas of flat, strong colour. His desire for intensity and simplicity, and passion for the exotic, drove him to seek the simple life—in 1895 he left his Danish wife and Western civilisation, and went to live in the South Sea Islands. This, one of his finest paintings, was done in 1897 and depicts a native girl called Paa'ura who, at the age of 14½, went to live with him.*

VAN GOGH: PEACH TREES IN BLOSSOM *In February 1888 Van Gogh suddenly left Paris for Arles and the warmth of a southern climate. Almost immediately the orchards of Provence became a foaming cascade of blossom and the next eight months were the happiest of his short life. In April he painted 15 orchards in blossom. This one he painted in the plain of Crau in the following spring. He used colour with brilliance and originality but with such conviction and sincerity that it works—the force of his expression is in his personal technique of dots, stripes and whorls rained on to the canvas with dramatic vehemence.*

MANET: A BAR AT THE FOLIES-BERGÈRE *In the 1860's Manet fought a lone battle against the artificiality and sentimentality of official art in Paris. He disregarded the mellow shading of the studio in favour of the harsher contrasts of light and shade in full light, and the use of full colour. He was an inspiration to the Impressionists—but himself desired more naturalism than is possible in the diffuseness of full Impressionism. Manet scandalised the public in his early days and it was just as much his defiance of the accepted way of painting as his subject matter which infuriated them. This painting, his last major work, was exhibited in 1882, and although it may lack the sparkle of his earlier works it is a compact design with the reflections of the barmaid and her customer.*

ITALIAN DRUG JAR *One of a set of jars that would have been displayed colourfully on a pharmacist's shelf. The inscription denotes that it contained the drug Zucaro Buglossato. Made in 1510-15 at Deruta in central Italy, the jar is traditionally shaped of majolica—Italian earthenware coated with opaque white tin-enamel and ornamented with metallic colours. The flowers and eagle on this piece are of tin-glazed enamel. Originally the name majolica was probably given by Italians to similar Spanish ware imported into Italy by ships sailing from Majorca —formerly called Majolica.*

CÉZANNE: MONT STE-VICTOIRE *Cézanne (1839–1906) was one of the leaders of the inevitable reaction against the sketchy methods and lack of structural form of the Impressionists. He worked out of the studio to achieve his identification of colour with form, and his calculated distortions of form to give fine compositions. Mont Ste-Victoire, which he could see from his studio near Aix-en-Provence, became a kind of holy mountain which he portrayed many times. In this distant view the components of the intervening landscape form an overall geometric pattern.*

# THE LONDON MUSEUM

The extensive collection of exhibits in the London Museum represents the life and history of London from the earliest times to the present day. The museum was founded and opened to the public in 1912 in the State Apartments at Kensington Palace. In 1913 it was moved to Stafford House (later renamed Lancaster House), and in 1951 was moved back to Kensington Palace until more permanent accommodation can be found for the collections. The main exhibition rooms are arranged chronologically, and the exhibits range from the crude flint implements of the Old Stone Age to the special exhibits illustrating the growth of the modern postal and fire services. Other rooms are devoted to royal gifts and loans, prints and drawings, the law, the theatre, and children's toys.

ROMAN JUG *This 10 in. high earthenware jug (right) was found in Southwark. It is inscribed with the words 'Londinii Ad Fanum Isidis' (At London, at the Temple of Isis), and probably belonged to a tavern near the temple. The jug dates from the early 1st century AD, and is one of the earliest examples of an inscription using the Roman name for London.*

FIRE ENGINE *The inhabitants of London presented this fire engine (above) to Frederick Hodges, a Lambeth distiller, in 1862 in appreciation of his efforts to fight local fires. Fire protection did not become a public responsibility until 1866 when the Metropolitan Fire Brigade (now the London Fire Brigade) was founded.*

THE CHEAPSIDE HOARD *This hoard of je (right), probably part of city merchants' stock-in hidden in Cheapside early in the 17th century, p a unique record of the taste in jewellery of the classes at that period. One of the most exquisite is a scent bottle or pommander (bottom righi chain) set with a sapphire, opals and diamond*

# NATIONAL GALLERY

Since its foundation, in 1824, the National Gallery has grown to be one of the greatest museums of art in the world. It is remarkable for the balance of its collections: all of the important national schools and almost all of the major old masters are represented. The richest collection of all is that of the Dutch masters, which includes 19 Rembrandts. The gallery, founded when the Government voted £60,000 to purchase and exhibit 38 paintings from the Angerstein Collection, moved to its present site, then newly built, in 1838. It now has more than 2000 paintings. As a matter of policy, drawings, water-colours and pieces of sculpture are not acquired; but an exception was made in the case of the Leonardo cartoon, which was purchased in 1962.

GOYA: DOÑA ISABEL COBOS DE PORCEL *The art of Goya (1746–1828) is one of astonishing versatility —his drawings, etchings, frescoes, and cartoons for tapestry, as well as about 500 oil paintings, include portrayals of daily life in Madrid, religious works, portraits, a savage indictment of the brutality of war, and finally horrific visions from the unconscious. The great period for his portraits was 1800 to 1808; acuteness of observation is matched by the beauty of his often restrained colour, and his handling of paint often foreshadows Impressionism. Goya painted Doña Isabel then; he captures her arrogance and radiant sensuality, and catches the play of light on skin and the gleam of satin through lace.*

BELLINI: THE AGONY IN THE GARDEN *With Bellini the Venetian painter's instinctive feeling for colour takes the form of an emotional reaction to light, as in this work of about 1464. In his brother-in-law Mantegna's earlier painting of the subject (also in the National Gallery) the figures merge into Mantegna's flinty world. Here the apostles are sleeping men in human attitudes— not fallen columns—and Christ towers against a sky flushed with magic dawn light.*

[L]ONARDO: CARTOON *Leonardo da Vinci (1452–1519) drew this [car]toon, a full-scale composition of the Virgin and Child with St Anne [an]d the infant St John the Baptist, before he left Milan, between 1497 and [14]99. It is universally admired as one of his most beautiful works. Leonardo's [fol]lower, Luini, carried out a painting from it, but there is none in existence [by] Leonardo himself. An unfinished painting, now in the Louvre in Paris, [sho]ws how he wanted to get away from the markedly vertical composition [of] the cartoon, and from the arrangement of having two heads on the same [lev]el. The Paris painting does not include St John the Baptist.*

THE WILTON DIPTYCH *Largely because of Henry VIII and Cromwell, few medieval panel paintings survive in England. These, painted about 1400, depict Richard II presented to the Virgin and Child by his patron saints. The English, French or Italian artist's delicate work resembles that of a manuscript illuminator.*

SEURAT: UNE BAIGNADE, ASNIÈRES *Seurat (1859–91) did not so much reject Impressionism as reduce it to order. His figures are precisely contoured and are arranged to obtain a perfect integration of space and forms. He analysed the exact proportions of colour and separated them into dots (points) of uniform size which are then blended optically by the spectator. This, his masterpiece, was the first of five major works on a large scale, and his 'pointillism' is not yet fully developed—composition is paramount.*

PIERO DELLA FRANCESCA: THE BAPTISM OF
CHRIST *Today Piero is widely regarded as the greatest
painter of the mid-15th century, although previously
held in low esteem. He was born in the small Umbrian
town of San Sepolero about 1415, but was known to
have worked in Florence in 1439. By 1442 he was
back in his native town, where he worked for the rest of
his life, making visits to Rome and the northern courts
of Ferrara and Rimini. His work holds a fine balance
between reality and abstraction. The pursuit of geometry and the development of perspective were his
particular interest, and he used pale, cool, flat colours
to give the effect of a fusion of light and colour. In
this picture, probably dating from the 1440's, Christ's
body seems almost to be carved out of light and has a
serenity—the keynote of Piero's art.*

DUCCIO: VIRGIN AND CHILD *Duccio (c. 1255–1319) has been called the last artist of the old world. He lived in Siena, where painting was conservative and decorative; in Florence at about the same time, art was vigorous and experimental, with a strong feeling for solidity and form. Duccio's painting was a late flowering of the Byzantine style, with its emphasis on flat pattern, against a sumptuous gold background. Another quality of Duccio's art, as of all Sienese painting, is the elegance of the draughtsmanship, exemplified in the central panel of this triptych by the graceful weaving line of the Virgin's headscarf.*

CARAVAGGIO: THE SUPPER AT EMMAUS *The Italian Caravaggio was one of the great rebels of art. His tempestuous life, punctuated by brawls, came to an untimely end when he was only 37. His painting shocked his contemporaries with its realism and its dramatic lighting. He chose the common people as his models, and is said to have once fished a corpse out of the Tiber to serve as a model for the Madonna. In this work, done about 1597, Christ is shown without any aura of holiness, and the disciples are rough peasant types. Caravaggio had a Flemish passion for incidental details—note the wormholes in the fruit.*

VAN EYCK: THE MARRIAGE OF ARNOLFINI *The Flemish artist Jan van Eyck, who died in 1441, perfected a new technique of painting in oils and varnish which allowed the building up of detail after acutely observed detail in brilliant colours, emphasising the beauty of surface and texture in fabric, fur, glass and metal. This famous double portrait, showing the symbolic marriage of the Bruges merchant Arnolfini and his* bride Giovanna Cenami, is full of elaborate symbolism —the single lighted candle symbolises Christ, the fruit stands for innocence, the dog for faithfulness, and the pattens Arnolfini has taken off show that he stands on holy ground. In the mirror between the espoused couple are two figures in a doorway, one of which must be van Eyck himself, for he has written on the wall, 'Jan van Eyck was here: 1434'.

# TATE GALLERY

Of all London's great art collections, the Tate Gallery is, to modern tastes, the most rewarding. It makes no attempt to cover the whole range of art, but concentrates on three distinct collections: British painting, modern foreign art and modern sculpture. The gallery, opened in 1897, was built by the sugar refiner Henry (later Sir Henry) Tate, who also gave to it works from his own collection of British paintings. The Tate sets out to cover all that is significant in British painting from the 16th century to the present day; it houses a number of superb Constables, some of the most powerful work of the visionary William Blake, as well as important Pre-Raphaelite and 20th-century works. But pride of place in the British section must go to its unparalleled collection of Turners—the Tate owns more than 280 of his oil paintings. The modern foreign collection began with the bequest of 39 paintings, mostly French, by Sir Hugh Lane in 1916. It now ranges from the French Impressionists to the American pop art of Roy Lichtenstein. The sculpture collection includes works by Rodin, Epstein, Barbara Hepworth, Butler, Giacometti and Henry Moore. The sculpture hall was the gift of the late Lord Duveen in 1937.

HOGARTH: THE GRAHAM CHILDREN *Hogarth (1697–1764) is often remembered only as a painter of social and political satire and as a vigorous campaigner against social ills. But he was also a superb portraitist with a very individual power of observation and exquisite sensibility in the technical handling of paint. This picture is a 'conversation piece'—an informal group portrait—a feature of English painting of 1730–1830. The four children of Daniel Graham, apothecary to Chelsea Hospital, are shown with their cat. The composition is admirably designed and the cherries held by the elder girl form an inspired accent of colour.*

MODIGLIANI: STONE HEAD *Amedeo Modigliani w one of the most fascinating sculptors of this centu although his sculpture is much less well known th his paintings. An Italian by birth, he went to Pa in 1906 and joined a group of avant-garde arti which included Picasso. He took up sculpture in 19c but in 1915 devoted himself again to painting un his early death in 1920. This powerful stylised he probably dates from 1912 or 1913, and was one of series of several stone heads which were origina conceived to form a sculptural ensemble. Those th survive are now widely scattered.*

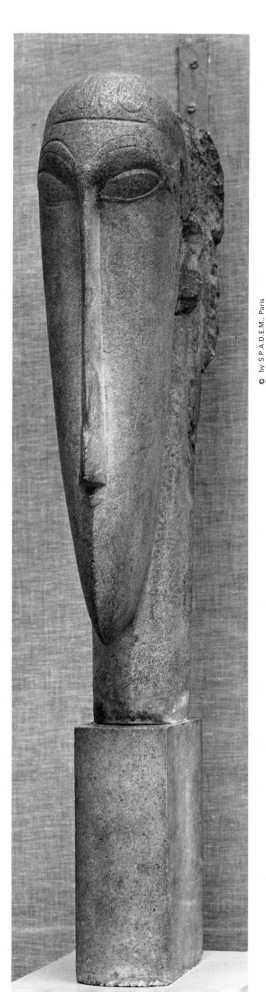

PICASSO: THREE DANCERS *In 1925 Picasso's career saw a turning point, marked by the 'Three Dancers'. The Classical spirit of his sculptural nudes and serene still-lifes of the early 1920's is exchanged for a mood of torment. His distortion of the human body is now emotional rather than intellectual, and the abandon of the three figures heralds a phase of expressionist violence. Images are given more than one meaning— the circle on the chest of the left dancer can be read as a breast or as an eye.*

KANDINSKY: FRAGMENT FOR COMPOSITION IV *The first abstract picture is traditionally a water-colour of 1910 by the Russian artist Kandinsky. In Munich in 1910–14, he was cautiously moving towards a whole-hearted abstraction and painted his 'Improvisations' and 'Compositions'. The former were direct expressions of the subconscious mind; for the latter he did a series of preparatory studies, and this is one. The forms are still vaguely based on reality—a castle, mounted Cossacks, birds. But these vestiges of representation are not the message of the picture—it produces an emotional effect merely by lines, shapes and colours.*

**331**

MATISSE: THE SNAIL *In 1950, at the age of 80, Matisse gave up oil painting (easel painting) because of his infirmities. For the last four years of his life he worked on a grand scale with cut-outs of sumptuous hand-coloured paper. These works have no perspective, but the flat, sharply defined areas of pure colour— unique in modern painting—are arranged to create forms that exist in space. This work is so named from the vaguely spiral disposition of paper pieces.*

MONDRIAN: COMPOSITION WITH RED, YELLOW AND BLUE *Mondrian (1872–1944) is now seen as one of the most influential and individual exponents of abstract art. But the style by which he is best known, shown in this work of about 1940, was reached only after ruthless self-discipline. In this ascetic style, with its black grid and colours on a brilliant white background, no disturbing element—a diagonal line, a brush stroke, the texture of wood or canvas—is permitted.*

BRAQUE: GUITAR AND JUG *Picasso and Braque were the joint inventors of Cubism—the use of arranged geometrical forms to represent what is seen. With Picasso the ideas, often expressed with lightning speed, are more important than the painting; but in Braque (1882–1963) painting is the reality—the technique is* deliberate and shows a craftsman's feeling for his material. After 1918, his liaison with Picasso over, he developed his own post-Cubist style. But in this work —one of a series of rich, sensuous still-lifes of the 1920's —the Cubist idiom is retained in the division of the jug into two halves to suggest volume.*

# VICTORIA AND ALBERT MUSEUM

Prince Albert, the Prince Consort, planned a great complex of museums and colleges at South Kensington. With money derived from the Great Exhibition of 1851, the South Kensington Museum, a collective museum of science and art, was erected. Opened in 1857, it incorporated the collections of the Museum of Ornamental Art opened at Marlborough House in 1852. The art departments grew rapidly to include fine and applied arts of all kinds, represented chiefly by post-Classical European art and that of the Near and Far East. Eventually, because of lack of space, the science exhibits were moved to the new Science Museum near by. In 1899 Queen Victoria laid the foundation stone of the present building, designed by Sir Aston Webb. She stipulated that the title be changed to 'Victoria and Albert Museum' and in 1909 Edward VII opened the new building; it now contains one of the world's outstanding collections of fine and applied arts.

THE SION GOSPELS COVER *A German manuscript cover, revealing an unusually high degree of craftsmanship in the use of repoussé—ornamental metalwork that has been hammered into relief from the reverse side. The book dates from about 1000 and has a beech-wood cover veneered with gold, its surface richly decorated with precious stones and cloisonné enamels. The centre panel depicting the seated figure of Christ is very likely 12th-century work and it is probable that some of the larger stones are also later additions. Much speculation surrounds the manuscript's origins and some authorities link it with the Gospels of Charlemagne, a book which belonged to the abbey of St Maurice d'Agaune, in Valais, Switzerland. It is more popularly supposed to have been made for the ancient church of Notre Dame de Valère, also in Valais. A contemporary inscription verifies that the manuscript was there during the 17th century and later transferred to the care of the Cathedral of Sion. In 1851 a dealer at Geneva bought the book from the cathedral authorities and later sold it to the Marquis de Ganay. It was eventually acquired by the Spitzer collection towards the end of the century and has been carefully restored. It is 10 in. high.*

THE SYON COPE *A cope, or large semicircular cloak, is the main vestment worn at numerous ecclesiastical ceremonies. The origins of the Syon cope are unknown, but the wealth of heraldic Arms surrounding it suggest that the cope was made in about 1300–20. It certainly once belonged to the nuns of the convent of Syon in Middlesex, whose community, founded in 1414–15, was exiled in Elizabeth I's reign and only returned to England about 1810. Embroidered on the cope in silver and silver-gilt thread and coloured silks are figures* *of the apostles and saints, including St Michael (above), six-winged seraphim, and two priests who may have been the donors. It is a good example of the medieval English embroidery known as 'Opus Anglicanum', renowned throughout Europe during the 13th and 14th centuries; the type of stitch used is peculiar to medieval embroidery, and was used particularly for metal threads which were pulled in little loops through to the back of the base material and caught with linen thread.*

**334**

THE ELTENBERG RELIQUARY *One of the finest surviving examples of Romanesque coppersmiths' work, this reliquary was made in Cologne, probably during the last quarter of the 12th century. By the time of the French Revolution it belonged to the Benedictine nunnery of Eltenberg in Holland. The nunnery was pillaged during the Revolutionary Wars, but the reliquary was saved by one of the nuns who hid it and other treasures in a chimney. The total effect of the reliquary is one of disciplined richness and magnificence; the principal decorative motif is a stylised floral scroll, but geometrical and scale patterns are also used.*

MEDICI PORCELAIN BOTTLE *The first European soft-paste porcelain was made in Florence under the patronage of the ruling Medici family in about 1570–80. The factory was set up to discover the porcelain formula after Marco Polo had brought back pieces of blue and white porcelain from China. Wares such as this bottle, made about 1580, were produced in soft-paste porcelain decorated under the glaze in mauvish-blue. This bottle is unmarked, but the pieces usually bore a mark incorporating the dome of Florence Cathedral and 'F' in underglaze blue.*

**335**

RAPHAEL: THE MIRACULOUS DRAUGHT OF FISHES *It is a miracle that Raphael's seven tapestry cartoons survive for they are painted in water-colour on a fragile jig-saw of paper pieces glued together. Raphael was at the height of his powers when Pope Leo X commissioned a set of ten cartoons, and seven of the finished tapestries were hung in the Sistine Chapel on Christmas Day, 1519. The cartoons are one of the noblest monuments of that peak of western Renaissance art which lasted 30 years, from Leonardo's painting of the 'Last Supper' until the sack of Rome in 1527. In them Raphael captured the effect of fresco on paper, for the cartoons had to be sent away to Brussels where the tapestries were woven. This one is particularly splendid.*

THE BURGHLEY NEF *Nefs—vessels shaped like ships —were a favourite subject for medieval and Renaissance goldsmiths. In France they were often used to mark the highest place at table, like the English great salts, and the Burghley Nef has a salt container fitted in the poop. It was made by the Parisian goldsmith, Pierre le Flamand, known to have been working about 1462.*

THE STUDLEY BOWL *A beautifully proportioned and decorated bowl and cover made of silver-gilt in England in the latter half of the 14th century. Made to hold porridge or similar food this piece of domestic silversmiths' work was once owned by the church at Studley Royal near Ripon, Yorkshire. The fine chased and engraved ornament covers both bowl and lid. On each part a black-letter alphabet is shown preceded by a cross and followed by various literary symbols and contractions of the type used in contemporary Latin manuscripts. Each alphabet is incorporated in a leafy wreath. On the cover knob is the letter 'a'. Together the pieces stand 5⅝ in. high and the whole testifies to the high level of technical and artistic perfection attained by English silversmiths in the Middle Ages.*

HILLIARD: AN UNKNOWN YOUTH LEAN AGAINST A TREE AMONG ROSES *An exqu miniature by Nicholas Hilliard (c. 1547–16 regarded as one of his best. Roughly 5½ by 2¾ in was painted on vellum about 1588, and is so min worked that even when enlarged it makes a fi executed picture. Hilliard trained as a goldsmith, as early as 1560 was painting miniatures, which probably worn as jewels. 1570 saw the first d portrait of Elizabeth I and Hilliard may have appointed her Limner (painter) and Goldsmith t Later, for 12 years he had the exclusive privileg painting James I and his family.*

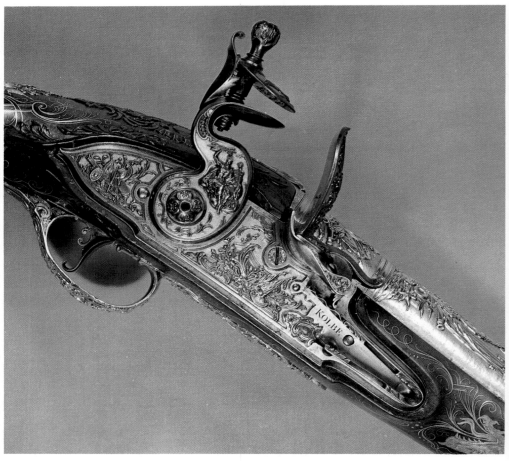

SILVER-MOUNTED GUN *This intricately decorated air-gun is said to have belonged to George II. It was made about 1735 by the German gunsmith Johann* *Gottfried Kolbe. The carved walnut stock is inlaid with silver and the steel stock is chiselled in relief with foliage and the figure of Jupiter brandishing a thunderbolt.*

PRESENTATION SWORD *This sword was presented by the East India Company to Lt.-Col. James Hartley for gallantry during the Mahratta War in 1779. It was made by James Morisset, and the hilt is solid gold.*

17TH-CENTURY GERMAN RAPIER *The rapier, with its hilt to protect the swordsman's hand, was developed in the 16th century. In its more elaborate forms it became a piece of masculine jewellery. This sword-hilt was made about 1610 by one of the German brothers Emmanuel and Daniel Sadeler of Munich. Their work is identical, and is often characterised by minute designs in chiselled relief.*

# WALLACE COLLECTION

The Wallace Collection is said to be the most valuable single gift ever made by an individual to any nation. It was built up mainly in Paris by the 3rd and 4th Marquesses of Hertford and by Sir Richard Wallace (1818–90), son of the 4th Marquess. In 1871, after the siege of Paris by the Prussians, Sir Richard came to live in England, bringing most of the collection over with him. It was bequeathed to the British nation by Sir Richard's widow, Lady Wallace, who died in 1897.

RUBENS: RAINBOW LANDSCAPE *In the landscapes Rubens painted at Steen—the Belgian château he bought in 1635—the rocks, torrents and serpentine movement of earlier landscapes give way to a lowland countryside, bathed in light of an unprecedented intensity. His superb draughtsmanship is seen in the painting's detail.*

From A. K. Snowman's '18th Century Gold Boxes of Europe' (Faber)

PRINCE HENRY'S SWORD *Medieval cross-hilted swords were briefly revived during the early 17th century when James I re-introduced the ancient ceremony of making Knights of the Bath. This sword was made about 1610 for Henry, Prince of Wales, who died in 1612.*

ENAMELLED GOLD BOXES *Part of a collection of 89 boxes largely built up by Richard Seymour-Conway, the 4th Marquess of Hertford, and added to by his son Sir Richard Wallace. The 'Fantaisie' box in the form of a coach seat (top right) is a great rarity, for work of this kind was never made in great quantity, and little of it has survived. It was made in 1756–7 by the Parisian goldsmith Aymé-Antoine Chollet. Below it is a shell-shaped box with white peacock-feather decoration, made in 1743–4 by Jean Ducrollay of Paris.*

**339**

**Long Ashton** *Som.*         *540Cg*
CHURCH OF ALL SAINTS A church of the 14th and
15th centuries with a west tower. The most interesting monument is that to Lord Chief Justice
Choke, who died in 1486. This has recumbent
effigies, heraldry, many angels and a canopy.

**Longbridge Deverill** *Wilts.*     *540Ee*
CHURCH OF SS PETER AND PAUL Of Norman
origin, the building has work of various periods.
There is a west tower, and inside on the north side
of the nave are Norman arches. At the end of the
south aisle is some Classical wood-panelling, and
a Norman font. Among several monuments there
is a medallion portrait by Sir Francis Chantrey,
and a memorial font by Alfred Gilbert of *c.* 1887.

**Long Crendon** *Bucks.*        *547Gc*
COURT-HOUSE A partly half-timbered, 14th-
century court-house or staple hall, which was
probably once used as a wool store; it has been
restored and repaired.

**Longford Castle** *Wilts.*       *540Fe*
A 16th-century residence, with later alterations,
built to a triangular plan. Furniture and paintings
are on display. It is surrounded by flower gardens.

**Longleat House** *Wilts.*       *540De*
A great early Renaissance house, begun for Sir
John Thynne in 1568. Thynne had bought the land
and original priory buildings at Longleat in 1541.
He at once set about building a new house, but
much was destroyed by fire in 1567. A year later,
the architect Robert Smythson arrived on the
scene and work on the present house began, but
was not finished when Thynne died in 1580.
Longleat, one of the great exploits of Elizabethan
architecture, is symmetrical, except for the great
hall, found to one side, as in most medieval houses;
at Wollaton (Nottinghamshire), Smythson's later
house, the hall is at the very centre of the house,
where in earlier buildings there had usually been an
open courtyard. Longleat has a flat, not gabled,

## LONGLEAT HOUSE

STATE DRAWING-ROOM *One of
the great Elizabethan houses, Longleat was designed by Robert Smythson for Sir John Thynne, Elizabeth
I's Lord High Treasurer. In 1789 a
descendant of Thynne was created
Marquess of Bath. In 1860, the 4th
Marquess, returned from a Grand
Tour, employed J. D. Crace to
Italianise the state rooms, Italian
craftsmen being imported.*

FIRST FOLIO OF SHAKESPEARE'S
PLAYS *Known as the First Folio,
and one of the most sought after of
all first editions, the first collected
edition of Shakespeare's plays
appeared in 1623. It contained 18
of the 19 plays already published
singly and another 18 published for
the first time.*

roof, with domed pavilions, and is characterised by the large number of windows in each of the four three-storey façades. Sir Jeffry Wyatville made alterations to the house in 1807–11. The magnificent state rooms contain fine furniture and paintings, and include a superb library. The mansion and colourful gardens are in the middle of a park, landscaped by Capability Brown.

**Long Marston Manor** *Yorks.*     558Db
A Tudor manor house (once a rectory), now re-fronted in Georgian style, containing relics of the Battle of Marston Moor, a decisive victory for the Parliamentarians which was fought on July 6, 1644. An obelisk in the grounds marks the site of the engagement.

**Long Meg and Her Daughters** *Cumb.*    557Jf
This stone circle is oval in plan, 120 yds by 100 yds in diameter. Of a former total of 59 stones, 27 are still standing, and perhaps a dozen more have disappeared. Long Meg herself is a single standing stone, some 12 ft high, on the south-west side.

**Long Melford** *Suffolk*     548Ce
Long Melford is the stateliest small town in Suffolk, with an unrivalled main street, long and wide. It has a magnificent church, a beautiful green, three 'great' houses and other worthwhile buildings.

On the green are: the church; Melford Hall, a large Elizabethan mansion of *c.* 1550, with turrets, gate-house and summer-house; and Holy Trinity Hospital, almshouses founded in 1573 (restored 1847). North of the church is Kentwell Hall, *c.* 1564, moated and with a great avenue of limes planted in 1678. To the south of the village is Melford Place, now mostly 18th century.
CHURCH OF THE HOLY TRINITY A huge 15th-century church, with magnificent windows, and a three-gabled Lady Chapel. The west tower is a replacement by G. F. Bodley, *c.* 1900, of one of the 18th century. A feature of the interior is the large amount of 15th-century stained glass. There are many brasses and monuments, including that by William Cure to Sir William Cordell (*d.* 1580). There is a carved alabaster panel of the Adoration of the Magi.

**Longnor** *Shrops.*     551Jb
CHURCH OF ST MARY THE VIRGIN A small and unaltered example of an Early English church, *c.* 1260, standing near Longnor Hall. The nave and chancel are in one, and there is iron Gothic tracery in the east window. There are 18th-century box-pews, reader's desk and pulpit, and galleries.

**Long Sutton** *Lincs.*     553Jc
CHURCH OF ST MARY This church has an excellent Early English tower with lead spire slightly set apart from the main building. The work on the interior includes some Norman fragments, and there is a handsome 15th-century south porch. Worth noticing is the medieval brass eagle lectern.

**Longthorpe Tower** *Hunts.*     547Jg
An interesting 13th-century fortified manor house. The two lower storeys have stone-vaulting. Some fascinating wall-paintings from the 14th century were discovered on the first floor *c.* 1946 and show, among other scenes, the Seven Ages of Man, the Labours of the Months, the Three Quick and the Three Dead.

**Long Wittenham** *Berks.*     546Fc
CHURCH OF ST MARY Not far from the Iron Age hill-top fort known as Wittenham Clumps (Sinodun Hill), St Mary's still has the original Norman chancel arch and 13th- and 14th-century additions.

OUR LADY OF PITY

*The great east window of this church was re-assembled in the 19th century, using the magnificent 15th-century stained glass that escaped destruction during the 16th and 17th centuries when much of the church's glass was destroyed. The window depicts the Virgin seated on a decorated throne, holding in her arms the body of Christ crowned with thorns; a detail is shown above. (Church of the Holy Trinity, Long Melford)*

There is much 17th-century woodwork—font cover, pulpit and a screen which, together with the stalls, came from Exeter College, Oxford. In the south aisle is a piscina which is also a monument, with a small figure of a knight.

**Looe** *Cornwall*     538Eb
Seaport town, divided into East Looe and West Looe by the R. Looe. It has many houses of medieval origin, and the 16th-century Old Guildhall has the original magistrates' bench and pillory.

**Loose** *Kent*     542Df
WOOL HOUSE A half-timbered house of the 15th century, once used for wool cleaning. (By appointment.)

**Loseley House** *Surrey*     542Af
Sir Thomas More's kinsman, Sir William More, built this Elizabethan mansion, set in a large park, in 1561–9; his descendants still live in the house, which incorporates stone from Waverley Abbey near Farnham. Inside are fine ceilings, panelling from Henry VIII's Nonesuch Palace, a unique chimney-piece carved from local chalk, fine furniture and tapestries.

**Lostwithiel** *Cornwall*     538Dc
CHURCH OF ST BARTHOLOMEW A church with an octagonal 14th-century spire, and a magnificently carved font of the same period. There are several mural monuments by minor sculptors.

## CARVED MISERICORD

*The comparatively austere interiors of medieval churches gradually changed during the 15th and 16th centuries, with a profusion of carved and painted furnishings. The clergy were no longer required to stand erect throughout the long services, and misericords —projections on the undersides of the hinged seats of the choir stalls—began to appear. These served as supports for standing clergy when the seats were turned up, and were often finely carved. Because they were less exposed to view than other church carvings, a far greater freedom of interpretation was permitted. (Church of St Laurence, Ludlow)*

**Lound** *Suffolk* 548Fh
CHURCH OF ST JOHN THE BAPTIST A pretty church with a round Norman tower, and a Perpendicular font with carved lions and angels. The rood and organ case, and the font cover, are early 20th-century works by Sir Ninian Comper.

**Louth** *Lincs.* 553Jf
There are a few remains of a Cistercian abbey, *c.* 1139, in Louth Park, an intricate pattern of streets and a number of good 17th- and 18th-century houses. Cromwell House was built *c.* 1600, and the Mansion House in the late 18th century. Most of the better houses are in Westgate, including the Mansion, built *c.* 1704 on a terrace above the pavement.

Thorpe Hall, at the west end of the town, has the remains of its west front, 1584. Most of the rest of Louth is 18th-century red-brick and hipped-roof construction, with Elizabethan terraces leading down to the river.
CHURCH OF ST JAMES A magnificent church, and one of the last great medieval Gothic masterpieces, it has one of the most famous spires in England; dating from the early 16th century, it rises to a height of 294 ft, with pinnacles and flying buttresses. Rebuilt by the local inhabitants in the 16th century, and restored by James Fowler during the 19th, the church contains some interesting woodcarving executed by local craftsmen during the 19th century.

**Lower Brockhampton House** *Herefs.* 546Bf
A small moated manor house in half-timber, which dates from the 14th century, with a detached gate-house of later date and the ruins of a 12th-century chapel.

**Lower Largo** *Fife.* 562Cg
ROBINSON CRUSOE STATUE Defoe's Robinson Crusoe was in real life Alexander Selkirk (1676–1721), who was put ashore on Juan Fernandez island by his shipmates in 1704, and rescued in 1709. A statuette to his memory is on the cottage where he was born.

**Lower Peover** *Cheshire* 552Be
CHURCH OF ST OSWALD A 16th-century timbered church with a massive sandstone tower. Inside, dark oak of the wooden columns, arches and exposed roof timbers is well set off against the whitewashed walls. The fittings, mainly 16th century, are distinguished, particulary the box-pews, screen, pulpit and cover on a Gothic font.

**Lowick** *Northants.* 547Hg
CHURCH OF ST PETER An impressive church, with large Perpendicular windows. The west tower is of the late 15th century and has an octagonal upper storey with pinnacles and flying buttresses. The 15th-century monuments include the effigies of Sir Ralph Greene and his wife, each under a vaulted canopy.

**Lowther Castle** *Westmld.* 557Jf
Mary, Queen of Scots stayed here as guest of Sir Richard Lowther; an alabaster memorial to Sir Richard is in the church. The castle, now in ruins, stands amid a 3000 acre park with a mausoleum containing Lowther family tombs. A tower of the castle dates from the 13th century, but the rest was rebuilt several times.

**Luddesdown Court** *Kent* 542Df
The lord of this flint-built Norman manor was Captain of the Fleet at the siege of Calais in 1347. Its great hall has an 11th-century fire-place and there is a red-brick chimney dated 1471. There are Tudor additions, and the house features a columbarium (pigeon loft) and bear pit.

**Ludham** *Norfolk* 554Dc
CHURCH OF ST CATHERINE The 14th- and 15th-century church contains a decorated sedilia and a hammerbeam roof to the nave. The octagonal font is carved with figures and lions, the screen has painted figures of saints. A mural of the Crucifixion is painted on the chancel arch.

**Ludlow** *Shrops.* 546Af
CHURCH OF ST LAURENCE The largest parish church in the county, it has a 135 ft high pinnacled central tower with tall windows and is over 200 ft long. The imposing exterior is of pale sandstone. The earliest remaining work is of *c.* 1300, but the general character of the church is in the Perpendicular style. Choir stalls date from 1447 and have especially interesting misericords and poppyheads. Medieval stained glass shows scenes from the life of St Laurence. Various monuments from the 16th to 18th centuries include some with recumbent or kneeling effigies. The church was restored by Sir Gilbert Scott in 1859 and by Sir Arthur Blomfield later in the 19th century.
MUSEUM Twenty thousand fossils from Shropshire and adjoining counties are the main feature of the museum's geological collection. Exhibits cover local history from prehistoric to Victorian times, with special reference to Ludlow Castle. The museum is in the Butter Cross, a mid-18th-century building.
READER'S HOUSE One of the many 17th-century houses of Ludlow still in their original state.

**Lullingstone Castle** *Kent* 542Cf
The original manor house stood on this site at the time of the Domesday survey. It was added to in

Tudor times, and was largely rebuilt in the 18th century, but the gateway dating from the reign of Henry VII remains. The castle contains fine Tudor panelling, paintings and a collection of armour. In the grounds is the Church of St Botolph, which was restored in the reign of Edward III.

**Lullingstone Villa** *Kent*       *542Cf*
Modern techniques of excavation have revealed much of this remarkable Roman villa. Apart from its quality as a country house it has what must be accepted as a private Christian chapel, together with many other finds which confirm this interpretation; there are also fine decorative features.

**Lumley Castle** *Durham*       *558Cg*
Originally a fortified castle (1389), Lumley was adapted to domestic use during the reigns of Elizabeth I and George I.

**Lundin Links** *Fife.*       *562Cg*
At one time there stood here a circle of standing stones. Today, three only remain, but their size is impressive. The shortest is 13 ft high and has 5 ft wide sides. The others stand 17 ft and 18 ft high.

**Lurgashall** *Sussex*       *541Je*
One of the best village greens in Sussex—wide, triangular and not too tidy; the cottages are spaced around it informally, leaving views into the lush countryside beyond.

**Luton** *Beds.*       *547Hd*
CHURCH OF ST MARY In spite of the industrial surroundings, this fine cruciform town church of the 13th to 15th centuries stands out as a magnificent building. There is a 13th-century font enclosed in a big pinnacled and gabled canopy, and the octagonal 14th-century baptistry is a fine piece of craftsmanship. There are also brasses and monuments.
MUSEUM AND ART GALLERY Originally a Victorian private residence, the Luton museum displays collections of considerable range. The local history collections include among the archaeological exhibits some important Saxon jewellery found in Luton and Dunstable; natural history, rural trades, crafts and folk life provide further information on the area. Also represented are the decorative arts of costume, domestic textiles, furniture and wood carvings (English and continental), pottery and glass (19th-century) and domestic furnishings. There are collections of musical instruments, candlesticks, spirit bottles and Palaeolithic implements, and a growing collection of paintings.

**Luton Hoo** *Beds.*       *547Hd*
'Hoo' is an Anglo-Saxon word meaning 'the spur of a hill'. This great mansion of the Wernher family has Adam associations, but little more than the façade remained after a fire in 1843. It is the contents which now matter, and these are incomparable. The tapestries include those woven at Beauvais (1711–22) depicting the Story of the King of China, the main feature of the dining-room. The collection of English porcelain and china has examples of Chelsea, Worcester, Staffordshire, Derby, Bristol, Liverpool, Swansea and Rockingham, and a few pieces from Dresden and China, as well as Limoges plate. The former chapel is a museum of sacred art. The racing interests of the Wernher's are indicated in the Brown Jack Room, named after their famous racehorse. There is also a collection of jewelled pieces by Fabergé, and the Russian Room contains robes worn at the Court of the Tsars, and personal mementoes of the Imperial family. Works of art include paintings by Rembrandt and Titian, and the unique *St Michael* by Bartoleme Bermejo (*c.* 1480). Although one section of Luton Hoo is occupied, the main part forms the museum. (See pp. 344–5.)

**Lydbury North** *Shrops.*       *551Ja*
CHURCH OF ST MICHAEL The handsome 15th-century nave roof here was not revealed until J. T. Micklethwaite's restoration work in 1901. The

MOSAIC FLOOR AT LULLINGSTONE ROMAN VILLA

*During reconstruction of the villa in the 4th century, this fine mosaic was laid. The foreground illustrates the Greek myth of the abduction of Europa by Zeus in the form of a bull. The Latin couplet above is from Vergil's 'Aeneid', and indicates the high level of literary education of the villa's upper-class owners.*

# LUTON HOO

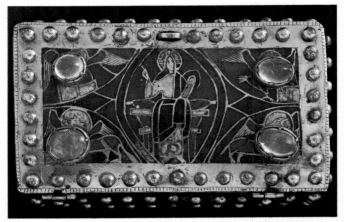

CASKET *This casket for relics is of copper gilt decorated with champlevé enamel. It is thought to have been made in Denmark in the late 12th century. The Danish goldsmith borrowed his subjects from similar caskets made in the Rhineland, but has followed Scandinavian tradition in making the figures part of a formalised design. The symbols of the Evangelists surrounding Christ are largely hidden by four rock crystals, added later in a typically medieval way; medieval donors of jewels given to honour the relics of a saint expected to see them on the casket even if it marred the design.*

CHELSEA PORCELAIN FIGURES *These unusual figures in Turkish costume were made about 1748 at the Chelsea factory which made fine porcelain from 1745 to 1765. The right-hand figure bears the rare blue anchor mark denoting that it was made during the peak of production when most of the figures were made.*

JACOPO SANSOVINO: ST JOHN THE BAPTIST *The magnificent art collections of the late Sir Julius Wernher at Luton Hoo include the finest group of Italian Renaissance bronze statuettes in private hands in Britain, and this is one of the rarest and most beautiful pieces. Jacopo Sansovino (1486–1570) was one of the most influential Italian Renaissance sculptors. By birth a Florentine, he worked in Rome, but after the sack of the city in 1527 moved to Venice, where he founded a new school of sculpture. Some of his finest work was done on a small scale in bronze.*

church's plan is cruciform, and it is of Norman origin; the west tower was added in the 13th century. There is a fine timbered south porch and early 17th-century box-pews and pulpit. Above the rood screen are the Commandments and Creed in painted lettering, dated 1615.

**Lyddington** *Rutland*         *553Gb*
CHURCH OF ST ANDREW Lyddington belonged to the medieval Bishops of Lincoln, and the 15th-century hall of their palace remains. The tower and chancel of the church are 14th-century work, but the nave and the aisles were rebuilt *c.* 1500 by one of the bishops. Among the medieval remains are glass, brasses and wall-paintings.

**Lydiard Mansion** *Wilts.*         *546Db*
Formerly the country seat of the St John family, whose splendid tombs are in the nearby church. Of medieval origin, the mansion was considerably altered when Georgian façades were added in 1743–9.

**Lydiard Tregoze** *Wilts.*         *546Db*
CHURCH OF ST MARY The style is mainly Perpendicular with alterations made *c.* 1633. The furnishings include an early 17th-century pulpit and some St John family pews of this date. There is a richly worked wrought-iron communion rail of *c.* 1700 and several medieval murals, but the main interest here centres on the many St John monuments,

RELIQUARY OF ST SEBASTIAN *One of the most impressive examples of German late 15th-century Gothic art in Britain, this reliquary was made to contain a saintly relic acquired by Abbot Georg Kastner for his Cistercian monastery of Kaisheim, near Donauworth in Swabia. Possibly designed by Hans Holbein the Elder about 1497, the reliquary is of silver and partly gilded, and came from the great goldsmithing centre of Augsburg, also in southern Germany. The elaborate pedestal creates an effective contrast to the simplicity of the figure of St Sebastian bound to the leafless tree trunk. The pedestal is decorated in relief with figures of Our Lady of Pity, saints, monks and abbots beneath the canopy of spiky foliage. The relic is set at the back, protected by crystal in an opening ornamented with precious gems.*

TRAY BY FABERGÉ *Nephrite, or Russian jade, was used a great deal by the royal goldsmith Peter Carl Fabergé (1846–1920) in his workshops at St Petersburg, Russia. This tray, made about 1900, is typical of his work, the dark nephrite contrasting with the gold handles with their enamel and diamond decoration.*

GERMAN PENDANT *An elaborate example of South German goldsmiths' work, this pendant was made about 1600 of enamelled gold, set with rubies, emeralds, diamonds and three pearl drops. It is really a piece of miniature sculpture, the gems being subsidiary elements in the design. A falconer stands against an openwork scrolled background, with a falcon on his wrist and two hounds at his feet—the modelling and enamelling of this miniscule group was the goldsmith's triumph.*

from the 16th century onwards, showing members of the family kneeling, lying or standing. One monument has doors painted with a heraldic genealogical tree, another has a gilded figure standing under a canopy, and yet another is by Michael Rysbrack.

**Lyme Park** *Cheshire*      552Cf
This estate was in the hands of the Legh family from 1397 until 1947. The present Elizabethan house was much altered by Giacomo Leoni *c.* 1720, when the exterior was extensively rebuilt, but the long gallery has remained unchanged since 1541. The state rooms contain fine panelling, wood carving and tapestries, and four Chippendale

chairs said to be covered with material from a cloak once worn by Charles I. The house is surrounded by a deer park and moorland.

**Lyme Regis** *Dorset*      540Bc
CHURCH OF ST MICHAEL The original Norman church had a tower between nave and chancel, but the present church was built to the east of the tower *c.* 1500; the old nave is now the west porch. Inside are a 17th-century oak lectern, many wall monuments, several windows with 19th-century stained glass, and a fine canopied pulpit dated 1613. PHILPOT MUSEUM The collections are devoted to local geology and history, and include old prints, documents, coins, and a fire engine of 1710.

## TOMB OF CHRISTOPHER ROPER

*The 2nd Lord Teignham lies with his feet resting on a lion and a red cloak over his armour. Beside him kneels his wife in widow's weeds. On the front of this tomb in the Roper Chapel are 17th-century carvings of Roper's two sons and five daughters by Epiphanius Evesham. (Church of SS Peter and Paul, Lynsted)*

**Lymington** *Hants.*                    541Gc
A centre of yachting. The town is most happily related to the broad estuary. From the cobbled Quay Hill, the way leads into the High Street, broad and straight, rising over a brow to the church at the far end.
CHURCH OF ST THOMAS THE APOSTLE The church has a south-east tower of 1670, crowned by a probably 18th-century cupola. There is some 13th-century work in the chancel and north chapel. The interior of the nave is mainly 18th

century with galleries on Tuscan columns. Features include an 18th-century font, a mid-19th-century stained glass window, and monuments by J. M. Rysbrack. One monument to a naval captain is by John Bacon.

**Lympne Castle** *Kent*                    542Fe
A rugged medieval castle with terraced gardens looking out over Romney Marsh and across the Channel to France. It was built *c.* 1360, 300 ft above the ruins of Stutfall Castle, a Roman coastal fort, and was restored in 1905.
LEMANIS (STUTFALL) A Kentish fort of the Saxon Shore, it guarded a harbour entrance, for in Roman times there was still an approach by sea to Lympne. Its structure marks it as one of the latest of the series. Since Roman times, the curtain wall has subsided on the slippery subsoil to give the present odd distribution of wall fragments.

**Lynsted** *Kent*                    542Ef
This village has many timbered Tudor cottages and an Elizabethan manor house.
CHURCH OF SS PETER AND PAUL Mainly Decorated and Perpendicular, with a wooden belfry and spire. There are several monuments by Epiphanius Evesham, and some interesting brasses.

**Lytes Cary** *Som.*                    540Ce
This manor house was the home of the Lyte family for 500 years. Here Sir Henry Lyte, botanist, wrote his *Niewe Herball* (a new history of plants) which was published in 1578 and was the most notable horticultural work of the time. The house and chapel were begun in 1343; the great hall was added in 1450, the quadrangle buildings in 1535.

**Lyveden New Bield** *Northants.*                    547Hg
Sir Thomas Tresham began this Renaissance house in *c.* 1600; its plan is cross-shaped to symbolise the Passion. However, Sir Thomas was a Papist and his family were involved in the Gunpowder Plot, so the house was never finished; only its shell remains. Lyveden Old Building is an Elizabethan farmhouse.

# M

**Macclesfield** *Cheshire*                    552Be
CHURCH OF ST MICHAEL A church which has had much rebuilding, but is of great interest for its tombs with effigies, from the 15th century onwards. William Stanton's monument to Lord Rivers (*d.* 1695) is especially worth noting.
WEST PARK MUSEUM Built and presented to the town of Macclesfield by the Brocklehurst family in 1898, the museum contains a collection of Egyptian antiquities, Victorian paintings with works by Landseer and others, a scold's bridle, a stuffed giant panda shot by Captain Brocklehurst on the borders of China and Tibet, and local and topographical items.

**Machynlleth** *Mont.*                    550Fb
Among the old houses here is the Royal House, where Owen Glendower (1359–1415) is said to have held a Welsh Parliament in 1405.

**Madeley** *Shrops.*                    552Ab
CHURCH OF ST MICHAEL Designed by Thomas Telford, the engineer (his other Shropshire church is St Mary Magdalene at Bridgnorth). The exterior is octagonal with a square west tower, but inside it is rectangular as the vestries cut off angles. The

original design had no chancel, but one was added in 1910. In the churchyard there are 19th-century tombs in the unconventional material of cast iron, two of them especially ambitious.

**Madingley** *Cambs.*                    548Af
CHURCH OF ST MARY MAGDALENE There is a west tower, with rebuilt spire, all mainly of the 13th and 14th centuries. The late 17th-century communion rails are from Cambridge. There are 15th- and 16th-century stained glass fragments, and monuments to members of the Cotton family, one perhaps by Edward Stanton, *c.* 1707. From a century later there is a large monument of a flag and anchor to an admiral by John Flaxman.
MADINGLEY HALL An Elizabethan mansion where Charles I hid and where Edward VII lodged when he was an undergraduate. Prince Albert fell ill there and died a few days later at Windsor. Today it belongs to Cambridge University. The nearby post-mill (in which the whole body of the mill revolves on the base), removed from Ellington, Huntingdonshire, to Madingley in 1936, is worth seeing. There are some old cottages with half-timbered work in the village.

**Madley** *Herefs.*                                      *546Ae*
CHURCH OF THE NATIVITY OF ST MARY THE
VIRGIN Some parts of the original Norman
building can still be seen in this 13th- and 14th-
century church. The contents include remains of
contemporary stained glass in the east window and
a mutilated monument of *c.* 1575 by John Guldo.

**Maes Howe** *Mainland, Orkney*                    *569Hf*
This is undoubtedly the finest chambered cairn in
north-western Europe and is still in fairly good
condition. It is a great domed mound of clay and
stones, 115 ft across and 24 ft high, encircled by a
wide, shallow ditch. The chamber, 15 ft square, is
lined with massive stone walling, and is entered by
a 36 ft long passage, again walled beyond the inner
doorway by great slabs, which also form its roof.
The roof of the chamber is corbelled, and corner
pillars aid in supporting the weight. The cairn has
been entered many times in the past. Several times
parties of Vikings have left runic inscriptions, the
language being Old Norse. One of these, surely
the first, records that they found a treasure,
doubtless of gold.

**Maesmawr Hall** *Mont.*                               *551Ga*
Montgomery is the Welsh county richest in
timber-framed houses. Maesmawr, a hotel, is a
good example of the style. Although timber-
framed houses may date from medieval times, the
majority fall into the 17th century, and a surprising
number, of which this house may be an example,
are of the early 18th century.

**Maesyronen Chapel** *Rad.*                          *545Je*
A Dissenters' chapel dating from 1679. Apart from
the lowering of the pulpit, the internal arrangements, including the communion table, are little
altered and preserve the atmosphere of humility
and domestic warmth lacking in more pretentious
larger chapels. The adjacent chapel house is earlier,
and the party wall contains fragments of an even
earlier cruck-truss, which would once have held a
primitive arch in position, part of a building once
occupying the site of the chapel.

**Maiden Bower** *Beds.*                               *547Hd*
A chalk quarry has shown that the bank of the hill-
fort was erected over the flat-bottomed ditch of a
causewayed camp. The hill-fort has a single bank
and ditch enclosing about 11 acres. When first dug,
this ditch was some 10 ft deep. Excavation of the
entrance on the south side has shown the post-holes
of a gate with a sentry-walk over it. From the air,
hut-circles have been seen within the fort.

**Maiden Castle** *Cheshire*                           *552Ad*
This is an Iron Age promontory fort, protected on
the south-east, where it joins the main hill-top, by
a double bank with a shallow ditch between. At
one end is the entrance, where the inner bank is
well inturned to make a tapering passage to the
gate. This inner bank is of stone laced with timber,
and the sandy outer bank has a stone revetment
which replaced an earlier one of timber. The other
sides are protected by steeply-scarped hill slopes.

**Maiden Castle** *Dorset*                             *540Dc*
This is perhaps the best known hill-fort in
England. Extensively excavated by Sir Mortimer
Wheeler, the long and varied history of the site is
well established. Concealed below the rampart of
the first Iron Age defences were those of a Neolithic causewayed camp of about 10 acres.
Towards the end of the Neolithic period, an enormous long barrow with quarry-ditches was built
on the hill-top and its line kinks where it crosses the
defences of the earlier camp. The first Iron Age
hill-fort, of 15 acres, occupied the eastern part of

LORD RIVERS'S TOMB

*This monument to Thomas, Earl Rivers of Rock
Savage, was erected in 1696 on the high altar of his
parish church. The tomb is baroque in style, and above
the figure of the earl is a massive canopy supported by
marble Corinthian columns from which hang curtains
in marble. Between them a long inscription sets out the
titles of Earl Rivers and his two wives. The church,
founded in the 13th century, was rebuilt in 1739 and
1898–1901. (Church of St Michael, Macclesfield)*

THE PROPHET EZEKIEL

*This is one of the figures in stained glass depicted on
three panels in the east window of this church, which
were taken from a fine 13th- or 14th-century Jesse
window. The prophet's hair and beard are worked in
gold stain against the red background and green vine
leaves of the Jesse tree. (Church of the Nativity of St
Mary the Virgin, Madley)*

# MAIDEN CASTLE

THE RAMPARTS *This Iron Age hill-fort was built on the site of a much earlier causewayed camp; Neolithic defences have been uncovered below the Iron Age* ramparts, *and there is a late Neolithic long barrow on the hill-top. The fort was captured and reduced by Vespasian's 2nd Roman Legion.*

IRON AGE OBJECTS *Both pots are of the second main Iron Age culture in Britain. Both have 'bead-rims' and the smaller one also has two countersunk handles. The pierced holes in the pot were intended to take a cord for suspension. Between the pots is a sample of slingstones found in the fort. The curved iron blades are probably primitive sickles. On the book are two bone combs of the first main Iron Age culture, and behind some beads. (Dorset County Museum, Dorchester)*

NEOLITHIC FINDS *These objects were all found at Maiden Castle. The smaller pot probably dates from the same period as the causewayed camp, while the larger one is contemporary with the great long barrow. The darker axe-head to the left is one of a small number made of epidiorite, or greenstone, a rock found in western Cornwall. The other axe-head, of chipped flint, has not been polished. On the book are several worked flint points. (Dorset County Museum, Dorchester)*

the hill. This comparatively insignificant fort was enlarged and remodelled again and again until, in the days of the last generation before the Roman conquest, the defences received their final refurbishing. The fort was one of the settlements reduced by Vespasian's 2nd Legion and, outside the east gate, the hastily buried skeletons of the inhabitants killed in the fight were found. Doubtless the chief *oppidum* (settlement) of the local tribe, the Durotriges, it was then superseded by Dorchester (Durnovaria), the Roman cantonal town, in the valley below. In the second half of the 4th century, a Romano-Celtic temple and priest's house, the foundations of which can still be seen, were built in the eastern part of the fort. It was near the gates of this hill-fort that great reserves of slingstones were found, proving that, in later Iron Age times, the sling was an important weapon.

**Maidenhead** *Berks.* 547Gb
This town on the Thames with its fine bridge was an important stage post in coaching days, on the main route from London to Bath. On the north-western outskirts is Boulter's Lock; the lock house was a flour mill in the 18th century.
HENRY REITLINGER BEQUEST In a typical Edwardian Thames-side house, the museum contains a wide selection of Chinese, Persian, Peruvian and European ceramics, as well as African and European sculpture, glass, paintings and drawings.

SCULPTURE AT THE CHURCH OF ST MARY, MALMESBURY

*Some of the finest carving to have survived from the 12th century. The figures of apostles surmounted by* *an angel were cleverly composed to fit into the lunette shape over the west wall porch of the abbey church.*

**Maiden Stone** *A'deen* 566Fe
An exceptionally fine and well preserved example of a Pictish symbol stone, still standing close by a minor road near Chapel of Garioch. It is of red granite, carved in relief with a varied series of men, fish and monsters.

**Maidstone** *Kent* 542Df
A former 'station' for Roman soldiers on the R. Medway, the town was of considerable importance in the Middle Ages. It possesses an archbishop's palace and several other fine buildings of those times. It has always been a market and route centre, giving rise to industrial and commercial activity; it is the administrative centre (county town) of Kent.
ARCHBISHOP'S OR OLD PALACE Built in 1348, the palace belonged to the Archbishops of Canterbury until Henry VIII's day. It contains a fine panelled banqueting hall. The palace stables—the old tithe barn—house a collection of carriages.
CHILLINGTON MANOR A former manor house, now a museum. It contains art and archaeological collections, and relics of William Hazlitt, the essayist, born in Maidstone in 1778.
CHURCH OF ALL SAINTS A fine, former collegiate church, built by Archbishop Courtenay in 1395 on the banks of the R. Medway beside the archbishop's palace, and mainly of the 14th and 15th centuries. There are several monuments, one by Joseph Nollekens, *c.* 1795; also misericords and brasses. The 19th-century restoration is by J. L. Pearson.
OLD COLLEGE The Master's House has links with a 14th-century ecclesiastical college, dissolved in 1547. It has been renovated and preserves a 16th-century staircase and archways. It is now a centre of the Kent Rural Music School. (By appointment.)

**Maldon** *Essex* 548Cc
BLUE BOAR INN The plain front conceals 15th-century stabling and 17th-century panelling inside. The 15th-century Swan Inn is also notable.

CHURCH OF ALL SAINTS The church was originally of the 13th century, but later additions include a unique triangular tower with a spire. The brick Gothic nave dates from 1728. The 14th-century south aisle is lavishly decorated, and there is a crypt. Monuments date from the 17th century.
MOOT HALL Sometimes called the D'Arcy Tower after its builder; a plain brick building of *c.* 1435, like a defensive tower with a higher stair turret. In the 19th century windows were added, and a porch with columns.
PLUME LIBRARY Founded in 1704 by Dr Plume, Archdeacon of Rochester, on the site of the ruined St Peter's Church. The embattled church tower is the library entrance.
ST GILES LEPER HOSPITAL The remains of a 12th-century chapel.
VICARAGE Built in the 15th century, timbered and gabled.

**Malmesbury** *Wilts.* 546Cb
Part of the 12th-century Benedictine abbey remains, its church being notable for a porch with splendid medieval carvings of the Apostles. The late medieval market cross survives.
CHURCH OF ST MARY The present church, dating from the mid-12th century, is a fragment of the original abbey church, which had transepts, a tall central spire and a western tower. All that is left is the nave with aisles. The nave was saved after the Reformation, and became the parish church. The south porch contains some of the best Romanesque sculpture in England. There is a 15th-century tomb with a reclining effigy, said to be that of King Athelstan. The Norman interior has 14th-century lierne vaulting.

**Malpas** *Cheshire* 551Jd
CHURCH OF ST OSWALD A spacious church, mainly of the 14th and 15th centuries, with large Perpendicular windows and a west tower. There are good timber roofs and screen work, stalls with misericords and a 13th-century chest with decorative iron binding.

BEN NICHOLSON *Au Chat Botté*

*This painting is of a shop window in the French town of Dieppe, with the name of the shop, Au Chat Botté, printed in bold letters across the glass. The French name (it means 'Puss in Boots') fascinated Nicholson and brought back memories of childhood fairy-tales. His picture of the shop was the culmination of a set of still-life studies produced between 1929 and 1932. Like his other works in different styles, it shows a coolness and a lyricism which is completely English, and a quality which he describes himself as 'musical and architectural'. Here the 'music' lies in the way he combines colour and form, and the 'architecture' in his use of space. The picture shows three planes: the window, reflections in the glass, and objects on the table inside. Nicholson later turned to abstract reliefs in the 1930's, and semi-abstract still-lifes in the 1950's. But this progress to non-figurative works has not altered his basic style—the 'music' and 'architecture'. (City Art Gallery, Manchester)*

**Malvern Link** *Worcs.* 546Be
DAVENHAM Gardens of botanical interest, with shrubs and alpine plants.

**Mam Tor** *Derbys.* 552Cf
This Iron Age hill-fort has an internal area of 16 acres; it is the largest in the Peak District, and comparable in size with many in south-western England. It has a ditch with internal bank and outer counterscarp bank and an entrance to the south-west. Here there is a fine inturned entrance passage some 100 ft long. There are also traces of a similar but smaller entrance at the north end of the enclosure. Two earlier Bronze Age round barrows lie within the enclosure.

**Manchester** *Lancs.* 552Bg
This great industrial city has for long been the centre of the cotton industry. Construction of the Ship Canal in 1894 converted it into the third largest port in England, while its modern airport is the second largest municipally-owned in the country. Manchester also has many cultural institutions and treasures.
CATHEDRAL The fine 15th-century collegiate church of St Mary was raised to cathedral status in 1848. It is a magnificent example of Perpendicular Gothic church building, with a suitable tower added in 1868, but its glory is its woodwork—the stalls with their intricate canopies and misericords, and the wooden pulpitum and parclose screens. Among the monuments is work by John Bacon the Younger, E. H. Baily and William Theed the Younger.
CHETHAM'S LIBRARY Founded in 1653, the library is the oldest public library in Europe. It contains printed books and manuscripts, including a fine

EPSTEIN *Bronze bust of C. P. Scott*

*Scott was perhaps the most famous of English editors. He was only 25 when he took charge of the 'Manchester Guardian' in 1872, and he transformed it from a local paper into one of the most influential in the world. He founded its liberal and progressive tradition, and under him it boldly championed many unpopular causes. Its opinions were quoted far outside its native city. This bust was presented to the city of Manchester in 1926 on his 80th birthday by a group of subscribers which included leading statesmen of the day, English and foreign. The choice of artist was fitting, since Jacob Epstein was himself, like Scott, a courageous innovator who was involved in controversy throughout most of his career. The bust captures with striking fidelity the pugnacious spirit of its subject. C. P. Scott died in 1932. (City Art Gallery, Manchester)*

collection of printed books of the 16th–18th centuries.

CITY ART GALLERY This Classical building, designed by Sir Charles Barry, architect of the Houses of Parliament, was originally opened to the public in 1829 as the headquarters of the Royal Manchester Institution. In 1882, it was given to the corporation, together with a number of pictures and other possessions which had been acquired over the years, for use as an art gallery. Its fine collection of paintings specialises in the development of the English School from the 16th century to the present day, and includes examples by most well-known British artists. There are also Italian, Flemish, Dutch and French paintings, as well as glass, sculpture, porcelain and silverware.

COURTS OF JUSTICE Rebuilt in 1957, they replace the bombed-out buildings of 1864.

FLETCHER MOSS (DIDSBURY) A former late-Georgian and early-Victorian parsonage which now houses the Manchester City Art Galleries Collection of English water-colours from Paul Sandby (1725–1809) onwards, including a group by J. M. W. Turner (1775–1851).

FREE TRADE HALL Rebuilt after bombing, it takes in much of the original stonework of 1843 and 1856, and dates from 1951 in its present form. Its large hall is 123 ft long, 78 ft wide, 60 ft high, with maximum accommodation for 2900 people.

GALLERY OF ENGLISH COSTUME The collection is of English costume from the 17th century to the present day. The building was formerly a country house of the 1760's.

HEATON HALL (PRESTWICH) This former residence of the Earls of Wilton was designed by James Wyatt in 1722. It contains an Etruscan room, an organ by Samuel Green, 18th-century furniture, and the Assheton Bennett Collection of English paintings and silver.

LIVERPOOL ROAD STATION Built in 1830, this is the oldest railway station in the world. The original building, which is scheduled as an ancient monument, is intact.

MANCHESTER UNIVERSITY Originally Owens College; its buildings, begun in 1870, are a free interpretation of 'French Gothic' and are noted as Victorian collegiate architecture.

PLATT HALL (RUSHOLME) A Georgian country house built in the 1760's. It contains a collection of English clothing from the 17th century to modern times.

PORTICO LIBRARY Opened in 1806, the library was designed in Classical style by Thomas Harrison, who also designed Chester and Lancaster Castles. Peter Mark Roget, compiler of *Roget's Thesaurus of English Words*, was its first secretary, and John Dalton (1766–1844), the physicist, was once a member. Its collections include rare historical works and ancient medical treatises.

QUEEN'S PARK ART GALLERY The gallery contains Victorian paintings and sculpture and a collection of dolls and dolls' houses of the 18th and 19th centuries. It is also the regimental museum of the Manchester Regiment and the 14th/20th King's Hussars.

TOWN HALL This magnificent Gothic Revival building was erected in 1868–77 to designs by Alfred Waterhouse (1830–1905), who was later architect of Eaton Hall in Cheshire. His design was chosen from 123 submitted in a competition held in 1867 by the Manchester authorities. One of the judges in the contest was George Edmund Street, the architect of the Royal Courts of Justice in London. The prominent feature of the main front of Waterhouse's building is a tall clock-tower with pinnacles, and flying buttresses supporting a spire.

### EGYPTIAN 7th-CENTURY COPTIC TUNIC

*Excavated from the Egyptian pyramids in the late 19th century, this Coptic tunic, dating from the 7th century AD, is one of several in the Whitworth collections. It is made of coloured wool, with white undyed linen and tapestry-woven arabesque decoration, some of its outlines being embroidered in the type of stitch known as Soumaq. Although the dry sand of the Egyptian burial grounds preserved textiles remarkably well, complete tunics are rare: tomb robbers and others often cut off the decorative bands.*
*(Whitworth Art Gallery, Manchester)*

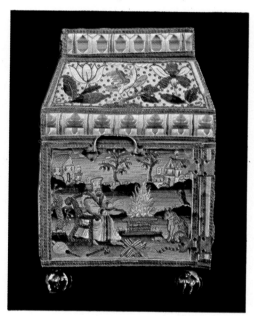

### EMBROIDERED BOX

*Well-bred young ladies of the 17th century embroidered boxes like this, in fine silk thread, for their personal belongings. (Whitworth Art Gallery, Manchester)*

WHITWORTH ART GALLERY, UNIVERSITY OF MANCHESTER Drawings, prints and textiles form the main collections. The drawings are by modern continental artists (including Van Gogh, Gauguin, Cézanne, Picasso, Klee); there are works by contemporary sculptors, by English artists (Gainsborough, Turner, the Pre-Raphaelites and others), and old masters. Prints include a large Japanese group and Italian and German Renaissance work.

WYTHENSHAWE HALL (NORTHENDEN) A half-timbered manor house, set in parkland, and the home of the Tatton family for over 500 years. It

**351**

## 15th-CENTURY STAINED GLASS

*King David, playing the harp, and King Solomon, who holds the tabernacle, are shown on this 15th-century east window, with their names behind them. The three lights of the window contain remains of the original Jesse tree, which has been partly restored. The use of white as a colour is unusual for stained glass of this period. (Church of St Margaret, Margaretting)*

contains 17th-century paintings and furnishings, and exhibits of Royal Lancastrian pottery and objects of local historical interest.

**Manorbier Castle** *Pemb.*     *544Dc*
One of the few Norman castles containing comfortable, spacious living quarters. The moated fortress was begun in the 12th century. Little remains of the outer ward, but the inner court remains intact. The vast gate-house, hall and chapel form the nucleus of the castle and, with the domestic buildings, have windows looking on to the inner court. The castle was never attacked. Because of its seclusion it has often been used by smugglers in the past.

**Mansfield** *Notts.*     *552Ee*
MUSEUM AND ART GALLERY The collection contains 150 water-colours of old Mansfield painted by A. S. Buxton—one-time principal of the Mansfield School of Art—and specimens of British birds and mammals. Two other galleries display loan collections of art, photography, sculpture, embroidery and other exhibitions.

**Mapledurham House** *Oxon.*     *547Gb*
Grounds running down to the Thames beside wooded hills are the background to the mansion used by John Galsworthy as one of the settings for *The Forsyte Saga* and by Kenneth Grahame for *The Wind in the Willows*. Old almshouses and a water-mill adjoin the recently restored Elizabethan manor of pink brick.

**March** *Cambs*     *548Ag*
CHURCH OF ST WENDREDA A magnificent Perpendicular church, with a west tower and tall spire. St Wendreda's is famous for its sumptuous double-hammerbeam roof in the nave, with angels everywhere, wings outstretched. There are early 16th-century brasses.

**Marford** *Flints.*     *551Jd*
An unusual and attractive village thought to have been designed by a Mr Boydell, agent for the Trevalyn Estate in the early 19th century. The most conspicuous feature is the fenestration; all the windows are curiously shaped, either as ogee eyelets, or in 'church-warden Gothic' style. A mile to

the north is the multi-gabled Elizabethan house, Trevalyn Hall, opposite a fine timber-framed water-mill.

**Margam** *Glam.*     *545Gb*
ABBEY The abbey was founded for the Cistercians in 1147 by Robert, Earl of Gloucester. The Norman church remains in part as the present parish church, though much of the east end has gone. The large 12-sided chapter house is in ruins.

**Margaretting** *Essex*     *548Bc*
CHURCH OF ST MARGARET In addition to its famous 15th-century Jesse window, the church has good timbering in its two porches and tower and a 15th-century octagonal font.

**Markenfield Hall** *Yorks.*     *558Cc*
A medieval moated manor of 14th-century origin, with 15th- and 16th-century additions

**Market Harborough** *Leics.*     *552Fa*
CHURCH OF ST DIONYSIUS A 13th–15th-century church, with notable window tracery, and a truly impressive west tower and broach spire. The interior is galleried.

**Markyate** *Herts.*     *547Hd*
MARKYATE CELL A neo-Elizabethan mansion (1825–6), incorporating a 12th-century priory for nuns, which Humphrey Bourchier turned into a Tudor manor house in 1539. There have been reports of ghostly nuns in the park. In the 18th century, Lady Ferrers, the infamous 'highwayman' lived there. She frequently disguised herself as a man and robbed stage-coaches. Not until she was shot dead was her true identity revealed.

**Marlborough** *Wilts.*     *540Fg*
A market town noted for its fine High Street, which is partly arcaded, and the famous public school.

**Marlow** *Bucks.*     *547Gb*
MARLOW PLACE A red-brick, baroque house built in 1720 for George II when Prince of Wales. (By appointment.)

**Marnhull** *Dorset*     *540Dd*
CHURCH OF ST GREGORY A good cruciform church with a west tower; it has 12th-century origins, but was refashioned and enlarged in the 15th and 19th centuries. The tower is mainly 15th century, but the top was added in the 18th. The font is Gothic.

**Marquess of Anglesey's Column**     *550Ee*
*Anglesey*
Erected in 1817 by the inhabitants of Anglesey and Caernarvon to commemorate the Marquess's military achievements in Spain and at the Battle of Waterloo, the column stands on the north coast of Anglesey, in view of Plas Newydd Mansion—the late 18th-century mansion in which the Marquess lived. It is crowned by a 12 ft bronze statue of the Marquess, wearing his uniform as Colonel of the 7th Hussars, executed by the then fashionable sculptor Matthew Noble. The overall height of the column is 112 ft.

**Marston Moretaine** *Beds*     *547He*
CHURCH OF ST MARY THE VIRGIN A pretty church, begun *c.* 1340, but practically rebuilt in 1445. It has a massive west tower set slightly apart from the main building. Inside can be seen carved bosses and angels on the roofs, interesting screen paintings, brasses, and a monument with recumbent effigy.

**Martley** *Worcs.*     *546Bf*
CHURCH OF ST PETER A fine church dating from Norman times, with later additions. Interesting

JOHN NOST *Perseus*

*John Nost left Belgium to settle in England in 1678, and became a successful sculptor, specialising in lead statues for gardens. Some of his works were direct copies, but others, like this one in the baroque style of his native Flanders, were original. It is one of a group completed in 1699–1705. (Melbourne Hall)*

THE PERGOLA AT
MELBOURNE HALL

*A beautiful example of English wrought-iron work, designed and made about 1706 by a local man, Robert Bakewell of Derby. Viewed from below, the graceful work shows the light touch and flair for design of this relatively obscure craftsman. Little is known of his life, but not long after making this arbour he was 'miserable poor'. However, other fine examples of his work exist at Okeover Hall in Derbyshire, All Saints Cathedral in Derby, and at the Radcliffe Camera in Oxford where he worked in 1744. The pergola stands at the far end of a pond in the Melbourne gardens, designed by the royal gardener under William III, Anne and George I—William Wise. At Melbourne, Wise designed in the manner of the French gardener André Le Nôtre, who laid out the gardens at Versailles.*

medieval mural paintings include one of St Martin, heraldry and animals. There is a mid-15th-century alabaster effigy of a recumbent knight.

**Marwick Head** *Mainland, Orkney*     569Hg
KITCHENER MEMORIAL On June 5, 1916, while outward bound from Scapa Flow to Russia, Field Marshal Earl Kitchener of Khartoum, Secretary of State for War, was drowned when the *Hampshire* struck a mine. The memorial stands at the point nearest to the place where the cruiser went down.

**Masham** *Yorks.*     558Cd
CHURCH OF ST MARY The west tower is Norman in its lower stages, and there is other Norman work at St Mary's; but much was added and altered, including the 15th-century spire. An important Saxon cross is in the churchyard, and there are many monuments from the early 17th century onwards.

**Matfield** *Kent*     542De
Matfield House, built in 1725, is a perfect early Georgian house, an expert piece of brickwork, of a deep plum colour. It stands behind wrought-iron gates, accompanied by stables with a gold and blue clock-face, and a pretty row of cottages, all facing across the duckpond to Matfield Green.

**Mathry** *Pemb.*     544Cd
LONGHOUSE An orthodox burial chamber. It is walled by no less than seven upright slabs which support a great capstone. The covering mound has long disappeared, and its outline cannot now be traced.

**Mawley Hall** *Shrops.*     546Bf
An 18th-century mansion, possibly designed by Francis Smith of Warwick, with period plaster-work and panelling.

**Maxstoke** *Warks.*     546Dg
CHURCH OF ST MICHAEL The church was probably built c. 1336, when a priory was founded here, and has no internal division between nave and chancel. The interior was remodelled during the 18th century.

**Maxstoke Castle** *Warks.*     546Dg
A splendid 14th-century moated castle built to a square plan, with curtain walls, angle-towers and parapets. The great hall dates from 1345.

**Maybole Castle** *Ayrs.*     561Gc
This former town house of the Earls of Cassillis (the Kennedy family) has notable oriel windows and romantic turrets.

**Mayfield** *Sussex*     542Ce
At the top of the village there are the remains of a palace of the Archbishops of Canterbury, with a grand 14th-century hall, and in the street several substantial houses, stone or half-timbered. The Middle House Hotel, one of the most spectacular pieces of decorative half-timbering in the Home Counties, is dated 1575. The imposing convent and school was once a 10th-century palace of the Archbishops of Canterbury.

**Medmenham Abbey** *Bucks.*     547Gb
The ruins of a 12th-century Cistercian abbey, made notorious by Sir Francis Dashwood as a meeting place for his Hell Fire Club in 1745—a congregation of young bloods whose motto was 'Do what you will' and whose orgies and rituals mocked all religion.

**Meigle Museum** *Perths.*     566Db
Here, in a small museum, is a fine collection of 25 Pictish symbol stones. These show a great range of different types.

**Meikleour House** *Perths.* 566Db
Noted for its beech hedge, planted in 1746, which is now nearly 90 ft high and 580 yds long.

**Meini Gwyr** *Carm.* 544Dg
The Prescelly range of mountains runs parallel to the coast and on the fringes of its southern slopes, which border Pembrokeshire's central valley, stand many isolated monuments. Among them this circle is unique in its design, for its stones are not set directly in the natural surface, but in a raised ring made to receive them.

**Melbourne** *Derbys.* 552Dc
CHURCH OF SS MICHAEL AND MARY An impressive, cruciform, Norman church, with two west towers, as well as one at the crossing. The interior is well preserved, with a triforium placed in front of the clerestory windows.

**Melbourne Hall** *Derbys.* 552Dc
A country mansion built on a site used by the Bishops of Carlisle since 1280, but developed by Sir John Coke (1563–1644) and transformed and further developed by his great-grandson, Sir Thomas Coke, between 1710 and 1744. Sir Thomas was Vice-Chamberlain to Queen Anne and George I, whose portraits hang in the drawing-room. Birthplace of Lord Melbourne, the 19th-century statesman, the Hall is now owned by the Marquess of Lothian. The gardens are laid out with long avenues, tunnels of yew, fountains, statuary, a shell grotto and a unique wrought-iron bird-cage pergola of 1725, by Robert Bakewell, a blacksmith. (See p. 353.)

**Melbury Sampford** *Dorset* 540Cd
CHURCH OF ST MARY Cruciform, with a central tower, St Mary's dates mainly from the 15th century, but was restored in 1878. It contains many monuments from the 15th century onwards, including recumbent men in armour, and a charming kneeling figure by sir Francis Chantrey (1821). There is also some 15th-century heraldic stained glass.

**Melford Hall** *Suffolk* 548Ce
Elizabeth I visited Sir William Cordell, her Master of the Rolls, in this fine mansion he had built between 1554 and 1578, in the year it was finished. Its two towers stand sentinel to the two wings that flank the main entrance court. The mansion houses the Hyde Parker Collection of Chinese porcelain, fine furniture and old masters.

**Mellerstain** *Ber.* 562Dd
The castellated country home of the Earl of Haddington, descendant of the Scottish poetess and heroine, Lady Grizel Baillie (1665–1746), who lived here. William Adam built the wings of the house in 1725 and his son, Robert, the central block *c.* 1765.

Inside the house are decorated plaster ceilings, old masters and much fine furniture; the library has a frieze of Classical figures over the bookshelves. The extensive grounds include a garden in the Italian style.

**Mellor** *Cheshire* 552Cf
CHURCH OF ST THOMAS An early 19th-century Gothic church that retains from an older building a Norman font, crudely carved with figures, and a beautiful 14th-century wooden pulpit.

**Mells** *Som.* 540Df
CHURCH OF ST ANDREW The 15th-century church has a tall tower with pinnacles. Inside are 16th-century benches and fragments of medieval stained glass. There are monuments by Burne-Jones and Sir Alfred Munnings.

THE LIBRARY AT MELLERSTAIN

*William Adam began this battlemented house in 1725, but built only the side wings. After a pause of some years his son Robert completed the house in the 1770's, and was responsible for the interior, a masterpiece of delicate Classical decoration and colour—pale blues, greens and white, with plaster decoration in low relief, of which he was so able a practitioner. Robert's genius as a designer is evident in the library with its fine Classical friezes, and its ceiling in the style of Angelica Kauffmann or Zucchi, with a painting of Minerva in the central medallion. The right-hand bust in the far corner is of Lady Grizel Baillie, wife of Mellerstain's first owner; it was carved by Louis Roubiliac in 1746 when she was 81.*

MELROSE ABBEY

*This abbey was founded by Cistercian monks on a site in the valley of the Tweed in 1136. The location was ideal for sheep farming, which produced a large part of the abbey's income, and nearby Berwick provided a convenient market for the monks to sell their wool. The house was close to the main road from England to Edinburgh, and so received visits from many eminent people whose donations made it one of the wealthiest abbeys in Scotland. But the situation soon became a source of danger in any dispute between the kings of England and Scotland. Melrose was sacked by Edward II in 1322 and by Richard II in 1385. The church had to be rebuilt (it continued in use until 1810), but the abbey never recovered from a final sacking in 1547.*

**Melrose Abbey** *Rox.*       562Dd
A Cistercian house founded by David I in 1136 for monks brought from Rievaulx in Yorkshire. Built of local red sandstone, it eventually became one of the richest abbeys in Scotland, but it was near the border where constant warring between England and Scotland occurred. In 1385 the troops of Richard II sacked the abbey seriously enough to warrant rebuilding of the church. This is now the main survival, largely because it was used as a parish church until 1810. It has many features of northern English architecture. For instance, the façades of the south and east arms compare with the west and east façades of York Minster (14th century). It was a splendid church, and its reconstruction lasted into the 16th century. The abbey was extensive—excavations have revealed most of the lay-out. But in 1547 Melrose was again sacked by the English, under the Duke of Somerset, and never recovered. A small museum in the Commendator's House, part of the abbey buildings, houses pottery and floor tiles found during excavations of the abbey site and adjoining grounds.

**Melton Mowbray** *Leics.*       552Fc
An ancient agricultural centre famous for its hunting, pork pies and Stilton cheese. It has two fine churches, several elegant 18th-century houses and some 19th-century civic buildings.
CHURCH OF ST MARY A large cruciform building, mainly 13th and 14th century, with a central tower about 100 ft high; the lower stage of this is 13th century, the upper *c.* 1500. There is an outstanding clerestory, but it has suffered badly from restoration. There is a set of 18th-century chandeliers, and an effigy of a cross-legged knight.

**Melverley** *Shrops.*       551Jc
CHURCH OF ST PETER Standing in fields by the R. Vyrnwy, an unusual black and white timber-framed church probably built in the 15th century. The interior is timbered too, with a primitive rood screen, and there is a western gallery from the late 16th century. The east window dates from the restoration in 1878.

**Menai Suspension Bridge**       550Ee
**and Britannia Tubular Bridge** *Caern.*
Thomas Telford was a well-known bridge engineer when he was asked, in the early 19th century, to design a bridge across the Menai Strait. This became his most famous and important work. The Menai road bridge is of cast iron, supported on each bank by a tremendous tower and suspended on metal chains over the channel. The bridge, which is nearly half a mile in length with a central span of about 600 ft, was begun in 1818 despite fierce opposition from local landowners, and was opened to traffic in 1826. The Britannia railway bridge was built farther up the strait by Robert Stephenson in the years 1846–50. Stephenson's problems were as great as those which had faced Telford, for a suspension bridge would be unable to carry heavy rail traffic. The bridge was eventually constructed of two great iron tubes supported by five huge piers. The red sandstone supports stand one at each bank and three in the strait. The central pier is built on a rock and is known as the Great Britannia Tower.

**Mendlesham** *Suffolk*       548Df
CHURCH OF ST MARY Of 13th-century origins, with later additions; the west tower and two porches have much flushwork decoration in flint and stone. There is a good font cover and pulpit of 1630. The upper room of the north porch contains an unusual feature—a parish armoury, with pieces of armour from the 15th to 17th centuries.

**Menstrie Castle** *Clack.*       562Af
The birthplace of Sir William Alexander (1567–1640), poet and statesman, later 'Lieutenant for the Plantations of New Scotland', otherwise known as Nova Scotia, commissioned by James VI

(James I of England) in 1621. The foundation of the colony of Nova Scotia was assisted by the creation of Scotian baronetcies; and the coats of arms of 107 baronets are displayed at the castle.

**Mere** *Wilts.*                                                    540De
CHURCH OF ST MICHAEL This is a large church of various dates, mostly Decorated though with later Perpendicular work, for example the tower, *c.* 1450. The octagonal font is Perpendicular, and the fine rood and chapel screens are of the same period. The stalls have misericords; there are brasses of 1398 and 1426, and good examples of 19th-century stained glass.

**Merevale** *Warks.*                                                546Eg
CHURCH OF ST MARY Originally built as the 'capella extra portam' (chapel outside the gate) of the Cistercian Abbey, which was founded in the mid-12th century and is now but fragmentary ruins near by. The church itself dates from the 13th century, but what can be seen now is mainly of the 14th and 15th centuries. Glass of this period includes a 14th-century Tree of Jesse window. There is a medieval organ loft from the abbey church, a 13th-century effigy, a 15th-century brass, an alabaster table-tomb and a Perpendicular screen.

**Mereworth Castle** *Kent*                                          542Df
Built in 1720–30 by Colin Campbell for the Hon. John Fane, this house is based on Palladio's Villa Capra at Vicenza, Italy. Chiswick House, the Earl of Burlington's home built about the same time, was modelled on the same villa. Like Chiswick, Mereworth is square; it has a central dome and on each side of the house is a large portico with Ionic columns. No chimneys are apparent from the outside, because Campbell cunningly conveyed all the flues through the thickness of the dome to an outlet at the top. The house contains fine plaster-work and paintings, and stands amid extensive grounds with fine gardens.

**Mersham** *Kent*                                                   542Ee
CHURCH OF ST JOHN THE BAPTIST A Norman church, later enlarged, with a west tower which has a pyramidal roof. There are some fragments of medieval glass. Among the monuments is one to Sir Wyndham Knatchbull, *c.* 1765, by William Tyler.

**Merthyrmawr** *Glam.*                                              545Gb
Most Welsh roofs are of slate, but in the Vale of Glamorgan there are one or two villages where thatch is used. Merthyrmawr, a small village near the mouth of the Ogmore, is one of the best preserved. It also has a medieval bridge, a ruined oratory containing pre-Conquest memorials, and within a short distance are the castles of Ogmore, with its splendid stepping-stones, and Candleston, standing on the edge of extensive sand dunes which have covered an area rich in prehistoric sites.

**Merthyr Tydfil** *Glam.*                                           545Hc
ART GALLERY AND MUSEUM (CYFARTHFA CASTLE) The neo-Gothic castle, built in 1825 by the Craw-shay family of ironmasters, has exhibits relating to the history and natural history of the district; there is a replica of a Welsh kitchen. The art collections include paintings, ceramics with examples of Swansea and Nantgarw china, coins, silver and medals.

**Methwold** *Norfolk*                                               554Bb
VICARAGE The house has a notable early 16th-century brick gable-end built on to a range of timber-framed houses. The gable is beautifully decorated in three tiers.

16th-CENTURY STAINED GLASS
WINDOW

*This church was rebuilt in the early 16th century by Sir Richard Assheton, lord of the manor, as a thank offering and memorial to the Battle of Flodden (1513) where he and his archers had distinguished themselves. The war memorial window, set up by Sir Richard in 1520, much altered, now stands in the south chancel. The line of 16 English archers kneeling in prayer is still recognisable, each dressed in blue with a long-bow on his shoulder. Above each bow is the archer's name. Sir Richard and his wife Anne are also included, and their chaplain, Henry Taylyer.*
*(Church of St Leonard, Middleton)*

**Michelham Priory** *Sussex*                                        542Cd
One of the largest private moats in the country surrounds the Augustinian priory, founded in 1229. A gate-house was built in the 14th century and the property was adapted as a Tudor farm-house in the late 16th century. It contains a collection of fine furniture, tapestries, Sussex ironwork, ancient stained glass, musical instruments, a doll's house, a forge and wheelwright's shop, and obsolete wagons.

**Mid Calder** *M'loth.*                                             562Be
In this 15th-century house in 1556 John Knox administered one of the first Protestant communions in the manner of the Reformed Scottish Church. Chopin stayed here in 1848.

**Middlesbrough** *Yorks.*                                           558De
DORMAN MEMORIAL MUSEUM AND MUNICIPAL ART GALLERY Collections devoted to the natural history, geology and archaeology of north-eastern Yorkshire are on display; there is also a group of model ships.
Temporary exhibitions are held in the art gallery, and there is also a small permanent collection of modern pictures.

**Middleton** *Lancs.*                                               552Bg
CHURCH OF ST LEONARD Rebuilt in the 16th century, the old tower has a gabled wooden belfrey cap, added in 1709. There is a window inserted by Sir Richard Assheton in 1520, recalling his command of local archers at Flodden Field (1513); also a 16th-century screen, and brasses.

**Middleton Hall** *Westmld.*  557Jd
A 15th-century manor house with walled court-yards. A Roman milestone was recently erected in a field near the hall, which notes the 53rd mile from Carlisle, and near by is an ancient cross called the Standing Stone of Whilprigg.

**Mid Howe** *Rousay, Orkney*  569Hg
The largest 'stalled cairn', 106¾ ft long by 42½ ft wide. The chamber is lined with drystone walling and the outer face with coursed slabs set slantwise. The chamber is 76 ft long and 7 ft wide, divided by upright slabs into 12 pairs of cells.

**Midhurst** *Sussex*  541Jd
In Tudor times Midhurst shared with Rye the privilege of making town tokens for use by private traders: the Midhurst Farthing had a weaver's shuttle as its device. A local quilt-maker founded the grammar school in 1672. Among its old boys are the statesmen Richard Cobden, the novelist H. G. Wells and Sir Charles Lyle, the geologist.

**Midmar Castle** *A'deen*  566Fe
A fine example of an early 17th-century Scottish baronial building with many turrets, said to have been built by Sir William Wallace.

**Midsummer Hill** *Herefs.*  546Be
A large Iron Age hill-fort lying towards the south end of the Malvern range. It is a 'contour' fort, its defences following the natural contours of the hill, and comprises a bank and ditch with counterscarp bank. The bank was faced with drystone walling, and some of the material came from internal quarry ditches. South of the fort on the adjoining hill are a long barrow and several round barrows of the Bronze Age.

**Mildenhall** *Suffolk*  548Bf
CHURCH OF SS MARY AND ANDREW A major church of Suffolk—very long and with a tall west tower. There is some 13th-century work in the chancel, but the remainder is mainly Perpendicular. The east window, *c.* 1300, has extraordinary and unique tracery design, and the magnificent roofs have angels and other carved

decoration. The font is of Purbeck marble, and there is a monument, with effigies, of *c.* 1620.

**Milford Haven** *Pembs.*  544Cc
A natural harbour, for centuries a middle-water fishing port, and now a major harbour for oil tankers too large to be accommodated elsewhere. Milford Haven was the departure point from which in 1172 the forces of Henry II set out to conquer Ireland. Lord Nelson laid the foundation stone of St Katherine's Church, and Lady Hamilton and her husband are buried in its churchyard.

**Millport** *Isle of Cumbrae*  561Ge
ROBERTSON MUSEUM AND THE AQUARIUM The museum is devoted to natural history, and the aquarium exhibits marine life found in the Clyde sea area.

**Millom** *Cumb.*  557Gd
CHURCH OF THE HOLY TRINITY A Norman and later church, near the castle. Inside are box-pews, and monuments to the Huddleston family, one of *c.* 1494 with alabaster effigies.

**Milton Abbas** *Dorset*  540Dd
ABBEY A magnificent 14th-century abbey church of transepts and choir, with a 15th-century tower. The Reformation put a stop to the work so that the nave was not built. Inside is the delightful monument, *c.* 1775, to Lord and Lady Milton by Agostino Carlini, with reclining effigies; it was designed by the architect Robert Adam.

**Milton Abbey** *Dorset*  540Dd
Milton Abbey was dissolved by Henry VIII, and the estate sold. Eventually Lord Milton bought it in 1752, and employed John Vardy, the former assistant of William Kent, to undertake rebuilding of the former monastic buildings. However, during the early 1770's Milton commissioned Sir William Chambers, one of the most outstanding architects of the 18th century, to build him a new Gothic house. After Milton and Chambers quarrelled in 1774, James Wyatt continued the work of building. He was responsible for most of the Classical interior decoration, with fine ceilings. Of the

MILTON ABBEY

*Two buildings in the Gothic style stand side by side at Milton Abbey. But three centuries separate them. The abbey church (centre) was erected in the 15th century, secularised after Henry VIII's dissolution, and bought in 1752 by Lord Milton. Work on the house (right) started 20 years later. Sir William Chambers,* *designer of Somerset House in London, first directed construction, and when he and Milton fell out in 1774, James Wyatt took over. One of the chimney-pieces is the work of Joseph Wilton; others are by Wyatt. The church, now only a fragment, contains two monuments, one—to Milton's wife—carved by Agostino Carlini.*

MINSTER LOVELL HALL

*The unluckiest owner of this house must surely have been Francis, 9th Baron Lovell, who started life a rich and powerful aristocrat and is said to have died in hiding in one of its vaults. Francis gambled his future on supporting the Yorkists in the Wars of the Roses—unlike his predecessor John, who was a Lancastrian. At first this change of sides brought rewards, and Francis was made a viscount by Richard III in 1483. Two years later, Richard and his supporters were defeated at the Battle of Bosworth. Francis never gained the favour of the new king, Henry VII, and after an unsuccessful rebellion in 1487 he is said to have gone into hiding in a vault at Minster Lovell Hall. Two centuries later, in 1708, workmen making alterations to the house found 'the entire skeleton of a man, as having been at a table which was before him with a book, paper, pen . . . all much mouldered and decay'. Minster Lovell Hall probably belonged to the Lovell family as early as the 12th century, but it was rebuilt in the 15th century.*

original abbey, the abbot's hall still survives. Next to the house is the 15th-century abbey church, but only part of this remains—the western side of what was the central tower has disappeared. The church contains much good vaulting under the tower and a carved altar screen. The abbey is now used as a school.

**Milton Hall** *Hunts.*                                  *547Jl*
Ancestral home of the Fitzwilliam family, the house has a late Elizabethan eastern front with many mullioned windows, while the garden front is in 18th-century Palladian style. The two-storied bay window of the Hall dates from the mid-16th century. The mosaic floor of the dairy was relaid here after being excavated in 1820 from ruined buildings near the parish church of nearby Castor; the buildings were once part of a Roman camp.

**Milton Manor** *Berks.*                                  *546Fc*
A small 17th-century manor house with Georgian wings. The chapel and library are in the neo-Gothic style. Among items on view is the telescope of John Benbow (1653–1702), Vice-Admiral of the Blue, 1701.

**Minstead** *Hants.*                                  *541Gd*
CHURCH OF ALL SAINTS The church was originally a 13th-century building, of which the chancel arch remains. During alterations in the late 18th century, the west tower was built and fittings added—including the three-decker pulpit, west gallery and pews. The square font is Norman, and is made of Purbeck marble, embellished with carvings of Christ.

**Minster** *Kent*                                  *542Eg*
CHURCH OF SS MARY AND SEXBURGA Norman and Gothic work survives in a small building that probably has Saxon origins. There is a good brass, and a monument to a medieval Warden of the Cinque Ports.

**Minster** *Kent*                                  *543Gf*
CHURCH OF ST MARY A beautiful cruciform church, with a west tower capped by a slender spire. The nave is Norman; there are misericords and several monuments. Tradition has it that the church is built on the site of a nunnery founded by Ermenburga *c.* 670.

**Minster Lovell** *Oxon.*                                  *546Ed*
CHURCH OF ST KENELM A cruciform church with a central tower, nearly all of the 15th century. The tower is narrower than the rest of the building, and the tower piers in the nave are set in, considerably narrowing the east end. There is some medieval stained glass, a Perpendicular font and good woodwork. The monument to the builder of the church, Lord Lovell, has an alabaster effigy, *c.* 1430.

**Minster Lovell Hall** *Oxon.*                                  *546Ed*
The ruins of Minster Lovell Hall stand in an attractive position on the banks of the R. Windrush. The ruins of the Hall never formed part of any religious establishment, although the owners of the property established a small religious foundation near by, which was subject to Ivry Abbey in Normandy and was therefore termed an 'alien priory'. The site of this priory is now lost. The remains are those of a 15th-century manor house. The chief fragments are of the hall and its porch, and part of the north and west sides of the court. The present ruined state of the Hall is the result of demolition *c.* 1750.

**Moat Hall** *Suffolk*                                  *548Ef*
A 15th-century building which has been restored. Here Lady Willoughby wrote her diary of the Civil War.

**Moat House** *Leics.*                                  *553Db*
Nothing remains of the 14th-century manor house (home of Sir Edmund de Appleby, who fought at the Battle of Crécy) except part of the moat, an old stone well, and a cobbled courtyard now beneath the present garden. The stone gate-house was rebuilt in the 15th century and a timber-frame building added to it to make a yeoman-type dwelling. In the grounds is a 16th-century dovecote, originally of stone but later restored in red brick.

**Mobberley** *Cheshire*                                  *552Be*
CHURCH OF ST WILFRID The origins are 13th century, but most of the work was done in the following two centuries. There is a good rood screen of *c.* 1500, a fine medieval nave roof and some old stained glass. The remains of a wall-painting show St Christopher. There is a tower screen dated 1683.

**Moccas** *Herefs.*                                  *546Ae*
CHURCH OF ST MICHAEL AND ALL ANGELS A Norman church of nave, chancel and apse, with

windows of *c*. 1300. Some stained glass dates from the 14th century, and there is a cross-legged knight on a monument of the same period.

**Moignes Court** *Dorset*                    540Dc
One fragment of this moated country house dates from 1280, and the windows and doorway are of the Early English period.

**Mold** *Flints.*                    551He
CHURCH OF ST MARY A spacious Perpendicular church, with a west tower rebuilt in 1773. Inside, there is sculptured decoration on capitals and panelling below the clerestory windows. Many memorials by Sir Henry Cheere, Benjamin and Solomon Gibson (brothers of the more famous John) and Michael Rysbrack.

**Monk Fryston** *Yorks.*                    558Da
CHURCH OF ST WILFRID The west tower is Saxon, but the rest of the church is mainly Early English and Decorated Gothic. There is a square Early English font, and fragments of medieval stained glass.

**Monkwearmouth** *Durham*                    558Dg
The monastery of Monkwearmouth was established in 674 and that at Jarrow, 6 miles to the north-west, in 684. Both were founded by Benedict Biscop, who had travelled widely in Europe; his churches are outstanding examples of the northern renaissance in architecture. By the 8th century the two monasteries were so famous that together they housed nearly 600 monks. Monkwearmouth is now almost completely submerged by the sea, but the parts of the church which survive provide a direct link with a remarkable period in English history. The most interesting part is at the west end, where the tower incorporates a lower porch dating from Biscop's time. The entrance, which is flanked by heavy stone balustrades, is tunnel-vaulted and is the earliest medieval vault in England. Above the entrance on the outside are the battered remains of a large standing figure carved in relief. This figure also dates from Biscop's time and is one of the earliest surviving pieces of large-scale architectural sculpture in Britain.

**Monmouth** *Mon.*                    546Ad
After many changes of ownership—from 1086 when William FitzBaderun acquired the town from the Breton Abbey of St Florent de Saumer, until 1387 when Henry V was born in the castle—Monmouth fell into decay in the Wars of the Roses. It became a Lancastrian holding until it was sold to the Earl of Worcester in 1630, and its fortunes then revived. The Shire Hall, in Agincourt Square, is a fine Georgian building erected in 1724 on the site of Old Market House. In the middle of its façade is a statue of Henry V. At one end of the Monnow bridge is a gateway which was constructed in the 13th century as a toll house and defence tower with portcullis. Great Castle House was built by the 1st Duke of Beaufort in 1673, and *c.* 1875 it became headquarters of the Royal Monmouthshire Royal Engineers; it has superb plaster ceilings. (By appointment.)
CHURCH OF ST MARY Originally a Norman church with Gothic enlargements, it was pulled down during the 18th century and rebuilt in a Classical style by Smith of Warwick. The 14th-century west tower was retained but given a tall slender spire. In *c.* 1880 G. E. Street Gothicised and enlarged the building. Monuments of the 18th and 19th centuries include work by James Paty the Younger of Bristol, and Sir Richard Westmacott. There are some 15th-century wall tiles and 19th-century glass by C. E. Kempe.

NELSON MUSEUM Among items commemorating Lord Nelson, Lady Hamilton and their contemporaries are collections of silver, china and glass, a model of the Battle of Trafalgar, ships, swords and naval equipment; also a collection of Nelson's letters, and items relating to local history.

**Montacute House** *Som.*                    540Cd
An Elizabethan house built in 1588–1601. It has fine windows and is surrounded by balustraded parapets. On the west side is a fine porch which dates from the early 16th century; this came from Clifton Maybank, a house a few miles away, when it was demolished in 1786. Carved statues of the Nine Worthies (Joshua, David, Judas Maccabeus, Hector, Alexander, Julius Caesar, Arthur, Charlemagne, Godfrey of Bouillon) stand in niches on the east front, originally the main entrance side of the house, and in the east forecourt are the original walled garden—a rare survival—and two domed pavilions. The house contains fine heraldic glass, plasterwork and panelling, portraits of the English School, and furniture. It was in the possession of the same family from 1601 to 1931.

**Montgomery** *Mont.*                    551Hb
CASTLE The castle stands on a spur overlooking the R. Severn, and was built by Henry III *c.* 1223 on the site of an earlier Norman motte and bailey. It has been a ruin since assaults by Parliamentarians in 1644 during the Civil War; only fragments of the walls and towers remain.

**Montrose** *Angus*                    566Fb
This is an ancient royal burgh with several treasures and curiosities. In the steeple of the Old Church is the Big Peter bell, cast in Rotterdam in 1676, which tolls the curfew at 10 p.m. each night. Also in the church is a chandelier shaped as a hearse, which was presented by a Swedish admiral in 1627. Chalices made by a superb craftsman, William Lindsay, stamped with the Tudor rose and made between 1671 and 1688, are still in use. Four of the books in the old Montrose library were printed before 1501. The old library was replaced in 1790, and a third or 'new' library now incorporates the contents of the previous buildings.

**Moor Park Mansion House** *Herts.*                    547Hc
A country mansion built in 1670 for the Duke of Monmouth who, in 1685, led a rebellion against James II, was defeated at Sedgemoor (Somerset), captured, and beheaded on Tower Hill. In 1727 Sir James Thornhill designed and added two flanking wings in Palladian style. Capability Brown landscaped the grounds. The estate is now a golf club.

**Moretonhampstead Almshouses** *Devon*                    539Gd
A row of thatched houses built of granite over an open colonnade facing the street; erected in 1637.

**Morley** *Derbys.*                    552Ed
CHURCH OF ST MATTHEW Of the Norman original, only some parts of the nave arcade remain; the remainder of the church is 14th and 15th century. Some of the stained glass dates from the 15th century. Many of the medieval monuments and brasses are dedicated to the Sacheverell family.

**Morpeth** *Northld.*                    563Gb
CHURCH OF ST MARY Mainly 14th century. There is a stained glass Tree of Jesse of the same date in the east window, and fragments of old glass in other windows.

**Morville** *Shrops.*                    546Bg
CHURCH OF ST GREGORY Making an attractive group with Morville Hall, this Norman church has a chancel arch as early as 1118, and most of the

# MONTACUTE HOUSE

MONTACUTE HOUSE *One of the most beautiful country houses of the reign of Elizabeth I, Montacute was built in 1588–1601 for Sir Edward Philips, who later became Speaker of the House of Commons during the reign of James I. It is possible that its designer was John Thorpe. The northern part of the ground floor comprises the great hall, one storey high, with a stone screen at one end; at the other end is a plaster panel* representing a hen-pecked husband who, having hit his wife with a shoe in desperation, is punished by the parish by being carried round tied to a pole—a procedure known as the 'Ride to Skimmington'. On the second floor of the house is a 180 ft long gallery extending the whole length of the building. There is much heraldic stained glass, especially in the windows of the library, formerly the great chamber.

18TH-CENTURY ENGLISH CHAIR *In England during the reigns of Queen Anne and George I there was a strong preference for simple furniture materials and designs. Natural walnut veneer, as in this chair, was preferred to marquetried wood, and the straight rectangular-shaped back contrasts with contemporary French baroque curves. The legs are en cabriole—a French term meaning 'to caper'—and the seat and back are covered with embroidery.*

EMBROIDERED HANGING *Originally hung in Stoke Edith, a great house in Herefordshire belonging to the Foley family, this embroidered hanging may well show the formal gardens of the house—burnt down in 1927. The styles of the clothes and wigs in the embroidery suggest that it was made about the 1720's, and the sunlit effect given by the shadows indicates a summer's day. It is embroidered in silk on linen, using both tent-stitch and chain-stitch.*

interior is 12th century. An interesting Norman tub font is carved with large faces; there is 12th-century ironwork on the south door. A chancel window has early 14th-century stained glass.

**Morville Hall** *Shrops.*                           *546Bg*
An Elizabethan house, altered and added to in the 18th century, with two projecting wings.

**Morwenstow** *Cornwall*                           *538Ee*
CHURCH OF ST MORWENNA Standing high above the sea, this is an impressive church with west tower and much still remaining of the original Norman building: the north arcade, the south doorway, and the font. There is also work of the 13th, 15th and 16th centuries, and some fine wagon-roofs. During the last century, the poet Robert Hawker was vicar here.

**Moseley Old Hall** *Staffs.*                           *552Bb*
An Elizabethan house where the Whitgreave family sheltered Charles II after the Battle of Worcester in 1651; the bed he used and his secret hiding place can be seen. The house contains fine furniture, and documents, portraits and other relics of the Whitgreaves.

**Mottisfont Abbey** *Hants.*                           *541Ge*
At the Dissolution of the monasteries this 12th-century Augustinian priory came into the hands of Lord Sandys, Chancellor to Henry VIII, and he converted it into a fine house for himself; the wall of the church nave forms the north front of the house. It was altered and redecorated during the 18th century. There are Gothic-style *trompe l'oeil* paintings by Rex Whistler in the drawing room.

**Moulton** *Lincs.*                           *553Jc*
CHURCH OF ALL SAINTS An impressive church, with a late Perpendicular tower and spire. There is fine work in the foliage capitals, and above the west window are canopied niches containing figures of saints. The font, which is 18th century, has figures of Adam and Eve.

**Mount Grace Priory** *Yorks.*                           *558De*
The ruins of a Carthusian priory, founded in 1397 for 20 monks who, according to their strict rule, lived in separate cells. The priory was dissolved under Henry VIII, but part was made into a house in 1654.

**Mow Cop** *Cheshire–Staffs.*                           *552Bd*
A sham castle crowns this hill on the Cheshire-Staffordshire border. It was built to enhance the landscape by Randle Wilbraham *c.* 1750, and comprises a ruined round tower and ragged curtain wall broken by archways. On the summit of the hill Hugh Bourne, a Staffordshire carpenter, began to hold open-air camp meetings in 1807 similar to the revivalist camp meetings then sweeping America, and out of these meetings Primitive Methodism was born.

**Muchalls Castle** *Kinc.*                           *567Gd*
Built in 1619 by the Burnetts of Leys, this fortified mansion is notable for its 17th-century elaborate plaster ceilings and fire-places.

**Much Cowarne** *Herefs.*                           *546Be*
CHURCH OF ST MARY A 13th- and 14th-century church consisting of nave and south aisle only—the arcade of the demolished north aisle can be seen from the outside. Among the monuments is a cross-legged knight of the late 13th century.

**Muchelney Abbey** *Som.*                           *540Ce*
The ruin of a medieval (15th-century) abbey; the abbot's quarters are still habitable. The parish church near by has 17th-century painted panels in the roof, and medieval tiles.

**Much Hadham** *Herts.*                           *548Ad*
An attractive village with a number of delightful small 16th- and 17th-century cottages alongside larger 18th-century dwellings. The Lordship in the main street is a large nine-bay house of *c.* 1740 with a number of later additions. The gabled dwellings opposite are 17th century and next to them is the Earl of Euston's chequered brickwork house, North Leys. Other good examples from this period are Woodham House with its fine doorway; the Old House with exposed timbers; Green Shutters near by and Gaytons, a large three-gabled brick house. Much Hadham Hall, a five-bay house of 1735 with a hipped-roof, is the dominant house of the village street. To the south lies the Hall's handsome stable range and arched carriageway. Moor Place, 1775, is a two-storied five-bay brick house with blank arcading on the ground floor. Inside there is a splendid three-flight staircase.

Other houses of interest around Much Hadham are Yewtree House, dated 1697, at Hadham Cross; the moated Grudds Farm and the sympathetically modernised Bucklers Farm at Perry Green. The rectory is a brick and plastered-timber Jacobean house.
CHURCH OF ST ANDREW Although originally of the 12th century, the church dates mainly from the 13th–15th centuries; there is an embattled west tower with spire, and the roofs are good. Contents include a 15th-century screen, stained glass of the 15th and 19th centuries, and brasses.
PALACE Stands near St Andrew's churchyard. It was the country home of the Bishops of London for over 800 years, and was the birthplace of Edmund Tudor, Henry VII's father. Built on the H-plan, and incorporating a much earlier house, the original timber-framed structure was clad with brickwork in the 17th century. At the same time a floor was inserted at mid-height in the great hall, situated at the centre of the H and originally open to the roof. The splendid staircase and interior panelling are Jacobean.

**Much Marcle** *Herefs.*                           *546Be*
CHURCH OF ST BARTHOLOMEW The nave was built in the 13th century, and has a clerestory of lancet windows. The tower is central, and the long chancel was lengthened late in the 13th century. The array of monuments, with effigies, includes one of the beautiful Lady Grandison, who died in 1347. There are several 19th-century stained glass windows by C. E. Kempe.

**Much Wenlock** *Shrops.*                           *552Ab*
Medieval town associated with the poet A. E. Housman. Its showpieces include Raynald's Mansion (1682) with fine galleries, the manor house (1577) and the timbered guildhall with panelled rooms and movable stocks.
CHURCH OF THE HOLY TRINITY Not far from Wenlock Priory, a Norman church with a Transitional west tower and later additions such as the 13th-century two-storied porch. In the chancel are vaulted sedilia and two sculptured heads. The pulpit is early 17th century.
WENLOCK PRIORY All the turbulence of early English history is recalled by these ruins. The original priory, founded in the 7th century by St Milburga, daughter of a Mercian king, was sacked by the Danes *c.* 896. A later college for priests, founded by Lady Godiva, was demolished at the time of the Norman Conquest; it was rebuilt by a Norman knight, Roger de Montgomery, in 1080 but was destroyed again by Henry VIII's soldiers. The buildings, including the ruined church and cloisters, date mainly from the 11th century and

WENLOCK PRIORY

The nunnery founded by St Milburga at Much Wenlock about 680 was destroyed by the Danes 200 years later, and refounded for monks about 1050. In 1080 the Norman Earl of Shropshire, Roger de Montgomery, established a third foundation, which survived until the Dissolution of the monasteries. The Cluniac priory was subject to the French monastery of La Charité-sur-Loire, and paid an annual tax to the mother house. There were many such 'alien priories'

in England—until the wars with France at the end of the 13th century, when the king began to penalise them for this allegiance. During the next century the property of the alien houses was continually being seized by the king, who also taxed them harshly. Eventually, in 1395, Wenlock Priory severed all links with La Charité and, in return for a large cash payment, was released from paying the king's special taxes.

are in Early English style with Norman arcades. Ruins of a 15th-century prior's lodging also survive.

**Mullion** *Cornwall* 538Ba
CHURCH OF ST MELAN In the village on the coast above Mullion Cove. Inside are many carved 16th-century bench ends and decorative work by the 20th-century stained glass artist F. C. Eden.

**Muncaster Castle** *Cumb.* 557Gd
Once a refuge of Henry VI, the castle has been the country seat of the Pennington family since the 13th century. It has fine views over the valley of the R. Esk.

**Munslow Aston** *Shrops.* 546Ag
THE WHITE HOUSE A three-period house with Norman dove-cote built on the site of an early Saxon manor. The house has a 14th-century hall, a black and white 16th-century wing, and 18th-century additions which include the hanging staircase; it is now a folklore museum.

**Mutford** *Suffolk* 548Fg
CHURCH OF ST ANDREW St Andrew's has a circular Norman west tower, and there are other Norman features. The carved font dates from c. 1380; there are benches, and an interesting wall-painting of St Christopher.

# N

**Nanteos** *Card.* 544Fg
A fine Georgian mansion, with rococo plaster-work, built between 1739 and 1757 by the Powell family. The name, by which an earlier house, now destroyed, had become known at the end of the 17th century, means Valley of the Nightingale. It contains fine period furniture and paintings, and a healing cup, said to be the original Holy Grail, and a good first-floor salon in the style of Isaac Ware, but of a much later date.

**Nantwich** *Cheshire* 552Ad
An ancient town, originally prosperous in Roman times because of its brine springs. A great fire

devastated the town in 1583, but it was rebuilt in rich Elizabethan style. The almshouses are notable and were built in 1640 by Sir Edmund Wright. On the outskirts of the town is Dorfold Hall (1616). CHURCHE'S MANSION A merchant's house, built 1577, half-timbered and with fine oak panelling. CHURCH OF ST MARY One of Cheshire's fine churches, cruciform, and with a central octagonal tower. The styles are Decorated and Perpendicular, and St Mary's was restored in the 19th century. The vaulted chancel contains magnificent late 14th-century choir stalls with canopies and delightful misericords. There is also a 15th-century stone pulpit.

**Narborough** *Norfolk* 554Bb
CHURCH OF ALL SAINTS The church has Norman origins with later additions. There are some pieces of 15th-century stained glass. There are monuments dating from *c.* 1300, to members of the Spelman family, many with effigies. That to Clement Spelman (*d.* 1672), which has been mistakenly attributed to Caius Gabriel Cibber, shows him standing dressed in the costume of the period. The story is that, being a proud man, he insisted on being interred standing up so that no one would be able to walk on him. In 1865 the monument was opened, and it was found that the coffin was indeed upright.

**Narborough Hall** *Norfolk* 554Bb
A house with a mainly Tudor façade of brick, later battlements and a late Georgian bay window. Near by are two attractive water-mills and in the park there is the beginning of the Devil's Dyke, an ancient earthwork about 2 miles long, running south.

**Navenby** *Lincs.* 553Gd
CHURCH OF ST PETER A fine church, except for the tower and spire, which are an 18th-century rebuilding. The Decorated east window is a good example of its kind. The Easter sepulchre, which stands on the north side of the chancel, is decorated with carvings of figures, including three Roman soldiers. The font, at the east end of the south aisle, has a carved cover designed by Charles Kirk of Sleaford, which was shown at the Great Exhibition of 1851.

**Naworth Castle** *Cumb.* 557Jg
A 14th-century castle with courtyard, great hall and oratory, and richly furnished with tapestries. It was used by Sir Walter Scott as the setting for 'The Lay of the Last Minstrel'.

**Nayland** *Suffolk* 548Ce
Nayland has many good 15th- and 16th-century houses, including the handsome White House and Queen's Head Inn.
ALSTON COURT In Church Street, a splendid half-timbered courtyard house, built *c.* 1450 and added to in 1524, incorporates part of an Edward IV house. Built by Thomas Payne, a wealthy cloth-maker, who married a Miss Parker of 'gentle blood'; he commemorated their alliance by putting their Arms into a notable series of heraldic glass. There is also a spectacular nine-light 16th-century window, a hooded doorway of 1700, and some richly carved woodwork in the dining-room, solar and great hall, which has exposed tie-beams and king-post. Elsewhere there is much brickwork and rich carving.

**Neath Abbey** *Glam.* 545Gc
The ruins of a Cistercian abbey founded in 1130. It was much enlarged during the 13th century. A fragment of the main gateway to the abbey precinct remains. Close by are the site of a Roman camp and a Norman castle.

**Needham Market** *Suffolk* 548Df
CHURCH OF ST JOHN THE BAPTIST One of the most superb hammerbeam roofs in England, such a daring piece of design and carpentry that it makes one wonder how it stays up.

**Neidpath Castle** *Peebl.* 562Bd
The ruins of the former fortress of the Border Frasers beside the R. Tweed, where James VI stayed in 1587. The castle was besieged by Cromwell's troops in 1650 but never surrendered. The original 15th-century tower-house was added to in the 17th century.

HALL CHAIR AT NEWBY HALL

*An 18th-century English entrance hall was really a luxurious waiting-room, far more a focal point of the house than the staircase. Hall chairs would be grouped around fires, and were often equipped with small leather cushions for the comfort of visitors. This mahogany chair shows how Robert Adam thought an entrance hall should be furnished—with simplicity in the style and a hint of luxury in the material.*

**Nether Winchenden House** *Bucks.* 547Gd
A Tudor mansion, with 18th-century additions by Sir Francis Bernard, Governor of New Jersey (1758) and Massachusetts Bay (1760) whose administration of British policy hastened the American War of Independence.

**Netley** *Hants.* 541Gd
ABBEY The abbey was founded during the first half of the 13th century by monks who came from the Cistercian abbey not far away across the water at Beaulieu. Like so many abbeys it is now a ruin, but much survives.

**Nettlestead** *Suffolk* 548De
CHACE, THE A 19th-century brick house; the gateway is nearly 18 ft high, has a rounded arch, fluted columns and is decorated with the Wentworth Arms.
HIGH HALL A fragment of an Elizabethan mansion. Of red brick with pillared porch, there is a panelled drawing-room with carved beams and cornice.

**New Alresford** *Hants.* 541He
The new town was laid out by the Bishop of Winchester in 1200. He also made the wide straight High Street, now quiet and tree-lined, and dammed the R. Itchen to make a reservoir, originally six times its present size.

**Newark-on-Trent** *Notts.* 552Fd
CHURCH OF ST MARY MAGDALENE One of the most impressive churches in the county, with a tall west spire about 250 ft high. The earliest part is the crypt, while the chancel with its tremendous east window is late 15th century. There are fragments of early glass, many monuments, rood screen and choir stalls, *c.* 1500.

## HIGH LEVEL BRIDGE, NEWCASTLE UPON TYNE

*Robert Stephenson designed this bridge, an engineering marvel of its day, to carry road and rail traffic on separate decks over the R. Tyne. It was completed in 1849, and is the finest example of an early cast-iron bridge still in use. The lower bridge in the foreground is a swing bridge built in 1876.*

MUSEUM AND ART GALLERY Housed in the former Magnus Grammar School, the museum exhibits archaeological items and relics of local history. These include the cheekpiece of a Roman cavalry helmet, Anglo-Saxon cremation urns, relics of the Civil War, and two interesting 17th-century coin hoards.

**New Barnet** *Herts.* 547Jc
ABBEY ART CENTRE AND MUSEUM A 14th-century tithe barn, removed from a site in Kent, houses the collection of the late William Ohly, sculptor and connoisseur of art. It contains fine examples of primitive and oriental art—mainly from Africa, America (American Indian), South America (Aztec and pre-Columbian) and the South Seas (including a book of Tapa bark brought back from Australia by a member of Captain Cook's crew);

### MUMMY FROM THEBES

*This mask is from the mummy of a young woman named Bakt-ent-hor, who was probably embalmed during the 21st or 22nd Dynasty of Egypt (1085–730 BC) when mummies were as life-like as possible, right down to rouge on the cheeks. It was bought in Qurna, Thebes, in 1820. (Hancock Museum, Newcastle upon Tyne)*

early Chinese and Egyptian pottery is also exhibited, and highly decorated Tibetan metalware.

**Newbury** *Berks.* 546Fb
At the foot of the Berkshire Downs, the town site has prehistoric links. Its prosperity dates from medieval times when 'Jack of Newbury' (John Winchcombe) extended the local cloth trade by establishing the first true factory in England—having 200 looms and employing over 1000 men, women and children.

Newbury was a battle area in 1643 and 1644; Donnington Castle was ruined in the Civil War. The Jacobean Old Cloth Hall is now a museum of local interests.
BOROUGH MUSEUM Housed in the former Cloth Hall, built in 1627 and restored in 1829, 1897 and 1902, the museum has collections of local archaeology from Palaeolithic to Roman times, and of geology and natural history including a display of moths and butterflies. There are also items dealing with the Civil War period in Newbury, and objects relating to the cloth industry and the Tudor clothier 'Jack of Newbury'.

**Newby Hall** *Yorks.* 558Cc
A country mansion, built in 1705, with alterations and additions by Robert Adam made in 1770–6. The furnishings include Gobelins tapestries and a collection of Classical statuary. It is surrounded by fine gardens. (See p. 363.)

**Newcastle upon Tyne** *Northld.* 558Cg
This important engineering city was once known as Pons Aelii, on the Roman Wall, a fragment of which is visible on the south side of Denton bank. The name Newcastle is derived from the Norman castle built in 1080 by Robert, eldest son of William the Conqueror, and replaced by the existing castle between 1172 and 1177.

During the early 19th century, many fine streets and squares in the city centre were constructed by builder Richard Grainger to the designs of John Dobson, the well-known architect.
CATHEDRAL The Cathedral Church of St Nicholas, a large and grand parish church, was given cathedral status in 1882; it has a famous tower whose lantern soars on flying buttresses. The building dates mainly from the 14th and 15th centuries.

The interior contains an ornate pinnacled font cover of *c.* 1500, and a brass lectern of the same date. There are many monuments to be seen, including ones by such sculptors as John Flaxman, E. H. Baily and W. Theed.

DEPARTMENT OF MINING ENGINEERING, THE UNIVERSITY Miners' lamps and miscellaneous mining relics are on display, along with water-colours by T. H. Hair of coal-mines in Northumberland and Durham from 1830 to 1840.

HANCOCK MUSEUM The nucleus of the collections originally belonged to Marmaduke Tunstall of Wycliffe, who died in 1790 leaving a large collection of stuffed animals and birds and a large number of ethnological specimens. These are mainly from the South Sea Islands and Africa, and many are thought to have been brought back by Captain Cook from his Pacific voyages. There is also a small collection of Egyptian mummy-cases, dating from the 22nd Dynasty. Other items of interest include the bird collection of the 19th-century zoologist John Hancock; a new botany gallery with automatic back-projection of local plants; a bird-song 'juke-box'; a new insect gallery; the 'Geological Alphabet' gallery; there are also some live exhibits and an aquarium.

HIGH LEVEL BRIDGE Built by Robert Stephenson in 1849, this 146 ft high bridge of cast-iron girders on masonry piers carries road and rail traffic on separate levels over the R. Tyne.

LAING ART GALLERY AND MUSEUM Oil paintings of the British School from the 18th century onwards, and water-colours illustrating the development of this art in England, are shown; also modern etchings and engravings, and early Japanese prints.

ROYAL NORTHUMBERLAND FUSILIERS REGIMENTAL MUSEUM A Peninsula Gold Medal and four Victoria Crosses are among the medals on display. Uniforms and arms worn and used by the Regiment, mainly since 1800, are also shown.

## New Lanark *Lanarks.* 562Ad
South of Lanark, in the gorge of the R. Clyde, are the textile mills of New Lanark. Here, in 1800, social reformer Robert Owen established his model town. Some of the original buildings are still used for making cord and canvas. (See p. 366.)

## Newland *Glos.* 546Ac
CHURCH OF ALL SAINTS This huge church in the Forest of Dean was mainly built during the 13th and 14th centuries; it also has later additions, and 19th-century restoration. The west tower is impressively pinnacled; inside, there are brasses and recumbent effigies of medieval knights and ladies.

## Newland *Worcs.* 546Ce
CHURCH OF ST LEONARD The mid-19th-century Gothic church replaced the original medieval one which was demolished. The interior is lavishly decorated, notably by paintings of biblical scenes on the walls.

## Newlyn *Cornwall* 538Aa
PASSMORE EDWARDS GALLERY Temporary exhibitions of works by modern artists are held in the gallery, which does not own a permanent collection. It was built in 1895 to enable the artists working in the locality to show their paintings to the public.

## Newmarket *Suffolk* 548Bf
The centre of racing and racehorse breeding; the Rutland Arms Hotel, with red-brick front, and courtyard with stables behind, and the Jockey Club, Georgian and rebuilt by Sir Albert Richardson in 1933, are worth noting. Newmarket Heath to the west (with the Devil's Dyke earthworks), and the race-course, form a pleasant setting for the town.

18th-CENTURY SILK DRESS

*The sea anemone shapes on this dress place it in a group of silks woven about 1700–12, whose outlandish patterns reflected the baroque taste of other arts. (Laing Art Gallery and Museum, Newcastle upon Tyne)*

DUTCH HOLSTER PISTOL

*Holster pistols were carried by horsemen on either side of their saddles. This one, made by the Utrecht gunsmith Pentermann in 1713, probably belonged to Thomas Wentworth, Earl of Stafford. (Laing Art Gallery and Museum, Newcastle upon Tyne)*

## Newport *Essex* 548Ae
Once an ancient market town, Newport is now an attractive village chiefly of a single street. On the main street, Monk's Barn is a 15th-century half-timbered house with brickwork and an oriel window with carving of the Virgin and angels below it. On the green are Crown House with pargetting and a shell-hooded doorway of 1692, and Martin's Farmhouse and barn of the 15th century. North of the village is Shortgrove House, of the late 17th or early 18th century.

CHURCH OF ST MARY THE VIRGIN Formerly collegiate, the church dates from the 13th to the 15th centuries. The west tower was built in 1858. The church contains a 13th-century font, a late 13th-century painted chest which may have been a portable altar, some 14th-century stained glass, a pre-Reformation lectern, and brasses.

## NEW LANARK

*A unique factory and model-village settlement founded by the social reformer Robert Owen after he became a partner in the New Lanark mills in 1800. Welfare schemes for his 2000 workers included reducing the working day to 10½ hours and the opening of a shop where they could exchange cash tokens (one is shown above) for low-priced goods of sound quality. For his workers' children, Owen set up some of the first infant schools in Britain—and abolished corporal punishment.*

**Newport** *Isle of Wight, Hants.* 541Gc
The most urbane town in the island, with a central square, and a town hall and guildhall, both by John Nash. The most important building is Carisbrooke Castle, on the outskirts to the south-west. It has a Norman keep, Norman curtain walls, and, at the lowest level, Elizabethan bastions.

**Newport** *Mon.* 545Jb
CATHEDRAL The Cathedral of St Woolos contains some magnificent Norman work with Gothic additions, especially the 15th-century aisles. There was mid-19th-century restoration, and more in 1913 revealed the fine woodwork of the roof.
MUSEUM AND ART GALLERY Local archaeological remains from the Romano-British town of Caerwent are the main attraction, and the museum also has a collection of Pontypool and Usk japan-ware. The art gallery specialises in early English watercolours, British 20th-century works and paintings by Welsh artists, including Augustus John, Sir Frank Brangwyn and Ceri Richards.

**New Shoreham** *Sussex* 542Bd
CHURCH OF ST MARY DE HAURA An impressive Norman church, with tower and transepts; the nave disappeared in the 17th century. There is an Early English vault to the chancel, a clerestory and flying buttresses. The interior has a lot of rich ornamental carving, with dog-tooth and foliage, and there is a Norman font with decoration.

**Newstead Abbey** *Notts.* 552Ed
The family of Lord Byron, the poet, lived here from 1540 until 1818, when he was forced to sell the property to pay his debts. The original priory was founded *c.* 1170; it was converted into a house known as Newstead Abbey by Lord Byron's ancestor, Sir John Byron, in the 1540's, but part of the old priory survives. In the 19th century the house was reconstructed in Gothic style to designs by John Shaw. It contains Byron relics, and the furniture collection includes some fine Tudor and Stuart pieces, together with some English armour of the same period. There is a collection of pictures. The grounds are noted for rare trees and shrubs.

**Newtimber Place** *Sussex* 542Bd
A 17th-century house, with water-filled moat, at the foot of the South Downs. The hall has some late 18th-century Etruscan wall-paintings.

**Newton Abbot** *Devon* 539Gc
BRADLEY MANOR A small 15th-century house of roughcast stone, with a great hall, buttery, solarium, and a chapel in Perpendicular style.

**Newton Kyme** *Yorks.* 558Db
CHURCH OF ST ANDREW Some Norman work remains, but St Andrew's is largely 14th century, with a small 15th-century west tower.

**Newtown** *Mont.* 551Ha
ROBERT OWEN MEMORIAL MUSEUM Dedicated to Robert Owen (1771–1858), whose ideas and factory community at New Lanark in Scotland did much to stimulate the Co-operative movement, the museum is housed in a building which was once his home, and displays books, pictures, documents and relics of his life.

**Niddry Castle** *W. Lothian* 562Bf
The ruins of a 15th-century castle to which Mary, Queen of Scots fled with Lord Seton in 1568 after her escape from Loch Leven Castle.

**Norbury** *Staffs.* 552Bc
CHURCH OF ST PETER A 14th-century church, with an 18th-century brick tower. St Peter's contains four stone sedilia in the chancel, and the tomb and brass of the church's founder, Ralph Le Botiller.

**Norman's Law** *Fife.* 562Ch
HILL-FORT This isolated hill, nearly 1000 ft high, stands close to the southern shore of the Firth of Tay over which, away to the Sidlaw Hills in the north, it gives a wide view. The defences of the fort crowning the hill are complex and represent various phases of construction, though the exact sequence is uncertain. The summit itself is enclosed by a solid stone wall; well outside this, and including a part of the lower slopes, is a second wall.
Later, a smaller oval area was enclosed in a 12 ft thick wall. This is thought to belong to the Dark Ages, but the dating is uncertain.

**Normanton** *Rutland* 553Gb
CHURCH OF ST MATTHEW The original church was built in 1764, and the tower was added in 1826 by Thomas Cundy; there are also additions of 1911, which replaced the Georgian nave and chancel with a style more in keeping with that of the tower. There is a medallion bust by Michael Rysbrack, *c.* 1733.

**Normanton** *Yorks.*                    558Da
CHURCH OF ALL SAINTS A big church in a mining
town, it has a Perpendicular exterior, but much
earlier work inside, including the north arcade of
*c.* 1300. Fragments of stained glass include a *Pietà*
that is probably 15th-century Flemish; there are
monuments of the 16th and 18th centuries.

**Normanton Down** *Wilts.*                    540Fe
This is one of the most remarkable barrow groups
in Britain. Many of them have been excavated in
the past and the contents, mainly of the Early
Bronze Age, show them to have been the graves of
people of importance of the 'Wessex culture'; one
of them, the Bush Barrow, may well have been
that of a paramount chief of his day. It seems
certain that these barrows were placed here to be
close to Stonehenge, which is surrounded for miles
by a concentration of fine barrows. A few of those
in this group have suffered some ploughing, but
most stand to a considerable height. Apart from a
single earlier long barrow, there are 26 round
barrows of bowl, bell, disc and saucer types.
Finds from the site are in Devizes Museum.

**Northampton** *Northants.*                    547Gf
The town has little to show of its long and eventful
history in Norman, Tudor and Elizabethan times,
as a great fire gutted the whole of the central
portion (600 houses) in 1675. The Eleanor Cross on
the London Road is one of the few survivors of the
crosses marking Queen Eleanor's funeral procession from Harby (Nottingham) to Westminster
(1290).
ABINGTON PARK MUSEUM A reconstruction of an
18th-century street, Northamptonshire lace,
exhibits of children's toys, agricultural and
domestic bygones, and collections of English and
Chinese porcelain are exhibited in a manor house
that was medieval in origin but much altered in the
17th and 18th centuries.
CENTRAL MUSEUM AND ART GALLERY Shoemak-
ing, the local industry, is the focus of a comprehensive collection that includes Queen Victoria's
wedding shoes, and ballet shoes of Nijinsky,
Ulanova and Fonteyn. Among the other varied
collections is the Irchester hoard of 42,000 3rd-
century coins, archaeological finds from the Iron
Age to medieval times, medieval pottery, paintings and furniture.
CHURCH OF ALL SAINTS A big church in the centre
of the town, rebuilt soon after the fire which
destroyed Northampton in 1675. A 14th-century
tower has a cupola of 1704 and there is an impressive west portico with Ionic columns. The elegant
interior has a crossing dome on Ionic columns and
retains the medieval crypt below the chancel. The
font and pulpit are of *c.* 1680.
CHURCH OF ST PETER A large, interesting Norman
church whose west tower was rebuilt in the 17th
century; the east end was also rebuilt, *c.* 1850.
There are Norman doorways, and the interior has
much ornate carving on arches and capitals.
CHURCH OF THE HOLY SEPULCHRE One of
England's rare Norman round churches, built *c.*
1110 and shaped like its prototype in Jerusalem. A
long 13th-century chancel and massive tower with
spire; the apse was added by Sir Gilbert Scott in
1860. The interior is dimly lit, and the circular nave
has piers. There is much 19th-century glass and a
good 17th-century brass.
NORTHAMPTONSHIRE REGIMENT MUSEUM The
history of the Regiment from 1741 to 1960 is told
in pictures and other exhibits, including weapons,
medals, uniforms, badges and silver.
TOWN HALL This large town hall was designed by
Edward William Bodwin in 1861–4 in the

Romanesque and Gothic tradition at a time when
the Gothic style was becoming unfashionable for
secular buildings. The two-storey hall building is
in Venetian Gothic style with a clock tower and a
gable flanked by two turrets. There is much
statuary on the façade, representing sovereigns and
patron saints of the United Kingdom. A newer
wing by Matthew Holding was added in 1889–92,
and is also much decorated with statuary. The
windows are richly ornamented; on the lower
floor sculptured groups depict scenes connected
with the history of the county, such as the trial of
Thomas à Becket at Northampton Castle in 1164,
Henry II granting the town its charter in 1189, and
the destruction by fire of most of Northampton in
1675.

**North Barningham** *Norfolk*                    554Cd
CHURCH OF ST PETER The church is mainly of the
Decorated period, and has good but damaged
piscina and sedilia, and a Perpendicular west
tower. Tiles and a stone circular window are laid
out in the nave floor. Various monuments are
dedicated to the Palgrave family, notably Sir
Austin (*d.* 1639) with two busts, and to his sister,
Mrs Pope (*d.* 1621), showing her kneeling beneath
a canopy with angels.

**North Berwick** *E. Loth.*                    562Df
BURGH MUSEUM Built in 1876 as a public school,
the museum has a natural history collection displaying birds, fish, butterflies, eggs and some animals. Medieval relics from the former 12th-
century Cistercian priory can be seen, along with
Scottish pottery, costumes and bygones. There are
also exhibits directly associated with the Royal
Burgh of North Berwick.

**Northborough** *Hunts.*                    547Jh
MANOR HOUSE The gate-house opens on to the
main street. Built *c.* 1320, with a porch added in
1500, and further alterations in the 17th century,
the house stands as a good example of a small
fortified stone-built dwelling. Gabled, with a
buttress on the south side, it has a Gothic chimney,
a crow-stepped angle, and three highly ornamented carved stone doorways to kitchen, buttery
and pantry.

**North Cerney** *Glos.*                    546Dc
CHURCH OF ALL SAINTS Largely Norman, this
cruciform church has a saddle-back west tower;
three windows have 15th-century glass, and the
stone pulpit is of the same period. Incised on the
outside south wall of the transept are two
grotesque animals known as *mantichora*, man-
eaters—creatures with the head of a man, the body
of a lion, the quills of a porcupine and the tail of a
scorpion.

**North Creake** *Norfolk*                    554Bd
CHURCH OF ST MARY The church, built *c.* 1300, has
a Perpendicular north tower with battlements, a
hammerbeam roof to the nave, and an elaborate
Easter sepulchre, sedilia and piscina. There is a
fading wall-painting above the chancel arch, and a
brass, *c.* 1500, in the chancel floor. Several fragments of the 15th-century rood and parclose
screens remain.

**North Elmham** *Norfolk*                    554Cc
The ruins of an early 11th-century Saxon cathedral
blend with the ruins of a manor house of 1386,
lying in a moated enclosure; the Saxon remains
can be distinguished by the large blocks of dark
brown stone. Elmham was the See of the Bishop of
the 'North Folk' from *c.* 800 or even earlier. The
See was moved to Thetford in 1075 and not long
after was finally settled in Norwich.

### 17th-CENTURY CUSHION

*This 'Turkey-work' cushion, decorated with the Arms of the city, is from a set given to Norwich Cathedral in 1651 by Thomas Baret, then mayor. Weavers adapted techniques copied from Turkish carpets, using European designs. (Castle Museum, Norwich)*

### THE READE SALT

*Alderman Peter Reade commissioned this salt, made by a Norwich silversmith in 1568, 'to serve the mayor and his successors for ever'. The shape, decoration and domed cover surmounted by a Roman warrior, show strong Renaissance influence. (City Hall, Norwich)*

CHURCH OF ST MARY The church is 13th to 15th century, though Norman fragments remain. The chancel is 16th century, and the pulpit dates from 1626. Features include a rood screen with many painted saints, and 14th-century stained glass.

**North End** *Essex*                                    548Ae
BLACK CHAPEL This little building is unusual for three reasons: few timber-framed church buildings survive; there are few old chapels left in Essex; and the priest's house is built into the church. Nave, chancel and the priest's dwelling are of the late 15th century, and there are some modern additions. The attractive interior has benches and

a screen of *c.* 1500, early 18th-century communion rails and 18th-century box-pews.

**North Foreland** *Kent*                               543Gg
LIGHTHOUSE When built in the 17th century, the tower was about half its present height and carried an open coal fire. In the 18th century attempts were made to enclose the fire in a glass lantern, but the result was so unsatisfactory that it had to be removed. At the end of the century the tower was raised to its present height and oil lamps fitted; later, some of the earliest experiments in electric lighting were made here.

**North Grimston** *Yorks.*                             558Fc
CHURCH OF ST NICHOLAS Though not large, the church has a good Norman chancel arch, and quite a large font of the same period, with rough carvings of the Last Supper, Descent from the Cross and St Nicholas.

**Northleach** *Glos.*                                  546Dd
CHURCH OF SS PETER AND PAUL A large and impressive building of the 15th century for the most part, the church has many of the characteristics of similar products of prosperous wool centres in the Cotswolds. It has a lofty west tower and a fine south porch with pinnacles and niches filled with statues. The clerestory over the chancel arch was built by John Fortey in the 15th century; his brass is in the floor of the nave. The stone pulpit is Perpendicular; the font has carvings of faces.

**North Lees Hall** *Derbys.*                           552Df
Originally built *c.* 1410, almost a ruin by the 20th century, the Hall has been restored since 1959. The tower walls with parapet are 3 ft thick, and original: the plasterwork is modern restoration to the period of 1594. The Hall was the home of the Eyre family: it is said to be the basis of Thornfield Hall in Charlotte Brontë's novel, *Jane Eyre*.

**North Leigh Villa** *Oxon.*                           546Ed
This is a fine Roman courtyard villa, excavated and preserved for inspection. It is of special interest in that it was shown to have been twice re-modelled after its first building, the earliest house on the site being a villa-residence of somewhat simpler type. It is large, the overall area being almost 300 ft in each direction. Its fine mosaics, like the best of those in Gloucestershire, appear to have been laid by men of the Cirencester workshop.

**North Luffenham** *Rutland*                           553Gb
CHURCH OF ST JOHN THE BAPTIST A church of the 13th and 14th centuries, with tower and spire, standing among trees away from the village. The window tracery is 14th century, the arcades 13th century. Remains of wall-paintings can be seen, and there is some medieval glass in the chancel.

**North Marden** *Sussex*                               541Jd
CHURCH OF ST MARY A tiny Norman church by a farm; it consists of nave and apse only, and there are perhaps only four such churches in England. The south doorway was carved in the 12th century, and the apse has a 13th-century piscina.

**North Newbald** *Yorks.*                              558Fb
CHURCH OF ST NICHOLAS A Norman cruciform church with a central tower, but no aisles. There are Norman doorways and windows; one of the doors has a carving of Christ in Majesty. Inside is a 13th-century font, with a 17th-century cover.

**North Runcton** *Norfolk*                             554Ab
CHURCH OF ALL SAINTS One of the finest 18th-century churches in Norfolk. It was built 1703–13, and is attributed to Henry Bell, designer of King's Lynn custom house. The west tower has a lantern.

The nave has a slight projection north and south, while the chapel, which projects on the south side of the chancel, is a late 19th-century addition. In the nave four Ionic columns support a dome, and there are other Ionic columns and pilasters. The panelling and reredos, designed by Henry Bell in 1684, come from St Margaret's, King's Lynn.

**North Stoneham** *Hants.*  541Gd
CHURCH OF ST NICHOLAS Rebuilt in the late 16th century, the church was restored in 1826 and again at the end of the 19th century. Several monuments include one of *c.* 1613 with reclining effigies, and another, *c.* 1787, by J. F. Moore to Admiral Lord Hawke, with a marble relief of a naval engagement. Fragments of heraldic glass date from 1826. The pulpit was designed by G. F. Bodley.

**Northwold** *Norfolk*  554Bb
A village of several attractive houses grouped around the church and, farther to the west, Manor Farm, with a gable-end dated 1635.

**Norton** *Durham*  558Df
CHURCH OF ST MARY In an attractive village, the church is cruciform, and a rewarding Saxon remnant, as the tower arches and windows survive. There is stained glass by C. E. Kempe, of 1896, and 14th-century effigies of a lady and knight.

**Norwich** *Norfolk*  554Db
Norwich began as a Saxon settlement 1000 years ago. It is the capital city of Norfolk, and is the market centre for a large part of East Anglia.

Norwich has a cathedral, 33 pre-Reformation churches, a Norman castle, a 15th-century guildhall and Georgian assembly rooms. As a medieval town it was built on an irregular pattern and there is no central square or main street, but cathedral and castle act as its centres.
BRIDEWELL MUSEUM Housed in a building which in part dates back to 1325, the collections illustrate the crafts and industries of Norfolk and Norwich. Agricultural equipment, boat-building and fishing, and the techniques of engineering, building and clockmaking are all represented; and weaving and leatherwork, two thriving local crafts, are illustrated from the tools to the finished products. Also on view are examples of land transport, together with a collection of early bicycles and tricycles.
CARROW ABBEY Carrow Abbey, or Priory, founded as a Benedictine nunnery *c.* 1146, is now a private house which includes the sumptuous prior-

PAINTED RETABLE

*The medieval retable, or altar-piece, in St Luke's Chapel (two panels are shown), was given to the cathedral by Bishop Despenser in 1380. Later converted into a table, it escaped destruction by the Puritans. Rediscovered in 1847, it was returned to the chapel in 1957. The centre panel shows the Crucifixion with the Virgin supported by St John; to the right is the Resurrection. (Norwich Cathedral)*

ess's lodging. Built shortly before the Dissolution for Prioress Isabella Wygun, it is a fine flint and brick building; the doorway has her rebus or sign, a Y and a gun, in the spandrels. Inside are hall, parlour and prioress's bedroom with moulded beams, doors, and a vast fire-place in the parlour. There are also fragmentary remains of the rest of the nunnery. Near by is Bracondale Manor House, with shaped gables and pedimented windows, dated 1578.
CASTLE The large keep of the Norman castle stands on a hill above the market-place. It was built in 1130, refaced in 1839 and was the county prison for 500 years. It became a Museum of Natural History in 1894 and includes a gallery of paintings by masters of the Norwich School.
CATHEDRAL The cathedral was begun in 1094 when Bishop Herbert de Losinga abandoned Thetford and made the more populous Norwich the centre of the diocese; it was complete by 1145. Subsequent changes included the replacement of the Norman roof by stone vaults (15th and 16th centuries) and the remodelling of the upper part of

ELM HILL, NORWICH
*Elm Hill is the most complete and best preserved of several streets in Norwich which still have a late medieval appearance, even though some of the buildings in them date from the 17th century.*

the choir and presbytery (14th century). The magnificent spire was added in the 15th century. The cathedral is surrounded by a close—the precinct of the medieval monastery, for the cathedral was served by monks. The close is entered by four gateways; three are elaborate land-gates, but the fourth is a water-gate (15th century) on the river at Pull's Ferry. Within the close the cloisters lie to the south of the cathedral; they belong to the 14th and 15th centuries and are unique in having a first floor running right round the cloister court. There is elaborate vaulting in the cloisters and the prior's door to the cathedral is of fine Decorated design (c. 1320). South of the cloisters lie the remains of the 12th-century refectory and infirmary. The former bishop's palace is to the north of the cathedral.

CHURCH OF ST GEORGE A church of the 15th and 16th centuries with a west tower, and a two-storey south porch. It has 18th-century furnishings which include the reredos, pulpit and west gallery on which is the organ of 1802. There are many monuments, including work by Thomas Green of Camberwell, Thomas Rawlins of Norwich and John Bacon the Younger.

CHURCH OF ST PETER MANCROFT The most impressive of Norwich's many interesting churches. It was begun in 1430, and consecrated in 1455. There is a richly decorated west tower, and a little lead spire with flying buttresses dating from 1895. The interior, with a long clerestory, is a hall without a chancel arch. The roof to the nave has hammerbeams concealed by false vaulting. Other features include a canopied font cover with carved supporting posts; an organ gallery, c. 1707; some 15th-century stained glass in the east window; and brasses and monuments.

CITY HALL Built in 1932–8 to the design of C. H. James and S. R. Pierce, this is one of the foremost public buildings erected between the wars. It has a 202 ft high tower. (See p. 368.)

EARLHAM HALL West of Norwich, at Earlham Hall, are the offices of the new University of East Anglia.

ELM HILL Elm Hill, which winds down from the church of St Peter Hungate (now a museum) to the R. Wensum, contains the huge chancel of the former Dominican convent (now St Andrew's Hall) and a series of attractively coloured timber-framed houses. The street is cobbled, and broadens in the middle into a small square or court. (See p. 369.)

MADDERMARKET Near the market-place is the Maddermarket, where red madder dye was sold, with the Maddermarket Shakespearian theatre built as a replica of an Elizabethan theatre. The assembly house, Norwich's best example of Georgian architecture, was re-opened in 1950 as a social and educational centre.

MARKET-PLACE The Norman market-place is surrounded by several notable buildings. On one side is the modern city hall (1938) with central library; on another side the small flint guildhall, built 1413 (with a council chamber dating from 1534), visited by Elizabeth I in 1578.

OLD MEETING HOUSE Norwich has two noted Nonconformist churches, the Old Meeting House (one of the earliest in England, 1693) and the Octagon with a neo-Classic interior.

PRIORY The cloisters, the largest now existing in England, are the most interesting remains of the pre-Reformation priory. Other priory buildings are now part of the grammar school (founded by Edward VI) where Nelson was a pupil. Nurse Edith Cavell, executed in 1915 for her part in helping Allied fugitives to escape, is buried in the cathedral close.

ROYAL NORFOLK REGIMENT MUSEUM Relics of the Regiment—uniforms, weapons and medals including a Victoria Cross—are displayed here.

ST PETER HUNGATE MUSEUM This collection of Church art is housed in a former parish church originating in the 15th century. A considerable amount of Norwich painted glass of the 15th and 16th centuries remains in the windows. The majority of the exhibits are English, mainly East Anglian, but there is also interesting continental material. The collection of manuscripts includes both English and European material of the 13th–16th centuries, many illuminated, and contains a number of service books and theological works. Outstanding among these is the Wycliffe Bible, c. 1380. Also on display are church vestments and altar frontals from the early 16th century; carved wood pieces including a set of six carved lime-wood panels (Flemish c. 1580) depicting the life of Christ; carved alabaster panels, monumental brasses, medieval decorative floor tiles, church furnishings and musical instruments.

STRANGERS HALL The house, which has 14th-century origins, was given to the city of Norwich, together with the owner's collection of furniture

## NOTTINGHAM CASTLE MUSEUM

VIRGIN AND CHILD *This alabaster statuette was excavated, with two others, at Flawford, near Nottingham, in the late 18th century. It had been buried to escape the wholesale destruction of church sculpture at the Reformation. Alabaster carvings, more often in the form of panels in high relief than of statuettes, were produced in large quantities in the Midlands (Nottingham was one of the main centres) from about 1350 until the Reformation put an end to this industry—for an industry it undoubtedly was. A flourishing export trade in alabasters was built up, and examples have been discovered in France, Spain, Portugal, Italy and even as far afield as Russia. This is an early example, dating from before 1370. In later years, as production increased, the quality of the workmanship declined considerably.*

GLASS BLES BOWL *The crown surmounting the lid of the Bles Bowl may mean that it was made for a royal occasion—perhaps to commemorate the accession of James II in 1685. The addition of lead oxide was the great English contribution to glass chemistry, and this bowl is a good example of English lead crystal.*

and historic domestic equipment, in 1922. Rooms are furnished in the style of different periods, from early Tudor to late Victorian. There are late 15th-century Flemish tapestries in the great hall and parlour, and mid-17th-century 'stumpwork' embroidery in the large bedroom; the Walnut Room contains marquetry furniture (1690–1720), and the Georgian dining-room a late 18th-century chandelier. There are also examples of the harp-lute and a late 18th-century tambourine in the Regency music room; a good collection of cooking equipment of the early 19th century in two kitchens; and an 18th-century dolls' house with contemporary dolls and furnishings in the toy room. In the coach house are the Lord Mayor's coach and a Panhard Levassor car of 1899, and in the cellar a collection of Norwich shop signs.

TOMBLAND By the cathedral is Tombland, the former Saxon market-place, now a Georgian square. Beyond that, across the R. Wensum, is Magdalen Street; this was the centre of the old weaving industry in Norwich, and is being repaired and restored by the Civic Trust. On this street is Gurney's Court, where the Quaker reformer Elizabeth Fry was born.

**Nostell Priory** *Yorks.*                     358Da
A country mansion, developed on a former priory site acquired by an Elizabethan merchant, and one of the first ventures in architecture by James Paine.

Work was begun in 1733 to the order of Sir Roland Winn. On his death in 1765 his son called in Robert Adam, who made both external and internal additions and alterations. The house contains fine pictures, paintings and Chippendale furniture. In the park is a lake and a motor-cycle museum.

**Notgrove** *Glos.*                     546Cd
A fine example of the transeptal gallery barrow, with two chambers on either side of the gallery and a fifth at the inner end. The gallery leads in from a forecourt. Beyond these chambers excavation revealed a further circular chamber of drystone walling (now concealed), an unusual feature in barrows of this type. The rubble of the mound was held in position by a double wall.

**Nottingham** *Notts.*                     552Ed
The county city of Nottinghamshire, with a turbulent history until modern times. The Romans ignored the original hamlet which the Angles later called Snot or Snotta, but the Danes made it a borough called Nottingham. The Normans erected a castle, and for an unknown cause there was a continuous feud between the Saxon townspeople and the Normans, crystallised in the legend of Robin Hood and his men, who used nearby Sherwood Forest as their base.

An agreement being reached in the 16th century, the town began to prosper, but the Civil

NYMANS GARDENS

*The gardens, which cover about 30 acres, are famous for their rare collection of trees and plants. Designed* *by Lt.-Col. L. C. R. Messel in the first years of this century, they comprise a series of separate gardens.*

War brought disaster, with the castle being destroyed by Cromwell's troops. In the 18th century the textile machinery inventions of Richard Arkwright, James Hargreaves and John Heathcoat opened the way to a vast increase in production, but also caused serious Luddite-type riots. These lasted for years, and their cause had hardly been settled when the proposed political reforms were strenuously blocked by the Duke of Newcastle. This led to violence at the Goose Fair of 1831, when the Duke's mansion, built on the site of the destroyed castle, was reduced to a smoking ruin as the Chartists brought havoc to the city.

From the time of the 1832 Reform Bill, Nottingham again became prosperous. In 1897 it became a city, and by the turn of the century one-third of the knitting frames in Britain were here, and Nottingham lace had achieved world-wide fame.

The medieval Goose Fair, once a prolonged week of merry-making, has now been reduced to three days in the first week of October, with amusements rather than trade as the main motif.

The University of Nottingham was established by royal charter in 1948 after 67 years as University College.

Robin Hood, as fact or fiction, is commemorated by four reliefs in the ruined castle wall, by frescoes in the cupola of the Council House, and also by a statue on Castle Green.
CHURCH OF ST MARY An imposing Perpendicular church, mainly of the 15th century, with a large central tower. There are many 19th-century windows by Ward & Hughes, Clayton & Bell, and others; also several monuments.
CITY MUSEUM AND ART GALLERY (NOTTINGHAM CASTLE MUSEUM) The painters Bonington and Sandby are the subjects of special collections.

There is a large collection of hand-made and machine-made lace and Lord Middleton's collection of Elizabethan and Jacobean embroideries. The ceramics section includes Nottingham 18th-century stoneware and Wedgwood pieces. The castle was built in 1674-9 on the site of a medieval castle, as a residence for the Dukes of Newcastle. It was much damaged by fire during riots over the Reform Bill in 1831, but was restored and adapted as a museum in 1878. (See pp. 370-1.)

**Nuneaton** *Warks.* *546Eg*
MUSEUM AND ART GALLERY Personal possessions of George Eliot, who lived in the district, are in the museum. Items of local interest are archaeological finds and 17th-, 18th- and 19th-century local maps. There are also collections of glass, pottery and silver, and of examples of native craftsmanship from the Far East, Africa and Australasia. The gallery contains a number of minor paintings.

**Nun Monkton** *Yorks.* *558Dc*
CHURCH OF ST MARY The church is formed from the nave of the 12th-century Benedictine nunnery that stood on this site. The east wall (pulled down at the Dissolution) was restored in 1873 and has windows with stained glass by William Morris.

**Nunney Castle** *Som.* *540Df*
The ruins of a rectangular moated castle begun in 1373 by Sir John de la Mare, whose family tombs are a feature of the nearby 13th-century church.

**Nunnington Hall** *Yorks.* *558Ed*
A manor house dating mainly from the 17th century, with panelled hall and staircase. The west wing dates from 1580.

**Nymans Gardens** *Sussex* *542Be*
About 30 acres of rare conifers, shrubs and plants.

# O

**Oakham** *Rutland* *553Gb*
CASTLE In the Norman banqueting great hall of this mansion is a remarkable collection of horseshoes left by royalty and peers of the kingdom. The church in Oakham has a Bible contemporary with the Magna Carta, and there are ancient punishment stocks in the town square.

Titus Oates (1649-1705) of the infamous Popish Plot was born here.
CHURCH OF ALL SAINTS An attractive country town surrounds this fine church, which has an impressive 14th-century west tower with spire of ashlar limestone. Inside there are a number of interesting sculptured capitals and arcades. Additions in the 15th century include the clerestory and Perpendicular windows.

**Oaksey** *Wilts.* *546Cc*
CHURCH OF ALL SAINTS A church of 13th-century origin, with 14th- and 15th-century additions and perhaps some Norman work. There is a Perpendicular clerestory but no north aisle. The screen and choir stall panels are 15th century. Large medieval wall-paintings of Christ of the Trades and of St Christopher were uncovered in 1933.

**Ockham** *Surrey* *542Af*
CHURCH OF ALL SAINTS A medieval church, with a fine east window and a 15th-century tower; it contains a brick mausoleum to the King family, which may have been designed by Nicholas

Hawksmoor. There is a carved monument to Lord King (d. 1734) by Michael Rysbrack.

**Oddington** *Glos.* *546Dd*
CHURCH OF ST NICHOLAS This is a fine church with its tower at the east end of the south aisle. Once Norman, it is now mainly Gothic in appearance. A large wall-painting of the Last Judgment covers the north wall, and the Arms of William IV are over the chancel arch. Its 17th-century canopied pulpit is supported on a single pillar. The church was carefully restored at the beginning of this century.

**Odell** *Beds.* *547Hf*
A lovely village with good limestone houses and cottages, and the mound of a vanished castle dating from the Domesday era.
CHURCH OF ALL SAINTS There is a massive pinnacled west tower to this 15th-century church, and the whole building is a good and complete example of the period. The interior has tall arcades and a medieval rood screen. Among the remaining stained glass is a particularly fine group of angels in the east window of the south aisle. There is a monument, *c.* 1807, by John Bacon the Younger.

**Odiham** *Hants.* *541Jf*
One of Hampshire's impressive broad streets. Here the houses are mostly colour-washed, and unusually low and set back behind sweeps of mown

MONUMENT TO
SIR SAMUEL ONGLEY

*The classical Roman costume in which Peter Schee-makers (1691–1770) and Laurent Delvaux (1695–1778) chose to dress this monument to Sir Samuel Ongley was typical of the taste of a time when both George I and George II were often represented as Caesar. Scheemakers, whose original design for the monument is now in the Victoria and Albert Museum, London, was born in Antwerp. He worked in Rome and then came to London. Among his other works are the monuments to Dryden and Shakespeare in Westminster Abbey. Delvaux, from Ghent, also enjoyed popularity as a sculptor. (Church of St Leonard, Old Warden)*

grass. Near the east end is Marycourt, an impressive Georgian house, and at the west end a Queen Anne mansion with Elizabethan work at the back.
CASTLE A picturesque ruin of Norman origin where Simon de Montfort imprisoned his captive, Prince Edward.
CHURCH OF ALL SAINTS This 13th- and 14th-century church, restored in the late 19th century, stands near some 17th-century almshouses. There is a round chalk font, and an early 17th-century pulpit and west gallery. The east windows are by John Hardman, 1858. Brasses date from the 15th and 16th centuries.

**Offa's Dyke**     *546Ac*
The north end of this great earthwork lies near Prestatyn at the seaward end of the Dee estuary, and passes through the counties of Flintshire, Denbighshire, Shropshire, Montgomeryshire, Radnorshire, Herefordshire and Gloucestershire,

to end at the mouth of the R. Wye opposite Chepstow. It is not absolutely continuous, and some of the gaps certainly represent areas where, when it was built, forest cover made the earthwork unnecessary.
All the evidence points to its having been constructed to the orders of Offa, the great Mercian king who reigned in the second half of the 8th century. It defined, for all men to see, the boundary between his kingdom and Welsh land.
Wat's Dyke, a similar but shorter earthwork, runs from Basingwerk on the Dee estuary to the Morda Brook, south of Oswestry. It lies, therefore, to the east of Offa's Dyke and is roughly parallel. Its date is not known, but it is generally thought to have been a somewhat earlier frontier-line in a difficult area, to be superseded later by the more ambitious work of Offa.

**Offord Darcy** *Hunts.*     *547Jf*
MANOR HOUSE Built *c.* 1610, the house was re-fronted in the 18th century to give it a three-storied elevation, although the top storey is merely a façade. It has a shell-hooded entrance doorway.

**Okehampton** *Devon*     *538Fd*
This small market town on the northern fringe of Dartmoor was originally a stage point, from Roman times onwards, for those crossing central Devon to and from Exeter. To protect travellers, Baldwin de Brionne built Okehampton Castle (now in ruins) shortly after the Norman Conquest. The town suffered badly in the plague of 1625. William Pitt, Earl of Chatham, was M.P. for Okehampton. Today, the town is a main centre for Dartmoor, 384 square miles of wild country-side with Yes Tor (2029 ft) and High Willhays (2039 ft) as high points.

**Old Bewick** *Northld.*     *562Fc*
A promontory hill-fort, protected on its south side by very steep scarp-slopes. On the opposite side, great curving ramparts enclose two areas which are further defended by a single bank and ditch lying farther to the north. These ramparts have been shown to have a clay core, to which the stonework is a facing. The western section contains circular huts, and the eastern was probably used to protect the flocks. Close to the fort on the south-east are several rocks with cup-and-ring decoration.

**Old Clee** *Lincs.*     *553Jg*
CHURCH OF THE HOLY TRINITY A cruciform church with a Saxon west tower. The Norman work includes both arcades, and the font. There is a tablet on one of the pillars referring to the dedication in 1192 of the chancel and transepts by St Hugh.

**Old Fletton** *Hunts.*     *547Jg*
CHURCH OF ST MARGARET A Norman church, which incorporates Saxon carvings in two buttresses of the chancel. There is a 16th-century font.

**Oldham** *Lancs.*     *552Bg*
ART GALLERY Early English water-colours, British paintings of the 19th century, and contemporary British art constitute the main part of this collection, which includes a bust of Sir Winston Churchill by Jacob Epstein (1946) and paintings by Walter Sickert and L. S. Lowry.

**Old Malton** *Yorks.*     *558Ec*
CHURCH OF ST MARY The remains of a large church of the Gilbertine priory, founded *c.* 1150. Now only the nave, part of the façade with a carved doorway, and the south-west tower exist. There are a few furnishings and some misericords.

**Old Oswestry** *Shrops.*       *551Jc*
This fine hill-fort was remodelled four times. A rectangle was enclosed by two banks with external ditches and an entrance at each end, the inner banks being here inturned. When rebuilt, a third bank was added to most of its circumference, followed by modifications of and additions to the defences of the west entrance. The last stage was marked by the addition of yet more banks and some re-modelling of the eastern entrance. The fort was occupied throughout the second half of the Iron Age and there was also some evidence of re-occupation during the Dark Ages.

**Old Sarum** *Wilts.*       *540Fe*
Here on a hill are the multiple earthworks of the forerunner of modern Salisbury. But only the outermost bank is of Iron Age date; later, because it stood at the crossing of important roads, it became the Roman Sorviodunum. Centuries later, the Norman invaders quickly realised its strength, and the inner earthworks are of Norman origin. Here a small town grew up and an early cathedral was built. Not until the 12th century, when the great cathedral of Salisbury began to grow up in the valley below, did the men of Sarum colonise the new site by the river.

**Old Shoreham** *Sussex*       *542Bd*
CHURCH OF ST NICHOLAS A basically Norman church with fragments of Saxon work, standing on the east bank of the R. Adur, not far from New Shoreham. The plan is cruciform, with a squat central tower. The carved tie-beam in the chancel is of *c.* 1300, and the blocked doorway in the north aisle dates from *c.* 1840; there was much restoration in the 19th century.

**Old Soar Manor** *Kent*       *542Cf*
A rare survival of the solar wing of an early medieval knight's house. With a chapel, it is partly of the 13th century.

**Old Warden** *Beds.*       *547Je*
CHURCH OF ST LEONARD A 15th-century church which contains good woodwork, much of it continental of the 16th and 17th centuries. There are several monuments, including a standing 18th-century figure in Roman costume by Peter Scheemakers and Laurent Delvaux. Scheemakers's design for the monument is in the Victoria and Albert Museum.

**Old Warden Aerodrome** *Beds.*       *547Je*
SHUTTLEWORTH COLLECTION A collection of historic aeroplanes, cars, bicycles and carriages. The aviation exhibits range from a genuine Bleriot of 1909, several First World War and inter-war types, both civil and military, to the Hurricane and Spitfire. Also on display are aero-engines, propellers, instruments and other related equipment. Most of the aeroplanes are in flying condition and they are demonstrated on special open days.

**Ombersley** *Worcs.*       *546Cf*
A delightful village with many timbered houses, including the King's Arms. Ombersley Court, a William-and-Mary house, has been refronted.

**Onibury** *Shrops.*       *551Ja*
CHURCH OF ST MICHAEL Like so many Shropshire churches, St Michael's is of Norman origin, but there is later work as well. The short west tower is battlemented; inside, the chancel arch is Norman, but the west gallery dates from Detmar Blow's restoration in 1902.

**Orchardleigh House** *Som.*       *540Df*
A 19th-century mansion, replacing a former manor house, standing in a great park with a lake.

ORFORD CASTLE

*Orford Castle was built by Henry II between 1165 and 1173 as part of a successful attempt to re-establish royal power in East Anglia. Of the original building only the keep survives. Its internal appointments were planned on a grand scale and include two superimposed halls with adjoining offices and a chapel. The castle was sufficiently important to be kept in reasonable repair throughout the 13th century, but by the beginning of the 14th century its military role had ceased to be great and in 1336 Edward III granted it in perpetuity to Robert of Ufford who, a year later, became Earl of Suffolk.*

On an island at the head of the lake is a 13th-century church where Sir Henry Newbolt, the poet, is buried.

**Orford** *Suffolk*       *548Ee*
CHURCH OF ST BARTHOLOMEW The church has a ruined 12th-century chancel, and a 14th-century nave and tower, the upper part of which collapsed in the 19th century. Inside are a font and screens.

**Orford Castle** *Suffolk*       *548Ee*
Of Orford Castle, the keep alone survives. The castle itself was of great military importance. It was built by Henry II between 1165 and 1173 as part of a successful attempt to re-establish royal power in East Anglia. The plan was entirely up to date: the bailey was surrounded by a curtain wall from which projected flanking turrets, and the keep was no longer of the rectangular plan but circular inside and polygonal outside. It, too, was defended by projecting turrets.

**Ormsby Hall** *Yorks.*       *558De*
A house built in the mid-18th century, with fine period plasterwork.

**Ormside** *Westmld.*       *557Je*
CHURCH OF ST JAMES The Norman church is situated on a conical knoll on the west side of the R. Eden, overlooking Roman Fell, and its strong western tower was probably intended for defence against marauding Scots. The chancel roof is 400 years old, and the Ormside Cup, a Saxon work in gold and enamel now at York, was excavated from the churchyard in 1823.

OSTERLEY PARK HOUSE

*The house at Osterley was originally built during the reign of Elizabeth I for Sir Thomas Gresham, the merchant who founded the Royal Exchange in the City of London. It eventually passed to the Childs, a great banking family, and in 1761 Robert Adam began a reconstruction of the house that was to take nearly 20 years. The rooms of the house retain their original decoration and furniture by Adam. The hall has a fine marble floor and the elegant library is decorated with painted panels by Antonio Zucchi. The gallery is about 130 ft long and contains Beauvais tapestries. In the tapestry room are Gobelins tapestries specially woven for it in 1775. Another room is decorated in Etruscan style, with tall columns and statuary. In the state bedchamber is a great domed bed designed by Adam about 1776.*

**Ormskirk** *Lancs.* 551Jg
CHURCH OF SS PETER AND PAUL The second of this Perpendicular church's two towers was added in 1540 to house bells from Burscough Priory after its dissolution. The monuments include rather worn 15th-century alabaster effigies to the 1st Earl of Derby and wife, also brought from Burscough.

**Orton Longueville** *Hunts.* 547Jg
CHURCH OF THE HOLY TRINITY A 13th- and 14th-century church, with a late 17th-century aisle. There are some fragments of medieval glass and a 16th-century wall-painting of St Christopher, a 15th-century font, a 13th-century knight's effigy, and a seated woman sculpted by Sir Francis Chantrey.

**Orton Waterville** *Hunts.* 547Jg
The name of this village is a corruption of the feudal family name of de Waltreville. Its 13th-century church has an Elizabethan carved pulpit. The stone-built Manor Farm was built in 1571, and retains its original mullioned windows.

**Osborne House** *Isle of Wight Hants.* 541Hc
Queen Victoria's favourite home, designed in the Palladian style by the Prince Consort and Thomas Cubitt; Victoria died here in 1901, and the state apartments, which are open to the public (the rest of the house is a convalescent home for officers and civil servants), contain many items of Victoriana.

**Osbournby** *Lincs.* 553Hd
CHURCH OF SS PETER AND PAUL The church is mainly Decorated, and has a Norman font. It contains much 15th-century woodwork, including a set of carved bench ends and poppy-heads.

**Ossian's Hall** *Perths.* 566Cb
A folly in the Hermitage, a wooded gorge of the R. Braan on the estate of the Dukes of Atholl near Dunkeld. A summer retreat was erected by the 3rd Duke in 1758.

**Osterley Park House** *Greater London* 547Hb
The first occupant of a house at Osterley was perhaps the richest English merchant of his age, Sir Thomas Gresham, the founder of the Royal Exchange and of Gresham's College. The building as it stands today, however, is mainly the creation of Robert Adam, between the years 1761 and 1780. Retaining the original square plan of the Elizabethan house, Adam placed the principal apartments on the first floor, or *piano nobile,* and raised the ground inside the court to that level, providing a wide flight of steps as an approach and throwing an Ionic portico across the open side of the square. The result is an unusual but superb expression of the classical Italian principles of the time. The interior is one of the finest and most complete by Adam; rejecting the heavy and imposing style favoured by his contemporaries, he used delicate decorations of low reliefs, friezes, pilasters, painted ornament and the so-called 'grotesque' style in stucco. Much of the original furniture remains in the rooms for which Adam designed it, some of it representing the best neo-Classical work. Paintings include a pair of large portraits by Hoppner, of Frederick Augustus, Duke of York, second son of George III, and his wife, Frederica Charlotta. Among the many fine tapestries in the house is a series from Arlington Court in Devon, woven in Beauvais between 1780

and 1793, depicting the four continents, a favourite theme of tapestry weavers since the end of the 17th century; and a set of Gobelins tapestries representing the loves of the gods after designs by Boucher.

**Oswestry** *Shrops.*         *551Jc*
To the west of this ancient town are the remains of Offa's Dyke which, running from the R. Wye to the R. Dee, was made *c.* AD 800 by Offa, King of Mercia, as a defence or political boundary. The town's charter was granted by Richard II; by the Act of Union with Wales (1535), Oswestry became English. In 1559 a local plague killed one-third of the inhabitants and in 1642 much of the town was destroyed in the Civil War. The town walls and gates were demolished in 1782. In 1860, the Cambrian Railway completely altered the town, leaving it with little of architectural note. It is, however, of interest to canal and railway historians: about 4 miles north, at Chirk, is a stone railway viaduct and an aqueduct with cast-iron trough 850 ft long and 100 ft high.

**Otham** *Kent*         *542Df*
STONEACRE A typical Kentish yeoman's half-timbered hall-house of the late 15th century. It was restored in 1923 and contains a great hall and a collection of furniture.

**Otley** *Suffolk*         *548Df*
OTLEY HALL A partly moated 15th-century timber and brick house of superb quality, with a fine diapered chimney-shaft on the hall building. The house has fine panelling, a good hall screen, heavily beamed ceilings in the hall and Jacobean wall decorations. In the same parish, Otley High House is a fine contemporary timber-framed building.

**Otterden Place** *Kent*         *542Ef*
A Tudor-style house, with 18th-century Georgian additions.

**Ousdale** *Caith.*         *569Kc*
BROCH Standing on a burn-side close to the sea; on one side, the steep slope to the stream gives ample protection, and on the other there is an 8 ft thick wall. Within this enclosure stands the broch itself, with a 14 ft thick wall and an internal space some 27 ft across. There is a double door and a guard-chamber in the thickness of the wall. Its condition is still good.

**Over Denton** *Cumb.*         *557Jh*
CHURCH A small Norman church, with Saxon details, which seems to have been built with Roman stones from Hadrian's Wall. The chancel arch is probably a rebuilt Roman arch.

**Overstone** *Northants.*         *547Gf*
CHURCH OF ST NICHOLAS A Gothic building of *c.* 1803, restored a century later. It has a west tower, box-pews, some 16th-century stained glass in the east window and two early 18th-century monuments by John Hunt.

**Overton Hill** *Wilts.*         *540Fg*
THE SANCTUARY This henge monument is the termination of 'The Avenue' leading from Avebury. In its latest form it consisted of two circles of sarsens, 130 ft and 45 ft in diameter. This structure dated from the very beginning of the Bronze Age. But it apparently had replaced a previous timber structure of Neolithic times, evidenced by six concentric circles of post-holes. An attempted reconstruction has shown that this was probably of more than one period, and that new holes were dug from time to time to hold replacing timbers as the old ones rotted.

After they had completed their examination of the site, the excavators erected concrete blocks in the former stone sockets and concrete pillars in the post-holes, so that the whole pattern is now visible for inspection.

OXBURGH HALL

*Though Oxburgh Hall dates from 1482, its great hall was demolished in the 18th century and few medieval fittings survive in the rest of the building. There is, however, an original fire-place in the so-called King's Chamber of the main gate-house. Henry VII is traditionally held to have stayed in the chamber when he visited Oxburgh in 1497. The parish church near the hall has two 16th-century terracotta monuments.*

**Ovingham** *Northld.*         *558Bg*
CHURCH OF ST MARY THE VIRGIN A mainly 13th-century church which has a plain tall Saxon west tower. The interior has painted royal Arms. Fragments of Saxon crosses were found here just after the Second World War. Thomas Bewick, the famous wood-engraver, was buried here.

**Owl House, The** *Kent*         *542De*
A 16th-century half-timbered cottage, formerly used by wool smugglers: only the extensive gardens, noted for roses, are open to the public.

**Owlpen Manor** *Glos.*         *546Cc*
A Cotswold stone house of 15th-century origin, with barn, mill and court-house. In the gardens are tall, clipped yews.

**Oxburgh Hall** *Norfolk*         *554Bb*
This property came into the possession of the Bedingfield family during the second half of the 15th century and the present house was begun in 1482 when Edmund Bedingfield received a licence to erect a fortified building. It is a fine building of brick, surrounded by a moat. There is an enormous gate-house, probably the largest 15th-century brick gate-house in England. Near the hall is a small chapel built in the grounds by Pugin in 1835. This is a curious Gothic Revival building furnished with a number of genuine medieval fittings. In a side aisle of the nearby parish church is the Bedingfield Chapel, containing two lavish terracotta monuments of the early 16th century.

# John Ruskin

## JOHN RUSKIN, THE PRE-RAPHAELITE PROPHET

'No other man that I met', wrote Carlyle, 'has in him the divine rage against iniquity, falsehood and baseness that Ruskin has, and every man ought to have.' John Ruskin was recognised early as an intellectual prodigy by his adoring parents, and his birthplace in Brunswick Square, London, is marked with a plaque. His passionate defence of Turner appeared in the first volume of *Modern Painters,* which he published, aged 24. Ruskin developed great skill in drawing while making illustrations for his books *The Stones of Venice* and *The Seven Lamps of Architecture.* He became the first Slade Professor of Fine Art, and his drawings can be seen at the Victoria and Albert Museum, the Ashmolean Museum, Oxford and the South London Art Gallery. As the early prophet of the Socialist movement, he swept a London street to show how it should be kept, and his advanced views on care of the aged, child education and taxation, appear in the 39 volumes of his collected works.

JOHN RUSKIN *from the water-colour by Sir Hubert von Herkomer.* (National Portrait Gallery)

BRANTWOOD, *Ruskin's house at Coniston in Lancashire, with his boat 'Jumping Jenny'. Ruskin bought the house, without seeing it, for £1500, as a favour to a friend who was short of money. The house can be visited.*

RUSKIN'S SEAL, *with his coat of arms and motto 'Today, today, today'. He sensed that man's spirit was being swamped by machine-age evils, 'the refusal of pleasure and knowledge for the sake of money'.*

RUSKIN'S CROSS *in Coniston churchyard commemorates the champion of the Pre-Raphaelites and the man who revolutionised our ideas of Italian painting. Sculpted from hard green stone by H. T. Miles.*

SKETCHBOOKS, paint-box and measuring tape belonging to Ruskin. 'It is as if an angel had come down to teach us how to draw', wrote a contemporary. The blue-lined notebook shows sketches of buildings in Venice, where he was overwhelmed with the glory of Renaissance architecture, extolled in 'The Stones of Venice'. (John Ruskin Museum, Coniston)

COLUMN HEAD in the University Museum, carved by Irish stone-cutters. WROUGHT IRON at the Museum.

EUPHEMIA CHALMERS RUSKIN, a detail from 'The Order of Release', painted by John Millais. Mrs Ruskin acted as the model, and her love affair with Millais led to the annulment of the Ruskins' marriage in July 1854. (Tate Gallery)

HANDBELLS, one of the simple forms of musical expression with which Ruskin experimented in an effort to discover an instrument which could be learnt quickly, played easily—and enjoyed—by children. (John Ruskin Museum, Coniston)

SLATE THRONE in the garden of Brantwood, Lancashire, where Ruskin, afflicted by madness in his last years, would sit for hours.

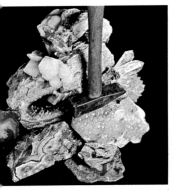

MINERAL SPECIMENS at the John Ruskin Museum, Coniston, from the collection he made. He presented the 'Edwardes Ruby' to the Natural History Museum, London, where it is permanently displayed.

# ASHMOLEAN MUSEUM

The oldest public museum in Britain. Its first buildings were opened in 1683, and the present ones, designed by Charles Cockerell, in 1845. The Department of Antiquities covers the great civilisations of the Mediterranean basin, and is particularly rich in Egyptian relics. The Chinese collection in the Department of Eastern Art is especially fine, and the Department of Western Art houses one of the best collections in England. It includes outstanding works of the Italian, French and English schools, and the collection of prints and drawings is world-famous.

UCELLO: THE HUNT *Of all 15th-century Italian painters, Ucello was the most learned in perspective and foreshortening. But it was not an arid discipline: he shows a masterly sense of design, a superb feeling for colour, and an irrational use of space. In 'The Hunt', painted about 1469, six years before he died, rider and hounds converge on a central point—the deer herd—a spot far in a forest divided equally by four trees. Everything—tree trunks, the paths of the hounds, the hunters' staves—leads to that point.*

RICCIO: PAN *Andrea Briosco, known as 'Riccio' (curly-head) was the leading member of a school of sculptors famous in Padua in the early 16th century for their work in bronze. This is one of his most beautiful works. The subject is typical, for the main source of his inspiration was the pastoral aspect of ancient mythology: nymphs, satyrs, shepherds, goats. From those elements he created sculptures which are often profoundly moving and which, through his treatment of them, attain the status of great works of art.*

**Oxford** *Oxon.*          546Fc

The town of Oxford is at least 300 years older than the university. In AD 879 King Alfred set up a mint there, and in 1068 William the Conqueror seized the town as a key point in his plan of conquest. The tower is all that remains of the chapel of the Norman castle built in 1071. Near by is the Mound, a grass-covered motte of Norman origin. The first school centre was University College, founded in 1249, 50 years after Henry II had granted Oxford its first charter. In 1258 the 'Mad Parliament' of Henry III took place at Oxford: Parliament openly rebelled against the king, confirmed Magna Carta, and vested the government of England in 24 councillors led by Simon de Montfort. Other colleges soon followed: Balliol (1263), Merton (1264), St Edmund Hall (1270), Exeter (1314), Oriel (1324), Queen's (1340); by which date Oxford University was fully established as a rival to Paris, Salamanca and other continental universities.

The Saxon tower of the church of St Michael-at-the-Northgate was once part of the northern fortifications of the city; the church stands on the site of the prison where the martyred Bishops Cranmer, Latimer and Ridley were held. The Martyrs' Memorial in St Giles was erected in 1841 to commemorate their deaths: a cross in Broad Street marks the spot where they were burnt at the stake. The central point of the city is Carfax, from the French *carrefour*, meaning cross roads, and from Carfax Tower there is an excellent panoramic view of the city.

Charles I held a Parliament at Oxford in 1644, and Charles II in 1665 and 1684.

The city was raised to county borough status in 1889. In the 1960's a ten-year programme of restoration and cleaning was initiated.

ASHMOLEAN MUSEUM Named after Elias Ashmole, antiquary and astrologer, the Ashmolean is housed in the same building as the Taylor Institution. This building was constructed in 1841 by C. R. Cockerell, RA, and paid for with money bequeathed to Oxford University by architect Sir Robert Taylor (d. 1835). The museum contains magnificent paintings by great masters of all periods. There are drawings by Michelangelo and Raphael, Dutch still-life and modern French paintings.

Also to be found here are fine examples of 16th- and 17th-century silver, bronzes, sculptures, tapestries and miniatures. There are snuff-boxes and watches, the Hill Collection of musical instruments and an extensive collection of coins.

LORRAINE: ASCANIUS SHOOTING THE STAG OF SYLVIA *Claude Gellée, usually known from the district of his birth as Claude Lorraine, painted this picture in 1682, the year of his death. He was 82. Lorraine spent most of his life in Rome and his pastoral landscapes have an intensely poetic quality. Light was his principal concern and his works follow the classical formula of a succession of layers going back in parallel planes to the* luminous distance. *The transition from foreground to background in this painting is effected by a distant bridge over which a herdsman drives his cattle. The scene in the foreground is taken from Vergil and shows Ascanius, the son of Aeneas, shooting the stag of Sylvia. But the figures add little of significance to the picture: it is the quality of the evening light which is all-important.*

THE ALFRED JEWEL *Alfred the Great, who died in 899, is generally agreed to have owned this jewel, for it bears the Anglo-Saxon inscription, 'Alfred had me made'. The jewel is gold decorated with cloisonné enamel, the technique of enamelling preferred for gold in the Dark Ages and early Middle Ages. It was found in Newton Park near the Island of Athelney, Somerset, in 1693. Its original purpose and the identity of the enamelled figure on it have been much discussed. The animal-headed socket to which the jewel is fixed shows that it once had a slender stem attached. The jewel might be the head of a pointer for following the lines of a manuscript and the figure might represent Sight.*

The Pomfret and Arundel marbles and many European antiquities, including items from Egypt, Crete and the Aegean, can be seen.

BODLEIAN LIBRARY One of the largest libraries in the world, with over 3,000,000 volumes. It includes the Selden Library and the library of Duke Humphrey (younger son of Henry V) who gave 600 manuscripts. Most of the works were destroyed during the Dissolution under Henry VIII: but Sir Thomas Bodley (1545–1613), a diplomat in the service of Queen Elizabeth I, restored the library in 1598–1603 and endowed it in 1611. The Bodleian was augmented in 1880 by the Radcliffe Science Library. Founded by Dr John Radcliffe (1650–1714), who left £40,000 to the university, the Radcliffe Camera, a circular building with great cupola, now serves as a reading room. The Schools Quadrangle (previously a teaching establishment) was absorbed by the Bodleian in 1882. In 1940 the New Bodleian building was completed at a cost of £1,000,000, much of which was contributed by the Rockefeller Trust. The three buildings are now served by an underground railway which connects the reading rooms to the bookstacks beneath. Of these buildings, only part of Duke Humphrey's Library and the New Bodleian are open to the public. (See p. 382.)

BOTANIC GARDENS These gardens are said to be the oldest in Britain. They were founded in 1621 by Henry Danvers, 1st Earl of Denby.

CATHEDRAL A magnificent Norman cathedral, with later additions which include the 13th-century central spire. The church was formerly that of an Augustinian priory, and was built during the 12th century to house the body of St Frideswide, a Saxon lady who died in 735. Her reconstructed shrine is in the presbytery. Cardinal Wolsey, who founded Christ Church College of which this church is part, demolished the western end when building the college. Happily, he was not able to rebuild all the present cathedral, and the splendid 15th-century lierne vault with octagonal pendants was spared. There are brasses, many monuments, 14th- and 17th-century glass and a 17th-century organ-case and pulpit.

The cathedral was restored in the 1870's by Sir Gilbert Scott, who replaced the east window by a more 'suitable' rose-window, an arcade and two smaller windows. Among the monuments of the 17th to 19th centuries is work by Jasper Latham, Sir Henry Cheere, William Tyler and E. H. Baily.

CHRIST CHURCH COLLEGE Founded in 1525 by Cardinal Wolsey, the college has a notable gateway surmounted by a great octagonal tower

DUKE HUMPHREY'S LIBRARY

*Duke Humphrey, youngest brother of Henry V, donated several hundred manuscripts to Oxford University and the library built to house them was completed in 1490. But during the Reformation it was virtually stripped of its books, and in 1598 Sir Thomas Bodley decided to spend the rest of his life refitting and restoring it. The ceiling bears the Arms of both the university and Bodley. (Bodleian Library, Oxford)*

KING ALFRED'S TRANSLATION OF
ST GREGORY'S *Pastoral Care*

*King Alfred's patronage of literature and learning extended to personal translation into Anglo-Saxon of a number of Latin texts. Most of them survive only as later copies, but this manuscript, of Pope Gregory the Great's 'Pastoral Care', is in his own hand. It was written between 890 and 897 and sent to Werfrith, Bishop of Worcester. The book was intended for the guidance of bishops and the text illustrated begins 'This book is for Worcester' and goes on 'When I remembered how the knowledge of Latin had formerly decayed throughout England and yet many could read English writing, I began, among various and manifold troubles of this kingdom, to translate into English the book which is called in Latin 'Pastoralis' and in English 'Shepherd's Care' . . . and I will send a copy to every bishopric in my kingdom.'*
*(Bodleian Library, Oxford)*

designed by Christopher Wren (built 1682), containing 'Great Tom', a 7 ton bell. (See p. 385.)
CHRIST CHURCH ART GALLERY The large collection from which the exhibits are selected includes drawings by Leonardo da Vinci, Raphael, Michelangelo, Holbein, Titian, Rubens, Van Dyck and Rembrandt. Portraits by Lely, Reynolds, Gainsborough, Millais and others, of distinguished former members of the college, are on show in the dining-hall of the college, which is often open to the public.
CHURCH OF ST MARY THE VIRGIN Oxford's famous university church, mainly of the 15th century but with a 13th-century north tower and bold 14th-century spire. The baroque south porch by Nicholas Stone was added *c.* 1637; it has barley-sugar columns and a standing figure of the Virgin in the ornate pediment; there are 18th-century iron gates in front. Inside, there is much of interest, including 15th-century choir stalls with tracery decoration, a canopied pulpit, and monuments and brasses.
CHURCH OF ST MICHAEL The pre-Norman tower dates from the early 11th century. The crude two-light windows have baluster pillars. The remainder of the church is 13th century and later, and there are several monuments and some medieval glass.
CHURCH OF ST PETER-IN-THE-EAST Originally Norman, with an impressive vaulted crypt below the chancel and a good Norman south doorway with beak ornament. The rest of the church with its north-west tower belongs to succeeding centuries. There is 15th-century glass, and several brasses and monuments.
DIVINITY SCHOOL This 15th-century Perpendicular Gothic building is the oldest lecture-room in the university, designed for the teaching of theology, the most important subject at Oxford in the Middle Ages. The foundations were laid in 1427, and the building was completed in 1483; it has hardly been altered since then, except for a Gothic doorway inserted in the north side in 1669. The fan-vaulting of the roof carries 455 bosses, many bearing the Arms of benefactors.
HOLYWELL MUSIC ROOM The oldest music room in Europe, belonging to the university's Faculty of Music. Except for a brief period in 1900–1, it has been in continuous use since 1748.
MAGDALEN COLLEGE Building of this college, founded in 1458 by William of Waynflete, began in the 1470's around the 13th-century St John's Hospital. The range along Long Wall Street including the tower at St Cross dates from 1470–3. The chapel was completed in 1474–5; it is T-shaped in plan with good proportions and graceful arches. The hall and cloister quadrangle were built in 1475. Founder's Tower, which dates from 1485–8, has profusely carved bay windows and fine vaulting beneath. The great bell-tower beside the road was built in 1492–1509. New Building (1733), facing the deer park, is a fine Georgian addition with a graceful pediment. Near by is Addison's Walk, named after a Magdalen man of Queen Anne's time who founded the *Spectator* magazine; the walk runs through the college grounds beside the R. Cherwell. (See p. 384.)
MERTON COLLEGE A college founded in 1264 by Walter de Merton, Bishop of Rochester. From this early period a number of buildings survive, but these lacked any close co-ordination in their planning. The hall was built before 1277 but was heavily restored in the 19th century. The bell-tower of the chapel (begun *c.* 1270) was not completed until 1450. During this time Mob Quad and afterwards the library were erected. Building has

OXFORD

## MUSEUM OF THE HISTORY OF SCIENCE

MOUNTED SPHERE *This Italian sphere was probably made in 1672–84 and demonstrates the planetary system of Heracleides of Pontus who lived in the 4th century BC. According to the system, Venus and Mercury revolve round the Sun, while the Moon, Sun, Mars, Jupiter and Saturn revolve round the Earth. Jupiter is shown with only four satellites and Saturn with only three.*

COMPOUND MICROSCOPE *This microscope was probably made by John Marshall (1663–1725), a famous optical instrument maker whose shop was at one time in Ludgate, London. The stand is of gilt, brass and iron, the tubes of pasteboard, covered with tooled leather and vellum, and the base is of ebony and walnut and weighted with lead. The microscope's accessories include six objectives of various powers, a stage with a glass plate and a brass trough 'to put on the Fish that the Circulation of the Blood may be seen', another stage to carry opaque objects, and stage forceps and tweezers. Marshall appears to have first produced his 'great Double-Constructed Microscope' in 1693.*

continued through the centuries; the new Warden's lodging was completed in 1963. Among the famous students of the college was William Harvey, who first demonstrated the circulation of the blood in the 17th century. (See p. 385.)

MERTON COLLEGE LIBRARY Open to the public, and older than the Bodleian, it was built in 1371–9 by William Humberville. It is sited on the southwest corner of Mob Quad, and housed on the first floor to avoid damp. It contains an astrolabe said to have belonged to Chaucer, who wrote a treatise about the instrument. Some books are still kept on chains, a custom once common to prevent their removal.

MUSEUM OF THE HISTORY OF SCIENCE The finest collection of early astronomical, mathematical and optical instruments in the world is held here. The old Ashmolean building in which it is housed is one of the best examples of 17th-century architecture in Oxford, and was the original home of the Ashmolean Museum, the oldest public museum in England. The museum was formally opened in 1683 to house the collection of the antiquary and astrologer, Elias Ashmole, one of the original Fellows of the Royal Society. Ashmole's collection consisted of rare geological, zoological, botanical and ethnological specimens from all over the world, together with a number of 'curiosities' typical of collections of the period.

One of the most distinguished parts of the present display is the series of Islamic and European astrolabes, once important instruments for astronomical calculation. Like many of the exhibits, these are interesting not only scientifically, but as

works of art; so too are a number of the sun-dials on display and three fine orreries—machines for representing by wheel-work the motions of the heavenly bodies. There is an almost complete series of early microscopes and other optical instruments, together with photographic apparatus. Also on display are clocks and watches; air-pumps, frictional electrical machines, early X-ray apparatus, and other instruments of physics; surgical and dental instruments, and a large number of drug-jars and other items relating to the history of pharmacy.

Of special interest for the history of science in Oxford is the penicillin material in the basement gallery, and H. G. Moseley's X-ray spectrometer—the first used in the spectroscopic analysis of elements. With this, Moseley discovered in 1914 the significance of atomic numbers, a fundamental contribution to the development of modern physics.

More recent relics are a blackboard used by Einstein and the prototype model of ZETA built in 1949 in the Clarendon Laboratory, Oxford, in an attempt to achieve a thermo-nuclear reaction.

There is also a comprehensive library of manuscripts, printed books and prints for students' use.

NEW COLLEGE The foundation stone of this college, the first complete complex of college buildings planned as a unit, was laid in 1380. The founder was William of Wykeham, Bishop of Winchester in 1367–1404, and most of his work survives, although much of it has been remodelled inside and substantial additions made. Wykeham's fine Gothic buildings, erected around the first

# OXFORD UNIVERSITY

The university, the oldest in Britain, probably dates from 1167 when Henry II, during a quarrel with Becket, ordered English students in Paris to return to England. His intention was to ensure that 'there may never be wanting a succession of persons duly qualified for the service of God in Church and State'.

GRINLING GIBBONS CARVING *This is part of the magnificent wooden reredos carved for the chapel of Trinity College by Grinling Gibbons about 1694. The original chapel, built in 1406, had fallen into disrepair by the 17th century, and under Dr Ralph Bathurst, who was president of the college from 1664 until 1704, a new chapel was built. The architect may have been Dean Aldrich, who was much influenced by Sir Christopher Wren. Besides the reredos there are lavishly carved stalls and screen. The chapel, begun in 1691, was completed three years later. (Trinity College)*

MAGDALEN COLLEGE TOWER *This is probably the best known piece of architecture in Oxford, since it is the sight which greets travellers by road from London as they cross Magdalen Bridge to enter the city. The college was founded in 1458 by William of Waynflete, Bishop of Winchester. Henry VI granted him St John's Hospital, a 13th-century building, and this formed the college nucleus. New building began in the 1470's with the chapel and hall, but the magnificent Gothic tower was not built until the end of the 15th century.*

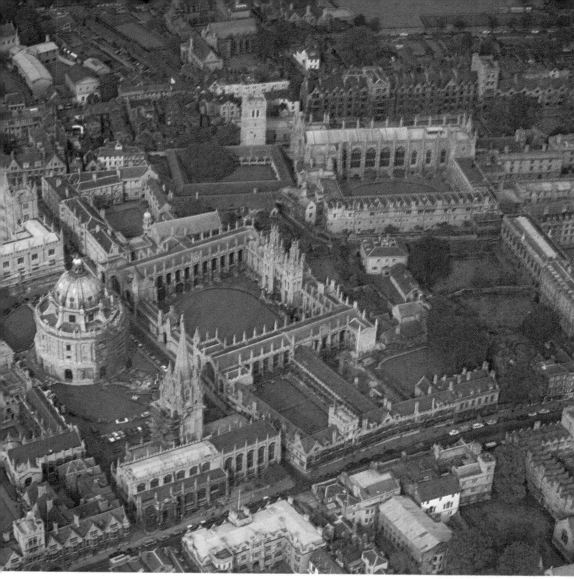

MERTON COLLEGE *Mob Quad, Oxford's oldest quadrangle (above), completed in 1304–11, contains not only the oldest library in England, but also the magnificent college chapel (left) which was built in 1270–1451. Many of the chapel windows retain their original 13th-century stained glass, and the tracery of the east window is particularly fine.*

NEW COLLEGE *The first stone of the college founded by William of Wykeham was laid in 1380. The quadrangle, completed in 1387, was one of the first to be built in Oxford and was designed to contain all the buildings necessary for collegiate life; on the north side are the chapel and hall, and on the east the founder's library.*

TOM TOWER, CHRIST CHURCH COLLEGE *Each evening the bell that once tolled the curfew for members of this college is still rung. At five minutes past nine Great Tom, cast in 1680, weighing over 6 tons, and hanging high in Wren's octagonal tower, chimes 101 over the quadrangle begun in 1525 by Cardinal Wolsey when he founded the college.*

RADCLIFFE CAMERA

*John Radcliffe, a well-known physician of William III's time, in his will left £40,000 for the erection of a library at Oxford University. It was decided to build the library between the Church of St Mary the Virgin and the Divinity Schools, but it was more than 20 years before the site was finally cleared. James Gibbs, the Scottish designer of St Martin-in-the-Fields, London, who had studied in Rome, was chosen as architect, and in 1737–48 he erected the great, circular, domed Radcliffe Camera or Library. His inspiration was probably derived from an earlier plan for a circular library at Trinity College, Cambridge, that was drawn up by Sir Christopher Wren. The Cambridge library was never built, but Gibbs's building was opened in 1749 with a ceremony at which Dr William King, the Vice-Chancellor of the University, gave a fiery pro-Jacobite speech—a flagrant act of disloyalty to the House of Hanover, the rulers of England since 1714 when George I came to the throne.*

GRAND STAIRCASE IN THE
RADCLIFFE CAMERA

*This graceful staircase was designed by James Gibbs, who also designed the library itself. The plasterers charged a total of £280 for their work on eight stucco ceilings in the building, including the grand staircase coves, entablatures and domed ceiling, all of which were made according to drawings by Gibbs. Gibbs also designed the staircase rail, which is made of Swedish iron, and in his estimate of the cost of the building, submitted to the trustees in 1746, he allowed £168 10s. for the ironwork.*

quadrangle, were largely completed by 1387. The gate-house, containing the Warden's lodging, was built in 1380. In the first quadrangle opposite the gate is the library. To the right is the living accommodation for scholars and fellows, and to the left the main community buildings—the chapel and hall (with kitchen beyond). The bell-tower and cloister attached to the chapel date from 1400. The land which Wykeham acquired for his college included a stretch of the medieval city wall which the college, by an ancient agreement with the city, is still obliged to keep in a good state of repair. The wall now survives as a picturesque boundary to one of the most attractive gardens in Oxford. (See p. 385.)

RADCLIFFE CAMERA A magnificent circular building erected in 1737–48 by James Gibbs. It rises from a powerful base which is strongly rusticated (has stone blocks firmly outlined to give an appearance of strength and solidity). The building above has pairs of tall Corinthian columns which support a parapet topped by urns. Capping all is the dome and lantern, the buttresses of which are not, as expected, in line with the columns but are deliberately placed between them. Originally intended as a science library, the Camera is now a reading room for the Bodleian Library. The two are linked by a tunnel with a conveyor belt for the speedy delivery of books from one to the other.

ROTUNDA In 1963, a rotunda, the first to be built in Oxford since the 18th century, was opened as a museum entirely devoted to dolls' houses and their contents—the only one of its kind in the world. The period covered is *c.* 1700–1855—though recently an Edwardian house (complete with billiard room and conservatory) has been added. The museum is not designed to interest children, and is only open on Sunday afternoons in summer.

SHELDONIAN THEATRE This building was erected as a university theatre and to house the University Press by Sir Christopher Wren in 1664–9. It is based on a Roman theatre and is roughly semicircular. Wren was faced with the problem of roofing a space some 70 ft by 80 ft, in wood. This he achieved with a complicated arrangement of beams and trusses supporting a flat ceiling. These are visible in the roof space which was used as a bookstore by the Press when the building was complete; the basement housed the printing presses. To save money, only the south front (the straight front) has Classical pilasters and columns; over the doorway there are the Arms of Archbishop Sheldon who gave the theatre to the university. Among those who assisted Wren was William Byrd, well known for the curious layers of knights he carved in Swinbrook church. Byrd, whose work included vigorously carved keystones on the curved side of the building, was paid £307 in 1666 for stone carving. Wren's original cupola was replaced by one designed by Edward Blore in 1838. On the south side of the theatre is a wall and railing with carved heads of philosophers.

TRINITY COLLEGE Founded in 1555; portions of the old Durham College (established 1380), which formerly occupied this site, are incorporated in the present buildings. Features are the Kettell Hall, a row of gabled buildings; the Garden Quadrangle designed by Wren in 1668; and the chapel built by Bathurst in 1691. (See p. 384.)

UNIVERSITY MUSEUM In 1854 a competition was held to choose a design for a University Museum, and that of Sir Thomas Deane and Benjamin Woodward was successful; work began the following year. Sir Henry Wentworth Acland, later Regius Professor of Medicine, was a supporter of the scheme and his friend John Ruskin,

## SHELDONIAN THEATRE

*Sir Christopher Wren was Professor of Astronomy at Oxford when Sir Gilbert Sheldon, Archbishop of Canterbury, requested him to design a theatre for the public ceremonies of the university. Sheldon provided all the money for the building, completed in 1664-9 and named after him. It is semicircular, and the flat ceiling was painted by Robert Streater with an allegory of 'Truth descending on the Arts and Sciences', and with a network of ropes to suggest the canvas awning of a Roman theatre open to the sky.*

an ardent advocate of the Gothic Revival, concerned himself in it from the start. On Ruskin's advice the columns, windows and doorways of the Venetian Gothic building were decorated with different motifs, each the design of the individual craftsman concerned. Ruskin himself put up one of the columns, but it had to be re-erected by more experienced and competent hands. Before the building was completely decorated, money for it was withheld, and consequently many of the capitals, bases and windows remain in a plain and unfinished state.

It contains the zoological, entomological, mineralogical and geological collections of the university, the earliest of which date from the late 17th century. In a rear gallery is the Pitt Rivers Museum containing ethnological specimens. To one side of the museum is a reconstruction of the abbot's kitchen at Glastonbury Abbey, which is now used as a laboratory.

**Ozleworth** *Glos.* 546Bc
CHURCH OF ST NICHOLAS The main feature of this church is the hexagonal Norman tower, which is thought to have Saxon origins, standing between the nave and sanctuary. There is a pretty south door ornamented with carved foliage. Restoration was carried out in the 19th century.

# P Q

**Packwood House** *Warks.* 546Df
A timber-framed Tudor house, built *c.* 1550, with additions made some 100 years later by John Fetherston. The house contains collections of needlework and tapestry, but is renowned chiefly for its yew tree garden (begun in 1650), fashioned to represent the Sermon on the Mount.

**Padworth** *Berks.* 546Fb
CHURCH OF ST JOHN THE BAPTIST An interesting church with a Norman nave and an apsed chancel. There are good north and south doors, an impressive chancel arch, and the remains of a medieval wall-painting of St Nicholas. One monument is dated 1711; another, by J. Wilton, 1776, has a mourning woman with an urn. A 19th-century stained glass window is by C. E. Kempe, 1891.

**Paignton** *Devon* 539Hc
OLDWAY A house in the neo-Classical style of 1874, with replicas of rooms at Versailles; it is set in Italian and grotto gardens.

**Painscastle** *Rad.* 545Je
In many great castles the original earthworks were swept away by the medieval masons, although they were to return to favour as a defence against catapults and gun-fire in later days. Painscastle gives a vivid impression of the appearance and layout of the traditional motte and bailey castle as shown on the Bayeaux Tapestry. Both the motte, or castle mound, and the bailey, which was big enough to contain a large garrison, are defended by deep double banks and ditches.

**Painswick** *Glos.* 546Cc
COURT-HOUSE Charles I used a room in this manor of Cotswold stone as a courtroom.

**Paisley** *Renf.* 561He
ABBEY The abbey was founded in 1163, and much of the present church dates from the 14th and 15th centuries, though the fall of the central tower destroyed the choir. Restoration was begun in the late 19th century. There is a monument with an effigy of a woman said to be Marjorie Bruce, Robert de Bruce's granddaughter. (See p. 388.)

**Pakenham Windmill** *Suffolk* 548Cf
An old mill, still used to grind corn.

**Papplewick** *Notts.* 552Ed
CHURCH OF ST JAMES Though the west tower is of the 14th century, the remainder of the building is Gothic of the late 18th century. The north gallery has a fire-place.

**Papworth St Agnes** *Cambs.* 547Jf
MANOR HOUSE One of the most interesting houses in the county, part medieval, part Elizabethan, with a combination of red brick and stonework. A straight gable at one end, a great chimney with star-shaped shafts, a six-light medieval window on an upper floor, and some good stucco work give the house great character. There are also some good ceilings inside. It was built in 1585 for Sir William Mallory, a descendant of Sir Thomas Mallory who wrote *Morte d'Arthur*. Most of the south front was rebuilt in 1660.

**Parc Cwm** *Glam.* 544Fc
This interesting Neolithic long barrow—or strictly cairn—standing near the centre of the Gower peninsula, has been the cause of some controversy. It has a horned forecourt leading to a gallery with two pairs of transeptal chambers, very like many of those in the Cotswolds. But the

mound is not long, being a fairly rounded oval, more like those of the western Atlantic type. Other examples, of both types are known in Gower and it may be, as some think, that Parc Cwm is a hybrid form.

**Parc Le Breos** *Glam.*                              *544Fc*
One of the best preserved passage-graves in Wales, recently re-excavated and consolidated. Although standing only a few feet high the remains show the ritualistic planning of these tombs. When excavated in 1869 the remains of 24 skeletons were found.

**Parc-y-Meirch** *Denb.*                          *551Ge*
DINORBEN This remarkable hill-fort stands not far from the sea, on a hill skirting the west side of the Vale of Clwyd. In places, the natural steep scarp-slopes of the hill need no defences. But they are not continuous, and the gentler slopes between are protected by enormous ramparts. The inner rampart came first and, for a time, was defence enough. But later in its history, the second outer rampart was added. In this, the entrance was inturned with stone-built guard-chambers on each side.

This fort was certainly occupied long before the Roman invasion. Apparently it was then abandoned for a time, to be restored and re-occupied in the Dark Ages.

**Parc-y-Meirw** *Pemb.*                           *544Ce*
In the hilly country inland from the coast lies this standing stone row. It is not an outstanding example of the type, but is a rarity in this part of Britain. Quite close to it stands yet another of the normal type of burial chamber, of uprights and capstone, known as Coetan Arthur.

EAST WINDOW, PAISLEY ABBEY

*The east window of Paisley Abbey, which was founded in 1163, is one of the largest and finest works by Douglas Strachan (1875–1950), the Scottish master of stained glass. From the west end of the abbey the window appears like a great tapestry stained with rich splashes of colour, but a closer inspection reveals the groups of figures and the carefully worked out design, which reaches its climax in the figure of Christ the King in the centre.*

**Parham** *Sussex*                                  *542Ad*
Sir Thomas Palmer (1540–1626), who sailed with Drake to Cadiz, began this Elizabethan mansion in 1577. The great hall has unusually tall mullioned windows and a plaster ceiling. The house contains Elizabethan, Jacobean and Georgian portraits. The grounds include fine walled gardens.
CHURCH OF ST PETER A small church in the grounds of the 16th-century house. Basically Perpendicular, it was restored in the early 19th century, when the interior was redecorated in Gothic style. There are box-pews and pretty ceilings. An unusual possession is the 14th-century lead font with lettering and heraldry.

**Parham Hall** *Suffolk*                            *548Ef*
A romantic survival of an early 16th-century timber-framed, high-gabled manor house, rising straight from the moat with figures of two 'wild men' on guard in the gateway.

**Partrishow (Patricio)** *Breckon.*                 *545Jd*
CHURCH A small remote church, mainly 15th-century, with a wonderful rood screen, which retains its gallery with delightful open-work tracery decoration.

**Patrington** *Yorks.*                              *559Ha*
CHURCH OF ST PATRICK A truly magnificent cruciform church, mainly of the 14th century, with a central tower and spire, among the best in England. There is a good Easter sepulchre, a restored medieval screen, and all around are many delightful carved details.

**Patrixbourne** *Kent*                              *542Fc*
CHURCH OF ST MARY This is a small church, with a south tower and spire; there is a Norman door under the tower which forms its porch, with carved ornament, and a tympanum with a carved figure of Christ. The west window is Norman; the glass includes some early work, and some 16th- and 17th-century Swiss windows. There are also some monuments.

**Pavenham** *Beds.*                                 *547Hf*
CHURCH OF ST PETER Although of 14th-century origin, with good examples of 14th-century canopied work remaining, the body of the church and its contents date from the 16th century. It is noted for its splendid 16th-century woodwork and carved panelling—reredos, gallery, lectern and screen. The nave roof, though only recently completed, harmonises well with the rest of the church.

**Paviland** *Glam.*                                 *544Eb*
GOAT'S HOLE CAVE This cave now opens into a cleft in the sea-cliffs of the Bristol Channel, and visitors must watch tide conditions when visiting it. When first occupied, the cliff was fronted by a coastal plain, which made access easy. It was first discovered by Dean Buckland, early in the 19th century; he made some small excavations, and found the first British Palaeolithic burial, a human skeleton associated with the bones of extinct animals. However, Dean Buckland's belief in Archbishop Ussher's Mosaic chronology, by which the Creation was estimated to have taken place only about 4000 years ago, would not let him accept this evidence of the antiquity of man. Further excavation was carried out in the early part of this century, and flint and bone implements, objects of ivory and other substances, all belonging to various cultural periods of the latter part of the Pleistocene Age, were discovered. Above these ancient traces of human occupation, other finds showed that even as late as Roman times, men had taken refuge in this cave.

PEMBROKE CASTLE

*On a splendid natural site, almost surrounded by the Pembroke R., this castle became a key fortress in the settlement of Wales in the late 11th century. The magnificent round keep and inner bailey date from about 1200. The 13th-century curtain walls are light, the steep banks to the river themselves forming a defence. The castle's dilapidated condition was largely the result of an epic siege by Cromwell's troops in 1648.*

**Pembridge** *Herefs.*     *546Af*
CHURCH OF ST MARY Originally a Norman building, the present church (nave with clerestory, aisles, transepts and chancel) is mainly of the 14th century, when the effigies and monuments were made; the pulpit, reader's desk and lectern are all early 17th century. The detached belfry was built in the late 14th century.

**Pembridge Castle** *Herefs.*     *546Ad*
A Welsh border castle of 13th-century origin, with a moat.

**Pembroke** *Pemb.*     *544Cc*
CASTLE Pembroke became important from the late 11th century onwards, first as a key point in the English settlement of Wales, and secondly as a 'staging post' on the journey to Ireland. In 1138, the Earldom of Pembrokeshire was raised to become a County Palatine, giving the holder of the title both supreme responsibility and supreme power.

The great castle, founded here in 1097 on a promontory in the Pembroke R. where steep banks afforded a strong defence, was a reflection of this power. The great circular vaulted keep dates from *c.* 1200 and is 75 ft high with 7 ft thick walls. The fine gate-house survives. In the adjoining tower Henry VII was born in 1457. The castle was taken by Parliamentarians in 1648 after a siege lasting six weeks when it was partially destroyed. The County Palatine survived until 1536 when it was abolished by Henry VIII. The castle reverted to the Crown but was granted privately by James I to a family who retained it up to 1928.

In spite of a considerable amount of recent restoration, it dates substantially from the 13th century.

**Pendennis Castle** *Cornwall*     *538Ca*
Like its counterpart, St Mawes Castle across the Carrick Roads from Falmouth, Pendennis Castle was a link in Henry VIII's coastal defence system. It was finished in 1546, three years after the completion of the fort at St Mawes. Similar to the other military fortifications, the castle consists of a central circular keep with semicircular bastions, enclosed by a curtain wall of further semicircular gun positions. The castle was enlarged at the end of the 16th century, but it suffered badly during the Civil War. While St Mawes had to capitulate after only one day's siege, Pendennis, in a better position, was able to hold out against the Cromwellian troops for five months, until supplies were exhausted. Pendennis Castle, which is now an ancient monument, has some fine barrack buildings dating from the 18th century.

**Pen Dinas** *Card.*     *544Fg*
This is a double Iron Age hill-fort with a considerable history of remodelling. It began as the North Fort, with an entrance at the south end, in a single bank, perhaps timber-faced, with a small ditch on the more vulnerable east side. Then came the South Fort, an independent enclosure with a stone-faced bank and a ditch with counterscarp bank on the east side. Finally, the two were linked by connecting defences, a slight revetted bank on the west and, on the east, a larger bank with ditch and counterscarp bank. A new entrance to the whole was made in this east side addition. It has since been somewhat disfigured by quarrying.

**Penfound Manor** *Cornwall*     *538Ee*
This is the oldest inhabited manor in Britain, part Saxon and Norman with Elizabethan and Stuart additions. It was mentioned in the Domesday Book.

**Penhurst** *Sussex*     *542Dd*
CHURCH A small, attractive Perpendicular church, which has missed the restorer's helping hand. The west tower has a pyramid roof, the nave a king-post roof, and the chancel a wagon-roof. The screen is 14th century, and much of the furniture 17th century, including the pulpit and lectern. There are fragments of medieval glass in the east window.

**Penkridge** *Staffs.*     *552Bb*
CHURCH OF ST MICHAEL AND ALL ANGELS A fine, former collegiate church, with work from the 13th century onwards. It has stalls, misericords and a number of 16th- and 17th-century monuments with effigies.

*After the death of his uncle, Lord Penrhyn, Mr Dawkins-Pennant engaged the architect Thomas Hopper to enlarge Penrhyn Castle. Hopper's fortress, the most gigantic example of the Norman Revival in Britain, was begun in 1827 and finished about 1846. The main feature of the interior is the great hall, three storeys high; it is arched and vaulted in a profusion of Norman decoration, and its north windows contain stained glass (dating from 1837) by Thomas Willement, representing the signs of the Zodiac.*

**Penmon Priory** *Anglesey* 550Ee
The foundation of the Priory Church of St Seriol probably goes back to the 6th century, but the earliest features—the font, and the cross in the deer park about 450 yds west of the church—date from *c.* 1000. The cruciform church has a nave of 1140, and this was followed some 20 years later by the square tower and transept. The large chancel dates from the early 13th century, although it has been partly rebuilt. The church contains the best-preserved Romanesque detail in North Wales: of particular interest are the crossing arches and wall arcades, the tympanum over the south door, and the font. South of the church is the prior's house (now a private house) and beyond this a fine three-storied building dating from the early 13th century, which contains the cellar, refectory and dormitory. The building is roofless, but has been consolidated.

On the opposite side of the road, to the south-east, is a charming square dove-cote with a stone roof which is crowned by an open hexagonal lantern through which the birds entered; this is post-Reformation and dates from *c.* 1600. There is an ancient cell and holy well some 80 yds north of the church.

PENSHURST PLACE

*Penshurst Place has one of the finest surviving 14th-century halls in England. The house was built for a London merchant, Sir John de Pulteney, in 1341.*

**Penrhyn Castle** *Caern.* 550Ee
The medieval house on this site, from which there are magnificent views of mountains and sea, was modernised by Samuel Wyatt for Lord Penrhyn *c.* 1782; this resulted in a mixture of typical 18th-century domestic architecture and Gothic. Lord Penrhyn died in 1818 and his nephew inherited the house; he employed Thomas Hopper to enlarge it and Hopper produced a massive Norman-style fortress in Mona marble. At the southern end is an immense square keep, 115 ft high and about 60 ft wide, which was probably based on the keeps of Rochester and Hedingham Castles. To the north-east is a massive circular tower called the Ice Tower.

The castle contains a collection of 1000 dolls from all parts of the world. Collections of locomotives and rolling stock, and of pottery, are also on view.

**Penrhyn Old Hall** *Caern.* 550Fe
Although described as an ancient house in 1536, the present Hall is Elizabethan and later; the small 15th-century cusped window, now re-set on the first floor, may be a fragment of the original building. Inside are two unusual carved fire-place beams and some Elizabethan wall-painting with pious inscriptions. The house was the home of a 16th-century Catholic family who were connected with a clandestine printing press set up in a cave near the Little Ormes Head.

**Penrice Castle** *Glam.* 544Fc
The ruins of a 12th-century Norman castle, with an 18th-century octagonal pigeon house close by.

**Penrith** *Cumb.* 557Jf
CHURCH OF ST ANDREW A medieval building rebuilt in *c.* 1720, but retaining the earlier west tower, which is probably of Norman origin. There are fragments of 15th-century glass, and 17th- and 18th-century fittings—font, pulpit, brass chandelier.

**Penshaw Monument** *Durham* 558Cg
A Doric temple, built in 1844 in honour of the 1st Earl of Durham (1792–1840), who in 1838 was Governor-General of the British Provinces in North America (now Canada).

**Penshurst** *Kent* 542Ce
Beside the great sandstone mass of Penshurst Place, this village has a handsome red-brick rectory which is typically Queen Anne. The lych-gate, with a house built over it, is the most picturesque corner of the village, increased to make a minute open-ended quadrangle in 1850, a most sensitive piece of Victorian development.

**Penshurst Place** *Kent* 542Ce
The birthplace of Sir Philip Sidney (1554–86), soldier, poet and statesman. The castellated Tudor mansion was greatly enlarged in Elizabethan times. It contains a great hall dating from 1360, fine 17th- and 18th-century furniture, portraits of the Sidney family and armour. The terraced formal gardens, poetically described by Sir Philip Sidney and Ben Jonson, were begun in 1560.

**Pentre Ifan** *Pemb.* 544De
The finest example of the Pembrokeshire burial chambers. Not only do the great uprights carry their capstone, estimated to weigh some 17 tons, but the upright slabs which formed the forecourt of the mound, long since lost, still stand to show that it was semicircular in plan; the stones seem to be more carefully graded than usual.

**Penzance** *Cornwall* 538Aa
NATURAL HISTORY AND ANTIQUARIAN MUSEUM The museum specialises in local history, showing bygones of West Cornwall, including some Bronze and Stone Age relics.

**Pen-y-Corddyn** *Denb.* 551Ge
This Iron Age hill-fort, like its neighbour Dinorben, a few miles away, stands on a hill close to the sea, and has an intermittent rampart linking the stretches of steep natural scarp where no rampart was needed. Here too the ramparts are of great strength, but the defences are simpler, and apparently not used over such a long period. The fort was built perhaps a century or more before the Roman invasion; the original defences were never remodelled, and the site was abandoned when the Romans penetrated this northern Welsh hill-country. There is no evidence that it was re-occupied after the breakdown of Roman control.

**Peover Hall** *Cheshire* 552Be
CHURCH OF ST LAURENCE The church that formerly stood on this site was rebuilt in 1811. But St Laurence's retains two earlier chapels with fine 15th- and 17th-century monuments with effigies of the Mainwaring family of the Hall. Also from the old church are a 15th-century font and a 17th-century pulpit.

**Pepperbox Hill** *Wilts.* 540Fe
On top of the hill stands Eyre's Folly, a six-sided brick tower with slate roof, built by Giles Eyre of Brickworth House in 1606.

**Pershore** *Worcs.* 546Ce
ABBEY The original abbey church, of which parts have survived to serve as the parish church, was probably established before the Norman Conquest. Only the eastern arm—with the presbytery—the south transept and the lantern tower remain. The nave and the Lady Chapel were destroyed in 1559 after the Dissolution, and the north transept collapsed in the 17th century. The presbytery itself was rebuilt after a fire in 1223, but the vaulting is early 14th century. The lantern tower rises on massive arches of the earlier Romanesque period, probably *c.* 1330.

**Perth** *Perths.* 566Ca
The brutal murder of James I, Scotland's poet king (1394–1437), in the Blackfriars monastery ended the status of Perth as capital of Scotland, and the Court moved to Edinburgh. Another epoch came to an end in Perth in 1559 when John Knox preached in the town his sermon 'vehement against idolatory' which led to widespread destruction and desecration of Roman Catholic monasteries in Scotland, priceless treasures being looted and destroyed. The Earl of Mar occupied the city for the Old Pretender in 1715, and in 1745 there was another Jacobite rising which severely suppressed. With this history few relics of the past remain, and these are mainly in the old streets known as 'Vennels'.

**Peterborough** *Hunts.* 547Jg
In AD 655, the King of Mercia founded a monastery on the site of the present cathedral. Henry VIII gave Peterborough city status in 1541: it was not until 1874 that it became incorporated as a municipal borough. The town hall was built in 1671.
CATHEDRAL Peterborough is one of the most complete and impressive Romanesque buildings in England. The church belonged to a Benedictine monastery, founded in the 7th century. Destroyed by the Danes in the 9th century, it was refounded

## PERSHORE ABBEY

*St Eadburga, the daughter of a 10th-century English king, is the most important saint venerated at Pershore Abbey. Offered the choice of necklaces and bracelets or a Bible and chalice by her father, to test her faith, the young Eadburga, who later became a nun, chose the Bible and chalice. The abbey, already an established institution by the end of the 10th century when it became a Benedictine house, was deprived of large parts of its estates by Edward the Confessor to help finance the building of Westminster Abbey. At the Dissolution part of the abbey was knocked down, leaving a lop-sided fragment of the original building which has been used as a parish church ever since. The vaulting of the presbytery is outstanding, with bosses deeply carved with naturalistic foliage.*

# PETERBOROUGH CATHEDRAL

Henry VIII gave Peterborough cathedral status in 1541; it had been one of the great Benedictine abbey churches, but the abbey was dissolved in 1539. The site was first consecrated in 655, when the King of Mercia founded a Benedictine monastery there. This was sacked by the Danes in 870, and a second monastery was destroyed by fire in 1116. The present building was started by the Abbot Jean de Seez two years later. Apart from its west front, Peterborough is an outstanding example of the Norman-Romanesque style. The Benedictines, conservative in their architecture, carried on building in this style up to the last decade of the 12th century—more than 20 years after England's first truly Gothic buildings had made their appearance.

WEST FRONT *Peterborough's crowning achievement, the unique west front, was created when a dramatic screen wall was placed in front of the old Romanesque façade. Originally it had been planned to finish off the nave with Romanesque twin towers, but the design was abandoned before these were completed. The Gothic front is dominated by three huge, deeply recessed arches, 81 ft high. For some unknown reason, the centre arch is much narrower than the other two, but the two corner towers prevent this narrowness from producing a cramped effect. The porch in the centre, in the late Gothic style, was added about 1370, probably to tie together the lofty supports of the arch and prevent them from spreading outwards.*

NAVE *Much of the original Norman fabric of Peterborough is preserved inside the cathedral, and the nave, completed under the Abbot Benedict between 1194 and 1197, is among the supreme surviving examples of the Romanesque style. The Peterborough monks owned the quarries producing the creamy-white Barnack stone from which it is built. The high wooden roof is richly decorated with paintings dating back to 1220, which have been carefully restored.*

TURNER *The Lake, Petworth: Sunset, Fighting Bucks*

*When Ruskin called James Turner's work 'the loveliest ever yet done by man in imagery of the physical world', he was implying the dominance of a quality in Turner's art which appeals today with increasing force —his concern with the vastness of nature and its physical properties of light and colour. After his father's* *death in 1829, at the invitation of his patron and friend Lord Egremont Turner had a studio at Petworth and did a large number of dazzling interior scenes there as well as landscapes in oils. This view of the lake, with a cricket match in progress and a herd of deer, was done about 1829–30. (Petworth House)*

in the 10th, a new church being built *c.* 965. This in turn was burnt in 1116 and the present church belongs to the subsequent rebuilding.

Of the domestic buildings of the monastery, a few parts survive, particularly of the abbot's and prior's lodgings and various gateways. The cloister walks no longer exist. The abbey was dissolved in 1539 and refounded as a cathedral in 1541.

MUSEUM AND MAXWELL ART GALLERY Located in a large Regency house, built as a private dwelling in 1816, the museum contains a unique collection of carved bonework and straw marquetry by prisoners from the Napoleonic Wars held in Norman Cross Barracks. The archaeological collection concentrates on the Romano-British and Anglo-Saxon periods, and the natural history and geology sections include fossil reptiles from the local clay. There are personalia relating to Mary, Queen of Scots, and John Clare, the rural poet. The art gallery has a small permanent picture collection and a representative selection of English ceramics.

**Peterhead** *A'deen* 567Hf
ARBUTHNOT MUSEUM The local history of Peterhead is illustrated by items in the museum. The marine section includes a collection of fishing boats showing development up to the present time, and exhibits relating to whaling and the Arctic. Other local industries represented include granite quarrying and dressing, and herring curing, which has died out. A collection of coins is also displayed.

**Petersfield** *Hants.* 541Je
The most handsome houses in this flourishing market town are Georgian. In the square at its centre stands an equestrian statue of William III, originally gilded.

**Petersham** *Greater London* 542Bg
The Georgian village still exists—a small church, and four massive town-style houses by a double-bend in the main road, where it skirts Richmond Park. The most handsome houses date from *c.* 1720. Sudbrooke Park, contemporary and even finer, designed by James Gibbs, is now the golf clubhouse.
CHURCH OF ST PETER A 13th-century church, largely rebuilt in the 18th century. There were additions in the 19th century, but Georgian fittings —font, pulpit, gallery, box-pews—remain.

**Petworth** *Sussex* 542Ad
Recorded in the Domesday Book, Petworth, a small town at the gateway of the Duke of Somerset's great house, has many Tudor and 17th-century houses. The gateway itself is spectacular, taller than most buildings in the town. An intricate knot of narrow streets develops round the tiny market-place, where the plain arcaded 18th-century town hall stands in contrast with an exuberant bank of 1901. At New Grove House (1620), Grinling Gibbons stayed while engaged on carvings for Petworth House.
PETWORTH HOUSE James Turner (1775–1851), the landscape artist, visited this great house to paint, and several of his pictures are here. It was raised by Charles Seymour, 6th Duke of Somerset, who, after his marriage to the Percy heiress, rebuilt the former Percy mansion between 1688 and 1696, retaining only the 13th-century chapel; the house was partly altered in the 19th century. The state rooms contain paintings by Holbein, Rembrandt, Hals, Van Dyck, Gainsborough and Reynolds. The Carved Room was decorated by Grinling Gibbons. (The park is open to the public but the gardens are not.)
SOMERSET LODGE A small 17th-century stone house, with mullioned windows and oak staircase.

**Pevensey** *Sussex* 542Dd
CHURCH OF ST NICHOLAS Pevensey has the remains of a Roman fort which were converted into a medieval castle, and the town was once a flourishing port; the church was probably originally Norman, but most of the present building is 13th century, with a clerestory. There is a large alabaster monument of 1616.

**Pevensey Castle** *Sussex* 542Dd
This Roman fort of the Saxon Shore stands guard on a harbour which is now silted up. It is not rectangular like most of its contemporaries, but oval in plan and is well provided with substantial external bastions. The military value of this coastal site was recognised after the Norman Conquest, and the castle was further strengthened by Robert, Count of Mortain. A keep was built in the south-east corner, and a smaller inner bailey was fortified within the Roman walls. These were used as defences for the outer bailey, and still stand for much of their length. Subsequent alterations were

PEVENSEY CASTLE

*The sea once lapped against the south and east sides of this castle. In William I's reign the Normans converted the remains of the original Roman sea fort into a fortress; it was an important part of their coastal defences and despite several sieges was never taken by assault. In 1264–5, while held by a favourite of Henry III, it was besieged by the forces of Simon de Montfort under the command of his son. Subsequently the castle fell into disrepair, for the sea receded and Pevensey ceased to be a castle commanding the coastline. It was temporarily fortified during the brief threat of the Spanish invasion in 1587 and 1588.*

limited to consolidating the inner bailey in the 13th century by substituting a stone curtain wall for the original palisade. During the 15th century the castle fell into disrepair and decay, a decline hastened by the sea gradually receding. Pevensey Castle reverted to military occupation during the Second World War, when it was fitted out as a Home Guard command post. Machine-gun posts were concealed within the ruins, but the medieval defences were never subjected to attack.

**Picardy Stone** *A'deen*                 566Ff
A Pictish symbol stone; it stands in a small enclosure close to a by-road 2 miles north-west of Insch. Its designs are those of the abstract symbol series, such as Z-rod, serpent, mirror and double disc.

**Pickering** *Yorks.*                 558Ed
CHURCH OF SS PETER AND PAUL A Norman church with much later rebuilding. The west tower is Early English, its spire added later. There is a fragment of Saxon carving, and much 15th-century mural painting, restored in the 19th century, with saints and scenes from the life of Christ. There are effigies of 14th-century knights.

**Pickering Castle** *Yorks.*                 558Ed
Richard II was kept a prisoner here in 1399 after being deposed by Parliament. The Norman castle of stone replaced an earlier motte and bailey castle. Repairs and additions were made in the late 12th and early 13th centuries, after which the castle comprised an oval inner ward, with domestic

buildings and chapel, surrounded by curtain walls with towers. Only the chapel, postern gate, dungeon and three towers of the curtain walls now remain.

**Piccotts End** *Herts.*                 547Hc
A 14th-century hall-house with wall-paintings of the period.

**Pimperne Barrow** *Dorset*                 540Ed
This large Neolithic long barrow stands close to the Salisbury–Blandford road and is still 15 ft high. It is more than 100 yds long and nearly 50 yds broad. Its quarry-ditches are also visible. It is probably one of the best preserved barrows of its type in the country.

**Pinkie House** *M'loth.*                 562Ce
A Jacobean mansion, incorporating a tower dating back to 1390. The long gallery has a splendid painted ceiling. The house is now part of Loretto College.

**Pitcaple Castle** *A'deen*                 566Ff
James Graham, Marquess of Montrose, who was captured while attempting to raise a rebellion against Charles II in 1650, was imprisoned here while awaiting execution. The 15th-century castle has a keep built on a Z-plan, and was reconstructed in the 19th century.

**Pitchford** *Shrops.*                 552Ab
CHURCH OF ST MICHAEL St Michael's has Norman remains—a doorway on the north of the chancel—and lancet windows of a later date. The reading desk and pulpit with sounding board are of the early 17th century. There is a fine oaken effigy of a cross-legged knight (perhaps John de Pitchford, d. 1285) and a series of monumental slabs with incised likenesses of four pairs of husbands and wives of the Pitchford family from 1529 to 1587.

**Pitchford Hall** *Shrops.*                 552Ab
A 16th-century black and white timbered mansion in a setting of trees and water, with superb gables and chimneys of the period. It was the home of the Ottley family for many generations: Sir Francis Ottley (1601–49) was nominated Sheriff of Shropshire by the Royalists in the Civil War.

**Pitmedden** *A'deen*                 567Gf
The garden was originally laid out in 1675 by the 1st Baronet of Pitmedden; it contains pavilions, sun-dials and fountains.

**Pittington** *Durham*                 558Cf
CHURCH OF ST LAWRENCE There is an impressive Norman north arcade, with twisted columns and zigzag ornament of *c.* 1175, with Saxon windows above, and a west tower. There was 19th-century restoration and rebuilding. Inside are 12th-century wall-paintings, and the effigy of a cross-legged knight, *c.* 1280.

**Pixley** *Herefs.*                 546Be
CHURCH OF ST ANDREW A small 13th-century church, surmounted by a Victorian bell-turret, with no division between nave and chancel. The rood screen is possibly of the 14th century.

**Plas Teg** *Flints.*                 551Jd
This fine early 17th-century mansion is square in plan with square towers at each corner surmounted by decorative lead roofs. It has a good Jacobean stair; it has recently been saved from demolition and restored for use as flats.

**Plas-yn-Rhiw** *Caern.*                 550Dc
A homestead of 10th-century origin, with Tudor and Georgian additions, recently restored. It has a sub-tropical garden.

**Plymouth** *Devon*         *538Fc*
Sir Francis Drake returned to Plymouth's natural harbour in September 1580 after circumnavigating the world. In 1620, the Pilgrim Fathers departed from it to settle in the New World. As a precaution against Roundhead trouble, Charles II built the great citadel which dominates city and harbour; its ramparts are 20 ft thick in places. The Elizabethan zone of Plymouth is known as the Barbican: the Mayflower Steps here commemorate the departure of the Pilgrim Fathers.
CITY MUSEUM AND ART GALLERY The Reynolds family portraits, Joshua Reynolds's diaries and the Cottonian Collection of pre-1800 paintings, drawings and printed books are among the displays in this museum. The paintings include old masters, contemporary works and the Clarendon Collection of portraits. The collection of fine silver, though small, includes the Drake Cup and the Eddystone Salt. Pottery and porcelain are represented, with emphasis on Cookworthy's Plymouth and Bristol hardpaste. There are also departments of archaeology and natural history.
EDDYSTONE LIGHTHOUSE (RE-ERECTED) On Plymouth Hoe is one of the world's most important 18th-century lighthouses. Some 14 miles south of Plymouth the Eddystone reef was the setting of the first true rock station, the earliest being wooden, built in 1698, followed in 1708 by a wood and stone building which survived until burnt in 1755. Four years later John Smeaton's tower showed its light, and this tower, rebuilt on the Hoe after the present lighthouse replaced it in 1882, was the first scientifically designed and jointed masonry structure to be built, serving as a model until the era of reinforced concrete.
ELIZABETHAN HOUSE A 16th-century house, restored in 1931 and with fine furniture of the 16th and early 17th centuries.

DOMENICO POGGINI *An Acrobat*

*Domenico Poggini (1520–90) was a Florentine artist who worked mainly as a goldsmith for the Grand Duke of Tuscany, but he also worked in marble and bronze. The brilliant quality of his bronzes is shown by this statuette and must owe much to his training as a goldsmith. (City Museum and Art Gallery, Plymouth)*

PORCELAIN SWEETMEAT DISH

*Made at Cookworthy's factory in Plymouth about 1770, this dish resembles three shells resting on coral. No other example with original matching spoons is known to exist. (City Museum and Art Gallery, Plymouth)*

**Plympton** *Devon*         *538Fc*
CHURCH OF ST MARY THE VIRGIN A large church dating from the early 14th and 15th centuries, with a prominent west tower. Monuments include one by Sir Francis Chantrey of *c.* 1840.

**Pocklington** *Yorks.*         *558Eb*
BURNBY HALL GARDENS Gardens with fine lily ponds.

**Polesden Lacey** *Surrey*         *542Af*
The writer of the plays *The School for Scandal* and *The Rivals*, Richard Brinsley Sheridan, lived in a house on this site, and his wife laid out part of the gardens, beautifully set amid downland woods. The present Edwardian house was adapted in 1906 from a Regency original built in 1824 to designs by Thomas Cubitt.

**Pollokshaws** *Lanarks.*         *561He*
POLLOK HOUSE A mansion designed by William Adam in 1752, situated in splendid grounds above the White Cart R. It contains paintings by Goya, El Greco, Hogarth and Raphael.

**Pont Cysyllte** *Denb.*         *551Hd*
This huge iron aqueduct, designed by Thomas Telford and completed in 1805, carries the Ellesmere Canal over the R. Dee. There is a towpath along the aqueduct for pedestrians.

**Pontefract** *Yorks.*         *558Da*
CASTLE MUSEUM Within the grounds of Pontefract Castle, the museum contains items of local interest, including various Roman articles, fragments of Norman pottery and siege coins made in the castle from silver given by Royalists during the Civil War.
KING'S OWN YORKSHIRE LIGHT INFANTRY MUSEUM Devoted to regimental relics, medals, uniforms, pictures and weapons relating to the King's Own Yorkshire Light Infantry.

**Ponteland** *Northld.*         *558Ch*
CHURCH OF ST MARY St Mary's has a Norman west tower, and a 13th-century chancel and north transept, with lancet windows. Inside are several fragments of 14th-century heraldic glass.

**Pontypridd** *Glam.*         *545Hc*
PONTYPRIDD BRIDGE The colliery town takes its name from this 140 ft single-arch bridge over the R. Taff. It was built by a local mason, William Edwards, in 1755, after two unsuccessful attempts. In order to save weight he pierced each of the spandrels with three cylindrical arched openings; the height of the arch is 36 ft.

## SIR FRANCIS DRAKE, THE GREAT CIRCUMNAVIGATOR

Drake, the Terror of the Spanish Main, was born at Crowndale, near Tavistock in Devon. His first command was a down-at-heel coastal vessel bequeathed him by the master to whom he was apprenticed. His early experiences in the West Indies gave Drake a hatred of Spain, but he gained revenge, and wealth, in 1572–3 by heading an expedition which snatched the King of Spain's treasure from the backs of mules plodding across the Isthmus of Panama. After sailing round the globe, Drake singed the King of Spain's beard by destroying 33 ships in Cadiz harbour in 1587. When the Armada sailed against England, a year later, he drummed them up the Channel to disaster. This indomitable sea captain became fatally ill on a last expedition to the Caribbean in 1596, and just before the end climbed into his armour 'To meet death like a gentleman'.

PORTRAIT of Drake painted in 1591 by an unidentified artist (National Maritime Museum, Greenwich). That year Drake diverted the waters of the R. Meve from Dartmoor to give Plymouth England's first municipal water supply.

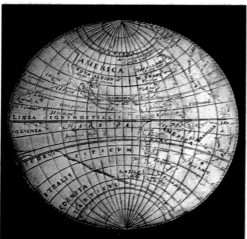

ASTROLABE, traditionally belonging to Drake. Of the five ships which left Plymouth in 1577, only the Golden Hind, under Drake's command, successfully navigated the Magellan Straits. (National Maritime Museum, Greenwich)

LODE-STONE, a natural magnet said to belong to Drake, and used to adjust compasses. (National Maritime Museum, Greenwich)

DRAKE'S MEDAL, cut in silver and based on the world map made by the great geographer, Mercator. (National Maritime Museum, Greenwich). Drake's course, marked by a dotted line, was taken because his ship was groaning with plunder, and he dared not sail it round Cape Horn.

BANNER *painted in gold on silk damask; it is one of the nine Drake used to dress his 'weather beaten bark', the Golden Hind, when the queen rode down to Deptford on April 4, 1581 to dine aboard and confer on him a knighthood after his voyage round the world. These banners are among the oldest in England. (Buckland Abbey)*

THE DRAKE CUP, *a New Year's gift from Queen Elizabeth I in 1582. The queen had told the Spanish Ambassador, who had complained about the 'master thief of the unknown world', 'The gentleman careth not if I disown him', but she had invested in Drake's expedition to break Spain's monopoly in the Pacific and happily received 400 per cent profit on her outlay. This piece is considered among the hundred best specimens of silver gilt in the country. (Plymouth City Museum)*

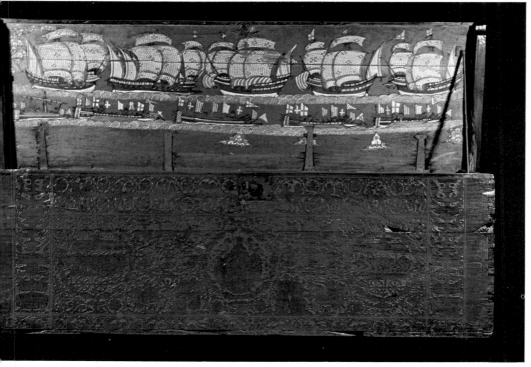

AK CHEST *in Berkeley Castle. It formed part of the furnishings of Drake's cabin aboard the Golden Hind, the ship which was to take him round the world. The ship was magnificently equipped, even the kitchen utensils being of* solid silver, *plundered from Spain. It was typical of Drake's rakish gaiety that an orchestra of four was engaged for the voyage which began in 1577 and took two years and ten months to complete.*

PORTCHESTER CASTLE

*There have been fortifications on this site to provide a defence against invaders from the sea since Roman times. The present castle was built in the 12th century inside the perimeter of a Roman fort. The small Church of St Mary, within the circle of the Roman walls, formed part of an Augustinian priory founded by Henry I in 1133, but the inconvenience of having Augustinian canons in the midst of the garrison probably led to their removal to Southwick about 1144–53. Two hundred years later, at the beginning of the Hundred Years War, the threat from the Continent revived and additions were made to the castle. By the end of the 14th century, under Richard II, Portchester had become a small but comfortable royal palace. It remained in the hands of the monarch until 1632.*

**Poole** *Dorset* 540Ec
OLD TOWN HOUSE The house was built as the headquarters of the pre-Reformation Guild of St George.

The exhibits displayed are devoted to local history and include pottery, china, arms, armour, ships and shipping. There is a dug-out canoe of the Bronze Age, which was raised from Poole Harbour in 1964.
POOLE MUSEUM All the collections are of local interest. The archaeology section includes Roman pottery and coins, the history section includes pottery, trade tokens, weapons and armour, and there are sections devoted to maritime history and local fauna.

**Portchester** *Hants.* 541Hd
CHURCH OF ST MARY Sited in one corner of the Roman castle, the church was originally monastic, as part of an Augustinian priory founded in 1133 by Henry I. It is a Norman building, once cruciform and with a central tower. The west front has a doorway, arcading and window above. The carved font is Norman. A monument of *c.* 1618 is by Nicholas Stone.

**Portchester Castle** *Hants.* 541Hd
A fine example of the later type of Saxon Shore fort, built within the last two decades of the 3rd century AD and occupied (on the evidence of coins found there) until *c.* AD 370. Its angular corners, with boldly projecting bastions and brick bonding-courses in the walls, are characteristic of this type of Roman fort. It was modified by its use as an outer curtain wall for a Norman castle, which was built in the north-west angle.

At the end of the 14th century Richard II began converting Portchester into a small palace and much of this building remains (in ruins) including the hall, kitchen and great chamber. In the outer bailey stands the 12th-century church of St Mary, which survived as a garrison chapel and parish church.

**Port Erin** *Isle of Man* 556Cc
MARINE BIOLOGICAL STATION A department of Liverpool University, for research into marine biology. Local marine fish and marine invertebrates are shown in the aquarium. There is also a fish hatchery.

**Port Glasgow** *Renf.* 561Gf
NEWARK CASTLE Begun in 1597 by Patrick Maxwell, the castle has a fine courtyard, hall and stepped gables. It was enlarged in the 17th century.

**Portland** *Dorset* 540Db
LIGHTHOUSE The present fine lighthouse, erected in 1906, is typical of the period, and replaced at least two other pairs of lights built since the early 18th century to warn sailors of this dangerous promontory. A tower of 1869 is now used as a bird observatory and field centre.

**Portmeirion** *Merioneth* 550Ec
In 1926 the Welsh architect Clough Williams-Ellis began what has developed into a combination of outdoor architectural museum and coastal holiday village. His first idea was to present a 'live' exhibition of architecture and landscaping inspired by the Italian village of Portofino, and Portmeirion is an integrated assembly of various buildings and monuments dating from 1610 onwards—a barbican gate-house, campanile, lighthouse and cloisters, for example. Sculpture, murals and ironwork are displayed among landscaped gardens —sub-tropical and other flowering plantations occupying a mile or so of the Portmeirion peninsula. A splendid collection of rhododendrons can be seen in the Gwyllt Gardens, with thousands of hydrangeas, and among the many varieties of trees are palms, cypresses, eucalyptus and magnolias, and various ferns and lilies.

**Portsmouth** *Hants.* 541Hc
Docks, arsenal and storehouse appropriate for a major naval base were established at Portsmouth by Henry VIII; it remains the chief Royal Navy seaport and, in the dockyard is Nelson's flagship *Victory* and the Victory Museum. A survivor of the Second World War air-raids is the house in Commercial Road where Charles Dickens was born in 1812, now a Dickens Museum.
CATHEDRAL This is the former parish church of St Thomas of Canterbury, which became a cathedral

in 1927, and dates from the late 12th century; the tower and other parts were rebuilt at the end of the 17th century. Further enlargements have been made since the 1930's which are still not yet complete. Among the 17th- and 18th-century monuments is one with an enormous urn to a murdered Duke of Buckingham, by Nicholas Stone, *c.* 1628.

CUMBERLAND HOUSE MUSEUM AND ART GALLERY (SOUTHSEA) Exhibits devoted to the natural history of southern Hampshire are displayed in the house, originally built in the late 18th century for the Comrades of the Portsmouth Garrison. Monthly exhibitions are held of local art, and modern and old masters, and there is a permanent collection of paintings of Portsmouth.

ROUND TOWER A medieval bastion guarding the harbour entrance; it is now used as a gallery for temporary exhibitions.

SOUTHSEA CASTLE Henry VIII founded and built the castle in 1546 as one of his chain of coastal forts for protection against French raids. It is now a museum with a collection illustrating the history of Portsmouth as a harbour and fortress; naval and military relics are included.

VICTORY MUSEUM The museum stands in the oldest part of the Portsmouth dockyard, on a site opposite Nelson's flagship the *Victory*. It was founded by the Society for Nautical Research as a complement to the *Victory* herself. There are relics of Lord Nelson, his officers and men, the *Victory* and naval life—Nelson's furniture, ship models, paintings, prints and figureheads. The centre-piece of the museum is a panorama, 42 ft long and 12 ft high, painted by the late W. L. Wyllie, depicting the Battle of Trafalgar when at its height at 2 p.m. on October 21, 1805. There is also a display of 73 models illustrating the battle, made for the Prince Consort *c.* 1860 by his own model maker.

**Port Sunlight** *Cheshire*                    551Jf

LADY LEVER ART GALLERY Paintings, principally of the British School; water-colours and engravings; miniatures, antique Renaissance and British sculpture; Chinese pottery and porcelain; cloisonné enamel; carved stones and crystals; Wedgwood china; and one of the best collections of English furniture, mainly of the 18th century, are displayed here.

**Potter Heigham** *Norfolk*                    554Ec

CHURCH OF ST NICHOLAS This thatched church, with a 14th-century round tower with octagonal top, is mainly Perpendicular, but in the chancel is an indication of a Norman window. The rood beam still exists, and a screen features painted saints. The octagonal font is built of brick.

**Potterne** *Wilts.*                    540Ef

CHURCH OF ST MARY A cruciform church with a central tower, mainly of the 13th century; the later additions do not spoil the essentially Early English character. The high standard of the 13th-century work was probably due to the fact that the Bishops of Salisbury had a manor house at Potterne. There are two fonts, one Saxon with Latin inscriptions, the other Perpendicular, and the wooden pulpit is also in the Perpendicular style. There is a monument by E. H. Baily, of 1821.

PORCH HOUSE A small, timbered house, dating from the 15th century.

**Poulton-le-Fylde** *Lancs.*                    557Hb

CHURCH OF ST CHAD All but St Chad's late Perpendicular tower were rebuilt 1752–3. The galleried interior has wall monuments, heraldic panels, and the remains of the 17th-century Hesketh family pew. The chancel was added in 1868.

**Powderham Castle** *Devon*                    539Hd

Built *c.* 1390, but much restored in the 18th and 19th centuries after damage in the Civil War. It contains some fine furniture, and portraits of the Courtenay family, Earls of Devon.

**Powerstock** *Dorset*                    540Cc

CHURCH OF ST MARY The impressive 12th-century chancel arch, with four rows of ornament, remains from the original Norman church. The 15th-century south doorway is flanked by carved figures in canopied niches.

**Powis Castle Gardens** *Mont.*                    551Hb

The medieval castle overlooks the Severn Valley. At the end of the 17th century the long terraced gardens below were laid out in the Dutch formal manner, and remain much the same over 250 years later. On the terraces, stone balustrades and lead statuary and vases form the background to colourful trees and shrubs. Yew pyramids, planted when the terraces were laid, are clipped in fanciful topiary-work. The terraces and the sheltered ground below them provide sites for such plants as winter's bark (*Drimys*), Brazilian feijoa and Chilean flame plants (*Embothrium*). In the park are fine specimen trees: a 180 ft Douglas fir is the tallest tree in Britain. (See p. 402.)

WEDGWOOD VASE

*This lilac jasperware vase is by Josiah Wedgwood, the greatest of English potters, and has white reliefs, by John Flaxman, of Apollo and the nine Muses. Flaxman, a well-known sculptor, first worked with Wedgwood in 1775, and was later closely associated with the Wedgwood factory—an enterprise which is still in existence. (Lady Lever Art Gallery, Port Sunlight)*

**Prescelly Hills** *Pemb.*                    544Dd

From the Prescelly Hills about 80 five-ton 'bluestones' were dragged and shipped the 240 miles to Stonehenge, where they were erected to form the inner horseshoe and middle ring enclosed by the circle of large sarsen stones. To the east of the 'quarry', on the summit of the eastern-most knoll of the Prescellys, is the 11 acre Iron Age hill-fort known as Moel Trigarn.

**Preston** *Lancs.*                    557Ja

LANCASTRIAN BRIGADE MUSEUM Uniforms, medals and arms are on display, including a French drum captured at Waterloo, and a Brown Bess musket of the type used at Waterloo.

**Preston-on-Stour** *Glos.*                    546De

CHURCH The west tower, 15th century, is all that remains of the old church; the rest was rebuilt in 1752. There is a monument by Thomas Scheemakers, designed by 'Athenian' Stuart, and mid-18th-century stained glass.

NELSON *by Lemuel Francis Abbott.* *(National Maritime Museum, Greenwich)*

## HORATIO LORD NELSON, ENGLAND'S FAVOURITE ADMIRAL

When England's most fêted and beloved admiral first joined the navy at the age of 12, his uncle wrote 'What has poor Horatio done, who is so weak, that he should be sent to rough it out at sea?' Two years later the boy was showing early signs of his unorthodox daring by clubbing polar bears with the butt-end of a musket, as shown in a picture at the National Maritime Museum, Greenwich.

Nelson first won fame as a Commodore in 1797. Acting without orders, he turned his ship out of the line of battle off Cape St Vincent, and with a cry of 'Westminster Abbey or glorious victory' he threw his small craft across the bows of the enemy, preventing the premature union of two portions of the Spanish fleet. In June of the same year Nelson was struck during a 'land' engagement and had to have his right arm amputated. While waiting for the stump to heal he sat for the portrait here shown.

In 1798 he was given a fleet of ships commanded by specially selected officers, who were to be known as 'The Band of Brothers' and whose portraits hang in Greenwich. They annihilated the French fleet at the mouth of the Nile, leaving Napoleon, the conqueror of all Europe, bottled up in Egypt. The grateful underwriters of Lloyds presented Nelson with a silver dinner service, pieces of which remain at Greenwich, at Nelson's Museum at Portsmouth and at the Nelson Room at Lloyds in the City of London.

ORDERS OF CHIVALRY *which Nelson wore at every opportunity; replicas were stitched on all his uniforms. (National Maritime Museum)*

NELSON'S CABIN *aboard the Victory, showing a map of the Trafalgar area lying on his own table. When Nelson, cheered by a large crowd as he left Portsmouth, joined the fleet off Cadiz* on September 28, 1805, it was transformed from a cluster of individual ships into an invincible fighting machine, and on October 21, quite destroyed the Franco-Spanish fleet.

THE VICTORY, *Nelson's flagship at Trafalgar, carrying 850 men and 100 guns. The ship, on view to the public, is now moored at Portsmouth and is still used as the Commander-in-Chief's flagship.*

NELSON FIRST MET LADY HAMILTON *when her husband, Sir William, was British Minister at Naples. She was beautiful—and notorious. Later, Nelson kept this pastel of her in his cabin on the Victory. He called it his 'guardian angel' and had it stowed in safety below decks before Trafalgar (National Maritime Museum, Greenwich). On the eve of the battle he wrote a last letter to Emma, which was found unfinished on his desk after his death. The letter begins 'My dearest beloved Emma the dear friend of my bosom the signal has been made that the enemy's combined fleet are coming out of port . . .' (Bristol Museum)*

NELSON'S DEATH-BED *on board the Victory, painted by Arthur William Devis. Nelson was hit by a sniper's bullet on the quarter-deck early in the action, but only died when victory was assured. His friend, Captain Hardy, standing above him, acceded to his last request to 'Kiss me, Hardy!' (National Maritime Museum, Greenwich)*

NELSON'S COLUMN, *towering 145 ft above Trafalgar Square, supports a statue of England's 'little Admiral' idealistically cast 18 ft high by E. H. Baily.*

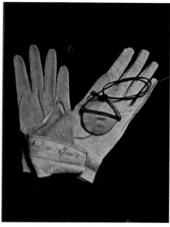

TWO LEFT HAND GLOVES, *and shield for his good eye. (National Maritime Museum, Greenwich)*

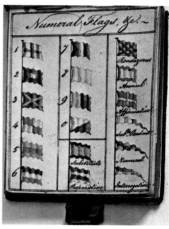

ADMIRAL POPHAM'S TELEGRAPHIC CODE, *used by Nelson at Trafalgar for his famous message to the fleet, 'England expects that every man will do his duty'. Nelson originally wished to put 'England confides', but there were no suitable flags. (National Maritime Museum, Greenwich)*

TOP ORNAMENT TO NELSON'S TOMB *beneath the cupola in St Paul's Cathedral. The ship's colours draped the coffin and before it was lowered to the crypt Nelson's sailors ripped them to pieces to keep as souvenirs. After his death many monuments throughout England were erected in evidence of the deep affection and respect his memory inspired.*

## POWIS CASTLE GARDENS

*These are some of the few formal gardens surviving in England; they were passed by in the 18th-century vogue for natural landscaping. The long garden terraces, designed in the Dutch manner, were added to the ancient castle overlooking the Severn Valley about 1690, and were later decorated with lead statuary.*

**Preston Pans** *E. Lothian*                    562Cf
HAMILTON HOUSE Built in 1628, the house was restored in 1937.

**Prestwold Hall** *Leics.*                    552Ec
A Georgian house, notable for its painted marble hall and corridor, and Chippendale furniture. Its rose garden contains 2000 trees.

**Priddy Circles** *Som.*                    540Cf
This complex consists of four circles, each about 200 yds across. They are set in a straight line almost a mile long, the circle at the north end being divided from the next by a gap wider than the average. Henge monuments normally have the ditch within the bank but these, like Stonehenge, have the ditches on the outside. There are many fine round barrows close to the site of the circles, doubtless the burials of the people who used these sacred sites.

**Princes Risborough** *Bucks.*                    547Gc
MANOR HOUSE A 17th-century red-brick mansion (near the church), noted for its Jacobean oak staircase and 18th-century wainscoting.

**Prior Park** *Som.*                    540Df
A Georgian mansion dating from *c.* 1735. In the grounds are lakes and a Palladian-style bridge.

**Probus** *Cornwall*                    538Cb
CHURCH OF ST PROBUS The impressive west tower here is the tallest in the county. Inside is a brass with figures, *c.* 1514, and a monument, a seated mourning woman of *c.* 1766.

**Puddletown** *Dorset*                    540Dc
CHURCH OF ST MARY A pleasant church, chiefly of 15th-century work, with a good interior. The panelled nave roof is 15th century; the gallery, box-pews and canopied pulpit are of the 16th century. The Norman font is carved with inter-laced decoration. In the south chapel are many monuments and brasses of the 15th and 16th centuries, and in the east window there is stained glass by Sir Ninian Comper.

**Pumpsaint** *Caern.*                    544Fe
ROMAN GOLD MINES About 8 miles south-east of Lampeter, on the hill-side on the east bank of the R. Cothi, are the remains of extensive Roman and later gold mines. At first open-cast trenches were used, up to 300 ft long and 50 ft deep, but later tunnels were dug to follow the seams. In 1935, when attempts were made to re-open the mine, a fragment of Roman water-wheel was recovered from an ancient level at a depth of 160 ft.

**Purton** *Wilts.*                    546Db
CHURCH OF ST MARY An interesting church whose striking feature is that it has two towers: the central one with a spire, and the west with pinnacles. Inside, many details indicate the Norman origins of the building, which was altered during the 13th–15th centuries. There are mural paintings, including a 14th-century Death of the Virgin, and several fragments of medieval stained glass.

**Purton Manor** *Glos.*                    546Bc
Once the home of Sir Walter Raleigh, the manor is noted for its massive doors with heavy latches, iron knockers and hinges a yard long. In the oak-panelled dining-room is a mantelpiece marked with the date 1618 and the initials D.T.M., said to be of Dorothy Throckmorton, into whose family Raleigh married.

**Puttenden Manor** *Surrey*                    542Cf
A black and white house begun in 1477 and later enlarged. It is notable for oak beams, open fire-places, four-poster beds, copper and wood baths, and fine gardens.

**Pyt House** *Wilts.*                    540Fe
A Georgian mansion in the Palladian style.

**Quainton** *Bucks.*          *547Gd*
CHURCH OF THE HOLY CROSS AND ST MARY A Decorated and Perpendicular church, rather heavily restored *c.* 1877, in a pleasant setting between a late 17th-century almshouse and a Georgian rectory. The importance of Quainton lies in its 17th- and 18th-century monuments: there is work by William Stanton (*c.* 1672), Thomas Stayner (1689) and Giacomo Leoni (after 1735).

The big monument to the Dormer family of *c.* 1730 is a puzzle-work; unsigned, it has been unconvincingly attributed to Louis Roubiliac (like the monument at Gayhurst). It shows Mr Justice Dormer and his wife grieving over the body of their dead son.

**Quarley Hill** *Hants.*        *540Fe*
An unfinished Iron Age hill-fort which reached the final stages of fortification before it was abandoned. It has a single bank-and-ditch defence, as well as a small counterscarp bank. Excavation made clear that, at the north-east entrance, work had proceeded so far that the post-holes for the timber gateway-structure had been dug, but never equipped with uprights. There was also evidence that these defences replaced a simple timber stockade of the Iron Age.

**Quatt** *Shrops.*          *546Bg*
CHURCH OF ST ANDREW The exterior is of 1763, with a red-brick tower, but the interior is medieval, of varying periods, and includes a Norman font. Portions of the Perpendicular rood screen remain. The pulpit and desk are dated 1629, and among the 17th-century monuments to the Wolryche family is one of 1614 with a baby lying beside its mother.

**Quebec House** *Kent*       *542Cf*
General James Wolfe, who was killed while commanding the British force which took Quebec in 1759, spent much of his childhood here. The brick house, dating from the early 16th century, was largely rebuilt in the 17th century and contains relics of the General.

**Queensferry** *W. Lothian*     *562Bf*
PLEWLANDS HOUSE A fine stone house, built in 1643 and restored in 1953. (Not open.)

**Quenington** *Glos.*        *546Dc*
CHURCH OF ST SWITHIN The two Norman doorways of this small church have elaborately carved tympana. That on the south door depicts the Coronation of the Virgin; on the north, probably the Harrowing of Hell.

# R

**Raby Castle** *Durham*       *558Bf*
A 14th-century fortress, with a great hall (136 ft long) in which some 700 knights could be mustered; at the western end is a minstrels' gallery in stone. The castle was altered in 1765 and again in the mid-19th century. It contains English, Dutch and Flemish paintings.

**Radburne** *Derbys.*       *552Dc*
CHURCH OF ST ANDREW This small church, with a tower at the north-west, is mainly of the 13th and 14th centuries. The benches came from Dale Abbey. As well as 15th-century monuments and slabs, there is a large architectural monument, of 1684, by Grinling Gibbons.

**Radcliffe** *Lancs.*        *552Bg*
LOCAL HISTORY MUSEUM Temporary displays of items of local history are on show, with frequently changing art exhibitions.

**Raglan Castle** *Mon.*       *546Ac*
The ownership of the land here can be traced back to the 11th century, but the existing castle was built mainly in the 15th century. Begun by Sir William ap Thomas, who died in 1445, it was completed by his son Sir William Herbert, created Earl of Pembroke in 1468. He was executed as a prominent Yorkist supporter in the following year. Ultimately, the property passed to Charles Somerset, created Earl of Worcester in 1574. The Somerset family's tenure ended with the Civil War siege of 1646, during which the castle was severely damaged and part of the keep deliberately destroyed. Large parts of the 15th-century building survive. This comprises a walled enclosure divided into two courts by a great hall set across the middle. Each court has its own gateway, and these entrances are each dominated from the outside by the keep, which lies just clear of the south wall of the main enclosure and is surrounded by a moat.

**Ragley Hall** *Warks.*       *546Df*
A country mansion begun in 1680; a portico and interiors designed by James Wyatt were added in 1780. The decorated great hall, by James Gibbs, has moulded 18th-century plasterwork. There are collections of paintings, china, furniture and books. It is set in a 500 acre park with extensive gardens and a lake; Capability Brown landscaped the grounds *c.* 1750.

THE RED SALOON AT RAGLEY HALL

*Ragley Hall was designed by Robert Hooke in 1680, but the house took many years to complete. James Gibbs (1682–1754) and James Wyatt (1746–1813) were both responsible for the decoration of some of the rooms. The Red Saloon is by Wyatt. The walls of the Saloon are papered in silk, and the ceiling was designed by Angelica Kauffmann (1741–1804); over the fireplace is van Haarlems' 'The Raising of Lazarus', painted on oak panels and dated 1602. The magnificent great hall, 70 ft long by 40 ft wide, was added by James Gibbs in about 1750; its finely executed plaster ceiling is 40 ft high.*

**Rainham** *Greater London* 548Ab
CHURCH OF SS HELEN AND GILES A late Norman church with nave, north and south aisles, chancel and west tower, dating from *c.* 1170. Some 13th- and 14th-century fragments of wall-paintings remain. There is a brass of *c.* 1480.
RAINHAM HALL A small red-brick house built in Wren style by John Harle, a merchant, *c.* 1730. It has wrought-iron gates and panelling of the period. (By appointment.)

**Rainsborough Camp** *Northants.* 546Fe
This oval fort, of nearly 6 acres, is surrounded by a bank, ditch and counterscarp bank. The main bank was revetted with a drystone wall. This is probably the best preserved of the hill-forts in the North-amptonshire uplands.

**Ramsey** *Hunts.* 547Jg
ABBEY Once the seat of Lord de Ramsey, the abbey was leased to the grammar school in 1938. The impressive gate-house, one of the most highly decorated specimens in England, is open to the public. Bodsey House, a mile and a half north, is moated; it has parts of a large 14th-century chapel, a superb 17th-century chimney-stack and a room with remarkable coved and panelled ceiling.
CHURCH OF ST THOMAS À BECKET A noble Norman church, a reminder of the abbey which was once here. There is a medieval oak pulpit, and a fragment of mural painting.

**Ranworth** *Norfolk* 554Db
CHURCH OF ST HELEN The church, which has a battlemented west tower and nave, and a two-storied north porch, possesses the county's finest screen, which is painted with saints and has its rood loft complete. There is also an exceptionally good 15th-century lectern.

**Ratcliffe-on-Soar** *Notts.* 552E
CHURCH OF THE HOLY TRINITY The 13th-centur west tower has a 14th-century spire. There are number of 16th-century and later monument with effigies to the Sacheverell family.

**Ravensburgh Castle** *Herts.* 547H
This is perhaps the best of the small group of hill forts in this area, strung along the edge of the chal Downs, close to the prehistoric Icknield Way Though to some extent tree-covered, the stee slopes of the hill-side and the defensive bank, ditc and counterscarp bank, together with intermitten additional works, are easily distinguishable. Ther were probably two entrances.

**Ravenstone** *Bucks.* 547G
CHURCH OF ALL SAINTS A generally Early Englis and Perpendicular church, which contains one o Buckinghamshire's three puzzling monument (the other two are at Gayhurst and Quainton): fine tomb to the 1st Earl of Nottingham (*d.* 1682 showing a black and white four-poster bed, on the Earl reclining in white, on a black slab, all i marble. The mystery is the identity of the sculptor it has been ascribed to Cibber, Catterns an William Stanton. The church also possesses som pleasing woodwork, including a fine pulpit.

**Raynham Hall** *Norfolk* 554E
One of the best houses of its date in Norfolk, buil *c.* 1620 (possibly by Inigo Jones) for Sir Roge Townshend. The interior was remodelled in th 18th century for the 2nd Viscount Townshen ('Turnip' Townshend, the agricultural reformer Still the home of the Townshend family.

**Reach** *Cambs.* 548A
A hamlet that once had seven churches, was Roman port, and marks the Fen end of the famou

CHURCH OF ST HELEN, RANWORTH

PAINTED SCREEN OF ST PAUL *This, the finest surviving rood screen in Norfolk, dates from 1485 and was probably painted by Flemish or German artists. It stretches right across the church with two wings that serve the side altars, and portrays twelve saints.*

SARUM ANTIPHONER *This manuscript, illuminate by the monks of Langley Abbey in 1400, was lost fo 300 years before being found in a private art collection The page shown, one of 285 made of sheepskin, is par of the order of service for the feast of Corpus Christ.*

Devil's Dyke. The old vicarage is a charming timber-framed and plastered house, probably *c.* 1500. Reach Lode is a waterway made by the Romans to connect with the Cam at Upware, and thence to the sea.

### Reading *Berks.* 547Gb
Reading lies at the extremities of the Berkshire Downs and the Chiltern Hills, where, because of the Kennet tributary, the Thames becomes a major river; like many other key geographical towns, it was a target for Danish raids (871 and 1006). With the Normans it rose in importance. Henry I founded the Benedictine abbey in 1121, and was buried there in 1136. Thomas à Becket consecrated a church in Reading in the presence of Henry II. Hugh Faringdon, the last abbot, was hanged before his own gateway in 1539 and the abbey dissolved. Henry VIII granted the first charter in 1542. Early in the 17th century the cloth trade declined; the Civil War further reduced trade in Reading, as did the meeting of William of Orange's troops with those of James II here in 1688. By 1700, the population had fallen to 7000. Prosperity came with the opening of the Kennet and Avon Canal in 1810, and the railway in 1840.

COLE MUSEUM As part of Reading University's Zoology Department, the museum is primarily a collection for students. It is noted for its fine display of dissections and microscopic slides demonstrating animal anatomy.

MUSEUM AND ART GALLERY Contains a comprehensive collection of Roman antiquities from neighbouring Silchester. Items of natural history, prehistoric and medieval metalwork and a collection of Delft are displayed. There are also art exhibitions, which are changed monthly.

MUSEUM OF ENGLISH RURAL LIFE Established in 1951 by Reading University as a centre of information and research on all aspects of country living, the museum contains farm implements, tools and domestic equipment. Collections of particular interest include farm wagons, ploughs, portraits of farm livestock, bee-keeping equipment (Bee Research Association Collection), English basketry, and a selection of bills and advertisements relating to rural life. Records include manuscripts, 70,000 photographs, prints, drawings and a general library.

A permanent exhibition is on view to the public; the study collections and records are available for reference on application to the Keeper.

MUSEUM OF GREEK ARCHAEOLOGY The greater part of the collection consists of Greek pottery, though there is also a smaller collection of Egyptian antiquities; part of Reading University.

### Reculver *Kent* 542Fg
Reculver (Regulbium) was the earliest fort of what later became the series known as the Saxon Shore. Though still complete at the beginning of the 18th century, erosion by the sea has eaten steadily into the northern part so that not more than about half the curtain wall remains. Recent excavation has shown that it was first occupied in the early years of the 3rd century AD, and guarded the northern entrance to the Wantsum Channel, now represented by the drained flats on the east side. In the centre of the enclosure stands a remnant of an early Saxon church.

CHURCH OF ST MARY Practically all that remains of this church, founded perhaps in the 7th century, on a Roman site, is the twin-towered west front. These towers are now preserved as aids to navigation. The encroaching sea has eaten away most of the low cliff on which the church stands.

### Redbourn *Herts.* 547Hd
CHURCH OF ST MARY The west tower and nave are Norman, with 14th- and 15th-century enlargements. The church contains a 15th-century rood screen, some brasses, and a monument of *c.* 1732 with a bust.

### Redgrave *Suffolk* 548Dg
CHURCH OF ST BOTOLPH A Decorated and Perpendicular church, with a font and 19th-century stained glass in the east window. There are first-rate monuments by Nicholas Stone, 1616, and Thomas Green of Camberwell, *c.* 1710.

LORD CHIEF JUSTICE HOLT'S MONUMENT

*Despite the growing 18th-century fashion for figures dressed in Classical robes, Thomas Green of Camberwell carved this marble monument in the traditional style. From 1689 until his death in 1709, Lord Justice Holt was Lord Chief Justice of the King's Bench, where he did much to discourage prosecutions for witchcraft. (Church of St Botolph, Redgrave)*

### Reepham *Norfolk* 554Gc
CHURCHES OF ST MARY AND ST MICHAEL Of the three parish churches which were enclosed in one churchyard, two are left; the third is only a wall. The parish church is St Mary's, of the 13th–14th centuries. There is a square Norman font, a brass, *c.* 1391, and a monument, *c.* 1337, to Sir Roger de Kerdiston, with a recumbent effigy lying on large pebbles. On the tomb-chest are weeping figures. The other church is St Michael's, the parish church of Whitwell, which has a Perpendicular west tower. The vestry is linked with that of St Mary's.

### Reigate *Surrey* 542Bf
CHURCH OF ST MARY MAGDALENE St Mary's has a large monument by an almost unknown sculptor, Joseph Rose the Elder. It dates from *c.* 1730, and has a large architectural background, in front of which reclines a man holding a celestial crown; on either side of him are life-size figures of Truth and Justice with their emblems.

**Rendcomb** *Glos.* *546Dd*
CHURCH OF ST PETER A late Perpendicular church; it was rebuilt at the beginning of the 16th century with a west tower. Inside there are good contemporary roofs and a 16th-century screen across the whole church; much of the glass is medieval, and there is some good 19th-century glass in the east window. The Norman font has carvings of the 12 Apostles.

**Repton** *Derbys.* *552Dc*
CHURCH OF ST WYSTAN An interesting church, with a Saxon chancel and a remarkable Saxon crypt. The remainder of the church is mainly of the 13th and 14th centuries, with west tower and spire, a 15th-century clerestory and porch, and monuments.
REPTON SCHOOL MUSEUM Housed in a 12th-century Augustinian priory, the museum illustrates the history of Repton village and school.

**Reynoldston** *Glam.* *544Fc*
ARTHUR'S STONE The peninsula of Gower, stretching several miles to the west of Swansea, has many fine monuments, of which this burial chamber is outstanding. It is in form a typical megalithic chamber, composed of uprights holding a capstone, and the mound has long since been lost. Its remarkable feature is the size of the capstone—a huge rock estimated to weigh no less than 25 tons.

**Rhuddlan Castle** *Flints.* *551Ge*
From here Edward I organised his administration of Wales, details of which were incorporated in the Statute of Rhuddlan (1284). Edward built the castle in 1277–82. It has concentric curtain walls, and twin gate-houses enclosing a square; a moat, fed by the sea, surrounded the building. In 1646, during the Civil War, the castle was besieged by Roundheads, and has been a ruin since then.

**Ribbesford** *Worcs.* *546Bf*
CHURCH OF ST LEONARD An interesting church with Norman remains, including a carved tympanum. The south piers of the nave are of wood; the glass in the west window was designed by Sir Edward Burne-Jones.

**Ribchester** *Lancs.* *557Jb*
The Roman fort of Bremetennacum, on the north bank of the R. Ribble, where it guarded the crossing of the road from Ilkley to the Fylde with the main highway from Manchester to Carlisle. Parts of it were excavated last century and can be seen; in a small museum are finds relating to life in a garrison in a wild part of the country.
MUSEUM OF ROMAN ANTIQUITIES All the items on display have been found in Roman Ribchester, and include Romano-British coarse-ware pottery and Samian pottery, coins, altar stones, brooches, lamps and a tombstone; there is also a replica of a bronze parade helmet and a model of the Ribchester Roman fort. In the museum grounds are a Roman well and an excavated granary.

ROMAN COINS

*An aureus, most valuable coin of Gratian's reign (367–383 AD), found on the site of the Roman fort at Ribchester. (Museum of Roman Antiquities, Ribchester)*

**Richards Castle** *Herefs.* *546Af*
CHURCH OF ST BARTHOLOMEW A church with a Norman nave, but also much later work. The detached bell-tower was added *c.* 1300. Some medieval stained glass remains, and 17th-century box-pews.

**Richards Castle** *Shrops.* *546Af*
CHURCH OF ALL SAINTS A late Victorian church of 1891–2, by R. Norman Shaw, the architect who designed New Scotland Yard. It stands on a hill, and a notable feature is the massive tower at the south-west. Shaw drew inspiration from a variety of Gothic periods for the style of the windows and other features.

THE ROMAN FORT OF RUTUPIAE
AT RICHBOROUGH

*One of the most remarkable monuments of the Roman occupation of Britain, the fort at Richborough was built at the end of the 3rd century. It was at the end of Watling Street—the road to London and North Wales—and also guarded the Wantsum Channel which separated the Isle of Thanet from the mainland. Richborough was a port and landing place of the Roman legions. Part of the north wall of the castellum remains and this is 460 ft long and 22 ft high. There is also a cruciform platform, 144 ft by 104 ft, which may once have been the base for a lighthouse. A series of defensive ditches surrounding the fortifications came to light during excavations carried out in 1926.*

## RIEVAULX ABBEY

Rievaulx Abbey's position, enclosed among the Yorkshire hills, is one of its most memorable features. Another is the austerity, for which the Cistercians were famous, of its early architecture. This can still be seen in the nave and transepts of the great church, the earliest large Cistercian church building in England.

But the chief glory of the abbey is now the choir of the church, part of substantial enlargements to the 12th-century building which were carried out in the 13th century. The choir, an unusually fine example of the architecture of northern England, was built in the period 1225 to 1230.

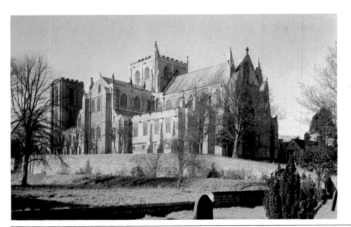

*An outstanding exception to the rule that cathedrals dating back to Saxon times have hardly a vestige of the original building apart from the foundations. Ripon's crypt is said to have been built about 670 for St Wilfrid, Bishop of York. The Gothic nave of master-builder Christopher Scune, built in 1502–22, is in subtle harmony with the sedate west front in the Early English style. The towers originally had spires, but the last of these was removed in 1664, some years after the central spire had fallen.*

## Richborough *Kent* 543Gf

Here stands Rutupiae, the key Roman fort of the Saxon Shore defences. Built probably in the last decade of the 3rd century, it is of the developed 'late' type, with square angles and elaborate external bastions. In its later days, it was garrisoned by a detachment of the 2nd Legion, brought from Caerleon in South Wales. It guarded the south-east entrance to the Wantsum Channel and all the many port activities spread out along the shores of that channel. (See p. 406.)

RICHBOROUGH CASTLE The castle stands on the site of the Roman fort Rutupiae, believed to have been the Romans' landing place in AD 43. Its collection of Roman pottery is generally acknowledged to be one of the best found on any site; over 50,000 coins were also found here, some of which are displayed. Also on view are bronze ornaments, weapons, Roman lamps and amphorae.

## Richmond upon Thames 547Jb
*Greater London*

Richmond Green is a spacious turfed square, like Kew, but without the church and without through traffic. Maids of Honour Row, on the south-west side, was built in 1724, and the Princess of Wales's maids of honour lived there.

## Richmond *Yorks.* 558Ce

Dominated by the hill-top ruins of an 11th-century castle, the town has alleyways known as 'wynds', one of the largest market squares in Britain and a theatre dating from 1788.

CASTLE This castle was probably built in the years following 1071 and was held for most of the Middle Ages either by the Crown or by the holder of the Honor of Richmond. It commands a fine natural site overlooking the valley of the R. Swale. Richmond is one of the few surviving castles with 11th-century walls. (Most of the existing military structures date from the 12th century.) It was built as a large enclosure bounded by stone walls. In the south corner are the remains of the original hall, the centre of the domestic apartments—a rare survival. The castle was originally entered from the town through a gate-tower, but in the second half of the 12th century this was walled up and the tower used as a base for the 100 ft stone keep.

GEORGIAN THEATRE A small theatre, built by Samuel Butler in 1788. There were no stage presentations from 1848 until 1943, when a production was staged as part of the 850th anniversary of·the Borough of Richmond. In 1960–2 the theatre was restored and re-opened.

GREEN HOWARDS MUSEUM The history of the Regiment from 1700 is illustrated by uniforms, medals, silver and trophies, campaign relics, documents, and contemporary pictures and prints.

## Rievaulx *Yorks.* 558D

RIEVAULX TERRACE Adjoining the ruins of th 12th-century Rievaulx Abbey, the terrace is vantage point for panoramic views of the Dale There are two 18th-century temples.

## Rievaulx Abbey *Yorks.* 558D

Rievaulx was founded in 1131. Its monks belonged to the Cistercian order, and the founding mission came from Clairvaux in France, one of th foremost Cistercian abbeys, ruled by St Bernard Within a few years it established its own colony The main buildings were completed in the 12t century and in the 13th century substantial enlargements were made; in the latter part of th 12th century there were said to be 140 monks and over 500 lay-brothers. But by the Dissolution (1539) there were only 22 monks and the lay brothers had probably vanished during the 14t century. Rievaulx is enclosed among the York shire hills. The early architecture has all the austerity for which the Cistercians were famous, an this may still be seen in the nave and transepts of th great church, the earliest large Cistercian church building in England. (See p. 407.)

## Ripley Castle *Yorks.* 558C

Both James I and Oliver Cromwell stayed in th crenellated house, the home of the Ingilby family since 1350. There is a 15th-century gate-house an a 16th-century tower. In 1780 alterations wer made, in the Gothic and Classical styles. The house contains fine furniture, panelling and ceiling paintings, armour and a secret hiding place. Ther is a walled garden in the grounds.

## Ripon *Yorks.* 558C

CATHEDRAL The present Diocese of Ripon wa only founded in 1836. In spite of such modernity the cathedral building contains parts which place amongst the oldest Christian buildings in th British Isles. A monastery was refounded on th site by the great Bishop Wilfrid of York in 66 From this foundation one small fragmen remains—a crypt beneath the central tower of th present church. This formed a relic chamber whic probably stood under the high altar of Wilfrid church. Architecturally, it is hardly spectacula but it is one of those few survivals which take on straight back to the earliest days of Christianity i northern England, and provides a physical lin with one of the most resounding personalities i the early history of the northern Church.

THE OLD HALL An 18th-century Dower Hous notable for its panelling and plasterwork.

## Rippington Hall *Hunts.* 547

An Elizabethan house with five stone chimney it has been recently restored.

**Rivenhall** *Essex* 548Cd
CHURCH OF ST MARY AND ALL SAINTS Though rebuilt in brick in 1838, the church possesses some of the best 12th-century glass in the country, which was brought from France by a former rector in 1840. There are also some 17th-century monuments.

**Roche** *Cornwall* 538Dc
CHURCH OF ST GONANDUS In spite of rebuilding in the 19th century, this church still possesses evidence of its Norman origins, such as a fine Transitional Norman font with a circular bowl ornamented with foliage and entwined snakes, and having at each corner a shaft topped by an angel's head (as does the font at Bodmin). On top of a nearby cliff is a 15th-century chapel, now ruined.

**Roche Abbey** *Yorks.* 552Ef
Ruins of a Cistercian abbey founded in 1147, beautifully sited in a valley of the R. Ryton. The Gothic transepts are the chief remains of the abbey church.

**Rochester** *Kent* 542Dg
Since before Roman times there has been a settlement here, at the ford across the R. Medway. The walled Roman town grew up beside the bridge which carried Watling Street (the Dover Road) across the river; much of the Roman wall foundations survive within the present city. The town grew in importance when it was made a bishopric by St Augustine in 604, and the present cathedral was begun in 1077 on the site of his church. Rochester, like adjoining Chatham, is closely associated with the life and works of Charles Dickens, who made his home at Gad's Hill on the north-west outskirts of the city.

The Norman castle dominates the town, cathedral and R. Medway, with a keep over 100 ft high, the finest and best preserved in England. It was begun *c.* 1120. In the High Street are the guildhall and Corn Exchange, both gifts to Rochester from Sir Cloudsley Shovel, in 1687 and 1706; there is splendid brickwork and plasterwork in the guildhall, and a colossal clock on the Corn Exchange overhanging the street; south of the cathedral stands Minor Canon Row, a terrace built in 1736, less pretentious than Shovel's buildings, and to the east of The Vines Inn is Restoration House, an interesting Elizabethan house, refaced in the 17th century with all sorts of decoration in cut brickwork.

CASTLE Set on a high chalk cliff above the river, the castle was mentioned in the Domesday Survey (1086). It was besieged by Simon de Montfort but never fell to direct attack. After 1610 the castle was dismantled and now only the keep and curtain walls remain. The massive square keep, internally arcaded, is the tallest in England, standing 120 ft high and 70 ft square; Archbishop de Corbeuil completed it in 1126.

CATHEDRAL Founded by St Augustine in 604, this abbey cathedral was partially destroyed by the Danes, but was rebuilt by Bishop Gundulph (1024–1108) who established an order of Benedictine monks here. It is basically Norman, the rest Early English, but has been much altered.

KING'S SCHOOL A fine Tudor building dating from the reign of Henry VIII.

RESTORATION HOUSE Built in 1587, the house was given its name when Charles II stayed here on May 28, 1660, on his way to London to take possession of his throne.

**Rockbourne** *Hants.* 540Fd
One of the best villages in a remote and completely rural part of Hampshire. There is a pretty street and, by the church, a rambling manor house, its earliest part dating from the 13th century.

**Rockingham** *Northants.* 547Gg
CHURCH OF ST LEONARD Restored during the 19th century, the church contains monuments dating from the 16th to the 19th century. There is a large work commemorating the 1st Earl of Rockingham (*d.* 1724) by Peter Scheemakers and his collaborator, Laurent Delvaux.

MONUMENT TO LORD HENNIKER

This marble monument to the 1st Lord Henniker, who died in 1806, was carved in the Victorian Romantic style by John Bacon the Younger (1777–1859), son of the famous sculptor John Bacon. (Rochester Cathedral)

**409**

## CHARLES DICKENS, THE LITERARY LION OF THE VICTORIAN ERA

'When I go back to the slow agony of my youth, I wonder how much of the histories I invented hangs like a mist of fancy over well-remembered facts', wrote Charles Dickens, whose birthplace in Commercial Road, Portsmouth, is preserved as a small museum. His father (the prototype for Mr Micawber) was imprisoned for debt and Charles was taken from school and put to work in a blacking factory. He taught himself shorthand, became a reporter to the House of Commons, and when his first comic sketch was published in *The Monthly Magazine,* wept with joy and pride. Dickens was 24 when the astonishing success of his monthly instalments of *The Posthumous Papers of the Pickwick Club* started him on a literary career. The essential humanity of his characters made his novels classics.

DICKENS'S DREAM *Part of an unfinished picture by R. W. Buss, it includes some of the many characters he created from seemingly futile and dull personalities, warming them with his genius into giants of wisdom and delight. (Dickens House)*

THE PICKWICK PAPERS *appeared in 19 monthly parts in 1836–7; it was paper-backed and sold at a shilling. The binders' order of 400 copies for the first issue rose to 40,000 for the 15th issue. This edition bound from the original parts. (Dickens House, 48 Doughty Street, London)*

THE GEORGE AND VULTURE, *a well-preserved inn of Lombard Street in the City where Dickens had Mr Pickwick stay. It was this middle-aged, bespectacled innocent whom Dickens, as a young reporter under the pseudonym of Boz, was employed to write about in a monthly magazine 'The Posthumous Papers of the Pickwick Club'. In a few issues he had perceived in this old man a romantic adventurer who would 'dance and jump, defy tyrants, experiment with life even act the knight errant'. The British public recognised Pickwick with delight and Dickens rose from obscurity to immense fame and popularity in one year.*

NANCY'S STEPS *on the south bank of the Thames, close to London Bridge, where the 'good bad' girl of 'Oliver Twist' kept the rendezvous which led to her murder. During the murder scene, which Dickens re-enacted so powerfully in his famous public readings, numbers of ladies regularly fainted and had to be carried from the hall.*

GRAVES AT COOLING *in Kent which Pip, in 'Great Expectations', says belonged to his parents and five young brothers. Dickens considered this novel his most perfect work, and much of the material is autobiographical, the hero's initials being the same as his own in reverse.*

THE FORGE AND COTTAGE *at Chalk in Kent, which were used by Dickens in 'Great Expectations' as the home of Pip, when the boy lived with blacksmith Joe Gargery and his wife. When writing this novel in 1860, Dickens was plagued with none of his usual doubts and misgivings.*

STUDY OF FORT HOUSE *in Broadstairs which Dickens bought in 1850. The study is on the first floor, 'about the size of a warm bath', and possessing a large window commanding a magnificent sea view. At this house he spent holidays with his wife and ten children until his marriage fell apart in 1858. The novelist's hysterical letters giving details of his matrimonial problems, which he insisted on having published in the daily press, shocked an adoring public, who regarded him as a pillar of security and Victorian morality. The house was renamed Bleak House by a subsequent owner, although the novel 'Bleak House' was not written here, nor was it the house described in the book. However, there are many interesting relics and manuscripts on view to the public.*

DICKENS'S WATCH, *a relic at the Rochester Museum. The novelist's headlong race against time ended with his premature death from overwork at the age of 58. He had asked to be buried privately and therefore the time of his funeral at Westminster Abbey was kept a close secret and only 13 people attended. It was not so much the furious pace of his writing that killed Dickens as the strain of giving a series of dramatic public readings from his works.*

QUILL PEN AND INKSTAND *at Dickens House, Bloomsbury, where the author wrote 'Oliver Twist'.*

SWISS CHALET *where Dickens did much of his later writing. It was given him by the actor Charles Fechter and rebuilt, plank by plank, among the cedar trees in the garden of Gad's Hill Place. Dickens had the walls lined with mirrors. (Rochester Museum, Kent)*

**Rockingham Castle** *Northants.*  *547Gg*
Built for William the Conqueror, the castle was used as a royal fortress until Queen Elizabeth I granted it to Edward Watson, whose descendants have lived here ever since. Here in 1095 William II (Rufus) was excommunicated by Archbishop Anselm. Charles Dickens was a frequent visitor. The present house and gardens are mainly Elizabethan, but the Norman gateway with crenellated round towers survives. The house contains fine furniture and a collection of paintings.

**Roker** *Durham*  *558Dg*
CHURCH OF ST ANDREW A massive church designed by E. S. Prior, built in 1906–7 with a solid-looking Gothic-inspired tower above the chancel. St Andrew's has Arts and Crafts Movement fittings: Morris & Co. wove the Burne-Jones tapestry behind the altar; there is a William Morris carpet; the altar cross is by Ernest Gimson; and there are tablets by Eric Gill.

**Rolleston** *Staffs.*  *552Dc*
CHURCH OF ST MARY The church is of mainly 14th-century work, and contains several fine monuments with effigies of the 16th and 17th centuries.

**Rollright Stones** *Oxon.*  *546Ed*
A circle of some 100 ft diameter is demarcated by 11 standing stones and, close by, there is a single standing stone, the King Stone, which probably had its place in the original design.
   A little to the east is the stone group known as the Whispering Knights. These form a rectangular chamber with a capstone and are the remnants of the megalithic structures formerly covered by a long barrow, all other traces of which have disappeared.

**Romaldkirk** *Yorks.*  *558Bf*
CHURCH OF ST ROMALD Late 12th-century church with 13th- to 15th-century additions; the low tower is Perpendicular, with a vaulted roof inside. An effigy of a knight, 1304, remains, and there is a Norman font and an 18th-century pulpit.

**Romsey** *Hants.*  *541Gd*
An ancient market town, the centre for the New Forest. Near the abbey is King John's House, a hunting lodge built in 1210; it has fine Norman dog-tooth carving.
ABBEY CHURCH OF SS MARY AND ETHELFLEDA The nunnery was founded in 907. The present cruciform church dates from later in the 10th century; it was enlarged by the Normans, and again during the 13th century. Among its treasures is a Saxon sculpture depicting the Crucifixion, and on an outside wall of the south transept is another Saxon carving of Christ Crucified. Among the monuments is an effigy of a 13th-century woman, and there is an early 16th-century painted reredos. The church was saved at the Dissolution, as it was bought by the town for about £100.

**Roslin** *M'loth.*  *562Ce*
ROSLIN CASTLE The 3rd Earl of Orkney built this castle, now in ruins, during the 14th century, and here the Scots defeated Edward I of England in his war with King Robert de Bruce.
ROSLIN CHAPEL The 15th-century chapel of a proposed collegiate church founded by William, Earl of Roslin and Orkney. It is noted for its superabundance of ornament, and the famous 'Prentice Pillar. This is purported to have been finished by an apprentice during his master's absence. The latter on his return was so enraged by this youthful skill that he hit the boy with a mallet and killed him.

**Rossendale** *Lancs.*  *552Bg*
RAWTENSTALL MUSEUM Situated in the former mansion of a Victorian mill-owner, the museum displays collections of natural history, Egyptian and Roman antiquities, ceramics and a collection of paintings. There is also a comprehensive collection of items of local history, including the craft of clog-making, and musical scores and instruments of the little-known music group who were called the 'Deighn Layrocks' (the Larks of Dean), and who flourished from the middle of the 18th century.

**Ross-on-Wye** *Herefs.*  *546Bd*
Though its origins are Roman, modern Ross owes much to John Kryle, known as the Man of Ross, born in 1637 and a natural town developer. He laid out the Prospect Gardens, raised a causeway to Wilton Bridge, created the first public water supply, and reconstructed the topmost 47 ft of the unsafe church spire. The Market House was built in 1670, a red sandstone structure, on arches. The Blake Memorial Gardens were laid down by Thomas Blake, first M.P. for the Forest of Dean. The almshouses in Church Street are more than 300 years old.
CHURCH OF ST MARY THE VIRGIN Large church dating from the 12th century, with 13th- and 14th-century and later additions. There are many monuments dating from the 16th century, with recumbent, kneeling or standing effigies; one of the latter shows a 17th-century soldier, Colonel Rudhall, in Roman armour.
WESTON HALL A red sandstone gabled house of *c.* 1595. The interior panelling dates from 1700. Contents include a painting by Robert Byng of horsemen and hounds in 1706.

**Rotherfield** *Sussex*  *542Ce*
CHURCH OF ST DENYS A large 13th-century church, with later additions and a west tower and shingled spire. The north porch of St Denys's has two storeys, vaulted inside, and the nave has a wagon-roof. The 13th-century wall-paintings include a Doom, and St Michael weighing souls; there are remains of Perpendicular screens. The font cover is dated 1533 and the pulpit is from the 17th century. In the east window is fine stained glass by William Morris and Sir Edwin Burne-Jones.

**Rotherfield Greys** *Oxon.*  *547Gb*
CHURCH Not a large building, and almost wholly rebuilt in the 19th century. It contains the magnificent canopied monument to Francis Knollys and his wife, erected by their son William in 1605. Kneelers around the base include William's first wife; he is on the canopy with his second wife.

**Rotherham** *Yorks.*  *552Ef*
CHURCH OF ALL SAINTS One of Yorkshire's grand parish churches, in an industrial town. The grimy exterior is in the Perpendicular style, with a central tower and tall spire. The interior, also mainly Perpendicular, has fan-vaulting under the tower, panelled nave and chancel ceilings, a south chapel screen, and tracery on stalls and bench ends. There is a 17th-century pulpit, and a monument of 1806 by John Flaxman. The church was restored in 1873–5 by Sir Gilbert Scott, who also designed some of the stained glass.
MUNICIPAL MUSEUM AND ART GALLERY The museum is housed in a small mansion built *c.* 1780 by John Carr of York for the Walker family (who founded the Rotherham iron trade), and which has been partly restored to 18th-century decorative style. Possibly the largest publicly-owned collection in Britain of Rockingham china can be

THE 'PRENTICE PILLAR, ROSLIN CHAPEL

*According to legend, the apprentice who carved this pillar was killed by his jealous master. The chapel was founded in 1446 by Sir William St Clair, dissolved in 1511, and left in disrepair until restored in 1842.*

seen, including one of the two famous 'Rhinoceros' vases. There are other examples of South Yorkshire pottery, a collection of gemstones, and Roman antiquities from the forts at Templeborough, including a granary re-erected in the museum grounds.

**Rothesay** *Island of Bute, Bute*  560Fe
ROTHESAY CASTLE The ruins of a 13th-century moated castle of the royal Stewarts. The castle is still a royal possession and the Scottish Dukedom of Rothesay is held by the eldest son of the monarch. Four round towers are linked by a curtain wall enclosing a circular courtyard and keep—such a plan, with a keep surrounded by an outer shell, is rare in Scotland. The gate-house and apartments were added by James IV and James V (of Scotland).

**Rothwell** *Lincs.*  553Hf
CHURCH OF ST MARY MAGDALENE A church interesting for its Saxon west tower and the Norman work inside—nave arcades with sturdy round columns and arches with zigzag ornament.

**Roughtinglinn** *Northld.*  562Fd
A small promontory fort, cut off from the main hill by from two to five ramparts. The internal area is less than 2 acres. To the east of the fort is a rockface with a remarkable display of cup-and-ring markings, many of which are elaborated.

**Rough Tor** *Cornwall*  538Dd
On Bodmin Moor are many different types of structure believed to belong to the second half of the Bronze Age, though none has been closely dated by excavation. Within a radius of about a mile of Rough Tor are two stone circles, a ruined stone fort and groups of enclosed fields with remains of their owners' circular huts.

The circles, Fernacre and Stannon, are about 150 ft and 140 ft in diameter and are remarkable for having been constructed of many irregular stones, instead of the usual matched ones. Each still has 70–80 stones, of which more than half are standing. The ruined 'fort' or defensive site is on the higher part of the Tor, and the settlement-group is on lower ground at the south-west end of the ridge.

413

**Rousham** *Oxon.* 546Fd
CHURCH OF SS LEONARD AND JAMES Standing by the manor house, an Early English and later Gothic church with a west tower. The lower part of the chancel arch is Norman, and the rest has been modified in a Gothic style; there is a 15th-century parclose screen, and the monuments include one with 16th-century figures facing each other in prayer.

**Rousham House** *Oxon.* 546Fd
A Royalist garrison used this mansion during the Civil War and shooting holes then made in the doors are preserved. The castellated house was built in 1635; it was enlarged *c.* 1730 when William Kent decorated the rooms and laid out the gardens—his only surviving landscape design—with temples, statues and hanging woods above the Cherwell.

**Rowlstone** *Herefs.* 546Ad
CHURCH OF ST PETER A 12th-century church with later additions. There is an early Norman nave, and the chancel arch and south doorway have good Romanesque carvings of birds and foliage. The tympanum over the south doorway represents Christ in Majesty.

**Royal Holloway College** *Surrey* 542Ag
This gigantic building, in the style of a French château, was made of stone and brilliant red brick, as one of the first women's colleges, in 1879–87. The Holloway Sanatorium, of 1884, is its companion piece, a mile to the south-west.

**Royal Leamington Spa** *Warks.* 546Ef
The medicinal value of the spring water here was discovered in the late 18th century and the town grew rapidly. Aylesford Well was opened up in 1813 by the 5th Earl of Aylesford. Many fine Regency houses like those at Bath were built and in 1814 the Royal Pump Room was opened. Queen Victoria granted the Royal prefix to the town name in 1838.
ART GALLERY AND MUSEUM The oil paintings, water-colours and drawings are mostly 20th century, though there are earlier works by Abraham Bloemart, Richard Wilson and Peter de Wint. Among the modern painters represented are Stanley Spencer, L. S. Lowry and Graham Sutherland. The collection of ceramics includes examples of medieval, Tudor, Delft, Wedgwood, Worcester, Liverpool and Derby ware, and there is a large collection of 18th-century drinking glasses.

**Royal Tunbridge Wells** *Kent* 542Ce
The wells near Tonbridge became known in the early 17th century as a health-giving spa, through the accidental discovery of its waters by Lord North while staying at nearby Eridge Castle. The place soon became fashionable, but at first there were so few buildings that when Henrietta Maria, Charles I's wife, went there, she was obliged to camp in the countryside. However, the Pantiles, the famous parade of galleried buildings with the spring at one end, was begun, and after the Restoration of Charles II there were further developments; Evelyn the diarist thought it a 'sweet place'. A church was begun in 1676 and soon enlarged. Inside it has a gallery and a splendidly rich plaster ceiling. The church is dedicated to the king's father, 'King Charles the Martyr'. A story is told that the first child baptised in its fashionable font was that of a gipsy-woman passing through the town. During the 18th century Tunbridge Wells flourished and was visited by such personalities as Dr Johnson, David Garrick, and Beau Nash. About 1830 Calverley Park, a series of terraced

RUFFORD OLD HALL

*Rufford Old Hall was built of wood in early Tudor times and added to between 1491 and 1523 by the owner, Thomas Hesketh. The 43 ft by 23 ft interior is richly carved. 'Speres'—short screens designed to cut down draughts—stand at the serving end of the hall and there is a moveable screen which was used to shield diners on the dais. This, one of the few such screens to survive intact, dates from about 1500. It is covered with intricate Gothic carving, including three extraordinarily elaborate finials.*

villas overlooking a private park, was built by Decimus Burton—a version of the idea John Nash had put into effect at Regent's Park in London.
MUSEUM AND ART GALLERY Items illustrating life in the town and surrounding district are displayed; there are collections of Tunbridge ware, dolls, 18th- and 19th-century toys, costumes and old prints. A group of Victorian paintings is included. Other sections relate to local geology, prehistory and natural history.

**Ruabon** *Denb.* 551Jd
CHURCH The many monuments include work by Joseph Nollekens, a large reclining figure by J. M. Rysbrack and, from the beginning of the 18th century, three life-size figures, one standing and two kneeling, by Robert Wynne of Ruthin.

**Rubers Law** *Rox.* 562Dc
The forts here show evidence of two periods of construction. They began by the enclosing of a considerable area with a wall lying well below the hill-top. Later, this was superseded by a smaller work, a wall enclosing only the top of the hill. It has been pointed out that some of the stones used in this later work show traces of being re-used Roman stone.

**Rudding Park** *Yorks.* 558Cb
This Regency mansion, set in a woodland park designed by Humphry Repton, contains collections of tapestries, porcelain, paintings and books, and an exhibition of figurines.

**Rudh an Dunain** *Skye, I'ness.* 564Ee
The cairn is 65 ft in diameter and 11 ft high. The eastern side has a concave forecourt, from which the entrance leads into an antechamber and a polygonal chamber.

A short distance to the south-east stands the galleried dun. It consists of a thick wall cutting off the tip of a headland and still stands some 9 ft high. The wall contains galleries.

**Rufford** *Lancs.* 551Jg
CHURCH OF ST MARY A small Victorian church, built in Gothic style in 1869 to replace an earlier building. There are many monuments to the Hesketh family, including one of *c.* 1458 showing 11 children; other monuments include one by John Flaxman (1817) and one with an effigy by Matthew Noble, *c.* 1874.
RUFFORD OLD HALL AND FOLK MUSEUM Presented to the National Trust in 1936 by the late Lord Hesketh, the Old Hall is a medieval timber-framed manor house with an ornate hammerbeam roof and screen. The great hall itself was built *c.* 1480, and the east wing in 1662—a good example of late Jacobean brick architecture. The folk museum was begun in 1936 and consists of ancient agricultural implements, domestic appliances and items of local craftsmanship. Domestic life during the Industrial Revolution is depicted, and period costumes and Victoriana are on show. The Hall contains 17th-century oak furniture including a magnificent Tudor tester bed, court and press cupboards, the Hesketh Collection of 16th-century arms and armour, old English coins, and Brussels and Mortlake tapestries. Some Neolithic tools and Roman remains can be seen, a display of antique porcelain, Staffordshire figures and china, some 17th- and 18th-century books and examples of book bindings. There is also a doll museum and dolls, a Georgian doll's house and a collection of children's games.

**Rufus Stone** *Hants.* 541Gd
A stone monument, erected in 1745 by Lord de la Warr, marks the probable spot where William II—called Rufus because of his ruddy complexion—was killed by an arrow in 1100. Rufus, 3rd son of William the Conqueror, became King of England in 1087; the English Chronicle records that he was 'loathesome to well nigh all his people'. The fatal arrow may have been shot by the Norman knight Sir William Tyrrall. Rufus was hastily buried at Winchester without any ceremony.

**Rug Chapel** *Merioneth.* 551Hd
A private chapel, built in 1637 by William Salisbury, an eccentric who, after a spell at sea to learn the 'arte of pyracy', reformed and was known as 'Hosannau Gleision' ('Blue-stockings'). The building was known as 'Envy Chapel', supposedly because of a conflict between the builder and the rector of Corwen. Salisbury was a descendant of an earlier William who first translated the New Testament into Welsh in 1567. A certain amount of repainting of the roof took place in the 18th century, but it, the carved painted frieze and much of the furnishing are interesting.

**Rumblingbridge** *Kinross.* 562Ag
The modern bridge spans a 120 ft chasm. Beneath it is an earlier bridge, which was built in 1713.

**Rushton Hall** *Northants.* 547Gg
John Tresham began the Hall *c.* 1500; extensive additions were made in 1590–1600 by Sir Thomas Tresham, who began Lyveden New Building. After the Gunpowder Plot the house passed out of the Tresham family and was enlarged in the 17th and 19th centuries.

**Ruthin** *Denb.* 551Hd
CHURCH OF ST PETER Basically a 14th-century church; parts of the building were demolished after the Dissolution, and restoration was carried out during the 18th and 19th centuries. The aisle roofs, which have carved bosses, are original 15th-century work; there are brasses and monuments, including one by Sir Richard Westmacott.
EXMEWE HALL A half-timbered mansion owned by Sir Thomas Exmewe, Lord Mayor of London in 1517. It was restored in 1928.
LORDSHIP COURT-HOUSE A half-timbered house built in 1404. Once gallows were part of the house, as is shown by a gibbet projecting from the façade.
NANTCLWYD HOUSE A 14th-century mansion with a half-timbered front, gabled portico, oak carvings and wainscoting. Its gallery has pre-Tudor heraldic crests.

RUTHWELL CROSS

*Depicting Mary Magdalene washing Christ's feet, this is probably the earliest and certainly the finest Northumbrian high cross. The reverse side shows Christ being worshipped by the beasts. The cross dates from the late 7th century and shows eastern Mediterranean influence. Two of its original four arms are missing.*

**Ruthwell** *Dumf.* 562Ba
CHURCH In an apse specially built for it in the church stands a Saxon cross, 18 ft high. It is one of the two best preserved Runic crosses that survive from the Anglo-Saxon period—the other is at Bewcastle in Cumberland.

**Rycote** *Oxon.* 546Fc
CHURCH OF ST MICHAEL AND ALL ANGELS A 15th-century domestic chapel, with a west tower. Inside is some early 17th-century woodwork including two large family pews; one is in two storeys with an organ.

## Rye *Sussex* 542Ed

The name comes from the Anglo-Saxon word for an island, for the town stands on high ground well above the surrounding flat country which has at times been submerged by the sea. In Norman times Rye was a port and became a Cinque Port in 1336. It was razed by the French in 1377 and silting of the harbour caused poverty in the town in the 13th and 14th centuries. With the decline of nearby Winchelsea, Rye revived in the 15th and 16th centuries, but from the late 16th century further silting of the harbour led to a decrease in importance; today Rye itself is no longer a port—the harbour at the mouth of the Rother is nearly 2 miles away. Rye was notorious for smuggling, which centred on the 13th-century Mermaid Inn. Baddings Tower, a defence post, was sold in 1430 to John de Ypres to raise money, and has since been known as Ypres Tower. The Gun Garden near by was originally the site of a defence battery but was converted to a bowling green in 1649. Lamb House, built in 1722–4, was once the home of the author Henry James. The town hall dates from 1742.

CHURCH OF ST MARY A large cruciform church on the top of a hill, around which huddles the town. The church is basically Norman with additions up to the 15th century. Outside, on the north transept, is a clock whose mechanism was made in 1561 (the exterior was renewed *c.* 1760). Inside are Perpendicular screens, the Arms of Queen Anne, stained glass of 1897 by William Morris's firm, and monuments by John Flaxman and John Bacon the Younger.

MERMAID STREET The houses in Mermaid Street are typical of the medieval town of Rye. In this street the Georgian houses incorporate building from the 13th century onwards; the Old Hospital, a half-timbered building from the 15th and 16th centuries, is particularly notable.

MERMAID STREET, RYE

*Mermaid Street, an 18th-century development, suggests the prosperity which Rye once enjoyed through membership of the confederation known as the Cinque Ports. After the sea receded and its harbour silted up, the town declined in importance.*

## Ryhall *Rutland* 553Gb

CHURCH OF ST JOHN THE EVANGELIST Dating from the 12th century, the church has a fine tower and spire of the 13th century, wide nave and aisles, and original north arcade. There are 14th-century sedilia, and a rebuilt chancel of the 15th century. Among the memorials is a tablet of 1696 to an infant genius, and 17th- and 18th-century monuments. In the wall of the north aisle are fragments of a medieval hermitage which was dedicated to the cult of St Tibba (the patron saint of falconers) who died here *c.* 690.

# S

## Saffron Walden *Essex* 548Ae

An ancient town, the 'Waledana' of the Ancient Britons; remnants of their extensive earthwork fortifications remain to the west and south of the town. A Saxon burial ground has also been discovered. The keep of the Norman castle, dating from the 12th century, still survives. Near by is a series of circular excavations—the best surviving earth maze in England. Such mazes were once numerous; their origin and use are obscure, but they were probably pre-Christian and connected with fertility rites. The town takes its name from the saffron crocus, the growing of which was the most important industry from the reign of Edward III until *c.* 1790. Saffron was used as a dye and as a medicine and condiment; it is still the symbol of the town. Fine timber-framed houses of the 15th and 16th centuries and brick, or brick and flint, houses from later periods abound in the town. There are also examples of the East Anglian decorative plasterwork known as pargeting. Though now principally a market town, Saffron Walden has recently developed some light industry.

CHURCH OF ST MARY THE VIRGIN Nearly 200 ft in length, the church is probably the finest in Essex. It has a west tower with big pinnacles, and an octagonal spire added in 1831. Rebuilt in the 15th and 16th centuries, the roofs are contemporary; the church contains the tomb of Lord Audley, a Chancellor to Henry VIII, 19th-century stained glass, and many brasses and monuments.

## St Albans *Herts.* 547Jc

In Market Place most of the older houses have been altered, but No. 29, dated 1637, and No. 30, probably of the same period, give an indication of the street's character in the 17th century. In High Street No. 17 has interesting plaster decoration work intended to imitate stonework and convey an impression of great strength. Hollywell Hill, running down to the R. Ver, is mainly Georgian, but the White Hart, a timber-framed building, much restored, dates from the 15th century. St Peter's Street has some good 18th- and 19th-century houses, in particular the Grange (No. 14), a mid-Georgian country house. In Hatfield Road, the Marlborough Almshouses, built in 1736 by Sarah, Duchess of Marlborough, form an effective three-sided courtyard composition. Attractive streets with good examples of medieval and Georgian houses are George Street, Fishpool Street and Romeland Hill. At the end of Abbey Mill Lane, by the river, there is the famous Fighting Cocks Inn. This small timber-framed structure, octagonal on plan, is said to be the oldest inn in

# ST ALBANS ABBEY

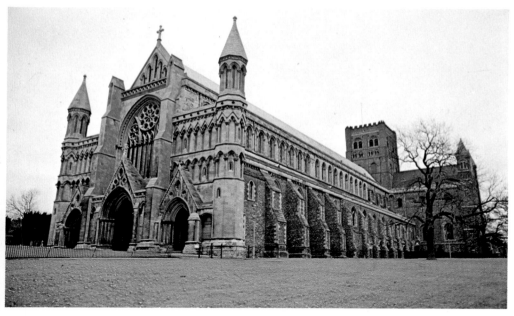

WEST FRONT *In the 12th and 13th centuries an extensive abbey, built around the shrine of St Alban, the first English martyr, existed; it was famous for its library, where Matthew Paris wrote his chronicle,* 'Historia Major'. *The present building is a fragment of the original abbey. Behind the reredos is the plinth on which St Alban's shrine once rested. A watching loft for monks appointed to guard it also survives.*

MURALS *When the Puritans' whitewash was removed from the abbey walls in 1877, a series of 13th- and 14th-century wall-paintings was discovered on the Norman nave piers.*

*On their west sides the Crucifixion is depicted, with a subject such as the Annunciation (left-hand picture). On the south sides saints such as Thomas à Becket are shown.*

SOUTH TRANSEPT *The Normans built much of the present abbey with its lofty arcades; the pillars in the triforium here are the only bits of the Saxon church they re-used.*

ROMAN MOSAIC FLOOR

*A magnificent multicoloured mosaic floor excavated at Verulamium in 1959. It dates from the 2nd century. In the centre a lion is depicted killing a stag—a subject in keeping with the 'other-world' ideas often used as themes for Roman domestic mosaics. (St Albans)*

ROMAN CASTOR POT

*This pot with figured relief work is an example of Castor ware, made in the district around Castor near Peterborough. Its decoration depicts hounds chasing a hare. Such scenes were popular with the hunt-loving Romanised Celts and the style was brought to Britain from the Continent. (Verulamium Museum, St Albans)*

England. Opposite is the 18th-century Silk Mill.
ABBEY The history of St Alban's Abbey is obscure from the 8th century until it emerged as a Benedictine community at the end of the 10th century. The abbey church and the gate-house are all that remain of the original buildings. The core of the church, which is the second longest in England, dates from the 11th century. It is dominated by a central tower of red Roman brick, pillaged from the Verulamium site near by. The original church was greatly enlarged to the west during the 13th century, and the Lady Chapel was added to the east side in the 14th century. At the Dissolution in 1539 the abbey church was taken over as a parish church, and the Lady Chapel was turned into a grammar school. In 1877 the present bishopric was created, at the same time the church was restored.
CHURCH OF ST MICHAEL The church has a Saxon nave and chancel, and this 10th-century work was opened during the 12th century when aisles were added. The saviour of the abbey, Lord Grimthorpe, restored this church at the end of the 19th century. There are 14th-century brasses, and a seated figure of Francis Bacon, who died in 1626.

CLOCK TOWER Built 1403–12, and situated in what was once the centre of medieval St Albans, this is one of the few belfries of that period to survive.
FRENCH ROW The first five houses are pre-Reformation, but a few others may date as far back as the 14th century. It is said that after King John of France was taken prisoner at Poitiers in 1356, he was for a time held in the Fleurs de Lys Inn which, despite considerable restoration, has its original timber framework.
ROMAN REMAINS The Roman *municipium* of Verulamium, one of the three destroyed by Boadicea during the Icenian revolt, was one of the finest towns in Britain. Rebuilt soon after its destruction, it had many excellent buildings and its full municipal status was a mark of its importance. Much of it is now covered, but the theatre—as distinct from an amphitheatre—with its colonnaded stage and auditorium, is still to be seen, as are many other remains. The fine museum close by also contains much material of importance. This Roman town was built partly over a former Belgic settlement, an *oppidum*, and in Prae Wood, just to the west, are remains of the north-west corner of its defences.

**St Andrews** *Fife.* 562Dg
At Magus Muir is the monument to Archbishop Sharp (1613–79), a pyramid of undressed rocks with an inscription in Latin describing his murder by Covenanters (Charles II's Presbyterian opponents). Near by are the Martyrs' Graves, of Covenanters routed and tortured by the Earl of Monmouth after the Battle of Bothwell Bridge, June 22, 1679. St Andrews has the oldest university in Scotland, founded in 1410. St Mary's College, founded in 1538, includes Old Parliament Hall above which the great mathematician and astronomer James Gregory (1638–75), inventor of the reflector telescope, carried out many experiments.
CATHEDRAL Founded during the 12th century, the cathedral was once large, but became ruinous after the Reformation. Beside it stands the ruined church and tower of St Regulus (or Rule), dating from the early 12th century.

**St Asaph** *Flints.* 551Ge
CATHEDRAL The smallest cathedral in England and Wales, smaller than many parish churches; it is cruciform, with a massive central tower. The earliest church was replaced by the Normans, but their work was destroyed by Edward I, and rebuilding began during the late 13th century. Part of the tower collapsed in the 18th century, and at the end of the 19th century the building was restored by George Gilbert Scott. There are some good 15th-century stalls; most of the glass is 19th century.

**St Bees** *Cumb.* 556Fe
CHURCH OF SS MARY AND BEGA A nunnery was founded here *c.* 650; destroyed by the Danes, it was refounded *c.* 1120. The present imposing cruciform Norman church dates from after this time, though the central tower was altered during William Butterfield's 19th-century restoration. There are some 19th-century monuments.

**St Benet's Abbey** *Norfolk* 554Dc
On the R. Bure, St Benet's is an early Benedictine monastery, possibly begun in AD 816. It was certainly re-established in 955, and was endowed under King Canute to become the great fortified abbey of St Benet-at-Holm. The few remaining ruins include the 15th-century west gate-house, dominated by a windmill. The outer walls (once enclosing 38 acres) and the church foundations are recognisable. The barn of Horning Hall Farm near by was the chapel of a hospice of the abbey.

## FIGURE OF THE GOD BES

*This ugly dwarf was an ancient Egyptian godlet of dance, music, mirth and children. When worn as an amulet, Bes was a talisman against serpents and other harmful creatures, and also against evil spirits. He was guardian of the home—but at one time also a god of war. This figure of blue glass paste, just over an inch high, dates from about 600 BC, from the Sais dynasty. (Pilkington Museum of Glass, St Helens)*

## GEORGE IV GLASS DECANTER

*A decanter made about 1801 for George, Prince of Wales, who was later George IV. The two coats of arms he used between 1801 and his accession in 1820 are engraved on the decanter. Its base and the stopper are decorated with bands of diamond shapes. Decanters of this shape are often known as 'ships' decanters' but by no means all of them were used on board ship. (Pilkington Museum of Glass, St Helens)*

**St Briavels Castle** *Glos.*     *546Ac*
Norman fortress, prison and manor court for the Forest of Dean, its Constable being Warden of the Forest of Dean. Arrowheads called 'quarrels' were manufactured at the castle in the Middle Ages—Henry III ordered 6000 in 1223. In 1310 the Constable was ordered to send 100 archers and 12 miners to assist in the siege of Berwick: the Forest miners were used to undermine the town walls. On Whit Sunday villagers of St Briavels are given bread and cheese, a ceremony commemorating a right obtained for them by the Countess of Hereford to gather wood.

**St Catherine's Point**     *541Gb*
*Isle of Wight, Hants.*
LIGHTHOUSE A unique structure, resembling a rocket on its launching pad, built *c.* 1314 as part of a penalty imposed by the ecclesiastical courts on a local landlord found guilty of wrecking.

**St Clere's Hall** *Essex*     *548Dd*
One of the few surviving 14th-century moated farmhouses with an aisled hall. The wings were altered in the 16th century.

**St. David's** *Pemb.*     *544Bd*
Small cathedral city. The 12th–14th-century cathedral of the patron saint of Wales is built of purple sandstone from local quarries: it is notable for its Irish oak nave roof and its 116 ft tower. Near by is the 14th-century bishop's palace, unoccupied for the past 300 years, and preserved as an ancient monument.
BISHOP'S PALACE The impressive cathedral close at St David's is bisected by a small stream, and most of the official and residential buildings are in the western half. St David's was always the richest of the Welsh dioceses, and the palace remains reflect this wealth. Grouped around three sides of a court-

yard are the remains of three separate halls and ancillary buildings dating from the 12th–15th centuries. Most impressive is the great hall on the south, which was built by Bishop Gower between 1327 and 1345. A unique feature of his work is the arcaded parapet, which here encircles all the earlier roof: this same curious detail is to be seen at his smaller palace at Lamphey in the south of the county, and also at Swansea Castle.

**St David's Head** *Pemb.*     *544Bd*
PROMONTORY FORT This small promontory fort is one of the most beautifully sited in Wales, being at the extreme end of St David's Head, with a magnificent view of Ramsey Island and Sound to the south-west. The defences, which may not be of only one period, consist of a strong stone rampart with two outer banks. Internally there are a number of stone huts and rock shelters, while the whole area between the fort and Carn Llidi is rich in prehistoric remains.

**St Donat's Castle** *Glam.*     *545Hb*
This castle is in fine condition, due to almost continuous habitation culminating in extensive restorations by William Randolph Hearst, the American millionaire, in 1925, and finally to its present use as the Atlantic College. Basically a concentric plan, it dates from the 13th and 14th centuries, although it must have had Norman beginnings, as did the little church in the vale immediately beneath it. Hearst's restorations were thorough and skilful; he introduced masonry details and woodwork from many parts of Britain.

**St Endellion** *Cornwall*     *538Dd*
CHURCH OF ST ENDELIENTA A church on a hilltop, with a Norman font, and some carved bench ends. There is a tomb-chest of *c.* 1400, which might be the shrine of St Endelienta.

**St Fagans Castle** *Glam.* *545Hb*
Only a low curtain wall remains of the original
13th-century castle; the wall now surrounds a
16th-century house, which is the Welsh Folk
Museum. Exhibits on the property include: a barn,
from Flintshire, period 1550–1600, removed and
re-erected; a wooden mill (1760) complete with
machinery, removed from Brecknockshire; a
wood-turner's shop; a basket-maker's shop; four
farmhouses, from Denbighshire (1570), Montgomeryshire (1600), Radnorshire (1730), Gower
(1730); a chapel dated 1777 from the Vale of Teifi;
and a cottage (1762) from Caernarvonshire.

**St Germans** *Cornwall* *538Ec*
CHURCH OF ST GERMANUS An imposing Norman
monastic church on the site of a Saxon cathedral.
There are two west towers, one of them octagonal
in its upper stages. Inside are fragments of stalls and
screen. The east window is by Burne-Jones. There
is a large monument by J. M. Rysbrack to Edward
Eliot, 1722.

**St Govan's Chapel** *Pemb.* *544Cc*
The chapel and well are dramatically set just above
high-water mark in a cleft in precipitous cliffs,
reached by a path from above. The tiny stone-
vaulted chapel probably dates from the 14th
century; at the side of its original stone altar is a
doorway leading to a small chamber in the rock
face. The well was frequented for cures as late as
the mid-19th century.

**St Helens** *Lancs.* *551Jf*
PILKINGTON MUSEUM OF GLASS The collection
traces the development of glass-making through
the ages; it includes an ancient Egyptian god-
figure, as well as examples of English and
continental craftsmanship. (See p. 419.)

**St Helier** *Jersey* *540Ea*
JERSEY MUSEUM AND BARREAU GALLERY Paintings by Millais, a Jersey artist, are included in the
collection, which is devoted to Jersey's natural
history, and its people's life from the earliest times.
There is a display of Jersey coins and bank notes
from the time of the Gauls to the German occupation during the Second World War.

**St Ives** *Cornwall* *538Ab*
ZENNOR FOLK MUSEUM Collections relate to the
local trades and industries of mining, quarrying,
fishing, farming, and the craft of the blacksmith.
There is a fine collection of old ploughs, an original
open hearth and a model of a typical Cornish tin
mine, with a mill and process plant. Also on view
are archaeological items of the region: stone axes,
stone tools, querns and models of archaeological
remains.

**St Ives** *Hunts.* *547Jf*
Once a village called Slepe, a slippery landing place
on the R. Ouse, St Ives became a manor of
Ramsey Abbey in 969. A priory cell of the abbey
was set up *c.* 1050 and dedicated to St Ivo, a Persian
bishop whose supposed remains were miraculously found in a nearby field. The priory supplanted the village, which thus acquired the name
of St Ives.

The six-arched bridge was built in 1415, but the
two southern arches were reconstructed in 1716. A
two-storey 15th-century miniature chapel is
preserved on the bridge. Only a ruined wall
remains of the priory, but the nearby parish church
dates from the 14th century. Its spire has been
rebuilt several times, most recently in 1918 after it
was hit by an aircraft.

The best house in St Ives is the Elizabethan
manor house by the bridge, with fine brick

ST MICHAEL'S MOUNT

*This rocky Cornish island is probably Ictis, from
which Mediterranean merchants obtained tin in the 1st
century BC. By Edward the Confessor's time it was
held by monks and, for about 100 years after, when it
was owned by the island abbey of Mont St Michel off*
*the Breton coast, it was an important centre for
pilgrimages. The present buildings date from the 12th
century but the Chapel of St Michael, with battlemented tower, was not begun until the 15th century. The
monastery was transformed into a mansion after 1659.*

chimneys. A great fire in 1680 destroyed 122 houses, and few built before that date have survived.

NORRIS LIBRARY AND MUSEUM The miscellaneous collection is entirely from the county of Huntingdonshire and ranges from pottery to fen skates.

**St Margaret's at Cliffe** *Kent*          *543Ge*
CHURCH OF ST MARGARET OF ANTIOCH A fine Norman church, with a squat, battlemented west tower. There is rich decorative detail inside in the carving over the nave arches, and on the exterior in the Norman arcading along the whole length of the nave. There is also a fine west doorway. The church was restored *c.* 1869.

**St Mawes Castle** *Cornwall*          *538Cb*
The coastal defences which Henry VIII erected as a precaution against a French invasion after the Dissolution stretched from the eastern Kent coast right round to Cornwall in the west. Near Falmouth, where the estuary of the R. Fal is wide, two forts were built: Pendennis Castle and, on the other side of the estuary, its counterpart, St Mawes Castle. The fort at St Mawes, on Roseland peninsula, was begun in 1540 and completed three years later. As it was intended as a military defence against attacks from the sea, the landward side was neglected; it took one day for Cromwellian troops to take the castle during the Civil War. Similar in style to Henry VIII's other coastal defence forts, the castle consists of a central circular keep with three semicircular bastions for the gun positions. An unusual feature is the display of heraldic decoration and various carved inscriptions, one of which runs round the keep below the battlement.

**St Michael Penkevil** *Cornwall*          *538Cb*
CHURCH OF ST MICHAEL Rebuilt by G. E. Street, 1862–6. Noteworthy for the monument to Admiral Boscawen (1763) by Rysbrack, and others to the Boscawen family by Joseph Nollekens later in the same century.

**St Michael's Mount** *Cornwall*          *538Aa*
A monastery built on an island, like its more imposing partner off the Brittany coast, Mont St Michel. The original buildings are of the 12th century, but after the Dissolution the monastery passed through many families until the present family, St Aubyn, came into possession during the later 17th century and converted it into a mansion.

**St Monance** *Fife.*          *562Dg*
CHURCH On a rock above the sea; dating from the 14th century, it consists of the choir, transepts and central tower with a small spire.

**St Neot** *Cornwall*          *538Dc*
The church stands near the St Neot R., a tributary of the R. Fowey, in a wooded valley. It is famous for its 15th- and 16th-century stained glass windows. Just outside the village is the holy well of St Neot, an Anglo-Saxon monk, supposedly of royal parentage and related to King Alfred; his relics were removed from St Neot in Cornwall to St Neots in Huntingdonshire.

**St Neots** *Hunts.*          *547Jf*
An old riverside market town of Saxon origin, with a number of good houses, including the Bridge Hotel, 1685, the Cross Keys Hotel of the same period, and some old houses that belonged to merchants, flanking the Hen Brook.

**St Nicholas** *Glam.*          *545Hb*
TINKINSWOOD This slightly wedge-shaped barrow, some 130 ft long by 57 ft wide, had a typical horned forecourt leading to the entrance. The stones of the cairn were held in position by dry-

15th-CENTURY STAINED GLASS

*The oldest stained glass in the church at St Neot dates from between 1480 and 1530, the windows depicting the stories of Adam (shown above), Noah, St George and Creation being the earliest. Although restored in 1829, they are important as showing the glazing of a remote church. Almost certainly produced locally, the windows show the work of English craftsmen before their traditional style was submerged in the Renaissance. (Parish Church, St Neot)*

stone walling, reinforced towards the west end by several parallel rows of upturned stones. The entrance led immediately into the chamber, which was constructed of several large slabs of stone on edge. These supported an enormous capstone, some 22 ft by 15 ft and estimated to weigh more than 40 tons. The gaps between the stones were filled by drystone walling. In addition, about half way along the length of the mound, on the north side, there was an enclosed chamber or 'pit', not approached from the side. The relationship of this barrow to the Cotswold group is very close.

**St Osyth** *Essex*          *548Dd*
CHURCH OF SS PETER AND PAUL The parish church is outside the walls of the abbey. Of 13th-century origin, it dates mainly from the 16th century when the nave and aisles were rebuilt in brick, with a plain hammerbeam roof. It contains some monuments with effigies, *c.* 1580.

**St Osyth's Priory** *Essex*          *548Dd*
The chapel and tower are of the 13th century, and the great gate-house was restored in the 15th century. The art collection includes ceramics and jade carvings.

**St Winnow** *Cornwall*          *538Dc*
CHURCH OF ST WYNNOCUS The church is in an attractive position on the bank of the R. Fowey. Originally Norman, it was later rebuilt. There are some fragments of medieval stained glass, 16th-century bench ends and a 17th-century pulpit. The 16th-century rood screen has been restored.

## SALISBURY CATHEDRAL

EXTERIOR *The glory of Salisbury Cathedral is its graceful spire, 404 ft high and the tallest in England. The cathedral is unique among English medieval cathedrals for it was planned as a single unit, and not built over several centuries as the others. Begun in 1220, the Early English Gothic building was finished 60 years later and only the spire was added afterwards —in 1334. The impressive west front, with its rows of niches with statues of saints, is just as the 13th-century builders left it.*

CHAPTER HOUSE *This magnificent octagonal building was constructed in 1263–84. It is 58 ft in diameter and round the walls are 49 seats for the members of the Chapter. The graceful central column (shown right) was renewed in 1856 when the building was carefully restored to its original splendour.*

**Salford** *Lancs* 552Bf
PEEL PARK MUSEUM AND ART GALLERY The art gallery has the largest public collection of paintings and drawings by L. S. Lowry in Britain, and the museum centres around 'Lark Hill Place'—a reconstruction of a small 19th-century street.
SCIENCE MUSEUM The building, erected in 1825 and designed by Sir Charles Barry, was converted for use as a museum in 1906. Its main collections are of natural history and mining technology, including a replica coal mine beneath the building, and associated material on mining. Also on view are good collections of birds and mammals.

**Salisbury** *Wilts.* 540Fe
CATHEDRAL The Norman cathedral was at what is now Old Sarum, where its plan can still be seen in

the grass, but at the start of the 13th century the See was moved to New Sarum, or Salisbury. The present cathedral is the only English one built in the Middle Ages as a single conception, and not piecemeal as were all the others. The foundations were laid in 1220, and about 60 years later this magnificent Early English cathedral was finished. Its spire was added in 1334. There are many interesting monuments, including the spectacular brass to Bishop Wyville, *c.* 1375, who is shown standing in a castle. The main decorative elements inside the cathedral are the dark columns of Purbeck stone which appear throughout the building—particularly dramatically in the Lady Chapel. In the 14th century Edward III granted a licence to build a wall round the cathedral and the houses of those who served it, and much of this wall surrounding the close survives. The close is still entered through medieval gateways, and many of the houses within it date from the Middle Ages, despite the Georgian exteriors; the bishop's palace and the old deanery were certainly built in the 13th century. To the south of the cathedral lies the magnificent 13th-century chapter house and cloisters.

CLOSE (NO. 68) Built in 1720, the house has a fine entrance hall and oak staircase, and an oak-panelled library with elaborate plaster ceiling. (By appointment.)

NORTH CANONRY A herbaceous garden in the cathedral precincts.

SALISBURY AND SOUTH WILTSHIRE MUSEUM Nearly all the finds from Stonehenge excavations are displayed. There are collections of natural history; guild and craft relics; a wide selection of medieval pottery from Old Sarum, Clarendon, Laverstock, Winterbourne, Mere and the New Forest; a Roman mosaic pavement from Downton, made *c.* AD 330; local costumes and bygones. There is also a collection of English pottery, china and glass.

THEOLOGICAL COLLEGE Built in the 17th century to designs by Wren, with extensions by William Butterfield in 1881, the college has a great staircase and interesting fire-places.

**Sall** *Norfolk*                     554Cc
CHURCH OF SS PETER AND PAUL An early 15th-century church, with a later 15th-century north transept. Among the families who contributed towards the cost of the building were the Boleyns. Both north and south porches are two-storied. The wide nave-roof and carved bosses in the chancel are decorated with angels. The seven-sacrament font was given in 1489, and is surmounted by a contemporary canopy on a pulley. The carved stalls have poppy-heads and misericords. There are many brasses, including a shrouded skeleton of 1454, and some original stained glass.

**Saltash** *Cornwall*                 538Fc
ROYAL ALBERT BRIDGE This bridge over the R. Tamar was the last built by the engineer Isambard Kingdom Brunel, who died in the year it was completed, 1859. The difficult crossing of the Tamar, with its deep, shifting course, had for many years delayed completion of the Great Western Railway's line from Bristol to Truro, but with Brunel's achievement London, Bristol and Cornwall were at last linked. The bridge is half suspension, the other half comprising a series of flattened tubular arches; its high brick piers straddle the town.

**Saltcoats** *Ayrs.*                  561Gd
NORTH AYRSHIRE MUSEUM The museum illustrates the history, industry—mainly shipping and coal mining—and domestic life of northern Ayrshire.

**Saltfleetby** *Lincs.*               553Jf
CHURCH OF ALL SAINTS Once a Norman church, but there has been much later rebuilding; the Early English tower had its Perpendicular top added during the 15th century. There are two pulpits, one Elizabethan, the other 17th century.

**Salt Island** *Anglesey*             550Df
Early in the 19th century Holyhead and Howth, north of Dublin, became the principal Irish packet ports. The engineer John Rennie was responsible for Holyhead's attractive harbour office, customs house and imposing Doric portico reminiscent of the lamented Euston 'arch'. On Salt Island pier stands his lighthouse; though disused, this most attractive little building has survived almost intact,

ROYAL ALBERT BRIDGE, SALTASH

*Isambard Kingdom Brunel, who helped his father Sir Mark Brunel engineer the Thames tunnel from Wapping to Rotherhithe, was appointed engineer to the new Great Western Railway in 1833. It was a time of great railway expansion; after linking London with Bristol, the company wanted to penetrate into remote Cornwall—but a stumbling block was the difficult crossing of the R. Tamar which marks the boundary with Devon. Brunel accepted the challenge. The deep and shifting bottom of the river presented him with enormous problems but he persevered and by 1859 his bridge was finished. On May 14 the Prince Consort rode across in a train, and the line was open through to Truro. Today this bridge, on which Brunel's name is proclaimed in large letters, is paralleled by the road bridge of 1963.*

and is complete with original lantern and gallery. Like the light at Howth, which it closely resembles, it was lit by gas.

**Saltram House** *Devon*              538Fc
The original 17th-century Tudor house, set in a fine landscaped park, was acquired by the Parker family in 1712, and remained in their possession until 1957. In the 1740's it was altered, and Georgian Classical façades were added to mask the remains of the older house. Much of the interior was also redesigned then. Later the saloon and dining-room were transformed by Robert Adam, who also designed an orangery for the gardens. The house is noted for its fine furniture, china and a collection of pictures including 14 portraits by Sir Joshua Reynolds. (See p. 424.)

**Sandal Magna** *Yorks.*              558Ca
CHURCH OF ST HELEN A cruciform church, with a central tower, mainly of the 14th and 15th centuries; the west end was lengthened in the 19th century. Inside there is a Perpendicular screen, a Restoration font of 1662 and monuments, including one by Edward Physick (1828).

**Sandford Orcas Manor** *Dorset*      540Dd
Built *c.* 1540 in classic Tudor style on earlier 11th-century foundations, the house contains period panels, furniture, woodwork, and collections of silver, china, glass and rugs.

**Sandiacre** *Derbys.*                552Ed
CHURCH OF ST GILES An interesting Norman church, with later additions, on a hill. The tall

## THE SALOON AT SALTRAM HOUSE

John Parker and his wife Lady Catherine came to live in this Tudor house, with views over Plymouth Sound, in the 1740's, and they set about redesigning it in Classical style. Fine plaster ceilings date from this time, and are traditionally ascribed to Italian workmen; they show many birds, cherubs and flowers representing the 'Art of Music' in the morning-room and the 'Seasons' in the Red Velvet Drawing-room. The entrance hall ceiling has a central panel showing Mercury in Flight. The chimney-piece here is probably by Thomas Carter, and has a central relief of 'Androcles and the Lion'. In about 1768 Robert Adam designed the saloon—one of the most beautiful neo-Classical rooms in the country. The great Axminster carpet was especially woven for it in 1770. The room contains a fine collection of paintings including works by Reynolds, Rubens, Gheeraerts and Murillo. The one over the fire-place is after 'The Andrians' by Titian in the Prado Museum, Madrid, and its exquisite frame may have been designed by Adam as part of the room's architecture. He probably also designed the candelabra which stand at each corner of the room. Adam also repaired damage caused by fire in 1778, and the dining-room is of this date.

424

14th-century chancel is almost as long as the nave, and has good tracery in the windows. The chancel arch is Norman.

**Sandleford Priory** *Berks.*        *546Fa*
At one time an Augustinian priory, it is now St Gabriel's School and has a 14th-century chapel. The oval drawing-room was restored in the 18th century, with work by Adam and Wyatt. Capability Brown landscaped the garden. (By appointment.)

**Sandling Park** *Kent*        *542Fe*
The park is noted for its formal and woodland gardens.

**Sandon** *Staffs.*        *552Cc*
CHURCH OF ALL SAINTS A church of the 13th to 15th centuries. It has a Norman font, a screen, and a 17th-century pulpit; noteworthy are monuments to the family of Erdeswick, and 17th-century wall-paintings of trees bearing heraldic shields.

**Sandon Hall** *Staffs.*        *552Cc*
Home of the Earl of Harrowby, the house is set in 50 acres of gardens, open to the public, with flowering shrubs, lawns, roses and rare trees.

**Sandown** *Isle of Wight, Hants.*        *541Hc*
ISLE OF WIGHT MUSEUM OF GEOLOGY More than 5000 fossils that have been found on the island are displayed. Diagrams, maps and models make the exhibits interesting to non-technical visitors as well as to geologists.

**Sandringham House** *Norfolk*        *554Ac*
A private country residence of the Queen; it was built by Edward VII when Prince of Wales in 1869–71. The grounds are open to the public when the Royal Family is not in residence.

**Sandwich** *Kent*        *543Gf*
Once a thriving port (one of the Cinque Ports), Sandwich is now over 2 miles from the sea, so much has the estuary of the R. Wantsum silted up. The little town is a network of narrow streets, punctuated by three huge churches, two of them never properly repaired after their towers collapsed in the 17th century. The tiny oblong square in front of St Peter's Church is the centre of the town's life today. High Street, to the east, is the most handsome street, but the best houses are in the north-west corner of the town: Manwood Court, built of typical Sandwich pale yellow brick in 1574, and the King's House, also 16th century. Off Strand Street is the picturesque, but mainly modern, tollhouse.
CHURCH OF ST CLEMENT A large and splendid church, mainly of the 14th and 15th centuries, but with a magnificent Norman central tower whose exterior has three tiers of arcading below the battlements. There is also a Norman doorway with carved decoration, and misericords. The site may have been the cemetery of nearby Roman Rutupiae (Richborough).

**Sapperton** *Glos.*        *546Cc*
DANEWAY HOUSE Linked, as its name implies, with Danish incursions in the 9th century, the present house dates from 1338 when it was owned by the Clifford family. It passed in 1603 to a distant descendant, Robert Hancox, whose family lived here until 1860. The building has 14th-, 17th- and 18th-century additions, including the twin-gabled wing, with entrance and sun-dial, which was added in 1710. (By appointment.)

**Sarnesfield** *Herefs.*        *546Ae*
CHURCH OF ST MARY A pretty Norman church of the 12th century. The west tower dates from the

following century and there is a 14th-century tie-beam roof in the nave. There are fragments of 14th- and 15th-century stained glass.

**Sawbridgeworth** *Herts.*        *548Ad*
CHURCH OF ST MARY THE GREAT A large church with a west tower, all mainly 14th century. The stained glass, 1864, is by Hardman. The octagonal font dates from *c.* 1400, the pulpit from the 17th century. There are many brasses and monuments, by Abraham Storey and others. One, unattributed but most interesting, is to Viscount Hewyt, *d.* 1689.

**Sawston Hall** *Cambs.*        *548Ae*
A formal country manor house built in 1553, home of the Huddleston family for more than 400 years; it contains family portraits, tapestries, oak panels, antiques and a priest's hiding hole. The long gallery is 100 ft long. A portrait of Mary Tudor is attributed to Guillim Stretes.

**Saxtead Green** *Suffolk*        *548Ef*
MILL A fine example of an East Suffolk post-mill (in which the whole body of the mill revolves on its base) of *c.* 1700 or earlier. The mill proper stands on a tall round house, with a long flight of steps leading to the hooded porch. It has four main sails, a fantail, and interesting machinery. (See p. 426.)

**Saxton** *Yorks.*        *558Db*
CHURCH OF ALL SAINTS The chancel arch and south doorway remain from All Saints' original Norman period. Later additions include the Perpendicular west tower. Inside, there are remains of a Saxon cross and a monument to two children by J. F. Moore (1783). In the churchyard there is an unusual survival—a tomb from *c.* 1461.

**Scarborough** *Yorks.*        *559Gd*
Anciently called Skardeburge, ravaged by the Danes under Harald Hardrada in 1066, incorporated by Henry II in 1181, and now a resort. The castle was built in the mid-12th century. The remains of a Roman signal-station of AD 370 can be seen in the castle yard.
ART GALLERY The permanent collection shows modern original prints, and oil paintings and water-colours by local artists. There are frequent temporary-loan exhibitions.
CASTLE The site of Scarborough Castle has been intermittently occupied since the Bronze Age. The headland on which it sits is a natural defensive site but the main defences now visible date from the 12th century. They were probably begun under William Le Gros, Count of Aumale, and included part of the present curtain wall. The main defensive feature of Scarborough is the keep, built in the reign of Henry II; it was probably completed between 1157 and 1167. Scarborough was an important strategic point on the east coast of England and remained in royal hands up to the reign of James I.
Throughout the 13th century it received attention, and King John spent the then enormous sum of £2000 on it. Many of the towers on the curtain wall probably date from this period. Thereafter, like many castles, it suffered a period of neglect, but in the late 14th century funds for its repair were placed on a regular basis and it survived the remainder of the Middle Ages intact.
CHURCH OF ST MARTIN A 19th-century church, by G. F. Bodley. It is built in Gothic style, and contains a spectacular display of decoration by Bodley himself and many of his Pre-Raphaelite friends. There is glass and mural painting by Burne-Jones; the chancel roof is by Philip Webb and William

SAXTEAD GREEN MILL

*There has probably been a windmill on this site since 1309 and it is certain that the present mill was worked by one Amos Webber in 1796; since then it was used continuously for producing flour until 1947. It is a fine post-mill—one in which the body carrying sails and machinery rotates on an upright post—and is 46 ft tall with a sail-span of 54 ft. The body is set on top of the roundhouse containing the millstones and other machinery. The 'fantail' at the rear automatically keeps the sails square into the wind.*

Morris; and Rossetti, Ford Madox Brown and others worked on the walls, pulpit and stained glass.

CHURCH OF ST MARY Due to severe damage in the Civil War, St Mary's is now only a fragment of the original cruciform church; the chancel has more or less disappeared, so that what was once a central tower now stands at the east of the building. Of the remaining medieval architecture, the most interesting pieces are the arcades, 12th- and 13th-century piers, and the series of chapels off the south aisle. There are many good monuments, including one of the 18th century by Roubiliac, and one, in the Bacon tradition, of the 19th century, by Edward Physick.

MUSEUM The museum was originally simply a rotunda, built by the Scarborough Philosophical Society in 1829 to a plan suggested by William Smith, 'the father of English archaeology'. The circular form was intended to display Smith's discovery of the stratification of rocks, and the wings were not added until 1860. The collection concentrates on the archaeology and bygones of the region of North-east Yorkshire—Mesolithic finds from Starr Carr, Iron Age finds from Castle Hill in Scarborough and Roman finds from the signal-station near the castle. Items of special interest are a Bronze Age oak trunk coffin, and pottery from the Iron Age, Roman and medieval times.

MUSEUM OF NATURAL HISTORY, WOOD END The museum shows material relating to the geology, fauna and flora of the region and is housed in the former seaside home of the Sitwell family.

ROMAN SIGNAL-STATION The castle stands on a headland on the north side of the town. In the narrow space between it and the cliff-edge are the preserved remains of this signal-station. The superstructure would have been a small square building surmounted by a tall tower. This station was one of five which lay along the Yorkshire coast between Saltburn and Filey. Built *c.* AD 370, they were intended to detect the approach of seafaring raiders, mainly Picts, from the north.

**Scarisbrick Hall** *Lancs.*                                         551Jg
A mansion built by the architects and neo-Gothic designers Augustus Charles Pugin (1762–1832) and his son Augustus Welby Pugin (1812–52). (By appointment.)

**Scilly Isles** *Cornwall*                                      538Af
The five main islands were occupied by the Phoenicians, whose principal interest was in the tin mines of Cornwall. In the days of sail, the Isles were a notorious navigation hazard: part of a British naval squadron under Sir Cloudsley Shovel in the *Association* was wrecked here in 1707.

**Scole** *Norfolk*                                              554Ca
WHITE HART INN One of the finest old coaching inns in England. Built of red brick in 1655, and resembling a mansion rather than an inn, it is crowned with five Dutch gables in front and more at the back. It has giant angle pilasters, square chimney-stacks with arched panels and, inside, a great oaken staircase. The Arms of the builder, John Peck, a Norwich merchant, are still visible over the door.

**Scone Palace** *Perths.*                                     566Ca
The present palace with castellated towers and battlements was built in 1803 on the site of an ancient abbey and palace dating back to the earliest days of recorded Scottish history. Here in 843 King Kenneth I brought the Stone of Destiny on which Scottish kings were crowned. This stone, the Stone of Scone or 'coronation stone', remained here until 1296 when Edward I took it to Westminster Abbey, London, to form part of Edward the Confessor's Chair, used in English coronation ceremonies. In the state rooms of the castle are collections of Vernis Martin vases, ivory statuettes, porcelain, French furniture and paintings.

**Scotney Castle** *Kent*                                       542De
Colourful landscape gardens surround the ruins of a moated round tower (Scotney Old Castle) built in 1377, and parts of a Tudor manor house.

**Scotstarvit Tower** *Fife.*                                   562Cg
The 17th-century residence of Sir John Scott (1585–1670), lawyer and Privy Councillor.

**Scrivelsby Court** *Lincs.*                                   553He
The Lion Gate at the entrance to the park of Scrivelsby Court is the emblem of the unique office of Hereditary Champion of England, which the Dymoke family have held since the time of Richard II. The Champion's duty was to appear mounted and in full armour at the coronation and challenge to the death any man who might deny the king's right to the throne. The ceremony was last performed in 1821. Old Scrivelsby Court has been pulled down and replaced by a newer and smaller Georgian house. The Lion Gate was rebuilt in the 19th century.

**Seaham** *Durham*                                             558Dg
CHURCH OF ST MARY The long nave of this church near the sea was perhaps built by the Saxons. The font is very old, from the early 13th century, and the chancel and west tower are also 13th century; the pulpit was made in the 16th century.

## SEATON DELAVAL HALL

SOUTH FRONT *Sir John Vanbrugh, the playwright who turned so successfully to architecture, began this great house about 1718 for Admiral George Delaval. It was completed about 1728, after the architect's death. The house, one of the great feats of architecture of the early 18th century, comprises a huge centre block between two arcaded and pedimented wings. At various times the house has suffered tragically by fire. In 1822 the centre block was gutted and for many years stood a gaunt ruin, but it was restored in 1959–62.*

DAVID AND GOLIATH *Although this is an 18th-century English lead copy of a 16th-century Italian marble statue, it is one of the most intriguing pieces of sculpture in England, since it is a unique record of a lost masterpiece. In the middle of the 18th century lead copies after famous statues, classical or modern, were a fashionable way of decorating gardens. When the original was modern, it was usually in an English collection, and there is therefore a strong possibility that the original of this vigorous group is standing somewhere neglected in England. The original must have been the work of the Florentine sculptor Vincenzo de' Rossi (1525–87), who is today a much underrated artist. If it is ever rediscovered, it should do much to rehabilitate him as a sculptor of considerable talent.*

**Seaton Delaval** *Northld.*      558Cl
CHURCH A pleasant little Norman church, which has chancel and apse arches with zigzag ornament. Inside are 14th-century effigies of a knight and lady.

**Seaton Delaval Hall** *Northld.*      558Cl
A splendid English baroque house, regarded by many as Sir John Vanbrugh's masterpiece. It was built *c.* 1718–28. The centre block, between two arcaded wings, is the main feature of the house and has quite different architecture to its two main fronts. That on the north is noted for its great Tuscan columns and strongly emphasised jointing of its stone facing. Above rises a high, pedimented storey. All the main forms are repeated on the south front, but here there is a giant portico of tall, fluted Ionic columns. The house contains fine furniture, portraits and ceramics. In the grounds are extensive gardens, an orangery, obelisks and statues.

**Sedbergh** *Yorks.*      557Jd
CHURCH OF ST ANDREW Originally a Norman building, but later additions are evident, notably the Transitional arcades, and the Perpendicular windows and tower. The pulpit is 18th century, and there are some brasses.

**Sedgefield** *Durham*      558Cf
CHURCH OF ST EDMUND Brasses of skeletons dating from 1630, and 13th-century effigies, vie for attention with the 18th-century organ and marble font at St Edmund's; but over all presides the elaborate, Gothically inspired rood screen of 1670. The choir stalls are also 17th century. The church is mainly Early English, with some later work; the west tower is Perpendicular.

**Sefton** *Lancs.*      551Jf
CHURCH OF ST HELEN The spire is 14th century and the rest mid-16th century. The interior is remarkable for the fine carved wooden fittings—stalls, font cover and canopied pulpit, and screens. Also remarkable are the many brasses and monuments to the Molyneux family, including a mailed effigy of *c.* 1296.

**Segontium** See Caernarvon.      550Ee

**Selborne** *Hants.*      541Je
CHURCH OF ST MARY A Norman church with nave arcade and later additions. Much of the remainder is mid-19th century. This restoration was made by a great-nephew of Gilbert White, the naturalist, who is buried in the churchyard, and is commemorated by a stained glass window depicting St Francis.

GILBERT WHITE MUSEUM AND THE OATES MEMORIAL MUSEUM Personal possessions of the naturalist Gilbert White and the Antarctic explorer Captain Oates are displayed in White's former home, The Wakes, a 17th-century house in 5 acres of grounds. There is an extensive library on natural history and polar exploration. Near by is Selborne Hill, where White made many observations recorded in *The Natural History of Selborne*.

## Selby *Yorks.* 558Eb
ABBEY The abbey was founded in the 11th century for the Benedictines, and its great church survived the Dissolution of the monasteries. It is a large, basically Norman, cruciform church, but was restored after a disastrous fire in 1906. There is a good Perpendicular font cover, and a 14th-century stained glass Jesse window.

## Sempringham *Lincs.* 553Hc
CHURCH OF ST ANDREW Only the nave arcades and doorways remain as good examples of Norman work in this former church of the nearby Gilbertine abbey. St Cuthbert's was much rebuilt in the 19th century, when the chancel was added.

## Sevenoaks *Kent* 542Cf
This big dormitory town for London keeps the top end of its High Street almost as it was in the 18th century (except for the traffic). Here is the church and, opposite, the Palladian Sevenoaks School, of 1727, based on a design by Lord Burlington. The Chantry, Old House and, further north, Red House, the best of all, are fine examples of gentlemen's houses of the reigns of William III and Queen Anne.

## Severn Bridge *Mon.* 546Ac
A majestic 3240 ft long suspension bridge, opened in 1966. The two towers are 44 ft high, the total width of the carriageway is 72 ft, and the total length of the bridge is 5240 ft. Unique in modern bridge design are the slender, widely spaced suspension wires, which hang in V-form to give extra rigidity to the platform.

## Shaftesbury *Dorset* 540Ee
ABBEY RUINS MUSEUM The museum contains objects found on the excavated site of Shaftesbury Abbey church—carved stones and medieval tiles—and has remains which may be those of Edward the Martyr. There are models of the church and Shaftesbury before 1539.
SHAFTESBURY AND DISTRICT HISTORICAL SOCIETY'S MUSEUM OF LOCAL HISTORY Shaftesbury's button industry is the subject of a main collection. Books and manuscripts on local history, local archaeological finds and collections of tools and crafts and Victoriana are also included. A manual fire engine dating from 1744, complete with leather hose and buckets, is preserved.

## Shalford Mill *Surrey* 542Ae
An 18th-century water-mill on the R. Tillingbourne.

## Sheffield *Yorks.* 552Df
Symbolic of the city's industries, Vulcan, god of the forge, crowns the 193 ft tower of the town hall, opened in 1897. The Cutlers' Hall, built in 1832, contains the unique silver collection of the Cutlers' Company founded in 1624, comprising at least one piece bearing the Sheffield hall mark for each year since 1773 when the Sheffield Assay Office was opened. The first annual Cutlers' Feast was held more than 300 years ago.
ABBEYDALE INDUSTRIAL HAMLET A late 18th-century scythe works, comprising a Huntsman crucible steel melting shop, forging hearths, tilt-hammers, grinding shop and workmen's cottages.

The machinery is operated by four water-wheels and is still in working order. The workshops are equipped, and the old warehouse block contains displays illustrating industrial development in the Sheffield area.
BEAUCHIEF ABBEY Only the west tower still stands of the 1175 foundation, but the ruins have been well preserved since the 17th century.
CATHEDRAL CHURCH OF SS PETER AND PAUL The cathedral is the former parish church, and is basically 15th century with tower and crocketed spire. Modern extensions with tower and lantern were consecrated in 1966, and there are plans to enlarge the building. There are many monuments from the 16th century.
CITY MUSEUM The first museum was opened in 1875; the present one, built in 1937, is a centre for information and research for North Derbyshire and South Yorkshire. It houses one of the world's largest cutlery collections, both Sheffield-made from the 14th century onwards and examples from the Stone Age to the present day from all over the world. There is also a large collection of Old Sheffield Plate. Other exhibits include Bronze Age pottery and antiquities collected from the Peak District in the 19th century by Thomas Bateman the antiquary, Derbyshire ornamental stonework, and local flora and fauna.
SHEPHERD WHEEL Two water-powered cutlery grinding shops dating back to the late 18th century. Shepherd Wheel, from which the establishment takes its name, is the only working example of a Sheffield cutlery master's grinding wheel to survive from this period. There was a wheel on the same site as early as 1584. (By appointment.)
YORK AND LANCASTER REGIMENTAL MUSEUM The history of the Regiment from 1758 to the present day is illustrated by medals, uniforms, weapons, pictures, photographs, books and manuscripts. Three Indian Mutiny Victoria Crosses and three First World War Victoria Crosses are among the medals.

## Sheffield Park Gardens *Sussex* 542Ce
Large gardens with five lakes linked by cascades, originally laid out by Capability Brown.

## Shellingford *Berks.* 546Ec
CHURCH OF ST FAITH A simple building without aisles; there is much Norman work, for example the south door and chancel arch. The windows are Decorated and Perpendicular Gothic, and some fragments of medieval glass remain. The Early English west tower has a spire added in 1625. There are several interesting monuments of the 17th to 19th centuries, including one by W. Tyler (1780) and one by John Flaxman (1802) of two Viscounts Ashbrook.

## Shepreth *Cambs.* 548Ae
DOCWRA'S MANOR A fine Queen Anne mansion and garden. (Interior not open.)

## Sherborne *Dorset* 540Dd
A small country town noted for its medieval buildings, its abbey, its school and two castles. Roger de Caen, Bishop of Old Sarum, began the abbey in the 12th century, and many additions were made until completion in 1490; some buildings were taken over by Sherborne School, which dates from 1550.
ABBEY CHURCH OF ST MARY The church of the former Benedictine abbey, which dates mainly from the 15th century; a Saxon doorway is still to be seen on the outside of the west wall of the north nave aisle. 'Great Tom', a tenor bell given to the abbey by Cardinal Wolsey, hangs in the tower.

## TILT-HAMMERS: ABBEYDALE INDUSTRIAL HAMLET, SHEFFIELD

*Constructed in 1785, these hammers forged scythe blades from steel made in the adjacent Huntsman furnace. They were driven by the water wheel, 18 ft in diameter, behind the large gear wheel.*

### ROCKINGHAM TRAY

*In 1826 Earl Fitzwilliam lent over £5000 to Thomas and John Wager Brameld, partners in the Brameld pottery at Swinton near Sheffield, and this gave a new lease of life to the factory. The Bramelds began selling porcelain as well as earthenware, and adopted the name Rockingham, and the griffin as their mark. In 1830 the Royal Dessert Service was made for William IV, but in 1842 the factory was forced to close because of financial difficulties. This small ornamental porcelain tray of about 1833 is painted in enamels with a view of Newstead Abbey, seat of Lord Byron, and is marked with the griffin. (City Museum, Sheffield)*

Inside the church there is a wealth of fan-vaulting. There are a number of fine monuments, including effigies of 13th-century abbots, but the most impressive is the large memorial by John Nost to the Earl of Bristol, *c.* 1698, with standing figures and mourning cherubs. There is a series of interesting carved misericords of the 15th century, and stained glass of the same period.

OLD CASTLE To the east of the town at Castleton is the castle built by Bishop Roger in 1107–39. It is one of the earliest castles with concentric walls of the 12th century. It was acquired by Elizabeth I, who leased it to Sir Walter Raleigh in 1592, and gave it to him in 1599. Raleigh attempted to modernise the property, but gave this up in order to build another castle, then known as the Lodge. The Old Castle suffered in the Civil War; it was badly battered by cannon in 1645, and dismantled by the Parliamentarians that same year.

SHERBORNE CASTLE Originated by Sir Walter Raleigh; the two wings of the H-plan were the work of the Earl of Bristol. Here in 1688 William of Orange issued his Proclamation to the English People.

**Sherburn in Elmet** *Yorks.*          *558Db*
CHURCH OF ALL SAINTS A large church with a west tower, in a commanding position on a hill.

Much survives of the late Norman work—the arcades, for example—and there is also Gothic work. A rare 15th-century cross-head is carved with figures of the Crucifixion.

**Sheringham Hall** *Norfolk*          *554Cd*
Built by Humphry Repton and his son, J. A. Repton, in 1812. It is noted for its rhododendron gardens. (By appointment.)

**Shifnal** *Shrops.*          *552Bb*
CHURCH OF ST ANDREW A large church built of the local sandstone, cruciform with a central tower. Originally Norman, there are many subsequent additions: the nave's hammerbeam roof and the chancel were probably added after a fire in 1591. There are 16th- and 17th-century monuments, and several stained glass windows of the mid-1800's. St Andrew's was restored by Sir Gilbert Scott *c.* 1876.

**Shillington** *Beds.*          *547He*
CHURCH OF ALL SAINTS The church has a wonderful hill-top site, typical of many in the Chilterns. Mainly the work of *c.* 1300, it has hardly been altered since, though the tower was rebuilt in the 18th century. There is a fine vaulted crypt under the chancel, partly built into the slope of the hill, and there are medieval screens and brasses.

SHIPLEY RELIQUARY

*This small reliquary or châsse is typical of those produced in large numbers at Limoges, central France, from the late 12th to the early 14th century. Typical of Limoges work are the rich blue background and the geometrical motifs containing brilliant bands of colour. Typical also are the gilt heads which were made separately and then applied, a method adopted probably for speed and cheapness.*

*Limoges was the most productive of all European enamelling centres from the late 12th to the late 13th century, and reliquaries, pyxes, crosses and other liturgical objects made there are found from Iceland to Cyprus, in great cathedrals and country churches. Because of this large-scale manufacture the châsses are very standardised and the scenes decorating them often bear no relation to the relics they enclose.*

*Limoges enamel is always champlevé on copper; where the copper is not enamelled it is gilt. In châsses of this type the metal plaques are sometimes fastened to a wood foundation. (Church of St Mary, Shipley)*

CHANCEL CHAIR

*The Norman church at Shobdon was rebuilt at the expense of Lord Bateman in 1752–6. He entrusted the work to the care of his brother Richard, a friend of Horace Walpole, the author and antiquary. The architect is unknown but he was a friend of Walpole's, perhaps William Kent or Richard Bentley. The church interior, all in pure Gothic style, has a striking blue and white colour scheme. This chair is one of a pair in the chancel and shows well the exquisite elaborate ornamental detail of the mid-18th century.*
*(Church of St John the Evangelist, Shobdon)*

**Shipley** *Sussex* 542A*c*
CHURCH OF ST MARY There is much fine Norman carving here and, in addition to the famous enamel reliquary, the notable Caryll monument.

**Shipton Hall** *Shrops.* 546A*j*
An Elizabethan manor house with a stone-walled garden.

**Shobdon** *Herefs.* 546A*j*
CHURCH OF ST JOHN THE EVANGELIST Once there was a 12th-century priory here, which was moved away. What remained of the church was rebuilt in 1752–6 (by a friend of Horace Walpole—the author and antiquary whose own house, Strawberry Hill, did much to popularise the 18th-century Gothic style), and is now a charming example of mid-18th-century Gothic. The chancel arch consists of a trio of ogee arches, with pendants instead of columns between them. There is a three-decker pulpit with a canopied sounding-board, and a monument of 1804 by Joseph Nollekens. There is some heraldic stained glass of 1753, but the font with carved lions dates back to the Norman church. In the park to the north, portions of the original church were erected as an architectural set-piece: the chancel arch, two Norman doorways and some now badly weathered sculpture.

**Shoreham-by-Sea** *Sussex* 542B*a*
MARLIPINS MUSEUM Housed in a building dating from the 12th and 14th centuries which was probably a feudal administrative headquarters of the port of New Shoreham, the museum specialises in the history of the ancient port and borough and the life of its people. Maritime exhibits include model ships and ship paintings, and there are local topographical prints and water-colours. A turret clock dated 1690 from the parish church

**Shorwell** *Isle of Wight, Hants.* 541G*c*
Perhaps the most characteristic of villages on the Isle of Wight, with many thatched cottages, three Elizabethan manor houses near by, and a splendid position under the ridge of Downs that bisects the island.
CHURCH OF ST PETER A mainly 15th-century church, with traces of earlier work, in a pretty village. It contains an interesting and unusual wall-painting of St Christopher. There is a 15th-century pulpit, and many memorials to the Leigh family, including one to Sir John Leigh with kneeling figures.

**Shottesbrook** *Berks.* 547G*b*
CHURCH OF ST JOHN THE BAPTIST A cruciform church in the Decorated Gothic style, its central tower topped by a steeple. There are two 14th-century tombs in the north transept, one of which is probably that of Sir William Trussell, who founded the church. Brasses of the 14th and 16th centuries remain, and there are several fragments of 14th-century stained glass. The font is also 14th century.

**Shotwick** *Cheshire* 551J*e*
CHURCH OF ST MICHAEL In a village where the Dee once flowed, a remote church with embattled west tower. Though mainly 14th century, a Norman doorway remains and inside there is a good three-decker pulpit, box-pews and a canopied church-warden's seat of 1673.

**Shrewsbury** *Shrops.* 551J*b*
ABBEY CHURCH OF THE HOLY CROSS Some Norman work is preserved in the abbey, founded *c.* 1080 by Roger de Montgomery. The font is reputedly made from a Roman capital, and the west tower has a fine Perpendicular window.

## ROMAN MIRROR FROM WROXETER

*Found during the excavations at the site of the Roman regional capital city of Uriconium (Wroxeter), five miles south-east of Shrewsbury, this silver mirror measures 11½ in. across. Apart from the handle it was cast in one piece, and was undoubtedly imported, the exquisite ornamentation suggesting that it came from an Italian workshop in the 2nd century or perhaps earlier. The handle is made of two loops of grooved silver wire, arranged to form a knot and soldered to the mirror back, the terminals being covered by four leaf-shaped ornaments; on each loop of wire are two six-petalled flowers. Leaves and fruits of the oak, apple and pine, with flowers, decorate the edge of the mirror back. (Rowley's House Museum, Shrewsbury)*

There are tombs and monuments dating from *c.* 1300 onwards, and remains of the 14th-century shrine of St Winifred. The chancel was designed by Pearson in 1887, and 19th-century stained glass can be seen.

ART GALLERY The collection consists mainly of paintings and drawings of the region by Turner, de Wint, David Cox, William Callow and others. Works by local artists are also on show.

CHURCH OF ST MARY The largest and most splendid of the several interesting churches in this medieval town; St Mary's is Norman, with Early English and later work. Its stained glass is especially important. There is a 14th-century Jesse window, and many windows with 15th- and 16th-century glass from Germany and the Netherlands, work by the craftsmen of Altenburg, Trier and Liège. There are several monuments, mainly of the 18th century.

CHURCH OF ST CHAD Old St Chad's Church dated from Norman times, but in 1788 the tower fell down. The fine 14th-century stained glass from its Jesse window was transferred to St Mary's Church. At first the intention was to rebuild St

Chad's on the same spot, but eventually the parish decided against this and the present site overlooking the Severn was obtained. George Steuart was chosen as architect and designed the circular church built in 1790–2. Years earlier James Gibbs had published his circular plan for the rebuilding of St Martin-in-the-Fields, London, and this could have been the source of Steuart's design. This comprises a square tower linked to the circular nave by a circular anteroom containing the stairs to the gallery. In its upper stages the tower becomes first octagonal, and then circular with detached columns supporting a cupola.

ROWLEY'S HOUSE MUSEUM A 16th-century timbered house containing a fine collection of antiquities from the Roman town of Viroconium (Wroxeter), as well as prehistoric and geological exhibits.

**Shugborough** *Staffs.* 552Cc
Seat of the Earls of Lichfield (the Anson family) containing the 2nd Earl's collection of 18th-century French furniture. The Staffordshire County Museum is housed in the former stable and

## SHUGBOROUGH

*The main block of this house was built for William Anson, father of Admiral Lord Anson. The admiral was responsible for the addition of a room in Chinese taste; in about 1747 he commissioned its decoration from drawings made in Canton by one of his officers. About 1760 Lord Anson's elder brother, Thomas, an ardent antiquarian, engaged James 'Athenian' Stuart to build the wings, and a sculpture gallery at right angles to the west front (shown below); the two wings have domed bows on the east side. Together Anson and Stuart laid out the park with much ornamental architecture in Classical style, including the Tower of the Winds (shown left). In 1803, in preparation for a visit by the Prince Regent, James Wyatt extended the west front of the main block to create an elegant saloon from what had been the dining-room. John Rossi provided the chimney-piece of the saloon and Peter Scheemakers carved the relief 'Et in Arcadio Ego'.*

kitchen wing of the house. In the park is a group of monuments based on the drawings *The Antiquities of Athens*, by James Stuart, painter and architect (1713–88), who introduced Greek-style architecture to England.

**Shute Barton** *Devon*      540Bc
A medieval castellated dwelling-house, built in 1390 with late 15th-century alterations. The gate-house, with mullioned windows, is early Jacobean, but the gazebo structures on its flanks date from after 1870. The kitchen has a huge fire-place; the hall, which is above the kitchen, has a trussed roof with curved wind-braces. (Interior by appointment.)

**Sibsey** *Lincs.*      553Jd
CHURCH OF ST MARGARET A Norman church near the Fen country—the nave arcades are particularly interesting. The west tower is Early English at its base and Perpendicular above. The south porch is dated 1699.

**Silbury Hill** *Wilts.*      540Fg
If this great mound really is a barrow, it is by far the largest in Britain. That it antedates Roman times is shown by the course of the east–west Roman road, which is sighted on to the mound and is then deflected to pass round it. Various excavations have been made to attempt to uncover its secret,

but so far they have failed. A new attempt has been planned and the mystery of Silbury may yet be solved.

**Silchester** *Hants.*      541Hj
This was the cantonal town known as Calleva Atrebatum and, though no internal buildings are today visible, the essential shape and defences of the area are clearly defined. There is an amphi-theatre, seen as an oval hollow, outside but close to the east end of the walled area. Its failure to become a town-site in post-Roman times has meant that, below the modern plough-soil, the bases of all its buildings are preserved.
CALLEVA MUSEUM Opened in 1951 as a contribu-tion to the Festival of Britain, the museum contains casts of some important archaeological finds, not-ably a freestone head of the god Serapis, a bronze eagle and an inscription found in a temple. A 2nd-century AD pottery jar containing cremated bones is also on view, with models of the west gate, a house and the church of the Roman town of Calleva Atrebatum. There is also an unusual collection of seeds found in old pits and wells on the site.
CHURCH OF ST MARY A medieval parish church, St Mary's has an early 18th-century pulpit, and medieval wall-paintings of masonry and flowers

SILBURY HILL

*The largest artificial mound in Europe, Silbury Hill is 130 ft high and covers 5½ acres. It stands near several prehistoric sites including Avebury and the West Kennet Long Barrow. Silbury is a mystery, for as yet no one has discovered what it is or why it was built. It may be a barrow—a prehistoric burial place. It was there before the Romans built their road from London to Bath, for the road makes a detour around the hill. At present excavations are in progress and exploratory tunnels are being dug into the hill.*

**Silkstone** *Yorks.*                    552Dg
CHURCH OF ALL SAINTS A Perpendicular, mainly 14th- and 15th-century church, with a west tower, replacing an earlier one. There are screens and a fine monument to Sir Thomas Wentworth and wife, *c.* 1675, attributed to Jasper Latham, a London mason-sculptor.

**Simonburn** *Northld.*                  558Ah
CHURCH OF ST MUNGO A 13th-century church rebuilt by Anthony Salvin in the mid-19th century. There is a fragment of a Saxon cross.

**Sissinghurst Castle** *Kent*           542De
The great Tudor and Elizabethan mansion of Sissinghurst Castle was little better than a derelict pile when in 1930 Harold Nicolson and his wife, Victoria Sackville-West, the authoress, acquired it. Round the restored buildings they created one of the loveliest gardens in England. The design is formal, and the main axis, which is a narrow walk between high yew hedges, cuts across the length of the site, widening in the centre to a rondel. The walk leads to small enclosures reminiscent of Elizabethan gardens. Prominent among the enclosures is the White Garden, planted with all silver-leaved and white-flowered plants and divided by low hedges of clipped box. Near the large rose garden, walled on one side and with a profusion of old-fashioned roses and flowering shrubs, is the Cottage Garden. This is reached from the far end of a long walk of pleached lime trees, and in it herbaceous plants grow among paving stones. Four Irish yews guard the entrance to the south cottage, which is covered by a yellow climbing rose. The small nut grove, underplanted with primulas and polyanthuses, is enclosed by formal yew hedges. (See p. 434.)

**Sissinghurst Court** *Kent*           542De
Extensive grounds with flowering trees, a rose garden, and yew gardens with lily ponds and fountains surround the 16th-century house.

**Sittingbourne** *Kent*                 542Ef
COURT HALL MUSEUM The collection, housed in a small manorial court-house of *c.* 1450, includes local archaeological specimens—Palaeolithic tools and Roman finds, and local bygones.

**Sizergh Castle** *Westmld.*            557Jd
The home of the Strickland family for 700 years, the castle comprises a 14th-century tower built as a shelter against Scots raiders, and additions made in the 15th, 16th and 18th centuries. It contains fine panelling and ceilings, pictures, furniture and Stuart and Jacobite relics.

**Skara Brae** *Mainland, Orkney*        569Hg
A Neolithic settlement of stone houses, preserved by being buried under blown sand. The houses are very closely grouped and each, internally, is roughly rectangular with rounded corners. These rooms contain furniture of stone 'planks' built into the main structure, which also includes box-beds, dressers, wall-cupboards and tanks for live fish. Some of the small finds from the excavation are preserved on the site.

**Skenfrith Castle** *Mon.*              546Ad
A Welsh border castle built by the Normans overlooking the Monnow Valley. It has a round keep surrounded by 13th-century walls with towers.

**Skipton** *Yorks.*                     558Bh
CASTLE A 13th-century fortification; perched on a rock, it was the stronghold of Robert de Clifford in 1309 and of the Clifford family for centuries. Its features include a great gateway with two round towers, a banqueting hall 50 ft long, a huge kitchen with a roasting and baking hearth, a dungeon, and a 'shell room' of sea-shells. The octagonal tower was built by the 1st Earl of Cumberland in 1536. The castle was the last stronghold of the Royalists in the North, but surrendered honourably in 1645 when it was 'slighted' (dismantled) by the Parliamentarians. Lady Anne Clifford (1590–1675) repaired and restored the castle.
CHURCH OF THE HOLY TRINITY A mainly Perpendicular church, with a simple west tower, standing by Skipton Castle. Inside are 14th-century sedilia with arches, screens of the 16th century, and a fine 17th-century font cover. There are 16th- and 17th-century monuments to the Cliffords, Earls of Cumberland.
CRAVEN MUSEUM The museum is concerned primarily with local history, natural history, and crafts. Antiquities include remains from Elbolton cave and an Iron Age sword.

**Skirza** *Caith.*                      569Me
BROCH Standing on a narrow spur of cliff above the sea, the approach to the broch from the main cliff-top is protected by a wide ditch. There is a wall, very thick in proportion to the enclosed space, the one being 14 ft thick and the other some

SISSINGHURST CASTLE GARDEN

A beautiful formal garden centred around the old tower of Sissinghurst Castle, created by Sir Harold Nicolson and his wife, Victoria Sackville-West the poetess and author, in the 1930's. From a derelict site, with husband as architect and wife as planter, after much experimentation a series of gardens took shape—each a faultless example of colour and form. A main walk between yew hedges leads from the tower, and to left and right are smaller enclosures, such as the White Garden with silver-leaved and white-flowered plants, and the rose garden. Near by is the Cottage Garden shown here, with a collection of old-fashioned plants.

22 ft across. The entrance is on the seaward side of the building and there is some evidence of minor additional structures.

**Sleaford** *Lincs.* 553Hd
CHURCH OF ST DENYS A grand church, dating from the 12th century; the west tower, with broach spire, was rebuilt in the 19th century. There is remarkable window tracery and an architecturally interesting interior, with brasses and several monuments, including one by Maximilian Colt of 1618, with alabaster effigies.

**Sledmere House** *Yorks.* 558Fc
A Georgian mansion, begun in 1751 and completed in 1787, with a great library (100 ft long) in Adam style. On view are Chippendale, Sheraton and French furnishings, porcelain and antique statuary; one room is uniquely decorated with Turkish tiles. The house stands in a landscaped park.

**Slinfold** *Sussex* 542Ae
The L-shaped group of Georgian cottages, chequered red and blue, behind white railings, is the best part of Slinfold.

**Smallhythe Place**
**(The Ellen Terry Memorial)** *Kent* 542Ee
Dame Ellen Terry, the actress, acquired this half-timbered house, dating from 1480, in 1902. It now contains items associated with Dame Ellen, Mrs Siddons, David Garrick and many other actors and actresses.

**Smarden** *Kent* 542Ee
One of the most unspoilt villages in the Weald of Kent: a short street of brick and weather-boarded cottages, leading up to the church; and, to the north-west, two big half-timbered houses, built by prosperous clothiers during the 17th century. One is dated 1671.

**Smedmore** *Dorset* 540Ec
An 18th-century manor, containing a collection of antique dolls.

**Smithills Hall** *Lancs.* 552Ag
A manor house with magpie façade. The great hall and adjoining rooms date from the 14th century; the remainder dates from the Tudor and later periods. The house was recently restored and contains fine Stuart furnishings.

**Snaith** *Yorks.* 558Ea
CHURCH OF ST LAURENCE A big church, originally Norman but rebuilt from the 13th to 15th centuries with west tower and battlements. Inside are various monuments from the 15th century onwards, including one to Viscount Downe (*d.* 1837) with a statue by Sir Francis Chantrey.

**Snarford** *Lincs.* 553Gf
CHURCH OF ST LAURENCE A small church begun in the 12th century, and worth visiting for three outstanding monuments: Sir Thomas St Pol (1582) with kneeling children, Sir George St Pol (1613) with recumbent effigies, and Robert, Earl of Warwick (1619) with alabaster medallion.

**Snowshill Manor** *Glos.* 546De
This manor house, dating from the 16th and 17th centuries, contains a collection of clocks, musical instruments, armour, scientific instruments, toys and dolls, bicycles, spinning wheels and fire-fighting equipment, over 15,000 items in all.

**Somerleyton Hall** *Suffolk* 548Fg
A 16th-century brick mansion, largely rebuilt in 1844. It contains carvings by Grinling Gibbons, tapestries and paintings. In the gardens is a maze.

**Somersby** *Lincs.* 553Je
MANOR FARM Built in 1722, with four towers and a castellated north front; the design is attributed to Sir John Vanbrugh.
SOMERSBY HOUSE The birthplace of Alfred, Lord Tennyson. Originally the rectory occupied by the poet's father, the Rev. George Tennyson, who designed the east wing extension in 'carpenter's Gothic'; it was built by his coachman, Howlins. The house has an elegant Georgian staircase.

**Sompting** *Sussex* 542Ad
CHURCH OF ST MARY THE VIRGIN A church with a Saxon tower, unique in England because of the four-gabled spire, known as a 'Rhenish helm'. There is some Saxon sculpture in the church, which was rebuilt during the 12th century by the Knights Templar. Their own vaulted chapel was made into a south transept during the 19th century. To the north of the church are the ruins of an extension made by the Knights Hospitaller.

**Southampton** *Hants.* 541Gd
A Norman walled and fortified city-port was built here. It was used for continental trade, and a vast influx of pilgrims taking the route via Winchester to the Becket shrine at Canterbury passed through the port. It was also a starting point for military forces bound for France, and the French frequently attacked the town, savagely so in 1338. A splendid civic centre has arisen out of the ruins resulting from the Second World War. Much of the old town, including the medieval walls, towers, and gates, and many Tudor and Georgian houses, still remains. The ancient ramparts are set with tablets commemorating events in Southampton's long history. Near by is the Pilgrim Fathers' Memorial, recalling their sailing on August 15, 1620.
BARGATE GUILDHALL The Bargate or Northgate was the most important gateway to medieval Southampton, where the town broker collected tolls on all merchandise entering or leaving the town. It was one of the seven main gateways, and dates from Norman times, its earliest feature being the half-round arch, *c.* 1175–1200. The guildhall, above this archway, was probably established *c.* 1400, and was originally used as the meeting place of the Guild Merchants and later of the Town Assembly. Now a local history museum, it includes among its exhibits two oak panels painted with the effigies of Sir Bevois, legendary hero of Southampton, and his giant squire Ascupart.
GOD'S HOUSE TOWER Originally part of the town's medieval fortifications, the tower is now a museum of archaeology, containing local pre-historic, Roman, Saxon and medieval finds. The oldest items displayed are a series of Old Stone Age (Palaeolithic) hand-axes from the gravel beds of the Southampton district, together with the teeth and bones of animals which inhabited the area during the Ice Ages and inter-glacial periods. There is a good collection of early medieval to late 17th-century pottery.
SOUTHAMPTON ART GALLERY Situated in the Civic Centre, it specialises in British paintings, but some French 19th-century and continental masters may also be seen. (See p. 436.)
TUDOR HOUSE A late 15th-century building with a Georgian wing, the house displays period furniture, tapestries, glass, domestic objects, costume and accessories, local topographical prints, paintings and drawings, and maritime exhibits. The garden, which is laid out in the formal style typical of the Tudor period, gives access to the remains of a Norman merchant's house of the 12th century, and contains a magnificent bronze cannon made for Henry VIII in 1542.
WOOL HOUSE Originally built during the 14th century as a medieval warehouse for wool prior to shipment, the Wool House is noted for its Spanish chestnut roof, which, apart from a few timber cross-ties, is of the same period as the main fabric. Carved on the beams are the names, with dates, of some of the French prisoners of war who were confined there during the 18th century. It is now used as a maritime museum.

**South Creake** *Norfolk* 554Bc
CHURCH OF ST MARY Mainly of the 15th century, the church shows signs of earlier work. Angels decorate the hammerbeam roof, and the octagonal font is of the East Anglian seven-sacrament type. Some early stained glass remains. Of the two brasses, one is a small effigy of a priest, *c.* 1400.

**Southend-on-Sea** *Essex* 548Ch
BEECROFT ART GALLERY European painting from the 17th century, with special emphasis on Dutch and Flemish painting of the 17th and 18th centuries and British schools from the 18th to the 20th century. A separate gallery of oil paintings, water-colours and drawings illustrates the history of Southend-on-Sea and shipping in the Thames Estuary. Temporary exhibitions of traditional and contemporary art are held every month.
PRITTLEWELL PRIORY MUSEUM The building itself incorporates the remains of a Cluniac priory founded *c.* 1110. These remains include the refectory of *c.* 1180, the half-timbered prior's chamber with its 14th-century roof, the cellars and the cloister garth. The foundations of the church, south transept and the east cloister wing are now being laid out in an individual garden.

The museum collections are housed in an early 19th-century wing, and cover the archaeology, history, social life and natural history of south-eastern Essex. They are particularly strong in the Iron Age and Romano-British periods.

SUTHERLAND *Red Landscape*

*The Englishness of English art finds in our time one of its purest exponents in Graham Sutherland. First he is English in his linear quality, which knits together with a wiry black thread the forms of his visionary landscapes, as in this 'Red Landscape'. Then he is English because landscape is the essence of his art—not landscape in the 18th-century sense, for he is not a scenic artist. He shuns perspective as it is not the look of the landscape but the feeling of it he is after. So his colour and luminosity are highly personal. His universe is one of strange forms and presences, of a hostile, sinister and mysterious Nature, of roots and thorns rather than fruits and flowers. These 'paraphrases of reality' as he has called them, are 'implications of the apparent tragedy of 20th-century civilization'. (Southampton Art Gallery)*

**South Harting** *Sussex* 541Jd
CHURCH OF SS MARY AND GABRIEL Impressive cruciform church, containing what may be Saxon work. The present building is mainly 14th century, restored after a fire in 1576. There is a central tower and broach spire, and a 13th-century font of Purbeck marble, with a 17th-century cover. There are several monuments, including, in the churchyard, a First World War memorial by Eric Gill.

**South Mimms** *Herts.* 547Jc
CHURCH OF ST GILES Basically 13th–15th century, with 16th-century additions; renovated *c.* 1877 by G. E. Street. There are 16th-century wood screens and stained glass, and some good tombs of the Fowyke family from the 15th and 16th centuries; also a 13th-century font.

**South Molton** *Devon* 539Gf
BOROUGH MUSEUM Housed in a building dating from 1620, the collection includes manuscripts and documents relating to local history, pewter—some of which, from Hanover, is dated 1585, and some marked Sandringham—weights and measures from the reign of William IV, a 1721 fire engine, a 1750 cider press, 18th-century wigmaking tools, and other items of agricultural or historical interest, including stocks and man-traps.

**Southport** *Lancs.* 551Jg
ATKINSON ART GALLERY A collection of early English water-colours and contemporary English paintings.
BOTANIC GARDEN MUSEUM Liverpool porcelain is a principal part of the collection. The 19th-century building has one room furnished in Victorian style. There are also local water-colours and relics, and a section devoted to British birds completes the collection.
CHURCH OF ST CUTHBERT The old parish church of Southport, rebuilt in 1730. The west tower and spire date from a few years later. St Cuthbert's was enlarged in the 19th century. There is a wall monument by Nollekens, *c.* 1791, showing carved

scientific instruments, an 18th-century font, and fine early 18th-century wood-carved reredos and panels by R. Prescott (from the demolished St Peter's, Liverpool).

**South Shields** *Durham* 558Ch
MUSEUM The museum contains a collection of model ships and lifeboats, notably an original model of the first lifeboat designed by William Wouldhave in 1789. The Sir Walter Runciman Natural History Collection can also be seen, and a collection of local glass.
ROMAN FORT AND MUSEUM The museum specialises in Roman antiquities—notably the South Shields Roman sword—and includes memorial stones, enamels, stamped roof tiles, bronze brooches, lead seals and Samian ware pottery.

**Southsea** *Hants.* 541Hc
ROYAL MARINES MUSEUM The museum was founded in 1955, with the aim of preserving objects related to the Royal Marines, past and present. The highlights are a medal collection which includes several Victoria Crosses, a display of military prints, portraits of former Royal Marine officers, a collection of military uniforms and a diorama of the action at Zeebrugge on April 23, 1918. The museum houses the offices of the Royal Marine historian, and there are many books, documents and photographs illustrating the history of the Marines.

**South Stack** *Anglesey* 550Df
Set on a small island connected to the mainland by an early suspension bridge reached by a descent of some 400 steps, South Stack presents a dramatic picture whatever the weather. The tower was built in 1809 and is little altered, although the station is now unmanned. One of the odd features of this site was devised in 1832: a small square revolving light was lowered to within 60 ft of the sea when fog obscured the lighthouse.

**Southwell** *Notts.* 552Fd
MINSTER The monastery was probably founded in the 10th century, perhaps even earlier. The church was begun in 1108, and has two western towers with reconstructed pyramidal roofs; the crossing tower is squat. The chancel is Early English of the 13th century, while late in the same century the chapter house was planned. This is famous for its carved foliage decoration. The church was raised to cathedral status in the late 19th century.

**Southwick** *Hants.* 541Hd
Once there was a mighty abbey here. Now the village has an Elizabethan church with a cluster of warm red cottages round it.

**Southwold** *Suffolk* 548Ff
A charming seaside town on a low cliff, once a centre for fishing and boat building, now a resort and holiday town. It has many open spaces, the greens being laid out to prevent further fires after a big fire in 1659. The town has flint and red-brick cottages, colour-washed houses and a white lighthouse. There is a museum containing local exhibits in the 'Dutch Cottage'.
CHURCH OF ST EDMUND, KING AND MARTYR A large, magnificent Suffolk church, with huge windows, a tall west tower, and a two-storey south porch. There is much flushwork decoration. Inside is a mutilated seven-sacrament font with 1930's cover, and a rood screen across the whole width of the church. There are also good stalls with carvings.
MUSEUM A 17th-century building, one of the earliest in the borough, houses a collection of local fossils, shells, birds, and relics, including some of the Southwold Railway.

## ITALIAN SALLET

*This late 15th-century helmet once hung over the tomb in Whaplode parish church (Lincs.) of Sir Anthony Irby, who died in 1625. An example of fine North Italian (probably Milanese) work, the skull is beaten out of a single piece of steel, and the whole decorated with strips of gilt copper. Originally the main surfaces would have been coloured blue. The helmet is a sallet, a popular 15th-century form of head armour. (Spalding Gentlemen's Society)*

**Sowerby** *Yorks* 558Dd
CHURCH OF ST PETER An 18th-century building in Classical style. There is a lively life-size statue of Archbishop Tillotson, who was born near by, by Joseph Witton (c. 1796). The original design for the statue is in the Victoria and Albert Museum.

**Spalding** *Lincs.* 553Hc
AYSCOUGHFEE HALL A 15th-century mansion restored in the 18th century, when it was the home of Maurice Johnson, who founded the Spalding Gentlemen's Society. It is now a natural history museum, including a collection of British birds.
CHURCH OF SS MARY AND NICHOLAS A church of varied styles, begun c. 1284, with additions of the 14th and 15th centuries. There is a Perpendicular hammerbeam roof with angels, Victorian stained glass and a screen of 1875.
SPALDING GENTLEMEN'S SOCIETY The society was founded at the beginning of the 18th century, and began with informal meetings at which a few local gentlemen gathered to discuss antiquities and read *The Tatler*. Its nature, however, soon became more formal, and its membership wider. Many notable 18th-century figures were among its members—Alexander Pope, George Vertue the engraver, Dr William Stukeley the antiquarian, Sir Isaac Newton and many noblemen. The Society's library was created by the gift of a volume from every new member, and through gifts, bequests and purchases it now contains extensive sections on archaeology, numismatics, local and natural history, heraldry and genealogy, as well as a large section on English and Scottish literature.
WHITE HORSE INN Built of stone and thatch, once the home of rich merchants, the Willesbys; it was then called Burguery House, and is perhaps the oldest dwelling in Spalding.

**Spean Bridge** *I'ness.* 565Hd
COMMANDO MEMORIAL Erected to the memory of Commando forces in the Second World War.

**Spetchley Park** *Worcs.* 546Ce
Some 20 acres of park with ornamental trees and shrubs, water fowl, and red and fallow deer.

**Spilsby** *Lincs.* 553Je
CHURCH OF ST JAMES Noteworthy for its monuments to the Berties and Willoughbys, from the 14th to the 17th centuries, many with effigies.

**Spofforth Castle** *Yorks.* 558Cb
The ruins of the former home of the Percy family, who received a licence to erect defences in 1308. The hall has 15th-century window tracery and a moulded doorway. The kitchens were part of the undercroft.

**Sprotborough** *Yorks.* 552Ef
CHURCH OF ST MARY Built between the 13th and 15th centuries, with a Decorated west tower. The furnishings include a rood screen, chancel stalls and carved bench ends. There is a brass of a knight (d. 1474), and other monuments.

**Spynie Palace** *Moray.* 566Dg
The ruins of a massive square fortress, built in the 15th century, and once the castle of the Bishops of Moray. The original tower was six storeys high.

**Stafford** *Staffs.* 552Bc
CHURCH OF ST CHAD A grand Norman church, with a superb chancel arch and impressive nave arcades.
MUSEUM AND ART GALLERY Items illustrating local history, social life, industry and art are on view; about 20 art exhibitions are held each year.

**Staindrop** *Durham* 558Be
CHURCH OF ST MARY Seven hundred years are chronicled in the impressive series of monuments at St Mary's, beginning with 13th-century effigies to the Earls of Westmorland, and continuing to the Duchess of Cleveland's memorial of 1859. Like much else in Co. Durham, the church's origins are Saxon; the west tower is Norman, and the transepts date from the 13th century. The font and stalls are in the Perpendicular style; the stained glass was made in the 19th century.

**Stalybridge** *Cheshire* 552Cf
ASTLEY CHEETHAM ART GALLERY Besides Egyptian, Greek and Roman antiquities and a collection of Italian, German, Flemish and Spanish pictures of the 13th–16th centuries, the gallery contains items on local history, geology and natural history.

**Stamford** *Lincs.* 553Gb
Stamford is one of the finest medieval towns in Europe. Recorded in the Domesday Book as a market, it later had a university and 17 churches, of which only six remain. During the Wars of the Roses, much of Stamford's architecture was destroyed by the Lancastrians. In 1566 Elizabeth I granted Lord Burghley the lordship of Stamford. The town became socially desirable in the 18th century due to the close proximity of the Great North Road. Much of the quality of Stamford's 17th- and 18th-century buildings is probably due to the famous architects who lived near by—the Adam brothers, Inigo Jones and John Thorpe, for example. The rich limestone strata on which Stamford is built accounts for the character of the town's architecture.
ALL SAINTS' PLACE The visual centre-point of the town. Nos. 1, 2, 3 and 16 are all good examples of 18th-century architecture.
BARN HILL A variety of Queen Anne, Georgian and Regency buildings. Barn Hill House, originally medieval, was rebuilt in the late 17th century and given a neo-Classical front c. 1843.
BASTION The Bastion in West Street is part of the original town wall, which once encircled Stamford. It has remained untouched for 700 years.
BRAZENOSE GATEWAY Situated opposite Stamford School is a relic of the Hall where rebellious students from Oxford tried to set up a rival university in the 14th century. The Whitefriar's Gateway, now the entrance to the infirmary, was part of the 14th-century White Friary.

### MONUMENT TO THE
### 5th EARL OF EXETER

*The Earl of Exeter was a leading patron of Italian sculpture, and while on a visit to Rome he commissioned a monument to himself and his wife from Pierre Monnot (1657–1733), a French sculptor whose most important work is the tomb of Pope Innocent XI in St Peter's, Rome. The Exeter monument was shipped to England in pieces and assembled in Stamford in 1704 by the English sculptor William Palmer; it is in the Roman baroque style and apart from the effigies of the earl and his wife in Classical dress, resembles the Papal tombs of the period. (Church of St Martin, Stamford)*

BROAD STREET Nos. 1, 3, 9, 14, 19, 25, 28, 30, 32 and 33 are 17th- and 18th-century houses. Browne's Hospital, *c.* 1480, founded by William Browne, a prosperous merchant, is one of the finest medieval hospitals (almshouses) surviving in England. The chapel contains a carved screen, original pews and early stained glass. The Audit Room has 16th- and 17th-century furniture.

BURGHLEY HOSPITAL AND ALMSHOUSES Originally founded by the Benedictine order in the 11th century. The semicircular arch, buttress and part of the river front all date from this period. In the 16th century Lord Burghley had it enlarged for the care of poor and aged people.

CASTLE Little remains at the foot of Castle Street other than the three blank 13th-century arches and part of the walling on the St Peter's Vale side. The castle mound and the base of a round tower were removed in 1935. The castle belonged to one of the barons who forced King John to sign the Magna Carta at Runnymede in 1215.

CHURCH OF ST MARTIN In a town with several good churches, St Martin's is probably best known, for its monuments to Lord Burghley (*d.* 1598) and to the Earl of Exeter by P. Monnot, 1703.

GEORGE HOTEL One of the original coaching inns, incorporating a 14th-century wooden screen in a lavatory. The remainder of the hotel includes building and decorations of the 17th, 18th and 19th centuries. Two rooms, labelled *London* and *York*, were formerly waiting-rooms for coach passengers. The crypt is part of the original Hospital of

the Knights of St John of Jerusalem, a military order primarily founded for the protection of pilgrims on their way to the Holy Land.

HIGH STREET Many well preserved 17th-century Georgian and Regency houses. St Martin's Church, 1480, was said to be a great favourite of Joseph Turner the painter and Sir Walter Scott the novelist; it has a 14th-century font and a large alabaster monument to Lord Burghley.

PRIORY ROAD In the west front of St Leonard's Priory are the remains of a Benedictine cell, *c.* 1082. Part of the original church, rebuilt in 1080 by the Norman architect of Durham Cathedral, still stands and has some well carved late Norman mouldings.

ROMAN RUINS The Romans had encampments to the north of Stamford at Casterton and to the south at Caster, with parts of the existing Ermine Street linking them. The old ford is marked accordingly by a stone pillar and carries a reference to Queen Boadicea.

ST GEORGE'S SQUARE Like other Stamford squares it has a village-like composition around its church. In the assembly rooms, 1725, is a large room with a coved ceiling and a great decorated chimney-piece. Nos. 14, 15, 17, 18, 19 and 20 are *c.* 1675; No. 21, which has a Doric doorcase, is *c.* 1740. The nearby Olive Branch Inn dates from 1666. The oldest house in Stamford, *c.* 1350 and still occupied, is in St George's Street and can be identified by its round stone chimney.

ST MARY'S HILL Some 17th- and 18th-century houses, with a Georgian town hall, *c.* 1777, and opposite this a Norman arch which probably led to the castle. Mr Scotney's antique shop near by was part of one of the six monasteries sacked in 1641, during the Civil War, and has a 13th-century crypt. Other crypts and passages below street level occur elsewhere in Stamford, all relics of religious houses. No. 11 St Mary's Hill incorporates the remains of a Norman dwelling, and Nos. 8 and 9, with timber-framed overhangs, are early 17th century, as are the warehouses facing the river. The large monumental archway to the works of Messrs C. Gray & Co. is late Classical, *c.* 1840.

ST PETER'S HILL A vista of bay windows, in a variety of shapes and sizes. Nos. 3 and 5 are from the 17th century. Stamford Institution, 1842, is in a Greco-Egyptian Revival style. In All Saints' Street No. 15 and the Wheatsheaf Inn were built *c.* 1630.

**Stand** *Lancs.*                                                552Bg
CHURCH OF ALL SAINTS Built *c.* 1825 by Sir Charles Barry, architect of the Houses of Parliament. Like them, All Saints is in a Gothic style with a tower.

**Stanford Hall** *Leics.*                                        552Ea
The home of the Cave family since 1430. The present William-and-Mary mansion was begun in 1697, and was much altered by the Smiths of Warwick in 1730–45. It contains a collection of Stuart paintings and relics, fine furniture, and family costumes from the time of Elizabeth I onwards. Part of the stables houses a collection of vintage motor-cycles and cars, and a full-size replica of the flying machine designed in 1898 by the aviation pioneer, Percy Pilcher. There is a walled rose garden, and a lake in the grounds.

**Stanstead Abbots** *Herts.*                                     548Ad
At the west end of the village street is an unusual red-brick house dating from 1752. It is an early example of sham-Gothic, with a circular stair turret and an embattled top. The Red Lion Inn, the Old Clockhouse and the Baesche Almshouses are all early 17th century.

CHURCH OF ST JAMES A mainly 15th-century church, with a timber south porch. The brick north chapel was added in 1577. The unspoilt interior has 18th-century furnishings, box-pews and three-decker pulpit. The monuments include early 19th-century work by John Bacon Junior and his partner Manning.

STANSTEAD BURY An attractive manor house near the Church of St James. Originally a 15th-century dwelling, it has been altered during each successive century.

**Stanton** *Glos.*                                    *546De*
CHURCH OF ST MICHAEL AND ALL ANGELS A cruciform church, with remains of Norman work, it has a west tower with spire, and a Perpendicular south aisle and porch. The pulpit is 17th century; and the rood screen, reredos, gallery and some of the stained glass are by Sir Ninian Comper.

**Stanton Drew** *Som.*                          *540Cf*
Here are three circles of standing stones. The central circle, the largest, is about 120 yds across and still has 27 standing stones visible. From it, an avenue, with several stones still standing, runs east to join another from the north circle. The latter is smaller in diameter, and here are eight stones. The remaining circle lies to the south-west and still has 12 stones. An adjunct of this circle-complex is the 'cove', a structural remnant standing behind the Druids Arms Inn. Its precise significance is not known.

**Stanton Harcourt** *Oxon.*               *546Ec*
CHURCH OF ST MICHAEL An impressive cruciform church, originally Norman. The central tower is Early English below and Perpendicular above, and most of the building is of these periods, for example the Early English chancel and screen. There are many monuments, mostly to 14th-century Harcourts; one of them shows a Lady Harcourt wearing the Order of the Garter. A fine standing figure of Lord Harcourt in peer's robes (*c.* 1832) is by R. W. Sievier.

**Stanton Moor** *Derbys.*                     *552De*
In an area of some 600 yds radius there lies a concentration of monuments, all apparently of the Middle Bronze Age. Near the north end of the area stands the embanked circle known as the Nine Ladies, with which the isolated standing stone, the King Stone, close by to the south-west, should probably be associated. Away to the west is Doll Tor, a free-standing stone circle. Many of its components are still upright, though two have fallen. There are also three circular rubble-banks, each with two opposed entrances and a few large stones which may once have stood upright.

There are 70 or more round cairns in the area, of various sizes. Some have been excavated but many more remain to be examined.

**Stanwell** *Surrey*                               *542Ag*
CHURCH OF ST MARY A church of 13th-century origin with work of the 14th and 15th centuries. There is a west tower and slender spire. An elegant monument of *c.* 1622 by Nicholas Stone shows Lord and Lady Knyvett kneeling, framed by marble curtains and Corinthian columns.

**Stanwick** *Yorks.*                               *558Ce*
HILL-FORT Though the first defences at Stanwick may be called a hill-fort, the subsequent additional fortifications make it unique in Britain.

The first structure is the Tofts, a 17 acre area protected by a single bank and external ditch; it belongs to the beginning of the 1st century AD.

About 50 years later, a 130 acre enclosure was attached on the north side, again defended by a

## MONUMENT TO LORD AND LADY KNYVETT

*This marble monument to Lord and Lady Knyvett was carved about 1622 by Nicholas Stone. Stone was master-mason to Charles I during most of the period that Inigo Jones was Surveyor-General, but he also worked as a sculptor. He is particularly noted for his monument to John Donne in St Paul's Cathedral. Stone received part of his early training in sculpture in Amsterdam and introduced the use of black and white marble into England. (Church of St Mary, Stanwell)*

single bank and ditch. This bank had a drystone facing and the ditch was 16 ft deep with a flat bottom.

About AD 72, an enormous addition was made on the south, nearly 600 acres being enclosed by a bank and ditch which linked with those of the second stage. This ditch was V-shaped and 15 ft deep; the bank also had drystone facing.

The history of the Roman conquest of Brigantian territory (the area occupied by the British tribe of the Brigantes—roughly from Cumberland and Durham in the north to Shropshire, Staffordshire and Derbyshire in the south), gives the clue to these developments. Shortly after AD 51, civil war developed between pro- and anti-Roman factions in the Brigantes. Some 20 years later, the whole tribe revolted and another year or two passed before they were finally reduced to submission.

**Stanydale** *Mainland, Shetland*        *568Ef*
TEMPLE AND HOUSES Called a temple because of its semi-sepulchral features, the chief of which is a 12 ft thick wall surrounding an oval area some 40 ft by 20 ft, though one end has a 'reversed' curve to its concave front, with an entrance in its middle.

Remains of several stone houses surround the temple and a further group stands near by.

**Stapleford** *Leics.*                             *552Fc*
CHURCH OF ST MARY MAGDALENE A Gothic Revival church was rebuilt by George Richardson in 1783 at the Earl of Harborough's expense. The interior has good contemporary furnishings, and inward-facing seats, as in a college chapel. Monuments include a brass of *c.* 1490 and, on the north side of the chancel, a large work in marble by Michael Rysbrack, *c.* 1732.

**Stapleford Park** *Leics.*                    *552Fc*
A mansion displaying a curious mixture of styles that resulted when the old wing, dated 1500 and decorated with sculptures depicting scenes from history, legend and the scriptures, was embellished with Flemish gables in 1633. The house was added to *c.* 1670 and in Victorian times. It contains pictures, tapestries, fine furniture and the Balston Collection of Staffordshire portrait figures of the Victorian age. A fine 18th-century parish church stands in the grounds, which contain a lake with herons and Canada geese, and a miniature passenger railway. (See p. 440.)

## VICTORIAN PORTRAIT FIGURES AT STAPLEFORD PARK

QUEEN VICTORIA, ALBERT AND CHILD *Staffordshire pottery figures were popular about 1840–90, and Queen Victoria was a favourite subject for pottery groups, especially during the period when her children were being born. Later, the outbreak of the Crimean War encouraged the production of figures of the queen with her allies, and the groups became larger so that incidents from the war could be portrayed. The figures were made from fine white earthenware, painted with bold enamel colours; gilt was often used for titles and decoration.*

NAPOLEON BONAPARTE *This 2 ft high Staffordshire pottery figure of Napoleon is the tallest of the known portrait figures. The Staffordshire figures, made for a popular market, were largely ignored by museums and collectors until the 1920's when Thomas Balston started a collection. Balston specialised in figures of famous personalities, and his collection of over 400 figures includes portraits of Queen Victoria and her family, of statesmen, soldiers, and theatrical personalities. It is on permanent display at Stapleford Park.*

**Staunton Harold** *Leics.*      552Dc
CHURCH One of the few churches built during Cromwell's Commonwealth; among the inscriptions inside is one over the west door recording that 'In the year 1653 When all things Sacred were throughout ye nation Either demolisht or profaned Sir Robert Shirley, Barronet, Founded this church, whose singular praise it is To have done the best things in ye worst times, and hoped them in the most calamitous'. The church has been little altered and its original fittings and communion plate are intact.
HALL A Georgian house (incorporating a 17th-century house) once owned by Group Captain G. L. Cheshire, V.C., an RAF hero who instituted the Cheshire Foundation Homes for the Incurably Sick. (By appointment.)

**Stebbing** *Essex*      548Bd
A village with some worthwhile houses: Church Farm of the early 16th century and Parsonage Farm, late 16th century; the Friends' Meeting House of 1674 with an 18th-century portico; and nearby moated Porter's Hall of c. 1600. There is also the mound of a vanished castle.
CHURCH OF ST MARY THE VIRGIN A 14th-century church, with west tower and spire. The rood screen is of stone and there is an 18th-century communion rail. The church contains a brass of c. 1390.

**Steeple Ashton** *Wilts.*      540Ef
CHURCH OF ST MARY THE VIRGIN A 15th-century church with a tall west tower, pinnacled and battlemented, which once had a tall stone spire, blown down in 1670. The chancel was rebuilt in

1853. Inside the church, there is a wooden roof to the nave, and the aisles and chapels are stone-vaulted, with big bosses; there are some medieval stained glass fragments, and several interesting monuments.

**Steeple Aston** *Oxon.*      546Fd
CHURCH OF SS PETER AND PAUL In this church is the large marble monument to Sir Francis and Lady Page, of c. 1730. The beautiful figures of the judge reclining behind his wife were carved by Henry Scheemakers, brother of the much more famous Peter; he was, nevertheless, an equally good sculptor.

**Steetley** *Derbys.*      552Ee
CHAPEL OF ALL SAINTS This small Norman chapel, only 52 ft by 15 ft, stands alone in a field and consists of a tiny nave, chancel and smaller apse, with arches between them. The chapel was derelict and roofless after the Commonwealth, but was restored by J. L. Pearson in 1880.

**Stein-A-Cleit** *Lewis*      568Cd
This cairn, some 50 ft in diameter, has suffered much robbing of its small stones, so that three great stone slabs which form part of the burial chamber stand up above the present top of the mound.
    Around the edge of the mound is set a series of 10 ft high upright slabs, and the whole is centred in an oval enclosure, 270 ft by 180 ft, of earth-set boulders placed close together.

**Stenness** *Mainland, Orkney*      569Hg
THREE STONE RINGS The Ring of Bookan is really a cairn of the Maes Howe type, but has been largely destroyed. The great surrounding ditch,

however, is still in existence. Half a mile to the north-east is the Ring of Brodgar, a henge monument. The external bank has now disappeared, but the circling ditch still exists and encloses an area 370 ft across, with two entrances. Inside the ditch is a ring of standing stones; there were originally 60, but of these only 27 remain. Their average height is about 7 ft, but there are great variations. On one of the stones there is a Norse Runic inscription.

A little to the south of Brodgar is the third ring, that of Stenness. This also is a henge, of which the bank and ditch are almost obliterated. It measures some 200 ft in diameter. Originally there stood, just within the ditch, a great ring of 13 stones, of which four only remain. The tallest of these is 17 ft high.

**Stevenage** *Herts.*                                         *547Jd*
MUSEUM The collection illustrates the archaeology, history and natural history of the Stevenage area.

**Stevington** *Beds.*                                         *547He*
Under the churchyard's east wall is a little spring called the Holy Well, visited by pilgrims in medieval times. The Fair Maid of Kent, wife of Edward III's eldest son, the Black Prince, is said to have died here in 1386.
STEVINGTON MILL Dating from 1770, the mill was restored in 1921, bought by Bedfordshire County Council in 1951 and again restored to commemorate the Queen's coronation in 1953. It is a splendid example of one of the few remaining windmills in the county.

**Stewkley** *Bucks.*                                         *547Gd*
CHURCH OF ST MICHAEL AND ALL ANGELS An impressive Norman church, essentially unchanged, with nave, central space with massive tower above, and chancel, but no aisles. There is much decorative carving of zigzags and dragons. G. E. Street did some restoration in 1862.

**Steyning** *Sussex*                                         *542Bd*
CHURCH OF ST ANDREW A magnificent Norman church, once collegiate (not under the authority of a bishop), of which only the nave remains. The chancel, transepts and central tower were demolished after 1577 and a west tower built instead—the present chancel arch rising to nearly 40 ft was the west arch of the original tower. The font, of carved marble, was made in the 12th century. In the south aisle are the Arms of Queen Anne.

**Stibbington Hall** *Hunts.*                                 *547Hg*
A country mansion built of Ketton stone *c.* 1625, to an E-shaped plan. It has a fine long gallery.

**Stilton** *Hunts.*                                          *547Jg*
At the 17th-century Bell Inn at Stilton, the famous cheeses, made in Leicestershire, were loaded on to coaches for London and the North. The Bell has a long range of stone-built bays and gables, with two massive chimney-stacks and an impressive coach entrance. One gable carries the date 1642 but the inn is probably earlier.

**Stirling** *Stir.*                                          *561Jf*
CASTLE A castle has crowned the precipitous rock set at the narrowing of the Forth Valley—the Gateway to the Highlands—since the Dark Ages.

STIRLING CASTLE

*The strategic position of Stirling Castle in the Forth Valley has always ensured it importance. By the 12th century it was among the most important castles of the Scottish kingdom. During the Scottish wars of Edward I, Stirling Castle was recognised as a key building for the command of the country, and was the subject of a siege in 1304 when it was heroically defended against the English king by Sir William Oliphant. It was recaptured by the Scottish king Robert de Bruce after the Battle of Bannockburn in 1314. The present building is largely a royal residence built in the 15th and 16th centuries. It was the scene of the coronation of Mary, Queen of Scots in 1543. In the ensuing civil wars, it changed hands several times but ceased to be a royal palace when James VI succeeded to the English throne.*

Alexander I of Scotland died here in 1124 and the castle was centuries old then. It was a residence and sometimes the capital of the Scottish kings until 1603, but was several times taken by the English. In 1297 William Wallace, Scottish patriot and hero, won it back, but it was retaken and occupied in 1304 until 1314. James III was born here in 1452; he later rebuilt the castle, adding the fine Parliament Hall, 124 ft long. James V built a carved palace within the castle precincts. James VI (later James I of England) was crowned here in 1567 and later rebuilt the Royal Chapel. The castle was held by Cromwell's troops in 1651.

WALLACE MEMORIAL, STIRLING

*In a niche high on this memorial tower stands Sir William Wallace, the Scottish patriot born in 1272. In 1297 he drove the English from Perth and defeated them at Stirling Bridge. Having been outlawed by Edward I in 1304, he was captured by treachery near Glasgow in 1305, brought to London, tried and executed.*

CHURCH OF THE HOLY ROOD A large church of the 15th century, in which Mary was crowned Queen of Scots at the age of nine months. The church had a chequered building history. It was divided into west and east churches in the mid-17th century after a parish argument, and it was not until just before the Second World War that it became one church again.
SMITH ART GALLERY AND MUSEUM The museum, founded in 1874, contains oil paintings and watercolours, weapons and implements from Oceania, Africa, India, China, Japan, local antiquities (particularly of the Bronze Age), local rocks, minerals and fossils as well as many items relating to local domestic history—including the oldest curling stone in Scotland, dated 1511, and a 15th-century measuring jug.
WALLACE MEMORIAL A pinnacled tower, 220 ft high, stands on top of Abbey Craig, and from a niche near its summit a bronze statue of William Wallace, clad in chain-mail, looks out over the scene of his victory in 1297. The monument was erected in 1867 and contains documents associated with Wallace.

**Stockbridge** *Hants.* 541Ge
The town is a single wide straight street, spanning the Test Valley between one sweep of upland and another, but there is a town hall, with a cupola, and two big inns, relics of the days when coaches changed horses here.

**Stockport** *Cheshire* 552Bf
MUNICIPAL MUSEUM On the ground floor of the museum is the large Blue John window, made from over 200 pieces of fluor spar (a native fluoride of calcium also known as Derbyshire spar) representing all the known varieties found in the caverns around Castleton, Derbyshire. The window and carved frame were the work of John Tym, curator of the museum when the window was finished in 1895.
There are relics of early man in the Stockport area, documents and items of local government from the 13th century to 1858, and a display of the manufacture of the felt hats for which Stockport is famous. A collection of ceramics includes Minton, Spode and Staffordshire porcelain, pieces of Derby, Worcester, Wedgwood and Coalport ware, and 18th-century tea and coffee services. A large natural history collection includes British birds, reptiles, amphibians, fishes, insects, seaweeds, fungi and non-flowering plants. A geology collection includes rocks, minerals and fossils, and a display showing the development of life from Cambrian times.
WAR MEMORIAL ART GALLERY L. S. Lowry's painting, *Crowther Street, Stockport,* and a bronze sculpture by Epstein, *Head of Yehudi Menuhin,* are the main exhibits in the gallery, which was built as a war memorial in the 1920's. The building is also used for travelling exhibitions.

**Stockton** *Wilts.* 540Ee
CHURCH OF ST JOHN THE BAPTIST Originally Norman, with later Gothic additions, the church has a west tower. An interesting feature inside is the solid wall which was built between the nave and chancel. The font is Norman and there are various monuments dating from the 14th to the 18th centuries.

**Stockton-on-Tees** *Durham* 558De
CHURCH OF ST THOMAS Sir Christopher Wren had a hand in the design of this pleasant church, built 1710–12. The font and pulpit are of about the same period, the latter borne on deliberately rough stone pillars.

**Stoke-by-Nayland** *Suffolk* 548Ce
CHURCH OF ST MARY A Perpendicular church, with a tall, ornamented west tower. There is a two-storey south porch; that on the north is 16th century, in brick. Inside is a carved Perpendicular font with figures; there are also screens, stalls, misericords and 19th-century stained glass. Many brasses and monuments remain from the 17th century.

**Stoke Charity** *Hants.* 541Ge
CHURCH OF ST MICHAEL Now standing alone, the church was once accompanied by the manor house. St Michael's is a small building with a bell-turret, and some Norman work. It contains many monuments and brasses, fragments of stained glass, a 13th-century mural painting, and a late 15th-century carved relief of the Mass of St Gregory.

**Stoke d'Abernon** *Surrey* 542Af
CHURCH OF ST MARY The church, of pre-Conquest origins, is famous for its brasses to the d'Abernons: that to Sir John (d. 1277) is the oldest brass in England. The 15th-century Norbury Chapel contains 17th-century monuments.

**Stoke Doyle** *Northants.* 547Hg
CHURCH OF ST RUMBALD Built in 1722–5, St
Rumbald's has a west tower with obelisks for
pinnacles. Pulpit, benches and other fittings are all
original. Monuments include a fine reclining
effigy of Sir Edward Ward (*d.* 1714) by John
Michael Rysbrack, and a mourning Grecian lady
of a century later by Sir Francis Chantrey.

**Stoke Dry** *Rutland* 553Gb
CHURCH OF ST ANDREW On a hillside in remote
country, this interesting little church dates from
Norman times, but has much later building.
Worth noting are the tombs of the Digby family,
who lived in Stoke Dry from the 15th to 17th
centuries, in particular the table-tomb of Kenelm
and Anne Digby. The chancel screen and wall-
paintings are 15th century. It was once said that the
Gunpowder Plot was hatched in the priest's
chamber over the north porch; the story is false,
but an Everard Digby was hanged for complicity
in 1606.

**Stoke Edith** *Herefs.* 546Be
CHURCH OF ST MARY THE VIRGIN The body of the
church was rebuilt in 1740, but the west tower and
spire of the 14th-century church remain. The
present building is of stuccoed brick, with Tuscan
columns. There is a three-decker pulpit, and 18th-
century pews. The monuments are 18th and 19th
century, except for two from the earlier building,
one an alabaster effigy of a 15th-century lady.

**Stoke-on-Trent** *Staffs.* 552Bd
CITY MUSEUM AND ART GALLERY (HANLEY) The
museum's main exhibits are Staffordshire, European, Near and Far Eastern and South American
pottery, making up a collection that is one of the
finest and largest in the world.

**Stoke Park Pavilions** *Northants.* 547Ge
A colonnade and two pavilions, built in 1630 by
Inigo Jones.

**Stoke Poges** *Bucks.* 547Hb
GRAY'S MONUMENT The scene at Stoke Poges
inspired Thomas Gray (1716–71) to write his
'Elegy Written in a Country Churchyard'. In 1799
this statue designed by James Wyatt was erected in
the churchyard to commemorate the poet.

**Stoke Prior** *Worcs.* 546Cf
CHURCH OF ST MICHAEL A good church dating
from the 12th century, with a 14th-century
octagonal carved font. The spire is recent.

**Stokesay** *Shrops.* 551Ja
CHURCH OF ST JOHN THE BAPTIST Situated by
Stokesay Castle, the church was begun by the
Normans, had later additions, and was largely
rebuilt in the 17th century after Civil War damage.
Nave and tower are from that period, and the
chancel roof and pulpit (which has a sounding
board) are also mid-17th century.

**Stokesay Castle** *Shrops.* 551Ja
A fortified manor house, parts of which date from
the 12th century. The buildings of the 'castle' are
arranged around a walled enclosure surrounded by
a moat. To the east side is the half-timbered 16th-
century gate-house. Opposite this lies the bulk of
the manor house, consisting of a great hall with
solar, and two towers, one at either end. The north
tower is the older, in spite of the 16th-century half-
timbering that surmounts it; its fabric may well go
back to the 12th century. In the 13th century the
great hall was built; it has well preserved windows
with simple tracery and a fine roof, although this
was probably remodelled later. Finally, there is the
great south tower and the solar between. These
were probably added soon after 1291 when the
owner received a licence permitting the building
of fortifications at Stokesay. Other buildings,
including a kitchen, were demolished in the early
19th century.

**Stone** *Kent* 542Cg
CHURCH OF ST MARY Tradition has it that the
building was erected by the masons of Westminster Abbey. It is the finest Gothic church in Kent
west of the R. Medway, with almost all the work
dating from the 13th century, and rich decoration
and clustered columns. There are traces of mural
paintings, a brass to John Lombard of 1408, and a
16th-century canopied monument to Sir John and
Lady Wyllshire.

**Stonehenge** *Wilts.* 540Fe
In Stonehenge, Britain possesses the finest Bronze
Age sanctuary in Europe. The monument as we
have it today (as it was when complete) was the last

STOKESAY CASTLE

*One of the most attractive small fortified houses in
England. It is a misnomer to call it a castle since its
fortifications are minimal and it could never have
resisted more than the casual marauder. In the 12th
century the property was owned by the de Saye family
from whom it takes its name. By 1281, however, it
had passed to a Laurence de Ludlow, whose descendants*

*held it until 1497. In the 17th century, it came into
the possession of the Craven family. The 'castle' is
a walled enclosure surrounded by a moat. On the east
side is the 16th-century gate-house, an ornamental
half-timbered structure. Opposite is the bulk of the
house, including the great hall, one of the oldest
surviving great halls in the country.*

stage in a long and complex history which began *c.* 1800 BC, at the very end of the Neolithic period, and was completed by *c.* 1400 BC, at the end of the Early Bronze Age. The phases of building are as follows:

Phase I, *c.* 1800 BC: Ditch and bank constructed, inside which was a ring of small pits, many containing cremation burials. A few upright stones were grouped to form an entrance. (The pits are now marked by concrete.)

Phase II, 1650–1500 BC: A double circle of bluestones, brought from the Prescelly Hills in Pembrokeshire, was erected, but never finished. The entrance was modified to suit the new orientation and 'The Avenue', leading up from the banks of the R. Avon, was constructed.

Phase IIIa, *c.* 1500 BC: The bluestones were taken down, the site levelled and the great sarsen stones we still see were brought from the Marlborough Downs, shaped and dressed, and erected as we see them today, in an outer ring with lintels and an inner horseshoe composed of five pairs of uprights with lintels. The entrance was again modified.

Phase IIIb, 1500–1400 BC: Some of the bluestones were dressed and set along the line of the present inner bluestone horseshoe. Further holes were dug outside the great circle but these were never used and the bluestones in the centre were removed.

Phase IIIc, *c.* 1400 BC: The bluestones were now reset as we see them, in a ring between the two lines of sarsens and in an inner horseshoe. Finally, at the very centre, the largest bluestone was apparently set upright. This has now fallen and is known as the Altar Stone.

Most of the missing stones have disappeared from the Middle Ages onwards, as farmers and others used the monument as a quarry until it was officially preserved.

**Stoneleigh Abbey** *Warks.*　　　　546Ef
An Italianate mansion built around the remains of an abbey, and completed in 1726. There is an Elizabethan wing and the 14th-century gate-house of the monastery survives. The house contains fine furniture and a collection of portraits.

**Stonor Park** *Oxon.*　　　　547Gc
A Tudor manor house set in a magnificent park. The medieval chapel has been in use continuously for over 800 years.

**Stony Littleton** *Som.*　　　　540Df
This is a chambered barrow of Cotswold type, restored for inspection. A wedge-shaped mound still stands some 10 ft high and this has a horned forecourt. Inside the entrance, the central gallery, some 40 ft long, leads to three pairs of side-chambers and one at the farther end. The roofing is formed by corbelling and not by capstones.

**Stopham** *Sussex*　　　　542Ad
A village at the confluence of the R. Arun and R. Rother, famed for its medieval bridge, originally built in 1309, repaired in the 16th century and again in 1865. The church contains brasses from 1428 of the Barttelot family, who from Norman times owned the lands on which the present Stopham House (18th century) stands.

**Stottesdon** *Shrops.*　　　　546Bg
CHURCH OF ST MARY A church containing much Norman work, and perhaps even some Saxon. There are Decorated windows with fine tracery, and a magnificent Norman font, mid-12th century, with carvings of animals, men and foliage.

**Stourhead** *Wilts.*　　　　540De
A Palladian house built in 1722 for Henry Hoare, the merchant banker. There are landscape paintings, and also furniture designed by the younger Chippendale.

## STONEHENGE

*Set in the middle of Salisbury Plain, near Amesbury in Wiltshire, Stonehenge is the finest Bronze Age sanctuary in Europe. It may have had a religious purpose and was built in several stages starting about 1800 BC when the outer ditch and bank were constructed. In 1650–1500 BC the great bluestones, brought all the way from the Prescelly Hills in South Wales, were erected in a double circle. About 1500 BC this circle was dismantled; the great sarsen stones were brought from the Marlborough Downs and erected as they are today—in an outer ring with lintels, and inner horseshoe comprising five pairs of uprights with lintels. Later the bluestones were re-erected between the two lines of sarsens and in an inner horseshoe.*

At the beginning of the 18th century a revolutionary change in garden design took place: in English landscape gardens the irregular, curving forms of nature replaced the regular geometrical designs in the French manner of Le Nôtre. Stourhead was one of the first examples of the innovation. The gardens were laid out in 1741 by the architect Flitcroft for Henry Hoare. The meres in the bleak valley were converted into a series of lakes, and the banks decorated with architectural ornaments amid groups of ornamental trees and flowering shrubs. (See p. 446.)

**Stow** *Lincs.*                                    *553Gf*
CHURCH OF ST MARY An interesting church dating from the Saxon period, with some Norman additions; it is a Greek cross in plan, with a low central tower. Inside, there are massive 11th-century arches, and a fine Norman chancel. The carving beneath the Early English font depicts a dragon, symbolising the defeated devil. In the north transept are the remains of a wall-painting representing St Thomas à Becket.

**Stowe** *Bucks.*                                    *547Ge*
A park and mansion produced for the Dukes of Buckingham by some of the best genius of the 17th and 18th centuries: Vanbrugh, Robert Adam, Grinling Gibbons and William Kent all worked on the house and landscaped park with lakes and temples; the Temple of Worthies by William Kent contains busts of heroes, poets and philosophers. In the grounds there is also a 13th-century church, all that remains of the village that was removed to make way for the church in 1713.

**Stowlangtoft** *Suffolk*                             *548Cf*
CHURCH OF ST GEORGE A good Perpendicular church with flushwork decoration. The roof is richer above where the rood was. Inside is a 14th-century font with carved figures; benches; and stalls with pretty carved figures instead of the more usual poppy-heads. There is a mural painting of St Christopher, and 17th-century monuments, one by John Johnson.

**Stranraer** *Wig.*                                  *556Bg*
WIGTOWN COUNTY MUSEUM Items of local archaeological and agricultural interest include a series of Bronze Age axes and an old wooden Scottish plough in use *c.* 1790. There are also personalia relating to Sir John Ross, the Arctic explorer, and bygones—mostly domestic equipment with some costume. In the church collection there are communion tokens, pewter plate and two 18th-century stone crosses.

**Stranraer Castle** *Wig.*                            *556Bg*
The castle, begun in the 15th century, stands in the middle of the town. It was the home of John Graham of Claverhouse—the persecutor of the Covenanters.

**Strata Florida** *Card.*                             *545Gf*
The remains of a remote Norman abbey founded for the Cistercians. The west doorway of the former church has unusual banded moulding, and there are some medieval tiles.

**Stratford-upon-Avon** *Warks.*                       *546Df*
Established as a market centre in 1196 by King John, it has continued as such until modern times: its annual Mop Fair (October 12), with traditional roast ox, is a direct survival of the ancient statute fair at which farm-workers were hired. In its early days the centre was comprised of three streets running parallel to the river and three at right angles to the river, and no basic change has taken place over the centuries. The buildings are predominantly Elizabethan and Jacobean, with picturesque 15th-century half-timbered work in Church Street; timber-framed examples of the 16th and 17th centuries in Chapel Street, High Street and Wood Street; and quite a number of 18th-century period buildings or refrontings with brick and stucco. Thus the whole town forms a natural backcloth to Shakespeare, his times and work. Interest in Shakespeare's background began shortly after his death in 1616. He had bought New Place in 1597, and to this he retired in 1610. He was buried, aged 52, in the chancel of the parish church of Holy Trinity. In 1769, the actor David Garrick organised the first Shakespeare celebrations, and thus started what soon became a literary pilgrimage, to such an effect that in 1847 the Shakespeare Birthplace Trust was formed to preserve this side of Stratford's heritage.

ANNE HATHAWAY'S COTTAGE At Shottery, a mile from the town. Its structure is of stone, timber-framing, wattle and brick, and in part dates to the 15th century.

CHURCH OF THE HOLY TRINITY By the R. Avon, this is the church where Shakespeare was baptised (1564) and buried (1616); his monument there is by Gerard Johnson. The building is cruciform and has a central spire, originally timber but rebuilt in 1763 by William Hiorn of Warwick. There is some Early English work, but the Perpendicular and Decorated periods predominate. In 1888 and 1898 restorations were made against which William Morris protested. The late 15th-century stalls have charming misericords and there are monuments of all periods (including those to Shakespeare's wife Anne Hathaway and to his daughter Susanna Hall), and work by Thomas Stanton, Michael Rysbrack and Sir Richard Westmacott.

The old font in which Shakespeare was baptised is near to the case in which is kept the parish register; this contains the entries for his baptism and burial.

CLOPTON BRIDGE Built by Hugh Clopton (*d.* 1496) who became Lord Mayor of London and built New Place (1483).

GUILD CHAPEL Built in 1269, it was much altered in 1450, and had later additions in the 15th century. The half-timbered range adjoining the chapel was built 1416–18. The original guildhall occupies the ground floor: above is a fine hall used by the grammar school since the suppression of the guild; Shakespeare studied here as a schoolboy.

HALL'S CROFT Home of Shakespeare's daughter Susanna and her husband Dr John Hall, it is an outstanding building of character with a splendid walled garden. It contains rare furniture and period exhibits.

HARVARD HOUSE Built by Alderman Thomas Rogers in 1596—his daughter Katherine married Robert Harvard of Southwark and their son John founded the famous American university. The house was presented to Harvard University in 1909. The adjoining Garrick Inn is of a similar date, as is the fine Elizabethan Old Tudor House adjacent.

MARY ARDEN'S HOUSE The Tudor farmhouse in Wilmcote village (3 miles north-west of the town) where Shakespeare's mother lived.

NEW PLACE The house to which Shakespeare retired in 1610; only the site and foundations remain. They are preserved in gardens reached through Nash's House. The adjoining Knot Garden is a replica of an Elizabethan garden.

ROYAL SHAKESPEARE THEATRE Built in 1932 to replace a theatre built in 1879 and destroyed by fire in 1926. It has a picture gallery and museum.

ROYAL SHAKESPEARE THEATRE PICTURE GALLERY
Portraits of Shakespeare, and portraits and caricatures of famous actresses and actors are displayed
with a collection of original costumes and designs
of sets used in productions from 1879 to 1968.
SHAKESPEARE STATUE (GOWER MEMORIAL) The
work of Lord Gower, it was presented to the town
in 1888, and has the figures of Hamlet, Lady Macbeth, Falstaff and Prince Hal, symbolising philosophy, tragedy, comedy and history.
SHAKESPEARE'S BIRTHPLACE A half-timbered
building of the early 16th century. In his lifetime it
was two separate buildings, one the family home,
the other an adjoining warehouse used by his
father John who was a glover and wool dealer.
SHRIEVE'S HOUSE Reconstructed and enlarged
after a fire in 1595: it was the home of William
Rogers, a serjeant-at-the-mace in Shakespeare's
time.
TOWN HALL Of Cotswold stone, it was built in
1769, but restored after a fire in 1946.

**Strelley** Notts. 552Ed
CHURCH OF ALL SAINTS There is a 13th-century
base to the west tower, but most of the building
dates from after its endowment in 1356 by Samson
de Strelley. The chancel is the best in the county.
There are numerous monuments to 14th–16th-
century members of the Strelley family, and a
good rood screen.

**Strensham** Worcs. 546Ce
CHURCH OF ST JOHN THE BAPTIST Standing on
high ground in a field close to the R. Avon, St
John's has a series of monuments to one family
from the 13th to the 19th century. One of them, in
marble, to Sir Francis Russell (d. 1705), is by
Edward Stanton, the mason-sculptor of Holborn
in London, whose father carved the monument to
the Earl of Coventry, c. 1700, which is at the
neighbouring Elmley Castle. On the west wall,
now set as a gallery front, is a painted rood loft
front with 23 saints.

**Strethall** Essex 548Ae
CHURCH OF ST MARY THE VIRGIN A small Saxon
church, with a 15th-century chancel and west
tower, an 11th-century chancel arch and a 15th-
century brass to a priest.

**Stretham** Cambs. 548Af
On the edge of the Fens, Stretham is notable for
its 20 ft high village cross, of c. 1400.
STRETHAM SCOOP-WHEEL ENGINE Only sur-
viving example of the type of machine used for
Fen-drainage in the early 19th century.

**Strome Castle** Ross 565Gf
The ruins of a medieval castle; it was destroyed by
English soldiers during a siege in 1602 following
numerous attempts to subdue it, and was never
rebuilt.

**Stroud** Glos. 546Cc
SUBSCRIPTION ROOMS Built in the early 19th
century, incorporating the George Room Art
Gallery, the building is architecturally interesting
for its porte-cochère with Tuscan columns and
balustraded balcony above.

STRETHAM ENGINE

*This scoop-wheel engine, built in 1831 by the Butterley
Company of Derbyshire, is the sole survivor of the
many similar beam engines installed in the early 19th
century to replace wind-pumps for Fen-drainage. The
engine, which has been restored, has a scoop-wheel
37 ft in diameter designed to lift water 4 to 5 ft into
the dyke at the rate of 124 tons a minute.*

**Studley Royal** Yorks. 558Cc
CHURCH OF ST MARY Built between 1871 and 1878
by William Burges; the style is elaborate Gothic,
with west tower and lofty spire, polychrome
marble, alabaster and mosaic. The founder, the
Marquess of Ripon (d. 1909), is entombed in the
south chapel. There is glass of the period.

**Studley Royal** 558Cc
**and Fountains Abbey Garden** Yorks.
Set in the steep-sided valley of the little R. Skell,
this is an incomparable water garden, laid out as
straight canals and geometrically-shaped pools.
There is superb statuary on the large stretches of
mown lawn; the Classical 'Temple of Piety' overlooks the Moon Pool and fountain. The road from
Ripon leads through a forest-like park and beside a
lake before entering the garden through handsome
gates. The water garden dates from c. 1727; it was
made for John Aislabie, notorious for his participation in the South Sea Company financial scandal.
The valley at the upper end of the river was
acquired by Aislabie's son when 'natural' garden
design was the vogue. It is crowded with giant
trees and, over the lake, a great tower rises above
the ruins of Fountains Abbey. (See p. 450.)

## THE PANTHEON AND LAKE AT STOURHEAD

*The English landscape garden was invented early in
the 18th century, and freedom of nature with its
irregular curving forms replaced the regular geometrical
designs in the manner of the French gardener,
Le Nôtre. When he inherited Stourhead in 1741,
Henry Hoare was one of the first to create such a
garden. With the help of Henry Flitcroft the architect,
he transformed a bare valley into a magnificent*
*landscape. The bottom of the valley became a series of
lakes, their banks planted with trees, and dotted with
temples and grottoes, mostly in Classical style. In the
19th century a variety of ornamental trees and great
stretches of flowering shrubs were planted. Unlike
Capability Brown's landscapes where form, shape and
the green of grass and trees predominated, at Stourhead
colour and variety has been the keynote.*

# ꟼⁱˢ Ghalƒꝛᵉ

## WILLIAM SHAKESPEARE, DRAMATIST TO THE WORLD

The Swan of Avon, as Ben Johnson named his friend, died a popular and successful dramatist, but his reputation has grown until today over a quarter of a million people visit his birthplace at Stratford-upon-Avon each year. Also on view at Stratford is New Place, the best house in the town when Shakespeare bought it in 1597, and Mary Arden's House and Hall's Croft. Dulwich College possesses the first reference to a performance of a Shakespeare play, *Henry VI, Part I*, in 1591 at the Rose Theatre, London. It was so popular it was repeated 14 times. At 30, Shakespeare had become an actor and the regular playwright of the Lord Chamberlain's players, and his name appears in the cast list of Ben Jonson's *Every Man in his Humour* at the Curtain Theatre in 1598 (British Museum). This theatre was inaccessible and old, so Shakespeare and his companions 'did in most forcible and ryotous manner take and carrye away from thence all the wood and timber' to build a new theatre across the river on Bankside, named the Globe, as shown in Visscher's *View of London* (British Museum).

WILLIAM SHAKESPEARE, *the Droeshout frontispiece of the First Folio, or the first collected edition of Shakespeare's plays, published in 1623. It is suspected of being a fake: a medical scientist noticed the portrait had two right eyes, and there are alleged to be two left sides to the coat. (British Museum)*

BAPTISM ENTRY *in Stratford Parish Register, April 26, 1564.*

STAIRS IN SHAKESPEARE'S BIRTHPLACE *at Stratford.*

SCHOOLROOM *in which he studied, at the King's New School, Stratford. To join the school he had to be 7 years old and able to read. In those days hardly anything but Latin grammar was taught and it can be seen from his plays that Shakespeare was made to read Vergil and Ovid.*

BAPTISMAL ENTRIES of Shakespeare's children. His marriage was not altogether happy and what little we know of his family life is through his children. Susanna was born on May 26, 1583, and the twins Hamnet and Judith on Feb. 2, 1585. (Register, Holy Trinity Church, Stratford)

ANNE HATHAWAY'S COTTAGE at Shottery, a mile from Stratford. It is thought the 18-year-old Shakespeare had to marry Anne, 18 years his senior, because she was pregnant.

CLOPTON BRIDGE over the R. Avon which the 22-year-old Shakespeare must have crossed on his way to London. It is likely he walked, and the journey would have taken 4 days.

PAINTED ROOM at the Crown Tavern in Oxford, where Shakespeare is said to have stayed on his journeys between London and Stratford. The painted walls were discovered in 1937.

GRAVE OF SHAKESPEARE placed within the sanctuary of Holy Trinity Church, Stratford. It is thought he died after a prolonged celebration with his fellow dramatists.

SHAKESPEARE'S SIGNATURE appears (above the seal at the left) on this mortgage for a London house close to the theatre. (British Museum)

THE TEMPLE OF PIETY AT STUDLEY ROYAL GARDENS

*Wild flowers and enormous trees abound in the steep valley of the R. Skell in which lies this garden—an abstraction of water, laid out in straight canals and geometrically shaped pools, punctuated by statuary and overlooked by the Classical Temple of Piety. John Aislabie, Chancellor of the Exchequer, started it all about 1727. Coming from Ripon the garden is entered beside the ornamented cascade, in the style of Louis XIV of France and his gardener, Le Nôtre. The upper gardens were laid out by Aislabie's son when the fashion in gardens had changed—here is a landscape of sinuous curving lines with an irregular shaped lake above which rise the magnificent ruins of Fountains Abbey.*

**Styal** *Cheshire*        552Bf
Quarry Bank Cotton Mill was erected in 1784 near a half-timbered farmhouse and cottages set in fine woodlands. Shortly afterwards the village of Styal was built near by—the whole forming a rare complete industrial community.

**Sudbury** *Suffolk*        548Ce
Sudbury is an ancient market town and the birth-place of Gainsborough. There are attractive medieval and 18th-century houses in the streets below Market Hill. The old Moot Hall is 15th century, with an oriel window and overhanging storey; also from the 15th century are the Chantry and Salter's Hall. Gainsborough's House of *c.* 1725 has a pillared doorway, and the Bull Inn and Ballingdon Hall (across the R. Stour) are both good buildings of *c.* 1590 and 1600.
CHURCH OF ST GREGORY The principal church of the town, it is Perpendicular, with a west tower, and large windows in the chancel built by Simon de Sudbury, Archbishop of Canterbury, who was murdered in 1387. There is a towering, beautiful font canopy, and misericords.
CHURCH OF ST PETER A Perpendicular church in a formerly prosperous town. The west tower has a small 19th-century spire. There are good rood and parclose screens.
GAINSBOROUGH'S HOUSE Birthplace of painter Thomas Gainsborough (1727–88), containing many pictures.

**Sudeley Castle** *Glos.*        546Dd
Catherine Parr, the sixth queen of Henry VIII, is buried here; in 1547, after Henry's death, she married her former lover, Lord Seymour of Sudeley, but died here in childbirth the following year. The castle was a headquarters of Charles I during the Civil War and was besieged in 1643 and again in 1644. The ruined banqueting hall dates from *c.* 1450; the chapel of the same date contains the tomb of Catherine Parr. The castle houses paintings, tapestries, fine furniture and stained glass. There is a good formal flower garden.

**Suie Hill** See Dungarry and Suie Hill.

**Sulgrave Manor** *Northants.*        546Fe
Ancestral home of George Washington, 1st President of the U.S.A., Sulgrave Manor is one of the few English country houses to fly the American flag. The design of the flag is believed to have been inspired by the Washington family Arms (three horizontal stars above two horizontal bars or stripes), which can be seen carved in a stone porch at the manor. The house, in coursed stone, was built by Lawrence Washington in 1560. Colonel John Washington, great-grandfather of George Washington, left Sulgrave Manor for Virginia in 1656. The house is a mixture of Elizabethan and Queen Anne architecture, but was partly altered and rebuilt in 1920–30. It contains portraits of George Washington, and some of his possessions.

**Sunderland** *Durham*        558Dg
The town's original name was Wearmouth; and in Saxon times it was a great centre of learning: the Venerable Bede received his early training at the monastery of St Peter. In its present form, largely expanded beyond the early boundaries, Sunderland is mainly a late 19th-century town.
CHURCH OF THE HOLY TRINITY A pleasant Classical church built in 1719; the apse was added in 1735. The interior is adorned with Corinthian columns, and the west screen (1724) bears the royal Arms. There is also a monument, *c.* 1838, with a life-size statue by Sir Francis Chantrey, the neo-Classical portrait sculptor who left a fortune (the Chantrey Bequest) to the Royal Academy.

MUSEUM AND ART GALLERY There are archaeological and natural history sections, model ships and pottery. The gallery has a collection of works by British artists; loan exhibitions are held.

**Sundridge Old Hall** *Kent*  542Cf
A medieval timbered hall-house, built *c.* 1458. The great hall, several storeys high and reaching from ground level to the roof, contains the original stone hearth. The house was restored in 1923. (Open to members of the National Trust by appointment.)

**Sutton-at-Hone** *Kent*  542Cg
ST JOHN'S JERUSALEM Henry III often stayed at the 13th-century Commandery (headquarters) of the Order of Knights Hospitaller of St John. The Commandery chapel survives, for it was incorporated in the house, built here in the 16th century, which was later the home of Abraham Hill (1635–1721), a founder and Treasurer of the Royal Society. The house was altered in the 18th century. A weeping willow, a descendant of the tree under which Napoleon was buried at St Helena, stands in the moated garden.

**Sutton Courtenay** *Berks.*  546Fc
CHURCH OF ALL SAINTS In a pretty village on the Thames, All Saints is basically Norman, with later additions. The broad tower is Norman, and so is the tub-shaped font with its Jacobean cover. Pulpit and box-pews are 17th century, and there are rood and parclose screens. Fragments of medieval glass are set haphazardly in the windows.

**Sutton End** *Sussex*  542Ad
Gardens with flowering shrubs and herbaceous borders.

**Sutton Rectory** *Sussex*  542Ad
Once a priest's house, the rectory retains its original medieval hall and timberwork. It is built of mud bricks, 12 in. by 9 in., a form extremely rare in England.

**Sutton Valance** *Kent*  542Df
A tiny town perched on a hill, which gives it its special character: the streets follow the contours, giving vast views of the Kent Weald. The many weather-boarded and brick cottages are typical of the area. At the east end of the village stand the overgrown ruins of a small Norman keep.

LUSTRE-WARE JUG

*A lustre-ware jug made about 1820 at the Sunderland pottery, also known as the 'Garrison', which operated from about 1807 to 1865. Lustre-ware was one of many local wares produced. It had a speckled appearance and was usually decorated with transfer patterns of local commemorative interest, one of the most popular subjects being the Wearmouth Bridge as on this jug. (Sunderland Museum and Art Gallery)*

SWANSEA PORCELAIN VASES

*These charming vases are probably by William Billingsley (1758–1828), a celebrated early 19th-century potter and porcelain painter. The vase on the left shows a view in Cumberland, that on the right Basingwerk Abbey; both vases have a view of Llangollen Vale on the other side. Billingsley was primarily a flower painter—he introduced a new technique for floral painting on pottery—and his landscapes are rare. After a series of unsuccessful ventures, he founded the famous Nantgarw factory, where most of the finest Welsh soft porcelain was made. He later moved to Swansea where he set up a factory between 1814 and 1817. (Glynn Vivian Art Gallery, Swansea)*

**Swaffham** *Norfolk*  554Bb
CHURCH OF SS PETER AND PAUL This 15th-century church has a steeple built *c.* 1510, clerestory, transepts, and south porch with hammerbeam roof. The nave ·has a superb double hammerbeam roof with angels. A 19th-century stained glass window is by Wailes, 1853.

**Swaffham Bulbeck** *Cambs.*  548Aj
Swaffham Bulbeck has an attractive old moated farmhouse, the Burgh Hall, *c.* 1650. On the back road to Quy, half hidden among the trees, lies Anglesey Abbey, from the early 12th century—the medieval part of which was incorporated in a mansion of *c.* 1600, and later restored.

Then come four notable smallish houses: the Lordship House, clunch-built, with lancet windows on one side and small mullioned windows on the other; the Merchant's House, dated 1711, a brick house with a Dutch gable; the Maltings opposite with a good shell-hood doorway dated 1697; and Abbey House of 1778, notable because the semi-basement is the vaulted undercroft of the old nunnery founded in 1190.

**Swaffham Prior** *Cambs.*  548Af
Swaffham Prior has many charming thatched cottages dominated by Baldwin Manor, standing right on the street. This Henry VIII half-timbered house has an impressive oversailing upper storey on a carved bressumer.

**Swanage** *Dorset*  540Ec
There are several old stone houses in the town, but most of it is modern. The town hall was erected in 1883, but the carved stone façade was designed by Wren in 1670 as the entrance to the Mercers' Hall, Cheapside, London, and re-erected in Swanage. Similarly, the Wellington Clock Tower was originally erected in Southwark, London, in 1854 in honour of the Iron Duke, but was also removed and re-erected in Swanage in 1867.

**Swansea** *Glam.*  544Fc
GLYNN VIVIAN ART GALLERY The museum contains collections of Swansea porcelain and Swansea pottery, the Deffett Francis Collection of prints and drawings, continental porcelain, a collection of glass including fine paperweights, and contemporary paintings, including some by the Welsh

SWEETHEART ABBEY

*Founded in 1273, Sweetheart Abbey is so named because of the great affection of the foundress, Dervorgilla, for her husband, John Balliol of Barnard Castle. On his death Dervorgilla kept his embalmed heart until her own death in 1290, when it was buried with her before the high altar of the abbey.*

LOCOMOTIVE 2516

*Built in 1897, locomotive number 2516 was one of 200 known as 'Dean Goods', a class of railway engines designed by William Dean, who was one of the foremost locomotive designers at the end of the 19th century. (Great Western Railway Museum, Swindon)*

artists Richard Wilson, Ceri Richards, Augustus John, Kyffin Williams, and bronzes by Epstein and Barbara Hepworth.

INDUSTRIAL MUSEUM OF SOUTH WALES Amongst many other industrial relics is a fireless locomotive, built during the First World War, designed to be used in an explosives factory.

**Sweetheart Abbey** *Kirkcud.* 556Fh
Sweetheart Abbey was founded in 1273, an unusually late date for a Cistercian foundation. In plan, however, the abbey kept to the normal Cistercian rules and a range for lay-brothers was included along the west walk of the cloister. Of the convent buildings little survives, but much of the church still exists. It is a long, low building dating from the period of the foundation. The central tower still stands, and there is still some of the window tracery and the vaulting in two of the chapels.

**Swinbrook** *Oxon.* 546Ed
CHURCH OF ST MARY THE VIRGIN An Early English and Perpendicular church famous for its extraordinary 16th- and 17th-century monuments to the Feltiplace family. Against the chancel north wall, they resemble canopied open cupboards with shelves: on three of the six shelves reclines a man in armour, resting on his elbow. The second group of three, the effigies in similar posture but without armour, is by William Byrd of Oxford, *c.* 1686.

**Swindon** *Wilts.* 546Db
GREAT WESTERN RAILWAY MUSEUM GWR locomotives on display include the *City of Truro* (which on May 9, 1904, averaged 70 mph from Exeter to Bristol), *Lode Star*, Hawsworth Pannier tank engine and a replica of the *North Star* (the first passenger train to run from Paddington to Maidenhead, in 1838). Smaller items include many fine model trains, signal apparatus, valve gear, tickets, directors' passes, etc. One room is devoted to the great 19th-century engineer and bridge builder Isambard Kingdom Brunel (1806–59), who literally laid the foundations of the Great Western Railway, and probably named it as well. The building was formerly a lodging for workmen building the Great Western Railway in the mid-19th century, and later became a Wesleyan church—hence the imposingly ecclesiastical entrance. It has been a museum since 1962.

MUSEUM AND ART GALLERY The work of modern artists, including Henry Moore, Ben Nicholson, Graham Sutherland and John Nash, is contained in modern surroundings—the art gallery was built in 1964, adjoining an 1820 building which houses coins, geological collections, musical instruments (including examples of the now obsolete serpent, a bass wind instrument some 8 ft long, and its later development, the ophicleide), and items of natural history—Wiltshire birds, and British mammals.

**Swine** *Yorks.* 559Gb
CHURCH OF ST MARY There was once a priory of Cistercian nuns here, and this church is the chancel of their former church, originally 12th century but enlarged in the 14th. There are misericords, a 16th-century screen and a 17th-century pulpit, while the tower and font are of the 18th century. There are many monuments with recumbent effigies.

**Swyncombe** *Oxon.* 547Gc
CHURCH OF ST BOTOLPH A small Norman church with nave, chancel and apse, in a rather remote setting. There is a Norman font, and a rood screen with loft dating from the early 20th century.

**Sycharth** *Denb.* 551Hc
This well preserved and unusually sited motte and bailey castle was one of the homes of the rebellious

Welsh leader Owen Glendower. Recent excavations have shown that he made alterations to the archaic structure, and evidence was found of its burning (during the absence of Glendower) by the 16-year-old Prince Henry in 1403.

**Sydenham Damerel** *Devon*                    *538Fd*
In this picturesque village is a bridge built in 1437. It is called Horsebridge, a corruption of its original name of Hautesbrygge.

**Sydenham House** *Devon*                    *538Fd*
An Elizabethan mansion, whose main feature is a splendid carved staircase.

**Sydling St Nicholas** *Dorset*                    *540Dc*
CHURCH OF ST NICHOLAS The church is mainly of the 15th century, with a west tower; the chancel was rebuilt in the mid-18th century. There are a number of minor but pretty 18th- and 19th-century wall monuments, a 12th-century font, and an 18th-century screen under the tower.

**Syon House** *Greater London*                    *547Jb*
Originally a nunnery founded by Henry V in 1415. At the Dissolution in 1534, the building passed to Edward Seymour, Duke of Somerset (Protector Somerset), brother of Jane Seymour, Henry VIII's third wife. Somerset converted the nunnery into a great castellated mansion. After his downfall in 1549 the property reverted to the Crown, but Elizabeth I gave it to the Earl of Northumberland. Repairs were made in the 17th century by Inigo Jones. In 1762, Hugh Smithson (later the 1st Duke of Northumberland) commissioned Robert Adam to renovate the interior. The house is planned as an open square with a great courtyard which Adam proposed to fill with an immense circular saloon, but the duke would not allow Adam to interfere with the levels or general arrangement of rooms within the house. Syon contains much fine furniture and a collection of pictures. It stands in extensive grounds landscaped by Capability Brown.

ANTE-ROOM AT SYON HOUSE

*One of several ornamental tables standing beneath panels depicting military trophies that Robert Adam designed for this room, the ante-room to the hall. Decorated in 1762–9, the room is an early version of the style developed by Adam, which later became noted for paler colours and more feminine ornament. But here he used brilliant colours, stucco panels and much gilt. The room is based on Diocletian's Palace at Spalato, and around the walls are 12 green marble columns, dredged from the R. Tiber and brought to Syon in 1765.*

# T

**Taliaris Park** *Carm.*                    *544Fd*
This was probably built in the 17th century for the Guynne family, who lived here until *c.* 1754. There is a notable Jacobean staircase rising from the ground to the third floor. The house also has 17th- and 19th-century additions.

**Talley Abbey** *Carm.*                    *544Fe*
The ruins of a 12th-century abbey, probably founded by Rhys ap Gruffyd, Prince of South Wales.

**Tamworth** *Staffs.*                    *552Db*
On a mound raised in late Saxon times is an imposing Norman castle with curtain wall and keep and, within the enclosure, Tudor and Jacobean domestic buildings. The town hall was built in 1701 by Thomas Guy (1645–1724), founder of Guy's Hospital, London, who was educated in Tamworth.
CASTLE Alfred the Great's daughter, Ethelfleda, raised the great mound on which the castle stands, in 913. Robert de Marmion, William the Conqueror's Royal Champion, was later granted the castle and built the Norman keep and curtain walls. The banqueting hall and other domestic offices date from the time of Henry VIII.

CASTLE MUSEUM The collection comprises Saxon and Norman coins, mainly from the Tamworth Mint, early printed books, Roman coins and glass, and local prints and water-colours.
CHURCH OF ST EDITHA A former collegiate church dating from the Normans, but mainly of 14th- and 15th-century work. There are several monuments, and stained glass made by William Morris to the design of Ford Madox Brown. The central tower has a unique double-spiral staircase.

**Tantallon Castle** *E. Lothian*                    *562Df*
Perched high on a rocky eminence overlooking the Firth of Forth, the castle played a considerable part in the medieval battles waged between the Crowns of England and Scotland. The existing remains consist of the castle proper, an outer bailey and various defensive outworks. The main curtain wall extends along only two sides of the courtyard, for impregnable cliffs protect the other two sides. The most impressive defences face inwards towards the headland, where the 14th-century fabric included a gate-house and the East and Douglas Towers. The gate-house was later altered when it was strengthened to accommodate more artillery. The north side of the courtyard contains

## TANTALLON CASTLE

*Perched on a high rock overlooking the Firth of Forth, Tantallon has had a lively and stormy history—throughout the Middle Ages it was the chief stronghold of the Douglas Earls of Angus. Although about midway between Edinburgh and the English border, the earls were frequently in open rebellion and receiving assistance from the English Crown. As a result the castle was besieged (unsuccessfully) by the royal Scots army in 1491 and 1528. However, during a third* *siege by Commonwealth forces in 1651, General Monk battered the walls with his guns, capturing the castle after a 12-day bombardment. This was the last time Tantallon served in a serious defensive role. In 1699 the Douglases sold it and the whole building fell into decay. All that now remains are parts of the castle proper, an outer bailey and various defensive outworks on two sides—the steep cliffs above the sea protected the other two sides.*

the remains of the chief domestic quarters—the great hall, living accommodation and kitchens.

**Tarporley** *Cheshire*          *552Ae*
CHURCH OF ST HELEN A medieval church, so rebuilt as to be nearly all 19th-century work. It contains some noteworthy memorials of the 17th and 18th centuries, with effigies of the Done and Crewe families.

**Tarvit House** *Fife.*          *562Cg*
A mansion, built in 1696 and rebuilt in 1906. It has a collection of furniture, tapestries, porcelain and paintings.

**Tattenhoe** *Bucks.*          *547Ge*
CHURCH OF ST GILES Deserted, and surrounded by traces of long-vanished buildings, St Giles's was built in 1540 with materials from a priory, and there are fishponds near by. Inside there are box-pews and a font made in the 18th century from 13th-century materials.

**Tattershall** *Lincs.*          *553Hd*
CHURCH OF THE HOLY TRINITY The church was entirely rebuilt between 1440 and *c.* 1480, and stands near the castle. Formerly a collegiate church, it has a west tower and, inside, a good 16th-century stone rood screen. There are 15th- and 16th-century brasses in the north transept; most of the original stained glass was removed in the 18th century, but the few remaining fragments can be seen in the east window.

**Tattershall Castle** *Lincs.*          *553Hd*
This great keep of a Norman castle is one of the most splendid and important examples of medieval brick building in the country: stone is used only for window and door frames, and a little for decoration. It was erected in the mid-15th century at a time when brick was becoming increasingly popular as a building material. The castle itself was founded in 1231 when the owner of the manor,

Robert of Tattershall, was granted a royal licence to put up a fortified building, but little remains except the keep.

**Tatton Park** *Cheshire*          *552Bf*
The home of the Egerton family since the late 16th century. The present house was begun in the late 18th century and was built around an earlier house dating from Charles II's time. The architect was Samuel Wyatt, who died in 1807 before building was complete. The house was furnished by Wyatt's nephew, Lewis. In the house are fine furniture, pictures, china, silver and glass.

Humphry Repton laid out the grounds, 54 acres of ornamental and woodland gardens, with the mile long Tatton Mere winding through them. He planned to have an ornamental lake, but this proposal was turned down. However, by chance the ground has subsided at the same spot and so today water is where Repton had visualised it.

One of the most prominent features of the formal gardens is the 400 yds long Broad Walk of tall trees leading to a replica (1811) of a Greek monument on the edge of the open park. An avenue of specimen trees leads to the Golden Brook, a pool-like stream bordered by conifers, shrubs and aquatic plants, and beyond is a Japanese garden, laid out at the beginning of the 20th century on a small islet; stonework, lanterns and Japanese plants surround a Shinto temple. Large undulating areas are densely planted with rhododendrons and azaleas, brilliant with flowers in spring and early summer, and later a blaze of autumn colour.

**Taunton** *Som.*          *540Be*
Mentioned in the Saxon Chronicle (AD 722), and acquired by the Bishops of Winchester in Norman times, Taunton was developed especially by Henry de Blois (founder of Glastonbury) who built the castle. It was the centre of rebellion when

Perkin Warbeck arrived with his Cornish rebels in 1497, and was again involved in strife in the Civil War. The Duke of Monmouth was proclaimed king in the market-place in 1685, and Judge Jeffreys tried 509 rebels in the great hall of the castle. In the strongrooms of the Somerset Record Office (Obridge Road) are about 2,000,000 documents dating from the mid-12th century. The castle (of 12th-century origin) was developed as a major military stronghold, with walls 13 ft thick. Its gateway dates from 1495 and the great hall is 120 ft long. Some of the municipal buildings were erected in 1522 by Richard Fox, Bishop of Winchester, and some, although built in Tudor style, are in fact from this century. The Tudor House (1578), however, is a splendid example of 16th-century domestic architecture, half-timbered and gabled. There are two sets of almshouses: one is Gray's, founded in 1635 by Robert Gray, of the Merchant Taylors of London, and has a series of triple-grouped tall chimneys; the second is Huish's, founded in 1615 by Richard Huish, also a London merchant.

SOMERSET COUNTY MUSEUM The museum is located in Taunton Castle, parts of which date from the 12th century, which has historic associations with the Bishops of Winchester, the Wars of the Roses, the Civil War, the Monmouth rebellion and Judge Jeffreys. Relics from local history include lake-village material from Glastonbury and Mease (including a dug-out boat) and a Roman mosaic from Low Ham. There is a Stringfellow steam aeroplane engine, a working beam engine, a geological and fossil collection and ceramics, portraits—including a full-length portrait of Charles I and his queen by Van Dyck—bygones and natural history, mainly birds of the county and, in aquaria, local freshwater fish.

**Taversoe Tuack** *Rousay, Orkney*          *569Hg*
One of Britain's two cairns with a two-storied chamber. The mound is 30 ft in diameter with a 19 ft long passage to the lower chamber, $12\frac{1}{4}$ ft long by 5 ft wide and $5\frac{1}{4}$ ft high. It is divided into four cells. The upper chamber, floored by the roof of the lower, has its own entrance-passage, 11 ft long. It has two compartments and a further recess opposite the passage.

**Tavistock** *Devon*          *538Fc*
CHURCH OF ST EUSTACE A large church, built when Tavistock was a prosperous wool-town in the 14th and 15th centuries. There is much 19th-century stained glass, and several monuments with figures.

**Teigh** *Rutland*          *553Gc*
CHURCH OF THE HOLY TRINITY The 14th-century west tower remains tacked on to the church, rebuilt in Gothic style by George Richardson in 1782. Inside, distinctive 18th-century features include box-pews facing each other, and a triple grouping of pulpit, reading desk and clerk's desk at the west end.

**Temple Newsam House** *Yorks.*          *558Ca*
An estate that once belonged to the Knights Templar, but later became a private home. Lord Darnley, second husband of Mary, Queen of Scots, was born here in 1545. The present Tudor and Jacobean mansion was largely rebuilt c. 1630 by Sir Arthur Ingram and much of the interior was redecorated in Georgian style c. 1740 by his descendant, the 7th Viscount Irwin. It now belongs to Leeds Corporation and contains collections of period furniture and silver, ancient ceramics, and pictures including prints by Hogarth. The grounds were landscaped by Capability Brown.

THE KEEP AT
TATTERSHALL CASTLE

*One of the most splendid examples of medieval brick building in Britain. During the tenure of the Cromwell family the original 13th-century castle at Tattershall was greatly enlarged. The main builder was Ralph, 3rd Lord Cromwell, who held the land from 1417 to 1456. He was a powerful and ambitious politician, Treasurer of England from 1433 to 1443. The keep was built by him; it was out of date as a defensive feature even in the 15th century, and was probably planned as a grandiose and palatial set of private apartments. Many of the interior fittings have been swept away, but a set of magnificent 15th-century fire-places, complete with heraldic adornments, still survive.*

TATTON PARK

*This house was begun for the Egerton family by Samuel Wyatt at the end of the 18th century. The Egertons had lived here since the late 16th century, and the house they built during the reign of Charles II remained the core around which Wyatt worked. Samuel Wyatt was the elder brother of James Wyatt, who became the fashionable architect at the turn of the century. Samuel produced a pleasant but not grand house whose main feature is the four-column portico, each column being made from a single huge block of stone from local Cheshire quarries. Samuel Wyatt died in 1807 before the work at Tatton was finished. He and his brother James had been assisted by a nephew, Lewis Wyatt, and he completed the work, including the entrance gateway and conservatory.*

## TEWKESBURY ABBEY

*One of the largest abbey churches to survive the Dissolution, Tewkesbury Abbey has been used as a parish church ever since, despite its enormous size. It has one of the finest sets of medieval tombs in England. The earliest parts date from the early 12th century, the magnificent tower from about 1150. During the 14th century a new vault was added to set off the tombs surrounding the choir. These belong to successive patrons of the abbey and commemorate some of the most powerful medieval families. In the 15th century the lordship of Tewkesbury was held by the Beauchamp family, including Warwick the King-maker. Many of the family are buried in the abbey, where they endowed the beautifully vaulted Warwick Chantry (right).*

**Temple Sowerby Manor** *Westmld.*     *557Jf*
An 18th-century red sandstone house, with some parts dating from the 16th century. The gardens are famous for their roses.

**Tenby** *Pemb.*     *544Dc*
The old centre of this attractive holiday town lay east of the town walls, which cut off a neck of land, at the tip of which stood the castle—strongly defended on three sides by the sea. From medieval times the sheltered harbour to the north served as an important link with Bristol and Ireland. The town grew beyond its walls with the coming of the railway in 1853 and its development as a holiday resort. The parish church dates from the 13th century, and by the 15th century had developed into an impressive building. There is an excellent museum at the entrance to Castle Hill. In the summer there are boat trips to Caldy Island, where there are two ancient churches which preceded the present priory, re-established in 1929.
CHURCH OF ST MARY A large church dating from the 13th century, with later additions. The tower and steeple are between the south aisle and chapel, and there is a 15th-century chancel roof with bosses. Among the monuments with figures is a 15th-century carved skeleton; from the 19th century is to be found work by Edward Physick and John Evan Thomas.
MUSEUM The building incorporates remains of a medieval castle. All the collections on display relate to Pembrokeshire, particularly to Tenby, and cover geology, archaeology, natural history and medieval history. They include the Smith Collection of local cave-animal remains with relics of mammoths, and the Lyons Collection of marine shells.
PLANTAGENET HOUSE An early 15th-century Tudor house. (Open to members of the National Trust by appointment.)
TUDOR MERCHANT'S HOUSE A house built *c.* 1500 and typical of that period. (Open to members of the National Trust by appointment.)

**Tenterden** *Kent*     *542Ee*
A market town, with a wide, tree-lined High Street, and the warm reds of its brick houses. There was clearly a local style of building here *c.* 1760–90, perhaps the work of one local builder, who left his mark on the town, and on the houses in their small parks dotted round it.

**Tetbury** *Glos.*     *546Cc*
CHURCH OF ST MARY MAGDALENE The old Norman church was pulled down, and replaced in 1781 by one to the design of Francis Hiorne. The tower and spire, however, date from the 15th century. The interior of the church is a fine 18th-century period piece, with box-pews, gallery and candelabra.

**Teversal** *Notts.*     *552Ee*
CHURCH OF ST CATHERINE Originally Norman, with later alterations. Remarkable 17th-century furnishings—box-pews, altar rails, pulpit, squire's pew and so on. Many monuments to the local Molyneux family; one of *c.* 1741 is by Sir Henry Cheere.

**Tewes** *Essex*     *548Be*
An unspoilt example of a 15th-century timber-framed manor house, *c.* 1480, with original oak-mullioned windows constructed before glass was used in this type of house. A porch and bay are 20th-century additions. Inside there is 17th-century furniture, a collection of wooden tea-caddies, snuff-boxes, and an early coffee grinder, as well as a collection of polychrome Worcester sauce-boats.

**Tewkesbury** *Glos.*     *546Ce*
Tewkesbury contains many inns and old timbered houses, including the House of the Golden Key and Ancient Grudge, as well as an abbey. In 1471 Edward IV defeated the Lancastrians at the Battle of Tewkesbury. About 6 miles from the town is Bredon Hill (980 ft). At the summit is a prehistoric camp known as the King and Queen Rocks. To the east of the town is the Tibble Stone, a boundary

stone probably dating from AD 600, which is referred to in Domesday Book and has been adapted as a modern signpost.

CHURCH OF ST MARY THE VIRGIN A surprising parish church: it is the former abbey church, bought by the townsfolk at the Dissolution for about £400, and is as big as a cathedral. It was attached to a Benedictine monastery and dates from the early part of the 12th century. The tall columns of the nave form one of the chief features of the Romanesque church and make it distinctly different from most other churches of that period. The striking central tower was probably built c. 1150.

The eastern parts of the church were almost entirely rebuilt in the 14th century, and a new vault was added to the nave. The most brilliant architectural feature is the vaulting of the presbytery in which the surface is decorated with patterns similar to those used in window tracery. The impressive interior has many tombs and monuments; especially interesting is the late 14th-century Despencer chantry chapel, on top of which kneels a small effigy of Edward le Despencer beneath its own canopy. There is also some 14th-century stained glass.

Of the monks' quarters, to the south of the church, little remains.

**Thame** *Oxon.* 547Gc
CHURCH OF ST MARY THE VIRGIN A magnificent cruciform church with a noble central tower, of Norman origins but with work of all Gothic periods: good windows, south porch, screens and an Early English font; also of interest are the brasses. Noteworthy among the monuments is one to Lord Williams of Thame (*d.* 1559) and his wife, in front of the altar.

**Thaxted** *Essex* 548Bd
Thaxted was one of the most prosperous towns in Essex, a centre of the wool trade. It has a large church with exceptionally tall spire, a timber-framed guildhall of 1475, and some noteworthy houses. The Recorder's House (now a restaurant) carries the Arms of Edward IV.
CHURCH OF ST JOHN THE BAPTIST The prosperity of Thaxted 500 years ago enabled the parishioners to build their spacious cruciform church with its 180 ft high spire. The pinnacled font cover, of the late 15th century, completely encases the font. There are 17th-century screens, many fragments of medieval stained glass, and two 20th-century windows by C. E. Kempe.

**Theddlethorpe** *Lincs.* 553Jf
CHURCH OF ALL SAINTS Largely a building of the 14th and 15th centuries, but with some earlier work. There are Perpendicular and good Decorated windows, and fragments of medieval glass remain. There is a brass of *c.* 1424, and screens of the 15th century. There are still some patches of early colour decoration on parts of the aisle walls. Among the 18th-century monuments is one by Andrew Carpenter, of *c.* 1727.

**Theobald's Park** *Herts.* 547Jc
London's Temple Bar (designed by Sir Christopher Wren in 1672) was removed from its original site in 1887, and re-erected at the entrance to the Park in 1888 by Sir Henry Meux.

**Therfield Heath** *Herts.* 548Ae
Here there is a 125 ft Neolithic barrow, still standing up to 8 ft high. It has a surrounding ditch and the mound was of piled turves coated with a crust of chalk. Just to the north is a group of eight bowl barrows. They vary greatly in diameter and are up to 12 ft high.

**Thetford** *Norfolk* 554Ba
An ancient town, once important, with a known history of more than 1000 years. It was the seat of the kings of East Anglia and a bishop's See from 1075 to 1091. Surrounding it are many relics of Stone Age cultures, and it stands on the ancient Icknield Way. In the Middle Ages and Tudor period it had as many as 20 parish churches and several monasteries. After the Dissolution the town's importance declined.

ANCIENT HOUSE MUSEUM A Tudor building houses a collection illustrating natural history and the history of man in Breckland (Norfolk). Finds from the Early Stone Age to the medieval period are included. More recent items are flint objects produced by the Brandon flint knappers, who still produce flints commercially. There is also a large collection of molluscs from the neighbouring brecks and meres.
BELL HOTEL Built in 1493, with fine timber work. Early wall-paintings and a section of the original wattle-and-daub wall tied with ropes of grass are preserved.
CAGE AND STOCKS In Cage Lane; erected in 1581 as a lock-up with stocks, it is a two-storied, gabled town gaol. In Old Market Street is the gaol of 1816.
CASTLE HILL The remaining mound of a motte and bailey castle demolished in 1173. The surrounding earthworks may be from the time of the Iceni, an Ancient British tribe.
CLUNIAC PRIORY OF OUR LADY These monastic remains are near the railway station; others are the Augustinian Priory of the Holy Sepulchre in Brandon Road; the Blackfriars in the grammar school, London Road; and the Benedictine Nunnery of St George, near the Euston road.
GREY GABLES A modern house incorporating the small cottage in which Thomas Paine, author of *The Rights of Man*, was born in 1737.
KING'S HOUSE Used as a hunting lodge by James I; it has an 18th-century front.
THETFORD WARREN LODGE A 15th-century flint-and-stone tower, perhaps a fortified game-keeper's house, in heathland near the Thetford to Brandon road.

**Thirlstane Castle** *Ber.* 562Dd
An imposing late 16th-century building incorporating a 14th-century fortress. It was altered in the late 17th century by Sir William Bruce, and contains fine plasterwork of that period and a collection of portraits by Lely, Romney and Aikmain. (By appointment.)

**Thirsk** *Yorks.* 558Dd
CHURCH OF ST MARY This is an impressive church in the Perpendicular style; built 1420, the chancel was added in 1470. There are still fragments of medieval glass in one or two windows, and the brass and screens are also worth noting. There is 19th-century restoration by G. E. Street.

**Thoresby Hall** *Notts.* 552Ee
The present large mansion, built in neo-Tudor style, is the third to be erected in Thoresby Park. The original country seat was built in 1683 for the 4th Earl of Kingston by William Talman, architect of the early work at Chatsworth. The mansion was destroyed by fire in 1745, and the only survivor was a sphinx, carved by Caius Gabriel Cibber. A few years later the house was rebuilt by John Carr of York in the Palladian manner, but in the 19th century this house was demolished. The owner, the 3rd Earl Manvers, a direct descendant of the 2nd Duke of Kingston, found Carr's house too small, and commissioned the architect Anthony Salvin to build the present mansion. (See p. 458.)

## THE GREAT HALL AT THORESBY HALL

*This large Victorian mansion was built by the architect Anthony Salvin to replace the smaller seat of the Earls of Manvers. Outstanding features of the house, on which Salvin worked from 1864 until 1875, include the large state apartments, the three-storied great hall with its lavish hammerbeam roof, and the entrance tower, which Salvin modelled on that of Burghley House in Huntingdonshire. The mansion is surrounded by the largest park in the Dukeries, and is enclosed in Sherwood Forest.*

**Thorington Hall** *Suffolk*     *548Ce*
An oak-framed, plastered and gabled house within retaining walls, built *c.* 1600, enlarged *c.* 1700, and restored in 1937. (By appointment.)

**Thorney** *Hunts.*     *547Jl*
Thorney village, only 15 ft above sea level, is the only village in Thorney Rural District, an area of 22,985 acres on the most northerly part of the Fenlands. Hereward the Wake made one of his last stands here against William the Conqueror. For a long time the village was the sole property of a single landlord, the Earls and Dukes of Bedford, who arranged the houses according to the status of employees on the estate.

At Toneham, south-west of the village, were the claypits, brick-yard and kiln used by the Duke of Bedford in building the estate houses of 19th-century Thorney.

CHURCH OF SS MARY AND BOTOLPH Remnants of the former Norman abbey church, with good early 12th-century arcades, and an impressive west front. The transepts, crossing tower and chancel have all gone, and the present east end is by Edward Blore (the architect who designed the Mall block of Buckingham Palace) in a Norman style of *c.* 1840.

THORNEY ABBEY The small island on which Thorney is built was used as a monastic settlement in the 7th century. This monastery was destroyed by the Danes in 870. The subsequent Norman abbey was dissolved in 1539 and left derelict until 1638, when part of the original was restored. Its west front has two tall 12th-century turrets surmounted by 15th-century octagonal tops, with a deeply recessed doorway of the same period between them, over which is a 17th-century window. Above this is a stone screen, extending from turret to turret, with nine canopied niches containing medieval statues. The chancel and transept were added in 1841 in imitation of Norman style.

THORNEY ABBEY HOUSE There are two houses here. The first is of the late 16th century, and the second, *c.* 1660, was the mansion house of the Dukes of Bedford, who voluntarily contributed their vast fortunes to drain the Bedford Level of the Fens.

Around the house spread 20,000 acres of land reclaimed from swamp and mere. The house is square, built of stone, with a hipped-roof and one great central chimney-stack. Inside, there is some good panelling in the dining-room, including a great carved fire-place surround, a broad staircase, and doorcases which may have been by Peter Mills, *c.* 1660.

**Thornhill** *Yorks.*     *558Ca*
CHURCH OF ST MICHAEL AND ALL ANGELS Originally 15th century, the church was restored and rebuilt in 1879 by G. E. Street. There are fragments of Saxon crosses, and many monuments with effigies, the most spectacular being the large 17th-century edifices to the Saviles. There is good 15th-century glass.

**Thornton Abbey** *Lincs.*     *553Hg*
The abbey was founded in 1139 for a community of Augustinian canons. Only parts of the chapter house and a fine gateway remain. One of the canons compiled a chronicle of Thornton Abbey from which it has been possible to date accurately the building of various parts of the monastery. The chapter house, which was begun in 1282, was paved in 1308, and must have been an impressive building. Licence to build the fine gateway was granted in 1382; it stood just inside the courtyard and had some military fortifications in the form of two round towers and an arcaded surrounding wall. It is faced partly in stone and partly in brick—an early example in England of this decorative use. The abbey is approached across a moat, spanned by a long bridge.

**Thorpe Hall** *Hunts.*     *547Jg*
A dignified mid-17th-century rectangular house, built by John Webb (a one-time pupil of Inigo Jones), during the Commonwealth period, for Chief Justice Oliver St John. It has two main floors, a high hipped-roof with dormers, and signs that suggest a Dutch influence on the later, east side. The entrance gates with piers carrying heraldic birds frame the house perfectly.

**Thorpe Market** *Norfolk*     *554Dc*
CHURCH OF ST MARGARET The church was built *c.* 1795 in the Gothic Revival style, and has open-work screens, porches on both sides, and at each corner of the building are turrets with little spires. The font is Perpendicular. One of the monuments is by Charles Regnart, 1796.

**Threave Castle** *Kirkcud.*     *556Eg*
The ruined stronghold of the Black Douglases, Lords of Galloway. It was built by Archibald the Grim, 3rd Earl Douglas, on an island in the R. Dee during the 14th century, and housed a Royalist garrison in the Civil War. The 14th-century tower-house is surrounded by walls built in the 15th century; these were more than 70 ft high and 8 ft thick.

The Threave Wildfowl Refuge is on the estate.

**Throwley** *Kent*      *542Ef*
CHURCH OF ST MICHAEL AND ALL ANGELS A large church for a sparsely populated parish, with 16th-century cottages adjoining. The tower between the south aisle and chapel is battlemented; its top stage was built in the 19th century. Traces of Norman work can be seen on the west door and on the blocked window under the tower in the nave. The monastic foundation of the church explains its unexpected misericords. There are fine late 16th- and 17th-century altar tombs with kneeling effigies of painted alabaster, among the earliest in the country, with heraldry, and a monument by the neo-Classical sculptor John Flaxman (1755–1826).

**Thrumpton Hall** *Notts.*      *552Ec*
A Stuart manor house begun *c.* 1610; it was altered and enlarged in 1660–9 and again in 1827–35, this time in Gothic style. A niece of one of its owners during the 19th century married a descendant of Lord Byron, the poet, and the house contains a number of Byron relics.

**Thungarton** *Notts.*      *552Fd*
PRIORY CHURCH OF ST PETER The Benedictine priory was founded in 1187, and the present parish church is a tiny fragment of what must have been quite a large building with two western towers.

**Tichborne** *Hants.*      *541He*
CHURCH OF ST ANDREW The church has a Norman chancel, an early 18th-century brick west tower, a Norman font, and fragments of medieval glass. Many monuments in the north aisle are dedicated to the local family, the Tichbornes, from the 17th to the 19th century. The box-pews are from the early 17th century.

**Tickencote** *Rutland*      *553Gb*
CHURCH OF ST PETER The huge Norman chancel arch, with its five rows of carving each in a different design, has long been famous. Much of the church was rebuilt in the late 18th century by Samuel Pepys Cockerell, but the vaulted chancel is largely original 12th-century work.

**Tickhill** *Yorks.*      *552Ef*
CHURCH OF ST MARY A large and impressive church, dating from the 13th century, when the base of the west tower was built. Rebuilding took place in the late 14th century, but the upper part of the tower was not completed until later, when the nave was rebuilt. There are remains of medieval glass, and monuments of the 15th–19th centuries.

**Tideswell** *Derbys.*      *552Ce*
CHURCH OF ST JOHN THE BAPTIST A cruciform church with a pinnacled west tower, almost all dating from the 14th century. It contains a Perpendicular font, some 19th-century stained glass, and many medieval monuments and brasses.

**Tilbury** *Essex*      *548Bb*
THURROCK LOCAL HISTORY MUSEUM The main collections are of local archaeological finds from Palaeolithic times, the Early and Late Bronze Age—including a Celtic founder's hoard—and Romano-British ceramics, glass, bronzes and ornaments, with a hoard of Roman silver coins of the 1st and 2nd centuries AD. There are also pre-Christian Saxon ceramics, domestic items, ornaments and weapons, and local social history is represented by items relating to the railways, fire-fighting and other services. Local engravings, water-colours and oil paintings can also be seen.

**Tilty** *Essex*      *548Bd*
CHURCH OF ST MARY THE VIRGIN This church was formerly the chapel outside the gate of the neighbouring Cistercian abbey. It has a 13th-century

## THE GATE-HOUSE AT THORNTON ABBEY

*One of the most splendid gate-houses to survive in England, probably designed for domestic use, possibly as a guest house. The upper floors contain a large hall and various small rooms including cloakrooms, and the impressive entrance façade is decorated with two rows of statuary. The Augustinian abbey appears to have been large and wealthy: at the time of the Dissolution one prior and 27 canons surrendered to the Crown. The abbey was turned into a secular college for canons for a few years during the reign of Henry VIII. The surviving walls of the fine octagonal chapter house are decorated with blank geometric tracery, and the vault sprang from a central column.*

nave and 14th-century chancel, with a five-light east window. It also contains brasses.

**Tintagel** *Cornwall*      *538Dd*
High on the cliff-top overlooking the sea lies Tintagel, well known for its association with the Arthurian legend, for here, so the story goes, King Uther Pendragon and Ygraine, Arthur's parents, first met. It was the site of a Celtic monastery, probably founded by St Juliot about the beginning of the 6th century. The foundations may still be seen. They were not grouped in any recognisable pattern, showing how different these early religious houses were from the later establishments, which may indicate that the first monasteries began as random gatherings of hermits, and only later became well organised.
TINTAGEL OLD POST OFFICE A small 14th-century stone house, with thick and uneven slate roof, built to the plan of a medieval manor house. It gets its name because it was a letter-receiving office for the district from 1844 until 1892.

**Tintagel Castle** *Cornwall*      *538Dd*
The castle at Tintagel was built in the 12th century, and considerable additions were made to it in the

following century. By the 16th century the central portion connecting the inner ward with the lower ward and part of the great hall had been washed away by the sea. The site then became derelict until interest in the Arthurian legend revived in the 19th century. Tennyson's poems popularised the legend and the ruins were repaired in 1852.

**Tintern Abbey** *Mon.*                    *546Ac*
The abbey was founded in 1131. Hardly anything is visible of the original foundation, for in the 13th and 14th centuries the abbey was extensively enlarged. Most of the ruined monastic buildings are well preserved, and the church itself is an impressive ruin. It was built on an axis slightly south of that of the first church, and the high altar was first used in 1288. The Cistercian architecture is simple: there is no triforium passage between clerestory and the main arcade, and large towers were forbidden by the rule of the Cistercian order.

**Tintinhull House** *Som.*                 *540Cd*
An elegant small manor house built in the late 17th century. It stands in a fine formal garden.

**Tiptofts Manor** *Essex*                  *548Be*
A moated house of *c.* 1330 with a rare surviving aisled hall. The exterior is timber-framed.

**Tisbury** *Wilts.*                        *540Ee*
CHURCH OF ST JOHN THE BAPTIST A cruciform 12th-century church, with a central tower which, until it fell in 1762, had a spire. Inside, the font cover, pulpit and pews are 17th century; the communion rail is made from parts of a rood screen.

**Titchfield** *Hants.*                     *541Hd*
In the main street there are Georgian brick cottages. Titchfield's outstanding building is the silvery-grey stone mansion built in Henry VIII's reign out of the buildings of the dissolved abbey. CHURCH OF ST PETER An interesting church, probably of Saxon origin. Among the monuments is one of *c.* 1615, attributed to Epiphanius Evesham, but the most striking is by Gerard Johnson to two Earls of Southampton, *c.* 1594, resplendent with effigies, shields, obelisks and heraldic beasts.

**Tittleshall** *Norfolk*                   *554Bc*
CHURCH OF ST MARY The west tower and chancel are Decorated, the nave Perpendicular, and the octagonal font Perpendicular. But the interest of Tittleshall is in its series of monuments to the Coke (Earls of Leicester) family. Nicholas Stone, the early 17th-century sculptor, carved that to Sir Edward Coke (*d.* 1634), with a recumbent effigy. Louis Roubiliac carved the busts of the 1st Earl and Countess of Leicester, *c.* 1760, and Joseph Nollekens sculpted the large marble relief showing Mrs Coke (*d.* 1800) leaning on a broken column, whilst above an angel sitting on clouds holds out his hand to her.

**Tiverton** *Devon*                        *539He*
BLUNDELL'S (OLD SCHOOL) The original building of the famous grammar school, built in 1604 by Peter Blundell, Clothier. The north-east façade is as described in the novel *Lorna Doone* by R. D. Blackmore.

TINTAGEL CASTLE

*Legend links this site—a rocky headland amid wild and romantic scenery—with King Arthur, a shadowy figure of the late 5th century who allegedly successfully led the native Celts against the invading Saxons during the breaking up of the Roman Empire. There is, however, no earlier evidence to support this link than the propagandist 12th-century writings of Geoffrey of Monmouth. The most interesting of the remains of earlier settlements on the site are those associated with the monastery which grew up around the cell of St Juliot, a Celtic missionary who came to Tintagel about 500. This community, which was housed in a series of small, rectangular stone huts scattered across the north-east side of the headland, was governed by no formal rule but formed a loose association of individuals serving God in varying ways. Tintagel became a royal castle attached to the Earldom of Cornwall, and among its distinguished lords was Edward III's son Edward, the Black Prince, who commissioned some of the surviving buildings.*

CHURCH OF ST GEORGE An early 18th-century Classical church, with a pleasant contemporary interior, galleried.

CHURCH OF ST PETER This large church, with its spectacular south aisle and porch, 1517, reflects the former prosperity of Tiverton, once a flourishing port. There is a 17th-century organ.

**Tixover** *Rutland* 553Gb

CHURCH A mainly Norman church with a tower, and inside an impressive tower arch (all *c.* 1140). The original medieval stone seats remain along the chancel walls. An early 17th-century marble monument to the lord of the manor has kneeling figures.

**Toddington** *Beds.* 547Hd

CHURCH OF ST GEORGE The church is built of Totternhoe stone and ironstone, with modern tile infilling; it is cruciform, with a central tower, and dates from the 13th to 15th centuries. The building is in keeping with the one-time prosperity of this hill-top town; inside are many monuments dating from the 14th century, including one to Lady Henrietta Wentworth, *c.* 1686, which has been attributed to both William Bushnell and William Stanton. The roof has carved angels and bosses. The three-storied priest's house on the north side is unique.

**Toddington** *Glos.* 546De

CHURCH OF ST ANDREW A Gothic Revival church by G. E. Street, 1873–9. There is a tall broach spire and, inside, two marble effigies of Lord and Lady Sudeley by J. G. Lough.

**Tolleshunt d'Arcy** *Essex* 548Cd

CHURCH OF ST NICHOLAS A 15th-century church with an embattled west tower. The nave ceiling was painted with a floral pattern in 1897. The church contains many brasses and monuments.

HALL A house of *c.* 1500 with a fine moat and four-arched brick and stone bridge dated 1585. A wing, remodelled in the 17th century, has outstanding 16th-century panelling of linenfold divided by ranges of carving. In the grounds is a large 16th-century dove-cote with tiled roof.

**Tolleshunt Major** *Essex* 548Cd

BECKINGHAM HALL An unusual brick wall surrounds a large courtyard and relatively small timber-framed and brick house of the mid-16th century. The large turretted gate-house is the central feature of the wall, and there are other turrets at each corner of the wall. Ornamental panelling from the Hall, dated 1546, is in the Victoria and Albert Museum.

**Tolpuddle** *Dorset* 540Dc

MARTYRS' TREE A seat commemorates the six agricultural labourers of Tolpuddle who were sentenced to transportation in 1834 for the 'crime' of demanding a wage increase.

**Tomen-y-mur** *Merioneth* 550Fd

In the wild mountain country a few miles to the south-east of the Snowdon range, the Roman fort of Tomen-y-mur stood on a spur of hill some 10 miles from the sea beyond Harlech. The site is complicated by the presence of the motte of an early medieval castle, standing inside the outline of the early fort. However, when the fort was rebuilt in stone in the 2nd century, its area was reduced, and the wall now running through the motte is the west wall of this second fort. By the path down to the stream are the remains of an amphitheatre, bath-buildings and a parade ground. The small square mounds along this track and beyond the stream are burial-mounds of members of the garrison.

## MONUMENT TO THE 1st EARL OF SOUTHAMPTON

*A fine Elizabethan monument to Thomas Wriothesley, 1st Earl of Southampton, and his wife and son. The four tall obelisks are characteristic of many tombs of the period. Wriothesley (1505–50), a secretary to Henry VIII, was knighted in 1540. At the Dissolution Henry gave him extensive lands including the Abbey of Titchfield, which Sir Thomas rebuilt as a sumptuous house. He was created Earl of Southampton in 1547. His grandson Henry, the 3rd Earl, was a patron of Shakespeare. (Church of St Peter, Titchfield)*

**Tong** *Shrops.* 552Bb

CHURCH OF ST BARTHOLOMEW A magnificent Perpendicular building dating from *c.* 1410, when the earlier church was rebuilt. The square central tower has a pinnacled and battlemented octagonal upper stage, and a short spire. The interior is dominated by superb tombs and monuments, but there is also a Perpendicular octagonal font, and much interesting woodwork, including screens, stall misericords and a Jacobean pulpit. There are monuments to the founders of the church, Sir Fulke and Lady Elizabeth de Pembruge, and to the Vernons of Haddon Hall, including those in the fan-vaulted Vernon Chapel (1515). (See p. 462.)

**Topcliffe** *Yorks.* 558Dc

CHURCH OF ST COLUMBA Although mainly a 19th-century rebuilding, the church still retains some of its original 14th-century work—a huge Flemish-type brass with two figures beneath a canopy containing many smaller figures of angels. There is some stained glass by Burne-Jones.

**Torhouse, Standing Stones of** *Wig.* 556Dg

A perfect circle of tall stones, about 60 ft in diameter, dating from the Bronze Age.

**Torphichen** *W. Lothian* 562Ae

CHURCH A hospital of the Knights of St John of Jerusalem once stood on this site. In the 16th century the remains were incorporated in the present church; the tower of this church was once part of the domestic buildings of the hospital and the nave was part of the hospital chapel.

**Torquay** *Devon* 539Hc

The town became prosperous in the Napoleonic Wars, as a centre for officers and their families awaiting orders to move overseas; their houses are features of the old town. There are also the remains of Torre Abbey, a 14th-century foundation.

CUP AND COVER MADE OF SILVER-GILT
AND ROCK CRYSTAL

*This splendid cup is one of the many items of domestic plate to have found their way into church treasuries all over England and Wales, usually as the result of benefactions made by devout parishioners. The cup has no maker's mark at all, and it would be difficult to date it precisely from its shape alone. The bowl with its spreading cover is formed round a cylinder of rock crystal (crystallised quartz) held in place by three straps in mid-16th-century fashion, while the stem has a short pillar and brackets more characteristic of the early 17th century. Fortunately the filigree decoration of scrolling and berried foliage seems to have been used solely by a distinguished London goldsmith who used the mark 'TYL' in monogram. This mark appears on two fine standing cups with similar filigree work which were made in 1611—one is in the Victoria and Albert Museum, London and the other is at Christ's College, Cambridge —and the cup at Tong is generally thought to have been made by the same goldsmith at about the same time. It stands to a height of just over 11 in. (Church of St Bartholomew, Tong)*

TORQUAY NATURAL HISTORY SOCIETY MUSEUM
Relics of early man (Old Stone Age to Iron Age)
and extinct mammals such as the mammoth and
woolly rhinoceros found in Kent's Cavern near
Torquay are included in the collections, which
have as their themes the geology, natural history
and folk culture of Devon.

**Toseland** *Hunts.*                               *547Jf*
TOSELAND HALL An almost perfect small Tudor
manor house of three bays with a central porch,
three gables, fine mullioned windows and graceful
ornamented octagonal chimney-stacks. It stands as
the centre-piece of a group of restored Elizabethan
buildings, including a thatched brick barn and
stables, giving an effective impression of what such
a manor house and its outbuildings might have
looked like in the time of Elizabeth I.

**Totnes** *Devon*                               *539Gc*
Totnes, on the R. Dart, existed in Norman times;
by the Middle Ages it had become a walled town
with four gates, two of which have survived. In
Fore Street is a Tudor merchant's house adjoining
the restored east gate. The guildhall houses the
council chamber, used since 1624, and the courtroom. The ruined castle stands by the remains of
the north gate.
CHURCH OF ST MARY An impressive mainly 15th-
century church, with a tall west tower. A stone
screen extending across the whole church is *c.* 1460,
and the pulpit is of the same period. There are
arcades and good roofs.
DARTINGTON HALL On the western outskirts of
Totnes. This medieval building is a centre for
practical experiments in farming, forestry and
small-scale industry. Its great hall was built in
1388–1400; the present roof was built of oak from
the estate and erected in 1932.

**Totternhoe** *Beds.*                               *547Hd*
Totternhoe has not only the great 500 ft high
earthwork—possibly a Bronze Age fort—but the
notable Cross Keys Inn, half-timbered, thatched
and with a fire-place dated 1433.
CHURCH OF ST GILES Begun in the 14th century
and completed in the 16th, St Giles's has a fine
exterior and a pinnacled skyline. The stone came
from the quarries in the village. Inside, the roof is
carved with bosses and figures, and there is interesting brass and a font, as well as some fragments of
medieval glass.

**Towyn** *Merioneth.*                               *550Eb*
NARROW-GAUGE RAILWAY MUSEUM Nine loco-
motives, a selection of rolling stock, name and
makers' plates, signalling equipment, posters,
coach fittings and crockery are among the major
exhibits at the museum, which is devoted to the
history of narrow-gauge railways throughout
Britain.

**Traprain Law** *E. Lothian*                               *562De*
This great hill-fort stands on an isolated hill-top
north of the Lammermuir Hills. Earlier excavations have shown that it was occupied from the
early part of the Iron Age right through into the
Dark Ages.
   From time to time, fresh defensive works were
raised. Sometimes these obscured the earlier ones
or modified them and the hill-top, as well as its
upper slopes, bears traces or parts of many of these
different systems.
   This fort, indeed, must have been the major
settlement of the Votadini tribe. For a time this
tribal area was within the sphere of direct Roman
rule, but after the Roman withdrawal from the
Antonine Wall to Hadrian's Wall, the Votadini

were apparently a Border tribe in close alliance
with Rome and in whose territory there were
many detached Roman forts. It was on Traprain
Law that the great hoard of looted silver from
Roman Britain, now in Edinburgh, was discovered.

**Traquair House** *Peebl.*                               *562Cd*
Mary, Queen of Scots and her second husband,
Lord Darnley, stayed here in 1566. The mansion,
whose origins are medieval, has remained unaltered since the 17th century. Its contents date
from the 12th century onwards: tapestries, glass,
embroideries, fine silver and relics of Mary, Queen
of Scots and the Jacobite rebellions. In the 18th-
century Brew-house attached to the main house,
Traquair Ale is made, and a licence to sell the
home-made brew has been granted to the owner
of the house.

**Trefignath** *Anglesey*                               *550De*
A fine megalithic chambered cairn, of the long
narrow Clyde-Carlingford type, seen mainly in
the north of Ireland and the south-west of Scotland. Though somewhat mutilated, the massive
stones of the forecourt, its entrance portal and the
internal chambers still form an imposing monument, and show to what lengths Neolithic man
would go to house worthily his family dead.

**Tremadoc** *Caern.*                               *550Ed*
A small village forming part of W. A. Maddocks's
scheme for reclaiming the Traeth Mawr. Built
round an open square and a road junction, it
included a town hall built in 1805, a hotel and
shops, with terraces of cottages facing the square.
At the approaches from Portmadoc is a Classical
Nonconformist chapel and a Gothic church, both
built between 1806 and 1810. The gate piers to the
church are said to be of Coade stone.

**Trencom Hill** *Cornwall*                               *538Ab*
A well preserved Iron Age hill-fort, with a stone
wall enclosing hut circles.

**Trent** *Dorset*                               *540Cd*
CHURCH OF ST ANDREW The church is of 13th-
century origin; additions include the 14th-century
south tower and spire, and a fine Perpendicular
rood screen, still with its vault. Among the
monuments is an effigy of a 14th-century knight.
There is 16th- and 17th-century foreign stained
glass. The pulpit is perhaps Dutch, of *c.* 1600, and
there are some 16th-century bench ends.

**Treowen** *Mon.*                               *546Ad*
This stone-built Tudor manor house, with
Jacobean porch, has an oak open-well staircase
four storeys high; there is also a four-storey spiral
staircase with solid oak treads. Plasterwork, panelling, doors and fire-places are original. (By
appointment.)

**Tre'r Ceiri** *Caern.*                               *550Dd*
Here, on an isolated hill overlooking the sea, stands
one of the most remarkable Iron Age hill-forts in
Britain. The inner area, protected by a strong
drystone wall, has a long irregular oval plan, and in
this are dozens of roughly circular stone huts.
Furthermore, the long north-western side has an
additional stone rampart which, starting close to
the south-west gate, gradually diverges in its
north-easterly course. Though technically belonging to the Iron Age tradition, Tre'r Ceiri appears
to have been occupied until the end of the Roman
period.

**Trerice** *Cornwall*                               *538Cc*
A manor house rebuilt in 1571 by John Arundell
on the site of an older house. The Elizabethan
plaster ceilings and fire-places can still be seen.

**Tresco** *Isles of Scilly, Cornwall* *538Af*
TRESCO ABBEY GARDENS The terraced gardens at Tresco Abbey are unique in the British Isles for their wealth of sub-tropical plants. They were made by Augustus Smith when he became Lord Proprietor of the Isles of Scilly in 1834. Round the ruins of Tresco Abbey, Smith planted trees to act as shelterbelts; behind these lie a series of protected terraces, planted with veronicas, acacias, fuchsias, pelargoniums and cinerarias. Mesembryanthemum, a native plant of South Africa, is much used as ground cover, and in the borders native and exotic plants grow side by side. Mediterranean and sub-tropical plants provide the gardens with brilliant colour, and there are Australasian tree-ferns and Mexican cacti. In early spring the gardens at Tresco Abbey are vivid with the cultivated daffodils which Augustus Smith found growing wild among the abbey ruins.
VALHALLA MARITIME MUSEUM Housed in a mid-19th-century building of rough sea-boulders and timber from wrecked ships, the collection includes examples of wood-carving from the 17th to the 20th century, many of which are restored figureheads or ornaments from ships wrecked off the Isles of Scilly.

### TRESCO ABBEY GARDENS

*These gardens with their Riviera plants are at their full glory in earliest spring—when mainland gardens are still winter-bound. They were begun around the ruins of Tresco Abbey by Augustus Smith in 1834. He first planted trees to withstand the gales and then constructed a series of sheltered terraces. Soon veronicas, acacias, fuchsias, cinerarias, palms and many other plants were flourishing out of doors all the year through. The daffodils at Tresco are superb—some are descended from those found among the abbey ruins, probably planted by the monks.*

**Tretower Court** *Brecon.* *545Jd*
One of the earliest and best fortified medieval manor houses in Wales, dating mainly from the 15th century. However, the ownership of the land here can be traced back to the 11th century. The present domestic buildings were preceded by a fortress—the keep—which stands adjacent. Inside, the keep is round, but outside the stonework is polygonal in plan. The main part of Tretower Court consists of a hall, with its attendant offices, built round a courtyard; a little of the masonry probably dates from *c.* 1300. The house has a picturesque open first-floor gallery looking on to the courtyard. The hall itself, the adjoining solar and the gate-house survive more or less intact. The 17th-century mystic poet Henry Vaughan used to live at Tretower Court.

**Trevalyn Hall** *Denb.* *551Jd*
A brick and stone cornered house, built by John Trevor (*d.* 1589) and his son, Sir Richard Trevor (*d.* 1637). Work on an E-shaped plan was begun in 1576, but the centre wing was never completed, the east and west wings being connected by a ground-floor passage in 1836. In an oak-panelled Jacobean gallery are portraits of the Trevors.

**Trotton** *Sussex* *541Je*
CHURCH OF ST GEORGE The church is mainly 14th century, and contains a contemporary wall-painting of the Last Judgment. Beautiful large brasses compensate for the lack of a chancel arch; one, to Lady Camoys (*d.* 1310), is perhaps the oldest monument of this kind to a woman. There are also brasses to Lord Camoys (*d.* 1419) and his wife, nearly life-size figures under pinnacled and battlemented canopies.

**Troutbeck** *Westmld.* *557He*
TOWNEND HOUSE A modest farmhouse, built *c.* 1625 by a yeoman farmer. His descendants, the Browne family, lived there until 1944, and the house contains carved woodwork and their books, papers and furniture.

**Trowlesworthy Warren** *Devon* *538Fc*
A Bronze Age moorland settlement, with six walled enclosures and circular huts. The enclosure-walls are remarkable for their massive construction.
    Not far away across the moor to the south by east there is a stone row and a stone circle, both Bronze Age. Across the streams to the east, the slopes of Lee Moor have more hut circles, enclosures and other structures, evidence of extensive occupation of the western valley-slopes of Dartmoor during the Bronze Age.

**Trumpington** *Cambs.* *548Af*
CHURCH OF SS MARY AND MICHAEL A 14th-century cruciform church, restored by William Butterfield in the late 19th century. There is a famous brass of *c.* 1289, the second oldest in England, to Sir Roger de Trumpington, showing a cross-legged effigy with trumpets on his shield.

**Trunch** *Norfolk* *554Dc*
CHURCH OF ST BOTOLPH Perpendicular church with a west tower, and another of Norfolk's hammerbeam nave roofs decorated with angels. However, Trunch is famous for its magnificent font canopy, of which type there are only three others in England. It stands on eight carved pillars, with much carving of foliage, and beneath the cover is a sort of fan-vault with a pendant. Above this are eight canopied niches, now without their statues. A large crocket finishes off the very top. St Botolph's also has a screen with painted saints of 1502, and several carved misericords to the stalls.

## MEMORIAL WINDOW BY CHAGALL

*The only stained glass by Marc Chagall—the contemporary Russian-born artist—in Britain, this magnificent window was dedicated in November 1967. It commemorates the 21-year-old daughter of Sir Henry and Lady d'Avigdor-Goldsmith who was drowned in 1963 while sailing. The window is constructed in 12 major pieces. The Crucifixion is depicted at the top. Below, floating in water, is the figure of the girl whose memorial the window is, and around her are mourning figures. She is also shown climbing the ladder to Heaven, symbolising hope. The red horse and rider symbolise happiness. (Church of All Saints, Tudeley)*

---

**Trundle, The** *Sussex*　　　　　　*541Jd*
The Iron Age hill-fort here overlies a Neolithic enclosure, but the two do not coincide; the inner Neolithic ditch lies within the Iron Age defences, and an outer Neolithic ditch, which is not circular, but whose ends overlap in a simple spiral, partly underlies and strays beyond the Iron Age structures. These latter comprise a substantial bank with external ditch and counterscarp bank. The two entrances are diametrically opposite and there is some evidence of the remodelling of the gates.

**Truro** *Cornwall*　　　　　　　　*538Cb*
CATHEDRAL The former 16th-century parish church of St Mary stood on the site of the cathedral, which was designed by John Loughborough Pearson, who also designed Chiswick parish church, London. All the old church was demolished except the south aisle, which was incorporated in the new building. This is in the Early English style, and work on it began in 1880. There are two western towers, with another over the point where nave and chancel meet, and all are crowned by stone spires—an unusual feature for an English church. By 1903 the 250 ft high central tower was finished as a memorial to Queen Victoria. The western towers, 204 ft high, were complete by 1910, and Edward VII allowed the south-western one to be named after him, while Queen Alexandra gave her name to that in the north-west.

COUNTY MUSEUM AND ART GALLERY Under the control of the Royal Institution of Cornwall since 1818, the gallery displays paintings by Rubens, Lely, Kneller, Hogarth, Gainsborough, Romney, Constable, Leighton, Millais and John Opie (The Cornish Wonder), Court portrait painter during George III's reign.

Life in Cornwall from the earliest times is illustrated by collections which include Bronze Age jewellery and funeral urns, items connected with tin and copper mining, ship models, vehicles, agricultural implements, coins and tokens. The art collections include English pewter, pottery and porcelain; Japanese ivories and lacquer; and a fine collection of Cornish minerals.

**Trusty's Hill** *Kirkcud.*　　　　　　*556Eg*
VITRIFIED FORT A small vitrified fort of the kind well represented in this part of Scotland. The vitrified wall encloses an almost rectangular area 90 ft by 60 ft. The south-east entrance lies between two natural rock-exposures. There are additional ramparts with ditches lying well away from the central enclosure. Pictish symbols are carved on one of the two natural rock-faces at the entrance.

**Tudeley** *Kent*　　　　　　　　*542Cf*
CHURCH OF ALL SAINTS This small church of brick and stone is mentioned in the Domesday Book. It contains a magnificent stained glass window by Marc Chagall which was dedicated in November 1967, when Chagall was in his 81st year.

**Turin Hill** *Angus*　　　　　　　*566Eb*
KEMP'S CASTLE This hill-fort was originally a large oval enclosure with two ramparts. Later, a smaller area within the earlier enclosure was surrounded by a stone wall. This fort was later abandoned, and a dun about 90 ft across was built. This rested in part on the inner wall of the fort. There are apparently two other similar duns on the hill-top.

**Turton Tower** *Lancs.*　　　　　　*552Bg*
A 12th-century house with 16th-century alterations. It contains the Ashworth Museum in the upper storey of a large, well preserved 15th-century tower.

**Turvey** *Beds.*　　　　　　　　*547He*
CHURCH OF ALL SAINTS A Saxon church; its 14th–15th-century additions were restored and 'improved' by Sir Gilbert Scott during the 19th century. There is a 12th-century font, a late 13th-century wall-painting, and many monuments, including one by John Hunt of Northampton, c. 1728. There are also a number of brasses, from the 15th century onwards.

**Tutbury** *Staffs.*　　　　　　　*552Dc*
CHURCH OF ST MARY The beautiful Norman church is that of the priory founded in the 11th century. It has an impressively decorated west front with a magnificent doorway. Inside are some good arcades.

**Twickenham** *Greater London*　　　*547Hb*
STRAWBERRY HILL Horace Walpole (1717–97) writer and Member of Parliament, fourth son of Sir Robert Walpole, settled here in 1747. He enlarged and rebuilt what had been a cottage, so that by 1776 it had become a 'little Gothic castle'. Here he set up a printing press, and the house became a fashionable centre of learning.

**Twickenham House** *Berks.*　　　　*546Fc*
Built in 1735 and considerably altered in 1760, this Georgian house has an unusual belvedere crowned

with a lead cupola and a ball finial. Its main internal feature is a staircase with Chinese lattice-pattern balustrade. The walled garden has a Gothic arbour.

**Ty Mawr** *Caern.*     *550Fd*
The birthplace of Bishop William Morgan (1540–1604), who first translated the Bible into Welsh in *c.* 1587.

**Tyberton** *Herefs.*     *546Ae*
CHURCH OF ST MARY A brick church of 1720, with a Norman doorway from an earlier building. John Wood of Bath carved the impressive reredos in 1728.

There are many 17th- and 18th-century monuments to members of the Brydges family, and the Arms of George I, dated 1720. Alterations were made to the church in the 19th century.

**Tydd St Mary** *Lincs.*     *553Jc*
CHURCH OF ST MARY This is a 14th-century church, with a later west tower and spire. Inside, the 12th-century arcades provide evidence of the

former church here. The chancel windows have fine tracery work, and there is some notable carving on the 15th-century font. There are several monuments, including one by J. M. Rysbrack, *c.* 1741.

**Tynemouth** *Northld.*     *558Ch*
PRIORY CHURCH As at many other places in Northumberland, a monastery existed here early in the 7th century, but raids by the Danes did great damage. The present church ruins date from *c.* 1090–1130.

**Tyttenhanger Park** *Herts.*     *547Je*
Built *c.* 1660 by an unknown architect, but perhaps the work of John Webb, a pupil of Inigo Jones—the architect who introduced Palladian architecture into England.

The superb staircase resembles those at Thorpe Hall near Peterborough, and Forde Abbey, Devon. The house has projecting wings, a noble entrance hall, some rich carving on the staircase and much good linenfold panelling.

# U V

**Uffington** *Berks.*     *546Ec*
CHURCH OF ST MARY A large cruciform church of *c.* 1250. The square central tower has an octagonal top storey, the south porch is large, and three transept chapels have unusual lancet windows. The 13th-century south door has ornamental hinges, and above the north door is a large circular window.

**Uffington Castle** *Berks.*     *546Ec*
The hill-fort is an 8 acre oval enclosure, with a single bank and counterscarp bank outside the ditch. The entrance lies on the north-west and the bank was apparently revetted with sarsen stones.

**Uffington White Horse** See White Horse.

**Unstan** *Mainland, Orkney*     *569Hf*
An almost circular mound, of the type known as 'stalled cairn'. This name derives from the construction of the chamber. From the entrance a passage leads to the chamber, which is 20 ft long by 6 ft wide. It is divided into compartments (the 'stalls') and a further small cell is also present.

**Upmarden** *Sussex*     *541Jd*
CHURCH OF ST MICHAEL A remote church on the South Downs, St Michael's has a very simple, atmospheric interior with brick floors, only a few pews, and a very plain font. The church has only a tower, nave and chancel—there are no aisles.

**Uppark** *Sussex*     *542Jd*
A red-brick house in Wren style, built to designs by William Talman in 1680–1700. From the mid-18th century until 1954 it was owned by the Fetherstonhaugh family. In *c.* 1750 alterations

were made to the interior, and the architect was possibly James Paine the Elder. Further alterations were made *c.* 1770, probably by Henry Keene. Most of the interior dates from this period, and has remained untouched to this day. There are fine portraits. The grounds were landscaped by Humphry Repton for Sir Harry Fetherstonhaugh at the beginning of the 19th century, and pastures now sweep right up to the walls of the house.

**Upton House** *Warks.*     *546Ee*
A country mansion built in the reigns of James II and William and Mary; it contains collections of Brussels tapestries, Sèvres porcelain, Chelsea figures, 18th-century furniture, and nearly 200 paintings by British, Dutch, Flemish, French, German, Italian and Spanish artists. In the grounds are fine terraced gardens. (See p. 468.)

**Urchfont** *Wilts.*     *540Ef*
CHURCH OF ST MICHAEL A long church, with a western pinnacled tower, built in the 14th century and added to in the 15th. The main feature of the interior is the chancel, which is vaulted. The nave roof dates from 1631. There is an Early English font; 19th-century stained glass; and a monument, *c.* 1753, by Peter Scheemakers.

**Usk** *Mon.*     *546Ac*
PRIORY CHURCH OF ST MARY The eastern part of this church has gone, but it was originally a Norman building, with central tower. Inside, the 15th-century screen extends the whole width of the building; it was restored in 1899. The 17th-century pulpit and the organ come from Llandaff Cathedral; there are also mural monuments.

## THE SALOON AT UPPARK

*Standing high on the South Downs. this charming Wren-style house of red brick with stone dressings was built during the last two decades of the 17th century for Lord Tankerville. It was designed by William Talman, the architect of Chatsworth in Derbyshire. The building remained untouched until it came into the possession of the Fetherstonhaugh family in the middle of the 18th century. Various alterations to the interior were made in 1750–70, probably first under*

*James Paine the Elder, and then under Henry Keene, who was famous for the beautiful Gothic transformation of Arbury in Warwickshire. The rooms of Uppark are delightful, for by lucky chance they retain many of the original flock wallpapers, damask curtains and other textiles dating from the 18th century. The saloon especially is a fine example of an elegant early Georgian interior. Its 'fragility' anticipated Robert Adam's work by more than a decade.*

UPTON HOUSE

STUBBS: THE HAYMAKERS *The passion for portraiture, so marked a feature of English taste in the 18th century, was not confined to the aristocratic landowner—it also extended to his country seat and the occupants of his stable. Of all the horse painters in this period, Stubbs was by far the greatest. But he is also a major figure in the English school, having a feeling for form and spatial organisation, and a Classicism that is most akin to French art. Stubbs had a strong spirit of scientific enquiry into the natural world, and the knowledge he gained was brought to bear on his numerous paintings of horses, and on his pictures of other animals. In addition, he often shows in his portraits—both human and animal—a fine sense for landscape. His pictures of farm labourers at work are important examples of the painting of English rural life—'The Haymakers' is one of these, dated 1783.*

SÈVRES PORCELAIN EWER *One of the few surviving pieces of Sèvres made with the rare yellow ground. It dates from 1756, the year the factory near Paris was moved to Sèvres from Vincennes, where it had been founded in 1738; its royal patronage continued until the revolution of 1789.*

---

**Uxbridge** *Greater London*      547Hb
HAMSON MUSEUM The collection is purely local in character, comprising photographs, prints, letters, portraits, records of local societies, manuscripts, histories and guides.

**Valle Crucis Abbey** *Denb.*      551Hd
A Cistercian abbey founded in 1201 by Madoc ap Gruffydd Maelor, Prince of Powys. Much of the church and the attached eastern range of the cloister still stands. The church belongs mainly to the 13th century. The square-ended presbytery is lighted by five lancet windows, forming a picturesque group when viewed from Llyn Eglwystl, the lake beside the abbey. At the west end, the façade, with its three Early English windows and later rose window above, also survives largely intact. Beneath is the richly carved west door.

The transepts still stand, and attached to the south transept lies the east range of the cloister. This was rebuilt in the 14th century and the chapter house remains, complete with its vaulting. Above was the dormitory, reached by a narrow staircase adjacent to the chapter house entrance.

**Vaynol Old Hall** *Caern.*      550Ee
This beautiful Elizabethan nucleus of the great Vaynol estate was replaced in the 18th century by the much larger Vaynol Hall. Consequently the older building did not receive the customary embellishment of the 18th and 19th centuries, and it is notable for the quality of its doors and mullioned windows, and particularly a massive oak stair which formed part of early 17th-century extensions. There is also a small private chapel of *c.* 1580, a beautiful garden and the largest barn in the county, dated 1605.

**Victoria Cave** *Yorks.*      559Ac
During the last phase of the Ice Age, this treble cave was a hyaena den only, and excavation of the lowest levels revealed only the bones of their prey. As the climate improved, Mesolithic man, perhaps *c.* 8000 BC, made his way to this part of the country, and for a time occupied the cave, where his characteristic implements have been found.

After this, the cave appears to have been deserted for many thousands of years until, during the Romano-British period, it was again occupied for a time.

**Vine House** *Glos.*      540Cg
The grounds contain a water garden and a landscaped garden.

**Vowchurch** *Herefs.*      546Ae
CHURCH OF ST BARTHOLOMEW The nave and chancel were built in the 14th century, and the timber bell-turret added just after 1522. There is a Norman window in the south wall and a Norman font. The roof of the nave and other woodwork,

including the screen, were renewed by the crafts-man John Abel in *c.* 1613.

## Vyne, The *Hants.*     *541Hf*
The name probably derives from a Roman vine-growing estate on the site, but the present Tudor mansion of brick and stone was built in 1500–20 for Lord Sandys, a Chancellor to Henry VIII; the chapel and panelled long gallery date from this period. In 1654 Chaloner Chute, Speaker of the House of Commons, altered the house, adding the Classical portico designed by John Webb. John Chute, a close friend of Horace Walpole, Britain's first Prime Minister's son, redecorated several rooms in rococo style and installed the Palladian staircase in the 1760's.

## Waddesdon Manor *Bucks.*     *547Gd*
A country mansion of French *décor* set in 160 acres of parkland, built for Baron Ferdinand de Rothschild in 1880–9. The contents include 18th-century furniture, carpets, Sèvres porcelain, and paintings by Gainsborough, Reynolds, Rubens, and Dutch and Italian schools. There is also a museum of small arms, and an aviary of 18th-century design. (See also p. 470.)

## Wadebridge *Cornwall*     *538Dc*
BRIDGE ON WOOL Reputedly built in 1470, with woollen bales as foundations, the bridge is claimed to be the oldest main road bridge in Britain still in everyday use.

## Wainfleet All Saints *Lincs*     *553Jd*
Once a port, but now 5 miles inland; Wainfleet School was founded in 1484 by William of Waynefleet, Bishop of Winchester, who also founded Magdalen College at Oxford.

## Wakefield *Yorks.*     *558Ca*
BRIDGE CHAPEL One of the few chapels on a bridge still surviving in England. It is Decorated Gothic, from the mid-14th century, but was restored in the 19th and 20th centuries, especially the west front. The bridge beneath is also medieval.
CATHEDRAL This was formerly the parish church of All Saints, and became a cathedral at the end of the last century. Mainly Perpendicular, it has a west tower and tall spire of the 15th century. Fittings include a rood screen of 1635, a font of 1660, stalls with misericords, and an 18th-century pulpit and organ-case. Among the monuments is one of *c.* 1714 with figures. Sir Gilbert Scott restored the cathedral.

## Walcot Hall *Shrops.*     *551Ja*
An 18th-century mansion in a great park, acquired by Clive of India (1725–94) for his retirement.

## Wall (Letocetum) *Staffs.*     *552Cb*
The remains of the Roman fort and settlement of Letocetum on Watling Street, just west of the intersection with Ryknield Street, have been excavated. The public baths clearly show an exer-cise hall, surrounded by a corridor with cold,

### SAVONNERIE CARPET

*The Savonnerie carpet factory near Paris was founded in 1627 in a former soap factory or 'savonnerie'. The workshops have produced carpets ever since despite bankruptcy, revolution and war. Many of the carpets were intended for the French royal palaces and were some of the most opulent ever made. Woven about 1670 during the reign of Louis XIV, this carpet, in baroque style so fashionable then, has Classical orna-ment, with acanthus scrolls and quivers of arrows all arranged symmetrically in a variety of colours. It was one of many made for the great gallery of the Louvre and was probably sold during the revolution of 1789, to reappear at Waddesdon a hundred years later. (Waddesdon Manor)*

CLODION *Youthful Votaries of Bacchus*

*Claude Michel, known as 'Clodion', was the greatest exponent of the French late 18th-century fashion for small terracotta groups and statuettes, and his skill in this racy, light-hearted medium amounts to genius. They were avidly collected a century later, and seven Clodion terracottas, collected by Baron Ferdinand de Rothschild, are at Waddesdon, his old home. The subject of this group, representing a youth with a wine pitcher, and a priestess of Bacchus leading a tiny reveller by the hand, is typical of Clodion—and so too is its freshness and vitality. (Waddesdon Manor)*

warm and hot baths along its south-west side, with hypocausts and furnaces. A museum near by houses other Roman relics found in the district.

**Wallingford** *Berks.*      546Fc
The town was destroyed by the Danish King Sweyn in 1006; the castle, built in 1071, is now in ruins: there are remains of the ramparts. In 1154 Henry II held a Parliament here and gave the town a charter in 1155. Life was disrupted by the plague in 1349, after which only 44 houses remained. In the Civil War, fighting raged through the town, and further disaster came from a fire in 1675, in which many medieval houses suffered. The war memorial in front of the town hall is encircled by cobble-stones taken from the old Bull Ring.

**Wallington** *Northld.*      562Fa
Built in 1688, altered in the 18th century and with a central hall added in the 19th century, the house is noted for its rococo plasterwork and decorative work by William Bell Scott, Ruskin and others. It contains furniture, Dutch blue and white porcelain and pictures, and stands in fine grounds.

**Walmer Castle** *Kent*      543Gf
One of several coastal forts erected by Henry VIII *c.* 1540—nearby Deal Castle was another. Walmer is quatrefoil in plan with a central two-storied tower, and was surrounded by a sea-filled moat. Its walls are more than 12 ft thick, with embrasures for cannon. It was taken by Parliamentarians in the Civil War. Early in the 18th century it was adapted for domestic use and became the official residence of the Lord Warden of the Cinque Ports. The

Duke of Wellington died here in 1852 and the castle contains a collection of his personal effects. The gardens were laid out *c.* 1805 by Lady Hester Stanhope, the niece of William Pitt and traveller in the Near East.

**Walpole St Peter** *Norfolk*      554Ac
CHURCH OF ST PETER The church dates mainly from the second half of the 14th century, and has a west tower, Perpendicular windows in aisles and clerestory, two-storey south porch with coats of arms, stone-vault and carved roof bosses, a 16th-century font with an early 17th-century cover, and a 17th-century screen across the west end. Part of the painted rood screen remains, together with a pulpit of 1620, box-pews, wall-paintings and fragments of stained glass.

**Walsall** *Staffs.*      552Cb
E. M. FLINT ART GALLERY Jerome K. Jerome, the author of *Three Men in a Boat*, was born in Walsall and the gallery contains items once belonging to him. The local history section reflects the trades which made Walsall an important centre in the Industrial Revolution: the leather industry is represented by a collection of saddlers' tools and there is a collection of harness furniture—bits, spurs and stirrups. The gallery contains a group of Victorian oil paintings including some by Charles Shayer and Erskine Nicol, and there is a growing collection of modern paintings.
LOCK MUSEUM (WILLENHALL) The only lock museum in England. Willenhall has been the home

THE EAST WALL AT
WALSINGHAM PRIORY

*In the Middle Ages Walsingham was one of the most famous pilgrimage centres in England. Legend tells how the pious Richeldis de Favarques in 1061 had a vision in which she was transported in spirit to Nazareth. There she was shown the house of the Holy Family and told to build a replica at Walsingham. She founded a chapel, the Shrine of Our Lady, which was served by a community of Augustinian canons from 1153. Walsingham's reputation for sanctity was revived in the 19th century, and it is now a focus of pilgrimages from both Anglican and Roman Catholic churches.*

of the lock and key industry since Elizabeth I's reign, and the museum contains English and continental locks dating from the 16th century to the present.

### Walsingham *Norfolk* 554Bc
A small town built around the ruins of the former Augustinian priory, once famous for its Shrine of Our Lady of Walsingham (founded 1061). Pilgrims came from all over Europe to worship here but the shrine was dissolved and its statue burnt at Smithfield in the Dissolution. Pilgrimages were revived in 1921. There are now two modern shrines, Anglican and Roman Catholic. The latter is in the ancient slipper chapel, a mile to the south-west of Walsingham, from which pilgrims walk barefoot to the Shrine of Our Lady.

### Walsingham Priory *Norfolk* 554Bc
Walsingham Priory was founded by Richeldis de Favarques for a community of Augustinian canons. By the 13th century the chapel containing the Shrine of Our Lady had become a revered place of pilgrimage. Both Henry III and Edward I paid many visits, and Walsingham's prosperity probably dates from this time. The visible ruins are from this and later centuries; the most striking fragment is the east wall of the 14th-century church. To the south lie the remains of the monastic buildings; the chief walls are those of the refectory, rebuilt at the end of the 13th century. Nothing remains of the original chapel, but it has been established as lying near the north aisle of the church and within the precinct wall. In 1931 an Anglican church was built adjacent to the former precinct wall of the priory. At Houghton St Giles the Roman Catholic church maintains a restored 14th-century chapel, known as the Slipper Chapel. It is supposed to have been one of the stations on the pilgrimage route to Walsingham.

### Waltham Abbey *Essex* 548Ac
ABBEY CHURCH OF THE HOLY CROSS AND ST LAURENCE The remnants of the former abbey church consist of a Norman nave, aisles, 14th-century south chapel and 16th-century west tower. The abbey was founded in 1030 and built by Harold before the Battle of Hastings. There is an early font and 17th-century pulpit. The reredos and new pulpit were designed by William Burges in 1876. The nave ceiling was painted by Sir E. J. Poynter and the east window is by Sir Edward Burne-Jones.

### Walton-on-Thames *Surrey* 542Af
CHURCH OF ST MARY The church, dating from Norman times, possesses a monument by the greatest of mid-18th-century sculptors in England, Louis Roubiliac. It is to Viscount Shannon, who died in 1740.

### Walton-on-the-Hill *Surrey* 542Bf
CHURCH OF ST PETER The church possesses a beautiful Norman lead font. Around the bowl is an arcade of round-headed arches, beneath each of which is a seated figure, either reading or with a hand raised in blessing.

### Wanborough *Wilts.* 546Db
CHURCH OF ST ANDREW The church possesses a west tower, and another, which is hexagonal and has a spire, at the east end of the nave. Most of the building dates from the 14th century, the monuments from the 15th century onwards.

### Wandlebury *Cambs.* 548Ae
Wandlebury crowns Cambridge's nearest hill-ridge, the Gogmagog Hills, a landmark in this flat countryside. The earthworks enclose a circular

JESSE WINDOW
AT WALTHAM ABBEY

*Restored in the 1860's, the abbey contains some of the finest 19th-century stained glass in the Jesse window. Dated 1861, it was designed by Sir Edward Burne-Jones who, with William Morris, Dante Gabriel Rossetti and others, formed the Pre-Raphaelite Brotherhood of artists and poets. The window has three lancets with Jesse himself represented at the base of the centre light. A vine grows from his body, each spray enclosing a figure or incident from the Bible. At the top is the Crucifixion, with the Nativity and Shepherds just below.*

area of some 15 acres, which was originally rather more, as the first defences, constructed in the first half of the Iron Age, were the outer bank with a 14 ft deep ditch and counterscarp. This bank was revetted with timber. After falling into disrepair, it was refortified within a century of the Roman conquest by the cutting of an inner V-shaped ditch, 18 ft deep, and the erection of an inner bank, the one now visible, entered by the south-eastern gap. Much of the outer bank has been thrown into the inner ditch, but traces are still visible.

### Wansdyke *Wilts.* 540Df
One of the finest linear earthworks in Britain, surpassed only, perhaps, by the later Offa's Dyke which traverses the Anglo-Welsh Border country. The best remaining parts of Wansdyke are in Wiltshire.

WARDOUR CASTLE
ADAM STAIRCASE

*Robert Adam was one of the first British architects to feature the staircase in his designs, and to use its theatrical qualities to emphasise different floor levels. The use of space in the staircase and the fragile appearance of the wrought-iron balustrade complement the house, built in 1768 by James Paine. The first Roman staircases were merely a necessary means of getting from one floor to another, and only with the Renaissance did they become one of the main decorative features of a building—the trend first appearing in England at the Queen's House, Greenwich.*

It is a single bank with a ditch on its north side. Its eastern end is rather obscure, but appears to be in the extreme east of the county near the border with Berkshire and Hampshire, not far from Hungerford. To the west it can be traced intermittently until it is lost for a few miles in Savernake Forest. It is then clearly visible, and at its modern best, as far as Morgan's Hill, near Calne. From here, south of Lacock, it is visible in part, resting on the Roman road to Bath, where it has left Wiltshire. It is lost near the town, but can be traced in Somerset from Stantonbury to Dundry Hill. It is thought to have continued to Portishead on the Bristol Channel, but there is little visible evidence of this.

Its position on the Roman road, and certain excavations, make it clear that it belongs to the early part of the Dark Ages, and it probably served the sub-Roman Britons of the south-west uplands as a defence against the earliest Anglo-Saxon invaders who were penetrating the upper Thames Valley.

**Wansford** *Hunts.*                    *547Hh*
THE BRIDGE The fine old bridge across the R. Nene has 12 arches: the seven northern arches date from 1577, the next three were rebuilt in 1672–4, and the last two added in 1795.

**Wanstead** *Greater London*                    *548Ac*
CHURCH OF ST MARY THE VIRGIN An 18th-century Classical church with a pediment, built in 1790 by Thomas Hardwick. The interior has

Corinthian columns, a pulpit with a sounding board resting on two palm-trees, *c.* 1790, box-pews and wrought-iron railings. The great monument to Sir Joshua Child (*d.* 1699), with reclining and standing figures, has been attributed to John Nost.

**Wantage** *Berks.*                    *546Ec*
Alfred the Great, King of the West Saxons, was born here in AD 849, and a statue to him was erected in the market-place in 1877. Robert Stiles, an Amsterdam merchant who settled in Wantage, built the attractive almshouses whose entry passage is paved with the knuckle-bones of sheep.

**Warboys** *Hunts.*                    *547Jg*
Fenland village, notorious for the trial of 'The Witches of Warboys': in 1593 an old lady, her husband and daughter were executed on charges of witchcraft based on evidence given by the five daughters of their next-door neighbour.

**Warburton** *Cheshire*                    *552Af*
CHURCH OF ST WERBURGH A secluded timber church with a brick tower of 1711, and rough-hewn timber pillars, probably of the 17th century, inside. The low screen dividing nave from chancel, and the pulpit, are also 17th century.

**Warden Manor** *Kent*                    *542Eg*
A small 15th-century mansion, now used as a hostel.

**Wardour Castle** *Wilts.*                    *540Ee*
The old castle, built originally by Lord Lovel in 1392, was acquired by the Arundell family in 1547, and modernised in 1578 by Roger Smythson. It was damaged and abandoned in the Civil War, and its ruins are still in the grounds, landscaped by Capability Brown, of the new 'castle', a Palladian mansion, built *c.* 1768 to designs by James Paine the Elder. At this time Paine was a leading architect in England and had just completed Worksop (Nottinghamshire) for the Duke of Norfolk. Paine's house consists of a three-storey central block with a two-storey wing on either side, containing the kitchen to the east and the chapel in the west wing. The entrance front is on the north side, and the principal doorway is surprisingly insignificant beneath a tall Venetian window. The castle is now a girls' boarding school.

**Ware** *Herts.*                    *548Ad*
The Bull Inn in Baldock Street and Nos. 8, 10, 12, 27 and 35 are good brick and half-timbered houses from the 16th and 17th centuries. The High Street presents an effective mixture of gabled and straight-fronted houses dating from the 16th century onwards. In Bluecoat Yard stands Bluecoat House, the 15th-century timber-framed manor house which was the Bluecoat School from 1574 until 1672. Opposite is an attractive range of timber-framed cottages built in 1698 for nurses and children. The Corn Stores in Star Street include an unusual 17th-century quadrangle of storehouses with outside ladders giving access to the upper floors and open timber roofs. Facing the bridges over the R. Lea and New R. is Amwell House, an elegant red-brick dwelling of *c.* 1730, which was once the home of John Scott, the Quaker poet. The Grotto, in Scott's Road, was once in the poet's garden. Built *c.* 1770, it has a complex arrangement of intricate passages and chambers lined with shells, quartz, fragments of glass and flint.
PRIORY Built from the remains of a Franciscan friary, founded by Thomas Wake, lord of the manor in 1338; now the council offices. Part of the original work dating from this period can be seen

# WARWICK CASTLE

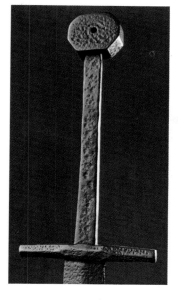

GUY OF WARWICK'S SWORD *Earl Guy of Warwick's remarkable exploits are the subject of a long medieval poem, his most distinguished feat being the defeat of the Danish giant Colbran to save the English Crown for King Athelstan, who reigned from 925 to 940. The sword, supposedly Guy's, is actually late 13th century; it is a typical cross-hilted weapon of its time, but over 5 ft long and designed for two hands. In Elizabeth I's time, there was an official 'Keeper of Guy of Warwick's Sword' who had an annual salary of £3.*

HORSE'S HEAD-DEFENCE *Associated since the 17th century with Guy of Warwick, this armour actually dates from about 1340 and is the earliest known surviving medieval horse-armour. Made of iron, it originally covered all the front and sides of the horse's head, including the ears. A series of holes over the nostrils gave ventilation, with similar ones over the eyes for vision, although this must have been very restricted. It may have belonged to Thomas, 1st Earl of Warwick, who fought at both Crécy (1346) and Poitiers (1356).*

PRINCE CHARLES'S TARGE *Traditionally this shield or targe is said to be one of 13 made for the Young Pretender, Prince Charles Edward Stuart. He gave them away as trophies to his supporters during the 1745 Jacobite rebellion, and this is thought to be the only one now in England. It is just under 20 in. across, and is of tooled leather stretched across a wooden frame. The silver decorations include the Medusa's head in the centre, and trophies of arms interspersed with crests in the circle around the edge of the shield.*

THE WARWICK VASE *Sir William Hamilton, husband of Lord Nelson's Emma, found this vase in a lake at Hadrian's villa in Tivoli near Rome, in 1770, while he was British Envoy in Naples. It was later bought by the Earl of Warwick. Dating from the 4th century AD,* *it is of white marble and 5 ft 6 in. high. The vase is dedicated to wine; its handles are twined vine stems whose leaves and tendrils spread round the upper band, with grape clusters falling from the lower rim. Satyr heads are carved below, over a slain panther.*

in the cloisters; elsewhere there are a number of 17th- and 18th-century additions.

**Wareham** *Dorset*                    *540Ec*
Though the town has existed since Saxon times, little of antiquity remained after a great fire in 1762 destroyed 133 houses and many of the principal buildings in the town centre. Edward the Martyr, King of the West Saxons, was murdered in nearby Corfe Castle and buried in Wareham in 978, before being moved to Shaftesbury.

**Warfield** *Berks.*                    *547Gb*
CHURCH OF ST MICHAEL An interesting church; though restored by G. E. Street in the 1870's, it is mostly Decorated Gothic, with the north aisle partly Early English. There is very pretty tracery in the Decorated east window, where 14th- and 19th-century glass is combined. There are good timbered roofs, and the 15th-century screen to the north chapel retains part of the rood loft. Some noteworthy monuments include one by John Bacon Junior, and Samuel Manning, *c.* 1825.

**Warham Camp** *Norfolk*                *554Bd*
Almost circular in plan, this Iron Age fort lies on the lowland coastal plain, bordered on its west side by the R. Stiffkey. Close to the stream there is a single defensive bank only, but the remainder of the 3½ acre area has two banks and ditches, the banks still standing higher than a man. Excavations have shown that it was constructed late in the Iron Age and lasted at least into early Roman times. It may originally have been constructed to resist the threat of Belgic conquest, and finally been used in the later stages of the Boadicean rebellion. The visible entrances are all modern.

**Warham St Mary** *Norfolk*             *554Bd*
CHURCH OF ST MARY Norman work includes a blocked north door, but the tower dates from the 14th century and the fittings are nearly all 18th century—for example, the three-decker pulpit. There is some early Renaissance German or Flemish stained glass with figures of popes, cardinals and kings, which is mixed with medieval English fragments.

**Warkton** *Northants.*                 *547Cg*
CHURCH OF ST EDMUND Important 18th- and 19th-century monuments to a Duke and three Duchesses of Montagu are set in theatrical-looking apses, with many figures, cherubs and urns. In one of them, a figure appears to have left the monument and stands in the church looking at it—though high pews spoil the effect. Two of the monuments (1752, 1753) are by the outstanding rococo sculptor Louis Roubiliac; others, more Classical, are by P. van Gelder after a design by Robert Adam (*c.* 1775), and Thomas Campbell (*c.* 1827).

**Warkworth** *Northld.*                 *563Cb*
CHURCH OF ST LAURENCE A Norman church, with a vaulted chancel of the 12th century and a west tower *c.* 1200 with a later spire. There is a monument to a knight of *c.* 1330.

**Warkworth Castle** *Northld.*          *563Cb*
For over four centuries, Warkworth Castle remained one of the most important castles in the north of England. Its origins are obscure but it may have been begun in the second quarter of the 12th century by Henry, son of David I of Scotland, who was created Earl of Northumberland in 1139. In 1157, however, the county of Northumberland was re-granted by Henry II to an Englishman, Roger de Stuteville, and his family fashioned the main outlines of the castle as it exists today. The

Percy family, who acquired it in 1332, built the unusual keep on the plan of a cross inscribed on a square (15th century); and they also began a large collegiate church whose foundations are still visible across the outer ward. It is not clear how much of this was actually built. Finally, some of the fine additions made to the great hall in the outer ward also survive, including the Lion Tower which forms its entrance porch.

**Warminster** *Wilts.*                  *540Ef*
A royal manor in Saxon times under the name of Guermistre, when it was also an important wool centre. The Jacobean-style town hall was built in 1830. The minster church is of the 14th century, rebuilt and altered in the 18th and 19th centuries. Nearby Lord Weymouth's School has its original (1707) buildings; pupils of former days include Dr Thomas Arnold, headmaster of Rugby School from 1828 to 1842.

**Warwick** *Warks.*                     *546Ef*
CASTLE One of the few medieval fortresses in England that are still inhabited. The castle, perched on a crag above the Avon, overlooks grounds laid out by Capability Brown; it is the home of the Earl of Warwick. The 14th-century curtain wall and massive tower defence system remain intact. The interior was largely rebuilt in the late 17th century and again *c.* 1770 following a fire. The great hall, dating from the 16th century, contains a collection of armour. The Cedar Room has Van Dyck portraits of Cavaliers, and in the Red Drawing-room are paintings by Velasquez and Rubens.
CHURCH OF ST MARY A most interesting church, of Norman origin, with an impressive 12th-century crypt. Much of the building was destroyed by fire in 1694, leaving only the 14th-century chancel and the Beauchamp Chapel. Rebuilt in 1698–1704, St Mary's most noticeable feature is the commanding pseudo-Gothic tower; nave and aisles are also in this style.

In the middle of the chancel is a monument to an Earl of Warwick and his wife, 1369; the alabaster effigies hold hands. The Beauchamp Chapel, a good specimen of late Gothic with decorative carving and fan-vaulting, contains the tomb of the donor, Richard Beauchamp (*d.* 1440).
COURT-HOUSE A civic building dating from *c.* 1725 which contains a fine Georgian ballroom.
DOLL MUSEUM (OKEN'S HOUSE) In an Elizabethan house is an interesting collection of many kinds of dolls—of wood, china, metal and wax; also automata—mechanical dolls—and musical dolls.
LORD LEYCESTER HOSPITAL AND CHAPEL OF ST JAMES The chapel of St James, built in 1123 over the west gate of the city, became the centre of the Guilds of the city. These were dispersed in 1546, and in 1571 Robert Dudley, Earl of Leicester (Leycester)—Elizabeth I's favourite—founded his hospital for 12 'poor and impotent' persons in the buildings of the Guilds near the chapel. The hospital is still run as a home for retired or disabled ex-servicemen.

The buildings, in black and white Elizabethan style, include a great hall, guildhall (now a museum) and chaplain's hall (now the Queen's Own Hussars Regimental Museum).
WARWICK COUNTY MUSEUM In a market hall constructed in 1670, the museum's collections concentrate on the history, natural history, archaeology and social history of Warwick and the surrounding area.

**Washford Abbey** *Som.*               *540Ae*
A Cistercian foundation, with a fine gate-house and original buildings; the church is no longer standing.

## CHURCH OF ST MARY, WARWICK

BEAUCHAMP CHAPEL STAINED GLASS *These windows show some of the most elaborate work that a 15th-century English glass painter could produce. John Prudde, King's Glazier and fashionable artist and craftsman, used every known resource and technique to achieve the most impressive effect. Coloured jewels are inset into the borders of the robes, and the tracery angels even hold real music. Prudde obtained his royal appointment in 1440 and the windows are dated 1447.*

MONUMENT TO ROBERT DUDLEY *Dudley lies clothed in armour and a cloak, a garter round his left knee, with his second wife Lettice beside him. He was a childhood companion of Elizabeth I and scandal was caused by their passionate attachment during the early years of her reign, culminating in the sudden death of Dudley's first wife Amy Robsart. Although the queen's infatuation cooled their friendship remained—Dudley was created Earl of Leicester in 1564 and was the predominant figure at Court until he died in 1588.*

## WARWICK COUNTY MUSEUM

FLINTLOCK BLUNDERBUSS BY NICHOLAS PARIS *Blunderbusses were designed to discharge a load of shot at fairly close quarters, and had barrels which flared at the muzzle in the incorrect belief that this spread the charge more quickly. This one came from Stoneleigh Abbey, near Warwick, where it was probably carried by one of the coach-guards. The barrel and mounts are of burnished brass, and the stock is of polished walnut. It was made about 1700 by an outstanding gunsmith of this time, Nicholas Paris of Warwick.*

SHELDON TAPESTRY MAP OF WARWICKSHIRE *Some of the first English maps to show roads were a set of tapestry maps first woven by Richard and Francis Hyckes in 1588 for Ralph Sheldon; they were re-woven for his son after 1647. The counties around Warwickshire are shown with great accuracy, the designs being based on Saxton's maps of England published in 1579. Weston, the Sheldon's home where the tapestries were woven, is shown under a panel.*

# WELLS CATHEDRAL

An attempt to remove the cathedral from Wells and re-establish it in the much larger city of Bath was made in 1090. The See had been established at Wells in 909 and the canons there fought to prevent its transfer. Eventually, in 1139, they won their struggle—the bishop remained at Wells but the See gained the dual title of 'Bath and Wells'. The cathedral nave, which has elaborate foliage carving on its capitals, was built in the late 12th and 13th centuries, while the east end and chapter house, with fine vaulting and window tracery, were almost entirely rebuilt in the early 14th century. In 1338 to 1340 the strengthening arches, which give the interior its distinctive appearance, were added where the nave and transepts meet. The cathedral contains a series of 13th-century tombs and a medieval clock dating from about 1390.

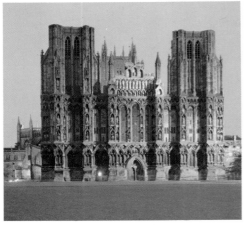

WEST FRONT *This, the glory of Wells, is really a screen built as a background setting for nearly 400 statues. It was constructed under Bishop Jocelin, who about 1230 enlarged the cathedral. He added the west towers, and to obtain extra space for the screen, the bases of these were placed outside the church and not as usually at the ends of the nave aisles. The two towers were then linked to the west end of the cathedral. The tower on the north side originally housed the Chapel of the Holy Cross; this is now the choir vestry. The southern tower formed a porch to the cathedral and was used by lay people.*

CHAPTER HOUSE *Bishop Ergum made additions to the cathedral, beginning about 1300, and the chapter house (shown on the right) dates from this time. Round the walls of the magnificent octagonal building, with its fine vaulting and window tracery, are the seats of the prebendaries or canons.*

WELLS CATHEDRAL CLOCK *With astronomical dial over 6 ft across and mechanical figures, this clock is in the north transept of the cathedral. In the centre the earth is represented with two circles that show the phase and age of the moon. From these, rings moving outwards show the days of the month, the minutes and the hours. The clock chimes the quarter-hours, and as each hour strikes the figures above the dial move—four knights on horseback engage in a jousting tournament and one of them is unseated. The cathedral records mention the clock as far back as 1392; the original mechanism continued in use until 1835 when it was replaced by a modern movement.*

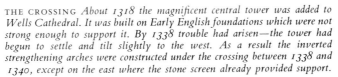

THE CROSSING *About 1318 the magnificent central tower was added to Wells Cathedral. It was built on Early English foundations which were not strong enough to support it. By 1338 trouble had arisen—the tower had begun to settle and tilt slightly to the west. As a result the inverted strengthening arches were constructed under the crossing between 1338 and 1340, except on the east where the stone screen already provided support.*

**Washington** *Durham* 558Cg
OLD HALL A Jacobean stone mansion of 1610, incorporating parts of an earlier medieval house; the seat of the Washington family, 1183–1613.

**Watermouth Castle** *Devon* 538Fg
A neo-Gothic mansion of 1825, built on a Norman site; it has a banqueting hall, minstrels' gallery, smugglers' tunnel, wine cellars and museum.

**Waterperry** *Oxon.* 546Fc
CHURCH OF ST MARY THE VIRGIN In the grounds of Waterperry House, an Early English church of Norman origin, with 14th- and 15th-century additions. The charming interior has box-pews, good medieval glass, and monuments including a 17th-century knight in armour facing his wife in prayer, and a mourning group by Sir Francis Chantrey, *c.* 1819.

**Waterston Manor** *Dorset* 540Dc
A Jacobean house, with later additions. It is said to be the Jacobean mansion mentioned by Thomas Hardy in *Far from the Madding Crowd.*

**Watford** *Herts.* 547Jc
CHURCH OF ST MARY A large church, with west tower and spirelet, 17th-century pulpit, and many brasses and monuments. Two of the monuments, to members of the Morrison family, are by Nicholas Stone, and have reclining effigies, allegorical figures, and big architectural surrounds.

**Wattisfield Potteries** *Suffolk* 548Cf
Bricks, tiles and earthenware have been manufactured here since pre-Roman times.

**Waverley** *Surrey* 541Jf
ABBEY Picturesque ruins, near the R. Wey, of the first Cistercian abbey founded in England (1128).

**Waxham Hall** *Norfolk* 554Ec
On the North Sea coast, Waxham Hall stands behind a long high flint wall and a 15th-century gateway. The flint and brick house, once the home of the Wodehouses, is now a farmhouse.

**Wayland Smith's Cave** *Berks.* 546Eb
This fine megalithic long barrow lies close to the Ridge Way, a little to the west of Uffington Castle. As most of the covering mound has disappeared, the chambers are clearly visible. One capstone is still in position, to give the semblance of a cave to its chamber. A pair of these flank the central gallery and a third terminates its inner end. It is a characteristic, though rather distant, member of the Cotswold group. Wayland the Smith figures in Scandinavian mythology, and his legend may have been brought to this area by the Norsemen, centuries after the barrow was built.

**Weaverthorpe** *Yorks.* 558Fc
CHURCH OF ST ANDREW A good Norman church, with tower. The font is also Norman. The building was restored *c.* 1872 by G. E. Street.

**Weldon** *Northants.* 553Ga
CHURCH OF ST MARY THE VIRGIN This church tower is a rare example of an inland lighthouse. In the 18th century the Gothic spire was removed and replaced by a 15 ft high, fully glazed, octagonal lantern. In this hung a chandelier, the light from which guided travellers through Rockingham Forest. Other examples of land lights were at York, and Dunstan Pillar near Lincoln.

**Wellingham** *Norfolk* 554Bc
CHURCH OF ST ANDREW Contains a rood screen dated 1532, with good figure painting of saints, among them St Sebastian, and St George fighting the Dragon, with onlookers from a city tower.

**Wellington Monument** *Som.* 540Ad
An obelisk, erected in 1817–18 in honour of the 1st Duke of Wellington, victor at Waterloo in 1815.

**Wellow** *Som.* 540Df
CHURCH OF ST JULIAN A large 15th-century church, with an impressive pinnacled west tower. Mural paintings and benches with poppy-heads remain; there are fine roofs in the nave and north chapel.

**Wells** *Som.* 540Cf
CATHEDRAL Most of Wells Cathedral, including the west front which displays the most extensive array of medieval sculpture to survive in the British Isles, dates from the late 12th and 13th centuries, although the three towers were not built until the late 14th and 15th centuries. Wells is a fine example of a medieval close which has survived more or less intact, and is still surrounded by the houses of cathedral dignitaries. To the north lies a row of lodgings built for the Vicars Choral. Adjoining the cathedral, also on the north side, is the chapter house, which is approached by a staircase and was originally used for daily meetings of the cathedral canons. To the south is the cloister and the partly ruined bishop's palace, surrounded by a moat. (See pp. 476–7.)
CHURCH OF ST CUTHBERT The west tower of this mainly 15th-century church is magnificent, with pinnacles and battlements; fragments of the original screens remain in the transepts, and there is a good 17th-century pulpit.

**Wells-next-the-Sea** *Norfolk* 554Bd
Wells, no longer quite next the sea, but on an estuary, is a little port with an attractive quay, extremely narrow streets and a pleasant series of Georgian houses on the green called the Buttland. Other good buildings are Ostrich House in Burnt Street, Marsh House in Marsh Lane, and the Ship Inn, possibly late 17th century, on the quay.

**Well Vale** *Lincs.* 553Je
An 18th-century Georgian house. The extensive grounds contain a fine Georgian church, gardens and landscaped park with lakes. (By appointment.)

**Welshpool** *Mont.* 551Hb
POWIS CASTLE Originally called the 'Red Castle', this Welsh border fortress of red limestone has been the home of the Powis family for over 500 years. The present castle was built in the 13th and 14th centuries on the site of a former stronghold; the long gallery was added in 1587 and its fine plaster ceiling made in 1592. The castle suffered considerable damage when it was taken by Roundheads in 1644, and much reconstruction, including the rebuilding of the west portals, great staircase and state rooms, was carried out in 1667. It contains fine murals by Lanscroon, paintings, furniture, tapestries and relics of Clive of India. The terraced gardens date from 1722, and have lead statues on a balustrade overlooking yews, ornamental trees and box hedges.

**Welwick** *Yorks.* 559Ha
CHURCH OF ST MARY The church was originally Norman, but was rebuilt during the 14th century. In the south aisle is the monument of a 14th-century priest. The pulpit is 17th century.

**Wendens Ambo** *Essex* 548Ae
CHURCH OF ST MARY THE VIRGIN The tower, with little spirelet, and nave are Norman; the chancel dates from *c.* 1300. Inside is a 16th-century font cover, a 15th-century pulpit, fragments of wall-paintings illustrating the life of St Margaret, *c.* 1330, and a brass, *c.* 1415.

**Wenham Hall** *Suffolk* 548De
A unique survival of a small fortified manor house, with hall, chapel, vault, stair-turret and embattled roofs. It is one of the earliest examples of home-made brickwork in England, and one of the best-preserved 13th-century dwellings. Primarily a house and not a keep, it is nonetheless a fortress.

**Wenhaston** *Suffolk* 548Ef
CHURCH OF ST PETER Originally Norman, but with later additions; the west tower has flushwork decoration. Inside is a large painting on wood, *c.* 1520, of the Last Judgment.

**Wensley** *Yorks.* 558Bd
CHURCH OF THE HOLY TRINITY The interest of this church is principally in the individual features. The Restoration font and cover, the early benches and box-pews and the 15th-century screen are note-worthy. There are also medieval wall-paintings, fragments of a Saxon cross and a Flemish-type brass of the late 14th century.

STATUE OF JAMES WOLFE

*General James Wolfe was born at Westerham in 1727 and this spirited bronze statue of him on the village green was erected in 1911. Wolfe was the victor at Quebec in 1759, but lost his life in the battle.*

**Wentworth** *Yorks.* 552Df
CHURCH OF THE HOLY TRINITY The new church is a Gothic building, erected during the second half of the 19th century from J. L. Pearson's design. The old church is now mainly ruined, except for its chancel and north chapel, which contains several 15th–17th-century monuments with effigies.

**Wentworth Woodhouse** *Yorks.* 552Df
This 18th-century house, quite large enough for a palace, has one of the longest fronts in Britain; the great park is now recovered from its post-war open-cast mining.

**Weobley** *Herefs.* 546Ae
CHURCH OF SS PETER AND PAUL The south door-way is in the original Norman style, but the rest of the church is mainly of the 13th and 14th centuries. Noteworthy is the north-west tower and spire, with pinnacles and flying buttresses. The oct-agonal font is early 14th century, and there are

monuments dating from the 14th century; also a marble statue in armour of Colonel John Birch of Cromwell's army (*d.* 1691).

**West Acre Priory** *Norfolk* 554Bc
The remains of an Augustinian priory, founded *c.* 1100. The ruined buildings, once as extensive as those of Castle Acre, lie on both sides of the R. Nar. The 14th-century gate-house stands, and there are fragmentary remains of a church and chapter house.

**West Bromwich** *Staffs.* 552Ca
OAK HOUSE A half-timbered house built in 1488, with a Jacobean wing (1635). Its most interesting feature is the lantern tower, reputed to be the only one of its kind in England. The rooms are panelled and carved, and contain Jacobean furniture. John Wesley's diary records that he preached from the courtyard during his pilgrimage through West Bromwich. In front of the house there is an Elizabethan garden.

**Westbury White Horse** See Bratton Castle.

**West Chiltington** *Sussex* 542Ad
CHURCH OF ST MARY A pretty church in an attrac-tive village, it has a shingled spire. St Mary's was originally Norman, with later additions in the 13th and 14th centuries. There is a 12th-century west doorway. Inside are many wall-paintings of the 12th to 14th centuries, showing scenes from the Passion and the life of the Virgin. There is an interesting very long squint between the south aisle and chancel.

**Westerham** *Kent* 542Cf
The statue of General Wolfe, the victor of the decisive battle between the French and English at Quebec in 1759, who was born at Westerham, dominates this village built round a sloping, roughly square green. The best houses are at the bottom of the hill to the east, Quebec House, early 17th century, and Grosvenor House, fine brick-work of Queen Anne's reign.
SQUERRYES COURT The Warde family has owned this William-and-Mary house for over 200 years. General James Wolfe (1727–59), a friend of the family, received his commission as lieutenant in the Marines in the garden in 1741; a cenotaph commemorates the event. The house was built in 1681 and contains a collection of Dutch paintings and family portraits, tapestries and fine furniture. Pictures and other objects of historical interest connected with General Wolfe are displayed in a small museum.

**West Hendred** *Berks.* 546Ec
CHURCH OF THE HOLY TRINITY A 14th- and 15th-century church, standing by a stream, with a Dec-orated west tower. Inside there are 17th-century furnishings (pulpit, font cover, communion rail), and many medieval tiles in the chancel and nave; also fragments of medieval stained glass.

**West Humble Chapel** *Surrey* 542Af
The ruins of a 12th-century chapel on what was once part of Pilgrim's Way.

**West Kennet Barrow** *Wilts.* 540Fg
One of the largest and finest Neolithic long bar-rows in Britain, a great chalk mound some 350 ft long, with a quarry ditch set well back. A kerb of sarsens surrounded the mound. A deep concave forecourt led to the entrance, held by a wall of large uprights. Inside, the gallery had two pairs of side chambers and a fifth at the end. Finally, after the last burial, the concave forecourt and the entrance were concealed by further uprights, pre-senting a very different false façade. (See p. 480.)

## WEST KENNET BARROW

*The finest example of many similar Neolithic long barrows, or burial chambers, on the Downs of North Wiltshire, the West Kennet barrow near Marlborough was excavated by Professors Stuart Piggott and R. J. C. Atkinson in 1955–6. The pottery (now in the Devizes Museum) dates from about 3000 to 1600 BC, when the barrow was used for burials by migrant peoples from the Continent who brought with them the knowledge of farming. The pots were probably used to store grain and milk. At the top is a bell beaker dating from about 2000 BC. The two bowls, at the right and front right, are of the Peterborough type, a late Neolithic culture, and Windmill type, made by early farmers in Britain about 2500–1800 BC. At the left is part of a Rinyo-Clactonian pot. The pieces of broken vessels date from various of these periods.*

**Westley Waterless** *Cambs.* 548Bf
CHURCH OF ST MARY The Early English and Decorated church once had a round tower, but this fell in the 19th century. There is a delicate early 14th-century brass to Sir John de Creke and his wife, with almost life-size figures, Sir John in armour.

**West Malling** *Kent* 542Df
The High Street of this small market town retains its 18th-century character. On market days stalls would have filled the lower, wider half of the street; professional people would have lived in the more prosperous houses higher up.

**Westonbirt Arboretum** *Glos.* 546Cc
The main arboretum is on the edge of Silk Wood Forest near Tetbury. The collection of trees and shrubs from many parts of the world was begun in 1829 by Robert Stainer Holford, squire of Westonbirt. The landscape architect, W. S. Gilpin, arranged the specimens and the arboretum has been developed and increased on a large scale ever since. Trees and shrubs are planted in groups; massed spring-flowering shrubs are displayed near huge conifers, and maple glades show autumn tints against trees with unusual barks. There are large banks of rhododendrons, magnolias and cherries. The long vistas and secluded bays, the old oaks and giant conifers are beautiful in all seasons.

**Weston Park** *Staffs.* 552Bb
Benjamin Disraeli was a frequent visitor to this country house, home of the Earls of Bradford for nearly 300 years, and some of his many letters may be seen. The mansion was built in 1671 and is a fine example of the Restoration style. It contains paintings by Holbein, Van Dyck, Bassano, Reynolds, Gainsborough and Lely; Gobelins and Aubusson tapestries; and fine 17th-century silver.

**Weston-super-Mare** *Som.* 540Bf
CHURCH OF ALL SAINTS Designed by G. F. Bodley between 1898 and 1902, with a later south aisle and chapel by F. C. Eden. Bodley designed the font and the pulpit.
MUNICIPAL MUSEUM The museum is mainly devoted to items of local significance. Archaeological finds from Worlebury British camp and Bream Down Roman temple sites are exhibited with a collection of agricultural and domestic bygones.

**Westonzoyland** *Som.* 540Be
CHURCH OF ST MARY The main feature of this large church, with its tall west tower (fan-vaulted on the inside), and its two-storied south porch, is the magnificent nave roof, carved with angels holding shields. In addition there are fragments of stained glass, and a monument to a priest that dates from *c.* 1300. Defeated rebels from the Battle of Sedgemoor were confined here in 1685.

**West Stow** *Suffolk* 548Cf
WEST STOW HALL The turreted brick gate-house of what was a large house built *c.* 1520 by Sir John Crofts, Master of the Horse to Mary Tudor, daughter of Henry VIII. The gate-house is connected with the house (little of the original survives) by a colonnade of *c.* 1590. Over the gateway are Mary Tudor's Arms and in a room inside amusing Elizabethan wall-paintings showing the Four Ages of Man.

**West Walton** *Norfolk* 553Jb
CHURCH OF ST MARY The church, one of the best in the county, dates from *c.* 1240. The tower is completely detached and stands some 60 ft from

the church itself; it has large arches on all four sides at ground level, with arches and belfry windows above, and later parapet and pinnacles. Inside the church are wall-paintings, carved bench ends and a Perpendicular font.

**Westwood Manor** *Wilts.*                          *542Df*
A 15th-century manor house, altered in 1610, with late Gothic and Jacobean windows, and Jacobean plasterwork. It contains a collection of fine furniture, and the garden includes modern topiary work.

**West Wycombe** *Bucks.*                          *547Gc*
A village of fine 17th- and 18th-century houses along the A40.
MAUSOLEUM Sir Francis Dashwood (1708–81), founder of the notorious 'Hell Fire Club', had this curious hexagonal, roofless monument built on the hill above the village in 1763. It is decorated with imposing vases and plastered columns, and one wall enshrines an 18th-century poet's heart. The caves in the hill are associated with the club which met at Medmenham Abbey.
WEST WYCOMBE PARK The Dashwood family came into possession of land at West Wycombe in 1698, and a three-storied brick house was erected; this was rebuilt in Palladian style *c.* 1750 by Sir Francis Dashwood. A two-storied Tuscan and Corinthian colonnade extends between the wings of the south front. The Ionic portico at the west was designed by Nicolas Revett *c.* 1770, and the Tuscan portico at the east was probably designed by John Donowell *c.* 1755. The house contains painted ceilings by Borgnis, tapestries, pictures and fine furniture.
The grounds were landscaped by Humphry Repton, and contain a swan-shaped lake and

temples, one of them designed by Revett. On top of the hill in the park, next to the parish church, is the mausoleum. Caves were excavated in the hill *c.* 1750, and these are reached through a flint ruin in Gothic style.

**Wetheral** *Cumb.*                          *557Hg*
CHURCH OF THE HOLY TRINITY A Gothic church, much altered and added to, but worth visiting for the large and important monument to Mrs Howard, of Corby, by Joseph Nollekens; it shows a young woman holding a baby, supported by Religion who points towards Heaven.
CASTLE CORBY Perched above the R. Eden, the remains date from the castle's dissolution during the Civil War. It incorporates an ancient pele tower and priory gate-house.
ST CONSTANTINE'S CELL Situated lower down in the village are three caves said to have been occupied by St Constantine.

**Wethersfield** *Essex*                          *548Bd*
CHURCH OF SS MARY MAGDALENE AND MARY THE VIRGIN Mainly of the 13th and 14th centuries, the church has a 15th-century nave and clerestory. Fragments of medieval stained glass exist. Monuments with effigies date from the 15th century, tablets from the 18th century.

**Weybridge** *Surrey*                          *542Af*
MUSEUM Local exhibits cover the history and archaeology of north-western Surrey, and there are displays of costume, trade and craft implements, and bygones.

**Weymouth** *Dorset*                          *540Dc*
TRINITY STREET (NO. 3) Built *c.* 1600–10, an early example of a pair of semi-detached houses (a style which did not become common until the late 19th

WESTONBIRT ARBORETUM

*Early in the 19th century wealthy landowners began to make arboreta—collections of trees. Robert Stayner Holford, squire of Westonbirt, was one of these and in 1829 began his collection. He employed the fashionable landscape architect of the day, W. S.*

*Gilpin. Today, with its long vistas and secluded bays, it is a place of great beauty at all seasons. Particular attention has been paid to autumn colouring, and the maple glade when at its most brilliant in mid-October shows the tremendous success attained.*

**481**

century). The furnishing is 17th-century through-out, including an elaborate piece of wrought iron representing the Tree of Jesse.

**Whalley** *Lancs.*       *558Ab*
CHURCH OF ST MARY Of Norman origin, St Mary's is now mainly a 13th-century building, but with Perpendicular additions. Splendid wood fittings include stalls and misericords from the nearby abbey, now ruined, screened family pews, and a magnificent organ of 1729, removed from Lancaster church at the beginning of the 19th century. There are monuments by Sir Richard Westmacott and John Fisher of York.

**Whaplode** *Lincs.*       *553Jc*
CHURCH OF ST MARY Little remains of the original Norman building except the chancel arch. The tower, which was begun in the 12th century and not completed until the 14th, stands in an uncommon position in the south aisle, at the east end. There are a number of monuments from the 13th century onwards, including the remarkable one of the late 16th century to the Irby family.

**Wharton Court** *Herefs.*       *546Af*
A 17th-century stone house, with moat.

**Wheatfield** *Oxon.*       *547Gc*
CHURCH OF ST ANDREW A Gothic church converted to Classical style in the mid-18th century. It has a good interior, with an altar table said to be by Chippendale, a family pew, pulpit and a large marble monument.

**Whissendine** *Rutland*       *553Gb*
CHURCH OF ST ANDREW This is a large church of the 14th and 15th centuries, with a tall, pinnacled west tower. The 16th-century rood screen in the south transept came from St John's College, Cambridge, in 1869. The 15th-century roof has carved figures.

**Whiston** *Northants.*       *547Gf*
CHURCH OF ST MARY The early 16th-century church stands on a hill-side away from the road, and has a west tower with fine carvings and gargoyles. There are timber ceilings, Perpendicular windows, and benches typical of the period; also monumental sculpture by Joseph Nollekens and William Pitts.

**Whitby** *Yorks.*       *558Fe*
A North Riding fishing port and holiday resort, whose history goes back to AD 664 when the Council of Whitby did much to establish Christianity in Britain. In 1768, Captain James Cook (1728–79), circumnavigator, sailed from Whitby in the *Endeavour* for Tahiti via Cape Horn; the 17th-century house in which he lived in Grape Lane is preserved.
ABBEY Perched on a high cliff overlooking the sea, Whitby has one of the most spectacular monastic sites in England. In view of the scanty knowledge of early monastic buildings, it is of interest that excavation has revealed traces of its 7th- and 8th-century origins, including the foundations of some of the small scattered cells in which the inmates lived.
    However, this monastery was sacked by the Danes in 867 and the present ruins belong to the monastery as it was refounded *c.* 1067. The main survival, the church, is a rebuilding of the 13th and 14th centuries. Two of the main façades (east and north) still stand to their full height.
CHURCH OF ST MARY Originally Norman, with many later alterations. There is a delightful 18th-century interior, with galleries, box-pews and a three-decker pulpit.

MUSEUM The section dealing with local history contains the 'Tempest Prognosticator', which once belonged to Dr George Merryweather and was used for forecasting the approach of thunderstorms. There are also relics of William Scoresby, a priest who was also a scientist and a whaler.

**Whitchurch** *Shrops.*       *552Ad*
Midway between Deva (Chester) and Uriconium (Wroxeter), Whitchurch was known to the Roman legions as Mediolanum. Under King Alfred, its site was west of the Hundred of Hodnet, and thus became known as Westune. The Normans erected a new church which was so striking that it was praised as the White Church, from which came the name Whitchurch.
    Many of the town streets have old names: Bargates, Bluegates, Watergate, Highgate, Newtown (built on the site of the old castle), Pepper Alley and Bull Ring—the town centre where the last bull was baited in 1802. Whitchurch is the birthplace of Sir Edward German (1862–1936), composer of *Tom Jones* and *Merrie England*.
CHURCH OF ST ALKMUND The original church collapsed in 1711 and was rebuilt in 1712–13 by William Smith of Warwick. St Alkmund's is large, with an impressive west tower, pinnacled and balustraded. The interior has tall columns and galleries; there is a 17th-century font decorated with a Tudor rose and the Prince of Wales's feathers, and monuments from the earlier church, including one to John Talbot, 1st Earl of Shrewsbury (*d.* 1453).

**Whitchurch Canonicorum** *Dorset*       *540Cc*
CHURCH OF ST CANDIDA AND HOLY CROSS This large and interesting church contains a rare parish church feature, a 13th-century shrine of St Wite, a Saxon female saint. The building is mainly 12th and 13th century, cruciform, with a Perpendicular west tower. The font is late 12th century, and there is an early 17th-century pulpit, fragments of 15th-century painted glass and a fine monument of *c.* 1611, with reclining armoured man.

**Whitcombe** *Dorset*       *540Dc*
CHURCH A Norman church with a 13th-century chancel. It contains a Norman font, the remains of a Saxon cross, and a 15th-century wall-painting of St Christopher.

**Whitehaven** *Cumb.*       *556Fe*
A town which benefited from the Wren-style planning initiated in 1690 by Sir John Lowther and followed by Sir James Lowther (1736–1802), 1st Earl of Lonsdale, who built Whitehaven Castle.

**White Horse** *Berks.*       *546Ec*
First cut in Iron Age times, though later attributed to King Alfred, who was supposed to have cut it after a victory over the Danes. But this is certainly the oldest of the 'white horses' which dot our chalk uplands. Very similarly shaped horses are seen on some of the pre-Roman coins of the local tribes. A prehistoric trackway—the Ridge Way—runs close past the hill-fort.

**Whithorn Priory** *Wig.*       *556Df*
The ruins of St Ninian's priory, which dates from the 12th century. The priory church was used as a parish church until the 19th century. The royal Arms of Scotland before the Union with England are carved on the 17th-century approach archway known as the Pend. A fine collection of carved stone crosses is housed in the museum. St Ninian, the first Christian missionary to Scotland, landed on the Isle of Whithorn, three miles to the south-east. There he built a chapel, the ruins of which can

## CHURCH OF ST MARY, WHITBY

*Whitby reached the height of its prosperity in the 17th and 18th centuries, and during this period this Norman church was renovated inside. Across the chancel arch the Cholmley pew, standing on four twisted columns with front decorated with wreaths and angels' heads, was erected in the late 17th century. The west gallery and organ were added in the 18th century, and the tall panelled pulpit dates from 1778. The church was filled with box-pews; the pews and galleries could hold a huge congregation—it is said that when two whalers from Whitby were lost in 1826 the Rev. Scoresby preached a memorial service to 3000 people.*

still be seen. To the south-west, on Port Castle Bay, is St Ninian's Cave, with sculptured stones and crosses.

**Whitkirk** *Yorks.* 558Cb
CHURCH OF ST MARY This Perpendicular church, with a chancel by G. F. Bodley, contains a number of monuments, including ones by Nollekens and Henry Westmacott; the most important is that to Viscount Irwin (*d.* 1688), designed by Edward Pierce and executed by John Nost. Also of interest is that to John Smeaton, the builder of the Eddystone lighthouse.

**Whittlesey** *Cambs.* 553Hb
Whittlesey has a few good buildings, for instance the manor house, of the 15th and 17th centuries; Grove House, late 17th century with a good hooded doorway; the Butter Cross, late 17th century with a tall pyramid on Tuscan columns and some mullioned windows; and the Black Bull Inn, *c.* 1650. No. 6 Gracious Street is an attractive mid-17th-century house.
CHURCH OF ST ANDREW A 13th- and 14th-century church, with a later west tower, with pinnacles. Much of the building has its original roof.

**Whitton Court** *Shrops.* 546Bf
A manor house built around a courtyard. It was begun in 1140 and includes a 14th-century black and white wing, and a red-brick south front added in 1621. The great hall contains the original oak panelling and a painted frieze (dated 1682) showing a hunting scene in the park.

**Whitwell** *Derbys.* 552Ee
CHURCH OF ST LAWRENCE The nave and west tower are Norman, the chancel and transepts 14th century. The font is Norman, and there is also a sedilia and what might be an Easter sepulchre.

**Wichenford Court Dove-cote** *Worcs.* 546Bf
A 17th-century half-timbered black and white dove-cote.

**Wicken** *Cambs.* 548Af
Wicken, notable for the unique, primeval un-drained Wicken Fen, has a small but dignified Hall, *c.* 1700, near the church. The thatched Sycamores or Old House, *c.* 1650 and facing the Middle

Green, was formerly a fishing and hawking box of Sir Henry Jermyn. Spinney Abbey, *c.* 1775, a mile out of the village, is a stone, twin-gabled structure which incorporates much of the Augustinian abbey of *c.* 1215. High Fen Farm, thatched and picturesque, has some good panelling and recessed cupboards inside. The reconstituted Fen draining-mill was presented by Lord Fairhaven.

**Wickham** *Berks.* 546Eb
CHURCH OF ST SWITHIN The Anglo-Saxon tower is of flint and mortar; papier-mâché elephants (shown at the Paris Exhibition of 1862) decorate the aisle roof. The interior is all 19th century, lavishly decorated (1845–9) by Benjamin Ferrey, who used carved angels to support the nave roof.

**Wickham** *Hants.* 541Hd
BRIDGE STREET Starts from the north-east corner of the square, and has good houses, one an un-usual 17th-century building, before it drops to the river; also a pair of big rural-industrial buildings: a Regency water-mill and a Victorian brewery.
THE SQUARE A most handsome piece of town-scape, with splendid Georgian houses of red and grey brick on three sides.

**Wickhambreaux** *Kent* 542Ff
The village is grouped around a grassy square with trees. The six houses, plus a water-mill, include the baroque early Georgian vicarage and the chequered post office, an Elizabethan building.

**Wickhambrook** *Suffolk* 548Bf
GIFFORD'S HALL A manor house of *c.* 1480, re-stored in 1908, timber-framed and gabled. There is a large timbered hall, great chamber with good fire-place, and much good oak woodwork throughout.

**Wickhamford** *Worcs.* 546De
In 1646, Parliamentary troops led by Colonel Henry Washington defeated Royalists in the siege of Worcester. Colonel Washington was of the same family as George Washington, 1st President of the U.S.A. The family Arms (three stars and two stripes) from which developed the American flag, are on the tomb of the colonel's daughter, Penelope, in the church at Wickhamford.

# WILTON HOUSE

WILTON HOUSE *Probably no house in England has been the scene of more distinguished gatherings than took place at Wilton under the presiding genius of Mary, wife of the 2nd Earl of Pembroke. She gathered around her the nation's outstanding intellectual, social* *and artistic talent—including her brother, Sir Philip Sidney, and Shakespeare himself. In 1647 a disastrous fire destroyed most of the Tudor house. It was rebuilt for the 4th Earl by Inigo Jones and his assistant, John Webb, in 1648–53.*

18TH-CENTURY SETTEE *Probably designed by William Kent—the first English architect to design the furniture for a specific architectural scheme—this settee of about 1730 is in the Double Cube Room at Wilton. The carved and gilded woodwork is in Italian style, and the crouching sphinxes may have been inspired by the French designer Jean Berain. Kent himself was usually responsible only for the design of the furniture, the actual carving being executed by first-rate craftsmen.*

JENSEN DESK *Gerreit Jensen, probably of Dutch descent, worked for four English monarchs in succession, starting with Charles II and ending with Anne. The many Dutch craftsmen who followed William III to England helped to raise the standard of English work and give it an international reputation. Made of metal, tortoiseshell and wood marquetry, this desk reflects the French Court style of the late 17th century and is a predecessor of the popular 18th-century English pedestal desk.*

**Widecombe-in-the-Moor** *Devon*    539Gd
A village set in a hollow on Dartmoor, which has become famous because of the traditional song 'Widecombe Fair'.
CHURCH HOUSE A 15th-century granite building near the church in the village.
CHURCH OF ST PANCRAS A large 14th-century church with a tall, pinnacled west tower of granite dominating the village. Inside are the remains of a rood screen with painted figure panels.

**Wideford Hill** *Mainland, Orkney*    569Hf
A cairn of Maes Howe type. A small cell opens from each of the three walls of this chamber, the fourth being broken by the entrance from the passage. The original diameter of the mound would be about 45 ft.

**Wiggenhall** *Norfolk*    554Ab
CHURCHES OF ST GERMAN, ST MARY THE VIRGIN AND ST MARY MAGDALENE Three neighbouring parish churches which, between them, have exceptional wood fittings in the way of benches, with poppy-heads and large carved figures of saints on the bench ends, remains of painted wood screens, and early 17th-century pulpits with hour-glass stands. St Mary Magdalene has some 15th-century stained glass. Not far away is the roofless ruin of the church of Wiggenhall St Peter.

**Wightwick Manor** *Staffs.*    552Bb
A half-timbered manor house, built 1887–93. It contains work by the most famous of the Pre-Raphaelite artists—wallpapers and fabrics by William Morris, a collection of water-colours by Ruskin, drawings by Burne-Jones, paintings by Millais, tiles by de Morgan, and Kempe stained glass. The gardens are mainly formal, with terraces, a lake and topiary work. They were designed by Alfred Parsons, the Victorian flower painter.

**Wigtown** *Wig.*    556Dg
During the persecution of the Covenanters (Presbyterians) by Charles II in 1685, two women Covenanters were bound to stakes on Wigtown sands and left to drown in the rising tide; their graves are in the churchyard. A memorial to these Wigtown martyrs stands on Windyhill.

DOUBLE CUBE ROOM *This elegant and beautifully proportioned Italianate state room on the south side of Wilton is the most important room in the house. It is 60 ft long, 30 ft wide and 30 ft high. Inigo Jones and John Webb designed it, as part of their reconstruction of the house after the fire of 1647, to house the Pembroke family's paintings by Rembrandt and Van Leyden, and family and royal portraits by Van Dyck. Over the fire-place is Van Dyck's portrait of Charles I's children. The ceiling is finely painted with the story of Perseus. About 1730 William Kent designed the suite of gilt and red velvet furniture for the room.*

PALLADIAN BRIDGE *The 9th Earl of Pembroke— the 'Architect Earl'—and Roger Morris, his clerk-of-works, built this elegant bridge in 1736–7. It spans the R. Nadder in the grounds at Wilton.*

**Wilderhope Manor** *Shrops.* 546Ag
Built of limestone in 1586, the manor is unaltered except for plaster ceilings added in the 17th century.

**Willington** *Beds.* 547He
WILLINGTON DOVE-COTE One of the earliest and most magnificent dove-cotes in the country, a tall, mid-16th-century stone-built structure; it has a two-tiered tiled roof with stepped gables at each end, and a dividing wall which carries up above the roof and is stepped like the end walls. Each part of the dove-cote is entered by a low Tudor doorway. It can hold 1400 pigeons.

The 16th-century barn near by, known as King Henry's Stables, is a sturdily built structure with buttresses, mullioned windows and stepped gable-ends.

**Wilmington** *Sussex* 542Cd
MUSEUM The only agricultural museum in the south of England. It displays old implements and farmhouse utensils, including ox-ploughs, yokes, man-traps and guns.

**Wilmington Long Man** *Sussex* 542Cd
On the north side of Windover Hill, this gigantic figure of a man is carved in outline in the chalk. It became somewhat overgrown and was renovated in the 19th century by a local man, who may have modified and weakened the original figure. Its age is not known. It has generally been thought to have been first cut in medieval times, but there are suggestions that it may have been as early as the mid-Saxon period.

**Wilton** *Wilts.* 540Fe
This small town, famous for its manufacture of carpets, felt and agricultural machinery, was once politically important: here in 838 King Egbert united the Kingdoms of Kent and Wessex. Today the town is the centre of the local sheep trade.

**Wilton House** *Wilts.* 540Fe
There had been an abbey at Wilton for centuries before it was dissolved by Henry VIII, who gave the lands to Sir William Herbert. Herbert held many powerful appointments; he was created 1st Earl of Pembroke in 1551 and built a house at

Wilton worthy of his standing. Tradition maintains that he consulted Hans Holbein—a porch, now detached from the house, is known as the Holbein Porch. Philip, 4th Earl of Pembroke, commissioned Isaac de Caus to construct a huge formal garden to the south of the house. In 1647 a fire destroyed much of the house and the earl asked the aged Inigo Jones to reconstruct it. Jones died in 1652 and his assistant, John Webb, completed the work; two of Webb's designs are in the Victoria and Albert Museum. In the grounds are a Palladian bridge by Roger Morris and a casino (dancing room) by Sir William Chambers. Much alteration to the building took place in the early years of the 19th century following the designs of James Wyatt. The house contains fine furniture and plasterwork, pictures and a collection of 7000 model soldiers of the 19th century.

**Wimbledon Common** *Greater London*      *547Jb*
CAESAR'S CAMP This is of interest as being a visible hill-fort within modern Greater London. It is a roughly circular 12 acre fort defended by a single bank and ditch. The entrance was probably on the west side. Originally, the ditch was more than 12 ft deep and the 30 ft wide bank was revetted on both sides with vertical timber palisades. The height of the bank was reduced in the 19th century.

**Wimborne Minster** *Dorset*      *540Ec*
CHURCH OF ST CUTHBERGA A large church, cruciform, with a central tower, and another at the west end. There are Norman tower arches, the nave arcade is Transitional Norman and 15th century, and there is also a magnificent choir with monuments and a crypt beneath. In the north aisle is a large wall monument, *c.* 1606, showing a reclining man in armour.

**Wimborne St Giles** *Dorset*      *540Ed*
ST GILES HOUSE The country home of the 1st Earl of Shaftesbury (1621–83), built *c.* 1650 but with interior alterations made *c.* 1750, to which period much of the furnishing belongs. There are also relics of the philanthropic 7th Earl (1801–85).

**Wimpole** *Cambs.*      *547Je*
CHURCH OF ST ANDREW Near Wimpole Hall; although of 14th-century origin, St Andrew's was almost completely rebuilt by Henry Flitcroft in 1749 and Gothicised in the late 19th century. There is a superb series of monuments, from 16th-century brasses onwards: work by Peter Scheemakers, Flaxman, Bacon the Elder, Banks and the Westmacotts may be seen.

**Wimpole Hall** *Cambs.*      *547Je*
Originally built by Sir Thomas Chichele or Chicheley (1618–99), but acquired and considerably extended by the 1st Earl Hardwick (1690–1764), Lord Chancellor in 1737. Its park has an avenue of elms, approximately 3 miles long and 100 yds wide. In this park is a sham castle built as an 18th-century folly.

**Winchcombe** *Glos.*      *546Dd*
CHURCH OF ST PETER Built between 1456 and 1474, this Perpendicular church has later 17th-century rebuilding and 19th-century restoration, and is typical of the 'wool' churches of the Cotswolds. The pinnacled west tower has a fine weather-cock, and there are gargoyles all round the church. Some of the glass is medieval; there is a late 17th-century organ-case and a brass candelabrum of 1753.

**Winchelsea** *Sussex*      *542Ed*
A new town was laid out on the heights above the marshes in 1283; of the original buildings only a

number of vaulted cellars are left, and the present houses are largely after 1900. The original grid plan is easy to make out, though a fraction of the planned lay-out was built on.
CHURCH OF ST THOMAS THE APOSTLE The church is a fragment, in fact only the 14th-century chancel of the original church. There are several 14th-century monuments, and a wall-painting of the same period. The modern stained glass of *c.* 1930 is by Douglas Strachan.

**Winchester** *Hants.*      *541Ge*
Winchester was a tribal centre long before the Romans came to Britain. Under the Romans Winchester became the fifth largest city in Britain. King Alfred made the town his capital. At the east end of the High Street is a statue of the king, erected in 1901 to commemorate the thousandth anniversary of his death. In Norman times Winchester was of unrivalled eminence; as late as the 13th century it was second only to London in importance, and an important centre for pilgrims from the Continent in the Middle Ages, who paid tribute at the shrine of St Swithin and then took the route to Canterbury.

The High Street formally ends with St Swithin's Bridge, an 18th-century successor to the original Saxon bridge across the R. Itchen. To the west, along the line of the river, in a district called The Weirs, are remains of the ancient city wall, built originally by the Romans. The walls lead to Wolvesey Castle, built by Henry de Blois in 1138 and demolished in the Civil War. Wren built an episcopal palace near by for Bishop Morley in 1684, and the remaining wing of this building is a residence for the Bishop of Winchester. The Plague Monument, erected in 1759 and rebuilt in 1821, commemorates the great plague in the city in 1666.

Outstanding post-medieval buildings are Serle's House in Southgate Street, a splendid example of the Queen Anne style; the Italianate library, built in 1836, in Jewry Street; and the new hotel immediately north of the cathedral.
CASTLE HALL At the western end of the old city are the remains of the former Norman castle which occupied this hill-top position. The great hall (1235) is Early English with Purbeck marble columns and stone window-seats, the finest and largest medieval hall in Britain after that at Westminster. Many notable Parliaments and trials were held here: in 1603, Sir Walter Raleigh heard his sentence of death, and in 1685 Judge Jeffreys held a 'Bloody Assize'. The Round Table of King Arthur hangs in the hall.
CATHEDRAL The present church was begun in 1079. At its west end it overlaps an earlier Saxon church in the immediate vicinity of the cathedral. In its present form Winchester Cathedral is, at 556 ft, the longest cathedral in Europe. The most complete remains of the early work are in the transepts, which are remarkable features of early Norman architecture. The arches have heavy plain mouldings, the capitals are undecorated, and the transepts themselves are unusual in featuring aisles that are continued across their end walls. In the 13th century the Norman church was extended to the east by the addition of the Lady Chapel. Most of the remaining church was subsequently remodelled, first under Bishop Edington (1345–66), but chiefly under William of Wykeham (1366–1404). The Norman masonry of the nave was carefully concealed in a casing of Perpendicular stonework. There is also a fine set of early 14th-century misericords, monuments of all periods, 19th-century stained glass, medieval

wall-paintings, and the important square black Tournai Norman font, with carved scenes from the life of St Nicholas.

The library of the cathedral has some notable treasures. These include a 10th-century copy of Bede's history, a 13th-century illuminated Bible and the first American Bible. (See also p. 488.)

CHURCH OF ST CROSS The cruciform Norman church of the former Hospital, with a central tower; there is later work as well. Parts of the 16th-century stalls remain, and some portions of 15th-century stained glass. There are screens and medieval wall-paintings. Among the monuments is one, c. 1790, by John Francis Moore, who was noted for his use of coloured marbles at a period when white and black were fashionable.

CITY MUSEUM Items representing local archaeology and history include parts of Roman mosaic floors, grave finds from the 1st century AD, a Saxon ivory panel, a stone on which is cut the name of King Alfred, coins minted in the city, medieval pottery and two original drawings for the palace which Wren started to build for Charles II in Winchester. Material from Hampshire includes prehistoric pottery and tools, Roman coins, a leaden canister which contained coins of William the Conqueror, and a few personal belongings of Jane Austen.

GUILDHALL A Gothic Revival building, dating from 1873 and containing numerous paintings from the 16th century onwards.

MIZ-MAZE The miz-maze on the top of St Catherine's hill may well be of prehistoric origin; its true purpose is now unknown, though this pattern of turf spirals is found elsewhere in Britain and abroad, and during the Middle Ages a maze or labyrinth was often marked on the floor of French cathedrals—at Amiens, for example, it was inlaid in white marble. The spirals may perhaps have been designed to guide dancers' feet in a ritual pattern, possibly connected with a fertility ceremony—although the religious use of specialised dances, to change the dancers' state of consciousness, still occurs, among the Dervishes for example.

PILGRIM'S HALL A 14th-century building with fine beamed roof.

ROYAL GREEN JACKETS MUSEUM The museum is concerned solely with the regimental history of the Green Jackets and the incorporated Rifle Brigade and the 43rd and 52nd King's Royal Rifle Corps.

ROYAL HAMPSHIRE REGIMENTAL MUSEUM Items connected with the Regiment and the campaigns in which it has taken part—uniforms, badges, medals including five Victoria Crosses, silver, old Colours, photographs and records, relics of the Gallipoli landings of April 1915—are displayed in Serle's House, which dates from 1735.

ST CROSS HOSPITAL A fine complex of medieval almshouses with high chimneys. Bishop Henry of Blois, half-brother of King Stephen, founded the hospital in 1136 for the maintenance of 13 poor men—nowadays aged men. In 1445, Cardinal Beaufort added a second foundation, for men of 'noble poverty'. The inmates of the Blois foundation have a black gown and medieval cap and wear a silver cross of St John on the left breast; those of the 'noble poverty' display a mulberry-coloured gown and their regulation dress includes a mulberry cardinal's hat and tassels. Both are familiar sights in Winchester. A wayfarer, of any sort, may apply at St Cross Hospital for the dole, a sliver of bread and a small portion of beer served in a horn mug with glass bottom.

TOWN CLOCK Above the main street, it was a gift to the city commemorating the Peace of Utrecht

## WINCHESTER CATHEDRAL

*The longest cathedral in Europe, begun when Winchester was the capital of England. The West Saxons had made their capital here during the 9th century and a Saxon church preceded the present building, though little evidence of it remains. The present church, begun in 1079 and now 556 ft long, overlaps the Saxon predecessor at its west end. During the Middle Ages Winchester was the richest See in England and became the ecclesiastical reward for a series of impressive men. William of Wykeham was twice Chancellor of England, under Edward III and Richard II. During his time as bishop much of the cathedral was remodelled (1366–1404) and the Norman masonry of the nave was carefully concealed in a casing of Perpendicular stonework. Cardinal Henry Beaufort (d. 1447), was a half-brother of Henry IV and played an important part in the negotiations with France in the last phases of the Hundred Years War.*

## VIRGIN AND CHILD

*A fragment of a unique Gothic statue of stone, dating from the late 15th century. The sculptor must have been familiar with the painting and sculpture of Flanders and Holland, but there is no reason to doubt that he was English. (Winchester Cathedral)*

## THE WINCHESTER BIBLE

*The finest ceremonial Bible produced in England in the 12th century was that written and illuminated for the cathedral priory of Winchester. It was probably begun between 1160 and 1170 and its decoration was conceived on so large a scale that although at least six artists worked on it over many years, it was never finished. The text was exceptionally accurate and a contemporary chronicler mentions that it was lent to Witham Priory at the special request of its founder, Henry II, so that the Witham monks could copy it. The left-hand initial shown is the 'B' beginning Psalm 1. King David slays the bear in the upper loop and the lion in the lower. The artist, because of his expert handling of figures in motion, is known as the 'Master of the Leaping Figures'.*
*(Winchester Cathedral Library)*

(1713). From the belfry turret of the adjacent old guildhall the curfew rings each night at 8 o'clock as it has done since Norman times.

TOWN CROSS At the centre of the High Street is a four-sided, 15th-century Gothic cross, restored in 1865. It has four figures: only St John the Baptist is original, the others—William of Wykeham, King Alfred and a supposed mayor of the city—were added during the restoration.

WESTGATE MUSEUM The museum is situated in the original west gate of the medieval city, and its exhibits relate mostly to Winchester's civic history. They include a large collection of medieval and post-medieval weights and measures, among which is a unique set of Edward III weights.

WINCHESTER COLLEGE One of the most famous public schools, it was founded in 1382 and its buildings retain a medieval atmosphere. Its great tower was built in 1481. The chapel has Perpendicular-style windows and the founder's (William of Wykeham's) fan tracery vaulting (used as a model by Henry VI for the chapel at Eton College). Its Jesse window is a copy of the original, and dates from 1822. In the centre of the cloister is Fromond's Chantry Chapel. A detached building known simply as 'School' dates from 1683; it bears on one wall an inscription in Latin meaning 'Learn, leave or be licked'. The school motto is 'Manners Makyth Man'.

### Windmill Hill *Wilts.*     540Fg
The top of this hill is surrounded by three rather irregular concentric ditches, all with characteristic causeways. The excavations on the site between the two World Wars first revealed these structures, and identified the camps as of Neolithic date. On the east of the camp is a group of round barrows.

### Windsor *Berks.*     547Hb
CASTLE The castle established by William the Conqueror probably consisted, as now, of a motte, or steep mound, and two large baileys enclosed by palisades. The stone fortifications were not built until the 12th and 13th centuries, and the defences are substantially those established by the end of Henry III's reign. Windsor was Edward III's favourite residence, and it was he who enlarged the existing royal apartments in the upper ward and established the Chapel of the Order of the Garter. Considerable additions to the castle were also made by Charles II, and an immense amount of restoration and embellishment was undertaken under George III, George IV and Queen Victoria. The exterior of the castle is largely the result of work carried out in the 19th century. The Round Tower, for example, is considerably higher than it was when originally built by Henry II, and many of the towers in the upper ward were either built or heightened during this period. (See also pp. 490–1.)

ST GEORGE'S CHAPEL, WINDSOR CASTLE This rich and complex building, begun in 1475, is the Chapel of the Order of the Garter. The proportions are noble, with a beautiful vault and stalls elaborately decorated with heraldry for the Garter Knights. There is much 16th-century sculpture, but the most theatrical piece is the 19th-century monument to Princess Charlotte of Wales by M. C. Wyatt, in which the Princess is shown, chaste but bare-breasted, ascending from her shrouded corpse. Adjacent is the amazing Albert Memorial Chapel, a shrine of *c.* 1870 taste, with Baron Triquetti's monument to the Prince Consort; more important is the art nouveau memorial by Sir Alfred Gilbert to the Duke of Clarence (*d.* 1892), completed in 1926.

WINDSOR GUILDHALL EXHIBITION The exhibition is concerned mainly with local history, from the Palaeolithic period to the present day. It has a collection of royal portraits dating from the time of Elizabeth I (who is shown in one wearing a jewelled anchor in her hair), many relics of Sir William Herschel the astronomer (1738–1822), and a series of diorama showing historical scenes of Windsor from the earliest times to George III's Jubilee celebrations in 1809. There is an exhibition of local natural history. Many of the exhibits, including ancient documents from the Borough Records, are changed annually and each year some special theme in Windsor's life and history is chosen for exhibition. The guildhall itself was built in 1689 by Sir Thomas Fitz, a surveyor of the Cinque Ports; on the north and south faces are statues of Queen Anne and Prince George of Denmark.

### Windsor Great Park *Berks.*     547Hb
The principal gardens in Windsor Great Park are the Savill and the Valley Gardens. Begun by Sir Eric Savill in 1931, the Savill Garden has rhododendrons, cherries, magnolias and camellias massed in woodland glades, and drifts of daffodils in the open spaces. Beside ponds and streams primulas and irises grow, and there are lilies, snowdrops and spring and autumn crocuses. In a formal garden, a wide turf path has broad herbaceous borders on either side; behind are beds devoted to particular plants—such as hybrid tea and old-fashioned roses. Behind the beds is a massive buttressed wall against which are trained climbing roses and tender shrubs. At the base of the wall are rockery beds with alpines. As the Savill Garden matured another area, the Valley Garden, to the south near Virginia Water, was developed in similar manner. Yet another valley to the south-east,

formed like an amphitheatre, was planted with thousands of brilliant Japanese Kurume azaleas, and is known as the Kurume Punch Bowl.

**Wing** *Bucks.* 547Gd
CHURCH OF ALL SAINTS An exceptionally interesting Anglo-Saxon church, it has one of the four Saxon apses in England and a crypt under it. The apse is seven-sided; the vaulted crypt has a hexagonal central chamber with a narrow passage around it. Four bays of the nave arcades are pre-Conquest; the easternmost, however, is 13th century. The west tower is 14th century, and the south aisle was rebuilt then. The lower windows were inserted in the 15th century and a clerestory added. The rood screen is 16th century, the pulpit early 17th century. All Saints is rich in monuments, and includes 15th-century brasses and two excellent tombs to the Dormer family, *c.* 1552 and *c.* 1590.

**Wingfield** *Suffolk* 548Dg
CHURCH OF ST ANDREW An ambitious church, with a clerestory to the chancel as well as to the nave, and a west tower. There are monuments to members of the de la Pole family from the 14th century, also font, screens, stalls and misericords.

**Wingham** *Kent* 542Ff
A long village, with the best houses close to the church; there is a half-timbered group opposite it, and handsome Queen Anne houses to the south and east.

**Winkworth Arboretum** *Surrey* 542Ae
The grounds cover 95 acres, and contain rare trees and shrubs and a lake.

**Winterborne Stoke Crossroads** *Wilts.* 540Fe
Like the perhaps even finer barrow group on Normanton Down, every type of Bronze Age barrow, as well as a long barrow, is present in a comparatively small area. Altogether, in addition to the long barrow, there are 22 round barrows.

**Winterborne Tomson** *Dorset* 540Ec
CHURCH OF ST ANDREW A small 12th-century church with an apsidal east end, and plastered roofs. The interior is simple, and has 18th-century box-pews, pulpit and canopy; the gallery was the medieval rood loft.

**Winterbourne Bassett** *Wilts.* 540Fg
CHURCH OF ST KATHERINE A good, mainly Decorated church, with a Perpendicular west tower. There is an Early English font, and 17th-century benches, pulpit and font cover among the fittings. A 13th-century coffin-lid, or tomb-slab, is carved with figures of a man and a woman holding hands.

**Winton House** *E. Lothian* 562Ce
Charles I paid a visit to this house in 1633, and the fine plaster ceilings were installed in his honour. It is said to be the 'Ravenwood Castle' of Sir Walter Scott's *The Bride of Lammermoor*. George Seton, 3rd Earl of Winton, built the mansion in Scottish Renaissance style in 1620; it has tall chimneys, carved and twisted.

**Wintringham** *Yorks.* 558Fc
CHURCH OF ST PETER A Norman church, with 14th-century enlargement, and a west tower and spire. Inside is a Norman font, medieval screens, 15th-century glass, and 17th-century pews and pulpit.

**Winwick** *Lancs.* 552Af
CHURCH OF ST OSWALD Mainly of the 14th century, with a west tower and large spire. The nave roof is panelled; the 19th-century chancel is by Pugin. There are brasses and monuments to the Gerard and Legh families; one, of *c.* 1690, may be by John Nost.

THE LIBRARY IN QUEEN MARY'S DOLLS' HOUSE

*This spectacular dolls' house was made and presented to Queen Mary in the 1920's as a token of national goodwill, and to provide a means of raising funds for charity. Sir Edwin Lutyens designed the building, which is a faithful replica of a 20th-century house—* *one-twelfth normal size—with all the intriguing details of a luxurious residence for a king and queen. In the library the books are arranged on Italian walnut bookshelves and most were written specially for the house by their famous authors. (Windsor Castle)*

# WINDSOR CASTLE

William the Conqueror began this stupendous royal fortress, perhaps about the time that the Tower of London was begun in 1078. The castle probably consisted, as now, of a motte and two large baileys, enclosed by palisades. The stone fortifications followed in the 12th and 13th centuries, and the defences are substantially those established by the end of Henry III's reign. Windsor has always been one of the favourite residences of the reigning monarch. Additions were made under Charles II, and much of the present fabric dates from the 19th century. The royal apartments, a series of grandiose rooms, were refurbished in the 17th and 19th centuries.

HANS HOLBEIN THE YOUNGER: SIR HENRY GUILDFORD *Holbein was the supreme portrait painter of the northern Renaissance. He first visited England in 1526 for 18 months; he returned in 1532. He probably entered the royal service soon after 1537 and did many portrait drawings as well as numerous portraits in oils for Henry VIII. It was during his first visit in 1527, that he painted 'Sir Henry Guildford'* ($30\frac{1}{2}$ by $26\frac{1}{8}$ in.) *one of the king's favourites, who held various posts at Court. Here we see him with the staff of the Comptroller of the Household. Holbein combines an intensity and dispassionate clarity of observation with an austerity of linear draughtsmanship which results in a unity of the details in the costume and jewellery and the fine modelling of the sitter's features.*

THE CASTLE FROM THE AIR *Windsor encloses nearly 13 acres and is the largest castle in England. Standing on a hill of chalk near the Thames, it was originally built to guard London's approaches. The castle has grown continuously since it was established by William the Conqueror. Edward III considerably enlarged the royal apartments in Upper Ward, and founded St George's Chapel. An immense amount of restoration and embellishment was undertaken under George III, George IV and Victoria, and much of what is seen today is the creation of this period—the great Round Tower as built by Henry II was much lower, and many towers in Upper Ward were built or heightened during the Gothic restorations by Sir Jeffry Wyatville in the early 19th century.*

ST GEORGE'S CHAPEL CHOIR *Edward III founded the Order of the Garter, with its own chapel, at Windsor in 1348. After 1475 the building was replaced by the existing chapel, one of the most sumptuous late Gothic buildings in England. In the choir are the exquisitely carved stalls of the Knights of the Garter, made about 1480, surmounted by their owners' banners.*

STALL-PLATE *This plaque, dating from about 1559, shows enamelling as it was practised on base metals in Elizabethan England. It is the stall-plate recording the creation of the 4th Duke of Norfolk a Knight Companion of the Order of the Garter. When a Knight Companion is created a plate showing his Arms, usually in enamel, and the date of his creation, is attached to his stall in the Chapel of the Order, St George's Chapel, and his crested helm and banner are displayed there. On his death, helm and banner are taken away but the stall-plate remains. The 4th Duke of Norfolk was involved in the Ridolfi plot to dethrone Elizabeth and put Mary, Queen of Scots in her place; for this he was attainted and executed. To be attainted meant degradation from the Order of the Garter and the stall-plate was removed from the chapel, probably in 1572; it was replaced in 1955. (St George's Chapel)*

**491**

**Wirksworth** *Derbys.* 552Dd
CHURCH OF ST MARY A large cruciform church, with a central tower and spire, dating from the 13th century. Sir Gilbert Scott restored it in 1872, adding the clerestory. A coffin-lid of *c.* 800 is carved with New Testament scenes. There are two fonts, one Norman, the other of 1662.

**Wisbech** *Cambs.* 553Jb
Wisbech is one of the few Fen towns with many houses of real architectural quality. The two Brinks on the R. Nene make one of the best Georgian scenes in England, but the typical grey brick of Cambridgeshire does not complement Georgian architecture quite as well as red brick. The North Brink has inherited a character chiefly from the Dutch, who continued the reclamation work started first by the Romans and finished by the Scottish civil engineers Telford and Rennie. Wisbech, once 4 miles away from the sea, is now 11 miles inland.

The Rose and Crown Hotel has early Tudor brick barrel-vaults and an elegant 18th-century staircase with buildings at the back dated 1801. There are early 18th-century houses in Norfolk Street and the Old Market. South Brink has houses of much the same character, particularly Nos. 7–8 which belonged to Sir Philip Vavasour. Wisbech's excellent museum has the original manuscript of Charles Dickens's *Great Expectations*.
CHURCH OF SS PETER AND PAUL A large and complex church in a once prosperous town, with work of the 12th century onwards. The tower on the north side is detached from the main building. There is 19th-century stained glass, and brasses and monuments, one by Joseph Nollekens; also the carved Arms of James I.
PECKOVER HOUSE Built on the North Brink *c.* 1726, is the finest house in Wisbech; the Peckover family, who also built Sibalds Home, were rich local bankers and the interior of the house reflects this wealth in the excellence of its rococo decoration work—in both wood and plaster.

**Wisley Gardens** *Surrey* 542Af
The Royal Horticultural Society's garden, near Ripley, Surrey. Here, new varieties of flowers, fruit and vegetables are tested, and established varieties are improved. Outstanding features are the rock garden and the mixed borders.

**Withcote** *Leics.* 552Fb
CHURCH This small 16th-century building serves as the chapel for the adjoining Withcote Hall. It is notable for the rich contemporary stained glass.

**Witherslack** *Westmld.* 557Hd
CHURCH OF ST PAUL A 17th-century Gothic church, built *c.* 1669 by John Barwick, Dean of St Paul's. Altered in 1768 and restored in 1873, St Paul's has 17th-century woodwork and stained glass.

**Withington** *Glos.* 546Dd
CHURCH OF ST MICHAEL AND ALL ANGELS In a Cotswold village, an interesting church with work from Norman to Perpendicular Gothic. There is a central tower, and a good Norman south doorway. A wall monument with kneeling figures is by Edward Marshall, 1651.

**Withyham** *Sussex* 542Ce
CHURCH OF ST MICHAEL AND ALL ANGELS The church was rebuilt between 1663 and 1672, after being struck by lightning. Its importance lies in its monuments to the Sackville family in their chapel of 1680, built to receive the monument to Thomas, a boy of 13 who died in 1677. This is by Caius

SACKVILLE MONUMENT

*Caius Gabriel Cibber, who lived from 1630 to 1700, was a Dane who studied in Rome and was much influenced by Bernini's works—traces of which can be seen in this monument. Carved in marble about 1674, it shows Sir Richard Sackville, 5th Earl of Dorset (1622–77) and his wife kneeling beside their dying son. Around the base of the tomb are the figures of their children who died in early childhood. (Church of St Michael and All Angels, Withyham)*

Gabriel Cibber, and is his only known important tomb, although he carved for Hampton Court, St Paul's Cathedral, Chatsworth and other late 17th-century buildings. Other monuments of the 18th and 19th centuries are by Joseph Nollekens, John Flaxman and Sir Francis Chantrey.

**Witney** *Oxon.* 546Ec
Witney prospered in the past from Cotswold wool, and the Witney blankets made from it. The R. Windrush provided power and clear water for washing the wool and a number of mills stand in and around the town. In Bridge Street is the Blanket Hall of *c.* 1740 where the merchants met to do business. The Butter Cross in the market-place dates from 1668. On Church Green, a tree-lined open space, are the church and the early 18th-century rectory at one end, and the 17th- and 18th-century houses of well-to-do clothiers down either side. On the west of the green an avenue of limes leads to the grammar school, built in 1660, the work of a local mason but already strongly influenced by the new Classicism of Inigo Jones and his followers.
CHURCH OF ST MARY THE VIRGIN A grand cruciform church, with central tower and spire, at one side of a large village green. The original Norman church was altered in the Early English and later Gothic periods; it contains a 14th-century brass with figures.

**Wiveton Hall** *Norfolk* 554Cd
A small manor house dated 1652, combined with a house in the same Jacobean style of *c.* 1909.

**Woburn Abbey** *Beds.* 547He
At the Dissolution in 1539 Henry VIII granted the land and buildings at Woburn to John Russell and made him 1st Baron Russell. In 1550 Russell was made 1st Earl of Bedford by Edward VI, and later the 5th Earl was created Duke of Bedford by

William III. The Russells did not live at Woburn until the 17th century, when they built themselves a house on the monastic site. The shell grotto in the north wing, reputed to have been designed by Isaac de Caux, dates from this time. Much of this house was destroyed during the 18th century when John Sanderson and later Henry Flitcroft were employed to remodel the abbey. At the end of the 18th century Henry Holland, architect of Carlton House, London, added the east front, the Chinese dairy, and other portions of the house, including the orangery which is now the picture gallery. After the Second World War the east front was found to be riddled with dry rot, and demolished. The mansion contains magnificent collections of pictures, including works by Canaletto, Rembrandt, Van Dyck, Gainsborough, Reynolds, Velazquez and Holbein; fine French and English 18th-century furniture; and 18th-century silver. In the park, landscaped by Humphry Repton, roam 11 varieties of deer, and American and European bison.

**Woden Law** *Rox.*                                562Ec
FORT AND ROMAN SIEGE WORKS The fort shows evidence, in its multivallate defences, of three structural phases. It. has, however, a still greater interest in that, outside the outermost defences there are the banks and ditches, forming different patterns, of Roman siege works. It is not thought that these were used in an attack on the fort, but that they are the results of a training exercise by a local garrison.

**Wollaton** *Notts.*                                552Ed
CHURCH OF ST LEONARD The church has a west tower and steeple, with a passage from north to south at ground level. There is a pretty, carved wood reredos with Corinthian columns, and many monuments, from *c.* 1471 to those by the younger John Bacon and Sir Richard Westmacott.

**Wollaton Hall** *Notts.*                           552Ed
This great mansion, now the home of the Natural History Museum of Nottingham, contains collections of exotic butterflies, British beetles and Wenlock limestone fossils. It is one of the most splendid examples of Elizabethan Renaissance architecture. The architect was Robert Smythson, who had worked for Sir John Thynne on the rebuilding of Longleat House in Wiltshire. Wollaton Hall, built 1580-8, was original for a period in which buildings planned around open courtyards were favoured. At Wollaton there was no courtyard, and the great hall was made the centre of the house. The hall rises like a great tower from the building and is ornamented with projecting round turrets at the four corners. A large tower ornamented with pinnacles is built at each of the four corners of the house itself. The facade and the sides are decorated with pilasters of the Ionic order, and the rather severe formality is broken by rich mouldings, numerous niches and huge windows.

**Wolterton Hall** *Norfolk*                         554Cc
Designed for Horace Walpole, the traveller, author and propagator of 18th-century Gothic taste, in 1727. It has state rooms and gardens and is the property of the present Lord Walpole. (By appointment.)

**Wolverhampton** *Staffs.*                          552Bb
Created a county borough in 1889, the town is now famous for its engineering but was originally a medieval wool centre. After a great fire in 1590 it switched to making locks and keys in the early 17th century, and also to buckle-making—in 1770 the town had 102 master buckle-makers in steel.

STATE SALON AT WOBURN ABBEY

*Woburn has been the home of the Russell family since the 17th century. The family, created Dukes of Bedford in 1694, was given the land and original monastic buildings there by Henry VIII at the Dissolution. The 17th-century house they built was largely demolished during the 18th century when John Sanderson and later Henry Flitcroft were commissioned to rebuild it. Flitcroft had had a brilliant career. He began as a joiner and then became an architectural draughtsman for William Kent; later he joined the Office of Works as a master carpenter and eventually became Comptroller there. At Woburn he reconstructed the west front with its magnificent state rooms which were finished about 1760.*

SÈVRES SOUP TUREEN

*Part of a magnificent Sèvres porcelain dinner service given by Louis XV to the Duchess of Bedford in 1763, when the Duke was English Ambassador at the signing of the Treaty of Paris. Made for 18 diners, most of the 183 pieces still survive. (Woburn Abbey)*

## SIR EDWARD ELGAR,
### ENGLAND'S TRIUMPHANT COMPOSER

At the age of ten Elgar was discovered sitting on a river bank, with a pencil and sheet of manuscript in his hand, trying to write down 'what the reeds are singing'. This early originality and self-reliance was fostered by a non-academic training and his orchestral techniques were self-acquired during music-making in his home town of Worcester. Elgar later gave up violin teaching to concentrate entirely on composition. In 1907 he was staying with friends when he pulled out a used envelope and scribbled down the outline of a march. 'Listen to this, this'll make them sit up!' he said, and moved to the piano to pick out for the first time 'The Pomp and Circumstance March in D major'. The subsequent unfolding of his genius revealed him as essentially a symphonic writer and his violin concerto and two symphonies give him a place among Britain's great composers.

THE ORDER OF MERIT *(1911) and other awards bestowed on Elgar. His was the first O.M. awarded to a musician. Elgar had been knighted in 1904, and was accepted as a peer among great continental musicians while still struggling for recognition in England. (Elgar's Birthplace, Broadheath, Worcester)*

TWO PHOTOGRAPHS OF ELGAR, *who liked nothing more than to be mistaken for a major-general, and a part of a handwritten manuscript.*

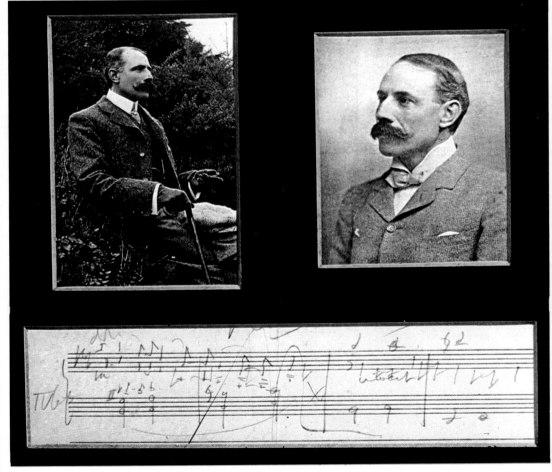

LADY ELGAR, *a pastel drawn prior to her marriage. Elgar's development owed much to his wife's belief in him. (Broadheath)*

ELGAR'S DESK *and the paraphernalia he used for composition. 'Gosh, man, I've got a tune in my head' was a typical expression of the delight he felt at the prospect of musical composition. His wife acted as his secretary, ruling out and copying most of his major scores.(Broadheath)*

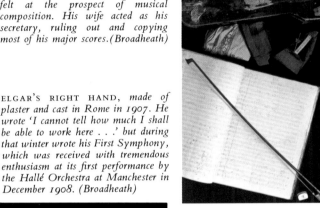

ELGAR'S RIGHT HAND, *made of plaster and cast in Rome in 1907. He wrote 'I cannot tell how much I shall be able to work here . . .' but during that winter wrote his First Symphony, which was received with tremendous enthusiasm at its first performance by the Hallé Orchestra at Manchester in December 1908. (Broadheath)*

ELGAR'S DIVERSE INTERESTS, *from chemistry to golf, cycling and poker-work, are here illustrated. An enthusiastic race-goer, bookmakers were awestruck with his infallible skill in picking losers. (Broadheath)*

SECOND SYMPHONY MANUSCRIPT *written 1910–11. Elgar called it 'a frank expression of the music bubbling from the spring within him'. Also shown: his violin case, bow, metronome, resin box and handkerchiefs. (Broadheath)*

BIRCHWOOD, *the cottage in Broadheath near Worcester, where Elgar was born. He grew up surrounded by music, his father being organist at St George's Roman Catholic Church, and owning a music shop in the town.*

ELGAR'S GRAVE *lies by the side of his wife's in St Wulstan's Church, Little Malvern. His life and work had paved the way for a renaissance of musical composing in England.*

## WOODHENGE

*A Neolithic defensive site on the Wiltshire Downs, recognised from an aerial photograph taken in 1925. A circular bank—220 ft in diameter—encloses a* *ditch and six concentric settings of timber uprights (perhaps roof supports) now marked by rows of concrete pillars.*

**Wolverton** *Hants.* 541Hf
CHURCH OF ST CATHERINE An elegant building of the early 18th century, this church suffered from Victorian insertion of mullions and tracery into the windows, and destruction of the chancel gates and the gallery. Much of the furniture and fittings, however, are original, such as the reading-desk, pews, reredos and pulpit.

**Woodbridge** *Suffolk* 548Ee
Woodbridge is a small town, half farming, half seafaring. It is full of good 15th-, 16th- and 18th-century houses dominated by Thomas Seckford's Dutch-like shire hall, *c.* 1575, with 19th-century additions. The lower part of the structure was originally open and formed a covered market. It was sealed off in 1803. The 'abbey', another building by this Elizabethan public benefactor, is Seckford's manor house in Church Street, *c.* 1654; the two-storey red-brick structure, with Flemish gables, is still in excellent repair. The King's Head Inn, timber-framed in Seckford Street, the Angel Inn, also timber-framed with overhangs, in Theatre Street, and the Bell Inn in New Street are notable inns of character. There are good Georgian houses in the Thoroughfare and better ones in Cumberland Street. The post office has Jacobean plaster ceilings and fire-places from an earlier house, with a staircase dated 1634. The unique feature of the town is the old steelyard or lever weighing-machine at the Bell Inn, for weighing hay, wool and hides. It is the only one in Suffolk and one of the few in England. Not far off, Seckford Hall, a Tudor mansion, is now a hotel.
CHURCH OF ST MARY A large church, with flushwork decoration, and a tall 15th-century west tower. Inside is a seven-sacrament font with a pinnacled canopy, and a rood screen with painted figures. There is modern stained glass in the east window, and an early 17th-century monument.

**Woodchester Roman Villa** *Glos.* 546Cc
The villa site, one of the largest in Britain, covers 26 acres and was excavated in 1796; it is generally kept covered with earth for preservation, but is occasionally opened up.

**Woodcroft Castle** *Hunts.* 547Jh
Built in 1280 and altered 200 years later, the small castle-house has an entrance gateway in the middle of the main front, with the porter's lodge on one side and the guard-room on the other; the south-west tower still stands in the remains of the moat. The room over the entrance is said to have been a chapel. Although it has no battlements or machicolations, the effect of a small, uncompromising fortress remains.

**Wood Hall** *Norfolk* 548Ae
An E-shaped house of 1579, brick-built with projecting porch and two wings. The porch has columns and pilasters, and there are mullioned windows.

**Woodhenge** *Wilts.* 540Fe
This monument lies immediately outside the Durrington Walls circle on its south-west side. It is certainly earlier than Stonehenge, as its origins lie well back in the Neolithic period. It is marked by a circular ditch inside its bank, some 220 ft in overall diameter. The centre, when excavated, showed six concentric circles of post-holes in the chalk, with others at the entrance. They may originally have been the major uprights of a roofed building.
When the excavations were completed, short concrete pillars were inserted in the post-holes, so that the pattern is visible on the surface. Woodhenge must form part of the complex of which Durrington Walls is the largest unit.

**Woodstock** *Oxon.* 546Ed
Woodstock is dominated by Blenheim Palace. West of the main road is the cobbled market-place, and a short street of 18th-century houses leads to a

small square outside the park gates. The rear of the rectory (visible from the park) and a house on the main road have heavy, baroque details that link them with Blenheim.

OXFORD CITY AND COUNTY MUSEUM, FLETCHER'S HOUSE Opened in 1966 to display crafts and industries, building and farming methods, and life in the Oxford area through the centuries.

**Wookey Hole Caves** *Som.*        *540Cf*
Caves in the Mendips, worn by the R. Axe over a period of 50,000 years. During the last phase of the Ice Age, the Hyaena Den was certainly a wild-animal den for much of the time, but men also used it at various periods. Their remains included many flint and bone tools, the ashes of fires and food debris.

A few yards north is Wookey Great Cave. Here the occupation was much later, during the Iron Age and the Romano-British period. The Witch of Wookey is a massive stalagmite, said by legend to be a petrified old woman.

WOOKEY HOLE CAVES MUSEUM Little or nothing is known of the prehistoric life in the Wookey Hole Caves, but much evidence of later occupants is on display in the museum. These were the Celtic tribes from the Continent, who lived there from 250 BC until AD 450, when the Romans evacuated Britain. Earlier remains were also found, including animal and human bones, cooking articles and examples of primitive jewellery. Finds of medieval pottery and Bristol Glass give evidence of 17th-century and later visitors; undoubtedly the stalactite grottoes were a major attraction even in those days.

**Woolaston Roman Villa** *Glos.*     *546Bc*
A large Roman villa of 20 rooms, excavated in 1934.

**Woolpit** *Suffolk*       *548Cf*
The last wolf in Suffolk is reputed to have been killed at Woolpit, which has a large brick-yard from which bricks were sent for the building of the U.S. President's residence, the White House in Washington. In folk-lore, Suffolk fairies are 'The Little Green Men of the Woolpit Brick-yard', so-called from the appearance there in the 11th century of two strange children, neither of them able to speak English, and each coloured green. In time they lost their colouring, and learnt to speak English, but were never able to explain where they had come from or how they arrived at Woolpit.

CHURCH OF ST MARY A Decorated and Perpendicular church, with a 19th-century spire. There is an ambitious south porch with niches for statues, roof-bosses and a marvellous hammerbeam roof. Inside is a 16th-century brass eagle lectern, and bench ends with carved figures and animals.

**Woolsthorpe Manor** *Lincs.*     *553Gc*
In the quiet orchard in front of the house Sir Isaac Newton, who was born here in 1642, watched an apple fall to the ground; this is reputed to have led him to his universal law of gravitation. A descendant of the apple tree can be seen today. The house was built in the early 17th century.

**Wootton Bassett** *Wilts.*     *546Db*
A mainly 18th-century town, with a half-timbered restored town hall (1700) in which are stocks, a ducking-stool and an ancient fire-engine.

**Wootton Lodge** *Staffs.*     *552Cd*
Splendid 17th-century mansion in the heart of the countryside; it was used by George Eliot as the setting of her novel, *Adam Bede*, written in 1859.

**Wootton Wawen** *Warks.*     *546Df*
CHURCH OF ST PETER The central tower is of Saxon origin, from the early 11th century, and the church built around it has work from the Norman period to the 17th century. Inside, the octagonal font is early 14th century, and there are two parclose screens of that era. There are fragments of earlier medieval wall decoration, and some pieces of 13th-century stained glass in the east window. A variety of monuments, some with effigies, range from an alabaster knight of the early 15th century to one with kneeling mourners of *c.* 1836.

**Worcester** *Worcs.*     *546Cf*
A cathedral city, granted its first royal charter in 1189 by Richard I. Its second and more detailed charter was given in 1227 by Henry III, whom the city supported in the Barons' Wars 35 years later. James I granted Worcester yet another charter in 1621, which declared it County of the City of Worcester, separate from the county of Worcestershire. The city has suffered from its loyalty to the Crown: it was plundered and burnt in 1041 as a reprisal for the death of King Hardicanute's tax-collectors whom the townspeople regarded as agents of an invader, and in the 12th century the city caught fire during King Stephen's military action against Matilda. In 1265, Prince Edward (later Edward I) used Worcester as a base from which to attack Simon de Montfort at the Battle of Evesham, and 400 years later the first battle of the Civil War was fought at Powick Bridge, 2 miles west of the town. Prince Rupert's cavalry routed the Parliamentary horse, but next day Parliamentary forces plundered the city and desecrated the cathedral. In 1651, Charles II's army confronted Cromwell's forces at the Battle of Worcester: the Royalists were overwhelmed and the king was forced to flee.

Worcester porcelain was first manufactured by a Dr Wall in 1751, but the business was sold in 1783 to Thomas Flight of Hackney, London. One of

WORCESTER PORCELAIN VASE

*The Worcester Porcelain Company was founded early in the 18th century and grew rapidly, taking over Benjamin Lund's factory at Bristol in 1752. From 1751 the Worcester factory was run by Dr Wall, and after his death in 1776, the works were continued under William Davis until 1783, when they were purchased by Thomas Flight. This vase is from the Flight, Barr and Barr period of about 1830; it has brilliant decoration known as the 'jewellery' type. From its beginnings the factory specialised in table-wares and ornamental vases. From 1770 the distinctive vivid colours which made the works famous were used, and the development of transfer printing progressed. The material was more reliable than that of contemporary factories because of the incorporation of Cornish soapstone. (Dyson Perrins Museum, Worcester)*

# WORCESTER CATHEDRAL

WORCESTER CATHEDRAL *In a superb position above the R. Severn, the cathedral is dominated by a magnificent 14th-century tower. But there have been buildings on this site since long before then. The See was founded in 680 when the large Diocese of Lichfield was divided. In the late 10th century the community of secular canons was refounded as a monastery by Bishop Oswald, later St Oswald, and this continued until the Dissolution. During the 1080's Bishop Wulfstan began rebuilding the existing Saxon church, and the oldest part of the* present cathedral, the stately Romanesque crypt, dates from that time. The Romanesque church was reconstructed in the late 12th and 13th centuries. Worcester has had numerous eminent bishops—St Wulfstan was a pious and much-respected figure, and alone of the Anglo-Saxon bishops survived the Norman Conquest for any considerable time (he died in 1096). In the cathedral a number of fine monuments includes that of King John, and the chantry of Prince Arthur, eldest son of Henry VII, who died in 1502.

CRYPT *The oldest part of the present cathedral, dating from 1084. The stately Romanesque structure was built by Bishop Wulfstan for the safeguarding and the worship of saints' relics. It was a church in itself, and is still used for services on the anniversary of St Wulfstan's death on January 19, 1095.*

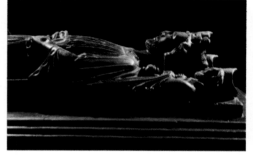

KING JOHN'S TOMB *This Purbeck marble effigy, once painted and jewelled, is the oldest royal effigy in England; it was probably made two years after the king's death in 1216. In 1797 the tomb was opened and the body found, wrapped in remains of a monk's cowl and an embroidered robe, with a sword and scabbard.*

the employees at the time was Robert Chamberlain, who left the firm to start a rival factory; this was so successful that in 1840 an amalgamation was arranged and in 1862 the Worcester Royal Porcelain Co. Ltd. was formed.

ASSEMBLY ROOM In Queen Anne style, the interior is hung with paintings. The lower hall contains suits of armour used at the Battle of Worcester, two brass cannons, and a helmet (called 'Branks') for punishing scolding women.

CATHEDRAL The cathedral occupies a memorable position overlooking the R. Severn. It is dominated by a fine 14th-century tower and much of the church belongs to this period. However, there have been buildings on this site for a far longer period. The See itself was founded in 680 when Theodore, Archbishop of Canterbury, separated off a part of the large Diocese of Lichfield. Its early history is obscure but in the late 10th century the community, formerly of secular canons, was re-founded as a monastery by Bishop Oswald, who was later canonised. It continued as a monastery until the Dissolution (1539). The earliest part of the present cathedral dates from the time of Bishop Wulfstan who, during the 1080's, began to rebuild the existing Saxon church. From his time survives a fine Romanesque crypt. Next in time comes one of the earliest circular chapter houses (c. 1120). In c. 1170 the west end of the nave was reconstructed in Transitional style. Finally, c. 1320, a complete replacement of the Romanesque church was undertaken, starting at the east end. A notable part of the cathedral is the 16th-century Prince Arthur's Chantry, built by Henry VII for his son who had died at Ludlow.

Among many things to see are fine misericords, one with a carved scene of a tournament, the monumental effigy of King John, and works by John Bacon the Younger, Sir Francis Chantrey, J. F. Moore, Joseph Nollekens, Louis Roubiliac, Thomas Stanton and other sculptors.

COMMANDERY The site of the former Commandery or Hospital of St Wulfstan—the headquarters of an order of knights from 1085 to 1540—was given to Richard Morrison in 1541, and on it he built a Tudor-style house, used as the headquarters of the Royalists in the Battle of Worcester. The original 15th-century timber hall was retained, and later an Elizabethan staircase and 17th-century panelling were installed.

DYSON PERRINS MUSEUM This collection of Worcester ceramics of all periods, housed in a converted Victorian school dating from 1843, is regarded as the most comprehensive of its kind in the world. It is based on the collection of the factory of the Royal Worcester Porcelain Company, and on the private collection of the late Dyson Perrins.

GUILDHALL Built 1721–3 to a design by Thomas White of Worcester, a pupil of Sir Christopher Wren. The façade is early Georgian; two statues flank the entrance, one of Charles I, the other of Charles II, and above the doorway, indicating the city's strong Royalist favour, is a carved head of Oliver Cromwell, nailed by the ears as a token of undying enmity from the 'Faithful City'. Between the two central windows is a statuette of Queen Anne. Five statues above an ornate coved cornice represent Justice, Peace, Plenty, Chastisement and Hercules.

SHIRE HALL With a massive Ionic portico, the city's legal centre: in its courtyard is a statue of Queen Victoria.

Other notable buildings include Nash House, with Elizabethan half-timbered façade and street overhang, and King Charles's House (1577) in

similar style. Edgar Tower, the gateway to the cathedral green, dates from the reign of King John, 1199–1216. Sir Edward Elgar (1857–1934), composer and Master of the King's Musick (1924–34), was born in Worcester: his museum, at nearby Broadheath, contains many mementoes and manuscripts. His compositions are a regular feature of the Three Choirs Festival.

**Worksop** *Notts.*      *552Ee*
PRIORY CHURCH OF SS CUTHBERT AND MARY A fine Norman west front with two towers, and an impressive late Norman nave. The priory was founded in 1103. The Early English Lady Chapel dates from the mid-13th century, with many lancets, although it has been rebuilt.

PUBLIC LIBRARY AND MUSEUM The museum contains items depicting local archaeology, history and natural history; of particular note are two Bronze Age decorated beakers found at Clumber Park, and a fragment of massive high-relief sculpture from the great altar of the Temple of Pergamon in Asia Minor, pillaged for the Earl of Arundel in the late 18th century, and once part of his collection of marble relics.

**Worlingham Hall** *Suffolk*      *548Eg*
The exterior was built in 1725; the interior dates from 1799–1800. A notable feature is an octagonal hall with double staircase. (By appointment.)

**Worstead** *Norfolk*      *554Dc*
CHURCH OF ST MARY The church was begun during the late 14th century, and has a west tower over 100 ft high. The west window is Decorated, with reticulated tracery. Other features include a hammerbeam nave roof, canopied font cover and much screen-work—the rood screen, with painted saints, dates from 1512. There are also box-pews and 15th- and 16th-century brasses.

**Worth** *Sussex*      *542Be*
CHURCH OF ST NICHOLAS Probably the most interesting cruciform Saxon church in England, with an apse and high chancel arch. The north-east tower was built by Anthony Salvin in 1871, when only protests saved much of the church from being pulled down and rebuilt. The font is from the 13th century and the 17th-century woodwork includes the west gallery of 1610.

**Wortham Manor** *Devon*      *538Ed*
A fortified manor house, of 11th-century foundation, with carved oak porch, oak panelled parlour, newel staircase, and a most unusual feature, a double hall—one great room above the other.

**Worthing** *Sussex*      *542Ad*
MUSEUM AND ART GALLERY Housed in a building given to the town by its first mayor—Alderman Alfred Cortis—the museum has a local archaeology collection including an Anglo-Saxon glass vase, a late Bronze Age cauldron, and a Romano-British bronze boar, perhaps a hunter's religious offering. There is a comprehensive selection of 19th-century dolls and late 19th-century mechanical toys, including a praxinoscope theatre of 1879, in which a series of reflected images create an impression of movement. Also displayed are items of costume from 1740 to 1940, English marked pottery and porcelain from 1770 to 1880, and a display of scale ship models including a Viking ship of c. AD 900. The art gallery has a collection of English art, specialising in early English water-colours with works by W. Holman Hunt and William Callow, among others.

**Worth Matravers** *Dorset*      *540Ed*
CHURCH OF ST NICHOLAS A Norman church, with west tower, and a noteworthy chancel arch

and south doorway. The chancel was altered during the 13th century and has a fine 14th-century east window. The interior suffered extensive restoration in the 19th century.

**Wothorpe Towers** *Hunts.* 547Hh
Wothorpe ruins, *c.* 1620, are all that remain of the cruciform house originally built for Thomas Cecil, eldest son of Lord Burghley, for use as a lodge until his great house Burghley, at Stamford, was completed. It fell into ruin during the 18th century; the towers, with an octagonal top storey, are still well preserved. A gateway with a stepped gable leads to the courtyard.

**Wotton** *Surrey* 542Af
CHURCH OF ST JOHN The 13th-century church retains its 11th-century tower. The north chapel is the burial place of the family of John Evelyn, the 17th-century diarist, who lived near by, and contains many monuments. St John's was restored during the 19th century.

**Wotton House** *Bucks.* 547Gd
A country mansion, built 1704–14, with interior alterations made in 1820.

**Wragby** *Yorks.* 558Da
CHURCH OF ST MICHAEL The church stands in Nostall Park, and contains much foreign glass of the 16th and 18th centuries. There are monuments by both Sir Francis Chantrey and John Flaxman.

**Wraxall** *Som.* 540Ce
CHURCH OF ALL SAINTS All that remains of the original Norman church is the south doorway; the rest of the church is mainly of the 14th and 15th centuries, with a pinnacled west tower. There is 19th-century glass by C. E. Kempe, and a coloured late 15th-century monument with recumbent effigies and shield-bearing angels.

GATES BY THE DAVIES BROTHERS

*Robert and John Davies made these wrought-iron gates about 1720, repeating elements of the chancel gates inside the church, made by Hugh Davies, who was their father. The brothers are said to have worked under the French smith Tijou and their work shows traces of his influence. (Church of St Giles, Wrexham)*

**Wrekin, The** *Shrops.* 552Ab
This great fort crowns an isolated hill commanding the Vale of the Upper Severn. The defences are rather complicated, but the basic structure is a bank enclosing a long oval of some 7 acres. The protection given by this bank is aided by artificial scarping of the hillside. At each end there are additional earthworks which increase the enclosed area by about half.

**Wrenbury** *Cheshire* 552Ad
CHURCH OF ST MARGARET A pleasant church, with an early 16th-century west tower, and 18th-century chancel, pulpit and west gallery. Among the 19th-century monuments are some by John Bacon the Younger and William Theed the Younger.

**Wrest Park** *Beds.* 547He
A mansion in French château style, now used by the National Institute of Agricultural Engineering. There is a fine formal garden beside the canal. (Interior not open.)

**Wrexham** *Denb.* 551Jd
CHURCH OF ST GILES A 14th-century church, with additions of the 15th and 16th centuries and a Decorated interior. It has one of the most glorious parish church towers in the British Isles —tall, massive, pinnacled and smothered in tracery. St Giles's is rich in 18th-century monuments, among them being work by William Stanton, Louis Roubiliac and P. M. Van Gelder. The chancel gates are by Hugh Davies, father of the makers of the wrought-iron gates to the church.
EXHIBITION HALL AND WREXHAM ROOM (PUBLIC LIBRARY) Items relating to Wrexham and the surrounding area, including books and manuscripts, are displayed in the Wrexham Room. Travelling exhibitions, including art exhibitions, are shown in the Hall.

**Writtle** *Essex* 548Bc
THE GREEN Writtle, on the outskirts of Chelmsford, has a most attractive green. To the south, with the church behind them, are Aubyns, a small timbered house of *c.* 1500 (much restored) and Mundays, 17th century, with shell-hooded front door. West of the village is Moor Hall, a moated 15th-century house.

**Wroxeter** *Shrops.* 552Ab
In the early days of the Roman conquest, a legionary fortress was established here. It covered the entrance to the Border hills along the Severn Valley and the link with the R. Trent frontier to the north-east. When the legion was moved to Chester, its military purpose was served and, in due course, it became the cantonal town, Viroconium Cornoviorum, of the Cornovii tribe. Parts of the Roman town are still visible and are in some places accessible for inspection.
CHURCH OF ST ANDREW The church incorporates Roman masonry. The font is probably made from a piece of a Roman column. The Normans built the church, but there is also later work: the pulpit and box-pews are Jacobean, and there are four impressive monuments, three with effigies, from 1555 to 1708.

**Wroxton** *Oxon.* 546Ee
CHURCH A spacious Gothic church, the west tower rebuilt in the 18th century. Inside are 17th- and 18th-century monuments, including an imposing one to Sir William Pope, *c.* 1631, with effigies under a canopy on black marble pillars. A monument by John Flaxman, *c.* 1802, in memory

of the politician Lord North (d. 1792), shows Britannia and a lion.

**Wroxton Abbey** *Oxon.* 546Ee
A Jacobean stone house, for centuries the home of the North family which included the 8th Lord North, who was Prime Minister in 1770–82. It was built in 1618 by Sir William Pope, the founder of Trinity College, Oxford, and incorporates remains of a 13th-century Augustinian priory.

**Wye** *Kent* 542Ef
The college, now an agricultural college, east of the church, was founded in 1450. To the south lies the town, the houses unusually uniform and small in scale, mostly 17th century (with grotesque figures in the porches) and Georgian brick.

**Wymington** *Beds.* 547Hf
CHURCH OF ST LAURENCE The church was begun in 1350, and John Curteys, who started the work, is buried in the chancel with his wife. There is a good ornamented tower and spire; the interior is rich and complex, with a fine nave roof of medieval timber. Altogether, with the remains of a 'Doom' painting, old pews and some fragments of colour on the capitals and arches, the building conveys a real idea of the luxuriant spirit of the 14th century. There are also brasses of knights and their ladies.

**Wymondham** *Norfolk* 554Cb
CHURCH OF SS MARY AND THOMAS OF CANTERBURY A fragment of the former abbey church, now with a tower at both east and west ends. The abbey was founded in 1107, and the church was a major Norman building of which the nave arcades remain. The founder intended the nave to be parochial but, as in other cases where a church was shared, there was perpetual disagreement. At Wymondham the dispute was over the tower, so the abbey built the octagonal tower, c. 1400, at the present east end, whilst c. 1448 the parish built the west tower, and the nave was sealed off by a roof-high wall. There is a Perpendicular clerestory, and beautiful hammerbeam roofs decorated with angels and star-bosses. After the Dissolution, stone from the ruined abbey was used to rebuild the south aisle, 1544–60. There is much else to see, including the ornate modern reredos, c. 1935, by Sir Ninian Comper.

**Wynnstay Hall** *Denb.* 551Jd
This modern building, styled as a Danish castle, replaces the Hall destroyed by fire in 1858. In its great hall, with its ornate ceiling and a solid oak carved fire-place, is a rare Snetzler organ made in 1774. Since 1950, the Hall has been a school.

# Y Z

**Yalding** *Kent* 542Df
Two tributaries join the R. Medway at Yalding, and two fine medieval stone bridges span them. The village rises gently to the north. The brick of the houses is varied in colour, especially the velvety-plum of the Old House, and the orangey Holborough House opposite. Both were built c. 1700, the period of the most adventurous brickwork in south-eastern England.

**Yardhurst** *Kent* 542Ee
A recently restored timbered house with a great hall, built c. 1450.

**Yarnton** *Oxon.* 546Fd
CHURCH OF ST BARTHOLOMEW The original Norman church was added to until the 17th century. It contains many interesting features: medieval glass, a 17th-century pulpit, screen, and fine monuments to the Spencer family in their chapel, also 17th century.

**Yate** *Glos.* 546Bb
CHURCH OF ST MARY An impressive Perpendicular west tower dominates this low-built church: it is buttressed and pinnacled, and has a large stair-turret. Inside is a brass of 1590 to a man, two wives and 11 children, and several wall monuments. There is also a 14th-century font.

**Yately** *Hants.* 541Jf
CHURCH OF ST PETER Of Saxon origin, with later rebuilding and additions, this church has a 13th-century Early English chancel and a 15th-century west tower of brick and timber. There is a 15th-century timber porch with figure of St John, several brasses, and fragments of an anchorite's cell. There are numerous brass candelabra and some 19th-century glass.

**Yatton** *Som.* 540Cf
CHURCH OF ST MARY The south porch of this impressive 14th- and 15th-century church is highly decorated. There are transepts and the tower is central. Inside are several monuments, one of them, a tablet of c. 1714, by the Bristol sculptor, Michael Signell.

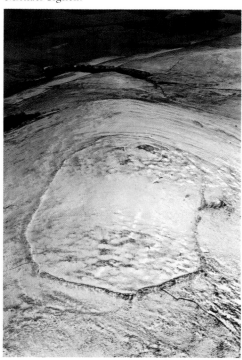

YEAVERING BELL

*Snow clearly picks out the stone rampart of this hill-fort on top of Yeavering Bell—one of the Cheviot Hills—which rises to 1182 ft. The rampart encloses nearly 14 acres and has three entrances.*

**Yaxley** *Hunts.* 547Jg
CHURCH OF ST PETER A cruciform church, with a west tower crowned by pinnacles and a flying-buttressed spire. Inside there is a 13th-century font, a 15th-century screen and stalls, and medieval wall-paintings.

**Yeavering Bell** *Northld.* 562Fc
A large fort for this part of the country, with an internal area of nearly 14 acres. A stone rampart encircles the hill-top along its contours and there are three entrances. The east entrance has a protecting outer wall. The south gate has a guard-chamber on each side. There are the visible foundations of many circular or oval huts. (See p. 501.)

**Yeovil** *Som.* 540Cd
BOROUGH OF YEOVIL MUSEUM, HENDFORD MANOR HOUSE Housed in a converted coach-house and stables once attached to Hendford Manor House, the museum specialises in items of local interest—archaeology from the Westland and Lufton sites, prints and engravings, and local industry. Also on view is the Henry Stiby Collection of fire-arms and an exhibition of costume.
CHURCH OF ST JOHN THE BAPTIST A large, late 14th-century town church; a fine Perpendicular building, with west tower, large windows, and transepts. The font is contemporary, as is the brass lectern, and there is a vaulted crypt under the chancel. Among the many monuments is one by Sir Richard Westmacott, *c.* 1855, with a life-size half-figure.

**Yeovilton** *Som.* 540Ce
FLEET AIR ARM MUSEUM The museum was opened at the Royal Naval Air Station in 1964, to celebrate 50 years of Naval flying. The history and development of this subject are covered from its origins in 1910 to the work of the present-day Fleet Air Arm.
Aircraft on display include the Sea Vampire—which carried out the first jet deck-landing in 1945—and Swordfish, Corsair, Martlet, Sea Fury, Walrus and Dragonfly planes, among others. There is also a unique collection of 1 : 24 scale models of important naval aircraft and many photographs. The histories of airships, aircraft carriers and carrier operations are shown, and a variety of weapons used or once used by naval aircraft. There is a collection of pilots' clothing and a special exhibition shows the various stages of ejection from a high speed jet.

**Yetminster** *Dorset* 540Cd
CHURCH OF ST ANDREW The chancel was built *c.* 1300, but the rest of the church, with a west tower, is 15th century. Inside, the roofs still retain some of their painted decoration. A brass with figures dates from *c.* 1531, and there are a number of wall monuments, mainly of the 17th and 18th centuries. Some of the benches are 15th century.

**Y Gaer Fawr** *Carm.* 545Gd
This is one of the largest hill-forts in Wales, the enclosed area being some 25 acres. Its single massive ramparts have collapsed; like others of its kind the defences did not include banks and ditches and had simple entrances. To the north is an annex with thinner walls.

**Ynys Y Pandy Slate Mill** *Caern.* 550Fd
This little-known building, which forms a most dramatic ruin against the sky, housed machinery for cutting and dressing slate from the quarries above Cwmstradlyn, which was brought down by tramway into the second floor. Finished slates were loaded on to a tramway leading out of the floor below, and eventually carried down to the sea at Portmadoc. This building is planned around a large water-wheel placed across the centre, with long side-shafts driving the machinery above.

**York** *Yorks.* 558Eb
The Romans came to York in AD 71, and set up a legionary fortress, originally with a wooden palisade, but shortly afterwards with stone walls. The Roman occupation lasted 340 years, and the city (raised to colony status) was visited by the Emperors Hadrian, Severus and Constantius. A small Christian community had assembled in the late 2nd century and their bishop went to the Council of Arles in AD 314. The See, overturned by the Saxons, was restored under the influence of Pope Gregory who created Paulinus archbishop in 625. The city then became a centre of learning with a Saxon equivalent of a university: its head, Alcuin, a Yorkshireman, was called by Charlemagne to run his palace school at Aachen in 782. The city changed its character with the coming of

POSSET CUP

*York, for centuries the chief city of northern England, possessed a fine collection of official plate and insignia. Many of these treasures were lost over the years, especially during the Civil War when the city probably had to sell its plate to raise money. Afterwards, city officials rebuilt the collection, some of the finest pieces being added in the 18th century. This fluted silver posset cup, one of a pair, bears the mark of the maker—Seth Lofthouse of London —and the year when it was made and given, 1702. The inscription says that it was given by the Lord Mayor of York in 1702 to replace a similar cup given by Leonard Besson, who twice held the office of mayor, in 1614 and 1626.
(Guildhall, York)*

the Danes who captured it in 876, and again radically when it was destroyed by fire in 1069, enabling the Normans to plan a new town. The Roman walled city became five times larger, and behind new defences the Normans established a major fortress between 1250 and 1300. Inside an area of 263 acres people were crammed tightly; and York city boundaries contained 40 churches, nine chapels, four monasteries, four friaries, 16 hospitals, and nine guildhalls for trade and fraternity. The city became a major wool centre, trading with the Continent.

With the decline of the wool trade and the Dissolution of the monasteries, York declined, but was revived in the 18th century when many of its medieval houses were pulled down to make way for Georgian dwellings; it further increased in prosperity in the 19th century when it became a railway centre, as it still is. Nevertheless, the medieval walls remained almost intact: the Multangular Tower dates from the beginning of the 4th century and—standing in the museum gardens—is a testimony to Roman stonework. Four great bars or gates commanded (as they still do) the main roads to the city: Micklegate bridged the road to the south, Bootham the road to the north, Monk the road to Scarborough, and Walmgate to Hull. These great gateways had almost every medieval device for defence, with drawbridges, portcullises, barbicans, watch towers, and guard-rooms. An existing royal charter of 1155–62 refers to an earlier one granted by Henry I which has been missing now for some 600 years.

St William's College was founded in 1461 for chantry priests; it is a half-timbered house with stone gateway. It was restored c. 1900 and is now the meeting place for the Northern Convocation. The Merchant Taylors' Hall dates from the 14th century and has been in the hands of the Craft of Tailors since at least 1415. The Merchant Adventurers built a great hall in 1357–68; it has a remarkable timber roof.

ASSEMBLY ROOMS Built by public subscription in 1736 to designs by the Earl of Burlington, they became a great centre of fashionable society. The central hall measures 112 ft by 40 ft, the roof being supported by 48 Corinthian columns, and resembles the Egyptian Room of the Mansion House in London.

CASTLE MUSEUM One of the leading folk museums of the country. Inside the building, life from Tudor to Victorian times is shown by a series of reconstructed streets. There are also period rooms, Jacobean to Victorian, and rooms dealing with trade and technical advances—showing microscopes, compasses, cameras and early electrical appliances. In the Green Gallery are Georgian and Victorian fans, card cases, watches, and domestic and personal ornaments. In the Chapel Gallery are unique collections of fire insurance marks, constables' truncheons and tipstaves, and an assortment of oddities from church alms boxes to Victorian blackboards. In the Music Gallery are such minstrel instruments as the serpent, bassoon and ophicleide, a virginal of 1651, a harpsichord of 1789, and a Johannes Player spinet, as well as harps and wind instruments. The Hearth Gallery has period fire-places, grates and hearth furniture.

CHURCH OF ALL SAINTS, NORTH STREET The arcades are c. 1350; the roofs to the south aisle and chancel c. 1450. The rood, parclose screens and vestry are 20th-century additions. It has some fine medieval glass and a variety of *objets d'art*.

CHURCH OF ALL SAINTS, PAVEMENT Mainly of the 15th century, the church lost part of its east end in the late 18th century as a result of an early road

'PRYKKE OF CONSCIENCE'
WINDOW

*Designed in the mid-15th century, this window shows that not all old stained glass was designed to illustrate biblical scenes. Intended as a warning of what was to come, it depicts the 'Last 15 Days of the World' in 15 subject panels. The scenes, with accompanying texts, are based on the 'Prykke of Conscience' written in the Northumbrian dialect by the English mystic Richard Rolle in 1325. This panel depicts the 8th day when rocks and trees are consumed; the 11th day when men emerge from their shelters and pray for help; and the 14th day when death comes to claim all mortals. (Church of All Saints, North Street, York)*

widening scheme. The west tower, with an octagonal lantern, was rebuilt during the first half of the 19th century. There is a fine canopied pulpit of the 17th century, and a 15th-century pulpit.

CITY OF YORK ART GALLERY Founded in 1879, it was re-opened in 1948 after rebuilding necessitated by bombing in 1942. In 1955 it was augmented by the Lycett Green Collection of 120 paintings by European masters of the 14th–19th centuries. The major European art movements from 1350 to 1800 are represented by works by Daddi, Guardi, Lely, Reynolds and Domenichino, among others. A selection of English paintings from 1890 to 1910 includes works by Whistler, Sickert and Wilson Steer; there is also a large collection of paintings by William Etty. There are collections of sculpture, engravings, Japanese colour prints, and Chinese and Korean ceramics. The Milner-White Collection of stoneware pottery includes work by Bernard Leach, Staite Murray and others. Topographical water-colours can be seen on request.

CLIFFORD'S TOWER The Normans raised two fortresses on artificial mounds, one each side of the river. That on the west has disappeared without a trace except for the mound or motte known as Baile Hill. The existing tower is 13th century, erected to replace the wooden Norman keep burnt down in the Jewish riots of 1190.

DEBTORS' PRISON Built in 1705 by Sir John Vanbrugh, and now an extension of the Castle Museum. It houses a collection of English costume, 1700–1920, and a collection of 19th-century toys. On the second floor is a military collection of the six Yorkshire line regiments: the West Yorkshires, East Yorkshires, Green Howards, Duke of Wellington's, York and Lancaster, and King's Own Yorkshire Light Infantry. In addition there is a collection of weapons covering four centuries— swords, lances, armour and fire-arms. Behind the Debtors' Prison, on the banks of the R. Foss, is Raindale Mill, a water-mill reconstructed in 1966.

GUILDHALL Built in 1448 by the city and the Guild of SS Christopher and George. It was largely demolished by fire-bombs in 1942. The restored guildhall opened in 1960. (See p. 502.)

KING'S MANOR Originally the residence of the Abbot of St Mary's. It was used as the centre for the Council of the North, which was abolished in 1641. In 1837 it became a school for the blind; the school was closed in 1957 and King's Manor is now part of the University of York.

MANSION HOUSE Built 1725–6: it houses a magnificent collection of silver, and is the home of the lord mayor. Behind it is the guildhall, built 1448, but largely destroyed by bombs in 1942 and carefully restored in 1960.

MINSTER When the mission of St Augustine came to convert England in 597, it carried instructions that the new church was to be governed from the former Roman capitals of London and York. The Archbishopric of London never materialised but that of York was successfully established by St Paulinus. The church itself was placed probably on the site of the Roman military headquarters and the present cathedral is the successor of this first

TOMB OF ARCHBISHOP DE GREY

*Archbishop Walter de Grey was Chancellor of England under Henry III; he died in 1255. Recently, when the canopied monument to him was dismantled, his stone coffin was found—the lid covered with a superb portrait of the archbishop. The coffin was sealed in the monument a few years after being painted and so the brilliant colours and gold leaf have retained their original splendour and freshness. (York Minster)*

tiny building. Evidence of the intermediate buildings may be seen in the crypt, in particular the surviving lower parts of some impressive late 12th-century piers and, at the lowest level, fragments of the Roman buildings underlying the whole site. The present cathedral, the largest Gothic church in England, dates from the 13th century, but building extended well into the 15th century. The last major additions, the western towers, were finished in 1474. The polygonal chapter house (built in 1286–1307) is outstanding: the huge vault span is unsupported by any central column; this was only made possible by building the vault in wood instead of stone.

ROMAN LEGIONARY FORTRESS York, the ancient capital of the North, began its effective life as Eburacum, when the new legionary fortress of the 9th Legion was sited here on the left bank of the Ouse in AD 71. More than once it was assaulted and severely damaged, and its defences were remodelled and renewed many times. One of these attacks took place about the beginning of the 4th century and the fine Multangular Tower, which can still be inspected, was the Roman response to it. This was the external bastion at the western angle, one end of the ornate face which fronted the Ouse. Across the river was the civilian settlement which, after a time, was raised to the dignity of a *colonia*. Other parts of the walls are to be found and a fine collection of small remains is in the Yorkshire Museum.

ST ANTHONY'S HALL Built 1446–53 with two storeys, it became a workhouse after 1551, and later a gaol, armoury and meeting place for minor guilds. The Hall is now the base of the Borthwick Institute, part of the University of York.

ST MARY'S ABBEY The 11th-century abbey is now only a ruin, but these remains are impressive, with much dating from the 13th century still visible.

TREASURER'S HOUSE A house built originally for the Treasurer to York Minster. Some 13th-century work survives in the vaults but the house is mainly 17th and 18th century with fine oak beams and furniture.

**Youlgreave** *Derbys.* 552De
CHURCH OF ALL SAINTS An impressive church, with a Norman nave and a tall Perpendicular west tower. Restoration in 1870 was by R. Norman Shaw. The circular Norman font has a separate basin projecting from one side. The church contains stained glass by Sir Edward Burne-Jones and several monuments with alabaster effigies.

**Yoxford** *Suffolk* 548Cf
COCKFIELD HALL A Jacobean house built in narrow red brickwork by Sir Arthur Hopton *c.* 1540. It has crow-stepped gables, massive chimney-breasts and some beautifully enriched chimney-shafts. The north wing, gate-house and a range of outbuildings are original; other parts were reconstructed in the 18th century. It was in the north wing that Katherine Grey, Lady Jane's sister, lived out the last days of her life after being incarcerated in the Tower on Queen Elizabeth's orders. This wing is still inhabited.

**Zennor Quoit** *Cornwall* 538Ab
This is a good example of an unusual type of megalithic tomb which originated in Brittany and is also found in the Penwith area of Cornwall. Divided into chamber and antechamber, it was originally covered by a large round cairn, but all trace of this has now disappeared, leaving the internal structure standing free. The capstone has probably slipped from its original position. The non-communicating antechamber was a 'dummy portal' or entrance which did not function.

# FAMOUS PEOPLE

## *Their works and whereabouts*

In the crumbling ruins of an old castle, the crude medical instruments used by the *Victory's* surgeon at Trafalgar, or the ivory-handled pen which Hardy used to write his novels, there is an intangible quality—something that evokes more than a mere sense of the past. It is as if these places and things have been endowed with a living presence by the men and women they represent, whether despotic ruler or humble craftsman. This section of the book lists the places associated with the people who have influenced the quality and character of our artistic heritage.

## ARCHITECTS

Architecture is said to be the youngest of the arts, since it was only comparatively late in man's nomadic existence that he sought a substitute for the cave or natural shelter. The architect, though, is more than a man who piles stone upon stone until he ends up with what is simply a more sophisticated cave. The great cathedrals of the land, the stately homes, even some of the factories, are massive if silent witnesses to the architect's passion to give a building grandeur, permanence and beauty—in other words, to make it a work of art—and at the same time make the space people live in a medium of expression.

**Adam Bros.**
*Bury St Edmunds, Suffolk*
*Stamford, Lincs.*

**Adam, James**
*Hertford, Herts.* Fore Street

**Adam, John**
*Banff, Banffs.*
*Downhill Castle, Lond.*

**Adam, Robert**
*Alnwick Castle, Northld.*
*Binley, Warks.* Church of St Bartholomew
*Brockhall, Northants.*
*Burton Constable, Yorks.*
*Castle Upton, Antrim*
*Culzean Castle, Ayrs.*
*Edinburgh, M'loth.* General Register House
*Fort George, I'ness.* Regimental Museum of The Seaforth Highlanders, The Queen's Own Cameron Highlanders and Queen's Own Highlanders

*Gifford, E. Lothian* Yester House
*Gunton, Norfolk* Church of St Andrew
*Headfort House, Meath.*
*Hopetoun House, W. Lothian*
*Kedleston Hall, Derbys.*
*Kimbolton Castle, Hunts.*
*London* Hyde Park Corner; Kenwood (Iveagh Bequest); Royal Hospital
*Mellerstain, Ber.*
*Milton Abbas, Dorset* Abbey
*Newby Hall, Yorks.*
*Nostell Priory, Yorks.*
*Osterley Park House, Greater London*
*Stowe, Bucks.*
*Syon House, Greater London*

**Adam, William**
*Aberdeen, A'deen.* Robert Gordon's College
*Aberfeldy, Perths.* General Wade's Bridge
*Banff, Banffs.* Duff House
*Chatelherault Lodge, Lanarks.*

*Haddo House, A'deen.*
*Mellerstain, Ber.*
*Pollokshaws, Lanarks.* Pollok House

**Ahrends, Peter**
*Dublin, Dublin* Trinity College

**Aitchison, George**
*London* Leighton House

**Allen, John**
*Jigginstown House, Kild.*

**Allen, W. Godfrey**
*London* Church of St Bride

**Allison, Sir Richard**
*London* Science Museum

**Anderson, John**
*Fermoy, Cork*

**Angus, George**
*Dundee, Angus* High School

**Archer, Thomas**
*Beningbrough Hall, Yorks.*
*Birmingham, Warks.* Cathedral
*Chicheley, Bucks.* Church of St
  Laurence
*Hale Park, Hants.*

**Ardwick, Thomas**
*Wanstead, Essex* Church of St Mary

**Ashlin, George**
*Ballintober Abbey, Mayo* Augustinian
  Friary
*Cobh, Cork*
*Dublin, Dublin* Church of SS
  Augustine and John
*Dungarvan, Waterford*
*Fermoy, Cork*
*Longford, Long.*
*Tralee, Kerry*
*Tulira Castle, Gal.*

**Ashton, Henry**
*Elton Hall, Hunts.*

**Atkinson, Thomas**
*Brandsby, Yorks.* Church of All
  Saints
*Coxwold, Yorks.* Church of St
  Michael

**Avery, Harry**
*Newtonstewart, Tyrone*

**Bachup, Tobias**
*Dumfries, Dumf.* Mid Steeple

**Baker, Henry Aaron**
*Derry, Lond.* Walker Monument
*Kells, Meath.*

**Barbon, Nicholas**
*London* Arts Council Gallery

**Bardwell, William**
*Glenstale Castle, Lim.*

**Barre, W. J.**
*Belfast, Antrim*
*Newry, Down*

**Barry, Sir Charles**
*Brighton, Sussex* Church of St Peter
*Cliveden, Bucks.*
*Halifax, Yorks.* Town Hall
*Harewood House, Yorks.*
*Kingston Lacy, Dorset*
*Leeds, Yorks.* Town Hall
*London* Houses of Parliament;
  Lancaster House
*Manchester, Lancs.* City Museum
*Salford, Lancs.* Science Museum
*Stand, Lancs.* Church of All Saints

**Barry, E. M.**
*London* Royal Opera House

**Bastard, John**
*Blandford Forum, Dorset* Almshouses;
  Church of SS Peter and Paul; Old
  House; Town Hall

**Bastard, John the Younger**
*West Wycombe Park, Bucks.*

**Bastard, William**
*Blandford Forum, Dorset*

**Batt, William**
*Belfast, Antrim*

**Baxter, John**
*Fochabers, Moray.*

**Bell, Henry**
*King's Lynn, Norfolk* Custom House;
  Tuesday Market-place
*North Runcton, Norfolk* Church of
  All Saints

**Bentley, John Francis**
*London* Church of St Botolph;
  Westminster Cathedral

**Bindon, Francis**
*Belan House, Kild.*
*Carnelly House, Clare*
*Clermont, Wicklow*
*Drogheda, Louth*
*Furness House, Kild.*
*Howth Castle, Dublin*
*Kilkenny, Kilk.*
*Limerick, Lim.*
*Newhall House, Clare*
*Russborough House, Wicklow*

**Blomfield, Sir Arthur**
*Alveley, Shrops.* Church of St Mary
*Bridgnorth, Shrops.* Church of St
  Mary Magdalene
*Halstead, Essex* Church of St Andrew
*Ludlow, Shrops.* Church of St
  Laurence

**Blore, Edward**
*Capesthorne, Cheshire*
*Castlewellan, Down*
*Oxford, Oxon.* Sheldonian Theatre
*Thorney, Cambs.* Church of SS Mary
  and Botolph

**Blow, Detmar**
*Breckles Hall, Norfolk*
*Onibury, Shrops.* Church of St
  Michael

**Bodley, G. F.**
*Brant Broughton, Lincs.* Church of St
  Helen
*Cuckfield, Sussex* Church of the Holy
  Trinity
*Leicester, Leics.* Cathedral
*London* Church of St John
*North Stoneham, Hants.* Church of St
  Nicholas
*Scarborough, Yorks.* Church of St
  Martin
*Weston-super-Mare, Som.* Church of
  All Saints
*Whitkirk, Yorks.* Church of St Mary

**Bodwin, Edward William**
*Northampton, Northants.* Town Hall

**Bonomi, Joseph**
*Great Packington, Warks.* Church of
  St James

**Boulger, James**
*Dublin, Dublin* St Andrew's

**Bowden, John**
*Belfast, Antrim* Church of St George
*Cavan, Cavan*
*Dublin, Dublin* Church of St Stephen
*Dundalk, Louth*

**Brandon, David**
*Hatfield, Herts.* Church of St
  Etheldreda
*Leicester, Leics.* Cathedral

**Brettingham, Matthew**
*Kedleston Hall, Derbys.*
*King's Lynn, Norfolk* Church of St
  Margaret

**Brettingham, R. F.**
*Hillsborough, Down*

**Brodrick, Cuthbert**
*Leeds, Yorks.* Town Hall

**Brooks, W.**
*Dudley, Worcs.* Church of St
Thomas the Apostle

**Brown, Capability**
*Claremont, Surrey*
*Slane, Meath* Castle

**Browne, Robert**
*Kew, Greater London* Church of St
Anne

**Browne, Wogan**
*Ballinlough Castle, Westmeath*
*Malahide Castle, Dublin*

**Bruce, Sir George**
*Culross, Fife* Palace

**Bruce, Sir William**
*Balcaskie House, Fife*
*Drumlanrig Castle, Dumf.*
*Edinburgh, M'loth.* Palace of
Holyroodhouse
*Hopetoun House, W. Lothian*
*Kinross, Kinross* Kinross House
*Thirlstane Castle, Ber.*

**Bryce, Robert**
*Blair Castle, Perths.*

**Burgess, William**
*Cardiff Castle, Glam.*
*Castell Coch, Glam.*
*Cork, Cork*
*Studley Royal, Yorks.* Church of St
Mary
*Waltham Holy Cross, Essex* Abbey
Church

**Burgh, Thomas**
*Celbridge, Kild.*
*Dublin, Dublin* Castle; Church of
St Werburgh; Steven's Hospital;
Trinity College
*Naas, Kild.*

**Burke, John**
*Granard, Long.*
*Longford, Long.*

**Burlington, Lord**
*Boynton Hall, Yorks.*
*Holkham Hall, Norfolk*
*London* Chiswick House
*Lismore, Waterford*
*Sevenoaks, Kent*

**Burton, Decimus**
*Dublin, Dublin* Phoenix Park
*Kew, Greater London* Palm House,
Royal Botanic Gardens
*London* Hyde Park Corner;
Regent's Park
*Royal Tunbridge Wells, Kent*

**Burton, Peter**
*Dublin, Dublin* Trinity College

**Butterfield, William**
*Alvechurch, Worcs.* Church of St
Lawrence
*Amesbury, Wilts.* Church of SS Mary
and Melor
*Baldersby, Yorks.* Church of St James
*Berkhamsted, Herts.* Church of St
Peter
*Canterbury, Kent* St Augustine's
Abbey
*Clyffe Pypard, Wilts.* Church of St
Peter
*Heytesbury, Wilts.* Church of SS Peter
and Paul
*Huddersfield, Yorks.* Churches of St
Thomas the Apostle and of St John
*London* Church of All Saints;
Church of St Mary Woolnoth

*St Bees, Cumb.* Church of SS Mary
and Bega
*Salisbury, Wilts.* Theological College
*Trumpington, Cambs.* Church of SS
Mary and Michael

**Byrd, William**
*Oxford, Oxon.* Sheldonian Theatre

**Byrne, Barry**
*Cork, Cork*

**Byrne, Patrick**
*Arklow, Wicklow*
*Dublin, Dublin* St Paul's, Arran
Quay; Trinity College

**Byrne, William**
*Loughrea, Gal.*

**Campbell, Colin**
*Ebberston Hall, Yorks.*
*London* Chiswick House
*Mereworth Castle, Kent*

**Campion, Henry**
*Danny, Sussex*

**Carr, James**
*London* Church of St James

**Carr, John**
*Boynton, Yorks.* Church of St Andrew
*Boynton Hall, Yorks.*
*Bradford, Yorks.* Bolling Hall
*Burton Constable, Yorks.*
*Cannon Hall, Yorks.*
*Harewood House, Yorks.*
*Kendal, Westmld.* Abbot Hall Art
Gallery
*Rotherham, Yorks.* Municipal
Museum and Art Gallery
*Thoresby Hall, Notts.*

**Carter, John**
*Debden, Essex* Church of St Mary the
Virgin and All Saints

**Casson, Sir Hugh**
*London* Regent's Park

**Castle, Richard**
*Ardbraccan House, Meath*
*Athlone, Westmeath*
*Ballinter House, Meath*
*Belan House, Kild.*
*Belvedere House, Westmeath*
*Carton Castle, Kild.*
*Cashel, Rock of, Tipp.* Cross of St
Patrick
*Celbridge, Kild.* Castletown
*Dublin, Dublin* Leinster House;
Rotunda; St Stephen's Green;
Trinity College; Tyrone House
*Duleek, Meath*
*Dunlavin, Wicklow*
*French Park House, Roscom.*
*Gill Hall House, Down*
*Hazelwood, Sligo*
*Ledwithstown House, Long.*
*Newbridge House, Dublin*
*Newry, Down*
*Powerscourt House, Wicklow*
*Rathbeale, Dublin*
*Russborough House, Wicklow*
*St Clerans House, Gal.*
*Sligo, Sligo*
*Strokestown House, Roscom.*
*Waterford, Waterford*
*Westport, Mayo*

**Cecil, William**
*Burghley House, Hunts.*

**Chambers, Sir William**
*Ampthill, Beds.* Avenue House
*Dublin, Dublin* Casino Marino;
Parnell Square
*London* Church of St Mary,
Marylebone Road; Somerset
House
*Lucan House, Dublin*
*Milton Abbey, Dorset*

*Rathfarnham Castle, Dublin*
*Slane, Meath* Castle
*Wilton House, Wilts.*

**Chesterfield, Lord**
*Dublin, Dublin* Phoenix Park

**Chiswell, R.**
*Debden, Essex* Church of St Mary the
Virgin and All Saints

**Clements, Nathanial**
*Beauparc, Meath*
*Dublin, Dublin* Phoenix Park
*Lodge Park, Kild.*
*Newberry Hall, Kild.*

**Cobden, Thomas A.**
*Carlow, Carlow*

**Cockerell, C. R.**
*Lampeter, Cards.* St David's
College
*Liverpool, Lancs.* St George's Hall

**Coke, Thomas**
*Holkham Hall, Norfolk*

**Cole, Sir Henry**
*London* Victoria and Albert
Museum

**Collcutt, T. E.**
*London* Imperial Institute Tower

**Comper, Sir Ninian**
*Chicheley, Bucks.* Church of St
Laurence
*Egmanton, Notts.* Church of St
Mary
*Eye, Suffolk* Church of SS Peter and
Paul
*High Melton, Yorks.* Church of St
James
*Lound, Suffolk* Church of St John
the Baptist
*Stanton, Glos.* Church of St Michael
and All Angels

**Cooley, Thomas**
*Armagh, Arm.*
*Belfast, Antrim* Clifton House
*Caledon House, Tyrone*
*Dublin, Dublin* City Hall; Four
Courts; Phoenix Park
*Kells, Meath*

**Corbett, W. E.**
*Limerick, Lim.*

**Cottingham, Lewis**
*Armagh, Arm.*

**Crawley, Benjamin**
*Castle Durrow, Laois*

**Cubitt, Thomas**
*Osborne House, Isle of Wight, Hants.*
*Polesden Lacey, Surrey*

**Cundy, Thomas**
*Normanton, Rutland* Church of St
Matthew

**Dalway, John**
*Carrickfergus, Antrim*

**Dance, George**
*Cork, Cork*

**Dance, George, the Elder**
*London* Church of St Botolph;
Mansion House

**Darley, Frederick**
*Dublin, Dublin* King's Inns; Trinity
College

**Davis, Whitmore**
*Charleville House, Wicklow*

**Deane, Butler William**
*Dublin, Dublin* Church of St Anne;
Kildare Street Club; Trinity
College
*Kilkenny, Kilk.*

**Deane, Kearnes**
*Cork, Cork*

**Deane, Sir Thomas**
*Cork, Cork*
*Dublin, Dublin* Leinster House
*Kilkenny, Kilk.* Castle; St Canice's
Cathedral
*Oxford, Oxon.* University Museum
*Tuam, Gal.* Protestant Cathedral

**de Courcy, John**
*Carrickfergus, Antrim.*

**de Lacy, Hugh**
*Carrickfergus, Antrim*

**de l'Orme, Philibert**
*London* Somerset House

**Dobson, John**
*Newcastle upon Tyne, Northld.*

**Donowell, John**
*West Wycombe Park, Bucks.*

**Drew, Sir Thomas**
*Belfast, Antrim*
*Dublin, Dublin* Cathedral of St
Patrick

**Ducart, Davis**
*Castle Hyde, Cork*
*Castletown House, Kilk.*
*Cork, Cork*
*Kilshannig House, Cork*
*Limerick, Lim.*

**Duff, Thomas**
*Armagh, Arm.*
*Belfast, Antrim* St Malachy's Catholic
Church; Old Museum
*Dundalk, Louth*

**Eden, F. C.**
*Weston-super-Mare, Som.* Church of
All Saints

**Edwards, William**
*Pontypridd, Glam.* Pontypridd
Bridge

**Elliot, Archibald**
*Glasgow, Lanarks.* Royal Bank of
Scotland and Royal Exchange
Square

**Elmes, Harvey Lonsdale**
*Liverpool, Lancs.* St George's Hall

**Ensor, George**
*Armagh, Arm.*

**Ensor, John**
*Dublin, Dublin* Northland House;
Royal Irish Academy; Rotunda;
Merrion Square

**Farrell, William**
*Belfast, Antrim* Old Museum
*Carrick on Shannon, Leit.*
*Portaferry, Down.*

**Fetherston, John**
*Packwood House, Warks.*

**Fitz, Sir Thomas**
*Windsor, Berks.* Windsor Guildhall
Exhibition

**Fitzwalter, Theobald**
*Nenagh, Tipp.*

**Flitcroft, Henry**
*Stourhead, Wilts.*
*Wimpole, Cambs.* Church of St
Andrew
*Woburn Abbey, Beds.*

**Fogarty, J.**
*Limerick, Lim.*

**Fontana, Carlo**
*Derby, Derbys.* Cathedral

**Forsyth, W.**
*Hillsborough, Down.*

**Fowke, Francis**
*Dublin, Dublin* Merrion Square
*London* Victoria and Albert Museum

**Fowler, James**
*Louth, Lincs.* Church of St James

**Galilei, Alessandro**
*Celbridge, Kild.* Castletown
*Drumcondra, Dublin*

**Gandon, James**
*Bishopscourt House, Kild.*
*Coolbanagher, Laois*
*Daingean, Offaly*
*Drumcondra, Dublin*
*Dublin, Dublin* Custom House; Four
  Courts; King's Inns; O'Connell
  Bridge; Old Parliament House;
  Phoenix Park; Rotunda
*Emo Castle, Laois*
*Longford, Long.*
*Port Laoise, Laois*
*Slane, Meath* Castle
*Waterford, Waterford*

**Garner, Thomas**
*Beaudesert, Warks.* Church of St
  Nicholas

**Gering, George**
*Danny, Sussex*

**Gibb, James**
*Bristol, Glos.* Church of All Saints
*Cambridge, Cambs.* Senate House
*Derby, Derbys.* Cathedral
*Ditchley Park, Oxon.*
*Kirkleatham, Yorks.* Church of St
  Cuthbert
*London* Church of St Clement Danes;
  Church of St Martin-in-the-Fields;
  Church of St Mary-le-Strand
*Oxford, Oxon.* Radcliffe Camera
*Petersham, Greater London*
*Raphoe, Don.*
*Shrewsbury, Shrops.* Church of St
  Chad

**Gibson, John**
*Charlecote, Warks.* Church of St
  Leonard

**Godwin, Edward**
*Dromore Castle, Lim.*
*London* Bedford Park

**Goldie, George**
*Limerick, Lim.*

**Goodhart-Rendel, H.**
*Idsworth, Hants.* Church of St Hubert

**Goodwin, Francis**
*Bilston, Staffs.* Church of St Leonard

**Gore, Sir Nathaniel**
*Ardtermon Castle, Sligo*

**Graham, James Gillespie**
*Elgin, Moray.* Gray's Hospital

**Grant, Sir Francis**
*Hughenden Manor, Bucks.*

**Gribbon, E. P.**
*Derry, Lond.*

**Griffiths, Sir Richard**
*Dublin, Dublin* Merrion Square

**Guy, Thomas**
*Tamworth, Staffs.*

**Hague, William**
*Letterkenny, Don.*

**Halfpenny, William**
*Boyle, Roscom.* Boyle Barrack

**Hamilton, David**
*Falkirk, Stir.* Steeple
*Glasgow, Lanarks.* Hutcheson's
  Hospital; Royal Bank of Scotland;
  Stirling's Library

**Hamilton, Gustavus, Viscount
Boyne**
*Stackallan, Meath*

**Hamilton, James**
*Belfast, Antrim*

**Hamilton, John**
*Barncluith, Lanarks.*

**Hamilton, Thomas**
*Ayr, Ayrs.* Town Hall

**Hannan, Nicholas**
*Limerick, Lim.*

**Hannan, William**
*Limerick, Lim.*

**Harding, James**
*Froyle, Hants.* Church of the
  Assumption

**Hardwicke, P. C.**
*Adare, Lim.* Adare Castle;
  Trinitarian Friary
*Limerick, Lim.*

**Hardwicke, Thomas**
*London* Church of St Mary,
  Marylebone Road; St John's
  Wood Chapel

**Hargrave, William**
*Cork, Cork*

**Harrison, Thomas**
*Manchester, Lancs.* Portico Library

**Haughy, Patrick**
*Strabane, Tyrone*

**Hawksmoor, Nicholas**
*Castle Howard, Yorks.*
*Easton Neston House, Northants.*
*Greenwich, Greater London* Church of
  St Alfege; Royal Naval College
*London* Christ Church; Church of St
  Anne; Church of St Mary Wool-
  noth; Westminster Abbey
*Ockham, Surrey* Church of All
  Saints

**Hayes, Samuel**
*Avondale, Wicklow*
*Monaghan, Mon.*

**Hennessey, M. S.**
*Limerick, Lim.*

**Hiorn, William**
*Stratford-upon-Avon, Warks.* Church
  of the Holy Trinity

**Hiorne, Francis**
*Tetbury, Glos.* Church of St Mary
  Magdalene

**Hobbs, Samuel**
*Cork, Cork*

**Holding, Matthew**
*Northampton, Northants.* Town Hall

**Holland, Henry**
*Althorpe, Northants.*
*Ampthill, Beds.* Avenue House
*Berrington Hall, Herefs.*
*Brighton, Sussex* Royal Pavilion
*Claremont, Surrey*
*Hale Park, Hants.*
*Woburn Abbey, Beds.*

**Hopper, Thomas**
*Gosford Castle, Arm.*
*Penrhyn Castle, Caern.*
*Slane, Meath* Castle

**Inwood, Henry**
*London* Church of St Pancras

**Inwood, Henry William**
*London* Church of St Pancras

**Ivory, Thomas**
*Blickling Hall, Norfolk*
*Carton Castle, Kild.*

*Dublin, Dublin* King's Hospital;
  Municipal Buildings
*Lismore, Waterford*
*Westport, Mayo*

**Jackson, Thomas**
*Belfast, Antrim* Old Museum; St
  Malachy's Catholic Church

**James, C. H.**
*Norwich, Norfolk* City Hall

**James, John**
*Greenwich, Greater London* Church
  of St Alfege

**Johnston, Francis**
*Armagh, Arm.*
*Ballymakenny, Louth*
*Charleville Castle, Offaly*
*Derry, Lond.*
*Drogheda, Louth*
*Dublin, Dublin* Castle; Church of St
  George; General Post Office; Old
  Parliament House; Phoenix Park
*Dundalk, Louth*
*Kells, Meath*
*Newry, Down*
*Slane, Meath* Castle
*Townley Hall, Louth*
*Tullamore, Offaly*
*Tullynally Castle, Westmeath*

**Johnston, John**
*Birr, Offaly* Castle

**Johnston, Richard**
*Castlecoole, Ferm.*
*Dublin, Dublin* Green Street
  Court-house; Rotunda

**Jones, Inigo**
*Ampthill, Beds.*
*Bodrhyddan Hall, Flints.*
*Castle Ashby, Northants.*
*Chilham Castle, Kent*
*Cobham, Kent* Cobham Hall
*Elstow, Beds.*
*Enfield, Greater London* Forty Hall
*Greenwich, Greater London* Queen's
  House; Royal Naval College
*Kirby Hall, Northants.*
*London* Banqueting House, White-
  hall; Queen's Chapel, St James's;
  St Paul's Cathedral; Somerset
  House
*Raynham Hall, Norfolk*
*Stamford, Lincs.*
*Stoke Park Pavilions, Northants.*
*Syon House, Greater London*
*Wilton House, Wilts.*

**Jones, Walter**
*Chasleton House, Oxon.*

**Joy, Robert**
*Belfast, Antrim* Clifton House

**Kay, Joseph**
*Hastings, Sussex* Pelham Crescent

**Keane, Joseph**
*Dublin, Dublin* Church of St Francis
  Xavier
*Galway, Gal.*
*Longford, Long.*

**Keble, John**
*Hursley, Hants.* Church of All Saints

**Keene, Henry**
*Dublin, Dublin* Trinity College
*Hartwell, Bucks.* Church
*Uppark, Sussex*

**Kempster, Christopher**
*Abingdon, Berks.* Town Hall

**Kent, William**
*Badminton House, Glos.*
*Holkham Hall, Norfolk*
*London* Chiswick House; Kensington
  Palace

*Milton Abbey, Dorset*
*Stowe, Bucks.*

**Kirby, J. J.**
*Kew, Greater London* Church

**Koralek, Paul**
*Dublin, Dublin* Trinity College

**Kryle, John**
*Ross-on-Wye, Herefs.*

**Lanyon, Sir Charles**
*Ballywalter, Down*
*Belfast, Antrim*

**Lanyon, John**
*Belfast, Antrim*

**Lawrence, Walter**
*Lawrencetown Arch, Gal.*

**Leeson, John**
*Dublin, Dublin* St Nicholas of Myra

**Leoni, Giacomo**
*Clandon Park, Surrey*
*Cliveden, Bucks.*
*Lyme Park, Cheshire*

**Leslie, James**
*Dundee, Angus* Custom House

**Lethaby, W. R.**
*Brockhampton-by-Ross, Herefs.*
  Church of All Saints

**Leuventhan**
*Youghal, Cork*

**Lightoler, Thomas**
*Burton Constable, Yorks.*

**Lilly, Charles**
*Downpatrick, Down* St Patrick's
  Cathedral
*Portaferry, Down*

**Lovel, Lord**
*Wardour Castle, Wilts.*

**Lovett Pearce, Sir Edward**
*Bellamont Forest, Cavan*
*Boyle, Roscom.* Boyle Barrack
*Cashel, Tipp.* Cashel Palace
*Celbridge, Kild.* Castletown
*Cuba Court, Offaly*
*Downpatrick, Down.*
*Drumcondra, Dublin*
*Dublin, Dublin* Castle; Henrietta
  Street; Old Parliament House
*Gloster, Offaly*
*Newry, Down*
*Palliser House, Dublin*
*Stillorgan, Dublin*
*Woodlands, Dublin*

**Lowther, Sir John**
*Whitehaven, Cumb.*

**Lutyens, Sir Edwin**
*Ashwell, Herts.*
*Barham, Kent*
*Breckles Hall, Norfolk*
*Lindisfarne Castle, Holy Island, Northld.*
*London* The Cenotaph

**Lyminge, Robert**
*Blickling Hall, Norfolk*
*Hatfield House, Herts.*

**Lynch, Nicholas**
*Galway, Gal.* Church of St Nicholas

**Lynn, W. H.**
*Belfast, Antrim* Castle

**McAllister, Alex**
*Belfast, Antrim*

**McCarthy, J. J.**
*Armagh, Arm.*
*Killarney, Kerry*
*Limerick, Lim.*
*Maynooth, Kild.*
*Monaghan, Mon.*
*Thurles, Tipp.*

**Mack, Robert**
*Dublin, Dublin* Powerscourt House

**Mackenzie, A. Marshall**
*Aberdeen, A'deen.* Marischal College

**Mackenzie, Thomas**
*Fochabers, Moray.*

**Mackintosh, Charles Rennie**
*Glasgow, Lanarks.* School of Art

**MacNamara**
*Letterkenny, Don.*

**Madden, Dominic**
*Tuam, Gal.*

**Malbie, Sir Nicholas**
*Roscommon, Roscom.* Castle

**Massingberd, Sir William**
*Gunby Hall, Lincs.*

**Matthews, James**
*Aberdeen, A'deen.* Music Hall

**Maufe, Sir Edward**
*Guildford, Surrey* Cathedral

**Maxwell, Patrick**
*Port Glasgow, Renf.* Newark Castle

**Meade, William**
*Youghal, Cork*

**Mendelsohn, Erich**
*Bexhill, Sussex* De La Warr Pavilion

**Micklethwaite, J. T.**
*Lydbury North, Shrops.* Church of St Michael

**Moffat, John**
*Dumfries, Dumf.* Mid Steeple

**Montgomery, Sir Hugh**
*Newtonards, Down.*

**Montgomery, John**
*Aberdeen, A'deen.* Mercat Cross

**Moore, John**
*Moore Hall, Mayo*

**Morris, Roger**
*Inveraray Castle, Argyll*
*Wilton House, Wilts.*

**Morrison, Sir Richard**
*Ballinasloe, Gal.*
*Ballyfin House, Laois.*
*Baronscourt, Tyrone*
*Carton Castle, Kild.*
*Cashel, Rock of, Tipp.* Cross of St Patrick
*Castle Freke, Cork*
*Clonmel, Tipp.*
*Galway, Gal.*
*Kilruddery, Wick*
*Luttrellstown Castle, Dublin*
*Lyons House, Kild.*
*Port Laoise, Laois*
*Roscommon, Roscom.*
*Thomastown Castle, Tipp.*
*Tullynally Castle, Westmeath*

**Morrison, William Vitruvius**
*Carlow, Carlow*
*Tralee, Kerry*

**Mottistone, Lord**
*London* Church of All Hallows; Church of St Mary Abchurch

**Mulholland, Roger**
*Belfast, Antrim* First Presbyterian Unitarian Church

**Mullen, Bernard**
*Birr, Offaly*

**Mulvany, J. S.**
*Athlone, Westmeath*
*Dublin, Dublin* Broadstone Railway Station, Dunleary
*Port Laoise, Laois*

**Murray, William**
*Derry, Lond.*
*Dublin, Dublin* St Stephen's Green
*Waterford, Waterford*

**Mylne, Robert**
*Belfast, Antrim* Clifton House
*Gatehouse of Fleet, Kirk.*
*Inveraray Castle, Argyll*

**Nash, John**
*Attingham Hall, Shrops.*
*Blaise Hamlet, Glos.* Blaise Castle House
*Brighton, Sussex* Royal Pavilion
*Caher Castle, Tipp.*
*Caledon House, Tyrone*
*Helmingham, Suffolk*
*Kentchurch Court, Herefs.*
*Killymoon Castle, Tyrone*
*Lissan Rectory, Tyrone*
*London* Buckingham Palace; Church of All Saints; Church of All Souls; Marble Arch; Royal Mews; Trafalgar Square
*Lough Cutra Castle, Gal.*
*Newport, Isle of Wight, Hants.*
*Shane's Castle, Antrim.*

**Newcomen, Sir Robert**
*Newtown Stewart, Tyrone*

**Newdegate, Sir Roger**
*Arbury Hall, Warks.*

**Norreys, Sir Thomas**
*Mallow, Cork* Castle

**O'Reilly, Terence**
*Waterford, Waterford*

**O'Shea Brothers**
*Dublin, Dublin* Kildare Street Club

**Owen, W. H.**
*Limerick, Lim.*

**Ower, C. and L.**
*Dundee, Angus* Custom House

**Paget, Paul**
*London* Church of All Hallows

**Pain Brothers**
*Adare, Lim.* Adare Castle
*Ash Hill Towers, Lim.*
*Doneraile, Cork*
*Dromoland Castle, Clare*
*Lough Cutra Castle, Gal.*
*Midleton, Cork*
*Port Laoise, Laois*
*Strancally Castle, Waterford*

**Pain, G. R.**
*Cork, Cork*
*Dungarvan, Waterford*
*Limerick, Lim.*
*Mitchelstown, Cork*

**Pain, James**
*Chatsworth, Derbys.*
*Doncaster, Yorks.* Mansion House
*Gibside, Durham* Chapel
*Kedleston Hall, Derbys.*
*Nostell Priory, Yorks.*
*Uppark, Sussex*
*Wardour Castle, Wilts.*

**Papworth, George**
*Kenure Park, Dublin*
*Kilcornan House, Gal.*
*Killeavy, Arm.*

**Park, Edward**
*Dublin, Dublin* St Stephen's Green
*Dundalk, Louth.*

**Parke, Robert**
*Dublin, Dublin* Old Parliament House

**Paxton, Sir Joseph**
*Lismore, Waterford*
*London* Hyde Park

**Pearson, J. L.**
*Appleton–le–Moors, Yorks.* Christ Church
*Burley on the Hill, Rutland* Church of the Holy Cross
*Crowland, Lincs.* Crowland Abbey
*Cullercoats, Northld.* Church of St George
*Dalton Holme, Yorks.* Church of St Mary
*Iwerne Minster, Dorset* Church of St Mary
*London* Church of St Augustine
*Maidstone, Kent* Church of All Saints
*Shrewsbury, Shrops.* Abbey Church of the Holy Cross
*Steetley, Derbys.* Chapel·of All Saints
*Wentworth, Yorks.* Church of the Holy Trinity
*Truro, Cornwall* Cathedral

**Pennethorne, Sir James**
*London* Public Record Office; Somerset House

**Penrose, F. C.**
*Escrick, Yorks.* Church of St Helen

**Pentland, George**
*Dysart House, Westmeath*

**Pentland, John**
*Multyfarnham, Westmeath*

**Pepys Cockerell, Samuel**
*Tickencote, Rutland* Church of St Peter

**Peto, Harold**
*Garinish Island, Cork*

**Pierce, S. R.**
*Norwich, Norfolk* City Hall

**Platt, Sir Roger**
*Kingston Lacy, Dorset*

**Playfair, William**
*Edinburgh, M'Loth.* Royal College of Surgeons of Edinburgh; Royal Scottish Academy
*Floors Castle, Rox.*
*Dollar, Clack.* Dollar Academy

**Pollen, John Hungerford**
*Dublin, Dublin* St Stephen's Green

**Porter, George**
*London* Church of St Mary Magdalene

**Preston, George**
*Cartmel, Lancs.* Priory Church of St Mary the Virgin

**Priestley, Michael**
*Ballymore, Don.*
*Lifford, Don.*
*Port Hall, Don.*

**Pugin, Augustus Welby**
*Adare, Lim.* Adare Castle
*Albury Park, Surrey*
*Birmingham, Warks.* Cathedral of St Chad
*Birr, Offaly*
*Bishopstone, Wilts.* Church of St John the Baptist
*Boston, Lincs.* Church of St Botolph
*Enniscorthy, Wex.*
*Gorey, Wex.*
*Killarney, Kerry*
*London* Houses of Parliament
*Maynooth, Kild.*
*Scarisbrick Hall, Lancs.*
*Waterford, Waterford*
*Wexford, Wex.*
*Winwick, Lancs.* Church

**Pugin, E. W.**
*Cobh, Cork*
*Fermoy, Cork*
*Tralee, Kerry*

**Rawlinson, Sir Robert**
*Liverpool, Lancs.* St George's Hall

**Reid, Robert**
*Edinburgh, M'Loth.* General Register House

**Rennie Bros.**
*London* Hyde Park

**Rennie, John**
*Dublin, Dublin* Dunleary
*London* London Bridge

**Repton, Humphrey**
*Sheringham Hall, Norfolk*

**Repton, J. A.**
*Sheringham Hall, Norfolk*

**Revett, Nicolas**
*West Wycombe Park, Bucks.*

**Richardson, Sir Albert**
*Ampthill, Beds.*
*Florence Court, Ferm.*
*Newmarket, Suffolk*

**Richardson, George**
*Stapleford, Leics.* Church of St Mary Magdalene
*Teigh, Rutland* Church of the Holy Trinity

**Robb, James**
*Waringstown, Down*

**Roberts, John**
*Waterford, Waterford*

**Robertson, David**
*Johnstown Castle, Wex.*

**Robertson, John**
*New Ross, Wex.*

**Robertson, William**
*Kilkenny, Kilk.* Castle
*Longford, Long.*

**Robinson, Sir Thomas**
*Glynde, Sussex* Church of St Mary the Virgin

**Robinson, Sir William**
*Clonmel, Tipp.*
*Dublin, Dublin* Royal Hospital, Kilmainham
*Kilkenny, Kilk.* Castle
*Kinsale, Cork*

**Rothery, William**
*Doneraile, Cork*
*Mount Ievers*

**Ruskin, John**
*Oxford, Oxon.*
*Wallington, Northld.*

**Saarinen, Eero**
*London* Roosevelt Memorial

**Salvin, Anthony**
*Alnwick Castle, Northld.*
*Capesthorne, Cheshire*
*Hodnet Hall Garden, Shrops.*
*Greystoke, Cumb.* Church of St Andrew
*Simonburn, Northld.* Church of St Mungo
*Thoresby Hall, Notts.*
*Worth, Sussex* Church of St Nicholas

**Sanderson, John**
*Dublin, Dublin* Trinity College
*Woburn Abbey, Beds.*

**Sandys, Francis**
*Belfast, Antrim* Church of St George

**Sandys, William**
*Hillsbrough, Down*

**Savage, James**
*London* Church of St Luke

**Savage, Roland**
*Kirkistown Castle, Down*

**Scott, Sir Gilbert**
*Aconbury, Herefs.* Church of St John
the Baptist
*Alford, Lincs.* Church of St Wilfrid
*Aylesbury, Bucks.* Church of St Mary
*Bangor, Caern.* Cathedral
*Bibury, Glos.* Church of St Mary
*Bradfield, Berks.*
*Brecon, Brecon* Cathedral
*Bridlington, Yorks.* Church of St Mary
*Cambridge, Cambs.* University
Library
*Chester, Cheshire* Cathedral
*Crowland, Lincs.* Crowland Abbey
*Dunsany, Meath*
*Easby, Yorks.* Church of St Agatha
*Eastnor, Herefs.* Church of St John
the Baptist
*Hillesden, Bucks.* Church of All
Saints
*Huddersfield, Yorks.* Churches of St
Thomas the Apostle and of St John
*Leicester, Leics.* Church of St
Margaret
*London* Albert Memorial; St Pancras
Station
*Ludlow, Shrops.* Church of St
Laurence
*Northampton, Northants.* Church of
the Holy Sepulchre
*Oxford, Oxon.* Cathedral
*Rotherham, Yorks.* Church of All
Saints
*Shifnal, Shrops.* Church of St Andrew
*Turvey, Beds.* Church of All Saints
*Wakefield, Yorks.* Cathedral
*Wirksworth, Derbys.* Church of St
Mary

**Scott, Giles Gilbert**
*Cambridge, Cambs.* Pembroke College
Chapel
*Glasgow, Lanarks.* University of
Glasgow
*Liverpool, Lancs.* Anglican Cathedral
*London* Guildhall
*t Asaph, Flints.* Cathedral

**Scott, H.**
*London* Victoria and Albert Museum;
Royal Albert Hall

**Scott, Michael**
*Dublin, Dublin* Bus Station (Busaras);
Church of St Francis Xavier

**Scott, Oldrid**
*Kinlet, Shrops.* Church of St John the
Baptist

**Sedding, E.**
*Crantock, Cornwall* Church of St
Carantoc

**Seddon, J. P.**
*Hoarwithy, Herefs.* Church of St
Catherine

**Semple, George**
*Carlow, Carlow*
*Graiguenamanagh, Kilk.*

**Semple, John**
*Abbeyleix, Laois*
*Dublin, Dublin* Mansion House; St
Mary's Chapel of Ease
*Tallaght, Dublin*

**Serlio, Sebastiano**
*Cambridge, Cambs.* Pembroke College
Chapel

**Shanahan, Michael**
*Belfast, Antrim* Church of St George

**Shaw, John**
*Newstead Abbey, Notts.*

**Shaw, Norman**
*Chipstead, Surrey* Church of St
Margaret
*London* Bedford Park; Church of St
Mark
*Richards Castle, Shrops.* Church of
All Saints
*Youlgreave, Derbys.* Church of All
Saints

**Sherrin, George**
*Ingatestone, Essex*

**Shiel, James**
*Killua House, Westmeath*
*Knockdrin Castle, Westmeath*
*Tullynally Castle, Westmeath*

**Simpson, Archibald**
*Aberdeen, A'deen.* Marischal College;
Music Hall
*Elgin, Moray* Anderson's Institution

**Slater, William**
*Limerick, Lim.*

**Sloane, Charles**
*Gravesend, Kent* Church of St George

**Smeaton, John**
*Coldstream, Ber.* Bridge over the
Tweed

**Smirke, Sir Robert**
*Dublin, Dublin* Phoenix Park
*London* British Museum;
Somerset House

**Smith, Francis**
*Derby, Derbys.* Cathedral
*Ditchley Park, Oxon.*
*Lamport Hall, Northants.*
*Mawley Hall, Shrops.*

**Smith, James**
*Glasgow, Lanarks.* Royal Bank of
Scotland and Royal Exchange
Square

**Smith, John**
*Aberdeen, A'deen* Robert Gordon's
College
*Dublin, Dublin* Church of St
Catherine; Trinity College

**Smith, W.**
*Belfast, Antrim*

**Smith, William, of Warwick**
*Monmouth, Mon.* Church of St
Mary
*Whitchurch, Shrops.* Church of St
Alkmund

**Smyth, John**
*Dublin, Dublin* Rotunda

**Smythson, Robert**
*Hardwick Hall, Derbys.*
*Longleat House, Wilts.*
*Wollaton Hall, Notts.*

**Smythson, Roger**
*Wardour Castle, Wilts.*

**Snowdon, Lord**
*London* Regent's Park

**Soane, Sir John**
*Aynhoe Park, Northants.*
*Baronscourt, Tyrone*
*Belfast, Antrim* Academical Institution
*Chillington Hall, Staffs.*
*Claremont, Surrey*
*London* Church of St John; Church
of St Peter; Soane Museum;
Royal Hospital

**Southampton, Earl of**
*Cowdray Park, Sussex*

**Spence, Sir Basil**
*Coventry, Warks.* Cathedral
*Falmer, Sussex*

# FAMOUS PEOPLE: ARCHITECTS

**Stapleton, H.**
*Dublin, Dublin* Belvedere House

**Stapleton, Michael**
*Dublin, Dublin* Ely House, Ely Place
*Maynooth, Kild.*

**Steuart, George**
*Attingham Hall, Shrops.*
*Baronscourt, Tyrone*
*Shrewsbury, Shrops.* Church of St Chad

**Stevens, Alexander**
*Bridge of Dun, Angus* Bridge over the R. South Esk

**Stevens, H. J.**
*Derby, Derbys.* Church of St Alkmund

**Stokes, Henry**
*Lismore, Waterford*

**Stone, Nicholas**
*Oxford, Oxon.* Church of St Mary the Virgin

**Stratford, Ferdinando**
*Newtonards, Down*

**Street, G. E.**
*Bloxham, Oxon.* Church of Our Lady
*Britford, Wilts.* Church of St Peta
*Clun, Shrops.* Church of St George
*Corsham, Wilts.* Church of St Bartholomew
*Cottesbrooke, Northants.* Church of All Saints
*Dublin, Dublin* Christ Church Cathedral
*Elford, Staffs.* Church of St Peter
*Haddo House, A'deen.*
*Kempsford, Glos.* Church of St Mary the Virgin
*Kildare, Kild.* St Brigid's Cathedral
*Kingston, Dorset* Church of St James
*Leicester, Leics.* Cathedral; Church of St Margaret
*Manchester, Lancs.* Town Hall
*Monmouth, Mon.* Church of St Mary
*St Michael Penkevil, Cornwall* Church of St Michael
*South Mimms, Herts.* Church of St Giles
*Stewkley, Bucks.* Church of St Michael and All Angels
*Thirsk, Yorks.* Church of St Mary
*Thornhill, Yorks.* Church of St Michael and All Angels
*Toddington, Glos.* Church of St Andrew
*Warfield, Berks.* Church of St Michael
*Weaverthorpe, Yorks.* Church of St Andrew

**Stuart, James 'Athenian'**
*Eastnor, Herefs.* Church of St John the Baptist
*Preston on Stour, Glos.* Church
*Shugborough, Staffs.*

**Sweetman, John**
*Dublin, Dublin* Pro-Cathedral of St Mary

**Talman, William**
*Chatsworth, Derbys.*
*Dyrham Park, Glos.*
*Little Stanmore, Greater London* Church of St Lawrence, Whitchurch
*Thoresby Hall, Notts.*
*Uppark, Sussex*

**Taylor, J.**
*Dublin, Dublin* Church of SS Micha and John
*Dundee, Angus* Custom House

**Taylor, Sir Robert**
*Belfast, Antrim* Belfast Bank Head Office
*Gorhambury, Herts.*
*Heveningham Hall, Suffolk*
*Oxford, Oxon.* Ashmolean Museum

**Telford, Thomas**
*Dunkeld, Perth.*
*Bridgnorth, Shrops.* Church of St Mar Magdalene
*Madeley, Shrops.* Church of St Michael

**Teulon, S. S.**
*Ampton, Suffolk* Church of St Peter

**Thomas, Sir Brumwell**
*Belfast, Antrim*

**Thompson, Alexander 'Greek'**
*Glasgow, Lanarks.* Caledonia Road Church; St Vincent Street Church

**Thornberry Brothers**
*Hillsborough, Down*

**Thornely, Sir Arnold**
*Belfast, Antrim*

**Thornhill, Sir James**
*Moor Park Mansion House, Herts.*

**Thoroton, John**
*Belvoir Castle, Leics.*

**Thorpe, John**
*Stamford, Lincs.*

**Thynne, Sir John**
*Longleat, Wilts.*
*Wollaton Hall, Notts.*

**Tinsley, William**
*Clonmel, Tipp.*

**Tite, Sir William**
*London* Royal Exchange

**Townsend, C. H.**
*London* Horniman Museum

**Townsend, Harrison**
*Great Warley, Essex* Church of St Mary the Virgin

**Tropenell, Thomas**
*Great Chalfield, Wilts.* Church of A Saints

**Vallancey, General Charles**
*Dublin, Dublin* Queen's Bridge

**Vanbrugh, Sir John**
*Audley End, Essex*
*Belfast, Antrim*
*Blenheim Palace Gardens, Oxon.*
*Carshalton, Surrey*
*Castle Howard, Yorks.*
*Claremont, Surrey*
*Dalkeith Palace, M'Loth.*
*Floors Castle, Rox.*
*Greenwich, Greater London* Royal Naval College; Vanbrugh Castle
*Grimsthorpe Castle, Lincs.*
*Iver, Bucks.* Iver Grove
*Kimbolton Castle, Hunts.*
*Seaton Delaval Hall, Northld.*
*Somersby, Lincs.* Manor Farm
*Stowe, Bucks.*
*York, Yorks.* Debtors' Prison

**Vardy, John**
*Milton Abbey, Dorset*

**Vaughan, Henry**
*Buncrana Castle, Don.*

514

# DIVINES

In cloister and cell, men of God kept spiritual values alive throug[h] what would otherwise rightly be known as the Dark Ages; they le[ft] behind a priceless heritage in manuscript and stone. As Churc[h] clashed with State, and the old faith with the new, many died f[or] their beliefs. Later, Nonconformism added its distinctive note [of] revivalism to worship in Britain.

**Aidan, St**
*Holy Island, Northld.* Lindisfarne Priory

**Alcock, Bishop**
*Cambridge, Cambs.* Jesus College
*Little Malvern, Worcs.* Church of St Giles

**Alcuin**
*York, Yorks.*

**Anselm, St**
*Bury St Edmunds, Suffolk*
*Chester, Cheshire*
*Rockingham Castle, Northants.*

**Augustine, St**
*Canterbury, Kent*

**Baldwin, Abbot**
*Bury St Edmunds, Suffolk*

**Barwick, John, Dean**
*Witherslack, Westmld.* Church of St Paul

**Beaufort, Cardinal**
*Winchester, Hants.* St Cross Hospital

**Becket, Thomas à**
*Berkhamsted, Herts.*
*Canterbury, Kent*
*Reading, Berks.*

**Bede, Venerable**
*Beverley, Yorks.* Minster, Church of St John of Beverley

**Bek, Bishop**
*Durham, Durham* Cathedral and Castle

**Beuno, St**
*Clynnog-Fawr, Caern.* Church of St Bueno

**Beverley, St John of**
*Beverley, Yorks.* Minster

**Biscop, Benedict**
*Monkwearmouth, Durham*

**Bolton, Theophilus**
*Cashel, Tipp.* Cashel Palace

**Bourchier, Thomas**
*Knole, Kent*

**Bourne, Hugh**
*Mow Cop, Cheshire–Staffs.*

**Buckland, Dean**
*Pavilland, Glam.* Goat's Hole Cave

**Bunyan, John**
*Ampthill, Beds.*
*Bedford; Beds.*
*Elstow, Beds.*

**Canice, St, of Aghaboe**
*Monahincha, Tipp.*

**Carswell, John**
*Carnasserie Castle, Argyll*

**Cartach, St**
*Rahan, Offaly*

**Cedd, St, Bishop**
*Bradwell-on-Sea, Essex* Church of Peter's On The Wall

**Chad, St, Bishop of Mercia**
*Lichfield, Staffs.* Cathedral

**Coke, Sir Thomas**
*Melbourne Hall, Derbys.*

**Colmcille, St**
*Derry, Lond.*
*Drumcliff, Sligo*

**Columba, St**
*Iona, Argyll*
*Kells, Meath*

**Cosin, John**
*Brancepeth, Durham* Church of Brandon

**Courtenay, Archbishop**
*Maidstone, Kent* Church of All Saints

**Cox, Archbishop**
*Castletown House, Kilk.*
*Kilkenny, Kilk.* St Canice's Cathedral

**Cranmer, Archbishop**
*Knole, Kent*

**Cronan, St**
*Roscrea, Tipp.*

**de Blois, Henry, Bishop**
*Farnham, Surrey* Castle
*Hursley, Hants.* Merdon Castle
*Taunton, Som.*
*Winchester, Hants.* St Cross Hospital

**de Caen, Roger, Bishop**
*Sherborne, Dorset* Old Castle

**de Cardeny, Robert, Bishop**
*Dunkeld, Perths.* Cathedral

**de Clinton, Roger, Bishop**
*Buildwas Abbey, Shrops.*

**Constantine, St**
*Wetheral, Cumb.* St Constantine's Cell

**de Corbeuil, Archbishop**
*Rochester, Kent* Castle

**de Leia, Peter, Bishop**
*St. David's, Pembs.* Cathedral a[nd] Bishop's Palace

**de Linton, Bernard, Abbot**
*Arbroath Abbey, Angus*

**de Losinga, Herbert, Bishop**
*Norwich, Norfolk* Cathedral

**de Luffa, Ralph, Bishop**
*Chichester, Sussex* Cathedral

**de Mapilton, Hugh, Bishop**
*Kilkenny, Kilk.* St Canice's
Cathedral

**Derry, Bishop of**
*Downhill Castle, Lond.*

**de Sudbury, Simon,
Archbishop**
*Sudbury, Suffolk* Church of St
Gregory

**de Valence, Aymer**
*Bampton, Oxon.*

**Diarmaid, St**
*Inchcleraun, Long.*

**Donne, John**
*London* Lincoln's Inn; St Paul's
Cathedral

**Doyle, Bishop**
*Carlow, Carlow*

**Drome, Jemmett, Bishop**
*Riverstown House, Cork*

**Edington, Bishop**
*Winchester, Hants.* Cathedral

**Endelienta, St**
*St Endellion, Cornwall* Church of St
Endelienta

**Etheldreda, St**
*Ely, Cambs.* Cathedral

**Faringdon, Hugh, Abbot**
*Reading, Berks.*

**Ferrar, Nicholas**
*Little Gidding, Hunts.*

**Finbar, St**
*Cork, Cork*

**Flambard, Ralph, Bishop**
*Christchurch, Hants.* Priory

**Fox, Richard, Bishop**
*Taunton, Som.*

**Foy, Bishop**
*Waterford, Waterford*

**Garan, St**
*Clonmacnoise, Offaly*

**Gower, Bishop**
*Lamphey, Pemb.* Bishop's Palace
*St David's, Pemb.* Bishop's Palace

**Gravesend, Bishop**
*Lincoln, Lincs.* Cathedral; Cathedral
Treasury

**Grosseteste, Bishop**
*Lincoln, Lincs.* Cathedral; Cathedral
Treasury

**Guthlac, St**
*Crowland, Lincs.* Abbey

**Hatfield, Bishop of**
*Durham, Durham* Cathedral and
Castle

**Hervey, Frederick Augustus,
Bishop**
*Ickworth, Suffolk*

**Huby, Abbot**
*Fountains Abbey, Yorks.*

**Hugh, St**
*Old Clee, Lincs.* Church of the Holy
Trinity

**Hughes, Father**
*Llanengan, Caern.* Church

**Ivo, St**
*St Ives, Hunts.*

**John the Baptist**
*Winchester, Hants.* Town Cross

**Kevin, St**
*Glendalough, Wicklow*

**Kildare, Bishop of**
*Great Connell Priory, Kild.*

**King, Bishop**
*Bath, Som.*

**Laisren, St**
*Inish Murray, Sligo*

**Laud, Archbishop**
*London* Church of St Katherine
Cree

**Lauder, Thomas, Bishop**
*Dunkeld, Perths.* Cathedral

**Leighton, Bishop**
*Culross, Fife* Bishop Leighton's
House

**Le Puiset, or Pudsey, Hugh,
Bishop**
*Durham, Durham* Cathedral and
Castle

**Leslie, John, Bishop**
*Raphoe, Don.*

**Lloyd, Bishop**
*Chester, Cheshire*

**Loftus, Adam, Bishop**
*Rathfarnham Castle, Dublin*

**Mabon, Dean**
*La Houge Bie, Jersey*

**Machale, John, Archbishop**
*Ballintober Abbey, Mayo* Augustinian
Friary

**Mackeilly, Archbishop**
*Cashel, Tipp.* Dominican Priory

**Magnus, St**
*Egilsay, Isle of Orkney*

**Marsh, Narcissus,
Archbishop**
*Dublin, Dublin* Cathedral of St
Patrick

**Mathew, Father**
*Cork, Cork*

**Milburga, St**
*Much Wenlock, Shrops.* Wenlock
Priory

**Milles, Bishop**
*Waterford, Waterford*

**More, Sir Thomas**
*London* Crosby Hall; Lincoln's Inn;
Tower of London; Westminster
Hall

**Morgan, William, Bishop**
*Ty Mawr, Caern.*

**Morley, Bishop**
*Winchester, Hants.*

**Morton, Archbishop**
*London* Lambeth Palace

**Morton, Bishop of Ely**
*Hatfield House, Herts.*

**Mungo, St**
*Glasgow, Lanarks.*

**Neot, St**
*St Neot, Cornwall*

**Ninian, St**
*Whithorn Priory, Wig.*

**Odo, Bishop**
*Dover, Kent*

**Odd, Dean**
*Clonmacnoise, Offaly* Cathedral

**O'Hedian, Archbishop**
*Cashel, Rock of, Tipp.*

**Oswald, Bishop**
*Worcester, Worcs.* Cathedral

**Otay, Thomas, Bishop**
*Kilkenny, Kilk.*

**Patrick, St**
*Armagh, Arm.*
*Dublin, Dublin* Cathedral of St Patrick
*Cashel, Rock of, Tipp.*

**Paulinus, St**
*York, Yorks.* Minster

**Peck, Robert**
*Higham, Norfolk* Market-place

**Percy, Thomas, Bishop**
*Bridgnorth, Shrops.*

**Phillips, Abbot**
*Kilcooly Abbey, Tipp.*

**Pococke, Bishop**
*Kilkenny, Kilk.*

**Rahere**
*London* Church of St Bartholomew
the Great

**Ralph, Bishop**
*Kildare, Kild.* St Brigid's Cathedral

**Ripley, John**
*Leeds, Yorks.* Abbey House Museum;
Municipal Offices

**Robinson, Primate**
*Armagh, Arm.*
*Ballymakenny, Louth*
*Dungannon, Tyrone*

**Ross, Provost**
*Aberdeen, A'deen.* Provost Ross's
House

**Rutherwyke, Abbot**
*Great Bookham, Surrey* Church of St
Nicholas

**St Calais, William of, Bishop**
*Durham, Durham* Cathedral and
Castle

**St Leger, Geoffrey, Bishop**
*Kilkenny, Kilk.* St Canice's Cathedral

**Schmidt, Father**
*London* Church of St Katherine Cree

**Sely, John, Bishop**
*Kilclief, Down*

**Sharp, Archbishop**
*St Andrews, Fife*

**Sheldon, Archbishop**
*Oxford, Oxon.*

**Stuart, Primate**
*Armagh, Arm.*

**Sudbury, Archbishop**
*Canterbury, Kent* Westgate Museum

**Sutton, Bishop**
*Lincoln, Lincs.* Cathedral Treasury,
Lincoln Cathedral

**Swithin, St**
*Winchester, Hants*

**Taylor, Jeremy, Bishop**
*Ballinderry, Antrim* Middle Church

**Tennyson, Rev. George**
*Somersby, Lincs.* Somersby House

**Tibba, St**
*Ryall, Rutland* Church of St John
the Evangelist

**Trevor, Richard, Bishop**
*Glynde Place, Sussex*

**Turnbull, William, Bishop**
*Glasgow, Lanarks.*

**Vyvyan, Prior**
*Bodmin, Cornwall* Church of St
Petrock

**Walter, Hubert, Archbishop**
*London* Lambeth Palace

**Waring, Rev. Holt**
*Waringstown, Down*

**Waynefleet, William of,
Bishop**
*Oxford, Oxon.* Magdalen College
*Wainfleet All Saints, Lincs.*

**Werburgh, St**
*Chester, Cheshire* Cathedral

**Wesley, John**
*Epworth, Lincs.* Old Rectory
*Gainsborough, Lincs.* Old Hall
*London* Wesley's House and
Chapel
*West Bromwich, Warks.* Oak House

**Wite, St**
*Whitchurch Canonicorum, Dorset*
Church of St Candida and Holy
Cross

**Wolsey, Cardinal**
*Great Wymondley, Herts.* Delamere
House
*Hampton Court, Greater London*
*Ipswich, Suffolk* Wolsey's Gateway
*Lincoln, Lincs.* Cardinal's Hat
*London* Banqueting House, White-
hall
*Sherborne, Dorset* Abbey Church of
St Mary

**Wren, Bishop**
*Cambridge, Cambs.* Pembroke College Chapel

**Wulfstan, Bishop**
*Worcester, Worcs.* Cathedral

**Wycliffe, John**
*Bristol, Glos.* Westbury College

**Wygun, Isabella, Prioress**
*Norwich, Norfolk* Carrow Abbey

**Wykeham, William of**
*Broughton Castle, Oxon.*
*Oxford, Oxon.* New College
*Winchester, Hants.* Cathedral;
Winchester College

**Wyville, Bishop**
*Salisbury, Wilts.* Cathedral

**York, Wilfrid of, Bishop**
*Ripon, Yorks.* Cathedral

# POLITICIANS AND LAWYERS

The two great contributions Britain has made to modern politics are representative government and the rule of law. Neither happened by chance or overnight: they were the work of generations of outstanding men. To visit Parliament or any law court in the land is to see these two massive principles operating through historical, often quaint, forms.

**Aislabie, John**
*Studley Royal and Fountains Abbey Garden, Yorks.*

**Alexander, Sir William**
*Menstrie Castle, Clack.*

**Anderson, Sir Edmund**
*Broughton, Lincs.* Church of St Mary

**Astor, Lord**
*Cliveden, Bucks.*

**Audley, Lord**
*Saffron Walden, Essex*

**Bernard, Sir Francis**
*Nether Winchenden House, Bucks.*

**Blake, Thomas**
*Ross on Wye, Herefs.*

**Blathwayt, William**
*Dyrham Park, Glos.*

**Bodley, Sir Thomas**
*Oxford, Oxon.* Bodleian Library

**Bonar Law, Andrew**
*Ashridge, Herts.*

**Boyle, Richard, Earl of Cork**
*Youghal, Cork*

**Bulwer Lytton, Sir Edward, 1st Lord Lytton**
*Knebworth House, Herts.*

**Carlisle, Earl of**
*Castle Howard, Yorks.*

**Cecil, Robert, 1st Earl of Salisbury**
*Hatfield House, Herts.*

**Cecil, William, Earl of Salisbury**
*Hertford, Herts.*

**Chaucer, Thomas**
*Ewelme, Oxon.* Church of St Mary the Virgin

**Chauncy, Henry**
*Hertford, Herts.* Lombard House

**Choke, Lord Chief Justice**
*Long Ashton, Som.* Church of All Saints

**Churchill, Sir Winston**
*Blenheim Palace, Oxon.*
*Chartwell, Kent*
*Ditchley Park, Oxon.*
*Oldham, Lancs.* Art Gallery

**Chute, Chaloner**
*Vyne, The, Hants.*

**Clive of India**
*Claremont, Surrey*
*Dorchester, Dorset* Dorset Military Museum
*Walcott Hall, Shrops.*
*Welshpool, Mont.* Powis Castle

**Clopton, Hugh**
*Stratford-upon-Avon, Warks.* Clopton Bridge

**Cobden, Richard**
*Midhurst, Sussex*

**Coke, Sir John**
*Melbourne Hall, Derbys.*

**Conolly, William**
*Celbridge, Kild.* Castletown

**Cordell, Sir William**
*Melford Hall, Suffolk* Church of the Holy Trinity

**Cortis, Alfred**
*Worthing, Sussex* Museum and Art Gallery

**Crichton, William**
*Crichton Castle, M'loth.*

**Cromwell, Oliver**
*Grantham, Lincs.*
*Huntingdon, Hunts.*
*Ripley Castle, Yorks.*

**Cromwell, Richard**
*Hursley, Hants.* Church of All Saints

**Crosby, Sir John**
*London* Crosby Hall; Church of St Helen's

**Curran, J. P.**
*Dublin, Dublin* Glasnevin Botanic Gardens

**Cuttle, John**
*Horham Hall, Essex*

**Dashwood, Sir Francis**
*Medmenham Abbey, Bucks.*
*West Wycombe, Bucks.* West Wycombe Park

**de Albini, William**
*Castle Rising, Norfolk* Castle

**de Breaute, Fulk**
*Bedford, Beds.*

**de Glanville, Ranulf**
*Butley, Suffolk* Butley Priory Gate-house

**de Rothschild, Baron Ferdinand**
*Waddesdon Manor, Bucks.*

**Digby, Kenelm**
*Stoke Dry, Rutland* Church of St Andrew

**Digges, Sir Dudley**
*Chilham Castle, Kent*

**Disraeli, Benjamin**
*Hughenden Manor, Bucks.*
*Knebworth House, Herts.*
*London* Lincoln's Inn
*Weston Park, Staffs.*

**Dobbs, Arthur**
*Castle Dobbs, Antrim*

**Dormer, Mr Justice**
*Quainton, Bucks.* Church of the Holy
Cross and St Mary

**Eisenhower, General Dwight D.**
*Culzean Castle, Ayrs.*

**Eliot, Edward**
*Saint Germans, Cornwall* Church of
St Germanus

**Exmewe, Thomas**
*Ruthin, Denb.* Exmewe Hall

**Eyre, Giles**
*Pepperbox Hill, Wilts.*

**Forbes, Duncan**
*Culloden, I'ness.*

**Fox, Sir Stephen**
*Fox's Hospital, Wilts.*

**Geffrye, Sir Robert**
*London* Geffrye Museum

**Gladstone, W. E.**
*Edinburgh* Mercat Cross
*Liverpool, Lancs.* Hornby Library
*London* Lincoln's Inn

**Gresham, Sir Richard**
*Fountains Abbey and Fountains Hall,*
*Yorks.*

**Hall, Sir Benjamin**
*London* Houses of Parliament

**Hampden, John**
*Aylesbury, Bucks.*

**Harvey, Bagenal**
*Bargy, Wex.* Castle

**Hatton, Sir Christopher**
*Kirby Hall, Northants.*

**Heathcote, Sir Gilbert**
*Normanton, Rutland* Church of St
Matthew

**Hill, Roland**
*London* National Postal Museum

**Hitler, Adolf**
*Dorchester, Dorset* Dorset Military
Museum

**Hopton, Sir Arthur**
*Yoxford, Suffolk* Cockfield Hall

**Jeffreys, Judge**
*Dorchester, Dorset*
*Exeter, Devon*
*Taunton, Som.*
*Winchester, Hants.* Castle Hall

**Knollys, Francis**
*Rotherfield Greys, Oxon.* Church

**Lincoln, Abraham**
*Hingham, Norfolk* Market-place

**Maitland, William**
*Lennoxlove, E. Lothian*

**More, Sir Thomas**
*London* Crosby Hall; Lincoln's Inn;
Tower of London; Westminster
Hall

**North, 8th Lord**
*Wroxton Abbey, Oxon.*

**O'Connell, Daniel**
*Derrynane Abbey, Kerry*
*Ennis, Clare*

**Onslow, Speaker**
*Guildford, Surrey* Church of the Holy
Trinity

**Owen, Robert**
*New Lanark, Lanarks.*
*Newtown, Mont.* Robert Owen
Memorial Museum

**Phelips, Sir Edward**
*Montacute House, Som.*

**Ponsonby, Speaker**
*Bishopscourt House, Kild.*

**Rhodes, Cecil**
*Bishops Stortford, Herts.*

**Richardson, Edward**
*Ricchill Manor House, Arm.*

**Roosevelt, F. D.**
*London* Roosevelt Memorial

**Sackville, Thomas**
*Knole, Kent*

**St John, Oliver**
*Thorpe Hall, Hunts.*

**Sandys, William**
*Mottisfont Abbey, Hants.*

**Scott, Sir John**
*Scotstarvit Tower, Fife*

**Stannard, Eaton**
*Wicklow, Wicklow*

**Trevor, John**
*Trevalyn Hall, Denb.*

**Walpole, Horace**
*Shobdon, Herefs.* Church of St John
the Evangelist
*Twickenham, Greater London*
Strawberry Hill
*Wolterton Hall, Norfolk*

**Washington, George**
*Sulgrave Manor, Northants.*

**Wellington, Duke of**
*Glasgow, Lanarks.* Stirling's
Library
*London* Hyde Park Corner; Royal
Exchange
*Walmer Castle, Kent*
*Wellington Monument, Som.*

**Wilkes, John**
*Aylesbury, Bucks.*

**Wolsey, Thomas**
*Hampton Court, Greater London*

# ROYALTY

England's monarchy has endured (apart from an 11-year break after Charles I lost his head) for more than 1000 years. The institution has adapted itself remarkably to the changing needs of the nation; and in turn, individual rulers as different in style as the hasty, avaricious Henry VIII and the formidably respectable Victoria have re-shaped their kingdom in their own images.

**Albert, Prince Consort**
*Balmoral Castle, A'deen.*
*London,* Albert Memorial; Royal Albert Hall; Victoria and Albert Museum
*Madingley, Cambs.* Madingley Hall
*Osborne House, Isle of Wight, Hants.*
*Portsmouth, Hants.* Victory Museum
*Windsor, Berks.* St George's Chapel, Windsor Castle

**Alexander I of Scotland**
*Stirling, Stir.* Castle

**Alexander II of Scotland**
*Balmerino Abbey, Fife*
*Eilean Donan Castle, Ross.*

**Alfred**
*Cricklade, Wilts.* Saxon burh
*Oxford, Oxon.*
*Wantage, Berks.*
*Winchester, Hants.* Town Cross

**Ap Rhys, Gruffydd**
*Tallie Abbey, Carm.*

**Arthur**
*Montacute House, Som.*
*Winchester, Hants.* Castle Hall

**Athelstan**
*Burnswark, Dumf.* Hill-fort and Roman siege works
*Malmesbury, Wilts.* Church of St Mary

**Beatrice, Princess**
*Brentford, Greater London* British Piano Museum

**Berthulf, King of Mercia**
*Bennington, Herts.*

**Black Prince, The**
*Canterbury, Kent* Cathedral
*Hellen's, Herefs.*

**Boadicea**
*Colchester, Essex*
*Stamford, Lincs.*

**Boleyn, Anne**
*Brighton, Sussex* Thomas-Stanford Museum
*Erwarton, Suffolk*
*Hever Castle, Kent*
*London* Tower of London

**Bolingbroke, Henry, Duke of Lancaster**
*Carreg-Cennen Castle, Carm.*
*Hertford, Herts.* Castle

**Bruce, Marjorie**
*Paisley, Renf.* Abbey

**Charlemagne**
*York, Yorks.*

**Charles Edward, Bonnie Prince Charlie**
*Carlisle, Cumb.* Castle
*Dunvegan, Isle of Skye, I'ness.*
*Lancaster, Lancs.*

**Charles, HRH Prince**
*Caernarvon, Caern.* Castle

**Charles I**
*Arreton, Isle of Wight, Hants.* Arreton Manor
*Birmingham, Warks.* Aston Hall
*Blithfield, Staffs.* Museum of Childhood and Costume
*Carisbrooke Castle, Isle of Wight, Hants.*
*Chester, Cheshire*
*Chirk Castle, Denb.*
*Enniskillen, Ferm.*
*Hadingley, Cambs.* Hadingley Hall
*London* St James's Palace; Westminster Hall
*Oxford, Oxon.*
*Painswick, Glos.* Court-house
*Royal Tunbridge Wells, Kent*
*Sudeley Castle, Glos.*
*Taunton, Som.* Somerset County Museum
*Winton House, E. Lothian*

**Charles II**
*Boscobel House, Shrops.*
*Chillington Hall, Staffs.*
*Dartmouth, Devon* Borough Museum
*Dunster, Som.* Castle
*Edinburgh, M'loth.* Palace of Holyroodhouse
*Harlington, Beds.* Harlington Manor
*Ipswich, Suffolk* Ancient House
*King's Lynn, Norfolk* Custom House
*London* Charles II Statue, Chelsea Hospital; Monument
*Moseley Old Hall, Staffs.*
*Oxford, Oxon.*
*Plymouth, Devon*
*Rochester, Kent* Restoration House

**Charlotte, Princess of Wales**
*Windsor, Berks.* St George's Chapel, Windsor Castle

**David I of Scotland**
*Cambuskenneth, Stir.* Abbey
*Dryburgh Abbey, Ber.*
*Hertford, Herts.* Castle
*Jedburgh, Rox.* Abbey
*Melrose Abbey, Rox.*
*Montacute House, Som.*

**David II of Scotland**
*Durham, Durham*

**de Bruce, King Robert of Scotland**
*Arbroath, Angus*
*Bannockburn, Stir.* Bore Stone
*Blair Castle, Perths.*

*Clackmannan, Clack.* Clackmannan
 Tower
*Drum Castle, A'deen.*
*Dunfermline, Fife*
*Dunstaffnage, Argyll.*
*Melrose Abbey, Rox.*
*Roslin, M'loth.* Chapel

**Edmund**
*Bury St Edmunds, Suffolk*

**Edward I**
*Beaumaris Castle, Anglesey*
*Caernarvon, Caern.* Castle
*Carlisle, Cumb.* Castle
*Conway, Caern.* Castle
*Criccieth, Caern.*
*Dirleton Castle, E. Lothian*
*Flint Castle, Flints.*
*Hardingstone, Northants.*
*Harlech Castle, Merioneth*
*Kidwelly Castle, Carm.*
*Linlithgow Palace, W. Lothian*
*Rhuddlan Castle, Flints.*
*Roslin, M'loth.* Chapel
*St Asaph, Flints.* Cathedral
*Scone Palace, Perths.*
*Walsingham Priory, Norfolk*

**Edward II**
*Berkeley Castle, Glos.*
*Caernarvon, Caern.* Castle
*Gloucester, Glos.* Cathedral

**Edward III**
*Dartmouth, Devon*
*London* Jewel Tower
*Salisbury, Wilts.* Cathedral
*Windsor, Berks.* Castle

**Edward IV**
*Hexham, Northld.*

**Edward VI**
*Christ's Hospital, Sussex*
*London* St Thomas's Hospital
*Norwich, Norfolk* Priory

**Edward VII**
*Belton, Kesteven, Lincs.*
 Belton House
*London* Marlborough House
*Madingley, Cambs.* Madingley Hall
*Sandringham House, Norfolk*

**Edward, Prince**
*Odiham, Hants.* Castle
*Worcester, Worcs.*

**Edward the Confessor**
*Bury St Edmunds, Suffolk*
*London* Royal Exchange

**Edward the Elder**
*Cricklade, Wilts.* Saxon burh

**Edward the Martyr**
*Shaftesbury, Dorset* Abbey Ruins
 Museum
*Wareham, Dorset*

**Elizabeth I**
*Basing, Hants.*
 Basing House Ruins
*Dublin, Dublin* Trinity College
*Hatfield House, Herts.*
*Huntingdon, Hunts.* Hinchinbrooke
*Kenilworth Castle, Warks.*
*Knole, Kent*
*London* Royal Exchange
*Melford Hall, Suffolk*
*Norwich, Norfolk* Market-place
*Stamford, Lincs.*
*Syon House, Greater London*
*Warwick, Warks.* Lord Leycester
 Hospital and Chapel of St James

**Elizabeth II**
*Balmoral Castle, A'deen.*
*Falkland, Fife* Falkland Palace
*London* Buckingham Palace;
 Royal Mews, Buckingham Palace
*Sandringham House, Norfolk*

**Elizabeth of Bohemia**
*Ashdown House, Berks.*

**Ermengarde**
*Balmerino Abbey, Fife*

**Ethelbald**
*Crowland, Lincs.* Crowland Abbey

**George I**
*London* Banqueting House, Whitehall; Kensington Palace

**George II**
*Hampton Court, Greater London*
*Marlow, Bucks.* Marlow Place

**George III**
*Kew, Greater London* Pagoda, Royal
 Botanic Gardens
*London* Buckingham Palace;
 Royal Academy
*Windsor, Berks.* Castle

**George IV**
*Dublin, Dublin* Mansion House
*London* Royal Mews, Buckingham
 Palace
*Windsor, Berks.* Castle

**George V**
*Edinburgh, M'loth.* Palace of
 Holyroodhouse
*Leeds, Yorks.* Municipal Offices

**George, Prince of Denmark**
*Windsor, Berks.* Windsor Guildhall
 Exhibition

**George, Prince of Wales**
*Brighton, Sussex* Royal Pavilion

**Grey, Lady Jane**
*London* Buckingham Palace; Tower
 of London

**Harold**
*Waltham Abbey, Essex*

**Henrietta Maria**
*Greenwich, Greater London* Queen's
 House
*London* Queen's Chapel, St James's
*Royal Tunbridge Wells, Kent*

**Henry I**
*Cardiff, Glam.* Castle, National
 Museum of Wales
*Reading, Berks.*

**Henry II**
*Orford Castle, Suffolk*
*Scarborough, Yorks.*
*Wallingford, Berks.*
*Warkworth Castle, Northld.*
*Windsor, Berks.* Castle

**Henry III**
*Chester, Cheshire* Castle
*London* Westminster Abbey
*Montgomery, Mont.* Castle
*Oxford, Oxon.*
*Sutton-at-Hone, Kent* St John's,
 Jerusalem
*Walsingham Priory, Norfolk*
*Worcester, Worcs.*

**Henry IV**
*Canterbury, Kent* Cathedral
*Kenilworth, Warks.* Castle

**Henry V**
*Monmouth, Mon.*
*Syon House, Greater London*

**Henry VI**
*Hexham, Northld.*
*Muncaster Castle, Cumb.*

**Henry VII**
*Cambridge, Cambs.*
 Trinity College
*London* Westminster Abbey
*Pembroke, Pemb.* Castle
*Worcester, Worcs.* Cathedral

**Henry VIII**
*Arreton, Isle of Wight, Hants.*
    Arreton Manor
*Berkhamsted, Herts.*
*Canterbury, Kent*
*Cowdray Park, Sussex*
*Durham, Durham* Grammar
    School
*East Barsham Hall, Norfolk*
*Elton Hall, Hunts.*
*Great Wymondley, Herts.* Delamere
    House
*Hampton Court, Greater London*
*Knole, Kent*
*London* Banqueting House,
    Whitehall; St James's Palace;
    St Bartholomew's Hospital;
    St Thomas's Hospital
*Milton Abbey, Dorset*
*Pembroke, Pemb.* Castle
*Peterborough, Hunts.*
*Portsmouth, Hants.*
*Walmer Castle, Kent*
*Wilton House, Wilts.*

**Henry, Prince**
*Sycharth, Denb.*

**Isabella**
*Hertford, Herts.* Castle

**James I of Scotland**
*Linlithgow Palace, W. Lothian*
*Perth, Perths.*

**James II of Scotland**
*Dryburgh Abbey, Ber.*

**James III of Scotland**
*Stirling, Stir.* Castle

**James IV of Scotland**
*Edinburgh, M'Loth.* Holyroodhouse
    Abbey; Palace of Holyroodhouse
*Rothesay, Isle of Bute, Bute* Castle

**James V of Scotland**
*Falkland, Fife*
*Rothesay, Isle of Bute, Bute* Castle
*Stirling, Stir.* Castle

**James VI of Scotland (James I of
    England)**
*Althorp, Northants.*
*Falkland, Fife* Falkland
    Palace
*Hatfield House, Herts.*
*Hoghton Tower, Lancs.*
*London* Apothecaries' Hall;
    Buckingham Palace
*Neidpath Castle, Peebl.*
*Pembroke, Pemb.* Castle
*Ripley Castle, Yorks.*
*Stirling, Stir.* Castle
*Thetford, Norfolk* King's
    House
*Worcester, Worcs.*

**John**
*Dorchester, Dorset*
*Eye, Suffolk*
*Ipswich, Suffolk*
*Lancaster, Lancs.* Castle
*Liverpool, Lancs.*
*Scarborough, Yorks.* Castle
*Stratford-upon-Avon, Warks.*

**John, King of France**
*St Albans, Herts.* French Row

**Katherine of Aragon**
*Brighton, Sussex* Thomas-Stanford
    Museum
*Buckden Palace, Hunts.*

**Kenneth I of Scotland**
*Scone Palace, Perths.*

**Knut**
*Bury St Edmunds, Suffolk*

**Loaghaire**
*Tara, Meath*

**Macbeth, King of Scotland**
*Dunsinane, Perth.*
*Iona, Argyll*

**McMurrough, Dermot, King of
    Leinster**
*Baltinglass, Wicklow*

**Maelor, Madoc Ap Gruffydd,
    Prince of Powys**
*Valle Crucis Abbey, Denb.*

**Maeve (Queen Mab)**
*Knocknarea, Sligo*

**Malcolm II of Scotland**
*Edinburgh, M'Loth.*

**Margaret, Princess**
*Glamis, Angus* Castle

**Margaret, Princess, daughter of
    Henry VII**
*Grantham, Lincs.* Grantham House

**Mary I**
*Daingean, Offaly*
*Elton Hall, Hunts.*
*Framlingham Castle, Suffolk*
*Lichfield, Staffs.*

**Mary II**
*Greenwich, Greater London* Royal
    Naval College

**Mary, Queen of Scots**
*Borthwick Castle, M'Loth.*
*Cadzow Castle, Lanarks.*
*Carlisle, Cumb.* Castle
*Dundrennan Abbey, Kirkcud.*
*Edinburgh, M'Loth.* Palace of
    Holyroodhouse
*Falkland, Fife* Falkland Palace
*Fotheringhay, Northants.*
*Hailes Castle, E. Lothian*
*Hermitage Castle, Rox.*
*Linlithgow, W. Lothian* Linlithgow
    Palace
*Loch Leven Castle, Kinross*
*London* Marlborough House
*Lowther Castle, Westmld.*
*Niddry Castle, W. Lothian*
*Peterborough, Hunts.* Museum and
    Maxwell Art Gallery
*Traquair House, Peebl.*

**Matilda**
*Worcester, Worcs.*

**O'Brien Domhnall, King of
    Munster**
*Canon Island, Clare*
*Corcomroe Abbey, Clare*
*Holycross, Tipp.*
*Kilcooly Abbey, Tipp.*

**O'Brien, Donat**
*Corcomroe Abbey, Clare*

**O'Conor, Cathel**
*Ballintober Abbey, Mayo* Augustinian
    Friary
*Knockmoy, Gal.*
*Roscommon, Ross.*

**Offa, King of Mercia**
*Offa's Dyke*
*Oswestry, Shrops.*

**Parr, Catherine**
*Kendal, Westmld.*
*Sudeley Castle, Glos.*

**Philip II, King of Spain**
*Daingean, Offaly*

**Richard I (Lionheart)**
*Butley, Suffolk* Butley Priory
    Gate-house
*Colchester, Essex*
*Worcester, Worcs.*

**Richard II**
*Blithfield, Staffs.* Museum of
    Childhood and Costume

*Hertford, Herts.* Castle
*Lichfield, Staffs.*
*Lincoln, Lincs.* Stonebow and
    Guildhall
*London* Westminster Hall
*Melrose Abbey, Rox.*
*Oswestry, Shrops.*
*Portchester Castle, Hants.*

**Richard III**
*Grantham, Lincs.*

**Rufus, Prince**
*Worcester, Worcs.*

**Seymour, Jane**
*Syon House, Greater London*

**Stephen**
*Worcester, Worcs.*

**Swynford, Katherine**
*Kettlethorpe Hall, Lincs.*

**Victoria**
*Balmoral Castle, A'deen.*
*Brighton, Sussex*
    Royal Pavilion
*Claremont, Surrey*
*Cowes, Isle of Wight, Hants.*
*Leeds, Yorks.* Town Hall
*London* Albert Memorial; Museum
    of Leathercraft; Royal Mews,
    Buckingham Palace; St James's
    Palace; St Thomas's Hospital;
    Victoria and Albert Museum

*Northampton, Northants.* Central
    Museum and Art Gallery
*Osborne House, Isle of Wight, Hants.*
*Windsor, Berks.* Castle

**William I (the Conqueror)**
*Battle Abbey, Sussex*
*Durham, Durham*
*Ely, Cambs.*
*Lincoln, Lincs.* Castle
*Oxford, Oxon.*
*Rockingham Castle, Northants.*
*Windsor, Berks.* Castle

**William II (Rufus)**
*Carlisle, Cumb.* Castle
*London* Westminster Hall
*Rockingham Castle, Northants.*
*Rufus Stone, Hants.*

**William III**
*London* Banqueting House, White-
    hall; Kensington Palace
*Petersfield, Hants.*
*Sherborne, Dorset* Castle

**William IV**
*Brighton, Sussex*
    Royal Pavilion
*Craigdarroch, Dumf.*

**William, King of Scotland**
*Arbroath Abbey, Angus*

**William the Lion**
*Dumfries, Dumf.*

# SCIENTISTS

Before there is any science, there must be a scientific approach; and in this sense, English science begins with Francis Bacon (1561–1626). He stressed that truth is not derived from authority, but is discovered through experiment and observation. The brilliant insights of Newton, the world-shaking theories of Darwin—even the work which led to the 'splitting' of the atom—followed, however indirectly, from this step.

**Acland, Sir Henry
Wentworth**
*Oxford, Oxon.* University
    Museum

**Anderson, Elizabeth Garrett**
*Aldeburgh, Suffolk*

**Banks, Sir Joseph**
*Horncastle, Lincs.*

**Cavendish, Sir Charles**
*Bolsover Castle, Derbys.*

**Crossley, Dr John**
*Abingdon, Berks.* Church of St
    Helen

**Curie, Mme**
*London* Wellcome Historical Medical
    Museum and Library

**Darwin, Charles**
*Downe, Kent* Down House

**Gray, Dr Alexander**
*Elgin, Moray.* Gray's Hospital

**Hall, Dr John**
*Stratford-upon-Avon, Warks.* Hall's
    Croft

**Herschel, Sir William**
*Windsor, Berks.* Windsor Guildhall
    Exhibition

**Hulse, Sir Edward**
*Breamore, Hants.* Breamore House

**Hunter, John**
*London* Apothecaries' Hall; Royal
    College of Surgeons

**Hutchinson, Sir Jonathan**
*Haslemere, Surrey* Educational
    Museum

**Lyon, Dr**
*Harrow, Greater London* Church of
    St Mary

**Milley, Dr Thomas**
*Lichfield, Staffs.*

**Newton, Sir Isaac**
*Grantham, Lincs.* Library and Museum
*Spalding, Lincs.* Spalding Gentlemen's
    Society
*Woolsthorpe Manor, Lincs.*

**Radcliffe, Dr John**
*Oxford, Oxon.* Bodleian Library

**Sloane, Sir Hans**
*Killyleagh, Down*

**Smith, William**
*Scarborough, Yorks.*

**Stukeley, Dr William**
*Spalding, Lincs.* Spalding Gentlemen's
Society

**Turner, Dr**
*Church Stowe, Northants.* Church of
SS Peter and Paul

**Van Giffen, Dr A. E.**
*Ballynoe Stone Circle, Down*

**Wall, Dr**
*Worcester, Worcs.*

# SCULPTORS

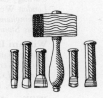

Sculptors approach their material in two different ways: either they
are explorers, searching out the forms they want in a block of marble
or a trunk of wood, and cutting away everything that is not part of
that form; or they are builders, making a shape grow from its core as
they add wax or clay. The hidden form or the undeveloped shape were
there before the sculptor got to work; the difference between him and
other men is that he sees them.

**Adams-Acton, John**
*Carlisle, Cumb.* Cathedral

**Adye, Thomas**
*Cuckfield, Sussex* Church of the
Holy Trinity
*Little Dunmow, Essex* Church of St
Mary

**Armstead, H. H.**
*Carlisle, Cumb.* Cathedral

**Bacon, John**
*Belton, Kesteven, Lincs.* Church of
SS Peter and Paul
*Berkswell, Warks.* Church of St
John the Baptist
*Bottisham, Cambs.* Church of the
Holy Trinity
*Hawstead, Suffolk* Church of All
Saints
*London* Somerset House
*Lymington, Hants.* Church of St
Thomas the Apostle
*Rye, Sussex* Church of St
Mary
*Tyrrelspass, Westmeath*
*Wimpole, Cambs.* Church of St
Andrew

**Bacon, John the Younger**
*Beverley, Yorks.* Church of St Mary
*Bradford, Yorks.* Cathedral
*Cottesbrooke, Northants.* Church of
All Saints
*Cuckfield, Sussex* Church of the
Holy Trinity
*Harefield, Greater London* Church of
St Mary
*Hawstead, Suffolk* Church of All
Saints
*Manchester, Lancs.* Cathedral
*Norwich, Norfolk* Church of St
George
*Odell, Beds.* Church of All Saints
*Stanstead Abbots, Herts.* Church of
St James
*Warfield, Berks.* Church of St
Michael
*Wollaton, Notts.* Church of St
Leonard
*Worcester, Worcs.* Cathedral
*Wrenbury, Cheshire* Church of St
Margaret

**Baily, E. H.**
*Baldock, Herts.* Church of St Mary
*Buckden, Hunts.* Church of St Mary
*Lichfield, Staffs.* Cathedral
*Manchester, Lancs.* Cathedral
*Newcastle upon Tyne, Northld.*
Cathedral
*Oxford, Oxon.* Cathedral
*Potterne, Wilts.* Church of St Mary

**Banks, Thomas**
*Ashbourne, Derbys.* Church of St
Oswald
*Bramley, Hants.* Church of St James
*Carlisle, Cumb.* Cathedral
*Flitton, Beds.* Church of St John the
Baptist
*Wimpole, Cambs.* Church of St
Andrew

**Behnes, W.**
*Clifton Campville, Staffs.* Church of
St Andrew
*London* St John's Wood Chapel

**Bernini, Pietro**
*London* Church of All Saints

**Bird, Francis**
*London* Church of St Leonard;
St Paul's Cathedral

**Boehm, Sir J. E.**
*Bedford, Beds.*
*Deene, Northants.* Church of St
Peter
*Eastnor, Herefs.* Church of St John
the Baptist
*Lewknor, Oxon.* Church of St
Margaret

**Bourdelle, Emile**
*Aberdeen, A'deen.* Art Gallery

**Burne-Jones, Sir Edward**
*Mells, Som.* Church of St
Andrew

**Bushnell, John**
*Ashburnham, Sussex* Church of St
Peter
*Babraham, Cambs.* Church of St Peter
*Boxted, Suffolk* Church of the Holy
Trinity

**Bushnell, William**
*Toddington, Beds.* Church of St George

**Byrd, William**
*Swinbrook, Oxon.* Church of St Mary the Virgin

**Campbell, Thomas**
*Warkton, Northants.* Church of St Edmund

**Carabelli, Casimiro**
*Ickworth, Suffolk*

**Carabelli, Donato**
*Ickworth, Suffolk*

**Caracchi, Joseph**
*London* Somerset House

**Carline, John**
*Hodnet, Shrops.* Church of St Luke

**Carlini, Agostino**
*Dublin, Dublin* Custom House
*London* Somerset House
*Milton Abbas, Dorset* Abbey

**Carpenter, Andrew**
*Amersham, Bucks.* Church of St Mary
*Bloxham, Oxon.* Church of Our Lady
*Leeds, Yorks.* Church of St Peter
*Theddlethorpe, Lincs.* Church of All Saints

**Carpentier, Andrew**
*Little Stanmore, Greater London* Church of St Lawrence, Whitchurch

**Carter, Thomas**
*Bramley, Hants.* Church of St James
*Celbridge, Kild.*

**Cartwright, Thomas**
*Cottesbrooke, Northants.* Church of All Saints

**Cass, Christopher**
*Great Barrington, Glos.* Church of St Mary the Virgin
*London* Church of St Martin-in-the-Fields

**Chantrey, Sir Francis**
*Armagh, Arm.*
*Ashley, Staffs.* Church of St. John the Baptist
*Bamburgh, Northld.* Church of St Aidan
*Bristol, Glos.* Church of St Mark
*Burley-on-the-Hill, Rutland* Church of the Holy Cross
*Charlton, Greater London* Church of St Luke
*Derby, Derbys.* Cathedral
*Edington, Wilts.* Church of SS Mary, Katherine and All Saints
*Farnworth, Lancs.* Church of St Luke
*Hackness, Yorks.* Church of St Peter
*Hodnet, Shrops.* Church of St Luke
*Ilam, Staffs.*
*Ingestre, Staffs.* Church of St Mary
*Lichfield, Staffs.* Cathedral
*London* Royal Exchange; St John's Wood Chapel
*Longbridge Deverill, Wilts.* Church of SS Peter and Paul
*Melbury Sampford, Dorset* Church of St Mary
*Orton Longueville, Hunts.* Church of the Holy Trinity
*Plympton, Devon* Church of St Mary the Virgin
*Snaith, Yorks.* Church of St Laurence
*Stoke Doyle, Northants.* Church of St Rumbald
*Sunderland, Durham* Church of the Holy Trinity
*Waterperry, Oxon.* Church of St Mary the Virgin

*Withyham, Sussex* Church of St Michael and All Angels
*Worcester, Worcs.* Cathedral
*Wragby, Yorks.* Church of St Michael

**Cheere, John**
*Aberdeen, A'deen.* Robert Gordon's College

**Cheere, Sir Henry**
*Abbots Langley, Herts.* Church of St Lawrence
*Amersham, Bucks.* Church of St Mary
*Frampton, Dorset* Church of St Mary
*Hillesden, Bucks.* Church of All Saints
*Hodnet, Shrops.* Church of St Luke
*Kirkleatham, Yorks.* Church of St Cuthbert
*Llandwrog, Caern.* Church of St Twrog
*Mold, Flints.* Church of St Mary
*Oxford, Oxon.* Cathedral
*Teversal, Notts.* Church of St Catherine

**Christmas, John**
*Ampton, Suffolk* Church of St Peter

**Cibber, Caius Gabriel**
*Cambridge, Cambs.* Trinity College Library
*London* Monument; St Paul's Cathedral
*Ravenstone, Bucks.* Church of All Saints
*Thoresby Hall, Notts.*
*Withyham, Sussex* Church of St Michael and All Angels

**Cobden, Thomas**
*Wexford, Wex.*

**Collins, Alan**
*Guildford, Surrey* Cathedral

**Colquhoun, James**
*Glasgow, Lanarks.* Hutcheson's Hospital

**Colt, Maximilian**
*Elmswell, Suffolk* Church of St John
*Hatfield, Herts.* Church of St Etheldreda
*Sleaford, Lincs.* Church of St Denys

**Comper, Sir Ninian**
*Wymondham, Norfolk* Church of SS Mary and Thomas of Canterbury

**Cox, Samuel**
*Abington, Northants.*

**Crutcher, Richard**
*Bletchingley, Surrey* Church of St Mary

**Cure, William**
*Cranford, Greater London* Church of St Dunstan
*Long Melford, Suffolk* Church of the Holy Trinity

**Degas, Edgar**
*Aberdeen, A'deen.* Art Gallery

**Delany, Edward**
*Dublin, Dublin* St Stephen's Green

**Delvaux, Laurent**
*Old Warden, Beds.* Church of St Leonard
*Rockingham, Northants.* Church of St Leonard

**Deval, John, Junior**
*Clyffe Pypard, Wilts.* Church of St Peter

**Dick, Sir William Reid**
*London* Roosevelt Memorial

**Dun, Thomas**
*Brent Eleigh, Suffolk* Church of St
Mary

**Epstein, Sir Jacob**
*Aberdeen, A'deen.* Art Gallery
*Bedford, Beds.* Cecil Higgins Art
Gallery
*Bury, Lancs.* Art Gallery and Museum
*Coventry, Warks.* Cathedral
*Llandaff, Glam.* Cathedral
*Oldham, Lancs.* Art Gallery
*Stockport, Lancs.* War Memorial Art
Gallery
*Swansea, Glam.* Glynn Vivian Art
Gallery

**Evesham, Epiphanius**
*Cuckfield, Sussex* Church of the
Holy Trinity
*Titchfield, Hants.* Church of St Peter

**Fisher, John**
*Whalley, Lancs.* Church of St Mary

**Flaxman, J.**
*Barlaston, Staffs.* Wedgwood
Museum Trust
*Basing, Hants.* Church of St Mary
*Bowness, Westmld.* Church of St
Martin
*Bradford, Yorks,* Cathedral
*Brecon, Brecon.* Cathedral
*Campsall, Yorks.* Church of St
Mary Magdalene
*Christchurch, Hants.* Priory Church
*Cuckfield, Sussex* Church of the Holy
Trinity
*East Dereham, Norfolk* Church of St
Nicholas
*Flamstead, Herts.* Church of St
Leonard
*Great Brington, Northants.* Church of
St Mary
*Great Gaddesden, Herts.* Church of
St John the Baptist
*Harrow, Greater London* Church of
St Mary
*Hatfield Broad Oak, Essex* Church of
St Mary the Virgin
*Ickworth, Suffolk*
*Inistioge, Kilk.*
*Ledbury, Herefs.* Church of St
Michael and All Angels
*Leeds, Yorks.* Church of St Peter
*London* Christ Church
*Madingley, Cambs.* Church of St
Mary Magdalene
*Newcastle upon Tyne, Northld.*
Cathedral
*Rotherham, Yorks.* Church of All
Saints
*Rufford, Lancs.* Church of St Mary
*Rye, Sussex* Church of St Mary
*Shellingford, Berks.* Church of St Faith
*Throwley, Kent* Church of St
Michael and All Angels
*Wimpole, Cambs.* Church of St
Andrew
*Withyham, Sussex* Church of St
Michael and All Angels
*Wragby, Yorks.* Church of St Michael
*Wroxton, Oxon.*

**Foley, J. H.**
*Birr, Offaly*
*Dublin, Dublin* City Hall

**Frampton, Sir George**
*London* Kensington Gardens

**Franceys, S.**
*Broughton, Staffs.* Church of St Peter

**Franceys, T.**
*Broughton, Staffs.* Church of St Peter

**Frink, Elizabeth**
*Eastbourne, Sussex* Towner Art
Gallery

**Gatley, Alfred**
*Disley, Cheshire* Church of St Mary
the Virgin

**Gibbons, Grinling**
*Bottesford, Leics.* Church of St Mary
*Conington, Cambs.* Church of St Mary
*Exton, Rutland* Church of SS Peter
and Paul
*Felbrigg, Norfolk* Church of St
Margaret
*Harefield, Greater London* Church of
St Mary
*London* Charles II Statue, Chelsea
Hospital; Church of St Mary
Abchurch; St Paul's Cathedral
*Petworth House, Sussex*
*Radburne, Derbys.* Church of St
Andrew

**Gibson, Benjamin**
*Mold, Flints.* Church of St Mary

**Gibson, John**
*Farnworth, Lancs.* Church of St Luke
*Fawsley, Northants.* Church of St
Mary

**Gibson, Solomon**
*Mold, Flints.* Church of St Mary

**Gilbert, Sir Albert**
*Bedford, Beds.*
*Windsor, Berks.* Windsor Castle, St
George's Chapel

**Gilbert, Alfred**
*Longbridge Deverill, Wilts.* Church of
SS Peter and Paul

**Gill, Eric**
*Guildford, Surrey* Cathedral
*Hadleigh, Suffolk* Church of St Mary
*Lapworth, Warks.* Church of St Mary
*Roker, Durham* Church of St Andrew
*South Harting, Sussex* Church

**Goscombe, John**
*Hatfield, Herts.* Church of St
Etheldreda

**Gott, J.**
*Gaddesby, Leics.* Church of St Luke

**Gower, Lord**
*Stratford-upon-Avon, Warks.* Shakespeare Statue, Gower Memorial

**Green, Thomas**
*Acton, Suffolk* Church of All Saints
*Dunstable, Beds.* Church of St Peter
*Knebworth, Herts.* Church of SS
Mary and Thomas of Canterbury
*Norwich, Norfolk* Church of St
George
*Redgrave, Suffolk* Church of St
Botolph

**Guelfi, G. B.**
*Deene, Northants.* Church of St Peter

**Guldo, John**
*Bosbury, Herefs.* Church of the Holy
Trinity
*Madley, Herts.* Church of the
Nativity of St Mary the Virgin

**Harrison, Charles**
*Dublin, Dublin* Kildare Street Club

**Henning, John**
*London* Hyde Park Corner

**Henning, John Junior**
*London* Hyde Park Corner

**Henning, Samuel**
*London* Hyde Park Corner

**Hepworth, Barbara**
*Aberdeen, A'deen.* Art Gallery
*Kingston upon Hull, Yorks.* Ferens Art
Gallery
*Swansea, Glam.* Glynn Vivian Art
Gallery

**Hickey, John**
*Abingdon, Berks.* Church of St Helen

**Hickey, William**
*Delgany Church, Wicklow*

**Hill, Vernon**
*Guildford, Surrey* Cathedral

**Hogan, John**
*Carlow, Carlow*
*Cloyne, Cork*
*New Ross, Wex.*

**Hohenlohelangenburg, Prince Victor of**
*Escrick, Yorks.* Church of St Helen

**Hollemans, Jasper**
*Great Brington, Northants.* Church of St Mary

**Hollins, Peter**
*Dudley, Worcs.* Church of St Thomas the Apostle

**Hollins, William**
*Dudley, Worcs.* Church of St Thomas the Apostle

**Horsnaile, Christopher**
*Ampney Crucis, Glos.* Church of the Holy Rood

**Horsnaile, Christopher the Elder**
*Dowdeswell, Glos.* Church of St Michael

**Houghton, John**
*Castle Lyons, Cork*

**Hughes, John**
*Loughrea, Gal.*

**Hunt, John**
*Overstone, Northants.* Church of St Nicholas

**Jagger, C.**
*London* Hyde Park Corner

**Johnson, Gerard**
*Bottesford, Leics.* Church of St Mary
*Stratford-upon-Avon, Warks.* Church of the Holy Trinity
*Titchfield, Hants.* Church of St Peter

**Johnson, John**
*Stowlangtoft, Suffolk* Church of St George

**Johnson, Nicholas**
*Bottesford, Leics.* Church of St Mary
*Exton, Rutland* Church of SS Peter and Paul

**Jones, Adrian**
*London* Hyde Park Corner

**Joseph, Samuel**
*Dudley, Worcs.* Church of St Thomas the Apostle

**Kelly, Oisin**
*Strabane, Tyrone*

**Kemp, G. M.**
*Edinburgh, M'loth.* Scott Monument

**Kempster, Christopher**
*London* Church of St Mary Abchurch

**Kidwell, William**
*Finglas, Dublin*
*Newmarket-on-Fergus, Clare*

**Kirk, Joseph**
*Ennis, Clare*

**Kirk, Thomas**
*Caledon House, Tyrone*

**Landseer, Sir Edwin**
*London* Trafalgar Square

**Latham, Jasper**
*Oxford, Oxon.* Cathedral
*Silkstone, Yorks.* Church of All Saints

**Leoni, Giacomo**
*Quainton, Bucks.* Church of the Holy Cross and St Mary

**Lough, J. G.**
*Crosthwaite, Cumb.* Church of St Kentigern
*Ledbury, Herefs.* Church of St Michael and All Angels
*Toddington, Glos.* Church of St Andrew

**Lucas, R. C.**
*Chilworth, Hants.* Church of St Denys
*Harlington, Greater London* Church of SS Peter and Paul

**McDowell, Patrick**
*Belfast, Antrim* Castle

**Manning, Samuel**
*Stanstead Abbots, Herts.* Church of St James
*Warfield, Berks.* Church of St Michael

**Marochetti, Baron**
*Belton, Kesteven, Lincs.* Church of SS Peter and Paul
*Glasgow, Lanarks.* Stirling's Library
*Leeds, Yorks.* Church of St Peter

**Marshall, Edward**
*Amersham, Bucks.* Church of St Mary
*Ightham, Kent* Church of St Peter
*Withington, Glos.* Church of St Michael and All Angels

**Marshall, Joshua**
*Chipping Campden, Glos.* Church of St James
*Connington, Cambs.* Church of St Mary
*Leicester, Leics.* Cathedral

**Middleton, John**
*Church Stowe, Northants.* Church of SS Peter and Paul

**Mills, Peter**
*Thorney Abbey, Hunts.*

**Monnot, P.**
*Stamford, Lincs.* Church of St Mary

**Moore, Henry**
*Aberdeen, A'deen.* Art Gallery
*Bedford, Beds.* Cecil Higgins Art Gallery
*Eastbourne, Sussex* Towner Art Gallery
*Kingston upon Hull, Yorks.* Ferens Art Gallery
*Swindon, Wilts.* Museum and Art Gallery

**Moore, J. F.**
*Bradford, Yorks.* Cathedral
*Cottesbrooke, Northants.* Church of All Saints
*Ettingdon, Warks.* Church of the Holy Trinity
*Hatfield Broad Oak, Essex* Church of St Mary the Virgin
*North Stoneham, Hants.* Church of St Nicholas
*Saxton, Yorks.* Church of All Saints
*Winchester, Hants.* Church of St Cross
*Worcester, Worcs.* Cathedral

**Morris, William**
*Scarborough, Yorks.* Church of St Martin

**Munnings, Sir Alfred**
*Mells, Som.* Church of St Andrew

**Murray, William**
*Caledon House, Tyrone*

**Nimmo, Alexander**
*Limerick, Lim.*

**Nixon, S.**
*London* St John's Wood Chapel

**528**

## Noble, Matthew
*Ashley, Staffs.* Church of St John the Baptist
*Flitton, Beds.* Church of St John the Baptist
*Hackness, Yorks.* Church of St Peter
*Holme Lacy, Herefs.* Church of St Cuthbert
*Leeds, Yorks.* Town Hall
*Marquess of Anglesey's Column, Anglesey*
*Rufford, Lancs.* Church of St Mary

## Nollekens, Joseph
*Abingdon, Berks.* Church of St Helen
*Armagh, Arm.*
*Cirencester, Glos.* Church of St John the Baptist
*Derby, Derbys.* Cathedral
*East Horndon, Essex* Church of All Saints
*Exton, Rutland* Church of SS Peter and Paul
*Felbrigg, Norfolk* Church of St Margaret
*Great Barrington, Glos.* Church of St Mary the Virgin
*Great Brington, Northants.* Church of St Mary
*Hillsborough, Down*
*London* Somerset House
*Maidstone, Kent* Church of All Saints
*Ruabon, Denb.* Church
*St Michael Penkevil, Cornwall* Church of St Michael
*Shobdon, Herefs.* Church of St John the Evangelist
*Southport, Lancs.* Church of St Cuthbert
*Tittleshall, Norfolk* Church of St Mary
*Wetheral, Cumb.* Church of the Holy Trinity
*Whiston, Northants.* Church of St Mary
*Whitkirk, Yorks.* Church of St Mary
*Wisbech, Cambs.* Church of SS Peter and Paul
*Withyham, Sussex* Church of St Michael and All Angels
*Worcester, Worcs.* Cathedral

## Nost, John
*Bradford-on-Avon, Wilts.* Church of the Holy Trinity
*Durisdeer, Dumf.* Church
*Sherborne, Dorset* Abbey Church of St Mary
*Wanstead, Essex* Church of St Mary the Virgin
*Whitkirk, Yorks.* Church of St Mary
*Winwick, Lancs.* Church of St Oswald

## Ohly, William
*New Barnet, Greater London* Abbey Art Centre and Museum

## O'Shea Brothers
*Dublin, Dublin* Trinity College

## Paolozzi
*Kingston upon Hull, Yorks.* Ferens Art Gallery

## Parker, Richard
*Bottesford, Leics.* Church of St Mary

## Paty, James
*Chepstow, Mon.* Church of St Mary

## Paty, James the Younger
*Monmouth, Mon.* Church of St Mary

## Paty, Thomas
*Chepstow, Mon.* Church of St Mary

## Physick, Edward
*London* St John's Wood Chapel
*Sandal Magna, Yorks.* Church of St Helen
*Scarborough, Yorks.* Church of St Mary
*Tenby, Pemb.* Church of St Mary

## Pickford, Joseph
*Ashby-de-la-Zouch, Leics.* Church of St Helen

## Pierce, Edward
*London* St Paul's Cathedral
*Whitkirk, Yorks.* Church of St Mary

## Pitts, William
*Whiston, Northants.* Church of St Mary

## Pozzo, Andrea
*Thurles, Tipp.*

## Rawlins, Thomas
*Norwich, Norfolk* Church of St George

## Read, Nicholas
*Lechlade, Glos.* Church of St Laurence

## Regnart, Charles
*Ledbury, Herefs.* Church of St Michael and All Angels
*Hadleigh, Suffolk* Church of St Mary
*Thorpe Market, Norfolk* Church of St Margaret

## Renard Goullet, Yann
*Dublin, Dublin* Custom House

## Rice, James
*Waterford, Waterford*

## Rodin, Auguste
*Aberdeen, A'deen.* Art Gallery

## Rose, Joseph the Elder
*Reigate, Surrey* Church of St Mary Magdalene

## Rossi
*London* Church of St Pancras

## Rossi, Felix
*Liverpool, Lancs.* Town Hall

## Roubiliac, Louis
*Armagh, Arm.*
*Canon Pyon, Herefs.* Church of St Lawrence
*Condover, Shrops.* Church of SS Mary and Andrew
*Derby, Derbys.* Cathedral
*Framlingham, Suffolk* Church of St Michael
*Gayhurst, Bucks.* Church of St Peter
*Lancaster, Lancs.* Church of St Mary
*London* Church of St Botolph, Aldersgate; Church of St Mary
*Quainton, Bucks.* Church of the Holy Cross and St Mary
*Scarborough, Yorks.* Church of St Mary
*Tittleshall, Norfolk* Church of St Mary
*Walton-on-Thames, Surrey* Church of St Mary
*Warkton, Northants.* Church of St Edmund
*Worcester, Worcs.* Cathedral
*Wrexham, Denb.* Church of St Giles

## Royleys of Burton-upon-Trent
*Breedon on the Hill, Leics.* Church of SS Mary and Hardulph

## Rysbrack, Michael
*Armagh, Arm.*
*Ashby-de-la-Zouch, Leics.* Church of St Helen
*Bradford-on-Avon, Wilts.* Church of the Holy Trinity
*Bristol, Glos.* Church of All Saints
*Clifton Campville, Staffs.* Church of St Andrew
*Derby, Derbys.* Cathedral
*Guildford, Surrey* Church of the Holy Trinity
*Hardingstone, Northants.* Church of St Edmund
*Hatfield, Herts.* Church of St Etheldreda

Lydiard Tregoze, Wilts. Church of St
Mary
Lymington, Hants. Church of St
Thomas the Apostle
Mold, Flints. Church of St Mary
Normanton, Rutland Church of St
Matthew
Ockham, Surrey Church of All Saints
Ruabon, Denb. Church
St Germans, Cornwall Church of St
Germanus
St Michael Penkevil, Cornwall Church
of St Michael
Stapleford, Leics. Church of St Mary
Magdalene
Stoke Doyle, Northants. Church of St
Rumbald
Stourhead, Wilts.
Stratford-upon-Avon, Warks. Church
of the Holy Trinity
Tydd St Mary, Lincs. Church of St
Mary

**Scheemakers, Henry**
Bandon, Cork
Kilkenny, Kilk. St Canice's
Cathedral
Steeple Aston, Oxon. Church of SS
Peter and Paul

**Scheemakers, Peter**
Abbots Langley, Herts. Church of St
Lawrence
Amersham, Bucks. Church of St Mary
Aylesbury, Bucks. Church of St Mary
Bradford, Yorks. Cathedral
Clifton Reynes, Bucks. Church of St
Mary the Virgin
Drumcondra, Dublin
Elgin, Moray Cathedral
Gloucester, Glos. Church of St
Mary-de-Crypt
Kirkleatham, Yorks. Church of St
Cuthbert
Ledsham, Yorks.
Old Warden, Beds. Church of St
Leonard
Rockingham, Northants. Church of St
Leonard
Urchfont, Wilts. Church of St
Michael
Wimpole, Cambs. Church of St
Andrew

**Scheemakers, Thomas**
Bungay, Suffolk Church of the Holy
Trinity
Eastnor, Herefs. Church of St John the
Baptist
Preston-on-Stour, Glos. Church

**Sheehan, David**
Castle Lyons, Cork

**Sheridan, Clare**
Brede Place, Sussex

**Sidnell, Michael**
Bredon, Worcs. Church of St Giles

**Sievier, R. W.**
Stanton Harcourt, Oxon. Church of St
Michael

**Signell, Michael**
Yatton, Som. Church of St Mary

**Smith, Nathaniel**
London Somerset House

**Smyth, Edward**
Derry, Lond. Walker Monument
Dublin, Dublin Castle; City Hall;
Custom House; O'Connell Bridge
Navan, Meath

**Smyth, John**
Derry, Lond. Walker Monument
Dublin, Dublin Castle

**Soldani**
Glynde Place, Sussex

**Stanton, Edward**
Ampney Crucis, Glos. Church of the
Holy Rood
Aylesbury, Bucks. Church of St Mary
Belton, Kesteven, Lincs. Church of SS
Peter and Paul
Faringdon, Berks. Church of All Saints
Fawsley, Northants. Church of St
Mary
Knebworth, Herts. Church of SS Mary
and Thomas of Canterbury
Lichfield, Staffs. Cathedral
Madingley, Cambs. Church of St
Mary Magdalene
Strensham, Worcs. Church of St John
the Baptist

**Stanton, Thomas**
Stratford-upon-Avon, Warks. Church
of the Holy Trinity
Worcester, Worcs. Cathedral

**Stanton, William**
Acton Round, Shrops. Church
Belton, Kesteven, Lincs. Church of SS
Peter and Paul
Besford, Worcs. Church of St Peter
Blithfield, Staffs. Church of St
Leonard
Croome D'Abitot, Worcs. Church of
St Mary Magdalene
Fawsley, Northants. Church of St
Mary
Flamstead, Herts. Church of St
Leonard
Harefield, Greater London Church of
St Mary
Haslingfield, Cambs. Church of All
Saints
London Church of St Paul
Macclesfield, Cheshire Church of St
Michael
Quainton, Bucks. Church of the Holy
Cross and St Mary
Ravenstone, Bucks. Church of All
Saints
Toddington, Beds. Church of St
George
Wrexham, Denb. Church of St Giles

**Stayner, Thomas**
Church Stowe, Northants. Church of
SS Peter and Paul
Quainton, Bucks. Church of the Holy
Cross and St Mary

**Steer, Wilson**
Bury, Lancs. Art Gallery and Museum

**Stewart, Richard**
Dublin, Dublin Church of St
Werburgh

**Stone, John**
Hessett, Suffolk Church of St Ethelbert

**Stone, Nicholas**
Acton Burnell, Shrops. Church of St
Mary
Ampton, Suffolk Church of St Peter
Berkhamsted, Herts. Church of St
Peter
Bramfield, Suffolk Church of St Mary
Charlton, Greater London Church of
St Luke
Church Stowe, Northants. Church of
SS Peter and Paul
Coxwold, Yorks. Church of St
Michael
Enfield, Greater London Church of St
Andrew
Great Brington, Northants. Church of
St Mary
Greenwich, Greater London Chapel,
Trinity Hospital
Hatfield, Herts. Church of St
Etheldreda
Hawstead, Suffolk Church of All
Saints
Kirby Hall, Northants.

ondon Church of St Helen's
ortchester, Hants. Church of St Mary
ortsmouth, Hants. Cathedral
edgrave, Suffolk Church of St
  Botolph
anwell, Surrey Church of St Mary
ittleshall, Norfolk Church of St Mary
Vatford, Herts. Church of St Mary

**torrs, John**
ork, Cork

**aylor, Sir Robert**
olne, Lancs. Church of St
  Bartholomew

**enerani, Pietro**
arnworth, Lancs. Church of St Luke

**heed, W.**
ewcastle upon Tyne, Northld.
  Cathedral

**heed, William the Younger**
Manchester, Lancs. Cathedral
Vrenbury, Cheshire Church of St
  Margaret

**hom, James**
yr, Ayrs.

**homas, John Evan**
arew Cheriton, Pemb. Church
alifax, Yorks. Town Hall
eeds, Yorks. Town Hall
enby, Pemb. Church of St Mary

**hornycroft, Hamo**
arlisle, Cumb. Cathedral

**ravers, Martin**
ompton Beauchamp, Berks. Church of
  St Swithin

**riquetti, Baron**
Vindsor, Berks. Windsor Castle,
  St George's Chapel

**yler, William**
hellingford, Berks. Church of St
  Faith
Aersham, Kent Church of St John the
  Baptist
Oxford, Oxon. Cathedral

**an Gelder, P.**
Varkton, Northants. Church of St
  Edmund
Vrexham, Denb. Church of St Giles

**an Nost, John**
Curraughmore House, Waterford

**ierpyl, Simon**
Oublin, Dublin Casino Marino

**Watts, George Frederic**
Compton, Surrey Watts Gallery

**Webb, Philip**
Scarborough, Yorks. Church of St
  Martin

**Weeke, H.**
Christchurch, Hants. Priory Church

**Weekes, Henry**
Amersham, Bucks. Church of St Mary

**Westmacott, Henry**
Whitkirk, Yorks. Church of St Mary

**Westmacott, J. S.**
Aughton, Lancs. Church of St Michael

**Westmacott, Sir Richard**
Arreton, Isle of Wight, Hants. Church
  of St George
Bicester, Oxon. Church of St Edburg
Blithfield, Staffs. Church of St Leonard
Cuckfield, Sussex Church of the Holy
  Trinity
Knutsford, Cheshire Church of St John
  the Baptist
London Royal Exchange
Monmouth, Mon. Church of St Mary
Ruthin, Denb. Church of St Peter
Stratford-upon-Avon, Warks. Church
  of the Holy Trinity
Whalley, Lancs. Church of St Mary
Wollaton, Notts. Church of St
  Leonard
Yeovil, Som. Church of St John the
  Baptist

**White, Thomas**
Alrewas, Staffs. Church of All
  Saints

**Wilton, Joseph**
Bicester, Oxon. Church of St Edburg
Dartrey Mausoleum or Dawson's Grove,
  Monag.
Padworth, Berks. Church of St John
  the Baptist
Sowerby, Yorks. Church of St Peter

**Wood, Francis Derwent**
London Hyde Park Corner

**Wyatt, M. C.**
Windsor, Berks. Windsor Castle,
  St George's Chapel
Escrick, Yorks. Church of St Helen

**Wynne, Robert**
Ruabon, Denb. Church

**Zadkine**
Aberdeen, A'deen. Art Gallery

# STAINED GLASS MAKERS

The belief that God once walked on the earth in the flesh is the
germinating idea from which springs the glory of stained glass windows.
Listed here are the names of those who have tried to equal the
anonymous genius of the medieval stained glass makers. In churches and
cathedrals throughout Britain, Christ and the saints (and sometimes
lesser men, such as nobles or rich merchants) are portrayed in trans-
parent radiance. Until light penetrates them the colours remain dead,
and the windows are thereby themselves symbols of man and his
contact with the divine.

**Backler, Joseph**
Dudley, Worcs. Church of St Thomas
  the Apostle

**Burlison & Grylls**
Aylesbury, Bucks. Church of St
  Mary

**Burne-Jones, Sir Edward**
Hatfield, Herts. Church of St
  Etheldreda

Ribbesford, Worcs. Church of St
  Leonard
Rotherfield, Sussex Church of St
  Denys
St Germans, Cornwall Church of St
  Germanus
Topcliffe, Yorks. Church of St
  Columba
Waltham Holy Cross, Essex Abbey
  Church of the Holy Cross

**531**

*Youlgreave, Derbys.* Church of All
Saints

**Chagall, Marc**
*Tudeley, Kent* Church of All
Saints

**Childe, A. E.**
*Loughrea, Gal.*

**Clarke, Harry**
*Cork, Cork*
*Letterkenny, Don.*

**Clayton & Bell**
*Appleton-le-Moors, Yorks.* Christ
Church
*Kenton, Devon* Church of All Saints
*Kings Langley, Herts.* Church of All
Saints
*London* Church of St Augustine
*Nottingham, Notts.* Church of St Mary

**Clayton, John**
*Etchingham, Sussex* Church of SS
Mary and Nicholas

**Comper, Sir Ninian**
*East Markham, Notts.* Church of St
John the Baptist
*East Meon, Hants.* Church of All
Saints
*Egmanton, Notts.* Church of St
Mary
*Harrow, Greater London* Church of
St Mary
*Langham, Rutland* Church of SS
Peter and Paul
*Puddletown, Dorset* Church of St
Mary

**Easton, Hugh**
*London* Church of St Luke

**Eden, F. C.**
*Blisland, Cornwall* Church of SS
Protus and Hyacinth
*Mullion, Cornwall* Church of St
Melan

**Forsyth, Moira**
*Guildford, Surrey* Cathedral

**Hardman, John**
*Odiham, Hants.* Church of All Saints

**Healey, Michael**
*Clongowes, Kild.*
*Letterkenny, Don.*
*Loughrea, Gal.*
*Rahan, Offaly*

**Hone, Evie**
*Clongowes, Kild.*
*Dublin, Dublin* King's Hospital
*Loughrea, Gal.*
*Rahan, Offaly*
*Tara, Meath*

**Kelly, Oisin**
*Rahan, Offaly*

**Kempe, C. E.**
*Abingdon, Berks.* Church of St Helen
*Aldwinkle, Northants.* Church of St
Peter
*Alfriston, Sussex* Church of St
Andrew
*Barsham, Suffolk* Church of the Holy
Trinity
*Berkhamsted, Herts.* Church of St
Peter
*Caistor, Lincs.* Church of SS Peter
and Paul
*Charlcote, Warks.* Church of St
Leonard
*Cholsey, Berks.* Church of St Mary
*Cuckfield, Sussex* Church of the Holy
Trinity
*Eastnor, Herefs.* Church of St John the
Baptist
*Edlesborough, Bucks.* Church of St
Mary

*Froyle, Hants.* Church of the
Assumption
*Glynde, Sussex* Church of St Mary
the Virgin
*Kempsford, Glos.* Church of St Mary
the Virgin
*Ledbury, Herefs.* Church of St Michael
and All Angels
*Leighton Buzzard, Beds.* Church of
All Saints
*Leominster, Herts.* Church of SS Peter
and Paul
*Monmouth, Mon.* Church of St
Mary
*Much Marcle, Herefs.* Church of St
Bartholomew
*Norton, Durham* Church of St Mary
*Padworth, Berks.* Church of St John
the Baptist
*Thaxted, Essex* Church of St John the
Baptist
*Wightwick Manor, Staffs.*
*Wraxall, Som.* Church of All
Saints

**McGoldrick, Hubert**
*Loughrea, Gal.*

**Mayer & Co.**
*Leominster, Herts.* Church of SS Peter
and Paul

**Morris & Co.**
*Armathwaite, Cumb.* Chapel of Christ
and Mary
*Beaudesert, Warks.* Church of St
Nicholas
*Hatfield, Herts.* Church of St
Etheldreda

**Morris, William**
*Bromham, Wilts.* Church of St
Nicholas
*Nun Monkton, Yorks.* Church of St
Mary
*Rotherfield, Sussex* Church of St
Denys
*Rye, Sussex* Church of St
Mary
*Tamworth, Staffs.* Church of St
Editha

**Piper, John**
*Liverpool, Lancs.* Roman Catholic
Cathedral

**Pollen, Patrick**
*Strabane, Tyrone*

**Pugin, A. W.**
*Kilpeck, Herefs.* Church of SS Mary
and David

**Pursar, Sarah**
*Cork, Cork*
*Loughrea, Gal.*

**Reyntiens, Patrick**
*Liverpool, Lancs.* Roman Catholic
Cathedral

**Rutherford, Rosemary**
*Guildford, Surrey* Cathedral

**Scott, Sir Gilbert**
*Rotherham, Yorks.* Church of All
Saints

**Strachan, Douglas**
*Winchelsea, Sussex* Church of St
Thomas the Apostle

**Wailes, William**
*Bishops Cannings, Wilts.* Church of
St Mary the Virgin
*Bishopstone, Wilts.* Church of St
John the Baptist
*Swaffham, Norfolk* Church of SS
Peter and Paul

**Ward & Hughes**
*Edlesborough, Bucks.* Church of St
Mary

**532**

*Kings Langley, Herts.* Church of All
Saints
*Nottingham, Notts.* Church of St Mary

**Whall, Christopher**
*Brockhampton-by-Ross, Herefs.* Church
of All Saints

**Willement, Thomas**
*Aylesbury, Bucks.* Church of St
Mary
*Charlecote, Warks.* Church of St
Leonard
*Leicester, Leics.* Church of St
Margaret

# THINKERS, MEN OF LETTERS
# AND THE THEATRE

Britain's poets, playwrights and her sturdy political thinkers—Keats,
Shakespeare and Adam Smith—have enriched the world. But
England's most characteristic contribution to literature is perhaps the
novel; and her most characteristic literary figure is Dr Johnson,
massive in his commonsense—a quality that can be sensed at the
house he lived in, off Fleet Street.

**Addison, Joseph**
*Lichfield, Staffs.*
*Oxford, Oxon.* Magdalen College

**Alexander, Sir William**
*Menstrie Castle, Clack.*

**Ashmole, Elias**
*Oxford, Oxon.* Ashmolean Museum

**Austen, Jane**
*Chawton, Hants.* Jane Austen's Home
*Winchester, Hants.* City Museum

**Bacon, Francis**
*Gorhambury, Herts.*
*London* Gray's Inn
*St Albans, Herts.* Church of St
Michael

**Baillie, Lady**
*Mellerstain, Ber.*

**Barnes, William**
*Dorchester, Dorset* Dorset County
Museum

**Barrie, Sir James**
*Dumfries, Dumf.*
*Kirriemuir, Angus*
*London* British Theatre Museum;
Kensington Gardens

**Beckford, William**
*Bristol, Glos.* Church of St Mark

**Beerbohm Tree, Herbert**
*London* British Theatre Museum

**Berkeley, George**
*Cloyne, Cork*

**Blackmore, R. D.**
*Tiverton, Devon* Blundell's

**Bodley, Sir Thomas**
*Oxford, Oxon.* Bodleian Library

**Borrow, George**
*Llangollen, Denb.*

**Boswell, James**
*Edinburgh, M'loth.* James Court

**Brontë, Anne**
*Haworth, Yorks.* Brontë Parsonage
Museum

**Brontë, Charlotte**
*Birstall, Yorks.* Oakwell Hall
*Haworth, Yorks.* Brontë Parsonage
Museum
*North Lees Hall, Derbys.*

**Brontë, Emily Jane**
*Haworth, Yorks.* Brontë Parsonage
Museum

**Browning, Robert**
*London* Carlyle's House

**Bulwer Lytton,
Sir Edward**
*Knebworth House, Herts.*

**Bunyan, John**
*Ampthill, Beds.*
*Bedford, Beds.*
*Elstow, Beds.*

**Byron, Lord**
*Newstead Abbey, Notts.*
*Thrumpton Hall, Notts.*

**Camden, William**
*Hadrian's Wall, Cumb.–Northld.*

**Carlyle, Thomas**
*Ecclefechan, Dumf.*
*Kirkcaldy, Fife*
*London* Carlyle's House

**Carroll, Lewis (Dodgson,
Charles)**
*Guildford, Surrey* Museum and
Muniment Room

**Chaucer, Geoffrey**
*Berkhamsted, Herts.*
*Oxford, Oxon.* Merton College
Library

**Churchill, Sir Winston**
*Chartwell, Kent*
*Ditchley Park, Oxon.*
*Oldham, Lancs.* Art Gallery

**Clare, John**
*Peterborough, Hunts.* Museum and
Maxwell Art Gallery

**Coleridge, Samuel Taylor**
*Coleridge Cottage, Som.*
*Grasmere, Westmld.*
Dove Cottage

**Conan Doyle, Sir Arthur**
*Grimspound, Devon*

**Coote, Thomas**
*Bellamont Forest, Cavan*

**Cotton, Sir Robert**
*London* British Museum

**Cowper, William**
*Berkhamsted, Herts.*
*East Dereham, Norfolk* Church of St Nicholas
*Liverpool, Lancs.* Hornby Library

**Curwen, Henry**
*Amersham, Bucks.* Church of St Mary

**Dalton, John**
*Manchester, Lancs.* Portico Library

**Davidson, John**
*Kirkoswald, Ayrs.* Souter Johnnie's Cottage

**Defoe, Daniel**
*Lower Largo, Fife* Robinson Crusoe Statue

**Diaghilev**
*London* British Theatre Museum

**Dickens, Charles**
*Barnard Castle, Durham*
*Broadstairs, Kent* Bleak House
*Knebworth House, Herts.*
*London* Carlyle's House; Cuming Museum; Dickens House; George Inn; Staple Inn
*Portsmouth, Hants.*
*Rochester, Kent*
*Rockingham Castle, Northants.*
*St Albans, Herts.*
*Wisbech, Cambs.*

**Donne, John**
*London* Lincoln's Inn; St Paul's Cathedral

**Drummond, William**
*Hawthornden, M'loth.*

**Dryden, John**
*Cotterstock Hall, Northants.*

**Duff, William**
*Elgin, Moray.* No. 7 High Street

**Dunne, J. W.**
*Blair Castle, Perths.*

**Eliot, George**
*Nuneaton, Warks.* Museum and Art Gallery

**Evelyn, John**
*Dyrham Park, Glos.*

**Fielding, Henry**
*London* Church of St Benet

**Flight, Thomas**
*Worcester, Worcs.*

**Fonteyn, Margot**
*Northampton, Northants.* Central Museum and Art Gallery

**Galsworthy, John**
*Mapledurham House, Oxon.*

**Garrick, David**
*Hendon, Greater London* Hendon Hall
*Lichfield, Staffs.*
*Royal Tunbridge Wells, Kent*
*Smallthye Place (The Ellen Terry Memorial), Kent*
*Stratford-upon-Avon, Warks.*

**Gay, John**
*Barnstaple, Devon* St Anne's Chapel Museum

**Gibbon, Edward**
*Buriton, Hants.*

**Graham, Kenneth**
*Mapledurham House, Oxon.*

**Granville Barker, Harvey**
*London* British Theatre Museum

**Gray, Thomas**
*Stoke Poges, Bucks.* Gray's Monument

**Gregory, James**
*St Andrews, Fife.*

**Gresham, Sir Thomas**
*London* Church of St Helen

**Hardy, Thomas**
*Dorchester, Dorset* Dorset County Museum; Old Shire Hall
*Hardy's Cottage, Dorset*
*Waterson Manor, Dorset*

**Harford, John**
*Blaise Hamlet, Glos.*

**Harvard, John**
*Stratford-upon-Avon, Warks.* Harvard House

**Hawker, Robert**
*Morwenstow, Cornwall* Church of St Morwenna

**Hazlitt, William**
*Maidstone, Kent* Chillington Manor

**Hearst, William Randolph**
*Gilling Castle, Yorks.*
*St Donat's Castle, Glam.*

**Hill, Abraham**
*Sutton-at-Hone, Kent* St John's Jerusalem

**Hope, Anthony**
*Leatherhead, Surrey*

**Housman, A. E.**
*Much Wenlock, Shrops.*

**Hume, David**
*Edinburgh, M'loth.* James Court

**Hurd, Richard**
*Hartlebury Castle, Worcs.*

**Irving, Sir Henry**
*Bournemouth, Hants.* Russell-Cotes Museum and Art Gallery
*London* British Theatre Museum

**James, Henry**
*Rye, Sussex*

**Jefferies, Richard**
*Coate, Wilts.* Richard Jefferies Museum

**Jerome, Jerome K.**
*Walsall, Staffs.* E. M. Flint Art Gallery

**Johnson, Dr Samuel**
*Dunvegan, Isle of Skye, I'ness.*
*Edinburgh, M'loth.* James Court
*Lichfield, Staffs.*
*Liverpool, Lancs.* Hornby Library
*London* Johnson's House; Middle Temple Hall; Staple Inn
*Royal Tunbridge Wells, Kent*

**Jonson, Ben**
*Hawthornden, M'loth.*
*Penshurst Place, Kent*

**Joyce, James**
*Dublin, Dublin* Dunleary

**Keats, John**
*London* Guy's Hospital; Keats House

**Kingsley, Charles**
*Bideford, Devon*

**Kipling, Rudyard**
*Bateman's, Sussex*

**Knox, John**
*Edinburgh, M'loth.* John Knox's House
*Mid Calder, M'loth.*
*Perth, Perths.*

**Lamb, Charles**
*London* Middle Temple Hall

**Lyte, Sir Henry**
*Lytes Cary, Som.*

**Lytton, Lytton**
*Knebworth, Herts.* Church of SS Mary and Thomas of Canterbury

**534**

**Martyn, Edward**
*Tulira Castle, Gal.*

**Miller, Hugh**
*Cromarty, Ross.* Hugh Miller's
Cottage

**Milton, John**
*Chalfont St Giles, Bucks.* Milton's
Cottage

**Moore, George**
*Moore Hall, Mayo*

**O'Casey, Sean**
*Dublin, Dublin* Abbey Theatre

**Paine, Thomas**
*Thetford, Norfolk* Grey Gables

**Pearse, Patrick**
*St Endas, Dublin*

**Pepys, Samuel**
*Brampton, Hunts.* Pepys's House
*Dyrham Park, Glos.*
*Huntingdon, Hunts.*
*London* Church of St Bride

**Pope, Alexander**
*Spalding, Lincs.* Spalding Gentlemen's
Society

**Potter, Beatrix**
*Hill Top, Lancs.*

**Roget, Peter Mark**
*Manchester, Lancs.* Portico Library

**Ruskin, John**
*Kirkby Lonsdale, Westmld.* Church of
St Mary the Virgin
*Oxford, Oxon.* University Museum

**Sackville, Thomas**
*Knole, Kent*

**Sackville-West, Victoria**
*Sissinghurst Castle, Kent*

**Salisbury, William**
*Rug Chapel, Merioneth*

**Scott, John**
*Ware, Herts.*

**Scott, Sir Walter**
*Abbotsford House, Rox.*
*Burleigh Castle, Kinross*
*Caerlaverock Castle, Dumf.*
*Carlisle, Cumb.*
*Castleton, Derbys.*
*Craig Nethan Castle, Lanarks.*
*Dryburgh Abbey, Ber.*
*Dunvegan, Isle of Skye, I'ness.*
*Edinburgh, M'loth.* Old Tolbooth
*Finlarig Castle, Perths.*
*Gifford, E. Lothian* Yester House
*Inveraray Castle, Argyll*
*Isle of May, Firth of Forth*
Lighthouse
*Kenilworth, Warks.* Castle
*Knockderry Castle, Cumb.*
*Stamford, Lincs.* High Street
*Winton House, E. Lothian*

**Shakespeare, William**
*Cawdor Castle, Nairns.*
*Clopton House, Warks.*
*Gawsworth Hall, Cheshire*
*London* Crosby Hall; Gray's Inn;
Guildhall; Middle Temple Hall;
Public Record Office
*Stratford-upon-Avon, Warks.* Church
of the Holy Trinity; Guild Chapel;
New Place; Royal Shakespeare
Theatre Picture Gallery

**Shaw, George Bernard**
*Ayot St Lawrence, Herts.* Shaw's
Corner

**Shelley, P. B.**
*Christchurch, Hants.* Priory Church
*London* Kensington Gardens

**Sheridan, Richard Brinsley**
*Polesden Lacey, Surrey*

**Siddons, Mrs Sarah**
*London* British Theatre Museum
*Smallthye Place (The Ellen Terry
Memorial), Kent*

**Sidney, Sir Philip**
*Penshurst Place, Kent*

**Smith, Adam**
*Kirkcaldy, Fife.* Museum and Art
Gallery

**Southey, Robert**
*Crosthwaite, Cumb.* Church of St
Kentigern

**Spenser, Edmund**
*Alton, Hants.*
*Doneraile, Cork*
*Enniscorthy, Wex.*

**Stevenson, R. L.**
*Isle of May, Firth of Forth* Lighthouse

**Swift, Jonathan**
*Celbridge, Kild.*
*Dublin, Dublin* Cathedral of St Patrick
*Howth Castle, Dublin*
*Kilkenny, Kilk.*

**Tennyson, Alfred Lord**
*Lincoln, Lincs.* Usher Art Gallery
*London* Carlyle's House
*Somersby, Lincs.* Somersby
House
*Tintagel Castle, Cornwall*

**Terry, Dame Ellen**
*Smallthye Place (The Ellen Terry
Memorial), Kent*

**Thackeray, William Makepeace**
*Clevedon Court, Som.*
*London* Carlyle's House; Middle
Temple Hall

**Thomas, Dylan**
*Laugharne, Carm.*

**Trollope, Anthony**
*Banagher, Offaly*

**Ulanova**
*Northampton, Northants.* Central
Museum and Art Gallery

**Walpole, Horace**
*Shobdon, Herefs.* Church of St John
the Evangelist
*Twickenham, Greater London*
Strawberry Hill
*Wolterton Hall, Norfolk*

**Wells, H. G.**
*Midhurst, Sussex*

**Wesley, Charles**
*Epworth, Lincs.* Old Rectory

**Wilde, Oscar**
*Enniskillen, Ferm.*

**Williams, Alfred**
*Coate, Wilts.* Richard Jefferies
Museum

**Wordsworth, Dorothy**
*Cockermouth, Cumb.*

**Wordsworth, William**
*Cockermouth, Cumb.*
*Edinburgh, M'loth.* White Hart Inn
*Grasmere, Westmld.* Dove
Cottage
*Hawkshead, Lancs.*

**Wycliffe, John**
*Bristol, Glos.* Westbury College

**Yeats, W. B.**
*Dublin, Dublin* Abbey Theatre
*Drumcliff, Sligo*
*Gort, Gal.*
*Sligo, Sligo* St Stephen's Green

# HOW TO USE
# THE MAPS

Continuity flaps have been used in the map section t
allow routes to be followed from page to page withou
interruption and to enable places on the flap to be seen
in relation to areas to both east and west. Each map
overlapped by the maps covering the regions to the nort
and south. Arrows in the margin indicate the number
of the pages on which the map is continued.

In production the continuity flaps have been folded ove
each other in groups; to use the maps divide the page
and fold each flap separately.

A uniform grid has been superimposed on each map
and the simple two-letter reference code is linked to th
entries in the gazetteers of Britain and Ireland.

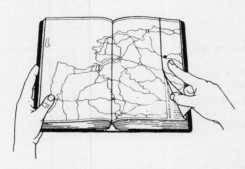

The continuity flaps provide
a link between adjacent maps. Close
the flap to see a point on it
in relation to the region to the west

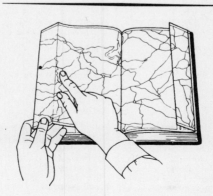

Open out the continuity flap
to see a place on it in relation to
the region to the east

# WHERE TO FIND THE TREASURES OF THE BRITISH ISLES

BASED ON ORDNANCE SURVEY

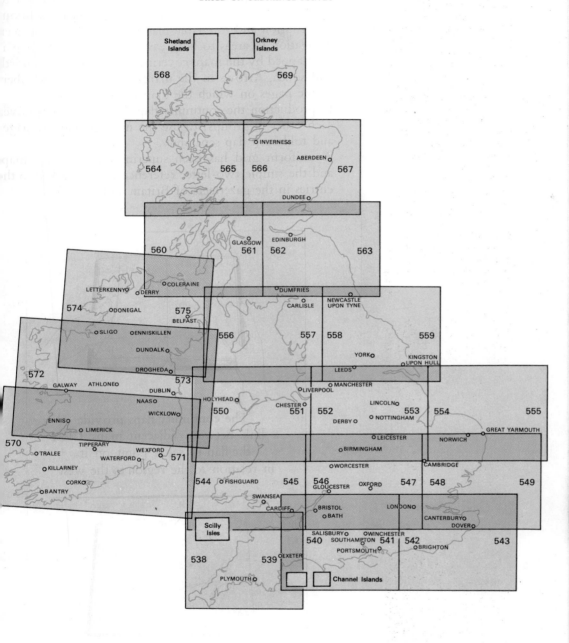

This incidence chart shows how the following 38 pages of maps, covering the whole of Britain and Ireland, have been arranged to maintain continuity and facilitate route-planning. The maps of England, Scotland and Wales are at a scale of 10 miles to 1 inch, which gives each full map spread a coverage of an area approximately 100 miles by 120 miles. The maps of Ireland are at a scale of 12.6 miles to 1 inch and cover an even greater area on each spread.

## SYMBOLS USED ON THE MAPS

### ROADS

MOTORWAY . . . . . . . . . . . .  M5

TRUNK OR 'A' ROAD . . . . . .  A4019

'B' ROAD . . . . . . . . . . . . . .

OTHER TARRED . . . . . . . . .

### BOUNDARIES

NATIONAL . . . . . . . . . . . . . —+—+—+

COUNTY . . . . . . . . . . . . . .

### SETTLEMENTS

TOWN . . . . . { READING
                Dorchester . . .

VILLAGE . . . . . . . . . . . . . . . . . Silchester o

### PHYSICAL FEATURES

LAKE . . . . . . . . . . . . . . . . . .

COASTLINE . . . . . . . . . . . . . . . .

### TREASURE SITES

CASTLE/HOUSE . . . . . . . . . .  ♟

GARDEN . . . . . . . . . . . . . . . . .  ✿

ECCLESIASTICAL
BUILDING . . . . . . . . . . . . . . . . .  ⛪

MUSEUM/ART GALLERY . . . . . . . . . . . . .  🏛

INDUSTRIAL MONUMENT . . . . . . . . . . .  ⊛

ARCHAEOLOGICAL SITE . . . . . . . . . . . .  ⁂

MONUMENT/MEMORIAL . . . . . . . . . . . .  ▮

OTHER NOTABLE
FEATURES . . . . . . . . . . . . . . . . . . . . .  ◆

TOWNS/VILLAGES OF ARCHITECTURAL
INTEREST *named in black* . . . . . . . . *Acton* o

537

The map shows part of Devon and Somerset with labels including:

Porthcawl, Tusker Rock, St Bride's Major, Cowbridge, Bonvilston, Wenvoe, Dinas Powis, CARDIFF, PENARTH, Beaupre, Wick, Llantwit Major, Rhoose, BARRY, St Donats Castle, Nash Pt, St Donats, Breaksea Pt, Flat Holm, Sand Pt, WESTON-SUPER-MARE, Steep Holme, Brean Down, Brean, Barrow Flats, BRISTOL CHANNEL, Lynton, Foreland Pt, Countisbury, Martinhoe, Brendon, Porlock, Allerford, Minehead, Watchet, BRIDGEWATER BAY, Stert Flats, Stockland Bristol, Burnham-on-Sea, Huntspill, Luccombe, Dunster, Timberscombe, Washford Abbey, Holford, Nether Stowey, Cannington, EXMOOR, Withycombe, Williton, Cleeve Abbey, Monksilver, Coleridge Cottage, Dodington Hall, Simonsbath, Exford, Luxborough, BRENDON HILLS, QUANTOCK HILLS, N Petherton, Withypool, Winsford, Exton, BRIDGWATER, Brayford, Brompton Regis, Brompton Ralph, Bishops Lydeard, Huish Champflower, Wiveliscombe, North Curry, N Molton, Molland, Dulverton, Morebath, Milverton, Norton Fitzwarren, Langford Budville, South Molton, Oakford, Cothay Manor, Wellington, TAUNTON, Hatch Beauchamp, Bampton, Holcombe Court, Corfe, Staple Fitzpaine, King's Nympton, Meshaw, Rackenford, Holcombe Rogus, Wellington Monument, Black Down Hills, Chulmleigh, Witheridge, Worlington, Sampford Peverell, Uffculme, Culmstock, Yarcombe, Combe St Nicholas, Chawleigh, Lapford, Morchard Bishop, Cheriton Fitzpaine, Bickleigh, Tiverton, Old Priest's House, Kentisbeare, Upottery, Stockland, Chardstock, Coldridge, Copplestone, Thorverton, Silverton, Cullompton, Bradninch, Broadhembury, Hembury, Crediton, Killerton Gardens, Broad Clyst, Talaton, Honiton, Axminster, Yeoford, Spreyton, Tedburn St Mary, Whitestone, A30, Rockbeare, Ottery St Mary, Sidbury, Colyton, Shute Barton, Seaton, Beer Hd, Dunsford, Chagford, Moretonhampstead Almshouses, Powderham Castle, EXETER, Topsham, Newton Poppleford, Otterton, Sidmouth, LYME BAY, Grimspound, Bovey Tracey, Kenton, A la Ronde, Bicton Gardens, Budleigh Salterton, Starcross, Chudleigh, Ideford, EXMOUTH, Dawlish, Bickington, Teignmouth, Ashburton, Newton Abbot, BABBACOMBE BAY, Kingskerswell, Kent's Cavern, TORQUAY, Buckfast Abbey, Buckfastleigh, Compton Castle, Oldway, Berry Pomeroy Castle, Totnes, PAIGNTON, TOR BAY, Harberton, Cornworthy, Berry Head, Dittisham, Brixham, Halwell, Royal Navy College, Kingswear, Dartmouth, Mew Stone, Stoke Fleming, Kingsbridge, Slapton, START BAY, Salcombe, Prawle Point, START POINT, Bolt Head

SIR FRANCIS DRAKE

## BUCCANEERS FOR THE QUEEN

Men of Devon were renowned among the sea-faring adventurers of the Elizabethan age. After the voyages of Columbus (1492) and Magellan (1520) had opened up new horizons, Spain and Portugal had the Pope's authority to divide any newly discovered lands between them. English sailors therefore had to find a north-west passage to the Orient or dispute the claims of Spain. With the support of Queen Elizabeth they took to the Spanish Seas.

**Sir John Hawkins,** born in Plymouth, sailed to West Africa, collected negroes and sold them in Hispaniola (San Domingo). A second trip was equally profitable (1564–5), but his third venture, in 1567, was disastrous: his convoy fell into the hands of a Spanish war fleet. Some of his men were tortured and killed; some were ransomed; others, including himself, escaped.

**Sir Francis Drake,** born near Tavistock, took part in Hawkins's misadventure of 1567. Intent on revenge and aware of the immense prizes to be won, he made several voyages to the West Indies. In 1577 Drake set sail for the Rio Plata, and in 1578 rounded Cape Horn. He sailed up the west coast of America, possibly getting as far north as Santa Barbara. Heading west across the Pacific, Drake began the long leg of the great circum-navigation that ended in Plymouth in 1581.

**Sir Walter Raleigh** was born near Budleigh Salterton and educated at Oriel College, Oxford. Raleigh voyaged to North America, and returned in 1586 with a far-reaching discovery—to-bacco. He attended Court for several years, but earned the queen's disfavour after a quarrel with her favourite Essex. James I was persuaded to let Raleigh undertake an expedition in search of gold, but the failure of this mission and an action against the Spanish settlement of San Tomas resulted in Raleigh being sent to the Tower—for the third time. After a summary trial, he was executed on October 29, 1618.

## SHIPSHAPE AND BRISTOL FASHION

For the seamen of Bristol trade was the motive for epic voyages, and their goal was to find the north-west passage to the fabulous East.

That was the lodestar for **John Cabot,** born Giovanni Caboto in Genoa, who settled in Bristol as a merchant. In 1497, he set sail in the *Matthew* and reached the Cape Breton Islands, but failed to find the north-west passage. His son Sebastian joined him on some of his voyages, but by 1512 had established a reputation as a cartographer, giving service in the art to Henry VIII. In 1519 **Sebastian Cabot** was made Pilot Major to Charles V, King of Spain. Returning to England in 1547, he promoted the Company of Merchant Venturers.

The activities of the Bristol seamen, whose skill gave to the English language the expression 'shipshape and Bristol fashion', fascinated **Richard Hakluyt,** descendent of a Leominster, Herefordshire, family.

In 1582 he published *Divers Voyages touching the Discovery of America,* enabling a wide circle of potential traders to familiarise themselves with North America. Hakluyt became Prebendary of Bristol in 1586, and evolved the theory that sea power meant trading ships, not warships and guns.

## TREASURE SITES

⚔ CASTLE/HOUSE
✿ GARDEN
🏛 ECCLESIASTICAL BUILDING
🏛 MUSEUM/ART GALLERY
⊕ INDUSTRIAL MONUMENT
❖ ARCHAEOLOGICAL SITE
❙ MONUMENT/MEMORIAL
◆ OTHER NOTABLE FEATURES
TOWNS/VILLAGES OF ARCHITECTURAL INTEREST *named in black*

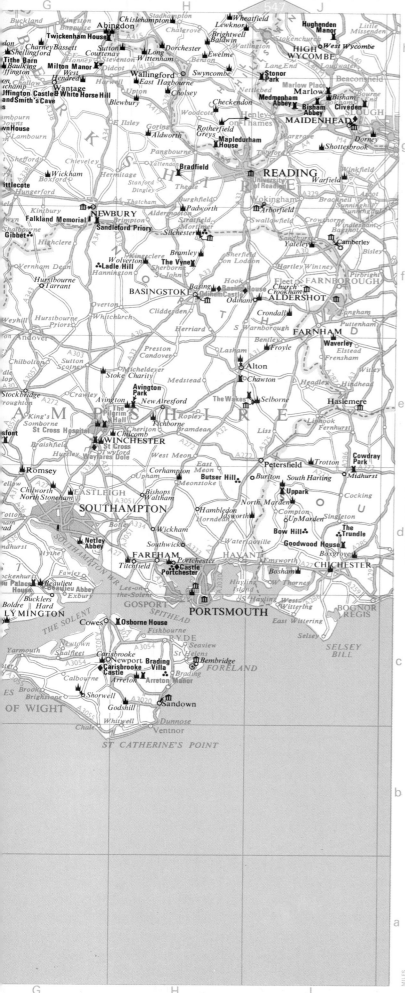

547

Buckland · Kingston Bagpuize · Chislehampton · Wheatfield · Lewknor · Hughenden Manor · Little Missenden · Stadhampton · Chatgrove · Brightwell Baldwin · Stokenchurch · West Wycombe · HIGH WYCOMBE · Loudwater · Abingdon · A415 · Charney Bassett · Sutton Courtenay · Long Wittenham · Dorchester · Benson · Ewelme · Lane End · Beaconsfield · Twickenham House · Steventon · Harwell · Didcot · Nettlebed · Marlow Place · Marlow · Bourne End · Tithe Barn · Milton Manor · West Hendred · Wallingford · East Hagbourne · Cholsey · Checkendon · Medmenham Abbey · Bisham Abbey · Cliveden · Ilffington Castle and Smith's Cave · Wantage · Blewbury · Woodcote · Rotherfield Greys · Henley-on-Thames · MAIDENHEAD · Dorney · Shottesbrook · wnHouse · Chieveley · Hermitage · Aldworth · Pangbourne · Yattendon · Mapledurham House · Wargrave · Winkfield · M4 · Wickham · Stanford Dingley · Bradfield · Theale · Burghfield · READING · Warfield · ittlecote · Hungerford · Thatcham · University of Reading · Wokingham · Bracknell · Sunninghill · Kintbury · BERKSHIRE · Shefford · E Ilsley · Gorings · Sunningdale · Falkland Memorial · NEWBURY · Aldermaston · Padworth · Arborfield · Swallowfield · Crowthorne · Bagshot · Shalbourne · Sandleford Priory · Brimpton · Stratfield Mortimer · Windlesham · Highclere · Silchester · Sherfield on Loddon · Yateley · Camberley · Bisley · Vernham Dean · Wolverton · Bramley · Hook · Fleet · Church Crookham · FARNBOROUGH · Pirbright · Hurstbourne Tarrant · Ladle Hill · The Vyne · Hartley Wintney · Weyhill · Hannington · Sherborne St John · Basing · Basing House · Odiham Castle · Odiham · ALDERSHOT · Overton · Whitchurch · BASINGSTOKE · Crondall · Tongham · Puttenham · Hurstbourne Priors · Cliddesden · Herriard · S Warnborough · FARNHAM · on Andover · Preston Candover · Bentley · Froyle · Waverley · Frensham · A303 · Chilbolton · Sutton Scotney · Micheldever · Stoke Charity · Lasham · Alton · Chawton · Medstead · Witley · Hindhead · Headley · Stockbridge · Crawley · HAMPSHIRE · Avington Park · Avington · New Alresford · The Wakes · Selborne · Haslemere · roughton · King's Somborne · The Pilgrim Hall · Tichborne · Ropley · Bramdean · Liss · Linhook · Fernhurst · Somborne · St Cross Hospital · Cheriton · Chilcomb · West Meon · Petersfield · Trotton · Cowdray Park · Braishfield · WINCHESTER · St Cross · Twyford · East Meon · South Harting · Midhurst · Romsey · Hursley · Wayfarers Dole · Corhampton · Meonstoke · Butser Hill · Buriton · Cocking · Chilworth · North Stoneham · Bishops Waltham · Upham · Uppark · Singleton · EASTLEIGH · A335 · Hambledon · Compton · Up Marden · SOUTHAMPTON · Botley · Wickham · Hornдean · Adsworth · Bow Hill · Goodwood House · The Trundle · Netley Abbey · Southwick · North Marden · Boxgrove · Waterlooville · CHICHESTER · FAREHAM · Titchfield · HAVANT · Emsworth · Bosham · Fawley · Portchester · Castle Portchester · Hayling Island · Thorney · Beaulieu · Hythe · GOSPORT · Lee-on-the-Solent · Hayling · West Wittering · Palace House · Bucklers Hard · LYMINGTON · THE SOLENT · Exbury · SPITHEAD · PORTSMOUTH · East Wittering · Boldre · Cowes · Osborne House · Fishbourne · RYDE · Selsey · SELSEY BILL · Yarmouth · Newtown · Shalfleet · Carisbrooke · Newport · Brading Villa · Seaview · St Helens · Bembridge · BOGNOR REGIS · Calbourne · Carisbrooke Castle · Arreton · Brading · Arreton Manor · FORELAND · OF WIGHT · Brook · Brighstone · Shorwell · A3020 · Godshill · Sandown · Whitwell · Dunnose · Chale · Ventnor · ST CATHERINE'S POINT

## SETTLEMENT OF A ROYAL SUCCESSION

During the Civil War, **Lucy Walter**, daughter of a Welsh Royalist, left England for the Hague where she became the mistress of the self-exiled **Charles II.** In 1649 she bore him a son, James. After the Restoration in 1660 Charles brought his son to England and made him **Duke of Monmouth.**

When the issue of the succession to the throne was raised, Charles supported his brother **James, Duke of**

DUKE OF MONMOUTH

**York,** affirmed that he had never married Lucy Walter and deprived the Duke of Monmouth of many of his posts. In 1683 a plot was hatched to assassinate Charles and the Duke of York, and though it is unlikely that Monmouth was involved he left England.

In 1685 Charles, who on his death-bed became a Roman Catholic, was succeeded by his brother James, also a Catholic. James's two daughters, Mary and Anne, were Protestants.

Knowing James's religion to be unpopular, Monmouth tried to dethrone him. With 82 followers, he landed at Lyme Regis on June 11, 1685, and issued a manifesto branding James as a Popish usurper and claiming his own legitimacy and right to the throne.

But when Monmouth marched north towards Bristol, a force of about 3000 was all he could muster. By the time he reached Taunton on June 20, where he was proclaimed king, his followers numbered 7000, but James's army barred the way to Bristol.

At Sedgemoor, north-east of Taunton, Monmouth made an ill-organised attack against the Royalists and was defeated. He was captured in the New Forest a few days later, and executed in the Tower of London on July 15, 1685.

Those who had rebelled with Monmouth were savagely punished by **Judge Jeffreys,** chief judge at the 'Bloody Assizes' in the West Country. About 300 rebels were drawn and quartered, 850 mercilessly whipped and 1000 transported to the West Indies. One of the court-rooms was at the rear of the Antelope Hotel, Dorchester, and Jeffreys stayed at a house (now a restaurant) in High West Street.

JUDGE JEFFREYS

James's policy of 'romanising' the country led to the hope that he would soon be succeeded by his Protestant daughter Mary who had married the Protestant **William of Orange** in 1677. However, a son, James Francis Edward Stuart, was born to the king in 1688 and became a Roman Catholic heir to the throne. As James II increased his tyranny, William was secretly invited to displace him. He landed at Brixham, Devon, in November 1688. James fled to France, leaving the way open for William.

Before accepting the Crown, William demanded that the throne should subsequently go to the issue of

WILLIAM AND MARY

his wife, **Mary of Orange,** the daughter of James II, and then to her sister Anne and her issue. William and Mary were crowned in April, 1689. Mary died in 1694, William in 1702, and **Queen Anne** reigned from 1702 to 1714.

---

## TREASURE SITES

| | | | |
|---|---|---|---|
| ♜ | CASTLE/HOUSE | ⊕ | INDUSTRIAL MONUMENT |
| ❀ | GARDEN | ♣ | ARCHAEOLOGICAL SITE |
| ⛪ | ECCLESIASTICAL BUILDING | ▮ | MONUMENT/MEMORIAL |
| 🏛 | MUSEUM/ART GALLERY | ◆ | OTHER NOTABLE FEATURES |

TOWNS/VILLAGES OF ARCHITECTURAL INTEREST *named in black*

G　　　　H　　　　J

h — 100

g — 90

MARGATE
North Foreland Lighthouse
*NORTH FORELAND*
Bleak House
Broadstairs
A255
RAMSGATE

Richborough

Sandwich

*Goodwin Sands*

Deal Castle
DEAL

80

f

Walmer
Castle *THE DOWNS*

St. Margaret's
at Cliffe

*SOUTH FORELAND*
Dover Lighthouse
VER

70

e

60

d

50

40

c

30

b

20

a

10
9
8
7
6
5
4
3
2
1
0

MILES

SCALE: ABOUT 10 MILES TO 1 INCH (1:625,000)

# CANTERBURY TALES: PRIESTS AND POETS

**Thomas à Becket** was not the first playboy to become a prelate in the 12th century. **Rahere,** Henry I's court jester, became a prebendary of St Paul's *c.* 1115 and later built the priory hospital of St Bartholomew in Smithfield, London, parts of which still stand.

RAHERE

Becket, Archbishop of Canterbury from 1162 to 1170, had studied in France and Italy as a young man and was a close companion of the worldly prince who became **Henry II.** When Becket assumed the responsibility and austerity of his high office at Canterbury his feud with the king ended in his death: in 1170 he refused the king's command to diminish the Church's privileges and Henry's expressed anger led four knights to murder Becket in the sanctuary of the cathedral.

Henry did solemn penance, being flogged by monks at Canterbury in 1174.

THOMAS À BECKET

Becket's shrine became a place of pilgrimage. Many pilgrims came by sea to Southampton, then on to Winchester, through Hampshire to the hills south of Guildford, and eastwards along the north of the Weald to Maidstone and Canterbury. Becket's shrine was broken up in 1538 during Henry VIII's Dissolution of the monasteries.

Though this put an end to the pilgrimage, an account of it survives in the works of **Geoffrey Chaucer,** who made the journey in 1386. Chaucer, son of a London vintner, had acquired an extensive knowledge of Italy, France and Flanders before becoming a customs official in London in 1382. He held several official posts before his death and burial in Westminster Abbey.

In his most famous work, *The Canterbury Tales,* 29 pilgrims assemble at the Tabard Inn in Southwark, London; to relieve the tedium of the journey to Canterbury each tells a story. In these tales, Chaucer drew extensively on his own experiences in England and abroad and recounted many well-known legends.

GEOFFREY CHAUCER

A worthy successor of Chaucer's, **Christopher Marlowe,** the Elizabethan playwright, was also connected with Canterbury. The son of a local shoemaker, he was educated at King's School (attached to the cathedral), and went to Corpus Christi, Cambridge.

*Tamburlaine,* written in 1587, was followed by *Dr Faustus, The Jew of Malta* and others. His plays influenced Shakespeare. Marlowe died after a drunken brawl in a Deptford tavern in 1593.

CHRISTOPHER MARLOWE

## TREASURE SITES

- ♜ CASTLE/HOUSE
- ✿ GARDEN
- ⛪ ECCLESIASTICAL BUILDING
- 🏛 MUSEUM/ART GALLERY
- ⊕ INDUSTRIAL MONUMENT
- ♣ ARCHAEOLOGICAL SITE
- ⌁ MONUMENT/MEMORIAL
- ◆ OTHER NOTABLE FEATURES

TOWNS/VILLAGES OF ARCHITECTURAL INTEREST *named in black*

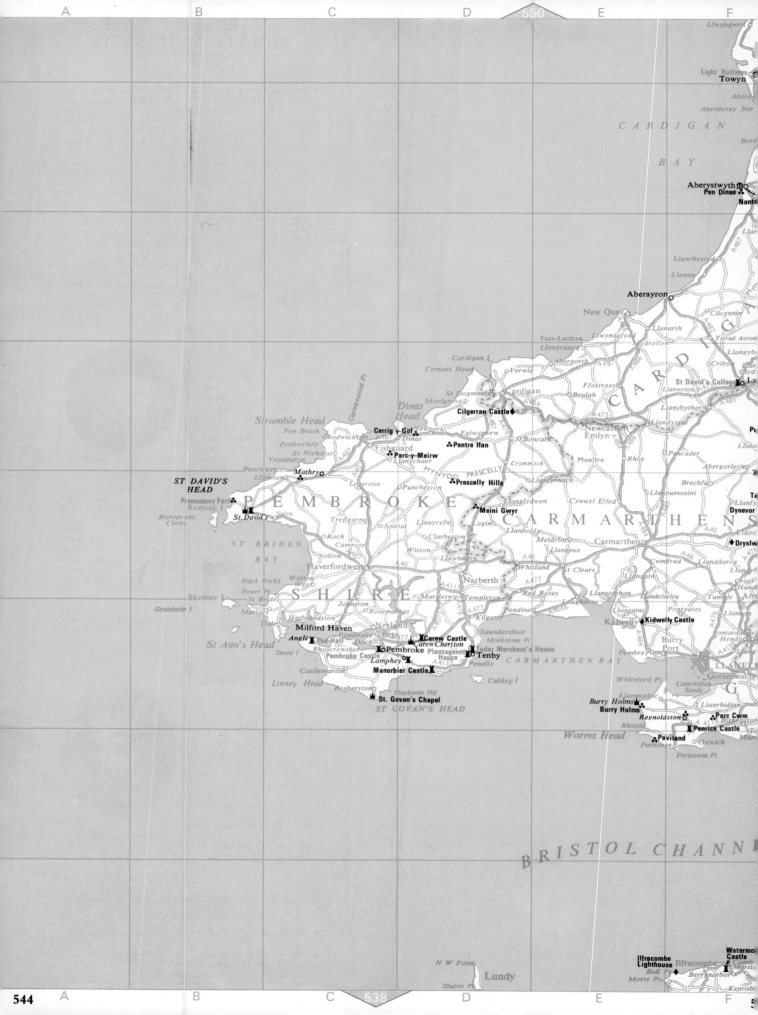

A       B       C       550       D       E       F

Llwyngwril

Light Railway
Towyn

Aberdo

Aberdovey Bar

C A R D I G A N

B A Y                                                     Bort

Aberystwyth🏛️
Pen Dinas⚲                                                Nante

Llar

Llanrhystyd

Llanon                        Llar

Aberayron○                    Cilcennin

New Quay○        Llanarth
Ynys-Lochtyn        Llwyndafydd   ydroilyn     Ystrad Aeron
Llangranog        Aberporth                    Llangyb

Cardigan I.                                    Cribyr    Llar
Cemaes Head        Verwig                                Clyd
St Dogmaels    Cardigan        Ffostrasol
Moylgrove                                      St David's College🏛️   La
Dinas                        Beulah                      Llanwenog
Head        Cilgerran Castle◆                            Llanybyther

Strumble Head                                 A 475    Llandyssul
Pen Brush    Carrewastlad Pt    Newport     Eglwyswrw      Newcastle
Cerrig-y-Gof⚲          Dinas    A 487              Emlyn    Llans
Goodwick                        Boncath
Penbwchdy        Fishguard    Pentre Ifan⚲              Moefre   Rhos    Pencader    Abergorlech   Ta
St Nicholas        Parc-y-Meirw⚲                Crymmych                              Llanfy
Ynysdeullyn    Llanychaer                                                Brechfa
Penclegyr                MYNYDD  PRESCELLY                              Llanpumsaint          Dynevor
Mathry○                    Prescelly Hills⚲    Llanfyrnach              Cynwyl Elfed   A 40
ST DAVID'S    Llanriant    Letterston   Puncheston                              Carmarthen    Drysl◆
HEAD                                Llanglydwen
Promontory Fort⚲            Spittal    Llanycefn    Meini Gwyr⚲              C A R M A R T H E N S
Ramsey I.        St.David's⚲    Roch    Clarbeston    Login      Llanboidy              A 40    Llanc
Bishops and        Salva    Camrose              Meidrim    Llanyrin              Llanddarog   Llandyt
Clerks        ST BRIDES        Wiston    Llawhaden    Whitland   St Clears   Cwmfrwd              Cros
BAY        Nolton                                                        Llansaint    Llandefaelog   Hand
Stack Rocks    Walton    Haverfordwest    A 40              Red Roses    Laugharne        Tumble   Am
Tower Pt        West                    Narberth        Pendine    A 4066              Pontyates   Llanne
Skomer I.    St Brides        Johnston        Martletwy    Templeton              Llansaint      Kidwelly    Kidwelly Castle◆
Grassholm I.        Marloes        Rosemarket    A 478    Kilgetty    Saundersfoot        Burry    Llanm
Dale                    Neyland              Monkstone Pt              Port
Herbrandston                        Carew Castle⚔    Tudor Merchant's House        Pembrey   LLANEL
Milford Haven⚔        Carew Cheriton◆              Penally   C A R M A R T H E N   B A Y              Gorseinon   G
Angle⚔    The Hall    Dock    Plantagenet        Tenby○⚔                        Whiteford Pt    Llanrhidian
St Ann's Head    Rhoscrowther    Pembroke⚔House   House                        Burry Holms⚲   Sands   Llanrhidian
Sheep I.    Pembroke Castle⚔    Lamphey◆    Penally                                Burry Holms⚲   Parc Cwm⚲
Castlemartin                Manorbier Castle⚔    Caldey I.                        Reynoldston   Penrice Castle⚔
Linney Head                                                        Rhossili        Oxwich
Bosherston    Stackpole Hd        Caldey I.              Worms Head        Paviland⚲
St Govan's Chapel⚲    Stackpole Hd                                        Porteynon   Oxwich   Mum
ST GOVAN'S HEAD                                                Porteynon Pt

B R I S T O L   C H A N N E

Ilfracombe        Waterma
N W Point    Lundy    Ilfracombe    Lighthouse    Ilfracombe    Castle
Bull Pt                        Comb
Morte Pt◆        Berrynarbor
Shutter Pt        Kentisb

544       A       B       C       538       D       E       F

# GLAMORGAN'S MEN OF IRON

Present-day mining in the coal and iron valleys of Glamorganshire, which now musters nearly half the total population of Wales and Monmouthshire, dates from the Industrial Revolution.

Foremost on the scene was **Anthony Bacon,** who between 1765 and 1784 developed Cyfarthfa. He arrived by mule at Merthyr Tydfil in 1763 and two years later acquired 4000 acres of the great mineral tract at Cyfarthfa for only £100 a year rent.

Bacon retired a rich man in 1784, to give pride of place as the greatest of all the Iron Kings to **Richard Crawshay** (1741–1810) founder of a dynasty. Crawshay came from Normanton, Yorkshire, learned his trade in London, and having won the then large sum of £1500 in a lottery used it to buy Cyfarthfa.

By 1803 the Crawshay works were turning out 70 tons of bar iron a week.

Meanwhile, **Richard Trevithick** (1771–1833) had been experimenting in Cornwall with steam locomotives. Hearing of these efforts, Samuel Homfray, another Iron King, bet Richard Crawshay £1000 that he could convey a load of iron by steam power from his works at Penydarren to the navigation canal 9 miles away—and he called on Trevithick to help him win his bet.

On February 22, 1804, Trevithick was ready for the first trial of his High Pressure Steam Tram. The course was the tram-way through Thomas Town, and Trevithick's unnatural monster conveyed not only the stipulated 10 tons of iron of the bet but 70 people as well —at 5 mph.

# A FAMILY ON THE BOARDS

While the Iron Kings were laying the basis for Welsh industry, one family—the Kembles—were laying the foundations of the modern theatre.

**Roger Kemble** (1721–1802) was one of the first actor-managers. He married Sarah Ward of Birmingham in 1753, and their first child, also called Sarah, was born

ROGER KEMBLE

in Brecon. Kemble ran a travelling company, in which all his children acted, and on one of their tours his daughter met William Siddons whom she married in 1773, when she was 18.

Appearing in a play at Cheltenham with her husband, **Sarah Siddons** attracted much attention, and was promptly engaged by David Garrick to play at Drury Lane. She failed to make much impression but on a return visit, after appearances at Manchester and Bath, she was launched on a spectacular career. She was painted by Sir Joshua Reynolds, and, though she was buried in Paddington churchyard in 1831, there is a statue of her by Sir Francis Chantrey in Westminster Abbey.

**John Philip Kemble** (1757–1823) displayed a remarkable virtuosity in his career; during his engagement at Drury Lane (1783–1802) he played more than 120 characters from Shakespeare's dramas. He was manager of the New Covent Garden Theatre and a friend of Sir Walter Scott.

**Charles Kemble** (1775–1854) made many stage appearances abroad; at his best in comedy, he was said to have a greater range than any other actor except Garrick.

**Stephen Kemble** (1758–1822) the least successful of the family, first appeared on the stage in Dublin. Later he took over the theatre in Edinburgh, but it failed financially.

---

## TREASURE SITES

| | | | |
|---|---|---|---|
| ⚔ | CASTLE/HOUSE | ⊛ | INDUSTRIAL MONUMENT |
| ❋ | GARDEN | ⚒ | ARCHAEOLOGICAL SITE |
| ⛪ | ECCLESIASTICAL BUILDING | ▮ | MONUMENT/MEMORIAL |
| ⛫ | MUSEUM/ART GALLERY | ◆ | OTHER NOTABLE FEATURES |

TOWNS/VILLAGES OF ARCHITECTURAL INTEREST *named in black*

SCALE ABOUT 10 MILES TO 1 INCH (1:625,000)

553

# PILGRIM'S PROGRESS, ADMIRAL'S FALL

A bronze statue at the north end of Bedford High Street commemorates a man whose career reached its peak when he was in prison—**John Bunyan,** author of *The Pilgrim's Progress*.

The son of a tinker and grandson of a brewer, he was born on the outskirts of Bedford and at 16 was conscripted in Cromwell's army and stationed at nearby Newport Pagnell. Two years later, a civilian again, he fell prey to religious remorse—black moments in which he saw his innocent pleasures of bell-ringing and dancing as heinous sins.

His sense of personal sin increased when his first child, a daughter, was born blind. Bunyan joined a Nonconformist church in 1653, and his first book, *Some Gospel Truths Opened,* appeared in 1656, the year his wife died leaving him four children. He then devoted himself more and more to studying the Bible, not the 1611 Authorised Version, but the earlier work of 1560 favoured by the Puritans.

JOHN BUNYAN

In November 1660 he was charged with 'holding a conventicle' (preaching without licence) and imprisoned in Bedford. He remained in prison for 12 years, during which time he wrote nine books, producing in 1672 a confession of his faith.

With the Declaration of Indulgence by Charles II later that year he was released and became a pastor of the Bedford church where his preaching had earlier caused trouble. When the Declaration was annulled, he was once more imprisoned, during which time he wrote the first part of *The Pilgrim's Progress from this world to that which is to come.*

By 1685 ten editions had been published and the work has since been translated into 108 languages and dialects. Three years later Bunyan died of a fever on Snow Hill, Holborn, and was buried in Bunhill Fields.

In Bedford Road at Elstow, Bunyan's Cottage is on the site of his former home; throughout the Bedford area there are places which are claimed to be the originals of such places as The Delectable Mountains in *The Pilgrim's Progress*.

THOMAS TOMPION

At Northill, a few miles from Bunyan's birthplace, **Thomas Tompion** made his name as the 'father of English watch-making'. He devised the first English watch with a balance spring and made clocks for the Royal Observatory, precision barometers and sundials. The clock he made for the Pump Room at Bath is still working over 250 years later.

At nearby Southill, **Admiral Byng** lies buried in the family mausoleum in the parish church. Byng survives as the inspiration of a French tag. An admiral in the Royal Navy in 1756, he was dispatched to prevent the French fleet from taking the island of Minorca, but was easily defeated. Recalled to face a court-martial at Portsmouth, he was found guilty of neglect of duty. He was shot on March 14, 1757.

ADMIRAL BYNG

Voltaire immortalised him by observing that in England it was necessary from time to time to shoot an admiral *pour encourager les autres*— 'to encourage the others'.

## TREASURE SITES

| | | | |
|---|---|---|---|
| ⚔ | CASTLE/HOUSE | ⊕ | INDUSTRIAL MONUMENT |
| ❀ | GARDEN | ⚲ | ARCHAEOLOGICAL SITE |
| ♜ | ECCLESIASTICAL BUILDING | ⚑ | MONUMENT/MEMORIAL |
| ⛪ | MUSEUM/ART GALLERY | ◆ | OTHER NOTABLE FEATURES |

TOWNS/VILLAGES OF ARCHITECTURAL INTEREST *named in black*

SCALE ABOUT 10 MILES TO 1 INCH (1:625,000)

7

TREASURE SITES

⚔ CASTLE/HOUSE     ⊕ INDUSTRIAL MONUMENT
✿ GARDEN     ✦ ARCHAEOLOGICAL SITE
▣ ECCLESIASTICAL BUILDING     ▮ MONUMENT/MEMORIAL
🏛 MUSEUM/ART GALLERY     ◆ OTHER NOTABLE FEATURES

TOWNS/VILLAGES OF ARCHITECTURAL INTEREST *named in black*

SCALE ABOUT 10 MILES TO 1 INCH (1:625,000)

548

# THE KIT-CAT CLUB: FACES FROM THE PAST

At the National Portrait Gallery in Trafalgar Square, London, are the portraits of some 3000 eminent Britons. Space is short and only a third of the portraits can be hung at any one time; but, given notice, gallery officials can produce any picture in the collection.

The gallery has bought or been given many collections, but none matches the extraordinary slice of history captured on canvas in what is known as the Kit-Cat Collection.

The object of the Kit-Cat Club was to bring together men of position, wit and social graces who were interested in Whig politics and literature. It included among its members eight dukes, 13 earls, two viscounts, three barons and three knights.

**Charles Seymour**, 6th Duke of Somerset, who lived from 1662 to 1748 and was a prominent Whig and supporter of the Hanoverian succession, probably founded the club, though **Jacob Tonson** (1656-1736), a publisher, was its first secretary and may well have been the real founder. Members met near his offices at Temple Bar at the house of Christopher Cat, pastry cook, whose mutton pies were known as kit-cats.

The original meetings at the tavern were succeeded by get-togethers at Tonson's house at Barn Elms, near Putney, or in summer months at the Flask Inn, Hampstead. The club probably broke up c. 1720-2; certainly in 1725 Sir John Vanbrugh wrote to regret that the happy meetings had stopped.

The portraits of club members were painted mainly between 1702 and 1717 by **Sir Godfrey Kneller**, Tonson's near-neighbour at Whitton, near Twickenham. Kneller painted 42 of them to a standard size of 28 in. by 36 in., so that the complete collection could be accommodated in the club-room at Tonson's house. The pose—a three-quarter figure, showing at least one hand—has become known as a kit-cat.

Among the members whose portraits appear in the Kit-Cat Collection are:

**Richard Temple** (1669-1749) 1st Viscount Cobham, who built the Palladian mansion at Stowe.

**John Montague** (1690-1749) 2nd Duke of Montague, Fellow of the Royal Society and Fellow of the Royal College of Physicians, Grand Master of the Grand Lodge of English Freemasons, patron of the arts.

**Spencer Compton** (1674-1743) Earl of Wilmington, Speaker of the House of Commons, 1715-27.

**John Vaughan** (1639-1713) 3rd Earl of Carbery, President of the Royal Society, 1686-9, patron of the poet Dryden.

**Charles Montague** (1661-1715) 1st Earl of Halifax, responsible for the Act which set up the Bank of England, President of the Royal Society, 1695-8, patron of Addison, Congreve and Prior.

**John Somers** (1651-1716) Baron Somers, President of the Royal Society, 1699-1703, patron of historical scholarship, art connoisseur, expert in English and continental law.

**William Congreve** (1670-1729) dramatist and pet of fashionable society.

**Sir Richard Steele** (1672-1729), an Irishman who edited the *London Gazette*, 1707-10; also connected with *The Tatler* and *The Spectator*.

**Sir Samuel Garth** (1661-1719) Fellow of the College of Physicians, Physician-General to the army, Physician-in-Ordinary to George I, friend of Dryden and Pope.

**Edmund Dunch** (1657-1719) descendant of Oliver Cromwell, Master of the Royal Household under Queen Anne and George I.

**Charles Sackville** (1638-1706) 6th Earl of Dorset, patron of Wycherley and Dryden, and the first protector of Nell Gwyn.

**Charles Dartiquenave** (1664-1737) epicure and wit, the most famous *bon vivant* of his time.

**Lionel Sackville** (1688-1765) 1st Duke of Dorset, considered the perfect English courtier.

**Charles Mohun** (1675-1712) one of Marlborough's generals, a notorious rake and duellist; twice tried for murder before he was 24, Mohun was killed in a duel with the Duke of Hamilton, who was also killed (as described in Thackeray's novel *Henry Esmond*).

**Thomas Wharton** (1648-1715) 1st Marquess of Wharton, rake and free-thinker who wrote the words of Purcell's famous song 'Lilliburlero'.

**Charles Lennox** (1672-1723) 1st Duke of Richmond and Lennox, son of Charles II and Louise de Kérouaille (Duchess of Portsmouth), Lord of the Bedchamber to George I.

JAMES I

Newmarket's prominence as a horse-racing centre began when **James I**, 'the wisest fool in Christendom', built a hunting lodge there, called the King's House, so that he could watch the racing on Newmarket Heath.

**Charles II** also went racing at Newmarket. He began the custom of awarding commemorative bowls or cups, each worth about 100 guineas. (William III later initiated the custom of awarding plates.)

Charles II's devotion to racing nearly led to disaster. With his brother James, Duke of York, and a party of friends he went to Newmarket in March, 1683. At Rye House, Broxbourne, Hertfordshire, followers of the Earl of Shaftesbury plotted to seize the royal brothers as they returned to London, with the intention of proclaiming the Duke of Monmouth king. But on March 22, during a race meeting, a fire which nearly destroyed Newmarket caused the royal party to depart hastily. The plot was foiled, and though it is doubtful whether they were implicated, Lord William Russell and Algernon Sidney were charged with treason and executed.

Formal racing, similar to today's, was introduced at Newmarket by Charles II in 1667. The Jockey Club, the ruling body of flat-racing, has been established there since 1750. Important races run at Newmarket include two of the 'Classics', the 2000 and 1000 guineas, and the 'Autumn Double', the Cesarewitch and the Cambridgeshire.

CHARLES SEYMOUR

SIR GODFREY KNELLER

WILLIAM CONGREVE

LIONEL SACKVILLE

## LONDON'S OLDEST THEATRES

English drama was at first inextricably bound up with religion. The first theatre licence was granted in 1574, and Shakespeare began his acting career in either the Theatre or the Curtain, both at Shoreditch, two or three years later. Some of his own plays were first presented at the Globe, a thatched-roof theatre, destroyed by fire in June, 1613.

The modern theatre owes a great deal to **James Burbage** (d. 1597) and his son Richard (1567-1619). James, a joiner, erected the Theatre in Finsbury Fields in 1576 and in 1596 acquired a house in South London, which he adapted as the Blackfriars Theatre. By 1588 **Richard Burbage** was an actor of repute who, having inherited his father's interest in the Blackfriars and Globe theatres, staged and acted in many contemporary plays. Another

DRURY LANE THEATRE

actor-manager of that time, **Edward Alleyn** (1566-1626), founded Dulwich College in 1619.

New theatres opened by licence granted by Elizabeth I were all closed by Parliament in 1642-60, but they re-opened with the Restoration, and in 1666 Nell Gwyn was starring at Drury Lane. The theatre was burnt down in 1672, rebuilt three times, partly destroyed by fire in 1809 and rebuilt again.

Covent Garden Theatre, now the Royal Opera House, which was opened in 1732, has a similar history: it has burnt down twice; and Her Majesty's Theatre in the Haymarket, originally the Italian Opera House, was totally destroyed twice, went bankrupt once, and was demolished in 1892-3 to make way for the present building.

CHARLES II

In Newmarket itself are Nell Gwyn's House and beside it Gwyn Cottage, reminders of Nell Gwyn's visits to the town with Charles II. They are amongst the few houses to survive two fires in 1683 and 1700. From selling oranges in Drury Lane **Nell Gwyn** (1651-87) became famous as a comedy actress. As Charles II's mistress she was a great favourite with the public, and it is said that her influence induced the king to found the Chelsea Hospital. She bore him two sons and is believed to have been faithful to Charles II, even rejecting suitors after his death.

The Skerries
Carmel Head
Point Lynas
Cemaes Bay
Amlwch

A5025
Llanfaethlu
Moelfre
Din Lligwy

South Stack Lighthouse
Holyhead
Caer Gybi
Trefignath
Bodedern
Llanerchymedd
Benllech

Penrhyn Mawr
Holy I.
ANGLESEY
A5
Talwrn
Penmon Priory
Hafotty
Penrhyn O
Gloddaeth
Conway Castle
Aberconwy
Plas Mawr
Conw

Rhoscolyn
Gwalchmai
Llangefni
A5025
Llangoed
Beaumaris Castle
Penmaenmawr

Rhosneigr
Llanfaelog
Menai Bridge
Beaumaris
Penrhyn Castle
Bangor
Llanfairfechar
Gilfach Garden

Aberffraw
Bryn Celli Ddu
Vaynol Old Hall
Marquess of
Anglesey's Column
Bryn Yr Hen Bobl
Llandegai
Cochwillan
Bethesda
Dolgarrog
Eglwy

Newborough
Bryn Siencyn
Port Dinorwic
Caernarvon Castle
Deiniolen
Llan
Gwydir Uchaf Chap
Gwydir

The Bar
Caernarvon
Segontium
Llanberis
Capel Curig
Betws-y-C

Rhostryfan
Hafodty
Capel C
Fedw Deg

Llandwrog
Glynllifon
Rhostryfan
Dolwyddelan
Dolwyddelan Castle

Llanllyfni
Talysarn
CAERNARVONSHI
Penmac

Bachwen
Clynnog-fawr
Beddgelert
Blaenau-Ffestinio

Trwyn y Gorlech
Tre'r Ceiri
Yr Eifl
Llanaelhaearn
A498
Ffestiniog Railway
Ffestinio

Carreg Ddu
Llithfaen
Ffynnon Gybi
Ynys y Pandy
Garreg
Tomen-y-M

Edern
Nefyn
Penarth Fawr
Tremadoc
Maentwrog

Garn Bodfean
Bodfuan
Chwilog
Criccieth
Portmadoc
Penrhyndeudraeth
Portmeirion

Tudweiliog
Dinas
Lleyn Peninsu
A497

Penrhyn Mawr
Sarn Meillteyrn
Pwllheli
Talsarnau
Trawsfynydd
Glyn Cywarch

Bodwrddan
Rhiw
Capel Newydd
Llanbedrog
Harlech Castle
Harlech
Rhinog Fawr

Aberdaron
Plas-yn-Rhiw
Llanengan
Abersoch
Llanbedr
Y Llethr

St Tudwal's Islands
MERIONET

Bardsey I.
Trwyn Cilan
Dyffryn Ardudwy
Carneddau Hengwm
Llanelltyd
Bont Newy

Llanaber
Barmouth
Dolgellau

The Bar
Fairbourne
CADER IDRIS

Llwyngwril
Castell-y-Bere
Llanfihangel y-pennant
Aberllef

Llanegryn
Abergynolwyn
Lle

Light Railway
Towyn
Machynlleth
Pennal

Aberdovey
Aberdovey Bar
Ysgubor-y-coe

Borth
Talybont
Elerch

Aberystwyth
Pen Dinas
Goginan
Dev

Nanteos
A44

Llanilar
Crosswood

Llanfihan
Lledrod
Ysbyty Ystwy

Map region (Blackpool, Liverpool, Wrexham, Shrewsbury, North Wales area with treasure site markers)

# LAND OF THE RED DRAGON

For nearly 600 years after William the Conqueror claimed Wales and made an invasion sortie in 1081, Welshmen fought for their independence. In Wales Britons had resisted domination by Romans, Saxons and Danes; now the running battle was against domination from London.

In 1114, Henry I began to build great Norman-style castles to contain the Welsh. When **Edward I** came to the throne he demanded the people's allegiance. **Llewelyn ap Griffith** (or Gruffydd), Prince of Wales, repeatedly refused the king's summons to Westminster. He was declared deposed and Wales was invaded in 1277.

In 1282 Llewelyn, with his brother David, took Hawarden and Rhuddlan castles. English forces closed in and Llewelyn was killed after the battle near Aberedw, and shortly afterwards David was executed. In March, 1284, the Statute of Wales was enacted at Rhuddlan, in effect appropriating nearly all Wales.

A month later Edward's

EDWARD II

queen, Eleanor of Castile, gave birth to a son at Caernarvon Castle, and the king informed the Welsh chiefs that this boy would be their future prince. Edward Plantagenet, Prince of Wales and Earl of Chester, succeeded to the throne in 1307 as **Edward II.**

After years of sporadic uprisings, **Owen Glendower** led the great rebellion of 1400. With aid from France, Glendower's forces took Carmarthen, Caerleon, Harlech, and besieged Caernarvon (1401). He continued to ravage English-held lands until he disappeared in 1415.

North Wales was again the scene of fierce fighting in 1645-9 when Cromwell's forces took castle after castle.

# ORIGIN OF MAN

Today, more than 100 years after **Charles Darwin** published *Origin of Species,* there is still controversy about its theories. To Victorians who believed in a literal interpretation of the Genesis, Darwin's theory of evolution was heresy.

CHARLES DARWIN

Darwin's statue is set in the gardens of the museum and library at Shrewsbury, the town where he was born and educated. He went to Edinburgh and Cambridge universities. In 1831 he set out in the *Beagle* on a scientific expedition to South

America and it was observations made in the Galapagos Islands that first suggested the theory of evolution to him. While secretary to the Geographical Society he published *The Zoology of the Voyage of the Beagle* in 1840.

In 1844, despite ill health, he set down his theory of the evolution of Man, but did not publish it, perhaps because he knew it would arouse controversy and opposition from theologians.

In 1858 another naturalist, Dr A. R. Wallace, sent Darwin a manuscript outlining a theory almost identical with his own. A joint paper was published (read before the Linnaen Society) on July 1, 1858, in which their theory of evolution was first given to the world, but Wallace acknowledged Darwin's prior claim to having originated the theory.

Darwin went on to write numerous works on plants and insects. He died in 1882.

## TREASURE SITES

| | | | |
|---|---|---|---|
| ♜ | CASTLE/HOUSE | ⊕ | INDUSTRIAL MONUMENT |
| ✿ | GARDEN | ⚶ | ARCHAEOLOGICAL SITE |
| ♜ | ECCLESIASTICAL BUILDING | ⌑ | MONUMENT/MEMORIAL |
| ⛪ | MUSEUM/ART GALLERY | ◆ | OTHER NOTABLE FEATURES |

TOWNS/VILLAGES OF ARCHITECTURAL INTEREST *named in black*

# MIDLANDERS AT HOME AND ABROAD

Izaak Walton, Thomas Cook and the Marquess of Curzon, born within 30 miles of each other in the Midlands, distinguished themselves in very different fields.

IZAAK WALTON

**Izaak Walton** was born in Stafford in 1593 and later moved to London where in 1614 he had an ironmonger's business in Fleet Street. He wrote verses in his spare time but his first literary work of note was an essay on the life of John Donne.

The work for which he became famous—*The Compleat Angler, or the Contemplative. Man's Recreation*—took 40 years to compile. Walton, who did not consider himself an expert fisherman, drew on the experience of amateurs all over Britain for the material in it. *The Compleat Angler* was published in 1653 and for the 5th edition in 1676 the original 13 chapters were expanded to 21, which included a treatise on fly-fishing by Charles Cotton of Beresford Hall, Staffordshire. Walton died at Winchester, and is buried in the cathedral there.

THOMAS COOK

**Thomas Cook,** pioneer of the travel agency business, was born at Melbourne, Derbyshire, in 1808, and in his early years was a gardener, wood turner, printer, lay reader and champion of the Baptist faith. He became a total abstainer, and in 1841 persuaded the Midland Counties Railway to let him organise a round trip to a temperance rally in Lough-borough for 570 people from Leicester. This, costing 1s. a head, was his first publicly-advertised excursion.

'Mr Cook's Voyages' caught on, and in 1856 he conducted his first foreign tour from Harwich to the Rhine, and back via Paris. The business moved to London in 1865, organising tours to the U.S.A. in 1866 and to Palestine in 1869.

A branch office was opened in Cairo in 1873 and, with government contracts for the Egyptian and Sudan campaigns, and the organisation of Moslem pilgrims from India to Mecca and Medina, the original local service became world-wide.

Thomas Cook died at Leicester in 1892.

**George Nathaniel Curzon** was born at Kedleston Hall, Derbyshire, in 1859, eldest of the 11 children of the 4th Lord Scarsdale. Educated at Eton and Balliol College, Oxford, at 27 he

GEORGE NATHANIEL CURZON

became M.P. for Southport which he represented until 1898. He had travelled in the East between 1887 and 1892, and his book *Problems of the Far East* appeared in 1894.

In 1899 he became Viceroy of India. He was at first greatly popular but, after clashes with Lord Kitchener, his influence in India waned and his relations with Whitehall grew bitter.

He returned home in 1905, became Chancellor of Oxford University in 1907 and entered the House of Lords in 1908. In 1916 he was appointed Lord President of the Council, and was a brilliant Foreign Secretary (1919–24), being created Marquess in 1921.

When Bonar Law retired in 1923, Curzon expected to become Prime Minister. Stanley Baldwin was chosen instead and Curzon retired from public life in 1924.

## TREASURE SITES

- ⚔ CASTLE/HOUSE
- ✿ GARDEN
- ⛪ ECCLESIASTICAL BUILDING
- 🏛 MUSEUM/ART GALLERY
- ⊛ INDUSTRIAL MONUMENT
- ⚘ ARCHAEOLOGICAL SITE
- ⌾ MONUMENT/MEMORIAL
- ◆ OTHER NOTABLE FEATURES

TOWNS/VILLAGES OF ARCHITECTURAL INTEREST *named in black*

## TREASURE SITES

- ⚜ CASTLE/HOUSE
- ✿ GARDEN
- ♜ ECCLESIASTICAL BUILDING
- 🏛 MUSEUM/ART GALLERY
- ✾ INDUSTRIAL MONUMENT
- ♣ ARCHAEOLOGICAL SITE
- ▌ MONUMENT/MEMORIAL
- ◆ OTHER NOTABLE FEATURES

TOWNS/VILLAGES OF ARCHITECTURAL INTEREST *named in black*

SCALE ABOUT 10 MILES TO 1 INCH (1:625,000)

MILES

Sutton on Sea

Huttoft

Chapel
St Leonards

Ingoldmells
Addlethorpe

A158

Croft     Skegness

Long Sands

Holme
next the Sea     Brancaster
Burnham     **Holkham Camp**
Hunstanton     Norton     **Holkham Hall**     *Blakeney*     *Cley-next-the-Sea*     Sheringham
Ringstead     Wells-     **Warham**     **Glandford**     Cromer
next-the-Sea     **St Mary**     **Sheringham Hall**     Overstrand
Heacham     North     **Warham**     *Binham Priory*     *Felbrigg*     Trimingham
Sedgeford     Creake     Camp     Binham     Holt
Snettisham     Docking     **Little**     North     Roughton     Mundesley
Great     South     Walsingham     Barningham     **Thorpe Market**     Bacton
Dersingham     Bircham     Creake     *Great Snoring*     Matlask     **Trunch**
Sculthorpe     Melton     Erpingham     **Gunton**     Happisburgh
Wolferton     Sandringham     **East Barsham**     Constable     **Wolterton Hall**     North
**Sandringham House**     Harpley     **Manor**     Fakenham     Saxthorpe     Walsham     Honing     Sea Palling
Breast     E &     Great     Hindolveston     **Blickling Hall**     Worstead     **Waxham Hall**
Sand     **Castle Rising**     W Rudham     Ryburgh     *Aylsham*     Stalham
Hillington     **Raynham Hall**     E Raynham     Guist     Sall     Smallburgh     Barton     Hickling     Horsey
Terrington     Great     **Wellingham**     Whissonsett     Foulsham     Reepham     Buxton     **Turf**     Ludham     Winterton-on-Sea
St Clement     Massingham     Grimston     Weasenham     **Tittleshall**     Bawdeswell     Cawston     Coltishall     Potter     Martham     Ormesby
**KING'S LYNN**     Gayton     North Elmham     **Alderford**     Wroxham     **Ludham**     **St Margaret**
A17     Litcham     Swanton     Morley     **Elsing**     Attlebridge     Horsham     **St Benet's**     Caister
Walpole     **North Runcton**     Middleton     **Beeston**     Lyng     St Faith     **Abbey**     **Castle**     **Caister-on-Sea**
St Peter     **Castle**     **East**     Ranworth     Filby     Caister-on-
Wiggenhall     **Acre**     **Dereham**     Costessey     Sprowston     Acle     Sea
St Mary     **West Acre**     Wendling     Honingham     **NORWICH**
the Virgin     **Wiggenhall St German**     **Priory**     Necton     Bawburgh     Blofield     Halvergate     Burgh     **GREAT**
Marshland     **Wiggenhall St Mary**     Shouldham     Shipdham     Barnham     **YARMOUTH**
**Wallington**     **Magdalene**     **Swaffham**     Broom     Hethersett     Castle
Outwell     Fincham     Ashill     Hingham     Newton     **Burgh Castle**
**Oxburgh Hall**     Cockley     **Great Cressingham Priory**     Flotman     Reedham     Fritton
Downham     Cley     Watton     **Cavick House**     Hales     Loddon     Belton
Market     Oxborough     Hilborough     **Wymondham**     Swardeston     Ferry     Loundn     Hopton
Stoke Ferry     Caston     Brooke     **Somerleyton**     Blundeston
Hilgay     Northwold     **Breckles Hall**     Ashwellthorpe     **Hall**     Corton
Welney     Methwold     **Attleborough**     Tacolneston     Newton     Haddiscoe
Southery     Tottington     Flotman     **Worlingham**     **LOWESTOFT**
Mundford     Long Stratton     Hempnall     **Hall**
Downham     E Wretham     New Buckenham     Pulham     **Bungay**     **Beccles**
Littleport     Feltwell     **Grime's Graves**     Kenninghall     A140     Barsham     Mutford
Hockwold     **East**     Harleston     Kessingland
Brandon     cum Wilton     **Harling**     Rumburgh
Beck Row     Lakenheath     A1066     Dickleburgh     Metfield     Wrentham
**The Chantry**     Elveden     **Thetford**     Garboldisham     Diss     Scole     Harleston     Halesworth
**Ely**     Southery     Barnham     Barningham     **Redgrave**     Hoxne     **Wingfield**     **Fressingfield**     **Wenhaston**     Wangford
**The King's School**     A11     Botesdale     **Wattisfield**     Mellis     Stradbroke     **Blythburgh**     **Southwold**
Isleham     Icklingham     Ampton     Bardwell     Stanton     Eye     Walberswick
**Stretham**     Soham     Mildenhall     Ingham     **Ixworth Roman**     Walsham le     **Thorpe**     Horham     **Heveningham**     **Bramfield**
Wicken     Fordham     Tuddenham     Ixworth     **Camp**     Willows     **Hall**     Laxfield     Dunwich

NORFOLK     SUFFOLK

554     548     556

Somewhere close to the R. Nene's outfall canal in Lincolnshire, just over the Norfolk border, a treasure beyond reckoning has been buried since it disappeared before its frantic owner's eyes on a misty October day in 1216.

Medieval England possessed both a State Treasury and an Exchequer, but the king had his own personal treasure as well. Much of this was, for safety, kept in widely separated abbeys, but a considerable amount always went with the king on his travels.

The Court was constantly on the move, with a baggage train of heavy carts that could travel at only about 2 miles an hour. The king would often leave the train to visit one of his caches while the train went on by the shortest route.

Thus in late September, 1216, **King John** (1167-1216) having been fêted and feasted at King's Lynn, decided to go to Swineshead via Wisbech and

KING JOHN

Spalding while his baggage train moved ponderously over an estuary separating Cross Keys—7 miles west of King's Lynn—from Long Sutton, about 4½ miles away.

The wagons could cross only when the tide was out, and they were partly across when the tide came swirling in and barred retreat. The wagon loaded

with the treasure was trapped in quicksands, and from the Lincolnshire bank John watched it slowly disappear.

Everything he valued most was lost in a matter of minutes. John was a noted connoisseur of jewellery and gems, and with this private collection went all his regalia, his ornamented plate, dozens of gold and silver flagons and goblets, candelabra, combs, clasps, crosses, charms, bracelets, rings and ornaments, the coronation robes and regalia, and the great crown, the golden wand, the golden dove and the bejewelled Sword of Tristram, all of which had belonged to his grandmother as Empress of Germany. Nothing has ever been recovered from the waters of the Wash.

At King's Lynn John had contracted dysentery. He died at Newark, having directed that his body be buried in Worcester Cathedral.

## REBELS AND REFORMERS

THOMAS PAINE

MRS ELIZABETH FRY

GEORGE BORROW

John's treasure had been in the Wash more than 330 years when **Robert Kett** won a brief moment of fame as the first of Norfolk's reformers. Kett's birth date is not known, but the year and manner of his death are still recalled by a tree called Kett's Oak at Ryston, 3 miles from Wymondham.

Edward Seymour, 1st Duke of Somerset, had been appointed Protector of England and had introduced an agrarian policy so unpopular that peasants throughout England rose against it.

In July 1549, Kett, the son of a Wymondham tanner, led one of the most serious uprisings. The Norfolk peasants particularly resented the fact that rich landlords used common land for grazing their sheep, and from a camp at Mousehold Heath, at the gates of Norwich, Kett led 16,000 men in a blockade of the city and slaughtered 20,000 sheep. The rising was put down by the Earl of Warwick and Kett was executed in December.

**Thomas Paine** (1737-1809), one of the fathers of socialism, was another Norfolk rebel. He was born at Thetford, where his house still stands.

The son of a staymaker and farmer, Paine became an excise officer but at the age of 35 was dismissed for agitating for more pay. He went to America

where in 1776 he published *Common Sense*, a work on the causes of the American War of Independence which brought him a number of official appointments.

He returned to England in 1787 and between 1790 and 1792 published *The Rights of Man*. This revolutionary work advocated social services such as provision for the aged poor, maternity and funeral grants, and the limitation of armaments by treaty.

It sold well over a million copies in England alone, but aroused such feeling among the authorities that Paine prudently fled to France where he was elected a member of the Convention, the French House of Representatives. He incurred further odium in England with *The Age of Reason* (1793) and not a little trouble in France. He returned to America in 1802 and died in New York.

**Mrs Elizabeth Fry** (1780-1845), a Quaker and preacher, was born in Norwich. At the age of 17, in the attic of her home, she taught the poor children of Earlham. The class soon numbered 60 and gained the nickname of 'Betsy's imps'. Earlham House is now part of the University of East Anglia.

She advocated prison improve-

ment, better conditions for convicts transported to Australia, and welfare services for the vagrants of London and Brighton. In 1817 she formed an association for safeguarding the interests of women in Newgate prison. Her extensive travels on the Continent lead to prison improvements there as well.

**George Borrow** (1803-81) traveller, linguist and author, was born the son of a recruiting officer at Dumpling Green, just south of East Dereham. He was educated at Edinburgh High School and then worked for a short time in a Norwich solicitor's office. He travelled extensively on the Continent, in Russia and the East, and eventually published in St Petersburg a work called *Targum* which contained translations from 30 languages. He became a traveller for the Bible Society in Russia and Spain and took a special interest in gypsies. In 1843 his *The Bible in Spain*, recounting his adventures as a salesman there, was an instant success and made his reputation. There followed *Lavengro* (1851), *The Romany Rye* (1857) and *Wild Wales* (1862). In 1840 he married and settled at Oulton Broad, Suffolk, dying there in 1881. The house in which he lived in Willow Lane, Norwich, can still be seen.

JOHN CROME

The 19th-century fashion for countryside paintings such as those done by John Constable in Essex led a group of painters to try to do the same thing for Norfolk. John Crome (1768-1821) is regarded as the founder of the Norwich School, but Robert Ladbrooke (1768-1842) who worked with him, was largely responsible for establishing the Norwich Society of Artists in 1803.

**John Crome,** who first exhibited at the Royal Academy in 1806, is noted for his tree paintings. A tree standing at the village of Poringland is said to be the original of the oak in his painting at the National Gallery, London, which also shows how Crome was influenced by the Dutch landscape painters—he particularly admired the work of Hobbema and Ruysdale. His son, John Bernay Crome, followed his father and also became a painter of the Norwich School.

**Robert Ladbrooke** exhibited landscapes at the Royal Academy between 1804 and 1815. His second son, Henry (1800-70) built a reputation for painting moonlight scenes, and his third son John (1803-79)—a pupil of Crome whose style he followed—exhibited at the Royal Academy, the British Institution and the Suffolk Street Gallery up to 1873.

**John Sell Cotman** (1782-1842), another painter of the Norwich School, specialised in water-colours, and interpreted landscapes as a series of flattened planes. After exhibiting in London from 1800 to 1806 he set up as a drawing master in Norwich in 1807 and from 1834 to 1842 was art master at King's College, London. He etched numerous plates of buildings and antiquities in Norfolk from 1811 to 1839. His eldest son, Miles Edmund Cotman, painted oils and water-colours of river and sea views. His other son, Joseph John Cotman, was a drawing master in Norwich in 1836 but became mentally deranged.

**James Stark's** most notable work is *Scenery of Rivers of Norfolk*, completed in 1834. **Joseph Stannard** exhibited with the Norwich Society between 1811 and 1816, and at the Royal Academy and British Institution between 1820 and 1829. **Henry Bright**, a water-colourist, exhibited at the Royal Academy between 1845 and 1850, and was elected a member of the Institute of Painters in Watercolours.

Cotman House is in St Martin-at-Palace Plain, Norwich, and works by all members of the Norwich Society can be seen in the art gallery section of the Norman castle in Norwich's city centre.

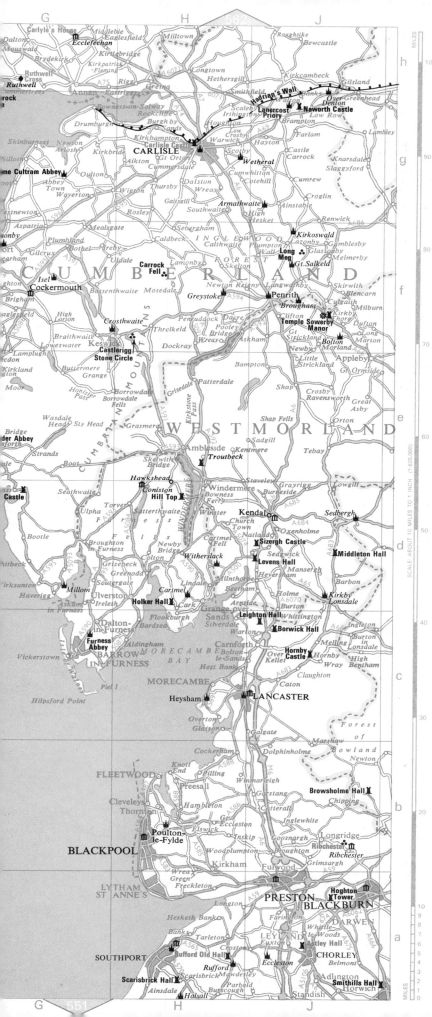

# LAKELAND'S ROMANTIC BROTHERHOOD

Romanticism dominated literature during the late 18th and early 19th centuries, and the landscapes of the Lake District were a source of inspiration to the romantic poets.

Foremost among the writers and poets who worked there was **William Wordsworth**, whose childhood in Westmorland is described in his poem 'The Prelude'. Born at Cockermouth he went to school at Hawkshead.

WILLIAM WORDSWORTH

In 1798 he wrote 'Lines Written above Tintern Abbey' and in the next year settled at Dove Cottage, Grasmere, with his sister and constant companion, Dorothy (1771–1855).

Fourteen years later he was given the office of Distributor of Stamps for Westmorland and moved to Rydal Mount, Grasmere. In 1843 he succeeded Robert Southey as Poet Laureate. He is buried in St Oswald's churchyard, Grasmere.

**Samuel Taylor Coleridge,** the son of a vicar at Ottery St Mary, Devon, met Robert Southey in 1793 at Jesus College, Cambridge, and two years later married Sarah Fricker, whose sister became Southey's wife in the same year.

The Coleridges lived with Wordsworth for a year at Nether Stowey and Alfoxden, in Somerset. Coleridge wrote 'Kubla Khan' in 1797, after waking from an opium-induced sleep, and 'The Ancient Mariner' a year later. He spent from 1800 to 1804 at Keswick, with the Wordsworths. Coleridge was not only an outstanding poet: his *Biographia Literaria* and lectures on Shakespeare are critical masterpieces.

**Robert Southey** was the son of a Bristol linen draper, and though expelled from Westminster School he went in 1792 to Balliol College, Oxford. He travelled to Portugal and Spain before settling in Keswick in 1807.

ROBERT SOUTHEY

In 1813 he published his *Life of Nelson* and was appointed Poet Laureate. His next major work was the *Life of Wesley,* published in 1820. He is buried in Crosthwaite churchyard.

# HUNTING COUNTRY

For 50 years **John Peel** hunted a pack of hounds from his native village of Caldbeck (Cumberland), where he was buried in 1854. His life-long friend, **John Graves,** wrote impromptu the song 'D'ye ken John Peel', noting that Peel's 'View halloo' would awaken the dead—as well as stir up the foxes. The melody is borrowed from an old air called 'Bonnie Annie'.

**Robert Surtees,** born in the village of Hamsterley, was a popular sporting writer who created the remarkable character of Jorrocks, the hunting hero of *Handley Cross,* published in 1843. He defined hunting as 'war without its guilt and only five-and-twenty per cent of its danger'.

ROBERT SURTEES

## TREASURE SITES

| | | | |
|---|---|---|---|
| ♟ | CASTLE/HOUSE | ⊕ | INDUSTRIAL MONUMENT |
| ♣ | GARDEN | ▲ | ARCHAEOLOGICAL SITE |
| ▲ | ECCLESIASTICAL BUILDING | ⚑ | MONUMENT/MEMORIAL |
| 🏛 | MUSEUM/ART GALLERY | ◆ | OTHER NOTABLE FEATURES |

TOWNS/VILLAGES OF ARCHITECTURAL INTEREST *named in black*

## Map labels (left side)

an Signal Station
orough Castle
RBOROUGH

Filey
Reighton
Burton
Fleming
Bempton
FLAMBOROUGH
HEAD
ynton Hall
Boyton
Flamborough
BRIDLINGTON
Burton Agnes
es Hall
Barmston
erton
ield
Skipsea
Beeford
N Frodingham
Atwick
Brandesburton
Hornsea
Sigglesthorne
wen
Withernwick
Lons
Riston
S Skirlaugh
Aldbrough
Garton
Burton Constable
Swine
Sproatley
Burton
Pidsea
Tunstall
Roos
Preston
Hedon
Halsham
Withernsea
KINGSTON
UPON HULL
Hollym
New Holland
Goxhill Priory
Ottringham
Patrington
Welwick
Easington
Halton
Thornton Abbey
Thornton
Curtis
Sunk
Island
Kilnsea
Immingham
Habrough
Keelby
GRIMSBY    SPUR HEAD

SCALE ABOUT 10 MILES TO 1 INCH (1:625,000)

# JARROW'S DARK AGE SCHOLAR

In the Saxon parish church of Jarrow, Newcastle-upon-Tyne, there is a chair used more than 1200 years ago by Bede, a monk who long after his death became known as the **Venerable Bede.**

Most of Bede's adult life was spent in Jarrow Abbey where, at a time when the ignorance of the Dark Ages held sway throughout Europe, he taught Latin, Greek and Hebrew. His major work, *Historia Ecclesiastica Gentis Anglorum*, a historical commentary on the Roman occupation of Britain and the succeeding years, interwoven with religious studies and arguments, was finished in 731.

Bede also wrote a treatise, unique in his time, called *De Natura Rerum*, in which he set out the extent of contemporary scientific knowledge. His fame spread to

VENERABLE BEDE

Europe and his works were published in both Paris and Basle, Switzerland, in the mid-16th century.

# CAPTAIN COURAGEOUS

One of the great navigators of history, **James Cook** was the son of a labourer at Marton in Cleveland, Yorkshire. Apprenticed at 12 to a haberdasher, he ran away to sea, first in the Baltic trade and then in the Royal Navy (1755).

Cook's interest in navigation began during General Woolfe's capture of Quebec when his ship took soundings in the St Lawrence R. Having surveyed the Newfoundland coast in 1762, he was made marine surveyor of Newfoundland and Labrador a year later.

JAMES COOK

His observations of a solar eclipse at Cape Ray led the Royal Society to invite him to join an expedition to observe the transit of Venus. He was commissioned lieutenant, and in 1768 sailed in *Endeavour* (370 tons), reaching Tahiti via Cape Horn in April, 1769. He then circumnavigated New Zealand in six months (discovering what is now called Cook

Strait) before probing New Guinea and Indonesia.

In 1771, he was promoted captain and put in charge of a second expedition, led by *Resolution* (460 tons) and escorted by a smaller ship, *Adventure*.

Cook sailed from Plymouth in July, 1772, to Madeira and then via the Cape of Good Hope, in search of a suspected Great Southern Continent. He crossed the Antarctic circle on January 16, 1773, wintering in the Society Islands, which he named in honour of the Royal Society.

In 1774 he probed far south, but failed to find land. He returned to Plymouth in 1775, proud that his new rules on hygiene and diet had saved his crew from fever and scurvy.

His next task was to search for the supposed North West Passage linking the north Atlantic with the north Pacific. He sailed from Britain for the Cape of Good Hope in July, 1776, discovered the Sandwich Islands in 1778, and headed for the American coast, probing northwards until baulked by a wall of ice. He charted the north and west coasts of America, and then turned for Hawaii, which he reached in 1779.

In a dispute with natives over ownership of a boat from his ships he was killed at Kealakekua Bay.

## TREASURE SITES

| | |
|---|---|
| ♜ CASTLE/HOUSE | ⊛ INDUSTRIAL MONUMENT |
| ✾ GARDEN | ⁂ ARCHAEOLOGICAL SITE |
| ⛪ ECCLESIASTICAL BUILDING | ⚑ MONUMENT/MEMORIAL |
| 🏛 MUSEUM/ART GALLERY | ◆ OTHER NOTABLE FEATURES |

TOWNS/VILLAGES OF ARCHITECTURAL INTEREST *named in black*

# SCOTTISH MEN OF VISION

Both Scottish and Victorian virtues found expression in men like David Livingstone, Keir Hardie and John Logie Baird. Each prized education, often hard-won, each fought determinedly for the cause he believed in, and each, except Baird, died having fallen short of the goal he glimpsed.

As a youth **David Livingstone** worked in a Glasgow cotton factory and educated himself by attending lectures at Anderson College and Glasgow University. He joined the London Missionary Society, and in 1840 he was sent to the Cape of Good Hope as a missionary.

Journeys into 'the interior', the largely unknown

DAVID LIVINGSTONE

territory to the north, led to his discovery in 1849 of Lake Ngami and the Zambezi R., and, between 1853 and 1856, to that of the Victoria Falls.

He was elected a Fellow of the Royal Society and awarded an honorary Oxford degree—but the London Missionary Society considered he had not paid enough attention to his missionary work. He resigned from its service the following year, joined the Foreign Office, and left Britain in 1858 to lead an expedition into East and Central Africa.

In 1859 he discovered Lake Shirwa and Lake Nyasa but five years later, following distorted reports of his activities, the Foreign Office recalled him. His book on the Zambezi and its tributaries led Sir Roderick Murchison, the geologist, to invite him to search for the source of the Nile.

The expedition began in 1865; after four years of great hardships Livingstone reached Ujiji and spent two years exploring the surrounding cannibal country.

His presumed disappearance caused an American newspaper to commission Henry Morton Stanley to locate him. The famous inquiry 'Dr Livingstone, I presume?' was uttered at Ujiji in 1871, where Stanley found Livingstone suffering from malaria.

Livingstone never found the source of the Nile. He died at a village in the Ilala country and his embalmed body was carried by mourning natives down the Zambezi. He was buried in Westminster Abbey.

**Keir Hardie** was at work in Lanarkshire pits near his birthplace, Legbrannock, at the age of ten. By 1880, when he was 24, his agitation for better conditions for miners had won him a place on the Lanarkshire pit-owners' black list.

In 1893 he founded the Independent Labour Party and in 1906 he became the first chairman of the Parliamentary Labour Party. Hardie began the Parliamentary Labour movement in Britain, but because his colleagues rejected his pacifist outlook at the start of the First World War, he died thinking himself a failure.

**John Logie Baird** was born at Helensburgh, the son of a minister. He studied electrical engineering at the Royal Technical College,

JOHN LOGIE BAIRD

Glasgow, and at 18 set up a small laboratory at Hastings, Sussex. Eighteen years of extensive experiments produced an elementary television apparatus in 1924, and two years later he demonstrated T.V. in a London attic to about 50 scientists. In 1929, after he proved that transatlantic transmissions were possible, the B.B.C. took an interest in his invention and made its first T.V. transmission in 1936—though it later decided to adopt a rival system. In 1941 Baird made successful transmissions in colour. He died in 1946.

## TREASURE SITES

&#9881; CASTLE/HOUSE     &#9883; INDUSTRIAL MONUMENT
&#9884; GARDEN     &#9880; ARCHAEOLOGICAL SITE
&#9878; ECCLESIASTICAL BUILDING     MONUMENT/MEMORIAL
&#127963; MUSEUM/ART GALLERY     &#9670; OTHER NOTABLE FEATURES
TOWNS/VILLAGES OF ARCHITECTURAL INTEREST *named in black*

SCALE ABOUT 10 MILES TO 1 INCH (1:625,000)

## Map labels (left)

farne Priory
and
sfarne Castle

Farne Islands

Bamburgh

Seahouses
ker N Sunderland
Beadnell

Chathill
tingham Newton-by-the-Sea
Charlton
Embleton
Dunstanburgh Castle
Craster
gton
Howick
Longhoughton
Alnwick Boulmer
Lesbury
ilnmouth
Shilbottle
Newton- Warkworth
on-the-
Moor Coquet Island
Amble
lington cklington
Felton Broomhill

West Chevington
harsley Widdrington
Ulgham Ellington Cresswell
lynemouth
Longhirst
INGTON Bothal
Newbiggin-by-the-Sea
Morpeth
Hepscott Cambois
LINGTON BLYTH
ngton
Cramlington
Seaton Seaton Delaval Hall
Burn Hartley
Mason Delaval
onteland WHITLEY BAY
Backworth Cullercoats
OSFOR WALLSEND TYNEMOUTH
CASTLE SOUTH SHIELDS
PON
YNE JARROW

3    G      H      J

558

# THE THOUGHTFUL REVOLUTIONARIES

Religion, mathematics, communications and the detective story : . . all have undergone drastic reshaping by Edinburgh men.

**John Knox,** founder of the Presbyterian Church, the established Church of Scotland, was born and spent most of his youth at Haddington, 16 miles east of Edinburgh. He attended

JOHN KNOX

Glasgow University, worked in Haddington as a notary between 1540 and 1543, and was then called to the ministry. In 1548, a year after he began preaching the new Protestant religion, he was captured at the fall of St Andrews Castle and imprisoned in France for a year.

Though he was made a royal chaplain in 1551, he fled to Dieppe in 1553 to avoid Mary Tudor's laws against Protestantism; he returned after five weeks there and a year later journeyed through France and Switzerland. Calvin, a leader of Protestantism, influenced his thinking.

In the same year he became pastor to the English congregation at Frankfurt, but within a year he had been charged with treason and ordered to leave. Back in Geneva in 1556, he began writing religious tracts, the most famous being *The First Blast of the Trumpet against the Monstrous Regiment of Women* (1558) which, not surprisingly, offended Elizabeth I and led to her lifelong bias against Scottish Protestantism.

In 1567 he persuaded the Scottish Parliament to approve the establishment of the Presbyterian Church. He was a minister in Edinburgh when he died in 1572.

**John Napier,** the mathematician, was born in the 16th-century castle of Merchiston, and became laird of the estates at Colinton and Merchiston. After St Andrews University,

Napier applied his talents to inventing machines of war (in particular, a primitive tank), and civil engineering devices, including a pump for extracting water from coal mines.

Then, as mathematics became his dominant interest, he devised logarithms, originally called artificial numbers. His thesis on them was published in 1614.

In *Rabdologia* (1615), Napier set out a method of computing by means of ivory pieces called 'numerating rods', which became known as 'Napier's Bones'. This was the earliest form of calculating machine.

**Alexander Graham Bell** revolutionised communications by inventing the telephone. Educated at Edinburgh and London Universities, he emigrated to Canada in 1870 and then went to the United States to work for the deaf. He became professor of vocal physiology at Boston University in 1873, and it was at Boston in 1875, the year after he became an American citizen, that he constructed his first telephone link— with Salem, 18 miles away.

At Edinburgh University **Arthur Conan Doyle** studied medicine under Dr Joseph Bell, who made an abiding impression on him. Doyle took up practice in Southsea, Hants, and there, in 1887, produced his first work of fiction, *A Study in Scarlet*, which featured Sherlock Holmes. In 1891 *The Adventures of Sherlock Holmes* appeared in the *Strand Magazine,* and brought Doyle universal acclaim.

ARTHUR CONAN DOYLE

Soon established as a highly successful author, he poured out stories about Sherlock Holmes as well as historical and adventure novels. Sir Arthur became deeply interested in spiritualism, and in 1926 published a history of the subject.

---

## TREASURE SITES

| | |
|---|---|
| ⚔ CASTLE/HOUSE | ⊕ INDUSTRIAL MONUMENT |
| ❀ GARDEN | ⁂ ARCHAEOLOGICAL SITE |
| ⛪ ECCLESIASTICAL BUILDING | ❙ MONUMENT/MEMORIAL |
| ⛫ MUSEUM/ART GALLERY | ◆ OTHER NOTABLE FEATURES |

TOWNS/VILLAGES OF ARCHITECTURAL INTEREST *named in black*

SCALE ABOUT 10 MILES TO 1 INCH (1:625,000)

# SCOTLAND
# BRAVE AND ROYAL

**Bonnie Prince Charlie** was not the first Stuart to pursue a claim to the throne of England. His father, **James Francis Edward Stuart**, son of the deposed James II, had tried in 1715. After the Battle of Culloden Charles, like his father, sought refuge in France. In the six months before he succeeded in reaching it he was greatly assisted by **Flora Macdonald**, the 24-year-old daughter of a farmer.

FLORA MACDONALD

Flora was born in Milton, South Uist, and met the Young Pretender at Benbecula (North Uist) on his flight from Culloden. She sailed with him to Port Kilbride near Uig on the Isle of Skye. After his escape she was caught, and taken to the Tower of London for trial, but released under the Act of Indemnity (1747). She married Allan Macdonald in 1750, emigrated to North Carolina in 1774, and returned to Scotland five years later. At Kilmuir, Isle of Skye, where Flora Macdonald was buried in 1790, stands the Celtic cross inscribed with lines in her memory by Dr Samuel Johnson.

The English Crown's links with Scotland were renewed in 1852 when **Queen Victoria** leased the property known as Balmoral in the north-west Highlands. She and the Prince Consort found such personal happiness at Balmoral that the property was bought outright. **Prince Albert's** alterations and adaptations set a fashion in Scottish baronial architecture, and the queen's regular visits to Balmoral set a pattern of Royal Family holidays which continues to this day.

# HIGHLAND HIGHWAYS

Following the Union of England and Scotland in 1707, **General George Wade** strengthened and enlarged the two key military bases at Fort William and Fort Augustus and introduced a network of improved roads. Ironically, they did Wade no good. In 1745, then 72, a Field Marshal, and commander-in-chief of the English armies, he was faced with putting down the second Jacobite rising, led by Prince Charles Edward Stuart, the Young Pretender.

Baffled by the speed with which Charles moved across the Highlands, Wade was replaced by the Duke of Cumberland. The rebellion came to an end with the Battle of Culloden in 1746. There are relics of the rising in the West Highland Museum at Fort William.

Wade's work was vastly extended by **Thomas Telford,** the son of a Dumfries shepherd. As a young man he worked as a mason in Edinburgh, then as a surveyor in London. The Chirk aqueduct in Shropshire, which he built between 1796 and 1801, brought him wide recognition.

THOMAS TELFORD

In 1804 he began the challenging task of linking the North Sea with the Atlantic by what became known as the Caledonian Canal. Some 23 miles of canal and 28 locks, added to the natural waters of Lochs Ness, Oich and Lochy, achieved his purpose. In the period up to 1818, Telford built 120 bridges, over 900 miles of roads and improved a score of major harbours.

## TREASURE SITES

- ⚔ CASTLE/HOUSE
- ✿ GARDEN
- ⛪ ECCLESIASTICAL BUILDING
- 🏛 MUSEUM/ART GALLERY
- ⊕ INDUSTRIAL MONUMENT
- ⚲ ARCHAEOLOGICAL SITE
- ⌶ MONUMENT/MEMORIAL
- ◆ OTHER NOTABLE FEATURES

TOWNS/VILLAGES OF ARCHITECTURAL INTEREST *named in black*

## Map labels

KINNAIRDS HEAD
Sandhaven
Rosehearty
Pennan
Fraserburgh
Inverallochy
Aberdour
St Combs
Memsie
Rathen
Loch of Strathbeg
Rattray Head
New Pitsligo
Strichen
New Leeds
Crimond
St Fergus
minestown
Fetterangus
Rora
Maud
Mintlaw
Longside
Peterhead
Deer
Stuartfield
Old Deer
Clola
Auchnagatt
Burnhaven
Boddam
Buchan Ness
Methlick
Hatton
Cruden Bay
Haddo House
Michael Muir
Tarves
Ellon
Collieston
Udn
Pitmedden
Castle
Newburgh
Foveran
wmachar
Balmedie
Belhelvie
Hatton Fintray
Dyce
Stoneywood
Bridge of Don
ucksburn
ABERDEEN
A944
Girdle Ness
Cults
Cove Bay
Portlethen
Downies
Skateraw
Muchalls Castle
Muchalls
Stonehaven
Dunnottar Castle
Catterline
Kinneff
Inverbervie
ourdon
haven

SCALE ABOUT 10 MILES TO 1 INCH (1:625,000)

# DRAMATIST, DUKE AND DREAMER

Fantasy, fact and something between the two centre on a few square miles of the southern Highlands.

**J. M. Barrie** supplied the fantasy with the work for which he is best known, *Peter Pan*. Born at Kirriemuir in 1860, Barrie began his career as a journalist,

J. M. BARRIE

first in Nottingham and then in London. An early book, *A Window in Thrums* (1889), a realistic picture of Kirriemuir, brought him fame.

But his true talent lay in drama: *Quality Street* (1901) and *The Admirable Crichton* (1902) preceded *Peter Pan* (1904). His last major work, the whimsical *Mary Rose*, was set on 'the island that wants to be visited', which is identified as at Loch Voshimid, Isle of Harris, Outer Hebrides.

Thirty-five miles from Barrie's birthplace is the magnificent ancestral home of the Murray family at Blair Atholl. **John Murray** was created Duke of Atholl in 1703. Secretary of State for Scotland from 1696 to 1698, and a Privy Councillor, he was Lord Privy Seal when, in 1705, he opposed the Union of England and Scotland so strongly that he was deprived of office.

However, he supported the government during the rising in 1715, and captured Robert Macgregor (Rob Roy), the Highlander who followed in the wake of the Jacobite rebels but did not join the Old Pretender.

Something not fantasy and yet not scientific fact came to Blair Atholl just before the First World War in the person of **J. W. Dunne.** Dunne's advanced ideas in aeronautics had interested Sir Hiram Maxim (the Maxim gun) and H. G. Wells at a time when aeroplanes were in their infancy.

The War Office sponsored secret experiments on the Blair Atholl estate, guarded by the duke's private army, the Atholl Highlanders. Dunne's concept of a swept-back aircraft wing was too far ahead of its time for acceptance.

Dunne's most amazing experiments were set down in *An Experiment With Time* (1927). For many years he

J. W. DUNNE

recorded each morning the dreams he had had during the night. He found that a significant number came true—one 14 years later.

Dunne built this material into a thesis on the nature of time and the unconscious which gave an explanation for the 'I have been here before' feeling many people experience.

# BIBLE REFERENCES

Cruden's *Biblical Concordance* is one of the first great works of reference in English. In the 1611 Authorised Version of the Bible there are 773,692 words, and Cruden's work—an index to its words and subjects—gives 225,000 references.

**Alexander Cruden,** who was born in Aberdeen in 1701, attended the local grammar school and Marischal College, now part of the university. Ill-health caused him to abandon study and take up teaching. He opened a book shop in the Royal Exchange, London, in 1732, and began the compilation of his reference book, which first appeared in 1737.

Cruden suffered from attacks of insanity, but between them earned his living as a proof reader and text corrector of learned works. He died on November 1, 1770 at Camden Place, Islington, London.

## TREASURE SITES

⚔ CASTLE/HOUSE     ⚙ INDUSTRIAL MONUMENT
✿ GARDEN     ⚘ ARCHAEOLOGICAL SITE
⛪ ECCLESIASTICAL BUILDING     ! MONUMENT/MEMORIAL
🏛 MUSEUM/ART GALLERY     ◆ OTHER NOTABLE FEATURES
TOWNS/VILLAGES OF ARCHITECTURAL INTEREST *named in black*

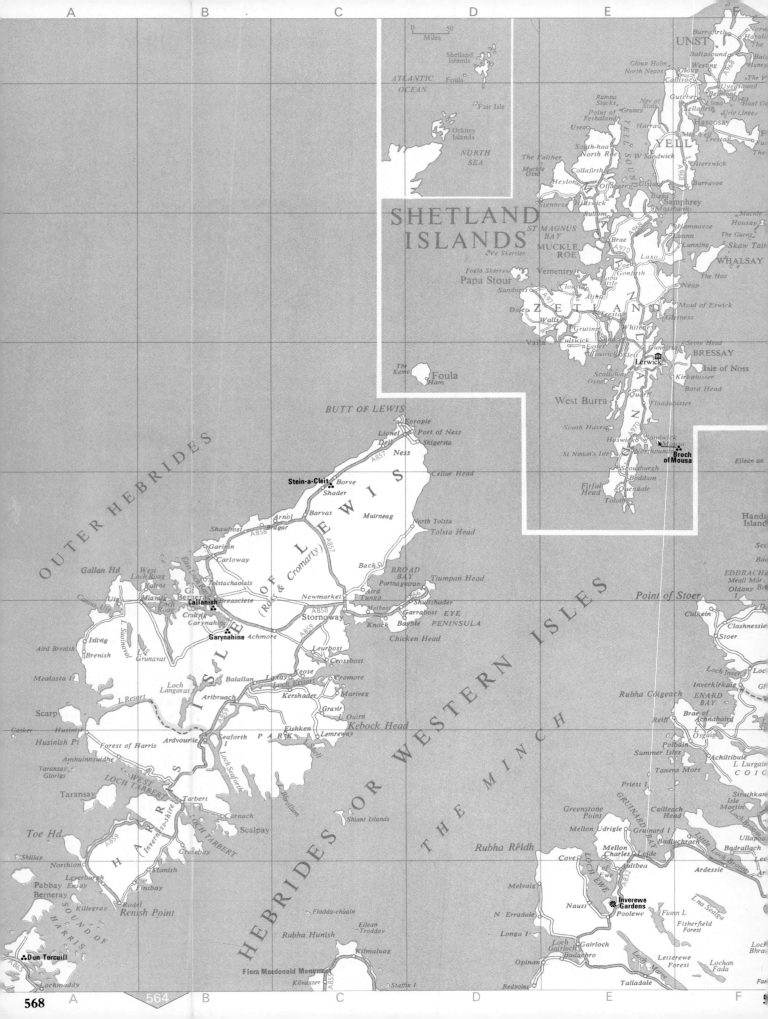

ATLANTIC
OCEAN

Fouls

Fair Isle

Orkney Islands

NORTH
SEA

UNST

Burrafirth
Harold

Saltasound
Westing
The

Gloup Holm
North Neans
Calliwoe

Gutcher
Belmont
Uyeasound
Uyea

Haaf Gr.

Ramna
Stacks
Point of
Fethaland

Nev of
Stula
Gruney

Sellafirth
Mid Yell

Hascosay
YELL

Otterswick

SHETLAND
ISLANDS

ST MAGNUS
BAY

MUCKLE
ROE

The Faither
Muckle
Ossa

Uyea
South-haa
North Roe
North Sandwick

Ollaberry

Stenness
Hillswick

Sullom

Brae
A970

Voe

Laxo

Buta
Mossbank

Flamnavoe
Lunna
The Guens

Skaw Tair

WHALSAY

Papa Stour

Foula Skerry

Vementry

Gonfirth

Yoe

Sandness

The Haa

The Kame
Foula
Ham

Dale
Walls
Vaila

Gruting

Culswick

Sand
Tresta
Whiteness

Clousta
Aith

Neap

Moul of Eswick

Gletness

West Burra

Scallow
Oxna

Sea Head
Gunnista

LERWICK

BRESSAY
Isle of Noss

Kirkabister

Bard Head

BUTT OF LEWIS

Eoropie
Port of Ness
Skigersta

South Havra

St Ninian's Isle

Housay
Hoswick
Sandwick
Northpunds

Broch
of Mousa

Eilean an

Lionel
Dell

Ness

Cellar Head

Stousburgh
Boddam
Quendale

Fitful
Head

Toloft

Stein-a-Cleit
Borve
Shader

Barvas

Muirneag

North Tolsta

LEWIS

Arnol
Shawbost
A858
Bridgar

Garinin

Carloway

Tolsta Head

Gallan Hd
West
Loch Roag

Kallos
Tolstachaolais

(ROSS & CROMARTY)

A857

Back

BROAD
BAY

Portnaguiran

HANDA
Island

Scot

EDDRACHA

Meall Mór
Oldany BA

Miavaig
Bernera

Crulivig
Garynahine
Achmore

Callanish
Breasclete

Newmarket

Aird
Tunga

A858

Stornoway
Melbost

Shulishader
Garrabost
EYE

Tiumpan Head

Point of Stoer

Loch
Roag

Uig

Loch

A859

Knock
Bayble

Chicken Head

PENINSULA

Culkein

Clashnessie
Stoer

Islivig
Brenish

Aird Brenish

L Suainaval

L Grunavat

Leurbost
Crossbost

Cromore

Loch Inver

Inverkirkaig

Loch
Langavat

Balallan
Laxay

Keose

Marivig

ENARD
BAY

Rubha Coigeach

Brae of
Achnahaird

Mealasta I

Aribruach

A859

Loch Frisort

Kershader

Gravir

L Ouirn

Reiff

Osgaig

Scarp

Husinish

Ardvourlie
Seaforth
I

PARK

Eishken
Lemreway

Kebock Head

Polbain
Summer Isles

Gasker

Husinish Pt

Forest of Harris

Loch Seaforth

Amhuinnsuidhe

WEST
LOCH TARBERT

Taransay
Glorigs

Taransay

HARRIS

Inverness-shire

Tarbert

LOCH TARBERT

Carnach

Scalpay

Blinottam

Shiant Islands

THE MINCH

Tanera More

Priest I

Cailleach
Head

Strathka
Isle
Martin
Loch Broo

Ullapo

Little Loch Broom

Toe Hd

Shillay

Northton
Leverburgh

Manish

Gredabay

Greenstone
Point
Mellon Udrigle
Gruinard I

GRUINARD BAY

Badluchrach

Badrallach

Ulla

Pabbay
Berneray

Ensay
Killegray

Finsbay

Rodel

Rubha Réidh
Cove
Mellon
Charles
of Laide
Aultbea

Loch Ewe

Ardessie

Lochan
Fada

Renish Point

SOUND
OF
HARRIS

Flodda-chùain

Rubha Hunish

Eilean
Trodday

N' Erradale
Melvaig

Nast
Poolewe

Inverewe
Gardens

Fisherfield
Forest

Lna Sealga

Loch
Bhra

Dun Torcuill

Lochmaddy

Kilmaluag

Flora Macdonald Monument

A855

Staffin I

Kilvaxter

Opinan

Loch
Gairloch
Badachro

Redpoint

Gairloch

Loch
Maree

Letterewe
Forest

Talladale

570

564

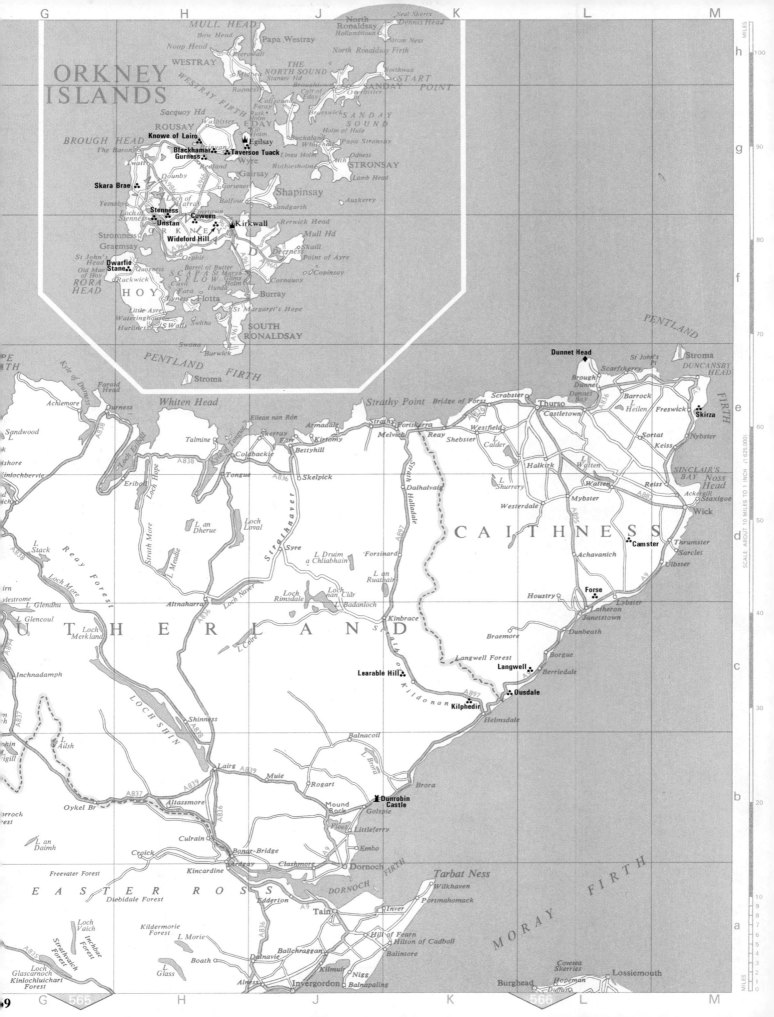

ORKNEY ISLANDS

MULL HEAD
Bow Head
Papa Westray
Noup Head
North Ronaldsay
Hollandstoun
Seal Skerres
Dennis Head
Drum Ness
WESTRAY
Pierowall
North Ronaldsay Firth
Northwaa
Midbea
Stanger Hd
THE NORTH SOUND
START POINT
WESTRAY
Rapness
Braeswick
SANDAY
Sacquoy Hd
Callsound
Faray
Cott of Eday
Overbister
Rusk Holm
Burn
SANDAY SOUND
BROUGH HEAD
ROUSAY
Knowe of Lairo
Egilsay
Till
EDAY
Buckaland
Whitehall
Papa Stronsay
Odness
The Barony
Blackhamar
Gurness
Taversoe Tuack
Pentland
Wyre
Linga Holm
STRONSAY
Twatt
Dounby
Gairsay
Rutheisholme
Lamb Head
Skara Brae
Gorseness
Shapinsay
Auskerry
Yesnaby
Loch of Harray
Sandgarth
Balfour
Stenness
Firth
Sandgarth
Cuween
Loch of Stenness
Unstan
Kirkwall
Rerwick Head
Stromness
Wideford Hill
ORKNEY
Mull Hd
Graemsay
A964
Orphir
Skaill
St John's Head
Deerness
Point of Ayre
Old Man of Hoy
Dwarfie Stane
Quoyness
Barrel of Butter
St Marys
Glims Holm
Copinsay
RORA HEAD
Rackwick
Cava
Fara
SCAPA FLOW
Holm
Cornquoy
HOY
Lyness
Flotta
Hunda
Burray
Little Ayre
Wateringhouse
Hurliness
S Walls
Switha
St Margaret's Hope
SOUTH RONALDSAY
Swona
Burwick
PENTLAND
Stroma
FIRTH

PENTLAND

Dunnet Head
Brough
Dunnet
St John's Pt
Stroma
DUNCANSBY HEAD
Whiten Head
Strathy Point
Bridge of Forss
Scrabster
Dunnet Bay
Barrock
Freswick
Eliean nan Rón
Armadale
Strathy
Portskerra
Thurso
Castletown
L Heilen
Skirza
Sandwood
Talmine
Skerray
Farr
Kirtomy
Melvich
Reay
Westfield
Sortat
Nybster
Achlemore
Durness
Farald Head
Bettyhill
Shebster
L Calder
Keiss
Kyle of Durness
Coldbackie
Halkirk
Watten
SINCLAIR'S BAY
Noss Head
Eribol
Tongue
Skelpick
Strath Halladale
L Shurrery
Watten
Reiss
Ackergill
Staxigoe
Loch Hope
Dalhalvaig
Westerdale
Mybster
A882
Wick
L an Dherue
Syre
Forsinard
CAITHNESS
Achavanich
Camster
Thrumster
Strath More
L Druim a Chliabhain
L an Ruathain
Houstry
Sarclet
L Stack
Attnaharra
Loch Naver
Loch nan Clàr
L Badanloch
Forse
Ulbster
L Glendhu
Reay Forest
Loch Rimsdale
Kinbrace
Braemore
Lybster
Inchnadamph
Loch More
Latheron
Janetstown
L Glencoul
L Merkland
Langwell Forest
Dunbeath
SUTHERLAND
Learable Hill
Langwell
Borgue
Berriedale
Strath Kildonan
Ousdale
Kilphedir
Helmsdale
Shinness
Balnacoil
L Ailsh
Lairg
Muie
L Brora
Dunrobin Castle
Oykel Br
Altassmore
Rogart
Brora
L an Daimh
Culrain
Mound Rock
Golspie
Croick
Bonar-Bridge
Fleet
Littleferry
Ardgay
Clashmore
Embo
Kincardine
DORNOCH FIRTH
Dornoch
Tarbat Ness
Freevater Forest
Wilkhaven
Portmahomack
EASTER ROSS
Edderton
Tain
Inver
Diebidale Forest
Kildermorie Forest
Hill of Fearn
Hilton of Cadboll
Loch Vaich
L Morie
Dalnavie
Balintore
Inchboe Forest
Boath
Kilmuir
Nigg
MORAY FIRTH
Strathvaich Forest
L Glass
Ballchraggan
Alness
Invergordon
Balnapaling
Burghead
Covesea Skerries
Hopeman
Lossiemouth
Duffus

MILES
100
90
80
70
60
50
40
30
20
10
MILES

SCALE ABOUT 10 MILES TO 1 INCH (1:625,000)

G 565    H    J    K 566    L    M

h
g
f
e
d
c
b
a

A     B     C     D     E     F

St Macdara's Island
Mweenish Island
Golam Head
Gorumna Island
Inveran
Spiddal
Barna
Oranmore
GALWAY
Athenry
Aughrim
Clontuskert
Lawrencetown
Kilreekill
Ballydavid
Killimor
Derryhive
Ca
Portumna Castle
Portu
Woodford
Craughwell
Kilcolgan
Tyrone House
Drumacoo
St Clerans House
Loughrea
Lough Rea
Dungory Castle
Corcomroe Abbey
Ardrahan
Tulira Castle
Pallas Castle
NORTH SOUND
GALWAY BAY
Tawin Island
Eddy Island
Kinvarra
Kilmacduagh
Kiltartan Castle
Gort
Lough Cutra
Lough Atorick
Newtown
Ballyvaghan
BLACK HEAD
Inishmore
Aran Islands
Inishmaan
Inisheer
SOUTH SOUND
Doolin Pt.
Lisdoonvarna
Cahercommaun
Lough Cutra Castle
SLIEVE AUGHTY MOUNTAINS
Lough Graney
Mountshannon
Cliffs of Moher
Hag's Head
Liscannor
Liscannor Bay
Lehinch
Lough Licken
Lough Inchiquin
Corrofin
Leamaneh Castle
Kilfenora
Lough Atedaun
Ennistimon
Dysert O'Dea
Feakle
Scariff
Tuamgraney
Inish Cealtra
Tuamgraney
Portro
NENAG
Mal Bay
Spanish Pt.
Milltown Malbay
Inagh
Mutton Island
Quilty
Kilmurry
C L A R E
ENNIS
Magh Adhair
Clarecastle
Tulla
Quin Abbey
Kilkishen
Bodyke
Broadford
Silver
Killaloe
Newhall House
Killone
Carnelly House
Newmarket on Fergus
Sixmilebridge
O'Briensbridge
Birdhill
Newport
Doonbeg
Cooraclare
Kilmihil
Urlanmore Castle
Mausoleum
Bunratty Castle
New Kildimo
Kilkee
Moyasta
Canon Island
Killadysert
Shannongrove House
King John's Castle
O'Connell Monument
Hermitage
Glenstal Cas
Cappame
Scattery Island
KILRUSH
Labasheeda
Forbes
Dromore Castle
Carrigogunnell Castle
LIMERICK
Cappa
Pallas Gree
(New)
Carrigaholt Castle
Carrigafoyle Castle
Carrigaholt
Kilconly Pt.
Tarbert
Loghill
Shanagolden
Askeaton
Cappagh Castle
Patrickswell
Caherconlish
LOOP HEAD
Ballylongford
Glin
Monaster-
nagalliaghduff
Garraunboy Castle
Adare
Groom
Monasternenagh
Herbertstown
Oola
MOUTH
OF
THE SHANNON
Ballybunnion
Glin Castle
Shanid Castle
Rathkeale
Disertoengus
Lough Gur
TIPPE
KERRY HEAD
Ballyduff
Listowel
Athea
Newcastle West
Ballingarry
Bruff
Ballygrennan Castle
Hospital
Ballyheige
Rattoo
Abbeydorney
Ardagh
Newcastle West Castle
Bruree
Causeway
Glenquin Castle
Kilmeedy
Ash Hill Towers
Duntryleague
Galbe
Illauntannig
Rough Pt.
Abbeyfeale
Springfield Castle
MULLAGHAREIRK
MOUNTAINS
Dromcollihy
Rath Luirc
(Charleville)
Kilmallock
Ballyland
BRANDON HEAD
BRANDON BAY
Ardfert
TRALEE BAY
Kilbolane Castle
Kilfinnane
Ballydavid Head
Sybil Pt.
Kilmalkedar
Caherdorgan
Reask
Gallarus Oratory
Camp
SLIEVE MISH MOUNTAINS
TRALEE
Castleisland
Newmarket
Freemount
Liscarroll
Liscarroll Castle
Buttevant
Mitchelstown
Glanfahan
Dingle
Anascaul
Inch
CASTLEMAINE HARBOUR
Castlemaine
Farranfore
Ballydesmond
Kanturk
Kanturk Castle
Doneraile
St. Leger Monument
Castletownroche
Glanworth
Sea Head
DINGLE BAY
Milltown
Killorglin
M U N S T E R
Boherboy
Lohort Castle
Castle Hyde
F
Leacanabuaile
Cahergal
Caharsiveen
Lough Caragh
K E R R Y
Rathmore
Banteer
Dromaneen Castle
MALLOW
NAGLES
MOUNTAINS
Barrymore Monument
Rathcormack
DOULUS HEAD
Valencia Island
Lough Derriana
Lough Chluain
Killarney
LOUGH LEANE
Ross Castle
Muckross House
Muckross
Lough Guitane
Millstreet
BOGGERAGH MOUNTAINS
C O R K
Kilshannig House
Watergr
BRAY HEAD
St. Finan's Bay
Lough Currane
Waterville
MACGILLYCUDDY'S REEKS
DERRYNASAGGART MOUNTAINS
Ballyvourney
Blarney
Riverstown House
M
BOLUS HEAD
Skellig Rocks
Great Skellig
Scariff Island
Staigue Fort
Kildreenagh
Kenmare
Kilgarvan
Ballyvourney
Macroom
Carrigadrohid
Dripsey
Coachford
Blarney Castle
CORK
Barryscourt Castle
CO
Hog's Head
Lamb's Head
Derrynane Abbey
KENMARE RIVER
Sneem
Carrigaphooca Tower
Ballincollig Castle
Douglas
Passage West
Cod's Head
Castletown Bearhaven
Allihies
Glengarriff
Garinish Island
Ballingeary
Inchigeelagh
Crookstown
Kilcrea Friary
Monkstown House
Ballinhassig
Carrigaline
DURSEY HEAD
Dunboy Castle
Bear Island
Bantry
Bantry House
BANTRY BAY
Whiddy Island
Adrigole
CAHA MOUNTAINS
Lauragh
SHEHY MOUNTAINS
Kealkill
Dunmanway
Enniskeane
Bandon
Inishannon
Belgooly
Crosshaven
Ro
Dursey Island
Muntervary or Sheep's Head
Durrus
Drimoleague
Ballynacarriga Castle
Kilbrittain Castle
Kinsale
DUNMANUS BAY
Skull
Ballydehob
Coppingers Court
Carrigillihy
Ross Carbery
Castle Freke
Timoleague Abbey
Timoleague
Clonakilty
Courtmacsherry
Ballinspittle
Kinsale Harbour
MIZEN HEAD
Crookhaven
Long Island
Sherkin Abbey
Baltimore
Calf Islands
Sherkin Island
Skibbereen
Castletownshend
Clonakilty Bay
Seven Heads
OLD HEAD OF KINSALE
CAPE CLEAR
Clear Island
Toe Head
GALLEY HEAD
Courtmacsherry Bay

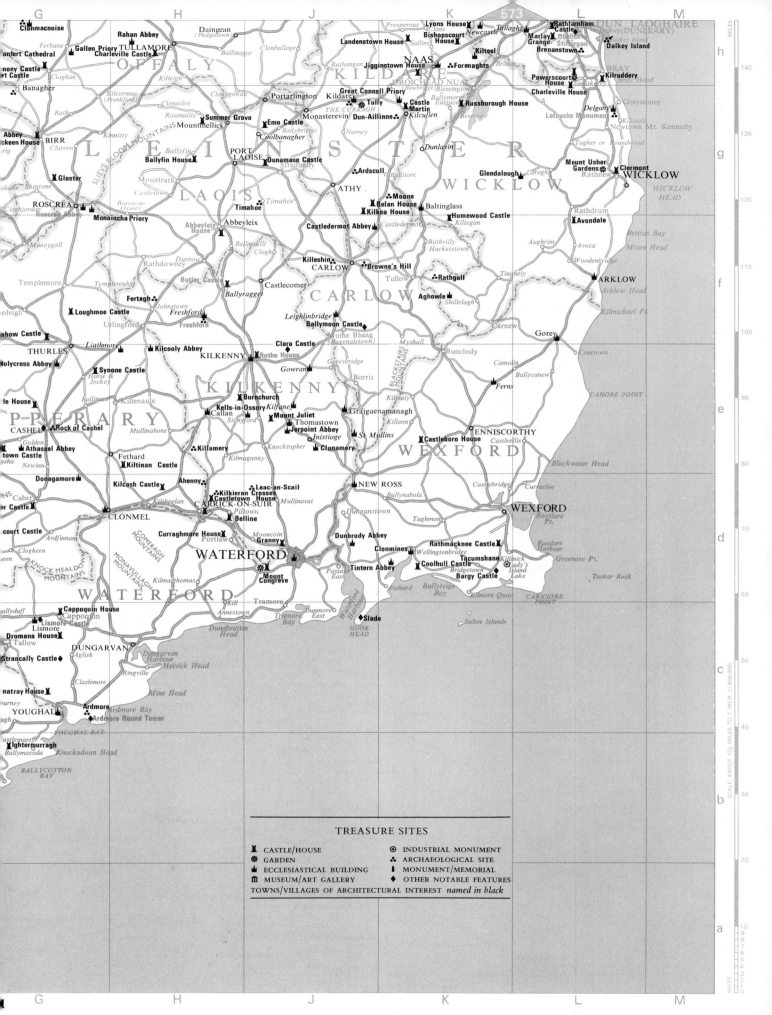

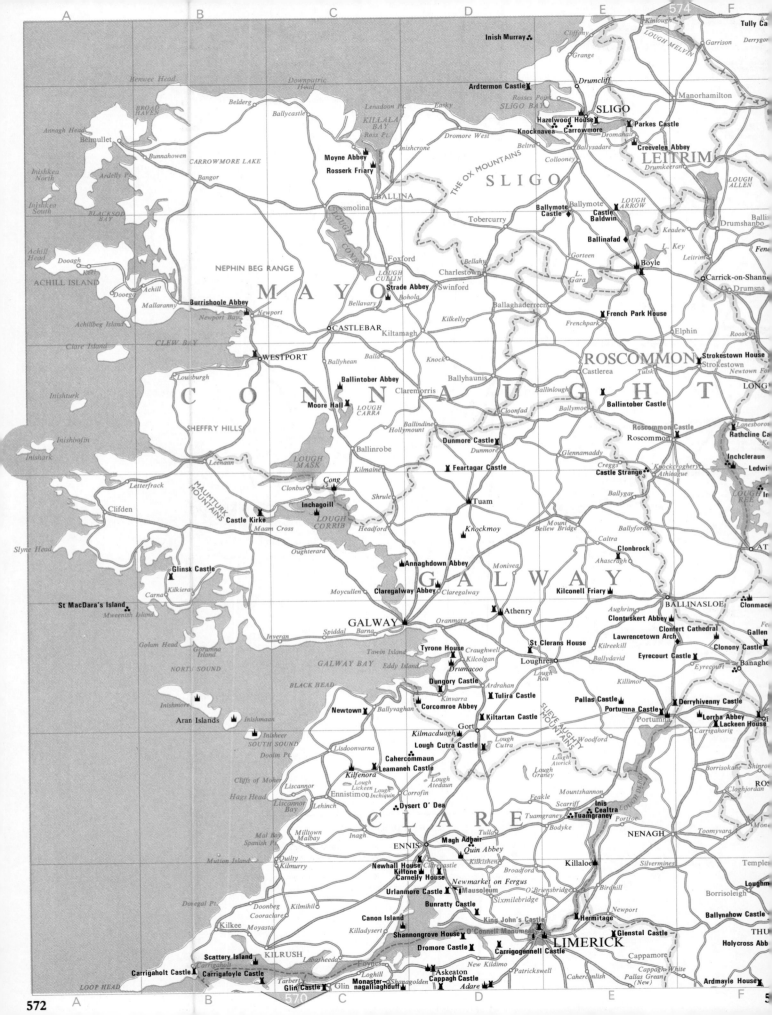

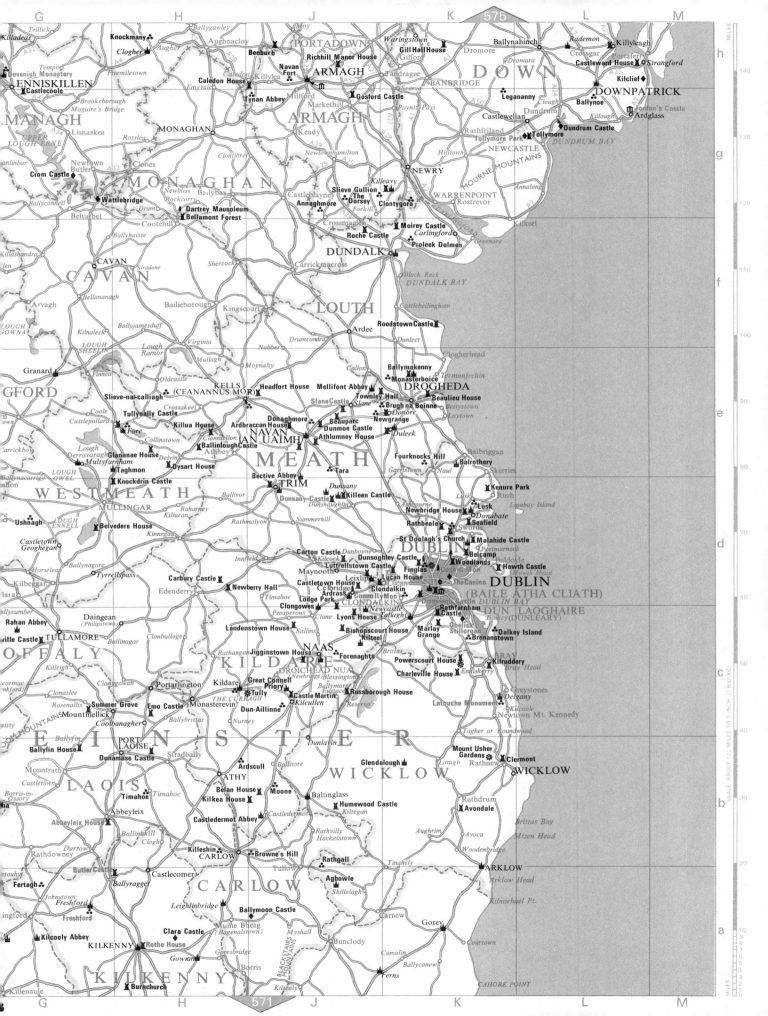

TREASURE SITES

- ⚔ CASTLE/HOUSE
- ❀ GARDEN
- ⛪ ECCLESIASTICAL BUILDING
- 🏛 MUSEUM/ART GALLERY
- ✿ INDUSTRIAL MONUMENT
- ⚘ ARCHAEOLOGICAL SITE
- ▌ MONUMENT/MEMORIAL
- ◆ OTHER NOTABLE FEATURES

TOWNS/VILLAGES OF ARCHITECTURAL INTEREST *named in black*

Rathlin Island

Fair Head

Ballintoy
Bushmills
◆ Dunluce Castle
Crannog
Carnanmore
Ballycastle
Moss-side
Dervock
Cushendun
LERAINE
t Sandel
Armoy
Cushendall
BALLYMONEY
Clogh Mills
Carnlough
Glenarm
Rasharkin
Clogh
Island Magee
Cullybackey
Broughshane
Ballygally Manor House
Gracehill
BALLYMENA
LARNE
Ahoghill
Ballynure
Ballycarry
Belaghy
Randalstown
Dalway's Bawn
Castle Dobbs
Whitehead
Toome
BALLYCLARE
Doagh
Browndod
Carrickfergus
Shane's Castle
Hill
Castle Upton
Castle
CARRICKFERGUS
Antrim
Templepatrick
ANTRIM
NEWTOWNABBEY
BELFAST LOUGH
Lyle's Hill
BANGOR
◆ Arboe
BELFAST
Cultra Manor
DONAGHADEE
LOUGH NEAGH
Crumlin
HOLYWOOD
Ballycopeland
Glenavy
Dundonald
Movilla Abbey
Ballinderry
Dunmurry
Comber
NEWTOWNARDS
Carrowdore Castle
LISBURN
Giant's Ring
Ballywalter
Home of
Greyabbey
Mount Stewart Gardens
Cutcavy
Crommlin
Kircubbin
Eglantine
Rowallane
Rubane
Moira
Saintfield
Hillsborough
Ballygowan
Kirkistown Castle
Waringstown
Dromore
Rademon
LURGAN
Gill Hall
Ballynahinch
Killyleagh
House
Dromara
Crossgar
Portaferry
Gilford
Richhill Manor House
DOWN
Castleward House
Strangford
RMAGH
Tandragee
BANBRIDGE
Kilclief
Scarva
Gosford Castle
Poyntz Pass
DOWNPATRICK
MAGH
Leganny
Clough
Ballynoe
Castlewellan
Dundrum
Jordan's Castle
arkethill
Castlewellan Park
Ardglass
Rathfriland
Tollymore
DUNDRUM BAY
Hilltown
NEWCASTLE
MOURNE MOUNTAINS
Killeavy
NEWRY
Annalong
The Dorsey
Slieve
WARRENPOINT
Gullion
Rostrevor
ghmore
Clontygora
Kilkeel
Crossmaglen
Moirey Castle
Carlingford
Roche Castle
Proleek Dolmen
Greenore
DUNDALK
kmacross
Black Rock
DUNDALK BAY
Castlebellingham
LOUTH
Ardee
Dunleer
Roodstown Castle
Clogherhead
Collon
Termonfechin
Ballymakenny
Mellifont Abbey
Monasterboice
Townley Hall
DROGHEDA
Slane
Beaulieu House
Brugh na Boinne
Bettystown
Beauparc
Donore
Dunmoe Castle
Newgrange
Laytown

MILES 100 90 80 70 60 50 40 30 20 10 9 8 7 6 5

SCALE ABOUT 10 MILES TO 1 INCH (1,625,000)

G H J

---

# THE MISSIONARY SAINTS

Just as Ireland's many legends have factual origins, so the accounts of its famous saints, often confusingly romanticised by time and imagination, deal with the story of real people involved in the teachings of Christianity.

It was **St Patrick**, the Apostle of Ireland, who was responsible for bringing Christianity to the country. Thought to have been born in a Roman villa in Monmouthshire in AD 389, Patrick lived a retiring and uneventful life until he was 16. He was then captured by Irish raiders and taken back to their country as a slave. For six years he worked a lonely life as a shepherd, finding his only comfort in prayer and meditation. Finally he managed to escape to the Continent. He spent the next 21 years of his life there in study, preparing for his later work as a missionary. In 432 he returned to Ireland as a consecrated bishop and started out on a life's mission of converting the heathen. He travelled extensively, built a number of churches and firmly established Christianity. When he died on March 17, 461, at the age of 72, he had impressed Rome sufficiently for the Papacy to raise Ireland's status to an ecclesiastical province.

Someone who was still only a child in his later years was **St Bridget**. Born near Dundalk in AD 452 and baptised by St Patrick, she was the daughter of a

ST BRIDGET

wealthy Leinster chieftain. Like her mother, however, she was one of her father's many slaves and worked long arduous hours on the farmland. Years later, by which time she had become a woman of considerable beauty, her father made many attempts to arrange a wealthy marriage.

But Bridget was adamant and her resolve to further the teachings of Christianity finally persuaded him to free her. With several female companions, Bridget set off for the monastery at Ardagh, there to study under Bishop Mel. Six months

later and now consecrated, Bridget and her companions returned home to found the convent of Kildare—'the place of the oak'. Stories are legion of the miracles performed by St Bridget as she travelled about the country, tending the sick, preaching the gospel and founding churches, schools and convents. She died at Kildare on February 1, 524.

The first two lines of an ancient Irish hymn dedicated to her, have a revealing eloquence about them:

*'Brigit, ever excellent woman, golden sparkling flame, lead us to the eternal Kingdom, the dazzling resplendent sun.'*

The Fleet Street church of St Bride's bears her name.

Of the many saints who travelled abroad **St Brendan** is one of the most interesting, although the stories of his famous seven-year voyage in search of the Land of Promise—the earthly paradise situated somewhere in the middle of the Atlantic—are perhaps more legendary than they are factual.

Born at Annagh in 484 on the south shore of Tralee Bay, he spent his early childhood in the care of a nun. Her religious influence prepared him for the higher studies he later pursued with Bishop Erc. Finally ordained by him as a priest, Brendan set off with great enthusiasm and energy to create two large monasteries: one at Ardfert in Tralee; the other well inland, up the R. Shannon, at Clonfert. All that remains of the latter is the famous Romanesque doorway to the church. A great seaman as well as a hillsman, Brendan covered what were then considered to be great distances, sailing not only to Scotland and the Hebrides but around the southern tip of Ireland to Wales and Brittany in his efforts to spread the influence of Christianity.

In later life he returned to his abbey at Clonfert and eventually died in 577 at the grand age of 93.

In the romantic life of his legendary voyages St Brendan's many experiences include the discovery of the Country of Perpetual Day where darkness never falls and seeing the Isle of Fleas where the insects outnumbered the grains of sand on the shoreline. He also celebrated Easter on the back of a whale, mistaking it for an island, and discovered Judas Iscariot suffering the punishment of Purgatory (except on Sundays and other religious occasions) on a tiny rock situated in the middle of the sea.

Irish history and Irish myth have long been the staple ingredients of Irish art but it was not until the latter part of the 19th century that a surge of creative writing used them to herald the famous Irish literary renaissance.

Before this period, the British occupation had almost killed continuity of tradition in the Irish way of life. Enthusiasm to restore the national language of Gaelic resulted in the formation of various literary and dramatic societies. Two of these were the Gaelic League by David Hyde in 1893 and the Irish Dramatic Movement in 1899. Two years later The Irish National Dramatic Society was formed and out of this grew the famous Abbey Theatre.

The Abbey Theatre's foundation was primarily due to the efforts of the poet **W. B. Yeats** who, with some financial assistance from England, purchased a property in Abbey Street, Dublin, and converted it to a theatre. It opened in 1904.

Yeats's other colleagues in the venture were originally **Edward Martyn** and **George Moore** but

GEORGE MOORE

being unable to go all the way with Yeats's visionary plans, first Martyn, then Moore, dropped out. They were replaced by the poet **AE (George Russell**, 1867–1935) and the playwright **Lady Gregory** (1852–1932).

Although the theatre originally set out to be nationalistic and draw on the wealth of Irish legends (which was Yeats's intention), its early presentations attacked many of the things the Irish held dear: mocking at marriage, ridiculing supposed miracles and pouring scorn on family relationships. For years afterwards its productions invariably provoked violent controversy at home, meanwhile earning a reputation abroad that was highly acclaimed.

After the period of civil strife ended in Ireland in 1924, dramatic emphasis shifted from the Abbey's productions to the Gate Theatre in Dublin. Founded by **Michael Mac Liammoir** and **Hilton Edwards**, the Gate presented a wider range of plays than the Abbey, embracing the work of international dramatists and subjects.

The Abbey meanwhile settled into the respectability of a national theatre, nourishing the best in Irish drama.

On the 17th July 1951, O'Casey's grim play *The Plough and the Stars* was presented at the Abbey. Its final act ends with a wild scene of insurrection and the burning of Dublin. A few hours after the curtain fell the theatre was a smoking ruin: gutted by a fire which consumed the stage props, scripts and costumes accumulated over nearly five decades. It was not until 1966 that the theatre re-opened.

W. B. YEATS

Ireland has probably reared more significant men of letters for its comparatively small size, than any other country in the English-speaking world. Of these, most seem to have been born in Dublin. The first outstanding native was **William Butler Yeats** (1865–1939). A far greater poet than dramatist (despite his activities in forming the Abbey), Yeats's early works—*The Land of Heart's Desire* (1894) and *Shadowy Waters* (1885–1906)—were symbolic, poetic dramas unrelated to contemporary life. As he developed, his writing became more intellectually obscure and an unfamiliar intensity revealed itself in his late plays, among them: *The Words upon the Window Pane* (1934) and *Purgatory* (1938).

His friend and companion, **Lady Gregory**, wrote no fewer than 27 short plays and poems. Her first two plays were written in collaboration with him: *The Pot of Broth* and *Cathleen ni Houlihan*.

This last was based upon the saga of Cuchulainn, which in turn bears a striking resemblance to the legendary labours of Hercules. She also translated a Molière play and her *Kiltartan Molière* was produced on the Irish stage.

A valuable recruit to the Abbey Theatre was **John Millington Synge** (1871–1909) whom Yeats had met in Paris. Synge, the son of a barrister, had studied at Trinity College, Dublin in 1892, and after visiting Germany and Italy decided to settle in Paris where he set himself to study Hebrew and French Drama. Ironically, it was Yeats who convinced him his real chance lay in Ireland. In 1903 Synge joined the Irish National Dramatic Society, and that same year wrote *The Shadow of the Glen*. By 1904 he was a director of the Abbey Theatre and in 1907 wrote his most famous work: *The Playboy of the Western World*. He died three years later, a reclaimed expatriate.

Another Dubliner, born in 1880, was the unschooled **Sean O'Casey**.

SEAN O'CASEY

The Abbey Theatre produced his first play, *The Shadow of a Gunman*, when he was 43 years of age. He followed this with *Juno and the Paycock*, a

drama of the Dublin slums, and its success established him as a foremost playwright. But his next play, titled *The Plough and the Stars*, is perhaps his finest. Those that followed were less successful and in 1928 the Abbey Theatre rejected *The Silver Tassie*. Living in England, O'Casey continued to write—*Within the Gates*, 1933; *Purple Dust*, 1940; *The Bishop's Bonfire*, 1955; he also produced an autobiography. He died in 1964.

In October 1856, the man many regard as the greatest wit of his time was born in Westland Row, Dublin: **Oscar Wilde**. Between 1887, when he was, for a short time, editor of the *Woman's World*, and his death in France in 1900, Wilde wrote plays—among them *Lady Windermere's Fan* and *The Importance of Being Earnest*: poems, criticisms, children's stories and the famous *De Profundis*, his final prose work cast as a letter to Lord Alfred Douglas. In this letter, written during his imprisonment for homosexuality, he claimed 'the Gods have given me almost everything', but it was society that provided the acclaim

OSCAR WILDE

he deserved and the final disaster he courted.

Two years younger than Wilde, **George Bernard Shaw** grew up in Dublin, then in 1876 moved to London. There, he wrote a number of unspectacular novels and from 1885 to 1894 was the music critic of the London *Star* and then *The World*. His first play, *Widowers' Houses*, was performed in 1892, and in 1909 the Abbey Theatre produced *The Shewing up of Blanco Posnet*, after the play had been banned in England because of Shaw's religious pronouncements. His best-known works include: *Arms and the Man* and *Candida*, 1894; *The Devil's Disciple* 1897; *Caesar and Cleopatra* 1898; *Man and Superman* 1903; *The Doctor's Dilemma* 1906; *Pygmalion* 1912; and *St Joan* 1924. In 1925 he was awarded the Nobel Prize for Literature. He died in 1950.

GEORGE BERNARD SHAW

Among the more recent Dublin dramatists few have made a greater impact than the late **Brendan Behan**. Born in 1923, he wrote an early

BRENDAN BEHAN

autobiography, *Borstal Boy*, which vividly illustrated his experiences in prison and his activities with the IRA. He then turned to playwrighting and his first work, *The Quare Fellow*, was produced in 1954. Four years later he followed this with another tragicomedy, *The Hostage*. As with *The Quare Fellow* he was largely assisted with the revision and expansion of the play by Joan Littlewood, founder of the Theatre Workshop. Unhappily Brendan Behan died at the early age of 41.

SAMUEL BECKETT

A far more complex playwright is the Anglo-Irishman **Samuel Beckett**. After a first-class academic grounding, which resulted in an exchange lectureship in Paris, he met and became associated with James Joyce and his contemporaries. Beckett's most widely acclaimed work is *Waiting for Godot*, which was produced in Paris in 1953 and later throughout the world. Beckett is now one of the world's foremost playwrights and novelists.

Although his close friend, **James Joyce**, did not write primarily for the theatre, the force of his dramatic invention influenced many of his creative counterparts. Born in Dublin in 1882, he travelled widely throughout Europe supporting himself by teaching. In 1914 he wrote a collection of short stories under the title *Dubliners*, and in the next 30 years

JAMES JOYCE

produced his greatest works, *Ulysses* and *Finnegans Wake*. He moved to Switzerland in 1940 and died in Zurich the following January.

# THE TREASURES OF IRELAND

---

*A unique and little-known*

*land that has preserved the inheritance*

*of over 3000 years of civilisation*

---

The hard facts of Ireland's history have made it dramatically different from the rest of the British Isles; accordingly Ireland is here given a separate section from England, Scotland and Wales. The story is a long, sad one of oppression by foreigners, cruel religious conflict at home and ordeal by famine; it is made bearable by the memory of a Golden Age when the Gaels, who made princes out of poets, carried the torch of Christianity through three dark centuries.

Monasteries, crosses, illuminated manuscripts and superb examples of religious metalwork still survive as reminders of that romantic period between the 6th and 9th centuries when Irish missionaries spread learning and culture across Europe. But the centuries that followed were so violent that an ancient church or monastery mentioned here must be presumed to be roofless unless otherwise stated.

Only in the middle of the 17th century was a condition of relative political stability assured, to permit the steady growth of urban civilisation. The towns, which often have a grandeur of lay-out which seems out of proportion to the size of their populations, are linked by a network of roads which again are unexpectedly large in scale.

After the famine and emigrations of the 1840's, the population fell by two million, and today is only four and a quarter million. One result of this is that the pace of life in Ireland seems easier than in Britain. When country houses and other occupied buildings are mentioned in this section, no implication is intended that they are all open to the public; but many people will still, in practice, prove ready to admit an interested visitor if asked courteously.

**Abbeyleix** *Laois* 573Gb
Laid out by the de Vesci family, with tree-lined streets and the Market House; the most interesting building is the church, with a front and spire by John Semple, altered and rebuilt by Thomas H. Wyatt in 1865.
ABBEYLEIX HOUSE Built for the 1st Viscount de Vesci in 1773–4, a square house entirely refaced in the 19th century. The interior has fine plasterwork designed by James Wyatt, and a dining-room with grisaille decoration by de Grée. (Not open.)

**Adare** *Lim.* 570Ee
ADARE CASTLE Only one wall survives of the original, nearly-square keep—surrounded by an inner bailey, a gate-house for a drawbridge and a fosse. The outer ward has a gate and two towers. The castle has two great halls by the river, the earlier and smaller being the first-floor hall, containing round-headed paired windows, dating from *c.* 1200, and the other being a 13th-century ground-floor hall. A FitzGerald stronghold.
An 18th-century mansion at Adare was joined by a new Tudor Revival manor, begun in 1832 by the 2nd Earl of Dunraven, with a magnificent long gallery and twin towers by the brothers Pain. The rest of the house was completed by P. C. Hardwicke, A. W. Pugin and Lord Dunraven himself, and was finished by 1876. It has fine paintings and furniture. (Grounds and house open to the public.)
AUGUSTINIAN BLACK ABBEY Founded in 1315 by the 1st Earl of Kildare, the structure dates mostly from the 15th century. The cloister-garth of *c.* 1470, with the FitzGerald saltire carved in the north spandrels of the east arcade, is pierced with triple openings; the cloister is small and square. In 1807 the ruins were adapted as a Protestant church and much unfortunate modification took place.
FRANCISCAN FRIARY Built by Thomas, 7th Earl of Kildare, and beautifully sited in the Adare Manor demesne. The church was finished *c.* 1484 and the rest probably by 1500. Notable cloister and sedilia.
TRINITARIAN FRIARY The sole example of a Trinitarian house in Ireland, founded in 1230 by Lord Ossory and enlarged in 1275. The whole building was remodelled, with the addition of a new nave aisle, to serve as the Catholic church, by P. C. Hardwick in the mid-19th century, for the 3rd Earl of Dunraven. Near by is a dove-cote.

**Aghowle** *Wicklow* 573Ja
The north, east and west walls survive of the early 12th-century church, whose most remarkable feature is its massive megalithic west doorway with a flat lintel and bold architrave.

**Ahenny (or Kilclispeen)** *Tipp.* 571Hd
Two superb 8th-century high crosses which are among the most important in the south-east. The north cross has fine abstract geometric and spiral ornaments on the shaft. A third cross, of which the base survives, is said to have been stolen.

**Annaghdown Abbey** *Gal.* 572Cd
The monastery traditionally founded by St Brendan of Clonfert. The cathedral, possibly a Premonstratensian church, has a Romanesque window and a Gothic north door. The ruins of an Augustinian priory of many dates and of a plain nunnery-church may also be seen. A small plain 15th-century church incorporates a late-Romanesque window with delicately carved chevron ornament.

**Annaghmore** *Arm.* 575Gd
A well-preserved court-cairn excavated in 1963–4, it has neat horizontal inter-filling between the upright stones.

**Antrim** *Antrim* 575He
The county town, site of an early monastery, whose Round Tower survives almost complete, with a cross in relief over the door and a restored conical cap. The ruins of Antrim Castle, burnt in 1922, remain; the embattled shell, by Sir Richard Morrison, incorporates an early 17th-century door. The most remarkable feature, though, is the garden, one of the rare examples of a French-style lay-out in Ireland.

**Aran Islands** *Gal.* 572Bc
There are three principal islands; Inishmore to the north-west, Inishmaan in the middle, and Inisheer to the south-east. On all three islands there are numerous early drystone forts and early Christian remains. The exact date of the great forts is unknown, but they are presumed to be of the Iron Age. St Enda, who is credited with the foundation of the Christian settlement, lived in the early 6th century, but it is doubtful whether the stone churches are so early; yet lack of timber makes it improbable that there were timber originals.
INISHEER Among the monuments are Creg.gankeel, an irregular large fort; a ruined 15th-century castle, set in a circular fort; a circular graveyard called Knockgrannia, near the landing-stage; St Cavan's Church, with a nave and chancel; Kilgobnet Church, small and primitive.
INISHMAAN The principal monument is Dun Conor, one of the finest of the great forts; it is oval, with an outer bailey and restored hut-sites within. Inishmaan also has one of the few Bronze Age tombs on the islands, 'Dermot and Grania's Bed', a name commonly given to chamber-tombs.
INISHMORE Kilronan, the principal town, is in Killeany Bay on the north-east coast. The major monument is the world-famous Dun Aengus, a huge drystone semicircular fort standing on the edge of a 300 ft cliff dropping sheer into the sea. To the north-west is Dun Onaght, a large ring-fort, also restored, and at Onaght village the so-called 'Seven Churches', with the remains of only two small churches, several early cross-slabs, and some 15th-century monastic remains. Near Kilmurvy village are Temple MacDuagh and Templenaneeve, both early churches, the former with a chancel. In the centre of the island, near the highest point, is Dun Oghil, a large stone ring-fort. West of it is the 15th-century church of the Four Beautiful Saints, and their grave. South of Kilronan is Killeany (Enda's Church). Here is the tiny Temple Benen, a well-preserved oratory built of enormous stones. A mile and half to the west is the promontory fort of Doocaher, also with a defensive line of spikes, and also restored, with clochans.

**Arboe** *Tyrone* 575Gd
HIGH CROSS At 18 ft 6 in., one of the tallest crosses in Ireland. Probably 10th century, it is carved with scenes from the Old and New Testaments.

**Ardbraccan House** *Meath* 573Je
A large stone house with wings, formerly the palace of the Bishops of Meath. The wings are by Richard Castle, and probably date from *c.* 1747. The main block is by James Wyatt. The parish church (1777) near by has a medieval bell-tower.

**Ardee** *Louth* 573Jf
An important strong-point on the north-west border of the medieval Pale. In the Main Street there is a castle, now a court-house, comprising a square keep of the 13th century. Hatch's Castle in Market Street is also 13th century. The Protestant church includes parts of a medieval church and has a medieval font.

## DUN AENGUS, INISHMORE, ARAN ISLANDS

*The most spectacular of the Aran Islands' many prehistoric monuments, this dramatically sited dry-stone fort encloses nearly 11 acres. It has three rings of defence, the central one reinforced with a line of jagged limestone uprights. The innermost rampart encloses an area about 150 ft in diameter.*

**Ardfert** *Kerry* 570Cd
FRANCISCAN FRIARY Founded in 1253 by Thomas
FitzMaurice, 1st Lord Kerry, and now in ruins.
The rectangular building has a row of lancets on
the south side of the choir. Near by are the
remains of Ardfert House, with a garden of formal
banks and an 18th-century Gothic arch. The
splendid mid-19th-century embattled lodge gates
of the demesne are in the village.
ST BRENDAN'S CATHEDRAL This roofless early
13th-century building has a fine chancel with a
row of nine lancet windows on its south side and
three tall lancets to the east.
TEMPLE NA HOE This early church has lost its
chancel, but the nave has angle columns with
carved capitals, a west door, a small decorated
south window and a carved chancel arch.

**Ardglass** *Down* 575Jc
This fishing village has five castles or fortified
houses as reminders of its importance in the Middle
Ages. Jordan's Castle is now a museum; Ardglass
Castle was Gothicised in 1790.

**Ardmayle** *Tipp.* 571Ge
A fine 17th-century wall with mullioned windows
survives here of the embattled house.

**Ardmore** *Waterford* 571Gc
The foundation of St Declan still contains some of
the most striking early Christian buildings in Ireland. The Round Tower, which is one of the tallest
and most complete, has an unusual degree of taper,
a set of string-courses marking the floors and its
original conical roof. Close by stands the 12th-
century cathedral, of which the west wall is decorated with two large blind arches each containing
small arcades with figure-sculpture, above which
is another arcade of 13 arches also containing
figure-sculpture.

**Ardrass** *Kildare* 573Jd
ST PATRICK'S CHAPEL A small, probably late-
medieval church, noteworthy for its traditional
Irish form of stone roof.

**Ardscull** *Kildare* 573Hb
The great mote around which the road from
Naas to Athy pivots may have been a prehistoric
burial mound; it was certainly fortified in Cromwellian times. Near by is the rath of Mullaghmast,
where a massacre took place in 1577.

**Ardtermon Castle** *Sligo* 574Bc
A semi-fortified house of the early 17th century, in
the form of a long rectangle with cylindrical angle-
towers and semicircular staircase-projection at the
back. The nearly-square fortified enclosure at the
back also has a cylindrical angle-tower.

**Arklow** *Wicklow* 573Kb
Handsome stone Catholic church of *c.* 1840 by
Patrick Byrne, with distinguished front including
a western tower and cupola. The domed interior
has good plasterwork.

**Armagh** *Arm.* 575Gc
The ecclesiastical capital of Ireland, seat of two
archbishops, traditionally founded by St Patrick.
The city occupies the site of an ancient earth-fort
within which lies the Protestant cathedral. The
first church on the site was built by St Patrick, but
the aspect of the present cathedral is an entirely
19th-century restoration by Lewis Cottingham.
The cathedral dominates the city; the churchyard
is the reputed burying-place of Brian Boru, who
drove the Norsemen from Ireland in the 11th
century, and there are monuments by Roubiliac,
Chantrey, Rysbrack and Nollekens. Famed as a
centre of learning, Armagh was repeatedly
plundered during the Middle Ages, and by the
16th century was little more than a village. It now
consists of the concentric circles of the ancient
settlement, side by side with the Mall, originally
the racecourse, and now surrounded for the most
part by fine houses. Much of its present attraction is
due to the influence of Primate Richard Robinson
(Lord Rokeby) who came to the See in 1765, and
remained there till his death in 1794. Apart from
the Protestant cathedral, the principal ancient relic
is the ruined church of the Franciscan friary in the
primate's demesne.

West of the Protestant cathedral is Vicar's Hill,
a row of 18th-century houses, and near them the
library, founded by Primate Robinson in 1771 to
house his notable collection of books and the diocesan records. It was designed by Thomas Cooley,
but harmoniously extended *c.* 1820. Beside it
stands the Infirmary of 1774 by George Ensor. At
the bottom of Abbey Street is the Shambles, or
Grain Market (1829). At the north-west end of the
Mall is the porticoed court-house of 1809 by
Francis Johnston, a native of Armagh and a
protégé of the primate, while the other end is
occupied by the gaol. The best terraces in the Mall
are Beresford Place, *c.* 1800, in red limestone, and
Charlemont Place, larger in scale and more
regular, in fine local limestone ashlar. The museum
on the north side of the Mall occupies a temple-like
school building of 1833. In Scotch Street is the
handsome town house of the Dobbin family, now
the Bank of Ireland, by Francis Johnston. In
College Hill is the Royal School, founded in 1608,
its present building of 1774 by Cooley, considerably enlarged. Opposite it on the hill is the charming Observatory founded by Primate Robinson

## MONUMENT TO SIR
## THOMAS MOLYNEUX

*This posthumous portrait of a
Physician-General to the British
forces in Ireland was commissioned
by his son from Roubiliac in 1752.
It first stood in the grounds of the
Molyneux house, Castle Dillon,
near Armagh (in a temporary
wooden shelter), and was not moved
to its present site for nearly 100
years. On the high base there is a
damaged relief by Roubiliac depicting Molyneux visiting the sick.
Another great work by Roubiliac,
a bust of Dean Swift, is in Trinity
College Library, Dublin.
(Armagh Protestant Cathedral)*

and designed by Thomas Cooley in 1788. On another hill to the north-west is the twin-towered Catholic cathedral begun by Thomas Duff of Newry in 1840 in the Perpendicular Gothic style, and completed in 1873 by J. J. McCarthy; the interior with its angel-roof is notable. St Mark's Protestant church, built by Primate Stuart *c.* 1830, is approached from the Mall by an avenue of trees; near by is the highly wooded demesne, now partially a golf course, of the bishop's palace, built by Primate Robinson to the design of Cooley in 1770. Beside it stands its detached chapel of 1781, with a notable Classical interior; the porticoed exterior is by Cooley and the interior, with splendid fittings, by Francis Johnston.

**Ash Hill Towers** *Lim.*                          *570Ed*
A Classical house with a central, pedimented, symmetrical block with a deep stable court and piers, built in 1781. The interior has Wyatt-type plasterwork. The rear facade was rebuilt in the Gothic Revival style of 1833, probably by the Pain brothers. (By appointment.)

**Askeaton** *Lim.*                          *570De*
One of the chief castles of the FitzGeralds of Desmond. Mostly 15th century, it comprises two courts on an island in the R. Deel. The most interesting feature is a magnificent 15th-century great hall with florid decorated windows.
FRANCISCAN FRIARY Founded before 1400, probably by Gerald, 4th Earl of Desmond, and restored in the 15th century by the 6th Earl. The cloister buildings lie, unusually, to the south of the church which, in consequence, has an aisled north transept; the refectory, again unusually, lies to the north and south, abutting on the south walk of the cloister. The beautifully carved cloister is among the earliest and finest in Ireland.

**Athassel** *Tipp.*                          *571Ge*
This Augustinian priory, founded in 1193 by the de Burgos, is one of the best of Irish monasteries. The church has an aisled nave, a tower (a 15th-century insertion) at the crossing of the transepts, with four eastward chapels and a short choir with lancets to north and south. The doorway dividing the nave from the choir is a striking feature with four orders of ornament. The dorter stands on a vaulted basement and the chapter house lies to the east of it. The refectory also stands on vaults, and there is a vaulted gate-house. Extensive precinct walls survive in large part.

**Athenry** *Gal.*                          *572Dc*
A 16th-century town cross has figures of St Mary and St John. The Protestant parish church has some fragments of its medieval predecessor, and near by is the ruined north gate of the town. Extensive sections of the town walls may also be seen.
ATHENRY CASTLE This castle of the de Berminghams is irregularly shaped, with a mid-13th-century keep in good condition. There is a fine early Gothic doorway with elaborate capitals.
DOMINICAN FRIARY OF SS PETER AND PAUL Founded in 1241 by Myler de Bermingham, but most of its present features date from the 14th century. It was partly rebuilt in 1423 after a fire, and was occupied as late as 1652. Good details.

**Athlone** *Westmeath*                          *572Fd*
An important bridge-head on the Shannon with a much altered 13th-century castle and some interesting early 19th-century fortifications on the west side of the river. The Renaissance-style Catholic church was built in 1937. North-east is the demesne of Waterstown, a house designed by Richard Castle, now in ruins though an octagonal

spired dove-cote and a hermitage remain in the landscape lay-out. Three miles north-east on the hill of Bealin is a high cross with spirals, a hunting scene and inscriptions.

**Athlumney House** *Meath*                          *573Je*
Adjoining the 15th-century Dowdall Castle is a fine gabled and mullioned 17th-century house.

**Athy** *Kild.*                          *573Hb*
The town contains White's Castle, built in 1575. There is also a court-house of *c.* 1800 with an additional modern storey; on the outside are rather crudely carved plaques representing the Scales of Justice and the Harp of Hibernia inside wreaths.

**Avondale** *Wicklow*                          *573Kb*
A square house of 1779, possibly designed by James Wyatt. It was built by Samuel Hayes, a notable amateur architect, and is famous as the birthplace and home of the Irish Nationalist Charles Stewart Parnell. Fine Wyatt plasterwork in the drawing-room incorporates mirrors in the decoration. (Open by appointment.)

**Ballinfad** *Sligo*                          *574Cb*
The castle of the Curlews at Ballinafad, built in *c.* 1519 to control an important pass, is a small keep with four massive cylindrical angle-towers.

**Ballinamantain** See Kiltartan.

**Ballinasloe** *Gal.*                          *572Ed*
A market town at the end of a branch of the Grand Canal, notable for the splendid mental hospital of 1838. There are also some good 18th-century houses. Near by is Garbally, originally the seat of the Trenches, Earls of Clancarty, in the grounds of which is a curious fluted obelisk. The house, by Sir Richard Morrison, is now a school and has a good library and art collection.

**Ballinatray House** *Waterford*                          *571Gc*
A large nine-bay pedimented block of 1795–7, magnificently sited in an enormous deer park by the R. Blackwater.

**Ballincollig** *Cork*                          *570Eb*
A tall medieval castle with a large bawn.

**Ballinderry** *Antrim*                          *575Hd*
MIDDLE CHURCH Bishop Jeremy Taylor began this church in 1664. It is a simple rectangle with square-headed, three-light windows with oak mullions and transoms, and retains part of its original Jacobean-style fittings.

**Ballinlough Castle** *Westmeath*                          *573He*
An early 18th-century house to which, *c.* 1760, a twin round-towered crenellated range was added.

**Ballintober** *Mayo*                          *573Ce*
AUGUSTINIAN FRIARY Founded by Cathal O'Conor in 1216. The church was originally cruciform and had no aisle, with a tower over the crossing. There are good Romanesque and early Gothic details on the windows and capitals. The choir is vaulted, and the transepts each have vaulted eastward chapels. It continued to be used for Catholic worship throughout the 17th and 18th centuries, and in 1846 the great John MacHale, Archbishop of Tuam, began its restoration. In 1889 George Ashlin re-roofed the chancel, crossing and transept, and there has recently been further sensitive restoration. The remains of a Jacobean tomb of the 1st Lord Mayo can be seen in the sacristy.

**Ballintober Castle** *Roscom.*                          *572Ee*
Built *c.* 1300 by the O'Conors; a large native copy of the Anglo-Norman castle at Roscommon.

*myself.*

## WILLIAM BUTLER YEATS, IRELAND'S POETIC GENIUS

The area around Sligo, in the west of Ireland, is known as Yeats Country because of its associations with the man who transmuted national legend into world poetry; a Yeats Summer School is held at Sligo every year. In his twenties, Yeats lived in London where 'he lived, breathed, ate, drank and slept poetry', striding about the streets reciting and flailing his arms. At 30, he was established as an imaginative writer with *The Celtic Twilight* (1893) and *Poems* (1895). Only a few broken walls remain of Coole Park in Galway where Yeats and Lady Gregory conceived the idea of a National Theatre. With her encouragement he developed into the colossus of the Abbey Theatre, Dublin.

'I shuddered', Yeats said, when he first saw this portrait, painted by Augustus John. 'Always particular about my clothes, never dissipated, never unshaven except during illness, I saw myself there as an unshaven, drunken bartender, and then I began to feel John had found something that he liked in me. He has found Anglo-Irish solitude, a solitude I have made for myself, an outlawed solitude.'
(Tate Gallery, London)

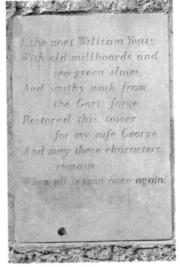

*I, the poet William Yeats,*
*With old millboards and*
*sea-green slates,*
*And smithy work from*
*the Gort forge,*
*Restored this tower*
*for my wife George,*
*And may these characters*
*remain*
*When all is ruin once again.*

THOOR BALLYLEE, *the roofless Norman tower built upon a small island in County Galway, which Yeats bought for £35 in 1917. He turned the place into a home, as the inscription upon it tells. The tower became the centre of Yeats's imagination, a symbol of mental solitude and questing. Publication of 'The Tower' in 1928, followed by 'The Winding Stair' in 1929, crowned his achievement as a poet. T. S. Eliot calls Yeats's work in his middle and later years 'a great and permanent example of a kind of moral as well as intellectual excellence'. The castle has been renovated and can be visited during summer months.*

MAUD GONNE, *beautiful and fiery Irish revolutionary, subject of much of Yeats's poetry, and the unrequited love of his youth. (By Sarah Purser at the Irish National Portrait Gallery)*

NOBEL MEDAL *for literature, awarded to Yeats in 1923, and a mark of his recognition as a lyric poet. It lies upon the manuscript of 'The Lake Isle of Innisfree'. (Sligo Museum, Eire)*

BRONZE *by Henry Moore in memory of Yeats, who became a Senator of the new Parliament of the Irish Free State in 1922 and founded, with Shaw, the Irish Academy of Letters. (St Stephen's Green, Dublin)*

THE POET'S HOME *in Woburn Walk, London, where Yeats lived for 24 years and, with his genius for friendship, entertained many intellectuals of his time.*

THE AUTOGRAPH TREE, *a copper beech at Lady Gregory's home, Coole Park, Galway. Lady Gregory's initials are surrounded by those of famous guests, including Yeats.*

> *Cast a cold eye*
> *on life, on death*
> *Horseman, pass by!*
> This epitaph, by the poet himself, is in Drumcliffe churchyard, Co. Sligo.

> *I will arise and go now, and go to Innisfree,*
> *And a small cabin build there, of clay and wattles made:*
> *Nine bean-rows will I have there, a hive for the honey-bee,*
> *And live alone in the bee-loud glade.*
> From 'The Lake Isle of Innisfree', Yeats's most famous poem.

**Ballycastle** *Antrim* 575Gg
The town consists of a long straight street leading from the 'diamond' to the sea. Marconi transmitted his first wireless message from a cottage here in 1905.
BUNAMARGY FRIARY Founded for the Franciscans *c.* 1500; it now stands in ruins, containing a mausoleum of the McDonnell family.
PROTESTANT CHURCH An attractive 18th-century building erected by the Boyd family in 1756; it has a western tower with a Venetian window and clock, a pedimented doorway and a stone spire.

**Ballycopeland** *Down* 575Jd
The little windmill is one of the only two in Ireland preserved by the State; the other is at Tacumshin.

**Ballyfin House** *Laois* 573Gb
A large, early 19th-century Classical house with Ionic portico designed by Sir Richard Morrison and his son for the Coote family. The gardens are by Lutyens. It is now a school.

**Ballygally Manor House** *Antrim* 575He
A Scottish tower-house built in 1625 by James Shaw, consisting of a rectangle with a north-east tower containing an entrance and spiral stairs.

**Ballygrennan Castle** *Lim.* 570Ee
A large castle with courtyards and a central keep with 16th-century mullioned windows, surrounded by 17th-century gabled and chimneyed buildings.

**Ballylee** See Gort.

**Ballymakenny** *Louth* 573Ke
Francis Johnston's first building designed in Gothic style. The church was completed in 1785–93 for Primate Robinson, in the style of Thomas Cooley; exquisite fittings and details.

**Ballymoon Castle** *Carlow* 571Jf
This keep-less castle is of unique, almost square form; it dates from the early 14th century, a period from which few buildings in Ireland survive.

**Ballymore** *Don.* 574Df
A good 18th-century church, probably designed by Michael Priestley of Lifford. It has a heavy moulded block Venetian window to the east, and retains its interior fittings.

**Ballymote Castle** *Sligo* 574Bb
The keep-less castle built by Richard De Burgh in *c.* 1300 has cylindrical angle-towers and D-shaped towers in the centres of the east and west walls. There was once a gateway of two such towers in the middle of the north front.

**Ballynacarriga** *Cork* 570Db
A 16th-century castle on a rock at the edge of a lake. The arched windows of the upper room on the top floor have interesting carvings and there is a sheila-na-gig (a female fertility figure) high up in the external wall.

**Ballynahinch** *Down* 575Hc
The assembly rooms have a Doric timber portico and date from the early 19th century.
ECHO HALL A good late 18th-century house with a first-floor central Venetian window.

**Ballynahow** *Tipp.* 571Gf
A 16th-century castle consisting of a five-storied circular tower, well preserved, the first and third storeys being vaulted over.

**Ballynoe Stone Circle** *Down* 575Jc
A regular circle of stones containing a horseshoe-shaped group of stones partly enclosing an oval mound, the whole about 100 ft in diameter. It was partly excavated in 1937–8 by Dr A. E. van Giffen.

**Ballyragget** *Kilk.* 571Hf
BUTLER CASTLE The 15th- and 16th-century Butler castle in the town retains its roof and the walled enclosure and ditch of its defences. In 1798 it served as a military barracks.

**Ballywalter** *Down* 575Jd
A large, *palazzo*-style house by Sir Charles Lanyon, built *c.* 1840 for the Mulholland family, later Barons Dunleath. (Not open to the public.)

**Balrothery** *Dublin* 573Ke
The tower of the Protestant church resembles that at Lusk, though here there was no Round Tower to serve as the starting point; it dates from *c.* 1500.

**Baltinglass** *Wicklow* 573Jc
A Cistercian house, founded by Dermot McMurrough, King of Leinster, before 1167. The church and remnants of the cloister survive.

**Banagher** *Offaly* 572Fc
Best known for its long bridge over the Shannon, and for having once been the home of Anthony Trollope, the novelist. It has a handsome house with a porch and curved pedimented door in the Main Street. By the Shannon are early 19th-century fortifications. Three miles to the north-east is Shannon Harbour, the western end of the Grand Canal, now totally deserted with numerous abandoned warehouses and a canal hotel.

**Bandon** *Cork* 570Eb
On the river of the same name, the town was founded in 1608 and bought shortly afterwards by the Great Earl of Cork. One of the earliest Protestant churches, that of Kilbrogin, was founded here in 1610. This church preserves the town stocks and whipping post. In St Patrick's Church, Ballymodan, is a monument by Scheemakers.

**Bantry House** *Cork* 570Cb
A house of many dates, from *c.* 1740 onwards, in red brick with stucco work and pilastered extensions magnificently sited in a notable garden. The 14-bay south front dates from 1840, but the house is mainly interesting for the paintings and furniture assembled by Richard, 2nd Earl of Bantry. A fine stable block has an entrance arch with a Corinthian lead-domed rotunda. (Open to the public.)

**Bargy** *Wex.* 571Kd
BARGY CASTLE At the head of Tacumshin Lough, a tower-house which was the home of Bagenal Harvey, a country gentleman hanged for his participation in the rising of 1798.

**Baronscourt** *Tyrone* 574Ee
An early 18th-century house, altered by George Steuart, later reworked by Sir John Soane, 1791–2, entirely revamped by Sir Richard Morrison, and recently modified. The seat of the Dukes of Abercorn since the 17th century. (Not open to the public.)

**Barryscourt Castle** *Cork* 570Fb
A large medieval castle rebuilt in 1585. There is an interesting chapel and a chimney-piece dated 1588.

**Beaulieu** *Louth* 573Ke
Almost the only wide-eaved, Dutch-inspired house to survive in Ireland, built in the 1660's by Sir Henry Tichborne, of rubble stone plastered with brick dressings. The interior contains notable wooden carvings in the hall, Carolean plasterwork and a fine early Georgian staircase.

**Beauparc** *Meath* 573Je
A house of 1755 of cut stone with wings and convex quadrants, possibly to the design of the amateur architect Nathaniel Clements.

**Bective Abbey** *Meath* 573Je
The original Cistercian abbey, founded by the King of Meath in the 12th century, was much rebuilt in the 15th century, and after the Dissolution was turned into a fortified house. The triple cloister arcades are of the 15th century, and the square chapter house, with a central column, is from the 13th century.

**Belan House** *Kild.* 573Jb
The ruined remains of the great house of Belan, built for Lord Aldborough by Richard Castle and Francis Bindon in 1743. There is a fine stable block and, in the surrounding fields, a Doric rotunda and several follies.

**Belcamp** *Dublin* 573Kd
A handsome house of *c.* 1786 with interior plasterwork.

**Belfast** *Antrim* 575Hd
Second city of Ireland and, since 1921, capital of Northern Ireland. It was a place of small importance until the middle of the 18th century, being overshadowed by Carrickfergus. It belonged to the Chichester family, later Earls of Donegall, who built a castle in the early 17th century on the Farset R., from which Belfast takes its name; the modern Castle Street commemorates its site. The broad High Street, continuing to the east, is the bed of the Farset R., which until the beginning of the 19th century was open between quays and flanked by the houses of a prosperous market town. A 12-arch bridge was built over the Lagan in 1682 on the site of the present Queen's Bridge, which replaced it in 1841. On the accession of the 5th Earl of Donegall in 1757, a policy of improving the town was begun.

By the 1770's Belfast was beginning to show symptoms of its future industrial development. In the 1780's, the local architect Roger Mulholland undertook the lay-out of regular streets such as Donegall Street and Donegall Place.

Sir Charles Lanyon was responsible for some of Belfast's most distinguished buildings. He was trained as a civil engineer and his earliest surviving structure in Belfast is the Queen's Bridge, now much altered. It was Lanyon who encased Sir Robert Taylor's assembly rooms in the Barry *palazzo* style in 1845. In the same year he began the Queen's College, now Queen's University, an elegant symmetrical red-brick Tudor building with stone dressings and central tower, well set back from University Road. Many unworthy additions have since been made to it at the back and sides. The head office of the Northern Bank, which Lanyon built in 1852, is an extraordinarily successful monumental effort with a central hall lit by clerestory windows with delicate glazing. Near the university, at the east end of University Square, is the Presbyterian Assembly's College (1853–5), in a style owing something to Vanbrugh and also to Soane; for many years it housed the new Parliament of Northern Ireland. The custom house, an E-shaped building, dates from 1857; it is in the *palazzo* style, and is considered by many to be Belfast's finest building.

Bedford Street, leading from Donegall Square to Dublin Road, is lined with the substantial mid-Victorian headquarters of linen manufacturers. Among them Nos. 9–15 have a most impressively windowed façade, the two upper storeys surmounted by a colossal Italianate cornice; it may well be the work of Sir Charles Lanyon. In the same street is the Ulster Hall of 1860 by W. J. Barre, whose most conspicuous Belfast building is the Albert Memorial clock-tower in Queen's Square. The head office of the Ulster Bank in

Waring Street, designed by James Hamilton and finished in 1860, is an exuberant work, especially the railings and lamp-standards. In the offices of the Belfast Gas Works in Ormeau Road, the staircase and entrance hall are rich with coloured tilework and pilasters; the exterior is by Sir Charles Lanyon's son John.

The public houses of Victorian Belfast are a study in themselves. Kelly's Wine Vaults are in the traditional style, though somewhat embellished for the tourists, and the Crown Liquor Saloon opposite the Great Northern Station is of unparalleled opulence, and still completely unspoilt. Other distinguished high-Victorian buildings include Alex McAllister's Gothic Oxford Street School.

The Ulster Brewery in Sandy Row, by Alex McAllister, has a good composition of barrels, sacks of grain and anchors in the segmental pediment. Another architect, William Batt, was responsible for perhaps the most notable building of high-Victorian Belfast, the National Bank of 1897, in High Street.

At the end of the 19th century, Belfast began to express its status with new public buildings. St Anne's Protestant Cathedral, on the site of the old parish church, was begun in 1898 by Sir Thomas Drew and W. H. Lynn and has been worked on ever since by a variety of people, as the changes of style show. The City Hall, begun in 1902 to the designs of Sir Brumwell Thomas, was completed in 1906. It is Edwardian baroque with a copper-covered dome visible for miles. The Presbyterian Church House and Assembly Hall in College Square East has an open-work steeple copied from St Giles's in Edinburgh. In 1902 the Sinclair Seamen's Church, built by Lanyon, was furnished with such maritime fittings as a Moby Dick corner pulpit, a binnacle as a lectern, ships' bells and a steering wheel. The establishment of the local Parliament in 1921 led to the building at Stormont of an enormous white Classical Parliament House designed by Sir Arnold Thornely.

SIDE TABLE: CORNER DETAIL

*One manifestation of Irish Palladianism (1730–60) was baroque furniture, detailed in the William Kent tradition. This grotesque animal mask, carved on the corner leg of a mahogany table, was typical of the period. (Ulster Museum, Belfast)*

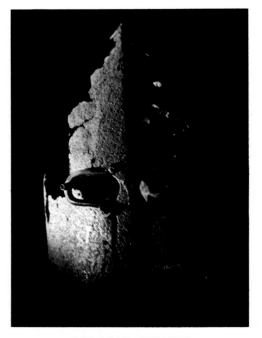

## CONICAL HELMET

*The origin of this rare brass-mounted helmet is obscure, but it is probably English and dates from the 14th century. It was found at Lough Henney in Co. Down with a mass of flat-sectioned chain-mail which may have been worn with it. (Ulster Museum, Belfast)*

## ARCHBISHOP COBBE GOBLET

*William III was popular with all Irish Protestants from about 1688, and this large ceremonial goblet, which belonged to Archbishop Cobbe (1687–1765), is engraved with a loyal toast and the figure of the king on horseback. (Ulster Museum, Belfast)*

BELFAST BANK, HEAD OFFICE The earliest public building now surviving, though much disguised; it started life as a market-house in 1769, and was converted in 1776 to assembly rooms with the addition of an upper storey by Sir Robert Taylor. Its present form is the result of much more drastic reshaping.

CASTLE Stands above the city, underneath Cave Hill. It was built in 1870 in the Scottish baronial style by Lanyon's partner W. H. Lynn, and has a tower reminiscent of Balmoral and a French Renaissance-style garden staircase of 1894. In the grounds there is a mortuary chapel containing a marble, life-size group of the Earl of Belfast on his death sofa (he died in Naples) by Patrick McDowell.

CHURCH OF ST GEORGE A building of 1816 by John Bowden of Dublin, incorporating the fine Corinthian portico of 1788 from Ballyscullion House, Co. Londonderry, built by Francis Sandys or Michael Shanahan for the Earl-Bishop of Derry.

CLIFTON HOUSE The second earliest public building in Belfast, 1774, otherwise known as the Poor House or the Charitable Institution. The composition is regular: a pedimented centre-piece, with single-storey wings pedimented at their ends in the Palladian manner; there is an octagonal tower with a stone spire. It is mostly the work of the local architect Robert Joy.

FIRST PRESBYTERIAN (UNITARIAN) CHURCH An elliptical church completed in 1783 by Roger Mulholland and showing the influence of the architect Francis Hiorns of Warwick. The exterior was crudely remodelled in 1833, but the interior survives with its gallery and nearly all its fittings.

OLD MUSEUM Built in 1831 by Thomas Duff of Newry and Thomas Jackson, in the Greek Revival style; it is the earliest building in Ireland to be built as a museum, and is now the headquarters of the Belfast Natural History and Philosophical Society.

ST MALACHY'S CATHOLIC CHURCH Completed in 1848 by Thomas Jackson, partner of Thomas Duff. Externally it has to be taken a little less than seriously, with its gawky octagonal turrets surmounting the battlemented gable, but the interior is the richest in Belfast. The altar is framed by an open-work screen and tracery, the style of which is re-echoed in the pulpit. The altar paintings are by one of the Tyrolean Piccioni family.

ULSTER MUSEUM Situated in the Botanic Gardens, it has an interesting archaeological collection of Neolithic axes and scrapers, and some Bronze Age pottery, spear-heads and bracelets. Local and natural history collections include early flax-spinning and weaving apparatus. The art gallery contains paintings by Lawrence, Sickert, Steer, Turner and a selection of works by Ulster and Irish artists. (See also p. 585.)

**Bellamont Forest** *Cavan*         *573Hg*
One of the finest Palladian houses in Ireland, Bellamont was designed by Sir Edward Lovett Pearce for his uncle by marriage, Thomas Coote, *c.* 1729–30. It is a nearly square red-brick 'villa' with a Doric portico. The house has been very little altered, and contains fine plaster ceilings.

**Belline** *Kilk.*         *571Hd*
A three-storey house, flanked by free-standing tower-like pavilions. In the grounds there is a rustic Doric temple, made of tree trunks *c.* 1790.

**Bellinter House** *Meath*         *573Je*
One of the last houses by Richard Castle, built *c.* 1750 and repeating the Powerscourt lay-out, with pavilions connected by straight arcades to the main block flanked by curved, gated quadrants. The interior has fine stucco decoration and a splendidly barbaric hall chimney-piece. The wooden spiral service staircase is also noteworthy. The house is now a convent.

**Belvedere House** *Westmeath*     573Gd
An important example of the Irish 'villa', built in 1742 for the Earl of Belvedere by Richard Castle, with a low but complex outline. It contains a fine staircase and rococo plasterwork of the highest quality. To the left of the house is Ireland's most important Gothic caprice, a large screen known as the Jealous Wall, built 1760. At the other end of the park is another fine piece of Gothic rustic work, an arch surmounted by an oriel window. Altogether, this is one of Ireland's most notable landscaping achievements. (House not open.)

**Benburb** *Tyrone*     574Fc
Built by Lord Wingfield *c.* 1615, it is an irregular quadrangular fort 200 ft above the R. Blackwater. The south-west corner is ruined. At two adjoining corners are square buildings of two storeys, one of which has a round tower with a spiral staircase.

**Birr** *Offaly*     572Fc
This well-planned town was laid out in the late 18th and early 19th centuries, with malls and a small square containing a column, formerly surmounted by a statue of the Duke of Cumberland. The Protestant church was designed in *c.* 1810 by John Johnston. The interior, with its slender Gothic pillars, plaster vaults and a corridor of galleries, is particularly attractive. The Catholic church, with its fine tower and spire, was built in 1817 to the design of Bernard Mullen. Also notable is an Ionic temple designed by Lord Rosse in 1828 in memory of his son; it serves as a school-house. In front stands the statue by Foley of William Parsons, 3rd Earl of Rosse, the astronomer. The Convent of the Sisters of Mercy, next door to the Catholic church, is by Augustus Welby Pugin.
BIRR CASTLE A 17th-century house built on the site of a castle. It still contains its late 17th-century yew-wood staircase, but the present aspect of the house is predominantly that of an early 19th-century 'castle', probably designed by John Johnston, of whom nothing outside Birr is known, and

## VICTORIAN GOTHIC CEILING

*A forest of pendants and tracery decorate this ceiling. The fan-vaults continue to the ground in the form of slender attached columns on the east wall of the church. (St Malachy's Catholic Church, Belfast)*

the 2nd Earl of Rosse, from 1808 to 1832. Its situation by the R. Brosna and its splendid garden, with 200-year-old box hedges over 30 ft high, magnolias and maple trees, make it one of the most ornamental estates in Ireland. The walls and barrel of the famous 'Great Telescope' which was, until 1915, the largest in the world—6 ft in diameter and 54 ft long—may still be seen in the grounds. (Gardens open to the public.)

**Bishopscourt House** *Kild.*     573Jc
A porticoed house of *c.* 1788 built for Speaker Ponsonby, who largely controlled the king's business in Ireland in the mid-18th century. It is probably the work of James Gandon.

**Blarney Castle** *Cork*     570Ec
Home of the Blarney Stone, said to confer eloquence on anyone who kisses it, the castle was built in 1446 by the McCarthys of Muskerry. It consists of an enormous machicolated keep with an angle-tower containing a staircase. On one side are the remains of a considerable 18th-century Gothic extension built by the Jefferyes family, who also laid out the elaborate landscape garden.

**Boher** *Offaly*     570Fe
The Catholic church here houses the bones of St Manchan in a shrine that is the largest Irish reliquary and one of the most important products of the post-Viking Irish revival. (See p. 588.)

**Boom Hall** *Lond.*     574Ef
Built *c.* 1770 for the 1st Earl of Caledon, of cut stone, it has a large cubical central hall and polygonal bay window on the east front. The house was named after the boom which the English placed across the R. Foyle to prevent supply ships reaching Derry during the 105-day siege of 1689.

**Bovevagh** *Lond.*     574Ff
In the churchyard is a house-shaped stone tomb, said to be that of a saint; a similar one is at Banagher.

**Boyle** *Roscom.*     572Ef
ABBEY Founded in 1161, it has one of the largest Cistercian churches in Ireland. The low crossing tower was an original feature, though it has since been heightened. The choir and eastward chapels are vaulted and the piers of the nave have interesting Transitional carvings.
BOYLE BARRACK A town house facing the R. Boyle, built to the designs of Sir Edward Lovett Pearce or his subordinate William Halfpenny. It is vaulted throughout and has a heavily pedimented front facing the river.

**Brenanstown or Glendruid** *Dublin*     573Kc
A fine portal dolmen with large granite capstone.

**Browndod** *Antrim*     575He
A cairn with four chambers to its gallery, on Donegore Hill. It was excavated in 1934.

**Browne's Hill** *Carlow*     571Jf
One of the largest dolmens in Europe, with a capstone estimated to weigh over 100 tons; two of the smaller supports have collapsed, and it stands in a hollow which may be original. Near by is a cut-stone Georgian house of *c.* 1763.

**Brugh na Boinne** *Meath*     573Ke
This is the most famous prehistoric cemetery in Ireland. It consists primarily of three great mounds close together in a loop of the R. Boyne: Dowth, which was pillaged in the 18th century, contains a passage-grave; Newgrange has a well-preserved cruciform chamber reached by a passage 62 ft long; Knowth, the entrance to which was found

### SHRINE OF ST MANCHAN

*This tomb-shaped box of yew wood with metal fittings contains the bones of St Manchan. It is one of the finest surviving products of the great revival of Irish metalwork in the early 12th century. Both the principal sides of the box have the same decoration: five bosses forming a cross and connected by short arms set with* *red and yellow cloisonné enamel. The borders at the base and the corners are also set with enamel. The reliquary was probably made in 1130 at the monastery of Clonmacnoise on the R. Shannon, Offaly. The row of cast bronze standing figures was added later in the 12th century. (Boher Catholic Church)*

in 1967, contains a similar chamber. Many of the stones in the three mounds are carved with intricate Bronze Age spiral and geometrical patterns, as are many of the massive kerbstones which surround and retain the structures. There are also outlying megaliths and secondary burials.

**Buncrana Castle** *Don.*      574Ef
One of Ireland's few surviving early 18th-century houses (1716), built by Henry Vaughan, with a panelled interior; it is now falling into decay. By the six-arched bridge leading up to the house is a late medieval tower-house of the Dohertys.

**Bunratty Castle** *Clare*      570Ef
Originally the chief seat of the O'Briens of Thomond, the castle is a late 15th-century keep with four angle-towers, the north and south of which are linked by high-level arches. The crenellations are modern and the whole castle and its interior was restored in 1956–8. Inside is a chapel with 17th-century stucco, and a collection of medieval furniture, paintings and sculptures collected by Lord Gort. (Open to the public.)

**Burnchurch** *Kilk.*      571He
A good 15th- and 16th-century tower-house, with stepped battlements and walls honeycombed with passages and chambers.

**Burncourt Castle** *Tipp.*      571Gd
The many-gabled, semi-fortified house was not quite finished when in 1650 its owner, Lady Everard, set it on fire to prevent it falling into the hands of the Cromwellians. Large corbels at second-floor level supported a timber walk.

**Burrishoole Abbey** *Mayo*      572Bf
A Dominican friary founded in 1469 on an inlet of the sea; the church with its tower and transept remains, as do some parts of the convent buildings.

**Buttevant** *Cork*      570Ed
A Franciscan friary founded in 1251 by David Og Barry. Most of the remains date from the 13th century, but many of the windows have been lowered and replaced in later centuries. There are eight round-headed windows on the south side of the choir, and beneath its east end is an unusual two-storied crypt. The cloister garth and the tower have gone. A mile to the south is Ballybeg, a fortified Augustinian priory founded in 1229 by Philip Barry; the belfry tower, cloister walls and dove-cote survive. The bell-rope holes in the tower are carved. Buttevant Castle, in ruins, is a good example of the early 19th-century castle style.

**Caher Castle** *Tipp.*      571Gd
One of the chief seats of the Butlers, Barons Caher, it stands on a rocky island in the R. Suir. It is the largest castle built in Ireland during the 15th and 16th centuries, and comprises two courts, a massive keep and a great hall. The Protestant church dates from 1817 and was designed by John Nash. Near by, beyond the castle, is Caher Park where there is a *cottage ornée* beside the Suir; it was probably designed by Nash, and the interior is decorated with wallpapers depicting the beauties of the Bosphorus by Dufour. Three miles to the north is Knockgraffon, a mote and bailey.

**Cahercommaun** *Clare*      570Dg
A large stone fort built on the edge of a cliff. Excavations in 1934 revealed that it was used as a dwelling in the 9th century, and traces of iron smelting were found. The fort has three concentric ramparts and contains souterrains, one of which leads outside the fort.

**Caherdorgan** *Kerry*      570Ad
Two ring forts, Caherdorgan South and North, each containing a group of clochans.

NEWGRANGE PASSAGE-GRAVE AT BRUGH NA BOINNE

One of the finest megalithic passage-graves in Ireland, situated in the Boyne Valley Cemetery, whose builders settled there some 4750 years ago. The chamber with three cells and the approach passage are walled with huge upright slabs and roofed with careful corbelling. The north cell (left) contains one of the finest and most intricately carved ceiling slabs, and a pair of flat stones one above the other, hollowed out into a basin shape; cremated remains may have been put into these. Part of one of the huge slabs is shown on the right. The patterns appear to have been cut before the stones were put in position, and may derive from Iberia.

**Cahergal** *Kerry* 570Ac
A stone ring-fort, about 85 ft in diameter, with flights of steps leading to the wall-top and two ruined chambers within the wall. Inside the fort are the remains of four huts.

**Caldragh** *Ferm.* 574Dd
An ancient churchyard near the west end of Boa Island on Lower Lough Erne. It contains a sculptured stone with two figures back-to-back, the chests bound with diagonal straps, dating from the 5th or 6th century.

**Caledon House** *Tyrone* 574Fc
The central block of this Georgian house, dating from 1779, is by Thomas Cooley, though the second floor was added in 1835; the colonnade and domed pavilion were built by Nash in c. 1812. The Doric column by William Murray carries a statue of the 2nd Earl of Caledon by Thomas Kirk. (Not open to the public.)

**Callan** *Kilk.* 571He
St Mary's Church was begun in c. 1460. It has a long aisle-less chancel, and incorporates a possibly older western tower; the arcades of the nave survive, and the chancel is in use as the Protestant parish church. Also in the town are the remains of the Augustinian friary of 1462, including a fine sedilia in the chancel. The Catholic church, dating from 1836, is a good early 19th-century building.

**Calliagh Birra's House.** See Slievegullion.

**Canon Island** *Clare* 570Dd
An Augustinian priory founded by Donal O'Brien, King of Munster, in the late 12th century, within an early cashel wall. The church, of the early 13th century, has a tower but no aisles or transepts, and there are two ranges of buildings dating from the 15th century.

**Cappagh Castle** *Lim.* 570Ee
A ruined 15th-century castle, originally of the Knights of Glin. It has a 70 ft high keep surrounded by a late 16th-century battlemented bawn with turrets at the eastern angles.

**Cappoquin House** *Waterford* 571Gc
A fine, cut-stone, balustraded house of c. 1770 by an unknown architect, overlooking the R. Blackwater.

**Carbury Castle** *Kild.* 573Hd
A picturesque Jacobean castle-like manor house, with graceful clustered chimneys. It stands beside a bailey; the mote has disappeared.

**Carlingford** *Louth* 573Kf
Like Ardglass, Carlingford is now a village, but was a town of importance in the Middle Ages. It is dominated by the massive D-shaped 13th-century castle, much altered and partly ruined. There are several medieval and 16th-century houses including Taaffe's Castle and the house called the Mint.

**Carlow** *Carlow* 571Jf
The court-house in Classical (Ionic) style is probably one of the finest in Ireland; it was built in 1830 to the design of William Vitruvius Morrison, and occupies a commanding position at the intersection of two streets. St Patrick's College, opened in 1795, is, with Maynooth, one of the earliest centres of Catholic education surviving, and has pleasant tree-planted walks. The Catholic cathedral, a building in the Gothic manner, complete with lantern, dates from c. 1820; it was designed by Thomas A. Cobden, and contains a good monument to Bishop Doyle by John Hogan.

**Carnanmore** *Antrim* 575Hg
A cairn, 75 ft in diameter, containing a partly exposed passage-grave.

**Carndonagh** *Don.* 574Eg
Opposite the church in the town stands a 7th-century cross carved with fine interlacing, similar to that at Fahan (Donegal), but more obviously cross-shaped and subtly carved. It is flanked by a pair of small carved stones, on each of which is carved a face. The cross is one of the oldest in Ireland.

**Carnelly House** *Clare* 570Ef
A square red-brick house, probably designed by Francis Bindon *c.* 1740. It has a heavily stuccoed salon incorporating a Corinthian 'tabernacle'.

**Carntighernagh** *Cork* 570Fe
A hill-top fort with an earlier chambered cairn close by.

**Carrickfergus** *Antrim* 575He
An old town, once an important port, on the shores of Belfast Lough. In 1778 the American captain John Paul Jones defeated the British warship *Drake* just off the shore. On a rocky peninsula projecting into the lough, this is probably the first true castle to be built in Ireland and is among the largest. It was built between 1180 and *c.* 1205 either by John de Courcy or Hugh de Lacy. The keep stands between the outer and inner courts at the south-west boundary of the site. The main landward entrance is guarded by four D-shaped towers of later date. The large cruciform parish church of St Nicholas has an elaborate monument to Sir Arthur Chichester and his family.

**Carrick-on-Shannon** *Leit.* 574Cb
Near the northern navigable limit of the Shannon, Carrick was given its charter by James I. There is a court-house of *c.* 1825 by William Farrell close by the remains of the gaol.

**Carrick-on-Suir** *Tipp.* 571Hd
The castle, a gabled and mullioned manor house, was built *c.* 1567 by the 10th Earl of Ormonde (Black Tom) in front of a 15th-century castle built by the Butlers, Earls of Carrick. Ormonde's building contains fine Elizabethan stucco decoration, the earliest surviving in Ireland. Beside the castle is the Tholsel, a tall square building with a clock-tower and lantern. Across the river in Carrick Beg, reached by a medieval bridge, is the Catholic parish church incorporating a tower and north wall of a 14th-century Franciscan friary. In the now disused Protestant church are two good monuments.

**Carrigadrohid** *Cork* 570Eb
The ruins of a gabled tower-house built in the 16th century by Dermot MacCarthy stand on a rocky island in the R. Lee, linked to either bank by medieval bridges.

**Carrigafoyle Castle** *Kerry* 570Ce
One of the chief strongholds of the O'Connors Kerry, an 80 ft tower-house on an inlet of the Shannon estuary. The O'Connors Kerry founded Lislaughton Abbey, on the other side of the inlet, in 1477.

**Carrigaholt Castle** *Clare* 570Ce
A partially restored tower-house and bawn.

**Carrigaphooca** *Cork* 570Db
A single tower, four storeys high, on a rock by the Sullane R. It was built without fire-places or chimneys, which suggests that it was erected before 1400.

**Carrigillihy** *Cork* 570Da
An excavation in 1950 revealed a ring wall around an Early Bronze Age homestead (circular) and early Christian homestead (rectangular) on the same site; the enclosing wall is 4 ft high in places.

**Carrigogunnell Castle** *Lim.* 570Ee
A stronghold of the O'Briens on the summit of a rock overlooking the R. Shannon; the remains, which include a shattered keep, bawn and chapel, date mainly from the 15th century.

**Carrowdore Castle** *Down* 575Jd
A castellated Georgian Gothic house built in 1818 for the family of de la Cherois Crommelin. The hall has fine Gothic stucco work.

**Carrowkeel** *Don.* 574Ef
A large group of passage-graves in association with a nearby group of 50 mysterious circular structures which may have been the walls of vanished dwellings.

**Carrowmore** *Sligo* 574Bc
A large group, formerly 80 but now 60, of passage-graves, thickly clustered together.

**Carton** *Kild.* 573Jd
Formerly the seat of the Dukes of Leinster, the head of the FitzGerald family, the present house replaced a Dutch-inspired winged manor house. In 1739–45 Richard Castle raised the house one floor, totally refaced it and constructed colonnades, pavilions and terminating pedimented arches in his typical Palladian mode. However, the house was turned back to front in the early 19th century by Sir Richard Morrison, spoiling Castle's original plan. The landscaped park possesses the balustraded bridge built after a design of Isaac Ware, and a shell house. There are also two gates by Thomas Ivory. (Not open to the public.)

**Cashel** *Tipp.* 571Ge
CASHEL PALACE Built *c.* 1731 for Theophilus Bolton, Archbishop of Cashel, to the designs of Sir Edward Lovett Pearce, and now a hotel. The interior possesses its contemporary panelled and Corinthian-columned hall, and one of its original twin staircases.
CASTLE Occupies the western half of the cathedral nave, and is in effect a tower-house, dating in its present form from Archbishop O'Hedian's time in the early 15th century. It is honeycombed with wall-passages.
CATHEDRAL Built in the 13th century, without aisles. There is a central tower; the choir is lit by five rows of lancet windows to north and south, being twice the length of the nave. The transepts have eastward chapels and wall-passages. The most notable tomb is that of Meiler McGrath, archbishop from 1571 to 1622.
CORMAC'S CHAPEL The largest, most elaborate and most complete of Irish-Romanesque buildings, in the angle between the choir and south transept. It was built by Cormac MacCarthy, king and bishop, and consecrated in 1134. It has a high stone-roofed nave and chancel and transeptal towers, one with a pyramidal stone roof; also an elaborate north porch and a decorated south doorway. Part of the east wall is a reconstruction of 1875. Within is a magnificent broken 11th-century sarcophagus with Scandinavian ornament.
CROSS OF ST PATRICK Stands south of the nave; it is of the 11th century, and unusual in having a rectangular frame linking the arms with the base, part of which survives.
In the town is the Dominican friary (13th–15th century), Quirke's Castle (15th century) and the new Protestant cathedral, begun in 1763 and completed (the west front and tower by Sir Richard Morrison) in 1788.
Near by are the ruins of Hore Abbey (Cistercian) of the 13th–15th century, and close to the Dublin road is the Charter School of 1744, possibly by Richard Castle.

ROCK OF CASHEL

*Dominating the town of Cashel from the north, the Rock was traditionally the seat of the kings of Munster and, until 1750, the See of the archbishopric of Munster. Amid the ruins of the 13th-century cathedral* *is Cormac's Chapel, a richly decorated Romanesque church built by the last great king-bishop Cormac MacCarthy, and consecrated in 1134. The 92 ft high Round Tower is even older than Cormac's Chapel.*

DOMINICAN FRIARY Founded by Archbishop MacKeilly in 1243, the long rectangular church has a south transept added *c.* 1270. The south side of the choir has a row of nine lancets.

ROCK OF CASHEL The rock rises 300 ft from the plain of Tipperary; its top is about 2 acres in area. Traditionally founded in AD 370 by Cormac, King of Munster, Cashel remained the principal stronghold of the kings of Munster until the 12th century. Visited by St Patrick in *c.* 450, it soon acquired religious significance which was to outshine and outlast its political significance, and many of the early kings were also bishops. In 1101 it became entirely ecclesiastical. The remains on the rock comprise the Round Tower, Cormac's Chapel, the roofless cathedral, the archbishop's castle, the hall of the Vicars Choral and the Cross of St Patrick, all splendidly grouped together. The 11th-century Round Tower is plain but very well built and complete, at the north-east corner of the north transept of the later cathedral. The buildings were burnt in 1647 by Murrough O'Brien, Earl of Inchiquin, with much bloodshed. The cathedral continued in use, and some restoration was done as late as 1730, but in 1749 the parish church of St John was constituted as the cathedral and the old buildings on the rock were thereafter allowed to decay.

**Castle Baldwin** *Sligo*        *574Cb*
A small semi-fortified house of the 17th century. It has gabled ends and was built to a simple rectangular plan with a small staircase projection giving it an L-shape.

**Castlebar** *Mayo*        *572Cf*
Founded in the 17th century by the Binghams (later Earls of Lucan), Castlebar is famous as the site of the battle known as Castlebar Races (1798) between the French General Humbert and General Lake, the British commander, who was soundly defeated. The gate-piers of the old Bingham

House survive. The most notable buildings in the town are the fine cut-stone 18th-century Linen Hall, with pedimented entrance, and opposite the court-house, the Methodist church and manse, unusually combined under one roof.

**Castleboro House** *Wex.*        *571Ke*
The ruined remains of an immense cut-stone house with wings. Built for the Carew family, and designed by Daniel Robertson of Kilkenny *c.* 1840.

**Castlecaulfeild House** *Tyrone*        *574Fd*
Originally called Ballydonnelly, the house was built by Sir Toby Caulfeild, ancestor of the Earls of Charlemont, and finished by 1619. It was burnt during the rising against the English in 1641. Soon afterwards, Castlecaulfeild was renovated and again lived in, but abandoned by 1700. The ruined house is of U-plan, and was originally three storeys high; it still has mullioned windows and some fine chimney-stacks.

**Castlecomer** *Kilk.*        *571Jf*
Castlecomer is an elegant town in spite of being a coal-mining centre at the heart of the Leinster coalfield. In 1635 the Wandesford family were granted the land there, and they developed the local mines and were responsible for laying out the spacious streets of the town as a copy of the town of Alsinore in Italy.

**Castlecoole** *Ferm.*        *574Ec*
Earlier houses were twice destroyed by fire during the 17th century. A new house was built at the beginning of the 18th century; later in the century the 1st Earl of Belmore asked Richard Johnston to prepare plans for a new house, but, perhaps not satisfied with the result, he called in James Wyatt who restyled Johnston's designs. The house has a central block with a four-columned portico, linked to side pavilions by tall colonnades; it contains fine decoration and furniture. (Open to the public.)

**Castledermot** *Kild.* 573Jb
A small town in which, amongst monastic remains, may be seen a Round Tower, two 10th-century high crosses, a Romanesque west doorway and church, a Franciscan friary and the tower of a priory of the Crutched Friars.

**Castle Dobbs** *Antrim* 575Je
A house built in the manner of Sir Edward Lovett Pearce in 1730 for Arthur Dobbs, Surveyor-General of Ireland and Governor of North Carolina; it incorporates later additions.

**Castle Durrow** *Laois* 573Gb
One of the few pre-Palladian houses in Ireland, the house was probably roughly designed by William Flower, its owner. It was finished in 1732, and survives intact except for the loss of its original dormer windows, and the later addition of a bay and porch. Opposite the front door is a Roman-Doric column.

**Castle Freke** *Cork* 570Da
The ruined remains of a Gothic Revival 'castle' built to designs by Sir Richard Morrison, *c.* 1830.

**Castle Hyde** *Cork* 570Fc
A late 18th-century house comprising a central block with wings incorporating oval rooms; it is possibly a late design by Davis Ducart. The columned hall leads to a splendid cantilevered staircase which, at the top floor, gives on to a wrought-iron bridge opening on to the garden, for the house backs on to the rocky bank of the R. Blackwater. The fine entrance gates have attendant sphinxes.

**Castle Kirke** *Gal.* 572Bd
The massive ruins of a mid-13th-century O'Conor-de Burgo castle stand on a small island in a north-western inlet of Lough Corrib.

**Castle Lyons** *Cork* 570Fc
In the churchyard is a pedimented mausoleum, with Corinthian columns, of James Barry, Earl of Barrymore, who died in 1747. The interior contains a monument by David Sheehan, and the angels on the entablature are by John Houghton.

**Castle Martin** *Kild.* 573Jc
An early 18th-century L-shaped house, notable chiefly for its wrought-iron gates and fine broken-pediment doorway.

**Castle Strange** *Roscom.* 572Ed
A ritual stone with fine La Tène ornament.

**Castletown** See Celbridge.

CHARLEVILLE CASTLE

*In Charleville Forest, with its grotto and serpentine walks, an Earl of Charleville built this whimsical family seat, complete with fine cut-stone detailing and a splendid fan-vaulted drawing-room.*

**Castletown House** *Kilk.* 571Hd
The masterpiece of the Sardinian architect, Davis Ducart, a richly detailed cut-stone house with pilastered centre-piece on both fronts, and arcaded wings placed cornerwise to the main block, terminating in octagonal domed pavilions. The interior has fine plasterwork by Patrick Osborne of Waterford. The house was built for Archbishop Cox of Cashel, begun in 1767 and finished in 1771.

**Castletowngeohegan** *Westmeath* 573Gd
Here is a conspicuous Anglo-Norman mote and bailey, and the remains of a medieval priory.

**Castle Upton** *Antrim* 575He
Originally a Plantation (English settlers') castle of 1619, which was remodelled for the Clotworthy family, later Viscounts Templeton, by Robert Adam in 1788–9. It has been much altered and damaged, but the Upton Mausoleum in the nearby churchyard, of 1783, remains in good condition.

**Castleward House** *Down* 575Jc
A strange house, built *c.* 1765–80 for the 1st Viscount Bangor by an unknown architect. Because of a disagreement over style between Lord and Lady Bangor, the south front is in Classical style with a pediment and a coat of arms above four central columns, and the north front is in Gothic style in three storeys with seven bays of pointed windows; on the battlements are urns at either end and three pinnacles in the centre. The mansion stands in fine grounds and gardens, and contains 18th-century furniture. There is also an exhibition of vehicles.

**Castlewellan** *Down* 575Hc
This small town consists of two squares, prettily planted with trees, laid out in the mid-18th century by the Annesley family. The market-house dates from 1764 and near by, in a park which is now a distinguished arboretum, is the 19th-century Blore-designed castle of the Annesleys. Some 2 miles south-west is the stone cashel of Drumena.

**Cavan** *Cavan* 573Gf
The county town in the old territory of Breffni, it is the seat of the Catholic Bishop of Kilmore. The cathedral of the diocese, a large building of 1942, has a west front with tower and spire closely modelled on St George's, Hardwicke Place, Dublin, flanked by small domes with a large dome over the crossing. The previous Catholic cathedral in the town, a modest Gothic building, was transported to Ballyhaise, where in a simplified form it was re-erected to serve as the parish church. The pedimented court-house, with a Doric porch and the royal Arms, is by John Bowden, who also designed the Protestant parish church of 1810. Three and a half miles south-west is Kilmore, the seat of the Protestant bishop, and 5 miles to the north-west is Clough Oughter, a circular tower-castle of the 14th–15th century on a small island. On the north-west of Lough Oughter, which is less a lake than a large number of peninsulas and islands, is Drumlane, with a truncated Round Tower and the ruins of a long, plain church.

**Celbridge** *Kild.* 573Jd
On the R. Liffey, dominated by large 18th-century mills, the town has, besides Castletown, an important early house, Oakley Park of 1720, possibly by Thomas Burgh, but much altered; also the Gothic Celbridge Abbey, the home of Esther van Homrigh—Vanessa in the works of Jonathan Swift. In the disused Protestant church is the magnificent monument by Thomas Carter, of *c.* 1730, with the recumbent figures of Speaker Conolly and his wife.

## CASTLETOWN, CELBRIDGE

*Speaker William Conolly began this, the largest 18th-century house in Ireland, in 1719. Sir Edward Lovett Pearce and Alessandro Galilei were probably the architects. When Conolly died in 1729 the house was still unfinished, and his widow continued in occupation until her death in 1752, without putting in the main staircase. The unfinished house then came into the hands of Tom Conolly and his wife, formerly Lady Louisa Lennox. They put in a Portland stone canti-levered staircase and employed the Francini brothers to complete the plasterwork of the staircase and hall in 1759–60.*

*The brothers had been responsible for the magnificent decoration in the saloon at Carton near by, where Louisa's sister Emily, Countess of Kildare was living, and where Louisa was largely brought up. Possibly only one of the Francinis was employed at Castletown, where the whole ornament is exquisite and highly Italianate, with swirls of light rococo and fanciful animals. A few of the frames contain figures (see right) and these are possibly portraits of Louisa and Tom's parents and relatives. Tom Conolly himself is portrayed in plaster, in pride of place near the foot of the staircase, and the smaller heads near to floor level represent the Four Seasons.*

CASTLETOWN The largest, most influential 18th-century house in Ireland, built in 1719–32, probably by Sir Edward Lovett Pearce and Alessandro Galilei, the Florentine architect, for Speaker William Conolly. The central block reiterates the Italian Renaissance town-palace façade, whereas the curved colonnaded quadrants are in the Palladian idiom. There is a magnificent entrance hall and staircase, the latter with plasterwork by the Francini brothers of 1759–60; the first-floor long gallery by Riley is in the Pompeian manner. At the end of a vista to the north of the house is probably the most fantastic of Irish follies, built in order to provide work during the hard year of 1741, by Conolly's widow. (Open to the public.)

**Charleville Castle** *Offaly*            *573Gc*
An extravagant and splendid 'castle' by Francis Johnston, built in 1801 for the Bury family, Earls of Charleville.

**Charleville House** *Wicklow*            *573Kc*
A cut-stone house built for the Monck family in 1797 by Whitmore Davis, in imitation of Lucan House. It has a raised centre-piece with engaged Ionic columns supporting a pediment.

**Clara Castle** *Kilk.*            *571Je*
The five-storied tower-house at Clara, with its small walled forecourt, is unusually complete and retains the oak timbers of the floors. There is a secret chamber in the thickness of the wall.

**Claregalway Abbey** *Gal.*            *572Dd*
A Franciscan friary founded by John de Cogan in the mid-13th century. It has a slender friars' tower with stepped battlements in good preservation. The transept and east window are 15th century, and the cloister has gone. There is a de Burgo tomb, possibly of the 14th century, and some interesting 18th-century tombstones.

**Clermont** *Wicklow*            *573Kb*
Built in 1731, almost identical to Furness, County Kildare, in red brick with wings, possibly to the designs of Francis Bindon. The interior has fine mantelpieces and elaborate plasterwork.

**Clogher** *Tyrone*            *574Ec*
The Cathedral of St Macartan was repeatedly rebuilt in the Middle Ages but now dates from the time of Bishop John Stearne, who built it at his own expense in 1745 in the Gothic style. It was remodelled in the Classical style in 1818.

**Clonamery** *Kilk.*            *571Je*
The ruined 10th- and 11th-century church has a fine massive west door with an incised cross above the lintel.

**Clonbrock** *Gal.*            *572Ed*
A large pedimented house of *c.* 1780.

**Clondalkin** *Dublin*            *573Kd*
The Round Tower, which retains its conical stone top, is the best preserved near Dublin.

**Clonfert Cathedral** *Gal.* 572Fc
ST BRENDAN'S CATHEDRAL A 13th-century building attached to a 12th-century façade, the portal of
which is perhaps the finest example of the Irish-
Romanesque style. It is the largest of its type in
Ireland and the pronounced slope of the jambs is
emphasised by the 15th-century work, which does
not slope, around the door.

**Clongowes** *Kild.* 573Jc
In the chapel are notable stained glass windows by
Michael Healey and Evie Hone.

**Clonkeen** *Lim.* 570Ee
The small church here has a decorated Romanesque doorway.

**Clonmacnoise** *Offaly* 572Fc
The monastic 'city' was founded by St Ciaran in
the 6th century, and was for long famous for its
learning, a centre of manuscript-making and
craftsmanship. It was repeatedly plundered by the
Vikings and Irish enemies and, after 1178, by the
English, whose sack of the place in 1552 proved
to be a death-blow. It remained deserted, though
used as a graveyard until modern times. All that
remains now is the large graveyard, in a lonely
site near the R. Shannon, and one outlying church.
Within the enclosure are seven churches, a Round
Tower (and another forming part of one of the
churches), three high crosses, and the largest
collection in Ireland of early grave-slabs, many
with inscriptions and ornaments of much beauty.
CATHEDRAL Originally a single chamber, with a
late Romanesque west door and a magnificent
15th-century north door built by Dean Odo, who

died in 1461. At about the same time a vaulted
three-aisled chancel was inserted into the east end.
A vaulted sacristy lies to the south. The Cross of
the Scriptures, alias King Flann's Cross, lies west of
the cathedral and has scenes from the life of Christ,
a Last Judgment, and horsemen and charioteers on
the base. The north cross (shaft only) has a curious
seated figure.
TEAMPULL CHIARAN A tiny church dedicated to
St Ciaran, heavily ruined and perhaps of the early
10th century.
TEAMPULL CHONOR An 11th-century church,
restored and now serving as the Protestant parish
church. The south cross, of the 9th or 10th century,
has vine-scroll ornament and a crucifixion.
TEAMPULL FINGHIN OR MACCARTHYS CHURCH
A nave and chancel church, the nave much ruined,
dating from the 12th century. It is unique in
having, south of the chancel, a round tower as
belfry, integral with the rest of the building. The
tower, which is complete with its conical top of
herring-bone masonry, is about half the usual size
for such structures. The chancel arch adjoins it.
Outside the present wall, to the west, stands the
truncated O'Rourke's Tower, with a later top.

The collection of inscribed and decorated grave-
slabs of the 8th–12th centuries is the largest and
most varied in the country, and many are of great
beauty. An ancient causeway leads eastwards from
the graveyard to the Nuns' Church. rebuilt by
Queen Dervorgilla and completed in 1167, in the
developed Romanesque style. West of the graveyard are the shattered remains of a possibly 13th-
century castle and a mote.

### WEST DOORWAY AT CLONFERT CATHEDRAL

*A Benedictine monastery on this site
was founded about 560 by St
Brendan, who is thought to have
reached America in the 6th century
and was nicknamed 'the Seafarer' or
'the Navigator'. The story of his
voyage across the Atlantic to the
'Promised Land of the Saints' or 'St
Brendan's Island' is told in one of
the greatest medieval sagas of
western Europe. The saga dates
from about 565–73 and appeared in
verse or prose in several languages,
including Latin, French, Irish,
Flemish, Welsh and Scottish Gaelic.
St Brendan died at Clonfert in about
578. The monastery was pillaged by
the Vikings in 844 and 845 during
the period of their great invasions of
the British Isles. It was burnt down
in 1016, 1164 and again in 1179.
Eventually, towards the close of the
12th century, the church was rebuilt
as a small Romanesque cathedral
dedicated to St Brendan, and its
west façade was incorporated in a
later building. In the superb, unique
west doorway, the pronounced slope
of the 12th-century jambs is
emphasised by the 15th-century
inner work which does not slope.
The cathedral was wrecked in the
16th century and has suffered at the
hands of later restorers; but it is
notable for the Transitional east
windows, the late medieval carvings
on the chancel-arch and the graceful
west doorway.*

**Clonmel** *Tipp.*    *571Gd*
The earliest building of note is the Franciscan church in Abbey Street, which incorporates a central tower dating from the 15th century and a 13th-century square well. The 19th-century Protestant church by J. Welland incorporates some medieval fragments, including a fine east window with Flamboyant tracery, identical to one at St Dominic's Friary at Cashel. At one end of O'Connell Street is the Main Guard, completed in 1674 and originally the seat of the Palatinate Court of Ormond, probably to the design of Sir William Robinson. The Methodist chapel is a fine Ionic temple by William Tinsley, and the Catholic parish church of St Mary, a Classical building dating from 1837–50 (though the steeple and portico date from 1875–80), contains a particularly rich interior, including a high altar by George Goldie. The court-house, of 1800, is by Sir Richard Morrison. Along the R. Suir is an array of warehouses, evidence of the former importance of trade by water here.

**Clonmines** *Wex.*    *571Kd*
The unique fortified church of Clonmines, in appearance like a small castle, consists of a vaulted ground floor, serving as the church, with a two-storied west end.

**Clonony Castle** *Offaly*    *572Fc*
This picturesque 16th-century tower and bawn was heavily restored in the early 19th century. It is pleasantly situated near the R. Brosna.

**Clontuskert Abbey** *Gal.*    *572Ec*
A small 15th-century Augustinian house with a west doorway closely recalling that of the cathedral of Clonmacnoise, and dated 1471. Fragments of a rood screen survive.

**Clontygora** *Arm.*    *575Gb*
An imposing horned cairn which originally had three chambers, of which the third and part of the second are destroyed; it was excavated in 1937. Near by is another cairn.

**Cloyne** *Cork*    *571Gb*
The Protestant cathedral of St Colman, for ever associated with the philosopher George Berkeley (1685–1753) is a cruciform building of the late 13th century. The nave and aisle were widened in 1856, and there is some good Classical woodwork at the west end. The monuments include one of Bishop Brinkley by Hogan, and a fragmentary font of 1611. The Round Tower stands in the village.

**Cobh** *Cork*    *570Fb*
Formerly called the Cove of Cork and, from 1849 until 1922, Queenstown, Cobh was an important naval base in the 18th century, and in the 19th a centre of the emigrant trade. The cathedral by E. W. Pugin and G. Ashlin dominates the town.

**Cong Abbey** *Mayo*    *572Cd*
The Augustinian friary, a royal foundation of the O'Conors, Kings of Connacht, dating from the early 13th century, but largely rebuilt. It retains a number of beautiful doorways showing distinct French influence, which are older than the present church. The scanty, reset remains of the cloister indicate that it had, perhaps, the first use of the dumb-bell pier which became almost universal throughout Ireland.

**Coolbanagher** *Laois*    *573Hc*
The Protestant parish church, with a west tower and spire, was built by James Gandon for the 1st Earl of Portarlington. The plaster ceiling has been replaced with an open timber one; the chancel is 19th century. The mausoleum is also by Gandon.

**Coolhull Castle** *Wex.*    *571Kd*
A late 16th-century structure remarkable for being an oblong of two storeys, rather than the usual tower-house type. The crenellations and round-headed windows are in good condition.

**Coppinger's Court** *Cork*    *570Da*
A semi-fortified house of the mid-17th century, it is shaped like a two-pronged fork, and has mullioned windows, tall gables and chimneys and elaborate machicolation for defence.

**Corcomroe Abbey** *Clare*    *570Dg*
Founded *c.* 1180, this Cistercian abbey dates mostly from the 14th and 15th centuries. It was originally a cruciform building without a tower; the present inadequate tower, inserted between the choir and nave, dates from the 15th century. The church has excellent masonry, delicate floral ornaments, and some effigies.

**Cork** *Cork*    *570Fb*
The third city of Ireland and second of the Republic was founded in the 6th–7th century by St Finbar. The name in Irish means marsh, and the Anglo-Norman walled town occupied a pair of islands among the many between the north and south channels of the R. Lee. Nearly all these islands have now been reclaimed and constitute modern Cork, though until comparatively recently, several of the channels between them, represented by modern streets such as Patrick Street, Grand Parade and South Mall, were still open water-courses. In the 1750's the walls of the rectangular medieval city between Grand Parade and Grattan Street were removed and the city began to assume its present form. The site of the Celtic monastic settlement is some distance to the south-west; St Finbar's cathedral, the masterpiece of William Burges, has three spires and a lavish interior in the French style.
   Among the earliest surviving buildings in Cork is South Gate Bridge of 1713, by Coltsman, and the Protestant Christ Church, a plain ashlar structure of 1720 by the same architect. The interior was remodelled and the west front built by G. R. Pain. In the churchyard is a remarkable effigy of a skeleton. The best-known building in the city is the Protestant church of St Anne Shandon (1722), on the high ground north of Pope's Quay; the tower is in diminishing stages, with a small cupola and a fish as a weathercock. Both tower and church have two sides in the silver Cork limestone, while the other two are in the dark red local stone. The quay-walls and bridges of Cork are also in the beautiful white limestone. The famous carillon of bells in St Anne's tower may be played by visitors. Close to St Anne's is the early 19th-century Butter Market and the L-shaped arcaded building of Skiddy's Almshouse (1718–19). The old red-brick custom house is a fine early 18th-century building with some panelled rooms still extant; it is encased in the relatively modern Crawford Municipal School of Art, whose art gallery has interesting pictures and sculpture. On the west side of North Main Street is St Peter's Protestant Church of 1783–8, in the northern porch of which is a monument with armorial bearings of Sir Matthew Down and his wife, of 1710. The church has a 17th-century font and, like Christ Church, has lost its spire. St Finbar's South, known as the South Chapel, is a remarkable Catholic city church of 1766, with its original nave and north transept with galleries.
   Of mid-18th-century buildings, the Cornmarket, probably by Coltsman, retains its ground-floor arcade only, three pediments and a central clock having been added in 1843. The Mayoralty House in Prospect Row, now the Mercy Hospital,

dates from 1765–73 and was designed by the Sardinian Davis Ducart, architect of the Limerick Custom House. Clarke's Bridge, by Samuel Hobbs, is of 1776.

The handsome single-arch Parliament Bridge is of 1806. Two families of architects, the brothers Pain and the Deanes, were responsible for most of the fine early 19th-century buildings in the city. Thomas Deane's first commission (in 1811, when he was 19) was the Commercial Buildings in the South Mall, adjoining the Imperial Hotel. Thomas and his brother Kearns are responsible for the early 19th-century riverside pedimented Savings Bank, on the continuation of the South Mall. Kearns Deane built the Ionic-porticoed St Mary's Dominican Church on Pope's Quay in 1832–9; the interior, with Corinthian columns and coffered ceilings, displays a 14th-century Flemish ivory figure of Our Lady of Grace from the Dominican friary in Youghal. The first building of their rivals, the Pains, was the dramatic Greek-Doric-porticoed gaol of 1818 (now part of University College). Like so many gaols of its period, it shows the influence of Piranesi and of George Dance. The front walls are slightly canted backwards from the portico and the columns are encased in a mantle, after the manner of the Temple of Segesta in Sicily.

In 1820, George Richard Pain reconstructed the interior of the Catholic church of St Mary Shandon; commonly called the North Chapel, it serves as the cathedral. St Patrick's, McCurtain Street, by George Richard Pain, is distinguished Corinthian, with a campanile. It dates from 1836, with a drastically remodelled interior of 1894. Both George Richard and James collaborated over the court-house of 1835, which has a superb Corinthian portico surmounted by sculpture; the interior was destroyed in 1891. A symptom of the battle of the styles is George Richard Pain's unusual Gothic-porticoed Father Mathew's Church (Holy Trinity Church) begun in 1832, with a spire and cupola completed by Coakly in 1880. The Ionic-porticoed Cork Steam Packet Company building in Penrose Quay is also by the brothers Pain. Sir Thomas Deane's last building was University College, built 1845–9 in the Tudor-Gothic collegiate style and modelled on an amalgam of Oxford colleges. Also in the college is the Honan Chapel, a full Hiberno-Romanesque Revival chapel of 1915 by James McMullan, with good glass by Henry Clarke and Sarah Pursar. Other distinguished 19th-century buildings are the finely detailed custom house of 1814 by William Hargrave and the Corinthian-porticoed Italianate Provincial Bank on the South Mall. At Glanmire is Riverstown House, and Lota, by Davis Ducart (1765), now a convent and much altered on the exterior, with a fine mahogany staircase and some interior plasterwork.

**Creevelea Abbey** *Leit.*       *574Cc*
A Franciscan friary, founded in 1508 by Margaret O'Brien and Eoghan O'Rourke—one of the last monasteries to be founded in Ireland. It was re-occupied for a period *c.* 1642 and later confiscated, but yet again occupied by the friars who roofed part of the church with thatch.

**Creevykeel** *Sligo*       *573Cd*
A magnificent 'lobster claw' cairn related to the 'Deer Park Monument'. It was excavated in 1935, and found to contain four cremated burials.

**Crom Castle** *Ferm.*       *574Eb*
On the lake in the park is an old Plantation castle built in 1611 and destroyed by fire in 1764. The outer bawn and two flankers survive; the castle of the Earls of Erne is by Blore and dates from 1830.

**Cuba Court** *Offaly*       *572Fc*
A ruined house of *c.* 1730 by, or in the style of, Sir Edward Lovett Pearce, with two fronts each with pediments and fine front staircase.

**Culcavy** *Down*       *575Hd*
A *cottage ornée* of *c.* 1826, complete with dome and trellis-worked balcony.

**Cullenswood** See Rathfarnham.

**Cultra Manor**       *575Jd*
**(Ulster Folk Museum)** *Down*
Collections here illustrate the past and present way of life and traditions of the people of Northern Ireland, and include furnishings, costumes, tools and equipment, vehicles and a group of photographs, documents and sound recordings. In the grounds are five traditional country buildings.

**Curraghmore House** *Waterford*       *571Hd*
The finest forecourt in Ireland (possibly to the designs of Francis Bindon, 1742–50), leads up to a much remodelled central block which contains interior decoration by James Wyatt, de Grée and Zucchi. (Not open to the public.) To the right of the house is the charming mid-18th-century Shell House, decorated by Lady Catherine Power and containing a statue of her by John van Nost. (The Shell House is open to the public on Thursday afternoons and Bank Holidays.)

**Cush** *Lim.*       *570Fd*
A complex of earth-forts, souterrains, tumuli and ancient fields on the west slope of Slievereagh.

**Cushendun** *Antrim*       *575Hf*
A picturesque village by the sea, mostly built by Clough Williams-Ellis, the architect of Portmeirion village in Wales.

**Daingean** *Offaly*       *573Hc*
Founded as Philipstown in the 16th century by Mary Tudor of England and her husband Philip II of Spain, to be the county town of King's County (Offaly), Daingean never took root, and in 1833 lost its function to Tullamore. The small court-house, though much disfigured, appears to be the work of James Gandon.

**Dalkey Island** *Dublin*       *573Kc*
St Begnet's Church is a small, early structure with typical lintelled west doorway and pilaster projections to both gables. The island also contains one of the Martello Towers, *c.* 1800, which are characteristic of the coast north and south of Dublin. In the Main Street of Dalkey village are two fortified houses of the 15th and 16th centuries; another stands above Bullock Harbour.

**Danganbrack** *Clare.*       *570Ef*
A fine, gabled early 17th-century tower with tall chimneys, one of the many tower-houses built by the MacNamara family in this area.

**Dartrey Mausoleum**       *573Hg*
**(or Dawson's Grove)** *Monag.*
The large Tudor Revival house has been totally demolished, but in the middle of a state forest is a notable mausoleum of 1770 by James Wyatt containing a large sculptural group by Joseph Wilton.

**Deerpark** *Sligo*       *574Cc*
The 'Deer Park Monument' (Leac Con Mhic Ruis), a long cairn formerly covering a central-court grave, with three galleries opening off the 50 ft court. One gallery-portal remains standing.

**Delgany Church** *Wicklow*       *573Kc*
The interior is chiefly notable for an enormous monument of 1789 to David La Touche, the banker, by William Hickey.

**Derry** *Lond.* 574Ef
Founded by St Colmcille in 546, on a steep hill near the mouth of the R. Foyle. The original site is now occupied by St Columb's Catholic Church in Longtower Street, a name which commemorates a former Round Tower there. In 1613 the town was granted by James I to a London company, the Irish Society, who presently laid it out and surrounded it with the existing wall.
BISHOP STREET The court-house of 1813–17 is by John Bowden and shows the same command of the Greek-Ionic order as his church of St Stephen, Mount Street, Dublin. The wings are surmounted by statues of Justice and Peace sculptured in Portland stone by Edward Smyth.
PROTESTANT CATHEDRAL Built in the southern quarter of the town in 1628–33, in an already archaic English style, sometimes called 'Planter's Gothic'. The west tower was crowned in 1778 by a spire erected by Frederick Augustus Hervey, the celebrated earl-bishop, but between 1805 and 1834 both tower and spire were totally rebuilt.
WALKER MONUMENT A Roman-Doric column of 1828 surmounted by a statue of Governor George Walker by John Smyth of Dublin; it commemorates the most famous event in the city's history, the siege of 1688–9. Near by is the Double Bastion and 'Roaring Meg', a large gun used in the siege. The siege is also commemorated by Bishop's Gate, and the triumphal arch designed by Henry Aaron Baker, James Gandon's pupil, in 1788, with Classical trophies and carved masks by Edward Smyth.

**Derryhivenny Castle** *Gal.* 572Ec
A well-preserved tower-house, erected in 1643, with a fortified enclosure and angle-towers; one of Ireland's last pure castles.

**Derrynane Abbey** *Kerry* 570Bb
The ancestral home of the O'Connells, now a museum dedicated to the memory of the Nationalist leader Daniel O'Connell.

**Devenish Island** *Ferm.* 574Dc
The Round Tower of Devenish Island, belonging to the monastic foundation associated with St Molaise, is one of the best built and best preserved in Ireland. It is remarkable not only for its fine ashlar masonry but also for the decorated frieze below the cap and the four carved heads facing the quarters of the compass. There are also the ruins of a small early church called St Molaise's House, with carved bases to its antae, the 'Great Church', and the 15th-century ruins of St Mary's Augustinian abbey.

**Disertoengus** *Lim.* 570Ee
A Round Tower 65½ ft high, with a Romanesque doorway; near by is a ruined church—and all was formerly enclosed by a cashel.

**Doe Castle** *Don.* 574Df
Doe Castle, surrounded by the sea and a rock-cut ditch, was the medieval castle of the MacSweeney Na Doe; it was restored in the 19th century.

**Donabate** *Dublin* 573Kd
On a peninsula between two inlets, an extremely attractive Protestant parish church of 1758 with curved gables and, at the west end, the octagonal private gallery of the Cobbe family with a corner fire-place and charming rococo plasterwork incorporating swans, the Cobbe family crest.

**Donaghmore** *Meath* 573Je
Just outside the town of Navan, the almost complete Round Tower of Donaghmore has a Romanesque doorway with a crucifixion above and human masks on either side of the architrave.

HIGH CROSS AT DONAGHMORE, COUNTY TYRONE

*Standing in the village street, this magnificent 9th- or 10th-century high cross is one of the finest in the north of Ireland. Although this type of sandstone weathers badly, the intricate wreathed carving on the sides and the scenes from the Old and New Testaments on the back and front are clearly defined. The New Testament panels in the photograph show the Appearance of the Angel to the Shepherds, Christ's Baptism, the Adoration of the Kings, the Wedding at Cana, the Feeding of the Five Thousand and the Transfiguration and Arrest of Christ.*

**Donaghmore** *Tipp.* 571Gd
The Romanesque church has a nave, small chancel and the remains of a decorated doorway and chancel-arch.

**Donaghmore** *Tyrone* 574Fd
St Patrick is said to have founded a church here, and a 13th-century monastery on the site contained elaborate shrines. All that now remains is a 9th–10th-century high cross carved with Biblical subjects, including the Fall of Adam and Eve and the Sacrifice of Isaac.

**Donegal Castle** *Don.* 574Cd
Donegal Castle consists of a keep, built by Red Hugh O'Donnell in 1505, to which was added one of Ireland's finest Jacobean gabled fortified houses, built by Sir Basil Brooke in 1610. The gigantic, elaborate chimney-piece is particularly remarkable.

**Doneraile** *Cork* 570Ed
Originally part of the estate of Edmund Spenser, the Elizabethan poet, it came into the possession of the St Leger family who built Doneraile Court, designed by William Rothery *c.* 1730 but since refaced. In the church (1816) are some fine St Leger monuments; the park entrance to Doneraile Court is a good Ionic triumphal arch, probably by the Pain brothers. Kilcolman Castle is where Spenser wrote parts of the *Faerie Queene*.

**Donore** *Meath* 573Ke
A 'ten-pound castle' (so-called because of a statute of 1429 subsidising the building of castles in the English Pale). It is a simple tower, built to the measurements required by the statute, having vaults over the two lower storeys and a turret incorporating a spiral stair.

**Dorsey, The** *Arm.* 575Gb
An elongated oval enclosure of the Iron Age, the largest of its type in Ireland; it must have been built to command the highway between Tara and the Navan fort.

**Downhill** *Lond.* 574Ff
The shell remains of the Earl-Bishop of Derry's irregular pilastered mansion. On the cliff the domed Mussenden Temple, fine gates, and a monument also survive. (Open to the public.)

**Downpatrick** *Down* 575Jc
This county town possesses some good late 18th-century terrace houses in English Street, Irish Street and Saul Street. The double bow-fronted judges' lodging is of *c.* 1840. Southwell School, a combined school and almshouse founded by Edward Southwell was probably designed by Sir Edward Lovett Pearce and finished by 1733. The parish church of 1560 is plain, with pedimented west tower.
ST PATRICK'S CATHEDRAL The present Protestant cathedral is a drastic remodelling, of 1798–1812, by Charles Lilly of Dublin, of what seems to have been a 13th-century choir. The carved capitals of the arcade, though much restored in plaster, embody some 13th-century work. The most attractive feature of the church is the woodwork of the pews which undulates in alternating curves and straight lines, with Gothic detailing.

**Dowth** See Brugh na Boinne.

DROMANA HOUSE LODGE

*Just off the road from Aglish to Cappoquin, on the Dromana House estate, is this romantic gate-house. It was built about 1840 on the lines of Brighton Pavilion in the style of the Mogul palaces of India—with an onion-shaped dome, slender spires, pointed arches and windows, and graceful filigree-like balustrades.*

**Drogheda** *Louth* 573Ke
The most important of the eastern seaboard towns between Dublin and Belfast is of Norse origin, walled and fortified by the Anglo-Normans. The church of the Augustinian friary is represented by its 15th-century tower which now spans a narrow street. All that remains of the Dominican friary is the so-called Magdalene Tower of the 15th century. St Laurence's Gate, a twin-towered 13th-century structure is, in fact, a barbican which stood before the gate. On the south bank of the Boyne is the Mill Mount, the mote of the Anglo-Norman castle, and other portions of the town walls survive here and there. St Peter's Church, rebuilt in 1753, with a later tower and spire by Francis Johnston, contains fine rococo plasterwork and several handsome monuments. In the church-yard there is a remarkable, macabre, 16th-century tomb-slab with the skeletons of Edward Golding and his wife. The Tholsel, a cupolaed building near the north end of the bridge, is by Francis Johnston and is now a bank. Other notable buildings include the custom house and the country club, both cut-stone pedimented structures at right angles to each other on the quay by the river. Other 18th-century houses are the grammar school, originally the Singleton House; the red-brick police barracks in Trinity Street, possibly by Francis Bindon; St Peter's Catholic church, which contains the embalmed head of Blessed Oliver Plunkett, martyred in 1681. Outside the town is Ball's Grove, with a fine Classical pedimented gate.

**Dromana House** *Waterford* 571Gc
The house was recently demolished; on the estate is the restored Hindu-cum-Gothic lodge.

**Dromaneen Castle** *Cork* 570Ec
A romantically sited strong-house on a rock on the south bank of the Blackwater. Access to the entrance court is by a fine Jacobean doorway.

**Dromoland Castle** *Clare* 570Ef
A splendid castle-house of 1826 by the brothers Pain; it replaced an 18th-century building of which the garden lay-out partially survives and includes a Doric rotunda and a gazebo on a hill. Now a hotel.

**Dromore Castle** *Lim.* 570Ee
The most important Gothic Revival castle in Ireland, built for the Earls of Limerick, 1867–70, by Edward William Godwin in the archaeological Gothic style based on Irish prototypes. The massing, and its situation on the rock overlooking various lakes, is unparalleled. Though the walls are enormously solid, the interior is entirely gutted.

**Drumacoo** See Tyrone House.

**Drumcliff** *Sligo* 574Bc
Of the monastery traditionally founded by St Colmcille, there remains a fine high cross with figure-sculptures from the Old and New Testaments, the shaft of a plain cross, and the stump of a Round Tower; the graveyard is the burial place of W. B. Yeats, the poet and dramatist.

**Drumcondra** *Dublin* 573Kd
The house, now a college, has two fronts; the south, of 1727, is by Sir Edward Lovett Pearce; the east front has an order of giant Corinthian pilasters of about the same date. On the lawn to the east is a temple, extremely Italian in character, and probably also by Pearce, or by Galilei. The church of St John the Baptist near by possesses a monument of 1740 to Marmaduke Coghill, the builder of Drumcondra House, by Peter Schee-makers. In the churchyard is buried James Gandon, the architect who designed some of Dublin's finest buildings.

**Dublin** *Dublin* 573Kd

A prehistoric burial site in Phoenix Park, 4000 years old, is Dublin's earliest monument. The site must have been important in Celtic times, since it had a ford and the natural harbour provided by the river mouth. Norse sea-rovers really founded the town, establishing a settlement in 841.

The Normans seized the little town in 1170 and erected a strong enclosing wall, and later a castle. The remains of this medieval city have since been largely rebuilt. After the Restoration of Charles II —and even more after the Hanoverian Settlement which was shortly accompanied by a Palladian movement headed by Sir Edward Lovett Pearce and his assistant Richard Castle—an amazing expansion began, culminating in the squares and houses of the Georgian era. Practically all the fine architecture of the city belongs to this period—an architectural heritage which remains basically intact.

ABBEY THEATRE The new building by Michael Scott, opened in 1966, succeeds the historic theatre of Yeats, Synge and O'Casey, destroyed by fire in 1951.

BELVEDERE HOUSE A large five-bay house in Great Denmark Street, facing down North Great George's Street, built in 1785 by Michael Stapleton, and lavishly adorned with his richest plasterwork. It has been a Jesuit college since 1841.

BROADSTONE RAILWAY STATION (now disused). The terminus of the old Midland Great Western line to Galway and Sligo, now used as a bus garage: a massive Greco-Egyptian block by J. S. Mulvany, 1841–50, with a long colonnade.

BUS STATION (BUSARAS) An imposing L-shaped building by Michael Scott of *c.* 1952; the first modern building to be erected in central Dublin.

CASINO MARINO Designed by Sir William Chambers for Lord Charlemont in 1765–71, it is a small pleasure-house, containing finely proportioned rooms, and is a miniature masterpiece of 18th-century architecture. No money was spared in its construction, Lord Charlemont bringing Simon Vierpyl, sculptor and builder, from Rome to work on the building. There are interesting underground passages and a fine view from the parapet. It is now a National Monument.

CASTLE Originally erected in 1204–28. The Record, or Wardrobe, Tower remains, with a machicolated parapet of 1813. The arcaded red-brick buildings of Upper Castle Yard (the cross-block reconstructed 1967) and the Bedford Tower (Genealogical Office and heraldic museum), with robust flanking gates, by Sir Edward Lovett Pearce who reconstructed the stone garden-front (recently reconditioned), contain the state apartments, including the Throne Room and St Patrick's Hall. They are still used for state functions, and possess many fine paintings, notably the ceiling of St Patrick's Hall by Vincent Waldré.

The Gothic Revival style Chapel Royal was designed by Francis Johnston and built in 1807–14. The exterior is richly decorated and the interior has fine Irish oak carving, plasterwork and stained glass. Originally a Protestant chapel for the Lords Lieutenant and Lords Deputy of Ireland who lived in the castle, the chapel was reconstructed in 1943 as the Catholic Church of the Most Holy Trinity.

CATHEDRAL OF ST PATRICK The present building dates from 1191, but it was extensively enlarged in the 13th century, and the tower added towards the end of the 14th century. It was advanced to cathedral status in 1213.

Jonathan Swift, the satirist, was Dean from 1713–45; his pulpit and tomb can be seen, as can the helmets, swords and banners of the knights of the now moribund Order of St Patrick. The cathedral is particularly rich in monuments, notably the five-storey Boyle monument.

To the east of the cathedral stands Marsh's Library, built by Archbishop Narcissus Marsh in 1707. It is the oldest public library in Ireland.

CHESTER BEATTY LIBRARY (See pp. 601–2.)

CHRIST CHURCH CATHEDRAL (PROTESTANT) A large cathedral founded in 1173 by Strongbow, the Norman Earl Richard Gilbert de Clare. The aisled six-bay nave was finished in 1234, and has been identified with the work of English masons of the school of Glastonbury. Soil subsidence caused the fall of the nave vaulting and south wall in 1562, and the north wall still leans about 2 ft out from the perpendicular. During the 16th and 17th centuries, the crypt was used as a tavern.

The cathedral's founder, Strongbow, is buried within, although it is doubtful whether the effigy said to represent him is genuine.

CHURCH OF SS AUGUSTINE AND JOHN This building by Pugin and Ashlin is among the finest Victorian Gothic designs in Dublin.

CHURCH OF ST ANNE This is a well designed church of 1720 by Isaac Wills; the present Romanesque front was added in 1868 by Deane and Woodward. Inside there is a finely carved wooden reredos and organ case.

CHURCH OF ST AUDOEN (PROTESTANT) This is Dublin's only surviving medieval parish church. The west door dates from 1190, and three of the bells are the oldest in Ireland, one cast in 1423.

CHURCH OF ST CATHERINE The present church was built in 1769 on a foundation dating from 1105. The architect was John Smith, and he designed a boldly-modelled Palladian elevation in mountain granite, which included pilasters, a central portico and a massive but unfinished tower.

CHURCH OF ST FRANCIS XAVIER Built in 1832 by Joseph Keane in the form of a Latin cross, with an Ionic portico. The interior of this Jesuit church has recently been redecorated under the direction of Michael Scott.

CHURCH OF ST GEORGE Francis Johnston designed this fine church in 1802; its 200 ft steeple was adapted from St Martin-in-the-Fields, London.

CHURCH OF ST MARY An early building, dating from *c.* 1700, having a tall, graceful interior remarkable for its fine west end. The handsome carved wooden case for the organ runs almost completely across the building, and embodies figure-sculpture, rare in such an early church.

CHURCH OF ST MICHAN Dedicated in 1095, but largely rebuilt in 1685, it is famous for its remarkable crypt, in which corpses are mummified. The church contains a fine early 18th-century organ.

CHURCH OF ST STEPHEN On an island site, it magnificently closes the vista along Upper Mount Street from Merrion Square. It was designed by John Bowden and completed by John Welland, with elements copied from Greek originals (1824).

CHURCH OF ST WERBURGH Reputed to be one of the oldest foundations in Dublin. The present building, by Thomas Burgh (1715), was re-modelled after a fire in 1759.

CITY HALL Built in 1769 by Thomas Cooley, who won an open competition for the design, it was formerly the Royal Exchange. Square in plan, it has three fronts decorated in the Corinthian order, and it is crowned by a finely lighted dome, supported by 12 columns, over the main hall. There are good sculptures by Smyth, Foley and others.

CIVIC MUSEUM Erected in 1765–71 for the Society of Artists. It has an octagonal exhibition hall, and was used as a municipal council chamber; it now houses a collection of Dublin relics.

# CHESTER BEATTY LIBRARY

When Sir Alfred Chester Beatty, the American mining millionaire, died in 1968, he left his priceless collection of manuscripts, and the library he had built to house them, to the Irish nation. The collection had taken over 40 years to assemble and agents in all parts of the world were employed. The oriental section is the largest; it contains manuscripts from India, Tibet, China and also Japanese sword guards, Chinese snuff bottles and rare Chinese jade books. Middle East items include Biblical papyri, among them the oldest known New Testament manuscript dating from 200–250. There are a number of Korans, some in scroll form, and many fine Western manuscripts.

ARMENIAN GOSPEL *Written in the 13th century for the Patriarch Constantine in Cilicia, the Armenian gospel shown here is one of four written about the same time. The photograph shows the beginning of St John's Gospel. On the left-hand page is a painting of the saint inscribed 'Saint John the Theologian'.*

THE THEBAID *This book of the poem 'The Thebaid' by the Latin poet Statius was copied in 1380–90, possibly by the Italian painter Altichiero. It has 12 miniatures, one at the beginning of each section, executed with extraordinary delicacy in grisaille (grey monotones) except for the deep blue of the sky, some green for trees, grass or water and red for blood or fire. The page reproduced is at the beginning of Book VI. Statius was born in Naples in AD 45 and proved himself to be the greatest poet in the Roman Empire. He received the golden crown for the victory in a poetical contest from the hand of the Emperor Domitian (AD 81–96). Proud of his powers of improvisation Statius (according to a description by Horace) once dictated 200 lines of poetry in an hour while standing on one leg. 'The Thebaid' is his best known work and took 12 years to write. It is an elaborate and typical story of the deadly strife of the Theban brothers, enlivened by dreams, miracles, single-combats, Homeric and Vergilian echoes and all the other familiar components of the Latin epic. Statius eventually retired to Naples in AD 94.*

CHINESE JADE BOOK *Painted by order of the Emperor Ch'ien Lung (1736–95), this jade book contains portraits and descriptions of the Buddha. The cover of the book shown here is of bronze, decorated with a repoussé dragon on an enamel ground. The entire contents of the book are painted in gold on jade.*

17TH-CENTURY COPY OF THE SHĀHNĀMAH *Written by Firdaussi, the Shāhnāmah is the national epic poem of Persia based on the collected legends of the ancient kings. In the 10th century, Mahmud ibn Sabuktagin commissioned Firdaussi to use the material, amassed from centuries of preparation, and write the poem. This is a page from a copy made for Shāh Abbas (1587–1629) by Muhammad Zaman, who had studied in Rome and acquired the art of perspective. The executioner is presenting the head of Iraj, youngest son of King Faridum, to his brothers Tur and Salm.*

CUSTOM HOUSE The masterpiece of James Gandon, with four decorated fronts; the south, facing the river, was begun in 1781 and embellished with splendid sculptures by Edward Smyth, notably the Arms of the Kingdom of Ireland on the four corners, and the scenes of 14 keystone-heads symbolising the rivers of Ireland. The pediment-sculpture on the south front of the friendly union of Britannia and Hibernia was designed by Carlini but executed by Smyth, who also did the statue of *Commerce* on the dome. During the fighting of 1921 the building was gutted by fire, but was soon afterwards restored. The memorial to the Dublin Brigade at the west front was carved by a Breton sculptor, Yann Renard-Goullet.

DOMINICK STREET No. 20 has the finest of Robert West's plaster. Now St Saviour's Orphanage.

DUNLEARY Since 1821 the packet-station for Holyhead, it has a splendid artificial harbour by John Rennie, a good railway-station, and a colonnaded yacht-club by J. S. Mulvany. An obelisk commemorates the state visit of George IV in 1821, after which the town was for 100 years called Kingstown. At Sandycove the Martello tower in which James Joyce lived is now the Joyce Museum.

ELY HOUSE (ELY PLACE) By Michael Stapleton, 1770, with the most remarkable staircase in Dublin and other splendid decoration in the Adam style.

FOUR COURTS Designed by James Gandon and incorporating on the west an office block of 1777 by Thomas Cooley, was begun in 1786. It has a frontage of 450 ft to the river, dominated by a great Corinthian portico of six columns, behind which rises a massive lantern and dome. Terminal pavilions are linked to the central block by rusticated arcades. The statues on the skyline are by Edward Smyth. The four High Courts radiate from the spacious circular hall under the dome.

GENERAL POST OFFICE Designed by Francis Johnston and completed in 1818, it has an impressive Ionic portico of six fluted columns, the pediment being surmounted by statues. It was the headquarters of the Irish Volunteers during the 1916 rising, and was shelled from the R. Liffey by a British gunboat. It has since been reconstructed.

GLASNEVIN BOTANIC GARDENS Founded in 1795 by the Royal Dublin Society; they cover some 50 acres and contain many rare plants, trees and shrubs. The palm houses were built by the iron-founder Richard Turner, who later built the palm house at Kew Gardens.

GREEN STREET COURT-HOUSE Built in 1792 by Richard Johnston, it has a central recessed portico of six columns, and is mainly notorious as the scene of many famous treason trials.

HARCOURT STREET RAILWAY STATION (now disused). By George Wilkinson (1859), with colonnaded entrance at an angle to the main block.

HENRIETTA STREET Leading to the King's Inns, this is the earliest street of really large houses in Dublin. No. 9, by Sir E. L. Pearce, has a splendid Palladian interior modelled on Lord Mountrath's house in Old Burlington Street, London (by Lord Burlington). No. 10 (Blessington House), also by Pearce, has been altered externally but has good interiors.

KILDARE STREET CLUB Erected in 1860 by the partnership of Deane and Woodward, with the O'Shea brothers, this brick Venetian *palazzo* is a most distinguished design. The whimsical carved beasts are by Charles Harrison.

KILMAINHAM GAOL Celebrated in Irish history, and recently reconditioned as a national monument by voluntary effort, its architect is unknown, but the entrance doorway with its powerful sculptural panel of chained serpents is noteworthy by any standards.

KING'S HOSPITAL Known also as the Blue Coat School, it is a delicate example of neo-Classical Palladianism, erected in 1780 by Thomas Ivory.

KING'S INNS This impressive building was one of the last commissions of James Gandon, and was designed in 1795, although it was not begun until 1802. The detailing shows Greek influence.

KINGSBRIDGE RAILWAY STATION (SEAN HUESTON STATION) A swaggering *palazzo* by Sancton Wood, 1845–61, flanked by cupolas.

LEINSTER HOUSE Now the Parliament House (Dail Eireann). One of the finest Dublin mansions, designed by Richard Castle for the Earl of Kildare in 1745. It has two formal fronts, and has been claimed as the prototype for the White House, Washington. Flanking the courtyard to Kildare Street are the later fine Renaissance-style buildings of the National Library and the National Museum by Sir Thomas Deane. In the National Library are over 500,000 volumes and an extensive Department of Manuscripts. The National Museum has a fine collection of archaeological and botanical objects, Irish antiquities forming a major part. (Both open to the public.)

MANSION HOUSE Though with a Victorian stucco front, it dates from 1705, and has been the residence of the Lord Mayor of Dublin since 1715.

MERRION SQUARE Laid out in 1762 by John Ensor, this is the second largest of Dublin's squares. Most of its brick houses contain the excellent stucco interiors characteristic of Georgian Dublin.

On the west side of the square is the lawn of Leinster House, flanked on the north by the National Gallery, designed by Lanyon, Fowke and Sir Richard Griffiths, and opened in 1864. It contains many outstanding examples from all European schools of painting. There is an Irish section and a National Portrait Gallery.

METAL BRIDGE An early single-arch cast-iron footbridge of 1816.

MOUNTJOY SQUARE Laid out for Lord Mountjoy, and finished in 1818, it is now sadly decayed. However, the Irish Georgian Society has taken over No. 50 as its Dublin headquarters, and has acquired other houses in the square for preservation. No. 47 was opened to the public in 1967, and was the first Dublin house to offer viewing facilities. The entrance hall has a fine ceiling.

MUNICIPAL BUILDINGS Adamesque, by Thomas Ivory in 1781; doubled in size in *c*. 1860.

NATIONAL GALLERY See Merrion Square.

NATIONAL MUSEUM See Leinster House.

NORTHLAND HOUSE (ROYAL IRISH ACADEMY) Built in 1770, probably by John Ensor. The plasterwork shows French arabesque influence.

O'CONNELL BRIDGE A reconstruction (1880) of Gandon's Carlisle Bridge of 1792.

OLD PARLIAMENT HOUSE Now the Bank of Ireland, it was begun in 1729 to the design of Sir Edward Lovett Pearce; the original building occupies three sides of a square, with an open colonnade round the three sides. This distinguished Ionic *piazza* was harmonised with the adjacent Trinity College by James Gandon in 1785. The House of Lords, by Pearce, survives intact with its tapestries and the silver-gilt House of Commons mace. In another room is the superb Venus ceiling from La Touche's Bank, installed in 1948. He extended the building eastwards and erected a magnificent Corinthian portico, joined to the earlier building by a plain quadrant screen. Further extensions were made westwards by Robert Parke, who balanced Gandon's work with a new west front featuring an Ionic portico. Francis Johnston remodelled the building, built the Cash Office, and harmonised the east and west quadrants.

# NATIONAL GALLERY

Public subscriptions enabled this fine gallery to be opened in 1864, in a building designed by Sir Charles Lanyon. The magnificent collections comprise more than 6000 paintings, over 1000 of them being on view. They include outstanding works from all the European schools, from 14th-century Florentine and Sienese paintings to the works of Irish artists of the 18th–20th centuries.

DANIEL MACLISE: THE MARRIAGE OF STRONGBOW AND AOIFE *Strongbow (Richard de Clare, Earl of Pembroke) led the Norman invasion of Ireland. In a canvas 16 ft by 10 ft, of which this is a detail, an Irish romantic gave vivid pictorial substance to his view that Irish freedom and values were lost for ever. First exhibited in 1854, the painting shows dejected Irish, and Strongbow trampling on an ancient Celtic cross.*

RUBENS: CHRIST AT THE HOUSE OF MARTHA AND MARY *The baroque style of the early 17th century introduced flamboyance and worldliness into painting. It developed early in Flanders, largely through the work of Rubens, Van Dyck and Jacon Jordaens, all of whom organised studios to undertake large series of commissions. In this work Rubens painted the figures, Jan Breughel was responsible for the sumptuous background landscape and Jan van Kessel for the birds, fruit and foreground accessories.*

FRA ANGELICO: THE ATTEMPTED MARTYRDOM OF
SS COSMAS AND DAMIAN *This panel is part of a
series of ten small scenes which formed a base to the
altar-piece 'Virgin and Child enthroned with angels
and saints', painted for the Church of San Marco in
Florence between 1438 and 1440. Now one of the most
precious possessions of the National Gallery of Ireland,
it depicts the attempt to burn the saints at the stake with*
*their three brothers; the flames turned away from the
victims and attacked the executioners. The scene is
depicted with a striking directness and clarity which are
typical of Fra Angelico's serene faith in the mysteries
of Christianity. The architecture in the background,
the foreshortening of the foreground figures and the
concept of space show how the artist had grasped the
treatment of perspective, a skill born in his own lifetime.*

PIETER CLAESZ: STILL-LIFE *The Dutch middle classes maintained
their homes with great pride in the 17th century, furnishing them dis-
creetly with articles of excellent craftsmanship. It was the century of
Rembrandt, Frans Hals, De Hooch and Vermeer, and paintings were in
great demand—the still-life was a favourite type. Pieter Claesz (1590–
1661) was a masterly exponent of the style; in this superb painting the
lemon and its peel and the pewter vase show how the artist was fascinated
by simple things—so that they take on an air of grandeur in his works.*

HORACE HONE: SELF-PORTRAIT
*As in England, miniature painting
flourished in Ireland in the 18th
century. Horace Hone was his
country's foremost exponent of the
art. He worked in both enamel and
water-colour—the technique used in
this fresh and confident likeness.*

603

# NATIONAL MUSEUM

Built in 1885–90 to designs by Sir Thomas Deane, the National Museum houses exhibits illustrating the history of the Irish people from earliest times, and the natural history of Ireland. The Irish Antiquities Division contains one of the most magnificent collections of national antiquities in Europe and is based on the Royal Irish Academy's superb collection. It represents every age from the Stone Age to medieval times, including prehistoric gold and early Christian art.

IRISH GOLD *Gold was discovered in the Wicklow Mountains about 1600 BC, and Ireland embarked on a period of great prosperity. The gold was exported as far as the Mediterranean, both in ingots and as decorative objects; these are still discovered in Ireland. The large collar (front left) was found in a field in 1932; thought to be worthless it was thrown into a hedge, but two years later its value was recognised. Made in 650 BC, it comes from Glensheen, Co. Clare.*

THE ARDAGH CHALICE *Dating from the 8th century, this bowl is the most important survival of early Irish Christian art. It is silver ornamented with silver gilt and enamel. The bands of decoration are of great intricacy; on the foot are plaques decorated with coloured glass. The chalice was found under a stone at Ardagh, Co. Limerick by a boy pulling up potatoes in 1868. Tradition has it that Mass was said secretly in the field during the 18th century.*

FRENCH IVORY PLAQUE: ST MARY OF EGYPT WITH ST ZOSIMUS AND THE CHRIST CHILD *This leaf of a diptych, barely 2½ in. high, is an exceptional product of the 14th-century Paris school of ivory carving. The subject is unusual. St Mary of Egypt was a courtesan of Alexandria in the 5th century. After a pilgrimage to Jerusalem she fled into the desert beyond the Jordan, and had lived there, naked apart from her long hair, without seeing a human creature for 47 years when she was discovered by the hermit Zosimus. During this time she had miraculously contrived to live on only three loaves of bread. Zosimus gave her communion—the scene depicted here. An angel flies down with a mantle to cover her nakedness. Visiting her again shortly afterwards, Zosimus found her dead, and buried her with the help of a lion.*

PARNELL SQUARE Second oldest of the great squares, and originally known as Rutland Square. Building began in the middle of the 18th century. Charlemont House by Sir William Chambers was originally one of the best of the city mansions, now incorporating the Municipal Gallery, with good selections of pictures, stained glass and sculpture.

PHOENIX PARK The largest city park in Europe; it contains various interesting buildings such as Gandon's Military Infirmary (1787), the enormous Wellington Testimonial (1817) by Sir Robert Smirke and Lord Chesterfield's Phoenix Column of 1747. Aras an Uachtarain, originally the house of its Ranger, was built by Nathaniel Clements and probably designed by him in 1751–2. It contains notable rococo plasterwork.

POWERSCOURT HOUSE This impressive mansion was built by Robert Mack for Viscount Powerscourt in 1771–4. The interior is delicately detailed.

PRO-CATHEDRAL OF ST MARY Designed by John Sweetman, this massive Greco-Doric edifice was begun in 1816 and has a portico.

QUEEN'S BRIDGE Perhaps the most graceful of the city's bridges, with three arches and a balustrade, by General Charles Vallancey, 1764–8.

ROTUNDA This complex of buildings in Parnell Square begins with the Maternity Hospital, the earliest in these islands, designed by Richard Castle in 1751 and most notable for the exuberant plasterwork of the chapel by Barthélemy Crémillion.

ROYAL HOSPITAL, KILMAINHAM Erected in 1680–7 to provide for aged war veterans, it was designed by Sir William Robinson in Franco-Dutch Classical style, and consists of a two-storied quadrangle with a stately tower and spire. The great hall is particularly impressive, and there are exceedingly fine wood carvings and the only important florid Carolean ceiling in Ireland.

ST ANDREW'S WESTLAND ROW A fine large Catholic town church of 1832–7 by James Boulger, with a Doric portico ingeniously tied in to the street façades. It contains many monuments.

ST MARY'S CHAPEL-OF-EASE Popularly known as the 'Black Church' this remarkable and important building was erected of black Dublin limestone in 1830 by the architect John Semple.

ST NICHOLAS OF MYRA A Classical church of 1832 by J. Leeson; entrance portico and domed tower.

ST PAUL'S ARRAN QUAY A riverside Catholic church by Patrick Byrne (1835–42). Its portico and cupolaed tower go well with the Four Courts.

ST STEPHEN'S GREEN Originally a common, this, the earliest of Dublin's squares, is also the largest. The buildings bounding the perimeter present an interesting variety of 18th- and 19th-century styles. They include: No. 85 by Richard Castle (1739) with Francini plasterwork, now united with its neighbour No. 86 by Robert West (1765); also with notable plaster is Newman House of University College; the University Church (1855–60) in Byzantine style by John Hungerford Pollen; the St Stephen's Green and United Services clubs and Nos. 16–17 all on the north side; a pair of houses (Nos. 119–20) on the west side by Richard Castle; the College of Surgeons (1806–27) by Edward Parke and William Murray. Iveagh House (Dept. of External Affairs) incorporates some good interiors of 1731 by Castle. In the gardens, laid out by Lord Ardilaun in 1880, are several monuments including one by Henry Moore in memory of W. B. Yeats.

STEEVEN'S HOSPITAL From a design by Thomas Burgh, it was started in 1720. It is the oldest public hospital in Ireland, and is arranged round an arcaded courtyard.

ROUBILIAC *Jonathan Swift*

*In 1738 the senior students of Trinity College decided to devote their entertainment money to commissioning a bust of the distinguished Dubliner Jonathan Swift, the great satirist and Dean of St Patrick's Cathedral. They chose Louis Francois Roubiliac, the leading sculptor of his time in Britain, for the assignment. The result, dated 1745, is the most vivid portrait of Swift that survives—although Roubiliac and Swift never met. (Trinity College Library, Dublin)*

TAYLOR'S HALL The last remaining guildhall in Dublin, dating from the reign of Queen Anne. The Hall, lit by circular-headed windows, has a carved wooden screen, and a marble fire-place.

TRINITY COLLEGE Founded in 1592 by Elizabeth I on the site of the Priory of All Hallows, the earliest surviving portion of the building, the Rubrics, dates from 1700. The impressive Palladian façade, built by Henry Keene and John Sanderson of London, dates from 1759. The quadrangles are bounded by many distinguished buildings—the chapel, the theatre (fine interiors), the Printing House, a miniature temple by Richard Castle, the Provost's House by John Smith using a façade of Palladio derived through Burlington, with intact interior including a splendid saloon with coffered ceiling, the dining-hall basically by Richard Castle, and the fine Venetian Revival museum buildings, designed in 1853 by Deane and Woodward with carvings by the O'Shea brothers. The great library, one of the copyright libraries, erected in 1712 to the design of Thomas Burgh, has 3000 ancient manuscripts, including the incomparable Book of Kells, the 7th-century Book of Durrow, and the Book of Armagh. The excellent New Library, built to an international competition-winning design by Ahrends, Burton and Koralek, adjoins it to the south-east. The Magnetic Observatory (now the Manuscript Room), is by Frederick Darley. (See also p. 606.)

TYRONE HOUSE Richard Castle built this notable Georgian mansion for Viscount Tyrone in 1740.

**Duleek** *Meath* 573Ke
There is a fine late 9th-century high cross in the churchyard and a sepulchral slab set in the churchyard wall. The tower and south aisle of the 15th-century Augustinian priory contain carved tombs, including the elaborate Bellew memorial.

## THE BOOK OF KELLS

*This famous illuminated copy of the Gospels is the greatest surviving masterpiece of early Irish art. It takes its name from the vanished monastery of Kells, in Co. Meath, which was founded by St Columba in the 6th century. However, the book is believed to have been written at St Columba's island monastery of Iona, off the coast of Scotland, in about 760–820 and carried to Kells by monks fleeing from the Viking invasions of the later 9th century.*

*The pages above are from St Matthew's Gospel, and the picture shows the arrest of Christ in the Garden of Gethsemane. On the left are the opening words of St Matthew's Gospel, Chapter 1, verse 18: 'Christi autem generatio', which, translated from the Latin is: 'Now the birth of Jesus Christ . . .' The XPI (Christ) monogram is ornamented with an intricacy and exuberance that present the eye with a feast of engaging detail. In addition to the standard motifs of Celtic art—interlaced ribbons, spirals and whorls repeated with subtle variations—the artist has included human heads, angels with spreading wings and, at the bottom of the letter P, two rats nibbling at the Eucharistic bread watched by a pair of cats—perhaps an allusion to the unpleasant fate in store for those who receive Holy Communion unworthily.*
*(Trinity College Library, Dublin)*

The wayside pillar erected by Dame Jennet Dowdall in 1601 is richly carved with angels and saints. Duleek House is a pedimented cut-stone house, with a good door by Richard Castle or his school.

**Dun Aillinne** *Kild.* 573Jc
This ceremonial hill-top site, said to be an early seat of the kings of Leinster, is enclosed by a large rampart and internal ditch.

**Dunamase Castle** *Laois* 573Hb
The Rock of Dunamase, conspicuously situated in a gap of the West Leinster Hills, is crowned by the much-ruined fragments of a large complicated castle of numerous medieval dates, destroyed by the Cromwellians in 1650.

**Dunboy** *Cork* 570Ba
This was the last stronghold in South-west Ireland to be taken by the Elizabethan forces during the

Nine Years War. The ruined 'castle' of the Puxleys is notable for its spectacular Victorian transverse arches.

**Dunbrody Abbey** *Wex.* 571Jd
A Cistercian friary founded by Hervey de Montmorenci in *c.* 1178 but built some 30 years later. It is one of the largest abbey churches in Ireland, cruciform with an added 15th-century crossing tower; for its size the church is relatively plain.

**Dundalk** *Louth* 573Kf
The Protestant church of St Nicholas, though much altered, is medieval in origin, with some 15th-century windows and a 14th-century tower. It was remodelled in 1685 and finally altered by Francis Johnston early in the 19th century. There are good monuments in the churchyard. The tower of the Franciscan friary, which dates from the 15th century, also survives.

**Dundonald** *Down* 575Jd
The fort here is an Anglo-Norman mote. In the churchyard is a fine Greco-Doric mausoleum of 1842, surmounted by a sarcophagus enclosed by six Ionic columns and a dome.

**Dundrum Castle** *Down* 575Hc
The cylindrical keep of Dundrum Castle is three storeys high, dates from 1230–40 and is surrounded by an irregularly curtained wall and a rock-cut fosse; it is among the earliest castles in Ireland. A gate-house leads to the lower ward, at the end of which stands a ruined Jacobean house.

**Dungannon** *Tyrone* 574Fd
Famous for its Volunteer Convention held in 1782, it is in origin an O'Neill stronghold. The Royal School, a Jacobean foundation, has buildings of 1786 which were erected by Primate Robinson. The Protestant church dates from 1790.

**Dungarvan** *Waterford* 571Hc
At the head of a spacious bay, it has the remains of a Norman castle now incorporated in the military barracks, and some broad quays, but is chiefly remarkable for its regular town plan and its attractive Grattan Square.

**Dungiven** *Lond.* 574Fe
The church of the Augustinian friary is a simple 12th-century structure remarkable mainly for the superb tomb of Cooey Na nGall O'Cahan, who died in 1385. He is in Irish costume, on an arcaded plinth containing six gallowglasses (mercenaries), the whole surmounted by a splendid Flamboyant pierced canopy.

**Dungory Castle** *Gal.* 572Dc
A 16th-century castle on a small island near the coast; it occupies the centre of an earlier earth-fort. The gabled tower adjoins one wall of an earlier hexagonal bawn. It has recently been entirely restored. (Open to the public.)

**Dunlavin** *Wicklow* 573Jc
Remarkable for its court- and market-house which stands in the middle of the square. It is a cruciform building with corner colonnades and fluted dome entirely built of masonry, probably to the design of Richard Castle in 1743.

**Dunluce Castle** *Antrim* 575Gg
On a rocky promontory jutting into the sea, Dunluce was built by Richard de Burgo c. 1300 and is one of the most spectacularly situated castles in Ireland. The 16th-century gate-house has Franco-Scottish corbelled turrets. In the outer court are the ruins of a Jacobean house which incorporates a great hall and kitchen. In 1639 some of the servants' quarters collapsed into the sea, taking a number of servants with them. Two earlier cylindrical towers remain.

**Dunmoe** *Meath* 573Je
A 13th-century castle altered in the 16th century. The adjoining church has a sacristy with a crypt underneath.

**Dunmore** *Gal.* 572De
The remains of a 13th-century castle with a square tower and added gables; and the 15th-century Augustinian friary church, also with a square tower, founded by Walter de Bermingham.

**Dunmurry** *Antrim* 575Hd
Now virtually a suburb of Belfast, it has a handsome Unitarian church of 1779; the church is a plain rectangle with an animated rhythm of windows and doorways on its entrance front.

**Dunsany** *Meath* 573Jd
Dunsany, the medieval castle of the Plunketts, Barons Dunsany, was remodelled in the 18th century, and has a splendid staircase with 18th-century Gothic ribbing and a drawing-room with plasterwork in the Stapleton manner. The stables are by Sir Gilbert Scott. There are also two good

## DUNDRUM CASTLE

*This ruined castle, standing on a high rock, was built in the 13th century by John de Courcy on the site of an ancient fort. The castle comprises a circular keep within irregular curtain walls, with a moat cut out of the rock. In the topmost storey of the keep is a series of continuous passageways cut in the wall. Its magnificent position made the castle a much sought after prize, and for centuries it was the scene of battles and sieges until it was eventually dismantled on the orders of Cromwell in 1652.*

entrance-lodges and a ruined church. The church of 1425–50, with crenellated parapets, has two western turrets and a wall dividing the nave from the chancel containing a rood. There is unusual tracery, typical of Fingall, the area north of Dublin. There is also a 16th-century high cross, a baptismal font carved with a Crucifixion and the Apostles, and a double-effigy tomb of the armoured Sir Thomas Plunkett and his wife.

**Dunsoghley** *Dublin*                        *573Kd*
The massive tower of Dunsoghley is on a small hillock in a marsh on the outskirts of Dublin. The four angle-towers rise above the main level of the keep which, unusually for Ireland, still retains the oak timbers of its roof.

**Duntryleague** *Lim.*                        *570Fd*
On a site which commands panoramic views are a ruined megalithic passage-grave, a circle of stones and a group of ruined barrows.

**Durrow Abbey** *Offaly*                        *573Gd*
The site of St Colmcille's monastery in which was written the famous Book of Durrow, now in Trinity College, Dublin. The 10th-century high cross and other smaller stones remain. The derelict Protestant church of *c.* 1700 has a splendid baroque west doorway.

**Dysart House** *Westmeath*                        *573He*
Built in 1757 by George Pentland for the Ogle family. Though relatively plain, the pedimented house has semicircular projections at both ends of the façade.

**Dysert O'Dea** *Clare*                        *570Df*
The remains of a two-cell Romanesque church, badly restored. It has a Round Tower but, most conspicuously, the fine mid-12th-century high cross, with a crucified Christ above the figure of a bishop, both in high relief.

**Eglantine** *Down*                        *575Hd*
A mid-19th-century house with a remarkable double staircase.

**Emo** *Laois*                        *573Hc*
A domed mansion with portico, designed by James Gandon for the 1st Earl of Portarlington, *c.* 1790, notable for Coade stone capitals and bas-relief panels. It is much altered internally. Gandon also designed Coolbanagher Church.

**Ennis** *Clare*                        *570Df*
The county town of Clare has a large Classical court-house of 1852 containing a statue by Joseph Kirk of Sir Michael O'Loghlen, Master of the Rolls, a column to the memory of Daniel O'Connell and some good 18th-century houses. But the principal relic of the town is a Franciscan friary, of O'Brien foundation in 1240, with features from the two following centuries; the MacMahon tomb in the friary church has a splendid relief of the Entombment dating from 1460.

**Enniscorthy** *Wex.*                        *571Ke*
An important Norman four-towered keep similar to those at Carlow and Ferns. St Aidan's Cathedral is a distinguished Gothic Revival work by Augustus Welby Pugin, 1843–8, the spire added to Pugin's plan in 1872–3.

**Enniskillen** *Ferm.*                        *574Dc*
In an important site on the Erne between the Upper and Lower Loughs, it has few ancient remains save the fragmentary Maguire Castle with a Scottish turret, and the 17th-century parish church, now the cathedral, which has a handsome font of 1666.

**Eyrecourt Castle** *Gal.*                        *572Fe*
Like Beaulieu, one of Ireland's few wide-eaved, Dutch-inspired houses of the late 17th century. The richly carved consoles of the cornice may still be seen. Extensive late 18th-century stables.

**Fahan Mura** *Don.*                        *574Ef*
The superlative erect slab has a cross with interlaced ornament and two stylised figures on its face. The projecting lugs seem to represent arms, and to be an early stage in the evolution of the high cross form. It has a Greek inscription.

**Fair Head Crannog** *Antrim*                        *575Hg*
In the little lake, Lough Na Crannagh, is a well preserved picturesque crannog, or lake-dwelling, with a drystone revetment.

**Feartagar Castle** *Gal.*                        *572Dd*
A 16th-century de Burgo castle: a well-preserved tower-house with corner machicolation, two staircases in the walls and a vaulted first floor.

**Fenagh** *Leit.*                        *574Db*
Both the churches at Fenagh have barrel-vaulted western ends, presumably to contain living quarters for the priest. The larger church has a very good east window of *c.* 1400.

**Fermoy** *Cork*                        *570Fc*
Laid out in 1791 by the Scottish immigrant John Anderson, it was a notable garrison town of the 19th century. The Protestant church dates from 1802 and has a grotesque medieval stoup.

**Ferns** *Wex.*                        *571Ke*
The remains of Ferns Cathedral, consisting of a 13th-century chancel, partly standing though unroofed, are far to the east of the present parish church-cathedral, which is a reduced reconstruction made in 1817 of a much larger aisled and cruciform medieval cathedral. The choir is puzzling, in being about 4 ft lower than the rest of the church, from which it is detached. Ferns Castle, the finest of the early 13th-century keeps, has cylindrical angle-towers, a type peculiar to Ireland. One of the corner towers has gone, and the principal feature is the vaulted chapel on the first floor of the south-east tower, the finest in any Irish castle.

**Fertagh** *Kilk.*                        *571Hf*
A fine round tower, in good condition, though damaged by fire in 1156. In the ruined church is a double effigy, the tomb of the FitzPatricks of Upper Ossory, the sides of which are decorated with window tracery and plans of lierne vaulting.

**Fethard** *Tipp.*                        *571He*
Though somewhat decayed, Fethard still has parts of its walls and four tower-houses, as well as the remains of an Augustinian friary of *c.* 1300, whose church has been re-roofed. The Protestant parish church has a medieval nave and west door, and several fine 14th-century windows.

**Finglas** *Dublin*                        *573Kd*
The church contains an excellent wall monument of 1700 by William Kidwell, to Sir William Fowler, the father of the 1st Lord Castle Durrow, builder of Durrow, County Leix.

**Florence Court** *Ferm.*                        *574Dc*
A somewhat bucolic house with wings of *c.* 1768 by Davis Ducart for Lord Mount Florence. Very good plasterwork. (Open to the public.)

**Fore** *Westmeath*                        *573He*
The ruined 9th- to 10th-century Church of St Fechin has pilaster projections and a massive west doorway with cross-inscribed lintel; it also has an early font and a reconstructed chancel arch of *c.*

1200. The extensive remains of the 13th-century priory are the only authenticated Benedictine remains in Ireland; there are fragments of a fine cloister and an Anglo-Norman tombstone. A conspicuous west tower of the 15th century and the north and south gate-houses of the medieval town survive, with other buildings and crosses.

**Forenaghts (Furness)** *Kild.*　　　*573Jc*
Near the ancient Woolpack Road from Dublin to the Curragh of Kildare is Long Stone, a 17 ft high granite standing stone, in the middle of Long Stone prehistoric enclosure, surrounded by an earth ring with two entrances. West of the stone is a roofless prehistoric burial chamber, where cremated bones, pottery and flints were found.

**Fourknocks** *Meath*　　　*573Ke*
This earthen mound was excavated in 1950 and found to contain a remarkable Neolithic to Bronze Age passage-grave. The chamber is now covered by a concrete dome, arranged to illuminate the carved stones.

**French Park** *Roscom.*　　　*572Ef*
One of the earliest red-brick, central block and wing houses in Ireland; it was probably built by Richard Castle *c.* 1729, and is now roofless.

**Freshford** *Kilk.*　　　*571Hf*
The Protestant church incorporates the west front of a Romanesque church, with double recessed doorway and gable.

**Furness House** *Kild.*　　　*573Jc*
Its central block is closely similar to Clermont in Wicklow, with wings, and was possibly designed by Francis Bindon in 1731. A column from Dangan in Meath has been erected in the park.

**Gallarus Oratory** *Kerry*　　　*570Ad*
A drystone chapel for private worship, a virtually unique survival of a method of building similar to that used in the Bronze Age burial chamber at Newgrange and in the more sophisticated mortared stone roofs at Killaloe, Kells and Glendalough. The system makes use of corbels, with inward-sloping bowed gables and side walls that merge imperceptibly into the roof.

**Gallen** *Offaly*　　　*572Fc*
Little remains of the famous 5th-century monastery, but a collection of grave-slabs similar to those at Clonmacnoise is preserved in the modern priory.

**Galway** *Gal.*　　　*572Cc*
Originally a Norman foundation, Galway was known as the City of the Tribes. Because of its remote situation and extensive trade with the Continent, it enjoyed virtual autonomy through much of the medieval period and became to all intents and purposes a city-state. The old Galway was built in the 16th–17th centuries and was notable for its fine architecture. Today little survives, but 16th-century Lynch's Castle (now the Munster and Leinster Bank), with its elaborate carved windows, is typical of the semi-fortified palaces of the aristocratic merchant families. Other fragments, such as the 'Spanish' Arch, survive throughout the town. In the Classical porticoed Franciscan church of 1836 are the remains of Sir Peter French's tomb, incorporating weepers in the Gothic tradition, and Renaissance ornamental detail.
CHURCH OF ST NICHOLAS The largest medieval church in Ireland, founded in 1230. It has a profusion of fine carving, much of it of the 15th and early 16th century, when Galway was at its most prosperous. The plan of the building is cruciform, and the south and north nave aisles were widened in 1500 and 1538–83 respectively, resulting in a

unique three-gabled west front. The central tower was added *c.* 1500, and the south transept was extended by Nicholas Lynch in 1561 and included a private chapel approached by private stairs. The carvings include gargoyles on the south aisle and, in the interior, the 16th-century font, 15th-century water stoup and the imported 15th-century reader's desk with its cusped tracery.

**Garinish Island** *Cork*　　　*570Cb*
In 1910, John Annan Bryce began to transform Garinish Island, a desolate rocky islet, into a unique island garden. Harold Peto, architect, horticulturist and landscape designer, laid out the garden in the Classical Italian style within a shelterbelt of trees; the formal garden gradually merges into meandering grass walks lined with naturalised trees, shrubs and flowers.

**Garraunboy** *Lim.*　　　*570Ee*
A fine mid-15th-century keep, symmetrically sited on a rock bawn, originally with D-shaped turrets at all four corners. The interior has numerous wall-recesses and ogee-headed windows, and there is a shot-hole over the main door.

**Giants' Ring** *Down*　　　*575Hd*
A circular ceremonial enclosure 750 ft in diameter, with a rampart about 12 ft high, in seven sections and with a small dolmen in the centre.

**Gill Hall** *Down*　　　*575Hc*
An early 18th-century house with a particularly fine front door and with dolphin-decorated spandrels to which two triple-storey rusticated window-bays have been added, probably by Richard Castle, who was certainly responsible for the groin-vaulted stables near by (*c.* 1731).

**Glananae House** *Westmeath*　　　*573He*
A late 18th-century house, probably by Samuel Woolley, who was certainly responsible for the Glananae triumphal arch now at Rosmead, in the same county. Good Wyatt-style plasterwork.

**Glanfahan** *Kerry*　　　*579Ac*
An extremely dense concentration of stone forts and clochans (bee-hive huts) on the south coast of the Dingle peninsula near Slea Head, including the impressive promontory fort of Dun Beag.

**Glencolumbkille** *Don.*　　　*574Be*
A complex site of prehistoric and early Christian remains, including a great cairn, a prehistoric chamber-tomb, ring-forts containing beehive huts, and many pillar-stones incised with crosses.

**Glendalough** *Wicklow*　　　*573Kb*
Among the most renowned, and in many ways the most picturesque, of the early monastic sites, Glendalough lies at the head of a narrow valley containing two lakes. Its foundation is attributed to St Kevin, who died early in the 7th century, but the present remains are mostly of the 10th–12th centuries. Among the earliest of these are Templenaskellig and 'St Kevin's Bed' on the south shore of the Upper Lake, accessible only by boat. The former, much reconstructed, has some early gravestones and a small enclosure. The 'Bed' is a cave. Reefert ('burial-place of the kings') Church, farther to the east, is possibly of the 10th century. Like Trinity Church, which it much resembles, it has a nave and chancel and stone brackets in place of pilasters to carry the ends of the barge boards.

East of the Lower Lake between Glendasan R. and the stream from the two lakes is the main monastic precinct, the north gateway of which, near the Royal Hotel, still survives, as does the paved causeway leading south from it. Within the present enclosure are the cathedral, the Round

## ST KEVIN'S CHURCH
## AT GLENDALOUGH

*The valley of Glendalough contains the site of one of Ireland's holy places, for it was here St Kevin settled, and died in 618. Around him grew up a community of followers who perpetuated his fame, and this has survived to the present day. Seven churches were built in the valley, and St Kevin's Church, with its belfry— a miniature version of the nearby Round Tower—is the most perfect. The original entrance at the west end is now blocked up and the present entrance was the chancel arch. Stone crosses and other carved stones from the valley are now stored inside. The belfry, one of the earliest examples of a belfry springing from a roof or gable, was probably added at a later date than the church itself. St Kevin's reputed burial-place is the Church of the Virgin, in the valley.*

Tower, the 'priests' house' and St Kevin's Cross. West of it, in a separate enclosure, is St Mary's Church and south of it St Kevin's. Of these buildings, St Mary's is probably the earliest, with an added Romanesque chancel and north door. The square-headed west doorway, with inclined jambs, has a saltire cross incised below its lintel. The cathedral, dedicated to SS Peter and Paul, is a complex building consisting basically of a 10th-century nave of exceptional width (30 ft) with antae, a fine west door, and a later chancel with a reconstructed chancel arch. Three early inscribed stones are fixed to the north wall. The Round Tower is among the most perfect in Ireland, its cap being a modern reconstruction using the original stones.

The so-called priests' house is a small building, perhaps a shrine or mortuary chapel, probably late 12th century, and most remarkable for the lintel over its south door. Though now fragmentary, it is known to have been triangular, with a seated figure in the centre receiving homage from two others carrying bell and crozier. St Kevin's Cross is a plain granite cross 11 ft high. St Kevin's Church was originally a single-cell church with barrel-vault, roof-croft and corbelled roof above it. Rising out of the west end of the roof is a miniature Round Tower. The whole probably dates from the 9th century. Several stone fragments including the market cross are kept inside. East of St Kevin's is the much ruined St Kierans, the smallest nave-and-chancel church recorded in Ireland.

East of this central group are two more churches: Trinity Church and St Saviour's. St Saviour's is the most elaborately decorated of the Glendalough churches and dates from the mid-12th century. It consists of a nave and chancel, with a domestic building adjoining it on the north.

Glendalough was repeatedly burnt and plundered in the 9th and 10th centuries, but from 1107 onwards was the See of a bishop, now united with the See of Dublin. In 1398 the English of Dublin sacked and destroyed it, but it remained a monastic centre until the end of the 16th century, and a place of pilgrimage until the middle of the 19th.

**Glenquin Castle** *Lim.*                    *570Dd*
A tall fortified tower, carefully restored in 1840.

**Glenstale Castle** *Lim.*                    *570Fe*
This massive pile includes a splendid re-creation of the medieval gate-house at Rockingham, England, and was designed by William Bardwell for the Barrington family in 1837.

**Glenveagh Castle** *Don.*                    *574Df*
A Scottish-style baronial castle by an unknown architect, in the centre of Ireland's only major deer forest; built for the Adair family in 1870.

**Glin Castle** *Lim.*                    *570De*
A Gothic castellated house of *c.* 1790–1812, which incorporates a fine double staircase and Wyatt-like plasterwork. A notable series of Gothic folly lodges surrounds the estate. It is the seat of the Knights of Glin (FitzGeralds).

**Glinsk** *Gal.*                    *572Bd*
Said to have been built by Ulick Burke, who died in 1708, Glinsk—a compact, three-storey, semi-fortified house—was more probably built by his predecessors. It has machicolations on the corners and a host of lofty chimneys.

**Gloster** *Offaly*                    *571Gg*
The central portion is a late 17th-century house with a superimposed order of pilasters on the garden front, to which have been added two extensions with windows and pedimented niches, possibly by Sir Edward Lovett Pearce *c.* 1730. He was probably responsible also for the richly stuccoed central saloon, with its arcaded gallery and flanking corridors. In the grounds, a triumphal arch flanked by obelisks is certainly by Pearce.

**Gorey** *Wex.*                    *571Lf*
The Loretto convent is by Augustus Welby Pugin, and dates from 1839–42. The Church of St Mark, in Norman style of the same date, is also by him. The Protestant parish church has fine stained glass by Harry Clarke and Catherine O'Brien.

**Gort** *Gal.*                    *572Db*
A town well laid out by the Vereker family of Lough Cutra, but principally associated with Augusta, Lady Gregory. Her house (now demolished) at Coole Park was a meeting place for such Irish poets and authors as W. B. Yeats and Sean O'Casey in the early years of the present century. Little now remains but a cedar avenue and a huge copper beech carved with initials of many literary visitors to Coole. Five miles to the north-east is Yeats's Tower at Ballylee.
BALLYLEE CASTLE The 16th-century tower where W. B. Yeats lived during the 1920's and wrote his book of poems *The Tower*. Yeats left the tower in 1929, after which it fell into ruin. It was restored as a Yeats Museum in 1965.

**Gosford Castle** *Arm.*                    *575Gc*
The first Norman Revival castle in these islands, designed by Thomas Hopper *c.* 1820.

**Gowran** *Kilk.*          *571Je*
The collegiate church of Gowran, *c.* 1275, has an aisled nave and long chancel. As at Callan, the chancel now serves as the Protestant church. The 14th- and 15th-century square keep stands between the nave and the chancel. The windows and other details of the church are of high quality.

**Gracehill** *Antrim*        *575Ge*
This Moravian settlement was founded in 1746 with separate houses for the brothers and sisters, grouped around a square, plain church with baroque woodwork to the doorways. It survives almost intact. The graveyard is behind the church.

**Graiguenamanagh** *Kilk.*     *571Je*
Almost the whole town is built inside the great Cistercian abbey founded by William the Marshall in *c.* 1207 and peopled with monks from Stanley in Wiltshire. The church is the largest Irish Cistercian example. The central tower fell in 1774 causing much damage; in 1813, the eastern parts were re-roofed to form the Catholic parish church. There was so much debris from the fall of the tower that the present floor level is 5 ft higher than the original, and architectural features are buried. There are good Transitional features, as at Kilkenny Cathedral. The seven-arched bridge over the Barrow is by George Semple (mid-18th century). The barracks in the town has an 18th-century doorway on which the local mason who made it has worked 13th-century dog-tooth ornament. There are two high crosses, one from Ballycogan with sculptured figures, including King David.

**Granard** *Long.*          *573Ge*
A gently curving street leads up to the Catholic Church of St Mary of 1861, built by John Burke, behind which may be seen the mote of Hugh de Lacy's castle, built in 1191.

**Granny** *Kilk.*           *571Jd*
A tower-house with an oriel window in good condition and one wall of its separate hall.

**Great Connell Priory**       *573Jc*
Of the great Anglo-Irish Augustinian priory founded in 1202, nothing remains save the magnificent mitred effigy of Walter Wellesley, Prior of Great Connell, and Bishop of Kildare, *c.* 1539.

**Great Skellig** *Kerry*       *570Ab*
The celebrated island of Skellig Michael, one of Europe's many rocky places associated with that saint, lies in the Atlantic 7 miles west of Bollus Head. There are nine buildings, two oratories, six dwelling huts and the church; all but the church are built of dry stone. The settlement seems to have been occupied by a community of hermits from the 9th until probably the 12th century. Access can be difficult, but the solitude, splendour and mystery of the scene is without parallel.

**Greencastle** *Don.*        *574Fg*
The keep at Greencastle, almost completed by 1261, is a long rectangle with four angle-towers and set-back gables. It is surrounded by the fragmentary remains of a bawn, which originally possessed four corner towers.

**Grey Abbey** *Down*       *575Jd*
A Cistercian abbey, founded in 1193 by John de Courcy; the church is aisle-less, with transepts and east chapels and an impressive west doorway of *c.* 1220. The east wall has two storeys, each of three lancets. The cloister was an elongated rectangle and the refectory, as at Askeaton, was endwise on. There are some good 17th- and early 18th-century Montgomery monuments, and a recumbent medieval tomb effigy.

ST STEPHEN WINDOW

*Harry Clarke, the son of a stained glass artist, sought to produce a more personal type of window than those produced in his father's Dublin studio. This window, dating from 1922, shows the influence of Clarke's work as a book illustrator and his interest in Aubrey Beardsley. The jewelled effect was achieved by abundant aciding. (Protestant Parish Church, Gorey)*

**Grianan of Aileach** *Don.*      *574Ef*
A large, well preserved, though much restored drystone circular fort, probably dating from the 5th to the 12th century. It consists of three outer rings of defences surrounding the fort proper, with three internal stepped terraces and stairways. There are galleries in the thickness of the wall.

**Hazelwood** *Sligo*       *574Cc*
Built in 1731, one of Richard Castle's earlier central block and wing houses on the shores of Lough Gill. Well detailed with William Kent-style interior decoration, it is now a mental home.

**Headfort House** *Meath*      *573Je*
A large, severe, oblong house notable for its rich
Robert Adam interior dating from 1770. Now a
boys' school.

**Hermitage** *Lim.*      *570Ff*
A late 18th-century pedimented house with Coade
stone enrichments, and the remnants of interesting
interior decoration; now in ruins, and picturesquely situated in a wooded park by the Shannon.

**Hillsborough** *Down*      *575Hd*
Founded in the mid-17th century by Colonel
Arthur Hill, who built a square fort with spear-
shaped bastions and gate-house here in the 1650's.
The fort has good wrought-iron gates and stone
piers with urns. The present gate-house is in the
18th-century Gothic style, and dates from 1758.
Much of the fort was remodelled at this time, and
a charming gazebo was constructed in the middle
of the north-east side by the 1st Lord Hillsborough.
His son, the 1st Marquess of Downshire, virtually
rebuilt the 17th-century Plantation church in 1773,
with a tower and spire, at the end of an avenue
framed by gate-lodges in the same style. The
interior of the church is remarkable for its Gothic
fittings, including box-pews, a hexagonal pulpit,
throne and organ by John Snetzler and some
monuments, one by Nollekens. Other notable
buildings include the court-house, originally the
market-house, which has a cupola, and dates from
1780, perhaps by W. Forsyth. Opposite is the
present Government House, originally the
Downshires' seat, designed by R. F. Brettingham
in 1795, with additions by William Sandys. In
front of it are elaborate gates of 1745, removed
from Richhill Castle, Co. Armagh, possibly by
the Thornberry brothers of Armagh.

**Holycross Abbey** *Tipp.*      *571Ge*
Founded in the 12th century by Donal Mor
O'Brien and named after a relic of the True Cross;
originally founded for the Tironian order, it passed
to the Cistercians at the end of the century. The
church has an aisled nave and choir with a vaulted
presbytery and transepts, and a massive central
crossing tower of the 15th century. The magnificent sedilia of the 15th century has meticulous
carving. Between the two chapels of the south
transept is a remarkable open-work structure,
popularly called 'the monks' waking place',
probably designed for the exhibition of the relic of

the True Cross; it has an elaborate foliated base and
twisted columns. The incidental carvings in the
church, such as the owl, are attractive.

**Howth Castle** *Dublin*      *573Kd*
A medieval castle of the St Lawrence family was
altered and made roughly symmetrical in 1738,
possibly by Francis Bindon. He was probably
responsible for the splendid pedimented front
door, and the compartment ceilings and chimney-
piece in the drawing-room. A large part of the
early 18th-century formal garden survives, with
30 ft high beech hedges. (Gardens open to the
public.)

**Humewood Castle** *Wicklow*      *573Jb*
With Dromore it ranks as Ireland's most successful
Gothic Revival high-Victorian essay in the castle
style. Designed by William White, 1867–8, with
extensive later additions including the immense
circular water tower. (Not open to the public.)

**Ightermurragh** *Cork*      *571Gb*
A cruciform 17th-century house, with four gables
and many fire-places, including one which records
the building of the house in 1641 by Edmund
Supple and his wife 'whom love binds in one'.

**Illauntannig** *Kerry*      *570Bd*
One of the largest of the Maharee Islands off the
north coast of Corkaguiny. A hermitage founded
by St Seanach in the 6th to 7th century, remains of
the monastery, small church, three clochans and
burial monuments survive in a massive drystone
cashel, part of which has fallen into the sea.

**Inchagoill** *Gal.*      *572Cd*
An island in Lough Corrib, about 5 miles south of
Cong, on which are the remains of an early
mortar-built oratory and a 12th-century Romanesque church. The doorway (rebuilt) is elaborately
carved with human heads and other ornaments.

**Inchcleraun** *Long.*      *572Fe*
In the north arm of Lough Ree is the island monastery founded by St Diarmaid. It contains a group
of churches, six in all, varying in age from the 10th
century to the 15th century.

**Inis Cealtra** *Clare*      *572Eb*
On an island in Lough Derg is the earliest group of
monastic remains in County Clare, containing an
earthen monastic enclosure, the ruins of four
churches, a small building called the 'Confes-
sional'—possibly a hermit's cell—a Round Tower,

HOLYCROSS ABBEY

*Once a place of pilgrimage, the abbey presents a view
of the great east window of the church, with reticulated
tracery, across the R. Suir. Some 4 miles south-west*
*of Thurles, the ruins include fragments of the 15th-
century cloister and its ranges, and the remains of the
infirmary and abbot's lodging.*

two high crosses and a cemetery full of early gravestones inscribed in Irish.

**Inishbofin** *Long.*      *572Fd*
A small island in the eastern arm of Lough Ree; it contains two churches and a few early gravestones. One church has a fine early Romanesque window.

**Inishmaine** *Mayo*      *572Ce*
An island in Lough Mask containing an Augustinian Transitional church of the late 12th century, with later transepts. On the west shore of the island is a twin-crypted sweat-house (used for sweat baths), with a high-pitched stone roof.

**Inismurray** *Sligo*      *573Bc*
This island site, 4 miles off the Sligo coast near Grange, is perhaps the most complete and perfectly preserved early monastic enclosure in Ireland. The monastic cashel, oval in outline, lies near the shore, in the middle of the south coast of the island, which was inhabited until very recently. It was founded by St Laisren and raided by the Vikings in 807. Within the cashel are a small stone-roofed church with pilasters, and three clochans, of which the largest is called the Schoolhouse, and two minor rectangular buildings, the larger called the Fire Temple and the smaller St Molaise's (Laisren) Chapel. There are also several paths and causeways as well as three open-air altars or tombs, and a covered holy well outside the east wall of the cashel. St Molaise's Chapel is a very small, stone-roofed oratory with a tiny east window. Against the outside of the south wall is a long stone bench. Over the west door is a small Greek cross. The larger church, south of it—sometimes called the 'Monastery', or the 'Men's Church'—has pilasters at its east end only, and is roofless. North of it are two pillar-stones, and east of it an open-air altar. Another altar lies to the south, and to the west a stone platform on which are the five Cursing Stones; they are inscribed with crosses and other devices, and an Englishwoman is said to have used them to curse Hitler. The Fire Temple and the Schoolhouse are close together in the subdivided west part of the enclosure. The former is of medieval date, but has an early cross on its lintel. The Schoolhouse is oval, of corbelled construction without mortar.

Another church, 'of the Women', and a grave-yard with some inscribed stones, lie south-east of the cashel. Several altars, cross-slabs and pillar-stones are found in isolated sites round the shores of the island.

**Inistioge** *Kilk.*      *571Je*
A well laid-out village, with tree-lined square and a fine 18th-century bridge over the R. Nore. It was built by the Tighe family of the Woodstock estate near by. The Protestant parish church incorporates parts of the medieval priory, and in the north tower is an effigy by Flaxman of the poetess Mary Tighe, the author of *Psyche*, who died in 1810.

**Isert Kelly** *Gal.*      *572Dc*
Standing in Castle Park is the 15th-century tower-house of the MacHubert Burke's castle; the windows of the second floor have arcaded embrasures, and inside is a carved chimney-piece dated 1604, with a Latin inscription.

**Jerpoint Abbey** *Kilk.*      *571Je*
The most interesting of the first generation of Cistercian houses. The silhouette of its tower with its characteristic Irish battlements, the elaboration and variety of the carvings of the cloister and other features, and its fine situation beside the Nore, combine to give it an unusual attraction. It was founded by Donal Mac Gillapatrick in 1180, but

the abbey was rebuilt in the 15th century when the conspicuous crossing tower was inserted. The cylindrical piers of the nave have Transitional capitals, as have the transept chapels. The richly carved piers of the cloister arcade, re-erected in recent years, are among the finest works of Irish medieval sculpture.

Also in the abbey, and connected with the cloister carving, are examples of altar tomb-sculpture; these carved effigies of saints have a kinship with figures of angels painted in 8th- and 9th-century Irish manuscripts. Just to the north-west is Newtown Jerpoint, in which are the ruins of St Nicholas's parish church; it has an unusual groin-vaulted rood gallery and a dwelling tower dating from the 15th century.

**Jigginstown House** *Kild.*      *573Jc*
The most ambitious of Thomas Wentworth, Earl of Strafford's Irish building ventures: a huge (380 ft long) uncompleted house, dating from before 1637. It is entirely built on a vaulted brick basement faced in stone on the exterior. The upper storeys, said to have been faced with marble, are incomplete, and today one can see only the chimney-stacks and the huge window-jambs of the first floor. It is superlatively well built, and is the earliest brickwork known in Ireland. The builder, John Allen, is reputed to have been a Dutch immigrant.

**Johnstown Castle** *Wex.*      *571Kd*
A magnificent group of buildings with many towers. It was designed in Gothic and Norman Revival styles by Daniel Robertson of Kilkenny in 1830–43. The castle, standing in grounds complete with a lake, is now an agricultural institute.

**Kanturk Castle** *Cork*      *570Ec*
In *c.* 1609 McDonagh McCarthy, Lord of Duhallow began, but never finished, this large compact semi-fortified house, resembling Burntcourt in plan. Both houses are related to English examples such as Lulworth and Mount Edgecumbe.

**Kells** *Meath*      *573He*
St Colmcille founded a monastery here in the 6th century. The Book of Kells, a magnificent illuminated copy of the Gospels in Latin, was written at the monastery of Kells in the 8th century; it is now preserved in Trinity College, Dublin. In the town are 'St Colmcille's House', a church of early stone-roof type, a Round Tower and five 10th-century high crosses, four in the churchyard and one in the middle of the town. The square bell-tower of the medieval church has a spire added by Thomas Cooley in 1783. The Catholic parish church and the court-house were designed by Francis Johnston. To the west, on the Hill of Lloyd, is the Taylour Column of 1791, in the form of a lighthouse, designed by Henry Aaron Baker.

**Kells-in-Ossory** *Kilk.*      *571Je*
An Augustinian fortified priory founded at the end of the 12th century by Geoffrey de Montemarisco. The ruins have all the appearance of a many-towered walled town. They consist of two courts and cover 5 acres, making this the largest monastic enclosure in Ireland. The ruined church with a Lady Chapel—originally cruciform with a large Cistercian-type tower now half demolished—is in the north-east angle. In the north transept is a slab with a pair of high-relief portrait heads. One and a half miles to the north-east is Kilree; the early church there has pilasters and a lintelled west doorway; there is also a Round Tower 98 ft high, and an 8th-century high cross decorated with spirals, frets and figures.

**Kenure Park** *Dublin*                               *573Kd*
A mid-18th-century house with two fine Robert
West rococo plaster state rooms, and a giant
Corinthian portico of 1842 by George Papworth.

**Kilbolane Castle** *Cork*                            *570Ed*
Two circular towers and two walls survive of the
13th-century castle built by the Cogans, and later
acquired by the Earls of Desmond. The water-
filled moat on the south-west side can still be seen.

**Kilbrittain Castle**                                 *570Eb*
A picturesque remnant of a Gothic Revival castle,
built around a medieval castle.

**Kilcash Castle** *Tipp.*                             *571Hd*
The stronghold of Kilcash stands on the southern
slopes of Slievenaman, north-west of Carrick-on-
Suir. It is a typical tower-house with very large
chimney-stacks and bartizans, at the side of which
are the remains of a great hall. Near by is a small
early church with a Romanesque south doorway.

**Kilclief** *Down*                                    *575Jc*
A tower-house of the 15th century, built by John
Sely, Bishop of Down, as a manorial residence
after 1413. There is a high arch between its two
eastern turrets. It was thatched in the 18th century.

**Kilconnell Friary** *Gal.*                           *572Ed*
A Franciscan friary founded in *c.* 1414 by William
Mor O'Kelly. It has a fine slender tower, but the
north range of the cloister buildings is missing. On
the eastern side of the south transept are three
chapels; the middle one dates from 1512. There is
evidence that galleries were inserted in the church
to accommodate increased numbers of monks in
the later Middle Ages. The glory of Kilconnell is in
the two canopied wall-tombs in the nave's north
wall. Both have arcaded bases, with tall pinnacles rising to the full height of the canopy. The
west tomb, one of the finest of Irish wall-tombs,
has six exquisitely carved saints on its base,
including St Louis and St Denis, and an inscription
to the unknown occupant.

**Kilcooly Abbey** *Tipp.*                             *571He*
A Cistercian abbey founded *c.* 1182 by Donal Mor
O'Brien, a daughter-house of Jerpoint. The
church, of *c.* 1200, is fairly small and has lost its
nave aisles. After almost total destruction in 1445,
Abbot Phillips (*d.* 1463) undertook the rebuilding.
The chancel was vaulted, the central tower added,
and galleries installed because of an increase in the
community; the transepts were also vaulted, and
an east window, with elaborate tracery, was inserted. The church's unique feature is the use of the
western piers of the crossing as niches for the seats
of the abbot and his deputy. Almost 2 miles south,
at Clonamicklon, are the remains of a large gabled
17th-century castle with a fortified enclosure.

**Kilcornan House** *Gal.*                             *572Dc*
A fine Tudor Revival house with a chapel incorporating a medieval tower; now a school.

**Kilcrea Friary** *Cork*                              *570Eb*
A Franciscan friary of neat and simple plan,
founded in 1463 by Cormac McCarthy and still
substantially complete. The cloister yard survives.
To the north-east of the chancel is a scriptorium,
well lit, for manuscript writing. Near by is
Cormac McCarthy's Castle, with a tower,
courtyard and turret.

**Kilcullen** *Kild.*                                  *573Jc*
The modern town is of small interest, but old
Kilcullen, 2 miles to the south-west, has the base of
a Round Tower, the remains of a Romanesque
church and parts of three stone crosses.

**Kildare** *Kild.*                                    *573Hc*
The early remains of Kildare include a fine Round
Tower 106 ft high, with a decorated Romanesque
doorway. The battlemented parapet is modern.
An enigmatic ruin in the churchyard is called St
Brigid's Fire House.
ST BRIGID'S CATHEDRAL Probably begun 1229 by
Bishop Ralph; it seems to have fallen into decay
during the 17th century, though a new chancel was
built *c.* 1686. The church remained a ruin until the
restoration by G. E. Street in 1875, which was
considerably more successful than most such
undertakings.

**Kildreenagh** *Kerry*                                *570Bb*
A small oval graveyard, containing in its north-
east corner a tiny oratory and in the north-west
corner a clochan. The rest of the enclosure is full of
small gravestones. There are other monuments of
this kind in the neighbourhood.

**Kilfane** *Kilk.*                                    *571Je*
This medieval church incorporates original priests'
quarters on the north side. The interior has a sedilia
and an extremely impressive knight holding an
armorial shield, of *c.* 1220.

**Kilfenora** *Clare*                                  *570Dg*
The cathedral, dedicated to St Fachtna, dates from
the 12th century, and now incorporates the small,
damaged Protestant church. The roofless chancel
possesses good Gothic altar-tombs and two primitive medieval episcopal effigies. In the churchyard
stands a magnificent 12th-century high cross. One
mile east is Ballykinvarga fort, a large cashel built
of great blocks of limestone with an encircling
bawn of pillar stones nearly 50 ft wide (forming a
*chevaux de frise*); there is also a 7 ft standing stone.

**Kilkea Castle** *Kild.*                              *573Jb*
An 1849 reconstruction of a basically medieval
castle; it has a haunted room which Gerald, the
famous Wizard Earl of Kildare, is supposed to visit
every seven years, riding a white horse.

**Kilkenny** *Kilk.*                                   *571Je*
In most respects the most interesting inland town
in Ireland. The early monastic settlement of St
Canice on top of the small hill beside the Nore,
now called Irish Town, has left its traces in the
Round Tower and a few stones incorporated in the
Gothic cathedral. A quarter of a mile to the south
on the same side of the Nore is the great Anglo-
Norman castle of William the Marshall, best
known as the principal seat of the Butlers, Earls,
Marquesses and formerly Dukes of Ormonde. The
medieval city, and the heart of the present town,
was a walled rectangle lying between these points,
with the castle at its south-east corner and its
northern boundary formed by the Bradoge R.,
which separates Irish Town from Kilkenny
proper. The main street, called successively The
Parade, High Street and Parliament Street, forms
the backbone of the town, and its mid-point is
marked by the Tholsel. Some fragments of the
walls survive, especially at the north-west corner,
near the Dominican 'Black Abbey'. A fine 18th-
century bridge by George Smith, Green's Bridge
of 1765, with five arches separated by piers
enriched with pedimented recesses, survives to the
east of Irish Town. In the churchyard is the
bishop's palace of 1735–6, plain, except for its
doorway. The interior has a fine carved and
panelled staircase. In the garden is the charming
pedimented robing-room, built by Bishop
Pococke in 1760. To the west of the churchyard is
the library, containing a notable collection of
16th- and 17th-century books; it was founded by

KILCONNELL FRIARY

*One of the most beautiful ruins in Ireland, Kilconnell Friary was founded about 1414 by William Mor O'Kelly for the Franciscans and built on the site of an earlier church. Little of the later cloister buildings, and* *the small cloister with its arcades springing from a low wall, remains. The friary was occupied by English soldiers for nine months in 1596, and in 1651 successfully withstood attack by Cromwell's troops.*

Bishop Thomas Otway in 1679. South of this is the mid-18th-century deanery.

The church of the Dominican friary—founded in 1226, re-roofed in the late 16th century and since 1840 again in use—has a typical long preaching transept of the 14th century and a square pedimented tower, inscribed as built by James Shortall, who died in 1537. In the adjoining convent are some good 15th- and 16th-century statuettes and statues. The Franciscan friary in Smithwick's Brewery consists principally of its crossing tower of *c.* 1350; some claustral buildings have recently been disentangled from the Brewery. St Mary's Church (now a parish hall) has a nave, transepts and a western tower; it is now partly embedded in the raised level of the churchyard. It contains a number of notable arcaded monuments of the 17th century. The Protestant parish church of St John, on the east bank of the Nore, is an 1817 reconstruction of the Lady Chapel of the 'new' Priory and Hospital of St John; it was founded *c.* 1211. Some distance south of this, in Maudlin Street, is a small medieval tower. Kilkenny is noteworthy for the possession of more late-medieval secular buildings than any other town in Ireland. Most of these are now fragmentary, but the Rothe House, a large elaborate town-house of 1594, restored in 1965, now houses the museum and library of the Kilkenny Archaeological Society. In Rose Inn Street is Shee's Almshouse, founded in 1581. There are scanty remains of Kyteler's Inn, associated with the most famous of Irish witchcraft trials in 1324. The south-west angle-tower of the town walls survives, near the junction of Ormonde Road and New Street.

Unlike most Irish towns of its size, Kilkenny retained practical and administrative importance right through the 17th century and into the 18th. Its 18th-century buildings are thus slotted into sites in the still-living medieval city. Most conspicuous of these is the Tholsel, built in 1761, possibly by the amateur architect-builder and marble-quarrier William Colles. It has a Roman-Doric arcade of five bays over the pavement, a council room on the first floor in which are kept the city muniments, and is surmounted by a three-storey octagonal lantern with a clock and pyramidal roof, a reconstruction of *c.* 1948 of its timber predecessor. A few hundred yards to the north is the court-house of 1794, standing on a vaulted basement now obscured by later work. It has a pedimented Doric centre-piece, with Wyatt windows lighting the main hall and columnar features surmounting the façade. The plan of the interior is a close copy of the vanished Gandon court-house in Waterford, and the external details show mannerisms of the school of Gandon. Opposite the castle garden is a fine terrace of 18th-century houses, one of which contained the Kilkenny theatre. Elsewhere in Kilkenny are numerous 18th-century houses, some characterised by the possession of adjoining twin doorways beneath a single fanlight or relieving arch.

On the east bank of the Nore, opposite the castle, is the building (1782) of Kilkenny College, founded in 1666, where Swift and Berkeley went to school; it has a handsome front door with large, Dublin-style fanlight. South of the castle is St James's or Switsir's Asylum, an elegant set of almshouses of 1803, with a swaggering statue of the founder, James Switsir. St Ciaran's College of 1836 is by William Deane Butler, as is the Catholic Cathedral of the Assumption, a short distance south of the 'Black Abbey' fronting James's Green and built from 1843 to 1857. Near by, on the river to the south, is Mill Mount, an interesting cruciform-plan house built by Christopher Colles, the owner of the marble quarries which supplied most of the mantelpieces found in mid-18th-century Irish domestic architecture. To the south-west is Castle Blunden, possibly designed by Francis Bindon, with a later pedimented porch.

CASTLE In its present form, it is a reconstruction in the medieval manner by William Robertson of 1826, and replaced practically all the remains of the late 17th-century Classical work except for the Corinthian pedimented entrance gate on the west side; this may be by Sir William Robinson, and is the earliest substantial fully Classical piece of architecture in the country. Three of the massive cylindrical towers are mainly 13th-century work. Opposite are the unusual castle stables, with their court in the shape of a horse-shoe; they have been recently sympathetically converted for the Kilkenny Design Workshops.

ST. CANICE'S CATHEDRAL Successor to a Romanesque church, as witness the adjacent Round Tower and a few re-used stones, it is the purest in style and one of the most attractive large Gothic churches in Ireland. It is cruciform, with an aisled nave and chapels north and south of the choir; further small chapels open eastward off the transepts, the southern one having been enlarged in the 14th century. The church was built between 1251 and 1286. The central tower fell in 1332 and was rebuilt shortly afterwards. The cathedral is remarkably rich in late medieval and 16th-century altar-tombs and similar monuments, many to the Ormonde-Butlers. In the south transept is a magnificent mid-18th-century tomb of Archbishop Cox, builder of Castletown House, and his wife, by Scheemakers.

**Kilkieran Crosses** *Kilk.*           *571Hd*
Across the valley from Ahenny stand the three crosses of Kilkieran. The west cross, though much damaged, is richly ornamented.

**Killadeas** *Ferm.*           *574Dc*
The graveyard contains remarkable carved stones.

**Killaloe** *Clare*           *570Ff*
The 13th-century Protestant Cathedral of St Flannan has an earlier Romanesque doorway built into the south wall. It is one of the most complete of the aisle-less medieval cathedrals in Ireland. In the churchyard is St Flannan's Oratory, a stone-roofed Romanesque building similar to those at Kells and Glendalough. Higher up the hill, in the churchyard of the Catholic church, is the reconstructed oratory of St Molua from the island of the same name in the Shannon, which was inundated when Ardnacrusha power station was built and the dam created. The little church, which has a chancel with a vaulted stone roof, was carefully taken apart and every stone correctly replaced. Near the town is the early 19th-century Protestant bishop's palace. One mile north is Beal Boru, a massive circular earthwork.

**Killamery** *Kilk.*           *571He*
A fine sandstone cross; the formal carving includes a heavily weathered hunting scene.

**Killarney** *Kerry.*           *570Cc*
The best-known of Irish beauty-spots, it has been admired for its mountain and lake scenery and its rich vegetation since the middle of the 18th century. Its man-made attractions are less numerous: the best of them is Muckross Abbey. The ruined Aghadoe Cathedral, just outside the town, is of some small interest. The Catholic cathedral, in the town, is perhaps the best in Ireland, and ranks among the principal works of A. W. Pugin. It was begun in 1842 and finished in 1855, the interior being completed by J. J. McCarthy, the foremost Irish church architect of the Gothic Revival.

ROSS CASTLE On an isthmus in Lough Leane is a good 15th-century tower-house with some later additions and a small bawn with flanker-towers.

MUCKROSS ABBEY Founded for Franciscan friars by Donal MacCarthy Mor, probably in *c.* 1340, on a site said to have been settled by St Finian in the 6th century. The buildings, ruined since a visitation of Cromwell's troops in 1652, date from the 15th century. The tiny cloister is filled by an enormous yew tree.

MUCKROSS HOUSE A gabled Victorian mansion (1843), in the heart of the Killarney lake district. The porch was added *c.* 1870 by William Atkins of Cork. The contents include objects of Irish historic interest—local carved period furniture, pictures, prints, maps and entomological specimens.

**Killeavy** *Armagh*           *575Gb*
On the eastern slopes of Slieve Gullion are two ruined churches, the earlier of which is pre-Romanesque and has a fine megalithic west doorway. The later church has sculptured heads flanking its east window. A mile to the south is a small symmetrical 'castle' of the same name, picturesquely situated, designed by George Papworth in 1836.

**Killeen** *Meath*           *573Jd*
The church at Killeen is believed to have been a model for that at Dunsany, which it much resembles, though it is slightly smaller and better in detail. The sedilia, with triple cusped arch, is finely carved.

**Killeen** *Meath*           *573Jd*
CASTLE A de Lacy castle of the 1180's, remodelled in 1802 by Francis Johnston and later further embellished by James Shiel. The interior has good Gothic-style plaster details.

BISHOP'S STONE, KILLADEAS

*Among the remarkable carved stones in the cemetery at Killadeas is this weathered monument to a bishop, dating from the 7th or 8th century. On the west side (above) the bishop is depicted full-face, while on the south side he is shown in profile with the emblems of his office—a crozier and a bell.*

**Killeshin** *Laois*           *573Hb*
After Clonfert and possibly Roscrea, Killeshin has probably the finest west doorway of the Irish-Romanesque style, though reset at some unknown date, with four recessed orders, and carving of unparalleled delicacy. It is probably of the early to mid-12th century. The north and west windows are round-headed with triangular gables.

**Killone** *Clare*           *570Df*
The Augustinian nunnery, probably dating from *c.* 1225, has a small cloister-court and a church with an eastern crypt. The east wall of the church has Transitional windows with small columns. A wall-passage pierces their jambs transversely.

**Killua House** *Westmeath* 573He
Basically an 18th-century house covered with a Gothic mantle, possibly by James Shiel *c.* 1830. It is now in ruins with its lodge, lake and follies, and its obelisk marking the alleged planting of the first potato in Ireland by Sir Walter Raleigh, is one of Ireland's most romantic demesnes.

**Killyleagh** *Down* 575Jc
A 17th-century house, its size was almost doubled in *c.* 1666, and Sir Charles Lanyon did further work on it in 1850. It retains its large walled bawn and entrance gate.

**Killymoon Castle** *Tyrone* 574Fd
A cut-stone 'castle', built by John Nash for the Stewart family *c.* 1803 and alleged to have cost £80,000.

**Kilmacduagh** *Gal.* 572Db
The cathedral is now ruined; its western half is 10th century, its eastern half probably 15th. There is some 12th-century work and late medieval transepts to the north and south. The outstanding features are the Flamboyant windows in the south chapel and the O'Shaughnessy altar-tomb. Near by stands a 112 ft Round Tower, leaning 2 ft out of the perpendicular.

**Kilmalkedar** *Kerry* 570Ad
The church is chiefly remarkable for its internal wall-colonnade of engaged columns. The west doorway has Romanesque decoration and the outer walls are sloping and show, internally, the beginning of a corbelled stone roof.

**Kilmallock** *Lim.* 570Ed
This originally walled town was founded by the FitzGerald family and was, until the 16th century, the chief seat of the White Knights. Many remnants survive, including Blossom's Gate, the only survivor of the four original medieval gates; the parish church of SS Peter and Paul, dating from the 13th–15th centuries and incorporating part of the Round Tower; the Dominican church founded in 1291 by Maurice FitzGerald, considerably enlarged in the 14th–15th century and possessing a notable 13th-century five-light window and a reticulated window of the 15th century. The last White Knight, Edmond FitzGibbon, betrayer of the Sugan, Earl of Desmond, is commemorated by a monument of 1608.

**Kilruddery** *Wick.* 573Kc
A Tudor Revival mansion built by Sir Richard Morrison for the Earl of Meath *c.* 1820 and now partly demolished. The interior contains a fine pair of Regency drawing-rooms with splendid plasterwork and scagliola columns. The greatest interest of the place lies in the survival of one of Ireland's late 17th- and early 18th-century formal gardens. At the garden front of the house are twin canals, a further pond terminating in a lime avenue. The whole lay-out is composed of cut banks, clipped hedges, and is peopled with many statues. To the right of the main vista is a miniature amphitheatre, a circular beech hedge, fountains, and to the east of the house a huge 19th-century rock garden.

**Kilshannig House** *Cork* 570Fc
A notable house with four wings by Davis Ducart, finished in 1765. The wings, though now partially ruined and lacking their domes, show many resemblances to Castletown House, also by Ducart. The interior contains plasterwork by the Francini brothers and a fine circular staircase.

**Kiltartan Castle** *Gal.* 572Dc
The ruins of an extensive 13th-century castle with a strongly defended courtyard.

**Kilteel** *Kild.* 573Je
The reconstructed remains of the Romanesque church are noteworthy for the figure-sculpture in the jambs of the chancel arch, the only instance of sculpture in this part of an Irish-Romanesque church. The subjects include Adam and Eve, Samson and Delilah, and David and Goliath. Close by stands a small tower-house castle.

**Kiltiernan** *Gal.* 572Dc
A monastic site with an early church, a good west door, and the remains of dry masonry; it is enclosed by a fragmentary cashel.

**Kiltinan Castle** *Tipp.* 571He
A castle of the Butlers, Barons Dunboyne, situated on a rock above a stream. Three of the angle-towers remain, two of which form a 19th-century house. It was taken by the Cromwellians in 1669.

**Kinsale** *Cork* 570Fb
A picturesque Irish seaport. The most important event in Kinsale's history was the double siege of 1601, with the Spaniards in the middle, the English under Mountjoy blockading them, and the Earls of Tyrone and Tyrconnell besieging them in turn. This resulted in the massacre of the Spaniards and the flight of the earls, and the James Fort on Rinnroin was then fortified by the English. In 1677 the huge Charles Fort on Rinncurran, on the opposite bank of Kinsale Harbour, was designed by Sir William Robinson, architect of the Royal Hospital, Dublin, and remained in military occupation until 1921. Most of the town dates from the 18th century and later, but the building called the Desmond Castle, or French Prison, is a 16th-century tower-house. Kinsale has one of the few medieval parish churches in Ireland still in use, St Multose; it is a substantial 13th-century cruciform building with aisles to north and south. At the north-west angle is a massive tower. The roofless south transept (Chapel of the Blessed Virgin) was built in 1550 by Geoffrey Galway, merchant of the town. The court-house of 1706 is a picturesque building with three curvilinear 'Dutch' gables, hung with slate, and a ground-floor arcade. It was restored in 1958–9 and is now a museum. The 18th-century houses of the town (though many are dilapidated and some have been destroyed) were, until recently, notable for the variety and richness of their fan-lights and ironwork, a few also being slate-hung, in the manner of south-western England. The buildings in Charles Fort include some fine robust 17th- and 18th-century pedimented gate-houses and doorways. On the hillside opposite the gate of St Multose churchyard, where there are some fine monuments, is the handsome cupolaed façade of the Catholic church of 1834. The chapel of the Carmelite friary is very similar and is probably by the same architect. The fishing village of Summercove nestles beneath the walls of Charles Fort.

**Kirkistown Castle** *Down* 575Jd
A tower-house with a large bawn which has twin towers at the western end; it was all built in 1622 by Roland Savage, and is still remarkably complete, having been restored in the 18th century.

**Knockdrin Castle** *Westmeath* 573 Hd
A good Gothic-style castle with an arcaded central hall, built *c.* 1830 by James Shiel for the Levinge family. There is also a baronial lodge.

**Knockmany** *Tyrone* 574Ed
A large circular cairn containing a grave; three of the side stones have Bronze Age decoration. There is a similar grave at Sess Kilgreen, 7 miles away to the north-east.

**Knockmoy** *Gal.*                              *572Dd*
A Cistercian abbey, founded in 1190 by King
Cathal O'Conor as a daughter-house of Boyle
Abbey. It is a transitional early Gothic building of
cruciform plan, chiefly remarkable for the remains
on the chancel wall of traces of painting. Their
subjects include the Holy Trinity and the Martyrdom of St Sebastian. There are also *graffiti* on the
plaster of the chancel walls.

**Knocknarea** *Sligo*                          *574Bc*
On the top of the 1000 ft Knocknarea Mountain is
the huge cairn known as Miosgaun Meabha,
reputedly the burial-place of Queen Maeve
(Queen Mab). It is 200 ft in diameter and 34 ft high,
and probably covers a Bronze Age grave; all
around are similar cairns.

**Knowth** See Brugh Na Boinne.

**Labbacallee** *Cork*                          *570Fc*
An early Bronze Age gallery grave, the largest and
finest of the wedge type in Ireland.

**Lackeen** *Tipp.*                             *571Gg*
A 16th-century four-storey tower-house; the
third storey is vaulted over. There is an extensive
walled bawn. In 1735 the famous Stowe Missal,
hidden for safety, was discovered during alterations.

**Landenstown House** *Kild.*                   *573Jc*
An unpretentious but pleasing house, with wings
joined by arches to a central block; built *c.* 1740.

**Lawrencetown Arch** *Gal.*                    *572Fc*
Walter Lawrence built a triumphal arch to commemorate the Irish Volunteers of 1782; it spans
a road through the devastated demesne.

**Leacanabuaile** *Kerry*                       *570Ac*
A 9th–10th-century stone ring-fort containing the
bases of four drystone huts, some circular and some
rectangular; there are two chambers in the rampart. It has been excavated and partially restored. A
quarter of a mile south-east is the stone ring-fort of
Cahergal, and 300 yds away another similar.

**Leac-an-Scail** *Kilk.*                       *571Jd*
A very fine portal dolmen, with a steeply sloping
capstone.

**Leamaneh Castle** *Clare*                     *570Dg*
The O'Brien castle of Leamaneh consists of a
tower of *c.* 1480 to which is joined a splendid 17th-
century high-gabled house of four storeys, with
rows of mullioned windows.

**Ledwithstown House** *Long.*                  *572Fe*
An extremely interesting, but now decayed, small
four-fronted square house with a pedimented
front, probably built by Richard Castle *c.* 1740.

LEGANANNY DOLMEN
*A coffin-shaped capstone with remarkable sharp edges
is poised on three graceful uprights. From an altitude
of 850 ft, this ancient chamber-tomb commands an
impressive view over the surrounding countryside.*

**Legananny** *Down*                            *575Hc*
One of the most impressive dolmens in Ireland,
standing on the southern slope of Slieve Croob.

**Leighlinbridge** *Carlow*                     *571Jf*
The attractively situated Protestant Cathedral of St
Laserian, in Old Leighlin, is largely 13th century,
with a central tower, a north chapel as wide as the
choir, and a north transept. The nave has hardly
any windows. The gateway of the churchyard is
early 18th-century work.

**Leixlip** *Kild.*                             *573Jd*
The medieval west tower of the later Protestant
church is a very complete priests' residence, a sort
of ecclesiastical tower-house. Leixlip Castle is
basically medieval, altered in the early to mid-18th
century by the Conolly family of Castletown. It is
remarkable for its octagon Gothic-style glazing.

**Letterkenny** *Don.*                          *574Df*
The Catholic Cathedral of St Eunan, built of
Mount Charles stone by Hague and MacNamara
in 1890–1901, has stained glass by Michael Healy
and Harry Clarke.

**Liathmore** *Tipp.*                           *571He*
Of the two churches at Liathmore, the smaller has
antae at both ends and the remains of a steep gable;
the larger incorporates a smaller, earlier church as
its chancel, with much complicated rebuilding.

**Lifford** *Don.*                              *574Ee*
The county town of Donegal, though hardly
more than a suburb of Strabane; it has a handsome court-house of 1745 by Michael Priestley.

**Limavady** *Lond.*                            *574Ff*
A plantation town, formerly a seat of the
O'Cahans, where the road crosses the R. Rose.
One and a half miles to the east is Drenagh, built
for the McCausland family, a chastely Classical
house representing one of Sir Charles Lanyon's
earliest architectural works.

**Limerick** *Lim.*                             *570Ee*
Like so many seaboard towns, Limerick is a Viking
foundation, fortified in the late 12th century by a
castle, which has a better claim than most to its title
King John's Castle. The city is divided into the old
medieval English Town on an island in the
Shannon, Irishtown on the mainland, and Newton
Pery, the regular late 18th-century development.
   The castle was nearly square; its north and south
walls survive, the former with round towers at
each end and a gateway of two D-shaped towers in
the middle, and the latter with only a south-west
tower standing. St Mary's Cathedral is among the
most interesting of Irish medieval cathedrals. It
was founded by King Donal Mor O'Brian in 1172,
and its nave, most of the west front and north
transept date from before 1195, when it had north
and south aisles to the nave; it has now further
chapels to the north and south, of later medieval
dates, making it in effect five-aisled. The arches
across the aisles are unique in Ireland. The 15th-
century tower, with 17th-century bells, is 120 ft
high and has four corner turrets embattled in the
Irish fashion. The whole cathedral was extensively
restored between 1857 and 1860 by William Slater
of London, though various other architects were
involved. The interior fittings include 15th-
century choir-stalls with misericords, unique in
Ireland, a Casslean tomb of Donogh O'Brian, Earl
of Thomand, of 1678, and several other tombs in
the chantry chapels; also the bishop's throne,
designed in 1831 by James Pain. Thomond
Bridge, of 1836, by the castle, is also by James
Pain. In Irishtown—across the river from the

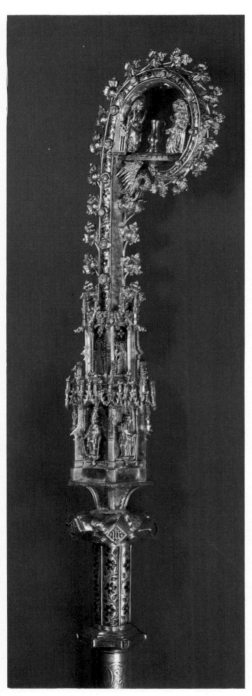

### THE LIMERICK CROZIER

*Made by the order of the Bishop of Limerick in the
early 15th century, this crozier and a mitre are still
owned by his successor and are the only medieval art
treasures in Ireland still in their ancient custody; both
are dated 1418. The crozier, made of gilded and
enamelled silver, is 6 ft 6 in. tall. It is the only medieval
Irish-made crozier in the continental form of a shepherd's crook—Irish pre-Norman croziers were staff-
like—and probably came from a large workshop of
silversmiths. Six niches around the base of the crook
contain exquisitely modelled figures representing the
Trinity, the Virgin, and saints; above are six
enamelled plates engraved with saints. The figures
inside the crook depict the Annunciation. (Treasury,
Catholic Cathedral of St John, Limerick)*

court-house, presenting a plain front facing
Charlotte's Quay and reserving its splendours for
the relatively inaccessible river front—is the
custom house. It was designed by Davis Ducart,
and built between 1765 and 1769. The river front is
composed of Corinthian pilasters and a channelled
ashlar basement flanked by arcaded wings. In
Patrick Street is the town hall of 1805, originally
the Mercantile Buildings. To the left, almost next
door, is a fine cut-stone Venetian door of Bruce the
Banker's house, (possibly by Francis Bindon), and
now ruined. Some distance to the east is the charming cut-stone St John's Square, dating from 1751,
consisting of ten houses and probably also designed
by Francis Bindon. Just off St John's Square is the
Catholic Cathedral of St John, 1856–61, by the
English architect P. C. Hardwicke, the tower and
spire by M. S. Hennessy of Limerick.

The centre of modern Limerick is the cross-
roads where Sarsfield Street, leading from the
balustraded Sarsfield Bridge (by James Pain,
dating from 1827) intersects O'Connell Street, the
backbone of the grid plan of Newtown Pery,
possibly laid out by Davis Ducart, which extends
to the south-west as far as the Crescent. This section of the town dates from well after 1750 and
owes its development to the Pery family, Earls of
Limerick. Most of the houses are in fact of *c.* 1790
onwards. The most distinguished houses in Newtown Pery include Lord Limerick's town house
and the old bishop's palace in Henry Street, the
Crescent, and Pery Square of *c.* 1840. In the middle
of the latter is the Spring-Rice Monument, by
Alexander Nimmo, and also in this area is the
Church of St Alphonsus Liguori of 1858–62 by
P. C. Hardwicke; near it is the public library,
art gallery and museum, and St Michael's Church
facing down Pery Square. Not far away is the
Limerick Protestant Orphans Society building of
1865 by William Fogerty of Limerick. In Baker
Street is St Saviour's Dominican church, started
by James Pain in 1817, but totally remodelled by
Maurice Hennessy, George Goldie and J. J.
McCarthy from 1860 onwards. Inside is a 17th-
century Flemish statue of the Virgin and Child. In
Glentworth Street is a Savings Bank by W. H.
Owen, in the form of a small Doric temple. Holy
Trinity Church, formerly the Church of the
Blind Asylum, has a recessed Ionic portico by
J. Fogarty, and the Franciscan Church of the
Immaculate Conception in Henry Street has an
attenuated Corinthian portico by W. E. Corbett
of 1876. On the Tipperary Road are the city gaol
building of 1821, with a Doric grand entrance, and
the lunatic asylum. Athlunkard Bridge on the
Killaloe Road, by James Pain, dates from 1830.
On the west bank of the Shannon, almost opposite
the castle, is the Treaty Stone on which the
Treaty of Limerick is alleged to have been signed.
The modern Church of our Lady of the Rosary,
on the Ennis Road, is adorned with stained glass
and sculpture by modern artists.

**Liscarroll Castle** *Cork*                          *570Ed*
The third largest 13th-century castle in Ireland,
consisting of an enormous rectangular bawn with
corner round towers and intermediate towers on
the south and north.

**Lismore** *Waterford*                              *571Ge*
The castle, strikingly situated high above the
Blackwater on the site of a medieval episcopal
building, subsequently the residence of the Boyles,
Earls of Cork, was later inherited by the Dukes of
Devonshire. It was extensively remodelled in 1850
by Sir Joseph Paxton and Henry Stokes. (Not open
to the public.) Below, spanning the Blackwater, is

the handsome inscribed mid-18th-century bridge by Thomas Ivory, the earliest of his works. The Protestant Cathedral of St Carthage was largely rebuilt in 1633 by Richard Boyle. It has an elegant spire of 1827, probably by G. R. Pain. The mid-16th-century tomb of the McGrath family in the nave is noteworthy. A few miles to the west, in woods north of the river, are the remarkable Gothic gates and Gothic castle bridge of Bally-saggartmore; the owner spent so much money on his gates and bridge that the house was never built.

**Lissan Rectory** *Tyrone*                        *574Fe*
An interesting example of John Nash's 'villa' style, built for the Rev. John Staples in 1807.

**Lodge Park** *Kild.*                              *573Jd*
The moderately-sized house is extended by four detached pavilions, giving an elongated five-part composition which is perhaps the most extreme example of this Irish Palladian style. It was probably designed by Nathaniel Clements and built 1775–7 for Hugh Henry, a rich banker.

**Lohort Castle** *Cork*                            *570Ec*
A remarkably well-preserved 15th-century tower-house, reduced in 1650 by the Cromwellians and restored in the 18th century. It was completely and elaborately refurbished in 1876.

**Longford** *Long.*                                *572Fe*
The fragmentary remains of the castle date from 1627 and form part of the military barracks. The most distinguished building in the town is the Classical Catholic St Mel's Cathedral, started in 1840 by Joseph B. Keane, and not completed until 1893 when the portico to the design of George G. Ashlin was added; the belfry of 1860 is by John Burke. In the Diocesan College near by is a collection of local antiquities. A few miles to the south-east is Carriglass Manor by William Robertson, of 1830, with distinguished Classical stables and an entrance arch by James Gandon.

**Lorrha** *Tipp.*                                  *571Gg*
The Dominican friary, built in 1269 by Walter de Burgo, has a long rectangular church with a stone screen in the centre. In the nave is a typical Jacobean armorial monument. The Augustinian church has a good Perpendicular doorway with ogee-shaped hood. There is also the elaborate base of a large cross with an animal frieze.

**Lough Cutra Castle** *Gal.*                       *572Db*
The most romantically situated and the finest surviving of John Nash's Gothic Revival castles in Ireland, begun *c.* 1816 and executed by the Pain Brothers. The Lismore Lodge is also by Nash. (Open to the public.)

**Lough Gur** *Lim.*                                *570Fe*
One of the richest concentrations of ancient remains in Ireland, including monuments from the Neolithic to the medieval period; among them is the largest stone circle in the country, numerous forts, house sites, pillar-stones, cairns, cultivation-terraces, crannogs and a good 15th-century tower-house.

**Loughmoe Castle** *Tipp.*                         *571Gf*
A 17th-century semi-fortified house added to a 15th-century tower, Loughmoe was a seat of the Purcells, whose monuments may be seen in the nearby church. There is a fine fire-place in a first-floor room, bearing armorials and initials.

**Loughrea** *Gal.*                                 *572Ec*
The Catholic Cathedral of St Brendan, by William Byrne of 1897–1903, though intrinsically of small merit, contains a rich collection of the best modern Irish ecclesiastical art, most notably stained glass by A. E. Childe, Sarah Purser, Hubert McGoldrick, Michael Healy and Evie Hone. The Virgin and Child in the chapel is by John Hughes, and there are embroideries designed by Jack Yeats. Part of the town gate, near the cathedral, is now a museum of ecclesiastical art; there is also a ruined church of the Carmelite friary of 1300. Four miles to the north-east is the famous Turoe Stone, covered with splendid La Tène abstract ornament.

TUROE STONE, NEAR LOUGHREA

*This rare Irish remnant of the Celtic Iron Age culture which originated at La Tène (Switzerland) and reached Ireland about the 3rd century BC, stands 4 ft high.*

**Lucan House** *Dublin*                            *573Jd*
An important medium-sized house, free-standing; like some other Irish houses, it is joined by an underground passage to the detached service buildings. It was built *c.* 1776 by the Rt. Hon. Agmondisham Vesey, an amateur architect, partly to his own designs but with some help from Chambers and, for the very fine decoration of the principal rooms, from James Wyatt and Michael Stapleton. It has an elevated central frontispiece with Ionic engaged columns and a pediment which was copied at Charleville, Co. Wicklow. The small demesne is attractively laid out by the Liffey, and contains a fine Coade-stone monument designed by Wyatt and a Gothic rustic hermitage. The house is now the official residence of the Italian Ambassador.

**Lusk** *Dublin*                                   *573Kd*
The mid-19th-century church in this pretty village is built on to a 15th-century tower which consists of a square body with three circular turrets at its angles, attached to an early Christian Round Tower which is thus used as the fourth angle-tower. The whole tower was in turn copied at Balrothery, 5 miles further north, though there is no pre-existing Round Tower. There are some good medieval and later tombs in the tower.

**Luttrellstown Castle** *Dublin*                   *573Kd*
Probably an early work by Sir Richard Morrison of *c.* 1800, the entrance front marred by a Victorian porch. The landscape garden—complete with

lake, Doric temple, series of waterfalls and Gothic ruin—is one of the most effective in Ireland. (Not open to the public.)

**Lyles Hill** *Antrim*     *575He*
A large hill-top enclosure of Neolithic date, unique in Ireland and well known as having given its name to a type of pottery found in it. A large cairn in the enclosure was revealed by excavation to be a rubbish dump.

**Lyons House** *Kild.*     *573Je*
Built in 1797 for Michael Aylmer by Sir Richard Morrison. Severely neo-Classical wings and colonnades were added *c.* 1810 by the first Lord Cloncurry. It contains notable landscape decoration in the dining-room, and the demesne contains the largest artificial lake in Ireland. The pedimented arch from Brownes Hill has been re-erected here. It is now an agricultural college.

**Magh Adhair** *Clare*     *570Ef*
An inauguration place of Kings of Thomond, sited in an amphitheatre of low hills. It consists of a large mound, 20 ft high, with a flat top 100 by 80 ft, and surrounded by a fosse and an external bank.

**Maghera** *Lond.*     *575Ge*
The most interesting feature of the ruined church is the unique carved lintel of the west doorway, depicting the crucified Christ surrounded by smaller figures. It has been assigned to an early date but is probably of the late 11th century.

**Malahide Castle** *Dublin*     *573Kd*
Seat of the Norman family of Talbot since medieval times, enlarged by twin towers and battlements *c.* 1765, possibly designed by the amateur architect Wogan Browne. (Not open.)

**Mallow** *Cork*     *570Ec*
Mallow was famous for its social life in the 18th and early 19th century, when it was a spa, and it still bears some signs of its former elegance.
MALLOW CASTLE Built by Sir Thomas Norreys *c.* 1600, it has a main front flanked by polygonal towers, a polygonal central porch and a polygonal projection at the back once containing the stairs and garderobes. Although the house has relatively large windows, it also has, as was usual at the time, clearly defensive features. Near by is the early 19th-century Tudor Revival manor house of the Jephson family, descendants of the Norreys. Six miles away are the ruins of Mourne Abbey, a fortified property of the Knights Templar.

**Marino, Casino** See Dublin.

**Markree Castle** *Sligo*     *574Bb*
An earlier house was refaced by Francis Johnston in the castle style in 1803. It has particularly fine gates and lodges, designed by John Goodwin in 1832.

**Marlay Grange** *Dublin*     *573Kc*
A seat of the La Touche family, of late 18th century date. It has good plasterwork and there are extensive stables.

**Maynooth** *Kild.*     *573Jd*
A well laid-out town, it is chiefly remarkable for being the seat of St Patrick's College, founded by the Irish Parliament in 1795 for the education of the Irish priesthood. Beside the old church at the entrance to the college are the shattered remains of the gate-tower and massive keep of the 13th-century castle. The earliest building of the college is Stoyte House, built by Michael Stapleton with additions of 1845 by A. W. Pugin, including a Gothic quadrangle culminating in J. J. McCarthy's college chapel, whose spire, the highest in Ireland, is in proportion not just to the chapel but to the

whole college. The college museum has a collection of antiquities and works of art. In the sacristy is Viavicenzi's *Flight into Eygpt*. On the Dublin road, to the right, is the Conolly Folly, closing the main vista to Castletown.

**Mellifont Abbey** *Louth*     *573Je*
At Mellifont, *c.* 1142, a band of Irish and French monks, at the instigation of St Malachy, founded the first monastery (Cistercian) of Classical European form in Ireland. This sounded the death knell not merely of the Celtic type of monastery, but of the whole native ecclesiastical system, and from Mellifont descend all other Cistercian monasteries in Ireland. The remains now visible on the banks of the little R. Mattock, on a typically secluded Cistercian site, consist of the foundations of the church, the chapter house, some remnants of the claustral buildings, and most conspicuous of all, about half an octagonal lavabo which occupies part of the cloister-garth. The church was consecrated in 1157. Part of the round-headed cloister arcade has been re-erected.

**Midleton** *Cork*     *570Fb*
Founded *c.* 1670 by the Brodrick family, later Earls of Midleton, it has in the Main Street a good mid-18th-century arcaded market house, complete with clock and cupola. The Protestant church, by the Pain brothers, dates from 1825.

**Mitchelstown** *Cork*     *570Fd*
Planned on a generous scale, with wide streets and squares, Mitchelstown is particularly remarkable for the group of almshouses called Kingston College for Decayed Gentlefolk, founded by the King family in 1780. The two-storey buildings, with a chapel set in the middle, are punctuated by pedimented features.

**Moira** *Down*     *575Hd*
The Protestant parish church, a simple rectangle with a western tower, built in 1723, has a distinguished west front with a pedimented doorway; the octagonal spire is a replacement of 1884. The altar rails have Gothic Revival ironwork.

**Moiry Castle** *Louth*     *575Gb*
Commanding the Gap of the North, it is a campaign fort of 1600–2, consisting of a square tower eccentrically set within a rectangular bawn; the exterior corners have many musketry loopholes.

**Monaghan** *Mon.*     *573Hg*
Incorporated in 1614 by James I, the town has some interesting buildings, including a distinguished ashlar pedimented market house of 1791–2, designed and signed by the amateur architect Samuel Hayes of Avondale for the first Lord Rossmore. The Catholic Cathedral of St Macartan is a distinguished Gothic Revival work of 1861–92, designed by J. J. McCarthy. The Cross of Clogher (14th–15th century) is kept in the Diocesan College.

**Monahincha** *Tipp.*     *571Gg*
An island monastery, now in the centre of a drained marsh; it was founded by St Canice of Aghaboe, but only the 12th-century church and a transeptal sacristy remain. The west doorway has inclined jambs and fine ornament, as has the chancel arch. This is a lovely little building, with a unique atmosphere.

**Monasterboice** *Louth*     *573Ke*
The three crosses at Monasterboice are perhaps the best known of the Irish high crosses. The north cross is fairly plain, except for a simple inscription and spiral composition on the west and east faces respectively; the shaft is modern. The south cross,

known as Muiredach's Cross, is dateable, for on the west face of the shaft is an inscription to Abbot Muiredach who died in 922. It is one of the finest of the earlier Irish figured crosses and the subjects include the Fall, the Murder of Abel, the Last Judgment, and SS Anthony and Paul in the desert. The summit of the cross is in the form of a shingle-roofed church. The west cross is exceptionally tall and carved with scriptural subjects. There is also a Round Tower, two early grave-slabs, two churches and a sun-dial.

**Monasterevin** *Kild.*                    *573Hc*
A handsome canal-town with well-built merchants' houses and warehouses of *c.* 1800. Beside the canal is an austere pedimented Charter School of *c.* 1740, now a warehouse. Moore Abbey is a large 18th-century castellated house with Gothic style windows. It is now a hospital.

**Monasternagalliaghduff**              *570De*
**or Old Abbey** *Lim.*
The ruins of this Augustinian nunnery comprise a long rectangular church with good pointed west door and, exceptionally, a walled cloister-court west of the church; other remains include gate-houses, a dove-cote and a fish-pond.

**Monasternenagh** *Lim.*               *570Ee*
A Cistercian abbey founded in 1148 by Turlough O'Brien; it is a daughter-house of Mellifont Abbey, and the remains are extremely fragmentary, but have some interesting late Romanesque and Transitional features—good carved capitals and round-headed west windows.

**Monea** *Ferm.*                       *574Dc*
In close proximity to one another at Monea are a crannog in the middle of a small lake, the early 17th-century Plantation castle, and an 18th-century or early 19th-century farmhouse, neatly representing three successive types of dwelling. The castle, which is the best Plantation castle in Ulster, is rectangular, with two Round Towers with Scottish corbelled projections.

**Monkstown House** *Cork*              *570Fb*
Built *c.* 1636 by Anastasia Archdeacon, and now a golf club. It is a gabled house with angle-machicolations and a good fire-place of 1636.

**Moone** *Kild.*                       *573Jb*
An unusually slender 9th-century granite high cross, pieced together in the 19th century. The panels contain extremely stylised figures of St Paul, St Anthony, the Flight into Egypt, the Twelve Apostles and the Multiplication of the Loaves and Fishes.

**Moore Hall** *Mayo*                   *572Ce*
The ruined shell of Classical Moore Hall stands on a peninsula in Lough Carra and is evocative of the scenes in George Moore's novels and autobiographical writings. John Moore, the builder of the house, was an active participant in the French-associated Connacht rising in 1798, as President of the 'Republic of Connacht', and later members of the family were also politically active.

**Mount Congreve** *Waterford*          *571Jd*
A Georgian house, seat of the Congreves, entirely refaced and remodelled in 1965, and containing an early 18th-century painted room. The gardens adjoining the R. Suir are prolific in sub-tropical flora. Although with an abundance in spring of rhododendrons and azaleas, the walled gardens offer herbaceous and shrub borders in mid-summer, a speciality of michaelmas daisies in September, and late-flowering shrubs as the season closes. (Open to the public.)

MUIREDACH'S CROSS

*During the Viking wars of the 9th and 10th centuries, in which so much Irish art was lost, carved crosses of durable stone appeared all over the country. Many survive, and this is the finest and most complete. It is 17 ft 8 in. tall and carved from a single piece of sandstone. The west face of the cross is shown and the bottom panel (below) depicts the Arrest of Christ. (Monasterboice)*

**Mount Ievers** *Clare*                *570Ef*
A remarkable example of the cubicle, almost doll's-house-like verticality found in many less distinguished Irish houses. The entrance front is of ashlar stone and the garden front of brick. It was designed by William Rothery in 1736 for Henry Ievers. (Not open to the public.)

**Mount Juliet** *Kilk.*                *571Je*
Built *c.* 1780 for the Earl of Carrick; it has rich Adam-style ornament in the principal rooms and is surrounded by a splendid demesne. (Not open.)

**Mountmellick** *Laois*                *573Hc*
A town whose sober neatness is evidence of its Quaker origin; it has some good 18th-century houses.

**Mount Sandel** *Lond.*                *575Gf*
One mile south of Coleraine, the earthen ring-fort stands 150 ft above the R. Bann, and was later adapted by the Anglo-Normans.

**Mount Stewart Gardens** *Down*     *575Jd*
On the narrow Ards Peninsula, the Dowager Marchioness of Londonderry began, in 1921, to transform the garden of her home, Mount Stewart. Today, a terrace leads to an Italian garden from which steps descend to the Spanish garden, so-called because the summerhouse tiles came from Spain. A paved garden in the form of a shamrock has a bed shaped like the Red Hand of Ulster, planted with red-leaved plants. The top of a cypress hedge is shaped to represent a hunting party. From the formal gardens, paths lead to 80 acres of gently undulating ground in which, because of high humidity and lack of frost, rare sub-tropical plants thrive. The Temple of the Winds is by James Stuart.

**Mount Usher Gardens** *Wicklow*     *573Kb*
The gardens at Mount Usher, on either side of the R. Vartry, are between the Wicklow Mountains and the sea; they were first laid out in 1868 by the Walpole family. Although the gardens specialise in rare and tender plants, including the dazzling blue Chilean crocus, large groups of native plants grow along the sides of the river.

**Moyne Abbey** *Mayo*     *572Cg*
A Franciscan friary on the shores of Killala Bay, begun *c.* 1460 by MacWilliam Burke and fairly complete, though burnt by Sir Richard Bingham in 1590. There is the usual slender central tower and a good cloister. The reader's desk in the projecting window of the refectory is worthy of note, as are the 16th-century *graffiti* on the plaster of the west nave wall. The west door has Renaissance detail.

**Muckross Abbey** See Killarney.

**Muckross House** See Killarney.

**Multyfarnham** *Westmeath*     *573Ge*
A distinguished Franciscan friary which incorporates in its church the nave, tower and south transept of its 13th-century predecessor, sacked in 1601 but occupied later in the century. One and a half miles to the south-west is Wilson's Hospital, a Protestant boys' school housed in an extremely important Palladian complex, designed by John Pentland *c.* 1760. The pedimented central block, surmounted by a cupola, has a central court with open arcading in the basement. The chapel has most of its original fittings, including a good door and a gallery. On either side, curved wings lead to pavilions in the true Palladian manner, making the arrangement reminiscent of a country house.

**Naas** *Kild.*     *573Jc*
The county town of Kildare, and formerly one of the royal seats of Leinster. The mote of the FitzGerald castle may still be seen. The Catholic parish church of SS Mary and David, in the Gothic style, is by Thomas Cobden of Carlow and dates from 1827. The towers and spire, of 1858, are modelled on St Andrew's Church, Ewerby, Lincolnshire.

At Oldtown, three-quarters of a mile to the north, is the last remaining pavilion of Ireland's first Palladian house, designed for himself by Colonel Thomas Burgh, Surveyor-General of Ireland, who died in 1730.

**Navan** *Meath*     *573Je*
The county town of Meath has the mote of its Anglo-Norman castle, but little else of interest except the earliest known sculpture (1792) by Edward Smyth—the Crucified Christ in wood, his only religious work—in the Catholic cathedral. The cathedral was built in 1836, with galleries on three sides, but has been spoilt by later embellishments.

**Navan Fort (Emain Macha)** *Arm.*     *575Gc*
An 18 acre hill-fort enclosed by a bank 800 ft in diameter, with central mound and the remains of a ploughed-out rath. Traditionally this was the seat of the Kings of Ulster.

**Nenagh** *Tipp.*     *570Ff*
The impressive cylindrical keep of Nenagh, the finest of its kind in Ireland, was built *c.* 1200 by Theobald FitzWalter. The present top storey and battlements are of *c.* 1860, but in general it is very well preserved. Fragments of its baily and drum towers and of a rectangular gate-house survive. There is also a good 19th-century court-house.

**Nendrum** *Down*     *575Jd*
The remains of the monastery of St Mochaoi were virtually unknown until Bishop Reeves described them in 1845. Excavation in 1922–4 exposed the remarkably complete plan of a monastic enclosure, with three concentric cashels, numerous small buildings (some of them circular), a graveyard, a church with nave and chancel, a sun-dial and the stump of a Round Tower, all dating from before the destruction of the monastery in 974. The monastic bell was found where it had evidently been hidden in a crevice in the wall and, together with many interesting finds—writing tablets and materials of the monastic school—is now in the Ulster Museum, Belfast.

**Newberry Hall** *Kild.*     *573Hd*
Built *c.* 1765 for Viscount Harberton and probably designed by Nathaniel Clements. It is a sister-house to Colganstown, but is built of brick and has curved sweeps leading to wings with central half-octagon projections, all of brick. There is good interior decoration in the rococo manner.

**Newbridge House** *Dublin*     *573Kd*
Designed by Richard Castle *c.* 1737. It has good plasterwork and a notable drawing-room picture gallery of *c.* 1745.

**Newcastle** *Dublin*     *573Jc*
The parish church has a tower-house style west tower and, reset in the east wall of the roofed nave, the fine curvilinear east window from the roofless chancel. The rectory close by is a handsome small house of the mid-18th century, with traces of an ornamental canal in the garden.

**Newcastle West** *Lim.*     *570De*
Formerly one of the chief seats of the Earls of Desmond; it has two halls, one 80 ft long, the other, known as Desmond's Hall, on a vaulted basement. They date from the late 15th century.

**Newgrange** See Brugh Na Boinne.

**Newhall House** *Clare*     *570Df*
A fine red-brick house, probably designed by Francis Bindon *c.* 1745. The entrance hall contains a cupboard masked as an elaborate organ case.

**Newmarket-on-Fergus** *Clare*     *570Ef*
In Kilnasoolagh church is a notable monument, with a recumbent figure and baroque trappings, of Sir Donough O'Brien, by William Kidwell and dating from 1717.

**New Ross** *Wex.*     *571Jd*
The large 13th-century ruined town church of St Mary was probably founded by William the Marshall, the effective founder of Anglo-Norman Ireland, and is among the earliest purely Gothic works in the country. As elsewhere, a much later Protestant church stands within the walls—in this case, in the nave. There are many interesting windows and tombs. The Tholsel is a distinguished cut-stone building of 1749, originally arcaded,

THE BOYNE MEDAL

*Perhaps the first medal to be awarded for individual gallantry, and a forerunner of the Victoria Cross, the Boyne Medal was struck by command of William III after the Battle of the Boyne in 1690; it was presented to Major A. P. Rogers of the Royal Inniskilling Fusiliers, who had rescued the king as he was about to* *be pulled off his horse by a southern Irish supporter of James II during the battle. Probably made by Jan Luder, the medal is of 18 carat gold and was made 'repoussé': two thin gold plates were deeply embossed and then fastened together at the rim. (Royal Inniskilling Fusiliers Regimental Museum, Omagh)*

rebuilt in 1806 by John Robertson, 'carpenter and architect' as a tablet records; it is surmounted by an octagonal and domed cupola. The early 19th-century Catholic Church of SS Mary and Michael possesses a *Pietà* by John Hogan.

**Newry** *Down*                                575Gc
St Patrick's Church, the earliest Protestant church to be built as such in Ireland, dates from 1578 and has been much altered since. The town has a regular plan beside the canal and the river, the Main Street punctuated by two small squares; it owes much to the canal from Lough Neagh, the earliest in the British Isles, which was begun in 1729 by Sir Edward Lovett Pearce and Richard Castle. There are still some 18th-century houses, with curvilinear gables of the Dublin type, in Boat Street. Other interesting Georgian houses exist in Trevor Hill and Upper Water Street. The east gate of the White Linen Hall of 1783 has good detailing, with a key-patterned frieze and plaques of a spinning wheel and an Irish harp on either side of the arch. The Bank of Ireland occupies a town house of 1826 attributable to Francis Johnston. The court-house dates from 1843, and beside the canal are many fine warehouses with their hoists.

**Newtown** *Clare*                                570Dg
A 16th-century tower, nearly round in plan; it rises from a square base on which is the entrance door. Ingeniously placed shot-holes protect its four sides.

**Newtownards** *Down*                              575Jd
The town mainly owes its origin to Sir Hugh Montgomery, who laid it out in the early 17th century, restored the priory church and built a polygonal market-house with pyramidal roof. The most distinguished building is the town hall, complete with cupola and pedimented portal, designed by Ferdinando Stratford of Bristol in 1765.

**Newtown Park** *Dublin*                          573Kc
A good Classical house of *c.* 1797. It has fine interior detailing. (Not open.)

**Newtownstewart** *Tyrone*                        574Ee
A well laid out town with a Plantation castle built in 1618 by Sir Robert Newcomen, with triple crow-stepped gables and mullioned windows.

**Omagh** *Tyrone*                                574Ed
The county town, with good Classical court-house.
ROYAL INNISKILLING FUSILIERS REGIMENTAL MUSEUM Displays of uniforms, arms, medals, colours and pictures trace the history of the Regiment.

**Pallas Castle** *Gal.*                           572Ec
A 16th-century tower-house with a bawn and gatehouse, all well preserved.

**Palliser House** See Rathfarnham.

**Parkes Castle** *Leit.*                          574Cc
On the shores of Lough Gill, the impressive 16th-century enclosure consists of a large bawn with two flanking towers, one of which forms part of the living quarters.

**Portaferry** *Down*                              575Jc
The town lies on the east side of the narrow entrance to Strangford Lough; the castle is a tower-house of the early 16th century. Portaferry House was designed by Charles Lilly in 1790 and completed by William Farrell in 1814, for the Nugent family; it has a good staircase, and Regency plaster decoration and fittings. The court-house dates from 1800.

**Portarlington** *Laois*                          573Hc
An interesting town, founded by John Ruvigny, Earl of Galway, in 1667, and populated with Huguenots (French Protestants). It has two Protestant churches of which the 'English' church is now disused; the graveyard of the 'French' church contains gravestones inscribed in French, some only about 100 years old. Many of the handsome 18th-century houses facing the R. Barrow turn their backs to the street in the French fashion. In the centre of the square is the simple but beautifully proportioned market-house of *c.* 1800.

**Port Hall** *Don.*                               574Ee
Built in 1746 for John Vaughan of Buncrana Castle, by Michael Priestley, the designer of Lifford Court-house, as an office, occasional dwelling and warehouse. It has recently been restored.

**Port Laoise** *Laois*                            573Hb
Formerly, and still by many, called Maryborough,

it is the county town of Laois. The Protestant church tower is topped by an obelisk spire designed by James Gandon. The court-house, by Sir Richard Morrison, fronts the massive rusticated and pilastered façade of the old gaol, perhaps also by Gandon.

**Portumna Castle** *Gal.*      *572Ec*
The huge semi-fortified house, perhaps the finest of its kind in Ireland, was built in 1618 at a cost of £10,000. It was entered via two spacious forecourts in succession, one of which has a fine Classical gateway with Tuscan columns and entablature, possibly the earliest of its type in Ireland, and now much overgrown. The castle was accidentally burnt in 1826. It still has an array of 'Jacobean' small gables, decorated with pedestals and balls, on all four fronts. There are remains of internal plasterwork. The house has massive corner towers, partly defensive, and the round-headed doorway is elaborately decorated. Portumna Abbey was furnished with a Cistercian cell, which became Dominican *c.* 1426; the church is aisle-less and has unusual tracery in its east window and in the south window of the transept. Two arcades of the small cloister have been re-erected.

**Poulnabrone** *Clare*      *572Cc*
A portal-grave with very large, thin flat capstone in the middle of a low circular cairn.

**Powerscourt House** *Wicklow*      *573Kc*
Together with its gardens and splendid estate, Powerscourt is one of the most impressive large houses in the Dublin area. It was built by Richard Castle around the core of an earlier semi-fortified house, the courtyard of which survives in the form of the 'Egyptian Hall' in the Burlington manner. Low arcades connect the central block to two-storey pavilions, beyond which are carved walls containing pedimented gateways and terminating in obelisks. The front is a composition of six Ionic pilasters carrying a pediment and voluted attic, and between them roundels containing busts.

The gardens (1400 acres), laid out in 1745 for the 2nd Viscount Powerscourt, are among the best in the world, with terraces, wooded demesne, deer park, a 400 ft waterfall and Japanese garden. The terraces were begun in 1745, and finally completed in 1867: the top terrace is 800 ft long (oriented east–west) and from it there is a descent by steps of grass slopes to a balustraded platform which has wrought-iron work from the balcony of a German castle. The descent continues to the Triton Pool, where statues of the winged horses of Fame and Victory stand. The gateway to the garden was once a cathedral door. (Open to the public.)

**Proleek** *Louth*      *573Kf*
The Proleek Stone, or Giant's Load, is a massive, almost spherical capstone balanced on three points.

**Quin Abbey** *Clare*      *570Ef*
Within the square enclosure of the great fortress built *c.* 1280, MacCon MacNamara founded in 1433 a Franciscan friary under licence from the Pope. The south curtain wall, and part of the east and west walls, were incorporated in the church, which has a tower separating the nave from the chancel, and a south transept with angle buttresses; to the north lies the cloister. The cloister arcades which support the building above have pointed arches in pairs between the buttresses; the capitals, shafts and bases are worked with resourceful variety. The friary survived well into the 19th century, and the last friar, who died in 1820, was buried in the north-east corner of the cloister. The Church of St Finghin near by is early 13th-century, with three lancet windows in its east wall.

**Rademon** *Down*      *575Jc*
The Presbyterian church of 1787 is a T-shaped building in plan, with arms of equal length. There are galleries in all three arms and a pulpit in the centre of the long wall. It has good fittings.

**Rahan** *Offaly*      *573Gc*
St Cartach founded three small churches at Rahan; the most remarkable early feature is the chancel arch, with bulbous bases and human-headed capitals, of the larger church, which is still in use as the Protestant parish church. A very early date has been claimed for this church, but other authorities assign it to *c.* 1100. The plan of the church is unique, in having had small chambers to the north and south of the vaulted chancel, and so is the circular Romanesque east window—but this has probably been reset. The small ruined church is a 15th-century rebuilding, incorporating a fine small early west doorway.

**Raphoe** *Don.*      *574De*
One of the last of the semi-fortified corner-towered block-shaped houses in Ireland. It was built in 1660 by the Protestant Bishop, John Leslie; the third storey, with battlements and bartizans, is probably late 18th century. The Gibbs entrance doorway must date from the early part of that century. The Cathedral of St Evnan (Protestant) incorporates some fragments of Romanesque and medieval buildings, and was rebuilt in 1700 with a 17th-century voluted porch. The tower is of 1738 and the lintels of two pre-Romanesque doorways may be seen.

**Rathbeale** *Dublin*      *573Kd*
A late 17th-century house, refaced and enlarged by curved walls and wings in the Palladian manner, probably by Richard Castle, in *c.* 1734. The interior has good plasterwork and decoration.

**Rathcline Castle** *Long.*      *572Fe*
A Butler house, of which a fine Classical gateway still exists.

POWERSCOURT HOUSE GARDENS

*Eight splendid terraces lead steeply southwards from the house to the Triton Pool, and beyond are views of the Wicklow Mountains and the conical dome of the Sugar Loaf Mountain. The terraces were begun in 1745 and completed in 1867. This view is from the highest one, 800 ft long. The third terrace, the focus of the whole design, is paved with black and white stones from the nearby beach at Bray, set in a striking geometrical pattern, and flanked by 18th-century bronze statues; the wrought-iron work is from the balcony of a castle in Hamburg. Winged horses of Fame and Victory stand guard beside the Triton Pool. The gardens' gate was once the door of Bamberg Cathedral, Germany.*

**Rathfarnham Castle** *Dublin*                573Kc
A large rectangular Elizabethan semi-fortified
house, built shortly before 1585 by Adam Loftus,
Archbishop successively of Armagh and Dublin,
later Chancellor of Ireland and first Provost of
Trinity College. In 1767 it was bought by the 2nd
Earl of Ely, who modernised it in 1770–1 with Sir
William Chambers as architect. It contains fine
neo-Classical decoration, and is now a Jesuit house.
PALLISER HOUSE A tall, red-brick house near
Rathfarnham Castle, built for the Palliser family
but most notable as the residence of George Grier-
son, the king's printer in Ireland. It was probably
built *c.* 1730 and is by Pearce or one of his
followers. It is now the central block of the
Loreto Convent.
ST ENDAS, CULLENSWOOD An 18th-century house
by an unknown architect. It is in neo-Classical
style with a Doric portico and low curved wings.

**Rathgall** *Wicklow*                573Jb
Unusually for eastern Ireland, this great fort is built
of dry stone, as in the west; it covers 18 acres and is
1000 ft in diameter, the central fort being 150 ft
across, though much ruined. Near by is another
large fort and a stone circle.

**Rathmacknee Castle** *Wex.*                571Kd
A picturesque 15th-century tower-house, with
stepped battlements and a well preserved five-
sided bawn. There is a bartisan on one corner of the
bawn wall.

**Rattoo** *Kerry*                570Ad
A Round Tower 92 ft high, with a restored roof and
the remains of a small church; in the churchyard
are some typical Kerry mausoleums and tombs.

**Reask** *Kerry*                570Ad
A late Celtic stone, with beautiful incised ornament—a cross supporting spirals.

**Richhill Manor House** *Arm.*                575Gc
An interesting mansion built by Edward Richardson, M.P., between 1655 and 1696; its Dutch
gables are of a kind formerly common in Ireland.

**Riverstown House** *Cork*                570Fc
An early 18th-century house built for Jemmett
Browne, Bishop of Cloyne; it is chiefly notable for
its splendid stucco decoration by the Francini
brothers in 1745.

**Roche** *Louth*                573Jf
ROCHE CASTLE Built in the late 13th century on a
rock overlooking a pass in the southern Armagh
hills; it consists of a large walled bailey separated
from the castle by a rock-cut fosse. The castle is
almost triangular in plan and there is a gate-house
and the remains of a great hall.

**Rockfleet** *Mayo*                572Bf
A typical 16th-century tower-house on the shores
of Clew Bay, chiefly interesting as being the only
known residence of the celebrated Grainne
Mhaille, or Grace O'Malley. In 1574 she beat off an
English seaborne attack against Carraig an
Chabhlaigh castle; 19 years later she appeared
before Elizabeth I and was granted a licence to
attack the queen's enemies.

**Roodstown Castle** *Louth*                573Kf
A 'ten-pound castle', so-called because of a statute
of 1429 which subsidised the building of castles
within the Pale, or English-controlled area. It
consists of a small tower with two turrets, and has
a particularly fine twin ogee-headed window.

**Roscommon** *Roscom.*                572Ee
The county town; it possesses a Classical court-
house with a tower and dome, attributed by some
to Sir Richard Morrison.

ROSCOMMON CASTLE A large keep-less castle built
in 1280 by Robert de Ufford, Justiciar of Ireland,
as a Crown fortress; it was later held by the
O'Conors. Its courtyard has D-shaped towers, a
square south gate, and a drawbridge. It was much
altered, notably by Sir Nicholas Malbie, who
*c.* 1580 made the many mullioned windows.

**Roscrea** *Tipp.*                571Gg
The early monastic remains of St Cronan consist of
a west front and gable of the church, an elegant
composition with a central gabled doorway,
flanked by four similar gabled recesses within
moulded pilasters, all probably of the early 12th
century. Across the road is the stump of a Round
Tower. There is also a figured 12th-century high
cross, the shaft decorated with interlaced vine
patterns, and on the west face a Crucifixion in
high relief. The town castle was built on an earlier
mote castle in 1280, which was granted in the
following year to Edmund Butler. A tall gate-
tower has stepped gables and chimneys dating
from the 17th century, and in the courtyard is the
nine-bay three-storey house of the Damer family,
built in the very early 18th century.

**Ross Abbey** *Gal.*                572Cd
The largest and best preserved friary in Ireland,
founded in 1351. The church, which lies south of
the cloister, has the usual slender tower between

HEROIC VIRTUE

*In 1734, the Francini brothers, Paul and Philip, burst
on the Irish scene. Nothing is known of their origins.
They introduced the use of the human figure into Irish
decorative plasterwork, and their example was immediately followed by the native craftsmen, who were
quick to learn the new techniques. The dining-room at
Riverstown House contains eight exquisite wall
plaques derived from Classical sources. There is also
a superb ceiling based on a painting by Poussin
entitled 'Time rescuing Truth from the assaults of
Discord and Envy', now in the Louvre in Paris. The
plasterwork was executed by the Francini brothers in
1745. There is apparently no theme linking the wall
decoration to that of the ceiling, and this wall plaque
depicts Heroic Virtue. (Riverstown House)*

the nave and chancel, and south of the nave is a double transept, as at Kilconnell, with an eastward chapel. West of it is Jenning's Chantry. The cloister is small and square and in remarkably good condition. A further court of similar dimensions lies to the north.

**Ross Carbery** *Cork*     *570Da*
St Fachtna's Protestant Cathedral is a cruciform building with a 17th-century tower; the north transept is probably medieval, but otherwise the building is mostly of the early 19th century.

**Ross Castle** See Killarney.

**Rosserk Friary** *Mayo*     *572Cg*
A small, very well-preserved friary of the third order of Franciscans, founded in 1441. The church lies south of the cloister and has a central tower and southern transept, with two chapels and a sacristy cupboard. The east window has cusped tracery like St Nicholas's, Galway.

**Rowallane Garden** *Down*     *575Jd*
South-east of Belfast, near Saintfield, this beautiful garden was created by Armytage Moore at the beginning of the century. His collection of exotic trees, shrubs and flowers from all over the world thrives in this mild climate, and many of the fine specimens were raised from seeds collected in China, Tibet and South America. There is a walled garden and nearly 50 acres of landscape garden.

**Rubane** *Down*     *575Jd*
A house formerly called Echlinville, built probably in the second quarter of the 18th century but largely rebuilt in 1850. From the early house survives the library, a four-bay pavilion with Ionic pilasters, Coade stone keystones and Gothic glazing. There is a small Classical bridge and a splendid pinnacled pebble house in the grounds.

**Russborough House** *Wicklow*     *573Jc*
Built by Richard Castle and Francis Bindon for the 1st Earl of Miltown from 1740 onwards, Russborough is the longest house in Ireland. It comprises a relatively small central block, with pedimented frontispiece joined by quadrant colonnades to long low wings, beyond which plain walls pierced by baroque gateways terminate in smaller pavilions which contain the kitchen and stable courts. The interior has lavish 18th-century decoration by the Francini brothers. (Not open.)

**St Clerans House** *Gal.*     *572Dc*
One of the 'villas' built to designs by Sir Richard Morrison *c.* 1810.

**St Doulagh's Church** *Dublin*     *573 Kd*
The chancel of St Doulagh's church dates from *c.* 1200 and has a high-pitched stone roof. The central battlemented tower is of the 15th century, while the body of the church is of the 19th century.

**St Macdara's Island** *Gal.*     *572Ac*
On this small island off the south-west Galway coast is an early Irish oratory, measuring internally 15 ft by 11 ft. It is built of massive stones, and its pilasters continue upwards to form the portions of the roof jutting out beyond the end walls. Much of its original stone roof still remains in position.

**St Mullins** *Carlow*     *571Je*
Situated on the R. Barrow, little remains of the monastery of St Moling save the stump of a Round Tower, a figured high cross and the ruins of some small churches and other buildings.

**Scattery Island** *Clare*     *570Ce*
An island in the Shannon estuary where St Seanan founded a monastery in the 6th century. Six churches and the tallest Round Tower in Ireland, 120 ft high, survive, as well as two enclosed graveyards with stone slabs, and a well.

**Seafield** *Dublin*     *573Kd*
A house probably built between 1720 and 1730 for the Arthur family, on the shores of the Malahide inlet. It has a Doric portico. The superb entrance hall has two storeys of pilasters, grisaille paintings, and a gallery with wrought-iron railings.

**Shane's Castle** *Antrim*     *575Ge*
The castle was originally rebuilt by John Nash in *c.* 1812, though the whole castle was burnt in 1816. Now only Nash's splendid greenhouse survives.

**Shanid** *Lim.*     *570De*
A castle dating from the end of the 12th century. Today only the remains of a polygonal battlemented tower stand on an impressive mote and fosse.

**Shannongrove** *Lim.*     *570Ee*
The earliest 18th-century house in County Limerick—the front door is dated 1709 and the rear 1723. The mason was John O'Brien. The central block, with red-brick chimneys, is flanked on either side by symmetrical wings, all in Dutch-Palladian style.

**Sherkin Abbey** *Cork*     *570Ca*
A Franciscan friary on Sherkin Island in Baltimore Bay. The abbey was founded in 1460–70 by the O'Driscolls, and has a typical Franciscan friary church with a cloister to the north of the nave, and a central tower and southern transept.

**Skellig's** See Great Skellig.

**Slade** *Wex.*     *571Jc*
The 15th- to 16th-century crenellated tower-house is well preserved and has a later oblong wing.

**Slane** *Meath*     *573Je*
The village was elegantly laid out, probably by Francis Johnston. There is a fine square with Georgian houses in the centre.
SLANE CASTLE One of the finest Gothic Revival castles in Ireland. The building incorporates an earlier castle. The structure of the present house is largely due to James Wyatt, who was called in by Lord Conyngham in 1785. Capability Brown, Chambers, Gandon, Francis Johnston and Thomas Hopper all designed parts of the building. (Not open to the public.)

**Slievegullion** *Arm.*     *575Gb*
On top of Slievegullion Mountain is the cairn known as 'Calliagh Birra's House'. This is a passage-grave; the chamber is polygonal.

**Slieve-na-calliagh** *Meath*     *573He*
The long ridge of low hills south-east of Oldcastle is surmounted by a remarkable series of 30 passage-graves (chambered tombs in which the chamber and passage leading to it form two distinct structural units). Many of the stones have Bronze Age ornament. There is also a ring-fort, a rectangular earthwork, a pillar-stone and a stone cross.

**Sligo** *Sligo*     *574Cc*
A county town founded in 1252 by Maurice FitzGerald, who also founded the Dominican friary now known as Sligo Abbey. The Church of St John, in Perpendicular Gothic Revival style by Richard Castle, was remodelled in 1812; the town has a tree-lined mall by the Garavogue River. Many places around Sligo, such as Lough Gill to the south-east, Drumcliff and Lissadell, are associated with the poetry of W. B. Yeats.

ABBEY The abbey contains much good 15th-century work, including a unique sculptured high altar, a good east window, a fragmentary 14th- to 15th-century rood screen, and a well-moulded cloister arcade. There are also some fine monuments, including the O'Craian tomb of 1506, with an elaborate canopy.

**Springfield Castle** *Lim.*    *570Ed*
A large, exceptionally well-preserved four-storied gabled tower-house dating from the 16th century.

**Stackallan** *Meath*    *573Je*
A house built for Gustavus Hamilton, Viscount Boyne, one of William III's generals. It has wide eaves and two formal fronts dated 1716. It is one of the rare survivors in Ireland of pre-Palladian style.

**Staigue Fort** *Kerry*    *570Bb*
One of the best preserved and most spectacular of the drystone ring-forts. It is situated in a hollow of the hills overlooking the Kenmare estuary. The walls are 13 ft high, terraced internally, and served by an elaborate system of stairways. There are two small chambers in the walls.

**Stillorgan** *Dublin*    *573Kc*
Of the great house and gardens of the Viscounts Allen, nothing now remains save the obelisk erected *c.* 1730 as a mausoleum designed by Sir Edward Lovett Pearce and now in the grounds of the hospice of the Order of St John of God. In the garden of a house north of the main road is a large underground brick grotto, also by Pearce.

**Strabane** *Tyrone*    *574Ee*
A town on the R. Foyle near Lifford. To the south-west, Urney Presbyterian Church dates from 1654, but was reconstructed in 1695. St Theresa's Catholic Church at Sion Mills, built in 1962–6 by Patrick Haughy, has carvings by Oisin Kelly and windows by Patrick Pollen.

**Strade Abbey** *Mayo*    *572Cf*
Founded as a Franciscan friary by Jordan de Exeter, Strade was transferred to the Dominican order in 1252–3. There are splendid figures on the high altar, a magnificent 15th- or 16th-century tomb with superb Flamboyant tracery and weepers on the plinth, and other sculptures representing Our Lord with the Five Wounds, a layman with an ear trumpet, two bishops and St Peter.

**Strancally Castle** *Waterford*    *571Gc*
Romantically situated on the banks of the Blackwater, at the foot of the Knockmealdown Mountains, this Gothic Revival house was built to designs by the Pain brothers.

**Strangford** *Down*    *575Jc*
A small port at the narrow entrance to Strangford Lough. It has a much-altered late 16th-century fortified town-house known as Strangford Castle, and a small tower close to the shore. Strangford House was built in 1789 and has some pleasant interior detailing.

**Strokestown House** *Roscom.*    *572Ee*
The central block of the house, now refaced, was originally 17th century, but it is likely that Richard Castle, very early in his career (*c.* 1730), added the curved quadrants and wings, which include splendid vaulted stables.

**Summer Grove** *Laois*    *573Gc*
An attractive small house of ashlar stones hardly larger than bricks. The main front has Venetian windows on the first floor over the door and a semicircular window in the pediment. The entrance hall, staircase hall and drawing-room have charming rococo ornament.

STAIGUE FORT

*In a hollow of the hills overlooking the Kenmare estuary, this drystone ring-fort has walls 13 ft high, terraced internally and served by an elaborate system of stairways. There are two small chambers within the thickness of the walls.*

**Swords** *Dublin*    *573Kd*
The village has a Round Tower 75 ft high; a 14th-century square tower, the only remains of a medieval monastery, opposite the present Protestant church; and a large castle or palace of the Archbishops of Dublin. This comprises a five-sided walled enclosure with a gateway, small tower and chapel of various dates from the 13th to the 15th century.

**Synone** *Tipp.*    *571Ge*
A circular castle of the 16th century, with machicolations and internal dome-like vaults.

**Tacumshane** *Wex.*    *571Ld*
Standing in the village is a small straw-thatched windmill (no longer working), one of only two in Ireland—the other is at Ballycopeland.

**Taghmon** *Westmeath*    *573He*
The church here, though disused, dates from the 15th century. It has a stone barrel-vault and an added four-storey west tower, which was used as living quarters and fortified. Originally there was a first-floor room over the western part of the nave.

**Tallaght** *Dublin*    *573Kc*
The site of the monastery of St Maelruan, founded in the 8th century. In the 14th century Tallaght became the country residence of the Archbishops of Dublin, who built a large manorial palace there; only one small tower survives of this building, which was demolished early in the 19th century. The church to the south stands detached from its medieval bell-tower, by John Semple.

**Tara** *Meath*    *573Je*
The hill at Tara, although little more than 500 ft high, commands a wide prospect. According to legend, the ancient kings of Tara, who ruled the northern half of the country, made their homes and were crowned here. The present names of the earthworks and monuments on the hill are traditional names only; they are probably not derived from true historical associations.
 The main part of the site is about 1000 yds from north to south. Near the centre is the Fort of the Kings, an oval enclosure about 1000 ft by 800 ft. Within the fort are two adjoining earthworks, the Royal Seat, a bivallate ring-fort, and Cormac's House, a high flat mound with two banks and ditches surrounding it. On top—and serving as a monument to the local dead of the 1798 rising against the English—is the standing stone now called the Lia Fail. Within the Fort of the Kings, near its northern edge, is the Mound of Hostages, on which the original Lia Fail—the inauguration

stone of the kings of Tara—is supposed to have stood; the present identity and whereabouts of this stone is not known. South of the Fort of the Kings is another smaller univallate fort, Laoghaire's Fort.

North of the Fort of the Kings, and partly encroached upon by the modern churchyard, is the trivallate earthwork called the Fort of the Synods; it has a small burial mound, the King's Chair, within its outer defences. North of the Fort of the Synods is the long narrow earthwork called the Banqueting Hall, 750 ft long and 90 ft wide. North-west of the Banqueting Hall is a group of three circular earthworks, the Sloping Trenches.

Tara was the centre of an influential pagan religious cult in the Iron Age. At that period there were timber houses on the site. The recent excavations at the Mound of the Hostages have established that it contains a Bronze Age burial relic dating from *c.* 2000 BC.

The Cross of Adamnan in the churchyard is a limestone pillar with a barely discernible carved figure. The modern statue of St Patrick, on Cormac's House, commemorates the saint's visit to the court of King Laoghaire.

**Thomastown** *Kilk.*      *571Je*
A formerly walled Anglo-Norman town.
PARISH CHURCH Of the 13th-century parish church, the north wall of the nave and the chancel arch remain. The chancel was used as a Protestant parish church until 1809. In the churchyard is the head of a high cross. In the Catholic parish church is the high altar from Jerpoint Abbey.

**Thomastown Castle** *Tipp.*      *571Ge*
A large, early 18th-century house with gate-house and formal garden, built by the Matthews family. It was completely refaced and extended by Sir Richard Morrison *c.* 1820. Today it is in ruins; near by is a huge walled garden. To the north-east are the ruins of Kilfane Church, with a 13th-century sedilia, traces of polychrome painting, a residential north tower, and a superb effigy of *c.* 1320 known as Long Cantwell.

**Thurles** *Tipp.*      *571Ge*
A town on the upper waters of the R. Suir. Thurles was largely the creation of the Butlers, who conquered the O'Fogartys of Eile, the former owners. The bridge is guarded by a small castle. Thurles is the seat of the Catholic Archbishop of Cashel, and the Cathedral of the Assumption by J. J. McCarthy (1865–72) has a good baroque altarpiece in the style of Andrea Pozzo. In St Patrick's College, site of the Synod of 1850, is St Caillian's Shrine of 1436. Brittas Castle, to the north, is a 19th-century reproduction of a medieval castle.

**Timahoe** *Laois*      *573Hb*
The 96 ft high 12th-century Round Tower has a fine Romanesque doorway with capitals and bases recalling Killeshin and Rahan.

**Timoleague Abbey** *Cork*      *570Ea*
A Franciscan friary, attractively sited on a peninsula in Courtmacsherry Bay, founded either in the 13th or 14th century. Its plan is irregular as a result of the shape of the peninsula. The buildings are mostly plainly finished. Features include a wall-passage on the east and south of the choir, and the large walled courtyard to the west, a bell-tower and dormitory. The library dates from the beginning of the 16th century. Only a small portion of the cloister remains, but the other buildings are intact.

**Tintern Abbey** *Wex.*      *571Kd*
A Cistercian abbey founded in 1200 by William the Marshall, it was a daughter-house of Tintern

Abbey in Monmouthshire, and most of the remains date from the late 13th century. Some of the presbytery detailing is based on that at Tintern Major. The nave survives, and the central tower at the crossing may be the original, although its upper part is 15th century. At the Dissolution, the abbey and lands were granted to the Colclough family, who turned the abbey into a dwelling house, and both the Tudor and Georgian-Gothic windows date from their occupation.

**Tollymore** *Down*      *575Hc*
The house, which was built for the Hamiltons, Earls of Clanbrassil, and later passed into the hands of the Earls of Roden, has been demolished. The grounds contain a series of follies and a grotto down by the river, dating from 1782.

**Townley Hall** *Louth*      *573Ke*
Designed in 1794 for Blayney Townley-Balfour by Francis Johnston, the house has a severe exterior of cut stone. There is a splendid central stone-cantilevered and domed staircase, and the principal rooms have fine joinery and plaster detail. The house is now occupied by the Agriculture Department of Trinity College.

**Tralee** *Kerry*      *570Cd*
The county town of Kerry owes its origin to the Earls of Desmond, of whose castle practically nothing survives. In the 16th century, after the rebellion led by the 15th Earl, the town was granted to Sir Edward Denny, whose family held it and its borough until the mid-19th century. The most distinguished building is the Classical courthouse by William Vitruvius Morrison. Its Ionic portico is approached by a flight of steps guarded by two Crimean and Indian Mutiny memorial canons; the courts are semicircular and flank the central hall. Day Place is an alley with fine Georgian houses. The church of the Dominican friary of the Holy Cross (founded in 1243) is by Edward Welby Pugin and George Ashlin.

**Trim** *Meath*      *573Jd*
The medieval town walls enclosed an extensive area; today remnants, including Sheep Gate, remain between Castle Street and Emmet Street. There are several fine 18th-century houses in the town and a column erected in 1817 to the honour of the Duke of Wellington, who spent his childhood in nearby Dangan. The gaol of *c.* 1800 has a fine gate-house. St Patrick's Church, a much-altered medieval church, has served as the Protestant cathedral of Meath since 1955. Across the R. Boyne is Talbot Castle, a fortified house of 1415, and Nangle Castle of about the same age. A little to the east rises the Yellow Steeple, the shattered remains of the splendid bell-tower of the Abbey of St Mary, founded in the 13th century; it was damaged by Cromwell's troops.

Just south-east of the town is Newtown Trim, with the ruins of the medieval Cathedral of SS Peter and Paul and its priory on the banks of the R. Boyne; it dates from 1206. Close by is the house of the Crutched Friars.
CASTLE The largest Anglo-Norman castle in Ireland, Trim covers more than 3 acres, bounded on one side by the R. Boyne. The castle was first built in 1172 by Hugh de Lacy, but in its present form dates from *c.* 1190. The irregular bailey has towers with a D-shaped plan, sally-ports and a barbican. The keep contains a hall and chapel. (See p. 630.)

**Tuam** *Gal.*      *572Dd*
The town was formerly the seat of a Protestant archbishop, but now has a Protestant bishop; it is still the centre of a Catholic archbishopric. The

Catholic Cathedral of the Assumption dates from 1827–37, and was designed by Dominic Madden. PROTESTANT CATHEDRAL A Gothic Revival building designed by Sir Thomas Deane in 1861. It incorporates the barrel-vaulted Romanesque chancel of a late 12th-century cathedral, the finely decorated chancel arch of which was the widest in Ireland. The chancel had long served as the porch of another church farther east which was used as a cathedral from the late 14th century onwards and which is now a chapter house. It contains elaborately carved Italian baroque choir stalls, dated 1740, which were presented to the diocese in 1882.

**Tuamgraney** *Clare*      570Ff
The Protestant church comprises a 12th-century eastern part, and a western portion of the mid-10th century with a lintelled and architraved doorway. Near the church are the ruins of a castle.

**Tulira Castle** *Gal.*      572Dc
A 17th-century tower-house, considerably added to in 1882 by George Ashlin. The interior contains a fine Gothic hall. The castle was the home of Edward Martyn (1859–1923), the dramatist and patron of the arts, who was influenced by William Morris, and was one of the initiators of the Irish stained glass revival. (Not open to the public.)

**Tullabeg** *Offaly*      573Gc
St Stanislaus College, a large country house now belonging to the Jesuit Fathers, has an oratory with fine stained glass by Evie Hone.

**Tullamore** *Offaly*      573Gc
Now the county town of Offaly, Tullamore is mainly the creation of the Burys, Earls of Tulla-more, who built Charleville Castle near by. The town has some good canal architecture, including a canal hotel. There is a splendid Ionic-porticoed court-house of *c.* 1835 and an 18th-century market-house. The Protestant church is by Francis Johnston, who was also the architect of Charleville.

**Tully** *Kild.*      573Jc
JAPANESE GARDENS The flowering shrubs, miniature trees and rockeries here were arranged by a Japanese designer in 1906, and completed four years later. The gardens are symbolic of the life of a human being and features include the Cave of Birth, Peace before the Hill of Mourning, and the Gates of Eternity.

**Tully Castle** *Ferm.*      574Dd
A Plantation castle. The square fortified enclosure contains a T-shaped strong-house.

**Turoe Stone** See Loughrea.

**Tullynally Castle** *Westmeath.*      573Ge
A 17th-century garrison house, Classicised in 1775 by Myers and transformed into a flamboyant Gothic castle by Francis Johnston from 1803 to 1806, with picturesque additions by James Shiel in 1825 and Sir Richard Morrison in 1842. Situated in a 1500 acre park and demesne, the castle has kitchen, museum and Duke of Wellington family relics. (House open at weekends.)

**Tynan** *Arm.*      574Fc
The four crosses of Tynan, one in the village and three on the estate of Tynan Abbey, have all been moved from their original sites. The village cross has a carved panel depicting the Fall of Adam and Eve, and was originally in the churchyard.

**Tyrone House** *Gal.*      572Dc
The burnt-out, ruined country house of the St George family, built in 1779 and splendidly situated on an inlet in Galway Bay. Facing it is Drumacoo church, with good 13th-century details, and the St George family mausoleum with cast-iron tracery.

**Tyrrelspass** *Westmeath*      573Gd
A formal landlord's village, laid out by the Roch-forts, Earls of Belvedere, around a semicircular green. Several of the houses are pedimented, and the Protestant church has a fine spire and a magnificent monument by John Bacon.

TRIM CASTLE

*The first castle at Trim, a fortress for the Norman invaders, was levelled by the Irish. This one dates from the end of the 12th century and the town of Trim grew up in its shelter. The square keep is 75 ft high and has a tower abutting the centre of each face, so that there are 20 sides in all. King John visited the castle—and confiscated it. Henry V was kept a prisoner there before his accession.*

## FINE SILVER AT WESTPORT HOUSE

*The bog-oak bowl with its intricately wrought cover (left) and the sugar sifter (centre) were made in Ireland for Colonel John Browne, owner of the first house on the site in the early 18th century. The group* *of slaves (right) are on the base of a 19th-century candelabrum—one of a superb pair presented to the 2nd Marquess of Sligo, Governor of Jamaica, for his part in the abolition of slavery in Jamaica.*

**Ullard** *Kilk.*                                              571Je
The ruined church has an unusual west doorway, partly reconstructed, with an inner arch at a lower level than the external one. High in the west gable above is a triangular-headed window with a small sculptured panel depicting two saints above it. Near by is a 9th-century cross.

**Ulster Folk Museum** See Cultra Manor.

**Urlanmore Castle** *Clare*                        570Ef
The building has a three-storied tower at one end and, at the other, a lower adjoining extension containing the remains of the first-floor hall. On the walls of the principal room in the tower are outline paintings of animals.

**Ushnagh** *Westmeath*                              573Gd
A place of sanctity or hosting site, and thought to have been the centre of Ireland in pagan times. It contains a large number of earthworks, including the remains of an elaborate house of the 2nd century AD and a souterrain. From this 600 ft hill, 20 of the counties of Ireland can be seen.

**Walpole Gardens** See Mount Usher.

**Waringstown** *Down*                               575Gd
Established in 1667 by the linen manufacturer William Waring, who built Waringstown House, a large U-shaped three-storied block with 18th-century two-storied pavilions added at the ends of the main front. The church, of 1681, is said to have been supervised by James Robb, chief mason of the king's works in Ireland. The west tower dates from 1750 and the church was enlarged in the 19th century. The pulpit and fittings, in 17th-century style, date from 1832.

**Waterford** *Waterford*                            571Jd
Among the most important Anglo-Norman foundations on the eastern seaboard, though owing its origin to the Vikings. It lies on the south bank of the R. Suir and consists of a long quay behind which are the narrow streets of the medieval walled town. The north-east corner of the town is marked by the massive cylindrical Reginald's Tower, probably 12th or 13th century, now a museum; other towers of the town wall survive.

The ruined Franciscan church, founded in 1240 and given to the Huguenots in 1695, has three lancets on its east wall and central tower. Fragments of other medieval buildings survive, such as the tower and belfry of the Dominican friary (Black Friars) in Arundel Square. The important

medieval cathedral, which resembled Christchurch, Dublin, was demolished in 1773 to be succeeded by the present splendid building (Protestant) by John Roberts, finished in 1779; it has a western Doric portico, tower and spire, an interior with a giant Ionic order, and fine original plasterwork; the macabre monument of James Rice in the north-west chapel, and other monuments, are noteworthy. Immediately south of it is the bishop's palace by Richard Castle, dating from 1741, latterly occupied by Bishop Foy's School. Other good 18th-century houses surround the cathedral. St Olave's Church, founded by Bishop Milles in 1734, is virtually intact, with bishop's throne, three-decker pulpit, black and white marble paving and scrolled pedimented reredos. John Roberts also designed the Catholic cathedral (a remarkable circumstance for the period) which dates from 1792, with double-aisled nave, a giant Corinthian order and plaster vaults. The façade is late 19th century. The cathedral has a splendid series of medieval vestments discovered during the demolition of the old Protestant cathedral in 1773 and presented by the then Protestant bishop to his Catholic counterpart. St Olave's, too, has its Catholic counterpart in St Patrick's Church of 1764, which is almost completely unaltered, with galleries carried on Doric columns. The present town hall, originally the assembly rooms, dates from 1782 and is also by John Roberts; it incorporates a 'play-house'. The decoration is simple, but there is a Waterford glass chandelier in the council chamber, installed in 1802. The present Ionic-porticoed court-house, in the People's Park, dating from 1849, is almost identical to the one in Tullamore. The Presentation Convent, by Augustus Welby Pugin, is a characteristic work begun in 1842.

**Wattlebridge** *Ferm.*                             574Eb
What appears to be a circle of numerous stones, 100 ft in diameter, is the kerb of a cairn removed early in the 18th century.

**Westport** *Mayo*                                  572Be
Perhaps the most elaborately planned of smaller Irish towns, laid out in 1780. The canalised river is the main feature of the plan, flanked by tree-lined quays and crossed by graceful bridges. Other streets ascend the slopes from an octagonal place containing a column. Near by is Westport House at the head of Clew Bay; it contains fine Wyatt plasterwork in the dining-room.

**Wexford** *Wex.* 571Kd
The county town owes its origin to the Vikings, but was captured by the Anglo-Normans. There are few remains of interest, but the Augustinian priory of SS Peter and Paul (called Selskar Abbey), comprises a square battlemented tower used as the belfry of the Protestant parish church, and a ruinous double nave. Near by, a fragment of the medieval town wall survives; there are also remains of St Mary's Church. St Peter's Catholic Church on Summer Hill is by Augustus Welby Pugin and was consecrated in 1840. Four and a half miles to the south-west is Johnstown Castle.

**White Island** *Ferm.* 574Dd
On Lough Erne, the remains of a small church with a Romanesque south doorway. Built into the wall are seven remarkable carved figures, probably of the 7th century, five of which represent sinister human beings.

**Wicklow** *Wicklow* 573Kb
A Viking foundation, now the county town, it has an 18th-century Protestant church with a square tower (1770), surmounted by a dome. The 19th-century open-work trusses, with their fan pattern, are curious. The interior retains its original Doric-columned gallery and to the left of the mid-19th-century chancel-arch is a fine mid-18th-century monument with a bust.

**Woodlands** *Dublin* 573Kd
One of the more interesting smaller houses in Ireland, Woodlands, traditionally associated with Jonathan Swift, was in fact built for his friend, the Rev. Jack Jackson, *c.* 1730, and must be by Sir Edward Lovett Pearce or one of his immediate school. The almost square plan contains a vaulted corridor leading from the front door to the centre of the house; a gazebo, or lantern, projects from the top of the pyramidal roof.

**Youghal** *Cork* 571Gc
The 13th-century collegiate Church of St Mary is among the few roofed medieval churches still in

FIGURES ON WHITE ISLAND

*Some of the incredible carved stone figures built into the walls of the ruined church. Probably dating from the 7th century, five represent sinister humans. The figure on the right holds two griffins by the neck; another carries the crozier and bell of a bishop.*

use. It is cruciform, with an aisled nave and a 15th-century long chancel. There is a massive fortified tower between the north transept and the nave. In the south transept is the monument of Richard Boyle, the Great Earl of Cork, to himself and members of his family, with fine effigies and remarkable wrought-iron work.

Dominating the centre of the town is the Clock Gate in South Main Street, a massive structure in limestone of four storeys above an archway with set-backs, surmounted by a domed lantern containing the clock. It was built in 1771, designed by William Meade. Near by is an altered 15th-century tower-house and, opposite, the Uniacke House (now the Presbytery) of 1706–15, built by a Dutch builder named Leuventhan; it has a steep central pediment with eaves-cornice and dormer. An even rarer survivor is the unique set of almshouses (1634) with pointed doorways and mullioned windows in North Main Street, where another early fragment, St John's Chapel, remains, with a small elaborate medieval window.

MONUMENT TO THE EARL OF CORK

*Richard Boyle, created Earl of Cork in 1620, erected this monument to commemorate himself and his family in about 1620. He wears armour and an earl's robes. His mother reclines over the main arch above the earl. On either side of him kneel his wives—his first wife,* *who died in childbirth, at his feet, and his second wife at his head. Below him nine children are represented. The children appear again, this time grown up, on Lady Cork's tomb in St Patrick's Cathedral, Dublin. (Church of St Mary, Youghal)*

# COLLECTIONS

## *Specialised collections in houses, museums and galleries*

The urge to collect has always been a strong characteristic of the British . . . Small boys eagerly fill stamp albums; playbills and punch ladles, seashells and swords set the scene in many of our homes, pubs and palaces.

This section of the book lists the collections, privately and publicly owned, which are notable for their special character or value. They demonstrate the diverse, cultivated and extravagant tastes of patrons and connoisseurs, the proud feeling for the past achievements of families and regiments, the scholarly and eccentric interests of learned men and dilletantes.

The collections are listed under subject headings, to assist the pursuit of specialised interests. They speak of the past as intimately as a diary and with an authority that the reflections of a historian could never possess.

## ARCHAEOLOGY AND ANTHROPOLOGY

The relics of man's earliest activities displayed in British museums come from all over the world and span some $1\frac{3}{4}$ million years. They show him in his role as a hunter and warrior, as farmer, ironsmith, potter, worshipper and artist. To study these collections is to understand the relationship—often surprisingly close—between 20th-century man and his prehistoric forebears.

**Aberdeen,** *A'deen.*
  University Anthropological Museum
**Abergavenny,** *Mon.*
  Abergavenny and District Museum
**Abingdon,** *Berks.*
  County Hall (Borough Museum)
**Ardoch Roman Camp,** *Perths.*
**Ashwell,** *Herts.*
  Village Museum
**Avebury,** *Wilts.*
  Alexander Keiller Museum

**Aylesbury,** *Bucks.*
  Buckinghamshire County Museum
**Barnet,** *Herts.* Museum
**Basing,** *Hants.*
  Basing House Ruins
**Basingstoke,** *Hants.* Willis Museum
**Batley,** *Yorks.* Bagshaw Museum
**Bedford,** *Beds.* Museum
**Bexhill,** *Sussex* Museum
**Bignor,** *Sussex* Roman Villa
**Birchington,** *Kent*
  Powell Cotton Museum

**Birchover,** *Derbys.*
Heathcote Museum
**Birmingham,** *Warks.*
Blakesley Hall (Yardley); City
Museum and Art Gallery; Weoley
Castle
**Blackburn,** *Lancs.*
Museum and Art Gallery
**Boroughbridge,** *Yorks.*
Aldborough Roman Site Museum
**Bournemouth,** *Hants.*
Rothesay Museum
**Bradford,** *Yorks.*
City Art Gallery and Museum
**Bridgwater,** *Som.*
Admiral Blake Museum
**Bridlington,** *Yorks.*
Art Gallery and Museum
**Bridport,** *Dorset*
Museum and Art Gallery
**Brighton,** *Sussex*
Museum and Art Gallery
**Bury,** *Lancs.*
Art Gallery and Museum
**Bury St Edmunds,** *Suffolk*
Moyses Hall Museum
**Caernarvon,** *Caern.*
Segontium Museum
**Cambourne,** *Cornwall*
Public Library and Museum
**Cambridge,** *Cambs.*
Scott Polar Research Institute;
University Museum of Classical
Archaeology
**Canterbury,** *Kent*
Roman Pavement; Royal Museum
(Beaney Institute)
**Carlisle,** *Cumb.* Tullie House
**Chichester,** *Sussex*
City Museum; Guildhall
Museum
**Christchurch,** *Hants.*
Red House Museum and Art
Gallery
**Cirencester,** *Glos.*
Corinium Museum
**Colchester,** *Essex*
Colchester and Essex Museum
**Dartford,** *Kent*
Borough Museum
**Derby,** *Derbys.*
Museum and Art Gallery
**Devizes,** *Wilts.*
Wiltshire Archaeological and
Natural History Society
**Dorchester,** *Dorset*
County Museum
**Dover,** *Kent*
Corporation Museum
**Dublin,** *Dublin*
Leinster House
**Dumfries,** *Dumf.*
Observatory (Burgh Museum)
**Dundalk,** *Louth*
**Durham,** *Durham*
Gulbenkian Museum of Oriental
Art
**Exeter,** *Devon*
Royal Albert Memorial Museum
and Art Gallery
**Farnham,** *Surrey*
Willmer House Museum
**Glandford,** *Norfolk*
Museum of Shells
**Glasgow,** *Lanarks.*
Hunterian Museum
**Gloucester,** *Glos.*
City Museum and Art Gallery
**Grantham,** *Lincs.*
Library and Museum
**Guildford,** *Surrey*
Museum and Muniment Room
**Harlyn,** *Cornwall*
Harlyn Bay Museum
**Haslemere,** *Surrey*
Educational Museum

**Hereford,** *Herefs.*
City Museum and Art Gallery
**Hertford,** *Herts.*
Museum
**Ilkley,** *Yorks.*
Manor House Museum and Art
Gallery
**Inverurie,** *A'deen.* Museum
**Ipswich,** *Suffolk* Museum
**King's Lynn,** *Norfolk*
Museum and Art Gallery
**Lancaster,** *Lancs.*
City Museum
**Leeds,** *Yorks.* City Museum
**Leicester,** *Leics.*
Jewry Wall Museum
**Lerwick,** *Shetland*
County Museum
**Lincoln,** *Lincs.*
City and County Museum
**London**
British Museum; Cuming
Museum; Guildhall Museum;
Passmore Edwards Museum
**Luton,** *Beds.*
Museum and Art Gallery
**Macclesfield,** *Lancs.*
West Park Museum
**Maidstone,** *Kent*
Chillington Manor
**Melrose,** *Rox.* Abbey
**Middlesbrough,** *Yorks.*
Dorman Memorial Museum and
Municipal Art Gallery
**Newark-on-Trent,** *Notts.*
Museum and Art Gallery
**Newbury,** *Berks.*
Borough Museum
**Newcastle upon Tyne,** *Northld.*
Hancock Museum
**Newport,** *Mon.*
Museum and Art Gallery
**Northampton,** *Northants.*
Central Museum and Art Gallery
**Nuneaton,** *Warks.*
Museum and Art Gallery
**Oxford,** *Oxon.*
Ashmolean Museum; Museum of
the History of Science
**Penzance,** *Cornwall*
Natural History and Antiquarian
Museum
**Peterborough,** *Hunts.*
Museum and Maxwell Art Gallery
**Plymouth,** *Devon*
City Museum and Art Gallery
**Pontefract,** *Yorks.*
Castle Museum
**Poole,** *Dorset*
Old Town House; Poole
Museum
**Reading,** *Berks.*
Museum and Art Gallery;
Museum of Greek Archaeology
**Ribchester,** *Lancs.*
Museum of Roman Antiquities
**Richborough Castle,** *Kent*
**Rossendale,** *Lancs.*
Rawtenstall Museum
**Rotherham,** *Yorks.*
Municipal Museum and Art
Gallery
**Rufford,** *Lancs.*
Rufford Old Hall
**St Ives,** *Cornwall*
Zennor Folk Museum
**Salisbury,** *Wilts.*
Salisbury and South Wiltshire
Museum
**Scarborough,** *Yorks.*
Museum
**Shaftesbury,** *Dorset*
Abbey Ruins Museum;
Shaftesbury and District Historical
Society's Museum of Local
History

**Sheffield,** *Yorks.* City Museum
**Shrewsbury,** *Shrops.*
Rowley's House Museum
**Silchester,** *Hants.* Calleva Museum
**Sittingbourne,** *Kent*
Court Hall Museum
**Skipton,** *Yorks.*
Craven Museum
**Southampton,** *Hants.*
God's House Tower
**Southend-on-Sea,** *Essex*
Prittlewell Priory Museum
**Southport,** *Lancs.*
Botanic Garden Museum
**South Shields,** *Durham*
Roman Fort and Museum
**Stevenage,** *Herts.*
Museum
**Stirling,** *Stir.*
Smith Art Gallery and Museum
**Stranraer,** *Wig.*
Wigtown County Museum

**Sunderland,** *Durham*
Museum and Art Gallery
**Taunton,** *Som.* County Museum
**Tenby,** *Pemb.* Museum
**Tilbury,** *Essex*
Thurrock Local History Museum
**Truro,** *Cornwall*
County Museum and Art Gallery
**Weston-super-Mare,** *Som.*
Municipal Museum
**Weybridge,** *Surrey* Museum
**Winchester,** *Hants.* City Museum
**Windsor,** *Berks.*
Windsor Guildhall Exhibition
**Wookey,** *Som.*
Wookey Hole Caves Museum
**Worksop,** *Notts.*
Public Library and Museum
**Worthing,** *Sussex*
Museum and Art Gallery
**Yeovil,** *Som.*
Borough of Yeovil Museum

# ARMOUR AND WEAPONS

Strength and pride, violence and skill: these are what weaponry proclaims. Its purpose is deadly, and its workmanship often as delicate as a goldsmith's or a lady embroiderer's. These are things upon which lives and freedom have depended, and collections of them have perhaps a greater vitality than anything else displayed to the public.

**Abbotsford House,** *Rox.*
**Abergavenny,** *Mon.*
Abergavenny and District
Museum
**Abingdon,** *Berks.*
County Hall (Borough Museum)
**Acton Round Hall,** *Shrops.*
**Barnstaple,** *Devon*
St Anne's Chapel Museum
**Birmingham,** *Warks.*
Museum of Science and Industry
**Blackburn,** *Lancs.*
Museum and Art Gallery
**Blair Castle,** *Perths.*
**Bodrhyddan Hall,** *Flints.*
**Bournemouth,** *Hants.*
Rothesay Museum
**Brecon,** *Brecon*
South Wales Borderers
Regimental Museum
**Brentwood,** *Essex*
Essex Regiment Museum
**Bridlington,** *Yorks.*
Bayle Museum
**Burnley,** *Lancs.*
East Lancashire Regimental
Museum
**Cambridge,** *Cambs.*
Fitzwilliam Museum
**Canterbury,** *Kent*
West Gate Museum
**Capesthorne,** *Cheshire*
**Chiddingstone Castle,** *Kent*
**Cotehele House,** *Cornwall*
**Delgatie Castle,** *A'deen.*
**Dorchester,** *Dorset*
Dorset Military Museum
**Dublin,** *Dublin*
Castle; Cathedral of St Patrick
**Eastnor Castle,** *Herefs.*

**East Riddlesden Hall,** *Yorks.*
**Edinburgh,** *M'loth.*
Castle; Scottish United Services
Museum
**Exeter,** *Devon*
**Fort George,** *I'ness.*
Regimental Museum of The
Seaforth Highlanders, The
Queen's Own Cameron
Highlanders and Queen's Own
Highlanders
**Hertford,** *Herts.*
Museum
**Inverary Castle,** *Argyll*
**Kedleston Hall,** *Derbys.*
**King's Lynn,** *Norfolk*
Queen Street and Saturday
Market
**Kingston upon Thames,** *Greater*
*London*
Queen's Royal Surrey Regiment
Museum
**Leatherhead,** *Surrey*
**Leeds,** *Yorks.*
Abbey House Museum
**Lincoln,** *Lincs.*
Stonebow and Guildhall
**Littlecote,** *Wilts.*
**London**
Armouries, Tower of
London; Imperial War
Museum
**Lullingstone Castle,** *Kent*
**Mendlesham,** *Suffolk*
Church of St Mary
**Monmouth,** *Mon.*
Nelson Museum
**Newcastle upon Tyne,** *Northld.*
Royal Northumberland Fusiliers
Regimental Museum

Newstead Abbey, *Notts.*
**Northampton,** *Northants.*
    Northamptonshire Regiment
    Museum
**Norwich,** *Norfolk*
    Royal Norfolk Regiment Museum
**Penshurst Place,** *Kent*
**Pontefract,** *Yorks.*
    King's Own Yorkshire Light
    Infantry Museum
**Poole,** *Dorset*
    Old Town House; Poole
    Museum
**Preston,** *Lancs.*
    Lancastrian Brigade Museum
**Ripley Castle,** *Yorks.*
**Rufford,** *Lancs.*
    Rufford Old Hall

**St Briavels Castle,** *Glos.*
**Sheffield,** *Yorks.*
    York and Lancaster Regimental
    Museum
**Snowshill Manor,** *Glos.*
**Southampton,** *Hants.*
    Tudor House
**Stirling,** *Stir.*
    Smith Art Gallery and Museum
**Waddesdon Manor,** *Bucks.*
**Warwick,** *Warks.*
    Castle
**Worcester,** *Worcs.*
    Assembly Room
**Yeovilton,** *Som.*
    Fleet Air Arm Museum
**York,** *Yorks.*
    Debtors' Prison

# CLOCKS AND WATCHES

Recording time has been one of man's keenest pursuits since he began
to question his place in the world, and this important activity has had
care lavished on it by artists as well as clockmakers. Among the time-
pieces displayed in Britain may be seen not only atomic clocks at
London's Science Museum, but also the jewelled masterpieces at the
Usher Art Gallery, Lincoln.

**Barnard Castle,** *Durham*
    Bowes Museum
**Basingstoke,** *Hants.*
    Willis Museum
**Bath,** *Som.* Victoria Art Gallery
**Bury St Edmunds,** *Suffolk*
    Angel Corner
**Christchurch,** *Hants.*
    Red House Museum and Art
    Gallery
**Colchester,** *Essex* Minories
**Dover,** *Kent*
    Corporation Museum
**Farnham,** *Surrey*
    Willmer House Museum

**Hampton Court,** *Greater London*
**Lincoln,** *Lincs.* Usher Art Gallery
**London**
    Science Museum; Victoria and
    Albert Museum; Wallace
    Collection
**Norwich,** *Norfolk*
    Bridewell Museum
**Oxford,** *Oxon.*
    Ashmolean Museum; Museum of
    the History of Science
**Rye,** *Sussex* Church of St Mary
**Shoreham-by-Sea,** *Sussex*
    Marlipins Museum
**Snowshill Manor,** *Glos.*

# COINS, MEDALS, TRADE TOKENS

Men have always lavished care and attention on the tokens of their
wealth and esteem. The coins and medals collected in Britain embody
2000 years of history. They provide a portrait gallery of monarchs
and a compendium of changing styles. They are also often objects of
beauty, examples of the designer's art as well as commemorations of
men and events. Trade tokens, social documents on a more mundane
level, are also included in these collections.

**Abingdon,** *Berks.*
    County Hall (Borough Museum)
**Barnstaple,** *Devon*
    St Anne's Chapel Museum

**Basingstoke,** *Hants.*
    Willis Museum
**Bath,** *Som.* Victoria Art Gallery
**Bedford,** *Beds.* Museum

**Birmingham,** *Warks.*
Assay Office
**Burford,** *Oxon.*
Tolsey Museum
**Cambridge,** *Cambs.*
Fitzwilliam Museum
**Canterbury,** *Kent*
Royal Museum (Beany Institute)
**Chester,** *Cheshire*
Grosvenor Museum
**Colchester,** *Essex*
Colchester and Essex Museum
**Gainsborough,** *Lincs.*
Old Hall
**Glasgow,** *Lanarks.*
Hunterian Museum
**London**
British Museum; Cuming
Museum; Wellcome Historical
Medical Museum and Library
**Lyme Regis,** *Dorset*
Philpot Museum

**Newark-on-Trent,** *Notts.*
Museum and Art Gallery
**Northampton,** *Northants.*
Central Museum and Art Gallery
**Norwich,** *Norfolk*
Strangers Hall
**Oxford,** *Oxon.* Ashmolean Museum
**Peterhead,** *A'deen.*
Arbuthnot Museum
**Poole,** *Dorset*
Museum
**Rufford,** *Lancs.*
Rufford Old Hall
**St Helier,** *Jersey*
Jersey Museum and Barreau
Gallery
**Swindon,** *Wilts.*
Museum and Art Gallery
**Tamworth,** *Staffs.*
Castle Museum
**Winchester,** *Hants.*
City Museum

# FOLK ART
# AND LOCAL HISTORY

The roots of art are in the country, not in the town. In collections all over Britain the ordinary art of the past can be seen: things made by men whose craftsmanship came from understanding the purpose of what they made, and whose decoration has the kind of freedom that an artist might spend years trying to achieve; the exhibits provide a quiet background to the high fashions and great art of urban life.

**Aberdeen,** *A'deen.*
Provost Skene's House
**Abergavenny,** *Mon.*
Abergavenny and District
Museum
**Aberstwyth,** *Card.*
University College, Aberystwyth
**Alton,** *Hants.* Curtis Museum
**Altrincham,** *Cheshire*
Art Gallery and Museum
**Arlington Mill,** *Glos.*
**Arreton,** *Isle of Wight, Hants.*
Arreton Manor
**Ashwell,** *Herts.*
Ashwell Village Museum
**Ayr,** *Ayrs.*
Carnegie Library, Museum and
Art Gallery
**Banbury,** *Oxon.*
Public Museum and Globe Room
**Barking,** *Greater London*
Valence House Museum
**Batley,** *Yorks.*
Bagshaw Museum
**Bedale,** *Yorks.*
Bedale Hall
**Bedford,** *Beds.*
Museum
**Beverley,** *Yorks.*
Art Gallery and Museum
**Bexhill,** *Sussex* Museum
**Birmingham,** *Warks.*
Blakesley Hall
**Blackburn,** *Lancs.*
Museum and Art Gallery
**Blaise Hamlet,** *Glos.*
Blaise Castle House

**Bournemouth,** *Hants.*
Rothesay Museum
**Bradford,** *Yorks.*
Bolling Hall; City Art Gallery
and Museum
**Bramber,** *Sussex*
St Mary's
**Bridgwater,** *Som.*
Admiral Blake Museum
**Bridlington,** *Yorks.*
Bayle Museum
**Bridport,** *Dorset*
Museum and Art Gallery
**Burton upon Trent,** *Staffs.*
Museum and Art Gallery
**Buxton,** *Derbys.*
Museum
**Camborne,** *Cornwall*
Public Library and Museum
**Chichester,** *Sussex*
City Museum
**Christchurch,** *Hants.*
Red House Museum and Art
Gallery
**Colchester,** *Essex*
Colchester and Essex Museum
**Cultra Manor,** *Down*
Ulster Folk Museum
**Derby,** *Derbys.*
Museum and Art Gallery
**Dorchester,** *Dorset*
Dorset County Museum
**East Looe,** *Cornwall*
Cornish Museum
**Ellisland Farm,** *Dumf.*
**Farnham,** *Surrey*
Willmer House Museum

**637**

**Filkins,** *Oxon*
  Filkins and Broughton Poggs
  Museum
**Forfar,** *Angus*
  Meffan Institute Museum
**Gainsborough,** *Lincs.* Old Hall
**Gawthorpe Hall,** *Lancs.*
**Glamis,** *Angus* Kirk Wynd
**Glenesk,** *Angus* Folk Museum
**Gloucester,** *Glos.*
  Folk Museum
**Godalming,** *Surrey*
  Borough Museum
**Great Yarmouth,** *Norfolk*
  Elizabethan Museum; Tolhouse
**Guildford,** *Surrey*
  Museum and Muniment Room
**Halifax,** *Yorks.* Shibden Hall
**Hall-I'-Th'-Wood,** *Lancs.*
**Haslemere,** *Surrey*
  Educational Museum
**Helston,** *Cornwall*
  Borough Museum
**Hereford,** *Herefs.*
  City Museum and Art Gallery
**High Wycombe,** *Bucks.*
  Museum and Exhibition Rooms
**Honiton,** *Devon*
  Honiton and Allhallows Public
  Museum
**Ilkley,** *Yorks.*
  Manor House Museum
**Inverurie,** *A'deen.* Museum
**Ipswich,** *Suffolk*
  Christchurch Mansion
**Kendal,** *Westmld.*
  Borough Museum
**La Hougue Bie,** *Jersey*
  Agricultural Museum; German
  Occupation Museum
**Leeds,** *York.*
  Abbey House Museum
**Leicester,** *Leics.*
  Newarke Houses Museum
**Lerwick,** *Shetland*
  Shetland County Museum
**Lewes,** *Sussex*
  Anne of Cleves House
**Lichfield,** *Staffs.*
  Art Gallery and Museum
**London**
  Cuming Museum; Museum of
  Leathercraft
**Lyme Regis,** *Dorset*
  Philpot Museum
**Macclesfield,** *Lancs.*
  Westpark Museum
**Manchester,** *Lancs.*
  Wythenshawe Hall, Northenden
**Merthyr Tydfil,** *Glam.*
  Art Gallery and Museum
**Monmouth,** *Mon.*
  Nelson Museum
**Munslow Aston,** *Shrops.*
  The White House
**Northampton,** *Northants.*
  Abington Park Museum
**North Berwick,** *E. Loth.*
  Burgh Museum
**Norwich,** *Norfolk*
  Castle; Strangers Hall

**Penzance,** *Cornwall*
  Natural History and Antiquarian
  Museum
**Peterhead,** *A'deen.*
  Arbuthnot Museum
**Poole,** *Dorset* Museum
**Portsmouth,** *Hants.* Southsea Castle
**Radcliffe,** *Lancs.*
  Local History Museum
**Reading,** *Berks.*
  Museum of English Rural Life
**Repton,** *Derbys.*
  Repton School Museum
**Rossendale,** *Lancs.*
  Rawtenstall Museum
**Rufford,** *Lancs.*
  Rufford Old Hall
**St Fagans Castle,** *Glam.*
**St Helier,** *Jersey*
  Jersey Museum and Barreau
  Gallery
**St Ives,** *Cornwall*
  Zennor Folk Museum; Norris
  Library and Museum
**Salisbury,** *Wilts.*
  Salisbury and South Wiltshire
  Museum
**Saltcoats,** *Ayrs.*
  North Ayrshire Museum
**Scarborough,** *Yorks.* Museum
**Shaftesbury,** *Dorset*
  Abbey Ruins Museum;
  Shaftesbury and District Historical
  Society's Museum of Local History
**Shoreham-by-Sea,** *Sussex*
  Marlipins Museum
**Sittingbourne,** *Kent*
  Court Hall Museum
**Southampton,** *Hants.*
  Bargate Guildhall
**Southend-on-Sea,** *Essex*
  Prittlewell Priory Museum
**South Molton,** *Devon*
  Borough Museum
**Stafford,** *Staffs.*
  Museum and Art Gallery
**Stevenage,** *Herts.* Museum
**Stockport,** *Cheshire*
  Municipal Museum
**Stranraer,** *Wig.*
  Wigtown County Museum
**Taunton,** *Som.*
  Somerset County Museum
**Tenby,** *Pemb.* Museum
**Thetford,** *Norfolk*
  Ancient House Museum
**Torquay,** *Devon*
  Torquay Natural History Society
  Museum
**Weston-super-Mare,** *Som.*
  Municipal Museum
**Weybridge,** *Surrey* Museum
**Windsor,** *Berks.*
  Windsor Guildhall Exhibition
**Woodstock,** *Oxon.*
  Oxford City and County
  Museum, Fletcher's House
**Wootton Bassett,** *Wilts.*
**Worksop,** *Notts.*
  Public Library and Museum
**York,** *Yorks.* Castle Museum

# GLASS

Twists of colour and air trapped in the clear material, engraved
patterns and scenes, the diamond sparkle of expert cutting: these are
some of the pleasures of glassware, and so are the fluid shapes of this
most fragile form of art, carefully protected in collections from
Aberdeen to Wookey in Somerset.

**Aberdeen,** *A'deen.* Art Gallery
**Aberystwyth,** *Card.*
  University College, Aberystwyth

**Alton,** *Hants.* Curtis Museum
**Arbury Hall,** *Warks.*
**Aynhoe Park,** *Northants.*

**Basing,** *Hants.*
  Basing House Ruins
**Bath,** *Som.*
  Holburne of Menstrie Museum;
  Victoria Art Gallery
**Bedford,** *Beds.*
  Cecil Higgins Art Gallery
**Berwick upon Tweed,** *Northld.*
  Museum and Art Gallery
**Brierley Hill,** *Worcs.*
  Museum
**Brighton,** *Sussex*
  Museum and Art Gallery
**Buckland Rectory,** *Glos.*
**Buxton,** *Derbys.* Museum
**Canterbury,** *Kent*
  Royal Museum (Beaney Institute)
**Chasleton House,** *Oxon.*
**Clevedon Court,** *Som.*
**Colchester,** *Essex*
  Colchester and Essex Museum
**Collacombe Manor,** *Devon*
**Dover,** *Kent*
  Corporation Museum
**Dublin,** *Dublin*
  Parnell Square
**Edinburgh,** *M'loth.*
  Huntly House
**Farnham,** *Surrey*
  Willmer House Museum
**Gilling Castle,** *Yorks.*
**Glasgow,** *Lanarks.*
  Provand's Lordship
**Gloucester,** *Glos.*
  City Museum and Art Gallery
**Great Yarmouth,** *Norfolk*
  Elizabethan Museum
**Guildford,** *Surrey* Cathedral
**Hereford,** *Herefs.*
  City Museum and Art Gallery

**Ipswich,** *Suffolk*
  Christchurch Mansion
**King's Lynn,** *Norfolk*
  Museum and Art Gallery
**London**
  Courtauld Institute Galleries;
  Wellcome Historical Medical
  Museum and Library
**Luton,** *Beds.*
  Museum and Art Gallery
**Maidenhead,** *Berks.*
  Henry Reitlinger Bequest
**Manchester,** *Lancs.*
  City Art Gallery
**Melton Mowbray,** *Leics.*
  Church of St Mary
**Monmouth,** *Mon.*
  Nelson Museum
**Montacute House,** *Som.*
**Norwich,** *Norfolk*
  Church of St Peter Hungate;
  St Peter Hungate Museum
**Nuneaton,** *Warks.*
  Museum and Art Gallery
**Royal Leamington Spa,** *Warks.*
  Art Gallery and Museum
**St Helens,** *Lancs.*
  Pilkington Museum of Glass
**Salisbury,** *Wilts.*
  Salisbury and South Wiltshire
  Museum
**Sandford Orcas Manor,** *Dorset*
**Southampton,** *Hants.* Tudor House
**South Shields,** *Durham* Museum
**Sudeley Castle,** *Glos.*
**Swansea,** *Glam.*
  Glynn Vivian Art Gallery
**Traquair House,** *Peebl.*
**Wookey,** *Som.*
  Wookey Hole Caves Museum

# GOLD, SILVER AND JEWELLERY

The men who work with precious stones and metals have special skills; they can afford no mistakes, and are the aristocrats of craftsmanship, whose services have always been only for the glory of the highest—God or the aristocracy. The fine collections now on view to the public in Britain—in stately homes, museums and palaces—make the pleasure of such things available to all.

**Abingdon,** *Berks.*
  County Hall (Borough Museum)
**Arlington Court,** *Devon*
**Aylesbury,** *Bucks.*
  Buckinghamshire County Museum
**Barnard Castle,** *Durham*
  Bowes Museum
**Barnstaple,** *Devon*
  Pentecost-Dodderidge Parlour
**Bath,** *Som.*
  Holburne of Menstrie Museum
**Berkeley Castle,** *Glos.*
**Berwick-upon-Tweed,** *Northld.*
  Museum and Art Gallery
**Birmingham,** *Warks.*
  Assay Office; City Museum and
  Art Gallery
**Bodmin,** *Cornwall*
**Brentwood,** *Essex*
  Essex Regiment Museum

**Bridlington,** *Yorks.*
  Bayle Museum
**Brighton,** *Sussex*
  Thomas-Stanford Museum
**Brodick Castle,** *Arran, Bute*
**Canterbury,** *Kent*
  Royal Museum (Beaney Institute);
  The Buffs Regimental Museum
**Capesthorne,** *Cheshire*
**Chacombe Priory,** *Oxon.*
**Colchester,** *Essex*
  Colchester and Essex Museum
**Dartford,** *Kent* Borough Museum
**Dover,** *Kent* Corporation Museum
**Drum Castle,** *A'deen.*
**Edinburgh,** *M'loth.*
  Castle; Regimental Museum of the
  Royal Scots
**Enfield,** *Greater London*
  Forty Hall

**Fort George,** *I'ness.*
Regimental Museum of The
Seaforth Highlanders, The Queen's
Own Cameron Highlanders and
Queen's Own Highlanders
**Glandford,** *Norfolk*
Museum of Shells
**Gloucester,** *Glos.*
City Museum and Art Gallery
**Greenock,** *Renf.*
McLean Museum and Art Gallery
**Grimsthorpe Castle,** *Lincs.*
**Harewood House,** *Yorks.*
**Haslemere,** *Surrey*
Educational Museum
**Heaton Hall,** *Lancs.*
**Hereford,** *Herefs.*
Churchill Gardens Museum
**Hodnet Hall,** *Shrops.*
**Ickworth,** *Suffolk*
**Ipswich,** *Suffolk* Museum
**Kedleston Hall,** *Derbys.*
**King's Lynn,** *Norfolk*
Guildhall of the Holy Trinity;
Queen Street and Saturday Market
**Leeds,** *Yorks.* City Art Gallery
**Lincoln,** *Lincs.*
Cathedral; Cathedral Treasury;
Stonebow and Guildhall; Usher
Art Gallery
**London**
British Museum; Courtauld
Institute Galleries; Geological
Museum; Mocatta Museum;
Royal Courts of Justice; Victoria
and Albert Museum; Wallace
Collection
**Luton Hoo,** *Beds.*
**Manchester,** *Lancs.*
City Art Gallery; Heaton Hall
**Merthyr Tydfil,** *Glam.*
Art Gallery and Museum

**Monmouth,** *Mon.*
Nelson Museum
**New Barnet,** *Greater London*
Abbey Art Centre and Museum
**Newstead Abbey,** *Notts.*
**Northampton,** *Northants.*
Northamptonshire Regiment
Museum
**Norwich,** *Norfolk*
St Peter Hungate Museum
**Nuneaton,** *Warks.*
Museum and Art Gallery
**Ormside,** *Westmld.*
Church of St James
**Oxford,** *Oxon.*
Ashmolean Museum
**Plymouth,** *Devon*
City Museum and Art Gallery
**Pontefract,** *Yorks.* Castle Museum
**Port Sunlight,** *Cheshire*
Lady Lever Art Gallery
**Richmond,** *Yorks.*
Green Howards Museum
**Rotherham,** *Yorks.*
Municipal Museum and Art
Gallery
**Sandford Orcas Manor,** *Dorset*
**Sheffield,** *Yorks.*
**South Molton,** *Devon*
Borough Museum
**Stranraer,** *Wig.*
Wigtown County Museum
**Tatton Park,** *Cheshire*
**Temple Newsam House,** *Yorks.*
**Tewes,** *Essex*
**Traquair House,** *Peebl.*
**Weston Park,** *Staffs.*
**Winchester,** *Hants.*
Royal Hampshire Regimental
Museum
**Woburn Abbey,** *Beds.*
**York,** *Yorks.* Mansion House

# INDUSTRY, MACHINERY
# AND TRANSPORT

The machine age began in Britain, and nowhere else are there finer
collections of the machines and vehicles that changed world history
than here. But there is more than historic appeal in the gleaming brass
and steel of these old machines; often they have a dramatic, almost
sculptural quality—as if their makers had had an intuition of the
changes they were about to make in the world.

**Arlington Mill,** *Glos.*
**Ashwell,** *Herts.*
Ashwell Village Museum
**Basingstoke,** *Hants.*
Willis Museum
**Batley,** *Yorks.* Bagshaw Museum
**Beaulieu,** *Hants.*
Beaulieu Abbey and Beaulieu
Palace House; Montagu Motor
Museum
**Bedford,** *Beds.* Museum
**Birmingham,** *Warks.*
Museum of Science and Industry
**Blithfield Hall,** *Staffs.*
**Bradford,** *Yorks.*
City Art Gallery and Museum
**Bradford-on-Avon,** *Wilts.*

**Bridgwater,** *Som.*
Admiral Blake Museum
**Bridlington,** *Yorks.*
Bayle Museum
**Brighton,** *Sussex* Motor Museum
**Burford,** *Oxon.* Tolsey Museum
**Bury St Edmunds,** *Suffolk*
Moyses Hall Museum
**Caister Castle,** *Norfolk*
**Capesthorne,** *Cheshire*
**Castleward House,** *Down*
**Crich,** *Derbys.*
Crich Tramway Museum
**Cromford Old Mill,** *Derbys.*
**Cultra Manor,** *Down*
Ulster Folk Museum
**Dartford,** *Kent* Borough Museum

**Dartmouth,** *Devon*
Borough Museum
**Derby,** *Derbys.*
Museum and Art Gallery
**Dudley,** *Worcs.* Central Museum
**East Looe,** *Cornwall*
Cornish Museum
**Eccles,** *Lancs.*
Monks Hall Museum
**Glamis,** *Angus*
Kirk Wynd (Angus Folk Museum)
**Glasgow,** *Lanarks.*
Hunterian Museum; Museum of
Transport (Eglinton Toll)
**Grantham,** *Lincs.*
Library and Museum
**Greenock,** *Renf.*
McLean Museum and Art Gallery
**Guildford,** *Surrey*
Museum and Muniment Room
**Haslemere,** *Surrey*
Educational Museum
**High Wycombe,** *Bucks.*
Museum and Exhibition Rooms
**Iron-bridge,** *Shrops.*
**Kingston upon Hull,** *Yorks.*
**Kirkcaldy,** *Fife*
Museum and Art Gallery
**La Hougue Bie,** *Jersey*
Agricultural Museum
**Lacock,** *Wilts.*
Lackham School of Agriculture:
Agricultural Museum
**Leeds,** *Yorks.*
City Museum
**Leicester,** *Leics.*
Belgrave Hall
**London**
Industrial Health and Safety
Centre; Museum of Leathercraft;
Royal Mews, Buckingham Palace;
Science Museum
**Lyme Regis,** *Dorset*
Philpot Museum
**Maidstone,** *Kent*
Archbishop's or Old Palace
**Michelham Priory,** *Sussex*
**Newcastle upon Tyne,** *Northld.*
Department of Mining
Engineering, The University
**Norwich,** *Norfolk*
Bridewell Museum; Strangers
Hall
**Nostell Priory,** *Yorks.*

**Old Warden Aerodrome,** *Beds.*
Shuttleworth Collection
**Penrhyn Castle,** *Caern.*
**Peterhead,** *A'deen.*
Arbuthnot Museum
**Reading,** *Berks.*
Museum of English Rural Life
**Rossendale,** *Lancs.*
Rawtenstall Museum
**St Fagans Castle,** *Glam.*
**St Ives,** *Cornwall*
Zennor Folk Museum
**Salford,** *Lancs.*
Science Museum
**Saltcoats,** *Ayrs.*
North Ayrshire Museum
**Shaftesbury,** *Dorset*
Shaftesbury and District Historical
Society's Museum of Local History
**Sheffield,** *Yorks.*
Abbeydale Industrial Hamlet;
Shepherd Wheel
**Snowshill Manor,** *Glos.*
**Southampton,** *Hants.*
Wool House
**South Molton,** *Devon*
Borough Museum
**Southwold,** *Suffolk*
Museum
**Stafford,** *Staffs.*
Museum and Art Gallery
**Stanford Hall,** *Leics.*
**Stockport,** *Cheshire*
Municipal Museum
**Stretham,** *Cambs.*
**Swindon,** *Wilts.*
Great Western Railway Museum
**Taunton,** *Som.*
Somerset County Museum
**Tilbury,** *Essex*
Thurrock Local History Museum
**Towyn,** *Merioneth*
Narrow-Gauge Railway Museum
**Truro,** *Cornwall*
County Museum and Art Gallery
**Walsall,** *Staffs.*
E. M. Flint Art Gallery;
Lock Museum, Willenhall
**Woodstock,** *Oxon.*
Oxford City and County Museum,
Fletcher's House
**Wootton Bassett,** *Wilts.*
**Yeovil,** *Som.*
Borough of Yeovil Museum

# LITERARY AND ARCHIVES

These collections take one into the private and public worlds of the men who have helped to make English the most widely spoken language in the world—its poets, novelists and dramatists. They live on many levels, perhaps struggling with a sonnet and the taxman at the same time, and their manuscripts and belongings, seen together, convey a fascinating impression of their ideas and life: sometimes complementary to each other, sometimes at variance. Throughout the British Isles, carefully preserved archives and charters are fascinating evidence of history in the making.

**Abingdon,** *Berks.*
County Hall (Borough Museum)
**Abbotsford House,** *Rox.*
**Alloway,** *Ayrs.* Burns Cottage

**Altrincham,** *Cheshire*
Art Gallery and Museum
**Barnstaple,** *Devon*
St Anne's Chapel Museum

**Beaulieu,** *Hants.*
  Montagu Motor Museum
**Bedford,** *Beds.*
**Bembridge,** *Isle of Wight, Hants.*
  Ruskin Galleries
**Birmingham,** *Warks.*
  Assay Office; Museum of Science
  and Industry
**Blackburn,** *Lancs.*
  Museum and Art Gallery
**Broughton Castle,** *Oxon.*
**Burford,** *Oxon.*
  Tolsey Museum
**Bury St Edmunds,** *Suffolk*
  Moyses Hall Museum
**Cambridge,** *Cambs.*
  Fitzwilliam Museum; Trinity
  College Library; University
  Library
**Chatsworth,** *Derbys.*
**Chawton,** *Hants.*
  Jane Austen's Home
**Coate,** *Wilts.*
  Richard Jefferies Museum
**Cockermouth,** *Cumb.*
**Dorchester,** *Dorset*
  Dorset County Museum
**Dublin,** *Dublin* City Hall;
  Northland House (Royal Irish
  Academy); Trinity College
**Dumfries,** *Dumf.*
  Observatory (Burgh Museum)
**Dunvegan,** *Isle of Skye, I'ness.*
**East Looe,** *Cornwall*
  Cornish Museum
**Ecclefechan,** *Dumf.*
  Carlyle's House
**Edinburgh,** *M'loth.*
  Lady Stair's House; National
  Library of Scotland; Scottish
  United Services Museum
**Elmore Court,** *Glos.*
**Elton Hall,** *Hunts.*
**Eye Manor,** *Herefs.*
**Glasgow,** *Lanarks.*
  Hunterian Museum
**Gort,** *Gal.*
**Guildford,** *Surrey*
  Museum and Muniment Room
**Hartlebury Castle,** *Worcs.*
**Hatfield House,** *Herts.*
**Haworth,** *Yorks.*
  Brontë Parsonage Museum
**Holkham Hall,** *Norfolk*
**Ingatestone,** *Essex*
  Ingatestone Hall
**Ixworth Abbey,** *Suffolk*
**Kilkenny,** *Kilk.*
**Kirkcaldy,** *Fife*
  Museum and Art Gallery
**Knebworth House,** *Herts.*
**Leeds,** *Yorks.* Thoresby Society

**Lincoln,** *Lincs.*
  Cathedral; Cathedral Treasury;
  Stonebow and Guildhall; Usher
  Art Gallery
**Liverpool,** *Lancs.* Hornby Library
**London**
  British Museum; British Theatre
  Museum; Carlyle's House;
  Cuming Museum; Dickens
  House; Guildhall; Johnson's
  House; Keats House; Lambeth
  Palace; Lincoln's Inn; Passmore
  Edwards Museum; Percival David
  Foundation of Chinese Art;
  Pharmaceutical Society's Museum;
  Public Record Office; Royal
  College of Music; Royal
  Geographical Society; Wellcome
  Historical Medical Museum and
  Library
**Lyme Regis,** *Dorset*
  Philpot Museum
**Maidstone,** *Kent*
  Chillington Manor
**Meigle,** *Perths.* Museum
**Mellerstain,** *Ber.*
**Monmouth,** *Mon.* Nelson Museum
**Montrose,** *Angus*
**Moseley Old Hall,** *Staffs.*
**Newstead Abbey,** *Notts.*
**Norwich,** *Norfolk*
  St Peter Hungate Museum
**Nuneaton,** *Warks.*
  Museum and Art Gallery
**Ragley Hall,** *Warks.*
**Rudding Park,** *Yorks.*
**Rufford,** *Lancs.*
  Rufford Old Hall and Folk
  Museum
**Selborne,** *Hants.*
  Gilbert White Museum and the
  Oates Memorial Museum
**Shaftesbury,** *Dorset*
  Shaftesbury and District Historical
  Society's Museum of Local History
**South Molton,** *Devon*
  Borough Museum
**Southsea,** *Hants.*
  Royal Marines Museum
**Tamworth,** *Staffs.*
  Castle Museum
**Thrumpton Hall,** *Notts.*
**Uxbridge,** *Greater London*
  Hamson Museum
**Walsall,** *Staffs.*
  E. M. Flint Art Gallery
**Winchester,** *Hants.*
  Cathedral; City Museum
**Wisbech,** *Cambs.*
**Wrexham,** *Denb.*
  Exhibition Hall and Wrexham
  Room (Public Library)

# MARITIME

Since Alfred the Great built a fleet of ships to defend Britain from Danish attack in the 9th century, Britain's security has rested largely on the skill and courage of her seamen. Her museums are rich in the romance and excitement of the sea: relics of great sailors can be seen, and great ships like the *Victory* at Portsmouth; finally the instruments of navigation on which life at sea depends convey their own excitement, even on dry land.

**Arlington Court,** *Devon*
**Birkenhead,** *Cheshire*
  Williamson Art Gallery and
  Museum
**Bournemouth**, *Hants.*
  Rothesay Museum
**Bridgwater,** *Som.*
  Admiral Blake Museum
**Bridlington,** *Yorks.*
  Bayle Museum

**Bridport,** *Dorset*
  Museum and Art Gallery
**Bucklers Hard,** *Hants.*
  Maritime Museum
**Claverton Manor,** *Som.*
  The American Museum in Britain
**Colchester,** *Essex*
  Colchester and Essex Museum
**Dartmouth,** *Devon*
  Borough Museum

**Dorchester,** *Dorset*
**Great Yarmouth,** *Norfolk*
  Maritime Museum for East Anglia
**Greenock,** *Renf.*
  McLean Museum and Art Gallery
**Greenwich,** *Greater London*
  National Maritime Museum
**Grimsby,** *Lincs.*
  Doughty Museum
**Ipswich,** *Suffolk*
  Christchurch Mansion
**Kingston upon Hull,** *Yorks.*
**Lerwick,** *Shetland*
  Shetland County Museum
**London**
  Science Museum
**Middlesbrough,** *Yorks.*
  Dorman Memorial Museum and
  Municipal Art Gallery
**Monmouth,** *Mon.*
  Nelson Museum
**Norwich,** *Norfolk*
  Bridewell Museum
**Peterhead,** *A'deen.*
  Arbuthnot Museum

**Poole,** *Dorset*
  Old Town House; Poole Museum
**Portsmouth,** *Hants.*
  Southsea Castle; Victory Museum
**St Ives,** *Cornwall*
  Zennor Folk Museum
**Saltcoats,** *Ayrs.*
  North Ayrshire Museum
**Shoreham-by-Sea,** *Sussex*
  Marlipins Museum
**Southampton,** *Hants.*
  Tudor House; Wool House
**Southend-on-Sea,** *Essex*
  Beecroft Art Gallery
**South Shields,** *Durham*
  Museum
**Sunderland,** *Durham*
  Museum and Art Gallery
**Tresco,** *Isles of Scilly*
  Valhalla Maritime Museum
**Truro,** *Cornwall*
  County Museum and Art
  Gallery
**Worthing,** *Sussex*
  Museum and Art Gallery

# MILITARY AND UNIFORMS

The regimental museums throughout Britain chronicle not only the
changing techniques of war—red jackets to commando camouflage,
sieges to ejector seats—but also its human aspect: the letters, documents
and medal citations displayed all tell the private story of wartime's
grief, heroism, action and fear.

**Abingdon,** *Berks.*
  County Hall (Borough Museum)
**Aldershot,** *Hants.*
  Airborne Forces Museum; Queen
  Alexandra's Royal Army Nursing
  Corps Museum; Royal Army
  Dental Corps Museum; Royal
  Army Medical Corps Historical
  Museum
**Arborfield,** *Berks.*
  Museum of the Corps of Royal
  Electrical and Mechanical
  Engineers
**Blair Castle,** *Perths.*
**Blithfield,** *Staffs.*
  Museum of Childhood and
  Costume
**Brecon,** *Brecon*
  South Wales Borderers Regimental
  Museum
**Brede Place,** *Sussex*
**Brentwood,** *Essex*
  Essex Regiment Museum
**Bridgwater,** *Som.*
  Admiral Blake Museum
**Burnley,** *Lancs.*
  East Lancashire Regimental
  Museum, Townley Hall
**Bury,** *Lancs.*
  Lancashire Regiment Museum
**Bury St Edmunds,** *Suffolk*
  Suffolk Regiment Museum
**Camberley,** *Surrey*
  Royal Army Ordnance Corps
  Museum
**Canterbury,** *Kent*
  The Buffs Regimental Museum

**Cardiff,** *Glam.*
  Welch Regiment Regimental
  Museum
**Carlisle,** *Cumb.*
  Border Regiment Museum; Castle
**Cefntilla Court,** *Mon.*
**Chatham,** *Kent*
  Museum of the Corps of Royal
  Engineers
**Chester,** *Cheshire*
  Castle; Cheshire Regiment
  Museum
**Chichester,** *Sussex*
  City Museum; Corps of Royal
  Military Police Museum
**Cothay Manor,** *Som.*
**Devizes,** *Wilts.*
  Wiltshire Regimental Museum
**Dorchester,** *Dorset*
  Dorset Military Museum
**Dublin,** *Dublin*
  Cathedral of St Patrick
**Dunrobin Castle,** *Suth.*
**Edinburgh,** *M'loth.*
  Regimental Museum of the Royal
  Scots; Scottish United Services
  Museum
**Exeter,** *Devon*
  Devonshire Regiment Museum
**Fort George,** *I'ness.*
  Regimental Museum of The
  Seaforth Highlanders, The Queen's
  Own Cameron Highlanders
  and Queen's Own Highlanders
**Gloucester,** *Glos.*
  Folk Museum and Regimental
  Museum

**Greenock,** *Renf.*
McLean Museum and Art Gallery
**Greenwich,** *Greater London*
National Maritime Museum
**Guildford,** *Surrey*
Women's Royal Army Corps
Museum
**Hereford,** *Herefs.*
City Museum and Art Gallery
**Hertford,** *Herts.* Museum
**Honiton,** *Devon*
Honiton and Allhallows Public
Museum
**Ipswich,** *Suffolk* Museum
**Kingston upon Thames,** *Greater
London*
Queen's Royal Surrey Regiment
Museum
**La Hougue Bie,** *Jersey*
German Occupation Museum
**Lancaster,** *Lancs.*
Lancaster City Museum
**Leicester,** *Leics.*
Newarke Houses Museum
**Lichfield,** *Staffs.*
Staffordshire Regimental Museum
**London**
Imperial War Museum; Museum
of Leathercraft; Royal Courts of
Justice
**Long Marston Manor,** *Yorks.*
**Manchester,** *Lancs.*
Queen's Park Art Gallery
**Monmouth,** *Mon.*
Nelson Museum

**Newcastle upon Tyne,** *Northld.*
Royal Northumberland Fusiliers
Regimental Museum
**Northampton,** *Northants.*
Northamptonshire Regiment
Museum
**Norwich,** *Norfolk*
Royal Norfolk Regiment Museum
**Old Warden Aerodrome,** *Beds.*
Shuttleworth Collection
**Pontefract,** *Yorks.*
King's Own Yorkshire Light
Infantry Museum
**Portsmouth,** *Hants.*
Southsea Castle; Victory Museum
**Preston,** *Lancs.*
Lancastrian Brigade Museum
**Richmond,** *Yorks.*
Green Howards Museum
**Sheffield,** *Yorks.*
York and Lancaster Regimental
Museum
**Southsea,** *Hants.*
Royal Marines Museum
**Warwick,** *Warks.*
Lord Leycester Hospital and
Chapel of St James
**Wilton House,** *Wilts.*
**Winchester,** *Hants.*
Royal Green Jackets Museum;
Royal Hampshire Regimental
Museum
**Yeovilton,** *Som.*
Fleet Air Arm Museum
**York,** *Yorks.* Debtors' Prison

# NATURAL HISTORY

The greatest craftsman and artist of all is Nature, the ultimate source
of inspiration. At London's Natural History Museum one can stand
beneath the great whale, dwarfed by an amazing ocean-going creature,
and only a few steps away marvel at the intricate delicacy of a hum-
mingbird's feathers or a sea shell's spiralling precision; but whatever
the size of the collection—one of the largest in the world or a small
village museum—Nature's astonishing virtuosity never fails: the
exhibits are always of the highest quality.

**Abingdon,** *Berks.*
County Hall (Borough Museum)
**Alton,** *Hants.*
Curtis Museum
**Batley,** *Yorks.*
Bagshaw Museum
**Bedford,** *Beds.* Museum
**Bexhill,** *Sussex* Museum
**Birchington,** *Kent*
Powell-Cotton Museum
**Birmingham,** *Warks.*
Cannon Hill; City Museum and
Art Gallery; Geology Depart-
mental Museum, University
**Bournemouth,** *Hants.*
Rothesay Museum
**Bradford,** *Yorks.*
City Art Gallery and Museum
**Bramber,** *Sussex*
Potter's Museum
**Bridport,** *Dorset*
Museum and Art Gallery
**Brighton,** *Sussex*
Museum and Art Gallery
**Burton upon Trent,** *Staffs.*
Museum and Art Gallery
**Buxton,** *Derbys.*
Museum
**Camborne,** *Cornwall*
Public Library and Museum
**Canterbury,** *Kent*
Royal Museum (Beaney Institute)
**Christchurch,** *Hants.*
Red House Museum and Art
Gallery

**Colne,** *Lancs.*
Museum
**Dartford,** *Kent*
Borough Museum
**Derby,** *Derbys.*
Museum and Art Gallery
**Dorchester,** *Dorset*
Dorset County Museum
**Dover,** *Kent*
Corporation Museum
**Downe,** *Kent*
Down House
**Dudley,** *Worcs.*
Central Museum
**Dumfries,** *Dumf.*
Observatory (Burgh Museum)
**Dunrobin Castle,** *Suth.*
**Erith,** *Greater London*
Museum
**Forfar,** *Angus.*
Meffan Institute Museum
**Glandford,** *Norfolk*
Museum of Shells
**Glasgow,** *Lanarks.*
Hunterian Museum
**Gloucester,** *Glos.*
City Museum and Art Gallery
**Godalming,** *Surrey*
Charterhouse School Museum
**Greenock,** *Renf.*
McLean Museum and Art Gallery
**Greenwich,** *Greater London*
Borough Museum
**Haslemere,** *Surrey*
Educational Museum

**Hereford,** *Herefs.*
City Museum and Art Gallery
**Hertford,** *Herts.*
Museum
**Hodnet Hall,** *Shrops.*
**Honiton,** *Devon*
Honiton and Allhallows Public
Museum
**Inverurie,** *A'deen.* Museum
**Ipswich,** *Suffolk* Museum
**Kendal,** *Westmld.*
Borough Museum
**Kew,** *Greater London*
Royal Botanic Gardens Museums
of Economic Botany
**King's Lynn,** *Norfolk*
Museum and Art Gallery
**Kirkcaldy,** *Fife*
Museum and Art Gallery
**Leeds,** *Yorks.*
City Museum
**Lincoln,** *Lincs.*
City and County Museum
**Liverpool,** *Lancs.*
City Museum
**London**
Broomfield House Museum;
Geological Museum; Horniman
Museum; Passmore Edwards
Museum; Queen Elizabeth's
Hunting Lodge
**Ludlow,** *Shrops.*
Museum
**Macclesfield,** *Lancs.*
Westpark Museum
**Mansfield,** *Notts.*
Museum and Art Gallery
**Merthyr Tydfil,** *Glam.*
Art Gallery and Museum
**Middlesbrough,** *Yorks.*
Dorman Memorial Museum and
Municipal Art Gallery
**Millport,** *Isle of Cumbrae*
Robertson Museum and the
Aquarium
**Newbury,** *Berks.*
Borough Museum
**Newcastle upon Tyne,** *Northld.*
Hancock Museum
**North Berwick,** *E. Loth.*
Burgh Museum
**Oxford,** *Oxon.*
Museum of the History of Science
**Peterborough,** *Hunts.*
Museum and Maxwell Art Gallery
**Plymouth,** *Devon*
City Museum and Art Gallery
**Port Erin,** *Isle of Man*
Marine Biological Station

**Portsmouth,** *Hants.*
Cumberland House Museum and
Art Gallery
**Reading,** *Berks.*
Cole Museum; Museum and Art
Gallery
**Rossendale,** *Lancs.*
Rawtenstall Museum
**Royal Tunbridge Wells,** *Kent*
**St Helier,** *Jersey*
Jersey Museum and Barreau
Gallery
**Salford,** *Lancs.*
Science Museum
**Sandown,** *Isle of Wight, Hants.*
Isle of Wight Museum of Geology
**Scarborough,** *Yorks.*
Museum of Natural History
**Selborne,** *Hants.*
Gilbert White Museum and Oates
Memorial Museum
**Sheffield,** *Yorks.*
City Museum
**Silchester,** *Hants.*
Calleva Museum
**Skipton,** *Yorks.* Craven Museum
**Southend-on-Sea,** *Essex*
Prittlewell Priory Museum
**South Shields,** *Durham*
Museum
**Southwold,** *Suffolk*
Museum
**Spalding,** *Lincs.*
Ayscoughfee Hall
**Stalybridge,** *Cheshire*
Astley Cheetham Art Gallery
**Stevenage,** *Herts.* Museum
**Stirling,** *Stir.*
Smith Art Gallery and Museum
**Stockport,** *Cheshire*
Municipal Museum
**Sunderland,** *Durham*
Museum and Art Gallery
**Swindon,** *Wilts.*
Museum and Art Gallery
**Taunton,** *Som.*
Somerset County Museum
**Tenby,** *Pemb.*
Museum
**Thetford,** *Norfolk*
Ancient House Museum
**Torquay,** *Devon*
Torquay Natural History Society
Museum
**Wollaton,** *Notts.*
Wollaton Hall Natural History
Museum
**Worksop,** *Notts.*
Public Library and Museum

# POTTERY

Since prehistoric man first watched rain collect in clay hollows, and learnt to make vessels out of this special kind of earth (perhaps some of it accidentally baked in his fire), clay has fascinated him, and he has put it to innumerable uses, as varied as the Greek amphorae in the British Museum and the Staffordshire figures of Victoria and Napoleon at Stapleford Park in Leicestershire.

**Aberdeen,** *A'deen.*
University Anthropological
Museum
**Aberystwyth,** *Card.*
University College, Aberystwyth
**Abingdon,** *Berks.*
County Hall (Borough Museum)
**Alton,** *Hants.*
Curtis Museum
**Antony House,** *Cornwall*
**Arbury Hall,** *Warks.*
**Ascott,** *Bucks.*
**Ashwell,** *Herts.*
Ashwell Village Museum

**Avebury,** *Wilts.*
Avebury Manor
**Aylesford,** *Kent*
**Barlaston,** *Staffs.*
Wedgwood Museum Trust
**Barnard Castle,** *Durham*
Bowes Museum
**Barnstaple,** *Devon*
St Anne's Chapel Museum
**Basing,** *Hants.* Basing House Ruins
**Bath,** *Som.*
Holburne of Menstrie Museum;
Victoria Art Gallery
**Batley,** *Yorks.* Bagshaw Museum

**Bedford,** *Beds.*
Cecil Higgins Art Gallery
**Berwick upon Tweed,** *Northld.*
Museum and Art Gallery
**Birkenhead,** *Cheshire*
Williamson Art Gallery and
Museum
**Birmingham,** *Warks.*
Aston Hall; City Museum and
Art Gallery
**Blair Castle,** *Perths.*
**Blenheim Palace,** *Oxon.*
**Bodrhyddan Hall,** *Flints.*
**Bootle,** *Lancs.*
Art Gallery and Museum
**Bournemouth,** *Hants.*
Rothesay Museum; Russell-Cotes
Museum and Art Gallery
**Bradford,** *Yorks.*
City Art Gallery and Museum
**Brighton,** *Sussex*
Museum and Art Gallery;
Thomas-Stanford Museum
**Bristol,** *Glos.* Church of St Mark
**Brodick Castle,** *Arran, Bute*
**Broughton Castle,** *Oxon.*
**Browsholme Hall,** *Lancs.*
**Burton Agnes Hall,** *Yorks.*
**Buxton,** *Derbys.* Museum
**Cambridge,** *Cambs.*
Fitzwilliam Museum
**Canterbury,** *Kent*
Royal Museum (Beaney Institute)
**Capesthorne,** *Cheshire*
**Cefntilla Court,** *Mon.*
**Chichester,** *Sussex*
City Museum
**Chorley,** *Lancs.* Astley Hall
**Clevedon Court,** *Som.*
**Colchester,** *Essex*
Colchester and Essex Museum;
Minories
**Derby,** *Derbys.*
Museum and Art Gallery
**Doddington Hall,** *Lincs.*
**Dover,** *Kent* Corporation Museum
**Durham,** *Durham*
Gulbenkian Museum of Oriental
Art
**Eccles,** *Lancs.* Monks Hall Museum
**Enfield,** *Greater London* Forty Hall
**Firle Place,** *Sussex*
**Gainsborough,** *Lincs.* Old Hall
**Garthewin,** *Denb.*
**Glandford,** *Norfolk*
Museum of Shells
**Gloucester,** *Glos.*
City Museum and Art Gallery
**Godalming,** *Surrey*
Charterhouse School Museum
**Godington Park,** *Kent*
**Goodwood House,** *Sussex*
**Great Yarmouth,** *Norfolk*
Elizabethan Museum
**Grimsby,** *Lincs.* Doughty Museum
**Guildford,** *Surrey*
Museum and Muniment Room
**Harewood House,** *Yorks.*
**Hereford,** *Herefs.*
City Museum and Art Gallery
**Hill Top,** *Lancs.*
**Ilkley,** *Yorks.*
Manor House Museum and Art
Gallery
**Ingatestone,** *Essex*
Ingatestone Hall
**Ipswich,** *Suffolk*
Christchurch Mansion
**King's Lynn,** *Norfolk*
Museum and Art Gallery
**Kirkcaldy,** *Fife.*
Museum and Art Gallery
**Leeds,** *Yorks.*
City Art Gallery
**Leicester,** *Leics.*
Museum and Art Gallery

**Lincoln,** *Lincs.*
Usher Art Gallery
**London**
British Museum; Courtauld
Institute Galleries; Fenton House;
Guildhall Museum; Mocatta
Museum; Passmore Edwards
Museum; Percival David
Foundation of Chinese Art; Royal
Courts of Justice; Southall District
Library; Victoria and Albert
Museum; Wallace Collection;
Wellcome Historical Medical
Museum and Library
**Luton,** *Beds.*
Museum and Art Gallery
**Luton Hoo,** *Beds.*
**Maidenhead,** *Berks.*
Henry Reitlinger Bequest
**Manchester,** *Lancs.*
City Art Gallery; Wythenshawe
Hall, Northenden
**Melford Hall,** *Suffolk*
**Merthyr Tydfil,** *Glam.*
Art Gallery and Museum
**Monmouth,** *Mon.*
Nelson Museum
**New Barnet,** *Greater London*
Abbey Art Centre and Museum
**Newport,** *Mon.*
Museum and Art Gallery
**Northampton,** *Northants.*
Abington Park Museum; Central
Museum and Art Gallery
**North Berwick,** *E. Loth.*
Burgh Museum
**Norwich,** *Norfolk*
St Peter Hungate Museum
**Nottingham,** *Notts.*
Castle Museum; City Museum
and Art Gallery
**Nuneaton,** *Warks.*
Museum and Art Gallery
**Penrhyn Castle,** *Caern.*
**Peterborough,** *Hunts.*
Museum and Maxwell Art Gallery
**Plymouth,** *Devon*
City Museum and Art Gallery
**Pontefract,** *Yorks.*
Castle Museum
**Poole,** *Dorset*
Old Town House; Poole Museum
**Port Sunlight,** *Cheshire*
Lady Lever Art Gallery
**Ragley Hall,** *Warks.*
**Reading,** *Berks.*
Museum and Art Gallery;
Museum of Greek
Archaeology
**Rossendale,** *Lancs.*
Rawtenstall Museum
**Rotherham,** *Yorks.*
Municipal Museum and Art
Gallery
**Royal Leamington Spa,** *Warks.*
Art Gallery and Museum
**Royal Tunbridge Wells,** *Kent*
**Rudding Park,** *Yorks.*
**Rufford,** *Lancs.*
Rufford Old Hall and Folk
Museum
**St Ives,** *Hunts.*
Norris Library and Museum
**St Osyth's Priory,** *Essex*
**Salisbury,** *Wilts.*
Salisbury and South Wiltshire
Museum
**Saltram House,** *Devon*
**Sandford Orcas Manor,** *Dorset*
**Scarborough,** *Yorks.*
Museum
**Scone Palace,** *Perths.*
**Seaton Delaval Hall,** *Northld.*
**Sledmere House,** *Yorks.*
**Southampton,** *Hants.*
God's House Tower

**Southport,** *Lancs.*
  Botanic Garden Museum
**Stapleford Park,** *Leics.*
**Stockport,** *Cheshire*
  Municipal Museum
**Stoke-on-Trent,** *Staffs.*
  City Museum and Art Gallery
**Sunderland,** *Durham*
  Museum and Art Gallery
**Swansea,** *Glam.*
  Glynn Vivian Art Gallery
**Tarvit House,** *Fife.*
**Tatton Park,** *Cheshire*
**Taunton,** *Som.*
  Somerset County Museum
**Temple Newsam House,** *Yorks.*

**Tewes,** *Essex*
**Truro,** *Cornwall*
  County Museum and Art Gallery
**Upton House,** *Warks.*
**Waddesdon Manor,** *Bucks.*
**Wallington House,** *Northld.*
**Wookey,** *Som.*
  Wookey Hole Caves Museum
**Worcester,** *Worcs.*
  Dyson Perrins Museum
**Worksop,** *Notts.*
  Public Library and Museum
**Worthing,** *Sussex*
  Museum and Art Gallery
**York,** *Yorks.*
  City of York Art Gallery

# SCIENTIFIC AND MEDICAL

Man's struggle for knowledge and against disease and pain has been with him as long as life itself; these collections record its triumphs, superstitions and failures, its heroes and heroines.

**Aldershot,** *Hants.*
  Queen Alexandra's Royal Army
  Nursing Corps Museum; Royal
  Army Dental Corps Museum;
  Royal Army Medical Corps
  Historical Museum
**Birmingham,** *Warks.*
  Museum of Science and Industry
**Brighton,** *Sussex*
  Museum and Art Gallery
**Cambridge,** *Cambs.*
  Scott Polar Research Institute;
  Whipple Museum of the History
  of Science
**Downe,** *Kent* Down House
**Eccles,** *Lancs.* Monks Hall Museum
**Edinburgh,** *M'loth.*
  Royal College of Surgeons of
  Edinburgh

**Helston,** *Cornwall*
  Borough Museum
**London**
  Geological Museum; Health
  Exhibition Centre, Royal Society
  of Health; Pharmaceutical
  Society's Museum; Royal College
  of Surgeons' Museum; Royal
  Geographical Society; Royal
  Hospital; Science Museum;
  Wellcome Historical Medical
  Museum and Library
**Ludlow,** *Shrops.*
  Museum
**Oxford,** *Oxon.*
  Museum of the History of Science;
  University Museum
**Snowshill Manor,** *Glos.*
**York,** *Yorks.*

# TEXTILES AND CLOTHING

Perhaps the most personal of the arts, textiles have been used since the earliest days of man's civilisation to protect himself—from the elements, and from cold stone floors or bare walls—and to distinguish one man from another: priest from king, peasant from lord. Mary, Queen of Scots embroidered to pass away the time of her imprisonment, and the well brought up Victorian lady sewed as an accepted element of her social accomplishment.

**Aberdeen,** *A'deen.*
  Art Gallery
**Abergavenny,** *Mon.*
  Abergavenny and District
  Museum
**Abingdon,** *Berks.*
  County Hall (Borough
  Museum)
**Acrise Place,** *Kent*
**Antony House,** *Cornwall*
**Barnard Castle,** *Durham*
  Bowes Museum

**Barnet,** *Greater London*
  Museum
**Basingstoke,** *Hants.*
  Willis Museum
**Bath,** *Som.*
  Museum of Costume
**Bedford,** *Beds.*
  Cecil Higgins Art Gallery
**Belton,** *Kesteven, Lincs.*
  Belton House
**Belvoir Castle,** *Leics.*
**Berkeley Castle,** *Glos.*

**Birmingham,** *Warks.*
  Aston Hall; City Museum and
  Art Gallery
**Blackburn,** *Lancs.*
  Museum and Art Gallery
**Blair Castle,** *Perths.*
**Blenheim Palace,** *Oxon.*
**Blickling Hall,** *Norfolk*
**Blithfield,** *Staffs.*
  Museum of Childhood and
  Costume
**Blithfield Hall,** *Staffs.*
**Boughton Monchelsea Place,** *Kent*
**Bradford,** *Yorks.*
  Bolling Hall
**Bramall Hall,** *Cheshire*
**Breamore,** *Hants.*
  Breamore House
**Brighton,** *Sussex*
  Thomas-Stanford Museum
**Browsholme Hall,** *Lancs.*
**Bucklers Hard,** *Hants.*
  Maritime Museum
**Burghley House,** *Hunts.*
**Cambridge,** *Cambs.*
  Fitzwilliam Museum
**Castle Ashby,** *Northants.*
**Castle Howard,** *Yorks.*
**Chasleton House,** *Oxon.*
**Chirk Castle,** *Denb.*
**Chorley,** *Lancs.* Astley Hall
**Christchurch,** *Hants.*
  Red House Museum and Art
  Gallery
**Clandon Park,** *Surrey*
**Colchester,** *Essex*
  Colchester and Essex Museum
**Cotehele House,** *Cornwall*
**Cullen,** *Banffs.* Cullen House
**Cultra Manor,** *Down*
  Ulster Folk Museum
**Denham Place,** *Bucks.*
**Doddington Hall,** *Lincs.*
**Dover,** *Kent*
  Corporation Museum
**Dublin,** *Dublin*
  City Hall; Old Parliament House
**Dunrobin Castle,** *Suth.*
**Dunster,** *Som.* Castle
**Durham,** *Durham*
  Gulbenkian Museum of Oriental
  Art
**Dyrham Park,** *Glos.*
**Eastnor Castle,** *Herefs.*
**Edinburgh,** *M'loth.*
  Palace of Holyroodhouse
**Elmore Court,** *Glos.*
**Exeter,** *Devon*
  Royal Albert Memorial Museum
  and Art Gallery
**Eye Manor,** *Herefs.*
**Farnham,** *Surrey*
  Willmer House Museum
**Forde Abbey,** *Som.*
**Gainsborough,** *Lincs.*
  Old Hall
**Gawthorpe Hall,** *Lancs.*
**Glasgow,** *Lanarks.*
  Provand's Lordship
**Gloucester,** *Glos.*
  City Museum and Art Gallery
**Glynde Place,** *Sussex*
**Grimsthorpe Castle,** *Lincs.*
**Guildford,** *Surrey*
  Cathedral
**Hale Park,** *Hants.*
**Ham House,** *Greater London*
**Hardwick Hall,** *Derbys.*
**Hereford,** *Herefs.*
  Churchill Gardens Museum
**Hinwick House,** *Northants.*
**Inveraray Castle,** *Argyll*
**Ipswich,** *Suffolk*
  Christchurch Mansion
**Kilbarchan,** *Renf.*
  Weaver's Cottage

**King's Lynn,** *Norfolk*
  Museum and Art Gallery
**Knole,** *Kent*
**La Hougue Bie,** *Jersey*
  German Occupation Museum
**Leeds,** *Yorks.*
  Abbey House Museum
**Leek,** *Staffs.* Art Gallery
**Lerwick,** *Shetland*
  Shetland County Museum
**Littlecote,** *Wilts.*
**London**
  British Theatre Museum;
  Guildhall Museum; London
  Museum; Museum of
  Leathercraft; Victoria and Albert
  Museum
**Loseley House,** *Surrey*
**Luton,** *Beds.*
  Museum and Art Gallery
**Luton Hoo,** *Beds.*
**Lyme Park,** *Cheshire*
**Manchester,** *Lancs.*
  Gallery of English Costume;
  Platt Hall, Rusholme; Whitworth
  Art Gallery
**Michelham Priory,** *Sussex*
**Newbury,** *Berks.*
  Borough Museum
**Newcastle upon Tyne,** *Northld.*
  Laing Art Gallery
**Northampton,** *Northants.*
  Abington Park Museum; Central
  Museum and Art Gallery
**North Berwick,** *E. Loth.*
  Burgh Museum
**Norwich,** *Norfolk*
  Bridewell Museum; St Peter
  Hungate Museum; Strangers Hall
**Nottingham,** *Notts.*
  Castle Museum; City Museum
  and Art Gallery
**Osterley Park House,** *Greater London*
**Oxford,** *Oxon.*
  Ashmolean Museum
**Packwood House,** *Warks.*
**Royal Tunbridge Wells,** *Kent*
**Rudding Park,** *Yorks.*
**Rufford,** *Lancs.*
  Rufford Old Hall and Folk
  Museum
**Sandford Orcas Manor,** *Dorset*
**Sawston Hall,** *Cambs.*
**Shaftesbury,** *Dorset*
  Shaftesbury and District
  Historical Society's Museum of
  Local History
**Somerleyton Hall,** *Suffolk*
**Southampton,** *Hants.*
  Tudor House
**Stanford Hall,** *Leics.*
**Stapleford Park,** *Leics.*
**Stranraer,** *Wig.*
  Wigtown County Museum
**Stratford-upon-Avon,** *Warks.*
  Royal Shakespeare Theatre
  Picture Gallery
**Sudeley Castle,** *Glos.*
**Tarvit House,** *Fife.*
**Traquair House,** *Peebl.*
**Upton House,** *Warks.*
**Waterford,** *Waterford*
**Welshpool,** *Mont.*
  Powis Castle
**Weybridge,** *Surrey* Museum
**Westerham,** *Kent*
  Squerryes Court
**Weston Park,** *Staffs.*
**West Wycombe,** *Bucks.*
  West Wycombe Park
**Worthing,** *Sussex*
  Museum and Art Gallery
**Yeovil,** *Som.*
  Borough of Yeovil Museum
**York,** *Yorks.* Debtors' Prison

# IOOO YEARS OF DESIGN

## *Details of architecture and decoration are the key to recognising period style*

Each period makes certain decorative elements its own. Gothic craftsmen used the pointed arch not only to vault their cathedral roofs, but to decorate their furniture. The Elizabethans covered walls, ceilings, silverware and furniture with strapwork ornament, and from the scholarship of the Georgian period evolved windows, chairs and staircases of Classical perfection. Victorian romantics harked back to the Middle Ages and to Greece and Rome to produce railway stations like cathedrals and town halls like temples. The details of architecture and decoration shown here enable the evolution of styles (described inside the continuity flaps) to be traced from Saxon times to the outbreak of the First World War, and the commentary at the top of each spread describes some of the historic events that helped to shape the appearance of things in Britain.

In this chronological style chart, subjects are grouped into horizontal bands across the pages, with continuity flaps linking the sequences from page to page. Under the flaps and across the heads of the pages background notes keep pace with the developments illustrated.

### ANGLO-SAXON

| | |
|---|---|
| EARLY SAXON KINGS | 978–1042 |
| EDWARD THE CONFESSOR | 1042–1066 |
| HAROLD II | 1066 |

Most buildings were of wood and few have survived. The stone-built churches are more interesting for their decoration than their form.

### NORMAN (ROMANESQUE)

| | |
|---|---|
| WILLIAM THE CONQUEROR | 1066–1087 |
| WILLIAM II | 1087–1100 |
| HENRY I | 1100–1135 |
| STEPHEN | 1135–1154 |
| HENRY II | 1154–1189 |

Characteristics of the style are round arches, barrel vaults, walls decorated with interlacing arches and arcades, highly decorated doorways, and an abundance of mouldings.

### EARLY ENGLISH

| | |
|---|---|
| RICHARD I | 1189–1199 |
| JOHN | 1199–1216 |
| HENRY III | 1216–1272 |
| EDWARD I | 1272–1307 |

Squat, bulky structures gave way to lighter, taller buildings.

### DECORATED

| | |
|---|---|
| EDWARD II | 1307–1327 |

Early English innovations were improved, resulting in larger windows, tracery work, and a superabundance of decorative features covering surfaces, gables and arches.

### PERPENDICULAR

| | |
|---|---|
| EDWARD III | 1327–1377 |
| RICHARD II | 1377–1399 |
| HENRY IV | 1399–1413 |
| HENRY V | 1413–1422 |
| HENRY VI | 1422–1461 |
| EDWARD IV | 1461–1483 |
| EDWARD V | 1483 |
| RICHARD III | 1483–1485 |
| HENRY VII | 1485–1509 |

A return to comparative simplicity. Buttresses were now deeper, allowing even larger windows, tracery was at its most elegant, the four-centred arch appeared, and fan-vaulting reached perfection.

### TUDOR

| | |
|---|---|
| HENRY VIII | 1509–1547 |
| EDWARD VI | 1547–1553 |
| MARY I | 1553–1558 |

The slow transition from Gothic to Renaissance. Large houses were built, many of them in the new building material—brick.

### ELIZABETHAN

| | |
|---|---|
| ELIZABETH I | 1558–1603 |

The growth of a new aristocracy and the wider distribution of wealth led to a vast increase in domestic building. The Renaissance brought a revival of Classical features. In the larger houses and palaces (often of a symmetrical E or H shape), galleries, grand staircases and carved chimneys appeared. Brick became the fashionable building material.

### JACOBEAN

| | |
|---|---|
| JAMES I (VI OF SCOTLAND) | 1603–1625 |

The period from 1603 to 1625 was marked by mannered, lively ornament and profusely decorated open surfaces. The great houses showed even greater symmetry and Inigo Jones began to build in the Palladian style, derived from the work of the Italian architect Andrea Palladio.

### STUART

| | |
|---|---|
| CHARLES I | 1625–1649 |
| COMMONWEALTH | 1649–1660 |
| CHARLES II | 1660–1685 |
| JAMES II | 1685–1688 |

The acceptance of Classical architecture was not complete until the time of Wren (1652–1723). Columns, cornices, pediments, architraved windows, and elegant proportions are characteristics of the period.

### QUEEN ANNE

| | |
|---|---|
| WILLIAM III AND MARY II | 1689–1702 |
| ANNE | 1702–1714 |

The age of the English baroque school, which tempered pure baroque's florid ornamentation and over-emphasis of detail with the Classical.

### GEORGIAN AND REGENCY

| | |
|---|---|
| GEORGE I | 1714–1727 |
| GEORGE II | 1727–1760 |
| GEORGE III | 1760–1820 |
| GEORGE IV | 1820–1830 |

The Georgian era brought a return to the beauty of form and proportion. For the middle classes terraced houses were built. Towards the end of the period Regency decoration emerged.

### VICTORIAN

| | |
|---|---|
| WILLIAM IV | 1830–1837 |
| VICTORIA | 1837–1901 |

The new rich class built to impress—and architects designed in styles ranging from pseudo-Egyptian to Elizabethan, but particularly Gothic Revival and Greek Revival. Mass schemes of squalid, insanitary houses were erected for the working classes. Steel and concrete, products of the Industrial Revolution, were largely ignored by architects, but exploited by engineers.

### EDWARDIAN

| | |
|---|---|
| EDWARD VII | 1901–1910 |

The trend in architecture from 1911 to 1914 was largely a continuation of the Victorian style. The art nouveau movement influenced decoration.

# THE MIDDLE AGES 1000-1300

## THE MARKS OF FASHION

The Norman Conquest removes England from Scandinavian influences and ties her politically, commercially and culturally to France and the Continent.

Norman castles overawe the people. The pointed arch, able to support stone roofs over more ambitious ground plans, is introduced. The Crusaders bring home

Arabic numerals, medicines, astronomy, arithmetic, the clock and a taste for luxuries. Heraldry becomes important as a 'badge of rank' in feudal society as w

### DOORS AND WINDOWS:

arches, porches, arcades and entrances

10th-century Saxon window, Worth Church, Sussex. Saxon windows are narrow, with thick baluster shafts

Saxon doorway, Brixworth Church, Northamptonshire

Norman doorway, Kilpeck, Herefordshire, c. 1140

Norman porch and staircase, Canterbury Cathedral

### DETAILS OF BUILDINGS:

vaults, ceilings, roofs, buttresses, columns, capitals, gargoyles

Carved Norman capital from the crypt, Canterbury Cathedral

Norman arcaded chapel, Tower of London

Carved doorway jamb, Kilpeck Church, Herefordshire

Decorated Norman capital, Leominster Priory, Herefordshire

Norman column chevron-incised Durham Cathe

### TOWERS, BRIDGES, STAIRS:

domes, spires, parapets, balustrades

Saxon tower, Sompting Church, Sussex, with unusual 'German Helm' roof. Saxon towers are narrow and simple in form and detail, with small windows

CHRIST IN MAJESTY—ELY CATHEDRAL. c. 1100

Church authority was the most constant factor in the Middle Ages, of which this awesome figure, symmetrical and deeply carved, is typical

Norman tower, Tewkesbury Abbey, Glos.

### FIRE-PLACES AND CHIMNEYS

stoves, fire-irons, kitchens

Central brick hearth with iron fire-dogs, Penshurst Place, Kent

Wall fire-place, Rochester Castle, Kent, c. 1130. An advance on the centre hea

### FURNITURE AND DOMESTIC ARTICLES:

beds, tables, chairs, clocks, bowls, mirrors, candlesticks

St Augustine's Chair, Canterbury Cathedral. Marble, probably 13th century. Archbishops of Canterbury have been enthroned in this chair for over 700 years

Saxon bucket with bronze bands, the top band decorated in relief; and a Saxon glass tumbler with spiral ornament

13th-century carved oak chests. One is a strongbox, with wrought iron clasps; the other a storage chest, pierced with holes for ventilation

### MEMORIALS, MONUMENTS AND MEMENTOES:

plaques, sculpture, tombs, ornaments

Saxon cross, 8th century. The interlaced carved motifs are also found in manuscripts of the period. Some crosses are carved with animal or human figures

Norman font, Eardisley Church, Herefordshire. The carving shows soldiers with spear and sword

Details from the edges of the Bayeux Tapestry, showing the stylised treatment of strange animals and plants

Norman tor in the Lady Cha Exeter Cathed It may represent Leof an early bishop of Exe The bishop's right han raised in bless

**[650]**

as in battle. Churches have reliquaries made for relics brought from abroad; pilgrimages and shrines become popular. English scholars returning from Paris and Bologna found the universities of Oxford and Cambridge. Edward I subjugates Wales and builds its great border castles. Merchant classes begin to emerge.

# SERMONS IN STONE

...ate tracery: rose window, ...incoln Cathedral, c. 1220. ...ew-style Gothic decoration

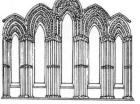

Multiple lancet window, Hereford Cathedral, 1220. Pointed, ornamented arches

West front portal, Salisbury Cathedral, 1234-58

Norman columns and vaulting, Canterbury Cathedral crypt

Multiple columns, foliated capitals

13th-century foliated capital from Lincoln Cathedral

Fortified gateway: Micklegate Bar, York

Shuttered window, Little Wenham Hall, Suffolk

Stone vault, Durham Cathedral

Fire-place with stone hood, c. 1200. The hood gives an improved draught

External stone castle staircase, 13th-century

Newel staircase, Dover Castle

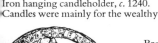

Iron hanging candleholder, c. 1240. Candles were mainly for the wealthy

Carved oak chair, for the head of the household

The Gloucester candlestick, made c. 1100 of bronze or bell-metal. The whole surface is ornamented with figures of men and monsters. Victoria and Albert Museum.

...he Great Seal of Henry II ...154-89). On it the ...ng is called 'Lord of ...ormandy and Aquitaine'

Bronze sanctuary door knocker from Durham Cathedral. Anyone who grasped the knocker was under the Church's protection

Early medieval dog-tooth ornament

**[651]**

**Solidity in stone.** Existing remains are from churches, cathedrals, abbeys and castles, which were built of stone. Houses and shops of less durable materials—wood, thatch and wattle—have vanished. Saxon windows are characterised by the thick baluster shaft dividing the two lights, set into rectangular blocks above and below.

The Normans brought with them from Normandy skilled masons and Caen stone. Their buildings are solid, with massive walls into whose thickness are constructed bedchambers and staircases. The semicircular arched openings of the deeply set doorways and windows are carved with chevron, billet and plant designs. By the late 12th century walls had become thinner, mouldings were rarely decorated, and the pointed arch replaced the round one. Lancet windows and simple tracery in the window head are typical.

**Columns and roofs.** The roofs of larger buildings are supported on columns or piers, with capitals, consisting of wider blocks of stone, set between support and arch. Norman capitals may be plain, or carved with beasts, devils, monsters, human figures or plaitwork. Columns are thick, and often incised in chevron (zigzag) or diamond patterns. Early medieval capitals are lighter and are often grouped above numerous shafts to form a multiple pier; and leaf decoration becomes more usual.

Roofs are generally of timber, open to the rafters, and based on collar and tie-beam construction. Some large churches from the 11th century have stone vaults in round or pointed arches with heavy, moulded ribs. As windows became larger in the early medieval period, buttresses were added to transfer the outward thrust of the roof to the ground.

**Towers and steeples.** Churches are the only surviving Saxon buildings, and usually only part of such churches remains—the tower, or a window or doorway. Saxon towers are characterised by slenderness and simplicity of form and detail. A group have strip decoration in stone.

Norman towers are low and solid. They originally had stumpy spires—simple, four-sided structures, which were later removed or rebuilt. The tower sides are decorated by arcading, panelling and narrow window slits. Early medieval towers are often capped by a spire of broach design, in which the awkward junction between square tower and octagonal spire is bridged by side pieces extending up the spire sides.

Towns were fortified by encircling walls, with entrance gateways at intervals, and were often dominated by castles as strongpoints.

**Stairs and fire-places.** Newel stairs of wood or stone were common in castles and churches of this date. They have a central post, with steps radiating spirally around it. They were suitable because they were narrow and easily built (not, as is often stated, because they were easily defensible), and took up little space in the wall thickness or the special turret in which they were constructed. There were also exterior steps, from floor to floor and, inside, ladders but no well.

Heating was provided by burning logs. One type of hearth was of brick or stone set in the middle of the floor. The logs were supported on iron fire-dogs, and the smoke escaped (when the wind was in the right direction) through a slatted opening (louvre) in the roof above. Other fire-places are of stone, with a round arch or hood above. Smoke escaped through a passage in the walls.

**Rare furniture.** Furniture was scanty, and items were costly and greatly prized. The decoration was simple, carved in animal, geometric and plant forms, sometimes with pierced holes. Indigenous woods were used, chiefly oak, to make chests, benches, tables, chairs and beds.

Chests and cupboards, made in solid panels, carved and pierced, were designed to hold linen, clothes, silver, pottery and food. Most benches and tables were of trestle, collapsible type, because dining was carried out in the hall which was also used for work and leisure purposes. There were few chairs; usually only the head of a large household had one. Bedsteads were simple, mainly wooden frames with an embroidered wool wall-hanging behind.

Lighting was by candles for the wealthy, or home-made rushlights in ordinary homes.

**Religious motifs.** Religion was the dominant theme of all decoration, from capitals and mouldings to silverware and pottery. One of the important surfaces to receive this vigorous, deeply cut carving was the tympanum—the solid wall panel beneath an arch. Such tympana frequently showed a religious subject, like the Day of Judgment.

In capitals, columns, fonts, doorways and window arches, motifs varied, but predominant were monsters, devils, animals and humans possessed by evil spirits, carved with great vigour and freedom of expression. In the 13th century these gave way to plain mouldings and beautifully carved leaf and plant forms. Norman mouldings were richly carved, chiefly with chevron ornament. Early medieval work is more restrained. Typical is the four-leafed dog-tooth ornament.

The Black Death kills possibly more than a third of the population in the mid-14th century. The resulting labour shortage inflates wages and accelerates the break-up of feudalism, which tied a labourer to his lord's land. The Wars of the Roses, costly in money as well as in blood, exhaust the old warlike aristocracy and strengthen the position of merchant class. Standards of comfort r the demand for privacy leads to Courtyard House replacing the H

The Judgment Portal, Lincoln Cathedral, 14th cent.

Decorated Gothic tracery, Exeter Cathedral, 14th cent.

South porch, Gloucester Cathedral, 1420

Perpendicular tracery, York Minster

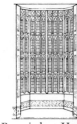

Rose window in curvilinear tracery, Lincoln Cathedral, 1325

Bay window, Horha Hall, Essex, 1510

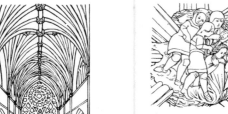

Sexpartite vault, Exeter Cathedral, 14th century

The Becket boss, depicting the murder of Becket, from Exeter vault

Carved capital from York Minster, c. 1310

Buttress waterspout, Thaxted Church, Essex

Nave vault, St. George's Chapel, Windsor Castle

Fortified gate-house, Hurstmonceux Castle, Sussex, c. 1440. Defence was still important

External domestic staircase found in cities. Superseded by the internal staircase

The Rokewode Mazer (drinking bowl), maplewood mounted in silver gilt, late 14th century. In front is the Pusey Horn, a Saxon relic mounted in silver gilt, early 15th century

## MISERICORD AT WORCESTER CATHEDRAL

As the 15th century replaced the 14th, decoration grew less severe and natural forms became popular motifs. A new light-heartedness produced such church carvings as this misericord, and an increasingly secular attitude is revealed in the use of heraldry as a decorative device

Tower, York Minster, 1432–74

Medieval bridge, wi sharp cutwaters. Sor bridges were fortifie

Abbot's kitchen, Glastonbury Abbey

Chimney-stac Oxburgh Hal Norfolk

Oak cradle, 15th century. Some cradles have curved rockers in place of a flat stand

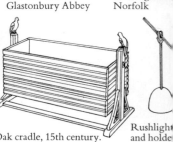

Rushligh and holde Used in th poorer ho

The Ramsey Abbey Censer, silver gilt, 1325–50. It imitates contemporary stone tracery, down to the smallest details

'Architectural' tomb of Bishop Bronescombe, Exeter Cathedral

The donor, stained glass, Merton Coll. Chapel, Oxford, c. 1300

Effigy of the Black Prince (1330–76) in Canterbury Cathedral, showing the new realism in Gothic sculpture

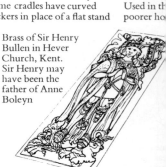

Brass of Sir Henry Bullen in Hever Church, Kent. Sir Henry may have been the father of Anne Boleyn

*House. Caxton introduces printing. In this age of humanism Renaissance scholarship flourishes. Holbein paints in Court. The Reformation removes educa-*

*tion from church control; grammar schools founded by Edward VII. The Dissolution of the monasteries and the sale of monastic lands endows a new ruling class*

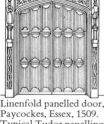

Linenfold panelled door, Paycockes, Essex, 1509. Typical Tudor panelling

Carved base of an oriel window, Hengrave Hall, Suffolk, 1538

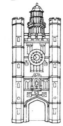

Gateway, Trinity Coll., Cambridge

Flying buttress, Henry VII Chapel, Westminster Abbey.

Complex fan vault, Bath Abbey, 1501–39

Hammerbeam roof, Rufford Old Hall, Lancashire, 1463–1505

Parapet, Lavenham Church, Suffolk, 15th century. Lavenham is one of the finest of the East Anglian wool churches

Fortified gate-house, Oxburgh Hall, Norfolk

Carving above the gate of St John's College, Cambridge

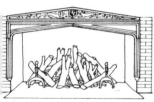

Domestic brick fire-place, c. 1505. Fire-places followed stylistic trends of the period, and reflected the greater attention paid to comfort

Baking ovens in the Tudor kitchen, Hampton Court Palace. The palace was begun by Cardinal Wolsey in 1515

Linenfold panelled armchair

The so-called 'Prince Arthur's cupboard', c. 1500

Elaborately decorated silver candle snuffers, 1547. Lighting was little changed from earlier times

Silver flask, 1546. Strapwork decoration

One of the King's Beast finials at Hampton Court

The Market Cross, Chichester, Sussex, 15th century

**[653]**

The royal Arms of Henry VIII in stained glass at Cowick Priory, Devon, c. 1540

Tudor linenfold panelling

## Three periods of Gothic.

The three periods covered by these 250 years are commonly known as Decorated, Perpendicular and Tudor Gothic, and their individual features can be seen in everything from architecture to furniture and ceramics.

Decorated work is of 14th-century date. Its chief feature is the equilateral pointed arch used above doorways, windows and arcades, and also used decoratively on tombs and furniture.

In window design tracery developed rapidly. The stonework was cut into geometric and curved shapes, cusped and moulded.

From c. 1375 Perpendicular Gothic took over. In it the vertical line is predominant—noticeable in window tracery and door panels.

By 1500 the last phase, Tudor Gothic, emerged, with its flat four-centred arches, and panelling which extended over all surfaces.

## Roof complexity.

In the 14th century capitals were naturalistic, most often in plant form. Perpendicular capitals returned to plain, moulded designs. The 14th-century timber roof was of king-post and tie-beam type; but in 1394 came the hammerbeam design at Westminster Hall. Here a horizontal beam carries the vertical hammer-post. Hammerbeam roofs were constructed well into the 16th century.

The stone vault is equally well represented, especially in cathedrals. The 14th-century vaults are ribbed designs, with radiating spokes terminating in bosses. Then emerged the lierne designs, with multiple tie ribs. The fan vault marked the final phase. These elegant, traceried vaults demanded ever-increasing abutment, and the sculptured finials of flying buttresses are their beautiful counterparts.

## Age of fortification.

The scope of military architecture was extended. The old idea of a strongpoint focussed on a central keep was abandoned in favour of curtain walling, with two or even three concentric rings of walls. These curtain walls were studded at regular intervals by defensive towers, and within the walls was space for a whole garrison or town with its livestock and provender. Castles, palaces, houses all had

fortified entrances, and many of these gate-houses remain. Bridges have multiple pointed arches and deep buttresses; most were also fortified and had chapels.

A number of architectural features received great attention and magnificent craftsmanship. One such feature is the tower or steeple. Perpendicular Gothic towers are very beautiful, with their soaring spires, traceried windows and decorative parapets.

## The chimney arrives.

Interior staircases, offering warmth and convenience, were becoming more usual, not only in churches, castles and large houses, but in smaller dwellings as well. Methods of heating, also, were slow to change, but the central hearth was disappearing, and fire-place designs were more varied, the arch following stylistic trends.

The Tudor fire-place illustrated is four-centred—that is, constructed

from four geometrical centres on two different curves, a flat one in the middle and a sharply angled one at the corners. The louvre in the roof above a central hearth gave place to decorative brick or stone chimneys by the later 15th century.

Inside the abbot's kitchen at Glastonbury Abbey the medieval ovens can still be seen; outside, the kitchen displays the architectural features of the Decorated period.

## Carved decoration.

There was still a minimum of furniture, even in large homes. Most furniture was made in carved oak, sometimes painted or gilded.

Carved decoration followed stylistic patterns, showing Decorated or Perpendicular cusped design, with vine and rose ornament interspersed with animal or figure decoration. Chests, carved or ornamented by ironwork in bands and scrolls, acted

as receptacles for clothes and linen and were also used for seating. Food cupboards (aumbries) differed from linen and plate cupboards only in that the Gothic decoration was pierced for ventilation.

The few chairs that existed were of box pattern, carved in Perpendicular Gothic design, with panels and cusps. A drawer in the box was used for storage. Lighting methods were unaltered.

## Decorated motifs.

Market crosses and impressive tombs, such as that of Bishop Bronescombe in Exeter Cathedral, present in architectural miniature the essential motifs of the Decorated period. The effigy of the Black Prince depicts the costume of the time—tight-fitting cotehardie with dagged edges, and metal plaque belt, worn low and patterned in heraldic motifs.

Misericord seat carvings illustrate

the vivid interpretation in carved wood of a sometimes ironic and realistic attitude to Christian sayings. Equally, the silver flask shows the beginnings of Elizabethan strapwork so soon to dominate Tudor design, while the Hampton Court King's Beast displays the proud lion of Henry VIII as a finial.

Also typical of this time is the linenfold oak panelling (so called because it represents folded strips of linen).

# ELIZABETHAN, JACOBEAN & EARLY STUART 1550-1630

The Elizabethan Age, more settled than the preceding years of dynastic and religious conflict, sees a dazzling expansion of trade. The merchant adventurers bring exotic items from Muscovy, the East and the New World—among them coconuts, ostrich eggs and tobacco. Private wealth increases; the nobility build palaces; the rich travel and collect pictures. Under the Stuarts some of England's finest glass and silverware is produced. The Union between England

Elizabethan window bay, Levens Hall, Westmorland. Strapwork ceiling

Carved wood door and doorcase, Levens Hall

Painted glass, Gilling Castle, Yorks., 1585

Entrance doorway, Hatfield, Herts., 1607-12

Oriel window c. 1610

Entrance porch, Audley End, Essex, c. 1610

Grotesque caryatid support in carved wood. Typical support for door lintels or mantelpieces

Elizabethan plaster frieze, Levens Hall, Westmorland

Plaster ceiling motif, 1599, reflecting maritime expansion

Strapwork ceiling London, 1599

### DETAIL OF BED HEAD BOARD, RUFFORD OLD HALL, LANCS:

Elizabethan half-timbering, Little Moreton Hall, Cheshire. The carved corner posts, window frames and gables are especially fine

President's Gallery, Queens' Coll., Cambridge

Plaster ornamental figure c. 1600. Interiors were full of such imagery, often copied from the Low Countries

Foreign lands, maritime adventure, exotic fruits and fabulous beasts begin to appear in ornament as new trade routes opened up and travellers' tales and discoveries filtered back to Europe. Often these elements appear amid a confusion of 'Classical' decoration, as builders and craftsmen used renaissance motifs on medieval structures, creating the strange but exuberant forms of Jacobean and Elizabethan work

Elizabethan dog-legged oak staircase. Built without a well

Elizabethan two-tiered chimney-piece, with figures

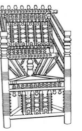
Jacobean carved oak newel post, Hatfield House, Hertfordshire, echoing Continental Renaissance work

Jacobean carved oak chest. Typical are the twisted guilloche carving, and the legs lifting the chest well off the floor

Jacobean carved oak bedstead, with curtains to keep out the draught

Turned chair, early 17th cent.

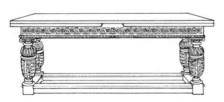
Elizabethan carved oak table. The construction is massive, with carving along the sides and stretchers to rest the feet. Bulbous legs reflect contemporary clothes

Goffering iron, for setting starched ruffs

Carved Jacobean pulpit, c. 1615.

Kneeling family effigies, from Culross, Fife. Such effigies accurately portray the costume of the age

Silver salt cellar, 1594

**[654]**

Carved wooden corbel, Queens' College, Cambridge

Cartouche ornamented with fantastic figures and strapwork from a map of the period

and Scotland is commemorated by the Union Jack. Charles I is a patron of painting and architecture; Van Dyck and Rubens paint at Court; Inigo Jones builds the Queen's House, Greenwich (1615) in the Roman manner. He visited Italy and brought back Palladio's 'Four Books of Architecture'— an influence for 200 years.

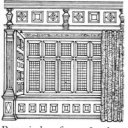

Bay window from a Jacobean drawing room, c. 1615-20

York Water Gate; London. Built as the river entrance to York House, in the Strand, c. 1626.

Debased Ionic columns, Cobham Hall, Kent

Ceiling with pendant bosses, Gilling Castle, Yorks.

Carved Jacobean wood panel, showing Bacchic musicians

Gate of Honour, Gonville and Caius Coll., Cambridge, 1573-8. Built by Dr John Caius, who had studied Renaissance building in Italy

Canongate Tolbooth, Edinburgh, 1592. Built of stone, like many Scottish buildings. A tolbooth was originally the place where taxes were collected

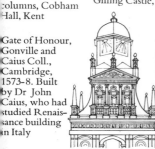

Half-timber entrance, Speke Hall, Lancs.

Jacobean staircase, Knole, Kent

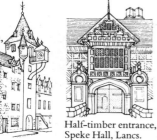

Decoration of the upper stage of a chimney-piece, 1623

Elizabethan kitchen fire-place, with weight-driven spit-jack

Jacobean cast-iron fire-dog

Jacobean oak court cupboard. Carved with mythological beasts

Child's high chair, c. 1625. Carved and turned oak, inlaid with holly and bog oak

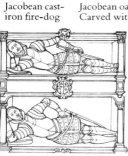

Recumbent family effigies, Swinbrook, Oxfordshire

**[655]**

Silver ewer, with all-over decoration, 1583

Detail from a silver salt of 1586

## Houses the main theme.

With the decline in ecclesiastical fortunes few churches were built, but houses of all sizes, from the mansions of the nobles to the half-timber or brick homes of the rising middle class, sprang up all over the country.

The most important exterior feature is the entrance porch, called a frontispiece. It has up to three stages, with columns to each storey and a wealth of carved stone decoration— strapwork (interlaced strap and panel designs), grotesque figures, fruit and flowers. Interior doors are beautifully panelled and carved, and have surrounding cases with columns and figures.

Windows became much larger; they are of casement type (opening on hinges), and often had coloured glass decoration. Bay and oriel windows are carved on the outside and have plasterwork ceilings inside.

## Ceilings and friezes.

Though a few open timber roofs were still constructed, the typical ceiling of this time is flat or coved, and made of plaster, or plaster panels between wood beams. Most examples are richly patterned all over in one of three methods: strapwork, ribbed, and pendant. The first two of these are similar, in that the whole ceiling is designed in panels of varying shapes; but one type is divided by wide decorated strap bands, and the other by moulded ribs. Pendant ceilings have ribs, which form downward-pointing clusters at regular intervals.

Friezes are also of plaster and richly ornamented. The plaster-work is white, and was originally painted and gilded on the enrichment—flowers and fruit, with vine and pomegranate predominating, heraldic features, human figures, animals, birds, pictorial scenes and grotesque figures.

## Craftsmen in timber and brick.

Elizabethan and Jacobean craftsmen excelled in the media of timber and brick. Wooden buildings were commonly of half-timber construction— that is, the structure is timber-framed but has plasterwork panels, giving the characteristic chequerboard appearance. The woodwork is deeply carved in the gable bargeboards, corner posts of the doorways and on all interior features. Walls are covered by carved or inlaid panelling. This inlay is in complex floral designs.

Brick construction was expanding, for timber supplies were becoming limited, and bricks were cheap and suited to the development of Renaissance styles. Flemish bond construction (alternate headers and stretchers) was introduced, as were gauged bricks, suitable for ornament.

Stone was often used where available, particularly in Scotland.

## Chimney-pieces and staircases.

Just as the entrance porch was the ornamental focal centre of the exterior of a house, so was the two-staged chimney-piece in individual rooms. Carved in wood, stone or marble, the lower stage includes the rectangular fire-place opening, flanked by columns, caryatid figures or flowers and fruits. Above is a centre-piece, either heraldic or pictorial, again flanked by columns and figures, with an elaborate cresting on top. Logs were still burnt, but coal was replacing them.

This is the age of staircase development. First came the Elizabethan dog-legged type, so-called because each short flight turns back in the opposite direction to the one below it. This evolved in Jacobean times into a proper stair and landing, set into a staircase well. Oak was the usual material. Later examples are carved with animal and human finials.

## The age of oak.

With larger homes, there were more rooms used for specific purposes and therefore more items of furniture, though chairs were still expensive. Oak was still the usual material; in fact, this period, up to the Restoration in 1660 when walnut was introduced, is designated the 'age of oak', for it was the time when the best furniture was produced in indigenous wood.

Decoration took the same forms as in architecture: leaves and fruit, especially acanthus and vine, strapwork, grotesques and animals.

A particular feature of the time is the bulbous leg used on tables, court cupboards (a prototype of the sideboard) and other large pieces of furniture, which has a clear affinity with the puffs and slashes of the contemporary costume. The bulbs were carved with acanthus decoration and glued on to the legs and posts.

## Animated effigies.

Sculptured tombs, memorials and effigies in churches became more animated. Medieval figures had been recumbent and depersonalised, though they were often beautiful. Elizabethan tombs were much more varied, and sculptors of note were employed.

The recumbent head of the family may be shown side by side with his wife, while the children kneel in a row or around the tomb, ranged according to size and age. As with the late medieval period, such effigies are a rich source for students of costume, portraying accurately and in detail the dress of the nobility and the middle class of their day.

Craftsmanship in silver, pottery and wood, from simple andirons to costly engraved silver tableware, displayed the same decorative motifs as everything else—above all, strapwork, and grotesque masks or figures.

# STUART 1630-1714

*Before the Civil War, Inigo Jones plans Covent Garden, the first of London's squares. During the war, fanatical Puritans attack religious images.*

*The most notorious, Richard ('Blue Dick') Culmer, smashes stained glass windows at Canterbury Cathedral. Roads are improved and the first regular stagecoaches*

*begin to run. Coffee houses open London and Oxford. The Restorati (1660) brings in French and Dutch ta with the returning exiles. The Great F*

Inigo Jones doorway, Wilton House, Wilts. Classical columns with broken pediment above, 1647–53

Window at Wilton, south facade

St Paul's Cathedral, south porch. Wren, 1675–1710

Decorated doorway head, Uppark, Sussex, by William Talman, 1688–9

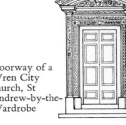

Doorway of a Wren City church, St Andrew-by-the-Wardrobe

Grinling Gibbons woodcarving in St Paul's Cathedral

Ceiling at Coleshill House, Berkshire, now destroyed. By Sir Roger Pratt, 1650–2

Part of a plaster frieze at St Michael's Mount, Cornwall, 1641

Wrought-iron screen by the iron-smith Jean Tijou at Hampton Court, c. 1690

Ceiling centre at Balls Park, Herts., c. 1650.

The dome of St Paul's Cathedral by Wren, begun in 1697. Wren had seen domes —the great Renaissance contribution to church architecture—in Paris

**GRINLING GIBBONS CARVING—PETWORTH HOUSE, SUSSEX**

The western towers of St Paul's Cathedral

Steeple, St Mary-le-Bow

Dragon weathervane, St Mary-le-Bow

Chimney-piece at Wilton, Wiltshire by Inigo Jones 1650

Staircase at Ham House London, 1638

Staircase finial, 1637

Chimney-piece, Gibbons style, 16

Restoration Stuart four-poster bedstead, c. 1675–80, hangings all of matching velvet

A love of nature, which was simply expressed in stone and wood carving in earlier periods, now appeared in the more sophisticated and naturalistic forms of the Classical Renaissance. Wren and master craftsmen such as Gibbons and the iron-smith Jean Tijou dominated the scene.

Side-table with barley-sugar legs, flat serpentine stretchers and marquetry decoration, c. 1685

Charles II chair in walnut, c. 1675

Silver snuffers, 1696

Wren pulpit at St Mildred, London, with cherubs and wreaths embellishing the sounding board

The Monument to the Great Fire of London. 1671–77

Monument to Dr Plot, a historian, 1698, at Borden, Kent. Memorials now reflect the occupations and achievements of those they commemorate

Staffordshire slipware plate, with naïve rampant lion design, 1660–80

Engraved silver tankard with flower design, hall-marked for York, 1657–8

Silver sweetmeat box c. 1640, height 1⅛ in

*(1666) destroys much of old London and gives Wren his chance of re-planning; spires and towers prick the skyline. Pineapples appear about 1670 and become a popular motif in stone and wood. The scientific revolution (Newton, Darby's blast furnace and Newcomen's steam engine) gains impetus.*

...indow at Petworth ...ouse, Sussex

Baroque window, Birmingham Cathedral, by Thomas Archer, 1709-15

Doorway at Morden College, Blackheath, 1695.

Detail of a wrought-iron gate at Trinity Coll., Cambridge, c. 1691

...usticated doorway, ...stle Ashby, Northants.

Temple Bar, by Wren, 1672; now at Theobald's Park, Herts.

Wren steeple, St Bride's, Fleet Street, made of Portland stone in 1701.

The bridge at Blenheim Palace, Oxon., by Sir John Vanbrugh, 1711. It spans the lake created by Capability Brown

St Philip's, Birmingham. Thomas Archer, 1709-15

...rought-iron scroll ...alustrade, 1695

Carved wood scroll balustrade, c. 1680

Enamelled brass andiron or 'fire-dog'

Staircase with barley-sugar balusters, 1700

Silver wall-sconce, 1703-4

...ng-case clock with ...ral marquetry, c. 1685

William-and-Mary winged settee with floral-patterned upholstery, walnut legs and stretchers, 1695

William-and-Mary chair, c. 1690

Silver case clock by Edward Webbe, 1676

...nt cover with carved ...erubs, All Hallows the Tower

High relief chest-tomb at Elmore, Glos., 1707

Sword-rest, All Hallows by the Tower

# THE PALATIAL AGE

**Wren's versatility.** Doorways and windows were designed in correct Classical form. The orders, with columns, bases, capitals and entablatures, flanked major openings and were surmounted by pediments with sculpture and cresting. Inigo Jones's work, as at Wilton, was beautifully designed. It did not, however, possess the infinite variety which was one of Wren's chief characteristics, and which is shown by the doors and windows of his churches in the City of London. Some are plain, with columns, some ornately carved, some have brackets to support the pediment. Other architects followed Wren's lead, though their work is often coarser and less vivid. The same decorative motifs appear again and again: cherubs (heads or whole bodies), acanthus leaf and other Classical forms like the egg and dart, scrolls, and swags of fruit and flowers.

**From strapwork to symmetry.** The all-over strapwork patterns of the Elizabethan plaster ceilings and friezes gave place to the centrally planned design. The dominant part was a deeply recessed panel—circular, oval or octagonal—whose wide border was elaborately moulded into flowers and fruit. The rest of the design was subordinate, but in similar vein. Up to c. 1700 the same characteristics were to be found in all ornamented surfaces. The motifs were chiefly floral or animal, as they had been for a long time, but the treatment was new.

Grinling Gibbons, Wren's famous carver, introduced an informal method of handling carving, especially in wood. His work was extremely realistic and three-dimensional, with the work cut almost free of the background, giving a pattern of strong light and shade, and full of vitality.

**Aftermath of the Fire.** The Fire of London necessitated the rebuilding of 53 churches destroyed, and these, together with St Paul's Cathedral, represented much of Wren's life-work.

The great dome of St Paul's is a London landmark, but more difficult to perceive nowadays are the steeples of the remaining City churches. These show the versatility of Wren, for no two are alike.

The interesting part of each steeple is the upper part; nearly all have plain tower sides below this. Until the office rebuildings of the 1950's and 1960's the scale of the steeples was unchallenged. They are Renaissance in general features, though many are reminiscent of Gothic spires.

The works of Hawksmoor and Archer initiated the brief span of English baroque at the end of the century.

**Chimney-pieces and staircases.** Chimney-pieces during the first half of the period are like the one at Wilton—though usually more modest. Still a two-storey feature, the chimney-piece extends as one unit from floor to cornice. The fire-place is rectangular, with metal basket and irons. The focal centre of the upper part is a mirror or painting, and both stages are decorated and framed by columns, figures, flowers and fruit.

The later type of design is more often in two parts: a fire-place below, and above it a separate mirror or painting.

Staircases evolved from the carved panel type of balustrade to the version with multiple balusters. The panel was in carved wood or wrought iron, with heavy carved newels and finials. By 1670-80 the barley-sugar twist motif was frequent in balusters. Wooden staircases had slenderer handrails and balusters.

**The age of walnut.** At the Restoration of 1660 the long 'age of oak', with its well-made but heavy designs, came to an end for fashionable homes, and the 'age of walnut' began, helped along by the influence of continental elegance experienced by the nobility in exile. Items became more numerous.

Walnut was used mainly as a veneer, glued in thin sheets on to an oak carcase. Oyster-shell and burr patterns were obtained by using the different parts of trunk, root and branch. Marquetry was introduced—a delicate type of inlay, using coloured woods. Fittings were of brass. The twisted barley-sugar leg was in fashion, as was the elaborately carved or serpentine stretcher.

Furniture was allied to costume, notably in severe designs (Cromwellian), complicated carved frames (Charles II), and very tall chairs and beds (William and Mary).

**Pulpits and candelabra.** The higher quality of craftsmanship and the predominant type of ornament were reflected in the monuments, fittings, silverware and ceramics of the day. Wren pulpits were of beautiful wood, carved either by Grinling Gibbons himself, or his assistants. The metalwork of screens and sword-rests, the stonework of tombs and the sculpture of memorials showed the same high standards.

Lighting was still by candle or rushlight, but the fittings were now varied and beautiful. Silver, glass and brass were used for candlesticks and wall sconces, while brass was most usual for the giant candelabra hanging from the centre of the ceiling panels. These candelabra now had many S-shaped branches attached to a central ball. The quality of silverware, pottery and glass was improving greatly.

**[657]**

*European Grand Tours become popular and the love of antiquity spreads. Foreign trade expands: custom houses and town halls are built. Duty reforms make im-* *ports cheaper; mahogany is used with home-grown woods for furniture. The art of wood-turning is discovered, affecting the shape of baluster-rails and furniture* *legs. Tea imports increase, potteries ex- pand and tea-pots appear. The rich buil  fake ruins to romanticise their gardens  Seaside building begins to develop a*

Palladian portico at Lyme Park, Cheshire, showing the taste of the times for Classical proportions. Leoni, 1726

Ornate ceiling, St Martin-in-the Fields. James Gibbs, 1722

St Martin-in-the-Fields. Gibbs, 1722

St George-in-the-East, London. Hawksmoor, 1715

Heavily ornamented fire-place at the Hall, Ditchley, Oxon. A painting framed in the overmantel is surmounted by near life-size figures. Gibbs, 1722

Brass candelabrum, 1727. Candles remain the only lighting system

Monument to Speaker Wright in Gayhurst parish church, Bucks., 1728

Guildhall, Worcs. White, 1722

Plasterwork, Hagley Hall, Worcs., 1758

All Souls, Oxford. Hawksmoor, 1730

ROCOCO MIRROR—HOWINGTON HALL, WARWICKSHIRE

The curves and shells of the rococo theme became dominant in decoration from 1740—lighter, freer, more elegant motifs replaced earlier florid forms with their festoons of flowers and fruit. This mirror reflects a patterned ceiling in the more formal style.

Doorcase with broken pediment, Claydon House, Bucks. The sophisticated rococo style originated in France

Classical ceiling at Houghton Hall, Norfolk. Plasterwork by Artari, architect Colin Campbell, 1730

Covered bridge in the Palladian style at Wilton Park, Wilts., built 1737 for its romantic contribution to the landsc as much as for its utility

Wrought-iron balustrade, Stoneleigh Abbey, Warks., 1720

Chimney-stacks in the Palladian manner

Rococo chimney-piece with mirror, 1750-60

Stone and wrought-iron staircase, 1720

Trivet and fir place, c. 1760

Tripod table with 'pie-crust' edge, 1760

Ribband-back Chippendale chair, mahogany, 1755

Marble-topped console table, with gilt eagle pedestal, c. 1730

Chippendale sconce, gilt pinewood, c. 1755

Four-poster bedstead i carved mahogany, c. 1

Carved oak staircase and unusually high decorated pulpit at St Martin-in-the-Fields, London. The work is attributed to Grinling Gibbons (1648-1721)

Headstone in Wisbech churchyard, Cambs., with rococo ornament and neo-Classic cherubs, 1767. The same forms were applied to furniture, buildings and household goods

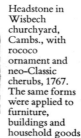

Chelsea porcelain, 'The Music Lesson', c. 1765

Scarborough. Stucco is used: partly to protect brickwork from the atmosphere, partly to simulate stonework. In poorer areas cottages are built in 'pairs' and be-

come the ancestors of semi-detached homes. Religious enthusiasm creates massive congregations and high-level pulpits to address them.

Palladian doorway, Houghton Hall, Norfolk, 1730

'Venetian' window, Holkham Hall, 1734

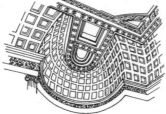

Window at Stoneleigh Abbey, Warks., 1720

Baroque portico, St Anne's Limehouse, 1720

Wall panels – carved, painted and gilded, 1760

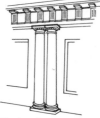

Doric columns at the Circus, Bath. Wood, 1754

Coffered ceiling at Holkham Hall, Norfolk. William Kent, 1734

Florid ornamental detail, pediment ornament, St George's, Hanover Square, London, 1714

The Wren tradition: St Mary-le-Strand, London. Gibbs, 1717

St George, Bloomsbury. Nicholas Hawksmoor, 1730

Stone parapet at Daventry Church. Hiorn, 1752

Imposing 'Palladian' staircase, Stourhead, with Classical statues

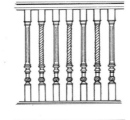

Mahogany staircase balustrade, Bath, c. 1728 (now removed)

Engraved silver tea-kettle and stand, with burner, 1730

Silver coffee pot, with flowers in relief, 1765

Red velvet and gilded wood settee. William Kent, c. 1740

The Scarborough coach, designed by Sir William Chambers in 1761, and an example of rococo at its most extreme. It cost £8000 to build

[659]

Owl in Chelsea porcelain, 1752

The mausoleum, Castle Howard, Yorks. Nicholas Hawksmoor, 1731

## SCHOLARSHIP IN DESIGN

**From Classicism to rococo.** Classicism prevailed in architectural detail. Porches, porticoes, doorways and windows display flanking columns, supporting central pediments. Doors are of beautiful polished wood: at first in oak or pine and two-panelled, but after the early 1740's more usually in mahogany and designed in six panels. Door furniture and panel edging is in brass or bronze.

Despite the overall influence of Italian-inspired Palladianism, two other forms of design existed. In the early years, baroque features were employed by architects like Hawksmoor or Vanbrugh. Hawksmoor's use of the baroque was monumental and uncompromising. In the mid-century years, light-hearted rococo decorative forms tended to oust severe Palladianism, replacing the correct Classicism with gayer, elegant curves.

**Fine plasterwork.** The ceiling continued to be the most important interior feature, whether in church or home. Plasterwork was of high quality, the best being created by Italian stuccoists. For example, the curved vault of St Martin-in-the-Fields, in London, was designed by James Gibbs and carried out by two Italians. Ceilings in most houses were flat, with a coving descending to the plaster frieze.

The Palladian school of architects, led by their patron Lord Burlington, included Colin Campbell, Giacomo Leoni and William Kent. Among the many English houses which they created, Houghton and Holkham, both in Norfolk, take pride of place. Kent, who was responsible for the Earl of Leicester's mansion at Holkham, introduced the custom of designing everything in the house—even down to the doorknobs.

**Unusual new churches.** London received many new churches from Sir Christopher Wren, but only as replacements for those lost in the Great Fire of 1666. In 1711 an Act of Parliament provided for the building of 50 new churches to cater for the needs of parishioners in London's expanding suburbs. Outstanding architects of the day contributed, designing fine buildings and unusual steeples different from Wren's.

James Gibbs gave us St Martin-in-the-Fields and St Mary-le-Strand, developing further the Wren tradition. Nicholas Hawksmoor built six churches—one in the City (St Mary Woolnoth), one in the West End (St George, Bloomsbury), and the remainder in the East End. Their great originality is seen especially in the steeples. All are different, but all possess a powerful monumentality, evincing Roman grandeur.

**Chimney-pieces and staircases.** The two-stage chimney-piece was seen until c. 1745-50. After this, rococo design began to take over. Many elegant chimney-pieces exist from the 1750's. These are more lightweight and project less from the wall. Everything about them is curved. The upper part incorporates many pieces of mirror and candle-holders; and the lower part is in carved, gilded pinewood.

The interior staircase became an important feature. Some are made entirely of wood, with barley-sugar balusters, and are set into wood-panelled stair wells. Others have stone steps with wrought-iron balustrade and mahogany handrail, set into a stucco-ornamented well. The principal entrance is often approached by an exterior stone staircase, with vase-shaped stone balusters or a wrought-iron balustrade.

**Kent and Chippendale.** In well-to-do homes, furnishings were becoming more comfortable, and lighting improved. Walls were panelled, stucco-decorated, or hung with silk or velvet. Until c. 1750 most of the furniture was in walnut or pine, or lacquered in imitation of Oriental designs, though mahogany imports increased after the 1720's.

William Kent and Thomas Chippendale are the paramount names in furniture in this half-century. Kent's designs set the pattern until c. 1740. His style is heavy, rich and baroque, with marble tops and gilded pedestals, often in the form of animals, birds and female figures.

The name Chippendale is synonymous with mahogany. His ribband and ladderback chairs and settees (1750's) are unmistakeable, as are the tripod stand and curved cabriole leg, with claw and ball foot.

**Famous ceramic names.** The quality of workmanship was rising, and there were scientific and technological advances in many crafts. This applied particularly to the ceramic industry. In the 18th century, many of the names famous in English ceramics became established—Bow, Chelsea, Derby and Worcester.

An incentive to producing new designs and techniques was the spread of the popularity for drinking tea and coffee. China tea services had long been imported from the East and later from Meissen. With the discovery of kaolin clay in Cornwall in the mid-century, porcelain manufacture began in England. Tea and coffee also influenced silver design: beautiful pots and kettles were made.

Architects did not confine themselves to buildings: Sir William Chambers even designed George III's coronation coach.

# LATE GEORGIAN & REGENCY 1765-1837

*Pattern-books disseminate designs to builders, cabinet makers and carpenters. Because of window-tax the number of windows in old and new houses is reduced.*

*Town-house entrances are dignified by being raised and provided with a short flight of steps, thus creating dark, dingy basements for the servants. The first town*

*planning is done at Bath by the Wood family. Sir Walter Scott's romantic literature evokes nostalgia for the Middle Ages and promotes Gothic Revivalism.*

Doorway by Robert Adam in St James's Sq., London, c. 1775

Corinthian capital designed for Luton Hoo, Bedfordshire, by Robert Adam

Telford's road bridge at Conway, with the medieval castle behind. The iron suspension bridge, built in 1826, has mock towers at the ends

Hooded bay window, with balconies, in Regency Sq., Brighton

Cut glass chandelier, c. 1770. To increase the light given out by the candles, glass was used— both chandeliers and wall mirrors

Late 18th-century door furniture. Such details were often architect-designed

### DETAIL OF CEILING BY ROBERT ADAM

The 18th-century custom of the European Grand Tour gave both patrons and artists a chance to study at first hand the Classical works in Italy and Greece which influenced all aspects of design. Robert Adam made this journey to Italy Greece and Dalmatia and his ceilings designs are an 18th-century Englishman's interpretation of what he saw.

Robert Adam doorway, Adelphi, London

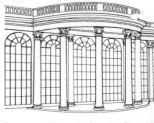

Orangery, Heveningham Hall, Suffolk by James Wyatt, 1790-1800

Faun and entablature from the anteroom, Syon House, London, by Robert Adam

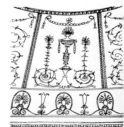

Stucco wall decoration by Adam. Kenwood, London

Ironbridge, Coalbrookdale, Shropshire. The world's first iron bridge, built across the Severn in 1779

Early Gothic Revival St Peter's, Brighton

Adam staircase, 20 St. James's Sq., London

Late 18th-century steel grate

Hooded iron balcony, Cheltenham, c. 1830

Adam fire-place, Syon House, London. Adam designed his houses down to the smallest detail of the fittings

Iron balustrade by Adam Kenwood, London

Chimney glass, to go above a fire-place. Adam style

Ladderback chair, c. 1775

Shield-back armchair, c. 1775. This period was the golden age of the chair

Serpentine-fronted chest, 1775. The flowing lines are in contrast to the square furniture of earlier periods

Hanging cabinet, lyre pattern, c. 1800

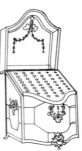

Veneered and inlaid knife box, c. 1770

Teapoy, c. 1820. A teapoy was a small table containing equipment for making tea

Ornamental clock designed by Adam

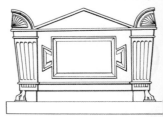

Classical tomb design, showing motifs used in architecture and furniture, such as the pediment and the animal foot

MacAdam's new roads and the end of foreign travel during the Napoleonic Wars, lead to increased travel at home and coaching inns. Technical develop-ments of the Industrial Revolution and a general increase in trade breed docks, warehouses and slums. Gas-lighting starts in Pall Mall.

# THE AGE OF ELEGANCE

Ionic archway by John Nash, Regent's Park, 1825. Part of a giant town-planning scheme

Window at Southgate Grove, London, by John Nash, 1797

Pelham Crescent, London, by Basevi, 1820-40

ling detail showing a Bacchic scene, by bert Adam. Harewood House, Yorkshire

Ceiling decoration in the Bank of England, by Sir Robert Taylor, reminiscent of Wedgwood designs

eek Revival: St ncras Church, 1822

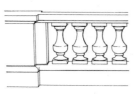

Parapet balustrade, from Tyringham House, Buckinghamshire, by Sir John Soane, c. 1796

Bridge designed for Syon House, Middlesex, by Robert Adam. A continuation of the Classical tradition

erpentine scroll alustrade, c. 1790

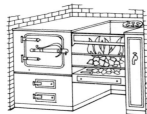

Cast-iron kitchen range, c. 1800. On the right is a boiler, with a tap for hot water

Dog turn-spit, c. 1800. The dog had to keep moving, so as not to lose balance

Regency convex mirror, c. 1810

Regency sabre-legged mahogany chair

Regency library table. Animal head and leg supports were common

Wedgwood and glass candlestick, c. 1800

val patera, a motif found in decor-on of all kinds, from architecture pottery, and especially common on neered furniture. Paterae are round oval, with varied central designs

Urn motif, from a tomb. This was used by Adam and others, on buildings and furniture

[661]

Wedgwood coffee-pot 1783, Jasper-ware. Wedgwood applied Classical design to everyday household articles

**Adam's work and influence.** The name of Robert Adam appears again and again in the field of architectural and domestic design. As he was rarely given the opportunity of designing a house from scratch, but had to re-adapt an existing one to current trends, his work is chiefly seen in de-tail or interior decoration.

Adam's own work belongs to the years 1760-92, but his influence was so extensive that the work of men like James Wyatt, Thomas Leverton and Henry Holland bears a close re-semblance to that of Adam. Doorway and window design is delicate and restrained. Adam utilised the exquisite wrought-iron work of his day on both railings and fanlights.

John Nash is noted for his Regency terraces and houses. His most am-bitious surviving works are the Regent's Park terraces, part of a planning scheme begun in 1812.

**Delicate decoration.** Interior de-coration was at its highest level in the years 1765-90—the period of Adam and Chambers. Stucco ornament de-corated the ceiling and many walls. Though still Classical, the treatment had changed and was now in delicate, low relief, rarely gilded but left white with pastel-coloured background. The overall design included circular, oval or octagonal paintings, generally figure compositions or landscapes, often painted by Angelica Kauffmann, one of the founder members of the Royal Academy of Arts and its first woman representative.

Wallpaper was gaining in popul-arity, and English papers were pro-duced at Battersea. Designs were more pictorial than our all-over pat-terns of today. They were repro-ductions of paintings by artists like Canaletto, or were based on current stucco designs.

**Advances in iron.** While the aes-thetic qualities of design slowly de-clined in the early 19th century, the Industrial Revolution was producing exciting new materials and methods. The advances of technique in the use of iron made Britain the foremost nation in industrial construction. This was the age of the great engineers, when Telford built bridges which were emulated all over the world.

The famous Ironbridge at Coal-brookdale was the first in this material —no structural masterpiece, but an experiment (still standing) in the use of iron. At Conway, Telford built a road bridge, and blended his castellat-ed towers with the medieval castle behind. The suspension bridges of early 19th-century engineers are among the most beautiful structures of the century.

Architecturally, churches fore-shadowed the coming Gothic Revival.

**Houses in terraces.** The first of the terraced groups of houses were built in 1730 in Bath. Others followed in London, Edinburgh, Bristol and Cheltenham; and during the Reg-ency, the newly fashionable seaside resorts laid out crescents, squares and sea-front terraces. In Brighton and Hove many such terraces have bow windows, extending the whole height of each house, with wrought-iron canopies and decorative balconies.

Ironwork was used increasingly for staircase balustrades, at first in straight flights but, at the turn of the century, in serpentine curves.

Adam and his colleagues continued Kent's custom of designing all the house furnishings, and the steel grates, kerbs and fire-irons of this period are some of the most beautiful ever made. Cooking was becoming easier with the introduction of the cast-iron cooking range.

**Furniture evolution.** The outstand-ing furniture designers of 1765-90 were Chippendale and Adam; in the later period, 1780-1810, Hepplewhite and Sheraton. In general, the earlier chairs have flat oval, shield, lyre, ribband, or ladderback forms; and the later ones concave oval, shield, or straight back designs. Earlier furni-ture is sturdy and generally carved. Later work is slenderer, especially the legs, and decorated more with inlay or painting. Regency furniture is heavier, often gilded, and with animal head and leg supports.

Though lighting was still only by candles, well-to-do homes now had hanging candelabra, wall sconces and standing girandoles, as well as simple candlesticks, in such quantity that the lighting power was considerable, though the room became odorous and hot. To increase the light, beauti-ful mirrors lined the walls.

**Wedgwood and his successors.** Porcelain was developed both tech-nically and artistically. At the same time, Wedgwood—an artist who was also a businessman—demonstrat-ed that the softer pottery could be made in as elegant a form as the more costly porcelain. Though Bow, Chelsea, Derby, and Worcester are household names, that of Wedgwood eclipses them. He was followed by similar men—Spode, Copeland and Minton—who made beautiful pottery available for all classes.

As in other fields, these years pro-duced the finest of workmanship, in silver and glass, in brass and ormolu for door and furniture fittings, and in household articles of all kinds. Even an everyday article like a knife-box was veneered for display. Many of them still exist, each one a work of art, to remind us of the quality of 18th-century craftsmanship.

# VICTORIAN 1837-1880

A widespread demand for a 'True Christian Architecture' promotes the main phase of Gothic Revivalism: Catholic emancipation and Anglican revival lead to huge church-building programmes. Railways change the face of the landscape. Prince Albert stages the Great Exhibition (1851); Paxton's Crystal Palace, derived from the greenhouse which gardening had made popular, suggests a new philosophy of building design. William Morris forms the Arts and Crafts Movement as

Entrance porch to Bridgewater House, London, by Charles Barry, c. 1849

Oriel window, St. Pancras Station

St Giles's Church, Cheadle, Staffs., by Pugin, 1841-6

Entrance porch, Highclere Castle, Hants., by Charles Barry, 1842-4

Decorative strapwork, St Mary and St Nicholas, Wilton, Wilts., by Wyatt and Brandon, 1840-6. This stone-built church shows Italian influence

Entrance doorway Keble Coll., Oxf

William Morris wallpaper, 1876. Morris's firm was famous for its fabrics and wallpapers designed by individual craftsmen

Capitals, Bristol Cathedral, by G. E. Street

Iron lamp standard, Embankment, London

Iron entrance gate, Kew Gardens, London, 1866

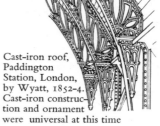

Cast-iron roof, Paddington Station, London, by Wyatt, 1852-4. Cast-iron construction and ornament were universal at this time

Base of a column with mouse carving, Natural History Museum, London, by Waterhou

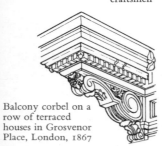

Balcony corbel on a row of terraced houses in Grosvenor Place, London, 1867

Clock tower, Houses of Parliament, Barry and Pugin

**VICTORIAN SALOON BAR WINDOW**

Machinery and new materials enabled the Victorians to imitate what they admired in other periods: inspired by romantic literature they made town halls look like temples and disguised cast iron as Gothic woodwork. The market for such techniques created by rising living standards is typified by the elaborate use of gilt, frosted and cut glass in their saloon bars.

Carved base of an oriel window, Prudential Assurance Building, Holborn by Alfred Waterhouse, 1878. This Gothic building is of red brick with terracotta decoration

Cast-iron and steel grate shown at the Great Exhibition, 1851

Fire irons

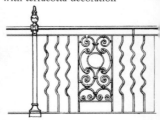

Balcony balustrade, Albert Hall Mansions, London, by Norman Shaw, 1

Bamboo stand for newspapers, 1879

Circular ottoman divided into four seats with buttoned upholstery, c. 1840. Buttoned upholstery was popular at this period

Brass gas lamp or chandelier, used in town houses by 1840

Iron plaque on the gates of the National Maritime Museum, Greenwich, by Philip Hardwick. One of the best examples of decorated cast-iron work

Artificial flowers protected from dust by a glass dome

'Medieval' sculptured detail, Scott Monument, Princes Street, Edinburgh, by Kemp, 1840-6. This Gothic memorial cost over £15,000

Royal lion, Victoria Tower, Houses of Parliament, by Barry and Pugin, c. 1835. Pugin designed most of the ornament

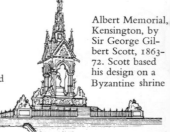

Albert Memorial, Kensington, by Sir George Gilbert Scott, 1863-72. Scott based his design on a Byzantine shrine

*eaction against the machine age. Mass-roduction ugliness increases. Britain is ow urbanised. Industry provides mass mployment but creates overcrowding in towns, with back-to-back slum housing. Land values soar and mansion-flats appear. The window-box becomes popular.*

# THE BATTLE OF STYLES

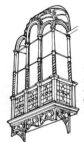

*rway, St Mary's hedral, Edinburgh* — *Lonsdale Square, Islington, 1838* — Oriel window, station master's office, Paddington Station, by Brunel and Wyatt — *Window, Scarisbrick Hall, Lancs., 1837*

*pital, St Mary and Nicholas, Wilton, Wyatt and Brandon* — *Lamp, Leeds Town Hall, by Brodrick, 1855-9* — Iron bracket supporting a cast-iron gallery, Coal Exchange, London, by Bunning, 1847-9. The Exchange has been demolished — *Decorated capitals, Natural History Museum, London, by Waterhouse*

*ail, Houses of liament, by Pugin* — Central clock tower, Leeds Town Hall, by Brodrick, 1855-9 — Cast-iron and wood seat with arms carved in the form of sphinxes, Embankment, London, 1865-70. The Victorians covered all surfaces with intricate decoration — Clock tower, Cardiff Castle, by Burges

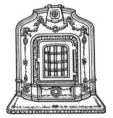

*Cast-iron balustrade for a aircase* — Cast-iron fire-place, 1875. The writhing forms, moulded in iron, typify design at this period — Cast-iron slow combustion stove, 1870

*Chiffonier, mirror back, electro-gilt, c. 1860* — Balloon-back dining chair with buttoned seat, 1850 — Brown glazed earthenware teapot — *Doulton tankard. Factory established in Lambeth, c. 1820*

*Clock, Paddington Station, by Brunel and Wyatt, 1852-4* — Silver bottle stand. Victorian silverware was generally over-decorated — Nelson's Column Trafalgar Square, London, by William Railton, 1839. The lions by Landseer were added later, in 1866

[663]

**Classical and Gothic.** The Gothic Revival flourished throughout the 19th century, and was at its strongest in the second half, when most buildings were in Gothic style. The spirit of the Revival was religious, exemplified by the work of Pugin, and nearly all churches were based on medieval originals. Earlier works are what the Victorians called 'English Middle Pointed' Gothic, but later all kinds of medieval work were copied.

Architects worked in both the Classical and Gothic styles. Sir Charles Barry, for example, architect of the Gothic Palace of Westminster, built many houses and public buildings in Classical style, as did also that ardent Revivalist, Sir Gilbert Scott. In civic building and terrace architecture the Classical tradition persisted, but Gothic cladding extended to railway stations, universities, town halls and hospitals.

**Iron for everything.** Ironwork, usually wrought iron, had been used in building for a long time, but during the 19th century its use became large-scale. After 1825, designs were less delicate and finely worked, and by 1830 iron was being used constructively as well as decoratively and became an essential building material. It was employed for columns, roofing and brackets, and structurally for tie-beams and arches.

Due to technical advances, cast iron became cheap and therefore widespread in its possible uses. By the second half of the century, it was used for everything from railings, gates and balconies to seats, bandstands, arcades and post-boxes. Though much of the work was coarse and poor in design, some excellent items were produced. Motifs were Classical and Gothic, and included animals and birds in complex ornamental schemes.

**Back to the Middle Ages.** There was a romantic air about many of the towers and steeples; even Classical ones on sober town halls had curving, baroque lines to the cupola. The most famous romanticised Gothic tower is the Clock Tower of the Palace of Westminster; its bell is called 'Big Ben' after Sir Benjamin Hall, Commissioner of Works. Cardiff Castle has another such turreted tower, while even a functional

building like the Natural History Museum in London has diminishing turrets in polychrome materials.

While ornament, both exterior and interior, is often crude, some is remarkably fine, though the appearance is always harder, more sharply defined and less sympathetically carved than the medieval inspiration. Terracotta work, as on the Prudential Assurance Building, London, was used as ornamentation on brick buildings.

**Accent on bric-a-brac.** From 1845 to 1885, Victorian interiors, particularly domestic ones, became darker, more over-furnished and filled with a quantity of bric-a-brac. Wallpapers and carpets were strongly patterned and coloured, and paintwork was dark. Windows were draped in layers of curtains. Chimney-pieces, tables and cabinets were shrouded in tasselled fabrics, especially red velvet, and even dressing tables coyly hid their

legs under frilled muslin with bows.

The fire-place was the focal centre of the room, providing heat from coal, which burnt in a cast-iron grate with marble and iron surround. Above the mantelpiece were shelves, cupboards and mirrors, stacked tightly with ornaments. After 1885 the pattern slowly changed towards lighter *décor*, smaller quantities of furniture and furnishing, and simpler ornamental design.

**Gaslight and button chairs.** By 1840 gas lighting was in general use in town houses. A metal chandelier hung from the ceiling, with three or four branches fitted with frosted globes in which the gas gently popped and purred in a flat flame. The carbon filament electric lamp was developed in 1860, but the change-over to electricity was slow. Oil lamps were in use all the century.

Most Victorian furniture design

is heavy and ornate. Mahogany was used chiefly, and the workmanship was excellent, as many pieces still in use testify. Items were large, especially dining tables, wardrobes, bedsteads and sideboards (chiffoniers). Buttoned upholstery was popular, as was horsehair covering and dark, rich colouring. Papier-mâché furniture contributed some of the most beautiful pieces of the century, as well as some of the most ugly.

**Miniatures and monuments.** From the quantity of knick-knacks produced, a great deal survives; and the early Victorian work at any rate is now becoming valuable in the antique market. Many of the small tables, work-boxes, porcelain groups, clocks and paperweights were beautifully made, and have a charm and attraction for us today. Silver, glass and china are of high quality, though they tend to be ornamented with

roses, violets and pictures of Windsor.

Of all the many memorials and monuments erected, probably the most controversial and typical is the Albert Memorial, which has been subjected to prejudiced comment—both for and against—ever since. Sir Gilbert Scott based his design for the monument to the Prince Consort on a Byzantine jewelled shrine, and the Memorial still gleams iridescently in the sunshine.

Art nouveau flourishes against a background of Edwardian material prosperity with its town halls and monumental commercial buildings. Voysey and Mackintosh experiment with functionalism in furniture and building design, and the first garden city is founded at Letchworth (1903) Free education is introduced; schools, libraries and art galleries are built. Photography influences painting. The petrol engine and the telephone arrive; an apparent security reigns.

Gateway at the Royal Holloway College for Women, Surrey, 1886. Built to an enormous rectangular plan, in the French château style

Newnham Coll. Cambridge

Detail of an entrance porch, Cardiff City Centre, 1906. Designed by Lanchester in neo-baroque style

Oriel window, Port Sunlight, Cheshire, c. 1905

Front door, Bedford Park, London, 1880's

Doorway at Queen's Gate, London, 1880 Norman Shaw

Detail of a wrought-iron gate at Newnham Coll., Cambridge

ART NOUVEAU FABRIC DESIGN BY G. H. NAFFELL, 1905

Design was freed from its Victorian confinement to surfaces as artists and designers tried to invest everything with an appearance of natural growth. Sinuous plant-like forms appeared everywhere and for a short while the distinction between the 'fine' and 'applied' arts almost disappeared.

Carving from the Cardiff City Centre, 1906. The stone crown symbolises the confidence of a patriotic, expansionist age

Tower Bridge, London, 1894, by Barry and Jones. The Gothic towers conceal a steel framework

Tower of the Law Courts, Cardiff. The design is Classical, and is based on French models of a few years earlier

Edwardian art nouveau staircase. A reaction against the complexity of Victorian decoration

Cooking range and grate, 1910. The cast-iron chimney piece is painted

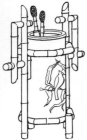

Bamboo umbrella stand. Bamboo furniture became popular in the 1870's, with the vogue for Japanese art

Washstand designed by William Burges for his house in Melbury Road, London. His Gothic designs were based on medieval furniture

Oak art nouveau table, by Charles Rennie Mackintosh, c. 1900

Electric light wall fitting, c. 1913. Oxidised copper tubing, with white glass shades

Oak chair with cane seat, c. 1900

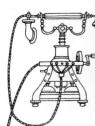

House telephone of the decade before the First World War

Racing cup and cover, 1868-9, partly frosted silver, parcel gilt. At the top is St George slaying the dragon. The side shows a battle scene

Cast-iron canopy of a bandstand on the Front at Brighton

Earthenware vase, c. 1900, by William de Morgan

Silver vase on a marble stand, 1900. The swirling lines of the decoration are typical of the art nouveau period

Granite drinking fountain, common in parks, c. 1890

# THE LANGUAGE OF EXPERTS

---

*The work of the men who have
helped to create and discover our heritage
and the terms they use*

---

Men who share the same training and skills and are engaged in a common enterprise tend to develop their own private language. Their words are their private shorthand and the 'passwords' which help to keep away outsiders.

Many of the words in this section are like that—words such as 'gadrooning' or 'hagioscope' or 'parvise', each representing an object which is reasonably familiar to the layman, but is not generally known to him by its name.

Other words have too much vigour to be confined by their original technical meaning, and have joined the mainstream of the language. The word 'hallmark', for instance, which nowadays means any distinguishing mark of genius, began its life as the official assaying mark stamped on gold and silver at the Goldsmiths' Hall in London; the word 'sterling', once an English silver penny, much in demand on the Continent, is now used generally to suggest high quality.

But even when words have developed in this way, the experts, from archaeologists to archbishops, still use them in their original technical meanings. One key to the work of experts is simply to understand the language they use.

# ARCHAEOLOGY

The last hundred years have seen archaeology reach the status of a precise science, drawing on almost every branch of learning. The clergy contributed much to its early development—William Stukeley (1687-1765), doctor and clergyman, did original research on Stonehenge and Avebury until he became involved in Druidic mysticism—but it was a clergyman who gave the budding science one of its severest handicaps. Archbishop Usher of Armagh published a Biblical Chronology in 1650, dating the Creation at 4004 BC. This generally accepted calculation distorted the researches of other archaeologists and even frightened those with some evidence of the earth's true chronology into keeping the results of their investigations to themselves.

Its foundations in Britain were laid in the 17th century by William Camden, Elias Ashmole and John Tradescant. Another outstanding figure was Sir Thomas Browne, whose *Urne Buriall*, published in 1658, aroused great interest and is still read. These 17th-century writers, however, were really archaeological philosophers, each working in his own narrow discipline as an individual, having little scientific knowledge and sharing little communal activity.

It was late in the 18th century before the modern concept of archaeology began to emerge, and not until the 19th century that it began to provide a scientific basis for future research. In 1868 a German, Heinrich Brugsch, using the brilliant investigations of the Frenchman Champollion and the eminent English physicist, Dr Thomas Young, finally deciphered the Rossetta Stone, the key to the understanding of Egyptian hieroglyphics.

In 1871, a ruthless archaeologist, Schliemann, rediscovered Troy, sweeping aside the relics of periods other than those which interested him. These excavations provided valuable material for the study of the Bronze Age in Asia Minor and therefore, because archaeology is partly concerned with comparative records, the study of the same period in Britain.

At the age of 24, in 1877, Flinders Petrie published *Inductive Metrology*, a milestone in the accurate measurement of antiquity; in the same year General Pitt-Rivers brought out his *Excavations in Cranbourne Chase*. He was the first archaeologist to use the technique of stratification.

The historians, geologists and scientists were now beginning to work with the archaeologists. T. H. Huxley and Charles Darwin were both influenced by the new archaeological thinking, and in turn influenced it themselves. In 1889 Sir Arthur Evans excavated Knossos, on the island of Crete, and made wide discoveries in the field of Minoan culture, including tablets inscribed in an unknown script, later to be known as Linear Script 'B'. This script was deciphered in 1952 by Michael Ventris, enabling the written records of Crete, a culture previously unknown, to be studied for the first time.

Today modern technology—photography, electronics, petrology and carbon-analysis—can often discover the characteristics of objects of which only the merest traces remain.

**Aerial photography** The sites of camps and ditches invisible from the ground may be seen from the air, and changes of colour in crops can provide clues to past disturbances in the sub-soil.

**Artifact** Any object fashioned by man.

**Barrow** A burial cairn. Barrows are divided into several types. *Long barrow*; built in the late Stone Age, this was a communal burial vault for a tribe or family, covered with earth or stones. Some were 200-300 ft long and 50 ft wide. There is a long barrow at Windmill Hill, Wiltshire, the site of a Neolithic camp. *Round barrows* date from the Bronze Age and fall into a number of distinctive shapes: *bowl barrows*, which resemble an upturned bowl; *bell barrows*, the shape of which suggests a slightly flattened bell. They are surrounded by a ditch and mound; *disc barrows* resemble a shield with a small mound forming the boss of the shield. A flat area, with ditch and mound at the outer edge, surrounded the whole.

**Bawn** A fortified court or outwork of a castle.

**Beaker People** Named after the drinking vessels they made, which were buried with them. They came to Britain from Russia and Spain by way of Germany and Holland.

**Bronze Age** 1800-550 BC.

**Cairn** A mound of stones covering a prehistoric grave or tomb.

**Causeway** A narrow path across ditches and earthworks along which the defenders could retire to their fort.

**Chamber** Stone-built burial chamber with access from exterior, usually covered with earth or stone or both.

**Cruciform chamber** One built in the shape of a cross.

**Chevaux de frise** A defensive setting of stakes or similar obstacles.

**Clochan** A corbel-roofed drystone hut, usually beehive shaped.

**Dolmen** A small rectangular or polygonal chamber set in a cairn with exterior access—a *barrow*.

**Dun** A fort, usually built of stone and heavily defended.

**Dyke** Ditch (see *Earthwork*).

**Earthwork** When ditches were dug, as additional protection, in concentric rings around camps and forts in prehistoric times (often filled with sharpened stakes or water), the soil from the excavation was piled up on the inside edge in banks. This presented the attacker with a steeper climb if he penetrated the ditch.

**Electrical resistivity** The points at which soil may have been disturbed can be recorded by passing electric current through the soil between two electrodes.

**Gallery-grave** An oblong chamber with no passage-way but frequently having a space in front of the entrance where funeral ceremonies may have taken place.

**Henge** A circle of wooden or stone uprights, enclosed by a bank of earth or stone and usually an internal ditch, forming part of ceremonial structures found in Britain and Ireland, of the late Neolithic or Bronze Age.

**Hypocaust** A hollow space under the floor of a building, which channeled heat from a furnace to heating panels of hollow tiles set in the walls. The Romans used this system for heating their houses and baths.

**Iron Age** 550 BC-AD 43.

**Mesolithic** 8000-3000 BC.

**Mosaic** Form of surface decoration used on floors and walls, composed of variously coloured fragments, usually square, of marble, glass, pottery, etc.

**Multivallate** Having many ramparts—used of a fortress.

**Neolithic** 3250-1800 BC.

**Palaeolithic** 300,000-8000 BC.

**Passage-grave** A tomb of the late Stone Age with a narrow passage leading into the burial chamber.

**Petrology** The study of rock formation and composition.

**Radio-carbon dating** When plants and animals die they cease to absorb the carbon needed to maintain life; the radioactive carbon they have also absorbed decays at a known rate, and by measuring their radioactivity archaeologists can date with considerable accuracy wood, charcoal, bone and other organic substances.

**Rath** An enclosure, usually of a circular form, made by a strong earthen wall and serving as a fort.

**Ridgeway** Roads or tracks used by prehistoric man to travel from hill-fort to hill-fort. These also have a religious significance because they converge from north, south, east and west on Avebury in Wiltshire, site of their most important temple.

**Ring fort** An area, usually circular, surrounded by banks and ditches, and containing dwellings.

**Sarsen** Local sandstone used in the uprights for one of the circles at Stonehenge.

**Souterrain** An underground chamber, store-room or passage.

**Spectrographic analysis** The use of a spectroscope (an instrument concerned with breaking down light into recognisable scientific colour values) to determine the chemical and molecular structure of a body, and thus to identify it.

**Trivallate** Having three ramparts.

**Vallum** The Latin word for an earth-rampart or wall, built for defence round a camp or fort.

**Vitrified fort** A stone fort whose walls in places have been melted or fused; found in Scotland.

# ARCHITECTURE

As well as the structural and decorative elements described below, an architect deals with certain constant factors in his effort to produce good buildings.

MATERIALS. Man first built with the material closest to hand. In ancient Mesopotamia it was mud, and with only mud bricks—no timber or large stones—Mesopotamians were obliged to discover the arch before they could roof their houses; the Greeks, living on a marble peninsula, used the largest slabs they could find as upright posts with slabs laid across them. From this evolved the typical Greek pillared building, and the post and lintel method of construction still used today.

The Romans discovered a local mineral which set like concrete when mixed with lime and water, enabling them to build larger structures than the Greeks and exploit the possibilities of the arch.

When mild steel and reinforced concrete became available in the mid-19th century, architects were able to make their buildings higher and wider, the openings in them larger, and reduce the walls to water-proof skins on steel and concrete frameworks.

CONTRAST. Architects use contrast to give their buildings character. Smooth and rough surfaces imply lightness and heaviness; sculpture and mouldings produce variations of light and shadow. An arched opening can give emphasis to a plain façade, and colour can create mood—warmth and nearness, coolness and distance; dark colours suggest weight, light colours the opposite

SCALE. Reactions to a building often depend on its scale. The enormous size of an Egyptian pyramid gave the Pharaoh who built it a safe tomb, and allowed him to dominate the living even after death. Gothic churches, with their lofty spires, implied aspirations to reach Heaven itself, and seen from afar gave comfort and inspiration to the villages around them. Inside, the high vaults shrouded in darkness created a feeling of humility and reverence. Today scale can imply security in a bank, or prestige in an office building.

FORM AND PROPORTION. The Greeks discovered that the circle and the square were pleasing to the eye. By experimenting with these and other geometrical shapes they arrived at a set of ideal proportions and using them as the basis of their designs achieved buildings of unsurpassed clarity and balance. These principles were revived in the Renaissance, and in England the Georgian architects came close to matching the excellence of Greek design.

**Abutment** The piece of solid masonry or brickwork on a *pier* or wall that supports the arch.

**Acanthus** A stylised representation of a plant with thick scalloped leaves, used as a decorative feature in the carving of Corinthian capitals.

**Angel beam** The end of a *hammerbeam* carved to represent a human or, often, an angel.

**Arcade** A range of arches supporting a wall or roof. Also a covered way between two rows of arches or between a row of arches and a solid wall.

**Ashlar** A wall of smooth-faced, precision-cut stones in regular courses, with fine jointing.

**Bailey** A fortified enclosure: the space within the outer walls of an ancient or mediaeval castle.

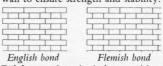

**Baluster** A carved column or upright post supporting a handrail.
**Balustrade** A series of *balusters*.
**Barbican** A fortified outer tower defending the entrance gate to a castle.
**Barge-board** A carved board, fixed to a *pitched roof* to hide the end of the rafters.

**Bartizan** An overhanging battlemented turret on a castle or church tower.
**Bas-relief** Carving which projects from the material from which it is formed.
**Bastion** A fortified projection occuring at intervals in a castle wall.
**Battlements** A square-toothed *parapet* used in medieval castles to protect archers.

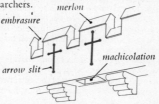

**Billet moulding** Norman ornamental *moulding*.
**Bolection moulding** See *Moulding*.
**Bond** The way in which bricks or masonry-blocks are arranged in a wall to ensure strength and stability.

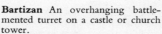

*English bond*     *Flemish bond*

**Brick-nogging** A timber partition with brickwork filling the space between the vertical timbers.
**Bressumer** A massive load-bearing beam used to span an opening.
**Broken-pediment** See *Pediment*.
**Cable moulding** An ornamental Norman *moulding*.

**Cantilever** A projecting beam supported at one end only.
**Capital** The carved or moulded feature at the head of a column on which the superstructure rests. See *Classical Orders*.
**Cartouche** An ornamental tablet representing a scroll of paper and usually bearing an inscription.
**Caryatid** A column in the form of a female figure.
**Castellation** *Battlements* used as a decorative feature.
**Chancel** The east end of a church where the altar is; the continuation of the *nave* beyond the *crossing*.
**Chapter-house** Assembly room for the governing body of a monastery or cathedral.
**Chevron** A carved zigzag *moulding* in Norman architecture usually seen around arches, doors and windows.
**Classical Orders** The Greeks, and later the Romans, introduced a set of architectural standards into their design for temples and public buildings. These standards or Orders regulated the proportions and relationships between the three principal parts of their buildings: the base (stylobate); the structural pillar (column); and the beams they carried (architrave).

The first three Orders, devised by the Greeks, were the DORIC, IONIC and CORINTHIAN. The first was the simplest and most widely used; the second rather more elegant and the third, used least, the most florid.

The Romans, less restrained than the Greeks, took these three Orders and adapted them to their own taste. They then added two further Orders, the TUSCAN and COMPOSITE. The Tuscan was a clumsy version of the Greek Doric, despite an attempt at simplification. The Composite, a combination of the Greek Ionic and Corinthian, was equally less satisfying due to a coarsening of detail and extravagant decoration.

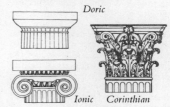

*Doric*

*Ionic*   *Corinthian*

**Clerestory** Windows near the ceiling in a high room or hall, which receive light from above the roofs of adjoining buildings.
**Clunch** A soft, white limestone, ideal for carving and often used for interior decorative work.
**Cob** Walling material of straw and unbacked-clay.
**Collar-beam roof** A timber beam connecting the mid-points of the sloping rafters of a *pitched roof*.
**Colonnade** A row of columns.
**Composite** See *Classical Orders*.
**Console** A large curved ornamental bracket generally occurring in Classical architecture.
**Coping** Brick or stone used to cap the top of a wall, to prevent weathering or for ornamental purposes.

**Corbel** A stone or brick projection from a wall to provide a horizontal support.

**Corinthian** See *Classical Orders*.

**Cove** A concave *moulding* usually seen at the junction of wall and ceiling.

**Coffering** Recessed panelling in ceilings, domes and vaults; used either for decoration or to reduce the weight in heavy construction work.

**Crenellation** See *Castellation*.

**Crocket** A carved decorative projection representing foliage on the edges of spires and canopies in Gothic architecture.

**Crossing** The central space at the intersection of the *nave* and *transept* in a church, usually directly beneath the tower.

**Crow-stepped gable** A series of steps in the *coping* of a gable.

**Crypt** An underground cell or burial-chamber beneath the chancel of a church, occasionally with an altar for worship.

**Cupola** A small spherical roof crowning a square, circular or polygonal area.

**Curtain wall** The length of wall between a castle's fortified towers; in modern use, a non-load-bearing wall.

**Cusps** Carved projections on the underside of a Gothic arch which separate the *foils*.

**Dado** The lower part of a wall when painted or decorated differently from that above.

**Diapered** A two-dimensional square or lozenge-shaped pattern on a wall. Brick diaper work is usually carried out with different coloured bricks.

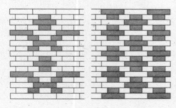

**Dormer** An upper floor window projecting through the side of a *pitched roof*.

**Doric** see *Classical Orders*.

**Dower-house** A house endowed for the use of a widow.

**Dressed stone** Smoothly finished stonework used externally at corners, doors and windows of brick and stone buildings.

**Drum-columns** Cylindrical sections forming a stone column.

**Embrasure** See *Battlements*.

**Entasis** A slight outward swelling on columns, devised by the Greeks to counteract the optical illusion which makes vertical parallel lines appear to curve inwards. An entasis is found on most Classical columns.

**Facade** The front or main face of a building.

**Fan vault** See *Vaults*.

**Fillet** A narrow rectangular strip that separates one moulding from another.

**Finial** An ornamental feature, often of timber, at the top of a *gable* on the ridge. Also used loosely for any small pinnacle finishing off a vertical feature.

**Flush-work** *Knapped flint* used with *dressed stone* to create decorative effects.

**Fluting** Shallow semicircular grooves cut into the surface of columns and *pilasters* for decoration.

**Foils** The inside arcs in *tracery* work between the *cusps*.

**Foliate** Leaf-shaped; *tracery* work with *foils* and *cusps*.

**Folly** A structure built solely for decorative effect, for example a Gothic-style ruin or tower.

**Frieze** The central division of an entablature. See *Classical Orders*. The frieze is also that part of a wall between the picture-rail and ceiling.

**Gable** The triangular area of wall beneath the roof at the end of a building.

**Gargoyle** A rain-water spout on a medieval building, directing water away from the face of the wall; carved with grotesque representations of beasts' heads.

**Gate-house** The tower over the fortified entrance of a castle's perimeter wall.

**Gauged-brickwork** Bricks cut and rubbed to shape, then mortared together with fine joints in an arch.

**Gazebo** A summer-house or tower situated in a garden to give maximum benefit from the view.

**Half-timbered** Buildings with a timber framework, often of oak, with other materials—bricks, tiles or lath-and-plaster—filling the spaces between the timbers.

**Hammer-beam** A timber bracket that supports a trussed roof. Hammer-beams eliminate the need for a *tie-beam*.

**Harl** The Scottish term for roughcast, or *pebble-dash*.

**Herringbone** Timber blocks, brickwork or similar materials laid diagonally, to create zigzag patterns on the *façade* of a building.

**Hipped-roof** A *pitched* roof sloping at the ends as well as the sides.

**Hood mould** A *moulding* which projects from the wall over an arch, door, or window to throw off rain-water.

**Hypocaust** Underground chamber in a Roman house which contained a furnace and distributed warm air to the rooms above.

**Ingle-nook** An enclosed seat built into the wall beside a fireplace.

**Ionic** See *Classical Orders*.

**Jamb** The straight side of an arch, door or window.

**Keep** The inner tower and defensive stronghold of a Norman castle.

**Keystone** The central wedge-shaped stone at the top of an arch.

**King-post** A roof which has an upright post between the ridge and the centre of the *tie-beam*.

**Knapped flint** Flint stones broken in half to present a roughly squared face when used in walls.

**Lancet** A tall, narrow, sharply-pointed window-opening found in Early English church architecture.

**Lavatorium** A Latin term describing a place for washing in.

**Lierne-rib** The short ribs between the principal ribs in a Gothic vault.

**Linen-fold** Decorative carving imitating the appearance of draped or folded cloth.

**Lintel** A horizontal length of stone, steel, timber or reinforced-concrete carrying the weight of the wall above a window or door.

**Loggia** A covered veranda open on at least one side; at the front of a building.

**Long-and-short work** Saxon stonework with the corner stones laid alternately upright and horizontal. Often seen in *stucco* work.

**Machicolation** A series of openings in the floor of projecting *parapets* in mediaeval castles, through which missiles were dropped on the enemy. See *Battlements*.

**Mansard** A roof with two slopes, the lower steeper than the upper.

**Mausoleum** An elaborate tomb, usually of monumental proportions.

**Merlon** One of the 'teeth' forming *battlements*.

**Mezzanine** An intermediate floor, usually between the ground and first floor level in a building.

**Motte** An artificial mound formed within castle walls, usually surmounted by the *keep*.

**Moulding** Ornamental carving on a wall's projections or recessions.

hood moulding

billet moulding

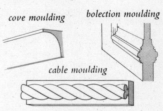

cove moulding

bolection moulding

cable moulding

**Mullion** A vertical bar of wood, stone or metal in a window.

**Nave** The main body of a church, excluding the *transept* and *chancel*.

**Newel** The central post of a winding staircase into which the steps are set. Also the posts at landing levels supporting the handrail.

**Oculus** A round window, also known as a 'bulls-eye' window.

**Oratory** Either a small chapel used for private prayer or a larger Roman Catholic church.

**Oriel-window** An upper-floor bay-window supported by *corbels*.

**Pallisade** A fence of stakes around a castle or defensive position.

**Pantile** An S-shaped roofing-tile.

**Parapet** The low wall projecting above the roof level of a house. In Renaissance buildings it was usually in the form of a *balustrade*.

**Pargetting** Plasterwork carved with ornamental patterns. Often seen on old cottages and houses.

**Pattern-book** A book of designs for architectural details based on the revived principles of Classical architecture.

**Pele or Peel tower** A fortified tower built in the 16th century as a defence against border raids.

**Pebble-dash** The finish given to external walls by applying small pebbles to the surface rendering while still wet. Often called rough-cast.

**Pediment** The triangular space formed by the ends of pitched roofs in Classical and Renaissance buildings; a feature that often surmounts the entrance porch. A BROKEN-PEDIMENT has part of its apex omitted; a familiar feature of baroque architecture.

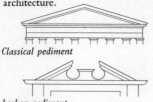

*Classical pediment*

*broken pediment*

**Piazza** a formal open space surrounded by buildings, and entered through archways.

**Pier** A vertical support; also the area of wall between windows.

**Pilaster** A flat rectangular pier or column, projecting slightly from a wall, largely used for decoration.

**Pinnacle** The terminating feature of a buttress or tower in Gothic architecture; usually pyramid-shaped and ornamented.

**Pitched roof** A sloping roof.

**Plinth** The projecting base of a wall or building.

**Pointing** After bricks have been laid, the joints between them are finished off with 'pointing'—a mixture of sand and cement. It is sometimes coloured to contrast with the remainder of the wall face.

**Portcullis** A heavy, gridded, defensive entrance-gate in a mediaeval castle, designed to be raised and lowered from inside.

**Porte-cochère** A large porch at the entrance of a house or mansion, big enough to receive a horse and carriage.

**Portico** A *colonnaded* space, with a covered roof, forming an entrance to a building.

**Quatrefoil** An opening carved into four leaf-shaped *foils*, occuring in Gothic architecture.

**Queen-post** A roof in which two uprights on a *tie-beam* support the rafters.

**Quoins** The external corner-stones of a brick or stone building.

**Random-rubble** Irregularly shaped stones used in wall construction.

**Ravelin** The part of a castle's advance defences, outside the curtain wall, whose two sides form an angle pointing towards the enemy.

**Refectory** The dining-hall in a monastery or convent.

**Retaining wall** A wall which resists the pressure from a mass of earth or water.

**Revetted** Faced with masonry; used of walls or banks.

**Rib** A projecting band on a vault or ceiling.

**Roof-truss** A system of lightweight timbers or lengths of steel for supporting a roof.

**Rose-window** A circular window in Gothic architecture, traceried to resemble a rose. Sometimes called a wheel-window because the *mullions* radiate from the centre like the spokes of a wheel.

**Rotunda** A circular building usually with a domed roof.

**Rough-cast** See *Pebble-dash*.

**Rustication** The rough finish given to projecting stonework in a Renaissance building by chiselling. The edges or margins of the stones were left smooth.

**Saddle-back roof** A pitched roof on a tower.

**Scagliola** Plasterwork painted to represent marble. Often seen on columns. It originated in Renaissance Italy.

**Shaft** The main part of a column.

**Shingle** Thin wood tiles used as a roof-covering—often made from cedar.

**Slype** A covered passage, usually between the transepts and chapter-house in a church, leading to the cloisters.

**Solar** A quiet study or private room in a sunny or exposed place in a medieval house.

**Spandrel** The triangular space between the underside of a staircase and the floor. Also the triangular space between the curved parts of two adjoining arches.

**Stairs** An arrangement of steps made of wood, stone or metal giving access to floors above or below. These may be in straight flights between landings or constructed in a continuous curve.

**Staple Hall** A covered market.

**Stepped-gable** See *Crow-stepped gable*.

**Strapwork** A form of ornament that imitates interlacing bands of leather.

**String-course** An ornamental band running horizontally across the face of a building.

**Stucco** Plaster used on the face of buildings to represent stonework. Also a general term describing rendered surfaces.

**Swag** An ornamental piece of carving resembling a garland or festoon of flowers, fruit or foliage, suspended at either end to form a loop and gathered up at the centre.

**Tie-beam** The horizontal beam connected to the feet of rafters to prevent them spreading out under the weight of the roof covering.

**Tile-hanging** The external surfacing of walls with overlapping rows of tiles on a timber framework; used in Elizabethan architecture and now becoming popular again. Slate-hanging follows the same principle.

**Tracery** Ornamental carving of *mullions* and *transoms* in Gothic windows.

**Transept** The short arms of a cross-shaped church.

**Transom** A horizontal bar in a window which, with the mullions, separates the panes of glass.

**Tuscan** See *Classical Orders*.

**Tympanum** The space between a *lintel* and the arch above it.

**Undercroft** A *vaulted* basement often found in monasteries.

**Vaults** Arched ceilings or roofs; vaulting is a method of roofing an area with a succession of load–bearing arches. They can be pointed or semi-circular, and usually intersect at right angles.

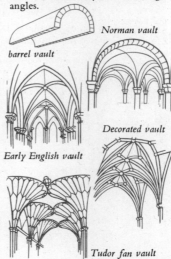

*Norman vault*

*barrel vault*

*Decorated vault*

*Early English vault*

*Tudor fan vault*

**Venetian-window** A triple window; the central window is arched, those on either side have flat or lintelled tops.

**Voussoirs** The wedge-shaped stones used to make an arch.

**Waggon-roof** A roof with curved braces but no *tie-beams*. When lined with boarding it resembles a covered wagon.

**Wattle-and-daub** Interlaced sticks of hazel or osier roughly plastered with a mixture of clay and chopped straw, sometimes reinforced with horse-hair as a binding agent.

**Wheel-window** See *Rose-window*.

# ARMS AND ARMOUR

The finest products of the armourer and weaponsmith have always been esteemed as much for their beauty as for their functional qualities. Artists as eminent as Dürer and Holbein have been responsible for their design, yet the most elaborately decorated pieces are not always the most pleasing. The art of the great armourers, like that of the great potters, lay in their ability to exploit the plastic potentialities of their material, and the plain armour of the 15th century, with its elegant lines and subtle curves, can be more satisfying than the elaborate parade armour of the next century. British weaponsmiths only achieved an international reputation in the 19th century, with the work of the London and Birmingham gun makers, but fine fire-arms were made here from the late 16th century onwards, and Henry VIII's armoury at Greenwich produced armour as good as that made on the Continent.

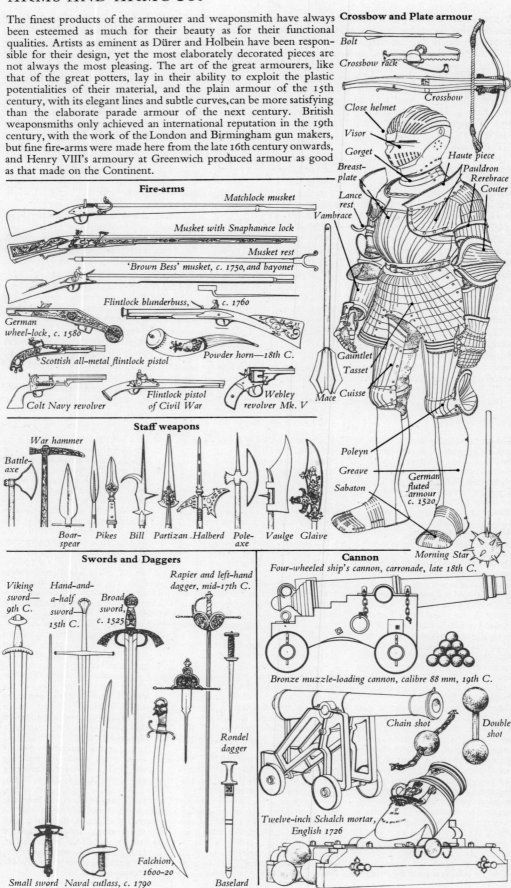

**Crossbow and Plate armour**

Bolt

Crossbow rack

Crossbow

Close helmet

Visor

Gorget

Breast-plate

Lance rest

Vambrace

Haute piece

Pauldron

Rerebrace

Couter

Gauntlet

Tasset

Cuisse

Mace

Poleyn

Greave

Sabaton

German fluted armour c. 1520

Morning Star

**Fire-arms**

Matchlock musket

Musket with Snaphaunce lock

Musket rest

'Brown Bess' musket, c. 1750, and bayonet

Flintlock blunderbuss, c. 1760

German wheel-lock, c. 1580

Powder horn—18th C.

Scottish all-metal flintlock pistol

Colt Navy revolver

Flintlock pistol of Civil War

Webley revolver Mk. V

**Staff weapons**

War hammer

Battle-axe

Boar-spear

Pikes

Bill

Partizan

Halberd

Pole-axe

Vaulge

Glaive

**Swords and Daggers**

Rapier and left-hand dagger, mid-17th C.

Viking sword— 9th C.

Hand-and-a-half sword, 15th C.

Broad sword, c. 1525

Rondel dagger

Small sword

Naval cutlass, c. 1790

Falchion, 1600-20

Baselard

**Cannon**

Four-wheeled ship's cannon, carronade, late 18th C.

Bronze muzzle-loading cannon, calibre 88 mm, 19th C.

Chain shot

Double shot

Twelve-inch Schalch mortar, English 1726

**670**

# CERAMICS

A great deal of English pottery from the 13th century onwards was derivative, but it nevertheless demonstrated peculiarly English characteristics. A peasant craft, it reflected the individual taste of the potter.

Most medieval pottery was made in monasteries; a red or buff body was covered with a green glaze. Slipware was already used in the middle ages, but earliest surviving signed examples were made at Wrotham in Kent early in the 17th century. This type of pottery was also made in Staffordshire by Ralph and Thomas Toft.

The famous Delft-ware, first made in England c. 1550, had an immediate success, and until the development of stoneware, was the most commonly used domestic ware. John Dwight of Fulham was the first potter granted a patent to produce stoneware, and in 1693 he sued the Dutch Elers brothers who worked in Staffordshire for infringement of his patent. The popularity of stoneware lasted until Staffordshire Saltglaze was invented by John Astbury in the 1730's, and the whitish finish of this ware prepared the way for the cream-coloured earthenware produced by Josiah Wedgwood, known as Queen's Ware.

During the 18th century the increasing demand for a finer and less durable ware was being satisfied by the manufacturers of fine porcelain.

Chelsea, famous for its figures and elegant tableware, was probably the first porcelain factory in the British Isles. Founded c. 1745, the factory was taken over by William Duesbury, owner of the Derby porcelain factory, who produced the porcelain known as Chelsea-Derby (1769-84).

During the same period Bow porcelain was being made in the East End of London by Thomas Frye, who took out a patent for it in 1744. Bow is best known for its figures and groups; typical colouring is dark crimson, emerald green and pale blue. The factory closed down in 1776.

The Worcester porcelain factory was founded in 1751 by a syndicate of 15 men, among whom was Dr John Wall and the brilliant chemist William Davis, who were responsible for the finest period of Worcester, from 1752-83. Worcester porcelain was resistant to heat, did not crack in hot water, and at the same time, was extremely fine with a thin, hard glaze. It is one of the few porcelains made in the 18th century that is still being made today.

During the 18th century porcelain was also produced at Caughley, Liverpool, Longton Hall, Plymouth and Bristol.

Towards the end of the century the development of Spode bone china—a compromise between hard and soft porcelain—resulted in an enormous commercial expansion. Spode predominated in the first quarter of the 19th century, until it was superseded c. 1820 by Rockingham, with its tendency to over-decoration. In 1851 the Great Exhibition popularised styles from all countries, especially Japan, and manufacturers, such as Coalport, Copeland and Minton, quickly adapted their designs to the current fashion. But towards the end of the century the formalised designs of Art Nouveau began to exert their influence, and despite popular taste 'in many Victorian servants' halls the tableware was still representative of the best of English pottery traditions, while above stairs the tables groaned under the fashionable nightmares of ceramic art'.

---

**Ceramics** The general term for objects fashioned from clay and hardened by fire, whether classed as earthenware, stoneware or porcelain. Variations of hardness and texture depending on the degree of heat used in firing are the main differences between the three types of ceramics. Soft earthenware is fired at 700°C,, while the hardest white porcelain is produced by firing the clay at 1350°C.

**Chelsea** See *Porcelain*.

**Delft** The general name applied to tin-glazed earthenware in northern Europe. It originated in Asia, and was first produced in Europe in Spain and Italy where it was called MAJOLICA; in France it was called FAIENCE; and in Holland and England DELFT, from the town where it was made in Holland. There is no technical difference between these three terms, only variations in style and decoration English Delft was first made at Lambeth in 1671.

**Faience** See *Delft*.

**Glaze** A coat of glass formed over the surface of pottery when fired, it consists of sand, flint or sandstone mixed with such fluxes as lead, potash or borax. This flux causes the glaze-mixture to melt at a lower temperature than that of clay. Its function is to make the pottery impervious to liquids, to give them a sheen, and to act as a basis or a protection for decoration. The glaze is coloured by adding metallic oxides, which are used instead of ordinary colours because they are not destroyed by the firing. Different colours are produced by varying either the temperature of the firing or the amount of oxygen in the kiln.

**Majolica** See *Delft*.

**Medici** See *Porcelain*.

**Meissen** See *Porcelain*.

**Porcelain** True, or 'hard-paste', porcelain is a hard, thin and translucent pottery made by fusing china-clay (*kaolin*) with china-stone (*petuntse* or 'hard-paste') at about 1350°C.–1400°C. It was first developed by the Chinese and appeared in the West in the 15th century. European imitations were made of 'soft-paste' porcelain which is really a form of hard earthenware made by adding a previously fired glassy mixture to white clay. This was the first European porcelain and was produced in Italy in the 1580's; it was known as MEDICI porcelain.

It was not until 1709 that true hard-paste porcelain was produced—by J. F. Bottger at MEISSEN in Germany. Later Dresden and Sèvres became the important centres. (Meissen-ware in England is usually called Dresden.)

The earliest dated English porcelain was CHELSEA made in 1745. It was a soft-paste variety, very glassy and translucent and made in the style of Meissen-ware.

**Salt-glaze** Stoneware glazed with salt, thrown in the kiln at the height of firing. The process was developed in the 1730's by John Astbury of Shelton who used Devonshire clay and calcined flint in order to produce a whiter and a harder pottery, which was called 'Staffordshire salt-glaze'. Salt-glaze, which could be reproduced rapidly and in quantity, immediately became popular for domestic use. By 1750, white salt-glaze was being made in at least 50 Staffordshire potteries; much of it was undecorated and none of it bears factory marks. It led the way to the cream-coloured earthenware which became more popular in the 1770's.

**Slipware** One of the first earthenwares. Made by peasant potters in Kent and Staffordshire in the 17th century, it was decorated with 'slip', a clay wash of a creamy consistency.

**Spode bone-china** A paste midway between hard and soft porcelain. White ash from burnt ox bones is used as the stabilising ingredient because it does not impair the translucency of the porcelain and makes it easier to work. Bone-china was first marketed by Josiah Spode c. 1800.

**Stoneware** In 1671 John Dwight of Fulham took out a patent for this ware which fired at a very high temperature, became extremely hard and impervious to fluids. The addition of salt to the kiln at the maximum temperature produced stoneware with a pleasant rough surface. This ware was often used in bottle-making in the 19th century.

**Wedgwood** Josiah Wedgwood (1730-95) revolutionised the potter's craft and made it into a flourishing industry. He produced the following wares: 1759, Green glaze 'cauliflower' wares; 1765, Queen's Ware, the first cream-coloured earthenware, which was fine, light and could be pierced, moulded or decorated with transfer printing; 1760-70, unglazed stonewares including Black Basalt, hard, fine and black, and Jasperware, hard, resembling porcelain, and made in different colours.

# FURNITURE

English furniture, from medieval times to the 17th century, was generally made of native oak, though other woods, elm and beech, were also used occasionally. Broadly speaking, Elizabethan, Jacobean and Cromwellian furniture was simply designed and solidly made and, since the oak was seasoned for ten to 20 years before use, lasted for centuries.

Decoration in the 14th and 15th centuries was simple, with Gothic ornament or the favourite *linenfold* pattern. In Elizabethan times it became more adventurous and was inlaid or carved with all kinds of motifs from geometric panels to festoons and swags. It was often painted and gilded, and even now there is still some colour visible on the 16th century Great Bed of Ware in the Victoria and Albert Museum.

In the 17th century the Puritan austerity of plain, unadorned furniture, produced a reaction in favour of more decorative woods and more flamboyant styles. With the Restoration, walnut came into its own and exotic woods were imported—kingwood from South America, amboyna from the West Indies, and ebony—to be used in *veneers*. Walnut was at the height of its popularity in the William and Mary period and at its best in Queen Anne's reign when it achieved an elegant simplicity of line, rarely surpassed since.

In the early Georgian period mahogany was being used, but sparingly as it was expensive. With the repeal in 1724 of the heavy duties on its import from the West Indies and Cuba, it immediately became popular with the cabinet-makers, and by 1750 had supplanted walnut in the public esteem.

Other exotic woods were imported in the late 18th century, among them satinwood, which became a minor vogue. This close-grained wood, of varying tones of yellow, with a gleam rather like satin, was often used for veneers. It was a favourite of Sheraton, who designed some of his finest pieces in it.

In the early 19th century furniture became heavier as the revived Classicism of the Regency became popular, and darker woods came into fashion, particularly rosewood. Imported from the West Indies and Ceylon, and called rosewood for its slight scent, it was dark brown with distinct, almost black, markings, and well suited to the period's style.

As the Victorian era progressed, the elegance of 18th-century line and ornament disappeared and furniture became larger, darker and more ponderous. One light-hearted production of the Victorian age was papier-mâché inlaid with mother of pearl and beautifully coloured. It was used for small objects like portable writing-desks and tables, and was highly decorative. It was in the smaller objects, rather than in their massive pieces of domestic furniture, that the Victorians were at their best.

**Cabriole Leg** A curved leg resembling the leg of an animal. It was a distinctive feature of William-and-Mary and Queen Anne furniture, and lasted well into the 1860's. The leg often terminated in an animal claw gripping a ball, hence the term *claw and ball foot*. A characteristic of English cabriole is a scallop shell carved on the shoulder of the leg. The fashion died out with the neo-Classical era when curves began to be supplanted by straight lines.

**Inlay** One of the earliest methods of decorating furniture. The art came to England via the Germans and the Flemish. The design was chiselled out of the wood, and into this recessed ground were fitted flat pieces of different coloured woods skilfully cut to fit the pattern. In early inlay, ebony, bog-oak and holly (white in colour) were used to give a black and white effect. The designs were usually geometric patterns or formalised flowers and foliage. Later, in the late 16th and early 17th century, inlaid pictorial effects were much in favour: views of buildings, courtyards and arches.

**Lacquer** A form of decoration made in the East by applying layers of resin, or lac, from the *Rhus vernicifera* insect, to the wood. Each layer was dried and rubbed down to obtain an absolutely smooth surface, and sometimes as many as 35 processes were used before the surface was ready for decoration. In the 17th century lac was unobtainable in Europe, so instead the wood was usually treated with a mixture of whitening and size and then coated with several layers of varnish, made of gum-lac, seed-lac or shell-lac. The ornament was outlined in gold size and the surface rubbed down with a dog's tooth or agate pebble. As lac began to be imported, European craftsmen improved their techniques to such an extent that they were able to produce a fair imitation of the hard polish of the Oriental craftsmen, and by the late 17th century their work had reached a high standard, though in the opinion of the connoisseurs not comparable with that from China and Japan.

**Linenfold** A decorative pattern carved on wood, its straight flat lines looking like folded linen. The design was Flemish in origin, and was popular in England in the 15th and 16th centuries, particularly as decoration on oak chests.

**Marquetry** A form of surface decoration closely allied to veneer, but distinct from inlay. The design is first cut and fitted into a thin sheet of wood or veneer; then the veneer, complete with the design in one flat sheet, is applied to the surface of the furniture. Marquetry became popular in the Restoration, when designs, inspired by the work of the Dutch, took the form of flowers and birds. Towards the end of the 17th century a more intricate version became fashionable known as *Seaweed* marquetry—the pattern suggested the delicate fronds of waving seaweed. In the Classical revival of the 18th century, marquetry was popular and motifs tended to be Greek—urns, festoons of leaves and flowers, and sometimes draped figures.

A large assortment of materials was used from natural woods of different colours — black through browns and yellows, to the white of sycamore or holly; and ivory, mother of pearl, bone, tortoiseshell, copper, brass and silver.

**Ormolu** The word comes from the French *bronze d'orée d'or moulu* (bronze gilded with ground gold). It is essentially French and was used in France as mountings in furniture and to make small useful objects like candlesticks. The ormolu used on English furniture was probably made by French craftsmen.

**Pembroke Table** A small table with hinged flaps which are supported by fly brackets, it came into use in the 1760's and was described as 'for a lady or gentleman to breakfast on'. Sheraton, who made designs for it, said it was called after the lady who first ordered it.

**Pie-Crust Table** A round table with a hinged top which could be folded flat against a wall, fashionable in the late 18th century. It had a carved scalloped edge rather like pastry crust on a pie. It was set on a single leg with three feet—a tripod—and often the legs were of the *cabriole* type with claw and ball feet.

**Pier Table** Designed to be used against a wall between windows, and frequently placed for decorative effect under a mirror.

**Piercing** Decoration in the form of holes, originally designed to let air into 'livery' cupboards where food or clothes were stored. In the early days of oak, small holes were pierced in the form of geometric patterns; these later evolved into more elaborate cut-outs.

Woven fabric was put on the inside to keep insects out. Pierced work has been much used in every age and particularly by Chippendale for chair backs.

**Splat** The centre support in the back of a chair, often elegantly shaped and decorated.

**Spoon-Back** A colloquial term used to describe a Queen Anne chair-back profiled to the curve of a spoon.

**Veneer** Thin sheets of wood applied to the surface of furniture for a decorative effect. Veneers first came into use after the Restoration in the late 17th century. The wood was chosen for its rarity and the beauty of its markings; at this time exotic woods like kingwood (from Brazil) ebony and amboyna were often laid on in veneers to form elaborate patterns created from the woods' natural markings. See also *Marquetry*.

# GARDENS

Until Tudor times gardens tended to be utilitarian, food-producing patches. But in Henry VIII's reign Cardinal Wolsey laid out a walled garden at Hampton Court with *arbours* and *alleys* and a *knot garden;* and Sir Thomas More had a garden in Chelsea about the same time 'full of lovely flowers and blossoming fruit trees'. All that survives of Tudor gardens now are the beautiful brick walls and the occasional building—at Montacute, Somerset, for example, where the courtyard still has garden pavilions of Elizabethan date.

Greenhouses, of a rudimentary sort, were used to house plants over the winter and these became the orangeries of the late 17th and early 18th century. Many of the original orangeries still exist, at Hampton Court, Kensington Palace and Kew among other places, often designed by the great architects of the period.

It was in 1621 that the first botanical garden was founded at Oxford, known as the Oxford Physic Garden, to which travellers brought back specimens from all over the world. The gardening family of Tradescants were responsible for introducing many exotic plants to England.

But it was in the Restoration that gardens began to change again and become elaborate. Travellers, and Royalists including Charles II, exiled on the Continent, came back with new ideas, particularly from France where the great André Le Nôtre had developed the formal garden laid out with paths, woods, lakes and 'fair prospects'.

The knot garden was supplanted by the *parterre*— a great level area in front of the house where designers could introduce fountains, statues, topiary and summer-houses, giving the garden a new spaciousness. Walks and avenues radiated from a central point, and vistas were all-important.

At this time seeds and plants were being imported from abroad: evergreens, bulbs and flowers from Holland; seeds and plants from the Near East and America. Greenhouses began to be artificially heated, and in 1804 the Horticultural Society of London, later the Royal Horticultural Society, was founded.

In the 18th century came the landscape garden, in which Nature, assisted by man, was allowed to dominate. The two great exponents of the new style were Capability Brown and Humphry Repton: geometric patterns and mathematical precision fell out of favour, paths and streams were permitted to wind and natural contours were made much of. Garden buildings—gazebos, temples, and ornate summer-houses—were placed to enhance the delights of Nature. Stourhead, in Wiltshire, and Stowe, in Buckinghamshire, are two fine examples of many surviving 18th-century gardens.

With 19th-century social changes came new kinds of gardens and gardeners—suburban gardens owned by the wealthy middle class. Books on gardening began to proliferate, and in 1838 J. C. Loudon produced *The Suburban Gardener and Villa Companion;* three years later the *Gardener's Chronicle* was published for the first time. The lawn mower was invented.

The botanical gardens at Kew, which had been collecting plants for over 100 years, now had emissaries all over the world sending back rare specimens.

In the 1860's William Robinson led a reaction against the park-like style of gardening, which resulted in the more natural 'wild' garden where shrubs like rhododendrons and azaleas could grow untended year after year. Robinson advocated great expanses of lawn and borders filled with roses, flowering shrubs and herbaceous plants. In this he started a trend which is still being followed.

**Alley** A broad walk or path cut through trees. The *allée* was a feature of formal French gardens in the 17th century, the trees on either side of the path being clipped to retain the formal effect. They were a usual feature in great English gardens in the early 18th century. *Pleached alleys* are tree-lined walks where the boughs are interlaced and arched over the walk beneath.

**Arboretum** A collection of trees planted together in one area, either to act as a feature in a landscaped garden or as a grove of special botanical interest. A *pinetum* is an arboretum consisting only of conifers.

Britain is said to have the finest arboreta in Europe, with particularly good specimens of conifers. One of the oldest pineta is at Dropmore, in Buckinghamshire, where there is a unique collection of trees grown from seed as far back as 1827.

**Arbour** A bower or shady retreat, usually covered with climbing plants grown over trellises. Arbours or 'herbers' were a feature of gardens as far back as the Middle Ages.

**Gazebo** A two-storied turret set on a wall or on a high point, where a fine view could be had of the surrounding landscape; it was popular in the 18th century when to sit and gaze was fashionable.

The bottom half was often used for storing garden tools while the upper room was reserved for admiring the view through the large windows. It was in fact an 18th-century version of the earlier summer-house.

**Grotto** A cave-like structure, a favourite feature of 18th-century gardens, often used to house collections of shells, minerals or fossils. Grottoes were often extremely elaborate, with statues and fountains and with rivers running through them.

**Ha-Ha** A boundary to a park or garden in the form of a wide, sunken ditch; it prevented animals from coming in or going out and was not visible from the surrounding landscape except at close quarters. The term is said to come from 'Ha', the expression of surprise it evoked when suddenly discovered. It was a favourite device of 18th- and early 19th-century designers, especially of Capability Brown, and contrived to deceive viewers into thinking the garden extended to the horizon.

**Knot garden** A series of small beds laid out in a formal manner, sometimes on a terrace, and edged with dwarf hedges. In the beds, dwarf clipped shrubs or herbs like rosemary, box and thrift were planted in complicated geometric patterns, or knots. The background to the pattern might be coloured earth or gravel and the effect might rely solely on the design the green plants made when seen from above. Where the pattern was less intricate, the empty spaces in the bed might be filled with topiary-work or flowers.

Knot gardens were fashionable in Elizabethan times and extremely popular throughout the 16th and early 17th century, when the more complicated the knots, the better.

**Mount** A raised place or small hill, usually man-made, designed to give a view of the estate. Elizabethan gardens of any importance all had a mount up which one could clamber 'to view a fair prospect'. At the top there was usually an *arbour* or sitting-place.

**Parterre** The level area in front of a house below the terrace or windows. It came to England in the 17th century from France, and was part of a movement to introduce the vista to English gardens; it replaced the Elizabethan *knot garden.*

**Pergola** A covered walk formed by climbing plants over trellis-work, probably coming originally from Italy, where shaded walks were a necessity. Pergolas were in fashion in Renaissance England, and have more or less remained so.

**Topiary** The training and clipping of trees and shrubs into ornamental shapes. Topiary is an ancient art which was probably introduced to England by the Romans. It was popular in Elizabethan gardens, when hedges were cut into shapes of birds, beasts and figures. It reached the height of fantasy in the 17th century: men on galloping horses, heraldic beasts, hunting hounds, any subject that struck the fancy, might be translated into topiary-work.

The 18th century saw a reaction against the cutting of trees into cones, globes and pyramids, and the fashion died out, but there is still topiary work to be seen all over Britain in old gardens.

# HALLMARKS

Gold and silver objects have been hallmarked in England for five or six hundred years. The object is to secure a uniform quality and to prevent fraud. The system is so reliable and complete that a collector can tell, with almost absolute certainty, the authenticity, maker and date of any piece of gold or silver which comes to hand, always providing he can read and interpret the hallmarks stamped upon it. Royal Plate and certain very small articles are exempt from hallmarking.

## The Maker's Mark
The maker's mark is usually the first in the series that makes up the hallmark. Since 1363, it has been compulsory for the maker to stamp his mark on a piece of silver plate before sending it to the Assay Office.

At first the marks were emblems, or symbols, such as the bird appearing on the Bacon Cup (1573–4) at the British Museum. Other symbols—a hart, a hand or a cross—were chosen at a time when most of the population were illiterate, as allusions to the name of the makers.

The conjoined letters, appear on a ewer (1597–8) at the Victoria and Albert Museum, show how the makers gradually gave up symbols and began using letters.

In the late 17th century several efforts were made to clarify makers' marks, and finally it became law in 1739 for makers to use the initial letters of their Christian and surnames. It was in response to this law that Paul de Lamerie, finest of London silversmiths, re-registered his mark. The crown indicates that he was under royal patronage. The practise of using makers' initials continues today, although the marks of firms and manufacturers have generally taken the place of the initials of individual craftsmen.

## The Assay Mark
The assay mark follows the maker's mark on most British silver. English silver, in particular, accounts for nine-tenths of the desirable antique silver in existence, and the lion symbol has been used since 1544, with very few changes. The device indicates that the metal has been passed by the Assay (testing) Office as sterling silver, that is, 92·5 per cent pure silver.

From the beginning the mark was 'lion passant guardant' with its head turned outward, full face. Since 1822 it has been a 'lion passant' looking straight ahead in the direction it is going. The lion was replaced for 23 years, 1697–1720, by the seated figure of Britannia and the standard of fine silver was raised to 95·84 per cent. This mark may still be used for fine silver today.

On Sheffield and Chester plate the assay mark has always been a 'lion passant regardant'. In Ireland, a crowned harp, in Edinburgh a thistle and in Glasgow a lion rampant denote sterling silver.

## Town Marks
Silver's fourth mark is the stamp of the Assay Office responsible for testing the article. Most English-made silver bears the mark of the London Assay Office. Silversmiths from all over Britain,. even in towns with Assay Offices, have always tended to

---

## THE DATE LETTER
The third symbol appearing on silver is a letter of the alphabet, surrounded by a shield. This indicates the date at which an object was assayed, which is almost invariably the date it was made. Date stamps on London-made silver, indicating the date to the nearest twelve-month, have been used without repetition for over 400 years. For 20 consecutive years the 20 letters from A to U (excluding J) are used, with the same style of letter and shield. After U has been reached, the style of letter and shape of the shield are changed. The following chart gives the letter style and shield design for each alphabet since 1558.

| | | | |
|---|---|---|---|
| 1558–1577 | | 1776–1795 | |
| 1578–1597 | | 1796–1815 | |
| 1598–1617 | | 1816–1835 | |
| 1618–1637 | | 1836–1855 | |
| 1638–1657 | | 1856–1875 | |
| 1658–1677 | | 1876, shield changed for rest of series 1877–1895 | |
| 1678–1696 no 'u' in this series | | | |
| 1696–1715 | | 1896–1915 | |
| 1716–1735 | | 1916–1935 | |
| 1736–1755 | | 1936–1955 | |
| 1756–1775 | | 1956–1975 | |

Other Assay Offices throughout England, Scotland and Ireland use different date marks.

### Birmingham marks
The whole alphabet is used, only excluding 'J'

1773–1797 shields differ

1798–1823 'j' used

1824–1848 in different style

1849–1874 'J' used in this series

1875–1899

1900–1924

1925–1949 'J' used in this series instead of 'I'

### Dublin marks since 1773
Whole alphabet used, with exception of 'J' and 'V'

1773–1796

1797–1820

1821–1845 'V' used in this series, italic 'e' alternative, and shields vary

1846–1870 'j' used instead of 'i', and 'v' used. Double 'f', 'g' and 'h'

1871–1895 'V' used in this series

1896–1915 ends at 'U'

1916–1941 'V' included in this series

1942–1967 this series used 'J' and 'V'

### Edinburgh marks since 1780
Whole alphabet used, with exception of 'J'

1780–1805 'I' and 'J' used in conjunction; double 'N', double 'O' and double 'R', shields differ

1806–1831 'j' used

1832–1856

1857–1881

1882–1905 no 'v' in this series

1906–1930

1931–1955

1956–

### Glasgow marks since 1819
Whole alphabet used

1819–1844

1845–1870

1871–1896

1897–1922

1923–1948

1949–1972 'J' and 'K' missing in this series

*Sheffield* and *Chester* date marks are irregular to list in chart form, but handbooks are available giving date marks for each separate year.

send their pieces to London for hall-marking, which complicates the identification of provincial silver. In Britain today the only remaining Assay Offices are at London, Birmingham and Sheffield, at Edinburgh and Glasgow, and in Dublin, although many other cities have had Assay Offices in the past.

 The leopard's head has been the London mark from the earliest times until the present day. The leopard was crowned from 1478 to 1821. The lion's head erased appears instead of the leopard's head on Britannia standard or fine silver 1697–1720, and is still valid for 95·84 per cent silver today.

A crown has been the Sheffield mark since 1773.

 An anchor has represented Birmingham since 1773. The City Arms represented Chester until the Assay Office was closed in 1962.

EDINBURGH   GLASGOW   DUBLIN

**Provincial Assay Offices which have closed**

Newcastle Assay Office used three castles as well as the London town mark from 1702 until closed in 1883.

Exeter used a three-towered castle (plus London town mark until 1777) from 1701 until closed in 1885.

York used five lions passant on a cross (plus London town mark until 1856). Norwich, Bristol, Salisbury, Lincoln, Coventry, Hull and Aberdeen also possessed Assay Offices.

**Other Marks**

A fifth mark, the sovereign's head, will be found on silver assayed between 1784 and 1890. During this period a duty was levied on gold and silver ware, and the monarch's head was stamped on the metal when the duty had been paid.

George III        William IV

George IV        Victoria

A mark commemorating the Jubilee of King George V and Queen Mary was used on silver plate from 1933 to 1935, and a coronation mark in 1952–3.

# SILVER

English silver dates back to at least the 7th century—the Venerable Bede records that St Oswald, King of Northumbria, was served food in a silver dish—though the oldest surviving piece, the Dolgelly chalice, was made in the 13th century. The Church was chief user of gold and silver in the middle ages, and it seems that by the time of the Norman invasion both were being made in some quantity, since the Normans looted 'vessels of silver and gold . . . of which the number and decoration would be hard to relate'.

Irish metalworkers used gold as long ago as the Bronze Age, when there was an established trade of Irish gold to central Europe. The Irish goldsmiths reached the peak of their craft in early Christian times, when they produced such masterpieces as the Ardagh chalice, now in the National Museum at Dublin.

In 1150 the Goldsmiths' Guild (which also included silversmiths) was founded, and about this time silver appeared on the tables of kings and barons. Much plate was destroyed during the sacking of the monasteries and the Civil War, and it is only from the late 17th century that English silver survives in quantity.

**Arabesque** A style of decoration characterised by flowing lines formed from elaborately intertwined leaves and flowers. This style, named after Mohammedan decoration, was much used on silver of the 16th century and on pierced work in the 18th century.

**Baroque** A general term used to describe the late Renaissance style of ornament, which combined scroll-work and naturalistic detail in a strong, flamboyant manner.

**Cartouche** A decoration in the form of a scroll, often used by engravers like a frame around coats of arms.

**Casting** The technique of shaping metal by pouring it molten into a mould. Small pieces, such as handles and finials, were often cast.

**Chasing** A way of decorating metal in high or low relief by incising the surface with punches of different shapes without actually removing any metal. In *repousse* or embossed chasing, parts of the design are raised into relief by hammering from the reverse side or from inside the article; the detail is then chased in by punch-work from the front. *Flat-chasing* gives decoration in very low relief and was frequently used, together with engraving, to decorate the borders of dishes, particularly in the 18th century.

**Cloisonne** A way of decorating metal with enamelling in which the various colours are separated by thin metal borders, called cloisons, fixed to the background of the work.

**Damascening** A technique of inlaying iron or steel with decoration in gold or silver.

**Enamelling** The decoration of the metal with coloured opaque or translucent glass. The enamel is crushed to a fine powder, then fused to the metal.

**Engraving** A method of decorating by cutting into the surface of the metal with a sharp tool which removes a thread of metal. Varied effects can be produced by using different tools.

**Etching** Decoration produced by using acid to eat into the surface of the metal. The technique was popular in Victorian times because it saved the labour of engraving.

**Filigree** Delicate work done with threads of silver or gold wire, finely interlaced and decorated with tiny balls of the metal. Where the balls alone are used for decoration, the work is known as *granulation*.

**Finial** The ornament at the top of the lid or cover of a dish. In the 18th century various shapes were popular —acorns early in the century, pineapples in the middle period and urns in the late, neo-Classical period.

**Flat-chasing** See *Chasing*.

**Flatware** The term used for tableware that has no cutting edge: spoons, forks, slices, etc.

**Flute** A decorative groove, derived from the columns of Classical architecture. In the late 17th century, fluting was often used alternately with *gadrooning* to form a corrugated surface.

**Gadrooning** A design consisting of a series of convex curves, stamped or cast, set vertically or slanting, and joined at their extremities. The pattern is typical of late 17th-century baroque ornament and was used extensively on the rims and bases of cups and on the borders of dishes.

**German silver,** also known as nickel silver; a tough white metal alloy consisting approximately of six parts of copper, three parts of zinc and one part of nickel.

**Granulation** See *Filigree*.

**Guilloche** A border consisting of ribbon-like bands twisting over each other in a continuous series; the spaces enclosed by the crossed lines often contain rosettes or wheel motifs.

**Moulding** A border formed from various combinations of parallel convex and concave forms, based on the mouldings used for decoration in architecture.

**Niello** Decoration made by filling *engraved* lines with a black mixture of lead, silver, copper and sulphur, and fusing it to the metal. The technique was much used in the second half of the 15th century.

**Pewter** An alloy of tin and varying proportions of copper, lead, antimony or bismuth.

**Pierced work** Decoration cut with a saw. It has been common since early times, but particularly fine pierced work was done in the William and Mary and Queen Anne periods.

**Raising** The silversmith's technique of forming a hollow vessel from flat sheet metal by hammering it on a wooden block.

**Repousse** See *Chasing*.

**Rococo** A general term used to describe the 18th-century style of ornament based on scrolls and shell forms. It is a lighter, more delicate style than the *baroque*.

**Sheffield Plate** Plate made of copper coated with silver. Invented by Thomas Boulsover, a Sheffield cutler, in 1743, it consists of a copper ingot fused between two silver plates and rolled out to the thickness required.

**Stamped work** Relief decoration produced by hammering the metal from the reverse into a sunken die.

# THE PARISH CHURCH

Britain's parish churches are living monuments as well as places of worship. For a thousand years of Christianity they have been the recording places of local history, and through the eloquence of their windows, carving and sculpture, the past can be felt and understood. The silverware, brasses, paintings and fabrics they contain are a vital part of our heritage—the treasures in daily use in Britain's villages and towns.

The ground plans below illustrate the typical growth of a parish church; the shaded parts of each drawing represent the additions that might have been made to the church in each period. In the exploded drawing, opposite, the most commonly mentioned parts of a church are illustrated and named.

1  *Alms box (for donations)*
2  *Altar*
3  *Angel*
4  *Apse*
5  *Aumbry (sacred vessels' cupboard)*
6  *Aumbry lamp*
7  *Battlement*
8  *Bell louvres*
9  *Boss (ornament at roof rib-junction)*
10 *Box-pew*
11 *Canopy over altar*
12 *Chancel*
13 *Chantry chapel*
14 *Choir (in west gallery)*
15 *Choir stalls*
16 *Church chest*
17 *Clerestory*

### NORMAN 12th century
A simple two-cell interior with an apse at the east end sufficiently large to accommodate the altar. Access doors are opposite each other in the north and south walls, and the windows are narrow slits.

### EARLY MEDIEVAL
13th–14th century
A population increase means more worshippers and the north aisle is extended. The altar space is likewise enlarged and a sedilia and piscina built in. A local family builds a chantry chapel on the south side and a porch is added for ceremonial purposes.

### LATE MEDIEVAL
15th–16th century
The north and south aisles are extended, the chantry chapel screened and a new tower erected. Above the south porch a priest's room is built. A rich merchant, or guild, donates a rood and screen while another finances a north chapel.

### POST-REFORMATION
17th–18th century. Bigger congregations necessitate galleried seating. The village choir sit in the west gallery. The chantry becomes the Squire's pew and the parvise a store. The north chapel is used by the village school and the chancel for quarterly communion services.

### VICTORIAN RESTORATION
19th century. A fashionable architect 'restores' the church resulting in new chancel stalls, pitch-pine pews, wrought-iron altar-rails and an eagle-lectern. The altar is raised and a marble reredos set behind it. A vestry is built on the north side.

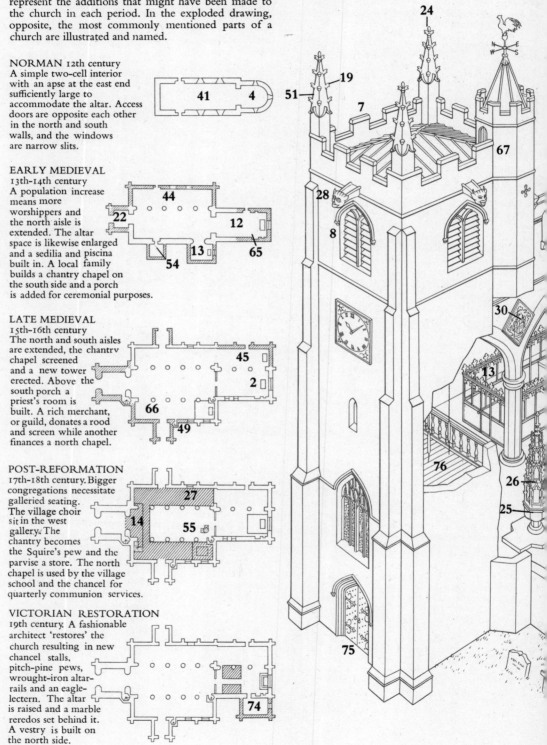

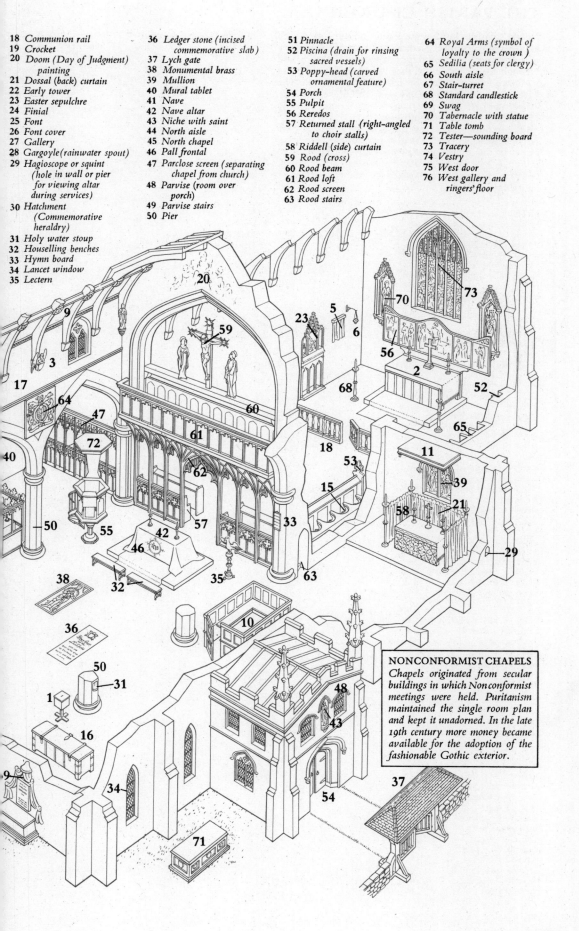

18 Communion rail
19 Crocket
20 Doom (Day of Judgment)
    painting
21 Dossal (back) curtain
22 Early tower
23 Easter sepulchre
24 Finial
25 Font
26 Font cover
27 Gallery
28 Gargoyle (rainwater spout)
29 Hagioscope or squint
    (hole in wall or pier
    for viewing altar
    during services)
30 Hatchment
    (Commemorative
    heraldry)
31 Holy water stoup
32 Houselling benches
33 Hymn board
34 Lancet window
35 Lectern

36 Ledger stone (incised
    commemorative slab)
37 Lych gate
38 Monumental brass
39 Mullion
40 Mural tablet
41 Nave
42 Nave altar
43 Niche with saint
44 North aisle
45 North chapel
46 Pall frontal
47 Parclose screen (separating
    chapel from church)
48 Parvise (room over
    porch)
49 Parvise stairs
50 Pier

51 Pinnacle
52 Piscina (drain for rinsing
    sacred vessels)
53 Poppy-head (carved
    ornamental feature)
54 Porch
55 Pulpit
56 Reredos
57 Returned stall (right-angled
    to choir stalls)
58 Riddell (side) curtain
59 Rood (cross)
60 Rood beam
61 Rood loft
62 Rood screen
63 Rood stairs

64 Royal Arms (symbol of
    loyalty to the crown)
65 Sedilia (seats for clergy)
66 South aisle
67 Stair-turret
68 Standard candlestick
69 Swag
70 Tabernacle with statue
71 Table tomb
72 Tester—sounding board
73 Tracery
74 Vestry
75 West door
76 West gallery and
    ringers' floor

**NONCONFORMIST CHAPELS**
*Chapels originated from secular
buildings in which Nonconformist
meetings were held. Puritanism
maintained the single room plan
and kept it unadorned. In the late
19th century more money became
available for the adoption of the
fashionable Gothic exterior.*

677

# SYMBOLS IN CHURCHES

The old churches and cathedrals of Britain were built for a devout but illiterate population. Statues, symbols, stained glass and painting were used to make each place of worship a colourful picture-book of Bible truth and Church history. Artists and craftsmen devoted their lives to this work, and ecclesiastics, noblemen and citizens vied with each other in building more and more elaborate and beautiful shrines. In spite of destruction by over-zealous reformers, much of beauty still remains, and a knowledge of the significance of some of the old emblems increases the pleasure of visiting an ancient church.

## Monograms

A monogram is two or more letters interwoven. The most ancient Christian symbol is the LABARUM, consisting of the two letters, chi and rho which begin the Greek word for Christ. This monogram is prominent in the decoration of Coventry Cathedral. A

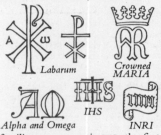

*Labarum*     *Crowned MARIA*

*Alpha and Omega*     *IHS*     *INRI*

familiar monogram is IHS, the first three letters of the Greek word for Jesus; it was often carved on church roof beams. A favourite medieval symbol is MR for Maria Regina, Mary Queen of Heaven, also MARIA as a monogram. One of the crypt chapel roofs at Canterbury Cathedral is decorated with crowned M's. INRI is not strictly a monogram but the initial letters of 'Iesus Nazarenus Rex Iudaeorum'—Jesus of Nazareth, King of the Jews.

Alpha and Omega, first and last letters of the Greek alphabet, signify that Christ is the Beginning and End.

## Numbers and Geometry

In medieval thought every number had its own mystical meaning, and numbers were easily translated into geometry. The equilateral triangle represents the Trinity; the three equal sides and angles symbolising the unity of three distinct persons. Two interwoven equilateral triangles form a six-pointed star, traditionally known as the Star of David; it is sometimes called the Creator's star, the six points representing the six days of Creation. The Triquetra is an ancient symbol whose three equal arcs express the Trinity, and whose continuous form symbolises eternity. It often appears on Celtic crosses. Baptismal fonts are often octagonal, eight being the number of Resurrection and new life.

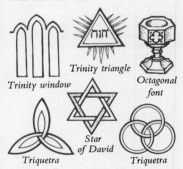

*Trinity window*     *Trinity triangle*     *Octagonal font*

*Triquetra*     *Star of David*     *Triquetra*

## The Cross

The Cross is a universal Christian symbol today, although the P-X monogram was used by the early Church. Monks and heralds evolved over fifty forms of the Cross. The most usual are:

The CRUCIFIX is a cross with Christ upon it. An early variety is the CHRISTUS REX (1), showing Christ crowned and robed. Later versions became more realistic. The ROOD (2)

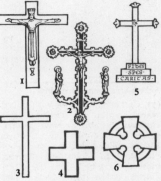

is the great crucifix that stands or hangs in the chancel arch. The attendant figures (St Mary, St John) are reminders of Calvary.

The LATIN CROSS (3) (Passion Cross) has a long upright. Many churches are built on a Latin Cross ground-plan. The GREEK CROSS (4) has all the arms equal. The Orthodox churches of the East are built on this plan, and so are many Nonconformist chapels. Five Greek crosses incised on most altars represent the five wounds of Christ. The CALVARY CROSS (5) is a Latin Cross mounted on three steps, symbolising Charity, Hope and (top) Faith. The CELTIC CROSS (6) or Iona Cross. The circle symbolises Eternity.

## Animal and Plant Symbols

In medieval times religious or spiritual meaning was attached to everything men observed in the world. Highly coloured natural history also served as a source of inspiration. The PHOENIX (7), the mythical bird believed to regenerate itself in the flames of its own funeral pyre was, for example, used to symbolise the Resurrection. The PELICAN (8), the bird that pierces its own breast to feed its young, symbolised the Sacrifice on the Cross, and the Holy Communion. Only a virgin, it was thought, could capture the UNICORN (9); fierce and swift, he would place his head on her lap and allow himself to be taken. This legend was taken as an allegory of the Incarnation of Christ in the Virgin Mary. The LAMB is a well-known symbol of Christ. The AGNUS DEI (10) 'Lamb of God', has a halo with a cross on it to indicate the Lord, and carries a banner of Victory. The DOVE (11) symbolises the Holy Spirit, and is carved on font covers to show the Spirit descending at Baptism. Seven Doves represent the Seven Gifts of the Holy Spirit. The LILY symbolises Purity because of its white flowers and is specially associated with the Blessed Virgin. It is usually

shown in the conventionalised form of the FLEUR-DE-LYS (12). The LILY CROSS (13)—Christ is shown not on a Cross but on a Lily with three stems. This means He bears our sins in the flesh of Mary His Mother. The ROSE (14) is emblematic of the two sides in the Wars of the Roses, but also symbolises Christ. The Vine and branches is based on Christ's words, 'I am the True Vine'; grapes and wheat represent the Eucharist. Palm branches symbolised victory amongst the Romans, and hence martyrs are shown carrying palms. POMEGRANATES (15), symbolise the unity of the Church, as many seeds in one fruit; also new life and hence the Resurrection. It was much used as a damask pattern. The Tree of JESSE (16) is used in many stained glass windows and carvings. The ancestry of Christ is shown in the form of a vine springing from Jesse, the father of King David. Kings and prophets are often added; Mary with the Holy Child is at the top, or a crucifix in some examples. The EVANGELISTS (17) are symbolised by the eagle (John), winged ox (Luke), winged lion (Mark) and winged man (Matthew). The FISH (18) was a secret sign used by early Christians. The initials of the Greek for 'JESUS CHRIST, SON OF GOD, SAVIOUR' make the Greek word for 'fish'.

## Symbols of God and the Trinity

To represent GOD directly was considered blasphemous, so a RAY OF LIGHT (19) or a HAND (20) was drawn; CIRCLES (21) or FISHES (22) symbolised the Trinity. In medieval times, THREE CROWNED FIGURES (23), the FATHER (24) with CRUCIFIX (25) were used.

## Symbols of the Passion

During the Middle Ages shields were used as decoration wherever possible. Emblems based on the Passion are frequently found on them and on screens, doors and bench ends, or held by angels in the roof-timbers.
(26) The Cross with the sheet used to lower Christ's body after His Crucifixion. (27) The Title (INRI). (28) The Crown of Thorns and Nails. (29) The Scourges. (30) The Seamless Robe, and the Dice. (31) The Ladder, and Sponge on Reed. (32) The Lantern, carried during the arrest in Gethsemane. (33) The Five Wounds. (34) The Cock that crowed after Peter's denial. (35) The Thirty Pieces of Silver, Judas's reward. (36) The Hammer and Pincers.

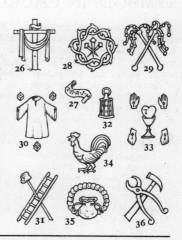

## Saints and their Emblems

(37) Catherine: Princess with spiked wheel, patron of teachers. (38) Dunstan: Archbishop with pincers, patron of goldsmiths. (39) George: knight killing dragon, patron of England. (40) John the Baptist: bearded, carrying 'Agnus Dei'. (41) Clement: Pope with anchor. (42) Jerome: Cardinal, with lion and book. (43) Denis: after execution, he walked carrying his head. (44) Stephen: Deacon carrying stones.

A saint's emblem is often the instrument of martyrdom, as with St Clement—tied to an anchor and thrown into the sea—or based on a legend, like the pincers with which St Dunstan nipped the Devil. (45) a long CROSS: held by an Apostle—Philip; held by a queen—Helena. Bishops hold the crozier, archbishops a cross. (46) LAMB held by female saint: Agnes. (47) Saltire CROSS: Andrew. (48) SWORD held by Apostle: Paul; otherwise a common emblem for martyrs; with archbishop: Thomas à Becket. (49) TOWER held by princess: Barbara. (50) KEYS: Peter; usually paired with Paul, as the Two Pillars of the Church. (51) Flaying KNIFE: Bartholomew. (52) GRIDIRON: Lawrence. (53) CHALICE with a dragon in it: John the Apostle. (54) Three gold BALLS: Nicholas, patron of bankers and pawnbrokers: also, as Santa Claus, of children. (55) ARROWS: held by a king—Edmund; by a young man—Sebastian. (56) SPEAR: Thomas the Apostle. (57) PIG and T-cross: Anthony the hermit. (58) SCALLOP-SHELL: James the Great. (59) SCYTHE held by a maiden: Sidwell, a West-country saint. (60) INVERTED CROSS: Peter. (61) WINDLASS: Erasmus. Other popular emblems for saints—a woman teaching Mary to read: Anne; a giant with the Christ-child, crossing a stream: Christopher; eyes on a plate: Lucy; dragon and cross: Margaret of Antioch.

## St Michael

He is shown in armour, trampling down the Devil, or with scales to weigh souls at Doomsday. 'Michael churches' are often on hill-tops and are thought to be remnants of a pre-Christian cult. The nine medieval Orders of angels are: Seraphim, Cherubim, Thrones, Dominions, Virtues, Powers, Principalities, Archangels and Angels.

## Symbolism in Church planning

Churches are orientated from rising to setting sun, a custom perhaps earlier than Christianity itself. The plan is very often a cross, and the chancel may show declination, representing the bowing of Christ's head on the Cross.

The nave (Latin navis, a ship) symbolises the voyage to Heaven. The north door, on the 'dark' side, is the Devil's Door, opened during the exorcism at Baptism. The font is near the main door, since entry to the church is by baptism. To reach the altar it is necessary to pass under the rood; so Heaven is reached by way of the Cross.

In the churchyard the lych gate (from the Saxon word for a corpse) shelters coffin and bearers. The evergreen yew trees symbolise eternity.

## Symbolism of Colours

The Church today uses colour chiefly to mark the liturgical seasons. Festivals—Christmas, Easter and Corpus Christi for example—are marked by WHITE vestments, altar-frontals and hangings; white also for the feasts of St Mary and for saints who were not martyrs. RED is the colour for Pentecost (Whit Sunday), Palm Sunday, Holy Cross Day, the Precious Blood, and martyrs. GREEN is used for the periods after Trinity and Epiphany. PURPLE is used in Advent and Lent; in many churches Lent is marked by unbleached linen to suggest penitence. BLUE is St Mary's colour. BLACK is for funerals and requiems. YELLOW was looked on as the colour of jealousy and treason; hence Judas is shown in yellow robes.

# ACKNOWLEDGEMENTS

The publishers wish to thank the following
people and organisations for their permission to reproduce
photographs belonging to them or of their property:

Her Majesty the Queen for gracious permission to reproduce the following subjects: Portrait of Queen Henrietta Maria by Van Dyck. *Caesar's Chariot* by Mantegna. The Gold State Coach. The Irish State Coach. The Ramillies Staircase at Marlborough House. Portrait of Sir Henry Guildford by Holbein. Queen Mary's Dolls' House.

And to: Aerofilms Ltd. J. Allan Cash. The Antique Dealer and Collectors Guide. Apollo Magazine Ltd. The Architectural Review. The Dean and Chapter of St Patrick's Cathedral, Armagh. Art-Wood Photography. The Ashmolean Museum, Oxford. His Grace the Duke of Atholl. The Barber Institute of Fine Arts, Birmingham. Barnaby's Picture Library. B. T. Batsford Ltd. His Grace the Duke of Bedford. Bedford Public Library. Captain Berkeley, Berkeley Castle. Birmingham Museum and Art Gallery. The Bowes Museum, Barnard Castle. Mrs Humphrey Brand. The Brantwood Trust. The Trustees of the British Museum. The Trustees of the British Museum (Natural History). The British Travel Association. Lord Brooke. The Trustees of Buckland Abbey, Plymouth. The Burlington Magazine Publications Ltd. The Burrel Collection, Glasgow Art Gallery and Museum. The Trustees of the Burns Monument and Museum, Kilmarnock. Camera Press Ltd. The Dean and Chapter of Canterbury Cathedral. The Royal Museum, Canterbury. The Chester Beatty Library, Dublin. The City of London School. The Colchester and Essex Museum. The Connoisseur. The Council for the Care of Churches. Country Life. The Courtauld Institute Galleries, London. The Provost and Chapter of Coventry Cathedral. Bernard Cox. The Daily Telegraph Ltd. Derby Museum and Art Gallery. The Devonshire Collection, Chatsworth; the Trustees of the Chatsworth Settlement. The Trustees of the Dickens House Museum and Library. Dorset Natural History and Archaeological Society, Dorchester. J. E. Downward. The Rector and Churchwardens of Dunstable Church. The Dean and Chapter of Durham. The Trustees of the Dyson Perrins Museum, Royal Porcelain Company Ltd, Worcester. The Trustees of Elgar's Birthplace. English Life Publications Ltd. The Marquess of Exeter. Faber and Faber Ltd. Ferens Art Gallery, Kingston upon Hull. The Syndics of the Fitzwilliam Museum, Cambridge. R. B. Fleming & Co. Ltd. Michael Frenchman. The Institute of Geological Sciences. Dr Georg Gerster. Gilchrist Studios Ltd. Glasgow Art Gallery and Museum. The Glasgow School of Art. P. M. Goodchild and Sons Ltd. The Trustees of the Goodwood Collection. Guy Gravett. The Green Studio Ltd, Dublin. The Gulbenkian Museum of Oriental Art, The University of Durham, Durham. The Hamlyn Group. The Governors of Harrow School. Eric Hartman. Lord Hastings. The Marquess of Hertford, Ragley Hall. The Cecil Higgins Art Gallery, Bedford. The John Hillelson Agency. The Museum of the History of Science, Oxford. The Holburne of Menstrie Museum, Bath. George Howard. The Hunterian Museum, University of Glasgow. Huntly House, Edinburgh. The Trustees, the Regimental Museum, the Royal Inniskilling Fusiliers. The Bank of Ireland, Dublin. The Irish Tourist Board. The Greater London Council as Trustees of the Iveagh Bequest, Kenwood. The Trustees of Dr Johnson's House. Dmitri Kastarina. A. W. Kerr. A. F. Kersting. The Trustees of the Lady Lever Art Gallery, Port Sunlight. The Museum of Leathercraft. Leatherhead Urban District Council. Leeds City Art Galleries. Lichfield City Council. The Dean and Chapter of Lincoln Cathedral. The Treasurers and Masters of the Bench of Lincoln's Inn. Viscount de l'Isle, Penshurst Place. The City of Liverpool Museums. The Trustees of the London Museum. The Rector of Long Melford. Madame Tussauds Ltd. Her Majesty's Stationery Office. Manchester City Art Galleries. The Mansell Collection. The Countess Manvers. His Grace the Duke of Marlborough. The Lord Methuen RA, FSA. The Rector of Middleton Parish Church. The Ministry of Public Building and Works. Tom Molland. The Municipal Gallery of Modern Art, Dublin. The Trustees of the National Gallery. The National Gallery of Ireland. The National Gallery of Scotland. The National Library of Scotland. The National Maritime Museum, Greenwich. The National Monuments Record. The National Museum of Antiquities, Edinburgh. The National Museum of Ireland. The National Museum of Wales. The National Portrait Gallery. The National Trust. The National Trust, Northern Ireland Committee. The National Trust for Scotland. Mrs F. R. Newens. His Grace the Duke of Norfolk. The Marquess of Northampton. His Grace the Duke of Northumberland. The City of Nottingham Museum and Art Gallery. Norwich City Council. City of Norwich Museums. George Ovens. The Oxford Preservation Trust. Nan Pattullo. The Earl of Pembroke. The Percival David Foundation of Chinese Art. The Dean and Chapter of Peterborough Cathedral. The Petworth Collection. Pictorial Colour Slides. Picturepoint. City Art Gallery, Plymouth. The Commander-in-Chief, Portsmouth. The Public Records Office, Corporation of London. Purnell and Sons Ltd. The President and Fellows of Queen's College, Cambridge. Radio Times Hulton Picture Library. George Rainbird Ltd. The Royal Academy of Arts. The Director, Royal Botanic Gardens, Kew. The Royal Scottish Museum. The Ruskin Museum, Coniston. Lord Salisbury. The Scottish National Portrait Gallery. The Scottish Tourist Board. Kenneth Scowen. Henk Snoek. The Council for the Preservation of Sheffield Antiquities. Sheffield City Museums. The Trustees of the Sligo County Museum. The Trustees of Sir John Soane's Museum. Soho Galleries Ltd. Somerset County Museum Governing Body. Southampton Art Gallery. S.P.A.D.E.M. George Spearman. The Earl Spencer. The Dean and Chapter of St David's Cathedral, Pembroke. The College Council of St John's College, Cambridge. Dr J. K. St Joseph. The Dean and Chapter of St Paul's Cathedral. The Vicar and Churchwardens of Holy Trinity Church, Stratford-upon-Avon. The Trustees of Shakespeare's Birthplace, Stratford-upon-Avon. The Sunday Times. Sunderland Museum and Art Gallery. His Grace the Duke of Sutherland. The Great Western Railway Museum, Swindon. The Tate Gallery. Temple Newsam House, Leeds. Thames and Hudson Ltd. The Thomas Coram Foundation for Children. Thomas Photos, Oxford. The Curator of Historical Relics, Museum of British Transport. Trans-Globe Film Distributors Ltd. The Board of Trinity College, Dublin. Tudeley Parochial Church Council. The Ulster Museum, Belfast. The Trustees of the University Museum, Oxford. The Victoria and Albert Museum. The Walker Art Gallery, Liverpool. Waltons Sound and Film Service. The Trustees of the Wallace Collection. The Warburg Institute. The County of Warwick Museum. The Earl of Warwick. Weidenfeld and Nicolson Ltd. Tom Weir. The Trustees of the Wellcome Historical Medical Museum and Library. The Duke of Wellington. The Dean and Chapter of Wells Cathedral. Major-General Sir Harold Wernher Bt, Luton Hoo. The Dean and Chapter of Westminster. The Westminster Press. The Whitworth Art Gallery, University of Manchester. Marcus Wickham-Boynton, Burton Agnes Hall. Simon Wingfield Digby, MP. Woodmansterne. The Dean and Chapter of Worcester Cathedral. The York Corporation. The Dean and Chapter of York.

The publishers also acknowledge
their indebtedness to the following books
which were used for reference or
as sources of illustrations:

*Age of Wren* by R. Dutton (Batsford); *Ancient Art of the Americas* by B. H. S. Bushnell (Thames & Hudson); *Architecture in Britain 1530–1830* by John Summerson (Penguin); *The Architecture of England* by D. Yarwood (Batsford); *Arms and Armour* by Vesey Norman (Weidenfeld and Nicolson); *Art in Britain under the Romans* by J. M. C. Toynbee (Oxford University Press); *Art Nouveau* by Mario Amaya (Dutton Vista); *Art Nouveau* by S. T. Schudi Madsen (World University Library); *Bartholomew's Gazetteer* (Bartholomew); *British Architects and Craftsmen* by S. Sitwell (Batsford); *Buildings of England* by Nikolaus Pevsner (Penguin); *Cambridge* by Michael Grant (Weidenfeld and Nicolson); *Castles* edited by Sir Hugh Casson (National Benzole Books); *Chambers's Biographical Dictionary* (Chambers); *Chambers's Encyclopaedia* (Newnes); *Clocks* by Simon Fleet (Weidenfeld and Nicolson); *The Complete Encyclopaedia of Antiques* by L. G. G. Ramsey (Connoisseur); *Concise Encyclopaedia of Architecture* by M. S. Briggs (Dent Dutton); *Concise History of Interior Decoration* by George Savage (Thames & Hudson); *Country Life Book of English Furniture* by E. T. Joy (Country Life); *Decorative Cast Iron Work in Great Britain* by R. Lister (G. Bell); *Dictionary of Art and Artists* by Peter and Linda Murray (Penguin); *18th Century Gold Boxes of Europe* by A. K. Snowman (Faber and Faber); *Embroidery and Tapestry Weaving* by Mrs Archibald H. Christie (John Hogg); *Encyclopaedia of the Arts* (Thames & Hudson); *English Cathedrals* by Martin Hurlimann (Thames & Hudson); *English Church Monuments 1510–1840* by K. A. Esdaile (Batsford); *The English Garden* by E. Hymans (Thames & Hudson); *The English Home* by D. Yarwood (Batsford); *English Needlework* by A. F. Kendrick (A. & C. Black Ltd.); *English Porcelain of the 18th Century* by J. L. Dixon (Faber and Faber); *English Stained Glass* by J. Baker (Thames & Hudson); *Encyclopaedia Britannica*; *Glass Through the Ages* by E. Barrington Haynes (Pelican); *Great Gardens of Britain* by P. Coats (Weidenfeld and Nicolson); *Great Houses of Britain* by N. Nicolson (Weidenfeld and Nicolson); *Great Interiors* by Ian Grant (Weidenfeld and Nicolson); *Guide to English Parish Churches* by John Betjeman (Collins); *Guns and Rifles of the World* by H. L. Blackmore (Batsford); *A History of Architecture on the Comparative Method* by Banister Fletcher (University of London, the Athlone Press); *Les Instruments des Sciences dans l'Art et l'Histoire* by H. Michel (Albert de Visscher); *Ireland Explored* by Wolfgang Retler (Thames & Hudson); *Irish Art during the Viking Invasion 800–1020 AD* by Francoise Henry (Methuen); *Irish Art in the Early Christian Period to AD 800* by Francoise Henry (Methuen); *London* by Nikolaus Pevsner (Penguin); *Monuments* edited by Sir Hugh Casson (National Benzole Books); *Oxford* by Felix Markham (Weidenfeld and Nicolson); *Pagan Celtic Britain* by Anne Ross (Routledge and Columbia); *The Penguin Dictionary of Architecture* by John Fleming, Hugh Honour, Nikolaus Pevsner (Penguin); *The Penguin Guide to London* by F. R. Banks (Penguin); *Picture Encyclopaedia of Art* (Thames & Hudson); *Porcelain* by H. Tait (Faber and Faber); *Regency Furniture* by M. Jourdain (Country Life); *The Shell Gardens Book* edited by Peter Hunt (Phoenix Rainbird); *The Shell Guide to Ireland* by Lord Killanin and Michael V. Duignan (Ebury Press and George Rainbird); *The Shell Guide to Britain and Northern Ireland* edited by Geoffrey Boumphrey (Ebury Press and George Rainbird); *Tides in English Taste 1619–1800* by B. S. Allen (Oxford University Press); *2000 Years of London* by Michael Hanson (Country Life); *Victorian Comfort* by J. Gloag (A. & C. Black Ltd.); *Webster's Biographical Dictionary* (G. and C. Merriam); *Worcester Porcelain* by F. Barrett (Faber and Faber); *Works in Architecture of R. and J. Adam* (Alec Tiranti Ltd.)

Among other people and organisations who contributed to the book were: Victor Ball; Bord Failte, Dublin; Helena Burke; Frank Dowling; Derek Hall; Illustration Research Services; Caroline Mackinlay; Bridget Morley ; Tower of London Armouries.